# AN INDEX
# TO BOOK REVIEWS
# IN THE HUMANITIES

VOLUME 14
1973

PHILLIP THOMSON
WILLIAMSTON, MICHIGAN

THIS VOLUME OF THE INDEX CONTAINS DATA
COLLECTED UP TO 31 DECEMBER 1973.

THIS IS AN INDEX TO BOOK REVIEWS IN
HUMANITIES PERIODICALS. BEGINNING WITH
VOLUME 12 OF THIS INDEX (DATED 1971), THE
FORMER POLICY OF SELECTIVELY INDEXING
REVIEWS OF BOOKS IN CERTAIN SUBJECT
CATEGORIES ONLY WAS DROPPED IN FAVOR
OF A POLICY OF INDEXING ALL REVIEWS IN
THE PERIODICALS INDEXED, WITH THE ONE
EXCEPTION OF CHILDREN'S BOOKS--THE RE-
VIEWS OF WHICH WILL NOT BE INDEXED.
EVERY PERIODICAL INDEXED DATED AFTER
1 JANUARY 1971 HAS HAD ALL REVIEWS IN-
DEXED. MANY OF THE PERIODICALS INDEXED
IN THIS VOLUME WITH EARLIER DATES HAVE
ALSO HAD ALL REVIEWS INDEXED, BUT IN THIS
VOLUME WE HAVE MADE NO ATTEMPT TO IDENTI-
FY THESE ISSUES IN THE LIST OF PERIODI-
CALS INDEXED BEGINNING ON PAGE III. IT
SHOULD THEREFORE BE ASSUMED THAT ALL
PERIODICALS SHOWN IN THAT LIST WITH DATES
EARLIER THAN 1971 WERE INDEXED UNDER THE
OLD RULES OF INCLUSION. THOSE RULES CAN
BE FOUND ON THIS PAGE IN ANY VOLUME OF
THIS INDEX SPINE-DATED 1970 OR EARLIER.

THE FORM OF THE ENTRIES USED IS AS
FOLLOWS:

        AUTHOR. TITLE.
            REVIEWER. IDENTIFYING LEGEND.

THE AUTHOR'S NAME USED IS THE NAME THAT
APPEARS ON THE TITLE-PAGE OF THE BOOK
BEING REVIEWED, AS WELL AS WE ARE ABLE
TO DETERMINE, EVEN THOUGH THIS NAME IS
KNOWN TO BE A PSEUDONYM. THE TITLE ONLY
IS SHOWN; SUBTITLES ARE INCLUDED ONLY
WHERE THEY ARE NECESSARY TO IDENTIFY A
BOOK IN A SERIES. THE IDENTIFYING LEGEND
CONSISTS OF THE PERIODICAL, EACH OF
WHICH HAS A CODE NUMBER, AND THE DATE
AND PAGE NUMBER OF THE PERIODICAL WHERE
THE REVIEW IS TO BE FOUND. PMLA ABBREVI-
ATIONS ARE ALSO SHOWN (WHEN A PERIODICAL
HAS SUCH AN ABBREVIATION, BUT SUCH AB-
BREVIATIONS ARE LIMITED TO FOUR LETTERS)
IMMEDIATELY FOLLOWING THE CODE NUMBER
OF THE PERIODICAL. TO LEARN THE NAME
OF THE PERIODICAL IN WHICH THE REVIEW
APPEARS, IT IS NECESSARY TO REFER THE
CODE NUMBER TO THE NUMERICALLY-ARRANGED
LIST OF PERIODICALS BEGINNING ON PAGE
III. THIS LIST ALSO SHOWS THE VOLUME
AND NUMBER OF THE PERIODICALS INDEXED.

REVIEWS ARE INDEXED AS THEY APPEAR AND
NO ATTEMPT IS MADE TO HOLD THE TITLE
UNTIL ALL THE REVIEWS ARE PUBLISHED.
FOR THIS REASON IT IS NECESSARY TO REFER
TO PREVIOUS AND SUBSEQUENT VOLUMES OF
THIS INDEX TO BE SURE THAT THE COMPLETE
ROSTER OF REVIEWS OF ANY TITLE IS SEEN.
AS AN AID TO THE USER, AN ASTERISK (*)
HAS BEEN ADDED IMMEDIATELY FOLLOWING ANY
TITLE THAT WAS ALSO INDEXED IN VOLUME 13
(1972) OF THIS INDEX.

AUTHORS WITH HYPHENATED SURNAMES ARE
INDEXED UNDER THE NAME BEFORE THE HYPHEN,
AND THE NAME FOLLOWING THE HYPHEN IS NOT
CROSS-INDEXED. AUTHORS WITH MORE THAN
ONE SURNAME, BUT WHERE THE NAMES ARE NOT
HYPHENATED, ARE INDEXED UNDER THE FIRST
OF THE NAMES AND THE LAST NAME IS CROSS-
INDEXED. WHEN ALPHABETIZING SURNAMES
CONTAINING UMLAUTS, THE UMLAUTS ARE
IGNORED. EDITORS ARE ALWAYS SHOWN IN
THE AUTHOR-TITLE ENTRY, AND THEY ARE
CROSS-INDEXED (EXCEPT WHERE THE EDITOR'S

SURNAME IS THE SAME AS THAT OF THE
AUTHOR). TRANSLATORS ARE SHOWN ONLY
WHEN THEY ARE NECESSARY TO IDENTIFY THE
BOOK BEING REVIEWED (AS IN THE CLASSICS),
AND THEY ARE NOT CROSS-INDEXED UNLESS
THE BOOK BEING REVIEWED HAS NO AUTHOR
OR EDITOR. CERTAIN REFERENCE WORKS
AND ANONYMOUS WORKS THAT ARE KNOWN PRIM-
ARILY BY THEIR TITLE ARE INDEXED UNDER
THAT TITLE AND THEIR EDITORS ARE CROSS-
INDEXED.

A LIST OF ABBREVIATIONS USED IS SHOWN
ON PAGE II.

ABBREVIATIONS

```
ANON ..............ANONYMOUS
APR ...............APRIL
AUG ...............AUGUST
BK ................BOOK
COMP(S) ...........COMPILER(S)
CONT. .............CONTINUED
DEC ...............DECEMBER
ED(S) .............EDITOR(S) [OR]
                      EDITION(S)
FASC ..............FASCICULE
FEB ...............FEBRUARY
JAN ...............JANUARY
JUL ...............JULY
JUN ...............JUNE
MAR ...............MARCH
NO. (OR #) ........NUMBER
NOV ...............NOVEMBER
OCT ...............OCTOBER
PREV ..............PREVIOUS VOLUME OF
                      THIS INDEX
PT ................PART
REV ...............REVISED
SEP ...............SEPTEMBER
SER ...............SERIES
SUPP ..............SUPPLEMENT
TRANS .............TRANSLATOR(S)
VOL ...............VOLUME
* (ASTERISK) ......THIS TITLE WAS ALSO
                      SHOWN IN THE VOLUME
                      OF THIS INDEX IM-
                      MEDIATELY PRECEDING
                      THIS ONE
```

THE PERIODICALS IN WHICH THE REVIEWS
APPEAR ARE IDENTIFIED IN THIS INDEX BY A
NUMBER. TO SUPPLEMENT THIS NUMBER, AND
TO PROMOTE READY IDENTIFICATION, PMLA
ABBREVIATIONS ARE ALSO GIVEN FOLLOWING
THIS NUMBER. EVERY ATTEMPT WILL BE MADE
TO INDEX THOSE ISSUES SHOWN HERE AS
"MISSING" IN A LATER VOLUME OF THIS
INDEX. EVERY PERIODICAL INDEXED IN THIS
VOLUME WITH A COVER DATE AFTER 1 JANUARY
1971 HAS HAD ALL REVIEWS APPEARING THERE-
IN INDEXED; MANY OF THE PERIODICALS
INDEXED WITH EARLIER COVER DATES HAVE
ALSO HAD ALL REVIEWS INDEXED, BUT THESE
ARE NOT INDICATED BELOW. IT SHOULD
THEREFORE BE ASSUMED THAT ALL PERIODICALS
SHOWN BELOW WITH COVER DATES EARLIER
THAN 1971 WERE INDEXED UNDER THE OLD
RULES OF INCLUSION.
    THE FOLLOWING IS A LISTING OF THE
PERIODICALS INDEXED IN VOLUME 14:

86(BHS) - BULLETIN OF HISPANIC STUDIES.
            LIVERPOOL. QUARTERLY.
            JAN72 THRU OCT72 (VOL 49
            COMPLETE)
89(BJA) - THE BRITISH JOURNAL OF AES-
            THETICS. LONDON. QUARTERLY.
            WINTER72 THRU AUTUMN72 (VOL
            12 COMPLETE)
90 - BURLINGTON MAGAZINE. LONDON.
            MONTHLY.
            JAN71 THRU DEC71 (VOL 113
            COMPLETE)
96 - ARTSCANADA. OTTAWA. BI-MONTHLY.
            FEB/MAR71 THRU DEC71/JAN72
            (VOL 28 COMPLETE)
97(CQ) - THE CAMBRIDGE QUARTERLY. CAM-
            BRIDGE, ENGLAND.
            SPRING/SUMMER70 THRU SUMMER/
            AUTUMN71 (VOL 5 COMPLETE)
98 - CRITIQUE. PARIS. MONTHLY.
            JAN70 THRU DEC71 (VOLS 26&27
            COMPLETE)
99 - CANADIAN FORUM. TORONTO. MONTHLY.
            JAN73 THRU NOV/DEC73 (VOL 52
            #624-626, VOL 53 #627-634/635)
            [VOL 53 BEGINS WITH APR73
            ISSUE]
102(CANL) - CANADIAN LITERATURE. VAN-
            COUVER, B.C. QUARTERLY.
            WINTER72 THRU AUTUMN72 (#51-
            54)
104 - CANADIAN-AMERICAN SLAVIC STUDIES/
            REVUE CANADIENNE-AMÉRICAINE
            D'ÉTUDES SLAVES. PITTSBURGH,
            PA. QUARTERLY.
            FALL72 & WINTER72 (VOL 6 #3&4)
            [ISSUES OF SPRING72 & SUMMER
            72 MISSING]
109 - THE CARLETON MISCELLANY. NORTH-
            FIELD, MINNESOTA. TWICE YEAR-
            LY.
            FALL/WINTER72/73 & SPRING/
            SUMMER73 (VOL 13 COMPLETE)
111 - CAMBRIDGE REVIEW. CAMBRIDGE, ENG-
            LAND. SIX YEARLY.
            23OCT70 THRU 2JUN72 (VOLS 92
            & 93 COMPLETE)
114(CHIR) - CHICAGO REVIEW. QUARTERLY.
            AUTUMN70 THRU WINTER72 (VOL
            22 COMPLETE, VOL 23 #1-3)
121(CJ) - CLASSICAL JOURNAL. QUARTERLY.
            OCT-NOV71 THRU APR-MAY72
            (VOL 67 COMPLETE)
122 - CLASSICAL PHILOLOGY. CHICAGO.
            QUARTERLY.
            JAN72 THRU OCT72 (VOL 67 COM-
            PLETE)
123 - CLASSICAL REVIEW. LONDON. THREE
            YEARLY.
            MAR72 THRU DEC72 (VOL 22 COM-
            PLETE)
124 - CLASSICAL WORLD. BETHLEHEM, PA.
            MONTHLY.
            SEP71 THRU APR-MAY72 (VOL 65
            COMPLETE)
127 - ART JOURNAL. NEW YORK. QUARTERLY.
            FALL71 THRU SUMMER72 (VOL 31
            COMPLETE)
128(CE) - COLLEGE ENGLISH. CHAMPAIGN,
            ILL. MONTHLY.
            OCT71 THRU DEC71 (VOL 33
            #1-3)
131(CL) - COMPARATIVE LITERATURE.
            EUGENE, OREGON. QUARTERLY.
            WINTER72 THRU FALL72 (VOL 24
            COMPLETE)

133 - COLLOQUIA GERMANICA. BERN, SWITZ-
            ERLAND. THREE YEARLY.
            1970/1 THRU 1971/3
134(CP) - CONCERNING POETRY. BELLINGHAM,
            WASHINGTON. TWICE YEARLY.
            SPRING70 THRU FALL71 (VOLS
            3&4 COMPLETE)
135 - CONNOISSEUR. LONDON & NEW YORK.
            MONTHLY.
            JAN70 THRU DEC71 (VOLS 173
            THRU 178 COMPLETE)
136 - CONRADIANA. ABILENE, TEXAS.
            THREE YEARLY.
            VOL 3 COMPLETE
139 - CRAFT HORIZONS. NEW YORK. BI-
            MONTHLY.
            JAN-FEB70 THRU AUG70, DEC70
            THRU OCT71 (VOL 30 #1-4 & 6,
            VOL 31 #1-5) [OCT70 ISSUE
            MISSING]
141 - CRITICISM. DETROIT. QUARTERLY.
            WINTER71 THRU FALL71 (VOL 13
            COMPLETE)
148 - CRITICAL QUARTERLY. LONDON.
            SPRING71 THRU WINTER71 (VOL
            13 COMPLETE)
149 - COMPARATIVE LITERATURE STUDIES.
            URBANA, ILL. QUARTERLY.
            MAR72 THRU DEC72 (VOL 9 COM-
            PLETE)
150(DR) - DALHOUSIE REVIEW. HALIFAX,
            N.S., CANADA. QUARTERLY.
            SPRING71 THRU WINTER71/72
            (VOL 51 COMPLETE)
151 - DANCE MAGAZINE. NEW YORK. MONTHLY.
            JAN70, MAR70 & MAY70 THRU
            DEC71 (VOL 44 #1, 3 & 5-12,
            VOL 45 COMPLETE) [ISSUES OF
            FEB70 & APR70 MISSING]
154 - DIALOGUE. MONTREAL. QUARTERLY.
            JUN70 THRU DEC71 (VOLS 9 &
            10 COMPLETE)
155 - THE DICKENSIAN. LONDON. THREE
            YEARLY.
            JAN71 THRU SEP71 (VOL 67
            COMPLETE)
157 - DRAMA/THE QUARTERLY THEATRE REVIEW.
            LONDON.
            SPRING70 THRU AUTUMN71
            (#96 THRU 102)
159(DM) - DUBLIN MAGAZINE. DUBLIN.
            QUARTERLY.
            SPRING70 THRU SPRING71 (VOL
            8 #3-7)
160 - DRAMA & THEATRE. FREDONIA, N.Y.
            VOL 8 #1-3, WINTER70/71 (VOL
            9 #2) & FALL71 (VOL 10 #1)
165 - EARLY AMERICAN LITERATURE. AMHERST,
            MASS. THREE YEARLY.
            WINTER73 THRU FALL73 (VOL 7
            #3, VOL 8 #1&2)
172(EDDA) - EDDA. OSLO. SIX YEARLY.
            1970/1 THRU 1971/6 (VOLS 70
            & 71 COMPLETE)
173(ECS) - EIGHTEENTH-CENTURY STUDIES.
            DAVIS, CALIF. QUARTERLY.
            FALL70 THRU SUMMER72 (VOLS
            4 & 5 COMPLETE)
175 - ENGLISH. LONDON. THREE YEARLY.
            SPRING70 THRU AUTUMN71 (VOLS
            19 & 20 COMPLETE)
177(ELT) - ENGLISH LITERATURE IN TRANSI-
            TION. TEMPE, ARIZ. QUARTERLY.
            VOLS 13 & 14 COMPLETE
179(ES) - ENGLISH STUDIES. AMSTERDAM.
            BI-MONTHLY.
            FEB71 THRU DEC71 (VOL 52 COM-
            PLETE)

363 - LITURGICAL ARTS. NEW YORK. QUAR-
TERLY.
NOV70 THRU AUG71 (VOL 39 COM-
PLETE)
368 - LANDFALL. CHRISTCHURCH, N.Z.
QUARTERLY.
MAR70 THRU DEC71 (VOLS 24 &
25 COMPLETE)
376 - THE MALAHAT REVIEW. VICTORIA,
B.C., CANADA. QUARTERLY.
JAN70 & JUL70 THRU OCT71
(#13 & #15-20) [ISSUE OF
APR70 MISSING]
377 - MANUSCRIPTA. ST. LOUIS, MO. THREE
YEARLY.
MAR72 THRU NOV72 (VOL 16 COM-
PLETE)
381 - MEANJIN. PARKVILLE, VICTORIA,
AUSTRALIA. QUARTERLY.
MAR71 THRU DEC71 (VOL 30 COM-
PLETE)
382(MAE) - MEDIUM AEVUM. OXFORD, ENGLAND.
THREE YEARLY.
1972/1 THRU 1972/3 (VOL 41
COMPLETE)
385(MQR) - MICHIGAN QUARTERLY REVIEW.
ANN ARBOR.
WINTER73 THRU FALL73 (VOL 12
COMPLETE)
390 - MIDSTREAM. NEW YORK. MONTHLY.
JAN70 THRU DEC71 (VOLS 16 &
17 COMPLETE)
391(JFI) - JOURNAL OF THE FOLKLORE IN-
STITUTE. BLOOMINGTON, IND.
THREE YEARLY.
VOL 17 COMPLETE [NO REVIEWS
INDEXED]
393(MIND) - MIND. LONDON. QUARTERLY.
JAN71 THRU OCT71 (VOL 80 COM-
PLETE)
396(MODA) - MODERN AGE. CHICAGO. QUAR-
TERLY.
WINTER72 THRU FALL72 (VOL 16
COMPLETE)
397(MD) - MODERN DRAMA. LAWRENCE, KANSAS.
QUARTERLY.
MAY70 THRU FEB72 (VOLS 13 &
14 COMPLETE)
398 - MODERN POETRY STUDIES. BUFFALO,
N.Y. SIX YEARLY, CHANGING TO
THREE YEARLY IN 1973.
VOL 3 #4-6 AND SPRING73 THRU
WINTER73 (73 ISSUES ARE
VOL 4 COMPLETE)
399(MLJ) - MODERN LANGUAGE JOURNAL. MIL-
WAUKEE, WISC. MONTHLY.
JAN71 THRU DEC71 (VOL 55 COM-
PLETE)
400(MLN) - MODERN LANGUAGE NOTES. BALTI-
MORE. SIX YEARLY.
JAN71 THRU DEC71 (VOL 86 COM-
PLETE)
401(MLQ) - MODERN LANGUAGE QUARTERLY.
SEATTLE, WASH.
MAR71 THRU DEC72 (VOLS 32 &
33 COMPLETE)
402(MLR) - MODERN LANGUAGE REVIEW. LON-
DON. QUARTERLY.
JAN72 THRU OCT72 (VOL 67 COM-
PLETE)
405(MP) - MODERN PHILOLOGY. CHICAGO.
QUARTERLY.
AUG70 THRU MAY72 (VOLS 68 &
69 COMPLETE)
406 - MONATSHEFTE. MADISON, WISC. QUAR-
TERLY.
SPRING72 THRU WINTER72 (VOL
64 COMPLETE)

410(M&L) - MUSIC & LETTERS. LONDON.
QUARTERLY.
JAN72 THRU OCT72 (VOL 53 COM-
PLETE)
412 - MUSIC REVIEW. CAMBRIDGE, ENGLAND.
QUARTERLY.
FEB72 THRU NOV72 (VOL 33 COM-
PLETE)
414(MQ) - MUSICAL QUARTERLY. NEW YORK.
JAN70 THRU OCT71 (VOLS 56 &
57 COMPLETE)
415 - MUSICAL TIMES. LONDON. MONTHLY.
JAN72 THRU DEC72 (VOL 113
COMPLETE)
418(MR) - THE MASSACHUSETTS REVIEW.
AMHERST, MASS. QUARTERLY.
WINTER-SPRING72 THRU AUTUMN
72 (VOL 13 COMPLETE)
424 - NAMES. POTSDAM, N.Y. QUARTERLY.
MAR70 THRU DEC71 (VOLS 18 &
19 COMPLETE)
430(NS) - DIE NEUEREN SPRACHEN. FRANK-
FURT AM MAIN. MONTHLY.
JAN70 THRU DEC71 (VOLS 69 &
70 COMPLETE)
432(NEQ) - NEW ENGLAND QUARTERLY. BRUNS-
WICK, MAINE.
MAR71 THRU DEC71 (VOL 44 COM-
PLETE)
433 - NEOPHILOLOGUS. GRONINGEN, THE
NETHERLANDS. QUARTERLY.
JAN70 THRU OCT71 (VOLS 54 &
55 COMPLETE)
439(NM) - NEUPHILOLOGISCHE MITTEILUNGEN.
HELSINKI. QUARTERLY.
1970/1 THRU 1971/4 (VOLS 71
& 72 COMPLETE)
441 - THE NEW YORK TIMES. DAILY.
1JAN73 THRU 31DEC73
442(NY) - THE NEW YORKER. WEEKLY.
6JAN73 THRU 31DEC73 (VOL 48
#46-52, VOL 49 #1-45) [VOL
49 BEGINS WITH 24FEB73 ISSUE]
445(NCF) - NINETEENTH-CENTURY FICTION.
BERKELEY, CALIF. QUARTERLY.
JUN70 THRU MAR72 (VOLS 25 &
26 COMPLETE)
447(N&Q) - NOTES & QUERIES. LONDON.
MONTHLY.
JAN71 THRU DEC71 (VOL 18 COM-
PLETE)
448 - NORTHWEST REVIEW. EUGENE, OREGON.
THREE YEARLY.
FALL70 THRU SUMMER71 (VOL 11
COMPLETE)
453 - THE NEW YORK REVIEW OF BOOKS.
BI-WEEKLY.
25JAN73 THRU 13DEC73 (VOL 19
#11/12 & VOL 20 #1-20)
454 - NOVEL. PROVIDENCE, R.I. THREE
YEARLY.
FALL71 THRU SPRING72 (VOL 5
COMPLETE)
462(OL) - ORBIS LITTERARUM. COPENHAGEN.
QUARTERLY.
VOL 26 COMPLETE
468 - PAKISTAN HORIZON. KARACHI. QUAR-
TERLY.
VOL 22 #1-3, VOL 23 #1&2,
VOL 23 #4 [VOL 21 #3&4, VOL
22 #4 & VOL 23 #3 MISSING]
470 - PAN PIPES. DES MOINES, IOWA.
QUARTERLY.
JAN66 THRU MAY66 & MAY 70
THRU MAY71 (VOL 58 #2-4,
VOL 62 #4 & VOL 63 COMPLETE)
[ISSUE OF MAR70 MISSING]

473(PR) - PARTISAN REVIEW. NEW YORK.
  QUARTERLY.
  1/1972 THRU FALL72 (VOL 39
  COMPLETE)
477 - PERSONALIST. LOS ANGELES. QUAR-
  TERLY.
  WINTER70 THRU AUTUMN71 (VOLS
  51 & 52 COMPLETE)
478 - THE PHILOSOPHICAL JOURNAL. EDIN-
  BURGH. TWICE YEARLY.
  JAN70 THRU JUL71 (VOLS 7 & 8
  COMPLETE)
479(PHQ) - PHILOSOPHICAL QUARTERLY. ST.
  ANDREWS, SCOTLAND.
  JAN71 THRU OCT71 (VOL 21 COM-
  PLETE)
480(P&R) - PHILOSOPHY & RHETORIC. UNI-
  VERSITY PARK, PA. QUARTERLY.
  WINTER70 THRU FALL71 (VOLS 3
  & 4 COMPLETE)
481(PQ) - PHILOLOGICAL QUARTERLY. IOWA
  CITY, IOWA.
  JAN71 THRU OCT71 (VOL 50 COM-
  PLETE)
482(PHR) - PHILOSOPHICAL REVIEW. ITHACA,
  N.Y. QUARTERLY.
  JAN71 THRU OCT71 (VOL 80 COM-
  PLETE)
483 - PHILOSOPHY. LONDON. QUARTERLY.
  JAN71 THRU OCT71 (VOL 46 COM-
  PLETE)
484(PPR) - PHILOSOPHY & PHENOMENOLOGICAL
  RESEARCH. BUFFALO, N.Y.
  QUARTERLY.
  SEP70 THRU JUN72 (VOLS 31 &
  32 COMPLETE)
485(PE&W) - PHILOSOPHY EAST AND WEST.
  HONOLULU. QUARTERLY.
  JAN70 THRU OCT71 (VOLS 20 &
  21 COMPLETE)
486 - PHILOSOPHY OF SCIENCE. EAST LAN-
  SING, MICH. QUARTERLY.
  MAR70 THRU DEC71 (VOLS 37 &
  38 COMPLETE)
487 - PHOENIX. TORONTO. QUARTERLY.
  SPRING71 THRU WINTER71 (VOL
  25 COMPLETE)
490 - POETICA. MÜNCHEN. QUARTERLY.
  JAN/APR70 THRU OCT71 (VOLS
  3 & 4 COMPLETE)
491 - POETRY. CHICAGO. MONTHLY.
  OCT72 THRU SEP73 (VOLS 121 &
  122 COMPLETE)
493 - POETRY REVIEW. LONDON. QUARTERLY.
  SPRING71 THRU WINTER72/73
  (VOLS 62 & 63 COMPLETE)
497(POLR) - POLISH REVIEW. NEW YORK.
  QUARTERLY.
  WINTER70 THRU AUTUMN71 (VOLS
  15 & 16 COMPLETE)
502(PRS) - PRAIRIE SCHOONER. LINCOLN,
  NEBRASKA. QUARTERLY.
  SPRING70 THRU WINTER71/72
  (VOLS 44 & 45 COMPLETE)
503 - THE PRIVATE LIBRARY. PINNER, MID-
  DLESEX, ENGLAND. QUARTERLY.
  SUMMER68, AUTUMN68, WINTER69
  & SPRING70 THRU WINTER71
  (VOL 1 #2&3, VOL 2 #4 & VOLS
  3&4 COMPLETE)
505 - PROGRESSIVE ARCHITECTURE. NEW YORK.
  MONTHLY.
  JAN70 THRU DEC71 (VOLS 51 &
  52 COMPLETE)
517(PBSA) - PAPERS OF THE BIBLIOGRAPHICAL
  SOCIETY OF AMERICA. NEW
  HAVEN, CONN. QUARTERLY.
  JAN-MAR72 THRU OCT-DEC72
  (VOL 66 COMPLETE)

518 - PHILOSOPHICAL BOOKS. LEICESTER,
  ENGLAND. THREE YEARLY.
  JAN72 THRU OCT72 (VOL 13 COM-
  PLETE)
529(QQ) - QUEEN'S QUARTERLY. KINGSTON,
  ONT., CANADA.
  SPRING71 THRU WINTER71 (VOL
  78 COMPLETE)
535(RHL) - REVUE D'HISTOIRE LITTÉRAIRE
  DE LA FRANCE. PARIS. SIX
  YEARLY.
  JAN-FEB70 THRU SEP-DEC71
  (VOLS 70 & 71 COMPLETE)
536 - RATIO. OXFORD, ENGLAND. TWICE
  YEARLY.
  JUN71 & DEC71 (VOL 13 COM-
  PLETE)
539(REN) - RENASCENCE. MILWAUKEE, WISC.
  QUARTERLY.
  AUTUMN68, WINTER69 & AUTUMN69
  THRU SUMMER72 (VOL 21 #1&2,
  VOLS 22, 23 & 24 COMPLETE)
  [SPRING69 & SUMMER69 MISSING]
541(RES) - REVIEW OF ENGLISH STUDIES.
  LONDON. QUARTERLY.
  FEB71 THRU NOV71 (VOL 22 COM-
  PLETE)
542 - REVUE PHILOSOPHIQUE DE LA FRANCE
  ET DE L'ÉTRANGER. PARIS.
  QUARTERLY.
  JAN-MAR70 THRU OCT-DEC71
  (VOLS 160 & 161 COMPLETE)
543 - REVIEW OF METAPHYSICS. NEW HAVEN,
  CONN. QUARTERLY.
  SEP70 THRU JUN71 (VOL 24 COM-
  PLETE)
544 - REVIEW OF NATIONAL LITERATURES.
  JAMAICA, N.Y. TWICE YEARLY.
  SPRING70 THRU FALL72 (VOLS
  1 THRU 3 COMPLETE)
545(RPH) - ROMANCE PHILOLOGY. BERKELEY,
  CALIF. QUARTERLY.
  AUG71 THRU MAY72 (VOL 25 COM-
  PLETE)
546(RR) - ROMANIC REVIEW. NEW YORK.
  QUARTERLY.
  FEB71 THRU DEC71 (VOL 62 COM-
  PLETE)
548(RCSF) - RIVISTA CRITICA DI STORIA
  DELLA FILOSOFIA. FIRENZE,
  ITALY. QUARTERLY.
  JAN-MAR70 THRU OCT-DEC71
  (VOLS 25 & 26 COMPLETE)
549(RLC) - REVUE DE LITTÉRATURE COMPARÉE.
  PARIS. QUARTERLY.
  JAN-MAR70 THRU OCT-DEC71
  (VOLS 44 & 45 COMPLETE)
550(RUSR) - RUSSIAN REVIEW. HANOVER,
  N.H. QUARTERLY.
  JAN71 THRU OCT71 (VOL 30 COM-
  PLETE)
551(RENQ) - RENAISSANCE QUARTERLY. NEW
  YORK.
  SPRING71 THRU WINTER71 (VOL
  24 COMPLETE)
555 - REVUE DE PHILOLOGIE. PARIS. TWICE
  YEARLY.
  VOL 45 COMPLETE
556(RLV) - REVUE DES LANGUES VIVANTES/
  TIJDSCHRIFT VOOR LEVENDE
  TALEN. BRUXELLES. SIX YEARLY.
  1970/1 THRU 1971/6 (VOLS 36
  & 37 COMPLETE)
557(RSH) - REVUE DES SCIENCES HUMAINES.
  LILLE, FRANCE. QUARTERLY.
  JAN-MAR70 THRU OCT-DEC71
  (#137 THRU 144)

563(SS) - SCANDINAVIAN STUDIES. QUARTER-
LY.
WINTER72 THRU AUTUMN72 (VOL
44 COMPLETE)
564 - SEMINAR. TORONTO. THREE YEARLY.
MAR70 THRU OCT71 (VOLS 6 &
7 COMPLETE)
565 - STAND. NEWCASTLE UPON TYNE, ENG-
LAND. QUARTERLY.
VOLS 11 & 12 COMPLETE
566 - THE SCRIBLERIAN. PHILADELPHIA.
TWICE YEARLY.
AUTUMN71 & SPRING72 (VOL 4
COMPLETE)
568(SCN) - SEVENTEENTH-CENTURY NEWS.
NEW YORK. QUARTERLY.
SPRING72 THRU FALL-WINTER72
(VOL 30 COMPLETE)
569(SR) - SEWANEE REVIEW. SEWANEE, TENN.
QUARTERLY.
WINTER72 THRU AUTUMN72 (VOL
80 COMPLETE)
570(SQ) - SHAKESPEARE QUARTERLY. NEW
YORK.
WINTER70 THRU AUTUMN71 (VOLS
21 & 22 COMPLETE)
571 - THE SHAVIAN. LONDON.
SUMMER70 & SPRING71 (VOL 4
#3&4)
572 - SHAW REVIEW. UNIVERSITY PARK, PA.
THREE YEARLY.
JAN70 THRU SEP71 (VOLS 13 &
14 COMPLETE)
573(SSF) - STUDIES IN SHORT FICTION.
NEWBERRY, S.C. QUARTERLY.
WINTER71 THRU FALL71 (VOL 8
COMPLETE)
575(SEER) - SLAVONIC AND EAST EUROPEAN
REVIEW. LONDON. QUARTERLY.
JAN72 THRU OCT72 (VOL 50 COM-
PLETE)
576 - JOURNAL OF THE SOCIETY OF ARCHITEC-
TURAL HISTORIANS. PHILADEL-
PHIA. QUARTERLY.
MAR70 THRU DEC71 (VOLS 29 &
30 COMPLETE)
577(SHR) - SOUTHERN HUMANITIES REVIEW.
AUBURN, ALA. QUARTERLY.
WINTER71 THRU FALL71 (VOL 5
COMPLETE)
578 - SOUTHERN LITERARY JOURNAL. CHAPEL
HILL, N.C. TWICE YEARLY.
SPRING73 & FALL73 (VOL 5 #2
& VOL 6 #1)
579(SAQ) - SOUTH ATLANTIC QUARTERLY.
DURHAM, N.C.
WINTER72 THRU AUTUMN72 (VOL
71 COMPLETE)
581 - SOUTHERLY. SYDNEY, AUSTRALIA.
QUARTERLY.
1971/3 & MAR72 THRU DEC72
(VOL 31 #3 & VOL 32 COMPLETE)
582(SFQ) - SOUTHERN FOLKLORE QUARTERLY.
GAINESVILLE, FLA.
MAR70 THRU DEC71 (VOLS 34 &
35 COMPLETE)
583 - SOUTHERN SPEECH JOURNAL [NAME CHANG-
ED TO SOUTHERN SPEECH COMMUNI-
CATION JOURNAL WITH FALL 71
ISSUE]. WINSTON-SALEM, N.C.
QUARTERLY.
FALL70 THRU SUMMER72 (VOLS
36 & 37 COMPLETE)
584(SWR) - SOUTHWEST REVIEW. DALLAS,
TEXAS. QUARTERLY.
WINTER72 THRU AUTUMN72 (VOL
57 COMPLETE)

589 - SPECULUM. CAMBRIDGE, MASS. QUAR-
TERLY.
JAN72 THRU OCT72 (VOL 47 COM-
PLETE)
590 - SPIRIT. SOUTH ORANGE, N.J. QUAR-
TERLY.
SPRING72 THRU WINTER73 (VOL
39 COMPLETE)
592 - STUDIO INTERNATIONAL. LIVERPOOL.
MONTHLY.
DEC69 THRU DEC71 (VOL 178
#917 AND VOLS 179 THRU 182
COMPLETE)
593 - SYMPOSIUM. SYRACUSE, N.Y. QUAR-
TERLY.
SPRING72 THRU WINTER72 (VOL
26 COMPLETE)
594 - STUDIES IN THE NOVEL. DENTON, TEX.
QUARTERLY.
SPRING70 THRU WINTER71 (VOLS
2 & 3 COMPLETE)
595(SCS) - SCOTTISH STUDIES. EDINBURGH.
TWICE YEARLY.
VOL 16 COMPLETE
596(SL) - STUDIA LINGUISTICA. LUND,
SWEDEN. TWICE YEARLY.
VOL 24 #1&2, VOL 25 #1
597(SN) - STUDIA NEOPHILOLOGICA. UPPSALA,
SWEDEN. TWICE YEARLY.
VOLS 42 & 43 COMPLETE
598(SOR) - THE SOUTHERN REVIEW. BATON
ROUGE, LA. QUARTERLY.
WINTER73 THRU AUTUMN73 (VOL
9 COMPLETE)
599 - STYLE. FAYETTEVILLE, ARK. THREE
YEARLY.
WINTER70 THRU FALL71 (VOLS
4 & 5 COMPLETE)
600 - SUMAC. FREMONT, MICH. THREE
YEARLY.
FALL69 THRU FALL71 (VOLS 2 &
3 COMPLETE, VOL 4 #1) [CEASED
PUBLICATION WITH FALL71]
606(TAMR) - TAMARACK REVIEW. TORONTO.
QUARTERLY.
#58 THRU #61
607 - TEMPO. LONDON. QUARTERLY.
WINTER70/71 (#95), SPRING71
(#96), #97 & #98
613 - THOUGHT. BRONX, N.Y. QUARTERLY.
SPRING70 THRU WINTER71 (VOLS
45 & 46 COMPLETE)
617(TLS) - TIMES LITERARY SUPPLEMENT.
LONDON. WEEKLY.
5JAN73 THRU 28DEC73 (#3696
THRU #3747)
619(TC) - TWENTIETH CENTURY. LONDON.
QUARTERLY.
VOL 178 #1044&1045, VOL 179
COMPLETE [#1043 IS MISSING]
627(UTQ) - UNIVERSITY OF TORONTO QUAR-
TERLY.
FALL70 THRU SUMMER71 (VOL 40
COMPLETE) [THE SUMMER ISSUES
OF THIS TITLE ARE NOT IN-
DEXED]
628 - UNIVERSITY OF WINDSOR REVIEW.
WINDSOR, ONT., CANADA. TWICE
YEARLY.
FALL70 THRU SPRING72 (VOLS
6 & 7 COMPLETE)
636(VP) - VICTORIAN POETRY. MORGANTOWN,
WEST VIRGINIA. QUARTERLY.
SPRING70 THRU WINTER71 (VOLS
8 &.9 COMPLETE)

*       *       *       *       *       *

EACH YEAR WE ARE UNABLE (FOR ONE REASON
OR ANOTHER) TO INDEX THE REVIEWS APPEARING
IN ALL OF THE PERIODICALS SCANNED. THE
FOLLOWING IS A LIST OF THE PERIODICALS
WHOSE REVIEWS WERE <u>NOT</u> INCLUDED IN THIS
VOLUME OF THE INDEX. EVERY ATTEMPT WILL
BE MADE TO INDEX THESE REVIEWS IN THE
NEXT VOLUME OF THE INDEX:

"ACC/DIRECTORY OF CRAFT COURSES."
M. LYON, 139:AUG71-6
AACH, H. - SEE VON GOETHE, J.W.
AARON, D. THE UNWRITTEN WAR.
Q. ANDERSON, 441:11NOV73-4
442(NY):26NOV73-199
AARON, H. SHELTER AND SUBSIDIES.
P. PASSELL & L. ROSS, 453:22MAR73-26
AARON, R.I. KNOWING AND THE FUNCTION OF
REASON.
D.G.C. MAC NABB, 518:MAY72-3
AARSLEFF, H. THE STUDY OF LANGUAGE IN
ENGLAND, 1780-1860.*
B.M.H. STRANG, 206:AUG70-438
AARTS, F.G.A.M., ED. THE PATER NOSTER OF
RICHARD ERMYTE.*
B. HILL, 47(ARL):[N.S.]VOL1-106
P. MERTENS-FONCK, 556(RLV):1971/5-640
ABBAGNANO, N. CRITICAL EXISTENTIALISM.*
(N. LANGIULLI, ED & TRANS)
D. LEMON, 154:JUN71-382
ABBEY, E. BLACK SUN.
T.J. LYON, 649(WAL):SUMMER71-157
ABBI, B.L. & S. SABERWAL, EDS. URGENT
RESEARCH IN SOCIAL ANTHROPOLOGY.
D.M. SPENCER, 318(JAOS):OCT-DEC71-558
ABBIATECI, A. & OTHERS. CRIMES ET CRIMI-
NALITÉ EN FRANCE SOUS L'ANCIEN RÉGIME,
17E-18E SIÈCLES.
R. DARNTON, 453:5APR73-25
ABBOTT, D.E. & OTHERS. WESTMINSTER ABBEY.
W.H. HONAN, 441:2DEC73-97
ABBOTT, H.P. THE FICTION OF SAMUEL
BECKETT.
617(TLS):12OCT73-1217
ABBOTT, S. & B. LOVE. SAPPHO WAS A
RIGHT-ON WOMAN.
M. LAMB, 441:25FEB73-39
ABBOUD, P.F. & OTHERS. ELEMENTARY MODERN
STANDARD ARABIC AND WRITING SUPPLEMENT.
R. ALLEN, 318(JAOS):APR-JUN71-340
ABDEL-MALEK, A. LA DIALECTIQUE SOCIALE.
617(TLS):23FEB73-205
ABDO, D.A. ON STRESS AND ARABIC PHONOL-
OGY.*
M.K. BRAME, 206:NOV71-556
ABÉ, K. DAI YON KAMPYO-KI.
270:VOL22#2-44
ABEL, A. & L. HERMANN. ESCHATOLOGIE ET
COSMOLOGIE.
J-P. AUDET, 154:DEC70-491
ABEL, T. THE FOUNDATION OF SOCIOLOGICAL
THEORY.
K. SYMMONS-SYMONOLEWICZ, 497(POLR):
WINTER71-118
ABELARDO, P. HISTORIA CALAMITATUM.
M. DAL PRA, 548(RCSF):JAN-MAR70-98
ABELARDO, P. SCRITTI DI LOGICA. (M.
DAL PRA, ED)
L.M.P., 543:JUN71-739
ABELLA, I.M. NATIONALISM, COMMUNISM,
AND CANADIAN LABOUR.
P. PHILLIPS, 99:MAY73-38
ABELLIO, R. DANS UNE ÂME ET UN CORPS.
617(TLS):15JUN73-660
ABELS, J. MAN ON FIRE.*
42(AR):SPRING71-136
639(VQR):SUMMER71-CXVII
ABERBACH, M. THE ROMAN-JEWISH WAR (66-
70 A.D.).
L. LEVINE, 328:SPRING71-244
ABERCROMBIE, D. ENGLISH PHONETIC TEXTS.
A.C. GIMSON, 47(ARL):VOL17FASC1-42
ABIAN, A. THE THEORY OF SETS AND TRANS-
FINITE ARITHMETIC.
B. ROTMAN, 316:MAR71-167

ABIR, M. ETHIOPIA: THE ERA OF THE
PRINCES.
V. LULING, 69:JAN71-67
ABLE, D. THE DWIGGINS MARIONETTES.
J.B. MYERS, 139:FEB71-10
"ABORTION: A WOMAN'S GUIDE."
J.E. BRODY, 441:8AUG73-29
ABOUCHAR, A. SOVIET PLANNING AND SPATIAL
EFFICIENCY.
F.E.I. HAMILTON, 575(SEER):JUL72-481
ABOUT, P.J. - SEE PLATO
ABRAHAM BAR HAYYA. THE MEDITATION OF
THE SAD SOUL. (G. WIGODER, TRANS)
J.K.B., 543:JUN71-740
ABRAHAM, L.U., ED. FESTSCHRIFT ERICH
DOFLEIN.
G. ABRAHAM, 415:JUN72-565
ABRAHAM, P. & OTHERS. ROMAIN ROLLAND.*
J. RELINGER, 535(RHL):MAY-JUN70-534
ABRAHAMI, I. THE GAME.
M. LEVIN, 441:26AUG73-31
ABRAHAMS, R.D. JUMP ROPE GAMES.
F.M. WILSON, 203:WINTER71-338
ABRAHAMS, R.D., ED. JUMP-ROPE RHYMES.
E. CRAY, 650(WF):OCT70-289
B.L. HAWES, 292(JAF):APR-JUN71-261
ABRAHAMS, R.D. POSITIVELY BLACK.
W.R. FERRIS, JR., 292(JAF):OCT-DEC71-
458
ABRAHAMS, R.D. - SEE RIDDLE, A.
ABRAHAMS, W., ED. PRIZE STORIES 1970:
THE O. HENRY AWARDS. PRIZE STORIES
1971: THE O. HENRY AWARDS.
S.F. PICKERING, 569(SR):SUMMER72-499
ABRAMS, C. THE LANGUAGE OF CITIES.*
C.P., 505:SEP71-178
ABRAMS, M.H. A GLOSSARY OF LITERARY
TERMS. (3RD ED)
173(ECS):FALL71-196
ABRAMS, M.H. NATURAL SUPERNATURALISM.*
A.R. CHISHOLM, 67:NOV72-279
T. MC FARLAND, 676(YR):WINTER72-279
C. ROSEN, 453:14JUN73-12
ABRAMS, M.H., GENERAL ED. THE NORTON
ANTHOLOGY OF ENGLISH LITERATURE. (REV)
H. KENNER, 441:30DEC73-6
ABRAMS, M.J. THE CANADA-UNITED STATES
PARLIAMENTARY GROUP.
A. BREWIN, 99:OCT73-36
ABRAMSON, D.E. NEGRO PLAYWRIGHTS IN THE
AMERICAN THEATRE, 1925-1959.*
J. FERGUSON, 397(MD):SEP70-231
ABREU, M.I. & C. RAMEH. PORTUGUÊS CON-
TEMPORÂNEO. (VOL 1)
E.R. SUTER, 238:SEP71-618
ABSE, D. FUNLAND AND OTHER POEMS.
A. MACLEAN, 362:16AUG73-223
617(TLS):27APR73-474
ABSE, L. PRIVATE MEMBER.
P. WHITEHEAD, 362:15NOV73-673
617(TLS):30NOV73-1463
ABŪ MA'SHAR. ALBUMASARIS, "DE REVOLU-
TIONIBUS NATIVITATUM."* (D. PINGREE,
ED)
D.R. DICKS, 303:VOL91-162
"THE ACADEMIC WHO'S WHO."
617(TLS):2FEB73-114
ACE, S. STAND ON IT.
M. LEVIN, 441:9DEC73-49
ACHEBE, C. BEWARE, SOUL BROTHER.
617(TLS):4MAY73-491
ACHEBE, C. GIRLS AT WAR AND OTHER STOR-
IES.*
P. ADAMS, 61:MAY73-123
A. BROYARD, 441:14MAR73-35
J. YARDLEY, 441:13MAY73-36
442(NY):14APR73-155

ACHESON, D.  PRESENT AT THE CREATION.*
  M. SYRKIN, 390:MAR70-74
ACHINSTEIN, P.  CONCEPTS OF SCIENCE.
  R.T. GRONTKOWSKI, 258:DEC70-667
ACHINSTEIN, P. & S.F. BARKER, EDS.  THE
  LEGACY OF LOGICAL POSITIVISM.
  T. GREENWOOD, 479(PHQ):JAN71-85
ACHLEITNER, F. & O. UHL.  LOIS WELZEN-
  BACHER, 1889-1955.
  F. HERMAN, 576:MAR71-93
ACKERMANN, R.J.  BELIEF AND KNOWLEDGE.
  617(TLS):2FEB73-133
ACKERMANN, R.J.  MODERN DEDUCTIVE LOGIC.
  R.P.M., 543:JUN71-740
ACKERSON, D., ED.  A PROSE POEM ANTHOL-
  OGY.
  G. KUZMA, 502(PRS):SPRING71-90
ACKLAND, V.  THE NATURE OF THE MOMENT.
  617(TLS):3AUG73-894
ACKRILL, J.L.  ARISTOTLE'S ETHICS.
  617(TLS):10AUG73-937
ACKROYD, P.R. & C.F. EVANS, EDS.  THE
  CAMBRIDGE HISTORY OF THE BIBLE.  (VOL 1)
  J.F. KELLY, 613:WINTER70-630
ACLAND, J.H.  MEDIEVAL STRUCTURE.
  617(TLS):24AUG73-980
"ACTA MUSEI NAPOCENSIS."  (VOL 6)
  M.D. PEYFUSS, 32:JUN72-485
"ACTAS DEL III CONGRESO ESPAÑOL DE ESTU-
  DIOS CLÁSICOS, III."
  C.J. RUIJGH, 361:VOL25#1-73
"ACTES DU VIIIE CONGRÈS."  [ASSOCIATION
  GUILLAUME BUDÉ]
  A.A. LONG, 123:MAR72-93
"ACTES DU PREMIER COLLOQUE FRANCO-JAPON-
  AIS POUR L'ENSEIGNEMENT DE LA LANGUE
  FRANÇAISE AU JAPON (21 AVRIL - 16 MAI
  1970)."
  H. BONNARD, 209(FM):OCT71-350
"ACTES DU QUATRIÈME CONGRÈS DES ROMANISTES
  SCANDINAVES (COPENHAGUE: 8-11 AOÛT 1967)
  DÉDIÉS À HOLGER STEN."
  P.F. DEMBOWSKI, 545(RPH):FEB72-336
LORD ACTON & R. SIMPSON.  THE CORRESPON-
  DENCE OF LORD ACTON AND RICHARD SIMP-
  SON.  (VOL 2) (J.L. ALTHOLZ, D. MC EL-
  RATH & J.C. HOLLAND, EDS)
  617(TLS):12OCT73-1251
ACTON, H.  MEMOIRS OF AN AESTHETE 1939-
  1969.*  (BRITISH TITLE: MORE MEMOIRS
  OF AN AESTHETE.)
  G.A. PANICHAS, 396(MODA):SUMMER72-317
ACTON, H.B.  KANT'S MORAL PHILOSOPHY.*
  J. KOPPER, 342:BAND62HEFT3-417
ACTON, H.B., ED.  THE PHILOSOPHY OF PUN-
  ISHMENT.*
  P.S.A., 154:JUN71-425
"THE ACTORS' ANALECTS."  (C. DUNN & B.
  TORIGOE, TRANS)
  R.H. BROWER, 293(JAST):MAY71-682
AD-DABIR, A.M.A.A.A.H. - SEE UNDER ḤĀJJĪ
  AD-DABIR, A.M.A.A.A.
ADAIR, P.M.  THE WAKING DREAM.
  I.H.C., 191(ELN):SEP71(SUPP)-38
"ADAM."  (L.R. MUIR, TRANS)
  M.D. LEGGE, 208(FS):JUL72-313
ADAM, C.  BIBLIOGRAFÍA Y DOCUMENTOS DE
  EZEQUIEL MARTÍNEZ ESTRADA.*
  H.J. BECCO, 263:APR-JUN72-163
ADAM, H.  MODERNIZING RACIAL DOMINATION.
  617(TLS):26JAN73-82
ÁDÁM, M., ED.  MAGYARORSZÁG KÜLPOLITIKÁJA,
  1938-1939.
  B.J. WINCHESTER, 32:MAR72-235
ADAM, M. - SEE GREGORY, A.
ADAMS, A. & N. NEWHALL.  THE TETONS AND
  THE YELLOWSTONE.
  T.J. LYON, 649(WAL):WINTER72-264

ADAMS, A.E. & J.S.  MEN VERSUS SYSTEMS.
  M. MC CAULEY, 32:JUN72-463
ADAMS, C.D. - SEE LYSIAS
ADAMS, D.K., ED.  THE MYSTERY AND DETEC-
  TION ANNUAL 1972.
  617(TLS):13APR73-427
ADAMS, F.B., JR. - SEE DICKENS, C.
ADAMS, G.B. & OTHERS.  ULSTER DIALECTS.
  H-H. SPEITEL, 47(ARL):[N.S.]VOL1-91
ADAMS, H.  THE INTERESTS OF CRITICISM.
  W.H. CLARK, JR., 290(JAAC):FALL70-130
ADAMS, H.  THE TRUTH ABOUT DRAGONS.
  639(VQR):SUMMER71-CIV
ADAMS, I.  THE TRUDEAU PAPERS.
  W.H. NEW, 102(CANL):SUMMER72-88
"JOHN ADAMS: A BIOGRAPHY IN HIS OWN
  WORDS."  (J.B. PEABODY, ED)
  G.F. SCHEER, 441:16DEC73-12
  442(NY):20AUG73-89
ADAMS, L.D.  THE WINES OF AMERICA.
  R.A. SOKOLOV, 441:2DEC73-84
ADAMS, M.  GOTTFRIED BENN'S CRITIQUE OF
  SUBSTANCE.
  R.W. LAST, 402(MLR):APR72-472
ADAMS, M., ED.  THE GERMAN TRADITION.
  J.M. LINDSAY, 67:NOV72-249
ADAMS, R.F.  WESTERN WORDS.
  K.W. PORTER, 650(WF):OCT70-291
ADAMS, R.M.  PROTEUS, HIS LIES, HIS TRUTH.
  C. LEHMANN-HAUPT, 441:26JAN73-37
  R.A. SOKOLOV, 441:21JAN73-2
ADAMS, R.P.  FAULKNER.*
  F. GADO, 597(SN):VOL42#1-240
ADAMS, T.W.  AKEL.*
  S.G. XYDIS, 32:JUN72-506
ADAMSON, A.H.  SUGAR WITHOUT SLAVES.
  617(TLS):23MAR73-318
ADAMSON, D. - SEE SENCOURT, R.
ADAMSON, J.  GROUCHO, HARPO, CHICO AND
  SOMETIMES ZEPPO.
  R. LASSON, 441:23SEP73-36
ADAMSON, R.  CANTICLES ON THE SKIN.*
  K.L. GOODWIN, 381:SEP71-365
ADCOCK, F.  HIGH TIDE IN THE GARDEN.*
  J.R. REED, 491:APR73-47
  R. SKELTON, 376:OCT71-136
  C.K. STEAD, 368:DEC71-457
ADDISON, J. & R. STEELE.  SELECTIONS FROM
  THE TATLER AND THE SPECTATOR.  (2ND ED)
  (R.J. ALLEN, ED)  CRITICAL ESSAYS FROM
  THE SPECTATOR BY JOSEPH ADDISON, WITH
  FOUR ESSAYS BY RICHARD STEELE.  (D.F.
  BOND, ED)
  J. MOWAT, 566:AUTUMN71-28
ADDISON, W.  ESSEX WORTHIES.
  617(TLS):24AUG73-986
ADELMAN, H.  THE HOLIVERSITY.
  I. DAVIES, 99:NOV-DEC73-16
ADEN, J.M.  SOMETHING LIKE HORACE.*
  A.W. HOFFMAN, 219(GAR):SUMMER70-248
  R.M. OGILVIE, 447(N&Q):FEB71-75
  R. PARKIN, 173(ECS):SPRING71-350
  R.W. ROGERS, 569(SR):AUTUMN72-645
  J. VOISINE, 549(RLC):JUL-SEP71-421
"ADINKIRA SYMBOLS."
  617(TLS):1JUN73-624
ADIZES, I.  INDUSTRIAL DEMOCRACY: YUGO-
  SLAV STYLE.
  D.D. MILENKOVITCH, 32:SEP72-726
ADKINS, A.W.H.  FROM THE MANY TO THE ONE.*
  G.B. KERFERD, 479(PHQ):JUL71-260
  J. ROBINSON, 319:JUL73-397
ADLARD, J.  STENBOCK, YEATS AND THE
  NINETIES.
  R. PYNSENT, 38:BAND89HEFT4-553
  H. SERGEANT, 175:SPRING71-26
ADLEMAN, R.H.  ALIAS BIG CHERRY.
  J. FLAHERTY, 441:14OCT73-44

2

ADLEMAN, R.H. & G. WALTON. THE CHAM-
PAGNE CAMPAIGN.
617(TLS):25MAY73-597
ADLER, A. MÖBLIERTE ERZIEHUNG.
H. BOESCHENSTEIN, 301(JEGP):OCT72-590
ADLER, A. & A. ZEMPLENI. LE BÂTON DE
L'AVEUGLE.
617(TLS):5OCT73-1192
ADLER, E. THOMAS LOVELL BEDDOES.
J. LUNDIN, 597(SN):VOL43#2-593
ADLER, G., WITH A. JAFFÉ - SEE JUNG, C.G.
ADLER, M.J. THE COMMON SENSE OF POLITICS.
S.R. RISKIN, 484(PPR):MAR72-426
ADLER, M.J. THE TIME OF OUR LIVES.
H.S., 543:SEP70-134
ADNÈS, A. ADENÈS, DERNIER GRAND TROUVÈRE.
W. ROTHWELL, 182:VOL24#13/14-538
ADORNO, T.W. GESAMMELTE SCHRIFTEN.
(VOLS 5, 7, 8 & 13) (VOL 7 ED BY R.
TIEDEMANN)
617(TLS):9MAR73-253
ADORNO, T.W. PRISMS.
E. TIMMS, 111:13NOV70-59
ADRADOS, F.R. ESTUDIOS DE LINGÜÍSTICA
GENERAL.
B. POTTIER, 361:VOL26#2-202
ADRIANI, A. - SEE PARLASCA, K.
ADRIANI, A. & OTHERS, EDS. HIMERA. (VOL
1)
J. BOARDMAN, 123:JUN72-294
A. NEUMANN, 182:VOL24#6-309
AELFRIC. HOMILIES OF AELFRIC.* (VOLS
1&2) (J.C. POPE, ED)
J.E. CROSS, 597(SN):VOL43#2-569
M.R. GODDEN, 38:BAND89HEFT2-251
P.M. VERMEER, 433:JUL70-319
"AELFRIC'S FIRST SERIES OF CATHOLIC HOMI-
LIES." (N. ELIASON & P. CLEMOES, EDS)
H. GNEUSS, 38:BAND88HEFT3-368
AESCHYLUS. AESCHYLI SEPTEM QUAE SUPER-
SUNT TRAGOEDIAE. (D. PAGE, ED)
617(TLS):9FEB73-161
AESCHYLUS. AGAMEMNON. (H. LLOYD-JONES,
ED & TRANS)
S. BENARDETE, 24:OCT72-633
D.J. CONACHER, 487:AUTUMN71-272
G. RONNET, 555:VOL45FASC2-333
AESCHYLUS. THE LIBATION BEARERS. THE
EUMENIDES. (H. LLOYD-JONES, ED & TRANS
OF BOTH)
S. BENARDETE, 24:OCT72-633
AESOP. THE FABLES OF AESOP PRINTED FROM
THE VERONESE EDITION OF MCCCCLXXIX IN
LATIN VERSES AND THE ITALIAN VERSION
BY ACCIO ZUCCO. THE FIRST THREE BOOKS
OF CAXTON'S AESOP CONTAINING THE FABLES
ILLUSTRATED IN THE VERONA AESOPUS OF
MCCCCLXXIX. THE WOODCUTS IN BLACK AND
WHITE ENGRAVED FOR THE FABLES OF THE
VERONESE AESOP OF MCCCCLXXIX AND RECUT
FOR THIS EDITION BY ANNA BRAMANTI.
617(TLS):7DEC73-1515
AETHELWULF. DE ABBATIBUS. (A. CAMPBELL,
ED)
C. VAN DE KIEFT, 433:JAN71-106
D. SCHALLER, 38:BAND89HEFT4-506
AFANASIEV, K.N., ED. IZ ISTORII SOVET-
SKOI ARKHITEKTURY, 1917-1925. IZ
ISTORII SOVETSKOI ARKHITEKTURY, 1926-
1932.
S.F. STARR, 576:MAY71-172
AFER, A.G.A. - SEE UNDER AMO AFER, A.G.
AFNAN, R.M. ZOROASTER'S INFLUENCE ON
ANAXAGORAS, THE GREEK TRAGEDIANS, AND
SOCRATES.
J-L. POIRIER, 542:APR-JUN71-225

AFSHĀR, I. INDEX IRANICUS (FIHRIST-I
MAQĀLĀT-I FĀRSĪ). (VOL 2)
A.A. KUDSI-ZADEH, 318(JAOS):JAN-MAR71-
147
AFSHĀR, I. & Ḥ. BANĪ-ĀDAM. KITĀBHĀYI
ĪRĀN. (VOL 1)
A.A. KUDSI-ZADEH, 318(JAOS):OCT-DEC71-
535
AGARD, F.B. & R.J. DI PIETRO. THE SOUNDS
OF ENGLISH AND ITALIAN. THE GRAMMATICAL
STRUCTURES OF ENGLISH AND ITALIAN.
K.V. TEETER & P. VALESIO, 545(RPH):
MAY72-401
AGEE, J. & W. EVANS. LET US NOW PRAISE
FAMOUS MEN.
J. CONDON, 97(CQ):AUTUMN70-200
AGER, D.E. STYLES AND REGISTERS IN CON-
TEMPORARY FRENCH.
P.M. CLIFFORD, 297(JL):OCT71-305
G. SCHWEIG, 430(NS):AUG71-442
AGGELER, W.F. BAUDELAIRE JUDGED BY
SPANISH CRITICS 1857-1957.
H.F. GRANT, 208(FS):OCT72-465
AGNON, S.Y. SHIRA.
B. HOCHMAN, 390:NOV71-68
AGOSTINI DE DEL RÍO, A., ED. FLORES DEL
ROMANCERO.
R.E. BARBERA, 238:MAR71-225
AGRAMONTE, R. MARTÍ Y SU CONCEPCIÓN DEL
MUNDO.
J.I. RASCO, 263:JUL-SEP72-299
AGRAWALA, V.S. - SEE GAṆAPATIŚĀSTRI, M.T.
AGRICOLA, E. SYNTAKTISCHE MEHRDEUTIGKEIT
(POLYSYNTAKTIZITÄT) BEI DER ANALYSE DES
DEUTSCHEN UND DES ENGLISCHEN.*
K. FAISS, 353:SEP70-105
AGRIPPA D'AUBIGNÉ. LES TRAGIQUES. (I.D.
MC FARLANE, ED)
A. BAÏCHE, 535(RHL):JUL-AUG71-690
Y. GIRAUD, 549(RLC):JUL-SEP71-416
AGUILAR, L.E. CUBA 1933.
617(TLS):12JAN73-35
AGUILAR, M.A. ECONOMÍA POLÍTICA Y LUCHA
SOCIAL.
H.B., 543:MAR71-533
AGUILAR PIÑAL, F. CARTELERA PRERROMÁN-
TICA SEVILLANA, AÑOS 1800-1836.
N.B. ADAMS, 240:JAN71-111
AGUILERA MALTA, D. SIETE LUNAS Y SIETE
SERPIENTES.
J. OTERO, 238:MAY71-404
AHERN, M.B. THE PROBLEM OF EVIL.
J. KLEINIG, 63:MAY72-95
J.L. MACKIE, 518:JAN72-1
AHERNE, B. A PROPER JOB.
H.H., 200:MAY70-287
J.P., 376:JAN70-114
AHLBERG, G. FIGHTING ON LAND AND SEA IN
GREEK GEOMETRIC ART.
F. BROMMER, 182:VOL24#5-223
AHLSTROM, S.E. A RELIGIOUS HISTORY OF
THE AMERICAN PEOPLE.*
J.M. CAMERON, 453:31MAY73-19
AHMAD, A. AN INTELLECTUAL HISTORY OF
ISLAM IN INDIA.
N.A. JAWED, 293(JAST):NOV70-201
A. SCHIMMEL, 318(JAOS):APR-JUN71-334
AHMAD, A. ISLAMIC MODERNISM IN INDIA AND
PAKISTAN: 1857-1965.
N.A. JAWED, 293(JAST):NOV70-200
AHMAD, A. - SEE GHALIB
AHMAD, A. & G.E. VON GRUNEBAUM, EDS. MUS-
LIM SELF-STATEMENT IN INDIA AND PAKIS-
TAN, 1857-1968.
A.A.A. FYZEE, 273(IC):APR71-137
AHMAD, Z. SINO-TIBETAN RELATIONS IN THE
SEVENTEENTH CENTURY.
M.C. GOLDSTEIN, 293(JAST):FEB71-438

3

AHMED-BIOUD, A., WITH H. HANAFI & H.
FEKI. 3200 REVUES ET JOURNAUX ARABES
DE 1800 À 1965.
D.H. PARTINGTON, 318(JAOS):OCT-DEC71-
540
AIGNER, D. DIE INDIZIERUNG "SCHÄDLICHEN
UND UNERWÜNSCHTEN SCHRIFTTUMS" IM
DRITTEN REICH.
R.E. CAZDEN, 517(PBSA):OCT-DEC72-448
617(TLS):11MAY73-532
AIKEN, C. COLLECTED POEMS. (2ND ED)
H. WITT, 502(PRS):FALL71-267
AINSA, F. LAS TRAMPAS DE ONETTI.
J. WALKER, 238:DEC71-976
AIRD, C. HIS BURIAL TOO.
N. CALLENDAR, 441:18NOV73-56
AITCHISON, R. FROM BOB TO BUNGLES.
D. AITKIN, 381:MAR71-118
AITKEN, A.J., R.W. BAILEY & N. HAMILTON-
SMITH, EDS. THE COMPUTER AND LITERARY
STUDIES.
617(TLS):8JUN73-636
AIYAR, S.P. THE COMMONWEALTH IN SOUTH
ASIA.
W. LEVI, 293(JAST):NOV70-247
AKAMATSU, P. MEIJI 1868.
H. BOLITHO, 441:11MAR73-3
AKASHII, Y. THE NANYANG CHINESE NATIONAL
SALVATION MOVEMENT, 1937-1941.
S. LEONG, 293(JAST):AUG71-878
AKENSON, D.H. EDUCATION AND ENMITY.
617(TLS):9NOV73-1364
AKHMATOVA, A. POEMS OF AKHMATOVA. (S.
KUNITZ & M. HAYWARD, EDS & TRANS)
J. BRODSKY, 453:9AUG73-9
H. MUCHNIC, 441:21OCT73-6
AKIN RABIBHADANA, M.R. THE ORGANIZATION
OF THAI SOCIETY IN THE EARLY BANGKOK
PERIOD, 1782-1873.
T. BUNNAG, 293(JAST):MAY71-728
AKIRA, T. - SEE UNDER TAKEDA AKIRA
AKRIGG, G.P.V. SHAKESPEARE AND THE EARL
OF SOUTHAMPTON.*
M. CRANE, 570(SQ):WINTER70-85
J.P., 376:JAN70-115
AKSTON, J.J. BEGINNING OF THE BEGINNING.
R. LEBOWITZ, 58:MAY72-30
AL-ANI, S.H. ARABIC PHONOLOGY.
D.H. OBRECHT, 350:SEP72-729
AL-'AZM, S.J. AL-NAQD AL-DHATI BA'D AL-
HAZIMA. NAQD AL-FIKR AL-DINI.
N. REJWAN, 390:APR71-72
AL-AZM, S.J. KANT'S THEORY OF TIME.
P. DUBOIS, 542:JUL-SEP70-353
M. KLEINSCHNIEDER, 342:BAND61HEFT3-
421
AL-AZM, S.J. THE ORIGINS OF KANT'S
ARGUMENTS IN THE ANTINOMIES.*
W.H. WERKMEISTER, 319:OCT73-561
AL-RĀZĪ, F.A. IMĀM FAKHR AL-DĪN AL-RĀZĪ'S
"ILM AL-AKHLĀQ." (M.Ṣ.Ḥ. MA'ṢŪMĪ, ED &
TRANS)
J. VAN ESS, 182:VOL24#23/24-839
AL-ZAMAKHSHARĪ. PĪSHROW-E ADAB (MUQADDI-
MAT AL-ADAB). (M.K. EMAM, ED)
G.M. WICKENS, 318(JAOS):OCT-DEC71-533
ALARD DE CAMBRAI. LE LIVRE DE PHILOSO-
PHIE ET DE MORALITÉ D'ALARD DE CAMBRAI.
(J.C. PAYEN, ED)
W. ROTHWELL, 208(FS):OCT72-440
P. ZUMTHOR, 433:OCT70-427
ALAYA, F. WILLIAM SHARP - "FIONA MAC-
LEOD:" 1855-1905.
A.J. SAMBROOK, 637(VS):JUN71-467
639(VQR):WINTER71-XXXVI
ALBARET, C., WITH G. BELMONT. MONSIEUR
PROUST.
617(TLS):21DEC73-1559

ALBÉRÈS, R-M. LE ROMAN D'AUJOURD'HUI
1960-1970.
M. CAGNON, 399(MLJ):MAR71-196
A. MARISSEL, 207(FR):OCT70-252
ALBERICCI, C. IL MOBILE LOMBARDO.
A.G-P., 135:APR70-277
ALBERIGO, G. CARDINALATO E COLLEGIALITA.
B. TIERNEY, 589:JAN72-99
ALBERS, J. INTERACTION OF COLOR.
R.D. ABBEY, 127:FALL71-110
ALBERS, W. & OTHERS. SOZIALPRODUKT,
ÖFFENTLICHE HAUSHALTE UND BILDUNGS-
AUSGABEN IN DER BUNDESREPUBLIK.
J-M. FLOQUET, 182:VOL24#5-201
ALBERTI, L.B. THE FAMILY IN RENAISSANCE
FLORENCE.
J.E. SEIGEL, 551(RENQ):SPRING71-53
ALBERTI, L.B. ON PAINTING AND ON SCULP-
TURE. (C. GRAYSON, ED & TRANS)
617(TLS):13APR73-429
ALBERTIN, L. LIBERALISMUS UND DEMOKRATIE
AM ANFANG DER WEIMARER REPUBLIK.
617(TLS):12OCT73-1230
ALBERTSEN, E. RATIO UND "MYSTIK" IM
WERK ROBERT MUSILS.*
R. VON HEYDEBRAND, 657(WW):SEP/OCT71-
358
ALBERTSON, C. BESSIE.
W. BALLIETT, 442(NY):24FEB73-128
S. BROWN, 362:16AUG73-222
G. DAVIS, 441:18FEB73-28
617(TLS):28DEC73-1593
ALBIA SALLES, I.B. LA RAÍZ DE LAS HORAS.
E.B. LABRADA, 37:OCT70-40
ALBINI, U. & A. LUPPINO, EDS. PAGINE
CRITICHE DI LETTERATURA GRECA.
R. WEIL, 555:VOL45FASC1-142
ALBINO, O. THE SUDAN.
J. BUXTON, 69:JAN71-68
ALBION, R.G. NAVAL AND MARITIME HISTORY.
(4TH ED)
617(TLS):19JAN73-73
ALBION, R.G., W.A. BAKER & B.W. LABAREE.
NEW ENGLAND AND THE SEA.
D. PIERCE-JONES, 70(ANQ):MAR73-110
DE ALBORNOZ, A. LA PRESENCIA DE MIGUEL
DE UNAMUNO EN ANTONIO MACHADO.*
G. RIBBANS, 86(BHS):JAN72-91
ALBOUY, P. - SEE HUGO, V.
ALBRECHT, K. NINETEENTH CENTURY AUSTRAL-
IAN GOLD & SILVERSMITHS.
C. OMAN, 135:SEP71-64
VON ALBRECHT, M. & E. ZINN, EDS. OVID.*
M.P.O. MORFORD, 122:APR72-139
ALBRECHT, R.C., ED. THE WORLD OF SHORT
FICTION.
J.W. STEVENSON, 573(SSF):SUMMER71-475
ALBUMASARIS - SEE UNDER ABŪ MA'SHAR
ALCAIDE, V.M.N. - SEE UNDER NIETO AL-
CAIDE, V.M.
ALCOTT, A.B. THE LETTERS OF A. BRONSON
ALCOTT.* (R.L. HERRNSTADT, ED)
W. WHITE, 646(WWR):SEP70-90
ALCOVER, M. LA PENSÉE PHILOSOPHIQUE ET
SCIENTIFIQUE DE CYRANO DE BERGERAC.
U. SCHULZ-BUSCHHAUS, 72:BAND209HEFT
1/3-215
ALDERMAN, G. THE RAILWAY INTEREST.
617(TLS):4MAY73-490
ALDERSON, W.L. & A.C. HENDERSON. CHAUCER
AND AUGUSTAN SCHOLARSHIP.*
P.L. HEYWORTH, 382(MAE):1972/3-273
H.H. SCHLESS, 481(PQ):JUL71-374
ALDISS, B. BILLION YEAR SPREE.
T. STURGEON, 441:23SEP73-39
ALDING, P. FIELD OF FIRE.
617(TLS):3AUG73-911

4

ALDINGTON, R. RICHARD ALDINGTON: SELECTED
CRITICAL WRITINGS, 1928-1960. (A. KER-
SHAW, ED)
M. POLI, 402(MLR):JUL72-625
ALDINGTON, R. LIFE FOR LIFE'S SAKE.
E. DELAVENAY, 189(EA):JAN-MAR70-97
ALDISS, B.W. BILLION YEAR SPREE.
617(TLS):9NOV73-1375
ALDISS, B.W. FRANKENSTEIN UNBOUND.
R. BLYTHE, 362:4OCT73-459
617(TLS):9NOV73-1377
ALDRED, C. TUTANKHAMUN'S EGYPT.
617(TLS):11MAY73-537
ALDRIDGE, A.O., ED. COMPARATIVE LITERA-
TURE.*
L.H. PEER, 219(GAR):SUMMER70-252
ALDRIDGE, A.O., ED. THE IBERO-AMERICAN
ENLIGHTENMENT.*
H. BERNSTEIN, 263:JAN-MAR72-45
A. DONOSO, 319:JUL73-413
J. LÓPEZ-MORILLAS, 149:DEC72-465
ALDRIDGE, J. A SPORTING PROPOSITION.
M. LEVIN, 441:9DEC73-47
ALDRIN, E.E., JR., WITH W. WARGA. RETURN
TO EARTH.
J. MC ELROY, 441:21OCT73-5
ALDWINCKLE, R. DEATH IN THE SECULAR
CITY.
617(TLS):5OCT73-1190
ALEGRIA, F. INSTRUCTIONS FOR UNDRESSING
THE HUMAN RACE.
E. FEINSOD, 114(CHIR):JAN-FEB71-156
ALEGRÍA, F. LA LITERATURA CHILENA DEL
SIGLO XX. (2ND ED)
D.R. REEDY, 238:SEP71-603
ALEJANDRO, C.F.D. - SEE UNDER DÍAZ ALE-
JANDRO, C.F.
ALEJO, A.E.D. & E. PRADO VELÁZQUEZ - SEE
UNDER DÍAZ ALEJO, A.E. & E. PRADO VEL-
ÁZQUEZ
ALEKSANDROV, V.A. ROSSIIA NA DAL'NEVOS-
TOCHNYKH RUBEZHAKH (VTORAIA POLOVINA
XVII V.).
R.H. FISHER, 32:MAR72-151
ALEKSANOV, P.A. V BOR'BE ZA SOTSIALIST-
ICHESKOE PEREUSTROISTVO DEREVNI
(KREST'IANSKAIA VZAIMOPOMOSCH', 1921-
1932 GG.).
D. ATKINSON, 32:DEC72-899
ALEVIZOS, T. & S., EDS & TRANS. FOLK
SONGS OF GREECE.
M.L. ARNOTT, 650(WF):JAN70-63
ALEXANDER, A. OPERANATOMY.
C. GRAHAM, 415:JAN72-45
ALEXANDER, A. GIOVANNI VERGA.*
J.W. KLEIN, 415:OCT72-976
ALEXANDER, C.H.O. FISCHER V. SPASSKY:
REYKJAVIK 1972. (D. BIRDSALL, ED)
617(TLS):6APR73-401
ALEXANDER, G. SILENT INVASION.
617(TLS):20JUL73-824
ALEXANDER, J.J.G. NORMAN ILLUMINATION AT
MONT ST. MICHEL, 966-1100.*
J. BECKWITH, 39:OCT70-314
C.R. DODWELL, 382(MAE):1972/2-137
H.B. GRAHAM, 377:MAR72-50
C.M.K., 135:AUG70-288
ALEXANDER, J.J.G. & A.C. DE LA MARE. THE
ITALIAN MANUSCRIPTS IN THE LIBRARY OF
MAJOR J.R. ABBEY.*
W.O.H., 135:JUL70-214
J.J. JOHN, 589:JAN72-100
ALEXANDER, M. DER DEUTSCH-TSCHECHOSLO-
WAKISCHE SCHIEDSVERTRAG VON 1925 IM
RAHMEN DER LOCARNO-VERTRÄGE.
S.B. WINTERS, 32:JUN72-473
ALEXANDER, M. - SEE "THE EARLIEST ENGLISH
POEMS"

ALEXANDER, S. THE HAND OF MICHELANGELO.
M. MILLER, 275(IQ):SUMMER71-108
ALEXANDRE, P. EXÉCUTION D'UN HOMME
POLITIQUE.
617(TLS):16FEB73-177
ALEXANDRE, P., ED. FRENCH PERSPECTIVES
IN AFRICAN STUDIES.
617(TLS):27APR73-480
ALEXANDRIAN, S. SURREALIST ART.*
B. REISE, 592:NOV70-214
"AL-FĀRĀBĪ'S BOOK OF LETTERS (KITĀB AL-
HURŪF) COMMENTARY ON ARISTOTLE'S META-
PHYSICS." (M. MAHDI, ED)
L.E. GOODMAN, 485(PE&W):APR71-220
"ALFARABI'S PHILOSOPHY OF PLATO AND ARIS-
TOTLE." (M. MAHDI, TRANS)
T. IZUTSU, 485(PE&W):APR70-196
ALFIERI, V. TRAGEDIE. (VOL 11) (R. DE
BELLO, ED)
G.G. FERRERO, 228(GSLI):VOL148FASC
464-616
ALFONSO, O.M. THEODORE ROOSEVELT AND THE
PHILIPPINES, 1897-1909.
P.W. STANLEY, 293(JAST):MAY71-740
ALFONSO, P. THE SCHOLAR'S GUIDE.* (J.R.
JONES & J.E. KELLER, EDS & TRANS)
S.G. ARMISTEAD & J.H. SILVERMAN,
582(SFQ):MAR71-93
ALFONZO, J.P.P. - SEE UNDER PÉREZ ALFONZO,
J.P.
ALFORD, B.W.E. W.D. AND H.O. WILLS AND
THE DEVELOPMENT OF THE U.K. TOBACCO
INDUSTRY 1786-1965.
J. VAIZEY, 362:5JUL73-23
617(TLS):3AUG73-898
ALFORD, M.H.T. & V.L. RUSSIAN-ENGLISH
SCIENTIFIC AND TECHNICAL DICTIONARY.
L. BERNHARDT, 399(MLJ):OCT71-403
ALGAROTTI, F. & S. BETTINELLI. OPERE.
(E. BONORA, ED)
P.Z., 228(GSLI):VOL148FASC462/463-465
ALGER, H., JR. SILAS SNOBDEN'S OFFICE
BOY.
J. SEELYE, 441:25MAR73-44
ALGREN, N. THE LAST CAROUSEL.
J.R. FRAKES, 441:11NOV73-20
ALHONIEMI, A. ÜBER DIE FUNKTIONEN DER
WOHIN-KASUS IM TSCHEREMISSISCHEN.
A. RAUN, 361:VOL26#1-108
ALI, S. DE LA PROJECTION.
Y. BRÈS, 542:JAN-MAR71-121
ALIGHIERI, D. - SEE UNDER DANTE ALIGHIERI
ALINEI, M.L. SPOGLI ELETTRONICI DELL'-
ITALIANO DELLE ORIGINI E DEL DUECENTO.*
(VOL 2, PT 1) (A. SCHIAFFINI, ED)
G. FRANCESCATO, 361:VOL25#3-326
G.C. LEPSCHY, 353:DEC70-118
ALIOTTA, A. IL NUOVO POSITIVISMO E LO
SPERIMENTALISMO.
E. NAMER, 542:JAN-MAR70-95
ALLABY, M. WHO WILL EAT?
617(TLS):12JAN73-46
ALLAN, A. & C. WOODWORTH. MISS ELIZABETH
ARDEN.
617(TLS):12OCT73-1240
ALLAND, A., JR. THE HUMAN IMPERATIVE.
P.B. MEDAWAR, 453:8MAR73-21
ALLARD, D.C. & B. BERN, COMPS. U.S.
NAVAL HISTORY SOURCES IN THE WASHINGTON
AREA AND SUGGESTED RESEARCH SUBJECTS.
D.F. HARRISON, 14:JUL71-314
ALLARD, M. LE PROBLÈME DES ATTRIBUTS
DIVINS DANS LA DOCTRINE D'AL-AŠ'ARĪ ET
DE SES PREMIERS GRANDS DISCIPLES.
R. LEMAY, 154:MAR71-190

ALLARD, S. RUSSIA AND THE AUSTRIAN STATE
  TREATY.
    H. HANAK, 575(SEER):JUL72-480
    R.J. RATH, 32:JUN72-462
ALLAUN, F., ED. NO PLACE LIKE HOME.
    617(TLS):6APR73-372
ALLBEURY, T. A CHOICE OF ENEMIES.
    R. BRYDEN, 362:18JAN73-90
    N. CALLENDAR, 441:18MAR73-41
    617(TLS):23FEB73-219
ALLCHIN, B. & R. THE BIRTH OF INDIAN
  CIVILIZATION.*
    L. ROCHER, 318(JAOS):JAN-MAR71-153
ALLDRIDGE, J.C. ILSE AICHINGER.
    K. BULLIVANT, 402(MLR):JUL72-711
    P. PROCHNIK, 220(GL&L):JUL72-401
ALLDRITT, K. THE MAKING OF GEORGE
  ORWELL.
    502(PRS):FALL70-278
ALLDRITT, K. THE VISUAL IMAGINATION OF
  D.H. LAWRENCE.
    E. BRANDABUR, 301(JEGP):JUL72-457
ALLEAU, R. ENIGMES ET SYMBOLES DU MONT-
  SAINT-MICHEL.
    R.H. BLOCH, 207(FR):MAR71-778
ALLEN, B. PRINT COLLECTING.
    G. WILLS, 39:NOV70-400
ALLEN, D. ANON AND VARIOUS TIME MACHINE
  POEMS.
    L. PHILLIPS, 491:FEB73-303
ALLEN, D. BATTLE FOR BRITAIN.
    617(TLS):9NOV73-1381
ALLEN, D. THE REASONABLENESS OF FAITH.
    R.E. SANTONI, 258:MAR70-157
ALLEN, D. - SEE O'HARA, F.
ALLEN, D.C. THE HARMONIOUS VISION.*
    J. GILLET, 549(RLC):JUL-SEP71-420
ALLEN, D.C. MYSTERIOUSLY MEANT.
    M. MURRIN, 301(JEGP):JAN72-119
    A. NAGEL, 481(PQ):APR71-310
    J. SEZNEC, 400(MLN):DEC71-946
    639(VQR):SUMMER71-CIX
ALLEN, E. STONE SHELTERS.
    W.C. KIDNEY, 505:JUN71-114
ALLEN, E.S. CHILDREN OF THE LIGHT.
    E. WEEKS, 61:DEC73-136
ALLEN, G.W. WILLIAM JAMES.*
    R. ASSELINEAU, 189(EA):JUL-SEP71-348
ALLEN, G.W. A READER'S GUIDE TO WALT
  WHITMAN.
    F. STOVALL, 646(WWR):DEC70-123
ALLEN, H.B. LINGUISTICS AND ENGLISH
  LINGUISTICS.
    H. GNEUSS, 38:BAND88HEFT1-99
ALLEN, H.B. & G.N. UNDERWOOD, EDS. READ-
  INGS IN AMERICAN DIALECTOLOGY.
    N. CONKLIN, 351(LL):DEC71-269
ALLEN, H.R. THE LEGACY OF LORD TREN-
  CHARD.
    617(TLS):19JAN73-71
ALLEN, H.R. THE QUEEN'S MESSENGER.
    617(TLS):6APR73-401
ALLEN, J.B. THE FRIAR AS CRITIC.
    B. COTTLE, 301(JEGP):JAN72-116
    V.M. LAGORIO, 377:JUL72-120
    B. SMALLEY, 382(MAE):1972/3-276
    639(VQR):AUTUMN71-CLXXII
ALLEN, J.D. - SEE COOKE, P.P.
ALLEN, J.J. DON QUIXOTE: HERO OR FOOL?*
    E.C. RILEY, 240(HR):OCT71-450
ALLEN, J.V. COWBOY LORE.
    W. GARD, 584(SWR):WINTER72-76
ALLEN, M. POE AND THE BRITISH MAGAZINE
  TRADITION.*
    J.R. MC ELRATH, JR., 577(SHR):SUMMER
    71-289
    R.S. MOORE, 219(GAR):WINTER71-481
                           [CONTINUED]

[CONTINUING]
    B.R. POLLIN, 445(NCF):DEC70-371
    S.L. VARNADO, 613:SPRING70-124
ALLEN, M. PORTRAIT PHOTOGRAPHY.
    617(TLS):7SEP73-1037
ALLEN, N.W., JR., ED. PROVINCE AND
  COURT RECORDS OF MAINE. (VOL 5)
    H.A. JOHNSON, 656(WMQ):JAN71-157
ALLEN, P.S. THE ROMANESQUE LYRIC.
    L.J. FRIEDMAN, 545(RPH):FEB72-365
ALLEN, R. A SHORT INTRODUCTION TO THE
  HISTORY AND POLITICS OF SOUTHEAST ASIA.
    L.W. PYE, 293(JAST):FEB71-500
ALLEN, R. THE SOCIAL PASSION.
    M. PRANG, 99:APR73-31
ALLEN, R.E. PLATO'S "EUTHYPHRO" AND THE
  EARLIER THEORY OF FORMS.*
    I.M. CROMBIE, 123:DEC72-330
    J. DYBIKOWSKI, 154:SEP71-565
    D.W. HAMLYN, 483:APR71-170
    R.K. SPRAGUE, 122:APR72-153
ALLEN, R.E., ED. STUDIES IN PLATO'S
  METAPHYSICS.
    J.V. BROWN, 154:DEC70-449
ALLEN, R.F. FIRE AND IRON.
    T.M. ANDERSSON, 301(JEGP):JAN72-100
    P. SCHACH, 563(SS):AUTUMN72-555
ALLEN, R.J. - SEE ADDISON, J. & R. STEELE
ALLEN, R.R. - SEE ERASMUS
ALLEN, S.S. SAMUEL PHELPS AND SADLER'S
  WELLS THEATRE.
    C.B. HOGAN, 676(YR):AUTUMN71-134
ALLEN, T.B. THE LAST INMATE.
    N. CALLENDAR, 441:21OCT73-49
ALLEN, W., ED. TRANSATLANTIC CROSSING.
    H.L., 131(CL):SUMMER72-269
ALLEN, W. - SEE BOIS, J.
ALLEN, W.E.D., ED. RUSSIAN EMBASSIES TO
  THE GEORGIAN KINGS (1589-1605).
    A.P. NOVOSELTSEV, 32:DEC72-880
ALLINGHAM, M. THE ALLINGHAM MINIBUS.
    617(TLS):18MAY73-562
ALLISON, A.F., COMP. THOMAS LODGE 1558-
  1625.
    617(TLS):13APR73-428
ALLISON, P. AFRICAN STONE SCULPTURE.
    E.L.R. MEYEROWITZ, 39:JUL70-81
    A. RUBIN, 54:SEP70-348
ALLISON, P. CROSS RIVER MONOLITHS.
    R. HARRIS, 69:OCT70-403
ALLISON, R.S. THE SEEDS OF TIME.
    617(TLS):23FEB73-222
ALLON, Y. THE MAKING OF ISRAEL'S ARMY.
    S.L.A. MARSHALL, 390:APR71-63
ALLOTT, A. NEW ESSAYS IN AFRICAN LAW.
    C.M. MC DOWELL, 69:OCT71-335
ALLOTT, K. - SEE BROWNING, R.
ALLOTT, M. - SEE KEATS, J.
ALLOWAY, L. VIOLENT AMERICA.
    W.D. CASE, 58:APR72-26
ALLROGGEN, G. E.T.A. HOFFMANNS KOMPOSI-
  TIONEN.
    G.A., 410(M&L):JAN72-84
ALLSOPP, B. ROMANESQUE ARCHITECTURE.
    J. BECKWITH, 39:OCT71-322
ALLSOPP, B. - SEE JONES, I.
ALLWORTH, E., ED. THE NATIONALITY QUES-
  TION IN SOVIET CENTRAL ASIA.
    617(TLS):26OCT73-1297
ALLWORTH, E., ED. SOVIET NATIONALITY
  PROBLEMS.
    D.B. SHIMKIN, 32:SEP72-700
    617(TLS):3AUG73-910
ALMARÁZ, F.D., JR. TRAGIC CAVALIER.
    W. GARD, 584(SWR):WINTER72-76
ALONSO, D. HIJOS DE LA IRA. (E.L.
  RIVERS, ED)
    C.B. MORRIS, 86(BHS):JUL72-314

6

ALONSO, J.M. THE PASSION OF ROBERT BRON-
SON.
J. RICHMOND, 473(PR):FALL72-627
ALONSO, L.R. EL CANDIDATO.
A.A. BORRAS, 238:SEP71-600
ALONSO, M. EVOLUCIÓN SINTÁCTICA DEL ES-
PAÑOL.
B. DUTTON, 47(ARL):VOL17FASC1-58
DE ALOYSIO, F. LEGGERE DEWEY.
E. NAMER, 542:JUL-SEP70-353
ALPATOV, M.W. ART TREASURES OF RUSSIA.
R.R. MILNER-GULLAND, 39:JAN71-73
ALPERA, L. LOS NOMBRES TRECENTISTAS DE
BOTÁNICA VALENCIANA EN FRANCESC EIXI-
MENIS.
J. GULSOY, 240(HR):APR71-233
ALPERA, L. - SEE MATUTE, A.M.
ALPERS, S. LEGENDS OF THE SOUTH SEA.
J. SIMPSON, 203:SUMMER70-151
ALPERS, K. BERICHT ÜBER STAND UND METH-
ODE DER AUSGABE DES ETYMOLOGICUM GENU-
INUM (MIT EINER AUSGABE DES BUCHSTABEN
L).*
E. DUKE, 303:VOL91-161
ALPERS, P.J. THE POETRY OF "THE FAERIE
QUEENE."*
J.E. HARTMAN, 599:SPRING70-163
ALPERS, P.J., ED. EDMUND SPENSER.
J. VOISINE, 549(RLC):JAN-MAR71-103
ALPERT, H. SMASH.
D. ADLER, 441:25NOV73-47
ALQUIÉ, F. LA CRITIQUE KANTIENNE DE LA
MÉTAPHYSIQUE.
J. KOPPER, 342:BAND61HEFT1-126
ALQUIÉ, F., ED. ENTRETIENS SUR LE SUR-
RÉALISME.
A.J. ARNOLD, 207(FR):APR71-976
ALQUIÉ, F., ED. LE SURRÉALISME.
M.A. CAWS, 188(ECR):SUMMER70-150
ALSDORF-BOLLÉE, A. & I. BURR. RÜCKLÄU-
FIGER STICHWORTINDEX ZUM ROMANISCHEN
ETYMOLOGISCHEN WÖRTERBUCH.
G. PLANGG, 430(NS):JUN70-308
ALSOP, S. STAY OF EXECUTION.
N. KOLTZ, 441:30DEC73-14
C. LEHMANN-HAUPT, 441:22NOV73-35
ALSTON, R.C. A BIBLIOGRAPHY OF THE ENG-
LISH LANGUAGE FROM THE INVENTION OF
PRINTING TO THE YEAR 1800. (VOLS 1,
5 & 8)
N.E. OSSELTON, 179(ES):FEB71-90
ALTBACH, P.G. STUDENT POLITICS IN BOMBAY.
J.P. HAITHCOX, 293(JAST):AUG71-912
ALTENHOFER, N. HOFMANNSTHALS LUSTSPIEL
"DER UNBESTECHLICHE."
L.M. FIEDLER, 657(WW):JAN/FEB70-62
M.E. GILBERT, 220(GL&L):JAN72-186
W. NEHRING, 52:BAND6HEFT1-113
ALTENHOFER, N. - SEE "HEINRICH HEINE"
ALTER, J.V. LES ORIGINES DE LA SATIRE
ANTIBOURGEOISE EN FRANCE. (VOL 2)
J. CROW, 208(FS):APR72-198
A. VARTANIAN, 207(FR):MAY71-1134
ALTER, R. AFTER THE TRADITION.
D.H. HIRSCH, 328:SPRING70-234
ALTER, R. FIELDING AND THE NATURE OF THE
NOVEL.
M. IRWIN, 541(RES):FEB71-89
T.E. MARESCA, 223:SEP70-289
H.K. MILLER, 149:MAR72-116
J. PRESTON, 184(EIC):JAN71-91
A. WRIGHT, 594:SUMMER70-239
ALTHAUS, H.P. ERGEBNISSE DER DIALEKTOLO-
GIE.
E.H. YARRILL, 182:VOL24#5-206
ALTHOLZ, J.L., D. MC ELRATH & J.C. HOL-
LAND - SEE LORD ACTON & R. SIMPSON

ALTHUSSER, L. POLITICS AND HISTORY.
617(TLS):15JUN73-667
ALTICK, R.D. VICTORIAN STUDIES IN SCAR-
LET.
P. COLLINS, 155:SEP71-174
J. ESPEY, 445(NCF):JUN71-126
T. FLANAGAN, 637(VS):JUN71-470
617(TLS):13APR73-427
ALTICK, R.D. & J.F. LOUCKS 2D. BROWN-
ING'S ROMAN MURDER STORY.*
R.O. PREYER, 637(VS):SEP70-98
ALTIERI BIAGI, M.L. GALILEO E LA TERMIN-
OLOGIA TECNICO-SCIENTIFICA.
W.T. ELWERT, 72:BAND209HEFT4/6-445
ALTIZER, T.J.J. THE NEW APOCALYPSE.
G.E. BENTLEY, JR., 627(UTQ):FALL70-86
ALTRUP, H.F. DIE FLACHENNUTZUNGSPLANUNG
IM JUNGSTEN WACHSTUMSPROZESS DEUTSCHER
GROSS-STADTE.
G. ALBERS, 182:VOL24#15/16-635
ALVA. WITH PEN AND BRUSH.
617(TLS):26OCT73-1325
ALVAR, M. EL ROMANCERO.
J.G. CUMMINS, 86(BHS):JUL72-295
ALVAREZ, A. SAMUEL BECKETT.
J. EPSTEIN, 441:25NOV73-6
ALVAREZ, A., ED. HUNGARIAN SHORT STORIES.
R.V. ADKINSON, 556(RLV):1970/1-107
ALVAREZ, A. THE SAVAGE GOD.*
M. PERLOFF, 295:NOV72-581
ALVAREZ, G.D.C. TOPÓNIMOS EN APELLIDOS
HISPANOS.*
P. BOYD-BOWMAN, 240(HR):JAN71-83
ALVIN, J. MUSIC FOR THE HANDICAPPED
CHILD.
M. SEARS, 470:MAY66-25
ALY, W. VOLKSMÄRCHEN, SAGE UND NOVELLE
BEI HERODOT UND SEINEN ZEITGENOSSEN.
(2ND ED REV BY L. HUBER)
E. ETTLINGER, 203:SUMMER70-155
AMABILE, G. BLOOD TIES.
R. DICKINSON-BROWN, 398:SPRING73-122
J. DITSKY, 99:AUG73-35
AMACHER, R.E. EDWARD ALBEE.*
W. WILLEFORD, 397(MD):FEB71-450
AMADI, E. SUNSET IN BIAFRA.
617(TLS):21DEC73-1556
AMADO, J. TENDA DOS MILAGRES.
M. SILVERMAN, 238:MAR71-206
AMADOU, R. - SEE MESMER, F-A.
AMALRIK, A. INVOLUNTARY JOURNEY TO
SIBERIA.*
J.A. ARMSTRONG, 550(RUSR):APR71-188
639(VQR):WINTER71-XXXIII
AMALRIK, A. WILL THE SOVIET UNION SUR-
VIVE UNTIL 1984?*
639(VQR):SPRING71-LXXIX
AMBROGIO, I. - SEE LENIN, V.I.
AMBROSE, A. & M. LAZEROWITZ, EDS. G.E.
MOORE: ESSAYS IN RETROSPECT.*
J.D. CARNEY, 484(PPR):DEC71-276
G.J. WARNOCK, 393(MIND):APR71-305
AMBROSE, A. & M. LAZEROWITZ, EDS. LUDWIG
WITTGENSTEIN: PHILOSOPHY AND LANGUAGE.*
C. LYAS, 518:OCT72-1
AMBROSETTI, G. LA FILOSOFIA SOCIALE DI
MAINE DE BIRAN.
E. NAMER, 542:JAN-MAR70-96
AMBROSI, J. & F. FRANCK. CROQUIS PARIS-
IENS.
B. EBLING, 207(FR):APR71-1000
AMBROSINI, M.L., WITH M. WILLIS. THE SEC-
RET ARCHIVES OF THE VATICAN.
J.W. MANIGAULTE, 14:OCT70-404
"AMERICAN BOOK-PRICES CURRENT, 1967."
(VOL 73) (E.P. HAZEN, G. MILNE & W.J.
SMITH, EDS)
A. MASON, 517(PBSA):OCT-DEC72-441

"AMERICAN BOOK-PRICES CURRENT, 1968."*
(VOL 74) (E.P. HAZEN, G. MILNE & P.H.
HEMINGSON, EDS)
J.W. BONNER, JR., 517(PBSA):APR-JUN72-
215
"AMERICAN BOOK-PRICES CURRENT 1970."
(VOL 76)
617(TLS):10AUG73-936
"THE AMERICAN HEALTH EMPIRE."
42(AR):SPRING71-135
"AMERICAN PAINTINGS IN THE MUSEUM OF FINE
ARTS, BOSTON."
W.H. GERDTS, 56:AUTUMN70-307
"AMERICAN REVIEW 16." (T. SOLOTAROFF, ED)
A. BROYARD, 441:31JAN73-43
AMÉRICO MAIA, P. A PROBLEMÁTICA MORAL NO
MODERNO ROMANCE BRASILEIRO.
F.P. ELLISON, 240(HR):OCT71-466
AMERY, J. APPROACH MARCH.
R. CROSSMAN, 362:15NOV73-672
617(TLS):16NOV73-1387
DE AMESCUA, A.M. - SEE UNDER MIRA DE
AMESCUA, A.
AMFITHEATROF, E. THE CHILDREN OF COLUM-
BUS.
A. DE CONDE, 441:20MAY73-48
AMICHAI, Y. NOT OF THIS TIME, NOT OF
THIS PLACE.
617(TLS):7DEC73-1512
AMIN, S. & C. COQUERY-VIDROVITCH. HIS-
TOIRE ÉCONOMIQUE DU CONGO 1881-1968.
H. DESCHAMPS, 69:APR71-176
AMIS, K. GIRL, 20.*
J.P. DEGNAN, 249(HUDR):SUMMER72-330
AMIS, K. THE GREEN MAN.*
J.C. FIELD, 556(RLV):1971/5-624
AMIS, K. ON DRINK.*
S. BROOK, 441:23DEC73-9
AMIS, K. THE RIVERSIDE VILLAS MURDER.
P. ADAMS, 61:OCT73-130
A. BROYARD, 441:26SEP73-45
J. CAREY, 362:5APR73-457
A. WILSON, 441:11NOV73-6
442(NY):80CT73-169
617(TLS):6APR73-393
AMIS, M. THE RACHEL PAPERS.
E. FEINSTEIN, 362:22NOV73-721
617(TLS):16NOV73-1389
AMMON, H. JAMES MONROE.
L.C. MILAZZO, 584(SWR):SPRING72-160
AMMONS, A.R. BRIEFINGS.*
L. LIEBERMAN, 676(YR):AUTUMN71-82
M.G. PERLOFF, 659:WINTER73-97
AMMONS, A.R. COLLECTED POEMS.*
J. ASHBERY, 453:22FEB73-3
X.J. KENNEDY, 61:MAR73-101
D. KENWORTHY, 31(ASCH):SUMMER73-514
J.C. OATES, 598(SOR):AUTUMN73-1014
AMMONS, A.R. TAPE FOR THE TURN OF THE
YEAR.
J. ASHBERY, 453:22FEB73-3
AMMONS, A.R. UPLANDS.*
M.G. PERLOFF, 659:WINTER73-97
AMO AFER, A.G. ANTONIUS GUILIELMUS AMO
AFER AUS AXIM IN GHANA. (B. BRENTJES,
B. THALER & U. BEWERSDORFF, EDS)
D.M. RIEPE, 484(PPR):SEP70-139
AMORÓS, A. - SEE PÉREZ DE AYALA, R.
AMORUSO, V. VIRGINIA WOOLF.
G. ROHMANN, 447(N&Q):OCT71-396
AMOUROUX, D., M. CRETTOL & J.P. MONNET.
GUIDE D'ARCHITECTURE CONTEMPORAINE EN
FRANCE.
617(TLS):20APR73-438
AMPHILOCHIUS. AMPHILOCHII ICONIENSIS
"IAMBI AD SELEUCUM."* (E. OBERG, ED)
J.D. FRENDO, 303:VOL91-158

AMSDEN, J. COLLECTIVE BARGAINING AND
CLASS CONFLICT IN SPAIN.
617(TLS):15JUN73-696
ANAHAREO. GREY OWL AND I.
617(TLS):2FEB73-133
"ANALYSE SPECTRALE ET FONCTION DU POÈME
BAROQUE."
J. BAILBÉ, 535(RHL):JUL-AUG70-700
ANANABA, W. THE TRADE UNION MOVEMENT IN
NIGERIA.
R.D. GRILLO, 69:JAN71-75
ANANIA, M. THE COLOR OF DUST.*
M. BUCCO, 649(WAL):SUMMER71-155
ANAN'ICH, B.V. ROSSIIA I MEZHDUNARODNYI
KAPITAL, 1897-1914.
O. CRISP, 32:DEC72-895
ANASTAPLO, G. THE CONSTITUTIONALIST.
I. DILLIARD, 31(ASCH):SPRING73-347
A.J. THOMAS, JR., 584(SWR):WINTER72-VI
ANASTAS, P. GLOOSKAP'S CHILDREN.
P. ADAMS, 61:MAY73-123
ANATOLE, C. & R. LAFONT. NOUVELLE HIS-
TOIRE DE LA LITTÉRATURE OCCITANE.
P. GARDY, 98:JUN71-508
ANATOLI, A. - SEE UNDER KUZNETSOV, A.
ANCESCHI, G., ED. IL BOIARDO E LA CRITI-
CA CONTEMPORANEA.
R. CESERANI, 228(GSLI):VOL148FASC461-
109
E. SACCONE, 400(MLN):JAN71-114
ANDERAU, A. GEORGE GASCOIGNES "THE AD-
VENTURES OF MASTER F.J."
G. LAMBRECHTS, 189(EA):OCT-DEC70-439
C. UHLIG, 38:BAND88HEFT1-135
ANDERSEN, D. & H. SMITH. A CRITICAL PĀLI
DICTIONARY.* (VOL 2, FASC 5)
C. CAILLAT, 260(IF):BAND75-299
ANDERSEN, D. & H. SMITH - SEE TRENCKNER,
V.
ANDERSEN, H.C. CONTES. (D. SOLDI, E.
GRÉGOIRE & L. MOLAND, TRANS)
P. HALLEUX, 556(RLV):1971/3-367
ANDERSEN, H.C. A VISIT TO PORTUGAL,
1866.* (G. THORNTON, ED & TRANS)
442(NY):22OCT73-176
ANDERSEN, T. MODERNE RUSSISK KUNST,
1910-1925.
S-F. STARR, 576:MAY71-174
ANDERSEN, W. CÉZANNE'S PORTRAIT DRAW-
INGS.*
H.C. MUENSTERBERGER, 58:FEB71-12
42(AR):SUMMER70-264
ANDERSEN, W., WITH B. KLEIN. GAUGUIN'S
PARADISE LOST.
R. LEBOWITZ, 58:MAR72-18
617(TLS):25MAY73-585
ANDERSON, C.L. POE IN NORTHLIGHT.
P.F. QUINN, 578:FALL73-81
ANDERSON, C.P., WITH M. VIORST. OUTSIDER
IN THE SENATE.
639(VQR):SUMMER71-CXVI
ANDERSON, D. THE TRAGIC PROTEST.
R. LAWRENCE, 175:SPRING70-33
ANDERSON, D.L. & W. BRADEN - SEE CHAN-
NING, E.T.
ANDERSON, D.M. THE ART OF WRITTEN FORMS.
R. NASH, 54:DEC70-427
ANDERSON, G. BRENNAN'S BOOK.
M. LEVIN, 441:25FEB73-49
ANDERSON, G.K. THE LEGEND OF THE WANDER-
ING JEW.
E. KNECHT, 535(RHL):JAN-FEB70-162
ANDERSON, H. - SEE GORDON, A.L.
ANDERSON, H. & L.J. BLAKE. JOHN SHAW
NEILSON.
A. STEWART, 71(ALS):MAY73-108
ANDERSON, J. THE INVENTION OF NEW JERSEY.
L. HART, 661:SUMMER/FALL71-85

ANDERSON, J. A. PHILIP RANDOLPH.
N.I. HUGGINS, 441:27MAY73-15
A.H. RASKIN, 441:3MAY73-47
ANDERSON, J., WITH G. CLIFFORD. THE
ANDERSON PAPERS.
A. MARLENS, 441:21OCT73-42
ANDERSON, J.K. MILITARY THEORY AND PRAC-
TICE IN THE AGE OF XENOPHON.*
A.M. SNODGRASS, 123:JUN72-194
639(VQR):SPRING71-LXXVI
ANDERSON, J.M. THE REALM OF ART.*
B.T., 543:MAR71-534
ANDERSON, K. PERMANENT GARDENS.
J.H. WILDMAN, 598(SOR):SUMMER73-748
ANDERSON, M. & OTHERS. A HANDBOOK OF
CONTEMPORARY DRAMA.
617(TLS):6JUL73-775
ANDERSON, P. THE BYWORLDER.
617(TLS):2FEB73-129
ANDERSON, Q. THE IMPERIAL SELF.
H.A. LARRABEE, 432(NEQ):SEP71-486
S. PAUL, 301(JEGP):JAN72-154
ANDERSON, R. AFTER.
M. ENGEL, 441:22JUL73-16
C. LEHMANN-HAUPT, 441:5JUL73-33
ANDERSON, R.R. SPANISH AMERICAN MODERN-
ISM.*
R.M. REEVE, 399(MLJ):DEC71-542
ANDERSON, S. A STORY TELLER'S STORY.*
(R.L. WHITE, ED)
R.N., 502(PRS):SPRING70-85
ANDERSON, S. & G. STEIN. SHERWOOD ANDER-
SON/GERTRUDE STEIN. (R.L. WHITE, ED)
K.T. REED, 70(ANQ):DEC72-61
441:8APR73-30
ANDERSON, W. THE BEER BOOK.
R. REIF, 441:24NOV73-29
ANDERSON, W.E.K. - SEE SCOTT, W.
ANDERSON, W.L. EDWIN ARLINGTON ROBINSON.*
J.K. ROBINSON, 598(SOR):SUMMER73-692
ANDERSON, W.S. THE ART OF THE "AENEID."*
G. DAVIS, 131(CL):WINTER72-93
D.O. ROBSON, 487:AUTUMN71-293
ANDERSON, W.S. - SEE "OVID'S 'METAMOR-
PHOSES'"
ANDERSSON, G. ARTE E TEORIA.
A. ILLIANO, 546(RR):OCT71-242
ANDERSSON, I. FRANZ BERWALD.
G.C. SCHOOLFIELD, 563(SS):WINTER72-150
ANDERSSON, T. FOREIGN LANGUAGES IN THE
ELEMENTARY SCHOOL.*
J.M. MOORE, 221(GQ):JAN71-113
ANDICS, E. METTERNICH UND DIE FRAGE
UNGARNS.
617(TLS):14SEP73-1048
ANDICS, E. - SEE AVERBUCH, R.A.
ANDIOC, R. SUR LA QUERELLE DU THÉÂTRE AU
TEMPS DE LEANDRO FERNÁNDEZ DE MORATÍN.
I.L. MC CLELLAND, 86(BHS):OCT72-408
ANDIOC, R. & M. - SEE DE MORATÍN, L.F.
ANDO, T. BUNRAKU: THE PUPPET THEATER.*
M. URY, 318(JAOS):OCT-DEC71-524
ANDOLF, S. LES PÉAGES DES FOIRES DE
CHALON-SUR-SAÔNE.
M. GONON, 597(SN):VOL43#2-612
ANDRADE, J.C. - SEE UNDER CARRERA AN-
DRADE, J.
ANDRÉ, J. - SEE PLINY
ANDRÉAS, B. & M. MOLNÁR, EDS. LA PREM-
IÈRE INTERNATIONALE.
W. MC CLELLAN, 32:DEC72-894
ANDREAS-SALOMÉ, L. CORRESPONDANCE AVEC
SIGMUND FREUD [TOGETHER WITH] JOURNAL
D'UNE ANNÉE (1912-1913).
Y. BRÈS, 542:APR-JUN71-189
ANDREASEN, N.J.C. JOHN DONNE.
G. THOMAS, 175:SPRING70-26

ANDRÉOTA, P. THE SWEET TASTE OF BURNING.
N. CALLENDAR, 441:21OCT73-49
ANDRÉSEN, B.S. PRE-GLOTTALIZATION IN
ENGLISH STANDARD PRONUNCIATION.*
A. WOLLMANN, 38:BAND89HEFT3-357
ANDRESKI, I. OLD WIVES' TALES.
G.I. JONES, 69:APR71-178
ANDRESKI, S. PROSPECTS OF A REVOLUTION
IN THE U.S.A.
617(TLS):14DEC73-1531
ANDRESKI, S. SOCIAL SCIENCES AS SORCERY.*
N.W. ALDRICH, JR., 231:JUL73-94
ANDREW, C. THÉOPHILE DELCASSÉ AND THE
MAKING OF THE ENTENTE CORDIALE.
R.A. COSGROVE, 50(ARQ):WINTER70-369
ANDREWS, A. INTENSIVE INQUIRIES.
617(TLS):13APR73-427
ANDREWS, K. ADAM ELSHEIMER, IL CONTENTO.
G. MARTIN, 39:DEC71-525
ANDREWS, K. NATIONAL GALLERY OF SCOT-
LAND: CATALOGUE OF ITALIAN DRAWINGS.*
J. SCHOLZ, 54:JUN71-253
ANDREWS, L. KALEIDOSCOPE.
617(TLS):2NOV73-1348
ANDREWS, W. ARCHITECTURE IN NEW ENGLAND.
617(TLS):10AUG73-937
ANDREY, B. & L. MILLET. LA RÉVOLUTION
UNIVERSITAIRE.
N. HAMPSON, 208(FS):JUL72-371
ANDREYEV, N. STUDIES IN MUSCOVY.
M. SZEFTEL, 32:JUN72-415
ANDRONOV, M. MATERIALS FOR A BIBLIOGRA-
PHY OF DRAVIDIAN LINGUISTICS.
L. LISKER, 318(JAOS):OCT-DEC71-556
ANDRZEJEWSKI, J. THE APPEAL.*
E. GLOVER, 565:VOL12#4-53
ÅNEMAN, C. OM UTVECKLINGEN AV GAMMALT
KORT "I" I ORD AV TYPEN "VIDJA" I NOR-
DISKA SPRÅK MED SÄRSKILD HÄNSYN TILL
SVENSKAN.
T.L. MARKEY, 563(SS):AUTUMN72-552
ANENE, J.C. THE INTERNATIONAL BOUNDARIES
OF NIGERIA.
A.H.M. KIRK-GREENE, 69:JUL71-260
ANGELELLI, I. STUDIES ON GOTTLOB FREGE
AND TRADITIONAL PHILOSOPHY.
E.M. GALLIGAN & M.D. RESNIK, 486:JUN
71-316
ANGELES, J. INTRODUCCIÓN A LA LITERATURA
ESPAÑOLA.
R.W. HATTON, 238:MAR71-226
ANGELUCCI, E. GREAT AEROPLANES OF THE
WORLD.
617(TLS):7DEC73-1521
THE MARQUESS OF ANGLESEY. A HISTORY OF
THE BRITISH CAVALRY 1816-1919. (VOL 1)
617(TLS):9NOV73-1365
ANGLO, S. MACHIAVELLI.*
639(VQR):WINTER71-XXXIII
ANGLO, S. SPECTACLE, PAGEANTRY, AND
EARLY TUDOR POLICY.*
G. WICKHAM, 541(RES):AUG71-333
ANGRAND, P. MARIE-ELIZABETH CAVÉ, DIS-
CIPLE DE DELACROIX.
G. LEVITINE, 54:DEC70-465
ANGULO IÑIGUEZ, D. & A.E. PÉREZ SANCHEZ.
HISTORIA DE LA PINTURA ESPAÑOLA: ESCU-
ELA MADRILEÑA DEL PRIMER TERCIO DEL
SIGLO XVII.
T. CROMBIE, 39:JUN71-526
ANGUS, S. ARSON AND OLD LACE.
N. CALLENDAR, 441:14JAN73-30
ANGUS-BUTTERWORTH, L.M. ROBERT BURNS AND
THE EIGHTEENTH-CENTURY REVIVAL IN SCOT-
TISH VERNACULAR POETRY.
G.A.M. WOOD, 175:SPRING70-27
ANGYAL, D. EMLÉKEZÉSEK.
G.F. CUSHING, 575(SEER):OCT72-609

ANISMAN, M.J. - SEE THACKERAY, W.M.
ANNENSKY, I.F. KNIGI OTRAZHENII I, II.
D. MC DUFF, 205(FMLS):APR70-200
R.D.B. THOMSON, 575(SEER):APR72-300
"ANNUAIRE DE L'INSTITUT DE PHILOLOGIE
ET D'HISTOIRE ORIENTALES ET SLAVES."
(VOLS 18 & 19)
W.B. EDGERTON, 32:MAR72-186
"ANNUAIRE XV 1961-1962." "ANNUAIRE XVI
1962-1963." [COMMISSION ROYALE BELGE
DE FOLKLORE, SECTION WALLONNE]
S.J. SACKETT, 650(WF):JAN70-65
"THE ANNUAL OF THE BRITISH SCHOOL AT
ATHENS." (NO. 67, 1972)
617(TLS):7SEP73-1036
ANOBILE, R.J., ED. A FLASK OF FIELDS.
P. ADAMS, 61:JAN73-100
ANOUILH, J. BECKET. (B.L. KNAPP & A.
DELLA FAZIA, EDS)
J. DECOCK, 207(FR):DEC70-435
ANOUILH, J. CHER ANTOINE OU L'AMOUR
RATÉ.
C. SAINT-LEON, 207(FR):OCT70-167
ANOZIE, S.O. CHRISTOPHER OKIGBO.
617(TLS):27JUL73-876
ANSART, P. MARX ET L'ANARCHISME.
C. SCHUWER, 542:APR-JUN71-226
ANSCOMBE, G.E.M. & G.H. VON WRIGHT - SEE
WITTGENSTEIN, L.
ANSELL, J. GOSPEL.
M. LEVIN, 441:8APR73-33
ANSELL, J. SUMMER.
J.C. OATES, 441:25NOV73-7
SAINT ANSELM. WHY GOD BECAME MAN [AND]
THE VIRGIN CONCEPTION AND ORIGINAL SIN.
(J.M. COLLERAN, ED & TRANS)
D.F.D., 543:JUN71-741
ANSHEN, R.N. - SEE TEILHARD DE CHARDIN,
P.
ANSTEINSSON, E. TEATER I NORGE.
V.A. BØRGE, 172(EDDA):1970/4-253
ANTHONI, E. FINLANDS MEDELTIDA FRÄLSE
OCH 1500-TALS ADEL.
J.S. MARTIN, 67:NOV72-259
ANTHONY, E. STRANGER AT THE GATES.
M. LEVIN, 441:23SEP73-48
ANTHONY, E.M., J.T. GANDOUR, JR. & U.
WAROTAMASIKKHADIT. FOUNDATIONS OF
THAI.* (BKS 1&2)
D.W. DELLINGER, 353:DEC71-123
"ANTIKEN AUS DEM AKADEMISCHEN KUNSTMUSEUM
BONN."
M. BIEBER, 182:VOL24#6-303
ANTIN, D. MEDITATIONS. CODE OF FLAG
BEHAVIOR. AUTOBIOGRAPHY. DEFINITIONS.
J. ROTHENBERG, 600:FALL71-134
ANTOINE, M. LE CONSEIL DU ROI SOUS LE
RÈGNE DE LOUIS XV.
R. HOWELL, JR., 182:VOL24#1/2-44
ANTON, F. ART OF THE MAYA.
M.K., 135:FEB71-138
ANTON, H. MYTHOLOGISCHE EROTIK IN KEL-
LERS "SIEBEN LEGENDEN" UND IM "SINNGE-
DICHT."*
J. ROTHENBERG, 680(ZDP):BAND90HEFT2-
294
ANTON, J.P., WITH G.L. KUSTAS, EDS.
ESSAYS IN ANCIENT GREEK PHILOSOPHY.
R.K. SPRAGUE, 122:OCT72-299
ANTON, K-H. - SEE PUJOL, J.
ANTONOVIČ, A.K. BELORUSSKIE TEKSTY, PIS-
ANNYE ARABSKIM PIS'MOM, I IX GRAFIKO-
ORFOGRAFIČESKAJA SISTEMA.
P. WEXLER, 215(GL):VOL11#1-43
ANTRIM, H.T. T.S. ELIOT'S CONCEPT OF LAN-
GUAGE.
S. STEPANCHEV, 27(AL):NOV72-505

ANTROBUS, J. WHY BOURNEMOUTH? AND OTHER
PLAYS.
P. ROBERTS, 565:VOL12#2-72
ANWAR, C. THE COMPLETE POETRY AND PROSE
OF CHAIRIL ANWAR. (B. RAFFEL, ED &
TRANS)
J.M. ECHOLS, 318(JAOS):OCT-DEC71-562
ANZOINO, T. PASOLINI.
617(TLS):12OCT73-1253
AOKI, H. NEZ PERCE GRAMMAR.
B. RIGSBY, 350:SEP72-737
N.S.H. SMITH, 361:VOL27#1-100
APEL, K-O. ANALYTIC PHILOSOPHY OF LANGU-
AGE AND THE GEISTESWISSENSCHAFTEN.
E. BUBSER, 260(IF):BAND75-220
APEL, W. HARVARD DICTIONARY OF MUSIC.*
(2ND ED)
M. PETERSON, 470:NOV70-43
APFEL, E. ANLAGE UND STRUKTUR DER
MOTETTEN IM CODEX MONTPELLIER.*
T. KARP, 317:SUMMER72-270
APGAR, V. & J. BECK. IS MY BABY ALL
RIGHT?
J.E. BRODY, 441:2FEB73-33
APOLLINAIRE, G. APOLLINAIRE ET "LA
DÉMOCRATIE SOCIALE." (P. CAIZERGUES,
ED)
C. TOURNADRE, 535(RHL):MAR-APR71-325
APOLLINAIRE, G. LES ONZE MILLE VERGES.
617(TLS):23NOV73-1417
APOLLONIO, U., ED. FUTURIST MANIFESTOS.
617(TLS):20APR73-438
APOSTOLSKI, M. & OTHERS, EDS. ISTORIJA
NA MAKEDONSKIOT NAROD. ISTORIJA MAKE-
DONSKOG NARODA.
W.S. VUCINICH, 32:JUN72-496
APPADORAI, A. ESSAYS IN POLITICS AND
INTERNATIONAL RELATIONS.
L.P. FICKETT, JR., 293(JAST):NOV70-247
APPEL, A., JR. - SEE NABOKOV, V.
APPIA, H. & O. METTAS. LE FRANÇAIS TEL
QU'ON LE PARLE AUJOURD'HUI.
J.L. SHEPHERD 3D, 207(FR):MAY71-1139
APPIAN. BELLORUM CIVILIUM LIBER V. (E.
GABBA, ED & TRANS)
P.J. CUFF, 313:VOL61-299
APPLE, A. SON OF GUYANA.
617(TLS):13JUL73-798
"THE APPLE OR ARISTOTLE'S DEATH." (M.F.
ROUSSEAU, TRANS)
J.J.R., 543:JUN71-761
APPLETON, S. THE PLENITUDE WE CRY FOR.
A. OSTRIKER, 441:11NOV73-42
APPLETON, T., COMP. A TYPOLOGICAL TALLY.
617(TLS):15JUN73-698
APRESJAN, J.D. ÈKSPERIMENTAL'NOE ISSLE-
DOVANIE SEMANTIKI RUSSKOGO GLAGOLA.
F.H.H. KORTLANDT, 361:VOL27#1-53
APTEKAR, J. ICONS OF JUSTICE.*
R.M. CUMMINGS, 447(N&Q):AUG71-318
B.E.C. DAVIS, 597(SN):VOL43#1-307
H. MEYER, 430(NS):AUG70-423
AQUILECCHIA, G. - SEE ARETINO, P.
AQUIN, H. THE ANTIPHONARY.
B. GODARD, 99:NOV-DEC73-33
AQUINAS, T. ON THE UNITY OF THE INTEL-
LECT AGAINST THE AVERROISTS (DE UNITATE
INTELLECTUS CONTRA AVERROISTAS). (B.H.
ZEDLER, TRANS)
A.A. MAURER, 154:DEC70-486
ARAGON. JE N'AI JAMAIS APPRIS À ÉCRIRE
OU "LES INCIPIT."
R. JEAN, 98:MAY71-421
ARAGON. PARIS PEASANT. (FRENCH TITLE:
LE PAYSAN DE PARIS.)
M. BOWRIE, 111:28MAY71-228

ARAGON, L. HENRI MATISSE.*
  A. BLUNT, 453:14JUN73-31
  F. STEEGMULLER, 61:JAN73-86
  617(TLS):16FEB73-170
ARANGO, J. THE URBANIZATION OF THE EARTH.
  L.J. CURRIE, 505:JUN71-102
ARANY, A.L. THE PHONOLOGICAL SYSTEM OF A
HUNGARIAN DIALECT.
  R. HETZRON, 353:JAN70-113
ARASARATNAM, S. INDIANS IN MALAYSIA AND
SINGAPORE.
  F.V. GAGLIANO, 293(JAST):MAY71-738
ARBASINO, A. IL PRINCIPE COSTANTE.
  617(TLS):16MAR73-303
ARBERRY, A.J. CLASSICAL PERSIAN LITERA-
TURE.
  R.C. CLARK, 544:SPRING71-182
ARBIB, M.A. BRAINS, MACHINES, AND MATHE-
MATICS.
  J.S. ULLIAN, 316:SEP70-482
ARBUS, D., ED. ALICE IN WONDERLAND. (R.
AVEDON, PHOTOGRAPHS)
  J. LAHR, 441:25MAR73-36
"DIANE ARBUS."* (D. ARBUS & M. ISRAEL,
EDS)
  S. SONTAG, 453:15NOV73-13
ARCE, J. - SEE CADALSO, J.
ARCE, J. - SEE DE JÁUREGUI, J.
ARCHARD, M. KIDS, BLOODY KIDS.
  617(TLS):12JAN73-49
"ARCHÉOLOGIE ET CALCULATEURS."
  R. PITTIONI, 182:VOL24#15/16-619
ARCHER, M. BRITISH DRAWINGS IN THE INDIA
OFFICE LIBRARY.
  H. FURBER, 318(JAOS):OCT-DEC71-558
  A. POWELL, 39:AUG70-154
ARCHIBALD, K. SEX AND THE PUBLIC SER-
VICE.
  E.H. MORTON, 529(QQ):SUMMER71-304
  R.N. WHITEHURST, 628:FALL71-86
ARCHIMEDES. ARCHIMÈDE, "DE LA SPHÈRE ET
DU CYLINDRE, LA MESURE DU CERCLE, SUR
LES CONOÏDES ET LES SPHÉROÏDES." (C.
MUGLER, ED & TRANS)
  P. LOUIS, 555:VOL45FASC2-350
"ARCHITECTURAL GRAPHIC STANDARDS." (6TH
ED)
  J.D. MORGAN, 45:MAR71-44
"THE ARCHITECTURE OF PAUL RUDOLPH."
  M.S., 45:SEP70-141
"THE ARCHITECTURE OF YORKE ROSENBERG
MARDALL, 1944-1972."
  617(TLS):9MAR73-264
"ARCHIVES DE JULES HUMBERT-DROZ." (VOL 1)
  R. CARR, 86(BHS):APR72-195
"ARCHIVES: MIRROR OF CANADA PAST."
  G.W., 102(CANL):AUTUMN72-116
ARDEN, J. TWO AUTOBIOGRAPHICAL PLAYS.
  A. RENDLE, 157:AUTUMN71-82
ARDEN, W. DEADLY LEGACY.
  N. CALLENDAR, 441:6MAY73-41
ARDIES, T. PANDEMIC.
  N. CALLENDAR, 441:20MAY73-22
ARDREY, R. THE SOCIAL CONTRACT.
  D. TERRILL, 396(MODA):FALL72-423
  D.M. WOLFE, 639(VQR):WINTER71-153
ARENDT, H. ON VIOLENCE.*
  H.M. CURTLER, 396(MODA):WINTER72-97
ARENDT, H. - SEE BENJAMIN, W.
ARENS, H. SPRACHWISSENSCHAFT. (2ND ED)
  E.F.K. KOERNER, 350:JUN72-428
ARETINO, P. SEI GIORNATE. (G. AQUILEC-
CHIA, ED) SCRITTI SCELTI. (G.G.
FERRERO, ED)
  M. POZZI, 228(GSLI):VOL147FASC460-587
"ARETINO'S DIALOGUES."* (R. ROSENTHAL,
TRANS)
  617(TLS):20APR73-440

ARETZ, I. EL TAMUNANGUE.
  E.T. STANFORD, 187:MAY73-318
ARÉVALO, T. RAFAEL ARÉVALO MARTÍNEZ.
  C.H. MONSANTO, 263:JUL-SEP72-290
AREY, J.A. THE SKY PIRATES.*
  617(TLS):20JUL73-841
ARGAN, G.C. THE RENAISSANCE CITY.
  J.S. ACKERMAN, 54:MAR71-115
ARGENIO, R. SAN PAOLINO DA NOLA CANTORE
DI MIRACOLI.
  P. LANGLOIS, 555:VOL45FASC2-373
"ARGENTIERI, GEMMARI E ORAFI D'ITALIA."
(VOLS 1-4)
  C. OMAN, 90:APR71-223
ARGUETA, M. EL VALLE DE LAS HAMACAS.
  K. SCHWARTZ, 238:DEC71-974
DE ARGUIJO, J. OBRA POÉTICA. (S.B.
VRANICH, ED)
  617(TLS):4MAY73-507
ARGYLE, B. AN INTRODUCTION TO THE AUS-
TRALIAN NOVEL 1830-1930.
  B. KIERNAN, 71(ALS):OCT73-209
ARGYLE, M. THE SOCIAL PSYCHOLOGY OF WORK.
  617(TLS):11MAY73-518
"ARGYLL: AN INVENTORY OF THE ANCIENT
MONUMENTS." (VOL 1: KINTYRE.)
  617(TLS):6APR73-370
ARIAS-LARRETA, A. LITERATURAS ABORÍGENES
DE AMÉRICA.* (9TH ED)
  P. BOYD-BOWMAN, 240(HR):OCT71-460
ARIEL FERNÁNDEZ, C. LÁGRIMA DE PIE.
  E.B. LABRADA, 37:OCT70-40
ARIMA TATSUO. THE FAILURE OF FREEDOM.
  W.F. SIBLEY, 244(HJAS):VOL31-247
  W. TSUNEISHI, 293(JAST):NOV70-193
ARISTIDES. PANATHENAIC ORATION AND IN
DEFENCE OF ORATORY. (C.A. BEHR, TRANS)
  617(TLS):24AUG73-986
ARÍSTIDES, J. ESTAR Y SER.
  J.P. AGUILAR, 263:APR-JUN72-171
ARISTOPHANES. THE ACHARNIANS; THE
CLOUDS; LYSISTRATA. (A.H. SOMMERSTEIN,
TRANS)
  617(TLS):21DEC73-1574
ARISTOPHANES. CLOUDS.* (K.J. DOVER, ED)
  P. CHANTRAINE, 555:VOL45FASC1-114
  M.J. O'BRIEN, 487:SUMMER71-168
ARISTOPHANES. ECCLESIAZUSAE. (R.G.
USSHER, ED)
  617(TLS):2FEB73-133
ARISTOPHANES. PLAYS. (P. DICKINSON,
TRANS)
  D.M. MAC DOWELL, 123:DEC72-406
ARISTOPHANES. WASPS. (D.M. MAC DOWELL,
ED)
  L.W. DALY, 124:SEP71-24
ARISTOTLE. ARISTOTE, "L'ÉTHIQUE À NICO-
MAQUE." (R-A. GAUTHIER & J-Y. JOLIF,
EDS & TRANS) (2ND ED; VOL 1, PT 1;
REV BY R-A. GAUTHIER)
  P. LOUIS, 555:VOL45FASC2-345
ARISTOTLE. ARISTOTELES' "POLITICA."
(A. DREIZEHNTER, ED)
  J. BARNES, 123:DEC72-339
  P. LOUIS, 555:VOL45FASC2-347
ARISTOTLE. ARISTOTLE'S "PHYSICS" BOOKS
I AND II. (W. CHARLTON, ED & TRANS)
  D.W. HAMLYN, 483:APR71-169
  P.M. HUBY, 123:JUN72-200
  C. MUGLER, 555:VOL45FASC2-344
  J. OWENS, 487:AUTUMN71-279
ARISTOTLE. ARISTOTLE'S "POETICS."* (L.
GOLDEN, TRANS; O.B. HARDISON, JR., ED)
  G.F. ELSE, 121(CJ):APR-MAY72-370
ARISTOTLE. ARISTOTLE'S "POLITICS."
(BKS 3&4) (R. ROBINSON, ED & TRANS)
  R. WEIL, 542:APR-JUN71-227

11

ARISTOTLE. DE GENERATIONE ANIMALIUM.
(WILLIAM OF MOERBEKE, TRANS; H.J. DROS-
SAART LULOFS, ED)
   J. LONGRIGG, 123:DEC72-409
ARISTOTLE. HISTORIA ANIMALIUM. (VOL 2)
(A.L. PECK, TRANS)
   P. LOUIS, 555:VOL45FASC2-347
ARISTOTLE. THE POETICS. (P.H. EPPS,
TRANS)
   J.J.R., 543:MAR71-534
ARISTOTLE. POLITIQUE D'ARISTOTE. (R.
WEIL, ED)
   J. BRUNSCHWIG, 542:APR-JUN71-229
ARKADIOU, M. CHARLES BAUDELAIRE, POULET-
MALASSIS. [IN GREEK]
   R. BOSER & C. PICHOIS, 535(RHL):
      MAR-APR71-314
ARLEN, M.J. AN AMERICAN VERDICT.
   B. DE MOTT, 61:OCT73-117
   T. FITZPATRICK, 441:30SEP73-27
   C. NEWMAN, 231:NOV73-116
   M. WATKINS, 441:21DEC73-33
ARLEN, M.J. EXILES.
   42(AR):SPRING70-131
ARLOTT, J., WITH R. COWAN & F. GIBSON.
ISLAND CAMERA.
   617(TLS):19JAN73-74
ARLT, W. EIN FESTOFFIZIUM DES MITTEL-
ALTERS AUS BEAUVAIS IN SEINER LITUR-
GISCHEN UND MUSIKALISCHEN BEDEUTUNG.
   H. TISCHLER, 589:OCT72-742
ARMATO, R.P. & J.M. SPALEK, EDS. MEDI-
EVAL EPIC TO THE "EPIC THEATER" OF
BRECHT.*
   G. COSTA, 545(RPH):MAY72-474
   P. WARNING, 52:BAND5HEFT2-210
ARMES, R. PATTERNS OF REALISM.
   617(TLS):28SEP73-1109
ARMFELT, N. CATCHING UP.
   K. CUNNINGHAM, 368:DEC71-463
ARMIN, R. THE COLLECTED WORKS OF ROBERT
ARMIN. (J.P. FEATHER, ED)
   617(TLS):22JUN73-723
ARMITAGE, C.M. & N. CLARK. A BIBLIOGRA-
PHY OF THE WORKS OF LOUIS MAC NEICE.
   617(TLS):19OCT73-1288
ARMOUR, L. THE CONCEPT OF TRUTH.*
   R. SQUIRES, 393(MIND):JAN71-154
ARMSTRONG, A. THE CHURCH OF ENGLAND,
THE METHODISTS AND SOCIETY.
   617(TLS):21SEP73-1093
ARMSTRONG, A.H., ED. THE CAMBRIDGE HIS-
TORY OF LATER GREEK AND EARLY MEDIEVAL
PHILOSOPHY.*
   P. LANGLOIS, 555:VOL45FASC1-179
ARMSTRONG, A.W. THIS DAY AND TIME.
   J.E. REESE, 50(ARQ):SUMMER71-178
ARMSTRONG, D.M. BELIEF, TRUTH AND KNOW-
LEDGE.
   617(TLS):24AUG73-971
ARMSTRONG, D.M. A MATERIALIST THEORY OF
THE MIND.*
   R.H. KANE, 543:DEC70-302
   J.A. SHAFFER, 262:SUMMER71-164
ARMSTRONG, E. RONSARD AND THE AGE OF
GOLD.*
   W.B. FLEISCHMANN, 188(ECR):WINTER70-
      339
   W.R. GAIR, 255(HAB):WINTER70-59
   J-M. KLINKENBERG, 556(RLV):1970/2-214
ARMSTRONG, H.F., ED. FIFTY YEARS OF
FOREIGN AFFAIRS.
   617(TLS):27APR73-459
ARMSTRONG, H.F. PEACE AND COUNTERPEACE.*
   R.W. LEOPOLD, 639(VQR):AUTUMN71-608
ARMSTRONG, I., ED. THE MAJOR VICTORIAN
POETS: RECONSIDERATIONS.*
   J.C. MAXWELL, 447(N&Q):NOV71-433

ARMSTRONG, J. THE PARADISE MYTH.*
   D.V.E., 191(ELN):SEP71(SUPP)-39
ARMYTAGE, W.H.G. 400 YEARS OF ENGLISH
EDUCATION.
   O. VÖLCKER, 182:VOL24#3-78
ARMYTAGE, W.H.G. THE GERMAN INFLUENCE
ON ENGLISH EDUCATION.
   K. SILBER, 220(GL&L):OCT71-81
ARNAOUDOV, M. LIČNOSTI I PROBLEMI V
EVROPEISKATA LITERATOURA.
   N. DONTCHEV, 535(RHL):MAY-JUN70-540
ARNAUD, E. & V. TUSÓN. GUIDE DE BIBLI-
OGRAPHIE HISPANIQUE.
   J. HORRENT, 556(RLV):1970/1-106
ARNAUDOV, M. IAVOROV.
   E. MOŽEJKO, 32:JUN72-502
ARNAULD, A. & P. NICOLE. LA LOGIQUE OU
L'ART DE PENSER.
   S. LUSIGNAN, 154:SEP71-620
ARNDT, W. - SEE PUSHKIN, A.S.
ARNDT, W.W. & OTHERS, EDS. STUDIES IN
HISTORICAL LINGUISTICS IN HONOR OF
GEORGE SHERMAN LANE.
   W. THOMAS, 260(IF):BAND74-191
ARNGART, O., ED. THE MIDDLE ENGLISH
"GENESIS AND EXODUS."*
   S.M. KUHN, 589:JAN72-103
   T.F. MUSTANOJA, 597(SN):VOL42#1-256
ARNHEIM, R. ENTROPY AND ART.
   W. CHARLTON, 89(BJA):SPRING72-192
ARNHEIM, R. VISUAL THINKING.*
   F.H. FORST, 186(ETC):MAR71-121
   T. MISCHEL, 484(PPR):SEP71-116
ARNOLD, A. FRIEDRICH DÜRRENMATT.
   J.C. HAMMER, 397(MD):DEC70-343
   G. MARAHRENS, 564:JUN71-158
ARNOLD, A.J. PAUL VALÉRY AND HIS CRIT-
ICS.*
   C.M. CROW, 208(FS):OCT72-476
ARNOLD, D. & N. FORTUNE, EDS. THE BEE-
THOVEN COMPANION.*
   A.E.F.D., 412:FEB72-60
ARNOLD, J. STUDENTS' GUIDE TO BASIC
FRENCH.
   J.D. GODIN, 207(FR):APR71-999
ARNOLD, K. JOHANNES TRITHEMIUS (1462-
1516).
   J.I.J., 568(SCN):SUMMER72-56
ARNOLD, M. GOD AND THE BIBLE. (R.H.
SUPER, ED)
   K. ALLOTT, 402(MLR):JAN72-176
ARNOTT, D.W. THE NOMINAL AND VERBAL
SYSTEMS OF FULA.
   P.F. LACROIX, 69:JUL71-262
ARNOTT, P. THE BYZANTINES AND THEIR
WORLD.
   617(TLS):28DEC73-1595
ARNOTT, P.D. AN INTRODUCTION TO THE
ROMAN WORLD.
   O. MURRAY, 123:DEC72-427
   S.E. SMETHURST, 529(QQ):AUTUMN71-481
ARON, R. RÉPUBLIQUE IMPÉRIALE.
   617(TLS):27APR73-463
ARONSON, A. PSYCHE AND SYMBOL IN SHAKE-
SPEARE.
   617(TLS):2FEB73-126
ARONSON, J. DEADLINE FOR THE MEDIA.
   C. LEHMANN-HAUPT, 441:23FEB73-33
   M.F. NOLAN, 441:4MAR73-26
ARP, J. ARP ON ARP.* (M. JEAN, ED)
   R. LEBOWITZ, 58:MAY72-30
ARPINO, G. RANDAGIO È L'EROE.
   617(TLS):18MAY73-562
"ARQUIVOS DO CENTRO CULTURAL PORTUGUÊS."
(VOLS 1&2)
   D-H. PAGEAUX, 549(RLC):APR-JUN71-257
ARRABAL, F. THÉÂTRE IV.*
   F. TONELLI, 207(FR):DEC70-406

12

ARRABAL, F. THÉÂTRE 8.
  R.C. LAMONT, 207(FR):APR71-949
ARRIVÉ, M. & J-C. CHEVALIER. LA GRAM-
MAIRE.
  M. GLATIGNY, 557(RSH):OCT-DEC71-663
ARRÓNIZ, O. LA INFLUENCIA ITALIANA EN EL
NACIMIENTO DE LA COMEDIA ESPAÑOLA.*
  E. COUGHLIN, 238:MAY71-393
  J.G. FUCILLA, 546(RR):OCT71-234
ARSLAN, E. GOTHIC ARCHITECTURE IN VEN-
ICE.
  617(TLS):23FEB73-215
"ART AND CONFRONTATION."
  J. ELDERFIELD, 592:JUL-AUG70-49
"ART FOR COMMERCE."
  617(TLS):7DEC73-1500
"ART GALLERY OF ONTARIO: THE CANADIAN
COLLECTION."
  R.L. BLOORE, 96:APR/MAY71-82
"THE ART OF ELIZABETH FRINK."
  617(TLS):16MAR73-284
"ART TREASURES IN GERMANY."
  58:SEP/OCT70-18
ARTAUD, A. COLLECTED WORKS. (VOL 2)
  P. ROBERTS, 565:VOL12#4-60
ARTAUD, A. VAN GOGH, LE SUICIDÉ DE LA
SOCIÉTÉ.
  R. LAPORTE, 98:FEB70-124
ARTAUD, A. LETTRES À GÉNICA ATHANASIOU.
  J. HENRIC, 98:JUL70-616
ARTAUD, D. LE NEW DEAL.
  A. MOULIN, 556(RLV):1971/5-651
ARTAUD, D. & A. KASPI. HISTOIRE DES
ETATS-UNIS.
  A. MOULIN, 556(RLV):1971/5-652
ARTHOS, J. MILTON AND THE ITALIAN CIT-
IES.*
  E. MERTNER, 38:BAND88HEFT2-265
ARTOU, J.C. & J.T. TERRATS. APPORTS
HISPANIQUES À LA PHILOSOPHIE CHRÉTIENNE
DE L'OCCIDENT.
  A. FOREST, 542:APR-JUN70-262
ARVIDSSON, R. FREDRIK BÖÖKS BIBLIOGRAFI
1898-1967.
  G.C. SCHOOLFIELD, 563(SS):SPRING72-287
"AS I CROSSED A BRIDGE OF DREAMS."* (I.
MORRIS, TRANS)
  J.I. ACKROYD, 67:MAY72-120
ASBELL, B. THE F.D.R. MEMOIRS.
  441:16SEP73-16
ASCH, M., J. DUNSON & E. RAIM, EDS. AN-
THOLOGY OF AMERICAN FOLK MUSIC.
  W. RHODES, 187:SEP73-544
ASCHAM, R. ENGLISH WORKS. (W.A. WRIGHT,
ED)
  B. COCHRANE, 67:MAY72-82
ASCHER, A. PAVEL AXELROD AND THE DEVEL-
OPMENT OF MENSHEVISM.
  617(TLS):24AUG73-983
ASCOLI, G. LA GRANDE-BRETAGNE DEVANT
L'OPINION FRANÇAISE DEPUIS LA GUERRE DE
CENT ANS JUSQU'À LA FIN DU XVIE SIÈCLE.
LA GRANDE-BRETAGNE DEVANT L'OPINION
FRANÇAISE AU XVIIE SIÈCLE.
  J. LOUGH, 208(FS):OCT72-448
ASENSIO, E. POÉTICA Y REALIDAD EN EL
CANCIONERO PENINSULAR DE LA EDAD MEDIA.
(2ND ED)
  E.L. RIVERS, 400(MLN):MAR71-302
VAN ASH, C. & E.S. ROHMER. MASTER OF
VILLAINY.* (R.E. BRINEY, ED)
  617(TLS):2FEB73-114
ASHBERY, J. THE DOUBLE DREAM OF SPRING.*
  A. HELMS, 473(PR):FALL72-621
ASHBERY, J. THREE POEMS.*
  A. HELMS, 473(PR):FALL72-621
  R. LATTIMORE, 249(HUDR):AUTUMN72-475
  R. MAZZOCCO, 453:13DEC73-45

ASHBY, T. THE ROMAN CAMPAGNA IN CLASSI-
CAL TIMES.
  R.M. OGILVIE, 123:JUN72-284
ASHE, G. THE FINGER AND THE MOON.
  617(TLS):24AUG73-969
ASHE, G. - SEE UNDER CREASEY, J.
ASHFORD, D. THE YOUNG VISITERS.
  A. FRIEDMAN, 441:15APR73-4
ASHFORD, J. THE DOUBLE RUN.
  N. CALLENDAR, 441:18NOV73-56
ASHLEY, J. JOURNEY INTO SILENCE.
  P. WHITEHEAD, 362:7JUN73-768
  617(TLS):8JUN73-647
ASHLEY, L.R.N., ED. NINETEENTH-CENTURY
BRITISH DRAMA.
  P.D. HERRING, 405(MP):AUG70-83
ASHLEY, L.R.N., ED. OTHER PEOPLE'S LIVES.
  J.W. STEVENSON, 573(SSF):SUMMER71-475
ASHLEY, M. OLIVER CROMWELL AND HIS
WORLD.
  617(TLS):12JAN73-49
ASHLEY, M. THE LIFE AND TIMES OF KING
JOHN.
  617(TLS):19JAN73-62
ASHLEY, M. THE LIFE AND TIMES OF
WILLIAM I.
  617(TLS):22JUN73-728
ASHLEY, R. HEROIN.
  P. STEINFELS & R.M. VEATCH, 441:
  4FEB73-6
ASHMAN, C. THE FINEST JUDGES MONEY CAN
BUY.
  M.M. BELLI, 441:18NOV73-42
ASHMOLE, B. ARCHITECT AND SCULPTOR IN
CLASSICAL GREECE.
  617(TLS):12JAN73-28
ASHMORE, H.S. FEAR IN THE AIR.
  S. MICKELSON, 441:25NOV73-42
ASHRAF, S.A., ED. THE NEW HARMONY.
  A. CLUYSENAAR, 565:VOL12#3-72
ASHTON, D. THE LIFE AND TIMES OF THE
NEW YORK SCHOOL.
  617(TLS):9NOV73-1362
ASHTON, D. THE NEW YORK SCHOOL.
  442(NY):9JUL73-71
ASHTON, D. A READING OF MODERN ART.
  T. HILTON, 592:MAR70-137
  F.D. MARTIN, 290(JAAC):SPRING71-421
ASHTON, D. - SEE PICASSO, P.
ASHTON, J. SOCIAL LIFE IN THE REIGN OF
QUEEN ANNE.
  P.A. SLACK, 447(N&Q):FEB71-77
ASHTON, T.L. - SEE LORD BYRON
ASIEGBU, J.U.J. SLAVERY AND THE POLITICS
OF LIBERATION (1787-1861).
  H. DESCHAMPS, 69:APR71-177
ASIMOV, I. BUILDING BLOCKS OF THE UNI-
VERSE. OF TIME AND SPACE AND OTHER
THINGS. THE GODS THEMSELVES.*
  T. STURGEON, 441:28JAN73-10
ASIMOV, I. THE EARLY ASIMOV. (L.P.A.
SHMEAD, ED)
  T. STURGEON, 441:28JAN73-10
  617(TLS):18MAY73-562
ASIMOV, I., ED. WHERE DO WE GO FROM
HERE?
  T. STURGEON, 441:28JAN73-10
ASINOF, E., W. HINCKLE & W. TURNER. THE
10-SECOND JAILBREAK.
  441:6MAY73-42
ASLANAPA, O. TURKISH ART AND ARCHITEC-
TURE.*
  T.T. RICE, 89(BJA):SPRING72-202
ASLANOV, M.G. & N.A. DVORJANKOVA, EDS.
AFGANSKO-RUSSKIJ SLOVAR' (PUŠTU).
  C.M. KIEFFER & S. SANA, 343:BAND13
  HEFT2-183

ASLIN, E.  THE AESTHETIC MOVEMENT.*
    B.G.B., 135:JUN70-135
    E. HOFFMANN, 90:JUN71-342
    R. MANDER, 39:MAR70-248
ASMUTH, B.  LOHENSTEIN UND TACITUS.
    J. SCHMIDT, 182:VOL24#17/18-669
ASPELIN, K.  TIMON FRÅN ATEN.
    W.A. BERENDSOHN, 182:VOL24#7/8-351
ASPILLERA, P.S.  BASIC TAGALOG FOR FOR-
    EIGNERS AND NON-TAGALOGS.*
    H. MC KAUGHAN, 399(MLJ):FEB71-118
ASPINALL, A. - SEE GEORGE IV
ASPLAND, C.W.  A SYNTACTICAL STUDY OF
    EPIC FORMULAS AND FORMULAIC EXPRES-
    SIONS CONTAINING THE -ANT FORMS IN
    TWELFTH CENTURY VERSE.*
    F. WHITEHEAD, 208(FS):APR72-181
ASSION, P.  DIE MIRAKEL DER HL. KATHARINA
    VON ALEXANDRIEN.
    B. HAAGE, 597(SN):VOL42#2-521
    E. MOSER-RATH, 196:BAND12HEFT2/3-259
DE ASSIS, J.M.M. - SEE UNDER MACHADO DE
    ASSIS, J.M.
ASTLEY, T., ED.  COAST TO COAST 1969-70.
    M. WILDING, 381:JUN71-259
ASTON, P.  THE MUSIC OF YORK MINSTER.
    W. SHAW, 415:DEC72-1189
ASTUDILLO Y A., R.  EL POZO Y LOS PARAÍ-
    SOS.
    R. SQUIRRU, 37:MAY70-41
ASTURIAS, M.A.  THE EYES OF THE INTERRED.
    P. ADAMS, 61:MAY73-123
    V. PERERA, 441:26AUG73-7
    M. WOOD, 453:19APR73-35
"AT FORSE RIKET MED BESTANDIGE OCH PRYD-
    LIGE BYGGNADER."
    L.K. EATON, 576:MAY70-200
ATHAS, D.  ENTERING EPHESUS.
    617(TLS):11MAY73-535
ATKIN, R.  MAINTAIN THE RIGHT.
    617(TLS):13JUL73-811
ATKINS, S., ED.  THE AGE OF GOETHE.
    D.S. GUILLOTON, 221(GQ):MAY71-427
    G.F. PROBST, 399(MLJ):MAY71-334
ATKINSON, A.B.  UNEQUAL SHARES.*
    617(TLS):27APR73-466
ATKINSON, B. & A. HIRSCHFELD.  THE LIVELY
    YEARS.
    J. HOUSEMAN, 441:25NOV73-50
ATKINSON, G. & A.C. KELLER.  PRELUDE TO
    THE ENLIGHTENMENT.
    A. MARTIN, 67:MAY72-95
    205(FMLS):JUL71-294
ATKINSON, H.  THE MAN IN THE MIDDLE.
    617(TLS):24AUG73-969
ATKINSON, M.  THE THAMES-SIDE BOOK.
    617(TLS):19OCT73-1289
ATLAS, S.  FROM CRITICAL TO SPECULATIVE
    IDEALISM.
    J.E. SCHLANGER, 542:JUL-SEP70-354
ATTERBURY, P. & A. DARWIN, EDS.  NICHOL-
    SON'S GUIDES TO THE WATERWAYS.  (VOL 4)
    617(TLS):15JUN73-700
"ATTI DEL CONVEGNO DI STUDI SU DANTE E LA
    MAGNA CURIA."
    M. POZZI, 228(GSLI):VOL147FASC457-133
"ATTI DEL CONVEGNO SUL SETTECENTO PAR-
    MENSE NEL 2° CENTENARIO DELLA MORTE DI
    C.I. FRUGONI."
    A.M. MUTTERLE, 228(GSLI):VOL147FASC
    460-598
"ATTI DEL CONVEGNO SUL TEMA: LA POESIA
    RUSTICANA NEL RINASCIMENTO (ROMA 10-13
    OTTOBRE 1968)."
    E. BIGI, 228(GSLI):VOL148FASC464-578
"ATTI DEL PRIMO SIMPOSIO INTERNAZIONALE
    DI PROTOSTORIA ITALIANA."*
    A. HUS, 555:VOL45FASC2-378

"ATTI DEL VII CONVEGNO DEL CENTRO PER
    GLI STUDI DIALETTÁLI ITALIANI."
    A. ALSDORF-BOLLÉE, 72:BAND209HEFT1/3-
    182
ATTWOOD, K.  FONTANE UND DAS PREUSSENTUM.
    T. ALT, 406:FALL72-307
ATWOOD, M.  THE EDIBLE WOMAN.*
    G.R. ELLIOTT, 648:OCT70-68
    B. MITCHELL, 296:FALL73-112
    R-S., 376:JAN70-108
ATWOOD, M.  THE JOURNALS OF SUSANNAH
    MOODIE.*  PROCEDURES FOR UNDERGROUND.*
    R-S., 376:JAN71-133
ATWOOD, M.  POWER POLITICS.*
    G. BOWERING, 102(CANL):SPRING72-91
    H. VENDLER, 441:12AUG73-6
ATWOOD, M.  SURFACING.*
    P. DELANY, 441:4MAR73-5
    E. GODFREY, 99:JAN73-34
    C. LEHMANN-HAUPT, 441:7MAR73-35
    D. MAHON, 362:24MAY73-696
    K. THOMPSON, 198:SPRING73-112
    E. WEEKS, 61:APR73-127
    442(NY):14APR73-154
    617(TLS):1JUN73-604
ATWOOD, M.  SURVIVAL.
    D. GUTTERIDGE, 99:MAY73-39
ATZESBERGER, M.  SPRACHAUFBAUHILFE BEI
    GEISTIG BEHINDERTEN KINDERN.
    V. RŪĶE-DRAVIŅA, 353:OCT71-117
AUBERT, R., ED.  CHURCH HISTORY IN FUTURE
    PERSPECTIVE.
    A.W. GODFREY, 363:MAY71-89
AUBÉRY, P.  POUR UNE LECTURE OUVRIÈRE DE
    LA LITTÉRATURE.
    J. ONIMUS, 557(RSH):OCT-DEC70-662
AUBINEAU, M. - SEE CHRYSOSTOM, J.
AUBOYER, J. & J-F. ENAULT.  LA VIE PUB-
    LIQUE ET PRIVÉE DANS L'INDE ANCIENNE
    (IIE SIÈCLE AV. J-C. - VIIIE SIÈCLE
    ENVIRON).  (FASC 1)
    J.E. VAN LOHUIZEN-DE LEEUW, 57:VOL
    33#1/2-150
AUBREY, J.  THREE PROSE WORKS.  (J.
    BUCHANAN-BROWN, ED)  AUBREY ON EDUCA-
    TION.*  (J.E. STEPHENS, ED)
    617(TLS):16FEB73-168
AUBRUN, M., ED & TRANS.  LA VIE DE
    SAINT ETIENNE D'OBAZINE.
    J. LECLERCQ, 382(MAE):1972/2-143
AUCHINCLOSS, L.  HENRY ADAMS.
    R. ASSELINEAU, 189(EA):JUL-SEP71-350
AUCHINCLOSS, L.  I COME AS A THIEF.*
    617(TLS):28SEP73-1100
AUCHINCLOSS, L.  MOTIVELESS MALIGNITY.
    I. BROWN, 157:AUTUMN70-67
    C.D. LINTON, 570(SQ):WINTER71-70
    C.B. LOWER, 219(GAR):FALL70-382
AUCHINCLOSS, L.  RICHELIEU.
    617(TLS):27JUL73-878
AUCHINCLOSS, L.  SECOND CHANCE.
    639(VQR):WINTER71-XIV
AUCLAIR, M.  ENFANCES ET MORT DE GARCIA
    LORCA.
    A. GARANT, 556(RLV):1970/1-106
AUDEMARS, P.  THE DELICATE DUST OF DEATH.
    617(TLS):18MAY73-562
AUDEN, W.H.  A CERTAIN WORLD.*
    42(AR):SUMMER70-263
AUDEN, W.H.  CITY WITHOUT WALLS.*
    T. EAGLETON, 565:VOL11#2-68
    J.H. JUSTUS, 598(SOR):WINTER73-261
    E. PUJALS, 202(FMOD):NOV71/FEB72-131
    H. SERGEANT, 175:SPRING70-29
AUDEN, W.H.  EPISTLE TO A GODSON.*
    D. DONOGHUE, 453:19JUL73-17
    R.B. SHAW, 491:SEP73-344
                              [CONTINUED]

AUDEN, W.H.  EPISTLE TO A GODSON.*  [CON-
    TINUING]
    V. YOUNG, 249(HUDR):WINTER72/73-665
    P.D. ZIVKOVIC, 109:SPRING/SUMMER73-147
    617(TLS):12JAN73-25
AUDEN, W.H.  FOREWORDS AND AFTERWORDS.
    (E. MENDELSON, ED)
    D. CAUTE, 362:23AUG73-256
    D. DONOGHUE, 453:19JUL73-17
    H. KENNER, 441:18MAR73-8
    617(TLS):12OCT73-1212
AUDEN, W.H.  SECONDARY WORLDS.*
    J.H. JUSTUS, 598(SOR):WINTER73-261
AUDEN, W.H. - SEE CHESTERTON, G.K.
AUDIBERTI, J.  L'EMPIRE ET LA TRAPPE.
    R.B. JOHNSON, 207(FR):DEC70-407
AUDRY, C.  L'AUTRE PLANÈTE.
    617(TLS):16FEB73-169
VON AUE, H. - SEE UNDER HARTMANN VON AUE
AUERBACH, E.  AN EYE FOR MUSIC.
    R. ANDERSON, 415:JUL72-672
AUERBACH, E.  GESAMMELTE AUFSÄTZE ZUR
    ROMANISCHEN PHILOLOGIE.*
    A.R. EVANS, JR., 545(RPH):NOV71-193
AUERBACH, E.  MIMESIS.
    S. LOTRINGER, 98:JUN70-498
AUGÉ, M.  LE RIVAGE ALLADIAN.
    C.L. GRANDMAISON, 69:APR71-166
AUGEROT, J.E. & F.D. POPESCU.  MODERN
    ROMANIAN.
    K. KAZAZIS, 32:JUN72-488
    E.D. TAPPE, 575(SEER):OCT72-637
AUGSTEIN, R.  JESUS: MENSCHENSOHN.
    617(TLS):6APR73-397
ST. AUGUSTINE.  ON EDUCATION.  (G. HOWIE,
    ED & TRANS)
    L.T., 154:SEP71-642
AUJAC, G. - SEE STRABO
AULOTTE, R.  PLUTARQUE EN FRANCE AU XVIE
    SIÈCLE.
    F. LASSERRE, 182:VOL24#7/8-361
AUNE, B.  RATIONALISM, EMPIRICISM, AND
    PRAGMATISM.
    W.J.L., 543:MAR71-535
AURICH, P.  DER DEUTSCH-POLNISCHE SEPTEM-
    BER 1939.
    V. MASTNY, 32:DEC72-918
AURIGEMMA, M.  ASPETTI DELLA LETTERATURA
    DEL PRIMO QUATTROCENTO.
    D.D., 275(IQ):SPRING-SUMMER72-117
AUSTEN, A.  T.S. ELIOT: THE LITERARY AND
    SOCIAL CRITICISM.
    M.L. RAINA, 295:FEB73-134
AUSTEN, R.A.  NORTHWEST TANZANIA UNDER
    GERMAN AND BRITISH RULE.
    R.G. ABRAHAMS, 69:APR71-169
AUSTER, H.  LOCAL HABITATIONS.
    G. LEVINE, 401(MLQ):SEP71-328
AUSTIN, A.  T.S. ELIOT.
    S. STEPANCHEV, 27(AL):NOV72-505
AUSTIN, C.  I LEFT MY HAT IN ANDAMOOKA.
    617(TLS):21DEC73-1574
AUSTIN, J.L.  HOW TO DO THINGS WITH WORDS.
    J. THOMSON, 316:SEP71-513
AUTHIER, D. - SEE TROTSKY, L.
"AUTOMATIC CARTOGRAPHY AND PLANNING."
    P. HALL, 46:SEP71-194
AUTY, R., J.L.I. FENNELL & J.S.G. SIM-
    MONS, EDS.  OXFORD SLAVONIC PAPERS.*
    (NEW SER, VOL 2)
    J. LEEPER, 39:JUN70-488
AUTY, R., L.R. LEWITTER & A.P. VLASTO,
    EDS.  GORSKI VIJENAC.
    G. DONCHIN, 575(SEER):APR72-327
AVALLE, D.S., ED.  "SPONSUS."
    L.J. FRIEDMAN, 545(RPH):MAY72-454

AVEDON, E. & B. SUTTON-SMITH.  THE STUDY
    OF GAMES.
    A.W. SMITH, 203:AUTUMN71-250
AVEDON, R. - SEE LARTIGUE, J.H.
AVELINE, C.  THE CAT'S EYE.
    N. CALLENDAR, 441:25FEB73-50
AVENA, A. - SEE PETRARCA, F.
AVERBUCH, R.A.  A MAGYAR NÉP SZABADSÁG-
    KÜZDELME 1848-49-BEN.  (E. ANDICS, ED)
    T. SPIRA, 32:JUN72-481
AVERY, C.  FLORENTINE RENAISSANCE SCULP-
    TURE.
    P. CANNON-BROOKES, 39:NOV71-420
AVERY, E.L.  THE LONDON STAGE, 1700-1729.
    C. PRICE, 570(SQ):WINTER71-67
AVERY, E.L. & A.H. SCOUTEN.  THE LONDON
    STAGE, 1660-1700.
    C. PRICE, 570(SQ):WINTER71-67
AVERY, G.C.  INQUIRY AND TESTAMENT.*
    H.L. KAUFMAN, 400(MLN):OCT71-747
AVI-YONAH, M. & OTHERS - SEE JONES, A.H.M.
"AVICENNA'S TREATISE ON LOGIC."  (F. ZA-
    BEEH, TRANS)
    R.E. ABU SHANAB, 319:JUL73-400
AVINERI, S.  HEGEL'S THEORY OF THE MODERN
    STATE.
    617(TLS):13APR73-426
AVIS, W.S.  A BIBLIOGRAPHY OF WRITINGS
    ON CANADIAN ENGLISH (1857-1965).
    W. STUCK, 430(NS):AUG71-449
AVNI, A.A.  THE BIBLE AND ROMANTICISM.*
    F. BASSAN, 207(FR):OCT70-257
    L.R. FURST, 220(GL&L):OCT71-63
    R.K. NEWMAN, 406:WINTER72-392
    L.M. PORTER, 131(CL):WINTER72-90
AVREKH, A.I.  STOLYPIN I TRET'IA DUMA.
    A. LEVIN, 32:JUN72-422
AVRICH, P., ED.  THE ANARCHISTS IN THE
    RUSSIAN REVOLUTION.
    617(TLS):27JUL73-865
AVRICH, P.  RUSSIAN REBELS 1600-1800.
    617(TLS):18MAY73-560
AVRIL, P.  POLITICS IN FRANCE.
    M. ROSS, 399(MLJ):JAN71-35
AXELBANK, A.  BLACK STAR OVER JAPAN.
    G. BARRACLOUGH, 453:14JUN73-27
    617(TLS):3AUG73-897
AXELOS, K.  VERS LA PENSÉE PLANÉTAIRE.
    ARGUMENTS D'UNE RECHERCHE.  LE JEU DU
    MONDE.
    G. DELEUZE, 98:APR70-344
AXTON, R. & J. STEVENS - SEE "MEDIEVAL
    FRENCH PLAYS"
AXTON, W.F.  CIRCLE OF FIRE.
    J.O. BAILEY, 599:WINTER70-81
AYALA, F.  EL RAPTO.  (P.Z. BORING, ED)
    R.W. HATTON, 238:SEP71-613
DE AYALA, R.P. - SEE UNDER PÉREZ DE
    AYALA, R.
AYAO, H. - SEE UNDER HOSHI AYAO
AYER, A.J., ED.  LOGICAL POSITIVISM.
    A. CHURCH, 316:JUN70-312
AYER, A.J.  METAPHYSICS AND COMMON
    SENSE.*
    D.D. TODD, 154:SEP70-258
AYER, A.J.  THE ORIGINS OF PRAGMATISM.*
    R.M. HERBENICK & P. TIBBETTS, 477:
    WINTER71-121
    R. RORTY, 482(PHR):JAN71-96
AYER, A.J.  RUSSELL AND MOORE.*
    V. HOPE, 518:MAY72-4
    A.R. LOUCH, 319:JAN73-130
AYER, A.J.  BERTRAND RUSSELL AS A PHIL-
    OSOPHER.
    617(TLS):23MAR73-330
AYERS, J.  THE BAUR COLLECTION: CHINESE
    CERAMICS.  (VOL 2)
    H.M. GARNER, 39:MAR71-225

15

AYERS, J. THE BAUR COLLECTION, GENEVA:
CHINESE CERAMICS. (VOL 3)
617(TLS):5OCT73-1168
AYERS, M.R. THE REFUTATION OF DETERMIN-
ISM.
R. BLANCHÉ, 542:APR-JUN70-258
K.W. RANKIN, 482(PHR):JAN71-106
AYERST, D., ED. THE GUARDIAN OMNIBUS
1821-1971.
617(TLS):10AUG73-922
AYLING, A., ED. A FURTHER COLLECTION OF
CHINESE LYRICS AND OTHER POEMS.
W. SCHULTZ, 50(ARQ):SPRING71-79
AYLING, R., ED. SEAN O'CASEY.*
S. COWASJEE, 159(DM):SUMMER/AUTUMN70-
121
AYLLÓN, C. & P. SMITH. SPANISH COMPOSI-
TION THROUGH LITERATURE.
H.J. FREY, 238:DEC71-992
AYNOR, H.S. NOTES FROM AFRICA.
S.A. GITELSON, 390:JAN71-75
AYRTON, M. FABRICATIONS.
V. CUNNINGHAM, 362:11JAN73-56
J. UPDIKE, 442(NY):5MAY73-147
617(TLS):11MAY73-537
AYRTON, M. THE MINOTAUR.
J. COTTON, 503:WINTER71-194
AYRTON, M. GIOVANNI PISANO SCULPTOR.*
D.A. STOTT, 592:NOV70-213
90:JUL71-432
AZEMA, J-P. & M. WINOCK. LA IIIE RÉPUB-
LIQUE.
L. LOUBERE, 207(FR):APR71-942
DE AZEREDO PERDIGÃO, J. CALOUSTE GUL-
BENKIAN - COLLECTOR.
E. LUCIE-SMITH, 592:JUL/AUG71-44
DE AZEVEDO, C. BAROQUE ORGAN-CASES OF
PORTUGAL.
P. WILLIAMS, 415:AUG72-777
DE AZEVEDO, L.A., J. CALHAU & L.C. SAR-
AIVA FEIJÓ. PORTUGUÊS PARA O CURSO
NORMAL, TERCEIRA SÉRIE.
J.R. KELLY, 238:SEP71-612
AZIZ, K.K. AMEER ALI.*
468:VOL22#1-58

BA SHIN, L. EARLY BURMESE CULTURE IN A
PAGÁN TEMPLE.
A.B. GRISWOLD & NAI PAN HLA, 57:VOL
33#3-228
VAN DEN BAAR, A.H. A RUSSIAN CHURCH
SLAVONIC KANNONIK, 1331-1332.*
E. KEENAN, 589:JUL72-563
BAASCH, K. DIE CRESCENTIALEGENDE IN DER
DEUTSCHEN DICHTUNG DES MITTELALTERS.
R.M. KULLY, 657(WW):JAN/FEB70-69
BABB, H.S. THE NOVELS OF WILLIAM GOLD-
ING.*
D.B. GRAY, 401(MLQ):SEP71-335
BABB, L. THE MORAL COSMOS OF "PARADISE
LOST."
E.F. DANIELS, 568(SCN):SPRING72-6
F. LYONS, 301(JEGP):JAN72-133
BABCOCK, C.M. - SEE WHITMAN, W.
"BABELIAN ILLUSTRATIONS/ILLUSTRATIONS
BABÉLIENNES."
R. MERCIER, 557(RSH):OCT-DEC70-665
BABINGTON SMITH, C. ROSE MACAULAY.*
617(TLS):12JAN73-41
BABINIOTES, G.D. HO DIA SYNTHESEOS
YPOKORISMOS EIS TEN ELLENIKEN.
R. BROWNING, 123:MAR72-124
BABLET, D. & J. JACQUOT, EDS. L'EXPRES-
SIONNISME DANS LE THÉÂTRE EUROPÉEN.
D. GRONAU, 182:VOL24#23/24-863
BABUT, D. PLUTARQUE DE LA VERTU ÉTHIQUE.
J.P. HERSHBELL, 24:OCT72-640

BABUT, D. PLUTARQUE ET LE STOÏCISME.
J.P. HERSHBELL, 24:JUL72-485
A.A. LONG, 123:MAR72-27
BABUT, D. - SEE PLUTARCH
BACH, E. AN INTRODUCTION TO TRANSFORMA-
TIONAL GRAMMARS.
D.L.F. NILSEN, 353:OCT71-107
BACH, E. & R.T. HARMS, EDS. UNIVERSALS
IN LINGUISTIC THEORY.*
H.E. BREKLE, 260(IF):BAND75-230
R.C. DOUGHERTY, 206:NOV70-505
J.R. HURFORD, 297(JL):APR71-132
BACH, H. & S. DUŠEK. SLAWEN IN THÜRINGEN.
K. TACKENBERG, 182:VOL24#19/20-745
BACHELARD, G. THE PHILOSOPHY OF NO. THE
POETICS OF REVERIE.
J.S. BOIS, 186(ETC.):JUN71-244
BACHELARD, S. A STUDY OF HUSSERL'S "FOR-
MAL AND TRANSCENDENTAL LOGIC."*
A.W. WOOD, 482(PHR):APR71-267
BACHMANN, I. SIMULTAN.
617(TLS):5JAN73-5
BACHMANN, J. & S. VON MOOS. NEW DIREC-
TIONS IN SWISS ARCHITECTURE.
J. GUBLER, 576:MAY71-181
BACIU, S. & K. MARTI, EDS & TRANS. DER
BU BIST IM EXIL.
A. CORREIA PACHECO, 37:JAN70-39
BACKÈS-CLÉMENT, C. LÉVI-STRAUSS.
L. FINAS, 98:NOV71-998
BACKHOUSE, S. SINGAPORE.
617(TLS):6APR73-368
BACQUE, J. THE LONELY ONES.*
J. MILLS, 648:JUN70-35
BACQUE, J. A MAN OF TALENT.
L. MONKMAN, 296:FALL73-91
BACULO, A.G. OTTO WAGNER.
N. PEVSNER, 46:FEB71-132
DE BADAJOZ, D.S. - SEE UNDER SÁNCHEZ DE
BADAJOZ, D.
BADALONI, N. ANTONIO CONTI, UN ABATE
LIBERO PENSATORE FRA NEWTON E VOLTAIRE.
E. GIANTURCO, 131(CL):FALL72-372
E. NAMER, 542:APR-JUN70-239
BADAWI, M.M. COLERIDGE: CRITIC OF SHAKE-
SPEARE.
617(TLS):18MAY73-558
BADEN, H.J. LITERATUR UND BEKEHRUNG.
K.S. WEIMAR, 221(GQ):JAN71-89
BADER, F. ÉTUDES DE COMPOSITION NOMINALE
EN MYCÉNIEN.* (VOL 1)
N.E. COLLINGE, 487:AUTUMN71-290
BADESLADE, J. & J. ROCQUE. VITRUVIUS
BRITANNICUS VOLUME THE FOURTH [TOGETHER
WITH] WOOLF, J. & J. GANDON. VITRU-
VIUS BRITANNICUS VOLUME IV AND VOLUME
V.
617(TLS):23FEB73-216
BADIAN, E. PUBLICANS AND SINNERS.
617(TLS):16FEB73-184
BADIN, G. TITRE PLURIEL SUJETS.
H.A. BOURAOUI, 207(FR):APR71-950
"LEO BAECK INSTITUTE YEAR BOOK XIV."
M.A. MEYER, 328:FALL70-504
BAEHR, R., ED. "ENEAS," ANTIKISIERENDER
ROMAN DES 12. JAHRHUNDERTS.
P.F. DEMBOWSKI, 545(RPH):AUG71-147
BAER, W. THE DEVELOPMENT OF THE BRAZIL-
IAN STEEL INDUSTRY.
F.J. MUNCH, 37:MAR71-37
BAETZHOLD, H.G. MARK TWAIN AND JOHN
BULL.
C.L. GRIMM, JR., 594:SPRING71-118
R. LEHAN, 445(NCF):SEP71-245
BAGLEY, D. THE TIGHTROPE MEN.
N. CALLENDAR, 441:12AUG73-12
S. HILL, 362:22MAR73-390
617(TLS):13APR73-427

16

BAGLEY, J.J. - SEE BLUNDELL, N.
BAGNOLD, E. ENID BAGNOLD'S AUTOBIOGRA-
PHY.
    639(VQR):WINTER71-XXXII
BAGOLINI, L. VISIONE DELLA GUISTIZIA E
SENSO COMUNE.
    H. PETZOLD, 480(P&R):SUMMER70-188
BAHLOW, H. DEUTSCHES NAMENLEXIKON.
    G.B. DROEGE, 424:MAR71-55
BAHM, A.J. THE HEART OF CONFUCIUS.
    E.J. COLEMAN, 485(PE&W):JUL70-329
BAHN, E. & M.L. A HISTORY OF ORAL INTER-
PRETATION.
    H.V. STEER, 583:SUMMER72-449
BAHNE, S., ED. ORIGINES ET DEBUTS DES
PARTIS COMMUNISTES DES PAYS LATINS
(1919-1923).
    J.W. HULSE, 32:MAR72-239
BAHNS, J. JOHANNES OTZEN 1839-1911.
    M. BRINGMANN, 683:BAND34HEFT4-320
BAHR, G.E. - SEE BRECHT, B.
BAHR, H. ZUR ÜBERWINDUNG DES NATURALIS-
MUS. (G. WUNBERG, ED)
    J. FINCK, 556(RLV):1971/3-359
    J.A. SOENEN, 433:OCT70-432
BAIER, K. & N. RESCHER, EDS. VALUES AND
THE FUTURE.
    L.A. ELIOSEFF, 290(JAAC):FALL70-133
BAIER-SCHRÖCKE, H. DER STUCKDEKOR IN
THÜRINGEN, VOM 16, BIS ZUM 18, JAHRHUN-
DERT.
    H. HUTH, 54:MAR70-106
DE BAÏF, J-A. JEAN-ANTOINE DE BAÏF;
POEMS. (M. QUAINTON, ED)
    G. CASTOR, 402(MLR):JAN72-185
    T.C. CAVE, 208(FS):OCT72-447
BAIGELL, M. A HISTORY OF AMERICAN PAINT-
ING.
    617(TLS):9NOV73-1362
BAILBÉ, J. AGRIPPA D'AUBIGNÉ, POÈTE DES
"TRAGIQUES."*
    R.J. FINK, 551(RENQ):AUTUMN71-388
    J. PINEAUX, 535(RHL):JAN-FEB70-120
BAILBÉ, J-M. LE ROMAN ET LA MUSIQUE EN
FRANCE SOUS LA MONARCHIE DE JUILLET.*
    J.S.P., 191(ELN):SEP71(SUPP)-65
BAILEY, D.R.S. - SEE UNDER SHACKLETON
BAILEY, D.R.
BAILEY, D.W. BRITISH MILITARY LONGARMS
1815-1865.
    617(TLS):23FEB73-212
BAILEY, H.C. LIBERALISM IN THE NEW
SOUTH, SOUTHERN SOCIAL REFORMERS AND
THE PROGRESSIVE MOVEMENT.
    W.W. ROGERS, 9(ALAR):APR71-156
BAILEY, H.C. EDGAR GARDNER MURPHY.
    M.B. HOWARD, JR., 9(ALAR):APR70-152
BAILEY, H.W. KHOTANESE TEXTS. (VOLS 1-3)
(2ND ED)
    R. SCHMITT, 343:BAND13HEFT2-217
BAILEY, J.O., ED. BRITISH PLAYS OF THE
NINETEENTH CENTURY.
    P.D. HERRING, 405(MP):AUG70-83
BAILEY, J.O. THE POETRY OF THOMAS
HARDY.*
    R. BENVENUTO, 637(VS):DEC70-220
    D.F. MOLDSTAD, 636(VP):WINTER71-462
    R.G. SCHWEIK, 177(ELT):VOL13#4-303
    W.F. WRIGHT, 502(PRS):WINTER70/71-363
BAILEY, P. A DISTANT LIKENESS.
    S. HILL, 362:14JUN73-808
    617(TLS):29JUN73-737
BAILEY, P. TRESPASSES.*
    42(AR):SPRING71-131
BAILEY, R. THE SQUATTERS.
    D.A.N. JONES, 362:8MAR73-313
    617(TLS):23MAR73-321

BAILEY, R.F. PRE-REVOLUTIONARY HOUSES
AND FAMILIES IN NORTHERN NEW JERSEY AND
SOUTHERN NEW YORK.
    R. LEWCOCK, 46:AUG70-131
BAILEY, R.W. & D.M. BURTON. ENGLISH
STYLISTICS.*
    D.C. FREEMAN, 206:NOV70-590
BAILEY, R.W. & L. DOLEŽEL. AN ANNOTATED
BIBLIOGRAPHY OF STATISTICAL STYLISTICS.
    H. KUČERA, 206:AUG71-455
BAILEY, S.D. CHINESE REPRESENTATION IN
THE SECURITY COUNCIL AND THE GENERAL
ASSEMBLY OF THE UNITED NATIONS.
    617(TLS):20APR73-434
BAILLÉN, C. CHANEL-SOLITAIRE.
    617(TLS):9NOV73-1381
BAILLIE, F. THE BEER DRINKER'S COMPANION.
    617(TLS):21DEC73-1574
BAILYN, B. THE IDEOLOGICAL ORIGINS OF
THE AMERICAN REVOLUTION.
    C.R. RITCHESON, 173(ECS):FALL70-95
BAIN, G. CHAMPAGNE IS FOR BREAKFAST.
    A. APPENZELL, 102(CANL):AUTUMN72-104
BAINBRIDGE, B. THE DRESSMAKER.
    E. FEINSTEIN, 362:27SEP73-426
    617(TLS):28SEP73-1101
BAINBRIDGE, B. HARRIET SAID...*
    G. GODWIN, 441:30SEP73-38
    442(NY):29OCT73-180
BAINES, J. & K. KEY. THE ABC OF HOUSE
AND CONSERVATORY PLANTS.
    617(TLS):23NOV73-1456
BAINTON, R.H. ERASMUS OF CHRISTENDOM.*
    J.C. OLIN, 613:SPRING70-155
BAIRD, J. THE DOME AND THE ROCK.*
    J.B. MEROD, 290(JAAC):WINTER70-276
BAKER, A. STOLEN SWEETS.
    A. BROYARD, 441:22OCT73-29
BAKER, A.R.H. & J.B. HARLEY, EDS. MAN
MADE THE LAND.
    617(TLS):16NOV73-1409
BAKER, C. THE GAY HEAD CONSPIRACY.
    N. CALLENDAR, 441:8JUL73-26
BAKER, C. HEMINGWAY. (NEW ED)
    617(TLS):30MAR73-357
BAKER, D.V. AN OLD MILL BY THE STREAM.
    617(TLS):14SEP73-1065
BAKER, E.C. A GUIDE TO RECORDS IN THE
WINDWARD ISLANDS.
    R.S. MAXWELL, 14:JAN70-86
BAKER, F. MORNING STAR. (A. BAKER, ED)
    617(TLS):12JAN73-48
BAKER, H.A., JR., ED. BLACK LITERATURE
IN AMERICA.
    639(VQR):AUTUMN71-CLXXII
BAKER, M. - SEE SEYMOUR, A.
BAKER, P. THE WILD BUNCH AT ROBBERS
ROOST.
    W. GARD, 584(SWR):SPRING72-V
BAKHTIN, M. RABELAIS AND HIS WORLD.*
    A.C. KELLER, 546(RR):FEB71-41
    W.W. KIBLER, 599:WINTER70-73
BAKHTINE, M. PROBLÈMES DE LA POÉTIQUE DE
DOSTOÏEVSKI.
    D. SALLENAVE, 98:DEC70-1008
BAKKER, D.M. SAMENTREKKING IN NEDER-
LANDSE SYNTACTISCHE GROEPEN.*
    A. SASSEN, 206:FEB71-143
BAKLANOFF, E.N., ED. THE SHAPING OF
MODERN BRAZIL.
    F.J. MUNCH, 37:MAR71-37
BAKUNIN, M. MICHEL BAKOUNINE ET SES
RELATIONS AVEC SERGEJ NEČAEV, 1870-
1872.* (A. LEHNING, ED)
    W. MC CLELLAN, 32:DEC72-893
BAKUNIN, M. BAKUNIN ON ANARCHY.* (S.
DOLGOFF, ED & TRANS)
    M. RAEFF, 676(YR):SUMMER72-625
    617(TLS):24AUG73-983

17

BALADI, N. LA PENSÉE DE PLOTIN.
  J.B. AYOUB, 154:JUN71-405
  J. GRENIER, 542:APR-JUN71-229
BALAKIAN, A. ANDRÉ BRETON.*
  H. CONANT, 127:FALL71-102
  J.H. MATTHEWS, 401(MLQ):SEP72-327
  A. WINDSOR, 89(BJA):SUMMER72-306
BALAKIAN, A. SURREALISM. (NEW ED)
  617(TLS):22JUN73-713
BALANDIER, G. POLITICAL ANTHROPOLOGY.
  639(VQR):SUMMER71-CXXXVII
BALASUBRAHMANYAM, S.R. EARLY CHOLA ART.
  (PT 1)
  P. CHANDRA, 293(JAST):FEB71-514
"THE BALAVARIANI." (D.M. LANG, TRANS)
  S. LEVITT, 318(JAOS):JAN-MAR71-160
BALD, R.C. JOHN DONNE.* (W. MILGATE,
  ED)
  H. FOLTINEK, 182:VOL24#4-157
  P. LEGOUIS, 541(RES):NOV71-490
  J.H. MC CABE, 613:SPRING71-133
  J.M. MUELLER, 405(MP):FEB72-231
  J.P., 376:JAN71-136
  S.G. PUTT, 175:AUTUMN70-102
  L. UNGER, 191(ELN):DEC71-141
BALDINGER, K., WITH J-D. GENDRON & G.
  STRAKA, EDS. DICTIONNAIRE ÉTYMOLOGIQUE
  DE L'ANCIEN FRANÇAIS. (FASC G1)
  R. HARRIS, 382(MAE):1972/3-294
BALDWIN, E. DIFFERENTIATION AND CO-OPER-
  ATION IN AN ISRAELI VETERAN MOSHAV.
  617(TLS):18MAY73-544
BALDWIN, J. TELL ME HOW LONG THE TRAIN'S
  BEEN GONE.
  J.C. FIELD, 556(RLV):1971/3-336
BALDWIN, J.W. MASTERS, PRINCES AND MER-
  CHANTS.*
  D. LUSCOMBE, 382(MAE):1972/1-56
  639(VQR):WINTER71-XL
BALDWIN, M. BURIED GOD.
  617(TLS):16NOV73-1405
BALDWIN, M.W., ED. A HISTORY OF THE
  CRUSADES. (VOL 1) (2ND ED)
  J.F. POWERS, 613:SPRING71-148
BALEWA, A.T. - SEE UNDER TAFAWA BALEWA,
  A.
BALFOUR, C. INCOMES POLICY AND THE PUB-
  LIC SECTOR.
  617(TLS):9FEB73-148
BALFOUR, C., ED. PARTICIPATION IN INDUS-
  TRY.
  617(TLS):19OCT73-1289
BALFOUR, C. UNIONS AND THE LAW.
  617(TLS):30NOV73-1469
BALFOUR, H. WINGS OVER WESTMINSTER.
  617(TLS):13APR73-417
BALFOUR, M. & J. FRISBY. HELMUTH VON
  MOLTKE.
  G.F. KENNAN, 453:22MAR73-3
  B.R. VON OPPEN, 441:15APR73-28
  617(TLS):23MAR73-311
BALINKY, A. MARX'S ECONOMICS.*
  P.C. ROBERTS, 550(RUSR):APR71-195
BALINT, M., P.H. ORNSTEIN & E. BALINT.
  FOCAL PSYCHOTHERAPY.
  617(TLS):23FEB73-200
BALKA, M. OUTPOST.
  M. LEVIN, 441:28JAN73-34
BALL, I. PITCAIRN.
  A. VILLIERS, 441:23SEP73-26
BALL, J. WILLIAM CASLON, 1693-1766.
  617(TLS):7DEC73-1519
BALL, P.M. THE CENTRAL SELF.*
  R. LANGBAUM, 636(VP):WINTER70-356
  F.N. LEES, 447(N&Q):OCT71-397
  J.R. MAC GILLIVRAY, 627(UTQ):FALL70-73

BALL, P.M. THE SCIENCE OF ASPECTS.
  K. ALLOTT, 402(MLR):APR72-404
  R. PARK, 89(BJA):SUMMER72-304
BALL, R.H. SHAKESPEARE ON SILENT FILM.
  R.A. FOAKES, 175:SPRING70-22
  C. HURTGEN, 570(SQ):SPRING70-177
BALLAIRA, G. - SEE TIBERIUS
BALLANCHE, P.S. LA VISION D'HÉBAL.
  (A-J-L. BUSST, ED)
  F.P. BOWMAN, 535(RHL):MAY-JUN71-517
BALLANTYNE, R.M. HUDSON'S BAY.
  S. ATHERTON, 296:SUMMER73-110
BALLARD, A.B. THE EDUCATION OF BLACK
  FOLK.
  F.M. HECHINGER, 441:7JUL73-19
BALLARD, J.G. CRASH.
  V. CUNNINGHAM, 362:28JUN73-873
  D.K. MANO, 441:23SEP73-7
  617(TLS):13JUL73-797
BALLARD, J.G. VERMILION SANDS.
  617(TLS):30NOV73-1466
BALLET, A.H., ED. PLAYWRIGHTS FOR TOMOR-
  ROW. (VOLS 5&6)
  A. RENDLE, 157:SUMMER70-75
BALLET, A.H., ED. PLAYWRIGHTS FOR TOMOR-
  ROW. (VOL 7)
  L. RUSSELL, 376:OCT71-134
BALLOU, S. THE BUILDING OF THE HOUSE.*
  W. GARRETT, 432(NEQ):JUN71-310
BALLY, C. & A. SECHEHAYE - SEE DE SAUS-
  SURE, F.
BALMAS, E. - SEE JODELLE, É.
BALME, M.G. THE MILLIONAIRE'S DINNER
  PARTY.
  617(TLS):15JUN73-699
BALOUS, S. L'ACTION CULTURELLE DE LA
  FRANCE DANS LE MONDE.
  H. GODIN, 208(FS):APR72-237
BALSDON, J.P.V.D. LIFE AND LEISURE IN
  ANCIENT ROME.*
  B. BALDWIN, 121(CJ):APR-MAY72-374
BALSEIRO, J.A. LA GRATITUD HUMANA.
  E. ECHEVARRÍA, 238:MAR71-202
VON BALTHASAR, H.U. HERRLICHKEIT. (VOLS
  2 & 3)
  A.A. ANDERSON, 182:VOL24#1/2-1
BALTY, J. LA GRANDE MOSAÏQUE DE LA
  CHASSE DU TRICLINOS.
  D.J. SMITH, 313:VOL61-291
DE BALZAC, H. LETTRES À MADAME HANSKA.
  (VOL 4) (R. PIERROT, ED)
  H.J. HUNT, 208(FS):OCT72-463
DE BALZAC, H. ALBERT SAVARUS. (W.G.
  MOORE, ED)
  D. ADAMSON, 208(FS):APR72-213
BAMBERGER, C., ED. THE CONDUCTOR'S ART.
  M. PETERSON, 470:MAR66-28
BAMBOROUGH, J.B. BEN JONSON.
  F.L. HUNTLEY, 551(RENQ):SUMMER71-275
  S.G. PUTT, 175:AUTUMN71-101
BAMBROUGH, R. REASON, TRUTH AND GOD.*
  N. SMART, 482(PHR):JUL71-402
BANAŠEVIĆ, N., ED. PROCEEDINGS OF THE
  FIFTH CONGRESS OF THE INTERNATIONAL
  COMPARATIVE LITERATURE ASSOCIATION:
  BELGRADE, 1967."* (FRENCH TITLE: ACTES
  DU VE CONGRÈS DE L'ASSOCIATION INTER-
  NATIONALE DE LITTÉRATURE COMPARÉE.)
  M. BELLER, 52:BAND6HEFT2-187
BANCQUART, M-C. & OTHERS - SEE BOUILHET,
  L. & L. COLET
BANDERA GÓMEZ, C. EL "POEMA DE MÍO CID."*
  H.T. OOSTENDORP, 433:APR71-210
BANDINELLI, R.B. - SEE UNDER BIANCHI BAN-
  DINELLI, R.

BANDMAN, B. & R.S. GUTTSCHEN, EDS. PHIL-
OSOPHICAL ESSAYS ON THE CURRICULUM.
PHILOSOPHICAL ESSAYS ON TEACHING.
J.F., 543:MAR71-555
BANDYOPADHYAYA, J. MAO TSE-TUNG AND
GANDHI.
617(TLS):7DEC73-1510
BANERJI, A.K. BANKURA.
J.H. BROOMFIELD, 293(JAST):AUG71-913
BANERJI, B. PATHER PANCHALI.
E. BENDER, 318(JAOS):JAN-MAR71-161
BANERJI, S.C. SMRTI MATERIAL IN THE
MAHĀBHĀRATA, BEING A COLLECTION OF
VERSES WHICH ARE IMPORTANT FROM THE
SOCIOLOGICAL POINT OF VIEW. (VOL 1)
617(TLS):23FEB73-221
BANG, I. & YI RYUK - SEE UNDER IM BANG &
YI RYUK
BANHAM, R. THE ARCHITECTURE OF THE WELL-
TEMPERED ENVIRONMENT.*
C.W. CONDIT, 56:SUMMER70-179
J.M. FITCH, 576:OCT70-282
BANHAM, R. LOS ANGELES.*
B. GOODEY, 46:SEP71-194
J.S. MARGOLIES, 44:NOV71-10
BANK, H. PRECIOUS STONES AND MINERALS.
G. WILLS, 39:MAY71-436
BANKS, R.F. MAINE BECOMES A STATE.
P. GOODMAN, 656(WMQ):JUL71-508
B.F. TOLLES, JR., 432(NEQ):JUN71-344
BANN, S., ED. CONCRETE POETRY.
D.H. SULLIVAN, 648:OCT70-69
BANN, S. EXPERIMENTAL PAINTING.
J. BENTHALL, 592:JUL-AUG70-50
BANN, S. & J.E. BOWLT, EDS. RUSSIAN
FORMALISM.
617(TLS):5OCT73-1164
BANNAN, A.J. & A. EDELENYI. DOCUMENTARY
HISTORY OF EASTERN EUROPE.
C. JELAVICH, 32:SEP72-702
BANTA, M. HENRY JAMES AND THE OCCULT.
617(TLS):30NOV73-1467
BANTA, M., WITH R. GOTTESMAN & D.J. NORD-
LOH - SEE HOWELLS, W.D.
BANTI, A. ARTEMISIA.
J-M. GARDAIR, 98:JAN71-89
BANTI, L. IL MONDO DEGLI ETRUSCHI.
D.E. STRONG, 313:VOL61-312
BANTOCK, G. EIRENIKON.
617(TLS):9MAR73-270
BANTOCK, M. GRANVILLE BANTOCK.*
P.J. PIRIE, 415:JUL72-670
J.A.W., 410(M&L):OCT72-438
BANTON, M. POLICE COMMUNITY RELATIONS.
617(TLS):10AUG73-934
BANVILLE, J. BIRCHWOOD.
M. LEVIN, 441:17JUN73-28
617(TLS):16FEB73-169
BAO RUO-WANG (J. PASQUALINI) & R. CHEL-
MINSKI. PRISONER OF MAO.
J.K. FAIRBANK, 453:1NOV73-3
BAQUERO GOYANES, M. ESTRUCTURAS DE LA
NOVELA ACTUAL.
A. CIORANESCU, 549(RLC):OCT-DEC71-620
BAR-ADON, A. & W.F. LEOPOLD, EDS. CHILD
LANGUAGE.
M. FULTON, 351(LL):DEC71-257
H.A. WHITAKER, 399(MLJ):DEC71-535
BAR-HILLEL, Y. ASPECTS OF LANGUAGE.
A. JAGGAR, 484(PPR):MAR72-429
BARANY, G. STEPHEN SZÉCHENYI AND THE
AWAKENING OF HUNGARIAN NATIONALISM,
1791-1841.*
L. PÉTER, 575(SEER):JAN72-122
BARATTA, G. L'IDEALISMO FENOMENOLOGICO
DI EDMUND HUSSERL.
E. NAMER, 542:OCT-DEC71-490

BARAZ, M. L'ÊTRE ET LA CONNAISSANCE
SELON MONTAIGNE.*
F.P. BOWMAN, 207(FR):MAR71-811
Y. DELÈGUE, 535(RHL):MAR-APR70-306
G. DREYFUS, 542:JUL-SEP70-356
C. EYER, 551(RENQ):AUTUMN71-385
D.M. FRAME, 546(RR):DEC71-293
BARBAGLI, D.A. - SEE PATRIZI, F.
BARBARISI, G. - SEE FOSCOLO, U.
BARBARO, E. DE COELIBATU - DE OFFICIO
LEGATI. (V. BRANCA, ED)
P. FLORIANI, 228(GSLI):VOL147FASC458/
459-449
A. SCAGLIONE, 405(MP):MAY72-338
BARBEAU, A.T. THE INTELLECTUAL DESIGN OF
JOHN DRYDEN'S HEROIC PLAYS.*
G. FALLE, 173(ECS):SPRING72-480
W.F.T. MYERS, 541(RES):AUG71-346
K.E. ROBINSON, 447(N&Q):DEC71-476
A.H. SCOUTEN, 481(PQ):JUL71-422
BARBER, C. LINGUISTIC CHANGE IN PRESENT-
DAY ENGLISH.
B.M.H. STRANG, 47(ARL):VOL17FASC1-55
BARBER, C. - SEE MIDDLETON, T.
BARBER, G., COMP. FRENCH LETTERPRESS
PRINTING.
J.W. JOLLIFFE, 208(FS):APR72-236
BARBER, J. SOUTH AFRICA'S FOREIGN POLICY
1945-70.
617(TLS):21SEP73-1076
BARBER, N. FROM THE LAND OF LOST CONTENT.
639(VQR):SUMMER71-CXXXIV
BARBER, N. THE LORDS OF THE GOLDEN HORN.
617(TLS):9NOV73-1359
BARBER, R. COOKING AND RECIPES FROM
ROME TO THE RENAISSANCE.
617(TLS):28DEC73-1583
BARBER, R. THE MIDNIGHTERS.
L. ELKIN, 287:MAY71-24
BARBERI, F. IL FRONTESPIZIO NEL LIBRO
ITALIANO DEL QUATTROCENTO E DEL CINQUE-
CENTO.*
R. MORTIMER, 551(RENQ):SPRING71-58
BARBEY D'AUREVILLY, J. EIN VERHEIRATETER
PRIESTER. (H. HOFER, ED)
R. KOPP, 535(RHL):JAN-FEB70-150
BARBIERI, F. CORPUS PALLADIANUM.* (VOL
2: LA BASILICA PALLADIANA.)
J.S. ACKERMAN, 54:JUN70-215
J. NEWMAN, 90:NOV71-675
BARBIERI, T. - SEE CARDUCCI, G.
BARBINA, A. BIBLIOGRAFIA DELLA CRITICA
PIRANDELLIANA, 1889-1961.
B.L., 275(IQ):SPRING-SUMMER72-123
BARBINA, A., ED. CONCORDANZE DEL "DECAM-
ERON."
M. MARTI, 228(GSLI):VOL148FASC462/
463-416
BARBOUR, D. LANDFALL.
D.G. JONES, 102(CANL):SUMMER72-81
P. STEVENS, 628:SPRING72-103
BARBOUR, D. A POEM AS LONG AS THE HIGH-
WAY.
D.G. JONES, 102(CANL):SUMMER72-81
BARBUDO, A.S. - SEE UNDER SÁNCHEZ BAR-
BUDO, A.
DE LA BARCA, P.C. - SEE UNDER CALDERÓN DE
LA BARCA, P.
BARCIA, J.R. & M.A. ZEITLIN - SEE UNDER
RUBIA BARCIA, J. & M.A. ZEITLIN
BARDÈCHE, M. MARCEL PROUST ROMANCIER.
(VOL 1)
G. TUPINIER, 535(RHL):SEP-DEC71-994
BARDEN, L., W.R. HARTSTON & R.D. KEENE.
THE KING'S INDIAN DEFENCE. (REV)
617(TLS):21SEP73-1093
BARDI, P.M. NEW BRAZILIAN ART.
G. CHAPMAN, 363:AUG71-120

19

BARDON, H. - SEE CATULLUS
BARDOS, J-P., ED. STENDHAL.
F.W. SAUNDERS, 208(FS):APR72-210
BAREA, A. THE FORGING OF A REBEL.
617(TLS):30MAR73-357
BARFOED, N. OMKRING NIELS LYHNE.
E. LUNDING, 462(OL):VOL26#2-158
BARGEBUHR, F.P. THE ALHAMBRA.
J. CORTÉS, 399(MLJ):JAN71-34
O. GRABAR, 54:JUN70-197
BAR HAYYA, A. - SEE UNDER ABRAHAM BAR
HAYYA
BARIK, H.C. A STUDY OF SIMULTANEOUS
INTERPRETATION.
75:4/1971-48
BARINEAU, É. - SEE HUGO, V.
BARING, A. UPRISING IN EAST GERMANY:
JUNE 17, 1953.
617(TLS):30NOV73-1470
BARKER, A. & M. RUSH. THE MEMBER OF
PARLIAMENT AND HIS INFORMATION.
M. HOPPE, 619(TC):VOL179#1046-54
BARKER, A.J. THE WAR AGAINST RUSSIA,
1854-1856.
J.S. CURTISS, 32:MAR72-155
W.B. WALSH, 550(RUSR):OCT71-395
BARKER, D. G.K. CHESTERTON.
R.R. LINGEMAN, 441:1SEP73-19
A. WILSON, 441:19AUG73-3
442(NY):8OCT73-170
617(TLS):17AUG73-943
BARKER, D. PROMINENT EDWARDIANS.
R.F., 189(EA):APR-JUN71-213
BARKER, E. AUSTRIA 1918-1972.
617(TLS):24AUG73-981
BARKER, G. IN MEMORY OF DAVID ARCHER.
617(TLS):21DEC73-1562
BARKER, G. POEMS OF PLACES AND PEOPLE.*
H. SERGEANT, 175:AUTUMN71-106
BARKER, J.A. A FORMAL ANALYSIS OF CON-
DITIONALS.
L.G., 543:MAR71-535
BARKER, M.A-A., H.J. HAMDANI & K.M.S.
DIHLAVI. AN URDU NEWSPAPER WORD-COUNT.
E. BENDER, 318(JAOS):JAN-MAR71-162
BARKER, N. & D. CLEVERDON, EDS. STANLEY
MORISON, 1889-1967.
D. CHAMBERS, 503:WINTER70-226
BARLA, G. KEMÉNY ZSIGMOND FŐBB ESZMÉI
1849 ELŐTT.
G. BARANY, 32:JUN72-480
BARLACH, E. DIE BRIEFE.* (VOLS 1&2)
(F. DROSS, ED)
617(TLS):5OCT73-1168
BARLAY, S. DOUBLE CROSS.
617(TLS):12OCT73-1235
BARLOW, D. DICK TURPIN AND THE GREGORY
GANG.
617(TLS):5OCT73-1182
BARLOW, D. - SEE STERNHEIM, C.
BARLOW, E. FREDERICK LAW OLMSTED'S NEW
YORK.
C. WISEMAN, 231:FEB73-105
BARLOW, F. EDWARD THE CONFESSOR.*
M. ALTSCHUL, 589:JUL72-508
BARLOW, S.A. THE IMAGERY OF EURIPIDES.
F. LASSERRE, 182:VOL24#7/8-363
BARLOW, W. THE ALEXANDER PRINCIPLE.
617(TLS):3AUG73-913
BARNABAS, A.P. CITIZENS' GRIEVANCES AND
ADMINISTRATION.
C.P. BHAMBHRI, 293(JAST):NOV70-209
BARNARD, E., ED. EDWIN ARLINGTON ROBIN-
SON.*
N. JOYNER, 577(SHR):SPRING71-201
W.R. ROBINSON, 219(GAR):SPRING71-105
BARNARD, F.M. - SEE VON HERDER, J.G.

BARNARD, G.C. SAMUEL BECKETT.*
A.W. BRINK, 529(QQ):SUMMER71-334
J. FLETCHER, 188(ECR):FALL71-67
R. MACLEAN, 157:SUMMER70-72
BARNARD, H.C. THE FRENCH TRADITION IN
EDUCATION.
D.F. BRADSHAW, 208(FS):OCT72-488
BARNARD, J., ED. JOHN KEATS.
617(TLS):16NOV73-1409
BARNES, H.E. THE UNIVERSITY AS THE NEW
CHURCH.
J.S. RYAN, 67:MAY72-121
BARNES, J. WHO IS CARLA HART?
M. LEVIN, 441:22APR73-28
BARNES, R. THE POSTAL SERVICE OF THE
FALKLAND ISLANDS.
617(TLS):27APR73-481
BARNES, T.R. POETRY APPRECIATION.
W. STUCK, 430(NS):OCT71-559
BARNET, R.J. ROOTS OF WAR.*
R.D. CUFF, 99:NOV-DEC73-48
BARNETT, A.D., ED. CHINESE COMMUNIST
POLITICS IN ACTION.
A.P.L. LIU, 318(JAOS):APR-JUN71-363
BARNETT, D. THE PERFORMANCE OF MUSIC.*
H.F., 410(M&L):OCT72-459
E. SAMS, 415:OCT72-975
BARNETT, G.L. EIGHTEENTH-CENTURY BRITISH
NOVELISTS ON THE NOVEL.*
J. VOISINE, 549(RLC):JAN-MAR71-114
BARNETT, R.D. & A. NIBBI. THE CAMBRIDGE
ANCIENT HISTORY. (REV) (VOL 2)
E. WILL, 555:VOL45FASC1-129
BARNEY, W.A. THE ROAD TO SECESSION.
W.K. SCARBOROUGH, 441:11MAR73-20
BARNHART, R. MARRIAGE OF THE LORD OF THE
RIVER.
T. LAWTON, 57:VOL33#4-350
BARNIKOL, E. BRUNO BAUER. (P. REIMER &
H-M. SASS, EDS)
617(TLS):13JUL73-813
BARNOUW, A.J. MONTHLY LETTERS ON THE CUL-
TURE AND HISTORY OF THE NETHERLANDS.
L. GILLET, 556(RLV):1971/5-653
BARNOUW, E. THE IMAGE EMPIRE.*
639(VQR):AUTUMN71-CLXXXVI
BARNS, C.G. THE SOD HOUSE.
R.V. FRANCAVIGLIA, 650(WF):JAN71-63
BARNSTONE, W., ED. EIGHTEEN TEXTS.
W.V. SPANOS, 659:SUMMER73-363
617(TLS):17AUG73-951
BARNSTONE, W., ED. SPANISH POETRY FROM
ITS BEGINNING THROUGH THE NINETEENTH
CENTURY.
M.D. TRIWEDI, 238:SEP71-616
205(FMLS):JUL71-298
BARNSTONE, W. - SEE MAO TSE-TUNG
BARNWELL, H.T. - SEE CORNEILLE, P.
BAROJA, J.C. - SEE UNDER CARO BAROJA, J.
BAROJA, P. EL ÁRBOL DE LA CIENCIA.
(G.C. FLYNN, ED)
R.W. HATTON, 238:MAY71-414
BAROJA, P. EL MUNDO ES ANSÍ. (D.L.
SHAW, ED)
E. RUGG, 238:DEC71-987
BARON, H. FROM PETRARCH TO LEONARDO
BRUNI.*
A. SCAGLIONE, 545(RPH):MAY72-469
A. TRIPET, 405(MP):AUG70-91
BARON, S.W. A SOCIAL AND RELIGIOUS HIS-
TORY OF THE JEWS. (VOLS 13 & 14)
T. OELSNER, 551(RENQ):SUMMER71-235
BARON, W. SICKERT.
F. AUERBACH, 362:14JUN73-807
J.R. MELLOW, 441:2DEC73-7
617(TLS):29JUN73-742

"LE BAROQUE AU THÉÂTRE ET LA THÉÂTRALITÉ
DU BAROQUE."
    J-P. CHAUVEAU, 535(RHL):MAR-APR70-306
BARR, A. RECONSTRUCTION TO REFORM.
    W. GARD, 584(SWR):WINTER72-76
BARR, J., ED. THE ENVIRONMENTAL HAND-
    BOOK.
    M. MIDDLETON, 46:JUL71-64
BARR, M-M.H., WITH F.A. SPEAR. QUARANTE
    ANNÉES D'ÉTUDES VOLTAIRIENNES.*
    J. VERCRUYSSE, 535(RHL):JAN-FEB70-131
BARR, P. TO CHINA WITH LOVE.
    617(TLS):5JAN73-16
BARR, R. THE DARK ISLAND.
    N. CALLENDAR, 441:22APR73-24
BARRABINI, V. L'ODISSEA A TRAPANI.
    J-B. HAINSWORTH, 123:DEC72-404
BARRACLOUGH, G. - SEE GRAUS, F. & OTHERS
BARRAL, P., ED. LES FONDATEURS DE LA
    TROISIÈME RÉPUBLIQUE.
    L.A. LOUBÈRE, 207(FR):OCT70-200
BARRATT, G.R.V. IVAN KOZLOV.
    617(TLS):13APR73-415
BARRATT, M. MICHAEL BARRATT.
    F. DILLON, 362:6DEC73-788
    617(TLS):30NOV73-1485
BARRATT BROWN, M. FROM LABOURISM TO
    SOCIALISM.
    617(TLS):30MAR73-343
BARRAX, G. ANOTHER KIND OF RAIN.
    639(VQR):SUMMER71-CVIII
BARRETT, A. - SEE "JACK LONDON AND WALT
    WHITMAN"
BARRETT, C. OP ART.
    N. LYNTON, 592:JUL-AUG70-63
BARRETT, D. CATALOGUE OF THE WARDROP
    COLLECTION AND OF OTHER GEORGIAN BOOKS
    AND MANUSCRIPTS IN THE BODLEIAN LIB-
    RARY.
    617(TLS):13APR73-428
BARRETT, D.D. DIXIE MISSION.
    L.P. VAN SLYKE, 293(JAST):MAY71-672
BARRETT, E.B. & B.R. HAYDON. INVISIBLE
    FRIENDS. (W.B. POPE, ED)
    617(TLS):13JUL73-796
BARRETT, M., ED. THE POLITICS OF BROAD-
    CASTING.
    J. LORD, 61:MAY73-109
BARRETT, M.E. AN ACCIDENT OF LOVE.
    M. LEVIN, 441:11NOV73-51
BARRETTE, P. - SEE "ROBERT DE BLOIS'S
    'FLORIS ET LYRIOPÉ'"
BARRETTE, P. & M. FOL. UN CERTAIN STYLE
    OU UN STYLE CERTAIN?*
    H. GODIN, 208(FS):JAN72-111
BARRIER, N.G. THE SIKHS AND THEIR LIT-
    ERATURE.
    H. SCHOLBERG, 293(JAST):MAY71-719
BARRIER, N.G. & P. WALLACE. THE PUNJAB
    PRESS, 1880-1905.
    B. RAMUSACK, 293(JAST):AUG71-914
BARRIOS, E., ED. BIBLIOGRAFÍA DE AZTLÁN.
    J. SOMMERS, 238:SEP71-610
BARRON, J.A. FREEDOM OF THE PRESS FOR
    WHOM?
    441:16SEP73-18
BARROS, J. THE LEAGUE OF NATIONS AND THE
    GREAT POWERS: THE GREEK-BULGARIAN INCI-
    DENT 1925.*
    R. CLOGG, 575(SEER):JAN72-135
BARROW, G.W.S. THE KINGDOM OF THE SCOTS.
    617(TLS):30NOV73-1483
BARROW, L.P. - SEE UNDER PIETROSI BARROW,
    L.
BARROW, R.H. - SEE SYMMACHUS
BARROW, T. ART AND LIFE IN POLYNESIA.
    617(TLS):6JUL73-786

BARRUCAND, D. LA CATHARSIS DANS LE
    THÉÂTRE ET DANS LA PSYCHOTHÉRAPIE.
    Y. BRÈS, 542:JAN-MAR71-121
BARRY, E. - SEE FROST, R.
BARRY, J.G. DRAMATIC STRUCTURE.
    F. HALL, 89(BJA):WINTER72-99
BARRY, J.V.W. THE COURTS AND CRIMINAL
    PUNISHMENTS.
    S. RAE, 368:JUN70-207
BARSALI, I.B. MEDIEVAL GOLDSMITH'S
    WORK.
    J. BECKWITH, 39:OCT70-314
BARSON, J. LA GRAMMAIRE À L'OEUVRE.
    N.J. LACY, 399(MLJ):FEB71-120
    M. PASCHAL, 207(FR):MAR71-819
BARSTON, R.P., ED. THE OTHER POWERS.
    617(TLS):6APR73-348
BARSTOW, S. & A. BRADLEY. A KIND OF
    LOVING.
    A. RENDLE, 157:SPRING71-77
BART, B.F. FLAUBERT.*
    J. BRUNEAU, 535(RHL):JAN-FEB70-147
    G. CORBIÈRE-GILLE, 207(FR):APR71-979
BARTENEV, I. & B. FYODOROV. NORTH RUS-
    SIAN ARCHITECTURE.
    617(TLS):23NOV73-1424
BARTER, A.R. LEARNING LANGUAGES.*
    G.P. ORWEN, 276:SUMMER71-270
BARTFELD, F. VIGNY ET LA FIGURE DE
    MOÏSE.
    M. SCHAETTEL, 557(RSH):APR-JUN70-330
    J. SUNGOLOWSKY, 207(FR):DEC70-455
BARTH, E. DIE GEWÄSSERNAMEN IM FLUSSGE-
    BIET VON SIEG UND RUHR.
    M. FAUST, 343:BAND13HEFT2-194
BARTH, J. CHIMERA.*
    J. HENDIN, 231:SEP73-102
    R. SALE, 249(HUDR):WINTER72/73-703
BARTH, J. THE END OF THE ROAD. THE
    FLOATING OPERA. THE SOT-WEEK FACTOR.
    GILES GOAT-BOY.*
    J. HENDIN, 231:SEP73-102
BARTH, J. L'ENFANT-BOUC.
    R. ASSELINEAU, 189(EA):JUL-SEP71-350
BARTH, J. LOST IN THE FUNHOUSE.*
    R.A. DAVISON, 573(SSF):FALL71-659
    J. HENDIN, 231:SEP73-102
BARTH, J.R. COLERIDGE AND CHRISTIAN
    DOCTRINE.*
    J.A. APPLEYARD, 401(MLQ):JUN71-206
    J.A. APPLEYARD, 613:AUTUMN70-456
    J.R.D. JACKSON, 529(QQ):SPRING71-155
    J.R. MAC GILLIVRAY, 627(UTQ):FALL70-73
    W.J.B. OWEN, 541(RES):AUG71-357
    M.F. SCHULZ, 405(MP):NOV71-142
    G. THOMAS, 175:AUTUMN70-105
BARTH, K. PROTESTANT THEOLOGY IN THE
    NINETEENTH CENTURY.
    617(TLS):5JAN73-18
BARTH, K. & R. BULTMANN. KARL BARTH -
    RUDOLF BULTMANN, BRIEFWECHSEL 1922 BIS
    1966. (B. JASPERT, ED)
    T.H.L. PARKER, 182:VOL24#17/18-650
BARTH, R.S. OPEN EDUCATION AND THE
    AMERICAN SCHOOL.
    R. GROSS, 441:25MAR73-40
BARTHELME, D. CITY LIFE.*
    E. SHORRIS, 231:JAN73-92
    42(AR):SPRING70-129
BARTHELME, D. SADNESS.*
    V. CUNNINGHAM, 362:6DEC73-793
    E. SHORRIS, 231:JAN73-92
    617(TLS):7DEC73-1495
BARTHELME, D. UNSPEAKABLE PRACTICES, UN-
    NATURAL ACTS.* SNOW WHITE. COME BACK,
    DR. CALIGARI.
    E. SHORRIS, 231:JAN73-92

BARTHES, R. MYTHOLOGIES.* (A. LAVERS,
ED & TRANS)
C. PRENDERGAST, 111:2JUN72-170
BARTHES, R. LE PLAISIR DU TEXTE.
617(TLS):22JUN73-713
BARTHES, R. S/Z.*
J. BAYLEY, 453:4OCT73-25
E. EGGEN, 172(EDDA):1971/3-181
BARTHES, R. & ERTÉ. ERTÉ.
617(TLS):12OCT73-1256
BARTHOLMES, H. BRUDER, BÜRGER, FREUND,
GENOSSE UND ANDERE WÖRTER DER SOZIAL-
ISTISCHEN TERMINOLOGIE.
J.E. HÄRD, 597(SN):VOL43#1-292
BARTHOLOMEUSZ, D. "MACBETH" AND THE
PLAYERS.
W. ANGUS, 529(QQ):SUMMER71-329
R.A. FOAKES, 175:AUTUMN70-98
H. SPANGENBERG, 430(NS):APR70-206
BARTLETT, C.J., ED. BRITAIN PRE-EMINENT.
R. KUBICEK, 637(VS):DEC70-209
BARTLETT, V. NORTHERN ITALY.
617(TLS):5OCT73-1151
BARTLETT, W.H. BARTLETT'S CANADA.*
(TEXT BY J. TYRWHITT)
J.P., 376:JAN70-116
BARTLEY, W.W. 3D. MORALITY AND RELIGION.
H. MEYNELL, 518:JAN72-3
BARTLEY, W.W. 3D. WITTGENSTEIN.
617(TLS):17AUG73-953
BARTÓK, B. BÉLA BARTÓK: LETTERS.* (J.
DEMÉNY, ED)
J.S.W., 410(M&L):JAN72-86
G. WATKINS, 385(MQR):FALL73-394
BARTÓK, B. RUMANIAN FOLK MUSIC.* (B.
SUCHOFF, ED)
B. KRADER, 317:SUMMER72-276
BARTON, R.M., ED. LIFE IN CORNWALL IN
THE LATE NINETEENTH CENTURY.
617(TLS):2FEB73-133
BARTONĚK, A. DEVELOPMENT OF THE LONG-
VOWEL SYSTEM IN ANCIENT GREEK DIALECTS.
W. KASTNER, 343:BAND13HEFT1-71
BARTONĚK, A., ED. STUDIA MYCENAEA.*
A. HEUBECK, 260(IF):BAND75-309
D.M. JONES, 123:DEC72-380
BARTOSZEWSKI, W. & Z. LEWIN, EDS. RIGHT-
EOUS AMONG NATIONS.*
J. MAURER, 497(POLR):AUTUMN70-108
BARTOSZEWSKI, W. & Z. LEWIN. THE SAMARI-
TANS. (A.T. JORDAN, ED)
J. MAURER, 497(POLR):AUTUMN70-108
BARTRAM, G. FAIR GAME.
A. BROYARD, 441:5NOV73-43
BARUZZI, A. & OTHERS, EDS. AUFKLÄRUNG
UND MATERIALISMUS IM FRANKREICH DES
18. JAHRHUNDERTS.
R. MORTIER, 535(RHL):MAR-APR70-315
BARVIS, M. MUTINY AT THE NORE.
A. RENDLE, 157:SPRING70-71
DE BARY, W.T., ED. THE BUDDHIST TRADITION
IN INDIA, CHINA, AND JAPAN.
R.J. MILLER, 293(JAST):NOV70-168
L. ROCHER, 318(JAOS):OCT-DEC71-547
DE BARY, W.T. & OTHERS. SELF AND SOCIETY
IN MING THOUGHT.
F.W. MOTE, 293(JAST):FEB71-434
BAR ZOHAR, M. THE THIRD TRUTH.
N. CALLENDAR, 441:19AUG73-13
BÄSCHLIN, D.L. SCHOPENHAUERS EINWAND
GEGEN KANTS TRANSZENDENTALE DEDUKTION
DER KATEGORIEN.
R. MALTER, 342:BAND61HEFT2-260
BASCOM, W. THE YORUBA OF SOUTHWESTERN
NIGERIA.
E. GILLIES, 69:JAN71-66
BASDEKIS, D. - SEE DE UNAMUNO, M.

BASHAM, A.L., ED. PAPERS ON THE DATE OF
KANIṢKA.
A.C. SOPER, 57:VOL33#4-339
BASIL THE GREAT. BASILE DE CÉSARÉE,
"SUR L'ORIGINE DE L'HOMME." (A. SMETS
& M. VAN ESBROECK, EDS & TRANS)
É. DES PLACES, 555:VOL45FASC1-158
BASKIN, L. BASKIN: SCULPTURE, DRAWINGS,
PRINTS.
M. WELISH, 58:FEB71-10
BASLER, O. EINIGES ZU SEBASTIAN SAILER.
C. MINIS, 680(ZDP):BAND90HEFT1-129
BASRI, S.A. A DEDUCTIVE THEORY OF SPACE
AND TIME.
G.G. BRITTAN, JR., 486:DEC71-610
BASS, B.M. & J.A. VAUGHAN. TRAINING IN
INDUSTRY.
617(TLS):17AUG73-961
BASS, G.F., ED. A HISTORY OF SEAFARING
BASED ON UNDERWATER ARCHAEOLOGY.
617(TLS):12JAN73-42
BASS, M.R. THE DOCTOR WHO MADE HOUSE
CALLS.
M. LEVIN, 441:14JAN73-24
BASSAN, F. POLITIQUE ET HAUTE SOCIÉTÉ À
L'ÉPOQUE ROMANTIQUE.*
G. DE BERTIER, 535(RHL):MAY-JUN71-518
N. KING, 208(FS):OCT72-461
F. LETESSIER, 557(RSH):OCT-DEC70-643
J.L. SHEPHERD 3D, 207(FR):MAR71-804
BASSAN, M. HAWTHORNE'S SON.
R.D. ARNER, 432(NEQ):MAR71-169
J.D. CROWLEY, 445(NCF):JUN71-121
BASSANI, G. BEHIND THE DOOR.*
R. ELLMANN, 453:15NOV73-23
D. MAHON, 362:21JUN73-840
BASSANI, G. THE GARDEN OF THE FINZI-
CONTINIS. FIVE STORIES OF FERRARA.
THE HERON.
R. ELLMANN, 453:15NOV73-23
BASSANI, G. DIETRO LA PORTA.
617(TLS):27JUL73-865
BASSANI, G. L'ODORE DEL FIENO.*
270:VOL22#4-80
BASSENGE, F. - SEE DIDEROT, D.
BASSO, A. IL CONSERVATORIO DI MUSICA
"GIUSEPPE VERDI" DI TORINO.
J.W.K., 410(M&L):APR72-197
BASTID, P. PROCLUS ET LE CRÉPUSCULE DE
LA PENSÉE GRECQUE.
R. LENOIR, 542:APR-JUN70-230
J. TROUILLARD, 542:APR-JUN70-228
BASTIDE, R. ANATOMIE D'ANDRÉ GIDE.
617(TLS):12OCT73-1257
BASTIDE, R. APPLIED ANTHROPOLOGY.
617(TLS):6JUL73-770
BASTIDE, R. THE SOCIOLOGY OF MENTAL DIS-
ORDER.
617(TLS):3AUG73-896
BASTOS, A.R. - SEE UNDER ROA BASTOS, A.
BATAILLE, G. MADAME EDWARDA.
L. FINAS, 98:MAR71-241
BATAILLE, G. OEUVRES COMPLÈTES. (VOLS
5&6) LITERATURE AND EVIL.
617(TLS):15JUN73-663
BATAILLE, M. LA COLÈRE BLANCHE.
R. LORRIS, 207(FR):DEC70-409
BÄTE, L. GOETHE UND DIE OSNABRÜCKER.
F.R. SCHRÖDER, 224(GRM):BAND21HEFT1-
117
BATE, P. - SEE RENDALL, F.G.
BATE, W.J. THE BURDEN OF THE PAST AND
THE ENGLISH POET.*
R.D. HUME, 481(PQ):JUL71-375
G.W. NITCHIE, 141:WINTER71-107
BATE, W.J. & A.B. STRAUSS - SEE JOHNSON,
S.

BATES, G.E. BYZANTINE COINS.
    G.C. MILES, 589:JAN72-107
BATES, H.E. THE VANISHED WORLD. (VOL 1)
    J.P., 376:JUL71-119
BATLLORI, M. - SEE FINESTRES, J.
BATLLORI, M. & C. PERALTA - SEE GRACIÁN,
    B.
BATSON, W., COMP. THE WILLIAM M. COLMER
    PAPERS, 1933-1962, 73RD THROUGH 87TH
    CONGRESS.
    P. MC CARTHY, 14:JUL71-315
BATTAGLIA, F. HEIDEGGER E LA FILOSOFIA
    DEI VALORI.
    E. NAMER, 542:APR-JUN70-255
BATTAGLIA, S., ED. GRANDE DIZIONARIO
    DELLA LINGUA ITALIANA. (VOL 6)
    M•F•, 228(GSLI):VOL147FASC460-630
BATTCOCK, G., ED. MINIMAL ART.*
    D. IRWIN, 39:JAN71-72
BATTEN, L. & OTHERS. BIRDWATCHERS' YEAR.
    617(TLS):2NOV73-1352
BATTENHOUSE, R.W. SHAKESPEAREAN TRAG-
    EDY.*
    J. BRITTON, 613:WINTER70-616
    R. GILL, 541(RES):NOV71-526
    H. LEVIN, 322(JHI):APR-JUN71-306
BATTERSBY, M. THE DECORATIVE THIRTIES.*
    P. WOLLEN, 592:NOV71-213
BATTERSBY, M. THE DECORATIVE TWENTIES.
    E. KAUFMANN, JR., 54:SEP70-340
BATTISTI, E. CIMABUE.*
    J. WHITE, 54:MAR70-96
BATTLES, F.L. & A•M• HUGO, EDS. CALVIN'S
    COMMENTARY ON SENECA'S "DE CLEMENTIA."
    J.R.G. WRIGHT, 123:MAR72-114
BATTS, M.S. & M.G. STANKIEWICZ, EDS.
    ESSAYS ON GERMAN LITERATURE IN HONOUR
    OF G. JOYCE HALLAMORE.*
    P•F• VEIT, 564:JUN70-175
    N•T•J• VOORWINDEN, 433:OCT70-435
BAUCH, K. STUDIEN ZUR KUNSTGESCHICHTE.
    E. SCHEYER, 56:SUMMER70-181
BAUDELAIRE, C. LES FLEURS DU MAL [AND]
    LES ÉPAVES. (VOL 1) (J. CRÉPET & G.
    BLIN, EDS; REV BY G. BLIN & C. PICH-
    OIS)
    L.J. AUSTIN, 535(RHL):JUL-AUG70-726
BAUDELAIRE, C. PETITS POÈMES EN PROSE.*
    (R. KOPP, ED)
    R. FAYOLLE, 535(RHL):MAR-APR70-328
"BAUDELAIRE: ACTES DU COLLOQUE DE NICE
    (25-27 MAI 1967)."
    J•S• PATTY, 535(RHL):MAR-APR70-326
BAUDRY, J-L. LA "CREATION."
    H. DAMISCH, 98:NOV71-950
BAUER & TROCHU. FRANZÖSISCH FÜR SIE 1.
    FRANZÖSISCH FÜR SIE 2.
    G. SCHWEIG, 430(NS):AUG71-446
BAUER, G.H. SARTRE AND THE ARTIST.*
    R. GOLDTHORPE, 208(FS):JAN72-95
    502(PRS):SPRING70-89
BAUER, H. DER INDEX PICTORIUS CALDERÓNS.
    A.L. MACKENZIE, 86(BHS):JAN72-78
BAUER, J. KAFKA AND PRAGUE.
    F. JONES, 32:SEP72-717
BAUER, W. THE PRICE OF MORNING.* (H.
    BEISSEL, ED & TRANS)
    R.H. WOOLLEY, 220(GL&L):JAN72-185
BAUER, W. & H. FRANKE. THE GOLDEN CAS-
    KET.
    C.W. CHEN, 399(MLJ):JAN71-43
BAUGH, A.C. CHAUCER.
    H. GNEUSS, 38:BAND88HEFT1-99
BAUM, R. THE PLANETS.
    617(TLS):31AUG73-1009
BAUMANN, G. JEAN PAUL.
    H-J. MODLMAYR, 402(MLR):JAN72-216

BAUMANN, W. THE ROSE IN THE STEEL DUST.*
    G. KNOX, 182:VOL24#5-210
    M•L• ROSENTHAL, 27(AL):MAY72-333
BAUMFIELD, B., ED. DO BOOKS MATTER?
    617(TLS):20JUL73-841
BAUMGARTNER, H•M• & W•G• JACOBS. J•G•
    FICHTE-BIBLIOGRAPHIE.
    C. CESA, 548(RCSF):APR-JUN70-208
    W. SCHWARZ, 484(PPR):SEP70-147
BÄUML, F•H•, ED. KUDRUN.*
    I•T• PIIRAINEN, 439(NM):1970/4-709
BÄUML, F•H• MEDIEVAL CIVILIZATION IN GER-
    MANY 800-1273.
    H. MARTIN, 406:SPRING72-66
BAUMSTIMLER, Y. AUTOMATISATION DU COM-
    PORTEMENT ET COMMUTATION.
    V. RÜFNER, 182:VOL24#9/10-397
BAUR, J•I•H• JOSEPH STELLA.
    D•M• SOKOL, 127:SPRING72-360
BAUSINGER, H. FORMEN DER "VOLKSPOESIE."*
    T•J• GARBÁTY, 650(WF):APR70-133
    E. KUNZE, 439(NM):1970/1-171
BAUSOLA, A. CONOSCENZA E MORALITÀ IN
    FRANZ BRENTANO.
    E. NAMER, 542:APR-JUN71-230
BAUSOLA, A. FILOSOFIA E STORIA NEL PEN-
    SIERO CROCIANO.
    E. NAMER, 542:OCT-DEC71-465
BAUSOLA, A. INDAGINI DI STORIA DELLA
    FILOSOFIA.
    E. NAMER, 542:APR-JUN70-259
    L•T•, 154:JUN71-425
BAUSOLA, A. LO SVOLGIMENTO DEL PENSIERO
    DI SCHELLING.
    E. NAMER, 542:APR-JUN70-247
BAUSOLA, A. METAFISICA E RIVELAZIONE
    NELLA FILOSOFIA POSITIVA DI SCHELLING.
    J.E. SCHLANGER, 542:APR-JUN71-231
BAWDEN, C•R• THE MODERN HISTORY OF MON-
    GOLIA.*
    J. FLETCHER, 244(HJAS):VOL31-306
BAXANDALL, M. GIOTTO AND THE ORATORS.
    J•I•J•, 568(SCN):SUMMER72-55
    R. WOODFIELD, 89(BJA):SPRING72-199
BAXANDALL, M. PAINTING AND EXPERIENCE
    IN FIFTEENTH CENTURY ITALY.
    617(TLS):19OCT73-1277
BAXTER, C. THE JANA SANGH.*
    F•J• CORLEY, 613:SUMMER71-317
BAXTER, J. A FOREIGN AFFAIR. A GIFT FOR
    GOMALA.
    G. VIDAL, 453:13DEC73-6
BAXTER, J.K. THE ROCK WOMAN.
    O. LEEMING, 368:MAR71-9
BAXTER, J.K. RUNES.
    617(TLS):18MAY73-548
BAYER, E. DEMETRIOS PHALEREUS DER
    ATHENER.
    J. BRISCOE, 123:MAR72-83
BAYER, W. THE GREAT MOVIES.
    W. MARKFIELD, 441:2DEC73-96
BAYES, R.H. HISTORY OF THE TURTLE.
    R.H. MILLER, 648:OCT70-81
BAYLEY, J. PUSHKIN, A COMPARATIVE COM-
    MENTARY.
    R. FREEBORN, 575(SEER):JAN72-117
    G. GIBIAN, 32:MAR72-188
    676(YR):AUTUMN71-XXXIV
BAYNES, J. THE JAKOBITE RISING OF 1715.
    G. HOLMES, 566:AUTUMN71-8
BAZELL, C•E• & OTHERS, EDS. IN MEMORY OF
    J•R• FIRTH.*
    J•W• LEWIS, 179(ES):JUN71-289
BAZHAN, M•P• & OTHERS, EDS. SOVIET
    UKRAINE.
    R•A• PIERCE, 529(QQ):WINTER71-638

23

BAZIN, A.  JEAN RENOIR.  (F. TRUFFAUT,
   ED)
   D. BROMWICH, 441:9SEP73-7
BAZIN, A.  WHAT IS CINEMA? (VOL 2) (H.
   GRAY, ED & TRANS)
   617(TLS):28SEP73-1109
BAZIN, G.  THE BAROQUE.*
   R.G. SAISSELIN, 54:SEP70-322
   J.R.F.T., 135:DEC70-291
BAZIN, G.  LE TEMPS DES MUSÉES.
   J-C. LEBENSZTEJN, 98:APR70-321
DE BAZIN, J.  INDEX DU VOCABULAIRE DES
   "MAXIMES" DE LA ROCHEFOUCAULD.  INDEX
   DU VOCABULAIRE DE "LA PRINCESSE DE
   CLÈVES."
   J. LANHER, 209(FM):OCT70-457
BAZIN, N.T.  VIRGINIA WOOLF AND THE
   ANDROGYNOUS VISION.
   J.C. OATES, 441:15APR73-7
   617(TLS):20JUL73-831
BAZYLOW, L.  DZIEJE ROSJI 1801-1917.
   A. POLONSKY, 575(SEER):JUL72-464
BEACHCROFT, T.O.  THE MODEST ART.
   A.M. WRIGHT, 405(MP):NOV70-220
BEAL, A.  D.H. LAWRENCE.
   E. DELAVENAY, 189(EA):JAN-MAR70-97
BEALS, C.  STORIES TOLD BY THE AZTECS
   BEFORE THE SPANIARDS CAME.
   K.M. BRIGGS, 203:SPRING71-85
BEAN, G.E. & T.B. MITFORD.  JOURNEYS IN
   ROUGH CILICIA 1964-1968.
   E.W. GRAY, 123:DEC72-398
BEAN, W.J.  TREES AND SHRUBS HARDY IN
   THE BRITISH ISLES.  (VOL 2)
   617(TLS):25MAY73-597
BEARDSLEY, A.  THE LETTERS OF AUBREY
   BEARDSLEY.*  (H. MAAS, J.L. DUNCAN &
   W.G. GOOD, EDS)
   M. EASTON, 135:OCT71-139
BEARDSLEY, M.C.  THE POSSIBILITY OF CRIT-
   ICISM.*
   M. RUDICK, 651(WHR):SPRING72-176
   K.L. WALTON, 311(JP):20DEC73-832
BEARDSLEY, T.S., JR.  HISPANO-CLASSICAL
   TRANSLATIONS PRINTED BETWEEN 1482 AND
   1699.
   J.G. FUCILLA, 551(RENQ):SUMMER71-260
   J.R. JONES, 238:SEP71-596
   A. PARDO V., 399(MLJ):APR71-254
   L.S. THOMPSON, 263:JAN-MAR72-47
BEARDSMORE, R.W.  ART AND MORALITY.
   H. OSBORNE, 89(BJA):SPRING72-189
BEARDSMORE, R.W.  MORAL REASONING.*
   R.F. ATKINSON, 393(MIND):JUL71-473
   P.D. EISENBERG, 482(PHR):JUL71-400
BEASLEY, W.G.  THE MEIJI RESTORATION.
   H. BOLITHO, 441:11MAR73-3
   617(TLS):21DEC73-1556
BEATON, C.  CECIL BEATON: MEMOIRS OF THE
   40S.
   W. ABRAHAMS, 61:APR73-112
   H. THOMPSON, 441:6MAY73-18
BEATON, C.  THE STRENUOUS YEARS.
   E.S. TURNER, 362:27SEP73-417
   617(TLS):5OCT73-1163
BEATON, L.  THE REFORM OF POWER.
   D.P. CALLEO, 441:25FEB73-44
BEATTIE, E.  A HANDBOOK OF CANADIAN FILM.
   P. HARCOURT, 99:NOV-DEC73-37
BEATTIE, J. & J. MIDDLETON, EDS.  SPIRIT
   MEDIUMSHIP AND SOCIETY IN AFRICA.
   P. FRY, 69:OCT70-393
BEATTY, R.G.  THE DDT MYTH.
   441:2SEP73-14
BEATY, N.L.  THE CRAFT OF DYING.
   M.B. MC NAMEE, 301(JEGP):OCT72-540

BEAUJEU, J., S. DELEANI & J-M. VERMANDER.
   INITIATION À LA LANGUE LATINE ET À LA
   CIVILISATION ROMAINE.
   A. ERNOUT, 555:VOL45FASC1-191
BEAUJOUR, E.K.  THE INVISIBLE LAND.*
   M.H. SHOTTON, 402(MLR):JAN72-239
BEAUJOUR, M.  LE JEU DE RABELAIS.*
   J-M. KLINKENBERG, 556(RLV):1971/3-355
BEAULIEU, V-L.  UN RÊVE QUÉBÉCOIS.
   A.E. POKORNY, 296:WINTER73-87
DE BEAUMARCHAIS, P.A.C.  BEAUMARCHAIS:
   CORRESPONDANCE.*  (VOLS 1&2) (B.N.
   MORTON, ED)
   J-P. DE BEAUMARCHAIS, 535(RHL):JUL-
   AUG71-705
BEAUMONT, C.W.  THE BALLET CALLED GISELLE.
   A. PAGE, 290(JAAC):SUMMER71-552
BEAUMONT, F.  THE KNIGHT OF THE BURNING
   PESTLE.  (A. GURR, ED)
   J.C. MAXWELL, 184(EIC):OCT71-382
BEAUMONT, F. & J. FLETCHER.  THE DRAMATIC
   WORKS IN THE BEAUMONT AND FLETCHER
   CANON.  (VOL 2) (F. BOWERS, ED)
   A. RENDLE, 157:SPRING71-77
BEAUMONT, F. & J. FLETCHER.  THE MAID'S
   TRAGEDY.  (A. GURR, ED)
   J.C. MAXWELL, 184(EIC):OCT71-382
BEAUMONT, F. & J. FLETCHER.  PHILASTER OR
   LOVE LIES A-BLEEDING.  (A. GURR, ED)
   M. HATTAWAY, 541(RES):MAY71-204
BEAURLINE, L.A. - SEE SUCKLING, J.
DE BEAUVOIR, S.  LA VIEILLESSE.*
   H.W. BRANN, 207(FR):DEC70-396
BEAVER, B.  LETTERS TO LIVE POETS.
   K.L. GOODWIN, 381:SEP71-369
BEAVER, P., ED.  THE WIPERS TIMES.
   617(TLS):28SEP73-1134
BEAVIS, R.W., ED.  18TH CENTURY DRAMA:
   AFTERPIECES.
   A. RENDLE, 157:SUMMER70-75
BEBEL, A.  AUGUST BEBELS BRIEFWECHSEL MIT
   KARL KAUTSKY.  (K. KAUTSKY, JR., ED)
   A. LASSERRE, 182:VOL24#11/12-503
BECARUD, J. & G. LAPOUGE.  ANARCHISTES
   D'ESPAGNE.
   J. GEORGEL, 98:MAY71-460
BECCARIA, G.L.  SPAGNOLO E SPAGNOLI IN
   ITALIA.*
   T.G. GRIFFITH, 402(MLR):APR72-430
BECH, G.  DIE ENTSTEHUNG DES SCHWACHEN
   PRÄTERITUMS.
   C. MINIS, 361:VOL26#1-103
BECH, G.  DAS GERMANISCHE REDUPLIZIERTE
   PRÄTERITUM.*
   I. RAUCH, 361:VOL24#4-367
BECK, C.M., B.S. CRITTENDEN & E.V. SULLI-
   VAN, EDS.  MORAL EDUCATION.
   R.F. DEARDEN, 518:OCT72-3
BECK, E.T.  FRANZ KAFKA AND THE YIDDISH
   THEATER.
   J. BORN, 406:WINTER72-394
   H. ZOHN, 301(JEGP):JAN72-87
BECK, J.H.  JACOPO DELLA QUERCIA E IL
   PORTALE DI S. PETRONIO A BOLOGNA.
   617(TLS):30NOV73-1475
BECK, J.H. - SEE DI JACOPO, M.
BECK, L.W.  EARLY GERMAN PHILOSOPHY.*
   W. CERF, 484(PPR):SEP71-122
   R. MALTER, 342:BAND61HEFT3-413
   M.J. SCOTT-TAGGART, 479(PHQ):JUL71-269
   G. TONELLI, 319:OCT73-549
BECK, L.W., ED.  KANT STUDIES TODAY.
   D.P. DRYER, 154:DEC71-847
   J. KOPPER, 342:BAND62HEFT3-418
   E. SCHAPER, 483:JUL71-278

BECK, L.W., ED. PROCEEDINGS OF THE THIRD
INTERNATIONAL KANT CONGRESS.
E. HUFNAGEL, 182:VOL24#23/24-833
K. WARD, 518:OCT72-6
W.H. WERKMEISTER, 319:OCT73-561
BECK, W. JOYCE'S "DUBLINERS."*
F.L. WALZL, 399(MLJ):JAN71-40
BECKER, A.L. - SEE BURLING, R.
BECKER, C. - SEE ZOLA, E.
BECKER, J. IRREFÜHRUNG DER BEHÖRDEN.
617(TLS):21DEC73-1557
BECKER, K.W. & F. MENDE - SEE HEINE, H.
BECKER, L. HENRY DE MONTHERLANT.
A. AMOIA, 207(FR):MAR71-798
J. FOX, 208(FS):JAN72-94
BECKER, L.C. ON JUSTIFYING MORAL JUDG-
MENTS.
617(TLS):29JUN73-753
BECKER, P.A. ZUR ROMANISCHEN LITERATUR-
GESCHICHTE. (M.E. BECKER, ED)
W-D. LANGE, 72:BAND209HEFT4/6-450
BECKER, S. DOG TAGS.
D.K. MANO, 441:23SEP73-7
BECKETT, J.C. CONFRONTATIONS.
617(TLS):9FEB73-155
BECKETT, S. LE DÉPEUPLEUR.
L. JANVIER, 98:MAY71-432
BECKETT, S. FIN DE PARTIE. (J. & B.S.
FLETCHER, EDS)
J. FOX, 208(FS):APR72-228
BECKETT, S. THE LOST ONES.* BREATH AND
OTHER SHORTS. NOT I. FIRST LOVE.
617(TLS):12OCT73-1217
BECKETT, S. TÊTES-MORTES. SANS.
A.C. MURCH, 98:JAN71-45
BECKETT, S. & OTHERS. OUR EXAGMINATION
OF HIS FACTIFICATION FOR IMCAMINATION
OF WORK IN PROGRESS.
C. MAC CABE, 111:2JUN72-174
BECKFORD, W. RECOLLECTIONS OF AN EXCUR-
SION TO THE MONASTERIES OF ALCOBAÇA
AND BATALHA.
617(TLS):22JUN73-724
BECKSMANN, R. DIE ARCHITEKTONISCHE RAH-
MUNG DES HOCHGOTISCHEN BILDFENSTERS.
M.H. CAVINESS, 54:DEC70-432
BECKWITH, J. EARLY CHRISTIAN AND BYZAN-
TINE ART.
M.V. ALPER, 58:APR71-18
BECKWITH, J. IVORY CARVINGS IN EARLY
MEDIEVAL ENGLAND.
617(TLS):16NOV73-1394
BÉCQUER, G.A. MAESE PÉREZ EL ORGANISTA.
E.M. MALINAK, 399(MLJ):OCT71-411
I. MOLINA, 238:MAR71-220
"BEDE'S ECCLESIASTICAL HISTORY OF THE
ENGLISH PEOPLE."* (B. COLGRAVE & R.A.B.
MYNORS, EDS & TRANS)
A.G. DYSON, 325:OCT71-341
BEDFORD, S. ALDOUS HUXLEY. (VOL 1)
C. SYKES, 362:1NOV73-601
617(TLS):9NOV73-1367
BEDIENT, C. ARCHITECTS OF THE SELF.
J.M. FLORA, 385(MQR):WINTER73-90
BEDINI, S.A. THE LIFE OF BENJAMIN BAN-
NEKER.*
B.G. DICK, 651(WHR):AUTUMN72-377
BEDRI, B. THE MEMOIRS OF BABIKR BEDRI.
T. ASAD, 69:APR70-184
VAN BEEK, M. AN ENQUIRY INTO PURITAN
VOCABULARY.*
C. BARBER, 597(SN):VOL42#1-265
G.H.V. BUNT, 179(ES):APR71-171
A.J. FRY, 433:OCT71-463
C. HANSEN, 215(GL):VOL10#1-40

BEEKES, R.S.P. THE DEVELOPMENT OF THE
PROTO-INDO-EUROPEAN LARYNGEALS IN
GREEK.
C.J. RUIJGH, 361:VOL26#2-181
BEELER, J. WARFARE IN FEUDAL EUROPE,
730-1200.
N. DOWNS, 589:OCT72-743
BEER, G. MEREDITH.*
R.B. HENKLE, 454:SPRING72-269
D. JOHNSON, 445(NCF):SEP71-242
R. LAWRENCE, 175:AUTUMN71-110
F. LÉAUD, 189(EA):APR-JUN71-205
DE BEER, G. MODERN COLLEGE SPANISH GRAM-
MAR.
J.R. SCHMITZ, 238:MAR71-222
BEER, G. THE ROMANCE.
205(FMLS):OCT70-420
BEER, J. BLAKE'S HUMANISM.*
G.E. BENTLEY, JR., 627(UTQ):FALL70-86
BEER, J. BLAKE'S VISIONARY UNIVERSE.*
R.M. BAINE, 219(GAR):SUMMER71-238
G. THOMAS, 175:SUMMER70-66
BEER, J. DIE GESCHICHT UND HISTORI VON
LAND-GRAFF LUDWIG DEM SPRINGER. (M.
BIRCHER, ED)
B.L. SPAHR, 133:1971/1&2-198
BEER, J.M.A. VILLEHARDOUIN, EPIC HISTOR-
IAN.
P.F. DEMBOWSKI, 546(RR):DEC71-289
BEERBOHM, M. LAST THEATRES 1904-10. (R.
HART-DAVIS, ED)
J.R. TAYLOR, 157:SUMMER71-79
BEERBOHM, M. MAX IN VERSE. (J.G. RIE-
WALD, ED)
V.S. PRITCHETT, 453:25JAN73-16
BEERBOHM, M. MORE THEATRES. (R. HART-
DAVIS, ED)
571:SUMMER70-107
BEERBOHM, M. A PEEP INTO THE PAST AND
OTHER PROSE PIECES.* (R. HART-DAVIS,
ED)
V.S. PRITCHETT, 453:25JAN73-16
BEESON, T. THE CHURCH OF ENGLAND IN
CRISIS.
617(TLS):18MAY73-559
BEESTON, A.F.L. ARABIC HISTORICAL PHRASE-
OLOGY.
F.J. CADORA, 318(JAOS):OCT-DEC71-537
BEESTON, A.F.L. WRITTEN ARABIC.*
J.A. BELLAMY, 215(GL):VOL10#1-18
"LUDWIG VAN BEETHOVEN: AUTOGRAPH MISCEL-
LANY FROM CIRCA 1786 TO 1799."* (J.
KERMAN, ED)
P.H.L., 414(MQ):APR71-323
"LUDWIG VAN BEETHOVEN: NEUN AUSGEWÄHLTE
BRIEFE AN ANTON SCHINDLER." (G. HERRE,
ED)
J.A.W., 410(M&L):JUL72-333
"BEETHOVEN-SYMPOSION, WIEN 1970: BERICHT."
G.A., 410(M&L):JUL72-327
BEGEMANN, E.H. & A-M.S. LOGAN. EUROPEAN
DRAWINGS AND WATERCOLOURS IN THE YALE
UNIVERSITY ART GALLERY: 1500-1900.
90:NOV71-692
BÉHAR, H. ROGER VITRAC, UN RÉPROUVÉ DU
SURRÉALISME.
M-C. DUMAS, 535(RHL):MAR-APR70-346
BEHLER, E. - SEE SCHLEGEL, F.
BEHLER, E. & R. STRUC - SEE SCHLEGEL, F.
BEHLMER, R. - SEE SELZNICK, D.O.
BEHN, H. - SEE GIDDINGS, R.W.
BEHRE, F. STUDIES IN AGATHA CHRISTIE'S
WRITINGS.*
I. POMMERENING, 38:BAND88HEFT2-240
BEHRMAN, L.C. MUSLIM BROTHERHOODS AND
POLITICS IN SENEGAL.
G. PARRINDER, 318(JAOS):OCT-DEC71-539

BEICHEL, U. ALEXANDRE VINET.
H. PERROCHON, 535(RHL):MAY-JUN70-531
BEIER, U., COMP. WHEN THE MOON WAS BIG
AND OTHER LEGENDS FROM NEW GUINEA.
617(TLS):23MAR73-333
BEIERWALTES, W., ED. PLATONISMUS IN DER
PHILOSOPHIE DES MITTELALTERS.
R.T. WALLIS, 123:MAR72-119
BEIKIRCHER, H. KOMMENTAR ZUR VI. SATIRE
DES A. PERSIUS FLACCUS.*
P. WHITE, 122:JAN72-59
BEILENSON, L.W. POWER THROUGH SUBVERSION.
K. GLASER, 396(MODA):SPRING72-213
BEILIS, A.S. STANOVLENIE MARKSISTSKOI
ISTORIOGRAFII V BOLGARII (S KONTSA XIX
V. DO SOTSIALISTICHESKOI REVOLIUTSII
1944 G.).
T.A. MEININGER, 32:SEP72-730
BEISSEL, H. - SEE BAUER, W.
BEISSNER, F. HÖLDERLINS GÖTTER.
G.L. JONES, 220(GL&L):OCT71-86
BEJA, M. EPIPHANY IN THE MODERN NOVEL.
J.M. FLORA, 385(MQR):WINTER73-90
BEKKER, H. THE NIBELUNGENLIED.*
M.S. BATTS, 564:OCT71-239
F.H. BÄUML, 589:APR72-278
D.R. MC LINTOCK, 382(MAE):1972/3-258
BEKKERS, J.A.F. - SEE MORRIS, J.
BELBEN, R. REUBEN, LITTLE HERO.
V. CUNNINGHAM, 362:31MAY73-728
617(TLS):29JUN73-736
BELCHER, W.J. & R.B. SIBSON. BIRDS OF
FIJI IN COLOUR.
617(TLS):5OCT73-1196
BELFORD, K. THE POST ELECTRIC CAVE MAN.
D. BARBOUR, 102(CANL):SPRING72-77
BELFRAGE, C. THE AMERICAN INQUISITION.
N. HENTOFF, 441:8JUL73-5
BELGARDT, R. ROMANTISCHE POESIE.
D.S. GUILLOTON, 301(JEGP):OCT72-575
E. MORNIN, 564:OCT71-242
R. PAULIN, 402(MLR):OCT72-944
BĚLIČ, O. ANÁLISIS ESTRUCTURAL DE TEXTOS
HISPANOS.
R.A. CARDWELL, 86(BHS):JUL72-293
BELIN, D.W. NOVEMBER 22, 1963.
G. & P.J. MC MILLAN, 441:18NOV73-35
BELITT, B. NOWHERE BUT LIGHT.
J.T. IRWIN, 598(SOR):SUMMER73-720
639(VQR):SPRING71-LVII
BELKNAP, G.N. OREGON IMPRINTS 1845-1870.
E. MOTTRAM, 354:JUN70-170
BELL, D. THE COMING OF POST-INDUSTRIAL
SOCIETY.
N. BIRNBAUM, 441:1JUL73-1
N. BLIVEN, 442(NY):17SEP73-151
C. LASCH, 453:180CT73-63
L. SILK, 441:2NOV73-45
BELL, D., ED. PALL MALL ENCYCLOPEDIA OF
ART.
592:JUL/AUG71-51
BELL, I.F. & J. GALLUP. A REFERENCE GUIDE
TO ENGLISH, AMERICAN, AND CANADIAN LIT-
ERATURE.
R.C. ELLSWORTH, 529(QQ):WINTER71-634
BELL, J.B. THE SECRET ARMY.*
R. DUNSTAN, 619(TC):VOL179#1046-53
BELL, K. NOT IN VAIN.
J.L. GRANATSTEIN, 99:NOV-DEC73-26
617(TLS):17AUG73-961
BELL, M. A PROBABLE VOLUME OF DREAMS.*
B. HAMLIN, 448:FALL70-111
T. HUGHES, 134(CP):SPRING70-67
BELL, M.D. HAWTHORNE AND THE HISTORICAL
ROMANCE OF NEW ENGLAND.*
L. LEARY, 432(NEQ):DEC71-664

BELL, Q. VIRGINIA WOOLF.* (VOLS 1&2
BOUND IN ONE VOL)
W. ABRAHAMS, 61:FEB73-93
J.W. BICKNELL, 295:FEB73-108
E. HARDWICK, 453:8FEB73-15
W. MAXWELL, 442(NY):3FEB73-88
BELL, R., G. FOWLER & K. LITTLE, EDS.
EDUCATION IN GREAT BRITAIN AND IRELAND.
617(TLS):9NOV73-1381
BELL, S.H. A MAN FLOURISHING.
617(TLS):24AUG73-969
BELLAMY, J. CRIME AND PUBLIC ORDER IN
ENGLAND IN THE LATER MIDDLE AGES.
617(TLS):15JUN73-668
BELLASIS, E. CHERUBINI.
B. DEANE, 415:MAY72-459
DU BELLAY, J. LES REGRETS ET AUTRES
OEUVRES POÉTIQUES, SUIVIS DES ANTI-
QUITEZ DE ROME.
Y. GIRAUD, 535(RHL):JAN-FEB70-116
BELLÉ, R. & A.F. HAAS. PERSONNAGES DE LA
LITTÉRATURE FRANÇAISE.
H.L. ROBINSON, 399(MLJ):FEB71-124
BELLELI, M.L. - SEE "GÉRARD DE NERVAL,
PROSA E POESIA"
BELLEVILLE, P. LAMINAGE CONTINU (CRISE
D'UNE RÉGION, ÉCHEC D'UN RÉGIME).
J-A. BOUR, 207(FR):DEC70-399
BELLEZZA, D. IL CARNEFICE.
617(TLS):7DEC73-1512
BELLEZZA, D. LETTERE DA SODOMA.
B. MERRY, 270:VOL22#3-69
BELLIDO, A.G. - SEE UNDER GARCÍA Y BEL-
LIDO, A.
BELLINATTI, G. & S. BETTINI. L'EPISTOL-
ARIO MINIATO DI GIOVANNI DA GAIBANA.*
E.B. GARRISON, 54:SEP70-313
BELLINZONI, A., JR. & T.V. LITZENBURG,
JR., EDS. INTELLECTUAL HONESTY AND
RELIGIOUS COMMITMENT.
M.S., 154:MAR71-212
BELLOC, H. BELLOC: A BIOGRAPHICAL AN-
THOLOGY.* (H. VAN THAL & J.S. NICK-
ERSON, EDS)
A. BORDEAUX, 189(EA):APR-JUN71-202
42(AR):SPRING71-133
BELLOC, H. COMPLETE VERSE.
A. BORDEAUX, 189(EA):APR-JUN71-203
"E.J. BELLOCQ: STORYVILLE PORTRAITS."
(J. SZARKOWSKI, ED)
42(AR):WINTER71/72-589
BELLONI, G.G. & L.F. DALL'ASIN. IRANIAN
ART.
R.D. BARNETT, 39:APR70-322
BELLOW, S. MR. SAMMLER'S PLANET.*
J. DITSKY, 628:FALL70-91
R.J. FEIN, 328:SPRING70-252
L. HABER, 287:JUN70-24
E. GROSSMAN, 390:AUG-SEP70-3
A. GUTTMANN, 659:SPRING73-157
BELLOWS, T.J. THE PEOPLE'S ACTION PARTY
OF SINGAPORE.
R.S. MILNE, 293(JAST):MAY71-739
BELOFF, M. THE INTELLECTUAL IN POLITICS
AND OTHER ESSAYS.
R. DUNSTAN, 619(TC):VOL179#1046-52
BELOFF, N. TRANSIT OF BRITAIN.
J. VAIZEY, 362:4JAN73-22
617(TLS):5JAN73-3
BEN-ISRAEL, H. ENGLISH HISTORIANS ON THE
FRENCH REVOLUTION.*
E.A. WALKER, 207(FR):OCT70-203
BENAMOU, M. WALLACE STEVENS AND THE
SYMBOLIST IMAGINATION.
617(TLS):6APR73-375
BENAMOU, M. & E. IONESCO, WITH M. CALLA-
MAND. MISE EN TRAIN.*
L.R. SCHUB, 207(FR):OCT70-149

BENARDETE, S. HERODOTEAN INQUIRIES.
    J.R. GRANT, 487:AUTUMN71-291
BENBOW, R.M., E. BLISTEIN & F.S. HOOK -
    SEE PEELE, G.
BENDER, E.J. BIBLIOGRAPHIE: CHARLES
    NODIER.*
        J. DECOTTIGNIES, 535(RHL):JUL-AUG71-
        711
        L. LIPSON, 207(FR):APR71-983
        A.R. OLIVER, 546(RR):FEB71-65
        A. VIATTE, 549(RLC):JUL-SEP70-426
        P.J. WHYTE, 208(FS):JAN72-86
BENDER, J.B. SPENSER AND LITERARY PIC-
    TORIALISM.
    617(TLS):1JUN73-620
BENDER, P. EAST EUROPE IN SEARCH OF
    SECURITY.
    617(TLS):9FEB73-154
BENDER, W. - SEE VON GRIMMELSHAUSEN,
    H.J.C.
BENDIX, E.H. COMPONENTIAL ANALYSIS OF
    GENERAL VOCABULARY.
        G.F. MEIER, 682(ZPSK):BAND23HEFT4-420
        F.C. SOUTHWORTH, 269(IJAL):OCT71-275
BENECKE, G.F. & K. LACHMANN - SEE HART-
    MANN VON AUE
BENEDETTI, A. DIARIA DE BELLO CAROLINO
    (DIARY OF THE CAROLINE WAR). (D.M.
    SULLIVAN, ED & TRANS)
        M.H. SAFFRON, 551(RENQ):WINTER71-519
BENEDETTI, M. CUENTOS COMPLETOS.
        H.D. OBERHELMAN, 238:DEC71-976
BENEDICT, M.L. THE IMPEACHMENT AND TRIAL
    OF ANDREW JOHNSON.
        I.F. STONE, 453:28JUN73-12
BENEDIKT, M. MOLE NOTES.*
        A. HELMS, 473(PR):FALL72-621
BENEDIKT, M. SKY.*
        A. HELMS, 473(PR):FALL72-621
        M.G. PERLOFF, 659:WINTER73-97
        639(VQR):SUMMER71-CVI
BENEDIKTSSON, H., ED. THE NORDIC LAN-
    GUAGES AND MODERN LINGUISTICS.
        Ö. DAHL, 350:SEP72-705
BENEDIKZ, B.S. THE SPREAD OF PRINTING:
    ICELAND.
        R. CAVE, 503:SUMMER70-99
        B. JUEL-JENSEN, 354:MAR71-73
BENEŠ, V.L. & N.J.G. POUNDS. POLAND.
        J.F. MORRISON, 497(POLR):SPRING71-117
        W.J. WAGNER, 32:SEP72-714
BENESCH, O. COLLECTED WRITINGS. (VOL 1)
    (E. BENESCH, ED)
        J.D. WELDON, 58:SUMMER71-11
        C. WHITE, 39:MAR71-229
BENEWICK, R. THE FASCIST MOVEMENT IN
    BRITAIN.
        617(TLS):30MAR73-343
BENEWICK, R., R.N. BERKI & B. PAREKH,
    EDS. KNOWLEDGE AND BELIEF IN POLITICS.
        617(TLS):14DEC73-1536
BÉNÉZÉ, G. L'ORDRE DES PENSÉES.
        R. BLANCHÉ, 542:OCT-DEC70-484
BENGIS, I. COMBAT IN THE EROGENOUS ZONE.*
        M. ELLMANN, 453:1NOV73-18
BENGTSON, H. INTRODUCTION TO ANCIENT
    HISTORY.*
        G.V. SUMNER, 487:SUMMER71-189
BENGTSSON, S. LA DÉFENSE ORGANISÉE DE
    LA LANGUE FRANÇAISE.
        A. ESKÉNAZI, 209(FM):OCT70-455
BÉNICHOU, P. CREACIÓN POÉTICA EN EL
    ROMANCERO TRADICIONAL.
        R.H. WEBBER, 240(HR):JUL71-316
BÉNICHOU, P. ROMANCERO JUDEO-ESPAÑOL DE
    MARRUECOS.*
        R.D. ABRAHAM, 240(HR):JUL71-318
        S.G. ARMISTEAD & J.H. SILVERMAN, 400
        (MLN):MAR71-295

BÉNICHOU, P. LE SACRE DE L'ÉCRIVAIN
    1750-1830.
        617(TLS):5OCT73-1160
BENITEZ, F. THE POISONED WATER.
        M. LEVIN, 441:12AUG73-20
BENJAMIN, W. GESAMMELTE SCHRIFTEN. (VOL
    3 ED BY H. TIEDEMANN-BARTELS; VOL 4 ED
    BY T. REXROTH)
        617(TLS):14DEC73-1539
BENJAMIN, W. ILLUMINATIONS.* (H.
    ARENDT, ED)
        J.P. STERN, 111:29JAN71-101
BENJAMIN, W. ÜBER LITERATUR.
        G. HARTUNG, 654(WB):7/1971-178
BENJAMIN, W. UNDERSTANDING BRECHT.
    CHARLES BAUDELAIRE.
        V. CUNNINGHAM, 362:6SEP73-319
BENKOVITZ, M.J. RONALD FIRBANK.
        J. HAFLEY, 50(ARQ):SPRING70-83
BENN, G. GOTTFRIED BENN: SELECTED POEMS.*
    (F.W. WODTKE, ED)
        B.K. BENNETT, 221(GQ):NOV71-614
        R.W. LAST, 402(MLR):OCT72-954
        205(FMLS):APR71-191
"GOTTFRIED BENN."* (E. LOHNER, ED)
        I. KOWATZKI, 221(GQ):JAN71-87
        F. STOCK, 52:BAND6HEFT1-106
BENN, M.B. - SEE HÖLDERLIN, F.
BENN, M.B. - SEE MÖRIKE, E.
BENNER, J.A. LONE STAR REBEL.
        W. GARD, 584(SWR):SPRING72-V
BENNETT, A. LETTERS OF ARNOLD BENNETT.
    (VOL 1) (J. HEPBURN, ED)
        D. ZEH, 38:BAND88HEFT1-153
BENNETT, A. A MAN FROM THE NORTH.
        617(TLS):28SEP73-1136
BENNETT, D. IRISH GEORGIAN SILVER.
        617(TLS):9MAR73-265
BENNETT, H.S. ENGLISH BOOKS AND READERS,
    1603 TO 1640.*
        P. EDWARDS, 354:SEP71-274
        T. LOGAN, 399(MLJ):MAR71-192
BENNETT, J. KANT'S ANALYTIC.
        L. GUILLERMIT, 53(AGP):BAND53HEFT2-
        198
BENNETT, J. LOCKE, BERKELEY, HUME.
        D.G.C. MAC NAB, 518:MAY72-7
BENNETT, J. & L. KIBBEE. THE BENNETT
    PLAYBILL.
        E.H. NASH, 200:AUG-SEP71-435
BENNETT, J.A.W. CHAUCER'S BOOK OF FAME.*
        R.W. FRANK, JR., 405(MP):NOV70-195
BENNETT, J.A.W. - SEE GOWER, J.
BENNETT, J.A.W. & G.V. SMITHERS, WITH N.
    DAVIS, EDS. EARLY MIDDLE ENGLISH VERSE
    AND PROSE.* (BOTH 1ST & 2ND EDITIONS)
        A.A. PRINS, 179(ES):AUG71-356
BENNETT, N.R. - SEE DODGSHUN, A.W.
BENNETT, R. & J. WATSON, COMPS. PHILA-
    TELIC TERMS ILLUSTRATED.
        617(TLS):9FEB73-161
BENNETT, R.M. THE ARCHER-SHEES AGAINST
    THE ADMIRALTY.
        617(TLS):13APR73-416
BENNETT, W.A. ASPECTS OF LANGUAGE AND
    LANGUAGE TEACHING.*
        R. GINZBURG, 215(GL):VOL10#3-206
BENNICH-BJÖRKMAN, B. FÖRFATTAREN I ÄMBE-
    TET.
        S. SWAHN, 172(EDDA):1971/4-254
        L. WENDELIUS, 563(SS):SPRING72-275
BENNICH-BJÖRKMAN, B. TERMEN LITTERATUR
    I SVENSKAN - 1750-1850.
        E. WALTER, 535(RHL):MAY-JUN71-514
BENOÎT. CHRONIQUE DES DUCS DE NORMANDIE
    PAR BENOÎT.* (C. FAHLIN, GENERAL ED)
    (VOL 3 ED & COMPLETED BY Ö. SÖDERGÅRD)
        B. HASSELROT, 597(SN):VOL42#2-516

27

BENOIT, F. ART ET DIEUX DE LA GAULE.
  D. REUILLARD, 98:APR70-384
BENOIT, F. LE SYMBOLISME DANS LES SANC-
  TUAIRES DE LA GAULE.*
  J.M.C. TOYNBEE, 313:VOL61-292
BENOIT, G. INTERMINABLE SANG.
  M. CRANSTON, 207(FR):APR71-951
BENOT, Y. DIDEROT.*
  F. ARCHAMBAULT, 154:MAR71-182
BENREKASSA, G. MONTESQUIEU.
  J.M. GOULEMOT, 535(RHL):JUL-AUG70-711
BENS, J. ADIEU SIDONIE.
  H. MICHOT-DIETRICH, 207(FR):DEC70-410
BENS, J. LE RETOUR AU PAYS (FRAGMENTS).
  L. JONES, 207(FR):DEC70-411
BENSE, M. ARTISTIK UND ENGAGEMENT. DIE
  REALITÄT DER LITERATUR. ZEICHEN UND
  DESIGN.
  617(TLS):12OCT73-1255
BENSON, J.J. HEMINGWAY.
  M. BRADBURY, 148:SUMMER71-185
BENSON, J.L. HORSE, BIRD AND MAN.
  J.M. COOK, 303:VOL91-206
  R.M. COOK, 123:DEC72-431
BENSON, T.W. & M.H. PROSSER, EDS. READ-
  INGS IN CLASSICAL RHETORIC.
  W.E. LAMPTON, 583:SPRING71-290
  617(TLS):13APR73-429
BENTHALL, J., ED. ECOLOGY, THE SHAPING
  ENQUIRY.
  617(TLS):12JAN73-46
BENTLEY, E. THEATRE OF WAR.
  617(TLS):25MAY73-588
BENTLEY, G.E. THE PROFESSION OF DRAMA-
  TIST IN SHAKESPEARE'S TIME, 1590-1642.
  617(TLS):2FEB73-126
BENTLEY, G.E., ED. THE SEVENTEENTH-
  CENTURY STAGE.*
  J.E.F., 502(PRS):SPRING70-87
  H.M. SPANGENBERG, 182:VOL24#13/14-542
BENTLEY, G.E., JR., ED. BLAKE RECORDS.*
  R.M. BAINE, 219(GAR):SUMMER71-238
  F.W. BATESON, 541(RES):MAY71-221
  D. BINDMAN, 90:APR71-218
  D.V.E., 191(ELN):SEP71(SUPP)-27
  K. GARLICK, 39:NOV70-398
  J.J. MC GANN, 405(MP):FEB72-261
  J.P., 376:JUL70-121
  M.F. SCHULZ, 173(ECS):SUMMER71-490
  G. THOMAS, 175:SUMMER70-66
BENTLEY, G.E., JR. - SEE BLAKE, W.
BENTLEY, N. THE EVENTS OF THAT WEEK.
  N. CALLENDAR, 441:28JAN73-20
BENTLEY, P. THE BRONTËS AND THEIR WORLD.
  M. ALLOTT, 637(VS):SEP70-104
BENTON, J.F. - SEE ABBOT GUIBERT OF
  NOGENT
BENTON, K. SPY IN CHANCERY.*
  N. CALLENDAR, 441:3JUN73-34
BENTWICH, H. IF I FORGET THEE.
  617(TLS):16MAR73-286
BENVENISTE, E. INDO-EUROPEAN LANGUAGE
  AND SOCIETY.
  617(TLS):17AUG73-961
BENVENISTE, É. LE VOCABULAIRE DES INSTI-
  TUTIONS INDO-EUROPÉENNES.*
  A.M. DAVIES, 123:DEC72-375
BENVENISTE, G. THE POLITICS OF EXPER-
  TISE.
  617(TLS):23FEB73-204
BENYOETZ, E. ANNETTE KOLB UND ISRAEL.
  B. KAHRMANN, 406:SPRING72-69
BERARDI, G. - SEE TENCA, C.
BERCKENHAGEN, E. ANTON GRAFF, LEBEN UND
  WERK.
  E. SCHEYER, 54:SEP70-331

BERCKMAN, E. THE HIDDEN NAVY.
  R. MITCHISON, 362:22MAR73-383
  617(TLS):5OCT73-1195
BERCKMAN, E. THE VICTORIAN ALBUM.
  M. LEVIN, 441:16SEP73-32
  617(TLS):26OCT73-1324
BERCKMAN, E. WAIT.
  617(TLS):23FEB73-219
BERCOVITCH, S., ED. TYPOLOGY AND EARLY
  AMERICAN LITERATURE.
  W.J. IRVIN, 165:SPRING73-83
BERENGUER, L. LEÑA VERDE.
  270:VOL22#4-88
BERENSEN, B. HOMELESS PAINTINGS OF THE
  RENAISSANCE.
  R.E., 135:JUL71-227
BERENT, E. DIE AUFFASSUNG DER LIEBE BEI
  OPITZ UND WECKHERLIN UND IHRE GESCHICHT-
  LICHEN VORSTUFEN.
  P. SKRINE, 402(MLR):OCT72-939
BERESFORD, A. THE LAIR.
  C. LEVENSON, 529(QQ):SUMMER71-309
BERESFORD-HOWE, C. THE BOOK OF EVE.
  P. GROSSKURTH, 99:NOV-DEC73-31
BERETTA, B. CONTRIBUTO ALL'OPERA NOVEL-
  LISTICA DI GIOVANNI SERCAMBI, CON IL
  TESTO DI 14 NOVELLE INEDITE.*
  G. GULLACE, 546(RR):OCT71-231
BERG, A. ALBAN BERG: LETTERS TO HIS
  WIFE.* (B. GRUN, ED & TRANS)
  G. WATKINS, 385(MQR):FALL73-394
BERG, K. STUDIES IN TUSCAN TWELFTH-
  CENTURY ILLUMINATION.*
  E.B. GARRISON, 54:SEP70-310
BERG, L. & P. CHAPMAN. THE TRAIN BACK.
  617(TLS):9MAR73-261
BERG, R., C. CHEMOUNY & F. DIDI. GUIDE
  JUIF DE FRANCE.
  S.D. BRAUN, 207(FR):OCT70-204
BERG, S. THE DAUGHTERS.
  J.R. REED, 491:APR73-47
  F. MORAMARCO, 651(WHR):SPRING72-194
BERG, S. THE QUEEN'S TRIANGLE.
  J. GALASSI, 491:MAR73-343
BERGAMINI, D. JAPAN'S IMPERIAL CONSPIR-
  ACY.*
  G. BARRACLOUGH, 453:31MAY73-9
BERGAMINI, G. - SEE CAVALCASELLE, G.B.
BERGENS, A. PRÉVERT.
  T. GREENE, 207(FR):DEC70-441
BERGER, A.A. THE COMIC-STRIPPED AMERICAN.
  R. LASSON, 441:9DEC73-40
BERGER, A.A. THE EVANGELICAL HAMBURGER.
  LI'L ABNER.
  J. ESKAY, 186(ETC.):MAR71-120
BERGER, B. & H. RUPP - SEE KOSCH, W.
BERGER, C. THE SENSE OF POWER.
  G.F.G. STANLEY, 529(QQ):SPRING71-145
BERGER, D.P., ED. FOLK SONGS OF JAPANESE
  CHILDREN.
  G.K. BRADY, 650(WF):JAN70-63
BERGER, H., ED. OSTAFRIKANISCHE STUDIEN
  ERNST WEIGT ZUM 60. GEBURTSTAG.
  A.H.J. PRINS, 69:OCT70-404
BERGER, J. ART AND REVOLUTION.*
  D. GERVAIS, 97(CQ):AUTUMN70-187
BERGER, J. G.*
  R. SALE, 249(HUDR):WINTER72/73-703
  G. STEINER, 442(NY):27JAN73-90
BERGER, J. NOTHING BUT THE TRUTH.
  B. SOUVARINE, 32:DEC72-902
BERGER, M. ISLAM IN EGYPT TODAY.
  A.A.A. FYZEE, 273(IC):JUL71-213
BERGER, R. IMPEACHMENT.
  P.B. KURLAND, 441:5AUG73-3
  I.F. STONE, 453:28JUN73-12

BERGER, T. REGIMENT OF WOMEN.
L. BRAUDY, 441:13MAY73-6
C. LEHMANN-HAUPT, 441:22MAY73-45
R. TODD, 61:SEP73-106
442(NY):16JUN73-109
BERGES, R. THE BACKGROUNDS AND TRADI-
TIONS OF OPERA.*
C. GRAHAM, 415:JAN72-45
BERGHAHN, K.L. FORMEN DER DIALOGFÜHRUNG
IN SCHILLERS KLASSISCHEN DRAMEN.
H. MOENKEMEYER, 406:WINTER72-415
BERGHAHN, K.L. - SEE SCHILLER, F.
BERGHAUS, P. & K. SCHNEIDER. ANGLO-
FRIESISCHE RUNENSOLIDI IM LICHTE DES
NEUFUNDES VON SCHWEINDORF (OSTFRIES-
LAND).
H. BECK, 38:BAND88HEFT1-128
VAN DEN BERGHE, C.L. DICTIONNAIRE DES
IDÉES DANS L'OEUVRE DE SIMONE DE BEAU-
VOIR.
R. GOLDTHORPE, 208(FS):JAN72-99
BERGIN, T.G. A DIVERSITY OF DANTE.
A.S. BERNARDO, 275(IQ):FALL70-105
C.E. TURNER, 546(RR):OCT71-231
BERGIN, T.G. PERSPECTIVES ON THE "DIVINE
COMEDY."
M. SHAPIRO, 545(RPH):NOV71-259
BERGMANN, A., ED. GRABBE IN BERICHTEN
SEINER ZEITGENOSSEN.
P.C. THORNTON, 402(MLR):APR72-469
G. WUNBERG, 433:APR70-204
BERGMANN, K. THE AGED.
617(TLS):23FEB73-200
BERGMANN, R. MITTELFRÄNKISCHE GLOSSEN.
H. STOPP, 680(ZDP):BAND89HEFT1-122
BERGMANN, R. STUDIEN ZUR ENTSTEHUNG UND
GESCHICHTE DER DEUTSCHEN PASSIONSSPIELE
DES 13. UND 14. JAHRHUNDERTS.
R. RUDOLF, 182:VOL24#23/24-860
BERGNER, H., ED. ENGLISH SHORT STORIES
OF THE NINETEENTH CENTURY.
W. FÜGER, 72:BAND209HEFT4/6-421
H.O., 430(NS):FEB71-108
BERGOM-LARSSON, M. DIKTARENS DEMASKERING.
W. MISHLER, 563(SS):SPRING72-280
BERGONZI, B. THE SITUATION OF THE NOVEL.
C.L. CHUA, 651(WHR):SPRING72-185
A. KETTLE, 541(RES):NOV71-520
BERGONZI, B. THE TURN OF THE CENTURY.
617(TLS):18MAY73-558
BERGSON, H. DURATION AND SIMULTANEITY.
J. MERLEAU-PONTY, 542:OCT-DEC71-445
BERGSON, H. ECRITS ET PAROLES. (R-M.
MOSSÉ-BASTIDE, ED)
E. AMADO LÉVY-VALENSI, 542:OCT-DEC71-
442
BERGSTEIN, E. ADVANCING PAUL NEWMAN.
A. BROYARD, 441:27NOV73-45
B. HAYES, 441:18NOV73-52
442(NY):24DEC73-78
BERGSTEIN, T. QUANTUM PHYSICS AND ORDI-
NARY LANGUAGE.
617(TLS):13APR73-425
BERGSTEN, B. - SEE NIVER, K.
BERGSTEN, B. - SEE NIVER, K.R.
BERKELEY, G. A TREATISE CONCERNING THE
PRINCIPLES OF HUMAN KNOWLEDGE, WITH
CRITICAL ESSAYS. (C.M. TURBAYNE, ED)
E.A.R., 543:DEC70-335
BERKHOF, A. DE COMMISSARIS GAAT UIT
STELEN.
J. GOFFART, 556(RLV):1971/6-786
BERKHOFER, R.F., JR. A BEHAVIORAL
APPROACH TO HISTORICAL ANALYSIS.
J.E. HANSEN, 484(PPR):MAR72-421
BERKMAN, A. PRISON MEMOIRS OF AN ANAR-
CHIST.
E. PAWEL, 390:MAY71-67

BERKMAN, R.L. & W.K. VISCUSI. DAMMING
THE WEST.
R. SHERRILL, 441:4MAR73-3
BERKOVITS, I. ILLUMINATED MANUSCRIPTS IN
HUNGARY: XI-XVI CENTURIES.* (REV BY A.
WEST)
M.L. D'ANCONA, 54:DEC71-520
BERLE, A.A. NAVIGATING THE RAPIDS.
(B.B. BERLE & T.B. JACOBS, EDS)
C. PHILLIPS, 441:9SEP73-47
442(NY):9JUN73-115
BERLEANT, A. THE AESTHETIC FIELD.*
D.J. CROSSLEY, 154:SUPP-1
T. MUNRO, 484(PPR):DEC71-278
B.T., 543:JUN71-741
BERLIN, B. TZELTAL NUMERAL CLASSIFIERS.
P. FRIEDRICH, 350:SEP72-742
BERLIN, B. & P. KAY. BASIC COLOR TERMS.
N.P. HICKERSON, 269(IJAL):OCT71-257
W.R. MERRIFIELD, 297(JL):OCT71-259
BERLIN, I. FOUR ESSAYS ON LIBERTY.*
J.A. BLAIR, 154:SEP70-266
BERLIN, I. & OTHERS. ESSAYS ON J.L.
AUSTIN.
617(TLS):16NOV73-1396
BERLIN, N. THE BASE STRING.
E.D. PENDRY, 597(SN):VOL42#2-469
BERLIOZ, H. LES GROTESQUES DE LA MUS-
IQUE.* (L. GUICHARD, ED)
P. CITRON, 535(RHL):JAN-FEB71-112
BERLIOZ, H. OEUVRES LITTÉRAIRES. (VOL
1) (L. GUICHARD, ED)
P. CITRON, 535(RHL):JAN-FEB71-110
BERMANGE, B. NO QUARTER [AND] THE INTER-
VIEW.
A. RENDLE, 157:SPRING70-71
BERMANT, C. THE LAST SUPPER.
J. HUNTER, 362:29MAR73-423
617(TLS):20APR73-451
BERMANT, C. TROUBLED EDEN.
H. MACCOBY, 390:FEB71-78
BERMEJO MARCOS, M. DON JUAN VALERA:
CRÍTICO LITERARIO.*
J. SCHRAIBMAN, 238:MAR71-196
BERNAL, O. LANGAGE ET FICTION DANS LE
ROMAN DE BECKETT.
J. FOX, 208(FS):JAN72-101
M.J. FRIEDMAN, 207(FR):OCT70-216
BERNANOS, G. JOURNAL D'UN CURÉ DE CAM-
PAGNE.* (E.M. O'SHARKEY, ED)
205(FMLS):APR70-204
BERNANOS, G. UN CRIME. (M. GUINEY, ED)
W. STAAKS, 207(FR):FEB71-594
BERNARD, J.F. TALLEYRAND.
G. DE BERTIER DE SAUVIGNY, 441:18FEB
73-21
T. LASK, 441:17MAR73-29
617(TLS):16NOV73-1390
BERNARD, L. THE EMERGING CITY.
639(VQR):SUMMER71-CXXVI
BERNARD, M. LE CHEVALÍER BLANC.
S. MAX, 207(FR):OCT70-168
BERNARD, P.P. JESUITS AND JACOBINS.
R.R. PALMER, 32:SEP72-707
BERNARDUS DE TRILIA. QUAESTIONES DIS-
PUTATAE DE COGNITIONE ANIMAE SEPARATAE.
(P. KÜNZLE, ED)
L. MOSER, 182:VOL24#3-74
BERNATH, M., H. JABLONOVSKI & W. PHILIPP
- SEE "FORSCHUNGEN ZUR OSTEUROPÄISCHEN
GESCHICHTE" (VOL 15)
BERND, C.A. - SEE STORM, T. & P. HEYSE
BERNDL, H., H. WEYHER & W. VON PÖLNITZ-
EGLOFFSTEIN, EDS. STIFTUNGEN AUS VER-
GANGENHEIT UND GEGENWART.
G. STRICKRODT, 182:VOL24#19/20-712

BERNDTSON, A. ART, EXPRESSION, AND
BEAUTY.*
M.B. QUINN, 613:AUTUMN70-445
BERNEN, S. & R. MYTH AND RELIGION IN
EUROPEAN PAINTING, 1270-1700.
617(TLS):30MAR73-361
BERNHARD, T. GARGOYLES.
42(AR):FALL/WINTER70/71-459
BERNINGER, H. & J-A. CARTIER. POUGNY
(IWAN PUNI). (VOL 1)
J.E. BOWLT, 32:DEC72-938
BERNSDORF, W., ED. WÖRTERBUCH DER SOZIOL-
OGIE. (2ND ED)
E.M. WALLNER, 182:VOL24#4-142
BERNSTEIN, B. CLASS, CODES AND CONTROL.*
(VOL 1)
617(TLS):29JUN73-745
BERNSTEIN, B., ED. CLASS, CODES AND CON-
TROL. (VOL 2)
J. VAIZEY, 362:15FEB73-215
617(TLS):29JUN73-745
BERNSTEIN, J. EINSTEIN. (F. KERMODE, ED)
C. LEHMANN-HAUPT, 441:30APR73-29
J. ZINMAN, 441:23SEP73-44
617(TLS):2NOV73-1341
BERNSTEIN, M.H. - SEE CHAPMAN, J.J.
BERNT, W. THE NETHERLANDISH PAINTERS OF
THE SEVENTEENTH CENTURY.
G. MARTIN, 39:JUN70-485
D.T., 135:NOV70-214
BEROFSKY, B. DETERMINISM.
C. BERRY, 518:OCT72-8
J. KIM, 311(JP):22NOV73-766
BÉROUL. THE ROMANCE OF TRISTRAN.* (VOLS
1&2) (A. EWERT, ED)
B. MERRILEES, 589:OCT72-744
BERR, S. AN ETYMOLOGICAL GLOSSARY TO THE
OLD SAXON HELIAND.
W.B., 681(ZDS):BAND27HEFT3-191
BERREMAN, G.D. HINDUS OF THE HIMALAYAS.
617(TLS):6JUL73-786
BERRIGAN, D. AMERICA IS HARD TO FIND.*
617(TLS):19JAN73-55
BERRIGAN, D. ENCOUNTERS.
W. DICKEY, 249(HUDR):SUMMER72-305
BERRIGAN, D. FALSE GODS, REAL MEN.
D. ROGERS, 613:AUTUMN70-453
BERRY, D.C. SAIGON CEMETERY.
A. OSTRIKER, 473(PR):SUMMER72-464
BERRY, F., ED. ESSAYS AND STUDIES 1969.
L.C. BONNEROT, 189(EA):JAN-MAR70-96
BERRY, J. & N.A. KOTEI. AN INTRODUCTORY
COURSE IN GA.
M.E.K. DAKUBU, 69:APR70-190
BERRY, L.E. - SEE FLETCHER, G.
BERRY, R. SHAKESPEARE'S COMEDIES.
617(TLS):24AUG73-982
BERRY, T.E. A.K. TOLSTOY.
W.E. HARKINS, 32:DEC72-937
BERRY, W. FARMING.*
P. CALLAHAN, 502(PRS):FALL71-273
T. EAGLETON, 565:VOL12#3-68
J.T. IRWIN, 598(SOR):SUMMER73-720
BERRY, W. THE HIDDEN WOUND.
P. CALLAHAN, 502(PRS):FALL71-273
639(VQR):WINTER71-XLII
BERRYMAN, J. DELUSIONS, ETC.*
G. BURNS, 584(SWR):SUMMER72-255
K. HARRISON, 109:SPRING/SUMMER73-111
R. LATTIMORE, 249(HUDR):AUTUMN72-481
W. MEREDITH, 491:MAY73-98
617(TLS):23FEB73-193
BERRYMAN, J. THE DREAM SONGS.*
J.H. JUSTUS, 598(SOR):WINTER73-261
BERRYMAN, J. HIS TOY, HIS DREAM, HIS
REST.*
J.C. FIELD, 556(RLV):1971/6-771
H. SERGEANT, 175:SPRING70-29

BERRYMAN, J. LOVE AND FAME.*
L.L. MARTZ, 676(YR):SPRING72-410
W. MEREDITH, 491:MAY73-98
A. OBERG, 598(SOR):WINTER73-243
M.G. PERLOFF, 659:WINTER73-97
639(VQR):AUTUMN71-CLXI
BERRYMAN, J. RECOVERY.
J. CAREY, 362:6DEC73-792
D. KALSTONE, 441:27MAY73-1
M. SCHORER, 61:AUG73-92
J. THOMPSON, 453:9AUG73-3
442(NY):9JUN73-114
617(TLS):30NOV73-1465
BERSANI, J. LES CRITIQUES DE NOTRE TEMPS
ET PROUST.
J. BOREL, 98:DEC71-1060
BERSANI, J., M. RAIMOND & J-Y. TADIE,
EDS. ETUDES PROUSTIENNES I.
617(TLS):13APR73-423
BERSANI, L. BALZAC TO BECKETT.
J. BAYLEY, 473(PR):SUMMER72-398
J. CULLER, 402(MLR):APR72-423
BERSELLI, A. L'OPINIONE PUBBLICA INGLESE
E L'AVVENTO DEL FASCISMO.
617(TLS):2MAR73-225
BERTACCHINI, R., ED. DOCUMENTI E PREFAZ-
IONI DEL ROMANZO ITALIANO DELL'800.
A.D.B., 228(GSLI):VOL148FASC461-158
W.T.S., 191(ELN):SEP71(SUPP)-164
VON BERTALANFFY, L. ROBOTS, MEN AND
MINDS.
A.C. MICHALOS, 486:SEP70-455
BERTAU, K. DEUTSCHE LITERATUR IM EURO-
PÄISCHEN MITTELALTER. (VOL 1)
617(TLS):12OCT73-1258
BERTAUX, P. HÖLDERLIN UND DIE FRANZÖ-
SISCHE REVOLUTION.
K. PEZOLD, 654(WB):1/1971-213
BERTELLI, I. CULTURA E POESIA.
M.P., 228(GSLI):VOL147FASC458/459-479
BERTELSEN, A. OCTOBER '43.
N. ASCHERSON, 453:14JUN73-3
BERTHOFF, A.E. THE RESOLVED SOUL.*
J.B. BROADBENT, 483:SUMMER71-188
J. CAREY, 541(RES):NOV71-496
R.A. FOAKES, 175:SPRING71-23
G.R. GUFFEY, 551(RENQ):SUMMER71-284
P. LEGOUIS, 401(MLQ):DEC71-437
639(VQR):SUMMER71-CX
BERTHOFF, W. FICTIONS AND EVENTS.*
L. LEARY, 579(SAQ):SPRING72-278
BERTHOLLE, L., ED. SECRETS OF THE GREAT
FRENCH RESTAURANTS.
617(TLS):28DEC73-1583
BERTINI, L. INDICI DEL CODICE DIPLOMAT-
ICO LONGOBARDO.
H.J. WOLF, 72:BAND209HEFT1/3-189
BERTO, G. ANONYMOUS VENETIAN.
617(TLS):26OCT73-1324
BERTOCCI, P.A. THE PERSON GOD IS.*
B. MILLER, 63:AUG72-198
BERTON, P. THE NATIONAL DREAM.*
G.F.G. STANLEY, 529(QQ):SUMMER71-327
BERTON, P. & A.Z. RUBINSTEIN, WITH A.
ALLOTT. SOVIET WORKS ON SOUTHEAST
ASIA.
R.A. KARLOWICH, 32:JUN72-451
BERTONASCO, M.F. CRASHAW AND THE BAR-
OQUE.
E.F. DANIELS, 568(SCN):SPRING72-9
W. VON KOPPENFELS, 72:BAND209HEFT4/6-
405
BERTONI, I. IL NEOILLUMINISMO ETICO DI
ANDRÉ LALANDE.
E. NAMER, 542:OCT-DEC71-492
BERTOTTI SCAMOZZI, O. LE FABBRICHE E I
DISEGNI DI ANDREA PALLADIO.
J. SCHULZ, 576:MAY70-199

BERTRAM, G. FAIR GAME.
N. CALLENDAR, 441:7OCT73-44
BERTRAND, M. L'OEUVRE DE JEAN PRÉVOST.*
A. DASPRE, 535(RHL):JAN-FEB70-158
BESCH, W. SPRACHLANDSCHAFTEN UND SPRACH-
AUSGLEICH IM 15. JAHRHUNDERT.
F. DEBUS, 433:JAN71-97
P. HEFTI, 657(WW):MAY/JUN70-205
M.Å. HOLMBERG, 597(SN):VOL42#1-287
BESCH, W. & OTHERS. VORARBEITEN UND
STUDIEN ZUR VERTIEFUNG DER SÜDWESTDEUT-
SCHEN SPRACHGESCHICHTE. (F. MAURER,
ED)
E. SKÁLA, 681(ZDS):BAND26HEFT1/2-125
BESCH, W., S. GROSSE & H. RUPP, EDS.
FESTGABE FÜR FRIEDRICH MAURER ZUM 70.
GEBURTSTAG AM 5. JANUAR 1968.
C. MINIS, 680(ZDP):BAND90HEFT1-126
BESER, S. LEOPOLDO ALAS, CRÍTICO LIT-
ERARIO.*
G. DAVIS, 546(RR):APR71-153
R.M. JACKSON, 400(MLN):MAR71-306
J.W. KRONIK, 240(HR):JUL71-329
J. LÓPEZ-MORILLAS, 149:JUN72-234
BESOMI, O. RICHERCHE INTORNO ALLA "LIRA"
DI G.B. MARINO.
A. DI BENEDETTO, 228(GSLI):VOL147
FASC460-594
BESPALOFF, A. GUIDE TO INEXPENSIVE
WINES.
R.A. SOKOLOV, 441:2DEC73-82
BESSER, G.R. BALZAC'S CONCEPT OF GEN-
IUS.*
C.F. COATES, 207(FR):APR71-983
P. LAURENT, 535(RHL):MAR-APR71-310
J.O. LOWRIE, 399(MLJ):FEB71-122
A. MICHEL, 557(RSH):OCT-DEC70-641
BESSET, M. WHO WAS LE CORBUSIER?*
P. SERENYI, 576:OCT71-255
BESSINGER, J.B., JR., ED. A CONCORDANCE
TO "BEOWULF."*
A. CRÉPIN, 189(EA):JUL-SEP70-274
L. WHITBREAD, 179(ES):OCT71-444
D. WOLFF, 38:BAND89HEFT4-508
BESSINGER, J.B., JR. & R.P. CREED, EDS.
FRANCIPLEGIUS. (BRITISH TITLE: MEDI-
EVAL AND LINGUISTIC STUDIES IN HONOR OF
FRANCIS PEABODY MAGOUN, JR.)
K.H. GÖLLER, 38:BAND88HEFT1-120
P. MERTENS-FONCK, 556(RLV):1971/4-486
BESSINGER, J.B., JR. & S.J. KAHRL, EDS.
ESSENTIAL ARTICLES FOR THE STUDY OF OLD
ENGLISH POETRY.*
A. CRÉPIN, 189(EA):JUL-SEP70-274
BEST, A.M. - SEE CHAPPUYS, C.
BEST, O.F. PETER WEISS.
T.K. BROWN, 406:SUMMER72-199
R. GRIMM, 301(JEGP):OCT72-591
BEST, R.H. & A.W. ROGERS. THE URBAN
COUNTRYSIDE.
617(TLS):12OCT73-1246
BEST, T.W. THE HUMANIST ULRICH VON HUT-
TEN.*
W. DIETZE, 654(WB):11/1970-221
J.E. ENGEL, 399(MLJ):MAY71-334
BESTERMAN, T., ED. STUDIES ON VOLTAIRE
AND THE EIGHTEENTH CENTURY. (VOL 60)
U. VAN RUNSET, 535(RHL):JUL-AUG70-713
BESTERMAN, T., ED. STUDIES ON VOLTAIRE
AND THE EIGHTEENTH CENTURY. (VOL 64)
R. BARNY, 535(RHL):JUL-AUG70-714
BESTERMAN, T., ED. STUDIES ON VOLTAIRE
AND THE EIGHTEENTH CENTURY.* (VOL 67)
U. SCHICK, 535(RHL):MAR-APR71-303
BESTERMAN, T., ED. STUDIES ON VOLTAIRE
AND THE EIGHTEENTH CENTURY. (VOL 70)
M.H. WADDICOR, 208(FS):APR72-202

BESTERMAN, T., ED. STUDIES ON VOLTAIRE
AND THE EIGHTEENTH CENTURY. (VOL 71)
617(TLS):21SEP73-1090
BESTERMAN, T., ED. STUDIES ON VOLTAIRE
AND THE EIGHTEENTH CENTURY. (VOL 73)
V. MYLNE, 208(FS):JUL72-335
BESTERMAN, T., ED. STUDIES ON VOLTAIRE
AND THE EIGHTEENTH CENTURY. (VOL 94)
617(TLS):19JAN73-59
BESTERMAN, T., ED. STUDIES ON VOLTAIRE
AND THE EIGHTEENTH CENTURY. (VOLS 96-
98)
617(TLS):20APR73-440
BESTERMAN, T. VOLTAIRE.*
A.J. KNODEL, 173(ECS):SUMMER71-471
P.H. MEYER, 207(FR):APR71-985
BESTERMAN, T. - SEE DE VOLTAIRE, F.M.A.
BESTHORN, R. TEXTKRITISCHE STUDIEN ZUM
WERKE HOLBACHS.
M. NAUMANN, 654(WB):10/1970-220
J. VARLOOT, 535(RHL):MAY-JUN71-513
BETANCUR, C. BASES PARA UNA LOGICA DEL
PENSAMIENTO IMPERATIVO.
A. NARANJO VILLEGAS, 263:APR-JUN72-
178
BETETA, R. JARANO.
37:OCT70-40
BETH, E.W. ASPECTS OF MODERN LOGIC.
B.E. EGYED, 154:DEC71-815
BETH, E.W. I FONDAMENTI LOGICI DELLA
MATEMATICA.
G. SANDRI, 316:JUN71-325
BETH, L.P. THE DEVELOPMENT OF THE AMERI-
CAN CONSTITUTION: 1877-1917.
I. DILLIARD, 31(ASCH):SPRING73-347
BETHELL, N. GOMUŁKA.*
A. BROMKE, 497(POLR):SPRING71-119
BETHELL, N. THE WAR HITLER WON.*
A. BULLOCK, 453:28JUN73-30
A.M. ROSENTHAL, 441:3JUN73-3
BETHGE, E. DIETRICH BONHOEFFER.
B. HEBBLETHWAITE, 111:23OCT70-33
BETHGE, E. - SEE BONHOEFFER, D.
BETJEMAN, J. COLLECTED POEMS.
W.H. PRITCHARD, 249(HUDR):SPRING72-127
BETJEMAN, J. GHASTLY GOOD TASTE.
R. EDWARDS, 39:APR71-341
BETJEMAN, J., ED. VICTORIAN AND EDWARD-
IAN LONDON FROM OLD PHOTOGRAPHS.
F.M. JONES, 637(VS):DEC70-221
BETTARINI, R. - SEE DA MAIANO, D.
BETTELHEIM, B. & OTHERS. THE SOCIAL
IMPACT OF URBAN DESIGN.
505:NOV71-130
BETTELHEIM, C. RÉVOLUTION CULTURELLE ET
ORGANISATION INDUSTRIELLE EN CHINE.
617(TLS):13APR73-407
BETTETINI, G. CINEMA: LINGUA E SCRIT-
TURA.
G.C. LEPSCHY, 353:OCT70-105
BETTS, D. BEASTS OF THE SOUTHERN WILD.
M. MEWSHAW, 441:28OCT73-40
BETTS, E. THE FILM BUSINESS.
617(TLS):14DEC73-1542
BETTS, R.R. ESSAYS IN CZECH HISTORY.*
F.G. HEYMANN, 589:APR72-282
BETZ, W. - SEE PAUL, H.
BEUMANN, E., ED. BAUHAUS AND BAUHAUS
PEOPLE.
S. SPECTOR, 58:SEP/OCT70-16
BEURDELEY, C. & M. GIUSEPPE CASTIGLI-
ONE.*
617(TLS):21SEP73-1077
BEVAN, B. JAMES DUKE OF MONMOUTH.
617(TLS):19OCT73-1289
BEVILLARD, M. GRAMMAIRE RAISONNABLE.
J.D. GODIN, 207(FR):APR71-1007

BEVIS, R.W., ED. EIGHTEENTH-CENTURY
DRAMA: AFTERPIECES.
J. DULCK, 189(EA):JUL-SEP71-337
BEWLEY, M. MASKS AND MIRRORS.*
C.A. BROWN, 613:SPRING71-125
BEYLE, T.L. & G.T. LATHROP, EDS. PLAN-
NING AND POLITICS.
505:JUN71-114
BEYNON, H. WORKING FOR FORD.
617(TLS):17AUG73-958
BEYSCHLAG, S. ALTDEUTSCHE VERSKUNST IN
GRUNDZÜGEN. (6TH ED)
H. TERVOOREN, 680(ZDP):BAND90HEFT1-
102
BEZZOLA, G. - SEE MONTI, V.
BHADURI, T.C. CHAMBAL.
617(TLS):16FEB73-172
BHARGAVA, P.L. INDIA IN THE VEDIC AGE.
L. STERNBACH, 318(JAOS):OCT-DEC71-545
BHAT, D.N.S. BORO VOCABULARY.
H.V. GUENTHER, 318(JAOS):OCT-DEC71-555
BHAT, D.N.S. TANKHUR NAGA VOCABULARY.
J.A. MATISOFF, 350:JUN72-476
BHATIA, J. THE LATCHKEY KID.*
W.H. NEW, 102(CANL):SUMMER72-88
BHATIA, P. ALL MY YESTERDAYS.
617(TLS):16FEB73-189
BHATNAGAR, G.S. EDUCATION AND SOCIAL
CHANGE.
617(TLS):29JUN73-757
BHATTACHARYA, H.S. - SEE VADIN DEVASURI
BHATTACHARYYA, B. EVOLUTION OF THE POL-
ITICAL PHILOSOPHY OF GANDHI.
D. DALTON, 293(JAST):NOV70-212
BIAGI, M.L.A. - SEE UNDER ALTIERI BIAGI,
M.L.
BIANCHI, M.D. EMILY DICKINSON FACE TO
FACE.
S. DONALDSON, 432(NEQ):MAR71-161
BIANCHI, U. IL DUALISMO RELIGIOSO.
R. WILDHABER, 182:VOL24#21/22-822
BIANCHI BANDINELLI, R. ROME.*
W.M. STERN, 124:APR-MAY72-279
J.M.C. TOYNBEE, 123:JUN72-296
BIARDEAU, M. BHARTRHARI.
H. QUELLET, 343:BAND13HEFT2-185
VON BIBERACH, R. DIE SIBEN STRASSEN ZU
GOT. (M. SCHMIDT, ED)
W.J. COURTENAY, 589:JAN72-149
"BIBLIOGRAFÍA DE LOS ESTUDIOS CLÁSICOS
EN ESPAÑA (1956-1965)."
P. LANGLOIS, 555:VOL45FASC1-194
"BIBLIOGRAFIA DI STORIA ANTICA E DIRITTO
ROMANO."
F. LASSERRE, 182:VOL24#11/12-495
"BIBLIOGRAFIA ISTORICĂ A ROMÂNIEI." (VOL
1)
E.M. WALLNER, 182:VOL24#11/12-499
"BIBLIOGRAPHICAL CONTRIBUTIONS." (VOL 1)
J. HORDEN, 354:DEC70-360
"BIBLIOGRAPHIE D'HISTOIRE DE L'ART."
E. ZIMMERMANN, 182:VOL24#1/2-30
"BIBLIOGRAPHIE INTERNATIONALE DE L'HUMAN-
ISME ET DE LA RENAISSANCE." (VOLS 4&5)
C.H. CLOUGH, 402(MLR):JUL72-607
"BIBLIOTHECA OSLERIANA."
F.N.L. POYNTER, 354:SEP70-271
BICKEL, A.M. THE SUPREME COURT AND THE
IDEA OF PROGRESS.
I. DILLIARD, 31(ASCH):SPRING73-347
BICKEL, L. RISE UP TO LIFE.
617(TLS):2MAR73-234
BIDDLE, G. TAHITIAN JOURNAL.
M.S. YOUNG, 39:JAN70-87
BIDDLE, G. VICTORIAN STATIONS.
617(TLS):30NOV73-1485

BIDDLE, M. & D. HUDSON, WITH C. HEIGHWAY.
THE FUTURE OF LONDON'S PAST.
617(TLS):23NOV73-1424
BIDWELL, C.E. A MORPHO-SYNTACTIC CHAR-
ACTERIZATION OF THE MODERN SLAVIC LAN-
GUAGES.*
L.L. THOMAS, 215(GL):VOL10#1-21
BIDWELL, C.E. OUTLINE OF SLOVENIAN
MORPHOLOGY.*
J. PATERNOST, 215(GL):VOL11#2-132
BIDWELL, C.E. THE STRUCTURE OF RUSSIAN
IN OUTLINE.*
C. JAMES, 399(MLJ):APR71-251
BIDWELL, R., COMP. BIDWELL'S GUIDE TO
GOVERNMENT MINISTERS. (VOL 1)
617(TLS):12OCT73-1235
BIEBUYCK, D. & K.C. MATEENE, EDS & TRANS.
THE MWINDO EPIC FROM THE BANYANGA
(CONGO REPUBLIC).*
G.R. HORNER, 292(JAF):APR-JUN71-249
R.G. WILLIS, 69:JUL70-280
BIEBUYCK, D.P., ED. TRADITION AND CREA-
TIVITY IN TRIBAL ART.
J.L. LEAHY, 290(JAAC):SUMMER71-564
BIEDERMANN, H. HANDLEXIKON DER MAGISCHEN
KÜNSTE VON DER SPÄTANTIKE BIS ZUM 19.
JAHRHUNDERT.
L. PIKULIK, 657(WW):NOV/DEC70-427
BIEGELEISEN, J.I. SCREEN PRINTING.
J. ORFF, 58:SUMMER71-12
BIEMEL, W. PHILOSOPHISCHE ANALYSEN ZUR
KUNST DER GEGENWART.
D.B. KUSPIT, 484(PPR):SEP70-148
BIEN, H. HENRIK IBSENS REALISMUS.
E. BEYER, 172(EDDA):1971/2-125
O.I. HOLTAN, 301(JEGP):APR72-311
BIENAIMÉ, D.R. GRÉVIN POETA SATIRICO E
ALTRI SAGGI SULLA POESIA DEL CINQUE-
CENTO FRANCESE.
M-R. LOGAN, 535(RHL):JUL-AUG70-697
BIENEFELD, M.A. WORKING HOURS IN BRITISH
INDUSTRY.
617(TLS):9FEB73-148
"BIENEK." (R. & M. MEAD, TRANS)
J. HART, 661:SUMMER70-113
BIER, W.C., ED. CONSCIENCE.
J.F. MOYNIHAN, 613:WINTER71-621
BIERMAN, A.K. & J.A. GOULD. PHILOSOPHY
FOR A NEW GENERATION.
A.W. MUNK, 484(PPR):SEP71-129
BIERMANN, W. FÜR MEINE GENOSSEN. DEUT-
SCHLAND, EIN WINTERMÄRCHEN.
617(TLS):23MAR73-319
BIGGER, C.P. PARTICIPATION.
R.S. BRUMBAUGH, 321:SUMMER70-158
BIGGS, R.D. ŠÀ.ZI.GA.
E. LEICHTY, 318(JAOS):OCT-DEC71-529
BIGI, E. LA GENESI DEL "CANTO NOTTURNO"
E ALTRI STUDI SUL LEOPARDI.
W.T.S., 191(ELN):SEP71(SUPP)-167
BIGLER, R.M. THE POLITICS OF GERMAN
PROTESTANTISM.
N. SONNE, 70(ANQ):MAY73-139
617(TLS):13JUL73-813
BIHALY, A. THE JOURNAL OF ANDREW BIHALY.
(A. TUTTLE, ED)
P. THEROUX, 441:9DEC73-32
BIHLER, H. & A. NOYER-WEIDNER, EDS.
MEDIUM AEVUM ROMANICUM.
J. HORRENT, 556(RLV):1971/4-481
BILES, J.I. TALK.
B. OLDSEY, 594:FALL71-346
BILL, E.G.W. A CATALOGUE OF MANUSCRIPTS
IN LAMBETH PALACE LIBRARY. (MSS. 1222-
1860)
617(TLS):2MAR73-248

BILL, E.G.W. UNIVERSITY REFORM IN NINE-
TEENTH CENTURY OXFORD.
617(TLS):18MAY73-552
BILLING, G. THE SLIPWAY.
F. BUSCH, 441:9DEC73-22
BILLINGTON, M. THE MODERN ACTOR.
J. ELSOM, 362:11JAN73-63
BILLINGTON, R. COCK ROBIN.
617(TLS):20APR73-437
BILLINGTON, R.A. FREDERICK JACKSON
TURNER.
I.R. DEE, 441:11MAR73-31
BILLINGTON, R.A., WITH W.M. WHITEHILL -
SEE TURNER, F.J. & A.F.P. HOOPER
BILLY, A. JOUBERT ÉNIGMATIQUE ET DÉLIC-
IEUX.
F.B. CONEM, 557(RSH):JUL-SEP70-480
BINDER, G. AENEAS UND AUGUSTUS.
S. LIEBERMAN, 124:JAN72-172
BINDMAN, D. EUROPEAN SCULPTURE.
P. CANNON-BROOKES, 39:OCT70-319
BINDSCHEDLER, M. & P. ZINSLI, EDS. GE-
SCHICHTE, DEUTUNG, KRITIK.
A. SUBIOTTO, 220(GL&L):OCT71-27
BING, S. ARTISTIC AMERICA, TIFFANY
GLASS, AND ART NOUVEAU.*
D.J. GORDON, 592:NOV70-216
BINGER, C. THOMAS JEFFERSON.
J.A. BEAR, JR., 656(WMQ):JUL71-512
J.V. JEZIERSKI, 432(NEQ):SEP71-501
BINGER, N.H. A BIBLIOGRAPHY OF GERMAN
PLAYS ON MICROCARDS.
J.K. FUGATE, 221(GQ):MAY71-423
E. SCHÜRER, 517(PBSA):JAN-MAR72-84
BINGHAM, C. THE LIFE AND TIMES OF EDWARD
II.
617(TLS):12OCT73-1259
BINGHAM, J. THE HUNTING DOWN OF PETER
MANUEL.
617(TLS):28SEP73-1104
BINGHAM, M. SHERIDAN.*
442(NY):10MAR73-135
BINGHAM, S. THE WAY IT IS NOW.*
J.P. DEGNAN, 249(HUDR):SUMMER72-330
617(TLS):23NOV73-1455
BINKLEY, L.J. CONFLICT OF IDEALS.
A.W. MUNK, 321:FALL70-238
J.S. WU, 258:JUN70-328
BINNI, W. SAGGI ALFIERIANI.
M. TURCHI, 228(GSLI):VOL148FASC464-
610
BINNI, W. - SEE RAMAT, R.
BINNI, W., WITH E. GHIDETTI - SEE LEOPAR-
DI, G.
BINNI, W. & N. SAPEGNO. STORIA LETTER-
ARIA DELLE REGIONI D'ITALIA.
F.S., 275(IQ):SPRING-SUMMER72-127
BINNICK, R.I. & OTHERS, EDS. PAPERS FROM
THE FIFTH REGIONAL MEETING OF THE CHI-
CAGO LINGUISTIC SOCIETY.
R.C. TURNER, 361:VOL26#2-199
BIOU, J. & OTHERS. LE MARQUIS DE SADE.
R.J. ELLRICH, 207(FR):FEB71-618
BIOY CASARES, A. DIARY OF THE WAR OF THE
PIG.
M. LEVIN, 441:28JAN73-34
M. WOOD, 453:19APR73-35
BIRCHER, M. JOHANN WILHELM VON STUBEN-
BERG (1619-1663) UND SEIN FREUNDES-
KREIS.
P.M. DALY, 564:JUN70-184
E. MANNACK, 433:APR70-202
B.L. SPAHR, 133:1970/1-127
BIRCHER, M. - SEE BEER, J.
BIRCHER, M. & H. STRAUMANN. SHAKESPEARE
UND DIE DEUTSCHE SCHWEIZ BIS ZUM BEGINN
DES 19. JAHRHUNDERTS.
J.L. HIBBERD, 220(GL&L):APR72-270

BIRD, A. ENGLISH HOUSE CLOCKS: 1600-
1850.
617(TLS):19OCT73-1277
BIRD, C. EVERYTHING A WOMAN NEEDS TO
KNOW TO GET PAID WHAT SHE'S WORTH.
M. BENDER, 441:15SEP73-35
BIRD, G. PHILOSOPHICAL TASKS.
617(TLS):23FEB73-218
BIRD, V. WARWICKSHIRE.
617(TLS):23MAR73-333
BIRDSALL, D. - SEE ALEXANDER, C.H.O.
BIRDSALL, V.O. WILD CIVILITY.*
C.B. HOGAN, 676(YR):AUTUMN71-134
R.D. HUME, 481(PQ):JUL71-375
BIRKE, J. - SEE GOTTSCHED, J.C.
VON BIRKEN, S. DIE TRUCKENE TRUNKENHEIT.
(K. PÖRNBACHER, ED)
B.L. SPAHR, 133:1971/1&2-197
BIRKENMAYER, S.S. A SELECTIVE BIBLIOGRA-
PHY OF WORKS RELATED TO THE TEACHING
OF SLAVIC LANGUAGES AND LITERATURES IN
THE UNITED STATES AND CANADA, 1942-
1967.
R. STURM, 399(MLJ):FEB71-116
BIRKINSHAW, P. THE LIVINGSTONE TOUCH.
617(TLS):7DEC73-1494
BIRKMAIER, E.M., ED. BRITANNICA REVIEW
OF FOREIGN LANGUAGE EDUCATION.* (VOL 1)
J.M. MOORE, 221(GQ):MAY71-433
R.L. POLITZER, 399(MLJ):MAR71-194
BÎRLEA, O. ANTOLOGIE DE PROZĂ POPULARĂ
EPICĂ.
V. NIŞCOV & H. STEIN, 196:BAND12HEFT
2/3-262
BIRLEY, R., ED. ETON COLLEGE LIBRARY.
R.A. SAYCE, 354:JUN70-176
BIRLEY, R. THE HISTORY OF ETON COLLEGE
LIBRARY.
P. MORGAN, 354:MAR71-79
BIRMINGHAM, J. THE VANCOUVER SPLIT.
M. ROGERS, 441:30SEP73-22
BIRMINGHAM, S. THE GRANDEES.
J. KUGEL, 390:AUG/SEP71-71
BIRMINGHAM, S. THE LATE JOHN MARQUAND.*
L. GURKO, 27(AL):JAN73-696
BIRMINGHAM, S. REAL LACE.
P. ADAMS, 61:NOV73-128
S. DARST, 441:18NOV73-16
BIRMINGHAM, S. THE RIGHT PLACES.
D. GODDARD, 441:17JUN73-22
BIRNBAUM, K.E. EAST AND WEST GERMANY.
617(TLS):30NOV73-1470
BIRNEY, E. THE BEAR ON THE DELHI ROAD.
617(TLS):26OCT73-1306
BIRNEY, E. RAG & BONE SHOP.*
D. BARBOUR, 150(DR):SUMMER71-289
BIRON, A.K. & V.V. DOROSHENKO. SOVET-
SKAIA ISTORIOGRAFIIA LATVII.
A. EZERGAILIS, 32:JUN72-455
BÎRSĂNESCU, Ş. PAGINI NESCRISE DIN ISTOR-
IA CULTURII ROMÂNEŞTI (SEC. X-XVI).
D.J. DELETANT, 575(SEER):OCT72-610
BIRSTEIN, A. DICKIE'S LIST.
P. ADAMS, 61:SEP73-118
A. BROYARD, 441:4SEP73-41
L. GOULD, 441:2SEP73-4
442(NY):22OCT73-174
BIRSTEIN, A. SUMMER SITUATIONS.*
J.P. DEGNAN, 249(HUDR):SUMMER72-330
BIRTWHISTLE, J. THE CONVERSION TO OIL OF
THE LOTS ROAD LONDON TRANSPORT POWER
STATION.
617(TLS):12JAN73-36
BIRÛKOV, B.V. KRUŠÉNIE MÉTAFIZIĆÉSKOJ
KONCÉPCII UNIVÉRSAL'NOSTI PRÉDMÉTNOJ
OBLASTI V LOGIKÉ.
I. ANGELELLI, 316:DEC70-571

BISANZ, A.J. DIE URSPRÜNGE DER SEELEN-
KRANKHEIT BEI KARL PHILIPP MORITZ.
  E.J. ENGEL, 402(MLR):OCT72-941
BISCHOFF, H. SETZUNG UND TRANSPOSITION
DES "-MENTE-"ADVERBS ALS AUSDRUCK DER
ART UND WEISE IM FRANZÖSISCHEN UND
ITALIENISCHEN MIT BESONDERER BERÜCK-
SICHTIGUNG DER TRANSPOSITION IN ADJEK-
TIVE.
  B. FOSTER, 208(FS):OCT72-501
  H. MEIER, 72:BAND209HEFT1/3-198
BISCHOFF, K. SPRACHE UND GESCHICHTE AN
DER MITTLEREN ELBE UND DER UNTEREN
SAALE.
  R. SCHMIDT-WIEGAND, 680(ZDP):BAND90
  HEFT1-140
BISHOP, E. THE COMPLETE POEMS OF ELIZA-
BETH BISHOP.*
  A. CLUYSENAAR, 565:VOL12#3-72
  H.T. KIRBY-SMITH, JR., 569(SR):SUM-
  MER72-483
BISHOP, E. & E. BRASIL, EDS. AN ANTHOL-
OGY OF TWENTIETH-CENTURY BRAZILIAN
POETRY.
  R. SCHRAMM, 651(WHR):AUTUMN72-389
  H. VENDLER, 441:7JAN73-4
BISHOP, F. ALLEN TATE.
  R. BUFFINGTON, 578:SPRING73-102
BISHOP, I. "PEARL" IN ITS SETTING.*
  R.E. KASKE, 38:BAND89HEFT1-135
  J. MAC QUEEN, 541(RES):MAY71-180
  R. WOOLF, 597(SN):VOL42#1-259
BISHOP, J. SOMETHING ELSE.
  W.H. PRITCHARD, 249(HUDR):WINTER72/73-
  685
BISHOP, M., ED. A CLASSICAL STORYBOOK.
  639(VQR):SPRING71-LVII
BISHOP, M. A MEDIEVAL STORY BOOK.
  Y. BRIDIER, 189(EA):OCT-DEC71-519
  639(VQR):WINTER71-XXVII
BISHOP, O.N. NATURAL COMMUNITIES.
  617(TLS):2MAR73-250
BISHOP, T., ED. L'AVANT-GARDE THÉÂTRALE.
  K.S. WHITE, 399(MLJ):FEB71-133
BISMUT, R. LA LYRIQUE DE CAMÕES.
  F. PIERCE, 86(BHS):JUL72-317
BISSELL, R. MY LIFE ON THE MISSISSIPPI.
  J. SEELYE, 441:9DEC73-16
  442(NY):24DEC73-80
BISSETT, B. NOBODY OWNS TH EARTH.*
  A. PURDY, 102(CANL):AUTUMN72-86
BISSINGER, A. DIE STRUKTUR DER GOTTESER-
KENNTNIS.
  C.A. CORR, 319:APR73-270
BISWAS, R.K. ARTHUR HUGH CLOUGH.
  617(TLS):12JAN73-43
BISWAS, S.C., ED. GANDHI.
  D. DALTON, 293(JAST):FEB71-493
BITTEL, K. HATTUSHA, THE CAPITAL OF
THE HITTITES.
  639(VQR):SUMMER71-CXXXVI
BITTERLING, K. DER WORTSCHATZ VON BAR-
BOURS "BRUCE."
  J.M. TEMPLETON, 597(SN):VOL43#2-579
BITTKER, B.I. THE CASE FOR BLACK REPARA-
TIONS.
  442(NY):10MAR73-135
  453:5APR73-37
BITTON, D. THE FRENCH NOBILITY IN CRISIS
1560-1640.
  J. DENT, 551(RENQ):SUMMER71-244
BITZER, G.W. BILLY BITZER.
  S. STERN, 441:16DEC73-25
BITZER, L.F. & E. BLACK, EDS. THE PROS-
PECT OF RHETORIC.
  W.W. BRADEN, 583:SPRING72-323

BIVAR, A.D.H. CATALOGUE OF THE WESTERN
ASIATIC SEALS IN THE BRITISH MUSEUM,
STAMP SEALS, II.*
  P.O. HARPER, 57:VOL33#1/2-144
BIVAR, A.D.H., ED. CORPUS INSCRIPTIONUM
IRANICARUM. (PT 3, VOL 6)
  R.N. FRYE, 318(JAOS):JAN-MAR71-145
BIVON, R. ELEMENT ORDER.
  R. RŮŽIČKA, 32:DEC72-947
BIXLER, N. BURMA.
  J. SILVERSTEIN, 318(JAOS):OCT-DEC71-
  564
BIZOS, M. - SEE XENOPHON
BJELOVUČIĆ, H. THE RAGUSAN REPUBLIC.
  T. STOIANOVICH, 32:MAR72-224
BJERKE, R., ED. FIFTEEN MODERN NORWEGIAN
STORIES.
  K.A. FLATIN, 563(SS):WINTER72-145
BJØNREBOE, J. FRIHETENS ØYEBLIKK.
  M. NAG, 270:VOL21#2-149
BJÖRKEGREN, H. ALEKSANDR SOLZHENITSYN.
  617(TLS):29JUN73-735
BJURSTRÖM, P. GERMAN DRAWINGS.
  617(TLS):9MAR73-265
BLACK, A. THE NATIVITY.
  A. RENDLE, 157:WINTER70-70
BLACK, A.J. MONARCHY AND COMMUNITY.
  P. RIESENBERG, 589:APR72-284
  J.A. WAHL, 377:NOV72-185
BLACK, C. THE LINLEYS OF BATH. (NEW ED)
  G. BEECHEY, 415:JAN72-49
BLACK, G. THE BITTER TEA.
  N. CALLENDAR, 441:14JAN73-30
  617(TLS):16MAR73-303
BLACK, M., ED. THE IMPORTANCE OF LAN-
GUAGE.
  L.B. CEBIK, 219(GAR):SUMMER70-252
  T.J. PACE, 480(P&R):WINTER70-66
BLACK, M. THE LABYRINTH OF LANGUAGE.*
  H.F. HARDING, 480(P&R):WINTER70-64
BLACK, M. MARGINS OF PRECISION.*
  R. CAMPBELL, 154:DEC71-805
BLACK, R.D.C. A CATALOGUE OF PAMPHLETS
ON ECONOMIC SUBJECTS PUBLISHED BETWEEN
1750 AND 1900 AND NOW HOUSED IN IRISH
LIBRARIES.
  J.H.P. PAFFORD, 78(BC):SPRING71-109
  M.C. REED, 354:MAR71-69
BLACK, R.D.C. - SEE JEVONS, W.S.
"THE BLACK PHOTOGRAPHERS ANNUAL 1973."
  S. SCHWARTZ, 441:2DEC73-95
BLACKABY, F., ED. AN INCOMES POLICY FOR
BRITAIN.
  P. OPPENHEIMER, 362:8MAR73-313
  617(TLS):12JAN73-45
BLACKBURN, P. IN. ON. OR ABOUT THE
PREMISES.
  R. VAS DIAS, 600:FALL69-153
BLACKBURN, S. REASON AND PREDICTION.
  617(TLS):18MAY73-550
BLACKER, H. - SEE UNDER NERO
BLACKETT, M. THE MARK OF THE MAKER.
  617(TLS):18MAY73-546
BLACKING, J. VENDA CHILDREN'S SONGS.
  A.M. JONES, 69:JUL70-295
BLACKSTONE, W.T. & G.L. NEWSOME, EDS.
EDUCATION AND ETHICS.
  J.W. BOWERS, 480(P&R):SUMMER71-188
BLACKWELL, R.J. DISCOVERY IN THE PHYSI-
CAL SCIENCES.
  H.J. BIRX, 484(PPR):JUN72-580
  M. RUSE, 154:DEC70-480
BLACKWOOD, C. FOR ALL THAT I FOUND THERE.
  G. ANNAN, 362:27DEC73-891
BLAGDEN, D. VERY WILLING GRIFFIN.
  617(TLS):14DEC73-1549
BLAINEY, G. THE CAUSES OF WAR.
  617(TLS):15JUN73-659

BLAIR, C., JR. SURVIVE!
  D.K. MANO, 441:19AUG73-7
BLAIR, P.H. - SEE UNDER HUNTER BLAIR, P.
BLAIR, W. - SEE TWAIN, M.
BLAISE, C. A NORTH AMERICAN EDUCATION.
  M. LEVIN, 441:11FEB73-31
  F. SUTHERLAND, 296:FALL73-105
BLAKE, N.F. CAXTON AND HIS WORLD.
  J. COTTON, 503:AUTUMN70-158
BLAKE, N.F. - SEE "THE HISTORY OF REYNARD
  THE FOX"
BLAKE, R. THE CONSERVATIVE PARTY FROM
  PEEL TO CHURCHILL.
  639(VQR):SUMMER71-CXXIII
  676(YR):AUTUMN71-XIV
BLAKE, W. THE POETRY AND PROSE OF WIL-
  LIAM BLAKE. (D.V. ERDMAN, ED)
  R.M. BAINE, 219(GAR):SUMMER71-238
BLAKE, W. TIRIEL. (G.E. BENTLEY, JR.,
  ED)
  M. PÜTZ, 38:BAND89HEFT2-265
BLAKEMORE, H. & C.T. SMITH, EDS. LATIN
  AMERICA.*
  P. VOSSELER, 182:VOL24#21/22-823
BLAMIRES, D. CHARACTERIZATION AND INDI-
  VIDUALITY IN WOLFRAM'S "PARZIVAL."
  P.W. TAX, 680(ZDP):BAND89HEFT1-117
  M.O. WALSHE, 220(GL&L):OCT71-16
BLAMIRES, D. DAVID JONES.*
  A.C.C. MURRAY, 148:WINTER71-380
  B. QUINN, 659:SPRING73-267
BLAMIRES, H. WORD UNHEARD.*
  H. SERGEANT, 175:AUTUMN71-106
BLANC, A. MONTHERLANT, UN PESSIMISME
  HEUREUX.
  M. RAIMOND, 535(RHL):JAN-FEB71-142
BLANCH, R.J., ED. STYLE AND SYMBOLISM IN
  "PIERS PLOWMAN."*
  A.D. WOOD, 541(RES):MAY71-182
BLANCHARD, A. TRÉSOR DE LA POÉSIE BAR-
  OQUE ET PRÉCIEUSE (1550-1650).
  H. LAFAY, 535(RHL):MAY-JUN71-496
BLANCHE-BENVENISTE, C. & A. CHERVEL.
  L'ORTHOGRAPHE.
  A. MEUNIER, 209(FM):JUL71-258
  N.C.W. SPENCE, 208(FS):OCT72-499
BLANCHET, A. - SEE BREMOND, H. & M. BLON-
  DEL
BLANCHOT, M. L'ENTRETIEN INFINI.
  F. COLLIN, 98:AUG-SEP70-747
BLANCHOT, M. LE RESSASSEMENT ÉTERNEL.
  J-P. LATTEUR, 98:OCT71-897
BLANCK, J. BIBLIOGRAPHY OF AMERICAN LIT-
  ERATURE. (VOL 5)
  S. NOWELL-SMITH, 354:SEP70-268
VON BLANCKENHAGEN, P.H. & C. ALEXANDER.
  THE PAINTINGS OF BOSCOTRECASE.
  C.M. DAWSON, 54:SEP70-307
BLAND, D. HISTORY OF BOOK ILLUSTRATION.
  (2ND ED)
  J. COTTON, 503:SUMMER70-97
  R. MC LEAN, 135:APR70-278
BLAND, P. THE MAN WITH THE CARPET-BAG.
  617(TLS):27APR73-474
BLAND, R.W. PRIVATE PRESSURE ON PUBLIC
  LAW.
  R. KLUGER, 441:30DEC73-5
BLANK, R. SPRACHE UND DRAMATURGIE.
  P. PÜTZ, 52:BAND6HEFT1-89
BLANK, W. DIE DEUTSCHE MINNEALLEGORIE.
  O. SAYCE, 402(MLR):JAN72-205
BLANKENSHIP, W.D. THE PROGRAMMED MAN.
  N. CALLENDAR, 441:2SEP73-18
BLANKFORT, M. I DIDN'T KNOW I WOULD LIVE
  SO LONG.
  M. LEVIN, 441:11FEB73-31
BLASSINGAME, J.W. THE SLAVE COMMUNITY.
  617(TLS):2MAR73-230

BLATT, T.B. THE PLAYS OF JOHN BALE.*
  G.K. HUNTER, 447(N&Q):DEC71-471
BLATTMANN, E. DIE LIEDER HARTMANNS VON
  AUE.
  L. OKKEN, 433:JUL71-347
  O. SAYCE, 220(GL&L):OCT71-20
  B. SOWINSKI, 657(WW):JAN/FEB71-71
  H. TERVOOREN, 680(ZDP):BAND89HEFT3-
  452
BLATTY, W.P. I'LL TELL THEM I REMEMBER
  YOU.
  G. BURNSIDE, 441:18NOV73-46
  G. WALKER, 441:6OCT73-21
BLAUKOPF, K. GUSTAV MAHLER.
  R. CRAFT, 453:29NOV73-10
  C.E. SCHORSKE, 441:7OCT73-3
BLAVIER-PAQUOT, S. LA FONTAINE.
  H.R., 430(NS):MAR70-154
BLAZER, J.S. DEAL ME OUT.
  N. CALLENDAR, 441:7OCT73-44
BLECUA, J.M. SOBRE POESÍA DE LA EDAD
  DE ORO (ENSAYOS Y NOTAS ERUDITAS).
  A. TERRY, 86(BHS):JUL72-301
BLECUA, J.M. - SEE LOPE DE VEGA
BLECUA, J.M. - SEE DE QUEVEDO Y VILLEGAS,
  F.G.
BLEGEN, C.W. & M. RAWSON. THE PALACE OF
  NESTOR AT PYLOS IN WESTERN MESSENIA.
  (VOL 1)
  D.G. MITTEN, 576:OCT71-263
BLEKASTAD, M. COMENIUS.
  J.J. TOMIAK, 575(SEER):JUL72-462
LADY BLESSINGTON. LADY BLESSINGTON'S
  "CONVERSATIONS OF LORD BYRON."* (E.J.
  LOVELL, JR., ED)
  J. BUXTON, 541(RES):FEB71-102
BLICKER, S. SHMUCKS.
  J. SHERMAN, 296:SPRING73-90
BLIN, G. LA CRIBLEUSE DE BLÉ.
  M-C. ROPARS, 535(RHL):SEP-DEC70-1099
BLIN, G. & C. PICHOIS - SEE BAUDELAIRE,
  C.
BLINDHEIM, M. NORWEGIAN ROMANESQUE DEC-
  ORATIVE SCULPTURE 1090-1210.
  G.J.H-S., 135:FEB70-126
BLINKENBERG, A. MONTAIGNE.
  L. GUSTAFSSON, 597(SN):VOL43#2-618
BLINKENBERG, A. & P. HØYBYE. DANSK-
  FRANSK SUPPLERINGSORDBOG.
  J. DUBOIS, 209(FM):APR70-169
BLISH, J. AND ALL THE STARS A STAGE.*
  617(TLS):2FEB73-129
BLISH, J. BEST SCIENCE FICTION STORIES
  OF JAMES BLISH.
  617(TLS):20APR73-451
BLISH, J. MIDSUMMER CENTURY.
  617(TLS):9NOV73-1377
BLISH, J., ED. NEBULA AWARD STORIES 5.*
  R. PHILLIPS, 573(SSF):FALL71-657
BLISHEN, E. THIS RIGHT SOFT LOT.
  J.C. FIELD, 556(RLV):1971/5-626
BLISS, A. AS I REMEMBER.*
  J.P., 376:OCT70-93
BLISS, A.J., ED. SIR ORFEO.* (2ND ED)
  K.R. BROOKS, 179(ES):OCT71-485
BLISS, I.S. EDWARD YOUNG.
  H. PETTIT, 191(ELN):JUN72-311
BLISTEIN, E.M., ED. THE DRAMA OF THE
  RENAISSANCE.
  T.P. LOGAN, 149:MAR72-90
BLIT, L. THE ORIGINS OF POLISH SOCIAL-
  ISM.*
  A. KATZ, 497(POLR):AUTUMN71-87
  L. ORTON, 32:DEC72-920
"BERNARD BLOCH ON JAPANESE."* (R.A.
MILLER, ED)
  J.J. CHEW, JR., 293(JAST):MAY71-688
                              [CONTINUED]

35

"BERNARD BLOCH ON JAPANESE."* (R.A.
MILLER, ED) [CONTINUING]
E.H. JORDEN, 215(GL):VOL11#3-188
H. AOKI, 318(JAOS):OCT-DEC71-523
BLOCH, D. ARISING.
617(TLS):8JUN73-633
BLOCH, M. THE ROYAL TOUCH.
P. BURKE, 362:9AUG73-177
617(TLS):15JUN73-668
BLOCH, P.A. SCHILLER UND DIE FRANZÖ-
SISCHE KLASSISCHE TRAGÖDIE.
N. OELLERS, 52:BAND6HEFT1-100
BLOCK, H.M. NATURALISTIC TRIPTYCH.
M. BRADBURY, 402(MLR):JAN72-160
J.L. GREEN, 399(MLJ):MAY71-324
BLÖCKER-WALTER, M. ALFONS I. VON PORTU-
GAL.
R.A. FLETCHER, 182:VOL24#6-311
BLOEM, J.C. ANTOLOGIA DE J.C. BLOEM.
(H. COLIN, ED)
J.A.S. TROMP, 202(FMOD):NOV70/FEB71-
170
BLOEMENDAL, F.A.H. & M. HIDES. SCOTLAND
IN CAMERACOLOUR.
617(TLS):2FEB73-133
BLOEMENDAL, F.A.H. & A.G. WARD. VENICE
IN CAMERACOLOUR.
617(TLS):2FEB73-133
BLOFELD, J. THE SECRET AND SUBLIME.
617(TLS):4MAY73-508
BLOIS, J. & M. BAR. NOTRE LANGUE FRAN-
ÇAISE.
M-L. MOREAU, 556(RLV):1971/2-235
"ROBERT DE BLOIS'S 'FLORIS ET LYRIOPÉ'" -
SEE UNDER ROBERT
BLOK, A. THE TWELVE AND OTHER POEMS.*
H. SERGEANT, 175:SUMMER71-65
BLOK, W. & OTHERS, EDS. STUDIA NEERLAN-
DICA.
C.F.P. STUTTERHEIM, 204(FDL):1971/1-
53
BLOKHINTSEV, D.I. THE PHILOSOPHY OF
QUANTUM MECHANICS.*
J. BUB, 486:MAR70-153
BLOM, E., COMP. EVERYMAN'S DICTIONARY OF
MUSIC.* (5TH ED REV BY J. WESTRUP)
L. SALTER, 415:MAY72-458
BLOMBERG, R. THREE PASTORAL NOVELS.
K. WHINNOM, 86(BHS):JUL72-298
BLONDEL, J. COMPARING POLITICAL SYSTEMS.
617(TLS):8JUN73-635
BLONDEL, M. LETTRES PHILOSOPHIQUES.
J. TROUILLARD, 542:OCT-DEC71-453
BLOODWORTH, D. ANY NUMBER CAN PLAY.*
M. LEVIN, 441:28JAN73-34
BLOODWORTH, D. AN EYE FOR THE DRAGON.
F.J. CORLEY, 613:AUTUMN71-479
BLOOM, A. GOD AND MAN.*
D. KNOWLES, 441:25FEB73-18
BLOOM, H. THE ANXIETY OF INFLUENCE.
J. HOLLANDER, 441:4MAR73-27
J. HOLLANDER, 491:AUG73-298
617(TLS):26OCT73-1308
BLOOM, H. BLAKE'S APOCALYPSE.*
R.M. BAINE, 219(GAR):SUMMER71-238
BLOOM, H. THE RINGERS IN THE TOWER.
G. BORNSTEIN, 385(MQR):SUMMER73-278
T. MC FARLAND, 676(YR):WINTER72-279
BLOOM, H. YEATS.*
J.D. BOULGER, 613:WINTER70-620
A.N. JEFFARES, 541(RES):NOV71-514
T. PARKINSON, 191(ELN):MAR72-234
H. SERGEANT, 175:SPRING71-26
42(AR):SPRING70-133
BLOOM, J.P., ED. THE TERRITORIAL PAPERS
OF THE UNITED STATES. (VOL 27)
D.R. BODEM, 14:APR71-191

BLOOM, W. GETTING THERE.
R. BRYDEN, 362:15FEB73-219
617(TLS):23FEB73-219
BLOOMFIELD, B.C. & E. MENDELSON. W.H.
AUDEN. (2ND ED)
617(TLS):27JUL73-883
BLOOMFIELD, L. THE MENOMINI LANGUAGE.
(C.F. HOCKETT, ED)
K.V. TEETER, 269(IJAL):JUL70-235
BLOOMFIELD, M.W. ESSAYS AND EXPLORA-
TIONS.*
A. DAVID, 589:JUL72-509
Y. MALKIEL, 545(RPH):AUG71-152
BLOSSER, S.S. & C.N. WILSON, JR. THE
SOUTHERN HISTORICAL COLLECTION.
W.W. WASSON, 14:JAN71-62
BLUESTEIN, G. THE VOICE OF THE FOLK.
A. REYES-SCHRAMM, 187:MAY73-319
BLUM, J.M. - SEE WALLACE, H.A.
BLUM, K. HUNDERT JAHRE EIN DEUTSCHES
REQUIEM VON JOHANNES BRAHMS.
M-M., 410(M&L):APR72-207
BLUM, L. L'OEUVRE DE LÉON BLUM. (VOL
3, PTS 1&2)
617(TLS):12OCT73-1229
BLUM, R. SOZIALE MARKTWIRTSCHAFT.
G. GAUDARD, 182:VOL24#4-143
BLUM, S.N. EARLY NETHERLANDISH TRIP-
TYCHS.
L. CAMPBELL, 589:APR72-288
C.M. KAUFFMANN, 39:DEC71-525
R. LEBOWITZ, 58:MAY71-16
R.M. WALKER, 551(RENQ):AUTUMN71-360
BLUME, B. - SEE RILKE, R.M.
BLUMENKRANZ, B., ED. HISTOIRE DES JUIFS
EN FRANCE.
617(TLS):16FEB73-185
BLUMENTHAL, T. SAVINGS IN POSTWAR JAPAN.
R. EVANS, JR., 293(JAST):MAY71-688
BLUND, J. IOHANNES BLUND TRACTATUS DE
ANIMA. (D.A. CALLUS & R.W. HUNT, EDS)
M.L. COLKER, 589:JAN72-108
M.B. CROWE, 382(MAE):1972/3-246
BLUNDELL, N. THE GREAT DIURNAL OF NICH-
OLAS BLUNDELL OF LITTLE CROSBY, LANCA-
SHIRE. (VOL 3) (J.J. BAGLEY, ED)
617(TLS):9MAR73-277
BLUNDEN, M. & G. IMPRESSIONISTS AND
IMPRESSIONISM.
C. LICHTBLAU, 58:DEC70/JAN71-12
BLUNT, A. SICILIAN BAROQUE.*
G. GANGI, 54:DEC70-460
J-L-M., 135:FEB70-124
BLUNT, A. SOME USES AND MISUSES OF THE
TERMS BAROQUE AND ROCOCO AS APPLIED TO
ARCHITECTURE.
617(TLS):10AUG73-937
BLUNT, W. THE DREAM KING.*
A. VON SCHUCKMANN, 39:NOV71-417
BLUNT, W. THE GOLDEN ROAD TO SAMARKAND.
442(NY):23JUL73-79
617(TLS):13JUL73-810
BLUSKE, M.K. & E.K. WALTHER. DAS ERSTE
JAHR. (2ND ED)
A.E. EHM, 399(MLJ):DEC71-529
BLY, R., ED. FORTY POEMS TOUCHING ON
RECENT AMERICAN HISTORY.*
S. MOORE, 385(MQR):SUMMER73-285
BLY, R. SLEEPERS JOINING HANDS.
D. CAVITCH, 441:18FEB73-2
J.C. OATES, 398:WINTER73-341
BLY, R. THE TEETH MOTHER NAKED AT LAST.
M-D., 502(PRS):SUMMER71-186
502(PRS):SPRING71-92
BLYTH, A. COLIN DAVIS.*
K. SPENCE, 415:DEC72-1191

BLYTH, H. CARO.*
P. ADAMS, 61:FEB73-103
A. BROYARD, 441:16FEB73-39
A. FREMANTLE, 441:18FEB73-6
442(NY):24FEB73-131
BLYTHE, P. STRESS DISEASE.
617(TLS):10AUG73-937
BLYTHE, R. AKENFIELD.
M. MUDRICK, 249(HUDR):SPRING72-142
BLYTHE, R., ED. ALDEBURGH ANTHOLOGY.
C. DRIVER, 362:12JUL73-60
617(TLS):13APR73-429
BO, D. - SEE PERSIUS
BOA, E. & J.H. REID. CRITICAL STRATE-
GIES.
617(TLS):9MAR73-272
BOADELLA, D. WILHELM REICH.
617(TLS):15JUN73-662
BOAK, D. ANDRÉ MALRAUX.
C.D. BLEND, 546(RR):FEB71-75
P.A. FORTIER, 188(ECR):WINTER70-345
J.D. GAUTHIER, 207(FR):OCT70-218
M. PICARD, 535(RHL):MAY-JUN70-538
BOARD, C. & OTHERS, EDS. PROGRESS IN
GEOGRAPHY. (VOL 4)
617(TLS):30MAR73-359
BOARDMAN, J. ARCHAIC GREEK GEMS.*
M-L. VOLLENWEIDER, 54:JUN71-240
BOARDMAN, J. ENGRAVED GEMS.*
R. HIGGINS, 39:AUG71-160
M-L. VOLLENWEIDER, 54:JUN71-240
BOARDMAN, J. GREEK GEMS AND FINGER
RINGS.
H.L. BLACKMORE, 135:NOV71-215
BOARDMAN, R. & A.J.R. GROOM, EDS. THE
MANAGEMENT OF BRITAIN'S EXTERNAL RELA-
TIONS.
617(TLS):8JUN73-635
BOAS, F.S., ED. FIVE PRE-SHAKESPEARIAN
COMEDIES.
I. BROWN, 157:SUMMER70-70
BOAS, G. THE HISTORY OF IDEAS.
L.B. CEBIK, 219(GAR):SUMMER71-241
J. FISHER, 322(JHI):OCT-DEC70-617
BOAS, G. VOX POPULI.
C.M.R., 543:DEC70-335
BOASE, A.M., ED. THE POETRY OF FRANCE.
(VOL 1)
G. GADOFFRE, 545(RPH):FEB72-355
BOASE, A.M., ED. THE POETRY OF FRANCE.
(VOL 2)
617(TLS):16NOV73-1405
BOASE, A.M., ED. THE POETRY OF FRANCE.*
(VOL 4)
J-M. KLINKENBERG, 556(RLV):1971/3-357
M. SCHAETTEL, 557(RSH):JAN-MAR70-176
BOASE, P.H., ED. THE RHETORIC OF CHRIS-
TIAN SOCIALISM.
R.L. HENDREN, 583:WINTER70-191
BOASE, T.S.R. CASTLES AND CHURCHES OF
THE CRUSADING KINGDOM.
J. FOLDA, 576:MAR70-64
BOBA, I. MORAVIA'S HISTORY RECONSIDERED.
S.H. THOMSON, 32:JUN72-453
BOBER, A., ED. THE OTHER ISRAEL.
P. COWAN, 441:21JAN73-4
BOBIK, J., ED. THE NATURE OF PHILOSOPHI-
CAL INQUIRY.
L.G., 543:JUN71-764
BOCCACCIO, G. OPERE MINORI IN VOLGARE.
(VOLS 1&2) (M. MARTI, ED)
M. TURCHI, 228(GSLI):VOL147FASC460-
579
BOCCACCIO, G. TUTTE LE OPERE. (V.
BRANCA, ED)
M.P., 228(GSLI):VOL148FASC462/463-461
V.S., 275(IQ):SPRING-SUMMER72-115

BOCCHETTA, V. HORACIO EN VILLEGAS Y EN
FRAY LUIS LEÓN.
D.L. BAUM, 238:DEC71-968
BOCCI, P. - SEE UNDER "CORPUS VASORUM
ANTIQUORUM" (ITALIA, FASC 41)
BOCK, F., ED & TRANS. ENGI-SHIKI, PRO-
CEDURES OF THE ENGI ERA. (BKS 1-5)
K. TANAKA, 293(JAST):FEB71-457
BODDY, F.A. FOLIAGE PLANTS.
617(TLS):13APR73-429
BODE, C. MENCKEN.*
C.A. BROWN, 613:AUTUMN70-450
W.D. TAYLOR, 399(MLJ):FEB71-133
BODE, C. - SEE MENCKEN, H.L.
BODEN, D. DAS AMERIKABILD IM RUSSISCHEN
SCHRIFTTUM BIS ZUM ENDE DES XIX. JAHR-
HUNDERTS.
V.A. TUMINS, 52:BAND6HEFT2-222
BODET, J.T. - SEE UNDER TORRES BODET, J.
BODICHON, B.L.S. AN AMERICAN DIARY
1857-8. (J.W. REED, JR., ED)
617(TLS):19JAN73-70
BODROGI, T. ART IN AFRICA.
F. WILLETT, 54:JUN71-277
BOECK, W. DER BAMBERGER MEISTER.
T.G. FRISCH, 54:SEP70-309
BOEHM, R. VOM GESICHTSPUNKT DER PHÄNOM-
ENOLOGIE.
R. SOKOLOWSKI, 484(PPR):SEP71-135
BOEHMER, G. ZUR ENTWICKLUNG UND REFORM
DES DEUTSCHEN FAMILIEN- UND ERBRECHTS.
(K.F. KREUZER, ED)
E.J. COHN, 182:VOL24#1/2-6
BOELEN, B.J. EXISTENTIAL THINKING.*
D.F.D., 543:MAR71-536
BOER, C. - SEE "THE HOMERIC HYMNS"
DEN BOER, W. SOME MINOR ROMAN HISTOR-
IANS.
617(TLS):26JAN73-95
BOERNER, P. TAGEBUCH.*
R-M., 191(ELN):SEP71(SUPP)-117
BOESCH, B. - SEE WIESSNER, E.
BOESIGER, W. LE CORBUSIER, LAST WORKS.
P. OLIVER, 592:JUL-AUG70-54
BOESSNECK, J. & OTHERS. DIE TIERKNOCHEN-
FUNDE AUS DEM OPPIDUM VON MANCHING.
E. KUHN-SCHNYDER, 182:VOL24#15/16-621
"BOETHII DACI OPERA." (J. PINBORG & H.
ROOS, WITH S.S. JENSEN, EDS)
A. ZIMMERMANN, 53(AGP):BAND53HEFT2-
195
BOETHIUS. THE THEOLOGICAL TRACTATES.
(H.F. STEWART, E.K. RAND & S.J. TESTER,
TRANS) THE CONSOLATION OF PHILOSOPHY.
(S.J. TESTER, TRANS)
617(TLS):16MAR73-305
BOETHIUS, A. & J.B. WARD-PERKINS. ETRUS-
CAN AND ROMAN ARCHITECTURE.
R. HIGGINS, 39:JAN71-74
BOËTHIUS, U. STRINDBERG OCH KVINNOFRÅGAN
TILL OCH MED GIFTAS I.
W. JOHNSON, 563(SS):AUTUMN72-571
BOETIUS, H. - SEE MORHOF, D.G.
BOETS, J. GEDICHTEN OM IN TE WONEN,
BESCHOUWINGEN BIJ EEN VEERTIGTAL NEDER-
LANDSE GEDICHTEN.
J. BARTHELS, 556(RLV):1971/5-652
BOGAN, L. A POET'S ALPHABET. (R. PHELPS
& R. LIMMER, EDS)
H. MORRIS, 569(SR):AUTUMN72-627
BOGAN, L. WHAT THE WOMAN LIVED. (R.
LIMMER, ED)
N. MILFORD, 441:16DEC73-1
442(NY):12NOV73-219
BOGDANOVICH, P. PIECES OF TIME.
G. WALKER, 441:17NOV73-29

BOGLE, D.  TOMS, COONS, MULATTOES, MAM-
MIES, AND BUCKS.
   M. WATKINS, 441:9JUN73-31
   441:26AUG73-8
BOGUCKA, M.  NICHOLAS COPERNICUS.
   617(TLS):29JUN73-744
BOHIGAS, O.  ARQUITECTURA MODERNISTA.
   R. BLETTER, 576:MAR70-68
   J.C. ROHRER, 54:SEP70-341
BOHLEN, C.E., WITH R.H. PHELPS.  WITNESS
TO HISTORY 1929-1969.
   G.A. CRAIG, 441:3JUN73-4
   C. LEHMANN-HAUPT, 441:24MAY73-49
   R. STEEL, 453:31MAY73-29
   E. WEEKS, 61:JUN73-119
   442(NY):16JUN73-110
   617(TLS):14DEC73-1531
BÖHM, D.  ZEITLOSIGKEIT UND ENTGLEITENDE
ZEIT ALS KONSTITUTIVE DIALEKTIK IM
WERKE VON GIOVANNI VERGA.
   O. RAGUSA, 546(RR):OCT71-211
BÖHM, F. & W. DIRKS, EDS.  JUDENTUM;
SCHICKSAL, WESEN UND GEGENWART.
   G. HEER, 182:VOL24#7/8-369
BÖHM, R.  WESEN UND FUNKTION DER STER-
BEREDE IM ELISABETHANISCHEN DRAMA.
   V.B. HELTZEL, 570(SQ):AUTUMN70-505
BÖHM, R.G.  GAIUSSTUDIEN.  (VOL 1)
   H.D. EVJEN, 24:APR72-364
BÖHM, R.G.  GAIUSSTUDIEN.  (VOL 2)
   W.M. GORDON, 123:MAR72-115
BÖHME, R.  ORPHEUS, DER SÄNGER UND SEINE
ZEIT.
   F. LASSERRE, 182:VOL24#9/10-430
BÖHMER, M.  UNTERSUCHUNGEN ZUR MITTEL-
HOCHDEUTSCHEN KREUZZUGSLYRIK.*
   L. OKKEN, 433:OCT71-455
BOHNE, H. & H. VAN IERSSEL.  PUBLISHING.
   C. CALLAHAN, 99:NOV-DEC73-56
BOHRER, K.H.  DER LAUF DES FREITAG.
   617(TLS):30NOV73-1468
BOIE, B.  HAUPTMOTIVE IM WERKE JULIEN
GRACQS.
   W.A. STRAUSS, 546(RR):FEB71-76
BOIME, A.  THE ACADEMY AND FRENCH PAINT-
ING IN THE NINETEENTH CENTURY.*
   R.E., 135:APR71-290
   A. FORGE, 592:MAR71-130
   B. LAUGHTON, 39:JUN71-529
   C. THOMPSON, 111:22OCT71-28
BOIREL, R.  LA RÉSOLUTION DES PROBLÈMES.
   R. BLANCHÉ, 542:OCT-DEC70-485
BOIS, J.  TRANSLATING FOR KING JAMES.*
(W. ALLEN, ED) [SHOWN IN PREV UNDER ED]
   J.A. DEVEREUX, 577(SHR):WINTER71-81
   J.R. MEYER, 551(RENQ):SPRING71-79
BOISSELIER, J.  MANUEL D'ARCHÉOLOGIE
D'EXTRÊME-ORIENT.  (VOL 1)
   S.J. O'CONNOR, 57:VOL33#1/2-151
BOKUN, B.  SPY IN THE VATICAN 1941-45.
   A. BROYARD, 441:20JUN73-45
BOLAM, D.W. & J.L. HENDERSON.  ART AND
BELIEF.
   F.D. MARTIN, 290(JAAC):SUMMER71-537
BOLBJERG, A.  VERBALSYSTEMET I NYDANSK.
   F.O. LINDEMAN, 260(IF):BAND74-313
BOLD, A., ED.  THE PENGUIN BOOK OF SCOT-
TISH VERSE.
   R. WILLIAMS, 565:VOL12#2-35
BOLD, A., ED.  THE PENGUIN BOOK OF SOC-
IALIST VERSE.
   J. WILLETT, 493:SPRING71-69
BOLD, A.  A PINT OF BITTER.
   A. CLUYSENAAR, 565:VOL12#4-68
BOLDT, G.  HITLER.
   A. BULLOCK, 453:28JUN73-30
   J.K. GALBRAITH, 441:22APR73-4

BOLELLI, T.  PER UN STORIA DELLA RICERCA
LINGUISTICA.
   L. ZGUSTA, 353:OCT71-95
"BOLETIM DO GABINETE PORTUGUÊS DE LEI-
TURA: ASPECTOS DO BARROCO."
   D-H. PAGEAUX, 549(RLC):OCT-DEC70-558
BOLINGER, D.  ASPECTS OF LANGUAGE.*
   D.J. ALLERTON, 297(JL):FEB70-125
   M. BALABAN, 353:SEP71-105
BÖLL, H.  GEDICHTE.
   617(TLS):12JAN73-36
BÖLL, H.  GROUP PORTRAIT WITH LADY.  (GER-
MAN TITLE: GRUPPENBILD MIT DAME.)
   A. BROYARD, 441:9MAY73-39
   V. CUNNINGHAM, 362:3MAY73-591
   D.J. ENRIGHT, 453:31MAY73-35
   E. LARSEN, 270:VOL22#1-14
   R. LOCKE, 441:6MAY73-1
   M. MADDOCKS, 61:JUL73-95
   617(TLS):1JUN73-604
BOLLACHER, M.  DER JUNGE GOETHE UND
SPINOZA.*
   H. MEYER, 405(MP):NOV71-172
BOLLACK, J.  EMPÉDOCLE II.  EMPÉDOCLE
III.
   G.B. KERFERD, 123:DEC72-325
   H. WISMANN, 98:MAY70-462 [& CONT IN]
   98:AUG-SEP70-774
BOLLACK, J., M. BOLLACK & H. WISMANN.  LA
LETTRE D'EPICURE.
   F.M. CLEVE, 319:APR73-255
   J.M. SNYDER, 124:MAR72-235
BOLLE, K.W.  THE FREEDOM OF MAN IN MYTH.
   J.Y. FENTON, 480(P&R):WINTER71-65
BOLLÈME, G.  LES ALMANACHS POPULAIRES AUX
XVIIE ET XVIIIE SIÈCLES.
   E.L. EISENSTEIN, 207(FR):MAR71-777
"BOLLETTINO DEL CENTRO PER LO STUDIO
DELL'INSEGNAMENTO ALL'ESTERO DELL'ITAL-
IANO."
   E.B., 228(GSLI):VOL147FASC460-631
BOLOGNA, F.  NOVITÀ SU GIOTTO.
   A. SMART, 39:FEB70-163
   D. WILKINS, 56:SPRING71-113
BOLSTER, R.  STENDHAL, BALZAC ET LE FÉMI-
NISME ROMANTIQUE.
   C.C., 191(ELN):SEP71(SUPP)-105
BOLT, C.  THE ANTI-SLAVERY MOVEMENT AND
RECONSTRUCTION.
   J.A. RAWLEY, 637(VS):MAR71-348
BOLTHO, A.  FOREIGN TRADE CRITERIA IN
SOCIALIST ECONOMIES.
   A. ABOUCHAR, 32:DEC72-908
   M. BORNSTEIN, 550(RUSR):OCT71-402
BOLTON, J.D.P.  GLORY, JEST AND RIDDLE.
   617(TLS):13JUL73-812
BOLTON, W.F. & D. CRYSTAL, EDS.  THE
ENGLISH LANGUAGE.*  (VOL 2)
   P.W. ROGERS, 529(QQ):AUTUMN71-474
BOMBACI, A. - SEE FUZŪLĪ
BOMBECK, E.  I LOST EVERYTHING IN THE
POST-NATAL DEPRESSION.
   R. LASSON, 441:7OCT73-16
BÖMER, F.  P. OVIDIUS NASO, "METAMOR-
PHOSEN".*
   E.J. KENNEY, 123:MAR72-38
BOMSDORF, F.  PROZESSMAXIMEN UND RECHTS-
WIRKLICHKEIT.
   P. PADIS, 182:VOL24#3-86
BON, A.  BYZANTIUM.
   617(TLS):18MAY73-565
BON, A.  LA MORÉE FRANQUE.
   P. TOPPING, 589:JUL72-511
BONALD, J.M.C. - SEE UNDER CABALLERO BON-
ALD, J.M.
BONANSEA, B.M.  TOMMASO CAMPANELLA.
   P.J.W. MILLER, 154:JUN71-363
   E. NAMER, 542:APR-JUN70-239

BORCHARDT, D.H. THE SPREAD OF PRINTING:
AUSTRALIA.
R. CAVE, 503:SUMMER70-99
K.I.D. MASLEN, 354:MAR71-75
"RUDOLF BORCHARDT: AUSWAHL AUS DEM WERK."
P. PROCHNIK, 220(GL&L):OCT71-85
"BORCHERS." (R. & M. MEAD, TRANS)
J. HART, 661:SUMMER70-113
BORCHERT, W. THE MAN OUTSIDE.*
P. LENTZ, 385(MQR):FALL73-390
"BORDAS ENCYCLOPÉDIE." (VOLS 1-5B) (R.
CARATINI, ED)
R. SHACKLETON, 208(FS):APR72-245
205(FMLS):OCT70-419
"BORDAS ENCYCLOPÉDIE." (VOL 6) (R. CARA-
TINI, ED)
R. SHACKLETON, 208(FS):APR72-245
BOREL, E. EMILE BOREL, PHILOSOPHE ET
HOMME D'ACTION. (M. FRÉCHET, ED)
P. LÉVY, 542:APR-JUN71-233
BOREL, J. LA DÉPOSSESSION.
617(TLS):13JUL73-803
BORER, M.C. TWO VILLAGES.
617(TLS):2NOV73-1352
BORER, M.C. A WEEK IN LONDON.
617(TLS):17AUG73-961
BORG, A. ARCHITECTURAL SCULPTURE IN
ROMANESQUE PROVENCE.
617(TLS):23FEB73-214
BORGEN, J. THE RED MIST.
617(TLS):7DEC73-1495
BORGEN, J. TRAER ALENE I SKOGER.
C.F. ENGELSTAD, 270:VOL21#2-146
BORGENICHT, M. ROADBLOCK.
N. CALLENDAR, 441:28OCT73-49
BORGER, R. & F. CIOFFI, EDS. EXPLANATION
IN THE BEHAVIOURAL SCIENCES.
Q. GIBSON, 63:MAY72-92
BORGES, J.L. THE ALEPH AND OTHER STOR-
IES.* (N.T. DI GIOVANNI, WITH J.L.
BORGES, EDS & TRANS)
D. LAGMANOVICH, 37:AUG71-41
J.C. MILLER, 573(SSF):SUMMER71-482
639(VQR):SPRING71-LVI
BORGES, J.L. BORGES ON WRITING. (N.T.
DI GIOVANNI, ED)
P. ADAMS, 61:AUG73-103
441:16SEP73-16
BORGES, J.L. DR. BRODIE'S REPORT.*
J.P. DEGNAN, 249(HUDR):SUMMER72-330
BORGES, J.L. OEUVRE POÉTIQUE, MISE EN
VERS FRANÇAIS.
M. BERVEILLER, 549(RLC):JAN-MAR71-133
BORGES, J.L. OTHER INQUISITIONS, 1937-
52. DREAMTIGERS.
A. TERRY, 362:23AUG73-253
BORGES, J.L. SELECTED POEMS, 1923-1967.*
(N.T. DI GIOVANNI, ED)
R. LATTIMORE, 249(HUDR):AUTUMN72-482
E. LUEDERS, 651(WHR):SUMMER72-291
A. TERRY, 362:23AUG73-253
BORGES, J.L. & A. BIOY CASARES. EXTRA-
ORDINARY TALES.
A. TERRY, 362:23AUG73-253
BORGES, J.L. & A. BIOY CASARES. LIBRO
DEL CIELO Y DEL INFIERNO.
H. GARCIA CÍD, 37:SEP71-40
BORING, P.Z. - SEE AYALA, F.
BORINSKI, L. ENGLISCHER HUMANISMUS UND
DEUTSCHE REFORMATION.
A-M. HARMAT, 189(EA):OCT-DEC70-437
BORK, S. MISSBRAUCH DER SPRACHE.
W.J. JONES, 220(GL&L):APR72-290
R.D. KING, 301(JEGP):JUL72-437
E.H. YARRILL, 182:VOL24#7/8-347
BORKOWSKI, L. - SEE ŁUKASIEWICZ, J.
BORLAND, H.H. SWEDISH FOR STUDENTS.*
205(FMLS):JUL71-295

BORLENGHI, A. DANTE E IL TRECENTO NELLA
CRITICA DEL NOVECENTO.
B.L., 275(IQ):SPRING-SUMMER72-113
VON BORMANN, A. NATURA LOQUITUR.*
A. HILLACH, 133:1970/2&3-330
L.R., 191(ELN):SEP71(SUPP)-126
BORMANN, E.G., ED. FORERUNNERS OF BLACK
POWER.
C.F. KARNS, 583:WINTER71-214
BORMANN, K. PARMENIDES.
F.M. CLEVE, 319:JUL73-394
BORN, N. DAS AUGE DES ENTDECKERS.
617(TLS):12JAN73-36
BORNECQUE, J-H. - SEE DAUDET, A.
BORNEMANN, E. SEX IM VOLKSMUND.*
W.B., 681(ZDS):BAND27HEFT3-191
BORNKAMM, G. EARLY CHRISTIAN EXPERIENCE.
W.A.J., 543:JUN71-742
BORNOFF, J., WITH L. SALTER. MUSIC AND
THE 20TH-CENTURY MEDIA.
N. GOODWIN, 415:DEC72-1189
BORNSTEIN, G. YEATS AND SHELLEY.
R.J. FINNERAN, 295:FEB73-129
H. SERGEANT, 175:SPRING71-26
T. WEBB, 541(RES):AUG71-376
639(VQR):WINTER71-XXVII
BOROS, M-D. UN SÉQUESTRÉ.
R. CHAMPIGNY, 400(MLN):MAY71-602
J.K. SIMON, 546(RR):FEB71-77
BOROWSKI, L.E., R.B. JACHMANN & A.C.
WASIANSKI. IMMANUEL KANT.
R. MALTER, 342:BAND61HEFT2-254
BORRAS, F.M. & R.F. CHRISTIAN. RUSSIAN
SYNTAX. (2ND ED)
N.J.C. GOTTERI, 402(MLR):JUL72-716
BORRELLI, L.V. - SEE UNDER VLAD BORRELLI,
L.
BORRELLO, A., ED. A CONCORDANCE OF THE
POETRY IN ENGLISH OF GERARD MANLY HOP-
KINS.
W.R. MUNDT, 598(SOR):AUTUMN73-1029
BORTZ, A. SOCIAL SECURITY SOURCES IN
FEDERAL RECORDS, 1934-1950.
W.W. PFLUG, 14:JAN71-60
BORY, J-F., ED. ONCE AGAIN.
D.H. SULLIVAN, 648:OCT70-69
BOS, G.F. & H. ROOSE - SEE DE GROOT, A.W.
BOSCH, R. & R. CERE. LOS FABULISTAS Y
SU SENTIDO HISTÓRICO.
L. FONTANELLA, 238:DEC71-970
BOSCO, U., ED. REPERTORIO BIBLIOGRAFICO
DELLA LETTERATURA ITALIANA: 1943-1947.
E.B., 228(GSLI):VOL147FASC458/459-477
BOSE, A. URBANIZATION IN INDIA.
H. SPODEK, 293(JAST):MAY71-705
BOSE, N.S. THE INDIAN AWAKENING AND
BENGAL.
D. KOPF, 293(JAST):FEB71-481
BOSI, A. HISTÓRIA CONCISA DA LITERATURA
BRASILEIRA.
G. SOBRAL, 263:OCT-DEC72-424
BOSINSKI, G. DIE MITTELPALÄOLITHISCHEN
FUNDE IM WESTLICHEN MITTELEUROPA.
R. PITTIONI, 182:VOL24#17/18-684
BOSL, K., ED. BOHEMIA: JAHRBUCH DES COL-
LEGIUM CAROLINUM. (VOL 10)
F.L. CARSTEN, 575(SEER):JAN72-128
BOSL, K., ED. BOHEMIA: JAHRBUCH DES COL-
LEGIUM CAROLINUM. (VOL 11)
F.L. CARSTEN, 575(SEER):OCT72-612
BOSL, K., ED. HANDBUCH DER GESCHICHTE
DER BÖHMISCHEN LÄNDER. (VOL 4)
F.L. CARSTEN, 575(SEER):JAN72-124
BOSL, K., ED. VERSAILLES, ST. GERMAIN,
TRIANON.
A. WAHL, 182:VOL24#21/22-814

BOSLOOPER, T. & M. HAYES. THE FEMININITY
GAME.
  P. ADAMS, 61:DEC73-138
BOSO. LIFE OF ALEXANDER III. (G.M.
ELLIS, TRANS)
  617(TLS):21SEP73-1093
BOSQUET, A. 100 NOTES POUR UNE SOLITUDE.
  G. BRÉE, 207(FR):DEC70-404
  R.R. HUBERT, 207(FR):DEC70-412
BOSS, D., ED. THE PRO FOOTBALL EXPERI-
ENCE.
  E. HOAGLAND, 441:2DEC73-3
BOSS, V. NEWTON AND RUSSIA.
  617(TLS):24AUG73-979
BOSSAGLIA, R. I FRATELLI GALLIARI PIT-
TORI.
  A.M. ROMANINI, 54:MAR70-105
BOSSE, M.J. THE INCIDENT AT NAHA.
  617(TLS):2FEB73-129
BOSSIÈRE, J. PERCEPTION CRITIQUE ET SEN-
TIMENT DE VIVRE CHEZ CHARLES DU BOS.
  C.G. HILL, 207(FR):DEC70-446
BOSTON, L.M. MEMORY IN A HOUSE.
  617(TLS):9MAR73-261
BOSTON, R. A THORN FOR THE FLESH.
  M. LEVIN, 441:27MAY73-18
BOSWELL, J. BOSWELL IN EXTREMES 1776-
1778. (C. MC WEISS & F.A. POTTLE, EDS)
  C. TRACY, 529(QQ):SUMMER71-322
  617(TLS):23MAR73-323
  639(VQR):SPRING71-LXV
BOSWELL, J. THE CORRESPONDENCE AND OTHER
PAPERS OF JAMES BOSWELL RELATING TO THE
MAKING OF THE "LIFE OF JOHNSON."* (M.
WAINGROW, ED)
  P.K. ALKON, 173(ECS):FALL71-189
  J.T. BOULTON, 402(MLR):JUL72-621
BOTEY, F. LO GITANO, UNA CULTURA "FOLK"
DESCONOCIDA.
  M. LAFFRANQUE, 549(RLC):JUL-SEP71-404
BOTKINE, V. LETTRES SUR L'ESPAGNE.*
(A. ZVIGUILSKY, ED & TRANS)
  R.W. TRUMAN, 86(BHS):JAN72-85
BOTTASSO, E. LE EDIZIONI POMBA 1792-
1849.
  M.F., 228(GSLI):VOL148FASC461-154
BOTTIGLIA, W.F., ED. VOLTAIRE.
  502(PRS):SPRING70-90
BOTTO, O., ED. CLASSICI DELLE RELIGIONI.
(VOLS 1&2)
  L. STERNBACH, 318(JAOS):OCT-DEC71-544
BOTTO, O., GENERAL ED. STORIA DELLE LET-
TERATURE D'ORIENTE.
  L. STERNBACH, 318(JAOS):OCT-DEC71-542
BOTTRELL, W. TRADITIONS AND HEARTHSIDE
STORIES OF WEST CORNWALL. (2ND ED)
  T. BROWN, 203:SPRING71-84
BOTVINNIK, M. BOTVINNIK'S BEST GAMES,
1947-1970.
  617(TLS):9MAR73-277
BOUCÉ, P-G. LES ROMANS DE SMOLLETT.
  L.M. KNAPP, 189(EA):OCT-DEC71-534
  617(TLS):26JAN73-98
BOUCHER DE BOUCHERVILLE, G. UNE DE PER-
DUE, DEUX DE TROUVÉES.
  A. POKORNY, 296:SUMMER73-117
BOUDAILLE, G. GUSTAVE COURBET.
  S. ROSENTHAL, 58:DEC70/JAN71-10
BOUDON, P. PESSAC DE LE CORBUSIER.
  P. SERENYI, 576:OCT71-255
BOUDON, R. A QUOI SERT DE LA NOTION
"STRUCTURE"?
  P. DUFOUR, 98:AUG/SEP71-805
BOUDOT, P. L'ONTOLOGIE DE NIETZSCHE.
  M. SERVIÈRE, 542:JUL-SEP71-385
BOUDOT, P. NIETZSCHE ET L'AU-DELÀ DE LA
LIBERTÉ.
  E. DIET, 542:JUL-SEP71-386

BOUDREAULT, M. RHYTME ET MÉLODIE DE LA
PHRASE PARLÉE EN FRANCE ET AU QUÉBEC.*
  P. DELATTRE, 545(RPH):AUG71-121
  A. HULL, 207(FR):OCT70-264
  W. ZWANENBURG, 361:VOL26#1-100
BOUEKE, D. MATERIALIEN ZUR NEIDHART-
ÜBERLIEFERUNG.
  H. REINITZER, 680(ZDP):BAND90HEFT1-
  117
BOUILHET, L. & L. COLET. LETTRES DE
LOUIS BOUILHET À LOUISE COLET.* (M-C.
BANCQUART & OTHERS, EDS)
  C. GOTHOT-MERSCH, 535(RHL):JAN-FEB70-
  145
BOUILLARD, H. BLONDEL ET LE CHRISTIAN-
ISME.
  A. FOREST, 542:OCT-DEC71-458
BOULANGER, D. FOUETTE, COCHER! LES DES-
SOUS DU CIEL.
  617(TLS):14DEC73-1529
BOULANGER, D. RETOUCHES.
  T. GREENE, 207(FR):OCT70-169
BOULBY, M. HERMANN HESSE.*
  P. GONTRUM, 400(MLN):APR71-438
BOULDING, K. BEYOND ECONOMICS.
  E.W. HARRIS, 186(ETC.):MAR71-115
BOULEZ, P. BOULEZ ON MUSIC TODAY.*
  639(VQR):AUTUMN71-CLXXXVI
BOULLE, P. EARS OF THE JUNGLE.* (FRENCH
TITLE: LES OREILLES DE JUNGLE.)
  E. WEEKS, 61:FEB73-102
BOULT, A.C. MY OWN TRUMPET.
  H. KELLER, 362:6DEC73-790
  617(TLS):30NOV73-1480
BOULTER, C.G. - SEE "CORPUS VASORUM
ANTIQUORUM"
BOULTON, J.T. - SEE DEFOE, D.
BOULWARE, M.H. THE ORATORY OF NEGRO
LEADERS: 1900-1968.
  C.L. TODD, 583:FALL71-107
BOUMAN, J.C. THE FIGURE-GROUND PHENO-
MENON IN EXPERIMENTAL AND PHENOMENO-
LOGICAL PSYCHOLOGY.
  V.J. MC GILL, 484(PPR):DEC70-301
BOUQUET, A. FÉTICHEURS ET MÉDECINES
TRADITIONNELLES DU CONGO (BRAZZAVILLE).
  J. VANSINA, 69:JAN71-71
BOURASSA, F. QUESTIONS DE THÉOLOGIE
TRINITAIRE.
  H. MUSURILLO, 613:WINTER71-619
BOURDEAUX, M. FAITH ON TRIAL IN RUSSIA.
  J.P. SCANLAN, 32:JUN72-442
BOURDEAUX, M. PATRIARCH AND PROPHETS.*
  H.A. STAMMLER, 550(RUSR):JUL71-301
BOURDIEU, P. ESQUISSE D'UNE THÉORIE DE
LA PRATIQUE PRÉCÉDÉ DE TROIS ÉTUDES
D'ETHNOLOGIE KABYLE.
  617(TLS):6JUL73-787
BOURDIEU, P. & A. DARBEL. L'AMOUR DE
L'ART.
  J-C. LEBENSZTEJN, 98:APR70-321
BOURDIN, J., ED. LE GOUVERNEMENT DE
VICHY, 1940-1942.
  617(TLS):21DEC73-1560
BOURDON, D. CHRISTO.*
  R. LEBOWITZ, 58:MAY72-30
BOURET, J. THE BARBIZON SCHOOL.
  J.R. MELLOW, 441:2DEC73-7
BOURGEOIS, B. L'IDÉALISME DE FICHTE.*
  J.D.C., 543:JUN71-743
BOURGY, V. LE BOUFFON SUR LA SCÈNE AN-
GLAISE AU XVIE SIÈCLE (C. 1495-1594).*
  E. WELSFORD, 551(RENQ):SPRING71-92
BOURIN, A. & J. ROUSSELOT. DICTIONNAIRE
DE LA LITTÉRATURE FRANÇAISE CONTEMPO-
RAINE.
  D.R. BRODIN, 207(FR):OCT70-163

BOURJAILY, V. BRILL AMONG THE RUINS.
P. WOLFE, 502(PRS):SUMMER71-174
BOURKE, V.J. HISTOIRE DE LA MORALE.
Y. MONGEAU, 154:DEC71-873
BOURKE-WHITE, M. THE PHOTOGRAPHS OF
MARGARET BOURKE-WHITE. (S. CALLAHAN,
ED)
617(TLS):11MAY73-530
BOURNE, M.A., J.B. SILMAN & J. SOBRINO.
EL ESPAÑOL.
J.W. ZDENEK, 238:DEC71-985
BOURNE, U. PORTUGUESE COOKERY.
617(TLS):1JUN73-625
BOURNEUF, R. SAINT-DENYS GARNEAU ET SES
LECTURES EUROPÉENNES.
P.M. GATHERCOLE, 207(FR):DEC70-475
D.M. HAYNE, 208(FS):JAN72-108
R. MERCIER, 557(RSH):OCT-DEC70-663
J.F.A. RICCI, 549(RLC):JAN-MAR71-127
A. VIATTE, 549(RLC):JUL-SEP70-427
BOURNIQUEL, C. & OTHERS. VAN GOGH.
R. LAPORTE, 98:FEB70-124
BOURSIN, J-L. & P. CAUSSAT. AUTOPSIE DU
HASARD.
R. BLANCHÉ, 542:OCT-DEC70-485
BOUSQUET, R. THE ORDEAL OF STANLEY STAN-
HOPE.
P.M. SPACKS, 249(HUDR):AUTUMN72-505
BOUTIÈRE, J. - SEE MISTRAL, F.
BOUTON, C.P. LES MÉCANISMES D'ACQUISI-
TION DU FRANÇAIS, LANGUE ÉTRANGÈRE CHEZ
L'ADULTE.
W.A. HENNING, 207(FR):MAR71-785
BOUTRUCHE, R. SEIGNEURIE ET FÉODALITÉ.
(VOL 2)
C.T. WOOD, 589:OCT72-747
BOUVIER, J. NAISSANCE D'UNE BANQUE: LE
CRÉDIT LYONNAIS.
J.M. LAUX, 207(FR):APR71-942
BOUYER, C. ODÉON EST OUVERT.
P. AUBERY, 207(FR):MAR71-774
BOVA, B., ED. HALL OF FAME. (VOL 2)
T. STURGEON, 441:22APR73-14
BOVENTER, H. RILKES ZYKLUS "AUS DEM
NACHLASS DES GRAFEN C.W."
B.L. BRADLEY, 400(MLN):OCT71-740
H.W. PANTHEL, 564:MAR71-77
BOVINI, G. RAVENNA.
J. CANADAY, 441:24APR73-35
BOWEN, B.C. THE AGE OF BLUFF.
D. DILLON, 584(SWR):SPRING72-158
BOWEN, E. EVA TROUT.
J.C. FIELD, 556(RLV):1971/6-766
BOWEN, I. ACCEPTABLE INEQUALITIES.
J.L. MC DOUGALL, 529(QQ):AUTUMN71-468
BOWEN, J.K. & R. VAN DER BEETS, EDS.
AMERICAN SHORT FICTION.
J.W. STEVENSON, 573(SSF):SUMMER71-475
BOWERING, G. AL PURDY.*
W.H. NEW, 102(CANL):AUTUMN72-90
BOWERING, G. TOUCH.*
A. PURDY, 102(CANL):AUTUMN72-86
BOWERING, P. ALDOUS HUXLEY.*
H.C. BOWERSOX, 405(MP):AUG70-122
BOWERMAN, M. EARLY SYNTACTIC DEVELOP-
MENT.
617(TLS):12OCT73-1220
BOWERS, F. SCRIABIN.*
R. HENDERSON, 415:JAN72-44
BOWERS, F., ED. STUDIES IN BIBLIOGRAPHY.
(VOL 20)
G.A. SMITH, 570(SQ):WINTER70-89
BOWERS, F., ED. STUDIES IN BIBLIOGRAPHY.
(VOL 22)
R. DONALDSON, 354:JUN70-158
BOWERS, F., ED. STUDIES IN BIBLIOGRAPHY.
(VOL 23)
R. DONALDSON, 354:SEP71-265

BOWERS, F., ED. STUDIES IN BIBLIOGRAPHY.
(VOL 26)
617(TLS):3AUG73-912
BOWERS, F. - SEE BEAUMONT, F. & J. FLET-
CHER
BOWERS, F. - SEE CRANE, S.
BOWERS, J. NO MORE REUNIONS.
M. LEVIN, 441:1APR73-33
442(NY):7APR73-150
BOWERS, J.Z. WESTERN MEDICAL PIONEERS IN
FEUDAL JAPAN.
K.H. HOWES, 293(JAST):FEB71-461
BOWERSOCK, G.W. GREEK SOPHISTS IN THE
ROMAN EMPIRE.*
J-P. CALLU, 555:VOL45FASC1-161
J.W. EADIE, 121(CJ):APR-MAY72-371
M. GRIFFIN, 313:VOL61-278
BOWERSOCK, G.W. - SEE PHILOSTRATUS
BOWIE, T., WITH OTHERS. EAST-WEST IN ART.
D.E. MUNGELLO, 485(PE&W):JUL70-325
BOWKER, J. JESUS AND THE PHARISEES.
617(TLS):7SEP73-1034
BOWKER, J. PROBLEMS OF SUFFERING IN
RELIGIONS OF THE WORLD.
J. NEUSNER, 318(JAOS):OCT-DEC71-531
BOWKER, J. THE SENSE OF GOD.
617(TLS):7DEC73-1516
BOWKER, J. THE TARGUMS AND RABBINIC LIT-
ERATURE.
F.F. BRUCE, 182:VOL24#3-83
BOWLBY, J. ATTACHMENT AND LOSS. (VOL 2)
E. FIRST, 441:25NOV73-31
D.W. HARDING, 362:19JUL73-90
617(TLS):23NOV73-1447
BOWLER, C., L. ANDREWS & F.W. WILLETTS.
NEW WRITERS 8.
J. SANKEY, 619(TC):VOL178#1045-58
BOWLES, C. PROMISES TO KEEP.
J.M. BURNS, 639(VQR):AUTUMN71-629
BOWLES, E.A., ED. COMPUTERS IN HUMANIS-
TIC RESEARCH.
G.J. BRAULT, 207(FR):FEB71-632
BOWLEY, M. STUDIES IN THE HISTORY OF
ECONOMIC THEORY BEFORE 1870.
617(TLS):7DEC73-1521
BOWMAN, F.P. - SEE CONSTANT, A.L.
BOWMAN, F.P. - SEE LÉVI, E.
BOWNESS, A., ED. THE COMPLETE SCULPTURE
OF BARBARA HEPWORTH 1960-69.
592:JUL/AUG71-51
BOWNESS, A., ED. IVON HITCHENS.
617(TLS):7DEC73-1502
BOWRA, C.M. ON GREEK MARGINS.
F.M. COMBELLACK, 122:APR72-147
BOWRA, C.M. PERICLEAN ATHENS.
C.W. FORNARA, 124:OCT71-66
617(TLS):23FEB73-209
BOWRA, C.M. POESIE DER FRÜHZEIT.
H. TRÜMPY, 657(WW):JUL/AUG70-277
BOWRING, J. THE KINGDOM AND PEOPLE OF
SIAM.
D.H. SAR DESAI, 318(JAOS):OCT-DEC71-
527
BOWSER, E., ED. FILM NOTES.
200:OCT70-500
BOXER, C.R. FIDALGOS IN THE FAR EAST
1550-1770. JAN COMPAGNIE IN JAPAN
1600-1817.
M.V. LAMBERTI, 318(JAOS):APR-JUN71-357
BOXER, C.R. FOUR CENTURIES OF PORTUGUESE
EXPANSION.
639(VQR):WINTER71-XXXIX
BOXER, C.R. THE PORTUGUESE SEABORNE
EMPIRE: 1415-1825.*
R. GRAHAM, 656(WMQ):APR71-329
BOXILL, R. SHAW AND THE DOCTORS.*
J.M. WARE, 177(ELT):VOL13#3-248

BOYANCÉ, P. ÉTUDES SUR L'HUMANISME
CICÉRONIEN.
A. ERNOUT, 555:VOL45FASC2-361
BOYD, A. & P. PORTER. JONAH.
617(TLS):2NOV73-1348
BOYD, B.C. & F.C. HARRIS. THE GREAT
AMERICAN BASEBALL CARD FLIPPING, TRAD-
ING AND BUBBLE GUM BOOK.
L. EISENBERG, 441:21OCT73-45
BOYD, E. & R. PARKES. THE DARK NUMBER.
617(TLS):26OCT73-1324
BOYD, M. THE LOVER.
P. MOORE, JR., 441:4MAR73-37
BOYD, M. THE TEA-TIME OF LOVE.
L. CANTRELL, 381:MAR71-125
BOYD, R. NEW DIRECTIONS IN JAPANESE
ARCHITECTURE.
R. BANHAM, 54:SEP70-344
BOYDEN, D.D. AN INTRODUCTION TO MUSIC.
412:MAY72-147
BOYDSTON, J.A., ED. GUIDE TO THE WORKS
OF JOHN DEWEY.
A. BERLEANT, 484(PPR):DEC71-285
W. MAYS, 518:OCT72-10
BOYER, F. LE MONDE DES ARTS EN ITALIE
ET LA FRANCE DE LA RÉVOLUTION ET DE
L'EMPIRE.
D. ADAMSON, 402(MLR):APR72-421
E. CHEVALLIER, 549(RLC):APR-JUN71-275
BOYER, P. MOTS D'ORDRE.
H. MICHOT-DIETRICH, 207(FR):APR71-969
BOYER, P. & N. SPERANSKI. MANUEL POUR
L'ETUDE DE LA LANGUE RUSSE. (NEW ED
REV BY W. WEISBEIN & A. VERBA)
R. BARTHELEMY-VOGELS, 556(RLV):1971/6-
787
BOYER, R.O. THE LEGEND OF JOHN BROWN.
G. HODGSON, 441:21JAN73-21
442(NY):10FEB73-115
BOYER, W. EDUCATION FOR ANNIHILATION.
L. MARSH, 99:SEP73-38
BOYLAN, B.R. BENEDICT ARNOLD.
G.F. SCHEER, 441:25NOV73-22
442(NY):30JUL73-71
BOYLAN, J., ED. THE WORLD AND THE 20'S.
A. WHITMAN, 441:8DEC73-39
BOYLE, H.J. THE GREAT CANADIAN NOVEL.*
B. SPROXTON, 296:FALL73-87
BOYLE, H.J. MEMORIES OF A CATHOLIC BOY-
HOOD.
G. BURNSIDE, 441:18NOV73-46
BOYLE, J.A. GRAMMAR OF MODERN PERSIAN.
Q.S.K. HUSAINI, 273(IC):OCT70-253
BOYLE, J.H. CHINA AND JAPAN AT WAR,
1937-1945.
G. BARRACLOUGH, 453:31MAY73-9
BOYLE, K. & J. VAN GUNDY, EDS. ENOUGH OF
DYING.
W. DICKEY, 249(HUDR):SUMMER72-296
BOYLE, R.H., J. GRAVES & T.H. WATKINS.
THE WATER HUSTLERS.
W. GARD, 584(SWR):SPRING72-V
42(AR):WINTER71/72-597
BOYLE, T.E. BRENDAN BEHAN.
G.E. WELLWARTH, 397(MD):SEP71-252
BOYLESVE, R. LES BONNETS DE DENTELLE.
P. MOREAU, 535(RHL):JAN-FEB70-156
BOYNTON, P. STONE ISLAND.
P. WOLFE, 441:19AUG73-20
BOZONIS, G.A. DOMĒ KAI MORPHĒ TOY PLATŌN-
IKOY DIALOGOY.
P-M. HUBY, 123:DEC72-408
BOŻYK, P., ED. INTEGRACJA EKONOMICZNA
KRAJÓW SOCJALISTYCZNYCH: PRACA ZBIOR-
OWA.
M. GAMARNIKOW, 32:MAR72-215
BOZZO, C.D. - SEE UNDER DUFOUR BOZZO, C.
BOZZOLI, A. - SEE CANTÙ, C.

BRAATEN, C. THE FUTURE OF GOD.
W.A.J., 543:JUN71-742
BRACE, G.W. THE STUFF OF FICTION.
J.P. LOVERING, 613:SUMMER70-303
BRACEGIRDLE, B., ED. THE ARCHAEOLOGY OF
THE INDUSTRIAL REVOLUTION.
617(TLS):31AUG73-999
BRACEGIRDLE, B. & P.H. MILES. THOMAS
TELFORD.
617(TLS):17AUG73-961
DE BRACH, P. LES AMOURS D'AYMÉE. (J.
DAWKINS, ED)
K. HÖLZ, 72:BAND209HEFT4/6-457
BRACHER, K.D. THE GERMAN DICTATORSHIP.*
639(VQR):AUTUMN71-CLXXX
BRACHIN, P., ED. ANTHOLOGIE DE LA PROSE
NÉERLANDAISE. (BELGIQUE II, 1940-1968)
A. WILLOT, 556(RLV):1970/1-110
BRACK, O.M., JR. & W. BARNES, EDS. BIB-
LIOGRAPHY AND TEXTUAL CRITICISM.
D.F. FOXON, 354:SEP70-266
BRACKENBURY, R. INTO EGYPT.
V. CUNNINGHAM, 362:26JUL73-125
617(TLS):13JUL73-797
BRACKERT, H. RUDOLF VON EMS.
H. RICHTER, 564:JUN71-157
BRACQUE, J. A MAN OF TALENT.
K. THOMPSON, 198:SPRING73-112
BRADBROOK, M.C. LITERATURE IN ACTION.*
K.L. GOODWIN, 71(ALS):OCT73-218
BRADBROOK, M.C. SHAKESPEARE THE CRAFTS-
MAN.
A. LANCASHIRE, 570(SQ):SPRING71-172
D. MEHL, 541(RES):FEB71-72
S-G. PUTT, 175:SUMMER70-64
BRADBURY, M. POSSIBILITIES.
F. KERMODE, 362:20SEP73-382
617(TLS):10AUG73-925
BRADBURY, M. & D. PALMER, EDS. METAPHYSI-
CAL POETRY.*
R.A. FOAKES, 175:SPRING71-23
G. WALTON, 541(RES):AUG71-344
639(VQR):SPRING71-LXV
BRADBURY, M. & D. PALMER, EDS. VICTOR-
IAN POETRY.
617(TLS):1JUN73-620
BRADBURY, R. DANDELION WINE.
T. BRADFORD, 114(CHIR):JAN-FEB71-160
BRADDOCK, J. SAPPHO'S ISLAND.
R. LAWRENCE, 175:SPRING71-28
BRADDON, R. SUEZ.
617(TLS):3AUG73-897
BRADDON, R. THE THIRTEENTH TRICK.
N. CALLENDAR, 441:30SEP73-18
BRADEN, S. THE MEMOIRS OF SPRUILLE
BRADEN.
P.C. DANIELS, 396(MODA):SPRING72-206
BRADEN, W.W., ED. ORATORY IN THE OLD
SOUTH, 1828-1860.
A. HILLBRUNER, 583:FALL70-89
G.F. SPARKS, 50(ARQ):SUMMER71-180
BRADFIELD, N. HISTORICAL COSTUMES OF
ENGLAND 1066-1968.
G. SQUIRE, 157:SPRING71-76
BRADFIELD, R.M. A NATURAL HISTORY OF
ASSOCIATIONS.
617(TLS):19OCT73-1274
BRADFORD, E. CHRISTOPHER COLUMBUS.
W. BEAUCHAMP, 441:23DEC73-10
BRADFORD, E. THE SHIELD AND THE SWORD.
442(NY):16JUL73-79
BRADFORD, R. SO FAR FROM HEAVEN.
E. ABBEY, 441:14OCT73-10
BRADFORD, S. PORTUGAL.
617(TLS):27JUL73-867

BRADLEY, F.H. THE PRESUPPOSITIONS OF
CRITICAL HISTORY. (L. RUBINOFF, ED)
H.B., 543:DEC70-336
R.E. ROBLIN, 484(PPR):SEP70-143
BRADLEY, M.Z. DARKOVER LANDFALL.
T. STURGEON, 441:22APR73-16
BRADSHAW, H. HENRY BRADSHAW'S CORRES-
PONDENCE ON INCUNABULA WITH J.W. HOL-
TROP AND M.F.A.G. CAMPBELL. (VOL 1)
(W. & L. HELLINGA, EDS)
C.F. BÜHLER, 354:SEP70-254
R. STOKES, 503:SUMMER71-96
BRADY, P. "L'OEUVRE" DE ÉMILE ZOLA.*
M. KANES, 405(MP):NOV70-209
BRADY, T. REHEARSAL.
S. HILL, 362:25JAN73-124
617(TLS):9FEB73-140
BRADY, V.P. LOVE IN THE THEATRE OF MARI-
VAUX.
H.T. MASON, 208(FS):JUL72-334
R. MERCIER, 557(RSH):JAN-MAR71-135
BRAET, H. L'ACCUEIL FAIT AU SYMBOLISME
EN BELGIQUE, 1885-1900.*
P. FORTASSIER, 557(RSH):APR-JUN71-330
BRAET, H. LE SECOND RÊVE DE CHARLEMAGNE
DANS "LA CHANSON DE ROLAND."
F. WHITEHEAD, 208(FS):APR72-181
BRAGG, M. THE HIRED MAN. WITHOUT A CITY
WALL.* THE SECOND INHERITANCE. FOR
WANT OF A NAIL.
R. PYBUS, 565:VOL11#3-68
BRAGG, M. A PLACE IN ENGLAND.*
D. BOLLING, 529(QQ):WINTER71-619
E. GLOVER, 565:VOL12#3-58
BRAHAM, A. VELÁZQUEZ.
617(TLS):1JUN73-625
BRAIBANTI, R., ED. POLITICAL AND ADMIN-
ISTRATIVE DEVELOPMENT.
J. RÖPKE, 182:VOL24#19/20-720
BRAINE, J. THE QUEEN OF A DISTANT COUN-
TRY.
A. BROYARD, 441:23MAY73-39
P. THEROUX, 441:27MAY73-16
442(NY):5MAY73-149
BRAMBLE, F. STONE.
D. MAHON, 362:24MAY73-696
617(TLS):8JUN73-634
BRANCA, V. BOCCACCIO MEDIEVALE. (3RD
ED)
G. TOURNOY, 568(SCN):SUMMER72-54
BRANCA, V. - SEE BARBARO, E.
BRANCA, V. - SEE BOCCACCIO, G.
BRANCA, V. & M.P. STOCCHI - SEE POLIZI-
ANO, A.
BRANCH, E.M. JAMES T. FARRELL.
C.C. WALCUTT, 27(AL):MAR72-166
BRANCH, E.M. - SEE TWAIN, M.
BRAND, G. DIE LEBENSWELT.
S.L. HART, 484(PPR):JUN72-589
G. NICHOLSON, 154:DEC71-850
BRANDABUR, E. A SCRUPULOUS MEANNESS.*
M.A. KLUG, 150(DR):WINTER71/72-592
D. O'BRIEN, 301(JEGP):APR72-282
R.S. RYF, 401(MLQ):MAR72-86
BRANDEL, M. THE MAN WHO LIKED WOMEN.*
S. HILL, 362:19APR73-520
617(TLS):27APR73-461
BRANDENBURG, H. STUDIEN ZUR MITRA.
S. BENTON, 303:VOL91-212
BRANDIS, T. MITTELHOCHDEUTSCHE, MITTEL-
NIEDERDEUTSCHE UND MITTELNIEDERLÄND-
ISCHE MINNEREDEN.*
D.R. MC LINTOCK, 220(GL&L):APR72-317
L. OKKEN, 433:OCT71-456
E. SCHMIDBERGER, 190:BAND65HEFT3-334
BRANDMÜLLER, W. DAS KONZIL VON PAVIA-
SIENA, 1423-1424. (VOL 1)
D.J. WILCOX, 589:APR72-291

BRANDNER, U. DREI UHR ANGST.
G. FISCHER, 270:VOL21#3-170
BRANDON, H. THE RETREAT OF AMERICAN
POWER.
G. SMITH, 441:3JUN73-3
617(TLS):19OCT73-1267
BRANDON, J.R., ED. ON THRONES OF GOLD.*
F. HALL, 89(BJA):WINTER72-99
A.C. SCOTT, 397(MD):MAY71-121
BRANDON, R. & C. DAVIES. WRONGFUL IMPRIS-
ONMENT.
617(TLS):20JUL73-837
BRANDON, W. THE MAGIC WORLD.
P. PAVICH, 649(WAL):SPRING71-72
BRANDSTETTER, A. - SEE "TRISTRANT UND
ISALDE"
BRANDT, T.O. DIE VIELDEUTIGKEIT BERTOLT
BRECHTS.*
K. DICKSON, 220(GL&L):OCT71-71
S. HOEFERT, 564:JUN70-183
J.W. ONDERDELINDEN, 433:JUL70-317
BRANDT, W.J. THE RHETORIC OF ARGUMEN-
TATION.
W.R. FISHER, 480(P&R):SPRING71-136
BRANDT-PEDERSEN, F. ANVENDT METRIK.
A.H. LERVIK, 172(EDDA):1970/5-313
BRANFMAN, F., COMP. VOICES FROM THE
PLAIN OF JARS.*
J. MIRSKY, 441:20MAY73-44
BRANIGAN, K. THE TOMBS OF MESARA.
J. BOARDMAN, 123:JUN72-255
BRANIGAN, K. TOWN AND COUNTRY.
617(TLS):12OCT73-1259
BRANKAČK, A. & OTHERS. SERBSKI BIOGRAF-
ISKI SŁOWNIK.
G. STONE, 575(SEER):OCT72-605
BRANNEN, N. & W. ELLIOTT - SEE "FESTIVE
WINE"
BRANNER, R., ED. CHARTRES CATHEDRAL.*
P. KIDSON, 46:NOV70-330
BRANSON, D. JOHN FIELD AND CHOPIN.*
H.F., 410(M&L):JUL72-326
N. TEMPERLEY, 415:JUL72-670
BRANT, I. THE FOURTH PRESIDENT.
M. BORDEN, 656(WMQ):JUL71-491
BRANT, I. IMPEACHMENT.*
I. DILLIARD, 31(ASCH):SPRING73-347
BRASHEAR, W.R. THE LIVING WILL.
E.E. SMITH, 636(VP):SPRING70-65
BRASHER, T.L. WHITMAN AS EDITOR OF THE
BROOKLYN "DAILY EAGLE."*
J.J. RUBIN, 646(WWR):MAR71-27
W. WHITE, 405(MP):MAY72-365
BRASHLER, W. THE BINGO LONG TRAVELING
ALL STARS AND MOTOR KINGS.
M. LEVIN, 441:12AUG73-20
M. WATKINS, 441:28AUG73-39
BRATHWAITE, E. THE COMPANION GUIDE TO
THE SOUTH ISLAND OF NEW ZEALAND.
617(TLS):20APR73-454
BRATHWAITE, E. ISLANDS.*
C. PEEK, 502(PRS):SPRING71-84
BRAUDEL, F. CAPITALISM AND MATERIAL LIFE
1400-1800.* (FRENCH TITLE: CIVILISATION
MATÉRIELLE ET CAPITALISME. [VOL 1])
K. THOMAS, 453:13DEC73-3
BRAUDEL, F. THE MEDITERRANEAN AND THE
MEDITERRANEAN WORLD IN THE AGE OF PHILIP
II.* (VOL 1)
J.H. ELLIOTT, 453:3MAY73-25
BRAUDY, L. NARRATIVE FORM IN HISTORY AND
FICTION.*
F.D. MC CONNELL, 481(PQ):JUL71-376
G.L. VOTH, 173(ECS):FALL71-172
BRAUKÄMPER, U. DER EINFLUSS DES ISLAM
AUF DIE GESCHICHTE UND KULTURENTWICK-
LUNG ADAMAUAS.*
A.H.M. KIRK-GREENE, 69:OCT71-343

BRAUN, A. CONRAD - DOTKNIECIE WSCHODU.
J.K. BOSWELL, 136:VOL3#1-110
BRAUN, E. & D. CAVAGNARO. LIVING WATER.
J. BONI, 649(WAL):SPRING71-74
BRAUN, H. CATHEDRAL ARCHITECTURE.
617(TLS):5JAN73-21
BRAUN, H. THE VERGIL WOODS.
J.L. WYANT, 502(PRS):SPRING71-80
BRAUN, K. & K. VÖLKER, EDS. SPIELPLATZ I.
617(TLS):11MAY73-521
BRAUND, H. DISTINCTLY I REMEMBER.
617(TLS):27APR73-481
BRAUNERT, H. UTOPIA.
H.C. BALDRY, 123:MAR72-121
BRAUNSWEG, J., WITH J. KELSEY. BRAUNS-
WEG'S BALLET SCANDALS.
617(TLS):28SEP73-1139
BRAUQUIER, L. FEUX D'ÉPAVES.
C. FRANÇOIS, 207(FR):DEC70-413
BRAUTIGAN, R. THE ABORTION.*
S. HILL, 362:25JAN73-124
617(TLS):2FEB73-113
BRAVO-VILLASANTE, C. GALDÓS VISTO POR
SÍ MISMO.
R.M. FEDORCHEK, 399(MLJ):DEC71-541
BRAY, J.J. POEMS 1961-1971.
S.E. LEE, 581:DEC72-302
BRAY, M. GUIDE TO THE FORD FILM COLLEC-
TION IN THE NATIONAL ARCHIVES.
A.F. MC CLURE, 14:JAN71-61
BRAY, W. & D. TRUMP, EDS. THE AMERICAN
HERITAGE GUIDE TO ARCHAEOLOGY.
R.S. STROUD, 124:NOV71-100
BRAZILL, W.J. THE YOUNG HEGELIANS.
L.D. EASTON, 484(PPR):DEC71-288
BREARLEY, K.T. & R-B. MC BRIDE. NOUVELLES
DU QUEBEC.
M. CAGNON, 399(MLJ):APR71-260
BREATHNACH, B. FOLKMUSIC AND DANCES OF
IRELAND.*
A. BRUFORD, 595(SCS):VOL16PT2-185
F. HOWES, 415:APR72-368
BRECH, U. - SEE KOBS, J.
BRECHER, E.M. & OTHERS. LICIT AND ILLICIT
DRUGS.*
P. STEINFELS & R.M. VEATCH, 441:
4FEB73-6
BRECHER, M. POLITICAL LEADERSHIP IN
INDIA.
W.H. MORRIS-JONES, 293(JAST):NOV70-203
BRECHT, A. THE POLITICAL EDUCATION OF
ARNOLD BRECHT.
639(VQR):SPRING71-LXX
BRECHT, B. ARBEITSJOURNAL. (W. HECHT,
ED)
617(TLS):23NOV73-1413
BRECHT, B. BERTOLT BRECHT COLLECTED
PLAYS. (VOL 1) (J. WILLETT & R. MAN-
HEIM, EDS)
A. RENDLE, 157:SUMMER70-75
BRECHT, B. DIE HEILIGE JOHANNA DER
SCHLACHTHÖFE. (G.E. BAHR, ED) DIE
MASSNAHME. (R. STEINWEG, ED)
617(TLS):28DEC73-1591
BRECHT, B. TALES FROM THE CALENDAR.
D.S. LOW, 220(GL&L):OCT71-55
BREDNICH, R.W., ED. JAHRBUCH FÜR VOLKS-
LIED-FORSCHUNG. (VOL 15)
E. ETTLINGER, 203:SPRING71-83
BREDNICH, R.W. & W. SUPPAN, EDS. GOTT-
SCHEER VOLKSLIEDER. (VOL 1)
B. NETTL, 187:SEP73-544
BRÉE, G. WOMEN WRITERS IN FRANCE.
A. BROYARD, 441:19DEC73-47
BRÉE, G. & P. SOLOMON. CHOIX D'ESSAIS
DU VINGTIÈME SIÈCLE.*
E.S. BROOK, 207(FR):OCT70-160
R. MERKER, 399(MLJ):APR71-261

BREEN, T.H. THE CHARACTER OF THE GOOD
RULER.
B.R. BURG, 432(NEQ):JUN71-339
R.L. BUSHMAN, 656(WMQ):OCT71-668
639(VQR):AUTUMN71-CLXXVII
BREGGIN, P. AFTER THE GOOD WAR.
M. LEVIN, 441:18FEB73-31
BREIN, F. DER HIRSCH IN DER GRIECHISCHEN
FRÜHZEIT.
J.M. COOK, 123:MAR72-119
BREKLE, H.E. & L. LIPKA, EDS. WORTBIL-
DUNG, SYNTAX UND MORPHOLOGIE.*
P. SALMON, 38:BAND89HEFT2-244
BRELICH, A. PAIDES E PARTHENOI.* (VOL 1)
M.J. COSTELLOE, 121(CJ):APR-MAY72-378
C. ROEBUCK, 24:APR72-358
C. SOURVINOU, 303:VOL91-172
BREMAN, P. & D. ADDIS. GUIDE TO VITRU-
VIUS BRITANNICUS.
617(TLS):23FEB73-216
BREMER, A.H. AN ASSASSIN'S DIARY.
A. BROYARD, 441:13APR73-43
G. VIDAL, 453:13DEC73-6
G. WILLS, 441:8APR73-4
BREMOND, C. LOGIQUE DU RÉCIT.
617(TLS):12OCT73-1236
BREMOND, H. & M. BLONDEL. CORRESPONDANCE.
(A. BLANCHET, ED)
P. MOREAU, 535(RHL):MAY-JUN71-463
DE BRÉMOND D'ARS, E. OEUVRE POÉTIQUE
1888-1958. (L.A. MAUGENDRE, ED)
J. ONIMUS, 535(RHL):MAR-APR70-345
BRENAN, G. ST. JOHN OF THE CROSS.
W.H. AUDEN, 453:1NOV73-8
617(TLS):24AUG73-977
BRENGELMAN, F. THE ENGLISH LANGUAGE.
K. SØRENSEN, 179(ES):OCT71-483
BRENGUES, J. - SEE DUCLOS, C.
BRENK, B. DIE ROMANISCHE WANDMALEREI IN
DER SCHWEIZ.
F. BUCHER, 54:DEC70-431
BRENNAN, M. IN AND OUT OF NEVER-NEVER
LAND.
E.N. HARBERT, 573(SSF):SPRING71-350
BRENNAN, M.M., ED & TRANS. BABIO, A
TWELFTH CENTURY PROFANE COMEDY.*
A.B. SCOTT, 447(N&Q):AUG71-311
BRENNER, A. THE WIND THAT SWEPT MEXICO.*
K.J. GRIEB, 263:JUL-SEP72-282
BRENNER, H., ED. ENDE EINER BÜRGERLICHEN
KUNST-INSTITUTION.
617(TLS):22JUN73-705
BRENT, M. MOONRAKER'S BRIDE.
M. LEVIN, 441:23DEC73-16
BRENT, P. THE EDWARDIANS.
617(TLS):23MAR73-333
BRENT, P. GODMEN OF INDIA.
617(TLS):2FEB73-127
BRENTANO, C. CLEMENS BRENTANO'S "PONCE
DE LEON." (S. SUDHOF, ED)
D.L., 191(ELN):SEP71(SUPP)-125
"CLEMENS BRENTANO." (W. VORDTRIEDE, WITH
G. BARTENSCHLAGER, EDS)
G.D. GREENWAY, 406:SPRING72-74
F. STOCK, 52:BAND6HEFT1-106
BRENTJES, B., B. THALER & U. BEWERSDORFF
- SEE AMO AFER, A.G.
BRENTON, H. REVENGE.
A. RENDLE, 157:SPRING71-77
BRERETON, G. FRENCH TRAGIC DRAMA IN THE
SIXTEENTH AND SEVENTEENTH CENTURIES.
617(TLS):7DEC73-1504
BRÈS, Y. LA PSYCHOLOGIE DE PLATON.
Y. LAFRANCE, 154:MAR71-134
BRESKY, D. THE ART OF ANATOLE FRANCE.*
M. SACHS, 207(FR):DEC70-447
BRESLER, F. SCALES OF JUSTICE.
617(TLS):20JUL73-837

BRESLIN, J. WORLD WITHOUT END, AMEN.
  H. GARDNER, 441:26AUG73-6
  H.E. SALISBURY, 441:24AUG73-37
  L.E. SISSMAN, 442(NY):8OCT73-168
BRESLIN, J.E. WILLIAM CARLOS WILLIAMS.*
  L. CASPER, 613:AUTUMN71-468
  B. DUFFEY, 659:SUMMER73-406
  P. MARIANI, 418(MR):AUTUMN72-669
  A.K. WEATHERHEAD, 401(MLQ):JUN72-172
  639(VQR):SPRING71-LXII
BRETNOR, R., ED. SCIENCE FICTION, TODAY
  AND TOMORROW.
  T. STURGEON, 441:4NOV73-76
BRETON, A. SURREALISM AND PAINTING.
  617(TLS):9FEB73-149
BRETON, S. PHILOSOPHIE ET MATHÉMATIQUE
  CHEZ PROCLUS.
  J. TROUILLARD, 542:APR-JUN70-229
BRETT, C.E.B. COURT HOUSES AND MARKET
  HOUSES OF THE PROVINCE OF ULSTER.
  617(TLS):7DEC73-1502
BRETT, R.L., ED. S.T. COLERIDGE.
  C. WALLACE-CRABBE, 67:NOV72-228
BRETT, R.L. FANCY AND IMAGINATION.
  205(FMLS):OCT70-420
BRETT-EVANS, D. - SEE STORM, T.
BRETT-JAMES, A. LIFE IN WELLINGTON'S
  ARMY.
  617(TLS):19JAN73-71
BREUER, D. DER "PHILOTHEUS" DES LAUREN-
  TIUS VON SCHNÜFFIS.
  A. MENHENNET, 220(GL&L):APR72-278
BREUER, H. - SEE FOERSTER, W.
BREUNIG, L.C. GUILLAUME APOLLINAIRE.*
  M. DAVIES, 208(FS):APR72-219
BREW, K. THE SHADOWS OF LAUGHTER.
  H. MAES-JELINEK, 556(RLV):1971/4-491
BREWER, D.S., ED. CHAUCER AND CHAUCER-
  IANS.
  P.M. VERMEER, 179(ES):FEB71-61
BREWER, J.H. THE CONFEDERATE NEGRO, VIR-
  GINIA'S CRAFTSMEN AND MILITARY LABOR-
  ERS, 1816-1865.
  S.D. JACKSON, 14:JAN70-83
BREWSTER, E. PASSAGE OF SUMMER.*
  R. COCKBURN, 255(HAB):FALL69-82
BREY MARIÑO, M., ED. ALFONSO X, REY DE
  CASTILLA.
  J.E. KELLER, 240(HR):JAN71-89
BREYER, S. BATTLESHIPS AND BATTLE-
  CRUISERS, 1905-1970.
  617(TLS):28DEC73-1595
BRIAND, J. LA BATAILLE DE LA SAMBRE.
  S. MAX, 207(FR):OCT70-170
BRICHFORD, M.J. SCIENTIFIC AND TECHNOLO-
  GICAL DOCUMENTATION.
  J. PINGREE, 325:APR71-252
BRIDGE, A. JULIA IN IRELAND.
  442(NY):10SEP73-133
BRIDGE, F.R. FROM SADOWA TO SARAJEVO.
  617(TLS):12JAN73-30
BRIDGES, H. AMERICAN MYSTICISM.
  R. BURR, 485(PE&W):JUL71-337
BRIDGES, R., ED. THE SPIRIT OF MAN.
  617(TLS):23FEB73-210
BRIDGMAN, R. GERTRUDE STEIN IN PIECES.*
  D. SUTHERLAND, 191(ELN):MAR72-235
BRIDOUX, A. ALAIN.
  C. SCHUWER, 542:OCT-DEC71-442
"DER BRIEFBOGEN IN DER WELT." (VOL 2)
  J.P. ASCHERL, 363:FEB71-61
BRIEGER, P., M. MEISS & C.S. SINGLETON.
  ILLUMINATED MANUSCRIPTS OF THE "DIVINE
  COMEDY."*
  J.J.G. ALEXANDER, 589:JUL72-514
  M.L. D'ANCONA, 54:MAR71-118
  P. BOYDE, 551(RENQ):AUTUMN71-357
                                [CONTINUED]

[CONTINUING]
  W.O.H., 135:SEP70-64
  C. HUTER, 354:DEC71-351
BRIEGLEB, K. LESSINGS ANFÄNGE 1742-1746.
  617(TLS):6JUL73-777
BRIEGLEB, K. - SEE HEINE, H.
BRIET, S. MADAME RIMBAUD.*
  A. ADAM, 535(RHL):MAR-APR70-334
BRIGANTI, G. THE VIEW PAINTERS OF EUR-
  OPE.
  R. EDWARDS, 39:MAR71-228
  S.J.F., 135:JAN71-55
  J.G. LINKS, 90:SEP71-554
  R. PAULSON, 173(ECS):SUMMER71-458
BRIGGS, A., JR. THE NOVELS OF HAROLD
  FREDERIC.
  S. GARNER, 594:FALL70-364
  R. LEHAN, 445(NCF):SEP70-251
BRIGGS, K.M. A DICTIONARY OF BRITISH
  FOLK-TALES.
  H. GLASSIE, 292(JAF):APR-JUN71-263
BRIGGS, P. WILL CALIFORNIA FALL INTO THE
  SEA?*
  J. SEELYE, 441:5AUG73-4
BRIGGS, S. & A., EDS. CAP AND BELL.*
  617(TLS):19JAN73-57
BRIGHAM, C.S. PAUL REVERE'S ENGRAVINGS.
  G. WILLS, 39:JAN70-86
BRIGHT, W., COMP. A LUISEÑO DICTIONARY.
  G.F. MEIER, 682(ZPSK):BAND23HEFT6-632
  W.R. MILLER, 269(IJAL):JAN71-55
BRIGHT, W., ED. SOCIOLINGUISTICS.*
  G.G. POČEPCOV, 353:MAY70-111
BRIGHTFIELD, M.F. VICTORIAN ENGLAND IN
  ITS NOVELS (1840-1870).*
  L. JAMES, 637(VS):DEC70-193
BRIGNANO, R.C. RICHARD WRIGHT.*
  N. SCHRAUFNAGEL, 502(PRS):WINTER70/71-
  361
  N.M. TISCHLER, 594:FALL70-365
BRILLIANT, R. THE ARCH OF SEPTIMIUS
  SEVERUS IN THE ROMAN FORUM.*
  P.P. BOBER, 54:JUN71-242
BRINER, A. PAUL HINDEMITH.
  E.H., 412:FEB72-59
  617(TLS):16MAR73-298
BRINEY, R.E. - SEE VAN ASH, C. & E.S.
  ROHMER
BRINGMANN, K. UNTERSUCHUNGEN ZUM SPÄTEN
  CICERO.*
  J.E. REXINE, 124:APR-MAY72-273
BRINK, C.O. HORACE ON POETRY.
  V. PÖSCHL, 124:DEC71-135
BRINKWORTH, E.R.C. SHAKESPEARE AND THE
  BAWDY COURT OF STRATFORD.
  617(TLS):9MAR73-277
BRINNIN, J.M. SKIN DIVING IN THE VIRGINS
  AND OTHER POEMS.*
  P.J. CALLAHAN, 569(SR):AUTUMN72-639
BRINNIN, J.M. THE SWAY OF THE GRAND
  SALOON.*
  G.W., 102(CANL):AUTUMN72-116
BRINSON, P. & C. CRISP. THE INTERNATIONAL
  BOOK OF BALLET.
  M. MARKS, 151:OCT71-96
BRISCOE, J. A COMMENTARY ON LIVY. (BKS
  31-33)
  617(TLS):29JUN73-757
BRISSAUD, A. CANARIS. (I. COLVIN, ED &
  TRANS)
  617(TLS):21DEC73-1570
BRISSENDEN, R.F., ED. STUDIES IN THE
  EIGHTEENTH CENTURY.*
  D.G., 173(ECS):WINTER71-212
  C.J. RAWSON, 447(N&Q):SEP71-355
BRISSENDEN, R.F. WINTER MATINS AND OTHER
  POEMS.
  S.E. LEE, 581:DEC72-302

BRISSON, J-P., ED. PROBLÈMES DE LA GUERRE
À ROME.
  J-C. RICHARD, 555:VOL45FASC2-382
  G.R. WATSON, 123:MAR72-133
BRISTOL, R.P. SUPPLEMENT TO CHARLES
EVANS' AMERICAN BIBLIOGRAPHY.*
  J.A.L. LEMAY, 165:SPRING73-66
BRISTOW, R.O. A FARAWAY DRUMMER.
  M. LEVIN, 441:8JUL73-22
BRISVILLE, J-C. LE RÔDEUR, NORA, LE
RÉCITAL.
  L. RIÈSE, 207(FR):MAR71-779
"THE BRITANNICA ENCYCLOPEDIA OF AMERICAN
ART."
  L. NOCHLIN, 441:2DEC73-4
BRITTAN, A. MEANINGS AND SITUATIONS.
  617(TLS):14SEP73-1052
BRITTAN, S. CAPITALISM AND THE PERMIS-
SIVE SOCIETY. IS THERE AN ECONOMIC
CONSENSUS?
  617(TLS):27JUL73-880
BRITTAN, S. STEERING THE ECONOMY.
  F.W. TOOBY, 619(TC):VOL179#1046-51
BRITTEN, B. KINDERKREUZZUG.
  H. KELLER, 362:6DEC73-790
BRITTON, K. PHILOSOPHY AND THE MEANING
OF LIFE.*
  G.M. PATERSON, 154:SEP71-575
  K. WARD, 483:JAN71-70
BROAD, C.D. INDUCTION, PROBABILITY, AND
CAUSATION.
  H.E. KYBURG, JR., 482(PHR):APR71-244
BROADBENT, J. "PARADISE LOST:" INTRO-
DUCTION.
  568(SCN):FALL-WINTER72-64
BROADBENT, J. - SEE MILTON, J.
BROADHEAD, H.D. TRAGICA.*
  P.T. STEVENS, 303:VOL91-146
BROCCIA, G. TRADIZIONE ED ESEGESI.
  D-C. INNES, 123:DEC72-404
BROCH, H. BARBARA UND ANDERE NOVELLEN.
(P.M. LÜTZELER, ED)
  617(TLS):3AUG73-911
BROCH, H. ZUR UNIVERSITÄTSREFORM. (G.
WIENOLD, ED)
  E.W. HERD, 220(GL&L):OCT71-82
"HERMANN BROCH - DANIEL BRODY: BRIEFWECH-
SEL 1930-1951."* (B. HACK & M. KLEISS,
EDS)
  W.A. REICHART, 406:SPRING72-85
BROCK, E. THE PORTRAITS AND THE POSES.
  617(TLS):3AUG73-894
BROCK, M. THE GREAT REFORM ACT.
  617(TLS):16NOV73-1388
BROCK, P. & H.G. SKILLING, EDS. THE
CZECH RENASCENCE OF THE 19TH CENTURY.
  J.F.N. BRADLEY, 575(SEER):JUL72-467
  F. PRINZ, 32:SEP72-715
BROCKARD, H. SUBJEKT, VERSUCH ZUR
ONTOLOGIE BEI HEGEL.
  J. FREUND, 542:APR-JUN71-236
  W. SCHWARZ, 484(PPR):MAR72-434
BRÖCKER, W. KANT ÜBER METAPHYSIK UND
ERFAHRUNG.
  W. STEINBECK, 342:BAND62HEFT2-257
BROCKETT, C.W., JR. ANTIPHONS, RESPON-
SORIES AND OTHER CHANTS OF THE MOZAR-
ABIC RITE.
  A.E. PLANCHART, 589:JUL72-517
  D-M. RANDEL, 414(MQ):JAN70-125
BRODER, D.S. THE PARTY'S OVER.*
  H. CLARK, 109:FALL/WINTER72/73-99
BRODERICK, J. AN APOLOGY FOR ROSES.
  617(TLS):9FEB73-141
BRODEUR, C. DU PROBLÈME DE L'INCONSCIENT
À UNE PHILOSOPHIE DE L'HOMME.
  R. LORRAIN, 154:JUN70-106

BRODEUR, P. DOWNSTREAM.*
  V. CUNNINGHAM, 362:8MAR73-315
  E.S. RABKIN, 385(MQR):SUMMER73-291
  617(TLS):30MAR73-340
BRODEUR, P. THE STUNT MAN.
  42(AR):SPRING70-130
BRODIN, D. MARCEL AYMÉ.*
  A. BERGENS, 546(RR):FEB71-74
BRODIN, G. TERMINI DIMOSTRATIVI TOSCANI.*
  I. BOSTRÖM, 597(SN):VOL43#1-280
BRODIN, P. & E. FRÉDÉRIC. GENS DE FRANCE
DANS L'HISTOIRE ET LA LITTÉRATURE.
  P.F. CHOLAKIAN, 399(MLJ):MAR71-191
BRODSKY, J. OSTANOVKA V PUSTYNE.*
  R. LOURIE, 550(RUSR):APR71-202
BRODSKY, J. SELECTED POEMS.
  A.A. COHEN, 441:30DEC73-1
BRODWIN, L.L. ELIZABETHAN LOVE TRAGEDY
1587-1625.
  617(TLS):29JUN73-752
BRODY, A. THE ENGLISH MUMMERS AND THEIR
PLAYS.
  J.W. ASHTON, 292(JAF):OCT-DEC71-452
BRODY, B. & N. CAPALDI, EDS. SCIENCE:
MEN: METHODS: GOALS.
  R.H. STOOTHOFF, 478:JUL70-176
BRODY, B.A., ED. READINGS IN THE PHIL-
OSOPHY OF SCIENCE.
  A. MUSGRAVE, 63:MAY72-89
BRODY, E. & R.A. FOWKES. THE GERMAN LIED
AND ITS POETRY.
  J.A.W., 410(M&L):OCT72-457
BRODY, H. INISHKILLANE.
  617(TLS):11MAY73-534
BROEKMAN, J.M. PHÄNOMENOLOGIE UND
EGOLOGIE.
  J. GRANIER, 542:OCT-DEC71-484
BROGAN, H. TOCQUEVILLE.
  617(TLS):27APR73-465
BROICH, U. STUDIEN ZUM KOMISCHEN EPOS.*
  D. ROLLE, 38:BAND89HEFT3-407
BROICH, U. - SEE COLLIER, J.
BROMBERT, V., ED. THE HERO IN LITERATURE.
  M. HANREZ, 207(FR):OCT70-256
BROMBERT, V. STENDHAL.*
  J.C. ALCIATORE, 188(ECR):FALL70-263
  R.M. CHADBOURNE, 207(FR):OCT70-232
  F.W.J. HEMMINGS, 593:WINTER72-376
BROMHEAD, P. THE GREAT WHITE ELEPHANT OF
MAPLIN SANDS.
  617(TLS):31AUG73-997
BRØNDSTED, M., ED. NORDENS LITTERATUR.
  617(TLS):23MAR73-320
BRONK, W. THE EMPTY HANDS.*
  M. CZARNECKI, 648:JUN73-37
BRONOWSKI, J. THE ASCENT OF MAN.
  J.W. BURROW, 362:6DEC73-783
BRONOWSKI, J. THE IDENTITY OF MAN.
  H.M. CURTLER, 396(MODA):SUMMER72-324
BRONSON, B.H. THE BALLAD AS SONG.*
  M. KARPELES, 203:SPRING71-77
  D.M. WINKELMAN, 292(JAF):JUL-SEP71-347
BRONSON, B.H. THE TRADITIONAL TUNES OF
THE CHILD BALLADS. (VOL 4)
  617(TLS):9FEB73-156
BRONTË, C. JANE EYRE. (J. JACK & M.
SMITH, EDS)
  R.A. COLBY, 405(MP):AUG71-77
  B. HARKNESS, 445(NCF):DEC70-355
  D. HEWITT, 447(N&Q):NOV71-429
BRONTË, C. JANE EYRE. (M. SMITH, ED)
  617(TLS):13JUL73-800
BRONTË, E. WUTHERING HEIGHTS.
  I. BAIN, 503:WINTER70-227
BRONZINI, G.B. IL MITO DELLA POESIA
POPOLARE.
  F.L. UTLEY, 545(RPH):MAY72-447

BRONZWAER, W.J.M. TENSE IN THE NOVEL.
  J. KILLHAM, 89(BJA):SPRING72-208
  R. PASCAL, 402(MLR):APR72-394
BROOK, G.L. THE LANGUAGE OF DICKENS.*
  A.R. TELLIER, 189(EA):APR-JUN70-222
  S. WALL, 184(EIC):JUL71-261
BROOK, G.L. VARIETIES OF ENGLISH.
  617(TLS):6APR73-398
BROOK-SHEPHERD, G. BETWEEN TWO FLAGS.
  617(TLS):29JUN73-734
BROOKE, C. THE TWELFTH CENTURY RENAIS-
  SANCE.
  B.M. PARSIL, 50(ARQ):SUMMER71-176
BROOKE, D. LORD JIM AT HOME.
  617(TLS):17AUG73-959
BROOKE, F. THE HISTORY OF EMILY MONTAGUE.
  L. SHOHET, 296:SUMMER73-101
BROOKE, J. - SEE WELCH, D.
BROOKE, N. SHAKESPEARE'S EARLY TRAGE-
  DIES.*
  R.A. FOAKES, 175:SPRING70-22
BROOKE-ROSE, C. A ZBC OF EZRA POUND.*
  H.N. SCHNEIDAU, 27(AL):NOV72-504
  H. WITEMEYER, 659:SPRING73-240
  M. WOOD, 453:8FEB73-7
BROOKES, G.H. THE RHETORICAL FORM OF
  CARLYLE'S "SARTOR RESARTUS."
  617(TLS):1JUN73-620
BROOKES, H.F. & C.E. GAWNE-CAINE - SEE
  KAFKA, F.
BROOKES, H.F. & H. ROSS. ENGLISH AS A
  FOREIGN LANGUAGE FOR SCIENCE STUDENTS.
  P. MICHEL, 556(RLV):1971/5-649
BROOKFIELD, H.C. COLONIALISM, DEVELOP-
  MENT AND INDEPENDENCE.
  617(TLS):5JAN73-22
BROOKFIELD, H.C. & D. HART. MELANESIA.
  P. VOSSELER, 182:VOL24#15/16-637
BROOKHOUSE, C., ED. "SIR AMADACE" AND
  "THE AVOWING OF ARTHUR."*
  R. BREUER, 38:BAND89HEFT3-379
BROOKNER, A. THE GENIUS OF THE FUTURE.
  T. CLARK, 592:NOV71-212
  R. WOODFIELD, 89(BJA):AUTUMN72-408
BROOKS, D. NUMBER AND PATTERN IN THE
  EIGHTEENTH-CENTURY NOVEL.
  617(TLS):19OCT73-1268
BROOKS, E. THIS CROWDED KINGDOM.
  617(TLS):4MAY73-496
BROOKS, G. REPORT FROM PART ONE.
  T.C. BAMBARA, 441:7JAN73-1
BROOKS, H.A. THE PRAIRIE SCHOOL.
  617(TLS):9MAR73-264
BROOKS, J. THE EXPERT.
  V. CUNNINGHAM, 362:8MAR73-315
  617(TLS):23MAR73-312
BROOKS, J. THE GO-GO YEARS.
  C. LEHMANN-HAUPT, 441:11OCT73-49
  L. WILLIAMS, 441:14OCT73-3
BROOKS, J.R. THOMAS HARDY.
  A. WELSH, 676(YR):SPRING72-459
BROOKS, M.Z. NASAL VOWELS IN CONTEMPOR-
  ARY STANDARD POLISH.*
  K. POLAŃSKI, 353:SEP71-115
BROOKS, P. THE HOUSE OF LIFE.*
  617(TLS):2NOV73-1341
BROOKS, P. THE NOVEL OF WORLDLINESS.*
  J. BAYLEY, 473(PR):SUMMER72-398
  M.S. GREENE, 173(ECS):SPRING71-332
  A.M. LABORDE, 188(ECR):SPRING70-91
  Y. SCALZITTI, 405(MP):FEB71-304
  E. SHOWALTER, JR., 173(ECS):SPRING72-
  467
  205(FMLS):JUL70-312
BROOKS, P.W. HISTORIC AIRSHIPS.
  617(TLS):15JUN73-699
BROOME, J. CONVOY IS TO SCATTER.
  617(TLS):27JUL73-884

BROPHY, B. THE ADVENTURES OF GOD IN HIS
  SEARCH FOR THE BLACK GIRL.
  M. WARNOCK, 362:6DEC73-785
  617(TLS):23NOV73-1417
BROPHY, B. IN TRANSIT.*
  J.C. FIELD, 556(RLV):1971/6-770
BROPHY, B. PRANCING NOVELIST.
  P.N. FURBANK, 362:29MAR73-421
  M. ROSENTHAL, 441:22JUL73-4
  617(TLS):30MAR73-347
BROSMAN, C.S. WATERING.
  J.I. FISCHER, 598(SOR):SUMMER73-710
BROSSARD, C. DID CHRIST MAKE LOVE?
  A.C.J. BERGMAN, 441:26AUG73-30
BROTHERSTON, G. MANUEL MACHADO.*
  C. CANNON, 240(HR):JAN71-115
  J. LÓPEZ-MORILLAS, 405(MP):MAY71-400
BROUÉ, P. & E. TÉMIME. THE REVOLUTION
  AND CIVIL WAR IN SPAIN.
  617(TLS):16MAR73-290
BROUGH, J. - SEE "POEMS FROM THE SAN-
  SKRIT"
BROUSSARD, L. THE MEASURE OF POE.
  H. BRADDY, 648:OCT70-73
BROUWERS, J. GROETJES UIT BRUSSEL.
  A. DIXON, 270:VOL21#3-171
BROWER, D.R. THE NEW JACOBINS.
  I.M. WALL, 207(FR):OCT70-194
BROWER, K. - SEE HAY, J. & R. KAUFFMAN
BROWER, R.A. HERO AND SAINT.
  P. MILWARD, 401(MLQ):SEP72-335
  E.M. WAITH, 676(YR):SPRING72-441
BROWN, A.F.J. ESSEX AT WORK, 1700-1815.
  D.J. JOHNSON, 325:APR71-244
BROWN, B.F. - SEE SONNINO, S.
BROWN, C. MANDELSTAM.
  J. BAYLEY, 362:6DEC73-781
BROWN, C.H. WILLIAM CULLEN BRYANT.*
  J.T. FLANAGAN, 579(SAQ):SUMMER72-440
  H.E. SPIVEY, 27(AL):NOV72-485
BROWN, D. THE FETTERMAN MASSACRE.
  617(TLS):6JUL73-780
BROWN, D.G. ACTION.*
  J.J.E., 543:MAR71-536
BROWN, E.G. REAGAN AND REALITY.
  639(VQR):WINTER71-XLI
BROWN, E.S. - SEE PLUMMER, W.
BROWN, F. AN IMPERSONATION OF ANGELS.
  U. WEISSTEIN, 397(MD):MAY70-107
BROWN, F. PÈRE-LACHAISE.
  A. BROYARD, 441:9AUG73-39
  V.S. PRITCHETT, 453:18OCT73-48
BROWN, G. IN MY WAY.
  P. JOHNSON, 441:7JAN73-6
BROWN, G.G. THE TWENTIETH CENTURY.
  617(TLS):23MAR73-331
BROWN, G.H. & OTHERS. DEVELOPMENT AND
  EVALUATION OF A SELF-INSTRUCTIONAL
  SPANISH COURSE.
  C.W. STANSFIELD, 238:SEP71-617
BROWN, G.M. MAGNUS.
  R. GARFITT, 362:20SEP73-384
  617(TLS):28SEP73-1101
BROWN, H. THE WILD HUNT.
  P. ADAMS, 61:MAR73-107
BROWN, H. & D. LUCE. HOSTAGES OF WAR.
  J. BUTTINGER, 453:14JUN73-20
BROWN, H.F., ED. PLANNING THE ACADEMIC
  LIBRARY.
  G. THOMPSON, 46:JUL71-64
BROWN, H.M. WHAT TO LOOK FOR IN CORNISH
  CHURCHES.
  617(TLS):13APR73-429
BROWN, H.M. & J. LASCELLE. MUSICAL
  ICONOGRAPHY.
  617(TLS):17AUG73-960
BROWN, H.O. JAMES JOYCE'S EARLY FICTION.
  H.B. STAPLES, 329(JJQ):SUMMER73-458

BROWN, I.  OLD AND YOUNG.
  R.J. SMITH, 157:SUMMER71-76
BROWN, I.  SHAKESPEARE AND THE ACTORS.
  R.A. FOAKES, 175:AUTUMN70-98
  J.C. TREWIN, 157:SUMMER70-69
BROWN, J.  TOWARDS A CHEMISTRY OF REEL
  PEOPLE.*
  D. BARBOUR, 102(CANL):SPRING72-77
"THE JOHN CARTER BROWN LIBRARY ANNUAL
  REPORTS 1901-1966."
  617(TLS):3AUG73-912
BROWN, J.F.  BULGARIA UNDER COMMUNIST
  RULE.
  N. OREN, 32:DEC72-933
BROWN, J.M.  THE ORDEAL OF A PLAYWRIGHT.*
  (N. COUSINS, ED)
  C.G. MASINTON, 397(MD):MAY71-123
BROWN, J.P.  THE LEBANON AND PHOENICIA.*
  (VOL 1)
  W.G. EAST, 303:VOL91-187
  N. JIDEJIAN, 318(JAOS):APR-JUN71-299
BROWN, J.R.  SHAKESPEARE AND HIS COME-
  DIES.
  P. MICHEL-MICHOT, 556(RLV):1970/1-101
BROWN, J.R.  SHAKESPEARE'S DRAMATIC
  STYLE.
  I. BROWN, 157:SPRING71-65
  J. RAMSEY, 401(MLQ):MAR72-69
BROWN, K.  ADVENTURES WITH D.W. GRIFFITH.
  (K. BROWNLOW, ED)
  P. ADAMS, 61:SEP73-118
  S. STERN, 441:16DEC73-25
BROWN, M.  THE POLITICS OF IRISH LITERA-
  TURE FROM THOMAS DAVIS TO W.B. YEATS.*
  T. KINSELLA, 295:FEB73-115
BROWN, M.B. - SEE UNDER BARRATT BROWN, M.
BROWN, M.B. & K. COATES, EDS.  TRADE
  UNION REGISTER: 3.
  617(TLS):30NOV73-1469
BROWN, M.E.  KENNETH BURKE.
  R. ASSELINEAU, 189(EA):JUL-SEP70-352
BROWN, M.E.  WALLACE STEVENS.
  W. BERTHOFF, 27(AL):NOV72-511
  J.N. RIDDEL, 401(MLQ):JUN72-213
  P. THOMAS, 648:JAN72-74
BROWN, M.H., ED.  PAPERS OF THE YUGOSLAV-
  AMERICAN SEMINAR ON MUSIC.*
  B. KREMENLIEV, 187:MAY73-323
BROWN, M.J.  ITINERANT AMBASSADOR.
  G.B. PARKS, 551(RENQ):WINTER71-552
BROWN, M.J.E.  CHOPIN: AN INDEX OF HIS
  WORKS IN CHRONOLOGICAL ORDER.  (2ND ED)
  G. ABRAHAM, 415:SEP72-868
BROWN, M.L., JR.  HEINRICH VON HAYMERLE.
  617(TLS):14SEP73-1048
BROWN, N.D.  DANIEL WEBSTER AND THE POLI-
  TICS OF AVAILABILITY.
  J.H. SILBEY, 432(NEQ):MAR71-151
BROWN, N.O.  CLOSING TIME.
  S. HAMPSHIRE, 453:18OCT73-8
  E.W. SAID, 441:9SEP73-31
BROWN, P.  RELIGION AND SOCIETY IN THE
  AGE OF SAINT AUGUSTINE.*
  W.H.C. FREND, 453:8FEB73-32
BROWN, P.L., ED.  CLYDE COMPANY PAPERS.
  (VOL 7)
  617(TLS):6JUL73-789
BROWN, R., ED.  KNOWLEDGE, EDUCATION,
  AND CULTURAL CHANGE.
  617(TLS):30MAR73-349
BROWN, R.  WATERFRONT ORGANISATION IN
  HULL 1870-1900.
  617(TLS):23MAR73-333
BROWN, R.A.  ORIGINS OF ENGLISH FEUDAL-
  ISM.
  617(TLS):22JUN73-728

BROWN, R.D.  REVOLUTIONARY POLITICS IN
  MASSACHUSETTS.
  C.W. AKERS, 432(NEQ):MAR71-143
  E. FONER, 453:22FEB73-35
  S.E. PATTERSON, 656(WMQ):JUL71-498
BROWN, R.E.  CARL BECKER ON HISTORY AND
  THE AMERICAN REVOLUTION.*
  T. COLBOURN, 432(NEQ):SEP71-498
  C. STROUT, 656(WMQ):APR71-338
BROWN, R.E.  HANS HENNY JAHNNS "FLUSS
  OHNE UFER."*
  D.E. JENKINSON, 220(GL&L):JAN72-195
BROWN, R.L. - SEE UNDER LAMONT BROWN, R.
BROWN, R.M.  THE HAND THAT CRADLES THE
  ROCK.
  W.H. PRITCHARD, 249(HUDR):SPRING72-119
BROWN, S.  THE HEYDAY OF SPIRITUALISM.
  R.E. CROUTER, 109:FALL/WINTER72/73-
  113
BROWN, S. & G. GÁL - SEE OCKHAM, WILLIAM
  OF
BROWN, S.C.  DO RELIGIOUS CLAIMS MAKE
  SENSE?*
  R. HEPBURN, 483:JAN71-68
  R.E. SANTONI, 258:SEP71-448
BROWN, S.C. - SEE THOMPSON, B.
BROWN, S.J.  ROBBER ROCKS.
  B. CHENEY, 577(SHR):FALL71-416
BROWN, V.P. & J.P. NABERS - SEE DUFFEE,
  M.G.
BROWN, W.  THE EARNINGS CONFLICT.
  617(TLS):16MAR73-300
BROWN, W.  ON THE COAST.
  617(TLS):4MAY73-491
BROWN, W.  PIECEWORK BARGAINING.
  617(TLS):17AUG73-958
BROWN, W.H., JR.  A SYNTAX OF KING AL-
  FRED'S "PASTORAL CARE."
  E.C. TRAUGOTT, 350:MAR72-182
BROWN, W.R.  IMAGEMAKER.*
  W.A. LINSLEY, 583:SPRING72-333
BROWNE, E.M.  THE MAKING OF T.S. ELIOT'S
  PLAYS.*
  M.J. LIGHTFOOT, 397(MD):DEC70-345
  T. ROGERS, 175:SUMMER70-67
BROWNE, G.A.  HAZARD.
  N. CALLENDAR, 441:5AUG73-10
BROWNE, J.R.  J. ROSS BROWNE: HIS LET-
  TERS, JOURNALS AND WRITINGS.  (L.F.
  BROWNE, ED)
  D.M. POWELL, 50(ARQ):SPRING70-82
BROWNE, M. - SEE CHORNOVIL, V. & OTHERS
BROWNE, R.B.  MELVILLE'S DRIVE TO HUMAN-
  ISM.
  H. COHEN, 27(AL):JAN73-685
  K.T. REED, 70(ANQ):OCT72-30
BROWNE, R.B. & OTHERS, EDS.  FRONTIERS OF
  AMERICAN CULTURE.*
  L. ATTEBERY, 650(WF):JAN71-64
BROWNE, R.B. & R. AMBROSETTI, EDS.  POPU-
  LAR CULTURE AND CURRICULA.
  G. CAREY, 292(JAF):APR-JUN71-262
BROWNE, R.B. & D. PIZER, EDS.  THEMES
  AND DIRECTIONS IN AMERICAN LITERATURE.*
  R.L.H., 502(PRS):FALL70-275
BROWNELL, A.H.  ARCHITECTURAL HARDWARE
  SPECIFICATIONS HANDBOOK.
  505:OCT71-152
BROWNING, E.B.  DIARY BY E.B.B.*  (P.
  KELLEY & R. HUDSON, EDS)
  G.B. TAPLIN, 636(VP):SUMMER70-168
BROWNING, R.  BROWNING, POETICAL WORKS
  1833-1864.*  (I. JACK, ED)
  L. BONNEROT, 189(EA):OCT-DEC70-450
  L.R. BURROWS, 67:MAY72-89
  R.E. FITCH, 85:FALL71-59
  J. UTZ, 72:BAND209HEFT1/3-165

BROWNING, R. THE COMPLETE WORKS OF ROB-
ERT BROWNING.* (VOL 1) (R.A. KING,
JR. & OTHERS, EDS)
    R.L. COLLINS, 636(VP):AUTUMN71-351
    M. PECKHAM, 85:FALL70-3
BROWNING, R. THE COMPLETE WORKS OF ROB-
ERT BROWNING. (VOL 2) (R.A. KING, JR.
& OTHERS, EDS)
    R.L. COLLINS, 636(VP):AUTUMN71-351
BROWNING, R. JUSTINIAN AND THEODORA.
    J.W. BARKER, 589:OCT72-748
    C. SCHULER, 122:JUL72-228
BROWNING, R. MEDIEVAL AND MODERN GREEK.*
    H.J. MASON, 487:SPRING71-90
BROWNING, R. SELECTED POEMS. (K. ALLOTT,
ED)
    L. BONNEROT, 189(EA):OCT-DEC70-448
BROWNING, R. & E.B. BARRETT. THE LETTERS
OF ROBERT BROWNING AND ELIZABETH BAR-
RETT BARRETT, 1845-1846.* (E. KINTNER,
ED)
    R.D. ALTICK, 405(MP):AUG71-76
    I. JACK, 541(RES):NOV71-506
BROWNJOHN, A. WARRIOR'S CAREER.*
    A. MACLEAN, 362:22MAR73-389
BROWNLOW, K. - SEE BROWN, K.
BROZOVIĆ, D. RJEČNIK JEZIKA, ILI JEZIK
RJEČNIKA? STANDARDNI JEZIK.
    L. MATEJKA, 32:JUN72-494
BRUANDET, P. INTRODUCING PHOTOGRAMS.
    617(TLS):9NOV73-1381
BRUCCOLI, M.J. F. SCOTT FITZGERALD: A
DESCRIPTIVE BIBLIOGRAPHY.
    617(TLS):30MAR73-360
BRUCCOLI, M.J. & J.R. BRYER, EDS. F.
SCOTT FITZGERALD IN HIS OWN TIME.
    B. KEETCH, 651(WHR):SPRING72-183
BRUCE, G. THE COLLECTED POEMS OF GEORGE
BRUCE.*
    A. CLUYSENAAR, 565:VOL12#4-68
BRUCE, J.G. & C.H. CURTIS. THE LONDON
MOTOR BUS.
    617(TLS):24AUG73-986
BRUCE, M., ED. THE RISE OF THE WELFARE
STATE.
    617(TLS):14SEP73-1052
BRUCE, M.L. ANNE BOLEYN.
    617(TLS):19JAN73-62
BRUCE, R.V. BELL.
    C. LEHMANN-HAUPT, 441:8MAY73-47
    D. MC CULLOUGH, 441:15APR73-3
    442(NY):23JUN73-91
BRUCH, J-L. LA PHILOSOPHIE RELIGIEUSE
DE KANT.
    J. KOPPER, 342:BAND61HEFT1-128
BRUCKER, H. COMMUNICATION IS POWER.
    C. LEHMANN-HAUPT, 441:23FEB73-33
    617(TLS):3AUG73-896
BRUCKNER, J. A BIBLIOGRAPHICAL CATALOGUE
OF SEVENTEENTH-CENTURY GERMAN BOOKS PUB-
LISHED IN HOLLAND.
    P.M. MITCHELL, 301(JEGP):OCT72-576
BRÜCKNER, W. BILDNIS UND BRAUCH.
    G. GROBER-GLÜCK, 680(ZDP):BAND90
    HEFT3-471
    H. TRÜMPY, 657(WW):MAR/APR70-142
BRUEGEL, J.W. CZECHOSLOVAKIA BEFORE
MUNICH.
    617(TLS):27JUL73-860
BRUEMMER, F. THE LONG HUNT.
    H. STEWART, 255(HAB):WINTER70-61
BRUFORD, A. GAELIC FOLK-TALES AND MED-
IAEVAL ROMANCES.
    E.S. IBARRA, 582(SFQ):JUN70-146
BRÜGEL/COLÓN. EL ESPAÑOL DE HOY.
    K.A. MÜLLER, 430(NS):NOV71-618

BRÜGGEMANN, D. VOM HERZEN DIREKT IN DIE
FEDER.
    R.M.G. NICKISCH, 680(ZDP):BAND90
    HEFT4-618
BRUHAT, J., J. DAUTRY & E. TERSEN. LA
COMMUNE DE 1871. (2ND ED)
    M. REBÉRIOUX, 98:NOV71-979
BRÜHL, C. STUDIEN ZU DEN LANGOBARDIS-
CHEN KÖNIGSURKUNDEN.*
    K.F. DREW, 589:JUL72-519
BRUMBAUGH, R.S. & R. WELLS, EDS. THE
PLATO MANUSCRIPTS.
    J.J.R., 543:DEC70-351
BRUMFITT, J.H. - SEE DE VOLTAIRE, F.M.A.
BRUMFITT, J.H. & J.C. HALL - SEE ROUSSEAU,
J-J.
BRUMM, U. AMERICAN THOUGHT AND RELIGIOUS
TYPOLOGY.
    C. FEIDELSON, 191(ELN):MAR72-220
    M.I. LOWANCE, JR., 656(WMQ):JAN71-145
BRUMMACK, J. DIE DARSTELLUNG DES ORIENTS
IN DEN DEUTSCHEN ALEXANDERGESCHICHTEN
DES MITTELALTERS.
    E. SCHRADER, 406:SPRING72-73
BRUN, J. L'UNIVERS TRAGIQUE DE KLEIST.
    R. LEROY, 1970/2-220
BRUN, R. LE LIVRE FRANÇAIS.
    R.D. PRATT, 503:SPRING70-44
    R.A. SAYCE, 354:MAR70-82
BRUNDAGE, J.A. MEDIEVAL CANON LAW AND
THE CRUSADER.*
    A.W. GODFREY, 363:MAY71-78
BRUNEAU, J. LE "CONTE ORIENTAL" DE
GUSTAVE FLAUBERT.
    617(TLS):17AUG73-950
BRUNEAU, J. - SEE FLAUBERT, G.
BRUNET, G. C-F. MEYER ET LA NOUVELLE.
    M.C. CRICHTON, 564:MAR70-79
BRUNET, J. ALBERT LABERGE, SA VIE ET
SON OEUVRE.*
    P.M. GATHERCOLE, 207(FR):MAR71-795
BRUNHOUSE, R.L. IN SEARCH OF THE MAYA.
    P. ADAMS, 61:JUL73-103
BRUNIUS, T. THEORY AND TASTE.
    A. BERLEANT, 484(PPR):JUN71-615
BRUNNER, F. & OTHERS. VOM WESEN DER
SPRACHE.*
    V. SKALIČKA, 353:FEB71-121
BRUNNER, J. AGE OF MIRACLES.
    617(TLS):9NOV73-1378
BRUNNER, O. NEUE WEGE DER VERFASSUNGS-
UND SOZIALGESCHICHTE. (2ND ED) PER
UNA NUOVA STORIA COSTITUZIONALE E
SOCIALE.
    S.W. ROWAN, 589:JAN72-110
BRUNS, G. KÜCHENWESEN UND MAHLZEITEN.
    J. BOARDMAN, 123:JUN72-291
BRUNSKILL, R.W. ILLUSTRATED HANDBOOK OF
VERNACULAR ARCHITECTURE.
    A. FENTON, 595(SCS):VOL16PT1-88
BRUNT, P.A. ITALIAN MANPOWER 225 B.C. -
A.D. 14.
    F.C. BOURNE, 124:NOV71-104
BRUS, W. THE MARKET IN A SOCIALIST
ECONOMY.
    617(TLS):6APR73-399
BRUSHWOOD, J.S. ENRIQUE GONZÁLEZ MARTÍN-
EZ.
    F. DAUSTER, 238:MAR71-208
BRUSSILOV, A.A. A SOLDIER'S NOTE-BOOK,
1914-1918.
    J.S. CURTISS, 32:SEP72-672
BRUSTEIN, R. REVOLUTION AS THEATRE.*
    T.R. EDWARDS, 473(PR):1/1972-121
BRUTUS. CLASS.
    W. SCHOTT, 441:27MAY73-6

BRUYLANT, A. ABN-GIDS VOOR DE HANDEL-
STAAL.
  M. ESCH-PELGROMS, 556(RLV):1971/4-509
BRUZZI, A. LA FORMAZIONE DELLE "MAXIMES"
DE LA ROCHEFOUCAULD ATTRAVERSO LE EDI-
ZIONI ORIGINALI.*
  J. LAFOND, 535(RHL):JAN-FEB70-123
BRYAN, A-M. & J. DUCHÉ. POUR PARLER.
  R.M. TERRY, 207(FR):MAR71-821
BRYAN, C.D.B. THE GREAT DETHRIFFE.*
  639(VQR):WINTER71-VIII
BRYANT, A. AMAZING GRACE.
  P.M. SPACKS, 249(HUDR):SPRING72-157
BRYANT, A. JACKETS OF GREEN.
  617(TLS):23MAR73-329
BRYANT, D.C., ED. ANCIENT GREEK AND
ROMAN RHETORICIANS.
  G.F. HOSTETTLER, 480(P&R):WINTER70-63
BRYANT, E. AMONG THE DEAD, AND OTHER
EVENTS LEADING UP TO THE APOCALYPSE.
  T. STURGEON, 441:22APR73-16
BRYANT, J.A., JR. EUDORA WELTY.
  R. ASSELINEAU, 189(EA):APR-JUN70-233
BRYANT, W. ESCAPE FROM SONORA.
  N. CALLENDAR, 441:8APR73-32
BRYHER. THE DAYS OF MARS.
  617(TLS):23FEB73-206
BRYLOWSKI, W. FAULKNER'S OLYMPIAN LAUGH.*
  F. GADO, 597(SN):VOL42#1-240
BRZEZINSKI, Z. BETWEEN TWO AGES.*
  H.W. HELD, 497(POLR):SUMMER71-101
  H.J. MORGENTHAU, 639(VQR):WINTER71-149
BRZEZINSKI, Z. THE FRAGILE BLOSSOM.*
  G. BARRACLOUGH, 453:14JUN73-27
BUBER, M. MARTIN BUBER: BRIEFWECHSEL AUS
SIEBEN JAHRZEHNTEN. (VOL 1) (G. SCHAE-
DER, ED)
  617(TLS):28DEC73-1577
BUBER, M. I AND THOU. (W. KAUFMANN,
TRANS)
  617(TLS):28DEC73-1577
  639(VQR):SPRING71-LXXXII
"MARTIN BUBER: L'HOMME ET LE PHILOSOPHE."
  S.J.B., 543:MAR71-554
BUBER, M. & A. GOES. MEN OF DIALOGUE:
MARTIN BUBER AND ALBRECHT GOES. (E.W.
ROLLINS & H. ZOHN, EDS)
  U. SIMON, 220(GL&L):JAN72-141
BUCCELLATI, G. CITIES AND NATIONS OF
ANCIENT SYRIA.
  Y.L. HOLMES, 318(JAOS):APR-JUN71-301
BUCHAN, A. POWER AND EQUILIBRIUM IN THE
1970'S.
  R. STEEL, 453:14JUN73-33
  617(TLS):23NOV73-1422
BUCHAN, D., ED. A SCOTTISH BALLAD BOOK.
  617(TLS):19OCT73-1289
BUCHAN, T. EXORCISM. POEMS 1969-1972.
  617(TLS):9MAR73-270
BUCHANAN, C. THE STATE OF BRITAIN.
  617(TLS):23FEB73-204
BUCHANAN, I. SINGAPORE IN SOUTHEAST
ASIA.
  617(TLS):6APR73-368
BUCHANAN, K. THE TRANSFORMATION OF THE
CHINESE EARTH.
  R. MURPHEY, 293(JAST):FEB71-449
BUCHANAN, P. A REQUIEM OF SHARKS.
  N. CALLENDAR, 441:18NOV73-56
BUCHANAN, R.A. INDUSTRIAL ARCHAEOLOGY IN
BRITAIN.
  617(TLS):31AUG73-999
BUCHANAN-BROWN, J. - SEE AUBREY, J.
BUCHANAN-BROWN, J. - SEE STEINBERG, S.H.
BUCHDAHL, G. METAPHYSICS AND THE PHIL-
OSOPHY OF SCIENCE.*
  J. KOPPER, 342:BAND62HEFT1-126
  W. VON LEYDEN, 483:JAN71-38  [CONT]

[CONTINUING]
  A.C. MICHALOS, 154:JUN70-111
  J.D. NORTH, 479(PHQ):APR71-184
  W. RÖD, 53(AGP):BAND53HEFT1-100
BUCHER, E., E.F.J. PAYNE & K.O. KURTH,
EDS. VON DER AKTUALITÄT SCHOPENHAUERS.
  W.H. WERKMEISTER, 319:OCT73-562
BUCHER, F. THE PAMPLONA BIBLES.*
  J. BECKWITH, 39:DEC71-524
BUCHNER, A. ANLEITUNG ZUR DEUTSCHEN
POETEREY - POET. (M. SZYROCKI, ED)
  H. RÜDIGER, 52:BAND6HEFT1-77
BUCHNER, A. FOLK MUSIC INSTRUMENTS OF
THE WORLD.
  A. APELIAN, 187:SEP73-545
BÜCHNER, G. DANTON'S DEATH. (H.J.
SCHMIDT, TRANS)
  J.C. BRUCE, 406:WINTER72-420
BÜCHNER, G. DANTONS TOD.* (R.C. COWEN,
ED)
  H.U. TAYLOR, 399(MLJ):OCT71-415
BÜCHNER, G. THE PLAYS OF GEORG BÜCHNER.
(V. PRICE, ED & TRANS) LEONCE AND
LENA, LENZ, WOYZECK. (M. HAMBURGER,
ED & TRANS)
  617(TLS):2MAR73-233
BUCHNER, H. PLOTINS MÖGLICHKEITSLEHRE.
  J. FREUND, 542:APR-JUN71-238
  R.T. WALLIS, 123:DEC72-343
BÜCHNER, K. STUDIEN ZUR RÖMISCHEN LIT-
ERATUR. (VOL 7)
  F. LASSERRE, 182:VOL24#1/2-37
BÜCHNER, K. STUDIEN ZUR RÖMISCHEN LIT-
ERATUR. (VOL 8)
  F. LASSERRE, 182:VOL24#1/2-37
  S. VIARRE, 555:VOL45FASC2-359
BUCHTHAL, H. HISTORIA TROIANA.
  C.D. SHEPPARD, 589:OCT72-750
BUCHWALD, A. COUNTING SHEEP.
  J.P., 376:APR71-130
BUCHWALD, A. I NEVER DANCED AT THE WHITE
HOUSE.
  G. BLAKE, 441:11NOV73-48
BUCK, A. DIE HUMANISTISCHE TRADITION IN
DER ROMANIA.
  S. PRETE, 52:BAND5HEFT3-322
BUCK, A., ED. ZU BEGRIFF UND PROBLEM DER
RENAISSANCE.
  F. SCHALK, 52:BAND6HEFT2-200
BUCK, S.H. TIBETAN-ENGLISH DICTIONARY
WITH SUPPLEMENT.
  T.V. WYLIE, 318(JAOS):JAN-MAR71-148
BUCKLAND, P. IRISH UNIONISM. (VOL 1)
  617(TLS):9FEB73-155
BUCKLAND, P. IRISH UNIONISM. (VOL 2)
  617(TLS):27JUL73-857
BUCKLE, R. NIJINSKY.*
  J. PERCIVAL, 415:FEB72-158
BUCKLEY, F.R. SERVANTS AND THEIR MASTERS.
  C.D.B. BRYAN, 441:4NOV73-73
BUCKLEY, J.H. THE TRIUMPH OF TIME.
  R. MAURICE, 186(ETC):JUN70-247
BUCKLEY, W.F., JR. CRUISING SPEED.
  H. REGNERY, 396(MODA):WINTER72-92
BUCKMAN, P., ED. EDUCATION WITHOUT
SCHOOLS.
  617(TLS):9NOV73-1381
BUCKNALL, B.J. THE RELIGION OF ART IN
PROUST.
  J.M. COCKING, 67:MAY72-101
BUCUR, M. DOCUMENTE INEDITE DIN ARCHIV-
ELE FRANCEZE PRIVITOARE LA ROMÂNI ÎN
SEC. AL XIX-LEA.
  A. CIORANESCU, 549(RLC):JUL-SEP71-427
BUCZKOWSKI, L. BLACK TORRENT.
  J.R. KRZYŻANOWSKI, 497(POLR):AUTUMN
  70-110

51

BUDDEN, J. THE OPERAS OF VERDI. (VOL 1)
617(TLS):14SEP73-1046
BUDDRUSS, G. - SEE THIEME, P.
BUDGEN, F. JAMES JOYCE AND THE MAKING
OF "ULYSSES."*
C. MAC CABE, 111:2JUN72-174
BUDGEN, F. MYSELVES WHEN YOUNG.
B.S. LLAMZON, 613:AUTUMN71-473
T.F. STALEY, 295:NOV72-576
BUDHRAJ, V.S. SOVIET RUSSIA AND THE
HINDUSTAN SUBCONTINENT.
617(TLS):24AUG73-986
BUDICK, S. DRYDEN AND THE ABYSS OF
LIGHT.*
P. HARTH, 481(PQ):JUL71-424
G. REEDY, 613:WINTER71-613
BUEB, B. NIETZSCHES KRITIK DER PRAKTIS-
CHEN VERNUNFT.*
E. DIET, 542:JUL-SEP71-386
BUECHNER, F. LION COUNTRY.*
639(VQR):SUMMER71-XCVII
BUECHNER, F. OPEN HEART.*
R. SALE, 249(HUDR):WINTER72/73-703
BUECHNER, F. WISHFUL THINKING.
E. FULLER, 441:13MAY73-20
BUEL, R., JR. SECURING THE REVOLUTION.
E. FONER, 453:22FEB73-35
BUELL, F. W.H. AUDEN AS A SOCIAL POET.
D. DONOGHUE, 453:19JUL73-17
617(TLS):3AUG73-894
BUELL, F. THESEUS AND OTHER POEMS.*
F.D. REEVE, 491:MAR73-348
BUELL, J. THE SHREWSDALE EXIT.*
E. ZIMMER, 296:SPRING73-91
DE BUENDÍA, I. TRIUNFO DE LLANEZA. (E.M.
WILSON, ED)
N.D. SHERGOLD, 86(BHS):OCT72-403
BUERKLE, J.V. & D. BARKER. BOURBON
STREET BLACK.
617(TLS):28DEC73-1593
BUERO VALLEJO, A. LA DOBLE HISTORIA DEL
DOCTOR VALMY. (A.M. GIL, ED)
M.T. HALSEY, 238:SEP71-614
BUFANO, A. CONCORDANZE DEI "CANTI" DEL
LEOPARDI.
A. STUSSI, 228(GSLI):VOL147FASC458/
459-465
BUFFA, J.L. TOPONIMIA ABORIGEN DE ENTRE
RIOS.
T.A. SEWARD, 215(GL):VOL10#3-223
BUFFIÈRE, F., ED & TRANS. ANTHOLOGIE
GRECQUE.* (PT 1, VOL 12)
D.A. CAMPBELL, 123:JUN72-183
BUFORD, T.O., ED. ESSAYS ON OTHER MINDS.
L.M. RICCI, 484(PPR):MAR72-425
639(VQR):SUMMER71-CXXXVI
BÜHLER, A. ART OF OCEANIA.
D.T., 135:JUL71-228
BÜHLER, C.F. - SEE DE PISAN, C.
BÜHLER, C.F. - SEE SCROPE, S.
BUHR, M. IMMANUEL KANT.
W. TEICHNER, 342:BAND62HEFT2-255
BUITENHUIS, P. THE GRASPING IMAGINATION.*
T.E. FLYNN, 150(DR):SPRING71-96
P. GROSSKURTH, 102(CANL):WINTER72-94
J.T. HORRELL, 651(WHR):WINTER72-82
D.K. KIRBY, 432(NEQ):JUN71-337
K. MC SWEENEY, 529(QQ):SPRING71-147
BUITENHUIS, P. HUGH MAC LENNAN.
B. NESBITT, 648:JAN71-68
BUKOWSKA-GROSSE, E. & E. KOSCHMIEDER,
EDS. POLNISCHE VOLKSMÄRCHEN.*
D. SIMONIDES, 196:BAND11HEFT1/2-158
BULGAKOV, M. THE MASTER AND MARGARITA.
E.H. LEHRMAN, 454:FALL71-92
BULL, D., ED. FAMILY POVERTY. (2ND ED)
617(TLS):23FEB73-222

BULL, W.E. TIME, TENSE, AND THE VERB.
J. PURCZINSKY, 215(GL):VOL11#1-35
"BULLETIN ANALYTIQUE D'HISTOIRE ROMAINE."
(VOLS 3 & 4)
J-C. DUMONT, 555:VOL45FASC1-189
"BULLETIN OF THE OPPOSITION."
617(TLS):23NOV73-1415
BULLINS, E. THE ELECTRONIC NIGGER AND
OTHER PLAYS.
A. RENDLE, 157:WINTER70-70
BULLINS, E. THE RELUCTANT RAPIST.
G. DAVIS, 441:30SEP73-24
442(NY):15OCT73-186
BULLITT, O.H. - SEE ROOSEVELT, F.D. &
W.C. BULLITT
BULLIVANT, K. - SEE GAISER, G.
BULLIVANT, R. FUGUE.
J.V.C., 410(M&L):APR72-194
M. TILMOUTH, 415:MAY72-463
BULLOCK, M. GREEN BEGINNING, BLACK END-
ING.*
J. REID, 102(CANL):AUTUMN72-110
BULLOUGH, G., ED. NARRATIVE AND DRAMATIC
SOURCES OF SHAKESPEARE. (VOL 7)
617(TLS):27APR73-458
BULMER, K., ED. NEW WRITINGS IN SF 21.
617(TLS):18MAY73-562
VON BÜLOW, I. DER TANZ IM DRAMA.
H.O., 430(NS):AUG70-421
BULTMANN, R. THE GOSPEL OF JOHN.
B. HEBBLETHWAITE, 111:19NOV71-57
BUMANN, W. DIE SPRACHTHEORIE HEYMANN
STEINTHALS, DARGESTELLT IM ZUSAMMENHANG
MIT SEINER THEORIE DER GEISTESWISSEN-
SCHAFT.
R.H. ROBINS, 206:AUG70-441
BUMKE, J. DIE ROMANISCH-DEUTSCHEN LIT-
ERATURBEZIEHUNGEN IM MITTELALTER.
H.R., 657(WW):NOV/DEC70-432
W. SCHRÖDER, 680(ZDP):BAND89HEFT3-448
BUMKE, J. DIE WOLFRAM VON ESCHENBACH
FORSCHUNG SEIT 1945.*
D.H. GREEN, 402(MLR):JAN72-203
BUMPUS, J.S. A DICTIONARY OF ECCLESIAS-
TICAL TERMS.
R.C. LA CHARITÉ, 582(SFQ):DEC70-379
BUMSTED, J.M. HENRY ALLINE 1748-1784.*
B. FERGUSSON, 150(DR):AUTUMN71-453
BUMSTED, J.M., ED. THE GREAT AWAKENING:
THE BEGINNINGS OF EVANGELICAL PIETISM
IN AMERICA.
E.S. GAUSTAD, 656(WMQ):APR71-314
BUNGERT, H. WILLIAM FAULKNER UND DIE
HUMORISTISCHE TRADITION DES AMERIKAN-
ISCHEN SÜDENS.
O.B. WHEELER, 27(AL):NOV72-513
BUNNAG, J. BUDDHIST MONK, BUDDHIST
LAYMAN.
617(TLS):21SEP73-1079
BUNSEKI-LUMANISA, A.F-K.K. - SEE UNDER
FU-KIAU KIA BUNSEKI-LUMANISA, A.
BUNTING, B. COLLECTED POEMS.
C. LEVENSON, 529(QQ):SUMMER71-309
BUNTING, B. - SEE FORD, F.M.
BUNTING, E., ED. THE ANCIENT MUSIC OF
IRELAND.
P. CROSSLEY-HOLLAND, 187:MAY73-325
BUNTING, J. THE EARLY CORRESPONDENCE OF
JABEZ BUNTING 1820-1829. (W.R. WARD,
ED)
617(TLS):9MAR73-277
BUNTING, J. THE LIONHEADS.*
617(TLS):27JUL73-851
BUNTING, J. SWITZERLAND INCLUDING LIECH-
TENSTEIN.
617(TLS):22JUN73-721

BUONO, F. BERTOLT BRECHT. ZUR PROSA
BRECHTS.
617(TLS):28DEC73-1591
BURCHARD, R.C. JOHN UPDIKE.*
W.T. STAFFORD, 295:NOV72-569
BURCHFIELD, R.W. - SEE "A SUPPLEMENT TO
THE OXFORD ENGLISH DICTIONARY" (VOL 1)
BURCKHARDT, J. BRIEFE.* (VOL 7)
T.J.G. LOCHER, 204(FDL):1970/2-141
F.M. WASSERMANN, 222(GR):MAY71-237
BURCKHARDT, S. THE DRAMA OF LANGUAGE.
H. LINDENBERGER, 173(ECS):WINTER71/72-
321
H. SALINGER, 149:DEC72-474
BURCKHARDT, S. SHAKESPEAREAN MEANINGS.*
R.A. FOAKES, 175:AUTUMN70-98
H. LINDENBERGER, 173(ECS):WINTER71/72-
321
BURD, V.A., ED. THE RUSKIN FAMILY LET-
TERS. (VOLS 1&2)
617(TLS):14DEC73-1537
BURD, V.A. - SEE RUSKIN, J.
BURDE-SCHNEIDEWIND, G. HISTORISCHE
VOLKSSAGEN ZWISCHEN ELBE UND NIEDER-
RHEIN.
R.L. WELSCH, 650(WF):APR71-144
VON BÜREN, E. ZUR BEDEUTUNG DER PSYCHOLO-
GIE IM WERK ROBERT MUSILS.
W. BRAUN, 406:FALL72-299
BURFORD, A. THE GREEK TEMPLE BUILDERS
AT EPIDAUROS.*
E.R. DE ZURKO, 219(GAR):SPRING71-116
C.H. GRAYSON, 303:VOL91-204
BURFORD, L. VICE AVENGED.
R. TRICKETT, 676(YR):AUTUMN71-121
BURG, D. & G. FEIFER. SOLZHENITSYN.*
D. CAUTE, 362:8FEB73-188
Z.A. MEDVEDEV, 453:17MAY73-32
BURGART, J-P. FAILLES.
V.A. LA CHARITÉ, 207(FR):FEB71-634
BURGER, A.S. OPPOSITION IN A DOMINANT-
PARTY SYSTEM.
P. WALLACE, 293(JAST):FEB71-489
BURGER, H.O., ED. ANNALEN DER DEUTSCHEN
LITERATUR. (2ND ED)
E. STOPP, 402(MLR):OCT72-934
BURGER, H.O. RENAISSANCE, HUMANISMUS,
REFORMATION.*
J. RIDÉ, 182:VOL24#5-212
BURGER, H.O., ED. STUDIEN ZUR TRIVIAL-
LITERATUR.
M.E. KEUNE, 221(GQ):JAN71-83
BURGER, H.O. & K. VON SEE, EDS. FEST-
SCHRIFT GOTTFRIED WEBER.
C. MINIS, 680(ZDP):BAND90HEFT3-450
BURGESS, A. JOYSPRICK.
617(TLS):15JUN73-669
BURGESS, A. ONE HAND CLAPPING.*
J.P. DEGNAN, 249(HUDR):SUMMER72-330
BURGESS, A. SHAKESPEARE.*
I. BROWN, 157:WINTER70-63
J.P., 376:JAN71-136
639(VQR):SPRING71-LXVIII
BURGESS, A. TREMOR OF INTENT.
G. AGGELER, 376:JAN71-90
BURGESS, C.F. - SEE GAY, J.
BURGESS, G.S. CONTRIBUTION À L'ÉTUDE DU
VOCABULAIRE PRÉ-COURTOIS.
B. FOSTER, 208(FS):OCT72-492
205(FMLS):JAN71-92
BURGESS, T. HOME AND SCHOOL.
617(TLS):9MAR73-271
BURGESS, T., ED. PLANNING FOR HIGHER
EDUCATION. THE SHAPE OF HIGHER EDUCA-
TION.
617(TLS):18MAY73-552
BÜRGIN, H. & H-O. MAYER. THOMAS MANN.*
K. SCHRÖTER, 222(GR):MAR71-129

BURGIN, R. CONVERSATIONS WITH JORGE
LUIS BORGES.
A. TERRY, 362:23AUG73-253
BURGOS, J., ED. "CIRCÉ," MÉTHODOLOGIE DE
L'IMAGINAIRE.
J. BELLEMIN-NOËL, 535(RHL):JUL-AUG71-
721
BURKE, E. THE CORRESPONDENCE OF EDMUND
BURKE.* (VOL 8) (R.B. MC DOWELL, ED)
J.T. BOULTON, 447(N&Q):SEP71-353
BURKE, E. REFLECTIONS ON THE REVOLUTION
IN FRANCE. (C.C. O'BRIEN, ED)
D.V.E., 191(ELN):SEP71(SUPP)-14
BURKE, E.E. - SEE MAUCH, C.
BURKE, K. COLLECTED POEMS: 1915-1967.
L.T. LEMON, 502(PRS):SPRING70-80
BURKE, K. THE COMPLETE WHITE OXEN.*
R. ASSELINEAU, 189(EA):JUL-SEP70-352
BURKE, K. A RHETORIC OF MOTIVES.
T. MELIA, 480(P&R):SPRING70-124
BURKE, K. THE RHETORIC OF RELIGION.
E.W. HARRIS, 186(ETC.):MAR71-119
BURKE, S.M. PAKISTAN'S FOREIGN POLICY.
617(TLS):18MAY73-543
"BURKE'S LANDED GENTRY." (VOL 3) (18TH
ED) (H. MONTGOMERY-MASSINGBERD, ED)
617(TLS):19JAN73-56
BURKHARD, A. GRILLPARZER IM AUSLAND.*
I.V. MORRIS, 220(GL&L):JAN72-167
P.K. WHITAKER, 133:1970/2&3-336
BURKHARD, M. - SEE SCHOTTEL, J.G.
BURKHART, C. CHARLOTTE BRONTË.
617(TLS):24AUG73-972
BURKHART, K.W. WOMEN IN PRISON.
L. OELSNER, 441:14OCT73-45
BURKHOLZ, H. THE SPANISH SOLDIER.
S. BLACKBURN, 441:28JAN73-7
BURKILL, T.A. THE EVOLUTION OF CHRISTIAN
THOUGHT.
H.B. TIMOTHY, 154:DEC71-854
BURKMAN, K.H. THE DRAMATIC WORLD OF
HAROLD PINTER.
A.P. HINCHLIFFE, 397(MD):FEB72-486
J. HURT, 301(JEGP):APR72-284
BURLAND, B. THE SAILOR AND THE FOX.*
617(TLS):14SEP73-1045
BURLEY, R. & F.C. CARRUTHERS. EDWARD
ELGAR.*
D. MC VEAGH, 415:NOV72-1086
BURLEY, W.J. DEATH IN A SALUBRIOUS
PLACE.
N. CALLENDAR, 441:13MAY73-39
617(TLS):23FEB73-219
BURLING, R. MAN'S MANY VOICES.
H. ROGERS, 320(CJL):FALL70-57
BURLING, R. PROTO-KAREN [TOGETHER WITH]
MATISOFF, J.A. LAHU AND PROTO-LOLO-
BURMESE. (A.L. BECKER, ED)
R.B. JONES, 293(JAST):NOV70-230
BÜRMANN, F. & J. MOREAU, EDS. NOUVELLES
POÉSIES FRANÇAISES.
R. AHRENS, 430(NS):DEC71-676
BURMEISTER, J. RUNNING SCARED.*
N. CALLENDAR, 441:23DEC73-16
BURN, M. OUT ON A LIMB.
617(TLS):16NOV73-1405
BURNET, J. L'AURORE DE LA PHILOSOPHIE
GRECQUE.
J. BERNHARDT, 542:APR-JUN71-239
BURNET, M. DOMINANT MAMMAL.*
P.B. MEDAWAR, 453:8MAR73-21
BURNETT, A.P. CATASTROPHE SURVIVED.*
B.M.W. KNOX, 122:OCT72-270
C. SEGAL, 124:APR-MAY72-275
E. SEGAL, 676(YR):SPRING72-452
BURNETT, B.G. POLITICAL GROUPS IN CHILE.
P. KELSO, 50(ARQ):AUTUMN71-281

BURNEY, C. MEMOIRS OF THE LIFE AND WRIT-
INGS OF THE ABATE METASTASIO.
J.A.W., 410(M&L):0CT72-448
BURNEY, F. THE JOURNALS AND LETTERS OF
FANNY BURNEY (MADAME D'ARBLAY). (VOL
3 ED BY J. HEMLOW, WITH P. BOUTILIER &
A. DOUGLAS; VOL 4 ED BY J. HEMLOW)
617(TLS):13JUL73-796
BURNFORD, S. ONE WOMAN'S ARCTIC.
617(TLS):16FEB73-190
BURNHAM, J. THE STRUCTURE OF ART.
J. BENTHALL, 592:JUL/AUG71-48
N. CALAS, 58:SEP/OCT71-27
H.P. RALEIGH, 290(JAAC):SUMMER71-541
BURNHAM, S. THE ART CROWD.
S. HUNTER, 441:25MAR73-5
C. LEHMANN-HAUPT, 441:27MAR73-49
BURNS, A. HISTORY OF NIGERIA. (8TH ED)
617(TLS):26JAN73-82
BURNS, E. THEATRICALITY.
617(TLS):1JUN73-622
BURNS, E. & T., EDS. SOCIOLOGY OF LIT-
ERATURE AND DRAMA.
617(TLS):11MAY73-537
BURNS, J.M. ROOSEVELT: THE SOLDIER OF
FREEDOM, 1940-45.*
H.E. BATEMAN, 50(ARQ):SPRING71-93
BURNS, R. AVEBURY.
617(TLS):9MAR73-270
BURNS, R. BURNS: POEMS AND SONGS. (J.
KINSLEY, ED)
D. HANNAH, 179(ES):AUG71-372
G.A.W., 581:MAR72-78
BURNS, R. THE POEMS AND SONGS OF ROBERT
BURNS.* (J. KINSLEY, ED)
D. HANNAH, 179(ES):AUG71-372
C. PRICE, 447(N&Q):FEB71-78
G.A.W., 581:MAR72-78
BURNSHAW, S. IN THE TERRIFIED RADIANCE.*
D. KENWORTHY, 31(ASCH):SUMMER73-514
R.B. SHAW, 491:SEP73-344
BURNSHAW, S. THE SEAMLESS WEB.*
C.S. BROWN, 131(CL):SUMMER72-277
C.M.R., 543:DEC70-337
BURRELL, M.C. WIDE OF THE TRUTH.
617(TLS):2FEB73-127
BURRIDGE, K. NEW HEAVEN, NEW EARTH.
L.G., 543:DEC70-338
BURROUGHS, P. THE CANADIAN CRISIS AND
BRITISH COLONIAL POLICY, 1828-1841.
617(TLS):9FEB73-159
BURROUGHS, P. ZEB.
A. BROYARD, 441:7AUG73-33
BURROUGHS, W., JR. KENTUCKY HAM.
R.P. BRICKNER, 441:29JUL73-5
A. BROYARD, 441:26JUN73-49
442(NY):20AUG73-91
BURROUGHS, W.S. EXTERMINATOR!
P. ADAMS, 61:SEP73-118
A.C.J. BERGMAN, 441:14OCT73-14
A. BROYARD, 441:21AUG73-27
442(NY):19NOV73-246
BURROW, J.A., ED. GEOFFREY CHAUCER.*
J. VOISINE, 549(RLC):JAN-MAR71-103
BURROW, J.A. RICARDIAN POETRY.
A.C. SPEARING, 111:2JUN72-177
R.M. WILSON, 175:AUTUMN71-96
R.M. WILSON, 402(MLR):JUL72-612
BURROW, J.W. - SEE VON HUMBOLDT, W.
BURROW, T. & M.B. EMENEAU. A DRAVIDIAN
ETYMOLOGICAL DICTIONARY. (SUPPLEMENT)
M. MAYRHOFER, 343:BAND13HEFT2-208
BURROWS, D., WITH R. GOTTESMAN & D.J.
NORDLOH - SEE HOWELLS, W.D.
BURROWS, J. LIKE AN EVENING GONE.
617(TLS):16NOV73-1407

BURSSENS, A. PROBLEMEN EN INVENTARISATIE
VAN DE VERBALE STRUCTUUR IN HET DHO
ALUR (NOORDOOST KONGO).*
J. KNAPPERT, 69:APR71-181
G.F. MEIER, 682(ZPSK):BAND24HEFT1/2-
135
BURSTON, W.H. JAMES MILL ON PHILOSOPHY
AND EDUCATION.
617(TLS):13JUL73-814
BURTON, A. THE CANAL BUILDERS.
617(TLS):16FEB73-183
BURTON, H. THE MORRO CASTLE.
P. ADAMS, 61:JUN73-124
BURTON, J. ANIMALS OF THE AFRICAN YEAR.
617(TLS):8JUN73-649
BURTON, M. THE SIXTH SENSE OF ANIMALS.
617(TLS):9FEB73-158
BURTON, N. & OTHERS - SEE MERTON, T.
BURTON, P. & J. LANE. NEW DIRECTIONS.
R. STACEY, 157:WINTER70-68
BURTON, R. THE LIFE AND DEATH OF WHALES.
617(TLS):18MAY73-565
BURTON, S.H. DEVON VILLAGES.
617(TLS):30MAR73-362
BURY, J.P.T. FRANCE: THE INSECURE
PEACE.
617(TLS):27APR73-465
BŮRZAKOVA, N. & OTHERS, COMPS. PŮTEVO-
DITEL NA TSENTRALNIIA DŮRZHAVEN
ISTORICHESKI ARKHIV.
T.A. MEININGER, 32:JUN72-504
BUSBY, R. PATTERN OF VIOLENCE.
617(TLS):3AUG73-911
BUSBY, R.J. A COMPANION GUIDE TO BRASSES
AND BRASS RUBBING.
617(TLS):13APR73-429
BUSCH, B.C. BRITAIN AND THE PERSIAN
GULF, 1894-1914.
R.G. LANDEN, 318(JAOS):APR-JUN71-336
BUSCH, F. I WANTED A YEAR WITHOUT FALL.
E. GLOVER, 565:VOL12#4-53
BUSCH, N. THE TAKEOVER.
M. LEVIN, 441:4MAR73-40
BUSCH, N.F. A CONCISE HISTORY OF JAPAN.
617(TLS):29JUN73-757
BUSH, D., J.E. SHAW & A.B. GIAMATTI, EDS.
VARIORUM COMMENTARY ON THE POEMS OF
JOHN MILTON.* (VOL 1)
J.W. BINNS, 402(MLR):JAN72-168
M.L. CLARKE, 123:JUN72-277
M.A. DI CESARE, 551(RENQ):WINTER71-587
I. SAMUEL, 401(MLQ):MAR72-78
639(VQR):SPRING71-LXV
BUSH, M.H. DORIS CAESAR.
D.T., 135:FEB71-139
BUSH, R. THE NATIONAL PARKS OF ENGLAND
AND WALES.
617(TLS):28DEC73-1595
BUSH, R. & J.B. MERIWETHER - SEE SIMMS,
W.G.
BUSH, V. PIECES OF THE ACTION.*
C.P. HASKINS, 639(VQR):WINTER71-141
BUSHELL, T.L. THE SAGE OF SALISBURY.
P. DUBOIS, 542(FR):APR-JUN71-239
BUSHMAN, R.L., ED. THE GREAT AWAKENING:
DOCUMENTS ON THE REVIVAL OF RELIGION,
1740-1745.
E.S. GAUSTAD, 656(WMQ):APR71-315
BUSI, F. L'ESTHÉTIQUE D'ANDRÉ SUARÈS.
W.T. STARR, 207(FR):FEB71-612
BUSIGNANI, A. GROPIUS.
617(TLS):7SEP73-1021
BUŠMIN, A.S. METODOLOGIČESKIE VOPROSY
LITERATUROVEDČESKIH ISLEDOVANIJ.
Z. KONSTANTINOVIĆ, 52:BAND5HEFT3-305
BUSST, A-J-L. - SEE BALLANCHE, P.S.
BUSTARD, R. SEA TURTLES.
617(TLS):11MAY73-537

BUTCHVAROV, P. THE CONCEPT OF KNOWLEDGE.*
    G. ENGLEBRETSEN, 154:SEP71-591
    M. STRATTON, 484(PPR):MAR72-431
BUTLER, B. A CHEYENNE LEGEND.
    617(TLS):9MAR73-270
BUTLER, C. NUMBER SYMBOLISM.
    H.N. DAVIES, 402(MLR):APR72-390
BUTLER, D. & M. PINTO-DUSCHINSKY. THE
    BRITISH GENERAL ELECTION OF 1970.
    R. BOARDMAN, 150(DR):WINTER71/72-594
BUTLER, F. THE STRANGE CRITICAL FORTUNES
    OF SHAKESPEARE'S "TIMON OF ATHENS."
    H.J. OLIVER, 570(SQ):WINTER70-90
BUTLER, G. A COFFIN FOR PANDORA.
    617(TLS):31AUG73-1007
BUTLER, H. TEN THOUSAND SAINTS.
    617(TLS):29JUN73-756
BUTLER, J. CABBAGETOWN DIARY.
    M. CZARNECKI, 648:OCT71-54
    M.J. EDWARDS, 102(CANL):WINTER72-91
BUTLER, J. THE GARBAGEMAN.*
    M.S. WILSON, 99:AUG73-32
BUTLER, S. CHARACTERS.* (C.W. DAVES, ED)
    A.H. DE QUEHEN, 627(UTQ):SPRING71-275
BUTLER, W. A GOD NOVEL.
    L.T. LEMON, 502(PRS):FALL71-268
BUTLER, W.E. THE SOVIET UNION AND THE
    LAW OF THE SEA.
    J.N. HAZARD, 32:MAR72-183
BUTLIN, M., ED. THE BLAKE-VARLEY SKETCH-
    BOOK OF 1819 IN THE COLLECTION OF
    M.D.E. CLAYTON-STAMM.*
    T. CROMBIE, 39:OCT70-319
    D. IRWIN, 90:JUN71-341
BUTLIN, M. WATERCOLOURS FROM THE TURNER
    BEQUEST, 1819-1845.*
    H.E. ROBERTS, 637(VS):SEP70-102
BUTOR, M. INTERVALLE. ILLUSTRATIONS III.
    617(TLS):3AUG73-911
BUTOR, M. LES MOTS DANS LA PEINTURE.
    J. KOLBERT, 207(FR):OCT70-205
    L. MARIN, 98:NOV70-909
BUTOR, M. RÉPERTOIRE III.
    J. DUBOIS, 556(RLV):1971/4-498
BUTOW, R.J.C. TOJO AND THE COMING OF THE
    WAR.
    R.L. BACKUS, 318(JAOS):JAN-MAR71-151
BUTT, J. POPE, DICKENS AND OTHERS.*
    (G. CARNAL, ED)
    S. MONOD, 189(EA):APR-JUN70-217
    C.J. RAWSON, 447(N&Q):JUL71-278
    M. WILDI, 179(ES):FEB71-87
BUTT, J. & I.F. CLARKE, EDS. THE VIC-
    TORIANS AND SOCIAL PROTEST.
    617(TLS):11MAY73-530
BUTTERFIELD, L.H. & M. FRIEDLAENDER, EDS.
    ADAMS FAMILY CORRESPONDENCE. (VOLS
    3&4)
    P. SHAW, 31(ASCH):AUTUMN73-686
BUTTERWORTH, E.A.S. THE TREE AT THE NAVEL
    OF THE EARTH.*
    J. FONTENROSE, 124:SEP71-26
    J.G. GRIFFITHS, 123:DEC72-430
BUTTERWORTH, W.E. STEVE BELLAMY.
    T.J. ROUNTREE, 9(ALAR):OCT70-288
BUTTI, E.A. L'AUTOMA - L'INCANTESIMO.
    (G. MANACORDA, ED)
    M.P., 228(GSLI):VOL147FASC460-635
BUTTKE, K. GESETZMÄSSIGKEITEN DER WORT-
    FOLGE IM RUSSISCHEN.
    H.W. SCHALLER, 430(NS):APR71-225
BUTTS, R.E., ED. WILLIAM WHEWELL'S
    THEORY OF SCIENTIFIC METHOD.
    H.T. WALSH, 486:JUN70-314
BUTTS, R.E. & J.W. DAVIS, EDS. THE
    METHODOLOGICAL HERITAGE OF NEWTON.
    I. BULWER-THOMAS, 479(PHQ):JUL71-267
    R.N.D. MARTIN, 483:OCT71-366 [CONT]

[CONTINUING]
    W. RÖD, 53(AGP):BAND53HEFT3-314
    617(TLS):1JUN73-615
BUTWELL, R. U NU OF BURMA.
    J. GUYOT, 293(JAST):NOV70-229
BUXTON, J. ELIZABETHAN TASTE.
    J.B. FORT, 189(EA):OCT-DEC70-438
BUXTON, J. RELIGION AND HEALING IN MAN-
    DARI.
    617(TLS):28DEC73-1578
BUYSSENS, E. LA COMMUNICATION ET L'AR-
    TICULATION LINGUISTIQUE.
    M. KOMÁREK, 353:OCT71-111
BUYSSENS, E. LES DEUX ASPECTIFS DE LA
    CONJUGAISON ANGLAISE AU XXE SIÈCLE.*
    R. HUDDLESTON, 361:VOL27#4-382
    I. SIMON, 556(RLV):1971/3-359
    A.R. TELLIER, 189(EA):JAN-MAR70-87
BUYSSENS, E. VÉRITÉ ET LANGUE.
    M-C. DELVAUX, 154:DEC71-861
    M. SANDMANN, 545(RPH):MAY72-471
BUZZATI, D. CRONACHE TERRESTRI. (D.
    PORZIO, ED)
    617(TLS):16FEB73-186
BYE, E. SPINN, MITT HJUL.
    E. HASLUND, 270:VOL22#2-47
BYLINKIN, N.P. & OTHERS. ISTORIIA SOV-
    ETSKOI ARKHITEKTURY, 1918-1957.
    S.F. STARR, 576:MAY71-172
BYNUM, T.W. - SEE FREGE, G.
BYRNE, E.F. PROBABILITY AND OPINION.
    I. THOMAS, 486:DEC71-616
BYRNE, E.F. & E.A. MAZIARZ. HUMAN BEING
    AND BEING HUMAN.
    J.L. CARAFIDES, 484(PPR):DEC71-283
    L. THIRY, 154:MAR71-160
BYRNE, F.J. IRISH KINGS AND HIGH-KINGS.
    617(TLS):28SEP73-1107
LORD BYRON. BYRON'S HEBREW MELODIES.
    (T.L. ASHTON, ED)
    F.W. BATESON, 453:22FEB73-32
LORD BYRON. BYRON'S LETTERS AND JOURNALS.
    (VOLS 1&2) (L.A. MARCHAND, ED)
    P. ADAMS, 61:DEC73-138
    C. RICKS, 362:27SEP73-415
    617(TLS):19OCT73-1265
LORD BYRON. DON JUAN. (T.G. STEFFAN,
    E. STEFFAN & W.W. PRATT, EDS)
    617(TLS):18MAY73-558


CABALLERO, C.F.S.F. - SEE UNDER FERNÁNDEZ
    CABALLERO, C.F.S.F.
CABALLERO BONALD, J.M., ED. NARRATIVA
    CUBANA DE LA REVOLUCIÓN.
    J.C. HANCOCK, 399(MLJ):APR71-258
CABALLERO CALDERÓN, E. EL NUEVO PRÍNCIPE.
    B. DULSEY, 238:MAR71-206
CABANNE, P. DIALOGUES WITH MARCEL DU-
    CHAMP.*
    G. EAGER, 651(WHR):WINTER72-87
    R. LEBOWITZ, 58:DEC71/JAN72-24
CABOCHE, L. - SEE PRIESTLEY, J.B.
CABOT, R. THE JOSHUA TREE.
    639(VQR):WINTER71-VIII
CACCAMO, D. ERETICI ITALIANI IN MORAVIA,
    POLONIA, TRANSILVANIA (1558-1611).
    A.J. SCHUTTE, 551(RENQ):WINTER71-532
CACCINI, G. LE NUOVE MUSICHE. (H.W.
    HITCHCOCK, ED)
    W.V. PORTER, 317:FALL72-483
CACERES, B. LE BOURG DE NOS VACANCES.
    M.G. ROSE, 207(FR):FEB71-635
CADALSO, J. NOCHES LÚGUBRES. (J. ARCE,
    ED)
    J.H.R. POLT, 202(FMOD):NOV70/FEB71-
    161

CADELL, E. ROYAL SUMMONS.
M. LEVIN, 441:7JAN73-35
CADOUX, R. VOUS ET MOI.
R.J. FULTON, 207(FR):APR71-998
CADWALLADER, S. & J. OHR. WHOLE EARTH
COOKBOOK.
617(TLS):19OCT73-1289
CADY, E.H. THE LIGHT OF COMMON DAY.
W.M. GIBSON, 579(SAQ):SUMMER72-442
R.S. MOORE, 27(AL):MAY72-338
CADY, E.H. - SEE HOWELLS, W.D.
CAESAR. DE BELLO GALLICO VI. (E.C.
KENNEDY, ED)
R. GLEN, 123:MAR72-98
CAFFERTY, B. SPASSKY'S 100 BEST GAMES.
617(TLS):9MAR73-277
CAFFREY, K. GREAT EMIGRATIONS 3.
617(TLS):21SEP73-1093
CAGE, J. M.
D. HENAHAN, 441:23SEP73-34
CAHEN, C. DER ISLAM. (VOL 1)
I.M. LAPIDUS, 318(JAOS):OCT-DEC71-538
"CAHIERS DADA-SURRÉALISME NO. 3."
H. BÉHAR, 535(RHL):JUL-AUG71-719
"CAHIERS DU MONDE HISPANIQUE ET LUSO-
BRÉSILIEN." (NO. 14)
B. MALMBERG, 596(SL):VOL25#1-65
CAHILL, S. & T. A LITERARY GUIDE TO IRE-
LAND.
R.M. KAIN, 329(JJQ):SUMMER73-460
CAHILL, S. & M.F. COOPER, EDS. THE
URBAN READER.
639(VQR):AUTUMN71-CLXXXVI
CAHN, S.M. FATE, LOGIC, AND TIME.*
P. FITZGERALD, 486:MAR71-122
CAHNMAN, W.J. & R. HEBERLE - SEE TOEN-
NIES, F.
CAILLOIS, R. L'ÉCRITURE DES PIERRES.
R. DROGUET, 98:AUG-SEP70-782
CAIN, C.W., GENERAL ED. AIRCRAFT IN
PROFILE. (VOL 2)
617(TLS):9FEB73-161
CAIN, G. BLUESCHILD BABY.
R. TRICKETT, 676(YR):AUTUMN71-121
CAIN, M.E. SOCIETY AND THE POLICEMAN'S
ROLE.
617(TLS):2MAR73-242
CAINE, S. BRITISH UNIVERSITIES.
R.C. ELLSWORTH, 529(QQ):SUMMER71-340
CAIRD, E. THE CRITICAL PHILOSOPHY OF
IMMANUEL KANT.
R. MALTER, 342:BAND61HEFT3-420
CAIRD, J. MURDER REMOTE.
N. CALLENDAR, 441:4FEB73-16
CAIRNS, D. RESPONSES.
M. STEINBERG, 441:7OCT73-40
617(TLS):26OCT73-1323
CAIRNS, F. GENERIC COMPOSITION IN GREEK
AND ROMAN POETRY.
617(TLS):12JAN73-28
CAIRNS, H., ED. THE LIMITS OF ART. (VOL
1)
P.M. BROWN, 123:MAR72-148
CAIRNS, H., ED. THE LIMITS OF ART. (VOL
3)
L.R. FURST, 220(GL&L):APR72-279
CAIZERGUES, P. - SEE APOLLINAIRE, G.
CALAFERTE, L. PORTRAIT DE L'ENFANT.
N.L. GOODRICH, 207(FR):OCT70-171
CALAM, J. PARSONS & PEDAGOGUES.
W.G. MC LOUGHLIN, 432(NEQ):SEP71-491
CALARCO, N.J. TRAGIC BEING.*
R.B. PALMER, 319:OCT73-575
M. TAYLOR, 255(HAB):WINTER70-49
CALDARINI, E. - SEE FÉNELON, F.
CALDER, R. LEONARDO AND THE AGE OF THE
EYE.
M.V. ALPER, 58:APR72-27

CALDERÓN, B.I. LA DOCTRINA GRAMATICAL DE
BELLO.
A.J. NARO, 206:NOV70-575
CALDERÓN, E.C. - SEE UNDER CABALLERO
CALDERÓN, E.
CALDERÓN DE LA BARCA, P. EL ALCALDE DE
ZALAMEA/L'ALCADE DE ZALAMEA. (R. MAR-
RAST, ED)
C.A. JONES, 240(HR):OCT71-453
CALDERÓN DE LA BARCA, P. PEDRO CALDERÓN
DE LA BARCA: LIFE IS A DREAM. (E.
HONIG, TRANS)
E.M. MALINAK, 399(MLJ):APR71-259
CALDERÓN DE LA BARCA, P. EL GRAN DUQUE
DE CANDIA. (G. SIEBENMANN, ED)
M. FRANZBACH, 224(GRM):BAND21HEFT4-
473
CALDERÓN DE LA BARCA, P. LA HIJA DEL
AIRE.* (G. EDWARDS, ED)
M. WILSON, 86(BHS):APR72-187
CALDERÓN DE LA BARCA, P. EL PLEITO MAT-
RIMONIAL DEL CUERPO Y DEL ALMA. (M.
ENGELBERT, ED)
J. HAHN, 400(MLN):MAR71-305
CALDERÓN DE LA BARCA, P. TAN LARGO ME LO
FIÁIS. (X.A. FERNÁNDEZ, ED)
L.C. PÉREZ, 593:FALL72-283
CALDERWOOD, J.L. SHAKESPEARIAN METADRAMA.
R.A. FOAKES, 175:AUTUMN71-98
B. KURTH, 376:OCT71-132
CALDWELL, E. ANNETTE.
M. LEVIN, 441:4NOV73-81
CALDWELL, H. MACHADO DE ASSIS.*
O. FERNÁNDEZ, 399(MLJ):APR71-255
J.C. KINNEAR, 86(BHS):JAN72-106
CALDWELL, J.C. AFRICAN RURAL-URBAN
MIGRATION.
J.W. GREGORY, 69:OCT70-400
CALDWELL, M. & LEK TAN. CAMBODIA IN THE
SOUTHEAST ASIAN WAR.
617(TLS):12OCT73-1235
CALHOUN, T.O. & J.M. POTTER - SEE MARVELL,
A.
CALÍ, P. ALLEGORY AND VISION IN DANTE
AND LANGLAND.
R.D.S. JACK, 402(MLR):APR72-396
CALISHER, H. EAGLE EYE.
P. ADAMS, 61:NOV73-128
F. LEVY, 441:11NOV73-38
442(NY):12NOV73-217
CALISHER, H. QUEENIE.
P.M. SPACKS, 249(HUDR):SPRING72-163
CALKINS, F. JACKSON HOLE.
E. WEEKS, 61:JUL73-102
CALLAGHAN, C.A. BODEGA MIWOK DICTIONARY.
G.F. MEIER, 682(ZPSK):BAND24HEFT5-441
CALLAGHAN, J. A HOUSE DIVIDED.
M. DEAS, 362:1NOV73-602
617(TLS):7SEP73-1029
CALLAGHAN, M. STRANGE FUGITIVE.
B. MITCHELL, 296:FALL73-112
CALLAHAN, D. ABORTION.
J.V. DOLAN, 613:SUMMER71-294
R.J. GERBER, 185:JAN72-137
CALLAHAN, R. THE EAST INDIA COMPANY AND
ARMY REFORM, 1783-1798.
617(TLS):8JUN73-653
CALLAHAN, S. - SEE BOURKE-WHITE, M.
CALLAN, R.J. MIGUEL ANGEL ASTURIAS.
T.B. IRVING, 263:APR-JUN72-172
D.L. SHAW, 402(MLR):APR72-449
E.R. SKINNER, 238:SEP71-604
CALLEBAT, L. SERMO COTIDIANUS DANS LES
MÉTAMORPHOSES D'APULÉE.*
A. ERNOUT, 555:VOL45FASC1-177
P.G. WALSH, 123:MAR72-128

56

CALLEO, D.P. & B. ROWLAND. AMERICA AND
THE WORLD POLITICAL ECONOMY.
R.L. HEILBRONER, 453:29NOV73-31
CALLISON, B. DAWN ATTACK.
M. LEVIN, 441:8APR73-33
CALLOT, E. L'INSTITUTION PHILOSOPHIQUE.
G. POTVIN, 154:JUN71-395
CALLOW, J.T. KINDRED SPIRITS.
A. WALLACH, 56:SPRING70-75
CALLUS, D.A. & R.W. HUNT - SEE BLUND, J.
CALMER, N. THE AVIMA AFFAIR.
N. CALLENDAR, 441:8JUL73-25
CALMEYER, P. DATIERTE BRONZEN AUS LURIS-
TAN UND KIRMANSHAH.
R. GHIRSHMAN, 57:VOL33#1/2-145
CALOGERO, G. LEZIONI DI FILOSOFIA.
(VOL 3)
M. RIESER, 319:OCT73-574
CALOGERO, G. STORIA DELLA LOGICA ANTICA.
(VOL 1)
E. NAMER, 542:APR-JUN70-231
CALVIN, J. A HARMONY OF THE GOSPELS
MATTHEW, MARK AND LUKE. (D.W. & T.F.
TORRANCE, EDS)
617(TLS):27JUL73-882
CALVIN, J. THREE FRENCH TREATISES.
(F.M. HIGMAN, ED)
D. COLEMAN, 208(FS):JUL72-319
M. SOULIÉ, 535(RHL):JUL-AUG71-690
CALVINO, I. IL BARONE RAMPANTE. (J.R.
WOODHOUSE, ED)
J.H. POTTER, 276:SUMMER71-278
CALVINO, I. IL CASTELLO DEI DESTINI IN-
CROCIATI.
617(TLS):14DEC73-1529
CALVINO, I. LE CITTÀ INVISIBILI.
617(TLS):9FEB73-140
CALVO, B. THE POEMS OF BONIFACIO CALVO.
(W.D. HORAN, ED)
F.M. CHAMBERS, 545(RPH):MAY72-451
CALVO, J.M.C. - SEE UNDER CASTRO Y CALVO,
J.M.
CALVO, L.N. - SEE UNDER NOVÁS CALVO, L.
CAM, H.M., ED. YEAR BOOKS OF EDWARD II.
(VOL 27, PTS 1&2)
J.M.W. BEAN, 589:JUL72-519
CAMACHO, G. LATIN AMERICA.
617(TLS):14DEC73-1532
CAMAJ, M. LA PARLATA ALBANESE DI GRECI.
S.E. MANN, 575(SEER):JUL72-450
CAMARIANO-CIORAN, A. ACADEMIILE DOMNEŞTI
DIN BUCUREŞTI ŞI IAŞI.
E.M. WALLNER, 182:VOL24#13/14-513
CAMBON, G. DANTE'S CRAFT.*
I. BRANDEIS, 131(CL):WINTER72-85
R. DOMBROWSKI, 405(MP):AUG71-59
J.M. FERRANTE, 551(RENQ):SPRING71-49
DE CAMBRAI, A. - SEE UNDER ALARD DE CAM-
BRAI
"CAMBRIDGE ANCIENT HISTORY." (3RD ED)
(VOL 1, PT 1)
J. BOARDMAN, 123:DEC72-379
CAMERANA, G. POESIE. (G. FINZI, ED)
M.P., 228(GSLI):VOL147FASC460-635
CAMERON, A. AGATHIAS.*
R.C. MC CAIL, 123:JUN72-205
CAMERON, A. CLAUDIAN.*
J.W. EADIE, 124:SEP71-29
P.G. WALSH, 123:DEC72-351
CAMERON, A. THE IDENTITY OF OEDIPUS THE
KING.*
J. PERADOTTO, 121(CJ):FEB-MAR72-282
CAMERON, A. POETRY AND PROPAGANDA AT THE
COURT OF HONORIUS.
P. COURCELLE, 555:VOL45FASC2-364
CAMERON, A. PORPHYRIUS THE CHARIOTEER.
617(TLS):10AUG73-932

CAMERON, A., R. FRANK & J. LEYERLE, EDS.
COMPUTERS AND OLD ENGLISH CONCORDANCES.*
R.D., 179(ES):JUN71-302
R.T. FARRELL, 382(MAE):1972/3-293
CAMERON, D. CONVERSATIONS WITH CANADIAN
NOVELISTS.
J.G. MOSS, 296:FALL73-115
CAMERON, I. MAGELLAN AND THE FIRST CIR-
CUMNAVIGATION OF THE WORLD.
W. BEAUCHAMP, 441:23DEC73-10
CAMERON, J. & W.A. DODD. SOCIETY,
SCHOOLS AND PROGRESS.
S. MILBURN, 69:JUL71-257
CAMERON, J.M. VICTORIAN PHOTOGRAPHS OF
FAMOUS MEN & FAIR WOMEN. (REV) (T.
POWELL, ED)
H. KRAMER, 441:2DEC73-4
CAMERON, K. - SEE DE RIVAUDEAU, A.
CAMERON, K.M. & T.J.C. HOFFMAN. THE
THEATRICAL RESPONSE.
E. ARGENT, 157:SPRING70-63
CAMERON, K.N. HUMANITY AND SOCIETY.
617(TLS):16NOV73-1404
CAMERON, K.N., ED. SHELLEY AND HIS CIR-
CLE, 1773-1822.* (VOLS 3&4)
J.R. MAC GILLIVRAY, 627(UTQ):FALL70-73
N. ROGERS, 78(BC):AUTUMN71-400
N. ROGERS, 541(RES):NOV71-502
C. WOODRING, 191(ELN):SEP71(SUPP)-53
CAMERON, R. VICE-ROYALTIES OF THE WEST.
T. CROMBIE, 39:APR71-344
CAMMANN, A. DEUTSCHE VOLKSMÄRCHEN AUS
RUSSLAND UND RUMÄNIEN.
H. LIXFELD, 196:BAND12HEFT1-98
CAMP, J., X.J. KENNEDY & K. WALDROP, EDS.
PEGASUS DESCENDING.*
42(AR):FALL71-441
CAMPANELLA, A.P., COMP. GIUSEPPE GARI-
BALDI E LA TRADIZIONE GARIBALDINA.
D. CARNEIRO, 263:OCT-DEC72-416
CAMPBELL, A. CHARTERS OF ROCHESTER.
617(TLS):5OCT73-1196
CAMPBELL, A. SEVEN STATES OF CONSCIOUS-
NESS.
617(TLS):21SEP73-1080
CAMPBELL, A. - SEE AETHELWULF
CAMPBELL, B., ED. SEXUAL SELECTION AND
THE DESCENT OF MAN 1871-1971.
617(TLS):7SEP73-1030
CAMPBELL, B. 35 YEARS ON THE JOB.
617(TLS):30NOV73-1485
CAMPBELL, C. VITRUVIUS BRITANNICUS OR
THE BRITISH ARCHITECT.
617(TLS):23FEB73-216
CAMPBELL, D. THE BRANCH OF DODONA AND
OTHER POEMS 1969-1970.
K.L. GOODWIN, 381:SEP71-371
S.E. LEE, 581:1971/3-227
CAMPBELL, J.C. FRENCH INFLUENCE AND THE
RISE OF ROUMANIAN NATIONALISM.
E. TURCZYNSKI, 32:DEC72-927
CAMPBELL, J.F. THE FOREIGN AFFAIRS FUDGE
FACTORY.
R.W. LEOPOLD, 639(VQR):AUTUMN71-608
CAMPBELL, J.W. THE BEST OF J.W. CAMPBELL.
617(TLS):18MAY73-562
CAMPBELL, K. BODY AND MIND.*
F. JACKSON, 63:MAY72-77
CAMPBELL, K. THUNDER ON SUNDAY.*
442(NY):17MAR73-132
CAMPBELL, M. CLOUD-WALKING.
K.M. BRIGGS, 203:AUTUMN71-253
CAMPBELL, O.J. & E.G. QUINN, EDS. A
SHAKESPEARE ENCYCLOPAEDIA.*
J.H.P. PAFFORD, 447(N&Q):OCT71-399
CAMPBELL, O.J., A. ROTHSCHILD & S.
VAUGHAN - SEE SHAKESPEARE, W.

57

CAMPBELL, R.N.  NOUN SUBSTITUTES IN MOD-
ERN THAI.*
  S. EGEROD, 361:VOL26#3-333
VON CAMPENHAUSEN, H.  THE FORMATION OF
THE CHRISTIAN BIBLE.
  617(TLS):29JUN73-755
CAMPION, E.  AMBROSIA.  (J. SIMONS, ED &
TRANS)
  568(SCN):FALL-WINTER72-82
DE CAMPOS, D.R. - SEE UNDER REDIG DE
CAMPOS, D.
CAMPS, F.E.  CAMPS ON CRIME.
  617(TLS):26OCT73-1307
CAMPS, W.A.  AN INTRODUCTION TO VIRGIL'S
"AENEID."*
  H.H. HUXLEY, 487:SPRING71-87
  S. VIARRE, 555:VOL45FASC1-170
CAMPTON, D.  ON STAGE AGAIN.
  A. RENDLE, 157:SPRING70-71
"CAMPUS AND FORUM: THIRD ANNUAL REVIEW,
1968-69."
  R.C. ELLSWORTH, 529(QQ):SUMMER71-340
CAMUS, A.  LA CHUTE.  (R. MULHAUSER, M.
KUPERSMITH & J. LUSSEYRAN, EDS)
  E.S. BROOK, 207(FR):MAR71-822
CAMUS, J-P.  HOMÉLIES DES ÉTATS GÉNÉRAUX
(1614-1615).  (J. DESCRAINS, ED)
  R. ZUBER, 535(RHL):JUL-AUG71-693
CANCIANI, F.  BRONZI ORIENTALI E ORIEN-
TALIZZANTI A CRETA NELL'VIII E VII
SEC. A.C.
  J. BOARDMAN, 54:SEP71-394
CÂNDEA, V. - SEE CANTEMIR, D.
CANGIOTTI, G.  PÌO BAROJA "OSSERVATORE"
DEL COSTUME ITALIANO.
  W. KRÖMER, 52:BAND6HEFT1-116
CANNING, J., ED.  GREAT EUROPEANS.
  617(TLS):27JUL73-884
CANNING, V.  THE RAINBIRD PATTERN.*
  N. CALLENDAR, 441:18MAR73-41
CANNON, G. - SEE JONES, W.
CANNON, J.  PARLIAMENTARY REFORM 1640-
1832.
  617(TLS):3AUG73-906
CANNON, M.  AN AUSTRALIAN CAMERA 1851-
1914.
  617(TLS):21DEC73-1573
CANNON, O. & J.R.L. ANDERSON.  THE ROAD
FROM WIGAN PIER.
  P. WHITEHEAD, 362:29MAR73-423
  617(TLS):13APR73-417
CANNON-BROOKES, P. & C.  GREAT BUILDINGS
OF THE WORLD: BAROQUE CHURCHES.
  J. LEES-MILNE, 39:MAY70-404
CANO, J.L.  LA POESÍA DE LA GENERACIÓN
DEL 27.*
  B. GICOVATE, 238:SEP71-598
CANO, J.L. - SEE DE CIENFUEGOS, N.A.
CANTACUZINO, S.  EUROPEAN DOMESTIC ARCHI-
TECTURE.
  46:JAN70-84
CANTELLI, G.  TEOLOGIA E ATEISMO.
  C. MARTELLI, 548(RCSF):OCT-DEC70-462
CANTEMIR, D.  DIVANUL.  (V. CÂNDEA, ED)
  M.H. IMPEY, 32:DEC72-926
CANTERA, J.  LA ENSEÑANZA DEL FRANCÉS A
HISPANOHABLANTES.
  G. SENZIER, 202(FMOD):NOV71/FEB72-142
CANTONI, A.  IL PROBLEMA TEILHARD DE
CHARDIN.
  E. NAMER, 542:OCT-DEC71-518
CANTOR, N.F. & P.L. KLEIN.  MEDIEVAL
THOUGHT.
  J.B., 543:DEC70-338
CANTOR, N.F. & P.L. KLEIN, EDS.  PLATO
AND ARISTOTLE.
  J.J.R., 543:JUN71-761

CANTÙ, C.  ROMANZO AUTOBIOGRAFICO.  (A.
BOZZOLI, ED)
  P.Z., 228(GSLI):VOL148FASC461-155
CANU, G.  CONTES MOSSI ACTUELS.
  T.H. PETERSON, 69:OCT71-347
CANZONERI, R.  BARBED WIRE AND OTHER
STORIES.
  J.L. HALIO, 598(SOR):SPRING73-455
ČAPEK, M.  THE PHILOSOPHICAL IMPACT OF
CONTEMPORARY PHYSICS.  (NEW ED)
  L.E. ROSE, 484(PPR):MAR72-428
CAPELL, A.  A SURVEY OF NEW GUINEA LAN-
GUAGES.
  K.J. FRANKLIN, 361:VOL25#3-333
CAPELLE, J. & G.  LA FRANCE EN DIRECT I.
  D. SCHLESINGER, 207(FR):MAR71-816
CAPITAN, W.H. & D.D. MERRILL, EDS.  META-
PHYSICS AND EXPLANATION.
  C. GINET, 482(PHR):OCT71-525
CAPIZZI, A.  SOCRATE E I PERSONAGGI FIL-
OSOFI DI PLATONE.
  F. LASSERRE, 182:VOL24#19/20-751
CAPLAN, H.  OF ELOQUENCE.*
  M. WINTERBOTTOM, 123:DEC72-363
CAPLAN, L.  LAND AND SOCIAL CHANGE IN
EAST NEPAL.
  F.J. MOORE, 293(JAST):NOV70-221
CAPONIGSI, A.R. - SEE "CONTEMPORARY SPAN-
ISH PHILOSOPHY"
CAPOTE, T.  THE DOGS BARK.
  L. HARRIS, 441:28OCT73-35
CAPOVILLA, G.  PRAEHOMERICA ET PRAEITAL-
ICA.
  A. SACCONI, 121(CJ):APR-MAY72-369
CAPOVILLA, L.F. - SEE POPE JOHN XXIII
CAPPARELLI, V.  IL TENORE DI VITA PITA-
GORICO ED IL PROBLEMA DELLA "OMOIOSIS."
  E. NAMER, 542:JAN-MAR70-97
CAPPUCCIO, C., ED.  CRITICI DELL'ETÀ
ROMANTICA.  (2ND ED)
  A.M. MUTTERLE, 228(GSLI):VOL147FASC
  457-145
  O.R., 191(ELN):SEP71(SUPP)-164
CAPRA, F.  THE NAME ABOVE THE TITLE.
  200:AUG-SEP71-433
CAPRETZ, P.J. - SEE PAGNOL, M.
DE CAPUA, A.G. & E.A. PHILIPPSON - SEE
"BENJAMIN NEUKIRCHS ANTHOLOGIE"  (VOL 2)
CAPUT, J. & J-P.  DICTIONNAIRE DES VERBES
FRANÇAIS.
  G. SCHWEIG, 430(NS):AUG71-443
  N.C.W. SPENCE, 208(FS):OCT72-496
CARADEC, F.  VIE DE RAYMOND ROUSSEL.
  617(TLS):13APR73-415
CARASSUS, E.  BARRÈS ET SA FORTUNE LIT-
TÉRAIRE.
  R. SAMUEL, 402(MLR):APR72-425
  205(FMLS):APR71-191
CARASSUS, E.  LE SNOBISME ET LES LETTRES
FRANÇAISES DE PAUL BOURGET À MARCEL
PROUST (1884-1914).
  S. JEUNE, 557(RSH):JAN-MAR70-174
CARATINI, R. - SEE "BORDAS ENCYCLOPÉDIE"
CARBALLIDO, E.  THE GOLDEN THREAD AND
OTHER PLAYS.  (M.S. PEDEN, ED & TRANS)
  M.F. HODAPP, 649(WAL):SPRING71-69
  L.F. LYDAY, 263:OCT-DEC72-425
CARBALLIDO, E.  THE NORTHER.*
  J.D. MC KEE, 649(WAL):SPRING70-65
CARBALLO, E., ED.  NARRATIVA MEXICANA DE
HOY.
  R.M. REEVE, 238:MAY71-403
CARBONARA NADDEI, M.  SPERMATA, NOYS,
CHRÈMATA NELLA DOTTRINA DI ANASSAGORA.
  C. MUGLER, 555:VOL45FASC1-150
CARDINAL, P.  LE MUTANT.
  M. NAUDIN, 207(FR):DEC70-414

CARDINAL, R. OUTSIDER ART.
 C. ROBINS, 441:8APR73-7
 617(TLS):16MAR73-284
CARDINAL, R. & R.S. SHORT. SURREALISM.*
 G. MELLY, 592:JUL-AUG70-56
CARDONA, G. ON HAPLOLOGY IN INDO-EURO-
 PEAN.
 A. BAMMESBERGER, 260(IF):BAND75-282
 R.S.P. BEEKES, 361:VOL26#2-210
CARDONE, D.A. L'OZIO, LA CONTEMPLAZIONE,
 IL GINOCO, LA TECNICA, L'ANARCHISMO.
 R.R., 154:JUN70-129
CARDUCCI, G. LETTERE DI GIOSUÈ CARDUCCI
 A MARIO MENGHINI. (T. BARBIERI, ED)
 M.F., 228(GSLI):VOL148FASC464-627
CARDUCCI, G. POESIE SCELTE. (P. TREVES,
 ED)
 M. FUBINI, 228(GSLI):VOL147FASC457-
 153
CARDUNER, J. LA CRÉATION ROMANESQUE CHEZ
 MALRAUX.*
 K. BIEBER, 454:FALL71-89
CARDWELL, D.S.L. THE ORGANISATION OF
 SCIENCE IN ENGLAND.
 617(TLS):11MAY73-531
CARDWELL, R.A. BLASCO IBÁÑEZ: LA BARRACA.
 617(TLS):5OCT73-1191
CARELESS, J.M.S., ED. COLONISTS AND CAN-
 ADIENS 1760-1867.*
 W.L. MORTON, 150(DR):WINTER71/72-602
CAREY, G.G. MARYLAND FOLKLORE AND FOLK-
 LIFE.
 D.J. WINSLOW, 292(JAF):OCT-DEC71-461
CAREY, J., ED. ANDREW MARVELL.*
 P. LEGOUIS, 189(EA):JAN-MAR71-92
 J. VOISINE, 549(RLC):JAN-MAR71-103
CAREY, J. MILTON.
 E. SAILLENS, 189(EA):OCT-DEC70-446
CAREY, J. THE VIOLENT EFFIGY.
 J. BAYLEY, 362:22NOV73-714
CAREY, J. - SEE HOGG, J.
CAREY, J. & A. FOWLER - SEE MILTON, J.
CARGO, R.T., ED. BAUDELAIRE CRITICISM
 1950-1967.*
 W.T. BANDY, 405(MP):MAY71-395
 C. PICHOIS, 535(RHL):MAR-APR71-313
CARILE, A. LA CRONACHISTICA VENEZIANA
 (SECOLI XIII-XVI) DI FRONTE ALLA SPAR-
 TIZIONE DELLA ROMANIA NEL 1204.
 F.C. LANE, 589:APR72-292
CARILE, P. LA "COMÉDIE DES ACADÉMISTES"
 DI SAINT-EVREMOND E IL CONTRASTO
 ESORDIO DELL'ACCADEMIA FRANCESE NELLA
 SATIRA LETTERARIA DEL TEMPO.
 H.T. BARNWELL, 208(FS):APR72-194
 J-P. COLLINET, 535(RHL):MAR-APR71-298
CARLETON, W.G. TECHNOLOGY AND HUMANISM.*
 639(VQR):SUMMER71-CXXXVII
CARLING, F. GJESTEN.
 E. STRAUME, 270:VOL21#2-141
CARLISLE, C.J. SHAKESPEARE FROM THE
 GREENROOM.*
 N. DENNY, 541(RES):AUG71-341
 R.A. FOAKES, 175:AUTUMN70-98
 R. WARREN, 447(N&Q):DEC71-474
CARLISLE, H. THE ROUGH-HEWN TABLE.
 J. KESSLER, 491:FEB73-292
CARLO, A.M. - SEE UNDER MILLARES CARLO, A.
DE CARLO, G. URBINO.
 J. GLOWCZEWSKI, 505:OCT71-134
CARLSON, C. SCIENTIFIC WORKS, ETC.
 R. WILLMOT, 296:FALL73-98
CARLSON, H.G. - SEE LAMM, M.
CARLSON, J. NO NEUTRAL GROUND.
 P. ADAMS, 61:APR73-128
 441:16SEP73-14
 442(NY):5MAY73-151
 617(TLS):27JUL73-850

CARLSON, L.H. - SEE GREENWOOD, J. & H.
 BARROW
CARLSSON, L. LE TYPE "C'EST LE MEILLEUR
 LIVRE QU'IL AIT JAMAIS ÉCRIT" EN ESPAG-
 NOL, EN ITALIEN ET EN FRANÇAIS.
 H. BONNARD, 209(FM):JAN71-72
CARLTON, C. A DESCRIPTIVE SYNTAX OF THE
 OLD ENGLISH CHARTERS.*
 C.J.E. BALL, 541(RES):NOV71-467
CARLTON, C. LA CORRESPONDANCE DE FLAU-
 BERT.*
 J.R. WILLIAMS, 207(FR):DEC70-450
CARLYLE, T. REMINISCENCES. (C.E. NOR-
 TON, ED)
 K. MILLER, 362:15MAR73-346
CARLYLE, T. & J.W. THE COLLECTED LETTERS
 OF THOMAS AND JANE WELSH CARLYLE.*
 (VOLS 1-4) (C.R. SANDERS, ED)
 W.S. DOWDEN, 301(JEGP):APR72-271
CARMACK, R.M. QUICHEAN CIVILIZATION.
 617(TLS):9NOV73-1374
CARMEN, A. & H. MOODY. ABORTION COUNSEL-
 ING AND SOCIAL CHANGE.
 J.E. BRODY, 441:8AUG73-29
DEL CARMEN, P.E.D. - SEE UNDER EULOGIO DE
 LA VIRGEN DEL CARMEN, P.
CARMICHAEL, H. NAKED TO THE GRAVE.
 N. CALLENDAR, 441:1APR73-34
CARMODY, F.J. PERCEVAL LE GALLOIS.
 J. GILLIS, 402(MLR):OCT72-882
CARNAL, G. - SEE BUTT, J.
CARNAP, R. THE LOGICAL STRUCTURE OF THE
 WORLD AND PSEUDO-PROBLEMS IN PHILOSO-
 PHY.*
 A. WEDBERG, 316:SEP71-551
CARNE, E-M. DIE FRAUENGESTALTEN BEI
 HARTMANN VON AUE.
 D.H. GREEN, 402(MLR):APR72-466
CARNEADES. KARNEADES, "FRAGMENTE, TEXT
 UND KOMMENTAR." (B. WIŚNIEWSKI, ED)
 G.B. KERFERD, 123:DEC72-410
CARNEGY, P. FAUST AS MUSICIAN.
 617(TLS):23NOV73-1421
CARNEIRO, D. BRASÍLIA E O PROBLEMA DA
 FEDERAÇÃO BRASILEIRA.
 R.M. LEVINE, 263:JAN-MAR72-51
CARNICELLI, D.D. - SEE PETRARCH
CARNOCHAN, W.B. LEMUEL GULLIVER'S MIRROR
 FOR MAN.*
 C.J. HORNE, 402(MLR):JAN72-170
 T.A. OLSHIN, 556(RLV):1970/5-551
 H.D. WEINBROT, 173(ECS):FALL70-109
CARO BAROJA, J. ENSAYO SOBRE LA LITERA-
 TURA DE CORDEL.
 191(ELN):SEP71(SUPP)-173
CAROFIGLIO, V. NERVAL E IL MITO DELLA
 "PURETÉ."
 J. GUILLAUME, 535(RHL):MAR-APR70-325
CARPENTER, C.A. BERNARD SHAW AND THE ART
 OF DESTROYING IDEALS.*
 P. GOETSCH, 430(NS):NOV71-616
 R.S. NELSON, 50(ARQ):SPRING70-87
 A.H. NETHERCOT, 397(MD):MAY70-100
CARPENTER, E. ESKIMO REALITIES.
 H. KENNER, 441:29JUL73-6
CARPENTER, E. OH, WHAT A BLOW THAT PHAN-
 TOM GAVE ME!
 H. KENNER, 441:29JUL73-6
 442(NY):27AUG73-92
CARPENTER, E. & K. HEYMAN. THEY BECAME
 WHAT THEY BEHELD.
 H. KENNER, 441:29JUL73-6
CARPENTER, R. THE ARCHITECTS OF THE PAR-
 THENON.
 J. WILTON-ELY, 39:MAR71-226
CARPENTIER, A. GUERRA DEL TIEMPO.
 G. FIGUEIRA, 263:OCT-DEC72-427

CARPER, J. NOT WITH A GUN.
M.J. GREEN, 441:4MAR73-38
CARR, D. - SEE HUSSERL, E.
CARR, D.W. RECOVERING CANADA'S NATION-
HOOD.
G. LAX, 99:APR73-33
CARR, E.H. & R.W. DAVIES. FOUNDATIONS OF
A PLANNED ECONOMY, 1926-1929. (VOL 1)
R.V. DANIELS, 32:JUN72-428
CARR, L. A CATALOGUE OF THE VANDER POEL
DICKENS COLLECTION AT THE UNIVERSITY OF
TEXAS.* (2ND ED)
S. NOWELL-SMITH, 354:JUN70-170
CARR, R., ED. THE REPUBLIC AND THE
CIVIL WAR IN SPAIN.
617(TLS):16MAR73-290
CARR, W. ARMS, AUTARKY AND AGGRESSION.
617(TLS):9NOV73-1365
CARRÀ, M. IVORIES OF THE WEST.
J. BECKWITH, 39:OCT71-322
CARRÀ, M., WITH P. WALDBERG & E. RATHKE.
METAPHYSICAL ART.*
R. LEBOWITZ, 58:MAY72-30
CARRAHER, R.G. ARTISTS IN SPITE OF ART.
617(TLS):4MAY73-495
CARRELL, P.L. A TRANSFORMATIONAL GRAMMAR
OF IGBO.
E.P. HAMP, 269(IJAL):JUL71-210
CARRER, L. SCRITTI CRITICI. (G. GAMBAR-
IN, ED)
U. CARPI, 228(GSLI):VOL147FASC460-621
CARRERA ANDRADE, J. EL VOLCÁN Y EL COLI-
BRI.
E.B. LABRADA, 37:MAY71-41
CARRÈRE, C. GEORGE SAND AMOUREUSE, SES
AMANTS, SES AMITIÉS TENDRES.
G. LUBIN, 535(RHL):MAR-APR70-324
CARRIER, R. LA GUERRE, YES SIR!*
J. MILLS, 648:OCT70-82
CARRIÈRE, J. L'EPERVIER DE MAHEUX.
617(TLS):6APR73-369
CARRIGHAR, S. HOME TO THE WILDERNESS.
E. WEEKS, 61:JUN73-122
"CARRINGTON: LETTERS AND EXTRACTS FROM
HER DIARIES." (D. GARNETT, ED)
R. EDWARDS, 39:FEB71-145
G.A. PANICHAS, 396(MODA):SUMMER72-317
P.M. SPACKS, 249(HUDR):SPRING72-157
J.J. WILSON, 418(MR):WINTER-SPRING72-
291
CARRINGTON, C. RUDYARD KIPLING.
J. WILLETT, 493:SPRING71-69
CARRINGTON, C. - SEE KIPLING, R.
CARRINGTON, J. "MEMORANDUMS FOR..."
(W.B. JOHNSON, ED)
617(TLS):7SEP73-1037
CARROLL, D., ED. GEORGE ELIOT: THE CRITI-
CAL HERITAGE.
G.M. HARVEY, 150(DR):AUTUMN71-430
CARROLL, D. THE MATINEE IDOLS.
617(TLS):15JUN73-699
CARROLL, J.M. BUFFALO SOLDIERS WEST.
W. GARD, 584(SWR):SPRING72-V
CARROLL, K. QUAKERISM ON THE EASTERN
SHORE.
J.A.L. LEMAY, 568(SCN):SUMMER72-48
CARROLL, P.N., ED. RELIGION AND THE COM-
ING OF THE AMERICAN REVOLUTION.
E.S. GAUSTAD, 656(WMQ):APR71-315
CARRUBA, O. DAS BESCHWÖRUNGSRITUAL FÜR
DIE GÖTTIN WIŠURIJANZA.
G. NEUMANN, 260(IF):BAND75-293
CARRUTH, H. FOR YOU.*
639(VQR):SUMMER71-CV
DES CARS, G. LA VIPÈRE.
P.J. JOHNSON, 207(FR):OCT70-172

CARSANIGA, G. GESCHICHTE DER ITALIENIS-
CHEN LITERATUR VON DER RENAISSANCE BIS
ZUR GEGENWART.
R.G. FAITHFULL, 402(MLR):APR72-432
CARSON, D. LAMENT.
F. BUSCH, 441:9DEC73-24
CARSON, R.W. ASPECTS OF CONTEMPORARY
SOCIETY IN "GIL BLAS."
617(TLS):13JUL73-816
CARSON, M.E. PABLO NERUDA.
617(TLS):11MAY73-532
CARSTEN, F.L. REVOLUTION IN CENTRAL
EUROPE, 1918-1919.*
I. DEAK, 32:DEC72-914
CARSTENSEN, B. SPIEGEL-WÖRTER SPIEGEL-
WORTE.
W.B., 681(ZDS):BAND27HEFT3-191
CARSWELL, J. FROM REVOLUTION TO REVOLU-
TION.
617(TLS):19OCT73-1279
CARSWELL, J. NEW JULFA.
J. BECKWITH, 39:JAN70-84
CARSWELL, J. & C.J.F. DOWSETT. KÜTAHYA
TILES AND POTTERY FROM THE ARMENIAN
CATHEDRAL OF ST. JAMES, JERUSALEM.
617(TLS):19JAN73-68
CARTER, A. DIRECT ACTION AND LIBERAL
DEMOCRACY.
617(TLS):14SEP73-1043
CARTER, A. JOHN OSBORNE.
T. ROGERS, 175:SUMMER70-67
CARTER, A.E. VERLAINE.*
L.D. JOINER, 188(ECR):FALL71-81
S·I. LOCKERBIE, 208(FS):JUL72-348
M. O'NEILL, 207(FR):FEB71-614
C. SCOTT, 447(N&Q):NOV71-439
G. ZAYED, 535(RHL):JAN-FEB71-122
CARTER, E.D., ED. ANTOLOGÍA DEL REALIS-
MO MÁGICO.
A.B. HENKIN, 238:MAR71-233
CARTER, F.W. DUBROVNIK (RAGUSA).
617(TLS):10AUG73-937
CARTER, G.A. - SEE HOBBS, J.L.
CARTER, H., ED. THE TYPE SPECIMEN OF
DELACOLONGE.
N. BARKER, 78(BC):SUMMER71-261
R. CAVE, 503:WINTER70-228
CARTER, H. A VIEW OF EARLY TYPOGRAPHY UP
TO ABOUT 1600.
F.J. MOSHER, 551(RENQ):SPRING71-60
CARTER, H.L. "DEAR OLD KIT."
E.W. TODD, 649(WAL):SPRING70-71
CARTER, J. WILD ANIMAL FARM.
617(TLS):13JUL73-817
CARTER, J.R. THE NET COST OF SOVIET
FOREIGN AID.
R.W. CAMPBELL, 550(RUSR):OCT71-409
CARTER, M. LA MAESTRA.
M. LEVIN, 441:15APR73-33
CARTER, R.E. - SEE CHRYSOSTOM, J.
CARTER, S. 3D. BLAZE OF GLORY.*
617(TLS):19JAN73-70
CARTER, T.P. MEXICAN AMERICANS IN
SCHOOL.
I.R. YOSHINO, 50(ARQ):WINTER70-366
CARTER, V.O. THE BERN BOOK.
N. BALAKIAN, 441:21JUL73-31
CARTER, W. BOLIVIA.
617(TLS):6APR73-368
CARTWRIGHT, A., L. HOCKEY & J. ANDERSON.
LIFE BEFORE DEATH.
617(TLS):3AUG73-913
CARTWRIGHT, M.T. DIDEROT CRITIQUE D'ART
ET LE PROBLÈME DE L'EXPRESSION.*
A. GUEDJ, 535(RHL):JAN-FEB71-98
J. MAYER, 557(RSH):JUL-SEP70-473
P.H. MEYER, 207(FR):OCT70-237

DE CARVALHO, J.G.H. - SEE UNDER HERCULANO
DE CARVALHO, J.G.
DE CARVALHO-NETO, P. THE CONCEPT OF
FOLKLORE.
A.L. CAMPA, 263:APR-JUN72-162
DE CARVALHO-NETO, P. HISTORIA DEL FOLK-
LORE IBEROAMERICANO.*
M.J. DOUDOROFF, 238:SEP71-602
DE CARVALHO-NETO, P. HISTORY OF IBERO-
AMERICAN FOLKLORE: MESTIZO CULTURES.
R.J. SMITH, 292(JAF):APR-JUN71-245
CARVER, P.L. THE LIFE OF A POET.
M. HAMMER, 189(EA):JUL-SEP70-302
CARVIC, H. MISS SEETON SINGS.
N. CALLENDAR, 441:1APR73-34
CARY, R. - SEE ROBINSON, E.A.
DELLA CASA, A. IL "DUBIUS SERMO" DI
PLINIO.
B. LOFSTEDT, 24:JUL72-494
CASANOVA, G. MÉMOIRES. (VOLS 1-3) HIS-
TOIRE DE MA VIE. MÉMOIRES. (VOLS 1-4)
F. ROUSTANG, 98:FEB71-175
CASARES, A.B. - SEE UNDER BIOY CASARES,
A.
CASCALES, C. L'HUMANISME D'ORTEGA Y
GASSET.
G. FABRE, 542:OCT-DEC71-510
CASERTA, P. & D. KNAPP. GOING DOWN WITH
JANIS.
D. WAKEFIELD, 61:SEP73-108
CASEY, J. THE LANGUAGE OF CRITICISM.
B. JEAN, 189(EA):JAN-MAR70-72
CASEY, J., ED. MORALITY AND MORAL REAS-
ONING.
T.D. CAMPBELL, 518:MAY72-9
CASEY, M. OBSCENITIES.*
R. LATTIMORE, 249(HUDR):AUTUMN72-477
A. OSTRIKER, 473(PR):SUMMER72-464
A. POULIN, JR., 398:VOL3#4-187
S. SPENDER, 453:8FEB73-3
CASH, A.H. & J.M. STEDMOND, EDS. THE
WINGED SKULL.
J. GRAY, 529(QQ):WINTER71-632
R. PAULSON, 402(MLR):APR72-403
CASH, J.H. & H.T. HOOVER. TO BE AN
INDIAN.
W.C. STURTEVANT, 441:18MAR73-38
CASH, T., ED. ANATOMY OF POP.
A. HIGGINS, 592:MAR71-131
CASINI, P. L'UNIVERSO-MACCHINA.*
617(TLS):1JUN73-615
CASMIR, F. & L.S. HARMS, EDS. INTERNA-
TIONAL STUDIES OF NATIONAL SPEECH
EDUCATION SYSTEMS. (VOL 1)
P.M. LARSON, 583:SPRING72-328
CASPER, L. A LION UNANNOUNCED.
M. TERRY, 584(SWR):WINTER72-83
CASSARA, E., ED. UNIVERSALISM IN AMERICA.
C-A. HOLBROOK, 432(NEQ):DEC71-670
CASSELS, L. CLASH OF GENERATIONS.
617(TLS):22JUN73-714
CASSIDY, F.G. & R.B. LE PAGE, EDS. A
DICTIONARY OF JAMAICAN ENGLISH.*
C. GOOD, 353:DEC70-112
CASSILL, R.V. DOCTOR COBB'S GAME.
42(AR):FALL/WINTER70/71-459
CASSIRER, E. DALL'UMANESIMO ALL'ILLUMIN-
ISMO. (P.O. KRISTELLER, ED)
M. DAL PRA, 548(RCSF):OCT-DEC70-457
CASSIRER, H.W. KANT'S FIRST CRITIQUE.
(2ND ED)
J. KOPPER, 342:BAND62HEFT1-139
CASSIRER, P. DESKRIPTIV STILISTIK. STIL-
EN I HJALMAR SÖDERBERGS "HISTORIETTER."
W. JOHNSON, 563(SS):WINTER72-148
CASSOLA, C. MONTE MARIO.
617(TLS):17AUG73-945

CASSON, L. SHIPS AND SEAMANSHIP IN THE
ANCIENT WORLD.
J.K. ANDERSON, 122:JUL72-215
F.J. FROST, 124:OCT71-64
CASSOU, J. & J. LEYMARIE. FERNAND LÉGER:
DESSINS ET GOUACHES.
617(TLS):27APR73-464
CASTANEDA, C. JOURNEY TO IXTLAN.*
617(TLS):15JUN73-663
CASTANEDA, C. A SEPARATE REALITY.*
N. BRAYBROOKE, 619(TC):VOL179#1049-54
CASTEDO, L. A HISTORY OF LATIN AMERICAN
ART AND ARCHITECTURE.*
T. CROMBIE, 39:APR71-344
R. SQUIRRU, 37:JAN70-38
CASTEIN, H. DIE ANGLO-IRISCHE STRASSEN-
BALLADE.
B.A. ROSENBERG, 568(SCN):SUMMER72-43
CASTELFRANCO, G. DONATELLO.
A.M. ROMANINI, 54:SEP71-401
CASTELLET, J.M. NUEVE NOVÍSIMOS POETAS
ESPAÑOLES.
J. GONZÁLEZ MUELA, 86(BHS):APR72-196
CASTELLI, E. L'INDAGINE QUOTIDIANA.
E. NAMER, 542:JAN-MAR70-98
CASTELLS, M.O. & P.Z. BORING. LENGUA Y
LECTURA.
E.M. DIAL, 238:MAY71-411
CASTEX, P-G. BAUDELAIRE CRITIQUE D'ART.
R. DEMORIS, 557(RSH):JUL-SEP71-484
A. FAIRLIE, 208(FS):JUL72-345
C. PICHOIS, 535(RHL):JAN-FEB71-114
CASTEX, P-G. "SYLVIE" DE GÉRARD DE NER-
VAL.
J. BELLEMIN-NOËL, 535(RHL):MAY-JUN71-
522
CASTEX, P-G. - SEE DE NERVAL, G.
CASTEX, P-G. - SEE DE VILLIERS DE L'ISLE-
ADAM, P.A.M.
CASTILLA DEL PINO, C. LA CULPA.
V. RÜFNER, 182:VOL24#9/10-385
CASTILLEJO, D. A COUNTER REPORT ON ART
PATRONAGE.
412:FEB72-67
DE CASTILLEJO, I.C. KNOWING WOMAN.
617(TLS):23MAR73-333
CASTILLO, H., ED. ESTUDIOS CRÍTICOS
SOBRE EL MODERNISMO.*
J-L. MARFANY, 86(BHS):JAN72-89
CASTILLO, H. & A.G., EDS. 3 NOVELAS
CORTAS Y 3 PIEZAS TEATRALES.
L.F. LYDAY, 238:SEP71-608
CASTLES, S. & G. KOSACK. IMMIGRANT
WORKERS AND CLASS STRUCTURE IN WESTERN
EUROPE.
617(TLS):24AUG73-965
CASTORINA, E. - SEE PETRONIUS
CASTREN, P. & H. LILIUS. GRAFFITI DEL
PALATINO. (VOL 2) (V. VÄÄNÄNEN, ED)
C-A. RALEGH RADFORD, 313:VOL61-286
J.M. REYNOLDS, 123:JUN72-295
CASTRO, A. TERESA LA SANTA Y OTROS EN-
SAYOS.
A. ADELL, 270:VOL22#4-89
CASTRO, A.A. & D.V. BENSON - SEE MARTÍ,
J.
CASTRO Y CALVO, J.M. - SEE PASTOR DÍAZ,
N.
CASWELL, H. SHADOWS FROM THE SINGING
HOUSE.
L. HENNIGH, 650(WF):JUL70-214
CATACH, N. L'ORTHOGRAPHE FRANÇAISE À
L'ÉPOQUE DE LA RENAISSANCE.
M. GLATIGNY, 535(RHL):JAN-FEB70-114
CATALÁN, D. POR CAMPOS DEL ROMANCERO.
R.E. BARBERA, 238:SEP71-597
J.G. CUMMINS, 86(BHS):JAN72-94

CATALÁN, D. SIETE SIGLOS DE ROMANCERO
(HISTORIA Y POESÍA).*
S.G. ARMISTEAD & J.H. SILVERMAN,
238:MAR71-195
"CATALOGUE DE L'EXPOSITION BERLIOZ."
P. CITRON, 535(RHL):JAN-FEB71-111
"CATALOGUE OF LITTLE PRESS BOOKS IN
PRINT, 1970, PUBLISHED IN THE UNITED
KINGDOM."
D. CHAMBERS, 503:SUMMER70-103
"THE CATALOGUE OF THE COLLECTION OF AN-
CIENT AND LATER COINS, THE PROPERTY OF
THE METROPOLITAN MUSEUM OF ART, SOLD BY
AUCTION BY SOTHEBY AND CO., A.G. ZUR-
ICH." (PTS 1&2)
M.J. PRICE, 453:19JUL73-15
"CATALOGUE OF THE DRAWINGS COLLECTION OF
THE ROYAL INSTITUTE OF BRITISH ARCHI-
TECTS." (VOL A)
A.A. TAIT, 90:APR71-227
CATANACH, I.J. RURAL CREDIT IN WESTERN
INDIA, 1875-1930.
T.R. METCALF, 293(JAST):AUG71-908
CATER, D. DANA, THE IRRELEVANT MAN.
639(VQR):WINTER71-XII
CATHCART, R.S. & L.A. SAMOVAR. SMALL
GROUP COMMUNICATION.
J.M. LAHIFF, 583:SUMMER71-406
CATHER, W. THE WORLD AND THE PARISH.
(W.M. CURTIN, ED)
M. FOX, 649(WAL):WINTER71-311
CATHERINE, R. LE STYLE ADMINISTRATIF.
(NEW ED)
P. LERAT, 209(FM):JAN70-73
CATHOLY, E. & W. HELLMANN, EDS. FEST-
SCHRIFT FÜR KLAUS ZIEGLER.
G. NEUMANN, 657(WW):JAN/FEB70-61
CATLIN, G. O-KEE-PA. (J.C. EWERS, ED)
M.E. ACKERMAN, 649(WAL):SUMMER70-164
CATTAN, H. PALESTINE, THE ARABS AND
ISRAEL.
468:VOL23#4-426
CATTAUI, G. PROUST ET SES MÉTAMORPHOSES.
617(TLS):13APR73-423
CATTELL, N.R. THE NEW ENGLISH GRAMMAR.
R.D., 179(ES):APR71-194
M. OPPENHEIMER, JR., 186(ETC.):SEP71-
371
A.R. TELLIER, 189(EA):JUL-SEP71-320
CATULLUS. CATULLI CARMINA.* (H. BAR-
DON, ED)
E.J. KENNEY, 123:JUN72-212
D.O. ROSS, JR., 24:OCT72-630
CATULLUS. THE POEMS. (K. QUINN, ED)
R.J. BAKER, 67:NOV72-212
W.C. SCOTT, 124:SEP71-30
CATULLUS. POEMS OF CATULLUS. (G.A. WIL-
LIAMSON, ED)
R. GLEN, 123:MAR72-98
CATULLUS. THE POEMS OF CATULLUS TRANS-
LATED. (P. WHIGHAM, TRANS)
M.L. CLARKE, 123:MAR72-107
"CATULLUS."* (C. & L. ZUKOFSKY, TRANS)
N. MOORE, 493:SUMMER71-179
CATULLUS & HORACE. ROMAN LYRIC POETRY:
CATULLUS AND HORACE.* (A.G. MC KAY &
D.M. SHEPHERD, EDS)
R. GLEN, 123:MAR72-98
M.O. LEE, 487:SUMMER71-177
W.S. THURMAN, 399(MLJ):APR71-262
CAUDILL, W.W. ARCHITECTURE BY TEAM.
505:NOV71-138
CAUDWELL, C. ROMANCE AND REALISM.* (S.
HYNES, ED)
G. WOODCOCK, 401(MLQ):MAR72-88
CAUSEY, A. PETER LANYON.
617(TLS):22JUN73-708
CAUSEY, A. - SEE "PAUL NASH'S PHOTOGRAPHS"

CAUTE, D. THE FELLOW-TRAVELLERS.
R. CROSSMAN, 362:25JAN73-120
P. ROSENBERG, 441:8APR73-23
617(TLS):6JUL73-765
CAUTHERY, P. STUDENT HEALTH.
617(TLS):14SEP73-1052
DELLA CAVA, R. MIRACLE AT JOASEIRO.
D. CARNEIRO, 263:JUL-SEP72-283
CAVADINI-CANONICA, T. LE LETTERE DI
SCIPIONE MAFFEI E LA BIBLIOTHÈQUE ITAL-
IQUE.
M. FUBINI, 228(GSLI):VOL148FASC462/
463-455
CAVAFY, C.P. PASSIONS AND ANCIENT DAYS.*
A. DECAVALLES, 661:WINTER/SPRING72-75
M. SAVVAS, 676(YR):WINTER72-308
"C.P. CAVAFY: SELECTED POEMS." (E.
KEELEY & P. SHERRARD, TRANS)
L. DURRELL, 441:21JAN73-2
CAVAILLÈS, J. PHILOSOPHIE MATHÉMATIQUE.
Y. GAUTHIER, 154:DEC71-818
CAVALCANTI, B. LETTERE EDITE E INEDITE.
(C. ROAF, ED)
M. POZZI, 228(GSLI):VOL147FASC457-136
CAVALCASELLE, G.B. LA PITTURA FRIULANA
DEL RINASCIMENTO. (G. BERGAMINI, ED)
617(TLS):17AUG73-944
CAVALIERO, G. THE ANCIENT PEOPLE.
617(TLS):16NOV73-1405
CAVE, R. & OTHERS. PRIVATE PRESS BOOKS
1971. (D. CHAMBERS, ED)
617(TLS):6APR73-400
CAVE, T., ED. RONSARD THE POET.
617(TLS):14SEP73-1051
CAVE, T. & M. JEANNERET. MÉTAMORPHOSES
SPIRITUELLES.
617(TLS):23MAR73-320
CAVE, T.C. DEVOTIONAL POETRY IN FRANCE,
C. 1570-1613.*
E. DU BRUCK, 546(RR):APR71-140
J. PINEAUX, 535(RHL):JUL-AUG70-699
205(FMLS):APR70-204
CAVELL, S. MUST WE MEAN WHAT WE SAY?*
R.J.B., 543:SEP70-134
CAVELL, S. THE WORLD VIEWED.
L. NELSON, JR., 676(YR):SUMMER72-610
CAVIGELLI, P. DIE GERMANISIERUNG VON BON-
ADUZ IN GESCHICHTLICHER UND SPRACHLICHER
SCHAU.*
L. SPULER, 400(MLN):APR71-443
CAVINA, A.O. CARLO SARACENI.*
R.W. BISSELL, 54:JUN71-248
CAVITCH, D. D.H. LAWRENCE AND THE NEW
WORLD.*
K. CUSHMAN, 405(MP):NOV71-152
E. DELAVENAY, 189(EA):APR-JUN71-208
P.R. GROVER, 402(MLR):JUL72-623
J.C.F. LITTLEWOOD, 184(EIC):APR71-195
K. MC LEOD, 541(RES):AUG71-378
L.A. RUFF, 613:AUTUMN70-458
CAWLEY, A.C., ED. CHAUCER'S MIND AND
ART.*
A. DAVID, 589:JUL72-522
CAWS, M.A. ANDRÉ BRETON.*
S. KANTARIZIS, 67:MAY72-119
J.H. MATTHEWS, 401(MLQ):SEP72-327
CAWS, M.A. THE POETRY OF DADA AND SUR-
REALISM.*
V.M. AMES, 290(JAAC):WINTER70-282
A. BALAKIAN, 401(MLQ):JUN72-208
J.A. DUNCAN, 402(MLR):APR72-427
CAWS, P. SCIENCE AND THE THEORY OF
VALUE.
R. GEORGE, 486:JUN71-319
CAWTE, E.C. RAPPER AT WINLATON IN 1955.
A. BRODY, 292(JAF):APR-JUN71-256
CAYLEY, M. THE SPIDER'S TOUCH.
617(TLS):3AUG73-894

CAYROL, J. HISTOIRE DE LA MER.
617(TLS):23FEB73-219
CAZALET-KEIR, T., ED. HOMAGE TO P.G.
WODEHOUSE.
617(TLS):2NOV73-1338
CAZAMIAN, L. THE SOCIAL NOVEL IN ENGLAND
1830-1850.
617(TLS):18MAY73-558
CAZAMIAN, L. & M. - SEE MEREDITH, G.
CAZEAUX, J. L'ECRITURE DE PROUST OU
L'ART DU VITRAIL.
617(TLS):13APR73-423
CAZZIOL, R. L'ARBRE À PALABRES. RÉCITS
AFRICAINS. ECRIVONS EN FRANÇAIS.
B. MULLER, 207(FR):MAR71-820
CECCHETTI, G. IL VERGA MAGGIORE.*
O. RAGUSA, 546(RR):OCT71-211
CECCHI, E. I CIPRESSI DI BOLGHERI. (E.
MONTALE & V. BRANCA, EDS)
E.B., 228(GSLI):VOL148FASC462/463-471
CECCHI, E. & N. SAPEGNO. STORIA DELLA
LETTERATURA ITALIANA.
R. BAEHR, 430(NS):MAY70-254
DE CECCHI DUSO, G. L'INTERPRETAZIONE
HEIDEGGERIANA DEI PRESOCRATICI.
E. NAMER, 542:OCT-DEC71-476
CECCHIN, S.A. PATRIOS POLITEIA.*
H.D. WESTLAKE, 123:MAR72-81
CECIL, D. THE CECILS OF HATFIELD HOUSE.
W. BEAUCHAMP, 441:23DEC73-10
P. BEER, 362:25OCT73-564
617(TLS):12OCT73-1205
CECIL, D. VISIONARY AND DREAMER.*
A.L. GRIFFIN, 637(VS):DEC70-213
A.S. ROE, 54:SEP71-421
CELAN, P. SPEECHE-GRILLE AND SELECTED
POEMS.* (J. NEUGROSCHEL, TRANS)
A.H. ROSENFELD, 390:NOV71-75
CELAN, P. STRETTE.
P. SZONDI, 98:MAY71-387
CELANT, G., ED. ART POVERA.*
C. HARRISON, 592:MAR70-136
CELATI, G. COMICHE.*
270:VOL22#3-67
CELL, G.T. ENGLISH ENTERPRISE IN NEW-
FOUNDLAND, 1577-1660.
K.R. ANDREWS, 656(WMQ):JAN71-138
CELL, J.W. BRITISH COLONIAL ADMINISTRA-
TION IN THE MID-NINETEENTH CENTURY.
R. KUBICEK, 637(VS):DEC70-209
CELLIER, L., ED. HOMMAGE À GEORGE SAND.
T.G.S. COMBE, 208(FS):JUL72-342
CELLIER, L. - SEE HUGO, V.
CELSIUS, O. UPPSALA UNIVERSITETSBIBLIO-
TEKS HISTORIA.
L.S. THOMPSON, 563(SS):SPRING72-267
CENDRARS, B. LICE.
617(TLS):13JUL73-798
CENDRARS, B. MORAVAGINE.
L.T. LEMON, 502(PRS):FALL71-268
ČEPAN, O., ED. LITTERARIA BD. XIII. LIT-
ERÁRNY BAROK.
D. TSCHIŽEWSKIJ, 72:BAND209HEFT1/3-
230
"CÉRAMIQUE CHINOISE." (VOLS 1&2)
P. JAQUILLARD, 57:VOL33#1/2-155
CERESA, A. LA FIGLIA PRODIGA.
B. MERRY, 270:VOL22#1-20
CERMAKIAN, M. LA PRINCESSE DES URSINS.
M. BATAILLON, 549(RLC):JAN-MAR71-110
D.A. WATTS, 402(MLR):JUL72-635
CERNUDA, L. CRÍTICA, ENSAYOS Y EVOCA-
CIONES. (L. MARISTANY, ED)
D.R. HARRIS, 86(BHS):JAN72-93
A. TERRY, 402(MLR):APR72-445
CERRUTI, M. NEOCLASSICI E GIACOBINI.
A.M. MUTTERLE, 228(GSLI):VOL147FASC
460-611

DE CERVANTES SAAVEDRA, M. MIGUEL DE CER-
VANTES SAAVEDRA, ACHT SCHAUSPIELE UND
ACHT ZWISCHENSPIELE, ALLE NEU UND NIE
AUFGEFÜHRT. (A.M. ROTHBAUER, ED)
H. RHEINFELDER, 430(NS):OCT71-558
DE CERVANTES SAAVEDRA, M. TWO CERVANTES
SHORT NOVELS. (F. PIERCE, ED)
R.S. RUDDER, 238:MAY71-413
CÉSAIRE, A. "UNE TEMPÊTE," ADAPTATION DE
"LA TEMPÊTE" DE SHAKESPEARE POUR UN
THÉÂTRE NÈGRE.
R. REGOSIN, 207(FR):APR71-952
CESBRON, J. JE SUIS MAL DANS TA PEAU.
H. FREYBURGER, 207(FR):FEB71-636
CESCINSKY, H. ENGLISH FURNITURE FROM
GOTHIC TO SHERATON.
D. FITZ-GERALD, 39:JAN70-88
CHAADAEV, P.Y. PHILOSOPHICAL LETTERS AND
APOLOGY OF A MADMAN.* (M-B. ZELDIN,
TRANS)
R.T. MC NALLY, 550(RUSR):JAN71-82
CHABER, M.E. BORN TO BE HANGED.
N. CALLENDAR, 441:2SEP73-18
CHABOD, F. DE MACHIAVEL À BENEDETTO
CROCE.
P. STADLER, 182:VOL24#3-108
CHACE, J. A WORLD ELSEWHERE.
H. BRANDON, 441:8APR73-26
CHADWICK, C. VERLAINE.
617(TLS):21DEC73-1562
CHADWICK, C. - SEE VERLAINE, P.
CHADWICK, H.M. & N.K. THE GROWTH OF LIT-
ERATURE.
A.C. PERCIVAL, 203:SPRING70-66
CHADWICK, J., J.T. KILLEN & J-P. OLIVIER,
EDS. THE KNOSSOS TABLETS. (4TH ED)
G.M. MESSING, 124:MAR72-238
CHADWICK, N.K. & V. ZHIRMUNSKY. ORAL
EPICS OF CENTRAL ASIA.*
R.C. DUNNE, 318(JAOS):JAN-MAR71-147
F.R. SCHRÖDER, 224(GRM):JAN70-106
CHADWICK, O. THE VICTORIAN CHURCH. (PT
2) (2ND ED)
K.S. INGLIS, 637(VS):MAR71-340
617(TLS):12JAN73-50
CHAFE, W.L. MEANING AND THE STRUCTURE
OF LANGUAGE.*
R.W. LANGACKER, 350:MAR72-134
CHAILLET, J. ETUDES DE GRAMMAIRE ET DE
STYLE.
D. BOUVEROT, 209(FM):OCT70-460
CHAILLEY, J. THE MAGIC FLUTE.* (H.
WEINSTOCK, TRANS)
P.J.B., 410(M&L):OCT72-434
DE CHAIR, S. FRIENDS, ROMANS, CONCU-
BINES.
617(TLS):23MAR73-316
CHAIX-RUY, J. LA FORTUNE DE G.B. VICO.
E. NAMER, 542:APR-JUN70-241
CHAIX-RUY, J. POUR CONNAÎTRE LA PENSÉE
DE NIETZSCHE.
J. GRANIER, 542:APR-JUN70-250
CHAIX-RUY, J. J.B. VICO ET L'ILLUMINISME
ATHÉE.
E. NAMER, 542:APR-JUN70-240
CHAKRABORTY, A. TRANSLATION IN MEDIEVAL
BULGARIA.
I.V. TALEV, 32:MAR72-232
CHAKRAVARTI, S.C. PHILOSOPHICAL FOUNDA-
TION OF BENGAL VAIṢṆAVISM.
J.B.L., 543:SEP70-135
G.J. LARSON, 485(PE&W):APR71-227
CHALINE, C. LONDRES.
J.C. FIELD, 556(RLV):1971/2-234
CHALKER, J. THE ENGLISH GEORGIC.*
C.E. RAMSEY, 481(PQ):JUL71-379
G.S. ROUSSEAU, 149:MAR72-109
P.M. SPACKS, 173(ECS):SPRING71-342

CHALMERS, E. INTERNATIONAL INTEREST
RATE WAR.
617(TLS):12JAN73-45
CHALMERS, W.W. & J.R. WILKIE. A SHORT
HISTORY OF THE GERMAN LANGUAGE.
K. SPALDING, 47(ARL):[N.S.]VOL2-158
CHAMBADAL, P. A LA RECHERCHE DE LA
RÉALITÉ PHYSIQUE.
R. BLANCHÉ, 542:OCT-DEC70-486
CHAMBERLIN, E.R. THE BATSFORD COLOUR
BOOK OF STATELY HOMES.
617(TLS):7SEP73-1037
CHAMBERS, D. - SEE CAVE, R. & OTHERS
CHAMBERS, D.S. THE IMPERIAL AGE OF VEN-
ICE, 1380-1580.
B.G. KOHL, 589:OCT72-753
CHAMBERS, G. THE BONNYCLABBER.
R. SUKENICK, 441:4MAR73-32
CHAMBERS, J.V. REMINISCENCES OF JUDGE
JOSEPH VERNON CHAMBERS. (M.C. CHAMBERS,
ED)
W.S. HOOLE, 9(ALAR):APR70-155
CHAMBERS, R. GÉRARD DE NERVAL ET LA
POÉTIQUE DU VOYAGE.*
J. BELLEMIN-NOËL, 535(RHL):MAY-JUN70-
523
F. CONSTANS, 557(RSH):JUL-SEP70-486
CHAMBERS, W. A TREATISE ON THE DECORA-
TIVE PART OF CIVIL ARCHITECTURE. (3RD
ED)
M. HECKSCHER, 576:OCT71-252
CHAMBERS, W.W. & J.R. WILKIE. A SHORT
HISTORY OF THE GERMAN LANGUAGE.*
D.R. MC LINTOCK, 220(GL&L):APR72-310
S.R. SMITH, 221(GQ):JAN71-117
205(FMLS):JAN71-93
CHAMBON, J. LA SENTINELLE.
B. STOLTZFUS, 207(FR):FEB71-637
CHAMISH, B. THE DEVIL WORE AN ANGEL'S
SUIT.
R. WILLMOT, 296:FALL73-98
CHAMPAGNE, A., ED. PETITE HISTOIRE DU
VOYAGEUR.
D. SWAINSON, 529(QQ):WINTER71-625
CHAMPION, L.S. THE EVOLUTION OF SHAKE-
SPEARE'S COMEDY.*
T.W. CRAIK, 551(RENQ):SUMMER71-273
CHAMPION, L.S. BEN JONSON'S "DOTAGES."
E. LEHMANN, 38:BAND89HEFT3-391
DE CHAMPLAIN, S. VOYAGES TO NEW FRANCE,
1599-1603. (M. MACKLEM, TRANS)
J.S. ERSKINE, 150(DR):WINTER71/72-601
DE CHAMPLAIN, S. VOYAGES TO NEW FRANCE,
1615-1618. (M. MACKLEM, TRANS)
J.S. ERSKINE, 150(DR):SPRING71-117
"CHAN-KUO TS'E."* (J.I. CRUMP, JR.,
TRANS)
W.A.C.H. DOBSON, 293(JAST):FEB71-429
D.R. KNECHTGES, 244(HJAS):VOL31-333
CHANCE, S. SEPTIMUS AND THE DANEDYKE
MYSTERY.
N. CALLENDAR, 441:14OCT73-47
CHANDLER, A. A DREAM OF ORDER.*
K. KROEBER, 637(VS):JUN71-462
R. LEHAN, 445(NCF):SEP71-245
CHANDLER, R.W. SPARKS AT SEA.
617(TLS):20APR73-454
CHANELES, S. THE OPEN PRISON.
D.J. ROTHMAN, 441:27MAY73-4
CHANEY, O.P., JR. ZHUKOV.
L. GOURE, 32:SEP72-679
CHANEY, W.A. THE CULT OF KINGSHIP IN
ANGLO-SAXON ENGLAND.*
R. BRENTANO, 589:OCT72-754
R. FRANK, 447(N&Q):JUL71-265
R.M. WILSON, 175:AUTUMN71-96

CHANG, G.C.C. THE BUDDHIST TEACHING OF
TOTALITY.
617(TLS):18MAY73-559
CHANG, J.K. INDUSTRIAL DEVELOPMENT IN
PRE-COMMUNIST CHINA.*
F.C. HUNG, 318(JAOS):JAN-MAR71-151
CHANG, R.T. FROM PREJUDICE TO TOLERANCE.
T.R.H. HAVENS, 293(JAST):FEB71-460
CHANG, R.T. HISTORIANS AND MEIJI STATES-
MEN.
B. TETERS, 293(JAST):AUG71-894
CHANG TEH-CHANG. CH'ING-CHI I KO CHING-
KUAN TI SHENG-HO.
A.Y-C. LUI, 302:JUL71-374
CHANNING, E.T. LECTURES READ TO THE
SENIORS IN HARVARD COLLEGE. (D.L.
ANDERSON & W. BRADEN, EDS)
G.A. HAUSER, 480(P&R):WINTER70-59
"LA CHANSON DE ROLAND."* (G. MOIGNET,
ED & TRANS)
I. SHORT, 545(RPH):AUG71-131
F. WHITEHEAD, 208(FS):APR72-181
205(FMLS):OCT70-419
"CHANSONNIER DES PREUX ALBANAIS."
C.R-M. PINSKY, 650(WF):JUL70-208
DE CHANTAL, R. MARCEL PROUST.
G. KAISER, 52:BAND5HEFT2-218
CHANTOUX, A., A. GONTIER & A. PROST.
GRAMMAIRE GOURMANTCHÉ.*
W.A.A. WILSON, 69:JAN70-97
CHANTRAINE, P. DICTIONNAIRE ÉTYMOLOGIQUE
DE LA LANGUE GRECQUE.* (VOL 1)
C.J. RUIJGH, 361:VOL25#3-302
CHANTRAINE, P. DICTIONNAIRE ÉTYMOLO-
GIQUE DE LA LANGUE GRECQUE.* (VOL 2)
J.W. POULTNEY, 24:OCT72-624
CHAO, Y.R. LANGUAGE AND SYMBOLIC SYS-
TEMS.*
C-C. CHENG, 206:AUG71-439
CHAPIN, C.F. THE RELIGIOUS THOUGHT OF
SAMUEL JOHNSON.
P.K. ALKON, 405(MP):NOV70-204
CHAPLIN, H.I. & S.E. MARTIN. A MANUAL
OF JAPANESE WRITING.
K.L.C. STRONG, 47(ARL):[N.S.]VOL1-110
CHAPMAN, G. THE PLAYS OF GEORGE CHAPMAN:
THE COMEDIES.* (A. HOLADAY, ED)
C.E. BAIN, 568(SCN):FALL-WINTER72-67
F.S. HOOK, 301(JEGP):JUL72-444
CHAPMAN, J.J. THE COLLECTED WORKS OF
JOHN JAY CHAPMAN.* (VOL 3) (M.H. BERN-
STEIN, ED)
W. WHITE, 646(WWR):SEP70-90
CHAPMAN, K.G. HOVEDLINJER I TARJEI
VESAAS' DIKTNING.
B. HUSEBY, 172(EDDA):1970/2-117
A. LIEN, 563(SS):WINTER72-142
CHAPMAN, K.G. TARJEI VESAAS.
A. LIEN, 563(SS):WINTER72-142
CHAPMAN, R. FAITH AND REVOLT.
R. LAWRENCE, 175:SUMMER71-70
E. NORMAN, 111:29JAN71-107
CHAPMAN, R. LINGUISTICS AND LITERATURE.
617(TLS):13JUL73-817
CHAPMAN, R.T. WYNDHAM LEWIS.
617(TLS):3AUG73-893
CHAPMAN, S.D. THE COTTON INDUSTRY IN THE
INDUSTRIAL REVOLUTION.
617(TLS):12JAN73-45
CHAPOTAT, G. VIENNE GAULOISE.
R. CHEVALLIER, 313:VOL61-293
CHAPPELL, P. THE GAUDY PLACE.
J. YARDLEY, 441:13MAY73-36
CHAPPELOW, A. SHAW - THE "CHUCKER-OUT."*
J-C. AMALRIC, 189(EA):APR-JUN71-210
A. BRADY, 109:SPRING/SUMMER73-125
T.F. EVANS, 572:MAY70-83
T. ROGERS, 175:SUMMER70-67

CHAPPUIS, A. THE DRAWINGS OF PAUL
CÉZANNE.
R. DOWNES, 441:29JUL73-7
CHAPPUYS, C. POÉSIES INTIMES.* (A.M.
BEST, ED)
S.M. CARRINGTON, 207(FR):DEC70-464
CHAR, R. LA NUIT TALISMANIQUE. ARRIÈRE-
HISTOIRE DU POÈME PULVÉRISÉ.
617(TLS):4MAY73-491
CHARBON, M.H. HISTORISCHE EN THEORET-
ISCHE WERKEN TOT 1800. (VOL 1)
617(TLS):20JUL73-840
CHARBONNEAUX, J., R. MARTIN & F. VILLARD.
CLASSICAL GREEK ART, 480-330 B.C.
J. CANADAY, 441:2DEC73-90
617(TLS):6APR73-401
CHARBONNEAUX, J., R. MARTIN & F. VILLARD.
HELLENISTIC ART, 330-50.
J. CANADAY, 441:2DEC73-90
617(TLS):26OCT73-1325
DE CHARDIN, P.T. - SEE UNDER TEILHARD DE
CHARDIN, P.
CHARDŽIEV, N. & V. TRENIN. DIE DICHTER-
ISCHE KULTUR MAJAKOVSKIJS (POETIČESKAJA
KUL'TURA MAJAKOVSKOGO).
D. TSCHIŽEWSKIJ, 72:BAND209HEFT4/6-479
CHARELL, R. HOW I TURN ORDINARY COM-
PLAINTS INTO THOUSANDS OF DOLLARS.
G. GOLD, 441:15DEC73-29
CHARITONIDIS, S. & OTHERS. LES MOSAÏQUES
DE LA MAISON DU MÉNANDRE À MYTILÈNE.
T.B.L. WEBSTER, 303:VOL91-210
CHARLES-PICARD, G., ED. LAROUSSE ENCY-
CLOPEDIA OF ARCHAEOLOGY.
P. ADAMS, 61:JAN73-100
CHARLESWORTH, M.J. PHILOSOPHY OF RELI-
GION.
D. BASTOW, 518:OCT72-12
CHARLESWORTH, M.P. THE ROMAN EMPIRE.
J-C. DUMONT, 555:VOL45FASC1-185
CHARLOT, J. & J. STOETZEL, EDS. QUAND
LA GAUCHE PEUT GAGNER...
617(TLS):30NOV73-1463
CHARLTON, W. AESTHETICS.*
E. SCHAPER, 483:OCT71-359
CHARLTON, W. - SEE ARISTOTLE
CHARNEY, M. STYLE IN "HAMLET."
R.A. FOAKES, 175:AUTUMN70-98
A.C. HARRISON, 583:SUMMER71-406
T.H. HOWARD-HILL, 541(RES):MAY71-191
A.C. KIRSCH, 570(SQ):WINTER71-71
CHARNEY, M. - SEE SHAKESPEARE, W.
CHARPIER, J. & P. SEGHERS. L'ART DE LA
PEINTURE.
P. DUFOUR, 98:AUG/SEP71-805
CHARRIÈRE, G. L'ART BARBARE SCYTHE.
P. GUERRE, 98:DEC71-1093
CHARRIÈRE, H. BANCO.
617(TLS):28SEP73-1104
CHARRIÈRE, H. PAPILLON.*
J.B. GORDON, 598(SOR):WINTER73-217
CHARTERS, A. KEROUAC.
J. DECK, 441:15APR73-23
442(NY):12MAY73-147
CHARTERS, A. NOBODY.
N.V. ROSENBERG, 650(WF):APR71-147
CHARTIER, A-M. - SEE DE LÉRY, J.
CHARYN, J. THE TAR BABY.
S. BLACKBURN, 441:28JAN73-7
DE CHASCA, E. EL ARTE JUGLARESCO EN EL
"CANTAR DE MÍO CID."*
H.T. OOSTENDORP, 433:APR71-210
CHASE, I. WORLDS APART.
617(TLS):25MAY73-597
CHASE, S. DANGER - MEN TALKING!
R. WANDERER, 186(ETC.):JUN71-247

CHASSANG, A. & C. SENNINGER. RECUEIL DE
TEXTES LITTÉRAIRES FRANÇAIS (XXE
SIÈCLE).
J. CANTERA, 202(FMOD):JUN71-332
CHASSÉ, C. THE NABIS AND THEIR PERIOD.*
A. NEUMEYER, 127:WINTER71/72-228
CHASTAGNOL, A. RECHERCHES SUR L'HISTOIRE
AUGUSTE.
A.R. BIRLEY, 313:VOL61-309
CHASTEL, A. THE MYTH OF THE RENAISSANCE,
1420-1520.*
R.M. QUINN, 50(ARQ):AUTUMN71-271
CHASTEL, A. & R. KLEIN - SEE GAURICUS, P.
CHÂTEAU, J. DU PIED AU BON SENS.
A. MONTEFIORE, 182:VOL24#11/12-453
DE CHATEAUBRIAND, F-R. VOYAGE EN ITALIE.*
(J-M. GAUTIER, ED)
R. LEBÈGUE, 535(RHL):JAN-FEB70-136
"CHATEAUBRIAND, LE VOYAGEUR ET L'HOMME
POLITIQUE."
R. LEBÈGUE, 535(RHL):JAN-FEB70-135
CHATHAM, J.R. & E. RUIZ-FORNELLS. DIS-
SERTATIONS IN HISPANIC LANGUAGES AND
LITERATURE.*
T.S. BEARDSLEY, JR., 238:SEP71-599
CHATMAN, S., ED. LANGUAGE AND LITERARY
STYLE.
G. STEINER, 111:5MAY72-143
CHATMAN, S. THE LATER STYLE OF HENRY
JAMES.*
S-J. KRAUSE, 27(AL):NOV72-494
CHATMAN, S. & S.R. LEVIN, EDS. ESSAYS ON
THE LANGUAGE OF LITERATURE.*
W. EMBLER, 186(ETC.):DEC70-501
CHATTERJI, S.K. BALTS AND ARYANS IN THEIR
INDO-EUROPEAN BACKGROUND.
R. ROCHER, 318(JAOS):JAN-MAR71-154
CHATTERJI, S.K. THE ORIGIN AND DEVELOP-
MENT OF THE BENGALI LANGUAGE.* (VOL 1)
K.K. SARKAR, 628:SPRING72-114
CHATTERJI, S.K. THE ORIGIN AND DEVELOP-
MENT OF THE BENGALI LANGUAGE. (VOL 3)
617(TLS):9FEB73-161
CHATTERTON, T. THE COMPLETE POEMS OF
THOMAS CHATTERTON. (D.S. TAYLOR, WITH
B.B. HOOVER, EDS)
G. LAMOINE, 189(EA):JUL-SEP71-338
CHATTOPADHYAYA, D. INDIAN ATHEISM (A
MARXIST ANALYSIS).
D-M. RIEPE, 484(PPR):DEC70-304
DE CHAULIAC, G. THE CYRURGIE OF GUY DE
CHAULIAC. (VOL 1) (M.S. OGDEN, ED)
THE MIDDLE ENGLISH TRANSLATION OF GUY
DE CHAULIAC'S TREATISE ON FRACTURES AND
DISLOCATIONS.* [SHOWN IN PREV UNDER
GUY] (B. WALLNER, ED)
S.M. KUHN, 589:JUL72-544
CHAURAND, J. HISTOIRE DE LA LANGUE FRAN-
ÇAISE.*
J. PICOCHE, 209(FM):OCT70-459
CHAUSSERIE-LAPRÉE, J-P. L'EXPRESSION
NARRATIVE CHEZ LES HISTORIENS LATINS.*
N.P. MILLER, 123:MAR72-64
CHAUVEL, J. COMMENTAIRE.
617(TLS):5OCT73-1152
CHAUVEL, S. LA VIE DOUCE.
M. SAKHAROFF, 207(FR):FEB71-638
DE CHAZAL, M. PLASTIC SENSE.
676(YR):SUMMER72-XVII
CHEADLE, W.B. CHEADLE'S JOURNAL OF TRIP
ACROSS CANADA 1862-1863.
L.R. RICOU, 296:SUMMER73-116
CHEATLE, S. STRAIGHT UP.
A. RENDLE, 157:AUTUMN71-82
CHEETHAM, A. RICHARD III.
617(TLS):16FEB73-189

CHEEVER, J. THE WORLD OF APPLES.
T.R. EDWARDS, 453:17MAY73-35
C. LEHMANN-HAUPT, 441:10MAY73-49
J. LEONARD, 61:JUN73-112
L. WOIWODE, 441:20MAY73-1
CHEICHEL, E. - SEE HAVIV, Y.
CHEJNE, A.G. THE ARABIC LANGUAGE.*
M.H. IBRAHIM, 350:SEP72-726
CHEKHOV, A. CHEKHOV - FOUR PLAYS. (D.
MAGARSHACK, TRANS)
A. RENDLE, 157:SUMMER70-75
CHEKHOV, A. LETTERS OF ANTON CHEKHOV.
(S. KARLINSKY, ED)
R. FULLER, 362:20SEP73-383
V.S. PRITCHETT, 453:28JUN73-3
R. SHELDON, 441:21OCT73-7
C. SIMMONS, 441:14JUL73-23
442(NY):23JUL73-78
617(TLS):21SEP73-1086
CHEKHOV, A. LETTERS OF ANTON CHEKHOV.
(A. YARMOLINSKY, ED)
P. ADAMS, 61:JUL73-103
W.H. AUDEN, 442(NY):3SEP73-62
V.S. PRITCHETT, 453:28JUN73-3
R. SHELDON, 441:21OCT73-7
C. SIMMONS, 441:14JUL73-23
CH'EN, J. - SEE MAO TSE-TUNG
CH'EN, J. & N. TARLING, EDS. STUDIES IN
THE SOCIAL HISTORY OF CHINA AND SOUTH-
EAST ASIA.
R. MURPHEY, 293(JAST):NOV70-163
E. WICKBERG, 318(JAOS):OCT-DEC71-521
CHENEY, D., ED. BROAD'S CRITICAL ESSAYS
IN MORAL PHILOSOPHY.
E. TELFER, 518:OCT72-14
CHENEY, S. - SEE DUNCAN, I.
CHERMAYEFF, S. & A. TZONIS. SHAPE OF
COMMUNITY.
K.W. DEUTSCH, 676(YR):AUTUMN71-101
CHERMENSKY, E.D. BURZHUAZIIA I TSARIZM
V PERVOI RUSSKOI REVOLIUTSII. (2ND
ED)
A. LEVIN, 32:SEP72-671
CHERNAIK, W.L. THE POETRY OF LIMITATION.*
B. O HEHIR, 405(MP):AUG70-100
C.F. WILLIAMSON, 597(SN):VOL43#1-312
CHERNOV, V. & M. GIRARD. SPLENDORS OF
MOSCOW AND ITS SURROUNDINGS.
G.H. HAMILTON, 32:MAR72-203
CHERRY, B. - SEE PEVSNER, N.
CHERRY, C. ON HUMAN COMMUNICATION. (2ND
ED)
P.W., 206:NOV70-594
DA CHERSO, F.P. - SEE UNDER PATRIZI DA
CHERSO, F.
CHERTOFF, M.S., ED. THE NEW LEFT AND THE
JEWS.
C. GERSHMAN, 287:NOV71-28
CHESLER, P. WOMEN AND MADNESS.*
F. HOWE, 31(ASCH):AUTUMN73-676
CHESNEAUX, J., F. DAVIS & N.N. HO, EDS.
MOVEMENTS POPULAIRES ET SOCIÉTÉS SEC-
RÈTES EN CHINE AUX XIXE ET XXE SIÈCLES.
Y-D.R. CHU, 293(JAST):AUG71-874
CHESNEY, K. THE ANTI-SOCIETY.* (BRITISH
TITLE: THE VICTORIAN UNDERWORLD.)
V.E. NEUBURG, 637(VS):MAR71-346
CHESTER, L. & OTHERS. WATERGATE.
617(TLS):30NOV73-1481
CHESTERTON, G.K. G.K. CHESTERTON: A
SELECTION FROM HIS NON FICTIONAL PROSE.
(W.H. AUDEN, ED)
L. CUNNINGHAM, 613:SPRING71-137
CHETHIMATTAM, J.B. CONSCIOUSNESS AND
REALITY.
E. COLEMAN, 485(PE&W):APR70-203
A.T. DE NICOLAS, 258:JUN71-262

CHETHIMATTAM, J.B. DIALOGUE IN INDIAN
TRADITION.
A.T. DE NICOLAS, 258:JUN71-262
CHEVALIER, J-C. HISTOIRE DE LA SYNTAXE.*
J. CHAURAND, 209(FM):JUL70-361
CHEVALIER, J-C. LA NOTION DE COMPLÉMENT
CHEZ LES GRAMMAIRIENS.
J. KRISTEVA, 98:FEB71-99
CHEVALIER, L. LABORING CLASSES AND
DANGEROUS CLASSES.
R.M. ANDREWS, 441:4NOV73-7
CHEVALIER, L. LES PARISIENS.
C.J. BEYER, 207(FR):OCT70-207
CHEVALIER, M. L'ARIOSTE EN ESPAGNE
(1530-1650).
A. CIORANESCU, 549(RLC):JAN-MAR71-104
CHEVALIER, M. LOS TEMAS ARIOSTESCOS EN
EL ROMANCERO Y LA POESÍA ESPAÑOLA DEL
SIGLO DE ORO.*
J.G. FUCILLA, 240(HR):OCT71-448
CHEVALLIER, R. LES VOIES ROMAINES.
617(TLS):20APR73-452
CHEW, A.F. AN ATLAS OF RUSSIAN HISTORY.
(REV)
R.A. FRENCH, 575(SEER):OCT72-633
CHEW, A.F. THE WHITE DEATH.
C.L. LUNDIN, 32:DEC72-900
CHEW, H.M. & M. WEINBAUM, EDS. THE LON-
DON EYRE OF 1244.
E. WELCH, 325:OCT71-342
CHI, W-S., ED. READINGS IN CHINESE COM-
MUNIST IDEOLOGY.
Y.J. CHIH, 318(JAOS):JAN-MAR71-150
CHIAPPELLI, F. NUOVI STUDI SUL LINGUAG-
GIO DEL MACHIAVELLI.
L. BLASUCCI, 228(GSLI):VOL148FASC464-
594
C.H. CLOUGH, 551(RENQ):WINTER71-527
CHIARI, J. THE NECESSITY OF BEING.
617(TLS):14DEC73-1536
CHIARINI, M. CLAUDE LORRAIN: SELECTED
DRAWINGS.*
M. KITSON, 90:APR71-224
CHIBA MASAJI. MATSURI NO HŌSHAKAIGAKU.
M. BAIRD, 293(JAST):FEB71-462
CHIBNALL, M. - SEE ORDERIC VITALIS
CHIDSEY, D.B. THE LOYALISTS.
G.F. SCHEER, 441:16DEC73-12
CH'IEN, T. - SEE UNDER T'AO CH'IEN
CHIEN YU-SHEN. CHINA'S FADING REVOLUTION.
S.B. THOMAS, 293(JAST):NOV70-184
CHIH-MING, C. - SEE UNDER CHOU CHIH-MING
CHILCOTE, R.H. REVOLUTION AND STRUCTURAL
CHANGE IN LATIN AMERICA.
H. KANTOR, 263:JUL-SEP72-280
37:SEP71-41
CHILD, H. - SEE JOHNSTON, E.
CHILDS, D. MARX AND THE MARXISTS.
617(TLS):15JUN73-667
"A CHIME OF WINDBELLS." (H. STEWART,
TRANS)
J. MALOF, 352(LE&W):VOL15#1-139
CHINERY, M. A FIELD GUIDE TO THE INSECTS
OF BRITAIN AND NORTHERN EUROPE.
617(TLS):23NOV73-1456
CHINIAKOV, A.G. BRATIIA VESNINY.
S.F. STARR, 576:MAY71-176
CHINOL, E. LA VITA PERDUTA.
617(TLS):11MAY73-517
CHIODI, P. L'ULTIMO HEIDEGGER. (2ND ED)
E. NAMER, 542:OCT-DEC71-476
CHIODI, P. L'ULTIMO HEIDEGGER. (3RD ED)
A.D.M., 543:MAR71-537
E. NAMER, 542:OCT-DEC71-477
CHIODI, P. - SEE KANT, I.
CHIOMENTI VASSALLI, D. VINCENZO MONTI
NEL DRAMMA DEI SUOI TEMPI.
M.P., 228(GSLI):VOL147FASC460-634

CHIRINO, P. THE PHILIPPINES IN 1600.
C.O. HOUSTON, 293(JAST):NOV70-240
CHISHOLM, A. PHILOSOPHERS OF THE EARTH.
442(NY):26MAY73-136
617(TLS):16MAR73-305
CHISHOLM, A.R. - SEE VALÉRY, P.
CHISHOLM, E. THE OPERAS OF LEOŠ JANÁČEK.
W. DEAN, 415:MAY72-460
J.T., 410(M&L):JAN72-74
CHISHOLM, S. THE GOOD FIGHT.
441:21OCT73-20
CHISSELL, J. SCHUMANN PIANO MUSIC.
617(TLS):27APR73-476
CH'IU-YUAN, H. - SEE UNDER HU CH'IU-YUAN
CHKLOVSKI, V. ZOO OU LA TROISIÈME
HÉLOÏSE.
R. MICHA, 98:JUL70-581
CHMIELEWSKI, E. THE POLISH QUESTION IN
THE RUSSIAN STATE DUMA.*
G.A. HOSKING, 497(POLR):WINTER71-123
M. SZEFTEL, 32:MAR72-161
CHOATE, S., WITH B.C. DE MAY. CREATIVE
GOLD AND SILVERSMITHING.
M. EASTHAM, 89(BJA):SPRING72-206
CHOAY, F. THE MODERN CITY.
J.E. BURCHARD, 54:MAR71-133
H.H. WAECHTER, 44:SEP71-76
CHOCHEYRAS, J. LE THÉÂTRE RELIGIEUX EN
SAVOIE AU XVIE SIÈCLE AVEC DES FRAGMENTS
INÉDITS.
G.A. RUNNALLS, 382(MAE):1972/3-280
CHOMSKY, C. THE ACQUISITION OF SYNTAX IN
CHILDREN FROM 5 TO 10.*
W. KAPER, 361:VOL26#4-422
J. MACNAMARA, 215(GL):VOL10#3-164
CHOMSKY, N. ASPECTS OF THE THEORY OF
SYNTAX.*
G.P. FAUST, 215(GL):VOL10#1-43
CHOMSKY, N. AT WAR WITH ASIA.
639(VQR):SUMMER71-CXXXIII
CHOMSKY, N. THE BACKROOM BOYS.
617(TLS):21DEC73-1565
CHOMSKY, N. FOR REASONS OF STATE.
S. HEAD, 453:9AUG73-26
C. LEHMANN-HAUPT, 441:2AUG73-39
R. TODD, 61:JUL73-97
S.S. WOLIN, 441:30SEP73-31
442(NY):30JUL73-72
617(TLS):21DEC73-1565
CHOMSKY, N. LANGUAGE AND MIND.*
J. BOUVERESSE, 98:DEC70-983
H.M. BRACKEN, 154:SEP70-236
E. PULGRAM, 399(MLJ):NOV71-474
CHOMSKY, N. & M. HALLE. THE SOUND PAT-
TERN OF ENGLISH.
K.J. KOHLER, 361:VOL26#1-73
C. ROHRER, 38:BAND88HEFT2-233
W. VIERECK, 430(NS):MAY71-277
CHOMSKY, N. & H. ZINN, EDS. CRITICAL
ESSAYS AND AN INDEX TO VOLS. 1-4 OF THE
SENATOR GRAVEL EDITION OF THE PENTAGON
PAPERS.
S. HEAD, 453:9AUG73-26
CHOPIN, K. THE COMPLETE WORKS OF KATE
CHOPIN.* (P. SEYERSTED, ED)
J. ESPEY, 445(NCF):SEP70-242
CHOPRA, P. INDIA'S SECOND LIBERATION.
617(TLS):23NOV73-1456
CHORNOVIL, V. & OTHERS. FERMENT IN THE
UKRAINE. (M. BROWNE, ED)
J.S. RESHETAR, JR., 32:DEC72-910
CHOU CHIH-MING, ED. T'AI-P'ING-YANG
HSÜEH-HUI YÜ FEI CHENG-CH'ING CHI-T'UAN.
L.H.D. GORDON & S. CHANG, 293(JAST):
NOV70-137
CHRIMES, S.B. HENRY VII.
617(TLS):19JAN73-62
CHRISMAN, H.E. - SEE HERRON, J.

CHRIST, R.J. THE NARROW ACT.
P.G. EARLE, 149:SEP72-354
R. LIMA, 546(RR):APR71-163
E. RODRÍGUEZ MONEGAL, 613:WINTER70-
623
M.E. VENIER, 400(MLN):MAR71-316
D.A. YATES, 238:MAR71-204
CHRISTADLER, M. DER AMERIKANISCHE ESSAY
1720-1820.
H.O., 430(NS):JUL71-392
CHRISTENSEN, E.M. EN FORTOLKNING AF
"HØJT FRA TRAEETS GRØNNE TOP."*
K. GULDAGER, 172(EDDA):1970/2-123
CHRISTENSON, R.M. & OTHERS. IDEOLOGIES
AND MODERN POLITICS.*
B. BECKETT, 619(TC):VOL179#1049-56
CHRISTGAU, R. ANY OLD WAY YOU CHOOSE IT.
J. ROCKWELL, 441:26DEC73-43
CHRISTIAN, H.A. LOUIS ADAMIC.
O. GRAHOR, 575(SEER):OCT72-628
CHRISTIAN, R.F. TOLSTOY: A CRITICAL IN-
TRODUCTION.*
J. FORSYTH, 205(FMLS):JAN71-28
"CHRISTIAN MARRIAGE IN AFRICA."
617(TLS):27APR73-482
CHRISTIANSEN, R. A REGIONAL HISTORY OF
THE RAILWAYS OF GREAT BRITAIN: THE WEST
MIDLANDS.
617(TLS):21DEC73-1574
CHRISTIE, A. POSTERN OF FATE.
N. CALLENDAR, 441:16DEC73-18
CHRISTIE, J.D. - SEE KNIGHT, W.F.J.
CHRISTIN, P. & P. LEFEBVRE. COMPRENDRE
LA FRANCE.
O. ANDREWS, JR., 399(MLJ):APR71-256
CHRISTOFF, P.K. AN INTRODUCTION TO NINE-
TEENTH-CENTURY RUSSIAN SLAVOPHILISM.
(VOL 2: I.V. KIREEVSKIJ.)
617(TLS):27APR73-468
CHRISTOFF, P.K. THE THIRD HEART.*
N.V. RIASANOVSKY, 550(RUSR):APR71-203
A. WALKER, 575(SEER):JAN72-138
CHRISTOPHER, M. THE ILLUSTRATED HISTORY
OF MAGIC.
W. ARNOLD, 441:16DEC73-7
CHRISTOPHERSON, D. THE UNIVERSITY AT
WORK.
617(TLS):18MAY73-552
CHRISTOW, S. TILLFELLET MARTIN.
S. LANGE-NIELSON, 270:VOL21#2-147
CHRISTY, J., ED. THE NEW REFUGEES.
A.M. BENVENUTO, 99:MAR73-46
CHROMAN, N. THE TREASURY OF AMERICAN
WINES.
R.A. SOKOLOV, 441:2DEC73-82
CHROMATIUS. CHROMACE D'AQUILÉE. "SER-
MONS."* (VOL 1) (J. LEMARIÉ, ED; H.
TARDIE, TRANS)
J. DOIGNON, 555:VOL45FASC2-371
CHRYSOSTOM, J. CODICES CHRYSOSTOMICI
GRAECI. (VOL 1 ED BY M. AUBINEAU; VOL
2 ED BY R.E. CARTER)
A. KEMMER, 182:VOL24#11/12-457
NÍ CHUILLEANÁIN, E. ACTS AND MONUMENTS.
617(TLS):27JUL73-864
CHUKOVSKY, K., ED. MASTERSTVO PEREVODA.
C. BROWN, 32:SEP72-736
"CHUNG-KUO HSIEN-TAI-SHIH TZU-LIAO TIAO-
CH'A MU-LU."
H. MAST 3D & LI YUN-HAN, 293(JAST):
FEB71-413
CHUPACK, H. ROGER WILLIAMS.
C. COVEY, 656(WMQ):APR71-345
CHURCH, G. & C.D. CARNES. THE PIT.*
J. STAFFORD, 453:5APR73-30
CHURCH, W.F. RICHELIEU AND REASON OF
STATE.
617(TLS):27JUL73-878

CHURCHILL, A. THE LITERARY DECADE.
M. BEEBE, 27(AL):NOV72-519
CHURCHILL, R.C. - SEE SAMPSON, G.
CHURCHILL, W.S. YOUNG WINSTON'S WARS.*
(F. WOODS, ED)
P. ADAMS, 61:APR73-128
CHURCHWARD, L.G. THE SOVIET INTELLIGENT-
SIA.
617(TLS):24AUG73-983
CHURTON, E. THE RAIL ROAD BOOK OF ENG-
LAND. (VOL 1)
617(TLS):22JUN73-725
CHYET, S.F. LOPEZ OF NEWPORT.
J.A. COHEN, 656(WMQ):JUL71-518
P.T. CONLEY, 432(NEQ):JUN71-346
CIAŁOWICZ, J. POLSKO-FRANCUSKI SOJUSZ
WOJSKOWY, 1921-1939.
P.S. WANDYCZ, 32:JUN72-470
CICERO. MARCUS TULLIUS CICERO: "BRUTUS."
(B. KYTZLER, ED)
F. LASSERRE, 182:VOL24#5-228
CICERO. CICÉRON, "LES PARADOXES DES
STOICIENS." (J. MOLAGER, ED & TRANS)
S.E. SMETHURST, 124:MAR72-238
CICERO. CICÉRON, "ORATIONES IN CATILI-
NAM."* (A. HAURY, ED)
J-C. DUMONT, 555:VOL45FASC2-357
CICERO. M. TULLI CICERONIS "PRO L. MUR-
ENA ORATIO."* (C. MACDONALD, ED)
R. GLEN, 123:MAR72-98
CICERO. M. TULLI CICERONIS: "PRO P.
QUINCTIO ORATIO." (T.E. KINSEY, ED)
617(TLS):19OCT73-1289
CICERO. RES PUBLICA. (W.K. LACEY &
B.W.J.G. WILSON, EDS & TRANS) [SHOWN
IN PREV UNDER EDS & TRANS]
S.M. TREGGIARI, 487:SUMMER71-194
CICERO. SELECTED POLITICAL SPEECHES.
(M. GRANT, TRANS)
J.M. SNYDER, 121(CJ):APR-MAY72-377
CICOUREL, A.V. COGNITIVE SOCIOLOGY.
617(TLS):10AUG73-926
DE CIENFUEGOS, N.A. POESÍAS. (J.L.
CANO, ED)
R.P. SEBOLD, 240(HR):JAN71-102
CIORANESCU, A. COLÓN, HUMANISTA.
J.S. CUMMINS, 86(BHS):JAN72-68
CIPOLLA, C.M. CRISTOFANO AND THE PLAGUE.
617(TLS):12OCT73-1223
CIPOLLA, C.M., ED. THE FONTANA ECONOMIC
HISTORY OF EUROPE. (VOLS 1, 3 & 4)
617(TLS):16MAR73-291
"CIRCLE." (J.L. MARTIN, B. NICHOLSON &
N. GABO, EDS)
A. BOWNESS, 592:JUL/AUG71-50
L. MARCH, 111:22OCT71-4
D. PIPER, 46:NOV71-323
CIRICI, A. L'ART CATALÀ CONTEMPORANI.
A.R. MILBURN, 86(BHS):APR72-201
CIRLOT, J-E. PICASSO: BIRTH OF A GENIUS.
A. BLUNT, 453:14JUN73-31
617(TLS):2FEB73-121
CIRRE, J.F. & M.M. ESPAÑA Y LOS ESPAÑ-
OLES.
F. SEDWICK, 238:MAY71-409
CISMARESCU, M. REFORMEN IM RECHTS- UND
JUSTIZWESEN RUMÄNIENS, 1965-1970.
K. GRZYBOWSKI, 32:SEP72-721
CITROEN, I.J., ED. TEN YEARS OF TRANS-
LATION.
V. RŪĶE-DRAVIŅA, 353:OCT71-121
CIXOUS, H. DEDANS.
D.F. JOURLAIT, 207(FR):OCT70-174
CIXOUS, H. THE EXILE OF JAMES JOYCE.*
(FRENCH TITLE: L'EXIL DE JAMES JOYCE
OU L'ART DU REMPLACEMENT.)
S. HAMPSHIRE, 453:18OCT73-8
[CONTINUED]

[CONTINUING]
J. MOYNAHAN, 441:11FEB73-21
C. ROSSMAN, 329(JJQ):SPRING73-360
CLACK, R.J. BERTRAND RUSSELL'S PHILOSO-
PHY OF LANGUAGE.
E. SIMPSON, 154:JUN70-103
CLADES, U. ROCCATAGLIATA CECCARDI.
P.Z., 228(GSLI):VOL148FASC462/463-469
CLAGETT, M. - SEE ORESME, N.
CLAIRMONT, C. THE JOURNALS OF CLAIRE
CLAIRMONT, 1814-1827.* (M.K. & D.M.
STOCKING, EDS)
J. BUXTON, 541(RES):FEB71-102
J.R. MAC GILLIVRAY, 627(UTQ):FALL70-73
CLAIRMONT, C.W. GRAVESTONE AND EPIGRAM.
J.M. COOK, 123:JUN72-292
J.G. PEDLEY, 54:DEC71-517
CLANCIER, G-E. LA POÉSIE ET SES ENVIR-
ONS.
617(TLS):12OCT73-1248
CLANCY, J.P. THE EARLIEST WELSH POETRY.
S. KNIGHT, 67:NOV72-216
CLAPHAM, J. SMETANA.*
J. TYRRELL, 415:AUG72-771
CLARAC, P. L'AGE CLASSIQUE, II, 1660-
1680.*
J. DUBU, 535(RHL):MAR-APR71-299
CLARE, J. BIRDS NEST.
617(TLS):22JUN73-726
CLARE, J. SELECTED POEMS AND PROSE OF
JOHN CLARE. (E. ROBINSON & G. SUMMER-
FIELD, EDS)
W.G. MÜLLER, 72:BAND209HEFT4/6-411
CLARENBACH, D. GRENZFÄLLE ZWISCHEN ARCH-
ITEKTUR UND PLASTIK.
E. SANTOMASSO, 576:OCT71-254
CLARK, A. ACES HIGH.
617(TLS):17AUG73-961
CLARK, A.H. ACADIA.
M. TRUDEL, 656(WMQ):APR71-325
CLARK, A.M. SIR WALTER SCOTT: THE FORMA-
TIVE YEARS.*
J. BODY, 549(RLC):OCT-DEC70-570
T. CRAWFORD, 541(RES):MAY71-223
F.R. HART, 445(NCF):JUN71-115
G.A.M. WOOD, 175:SPRING70-27
CLARK, C., ED. THE PETERBOROUGH CHRON-
ICLE 1070-1154.* (2ND ED)
R.H. ROBBINS, 72:BAND209HEFT1/3-149
CLARK, C.E. THE EASTERN FRONTIER.
D.E. LEACH, 656(WMQ):APR71-336
R.F. UPTON, 432(NEQ):JUN71-331
CLARK, D.R. & G. MAYHEW - SEE YEATS, W.B.
CLARK, E. BALDUR'S GATE.*
J.L. HALIO, 598(SOR):SPRING73-455
CLARK, E. CORPS DIPLOMATIQUE.
617(TLS):24AUG73-968
CLARK, E. & N. HORROCK. CONTRABANDISTA!
617(TLS):12OCT73-1259
CLARK, G.K. - SEE UNDER KITSON CLARK, G.
CLARK, J.R. FORM AND FRENZY IN SWIFT'S
"TALE OF A TUB."*
R. LAWRENCE, 175:SPRING71-28
H.K. MILLER, 149:MAR72-114
C.J. RAWSON, 541(RES):MAY71-214
R. QUINTANA, 597(SN):VOL43#1-314
G.D. STOUT, JR., 301(JEGP):JAN72-135
E. TUVESON, 481(PQ):JUL71-486
B. WOODWARD, 290(JAAC):SPRING71-426
CLARK, K. CIVILIZATION.
R.E., 135:SEP70-62
T.A. HEINRICH, 96:OCT/NOV71-73
T. HILTON, 592:MAR70-125
D. SUTTON, 39:APR70-320

CLARK, K. THE DRAWINGS OF LEONARDO DA
VINCI IN THE COLLECTION OF HER MAJESTY
THE QUEEN AT WINDSOR CASTLE.* (2ND ED,
REV WITH THE ASSISTANCE OF C. PEDRETTI)
A.M. BRIZIO, 54:DEC71-528
D.T., 135:MAR70-202
CLARK, K. PIERO DELLA FRANCESCA. (2ND
ED)
O.V.O., 135:MAY70-48
G. ROBERTSON, 56:AUTUMN71-356
CLARK, K. LEONARDO THE ATOMIST. (REV
WITH THE ASSISTANCE OF C. PEDRETTI)
C. GOULD, 39:NOV71-421
CLARK, K. REMBRANDT AND THE ITALIAN
RENAISSANCE.
S. ALPERS, 54:SEP70-326
CLARK, K. THE ROMANTIC REBELLION.
617(TLS):28DEC73-1585
CLARK, M. DISQUIET AND OTHER STORIES.
M. WILDING, 381:JUN71-265
CLARK, R. SIR EDWARD APPLETON.
617(TLS):2MAR73-234
CLARK, R. CRIME IN AMERICA.
L. RADZINOWICZ, 639(VQR):SUMMER71-459
CLARK, R.J., ED. THE ARTS AND CRAFTS
MOVEMENT IN AMERICA 1876-1916.
617(TLS):28DEC73-1585
CLARK, R.J.B. - SEE MÉRIMÉE, P.
CLARK, R.W. THE ALPS.
W.H. HONAN, 441:2DEC73-97
617(TLS):21DEC73-1574
CLARK, R.W. EINSTEIN.
J. MADDOX, 362:6SEP73-317
617(TLS):2NOV73-1341
CLARK, T. AIR.*
M.G. PERLOFF, 659:WINTER73-97
CLARK, T. STONES.
N. MEINKE, 448:SPRING71-92
CLARK, T.J. THE ABSOLUTE BOURGEOIS.
IMAGE OF THE PEOPLE.
M. PODRO, 362:1NOV73-594
C. THOMPSON, 441:2SEP73-6
CLARKE, A. THE CELTIC TWILIGHT AND THE
NINETIES.
R.F., 189(EA):APR-JUN71-211
R.S., 376:JAN70-114
CLARKE, A. THE ECHO AT COOLE.*
S. FAUCHEREAU, 98:MAY70-438
CLARKE, A. THE IMPURITANS.
617(TLS):7SEP73-1020
CLARKE, A. A SERMON ON SWIFT AND OTHER
POEMS.
E.N. CHUILLEANÁIN, 159(DM):SPRING70-
111
S. FAUCHEREAU, 98:MAY70-438
CLARKE, A. STORM OF FORTUNE.
L. SHIRINIAN, 296:FALL73-96
442(NY):20AUG73-89
CLARKE, A. WHEN HE WAS FREE AND YOUNG
AND HE USED TO WEAR SILKS.*
M. LEVIN, 441:9DEC73-48
D. STEPHENS, 102(CANL):AUTUMN72-84
CLARKE, A.C. RENDEZVOUS WITH RAMA.
J. LEONARD, 441:22AUG73-29
T. STURGEON, 441:23SEP73-38
617(TLS):9NOV73-1377
CLARKE, C. RIVER OF DISSOLUTION.*
E. DELAVENAY, 189(EA):APR-JUN71-207
CLARKE, D.A. HIERARCHIES OF PREDICATES
OF FINITE TYPES.
P.G. HINMAN, 316:MAR71-146
CLARKE, D.C. AGUDIECISM, THEMATICS AND
THE NEWEST NOVEL.
R.S. MILLS, 86(BHS):JAN72-105
K. SCHWARTZ, 238:MAY71-400
CLARKE, D.C. ALLEGORY, DECALOGUE, AND
DEADLY SINS IN "LA CELESTINA."*
D.S. SEVERIN, 545(RPH):MAY72-479

CLARKE, D.L., ED. MODELS IN ARCHAEOLOGY.
617(TLS):12JAN73-42
CLARKE, J.F. BIBLE SOCIETIES, AMERICAN
MISSIONARIES AND THE NATIONAL REVIVAL
OF BULGARIA.
C.S. CALIAN, 32:JUN72-500
CLARKE, J.H. - SEE ROGERS, J.A.
CLARKE, M. A COLONIAL CITY. (L.T. HER-
GENHAN, ED)
S. MURRAY-SMITH, 71(ALS):MAY73-104
CLARKE, R.A. SOVIET ECONOMIC FACTS 1917-
1970.
617(TLS):2FEB73-116
CLARKE, R.O., D.J. FATCHETT & B.C.
ROBERTS. WORKERS' PARTICIPATION IN
MANAGEMENT IN BRITAIN.
617(TLS):16MAR73-300
CLARKE, S. & A.H. - SEE SÁNCHEZ FERLOSIO,
R.
CLARKE, T.W., ED. THE NOVEL IN INDIA.
S.K. JAIN, 628:SPRING72-116
CLARKE WILSON, D. HILARY.
617(TLS):12JAN73-49
CLARKSON, A. TRUE TO YOU IN MY FASHION.
102(CANL):WINTER72-103
CLARKSON, P.S. & R.S. JETT. LUTHER MARTIN
OF MARYLAND.
R.M. IRELAND, 656(WMQ):JAN71-160
CLARKSON, S. CITY LIB.
L. AXWORTHY, 99:JAN73-26
CLARKSON, S., ED. VISIONS 2020.
A. LOWER, 529(QQ):SPRING71-162
CLARYS-PAUWELS, L. NEDERLANDSE HANDELS-
CORRESPONDENTIE.
M. ESCH-PELGROMS, 556(RLV):1971/4-509
CLAUDEL, P. & A. MEYER. CLAUDEL ET
L'AMÉRIQUE, II.* (E. ROBERTO, ED)
A. BLANC, 535(RHL):MAR-APR70-342
CLAUDIAN. DE RAPTU PROSERPINAE.* (J.B.
HALL, ED)
W. BARR, 313:VOL61-310
A. HUDSON-WILLIAMS, 123:MAR72-42
CLAYRE, A. THE IMPACT OF BROADCASTING.
617(TLS):14DEC73-1542
CLAYTON, B. THE SAVAGE IDEAL.
617(TLS):9FEB73-159
CLAYTON, J.J. SAUL BELLOW.*
R.H. FOSSUM, 594:SPRING70-99
CLEARY, J. RANSOM.
N. CALLENDAR, 441:13MAY73-38
617(TLS):16MAR73-303
CLEAVELAND, G., WITH G. FITZPATRICK. THE
MORLEYS.
W. GARD, 584(SWR):WINTER72-76
CLEAVER, V. & B. THE WHYS AND WHEREFORES
OF LITTABELLE LEE.
J. YARDLEY, 441:4MAR73-6
CLEEVE, B. THE DARK SIDE OF THE SUN.
617(TLS):28DEC73-1581
CLEEVE, B. TREAD SOFTLY IN THIS PLACE.
M. LEVIN, 441:14OCT73-48
CLEMENS, D.S. YALTA.*
639(VQR):AUTUMN71-CLXXX
CLEMENT OF ALEXANDER. CLÉMENT D'ALEXAN-
DRIE, "LE PÉDAGOGUE." (BK 3) (C. MON-
DÉSERT & C. MATRAY, TRANS; H-I. MARROU,
ED)
É. DES PLACES, 555:VOL45FASC2-354
CLEMENTE, G. LA "NOTITIA DIGNITATUM."
S.I. OOST, 122:JUL72-224
CLEMENTS, A.L. THE MYSTICAL POETRY OF
THOMAS TRAHERNE.*
J.R. MULDER, 191(ELN):DEC71-143
S.G. PUTT, 175:AUTUMN70-102
CLEMENTS, R.J. - SEE DONADONI, E.
CLEMENTS, R.J. - SEE "MICHELANGELO: A
SELF-PORTRAIT"

CLEMENTS, W.M. THE TYPES OF THE POLACK JOKE.
    M.E. BARRICK, 292(JAF):APR-JUN71-258
CLEMOES, P. & K. HUGHES, EDS. ENGLAND BEFORE THE CONQUEST.*
    H.E. HALLAM, 67:NOV72-218
CLENDENNING, J. - SEE ROYCE, J.
DE CLERCQ, C. - SEE RAIMBAUD
CLEUGH, M.F. DISCIPLINE AND MORALE IN SCHOOL AND COLLEGE.
    J. HENNINGSEN, 182:VOL24#15/16-583
CLEVELAND, J. THE POEMS OF JOHN CLEVELAND.* (B. MORRIS & E. WITHINGTON, EDS)
    R. ELLRODT, 189(EA):OCT-DEC71-526
    J. HORDEN, 38:BAND88HEFT3-392
CLEVERLEY, G. MANAGERS AND MAGIC.
    P. ADAMS, 61:MAR73-107
CLIFFORD, D. COLLECTING ENGLISH DRAWINGS.
    R.E., 135:DEC70-292
CLIFFORD, D. THE PAINTINGS OF P.A. DE LASZLO.
    T. CROMBIE, 39:MAR70-248
CLIFFORD, D. & T. JOHN CROME.*
    R.R. WARK, 54:JUN70-219
CLIFFORD, F. AMIGO, AMIGO.
    N. CALLENDAR, 441:16SEP73-30
    442(NY):31DEC73-60
    617(TLS):26OCT73-1324
CLIFFORD, J.L. FROM PUZZLES TO PORTRAITS.
    K. ALLOTT, 402(MLR):JUL72-610
    R.E. KELLEY, 481(PQ):JUL71-380
    R. LAWRENCE, 175:AUTUMN71-110
    M.R. MAHL, 173(ECS):WINTER71/72-356
    M. WAINGROW, 191(ELN):MAR72-240
CLIFFORD, J.L. & D.J. GREENE. SAMUEL JOHNSON.
    H.N. DAVIES, 354:DEC71-359
    R.E. KELLEY, 481(PQ):JUL71-445
    C. TRACY, 529(QQ):AUTUMN71-467
    M. WAINGROW, 173(ECS):SUMMER72-636
CLIFFORD, P.M. INVERSION OF THE SUBJECT IN FRENCH NARRATIVE PROSE FROM 1500 TO THE PRESENT DAY.
    617(TLS):12OCT73-1220
CLIFTON, L. GOOD NEWS ABOUT THE EARTH.*
    R.J. MILLS, JR., 491:MAY73-105
CLIFTON, L. GOOD TIMES.
    A.C. CARVER, 502(PRS):FALL71-272
CLIGNET, R. MANY WIVES, MANY POWERS.
    J. GOODY, 69:JUL71-258
CLINCH, N.G. THE KENNEDY NEUROSIS.
    R. CLAIBORNE, 441:25FEB73-36
    R. COLES, 453:8MAR73-25
CLINE, C.L. - SEE MEREDITH, G.
CLIVE, H.P. - SEE MARGUERITE DE NAVARRE
CLIVE, J. MACAULAY. (BRITISH TITLE: THOMAS BABINGTON MACAULAY.)
    P. ADAMS, 61:APR73-128
    O.D. EDWARDS, 441:1APR73-1
    C. LEHMANN-HAUPT, 441:29MAR73-51
    H.R. TREVOR-ROPER, 453:3MAY73-3
    J. VINCENT, 362:28JUN73-868
    442(NY):14APR73-155
    617(TLS):29JUN73-733
CLIVE, J. & T. PINNEY - SEE MACAULAY, T.B.
CLOETE, S. THE GAMBLER.
    617(TLS):16NOV73-1391
CLOETE, S. A VICTORIAN SON.*
    N. WEYL, 396(MODA):FALL72-433
    441:7OCT73-41
CLOGG, R. & G. YANNOPOULOS, EDS. GREECE UNDER MILITARY RULE.
    617(TLS):9MAR73-255

CLOSS, A., ED. TWENTIETH-CENTURY GERMAN LITERATURE.*
    K. GUDDAT, 399(MLJ):FEB71-114
    D.S. LOW, 220(GL&L):OCT71-49
CLOTHIER, C. BEHIND HESLINGTON HALL.
    617(TLS):31AUG73-996
CLOUGH, E.A. A SHORT-TITLE CATALOGUE ARRANGED GEOGRAPHICALLY OF BOOKS PRINTED AND DISTRIBUTED BY PRINTERS, PUBLISHERS AND BOOKSELLERS IN THE ENGLISH PROVINCIAL TOWNS AND IN SCOTLAND AND IRELAND UP TO AND INCLUDING THE YEAR 1700.
    P. MORGAN, 354:JUN71-175
CLOUZOT, M. THE WALLED CITY.
    G. WALKER, 441:23DEC73-14
CLUBB, L.G. ITALIAN PLAYS (1500-1700) IN THE FOLGER LIBRARY.*
    C. FAHY, 354:SEP70-255
CLUBB, O.E. CHINA AND RUSSIA.*
    C.M. FOUST, 32:DEC72-892
CLUBBE, J. VICTORIAN FORERUNNER.*
    A. EASSON, 447(N&Q):NOV71-424
    C.H. KETCHAM, 50(ARQ):WINTER70-367
    W.G. LANE, 405(MP):MAY71-390
CLUBBE, J. - SEE HOOD, T.
CLURMAN, H. ON DIRECTING.*
    442(NY):27JAN73-94
CLUTTERBUCK, R. PROTEST AND THE URBAN GUERRILLA.
    M. CALVERT, 362:5APR73-457
CLUTTERBUCK, R. RIOT AND REVOLUTION IN SINGAPORE AND MALAYA 1945-1963.
    617(TLS):1JUN73-606
CLUTTON-BROCK, G. & M. COLD COMFORT CONFRONTED.
    617(TLS):19JAN73-73
CLUYSENAAR, A. NODES.
    J. SAUNDERS, 565:VOL12#4-63
COATES, K., ED. ESSAYS ON SOCIALIST HUMANISM.
    617(TLS):30MAR73-343
COATES, R.D. TEACHERS' UNIONS AND INTEREST GROUP POLITICS.
    617(TLS):18MAY73-552
COATS, A.M. THE BOOK OF FLOWERS.
    617(TLS):2NOV73-1335
COBB, R. THE POLICE AND THE PEOPLE.
    R. DARNTON, 453:5APR73-25
    N. HAMPSON, 208(FS):JUL72-371
    J.H. STEWART, 207(FR):APR71-945
COBB, R. REACTIONS TO THE FRENCH REVOLUTION.* A SECOND IDENTITY.
    R. DARNTON, 453:5APR73-25
COBBAN, A., ED. THE EIGHTEENTH CENTURY.
    J.D. GRIFFIN, 58:NOV70-I5
COCHISE, N., WITH A.K. GRIFFITH. THE FIRST HUNDRED YEARS OF NIÑO COCHISE.*
    W. GARD, 584(SWR):SPRING72-V
    W.C. STURTEVANT, 441:18MAR73-38
COCHRANE, I. A STREAK OF MADNESS.
    617(TLS):4MAY73-488
COCKBURN, C. THE DEVIL'S DECADE.
    C. DRIVER, 362:18OCT73-527
    617(TLS):12OCT73-1240
COCKBURN, H. MEMORIALS OF HIS TIME.*
    K. MILLER, 362:15MAR73-346
COCKBURN, R.H. THE NOVELS OF HUGH MAC LENNAN.*
    B. NESBITT, 648:JAN71-68
COCKE, R. PIER FRANCESCO MOLA.*
    F. AMES-LEWIS, 89(BJA):SUMMER72-308
COCKS, B. THE EUROPEAN PARLIAMENT.
    617(TLS):19JAN73-56
COCKSHUT, A.O.J. THE ACHIEVEMENT OF WALTER SCOTT.*
    A.R. BURKE, 50(ARQ):AUTUMN70-278
    D. CAMERON, 529(QQ):SPRING71-153
                  [CONTINUED]

COCKSHUT, A.O.J. THE ACHIEVEMENT OF
WALTER SCOTT.* [CONTINUING]
  T. CRAWFORD, 541(RES):MAY71-223
  F.R. HART, 445(NCF):JUN71-115
  J.R. MAC GILLIVRAY, 627(UTQ):FALL70-73
  E. WAGENKNECHT, 594:SPRING71-103
  G.A.M. WOOD, 175:SPRING70-27
COCTEAU, J. COCTEAU'S WORLD. (M. CROS-
LAND ED)
  442(NY):5MAY73-152
  617(TLS):12JAN73-33
COCTEAU, J. JOURNAL D'UN INCONNU.
FAIRE-PART. CAHIERS JEAN COCTEAU, I.
  C. HODIN, 98:OCT70-839
COCTEAU, J. PROFESSIONAL SECRETS. (R.
PHELPS, ED)
  617(TLS):12JAN73-33
CODINO, F. EINFÜHRUNG IN HOMER.
  J.B. HAINSWORTH, 123:JUN72-268
CODRESCU, A. LICENSE TO CARRY A GUN.
  R. BROTHERSON, 661:SPRING71-69
CODY, J. AFTER GREAT PAIN.*
  N. BAYM, 301(JEGP):APR72-287
  A. GELPI, 27(AL):MAR72-157
  C. GRIFFITH, 598(SOR):SPRING73-468
CODY, R. THE LANDSCAPE OF THE MIND.*
  J.A. BARISH, 184(EIC):OCT71-390
COE, B. GEORGE EASTMAN AND THE EARLY
PHOTOGRAPHERS.
  617(TLS):21DEC73-1573
COE, R.N. IONESCO.
  R. HAYMAN, 157:AUTUMN71-79
COE, R.N. THE VISION OF JEAN GENET.
  M. DE ROUGEMONT, 535(RHL):JAN-FEB70-
  161
  T.A. SHEALY, 207(FR):OCT70-217
COE, R.N. - SEE STENDHAL
COE, T. WAX APPLE.
  617(TLS):13APR73-427
COFFEY, B. BLOOD RISK.
  N. CALLENDAR, 441:15APR73-35
COFFEY, M. MARCELLA.
  A.K. SHULMAN, 441:11NOV73-38
COFFIN, A.B. ROBINSON JEFFERS.*
  D.V. FULLER, 50(ARQ):SUMMER71-186
  S.P. MOSS, 579(SAQ):SPRING72-276
  M.D. UROFF, 301(JEGP):JAN72-158
COFFIN, T.P., ED. OUR LIVING TRADITIONS.
  T. BROWN, 203:SPRING71-75
COGLEY, J. CATHOLIC AMERICA.
  W. ARNOLD, 441:11MAR73-36
  E.B. FISKE, 441:31MAR73-33
COGNY, P. MAUPASSANT.*
  F. FLAGOTHIER, 556(RLV):1971/5-637
COHEN, A. ISRAEL AND THE ARAB WORLD.
  Y. ARGAMAN, 390:JAN71-69
COHEN, A.A. IN THE DAYS OF SIMON STERN.
  C. LEHMANN-HAUPT, 441:5JUN73-35
  C. OZICK, 441:3JUN73-6
  442(NY):16JUL73-79
COHEN, B.B., ED. THE RECOGNITION OF
NATHANIEL HAWTHORNE.
  E. STOCK, 445(NCF):MAR71-482
COHEN, E.H. WORKS AND CRITICISM OF
GERARD MANLEY HOPKINS.
  E.W. MELLOWN, 405(MP):MAY71-396
  W.R. MUNDT, 598(SOR):AUTUMN73-1029
  J. PICK, 636(VP):SUMMER70-176
COHEN, H., ED. LANDMARKS OF AMERICAN
WRITING.
  D.J. YANNELLA, JR., 399(MLJ):JAN71-44
COHEN, I.B. INTRODUCTION TO NEWTON'S
"PRINCIPIA."
  C. WILSON, 319:JAN73-120
COHEN, J., ED. THE ESSENTIAL LENNY
BRUCE.
  617(TLS):26OCT73-1303

COHEN, J. STRUCTURE DU LANGAGE POÉTIQUE.
  M. DÉCAUDIN, 535(RHL):SEP-DEC70-1096
COHEN, J.A., ED. CONTEMPORARY CHINESE
LAW.
  W-S. P'AN, 293(JAST):AUG71-880
COHEN, J.A., ED. THE DYNAMICS OF CHINA'S
FOREIGN RELATIONS.
  C-T. HSÜEH, 293(JAST):MAY71-671
COHEN, J.S. - SEE MOLES, A.
COHEN, L. THE ENERGY OF SLAVES.
  C. BEDIENT, 441:18FEB73-26
  617(TLS):5JAN73-10
COHEN, L.J. THE DIVERSITY OF MEANING.
  J. BENNETT, 316:JUN71-316
COHEN, L.J. THE IMPLICATIONS OF INDUC-
TION.*
  R. BLANCHÉ, 542:OCT-DEC70-486
COHEN, M. THE MONDAY RHETORIC OF THE
LOVE CLUB AND OTHER PARABLES.
  617(TLS):3AUG73-911
COHEN, M. TOUJOURS DES REGARDS SUR LA
LANGUE FRANÇAISE.
  G. GOUGENHEIM, 209(FM):JUL71-257
  P. RICKARD, 208(FS):OCT72-497
COHEN, M. TRAITÉ DE LANGUE AMHARIQUE
(ABYSSINIE). (2ND ED)
  A.K. IRVINE, 315(JAL):VOL10PT2-59
COHEN, P.J. SET THEORY AND THE CONTINU-
UM HYPOTHESIS.
  K. KUNEN, 316:DEC70-591
COHEN, R. GIRAUDOUX.*
  F.G.B., 502(PRS):SUMMER71-185
COHEN, R. THE UNFOLDING OF "THE SEA-
SONS."*
  M. GOLDEN, 191(ELN):DEC71-146
  W.P. JONES, 481(PQ):JUL71-492
  P-M. SPACKS, 401(MLQ):MAR71-113
COHEN, R. & J. MIDDLETON, EDS. FROM
TRIBE TO NATION IN AFRICA.
  L. MAIR, 69:JUL71-253
COHEN, R.S. & R.J. SEEGER, EDS. BOSTON
STUDIES IN THE PHILOSOPHY OF SCIENCE.
(VOL 6)
  L.G., 543:SEP70-145
  D. SALT, 486:SEP71-453
  F. WILSON, 154:SEP71-584
COHEN, R.S. & M.W. WARTOFSKY, EDS. BOS-
TON STUDIES IN THE PHILOSOPHY OF SCI-
ENCE. (VOL 4)
  W.R. SHEA, 154:SEP70-271
COHEN, R.S. & M.W. WARTOFSKY, EDS. BOS-
TON STUDIES IN THE PHILOSOPHY OF SCI-
ENCE.* (VOL 5)
  V.F. LENZEN, 484(PPR):SEP70-134
  W.R. SHEA, 154:SEP70-271
COHEN, S. THE DIANE GAME.
  N. CALLENDAR, 441:30DEC73-19
COHEN, S. TELL US, JERRY SILVER.
  M. LEVIN, 441:25NOV73-49
COHEN, S.B., ED. OXFORD WORLD ATLAS.
  617(TLS):10AUG73-937
COHEN, S.F. BUKHARIN AND THE BOLSHEVIK
REVOLUTION.
  H.E. SALISBURY, 441:25NOV73-4
COHEN, S.J. - SEE "DORIS HUMPHREY: AN
ARTIST FIRST"
COHN, A. THE COLLECTOR'S 20TH-CENTURY
MUSIC IN THE WESTERN HEMISPHERE.
  M. HARRISON, 415:DEC72-1192
COHN, N., ED. THE PURSUIT OF THE MILLEN-
IUM.
  42(AR):SPRING70-133
COHN, N. ROCK FROM THE BEGINNING.
  M. PETERSON, 470:JAN71-45
COHN, R. EDWARD ALBEE.*
  W. WILLEFORD, 397(MD):FEB71-450

COHN, R. CURRENTS IN CONTEMPORARY DRAMA.
    E. BIANCO, 160:VOL8#2-150
    J. FUEGI, 149:MAR72-85
    C.J. GIANAKARIS, 397(MD):MAY71-116
    B.L. KNAPP, 207(FR):OCT70-253
COHN, R. DIALOGUE IN AMERICAN DRAMA.
    J.H. RALEIGH, 27(AL):MAR72-174
COHN, R., G. ARMSTRONG & A. HIKEN, EDS.
  CLASSICS FOR CONTEMPORARIES.
    M. RIENZI, 397(MD):MAY70-109
COHN, R.G. MALLARMÉ'S MASTERWORK.
    L.J. AUSTIN, 535(RHL):JAN-FEB70-151
COHN, S.H. ECONOMIC DEVELOPMENT IN THE
  SOVIET UNION.*
    P.C. ROBERTS, 550(RUSR):APR71-195
COINDREAU, M.E. THE TIME OF WILLIAM
  FAULKNER.* (G.M. REEVES, ED & TRANS)
    S.C. MOORE, 219(GAR):WINTER71-505
COIRAULT, Y. LES MANUSCRITS DU DUC DE
  SAINT-SIMON.
    H. HIMELFARB, 535(RHL):JUL-AUG71-702
COISSORO, N. THE CUSTOMARY LAWS OF SUC-
  CESSION IN CENTRAL AFRICA.
    R.P. WERBNER, 69:APR71-176
COKE, P. THE TAXPAYERS WALTZ.
    A. RENDLE, 157:AUTUMN70-77
COKE, V.D. THE PAINTER AND THE PHOTO-
  GRAPH FROM DELACROIX TO WARHOL.*
    617(TLS):9MAR73-275
COKER, W. MUSIC AND MEANING.
    F.H., 410(M&L):OCT72-437
COLBERT, J.G., JR. LA EVOLUCIÓN DE LA
  LÓGICA SIMBÓLICA Y SUS IMPLICACIONES
  FILOSÓFICAS.
    J. FERRATER MORA, 316:JUN71-324
COLBY, U. - SEE VON GOETHE, J.W.
COLBY, V. THE SINGULAR ANOMALY.
    K.M. ROGERS, 637(VS):JUN71-463
    G.B. NEEDHAM, 445(NCF):MAR71-497
COLDSTREAM, J.N. & G.L. HUXLEY, EDS.
  KYTHERA.
    617(TLS):1JUN73-618
COLE, B. PATHETIC FALLACIES.
    617(TLS):17AUG73-946
COLE, B. THE VISITORS.*
    T. EAGLETON, 565:VOL12#2-59
COLE, H. HAWKWOOD AND THE TOWERS OF PISA.
    617(TLS):8JUN73-634
COLE, H.S.D. & OTHERS, EDS. THINKING
  ABOUT THE FUTURE.
    617(TLS):14SEP73-1041
COLE, J.P. & F.C. GERMAN. A GEOGRAPHY OF
  THE USSR. (2ND ED)
    R.A. FRENCH, 575(SEER):OCT72-634
COLE, M. THE LIFE OF G.D.H. COLE.
    P. JOHNSON, 441:7JAN73-6
COLE, R. SAHARA SURVIVAL.
    N. CALLENDAR, 441:24JUN73-34
COLE, R.A. EXODUS.
    617(TLS):1JUN73-625
COLECCHIA, F. PAISAJES Y PERSONAJES
  LATINOAMERICANOS.
    M.W. COATES, 238:DEC71-989
COLEGATE, I. AGATHA.
    E. FEINSTEIN, 362:25OCT73-572
    617(TLS):5OCT73-1157
COLEMAN, A. OTHER VOICES.*
    J. CRISPÍN, 202(FMOD):FEB70-227
    A. TERRY, 402(MLR):APR72-445
COLEMAN, B.I., ED. THE IDEA OF THE CITY
  IN NINETEENTH-CENTURY BRITAIN.
    617(TLS):23NOV73-1424
COLEMAN, E.G., ED. THE TEMPERANCE SONG-
  BOOK.
    F. HOWES, 415:JUN72-566
COLEMAN, F.X.J. THE AESTHETIC THOUGHT OF
  THE FRENCH ENLIGHTENMENT.
    A.M. LABORDE, 319:JAN73-124

COLEMAN, G.C. RABELAIS.
    A. YLLERA, 202(FMOD):NOV71/FEB72-135
COLEMAN, L. BEULAH LAND.
    R.R. LINGEMAN, 441:21OCT73-47
    G. WALKER, 441:1DEC73-37
COLEMAN, M.M. FAIR ROSALIND.
    B. BANDEL, 570(SQ):AUTUMN71-409
COLEMAN, V. LIGHT VERSE.*
    D.H. SULLIVAN, 648:OCT70-69
COLERIDGE, S.T. THE ANCIENT MARINER AND
  OTHER POEMS. (A.R. JONES & W. TYDEMAN,
  EDS)
    617(TLS):26OCT73-1325
COLERIDGE, S.T. COLERIDGE'S VERSE.* (W.
  EMPSON & D. PIRIE, EDS)
    C. ROSEN, 453:14JUN73-12
COLERIDGE, S.T. THE COLLECTED WORKS OF
  SAMUEL TAYLOR COLERIDGE: LAY SERMONS.
  (R.J. WHITE, ED)
    617(TLS):16FEB73-187
COLERIDGE, S.T. THE COLLECTED WORKS OF
  SAMUEL TAYLOR COLERIDGE: LECTURES 1795
  ON POLITICS AND RELIGION. (L. PATTON
  & P. MANN, EDS)
    W.J.B. OWEN, 541(RES):NOV71-500
    M.F. SCHULZ, 173(ECS):SPRING72-490
COLERIDGE, S.T. THE COLLECTED WORKS OF
  SAMUEL TAYLOR COLERIDGE: THE FRIEND.*
  (B.E. ROOKE, ED)
    C. CLARKE, 148:SPRING71-88
    W.J.B. OWEN, 541(RES):FEB71-95
    I.A. RICHARDS, 627(UTQ):FALL70-102
    M.F. SCHULZ, 405(MP):NOV71-142
COLERIDGE, S.T. THE COLLECTED WORKS OF
  SAMUEL TAYLOR COLERIDGE: THE WATCHMAN.*
  (L. PATTON, ED)
    I.H.C., 191(ELN):SEP71(SUPP)-41
    C. CLARKE, 148:SPRING71-88
    W.J.B. OWEN, 541(RES):AUG71-357
    M.F. SCHULZ, 173(ECS):SPRING72-490
    S.M. TAVE, 405(MP):FEB72-266
COLES, R. ERIK H. ERIKSON.
    D.W. HARDING, 362:19JUL73-90
    617(TLS):26OCT73-1318
    639(VQR):SPRING71-LXXII
COLES, W.A. - SEE VAN BRUNT, H.
COLETTE. LE BLÉ EN HERBE. (C. PICHOIS,
  ED)
    S.M. BELL, 208(FS):JUL72-359
COLETTE. COLETTE: LETTRES À SES PAIRS.
  (C. PICHOIS & R. FORBIN, EDS)
    617(TLS):8JUN73-647
COLETTE. LA MAISON DE CLAUDINE. (H.
  SHELLEY, ED)
    A.J. WELTON, 207(FR):FEB71-595
COLETTE. THE THOUSAND AND ONE MORNINGS.
  THE EVENING STAR.
    617(TLS):13APR73-413
COLGRAVE, B. & R.A.B. MYNORS - SEE
  "BEDE'S ECCLESIASTICAL HISTORY OF THE
  ENGLISH PEOPLE"
COLICCHI, C. - SEE SACCHETTI, R.
COLIE, R.L. "MY ECCHOING SONG."*
    J. CAREY, 541(RES):NOV71-496
    K.S. DATTA, 551(RENQ):WINTER71-579
    R.A. FOAKES, 175:SPRING71-23
    M. MC CANLES, 141:SPRING71-201
    J.M. WALLACE, 401(MLQ):SEP71-320
COLIN, H. - SEE BLOEM, J.C.
COLISH, M.L. THE MIRROR OF LANGUAGE.
    J. DAVIS, 480(P&R):WINTER71-64
    E.P. MAHONEY, 319:APR73-258
    V.G. POTTER, 258:JUN71-273
COLLAER, P., ED. MUSIC OF THE AMERICAS.
    617(TLS):2FEB73-118
COLLART, J. - SEE PLAUTUS
COLLERAN, J.M. - SEE SAINT ANSELM

COLLETTI, L. FROM ROUSSEAU TO LENIN.
617(TLS):15JUN73-667
COLLI, G. & M. MONTINARI - SEE NIETZSCHE,
F.W.
COLLIER, B. THE LION AND THE EAGLE.
617(TLS):23MAR73-328
COLLIER, C. ROGER SHERMAN'S CONNECTICUT.
M.M. KLEIN, 432(NEQ):DEC71-673
COLLIER, J. MILTON'S "PARADISE LOST."
L. BRAUDY, 441:5AUG73-6
J. UPDIKE, 442(NY):20AUG73-84
COLLIER, J. A SHORT VIEW OF THE IMMORAL-
ITY AND PROFANENESS OF THE ENGLISH
STAGE. (U. BROICH, ED)
G.R. HIBBARD, 179(ES):APR71-193
COLLIER, R. DUCE!
617(TLS):2MAR73-225
COLLIN, B. PERPÉTUEL.
A-C. DOBBS, 207(FR):DEC70-414
COLLIN, F. MAURICE BLANCHOT ET LA QUES-
TION DE L'ÉCRITURE.
J.C. BLEGEN, 400(MLN):DEC71-952
COLLINDER, B. KRITISCHE BEMERKUNGEN ZUM
SAUSSURE'SCHEN COURS DE LINGUISTIQUE
GÉNÉRALE.
H.M. HOENIGSWALD, 206:FEB71-136
COLLINDER, B. SPRACHVERWANDTSCHAFT UND
WAHRSCHEINLICHKEIT.
H.M. HOENIGSWALD, 206:MAY70-281
COLLINET, J-P. LE MONDE LITTÉRAIRE DE LA
FONTAINE.
J.D. BIARD, 208(FS):JUL72-326
COLLINGWOOD, R.G. THE ARCHAEOLOGY OF
ROMAN BRITAIN.* (REV BY I. RICHMOND)
R. HIGGINS, 39:AUG71-162
COLLINS, A. A DISCOURSE CONCERNING RIDI-
CULE AND IRONY IN WRITING (1729).
566:AUTUMN71-26
COLLINS, D.M. THE MENDING MAN.
R. WILLMOT, 296:FALL73-98
COLLINS, F., JR. THE PRODUCTION OF
MEDIEVAL CHURCH MUSIC-DRAMA.*
M. AUGEN, 385(MQR):SUMMER73-296
COLLINS, J. INTERPRETING MODERN PHILOSO-
PHY.
W.T. DEININGER, 319:JUL73-410
COLLINS, M. THE SILENT SCREAM.
N. CALLENDAR, 441:16DEC73-18
COLLINS, P. ARCHITECTURAL JUDGEMENT.
J. VOELCKER, 89(BJA):WINTER72-100
COLLINS, P. CHANGING IDEALS IN MODERN
ARCHITECTURE: 1750-1950.
T.M. BROWN, 54:SEP70-346
COLLINS, P. DICKENS AND CRIME.
S. MONOD, 189(EA):APR-JUN70-219
COLLINS, P. DICKENS: "BLEAK HOUSE."
T. BLOUNT, 155:SEP71-168
COLLINS, P., ED. DICKENS, THE CRITICAL
HERITAGE.
I. RANTAVAARA, 155:MAY71-109
S. WALL, 184(EIC):JUL71-261
COLLINS, R.O. LAND BEYOND THE RIVERS.
639(VQR):AUTUMN71-CLXXX
COLLIOT, R. ADENET LE ROI: "BERTE AUS
GRANS PIÉS."*
L.T. TOPSFIELD, 382(MAE):1972/1-62
COLLIS, J.S. THE VISION OF GLORY.
617(TLS):23FEB73-222
COLLISHAW, R., WITH R.V. DODDS. AIR
COMMAND.
617(TLS):14DEC73-1549
COLLISON, R. THE STORY OF STREET LITERA-
TURE.
617(TLS):2MAR73-248
COLLON-GEVAERT, S., J. LEJEUNE & J.
STIENNON. A TREASURY OF ROMANESQUE
ART.
J. CANADAY, 441:21SEP73-45

"COLLOQUIUM ERASMIANUM."
N-M. EGRETIER, 551(RENQ):SPRING71-75
COLMCILLE, M. FIRST THE BLADE.
L. ROTHENHEBER, 318(JAOS):JAN-MAR71-
159
COLODNY, R.G., ED. THE NATURE AND FUNC-
TION OF SCIENTIFIC THEORIES.
A. MERCIER, 182:VOL24#13/14-519
W.R. SHEA, 154:JUN71-361
COLOMBO, A. SULLA FENOMENOLOGIA E LA
RIVELAZIONE DELLA COSE.
E. NAMER, 542:APR-JUN70-254
COLOMBO, J.R. THE GREAT SAN FRANCISCO
EARTHQUAKE AND FIRE.*
C.X. RINGROSE, 102(CANL):SPRING72-87
COLOMBO, J.R., ED. HOW DO I LOVE THEE?
P. STEVENS, 628:SPRING72-103
COLOMBO, J.R. NEO POEMS.* JOHN TORONTO,
NEW POEMS BY DR. STRACHAN.
R.S., 376:JAN71-132
COLONNA, G. BRONZI VOTIVI UMBRO-SABELLICI
A FIGURA UMANA. (VOL 1)
D. RIDGWAY, 313:VOL61-290
DE COLONNA, G. - SEE UNDER GUIDO DE
COLONNA
COLQUHOUN, A.R. AMONGST THE SHANS.
F.N. TRAGER, 293(JAST):MAY71-723
COLQUHOUN, K. THE SUGAR COATING.
R. BRYDEN, 362:5JUL73-25
617(TLS):20JUL73-825
COLUMELLA. COLUMELLE, "DE L'AGRICUL-
TURE."* (BK 10) (E. DE SAINT-DENIS,
ED & TRANS)
A. ERNOUT, 555:VOL45FASC1-174
COLVILLE, D. VICTORIAN POETRY AND THE
ROMANTIC RELIGION.
K.C., 191(ELN):SEP71(SUPP)-19
K. KROEBER, 637(VS):JUN71-462
COLVIN, H. & J. HARRIS, EDS. THE COUNTRY
SEAT.
B. GUINNESS, 46:NOV70-327
J.L-M., 135:AUG70-289
N.N., 90:FEB71-101
F.J.B. WATSON, 39:JUL70-82
COLVIN, I. - SEE BRISSAUD, A.
COMAROFF, J.L. - SEE PLAATJE, S.T.
COMBE, T.G.S. & P. RICKARD, EDS. THE
FRENCH LANGUAGE.*
A.H. DIVERRES, 402(MLR):JAN72-182
COMBELLACK, F.M. - SEE QUINTUS OF SMYRNA
"LA COMEDIA THEBAIDA." (G.D. TROTTER &
K. WHINNOM, EDS)
D.W. MC PHEETERS, 240(HR):JUL71-319
205(FMLS):OCT70-419
COMES, S. ADA NEGRI DA UN TEMPO ALL'-
ALTRO.
M. PUCCINI, 275(IQ):SPRING71-143
COMETTI, E. - SEE DAL VERME, F.
"THE COMMON BIBLE." (REVISED STANDARD
VERSION)
617(TLS):2MAR73-243
COMMONS, J.R. THE ECONOMICS OF COLLEC-
TIVE ACTION. (K.H. PARSONS, ED)
185:OCT70-86
COMPAGNONE, L. LE NOTTI DI GLASGOW.
270:VOL22#2-40
"COMPLETE CATALOGUE OF THE LIBRARY OF JOHN
QUINN SOLD BY AUCTION IN FIVE PARTS."
J. CARTER, 354:MAR71-68
COMPTON, M. POP ART.
A. HIGGINS, 592:MAR71-131
D. IRWIN, 39:APR71-342
CONANT, K.J. CLUNY, LES ÉGLISES ET LA
MAISON DU CHEF D'ORDRE.
R. BRANNER, 54:JUN71-246
CONANT, R.W. THE PROSPECTS FOR REVOLU-
TION.
D.E. APTER, 639(VQR):SUMMER71-445

CONARROE, J. WILLIAM CARLOS WILLIAMS'
"PATERSON."*
B. DUFFEY, 659:SUMMER73-406
P. MARIANI, 418(MR):AUTUMN72-664
A.K. WEATHERHEAD, 401(MLQ):JUN72-172
639(VQR):SPRING71-LXIV
CONAWAY, J. JUDGE.
M. IVINS, 441:21OCT73-4
DE CONDÉ, J. JEAN DE CONDÉ: LA MESSE
DES OISEAUX ET LE DIT DES JACOBINS ET
DES FREMENEURS. (J. RIBARD, ED)
J.C. LAIDLAW, 382(MAE):1972/1-71
B.S. MERRILEES, 589:JAN72-111
CONDEESCU, N.N. INITIATION À LA PHILOLO-
GIE FRANÇAISE.
O. NANDRIS, 209(FM):JAN71-77
CONDIT, C.W. AMERICAN BUILDING.
M.M. ROTSCH, 576:OCT70-284
CONDLIFFE, J.B. TE RANGI HIROA.
617(TLS):9NOV73-1368
CONDON, R. AND THEN WE MOVED TO ROSSE-
NARRA.
442(NY):2JUL73-76
CONE, J.H. THE SPIRITUALS AND THE BLUES.
V.E. BUTCHER, 187:JAN73-132
CONEY, M. MIRROR IMAGE.
617(TLS):9NOV73-1378
CÔNG-HUYÊN-TÔN-NÙ, N-T. VIETNAMESE FOLK-
LORE.
H. GLASSIE, 292(JAF):OCT-DEC71-468
CONGAR, Y. THE REVELATION OF GOD.
J.M.S., 543:JUN71-743
CONKLIN, D.W. AN EVALUATION OF THE
SOVIET PROFIT REFORMS.
G. GROSSMAN, 32:MAR72-185
CONKLIN, J.E. ROBBERY AND THE CRIMINAL
JUSTICE SYSTEM.
A. HACKER, 453:19APR73-9
CONLEY, J., ED. THE MIDDLE ENGLISH
"PEARL."
R.D., 179(ES):JUN71-303
S.S. HUSSEY, 447(N&Q):JUL71-266
CONLON, P.M. PRÉLUDE AU SIÈCLE DES
LUMIÈRES EN FRANCE.* (VOL 1)
T.E.D. BRAUN, 207(FR):MAR71-808
M. LEVER, 535(RHL):MAY-JUN71-506
J. LOUGH, 208(FS):APR72-197
CONLON, P.M. PRÉLUDE AU SIÈCLE DES
LUMIÈRES EN FRANCE. (VOL 2)
A. MARTIN, 67:MAY72-95
CONN, S. AMBUSH.
W. WALLIS, 502(PRS):FALL71-278
CONN, S. AN EAR TO THE GROUND.
A. MACLEAN, 362:22MAR73-389
617(TLS):5JAN73-10
CONNELL, E.S., JR. POINTS FOR A COMPASS
ROSE.
T.R. EDWARDS, 453:17MAY73-35
H. MITGANG, 441:30JUN73-37
P. WEST, 441:29APR73-7
CONNELLY, T.L. AUTUMN OF GLORY.
639(VQR):SUMMER71-CXXII
CONNOLLY, E. LEOPOLDO PANERO.*
A.M. FAGUNDO, 238:MAR71-199
CONNOLLY, R. A GIRL WHO CAME TO STAY.
S. HILL, 362:22MAR73-390
CONNOR, T. IN THE HAPPY VALLEY.*
A. CLUYSENAAR, 565:VOL12#4-68
D. TIPTON, 619(TC):VOL179#1047-46
CONNOR, W.R. THE NEW POLITICIANS OF
FIFTH-CENTURY ATHENS.*
F.J. FROST, 122:JUL72-199
T. KELLY, 124:DEC71-137
CONNORS, D.F. THOMAS MORTON.*
S. BERCOVITCH, 551(RENQ):SPRING71-103
J.J. MC ALEER, 613:AUTUMN70-446

CONOLLY, J. TREATMENT OF THE INSANE
WITHOUT MECHANICAL RESTRAINTS. (R.
HUNTER & I. MACALPINE, EDS)
617(TLS):28SEP73-1137
CONQUEST, N. THE GUN AND THE GLORY OF
GRANITE HENDLEY.
C. BAKER, 649(WAL):WINTER71-307
CONQUEST, R. THE GREAT TERROR.*
617(TLS):16NOV73-1397
CONQUEST, R. THE NATION KILLERS.
D. VON MOHRENSCHILDT, 550(RUSR):JUL
71-310
CONQUEST, R. - SEE SHECKLEY, R.
CONQUEST, R. - SEE YAKIR, P.
CONRAD, B. MY FATHER: JOSEPH CONRAD.
J.S. LEWIS, 177(ELT):VOL13#3-246
A.T. SCHWAB, 136:VOL3#1-123
CONRAD, J. JOSEPH CONRAD'S LETTERS TO
R.B. CUNNINGHAME GRAHAM.* (C.T. WATTS,
ED)
J. ESPEY, 445(NCF):JUN70-124
I. VIDAN, 177(ELT):VOL13#1-77
CONRAD, J. NOSTROMO.
I. BAIN, 503:WINTER70-227
CONRAD, J. THE SISTERS. (U. MURSIA, ED)
J.S. LEWIS, 177(ELT):VOL13#3-245
CONRAD, P. THE VICTORIAN TREASURE-HOUSE.
J. BAYLEY, 362:5JUL73-24
617(TLS):6JUL73-768
CONRAD, T. ZUR WESENSLEHRE DES PSYCHIS-
CHEN LEBENS UND ERLEBENS.
W.J.H. STEIN, 484(PPR):DEC70-313
CONROY, P.V., JR. CRÉBILLON FILS: TECH-
NIQUES OF THE NOVEL.
617(TLS):20APR73-440
"CONSERVATION IN ACTION."
617(TLS):2FEB73-133
CONSTABLE, G. & B. SMITH, EDS & TRANS.
LIBELLUS DE DIVERSIS ORDINIBUS ET
PROFESSIONIBUS QUI SUNT IN AECCLESIA.
617(TLS):2FEB73-128
CONSTANT, A.L. ELIPHAS LÉVI, VISIONNAIRE
ROMANTIQUE.* (F.P. BOWMAN, ED)
A. BECQ, 535(RHL):MAR-APR71-308
CONSTANT, B. ACTES DU CONGRÈS DE LAU-
SANNE.
P. MOREAU, 557(RSH):JUL-SEP70-479
CONSTANTIN, M.M. GOD AND THE OTHERS.
M. LEVIN, 441:21JAN73-24
CONSTANTINE, K.C. THE MAN WHO LIKED TO
LOOK AT HIMSELF.
N. CALLENDAR, 441:23DEC73-16
CONSTANTINE, K.C. THE ROCKSBURG RAILROAD
MURDERS.
N. CALLENDAR, 441:11FEB73-30
CONSTANTINESCU, N.A. DICȚIONAR ONOMASTIC
ROMÎNESC.
E.P. HAMP, 215(GL):VOL11#1-61
CONSTANTINI, H. HÁBLENME DE FUNES.
K. SCHWARTZ, 238:DEC71-973
CONSTANTINOV, G. MOETO POKOLÉNIE V LIT-
ERATURATA. (PT 1)
N. DONTCHEV, 270:VOL21#1-118
CONTAG, V. CHINESE MASTERS OF THE SEVEN-
TEENTH CENTURY.
M. SULLIVAN, 39:MAY70-402
CONTAG, V. & WANG CHI-CH'IEN. SEALS OF
CHINESE PAINTERS AND COLLECTORS OF
THE MING AND CH'ING PERIODS.
CHUANG SHEN, 302:JUL71-376
CONTAT, M. & M. RYBALKA. LES ÉCRITS DE
SARTRE.
M. DUFOUR, 154:SEP70-279
E. MOROT-SIR, 207(FR):FEB71-603
"CONTEMPORARY ITALIAN VERSE." (G. SINGH,
TRANS)
L. REBAY, 276:AUTUMN71-405.

"CONTEMPORARY SPANISH PHILOSOPHY." (A.R. CAPONIGSI, TRANS)
S. BACARISSE, 86(BHS):JAN72-95
CONTI, G.G. - SEE UNDER GADDA CONTI, G.
CONTINI, G. ALTRI ESERCIZI.
617(TLS):12OCT73-1225
CONTINI, G. LETTERATURA ITALIANA DELLE ORIGINI.
A.L. LEPSCHY, 402(MLR):OCT72-917
L.T., 275(IQ):SPRING-SUMMER72-111
CONTINI, P. THE SOMALI REPUBLIC.
V. LULING, 69:OCT71-340
"CONTRIBUTI ALLA STORIA DEL LIBRO ITAL-IANO: MISCELLANEA IN ONORE DI LAMBERTO DONATI."
C. FAHY, 354:SEP71-269
"CONTRIBUTI DELL'ISTITUTO DI ARCHEOLOGIA." (VOLS 1 & 2)
D.E. STRONG, 123:MAR72-144
"CONVEGNO DI STUDI IN ONORE DI LODOVICO ZUCCOLO NEL QUARTO CENTENARIO DELLA NASCITA (FAENZA, 15-16 MARZO 1969)."
R. ALONGE, 228(GSLI):VOL148FASC462/463-452
COOK, A. THE CHARGES.
L. MUELLER, 491:AUG73-293
COOK, A. PRISMS.
H. OPPEL, 38:BAND88HEFT2-279
COOK, A.B. 3D. INTRODUCTION TO THE ENG-LISH LANGUAGE: STRUCTURE AND HISTORY.
E.A. EBBINGHAUS, 215(GL):VOL10#3-181
COOK, B. THE BEAT GENERATION.
L. LEARY, 27(AL):MAY72-336
COOK, J.M. THE TROAD.
617(TLS):7SEP73-1036
COOK, J.W. & H. KLOTZ. CONVERSATIONS WITH ARCHITECTS.
R. JELLINEK, 441:26AUG73-4
617(TLS):14SEP73-1047
COOK, O. THE ENGLISH HOUSE THROUGH SEVEN CENTURIES.
A.C-T., 135:APR70-277
J. WILTON-ELY, 39:APR70-318
COOK, P., ED. ARCHIGRAM.
617(TLS):23FEB73-203
COOK, R. THE MAPLE LEAF FOREVER.*
J.M. BECK, 150(DR):SUMMER71-288
COOK, R.I. JONATHAN SWIFT AS A TORY PAMPHLETEER.
P. DANCHIN, 179(ES):JUN71-272
COOK, S. SIGNS OF LIFE.
617(TLS):17AUG73-946
COOK, W.A. INTRODUCTION TO TAGMEMIC ANALYSIS.
R. HUDDLESTON, 297(JL):OCT71-291
V.B. PICKETT, 215(GL):VOL11#2-104
COOK, W.L. FLOOD TIDE OF EMPIRE.
617(TLS):11MAY73-533
"ALISTAIR COOKE'S AMERICA."
617(TLS):30NOV73-1481
COOKE, J.R. PRONOMINAL REFERENCE IN THAI, BURMESE, AND VIETNAMESE.*
N.D. HOA, 215(GL):VOL10#1-68
COOKE, M.G. THE BLIND MAN TRACES THE CIRCLE.*
K.A. BRUFFEE, 405(MP):AUG70-115
J.R. MAC GILLIVRAY, 627(UTQ):FALL70-73
COOKE, P.P. PHILIP PENDLETON COOKE: POET, CRITIC, NOVELIST. (J.D. ALLEN, ED)
D.R. NOBLE, JR., 577(SHR):FALL71-412
COOKE, W. EDWARD THOMAS.
R.P. DRAPER, 148:SPRING71-92
R. LAWRENCE, 175:SUMMER71-70
J.P., 376:JUL70-112
COOKSON, W. - SEE POUND, E.

COOLEY, J.K. GREEN MARCH, BLACK SEPTEM-BER.
617(TLS):20JUL73-824
COOLEY, L.F. CALIFORNIA.
M. LEVIN, 441:21OCT73-50
COOLIDGE, C. SPACE.*
M.G. PERLOFF, 659:WINTER73-97
COOLIDGE, C. YOUR SON, CALVIN COOLIDGE. (E.C. LATHEM, ED)
A.F. MC CLURE, 14:JAN70-93
COOLIDGE, J.S. THE PAULINE RENAISSANCE IN ENGLAND.
E. EMERSON, 568(SCN):SUMMER72-43
COOMBES, H., ED. D.H. LAWRENCE.
617(TLS):9NOV73-1369
COOMBS, O., ED. WE SPEAK AS LIBERATORS.
G. FOX, 529(QQ):SPRING71-160
COOPE, R. SALOMON DE BROSSE.
617(TLS):23FEB73-216
COOPER, A. - SEE "LI PO AND TU FU"
COOPER, C. CONRAD AND THE HUMAN DILEMMA.
R.F. HAUGH, 136:VOL3#1-128
COOPER, D. BRAQUE: THE GREAT YEARS.
617(TLS):27JUL73-879
COOPER, D. THE CUBIST EPOCH.
R. LEBOWITZ, 58:MAY71-14
D.M. SOKOL, 127:FALL71-102
COOPER, E. A HISTORY OF POTTERY.
617(TLS):2FEB73-133
COOPER, H.S.F., JR. 13: THE FLIGHT THAT FAILED.
J. MC ELROY, 441:11MAR73-4
COOPER, I.S. THE VICTIM IS ALWAYS THE SAME.
J.E. BRODY, 441:29SEP73-29
C.P. SNOW, 441:12AUG73-3
COOPER, J. JOLLY SUPER TOO.
617(TLS):7DEC73-1521
COOPER, J. CATHERINE SPENCE.
B.H. BENNETT, 71(ALS):OCT73-220
COOPER, J.P., ED. WENTWORTH PAPERS 1597-1628.
617(TLS):21SEP73-1093
COOPER, J.R. THE ART OF "THE COMPLEAT ANGLER."
K.R. GROS LOUIS, 599:WINTER70-69
COOPER, L. TEA ON SUNDAY.
617(TLS):3AUG73-911
COOPER, M. BEETHOVEN: THE LAST DECADE, 1817-1827.*
E.C. KROHN, 377:MAR72-56
COOPER, P. THE AUTOBIOGRAPHICAL MYTH OF ROBERT LOWELL.*
K.H. BALDWIN, 651(WHR):WINTER72-79
G.S. FRASER, 473(PR):FALL72-602
L. PRATT, 502(PRS):WINTER71/72-361
W.B. RIDEOUT, 659:SUMMER73-384
H. SERGEANT, 175:SUMMER71-65
COOPER, S. J.B. PRIESTLEY.
G. NIGOT, 189(EA):OCT-DEC71-540
COOPER, W. LOVE ON THE COAST.
R. BRYDEN, 362:15MAR73-348
617(TLS):16MAR73-285
COOPERMAN, S. CAPPELBAUM'S DANCE.*
R. GUSTAFSON, 529(QQ):SPRING71-140
COPE, J. ALLEY CAT.
617(TLS):13JUL73-797
COPELAND, J.I. - SEE GREEN, F.M.
COPERNICUS, N. COMPLETE WORKS. (VOL 1) (P. CZARTORYSKI, ED)
617(TLS):2MAR73-232
COPI, I.M. INTRODUCTION TO LOGIC. (3RD ED)
A. BORGERS, 316:MAR70-166
COPI, I.M. THE THEORY OF LOGICAL TYPES.*
H.S. STANILAND, 518:MAY72-11
COPLANS, J. ELLSWORTH KELLY.
L. NOCHLIN, 441:2DEC73-40

COPLESTON, F.C. A HISTORY OF MEDIEVAL
PHILOSOPHY.*
L. VELECKY, 518:OCT72-16
COPLEY, F.O. LATIN LITERATURE: FROM THE
BEGINNINGS TO THE CLOSE OF THE SECOND
CENTURY A.D.*
L.C. CURRAN, 121(CJ):FEB-MAR72-285
COPPENS, J., ED. SCRINIUM ERASMIANUM.
(VOL 1)
S. MANDEVILLE, 551(RENQ):SPRING71-77
COPPER, B. SONGS AND SOUTHERN BREEZES.
617(TLS):2NOV73-1352
COPPER, B. THE VAMPIRE.
617(TLS):20APR73-452
COQUIN, F-X. LA GRANDE COMMISSION LÉGIS-
LATIVE, 1767-1768.
M. RAEFF, 32:SEP72-663
CORBEIL, J-C. LES STRUCTURES SYNTAXIQUES
DU FRANÇAIS MODERNE.*
E. ROULET, 343:BAND13HEFT2-173
CORBETT, E.P.J., ED. RHETORICAL ANALY-
SES OF LITERARY WORKS.
T.W. BENSON, 480(P&R):SPRING70-128
CORBETT, P.B. PETRONIUS.*
G. SCHMELING, 399(MLJ):NOV71-482
"CORBIÈRE." (T. SAVORY, TRANS)
J. HART, 661:SUMMER70-113
CORBIN, H. EN ISLAM IRANIEN. (VOLS 3&4)
617(TLS):13APR73-422
CORBOZ, A. INVENTION DE CAROUGE 1772-
1792.*
R. POMMER, 576:OCT71-251
CORBUSIER, W.T. VERDE TO SAN CARLOS.
W. GARD, 584(SWR):SPRING72-V
CORDASCO, F. & E. BUCCHIONI. THE PUERTO
RICAN EXPERIENCE.
J.M. GARCIA-PASSALACQUA, 441:7OCT73-
24
CORDELL, A. IF YOU BELIEVE THE SOLDIERS.
617(TLS):28SEP73-1101
CORDER, J.W. USE OF RHETORIC.
R. CONVILLE, 583:SPRING72-330
CORDERO, F. AGAINST THE CATHOLIC SYSTEM.
617(TLS):16MAR73-305
CORDERO, F. PAVANA.
617(TLS):18MAY73-562
CORDES, G., ED. EIN NEUWERKER KOPIALBUCH
AUS DEM ANFANG DES 15. JAHRHUNDERTS.
N.T.J. VOORWINDEN, 433:APR70-198
CORDIER, A.W. & W. FOOTE, EDS. PUBLIC
PAPERS OF THE SECRETARIES-GENERAL OF
THE UNITED NATIONS. (VOL 2: DAG HAM-
MARSKJÖLD, 1953-1956.)
617(TLS):20APR73-433
CORIPPUS. FLAVII CRESCONII CORIPPI "IO-
HANNIDOS" LIBRI VIII.* (J. DIGGLE &
F.R.D. GOODYEAR, EDS)
A. HUDSON-WILLIAMS, 123:JUN72-219
CORLU, A. - SEE PLUTARCH
CORMACK, A.J.R., ED. SMALL ARMS IN PRO-
FILE. (VOL 1)
617(TLS):23FEB73-212
CORMAN, C. LIVINGDYING.
A. OSTRIKER, 473(PR):SPRING72-270
CORMAN, C. - SEE PONGE, F.
CORMEAU, C. HARTMANNS VON AUE "ARMER
HEINRICH" UND "GREGORIUS."
M.O. WALSHE, 220(GL&L):OCT71-16
CORNEILLE, P. POMPÉE. (H.T. BARNWELL,
ED)
D.L. ANDERSON, 568(SCN):FALL-WINTER72-
69
CORNEILLE, P. SURÉNA, GÉNÉRAL DES PAR-
THES. (J. SANCHEZ, ED)
P.J. YARROW, 208(FS):JUL72-324
CORNELISEN, A. VENDETTA OF SILENCE.*
TORREGRECA.
M. MUDRICK, 249(HUDR):SPRING72-142

CORNELIUS, F. GEISTESGESCHICHTE DER
FRÜHZEIT II. (PT 2)
E. NEU, 260(IF):BAND75-254
CORNELL, K. THE POST-SYMBOLIST PERIOD.
S.I. LOCKERBIE, 208(FS):JUL72-350
CORNER, B.C. & C.C. BOOTH - SEE FOTHER-
GILL, J.
CORNEVIN, R. LE THÉÂTRE EN AFRIQUE
NOIRE ET À MADAGASCAR.
M. URBAIN-FAUBLÉE, 69:OCT71-347
CORNFORTH, M. MARXISM AND THE LINGUISTIC
PHILOSOPHY.
A. LINGIS, 206:FEB71-131
CORNFORTH, M. THE OPEN PHILOSOPHY AND
THE OPEN SOCIETY.*
J.J. JENKINS, 478:JAN70-88
CORNING, H.M. THIS EARTH AND ANOTHER
COUNTRY.
P. GOW, 134(CP):SPRING71-55
CORNMAN, J.W. MATERIALISM AND SENSA-
TIONS.*
P. JONES, 518:MAY72-14
CORNMAN, J.W. METAPHYSICS, REFERENCE AND
LANGUAGE.
M. HOLLIS, 206:FEB70-106
"CORNMARKET CAREERS FOR SCHOOL LEAVERS
1973."
617(TLS):13APR73-429
CORNWALL, B. THE BUSH REBELS.
617(TLS):2MAR73-244
CORNWELL, J. COLERIDGE, POET AND REVOLU-
TIONARY 1772-1804.
617(TLS):13APR73-415
"CORPUS INSCRIPTIONUM LATINARUM." (VOL 4)
J. ANDRÉ, 555:VOL45FASC2-355
"CORPUS VASORUM ANTIQUORUM." (ITALIA,
FASC 41, PT 1 ED BY L. VLAD BORRELLI;
PT 5 ED BY P. BOCCI)
B.A. SPARKES, 303:VOL91-207
"CORPUS VASORUM ANTIQUORUM." (U.S.A.
FASC 15) (C.G. BOULTER, ED)
617(TLS):16FEB73-184
CORRALES EGEA, J. BAROJA Y FRANCIA.
P. REDONDO, 202(FMOD):JUN70-345
CORRIGAN, B., ED. ITALIAN POETS AND
ENGLISH CRITICS, 1755-1859.*
D.J. DONNO, 276:AUTUMN71-390
CORRIGAN, F. SIEGFRIED SASSOON.
617(TLS):7DEC73-1507
CORRIGAN, R.W., ED. LAUREL BRITISH
DRAMA: THE NINETEENTH CENTURY.
P.D. HERRING, 405(MP):AUG70-83
CORRIGAN, R.W., ED. ARTHUR MILLER: A
COLLECTION OF CRITICAL ESSAYS.
502(PRS):WINTER71/72-370
CORSARO, F. LACTANTIANA.
P. COURCELLE, 555:VOL45FASC2-371
CORSARO, F. - SEE LACTANTII, L.C.F.
CORSI, G., ED. POESIE MUSICALI DEL TRE-
CENTO. RIMATORI DEL TRECENTO.
M. MARTI, 228(GSLI):VOL148FASC462/
463-370
CORSI, M. INTRODUZIONE AL LEVIATONO.
A. PACCHI, 548(RCSF):APR-JUN70-202
CORSON, R. FASHIONS IN MAKEUP.
617(TLS):19JAN73-68
CORTÁZAR, J. ALL FIRES THE FIRE.
P. ADAMS, 61:OCT73-130
M. WOOD, 441:9SEP73-4
CORTÁZAR, J. LIBRO DE MANUEL.
617(TLS):12OCT73-1208
CORTÁZAR, J. 62: A MODEL KIT.*
M. WOOD, 453:19APR73-35
CORTELAZZO, M. L'INFLUSSO LINGUISTICO
GRECO A VENEZIA.
G.C. LEPSCHY, 382(MAE):1972/1-87

CORTÉS, H. LETTERS FROM MEXICO. (A.R.
PAGDEN, ED & TRANS)
617(TLS):2FEB73-120
CORTI, M. - SEE LEOPARDI, G.
CORTINA, J.R. EL ARTE DRAMÁTICO DE
ANTONIO BUERO VALLEJO.
C.C. DE COSTER, 397(MD):FEB71-456
J-L. MARFANY, 86(BHS):JAN72-97
CORTLAND, P. A READER'S GUIDE TO FLAU-
BERT.
E. ZAPPULLA, 207(FR):OCT70-227
"PIETRO DA CORTONA, MOSTRA DOCUMENTARIA."
A. BLUNT, 90:NOV71-672
CORVEZ, M. LA PHILOSOPHIE DE HEIDEGGER.
P. AUBENQUE, 542:OCT-DEC71-474
CORVINGTON, G., JR. PORT AU PRINCE AU
COURS DES ANS. (VOL 1)
M-A. LUBIN, 263:JAN-MAR72-52
COSELL, H., WITH M. HERSKOWITZ. COSELL.
C. LEHMANN-HAUPT, 441:17OCT73-47
COSGRAVE, P. THE PUBLIC POETRY OF ROBERT
LOWELL.*
G.S. FRASER, 473(PR):FALL72-602
COSMAS INDICOPLEUSTES. COSMAS INDICO-
PLEUSTES, "TOPOGRAPHIE CHRÉTIENNE."
(W. WOLSKA-CONUS, ED & TRANS)
P.J. ALEXANDER, 589:JUL72-574
COST, M. A KEY TO LAURELS.
442(NY):24FEB73-129
COSTA, C. PANORAMA DA HISTÓRIA DA FIL-
OSOFIA NO BRASIL.
A.M., 543:JUN71-744
COSTA, C.D.N. - SEE SENECA
DA COSTA, M.G., C.F. BECKINGHAM & D.M.
LOCKHART - SEE UNDER GONÇALVES DA
COSTA, M., C.F. BECKINGHAM & D.M. LOCK-
HART
COSTELLO, D.F. THE DESERT WORLD.*
W. GARD, 584(SWR):AUTUMN72-330
COSTELLO, M. THE MURPHY STORIES.
R.V. CASSILL, 441:25FEB73-3
DE COSTER, C.C. BIBLIOGRAFÍA CRÍTICA DE
JUAN VALERA.
A. NOUGUÉ, 182:VOL24#17/18-671
COSTES, A. ALBERT CAMUS ET LA PAROLE
MANQUANTE.
617(TLS):12OCT73-1252
COTEANU, I., ED. ISTORIA LIMBII ROMÂNE.
(VOL 2)
R. BROWNING, 123:MAR72-128
COTEANU, I. & I. DĂNĂILĂ. INTRODUCERE
ÎN LINGVISTICA ŞI FILOLOGIA ROMÂNEASCĂ.
J. KRAMER, 72:BAND209HEFT1/3-177
E.M. WALLNER, 182:VOL24#11/12-474
COTEANU, J. OÙ EN SONT LA PHILOLOGIE ET
LA LINGUISTIQUE ROUMAINES.
O. NANDRIS, 209(FM):APR70-171
"COTEANU ŞI COLABORATORII."
L. FASSEL, 597(SN):VOL43#1-266
COTLOW, L. THE TWILIGHT OF THE PRIMITIVE.
617(TLS):7DEC73-1521
COTRONEO, G. CROCE E L'ILLUMINISMO.
G. OLDRINI, 548(RCSF):OCT-DEC71-468
COTTER, J.F. INSCAPE.
W.R. MUNDT, 598(SOR):AUTUMN73-1029
COTTERELL, G. AMSTERDAM.
617(TLS):24AUG73-975
COTTIN, M. - SEE GAUTIER, T.
COTTLE, B. THE TRIUMPH OF ENGLISH, 1350-
1400.
A. HUDSON, 541(RES):FEB71-110
COTTLE, T.J. THE ABANDONERS.
T. SOLOTAROFF, 441:4MAR73-8
COTTLE, T.J. TIME'S CHILDREN.
676(YR):WINTER72-XIII
COTTON, J. OLD MOVIES AND OTHER POEMS.
R.J. MILLS, JR., 491:MAY73-105
COTTON, J.P., JR. - SEE MARSHALL, J.

COTTRELL, A.P. WILHELM MÜLLER'S LYRICAL
SONG-CYCLES.
E. LOEB, 401(MLQ):JUN72-201
R. TAYLOR, 564:OCT71-247
COTTRELL, L. READING THE PAST.
617(TLS):13JUL73-812
COTTRELL, R.D. BRANTÔME.*
K.M. HALL, 208(FS):JUL72-322
L.M. HELLER, 399(MLJ):MAR71-183
C.E. RATHÉ, 207(FR):MAY71-1132
COUFFIGNAL, R. "AUX PREMIERS JOURS DU
MONDE," LA PARAPHRASE POÉTIQUE DE LA
GENÈSE DE HUGO À SUPERVIELLE.
A. BLANC, 535(RHL):JUL-AUG71-720
E.K. KAPLAN, 207(FR):MAR71-802
COULEAU, J. LA PAYSANNERIE MAROCAINE.
P. SALMON, 182:VOL24#1/2-9
COULET, H. LE ROMAN JUSQU'À LA RÉVOLU-
TION.* (VOLS 1&2)
E. SHOWALTER, JR., 173(ECS):SPRING72-
467
COULETTE, H. THE FAMILY GOLDSCHMITT.
F.D. REEVE, 491:MAR73-348
COULOS, J., ED. YOUTH AND MATURITY.
J.W. STEVENSON, 573(SSF):SUMMER71-475
COULSON, G. SPEECH PRACTICE.
C. LAMBERT, 157:SUMMER70-73
COULSON, W.R. GROUPS, GIMMICKS, AND
INSTANT GURUS.
J. STAFFORD, 453:5APR73-30
COUNTS, D. A GRAMMAR OF KALIAI-KOVE.
A. CAPELL, 350:MAR72-230
COUPER, J.M. THE BOOK OF BLIGH.
S.E. LEE, 581:1971/3-227
COUPEZ, A. & T. KAMANZI. LITTÉRATURE DE
COUR AU RWANDA.
M. D'HERTEFELT, 69:OCT70-386
COURCELLE, J. & P. ICONOGRAPHIE DE SAINT
AUGUSTIN.
A. ERNOUT, 555:VOL45FASC1-180
COURCELLE, P. LATE LATIN WRITERS AND
THEIR GREEK SOURCES.*
J. ANDRÉ, 555:VOL45FASC1-180
COURLANDER, H. THE FOURTH WORLD OF THE
HOPIS.
W. GARD, 584(SWR):WINTER72-76
COURLANDER, H. TALES OF YORUBA GODS AND
HEROES.
P. ADAMS, 61:JAN73-100
"LE COURONNEMENT DE LOUIS." (A. LANLY,
TRANS)
C. RÉGNIER, 209(FM):JUL70-370
COURSE, E. THE RAILWAYS OF SOUTHERN ENG-
LAND: THE MAIN LINES.
617(TLS):30NOV73-1485
DE COURTAIS, G. WOMEN'S HEADDRESS AND
HAIRSTYLES IN ENGLAND FROM A.D. 600 TO
THE PRESENT DAY.
617(TLS):6JUL73-789
COURTECUISSE, J. L'OEUVRE ORATOIRE FRAN-
ÇAISE DE JEAN COURTECUISSE. (G. DI
STEFANO, ED)
W. ROTHWELL, 208(FS):JAN72-64
COURTNEY, F.T. FLIGHT PATH.
617(TLS):13JUL73-817
COUSIN, G. BLACK OPERA (AND) THE GIRL
WHO BARKS LIKE A DOG.
P. ROBERTS, 565:VOL12#2-72
COUSINS, E.H., ED. HOPE AND THE FUTURE
OF MAN.
617(TLS):21DEC73-1571
COUSINS, N. - SEE BROWN, J.M.
COUSTILLAS, P. - SEE GISSING, G.
COUSTILLAS, P. - SEE HICK, P.
COUSTILLAS, P. & C. PARTRIDGE, EDS. GIS-
SING: THE CRITICAL HERITAGE.
617(TLS):2FEB73-112

77

COUTINHO, A. AN INTRODUCTION TO LITERA-
TURE IN BRAZIL.*
  W. ROTH, 52:BAND5HEFT3-309
COUTTS-SMITH, K. THE DREAM OF ICARUS.*
  J. ELDERFIELD, 592:JUL-AUG70-49
  A.G., 135:JUN70-133
COUTURIER, F. MONDE ET ÊTRE CHEZ HEI-
DEGGER.
  P. XENOPOULOS, 154:DEC71-786
COUVE DE MURVILLE, M. UNE POLITIQUE
ÉTRANGÈRE 1958-1969.
  617(TLS):12JAN73-37
COUZYN, J. FLYING.
  W.G. SHEPHERD, 493:SUMMER71-204
COUZYN, J. MONKEYS' WEDDING.
  A. MACLEAN, 362:22MAR73-389
COVIN, K. MANY BROKEN HAMMERS.
  R.M. BROWN, 102(CANL):AUTUMN72-93
COWAN, H.J. ARCHITECTURAL STRUCTURES.
  505:NOV71-138
COWAN, J.C. D.H. LAWRENCE'S AMERICAN
JOURNEY.*
  L.D. CLARK, 50(ARQ):SUMMER71-184
  D.M. MONAGHAN, 150(DR):SUMMER71-278
COWAN, J.L. PLEASURE AND PAIN.*
  A. PALMER, 393(MIND):APR71-308
COWAN, M.H. CITY OF THE WEST.
  U. BRUMM, 38:BAND89HEFT3-406
COWARD, N. SIR NOEL COWARD: HIS WORDS
AND MUSIC. (L. SNIDER, ED)
  P. ADAMS, 61:SEP73-118
COWDREY, H.E.J. THE CLUNIACS AND THE
GREGORIAN REFORM.*
  A. STACPOOLE, 382(MAE):1972/2-174
COWDREY, H.E.J. - SEE POPE GREGORY VII
COWELL, H. & S. CHARLES IVES AND HIS
MUSIC.
  M. PETERSON, 470:MAY71-35
COWEN, R.C. HANDBUCH DER DEUTSCHEN LIT-
ERATURGESCHICHTE: BIBLIOGRAPHIEN.*
(VOL 9)
  F.D. HIRSCHBACH, 221(GQ):NOV71-601
COWEN, R.C. - SEE BÜCHNER, G.
COWEN, R.C. - SEE GRABBE, C.D.
COWEN, R.C. - SEE GRILLPARZER, F.
COWLES, V. THE ROMANOVS.
  R.T. FISHER, JR., 32:DEC72-883
COWLES, V. THE ROTHSCHILDS.
  E. WEEKS, 61:NOV73-124
  617(TLS):14DEC73-1533
COWLES, V. THE RUSSIAN DAGGER.*
  G. TOKMAKOFF, 550(RUSR):JAN71-93
COWLEY, A. SELECTED POETRY AND PROSE.
(J.G. TAAFFE, ED)
  O.S. REDD, 568(SCN):SPRING72-10
COWLEY, J. MAN OF STRAW.
  D. MC ELDOWNEY, 368:SEP71-304
COWLEY, J. OF MEN AND ANGELS.*
  617(TLS):31AUG73-993
COWLEY, M. A SECOND FLOWERING.
  W. STYRON, 441:6MAY73-8
  442(NY):23JUN73-90
COWLING, M. THE IMPACT OF LABOUR, 1920-
1924.
  H. PELLING, 111:7MAY71-180
COWPER, R. CLONE.
  617(TLS):2FEB73-129
COWPER, R. TIME OUT OF MIND.
  617(TLS):9NOV73-1378
COX, C.B. & A.E. DYSON, EDS. THE TWENTI-
ETH-CENTURY MIND.
  617(TLS):20APR73-435
COX, C.B. & M. SCHMIDT, EDS. POETRY
NATION.
  617(TLS):23NOV73-1452
COX, H. THE FEAST OF FOOLS.*
  W.J. GAVIN, 613:SPRING71-142

COX, H. THE SEDUCTION OF THE SPIRIT.
  J.M. CAMERON, 453:31MAY73-19
  E.B. FISKE, 441:20AUG73-29
  A.M. GREELEY, 441:16SEP73-7
COX, R.L. BETWEEN EARTH AND HEAVEN.
  D.J. CAHILL, 613:WINTER70-618
  R.A. FOAKES, 175:AUTUMN70-98
  A.D. NUTTALL, 541(RES):AUG71-382
  A.C. YU, 405(MP):FEB72-275
COXE, G.H. THE SILENT WITNESS.
  N. CALLENDAR, 441:11FEB73-30
COYSH, A.W. BLUE-PRINTED EARTHENWARE
1800-1850.
  617(TLS):2FEB73-133
COZZA, A. TOBIAS SMOLLETT.
  P-G. BOUCÉ, 189(EA):JAN-MAR71-96
COZZENS, J.G. MORNING, NOON AND NIGHT.*
  502(PRS):FALL71-279
COZZI, G. & L. - SEE SARPI, P.
CRACKANTHORPE, H. COLLECTED STORIES
(1893-1897).
  H.E. GERBER, 177(ELT):VOL13#4-307
CRACRAFT, J. THE CHURCH REFORM OF PETER
THE GREAT.
  L.R. LEWITTER, 575(SEER):APR72-276
  A.V. MULLER, 32:MAR72-153
CRADDOCK, J.R. LATIN LEGACY VERSUS SUB-
STRATUM RESIDUE.
  L.F. SAS, 240(HR):OCT71-443
CRADDOCK, J.R. & Y. MALKIEL - SEE GEORGES,
E.S.
CRADDOCK, P.B. - SEE GIBBON, E.
CRAFT, R. STRAVINSKY.*
  R. EVETT, 61:JAN73-91
"CRAFT SHOPS/GALLERIES U.S.A."
  M. LYON, 139:AUG71-6
CRAGG, K. THE MIND OF THE QUR'ĀN.
  617(TLS):27JUL73-882
CRAIG, A.M. & D.H. SHIVELY, EDS. PER-
SONALITY IN JAPANESE HISTORY.
  G.A. DE VOS, 244(HJAS):VOL31-294
  P.K. FROST, 293(JAST):AUG71-893
  E. SATŌ, 285(JAPQ):JUL-SEP71-347
  639(VQR):AUTUMN71-CLXXXIV
CRAIG, C. CHRISTOPH MARTIN WIELAND AS
THE ORIGINATOR OF THE MODERN TRAVESTY
IN GERMAN LITERATURE.*
  W.H. CLARK, 399(MLJ):DEC71-530
  E.E. REED, 221(GQ):MAY71-407
CRAIG, D. BOLTHOLE.
  617(TLS):2FEB73-129
CRAIG, D. KNIFEMAN.
  N. CALLENDAR, 441:11MAR73-50
CRAIG, D. & J. MANSON - SEE MAC DIARMID,
H.
CRAIG, J. POWER PLAY.
  M. LEVIN, 441:22APR73-28
CRAIG, J. ZACH.
  617(TLS):19OCT73-1270
CRAIG, M. & THE KNIGHT OF GLIN. IRELAND
OBSERVED.
  D. ROHAN, 159(DM):SPRING71-118
CRAIG, R.B. THE BRACERO PROGRAM.
  W. GARD, 584(SWR):SPRING72-V
CRAIG, W. ENEMY AT THE GATES.
  J. ERICKSON, 441:19AUG73-14
CRAIGHEAD, E.S. & F. CRAIGHEAD'S MOBILE.
(C. DELANEY, ED)
  F.L. OWSLEY, JR., 9(ALAR):JUL71-220
CRAIK, W.A. THE BRONTE NOVELS.*
  M. ALLOTT, 637(VS):SEP70-104
  S. MONOD, 189(EA):JUL-SEP70-344
CRAMER, T. "LOHENGRIN."
  F.H. BÄUML, 301(JEGP):OCT72-570
CRAMPTON, E. A HANDBOOK OF THE THEATRE.
  617(TLS):14DEC73-1549

CRANDALL, C., ED. SWETNAM THE WOMAN-
HATER.*
J.C. MAXWELL, 447(N&Q):DEC71-479
CRANE, M., ED. SHAKESPEARE'S ART.
617(TLS):21DEC73-1555
CRANE, R.S. THE IDEA OF THE HUMANITIES.*
(W. BOOTH, ED)
E.N. TIGERSTEDT, 597(SN):VOL42#2-481
CRANE, S. THE WORKS OF STEPHEN CRANE.*
(VOLS 1&7) (F. BOWERS, ED)
L. HOWARD, 445(NCF):SEP70-232
D. PIZER, 405(MP):NOV70-212
CRANE, S. THE WORKS OF STEPHEN CRANE.*
(VOL 4) (F. BOWERS, ED)
G. MONTEIRO, 27(AL):MAR72-161
CRANE, S. THE WORKS OF STEPHEN CRANE.*
(VOL 9) (F. BOWERS, ED)
D. AARON, 27(AL):MAY72-332
CRANE, W. OF THE DECORATIVE ILLUSTRATION
OF BOOKS OLD AND NEW.
617(TLS):26JAN73-103
CRANSTON, M. THE MASK OF POLITICS AND
OTHER ESSAYS. WHAT ARE HUMAN RIGHTS?
617(TLS):13APR73-426
CRAPANZANO, V. THE FIFTH WORLD OF FOR-
STER BENNETT.*
W.C. STURTEVANT, 441:18MAR73-36
CRAPULLI, G. MATHESIS UNIVERSALIS.
A. MERCIER, 182:VOL24#4-129
CRASHAW, R. THE COMPLETE POETRY OF
RICHARD CRASHAW.* (G.W. WILLIAMS, ED)
P.K. SUNDARARAJAN, 648:JAN71-66
CRATHORNE, N. TENNANT'S STALK. (COM-
PLETED BY K. ELLIOT & J. DUGDALE)
E. TENNANT, 362:3MAY73-590
617(TLS):8JUN73-643
CRAVEN, W. SCULPTURE IN AMERICA.
M.B. COWDREY, 54:MAR71-130
CRAWFORD, J. MY WAY OF LIFE.
P.M. SPACKS, 249(HUDR):SPRING72-157
CRAWFORD, M. & S. WHAT WE EAT TODAY.
617(TLS):8JUN73-649
CRAWFORD, W.H. & B. TRAINOR, EDS. ASPECTS
OF IRISH SOCIAL HISTORY, 1750-1800.
H.A. HANLEY, 325:OCT71-347
CRAWFORD, W.R. BIBLIOGRAPHY OF CHAUCER,
1954-63.
P.M. VERMEER, 179(ES):APR71-164
CRAWLEY, A. THE RISE OF WESTERN GERMANY
1945-1972.
617(TLS):14SEP73-1048
CRAWLEY, C.W., ED. THE NEW CAMBRIDGE
MODERN HISTORY. (VOL 9)
R. MARX, 189(EA):APR-JUN71-215
CRAWLEY, S.W. & R.M. DILLON. STEEL
BUILDINGS.
505:JUN71-118
CRAWLEY, T.E. THE STRUCTURE OF "LEAVES
OF GRASS."*
D.K. KIRBY, 646(WWR):DEC71-140
639(VQR):SUMMER71-CXI
CREAGH, P. TO ABEL AND OTHERS.
A. CLUYSENAAR, 565:VOL12#2-63
R.S., 376:JAN71-130
CREASEY, J. (AS G. ASHE) A LIFE FOR A
DEATH.
A. BROYARD, 441:1AUG73-31
"CREATIVE CANADA." (VOL 1)
J.R. SORFLEET, 296:SPRING73-94
G.W., 102(CANL):AUTUMN72-116
"CREATIVE CANADA." (VOL 2)
J.R. SORFLEET, 296:SPRING73-94
CREED, R.P., ED. OLD ENGLISH POETRY.*
H. BERGNER, 38:BAND88HEFT3-359
P.M. VERMEER, 179(ES):AUG71-348
CREEDY, J., ED. THE SOCIAL CONTEXT OF
ART.*
A. HIGGENS, 592:NOV70-209

CREEL, H.G. THE ORIGINS OF STATECRAFT
IN CHINA. (VOL 1)
D.N. KEIGHTLEY, 293(JAST):MAY71-655
CREELEY, R. A DAY BOOK.
C. RICKS, 441:7JAN73-5
CREELEY, R. PIECES.*
M. BUCHOLTZ, 600:WINTER/SPRING70-237
CREGAN, D. MINIATURES.
A. RENDLE, 157:AUTUMN70-77
CRELLIN, J.K. MEDICAL CERAMICS.
M.A., 135:MAR70-201
CREMIN, L.A. AMERICAN EDUCATION: THE
COLONIAL EXPERIENCE, 1607-1783.
R. VASSAR, 656(WMQ):OCT71-679
DE CRENNE, H. - SEE UNDER HELISENNE DE
CRENNE
CRÉPET, J. & G. BLIN - SEE BAUDELAIRE, C.
CRÉPIN, A. HISTOIRE DE LA LANGUE
ANGLAISE.
H. KOZIOL, 72:BAND209HEFT4/6-394
DE CRESPIGNY, R. THE LAST OF THE HAN.
R.K. NORRIS, 302:JAN71-175
CRESPO, F. TRÊS MOMENTOS NA LÍRICA POR-
TUGUESA.
R.C. WILLIS, 86(BHS):JAN72-99
CREWS, F., ED. PSYCHOANALYSIS AND LITER-
ARY PROCESS.
A.W. BRINK, 529(QQ):SPRING71-148
L.F. MANHEIM, 141:SPRING71-209
CREWS, H. CAR.*
R. BRYDEN, 362:18JAN73-90
617(TLS):2FEB73-129
CREWS, H. THE HAWK IS DYING.
P. ADAMS, 61:APR73-128
S. BLACKBURN, 441:25MAR73-47
C. LEHMANN-HAUPT, 441:21MAR73-49
CRIBIER, F. LA GRANDE MIGRATION D'ÉTÉ
DES CITADINS EN FRANCE.
P. VOSSELER, 182:VOL24#1/2-55
CRICHTON, R. THE CAMERONS.*
E. WEEKS, 61:JAN73-98
617(TLS):13APR73-409
CRICHTON SMITH, I. THE BLACK AND THE
RED AND OTHER STORIES.
V. CUNNINGHAM, 362:8NOV73-638
617(TLS):19OCT73-1269
CRICHTON SMITH, I. LOVE POEMS AND ELE-
GIES.*
A. MACLEAN, 362:22MAR73-389
CRICHTON SMITH, I. SELECTED POEMS.
T. EAGLETON, 565:VOL12#2-59
CRICHTON SMITH, I. SURVIVAL WITHOUT
ERROR.
R. PYBUS, 565:VOL12#1-68
CRINKLEY, R. WALTER PATER: HUMANIST.
F.E. COURT, 177(ELT):VOL14#3-178
G. MONSMAN, 637(VS):JUN71-468
CRINÒ, A.M., ED. UN PRINCIPE DI TOSCANA
IN INGHILTERRA E IN IRLANDA NEL 1669.
P. ZAMBELLI, 548(RCSF):JAN-MAR71-102
CRIPPA, R. PROFILO DELLA CRITICA BLON-
DELLIANA.
E. NAMER, 542:OCT-DEC71-460
"CRITICAL ESSAYS ON MILTON."
J. GURY, 549(RLC):JUL-SEP71-419
CRITTALL, E., ED. A HISTORY OF WILT-
SHIRE. (VOL 1, PT 2)
617(TLS):15JUN73-668
"CROATICI AUCTORES QUI LATINE SCRIPSER-
UNT." (VOLS 1&2)
D. TSCHIŽEWSKIJ, 72:BAND209HEFT1/3-
226
CROCE, A. THE FRED ASTAIRE AND GINGER
ROGERS BOOK.*
M. WOOD, 453:29NOV73-6
CROCE, A. - SEE DE SANCTIS, F.

79

CROCE, B. HISTORY OF THE KINGDOM OF
NAPLES.
A. LANDI, 275(IQ):SPRING71-144
CROCE, E. IN VISITA.
617(TLS):12OCT73-1208
CROCKER, L. ED. HARRY EMERSON FOSDICK'S
ART OF PREACHING.
W.E. LAMPTON, 583:SPRING72-332
CROCKER, L.G. JEAN-JACQUES ROUSSEAU.*
(VOL 1)
G. MAY, 546(RR):DEC71-305
R. MERCIER, 557(RSH):JUL-SEP71-476
J. STAROBINSKI, 453:29NOV73-20
CROCKER, L.G. JEAN-JACQUES ROUSSEAU.
(VOL 2)
J. STAROBINSKI, 453:29NOV73-20
CROCKER, L.G. ROUSSEAU'S SOCIAL CON-
TRACT.*
J-L. LECERCLE, 535(RHL):JAN-FEB70-133
P.H. MEYER, 546(RR):APR71-147
J. SAREIL, 188(ECR):WINTER70-329
CROCKER, W.C. TALES FROM THE COFFEE
HOUSE.
617(TLS):31AUG73-1009
CROFT-COOKE, R. THE DOGS OF PEACE.
617(TLS):11MAY73-537
CROMBACH, M. "BOCADOS DE ORO."
W. METTMANN, 72:BAND209HEFT1/3-201
CROMBIE, A.C. & M.A. HOSKIN, EDS. HIS-
TORY OF SCIENCE. (VOL 10, 1971)
617(TLS):16MAR73-305
CROMPTON, L. SHAW THE DRAMATIST.*
B.B. WATSON, 397(MD):SEP70-233
S. WEINTRAUB, 405(MP):NOV70-215
CROMPTON, L., WITH H. CAVANAUGH - SEE
SHAW, G.B.
CRONIN, V. A CONCISE HISTORY OF ITALY.
617(TLS):3AUG73-895
CRONJE, S. THE WORLD AND NIGERIA.*
617(TLS):2MAR73-244
CRONKHITE, G. PERSUASION.
L.L. BARKER, 583:WINTER70-189
CRONNE, H.A. & R.H.C. DAVIS, EDS. REGES-
TA REGUM ANGLO-NORMANNORUM 1066-1154.
(VOL 4)
C.A.F. MEEKINGS, 325:OCT71-337
CROOK, J.M. THE REFORM CLUB.
617(TLS):26OCT73-1325
CROOK, J.M. - SEE EASTLAKE, C.
CROS, E. PROTÉE ET LE GUEUX.*
J. JOSET, 556(RLV):1971/3-363
CROSBY, D.H. & A.F. GOESSL - SEE VON
KLEIST, H.
CROSBY, J. THE LITERARY OBSESSION.
R. BRYDEN, 362:10MAY73-623
617(TLS):1JUN73-604
CROSBY, J.O. EN TORNO A LA POESÍA DE
QUEVEDO.*
H. IVENTOSCH, 546(RR):FEB71-45
CROSBY, T., ED. HOW TO PLAY THE ENVIR-
ONMENT GAME.
617(TLS):4MAY73-496
CROSBY, T. THE NECESSARY MONUMENT.
P. OLIVER, 592:JUL-AUG70-54
CROSLAND, M. COLETTE.
A. BROYARD, 441:27DEC73-35
M. GALLANT, 441:9DEC73-3
442(NY):31DEC73-59
617(TLS):13APR73-413
CROSLAND, M. - SEE COCTEAU, J.
CROSS, A.G. N.M. KARAMZIN.
H.W. DEWEY, 32:JUN72-420
I.P. FOOTE, 402(MLR):OCT72-958
J.D. GOODLIFFE, 67:NOV72-254
CROSS, J.L. LONDON MISSION.
J.A. COMBS, 656(WMQ):JAN71-151

CROSS, K.G.W. & R.T. DUNLOP. A BIBLIOG-
RAPHY OF YEATS CRITICISM, 1887-1965.*
R.J. FINNERAN, 295:FEB73-129
CROSS, M. & R. BOTHWELL, EDS. POLICY
BY OTHER MEANS.
W.A.B. DOUGLAS, 99:OCT73-34
CROSS, R.K. FLAUBERT AND JOYCE.*
639(VQR):AUTUMN71-CLXVIII
CROSSLEY, A., ED. THE VICTORIA HISTORY
OF THE COUNTIES OF ENGLAND: A HISTORY
OF THE COUNTY OF OXFORD. (VOL 10)
617(TLS):5JAN73-19
CROSSLEY-HOLLAND, K. PIECES OF LAND.
617(TLS):20APR73-450
CROSSLEY-HOLLAND, K. THE RAIN-GIVER.
A. MACLEAN, 362:22MAR73-389
617(TLS):16FEB73-183
CROUCH, M. THE CREAM OF KENT.
617(TLS):26OCT73-1325
CROUSE, T. THE BOYS ON THE BUS.
G. WILLS, 453:4OCT73-3
442(NY):17DEC73-153
CROUZEL, H. - SEE SAINT GREGORY
CROUZET, M. UN MÉCONNU DU RÉALISME:
DURANTY (1833-1880).
P. BONNEFIS, 535(RHL):JAN-FEB70-144
CROVI, R. ELOGIO DEL DISERTORE.
617(TLS):5OCT73-1176
CROW, C.M. PAUL VALÉRY AND MAXWELL'S
DEMON.
617(TLS):5JAN73-21
CROW, J. - SEE "LES QUINZE JOYES DE MARI-
AGE"
CROW, J.A. THE EPIC OF LATIN AMERICA.
T.E. LYON, 263:JUL-SEP72-275
CROWDER, M. REVOLT IN BUSSA.
617(TLS):30NOV73-1479
CROWDER, M. THE STORY OF NIGERIA. (NEW
ED)
617(TLS):30NOV73-1479
CROWE, B. THE PLAYGROUP MOVEMENT.
617(TLS):23NOV73-1456
CROWLEY, A. WHITE STAINS. (J. SYMONDS,
ED) MAGICK. (J. SYMONDS & K. GRANT,
EDS)
617(TLS):27JUL73-871
CROWLEY, E.T. & R.C. THOMAS, EDS. ACRO-
NYMS AND INITIALISMS DICTIONARY. (3RD
ED)
K.B. HARDER, 424:SEP71-218
CROWSON, P.S. TUDOR FOREIGN POLICY.
617(TLS):12OCT73-1260
CROZET, R. L'ART ROMAN EN SAINTONGE.
J. BONY, 589:OCT72-755
A. REINLE, 182:VOL24#1/2-32
CROZIER, A. THE NOVELS OF HARRIET
BEECHER STOWE.*
B.C. BACH, 613:SPRING70-127
R. LEHAN, 445(NCF):SEP70-250
C. PÉROTIN, 189(EA):JAN-MAR71-106
CROZIER, B. DE GAULLE: THE WARRIOR.
M. HOWARD, 231:DEC73-116
617(TLS):5OCT73-1152
CROZIER, B. THE FUTURE OF COMMUNIST
POWER.
L. CLARK, 619(TC):VOL179#1046-54
CROZIER, W.P. OFF THE RECORD. (A.J.P.
TAYLOR, ED)
R. CROSSMAN, 362:30AUG73-285
617(TLS):10AUG73-922
CRUCITTI ULLRICH, F.M. SCIPIONE MAFFEI
E LA SUA CORRISPONDENZA CON LOUIS BOUR-
GUET.
M. FUBINI, 228(GSLI):VOL148FASC462/
463-455

CRUICKSHANK, J., ED. FRENCH LITERATURE
AND ITS BACKGROUND.* (VOL 1)
D.M. FRAME, 546(RR):APR71-138
J-Y. POUILLOUX, 535(RHL):JAN-FEB70-
115
CRUICKSHANK, J., ED. FRENCH LITERATURE
AND ITS BACKGROUND.* (VOL 2)
M. CARDY, 188(ECR):SPRING70-85
L. VAN DELFT, 207(FR):OCT70-259
E. HARTH, 546(RR):DEC71-295
J. MOREL, 535(RHL):MAY-JUN70-512
CRUICKSHANK, J., ED. FRENCH LITERATURE
AND ITS BACKGROUND.* (VOL 4)
A. FAIRLIE, 208(FS):APR72-209
M. O'NEILL, 188(ECR):SPRING70-86
CRUICKSHANK, J., ED. FRENCH LITERATURE
AND ITS BACKGROUND.* (VOL 6)
J.M. COCKING, 208(FS):OCT72-481
CRUM, M., ED. FIRST-LINE INDEX OF ENGLISH
POETRY 1500-1800 IN MANUSCRIPTS OF THE
BODLEIAN LIBRARY, OXFORD.*
R. KRUEGER, 541(RES):FEB71-69
CRUM, M., ED. FELIX MENDELSSOHN BARTHOL-
DY.
E. SAMS, 415:NOV72-1089
CRUMMEY, D. PRIESTS AND POLITICIANS.
617(TLS):1JUN73-609
CRUMMEY, R.O. THE OLD BELIEVERS AND THE
WORLD OF ANTI-CHRIST.*
S. FEINSTEIN, 481(PQ):JUL71-352
S.A. ZENKOVSKY, 550(RUSR):JUL71-302
CRUMP, G.M., ED. POEMS ON AFFAIRS OF
STATE.* (VOL 4)
E. SPÄTH, 38:BAND89HEFT3-398
CRUMP, G.M. - SEE STANLEY, T.
CRUMP, J.I., JR. - SEE "CHAN-KUO TS'E"
CRUNDEN, R.M. FROM SELF TO SOCIETY,
1919-1941.
H.B. GOW, 396(MODA):FALL72-432
CRUSO, T. MAKING THINGS GROW OUTDOORS.
617(TLS):27APR73-481
CRUTCHLEY, B. - SEE MORISON, S.
CRYMES, R. SOME ASPECTS OF SUBSTITUTION
CORRELATIONS IN MODERN AMERICAN ENG-
LISH.
A.R. TELLIER, 189(EA):JAN-MAR70-88
CRYSTAL, D. LINGUISTICS.*
B. BLAKE, 67:NOV72-268
CRYSTAL, D. PROSODIC SYSTEMS AND INTON-
ATION IN ENGLISH.
B. CARSTENSEN, 430(NS):SEP71-504
G.A.C. HUBERS, 361:VOL26#4-370
205(FMLS):OCT70-420
CRYSTAL, D. & D. DAVY. INVESTIGATING
ENGLISH STYLE.*
N.L. FAIRCLOUGH, 361:VOL27#2/3-288
R. FOWLER, 599:FALL71-300
R. GLÄSER, 682(ZPSK):BAND24HEFT5-437
G. HOUGH, 597(SN):VOL43#2-600
CSAPODI, C. & K. CSAPODI-GÁRDONYI, EDS.
BIBLIOTHECA CORVINIANA.*
C.H. CLOUGH, 78(BC):SUMMER71-253
M.L. D'ANCONA, 54:DEC71-520
CSÉCSY, M. DE LA LINGUISTIQUE À LA
PÉDAGOGIE: LE VERBE FRANÇAIS.
A. VALDMAN, 207(FR):MAR71-787
CSORBA, G. A LÉLEK ÉVSZAKAI.
G. RABA, 270:VOL21#3-174
CUADRA, P.A. POESÍA ESCOGIDA.*
R. SQUIRRU, 37:JAN70-41
ČUBRILOVIĆ, V., ED. OSLOBOĐENJE GRADOVA
U SRBIJI OD TURAKA 1862-1867. GOD.
G. STOKES, 32:JUN72-491
CUCCIOLI MELLONI, R. RICERCHE SUL PITA-
GORISMO. (VOL 1)
G.B. KERFERD, 123:MAR72-57
C. MUGLER, 555:VOL45FASC1-149

CUCUEL, G. LA POUPLINIÈRE ET LA MUSIQUE
DE CHAMBRE AU XVIIIE SIÈCLE.
L. SALTER, 415:FEB72-157
CUDWORTH, C. HANDEL.*
A. HICKS, 415:AUG72-771
CUGUSI, P. EPISTOLOGRAPHI LATINI MINORES.
(VOL 1)
A.S. GRATWICK, 123:DEC72-359
CULLEN, P. SPENSER, MARVELL, AND RENAIS-
SANCE PASTORAL.*
P. LEGOUIS, 189(EA):OCT-DEC71-526
CULLOP, C.P. CONFEDERATE PROPAGANDA IN
EUROPE 1861-1865.
F.L. OWSLEY, JR., 9(ALAR):JAN70-77
CULLY, K.B. DOES THE CHURCH KNOW
HOW TO TEACH?
R.L. FARICY, 613:SUMMER71-301
CULMER, W.H. BILLY THE CARTWHEELER.
L.C.S., 155:JAN71-55
CULOT, J-M. & OTHERS, EDS. BIBLIOGRAPHIE
DES ÉCRIVAINS FRANÇAIS DE BELGIQUE.
(VOLS 1-3)
J. HANSE, 535(RHL):JUL-AUG70-739
CULVERWELL, N. AN ELEGANT AND LEARNED
DISCOURSE OF THE LIGHT OF NATURE.
(R.A. GREENE & H. MAC CALLUM, EDS)
G.D. MC EWEN, 568(SCN):FALL-WINTER72-
64
CUMBERLEGE, M. RUNNING TOWARDS A NEW
LIFE.
617(TLS):9MAR73-270
CUMMING, R.D. HUMAN NATURE AND HISTORY.
R.J.B., 543:SEP70-135
A. HOLLOWAY, 479(PHQ):APR71-185
CUMMINGS, E.E. COMPLETE POEMS, 1913-
1962.
G. STADE, 441:22JUL73-17
CUNARD, N. THESE WERE THE HOURS. (H.
FORD, ED)
R.S., 376:JUL70-120
CUNG-YUAN, C. ORIGINAL TEACHINGS OF
CH'AN BUDDHISM.
P.J.H., 543:JUN71-744
CUNLIFFE, B. FISHBOURNE.
D. HENRY, 122:OCT72-307
R.L. VANN, 576:DEC71-339
CUNLIFFE, B. THE REGNI.
617(TLS):10AUG73-932
CUNLIFFE, B. ROMAN BATH DISCOVERED.
R. HIGGINS, 39:AUG71-162
CUNNINGHAM, E.V. MILLIE.
N. CALLENDAR, 441:27MAY73-19
CUNNINGHAM, I.C. - SEE HERODAS
CUNNINGHAM, J.V. THE COLLECTED POEMS AND
EPIGRAMS.*
J. ATLAS, 491:JAN73-229
L. STALL, 598(SOR):AUTUMN73-1044
CUNNINGHAM, R. THE PLACE WHERE THE WORLD
ENDS.
441:7OCT73-41
CUNNINGHAM, S., ED. BROADSIDE.
J.O. WEST, 650(WF):JAN70-62
CUNQUEIRO, A. MERLÍN Y FAMILIA.
J-A. FLIGHTNER, 238:MAY71-396
CUNQUEIRO, A. LAS MOCEDADES DE ULISES.
(2ND ED)
J-A. FLIGHTNER, 238:DEC71-971
CUNYNGHAM-BROWN, S. THE TRADERS.
617(TLS):6APR73-368
CUOMO, G. THE HERO'S GREAT GREAT GREAT
GREAT GREAT GRANDSON.
L. ROOKE, 376:OCT71-139
CUPITT, D. CRISIS OF MORAL AUTHORITY.
617(TLS):27APR73-479
CURI, U. I PRESOCRATICI, TESTIMONIANZE
E FRAMMENTI, CLASSICI DI FILOSOFIA.
L.M.P., 543:MAR71-538

CURLEY, E.M. SPINOZA'S METAPHYSICS.*
  D.J., 543:SEP70-136
  W. VON LEYDEN, 479(PHQ):JUL71-264
CURRAN, C.P. JAMES JOYCE REMEMBERED.*
  G. SOLMECKE, 38:BAND89HEFT1-154
CURRAN, S. SHELLEY'S "CENCI."*
  K.N.C., 191(ELN):SEP71(SUPP)-54
"CURRENT TRENDS IN LINGUISTICS." (VOL 3)
  M. DOHERTY, 682(ZPSK):BAND23HEFT6-619
CURREY, C.B. CODE 72 - BEN FRANKLIN.
  J.C. BOSWELL, 165:SPRING73-78
  J.H. PLUMB, 453:19APR73-4
CURREY, C.B. ROAD TO REVOLUTION.
  J.H. PLUMB, 453:19APR73-4
CURRY-LINDAHL, K. CONSERVATION FOR SUR-
  VIVAL.
  617(TLS):12JAN73-46
CURSCHMANN, M., ED. TEXTE UND MELODIEN
  ZUR WIRKUNGSGESCHICHTE EINES SPÄTMIT-
  TELALTERLICHEN LIEDES (HANS HESELLOHER,
  "VON ÜPPIGLICHEN DINGEN").
  O. SAYCE, 402(MLR):JAN72-206
  R.J. TAYLOR, 220(GL&L):APR72-309
CURTI, C. OSSERVAZIONI SUL "QUIS DIVES
  SALVETUR" DI CLEMENTE ALESSANDRINO.
  P. LANGLOIS, 555:VOL45FASC1-160
CURTIN, P.D., ED. AFRICA REMEMBERED.
  D. BEN-AMOS, 650(WF):JUL70-215
CURTIN, P.D. THE ATLANTIC SLAVE TRADE.
  H. DESCHAMPS, 69:OCT70-395
CURTIN, S.R. NOBODY EVER DIED OF OLD
  AGE.
  A. BROYARD, 441:20FEB73-31
  E. HOAGLAND, 441:4FEB73-4
  442(NY):20JAN73-103
CURTIN, W.M. - SEE CATHER, W.
CURTIS, A. SWEELINCK'S KEYBOARD MUSIC.*
  E.A. BOWLES, 551(RENQ):AUTUMN71-366
CURTIS, D. DARTMOOR TO CAMBRIDGE.
  617(TLS):16NOV73-1387
CURTIS, D. EXPERIMENTAL CINEMA.
  P. GIDAL, 592:JUL/AUG71-42
CURTIS, E.S. THE NORTH AMERICAN INDIANS.
  S. SCHWARTZ, 441:2DEC73-94
CURTIS, E.S. PORTRAITS FROM NORTH AMERI-
  CAN INDIAN LIFE.*
  617(TLS):23NOV73-1425
CURTIS, J-L. UN MIROIR LE LONG DU CHE-
  MIN.
  D.F. JOURLAIT, 207(FR):MAY71-1121
CURTIS, L.P., JR. - SEE LECKY, W.E.H.
CURTIS, R.L. TRISTAN STUDIES.*
  R.J. CORMIER, 207(FR):OCT70-251
CURWEN, S. THE JOURNAL OF SAMUEL CURWEN,
  LOYALIST. (A. OLIVER, ED)
  617(TLS):14SEP73-1049
CUSAC, M.H. NARRATIVE STRUCTURE IN THE
  NOVELS OF SIR WALTER SCOTT.
  T. CRAWFORD, 541(RES):MAY71-223
  F.R. HART, 445(NCF):JUN71-115
CUSHION, J.P. POTTERY AND PORCELAIN.
  617(TLS):2FEB73-133
CUTLER, I. MANY FLIES HAVE FEATHERS.
  617(TLS):23NOV73-1452
CUTLER, J.H. ED BROOKE.
  M.F. NOLAN, 441:11FEB73-14
CUTT, T. - SEE PLAUTUS
CUTTLER, C.D. NORTHERN PAINTING FROM
  PUCELLE TO BRUEGEL.*
  R.A. KOCH, 54:JUN70-202
  A. SMITH, 90:JUL71-412
  C. TALBOT, 56:WINTER71-485
CUTTS, J.P. THE SHATTERED GLASS.*
  R.A. FOAKES, 175:SPRING70-22
CUYLER, L. THE EMPEROR MAXIMILIAN I AND
  MUSIC.
  617(TLS):7DEC73-1517

CZAPLICKA, M. ABORIGINAL SIBERIA.
  293(JAST):NOV70-246
CZARTORYSKI, P. - SEE COPERNICUS, N.
CZIKOWSKI, E., I. IDZIKOWSKI & G. SCHWARZ,
  EDS. MAXIM GORKI IN DEUTSCHLAND.
  J. PERUS, 549(RLC):JUL-SEP70-428


DABEZIES, A. VISAGES DE FAUST AU XXE
  SIÈCLE.
  H. HENNING, 52:BAND6HEFT1-111
DACLIN, M. LA CRISE DES ANNÉES 30 À
  BESANÇON.
  D.B. GOLDEY, 208(FS):JUL72-372
DACOS, N. LA DÉCOUVERTE DE LA DOMUS
  AUREA ET LA FORMATION DES GROTESQUES
  À LA RENAISSANCE.
  C.H. CLOUGH, 39:JUL71-77
  J. SCHULZ, 551(RENQ):WINTER71-541
MARQUIS D'ADHÉMAR. LE MARQUIS D'ADHÉMAR:
  LA CORRESPONDANCE INÉDITE D'UN AMI DES
  PHILOSOPHES À LA COUR DE BAYREUTH. (E.
  MASS, ED)
  617(TLS):21SEP73-1090
DAEMMRICH, H.S. & D. HAENICKE, EDS. THE
  CHALLENGE OF GERMAN LITERATURE.
  C. CRAIG, 651(WHR):SPRING72-173
DAENEN, C. & H. DE JONGHE. NEDERLANDSE
  SPRAAKKUNST.
  J.P. WILLEMS, 556(RLV):1971/5-654
DAGAN, A. MOSCOW AND JERUSALEM.
  O.M. SMOLANSKY, 32:MAR72-176
DAGENS, B., ED & TRANS. MAYAMATA. (PT
  1)
  O. VON HINÜBER, 182:VOL24#15/16-616
D'AGOSTINO, N. L'ORDINE E IL CAOS.
  P.K., 566:AUTUMN71-7
DAHINDEN, J., ED. URBAN STRUCTURES FOR
  THE FUTURE.
  617(TLS):23FEB73-204
DAHL, H., ED. GOETHES AMTLICH SCHRIFTEN.
  N.H. SMITH, 182:VOL24#6-295
DAHL, L. LINGUISTIC FEATURES OF THE
  STREAM-OF-CONSCIOUSNESS TECHNIQUES OF
  JAMES JOYCE, VIRGINIA WOOLF AND EUGENE
  O'NEILL.*
  A. BRUTEN, 447(N&Q):JUL71-278
DAHL, L. NOMINAL STYLE IN THE SHAKE-
  SPEAREAN SOLILOQUY.
  A. BRUTEN, 447(N&Q):APR71-158
  I. KOSKENNIEMI, 439(NM):1970/3-525
  K. WIKBERG, 597(SN):VOL43#1-310
DAHL, Ö. TOPIC AND COMMENT.
  J. FIRBAS & K. PALA, 297(JL):APR71-91
DAHL, O-C. CONTES MALGACHES EN DIALECTE
  SAKALAVA.
  M. URBAIN-FAUBLÉE, 69:OCT70-402
DAHL, R.A. POLYARCHY.
  A.A. ROGOW, 639(VQR):AUTUMN71-615
DAHLBERG, E. THE CARNAL MYTH.
  M. LYON, 502(PRS):SPRING70-81
DAHLBERG, E. THE CONFESSIONS OF EDWARD
  DAHLBERG.*
  42(AR):SPRING71-134
DAHLE, W. DER EINSATZ EINER WISSEN-
  SCHAFT.
  W. BAUSENHART, 433:OCT71-457
DAHLHAUS, C., ED. RICHARD WAGNER.
  R.H., 410(M&L):OCT72-460
DAHLHAUS, C. WAGNERS KONZEPTION DES
  MUSIKALISCHEN DRAMAS.
  R.H., 410(M&L):OCT72-460
DAHLMANN, F.C. & G. WAITZ. QUELLENKUNDE
  DER DEUTSCHEN GESCHICHTE. (10TH ED)
  (VOL 1) (H. HEIMPEL & H. GEUSS, EDS)
  G. GRANIER, 182:VOL24#1/2-46

DAHM, B. HISTORY OF INDONESIA IN THE
TWENTIETH CENTURY.
F.J. CORLEY, 613:WINTER71-635
DAHM, B. SUKARNO AND THE STRUGGLE FOR
INDONESIAN INDEPENDENCE. (REV)
J.D. LEGGE, 293(JAST):NOV70-235
DÄHNERT, U. DIE ORGELN GOTTFRIED SILBER-
MANNS IN MITTELDEUTSCHLAND.
S. JEANS, 415:JAN72-50
DAHRENDORF, R. KONFLIKT UND FREIHEIT.
617(TLS):28DEC73-1592
DAICHES, D. THE LAST STUART. (BRITISH
TITLE: CHARLES EDWARD STUART.)
A. BELL, 362:12APR73-486
442(NY):16JUN73-111
617(TLS):18MAY73-561
DAICHES, D. MORE LITERARY ESSAYS.*
L. BONNEROT, 189(EA):OCT-DEC71-543
J.K. ROBINSON, 598(SOR):SUMMER73-692
DAICHES, D. SOME LATE VICTORIAN ATTI-
TUDES.
E. ENGELBERG, 637(VS):DEC70-205
DAICHES, D. ROBERT LOUIS STEVENSON AND
HIS WORLD.
617(TLS):14DEC73-1549
DAIM, W. THE VATICAN AND EASTERN EUROPE.
B.R. BOCIURKIW, 32:MAR72-209
DAIN, P. THE NEW YORK PUBLIC LIBRARY.*
E. MOERS, 453:3MAY73-31
DAKIN, J.C. EDUCATION IN NEW ZEALAND.
617(TLS):21SEP73-1089
DAL, E. SCANDINAVIAN BOOKMAKING IN THE
TWENTIETH CENTURY.
R. CAVE, 503:AUTUMN70-165
D'ALBERTI, S. PIRANDELLO ROMANZIERE.*
O. BÜDEL, 546(RR):OCT71-243
DALE, C. INNOCENT PARTY.
R. BLYTHE, 362:1NOV73-605
617(TLS):5OCT73-1157
DALE, J.S. GARBORGSTUDIAR.
G. BØ, 172(EDDA):1970/5-311
DALE, P. MORTAL FIRE.*
T. EAGLETON, 565:VOL12#1-77
DALESKI, H.M. DICKENS AND THE ART OF
ANALOGY.
W.F. AXTON, 401(MLQ):JUN72-203
S. GILL, 447(N&Q):NOV71-425
M.S. HELFAND, 454:WINTER72-186
M. PRICE, 676(YR):WINTER72-271
G. SMITH, 155:JAN71-49
H.P. SUCKSMITH, 445(NCF):DEC71-352
G. THOMAS, 175:SPRING71-25
P. THOMSON, 541(RES):NOV71-509
S. WALL, 184(EIC):JUL71-261
D'ALESSIO, R.H. - SEE UNDER HENZO D'ALES-
SIO, R.
DALEY, R. TARGET BLUE.
M.P. NICHOLS, 441:27MAY73-3
DALGARD, O. INGE KROKANN.
L. MAEHLE, 172(EDDA):1971/1-61
DALI, S. HIDDEN FACES.
D.J. ENRIGHT, 362:13SEP73-352
617(TLS):7SEP73-1017
DALLAS, K., COMP. THE CRUEL WARS.
617(TLS):1JUN73-625
DALLA VALLE, D. LA FRATTURA.
L.H. PEER, 149:SEP72-338
DALLIN, A. & G.W. BRESLAUER. POLITICAL
TERROR IN COMMUNIST SYSTEMS.*
J.S. ROUCEK, 550(RUSR):APR71-203
DAL MONTE, M.T. CHRISTIAN JOSEPH JAGE-
MANN.
F. STOCK, 52:BAND6HEFT3-332
DAL PRA, M. - SEE ABELARDO, P.
DAL PRA, M. - SEE MARCUSE, H.
DALTON, M. A.K. TOLSTOY.
W.E. HARKINS, 32:DEC72-937

DAL VERME, F. THE JOURNAL AND LETTERS OF
COUNT FRANCESCO DAL VERME, 1783-1784.
(E. COMETTI, ED & TRANS)
E.S. FALBO, 275(IQ):SUMMER71-101
DALY, J. DESCRIPTIVE INVENTORY OF THE
ARCHIVES OF THE CITY AND COUNTY OF
PHILADELPHIA.
M.K. GORDON, 14:OCT71-390
DALY, J. EDUCATION OR MOLASSES?
B. HENDLEY, 154:JUN71-386
DALY, L.W., ED. BRITO METRICUS.
G.M. MESSING, 589:APR72-298
DALY, L.W. CONTRIBUTIONS TO A HISTORY OF
ALPHABETIZATION IN ANTIQUITY AND THE
MIDDLE AGES.
S.M. KUHN, 589:APR72-300
DALY, M. BEYOND GOD THE FATHER.
M. ELLMANN, 453:1NOV73-18
DALZELL, R.F., JR. DANIEL WEBSTER.
D.H. DONALD, 441:4FEB73-4
DAMASE, J. SONIA DELAUNAY.
J.R. MELLOW, 441:2DEC73-10
DAMERAU, N. POLNISCHE GRAMMATIK.*
I. KUNERT, 343:BAND13HEFT1-106
DAMIANI, B.M. - SEE DELICADO, F.
DAMM, B. GEOLOGIE DES ZENDAN-I SULEIMAN
UND SEINER UMGEBUNG, SÜDÖSTLICHES BAL-
QASH-GEBIRGE, NORDWEST-IRAN.
A.F. DE LAPPARENT, 182:VOL24#1/2-57
DAMON, S.F. A BLAKE DICTIONARY.
G.E. BENTLEY, JR., 627(UTQ):FALL70-86
R.C. ELLSWORTH, 529(QQ):WINTER71-635
DAMOURETTE, J. & E. PICHON. ESSAI DE
GRAMMAIRE FRANÇAISE. (VOLS 5&6)
J. CHAURAND, 209(FM):JUL71-264
DAMOURETTE, J. & E. PICHON. DES MOTS À
LA PENSÉE.
J. CHAURAND, 209(FM):APR70-161
DAMROSCH, L., JR. SAMUEL JOHNSON AND THE
TRAGIC SENSE.
617(TLS):1JUN73-613
DANA, R. THE POWER OF THE VISIBLE.
E. OCHESTER, 398:SPRING73-119
DANAHER, K. THE PLEASANT LAND OF IRE-
LAND.
E. ETTLINGER, 203:SPRING71-78
DANAHER, K. THE YEAR IN IRELAND.
617(TLS):16MAR73-305
D'ANCONA, P.D. & E. AESCHLIMANN. THE ART
OF ILLUMINATION.*
I. TOESCA, 39:MAR70-249
DANDEKAR, R.N., ED. PROCEEDINGS OF THE
TWENTY-SIXTH INTERNATIONAL CONGRESS OF
ORIENTALISTS. (VOL 3)
E. BENDER, 318(JAOS):OCT-DEC71-566
DANDEKAR, R.N. & A.M. GHATAGE, EDS. PRO-
CEEDINGS OF THE SEMINAR IN PRAKRIT
STUDIES (JUNE 23-27, 1969).
E. BENDER, 318(JAOS):OCT-DEC71-565
D'ANDLAU, B. LA JEUNESSE DE MADAME DE
STAËL (DE 1776 À 1786).
F.P. BOWMAN, 402(MLR):OCT72-913
DANG THAI MAI. VAN THO CACH MANG VIET-NAM
DAU THE KY XX.
D.G. MARR, 293(JAST):MAY71-733
D'ANGELO, E. THE PROBLEM OF FREEDOM AND
DETERMINISM.
H.R. SHUFORD, JR., 480(P&R):SUMMER71-
193
DANIEL, G. & J.D. EVANS. THE WESTERN
MEDITERRANEAN. (REV)
J.D. MUHLY, 318(JAOS):APR-JUN71-326
DANIEL, G.B., JR., ED. RENAISSANCE AND
OTHER STUDIES IN HONOR OF WILLIAM LEON
WILEY.*
G. FASANO, 535(RHL):MAR-APR70-303
DANIELL, J. EXPERIMENT IN REPUBLICANISM.
R.D. BROWN, 432(NEQ):SEP71-495

DAVID, C. L'ÉTAT AMOUREUX.
  Y. BRÈS, 542:APR-JUN71-207
DAVIDOFF, L. THE BEST CIRCLES.
  617(TLS):30NOV73-1473
DAVIDSON, D., ED. RESTORATION COMEDIES.
  A. RENDLE, 157:SUMMER70-75
DAVIDSON, D., M.C.S. OLIPHANT & J.B.
  MERIWETHER - SEE SIMMS, W.G.
DAVIDSON, E.H. JONATHAN EDWARDS.
  N.S. FIERING, 656(WMQ):OCT71-655
DAVIDSON, E.P. FOR ALWAYS ONLY.
  M. LEVIN, 441:16SEP73-32
DAVIDSON, G. ALL THINGS ARE HOLY.
  A.M. SAMPLEY, 502(PRS):SUMMER71-177
DAVIDSON, M. THE WORLD, THE FLESH AND
  MYSELF.
  617(TLS):8JUN73-647
DAVIDSON, M.B. & OTHERS. THE AMERICAN
  HERITAGE HISTORY OF THE ARTISTS' AMERI-
  CA.
  L. NOCHLIN, 441:2DEC73-4
DAVIDSSON, Å. UPPSALA UNIVERSITETSBIB-
  LIOTEK 1620-1970.
  L.S. THOMPSON, 563(SS):SPRING72-267
DAVIE, D. COLLECTED POEMS 1950-1970.*
  P. BEER, 362:1MAR73-280
  T. GUNN, 441:7JAN73-5
  D. KENWORTHY, 31(ASCH):SUMMER73-514
  W.A. PRITCHARD, 491:AUG73-289
DAVIE, D. ESSEX POEMS.
  R. FULTON, 565:VOL11#2-64
DAVIE, D. THOMAS HARDY AND BRITISH
  POETRY.
  P. BEER, 362:1MAR73-280
  T. GUNN, 441:7JAN73-5
  617(TLS):13JUL73-793
DAVIE, D. SIX EPISTLES TO EVA HESSE.
  A. CLUYSENAAR, 565:VOL12#1-72
DAVIE, M. CALIFORNIA.
  C. LEHMANN-HAUPT, 441:21FEB73-45
  J. SEELYE, 441:5AUG73-4
DAVIES, A.T. ANTI-SEMITISM AND THE
  CHRISTIAN MIND.
  M.H. ELOVITZ, 328:WINTER71-124
DAVIES, C.S. & J. LEVITT. WHAT'S IN A
  NAME?
  K.B. HARDER, 424:MAR71-60
DAVIES, D. A DICTIONARY OF ANTHROPOLOGY.
  617(TLS):9MAR73-258
DAVIES, G. NATIONAL GIRO.
  617(TLS):30NOV73-1485
DAVIES, J.G., ED. A DICTIONARY OF LIT-
  URGY AND WORSHIP.
  617(TLS):20APR73-448
DAVIES, J.G. EVERY DAY GOD.
  617(TLS):27APR73-479
DAVIES, J.K. ATHENIAN PROPERTIED FAM-
  ILIES 600-300 B.C.
  M.E. WHITE, 124:MAR72-237
  617(TLS):23FEB73-209
DAVIES, J.V., ED. LAWRENCE ON HARDY AND
  PAINTING.
  617(TLS):15JUN73-699
DAVIES, L. FRANCK.
  617(TLS):20JUL73-830
DAVIES, L. CÉSAR FRANCK AND HIS CIRCLE.*
  E.L., 410(M&L):JUL72-336
DAVIES, L.P. WHAT DID I DO TOMORROW?
  N. CALLENDAR, 441:1APR73-34
DAVIES, M. CARLO CRIVELLI.
  617(TLS):1JUN73-625
DAVIES, M. THE NATIONAL GALLERY, LONDON.
  (VOL 3)
  E. YOUNG, 39:SEP71-246
DAVIES, M. ROGIER VAN DER WEYDEN.*
  A. MARTINDALE, 362:30AUG73-278

DAVIES, P. & OTHERS. THE TRUTH ABOUT
  KENT STATE.
  B. DE MOTT, 61:OCT73-115
  T. POWERS, 441:2SEP73-1
DAVIES, R. FIFTH BUSINESS.*
  E. CAMERON, 529(QQ):SPRING71-139
  R. SALE, 453:8FEB73-21
DAVIES, R. HUNTING STUART AND OTHER
  PLAYS.
  G. JOCELYN, 99:FEB73-44
  E. MULLALY, 198:SPRING73-111
DAVIES, R. THE MANTICORE.*
  R. BRYDEN, 362:12APR73-489
  M. DYMENT, 296:WINTER73-83
  G. JOCELYN, 99:FEB73-44
  R. SALE, 453:8FEB73-21
  617(TLS):13APR73-409
DAVIES, R. PRINT OF A HARE'S FOOT.
  T.F. STALEY, 295:NOV72-576
DAVIES, R. - SEE LEACOCK, S.
DAVIES, T. WHEN THE MOON RISES.
  617(TLS):31AUG73-1009
DAVIN, D. BRIDES OF PRICE.*
  C. LEHMANN-HAUPT, 441:1FEB73-37
  M. LEVIN, 441:4MAR73-39
  442(NY):3FEB73-99
DAVIN, D. NOT HERE, NOT NOW.
  M. BEVERIDGE, 368:SEP70-296
DAVIS, A.F. AMERICAN HEROINE.
  R.R. SCHERMAN, 441:28OCT73-6
DAVIS, B.H. A PROOF OF EMINENCE.
  617(TLS):23NOV73-1451
DAVIS, C.C. THAT AMBITIOUS MR. LEGARÉ.*
  J.O. EIDSON, 27(AL):JAN73-681
DAVIS, C.T. - SEE ROBINSON, E.A.
DAVIS, D.B., ED. THE FEAR OF CONSPIRACY.
  42(AR):SPRING71-137
DAVIS, D.B. WAS THOMAS JEFFERSON AN
  AUTHENTIC ENEMY OF SLAVERY?
  639(VQR):SPRING71-LXXIV
DAVIS, D.S. THE LITTLE BROTHERS.
  N. CALLENDAR, 441:18NOV73-56
DAVIS, E. VISION FUGITIVE.
  M. MONTGOMERY, 219(GAR):WINTER70-508
  H. WITEMEYER, 659:SPRING73-240
DAVIS, E.G. THE FIRST SEX.
  617(TLS):30NOV73-1473
DAVIS, G. BANDAGING BREAD AND OTHER
  POEMS.*
  J. GALASSI, 491:MAR73-343
  J.T. IRWIN, 598(SOR):SUMMER73-720
  639(VQR):SPRING71-LXI
DAVIS, G. I CAME TO KILL. WHERE MURDER
  WAITS.
  G. VIDAL, 453:13DEC73-6
DAVIS, G. KINGDOM COME.
  M. LEVIN, 441:18MAR73-40
DAVIS, H. - SEE SWIFT, J.
DAVIS, H.E. LATIN AMERICAN THOUGHT.
  A. DONOSO, 319:JUL73-413
DAVIS, J. THE FIRST-BORN AND OTHER
  POEMS.
  K.L. GOODWIN, 381:SEP71-373
  S.E. LEE, 581:1971/3-227
DAVIS, J. LIFE SIGNS.
  S. BLACKBURN, 441:24JUN73-16
  C. LEHMANN-HAUPT, 441:28MAY73-13
  442(NY):9JUL73-70
DAVIS, J.G. OPERATION RHINO.*
  442(NY):28APR73-147
DAVIS, L., WITH R. GALLAGHER. LETTING
  DOWN MY HAIR.
  D. ADLER, 441:18NOV73-30
DAVIS, M. BEIT YISRAEL BA-AMERIKAH.
  J. KABAKOFF, 328:SUMMER71-372

DAVIS, M., ED. THE PUBLICATIONS OF THE
STUDY CIRCLE ON DIASPORA JEWRY IN THE
HOME OF THE PRESIDENT OF THE STATE OF
ISRAEL. (VOL 3)
J. RIEMER, 287:MAR71-28
DAVIS, N., ED. NON-CYCLE PLAYS AND
FRAGMENTS.*
R. AXTON, 382(MAE):1972/2-157
D.C. BAKER, 191(ELN):JUN72-293
A.C. CAWLEY, 447(N&Q):FEB71-71
DAVIS, N., ED. PASTON LETTERS AND PAPERS
OF THE FIFTEENTH CENTURY. (PT 1)
N.F. BLAKE, 72:BAND209HEFT1/3-150
G.C. BRITTON, 447(N&Q):DEC71-465
R.M. WILSON, 402(MLR):OCT72-867
DAVIS, N. - SEE "SIR GAWAIN AND THE GREEN
KNIGHT"
DAVIS, N. & C.M. KRAAY. THE HELLENISTIC
KINGDOMS.
617(TLS):27JUL73-859
DAVIS, O. THE SCENT OF APPLES.
M. LEVIN, 441:21JAN73-22
DAVIS, R. ENGLISH OVERSEAS TRADE 1500-
1700.
617(TLS):11MAY73-533
DAVIS, R. THE RISE OF THE ATLANTIC
ECONOMIES.
617(TLS):2NOV73-1350
DAVIS, R., ED. SPACE 1.
617(TLS):9NOV73-1378
DAVIS, R.B. LITERATURE AND SOCIETY IN
EARLY VIRGINIA, 1608-1840.
A. TURNER, 578:FALL73-111
DAVIS, R.W. POLITICAL CHANGE AND CONTIN-
UITY 1760-1885.
617(TLS):23FEB73-221
DAVIS, W. THE LANGUAGE OF MONEY.
441:8APR73-30
DAVIS, W.R. IDEA AND ACT IN ELIZABETHAN
FICTION.*
H. BONHEIM, 430(NS):OCT71-559
A.R. CIRILLO, 405(MP):AUG71-65
K. DUNCAN-JONES, 447(N&Q):JUN71-233
J. ROBERTSON, 541(RES):MAY71-190
DAVISON, D. DRYDEN.
P. ROBERTS, 541(RES):FEB71-107
DAVISON, D., ED. THE PENGUIN BOOK OF
EIGHTEENTH-CENTURY ENGLISH VERSE.
617(TLS):5OCT73-1173
DAVISON, N.J. EDUARDO BARRIOS.
D.L. SHAW, 402(MLR):APR72-449
DAVISON, P. HALF REMEMBERED.
H. BEVINGTON, 441:16SEP73-6
DAVISON, P., SER ED. THEATRUM REDIVIVUM.
617(TLS):22JUN73-726
DAWE, B. BEYOND THE SUBDIVISIONS.
K.L. GOODWIN, 381:SEP71-369
DAWES, F. NOT IN FRONT OF THE SERVANTS.
617(TLS):14SEP73-1057
DAWKINS, C. THE LIVE GOAT.
R. TRICKETT, 676(YR):AUTUMN71-121
DAWKINS, J. - SEE DE BRACH, P.
DAWSON, C. HIS FINE WIT.*
J. ESPEY, 445(NCF):JUN71-125
D.N. GALLON, 541(RES):MAY71-226
J.E.J., 191(ELN):SEP71(SUPP)-49
R. LAWRENCE, 175:AUTUMN70-107
DAWSON, F. A GREAT DAY FOR A BALLGAME.
A.C.J. BERGMAN, 441:26AUG73-28
DAWSON, O.L. COMMUNIST CHINA'S AGRICUL-
TURE.
C-Y. CHENG, 293(JAST):NOV70-185
DAWSON, S.W. DRAMA AND THE DRAMATIC.*
J.R. BROWN, 157:SPRING71-67
205(FMLS):OCT70-420

DAY, D. MALCOLM LOWRY.
A. ALVAREZ, 441:4NOV73-3
W. GASS, 453:29NOV73-26 [& CONT IN]
453:13DEC73-28
C. LEHMANN-HAUPT, 441:8NOV73-51
442(NY):12NOV73-217
DAY, D. MEDITATIONS. (S. VISHNEWSKI,
ED)
M. LAVANOUX, 363:FEB71-59
DAY, D. & A. ERSKINE - SEE FAULKNER, W.
DAY, J.R. THE STORY OF THE LONDON BUS.
617(TLS):24AUG73-986
DAY, P. JOHN MULGAN.
R. GROVER, 368:MAR70-95
DAY, R.A. TOLD IN LETTERS.*
D. BANK, 597(SN):VOL42#2-474
DAY, R.B. LEON TROTSKY AND THE POLITICS
OF ECONOMIC ISOLATION.
617(TLS):24AUG73-983
DAY LEWIS, C. THE WHISPERING ROOTS AND
OTHER POEMS.*
P. GOW, 134(CP):SPRING71-55
J. SAUNDERS, 565:VOL11#4-68
DAYAN, R. & H. DUDMAN. ...OR DID I
DREAM A DREAM?
617(TLS):13JUL73-799
DEAK, I. WEIMAR GERMANY'S LEFT-WING
INTELLECTUALS.
J. THOMAS, 220(GL&L):OCT71-45
DEAKIN, F.W.D. THE EMBATTLED MOUNTAIN.
P. AUTY, 575(SEER):OCT72-623
G. STOKES, 32:SEP72-725
DEAL, B.H. THE CRYSTAL MOUSE.
M. LEVIN, 441:18FEB73-31
DEAN, B. MIND'S EYE.
P. BLACK, 362:22NOV73-716
617(TLS):20JUL73-827
DEAN, B. SEVEN AGES.
R.J. SMITH, 157:SUMMER71-76
DEAN, L.F., ED. TWENTIETH CENTURY INTER-
PRETATIONS OF "JULIUS CAESAR."
J.W. VELZ, 570(SQ):WINTER71-73
DEAN, W. THE INDUSTRIALIZATION OF SÃO
PAULO, 1880-1945.*
F.J. MUNCH, 37:MAR71-37
DEANE, B. CHERUBINI.
A.F.L.T., 412:MAY72-150
DEANE, S. GRADUAL WARS.
617(TLS):16FEB73-183
DEANE, S. - SEE HOLCROFT, T.
DEARDEN, J.S. FACETS OF RUSKIN.
M.L., 135:JUN70-135
DEARDEN, R.F., P.H. HIRST & R.S. PETERS,
EDS. EDUCATION AND THE DEVELOPMENT
OF REASON.
I. GREGORY, 518:OCT72-19
DEARNLEY, M. THE POETRY OF CHRISTOPHER
SMART.*
J.N.R. SAUNDERS, 447(N&Q):FEB71-76
DEARNLEY, M. THAT WATERY GLASS.
617(TLS):28DEC73-1581
DEASY, L. TOWARDS IRELAND FREE.
617(TLS):21DEC73-1556
DEBAUVE, J.L. LAFORGUE EN SON TEMPS.
617(TLS):27JUL73-864
DEBAUVE, J.L. - SEE LAFORGUE, J.
DE BELLIS, J. SIDNEY LANIER.
T.D. YOUNG, 578:FALL73-101
DE BELLO, R. - SEE ALFIERI, V.
DEBENEDETTI, G. IL ROMANZO DEL NOVECEN-
TO.*
L.T., 275(IQ):SPRING-SUMMER72-122
DEBENEDETTI, G. NICCOLÒ TOMMASEO.
617(TLS):25MAY73-578
DEBICKI, A.P. ESTUDIOS SOBRE POESÍA
ESPAÑOLA CONTEMPORÁNEA.*
P.W. SILVER, 240(HR):JUL71-340
J.M. VALVERDE, 546(RR):APR71-160

DEBIDOUR, V-H. SIMONE WEIL OU LA TRANS-
PARENCE.
J-F. THOMAS, 542:OCT-DEC71-522
DE BILIO, B. VENDETTA CON BRIO.
N. CALLENDAR, 441:22JUL73-12
DEBRAY, R. THE BORDER AND A YOUNG MAN IN
THE KNOW.
502(PRS):SPRING70-88
DEBRAY, R. PRISON WRITINGS.
617(TLS):17AUG73-949
DEBRAYE-GENETTE, R., ED. FLAUBERT.
B.F. BART, 399(MLJ):APR71-261
M. TILLETT, 208(FS):JUL72-346
DEBRECZENY, P. & J. ZELDIN, EDS & TRANS.
LITERATURE AND NATIONAL IDENTITY.*
L.J. SHEIN, 550(RUSR):JUL71-311
DEBRIS, J-P. & A. MENRAS. RESCAPÉS DES
BAGNES DE SAIGON.
J. BUTTINGER, 453:14JUN73-20
DEBRUNNER, A. - SEE HOFFMANN, O.
DE BRUYNE, E. THE ESTHETICS OF THE MID-
DLE AGES.*
G. BOAS, 290(JAAC):FALL70-131
DE CARLO, G. URBINO - LA STORIA DI UNA
CITTÀ E IL PIANO DELLA SUA EVOLUZIONE
URBANISTICA.
N. MILLER, 576:MAR71-92
DECARY, R., WITH M. URBAIN-FAUBLÉE. LA
DIVINATION MALGACHE PAR LE SIKIDY.
J. FAUBLÉE, 69:OCT70-402
DECKERS, M-C. LE VOCABULAIRE DE TEILHARD
DE CHARDIN.*
A. FUSS, 209(FM):JUL70-364
DECOCK, J. LE THÉÂTRE DE MICHEL DE
GHELDERODE.
R. LORRIS, 207(FR):MAY71-1129
DÉCOUFLÉ, A. LA COMMUNE DE PARIS.
M. REBÉRIOUX, 98:NOV71-979
D-B. WEINER, 207(FR):MAY71-1120
DE CRESCENZO, G. FRANCIS HUTCHESON E IL
SUO TEMPO.
L. TURCO, 548(RCSF):JAN-MAR70-104
DE CRESPIGNY, R. THE RECORDS OF THE
THREE KINGDOMS.
C-Y. CHEN, 293(JAST):MAY71-658
DÉCSY, G. YURAK CHRESTOMATHY.
E.K. RISTINEN, 350:MAR72-206
DECTER, M. THE LIBERATED WOMAN AND OTHER
AMERICANS.
P.M. SPACKS, 249(HUDR):SPRING72-160
DECTER, M. THE NEW CHASTITY AND OTHER
ARGUMENTS AGAINST WOMEN'S LIBERATION.*
617(TLS):30NOV73-1473
DEDIJER, V. LE DÉFI DE TITO.
F. FEJTÖ, 98:MAR71-267
DEDIO, A. DAS DRAMATISCHE WERK VON LADY
GREGORY.*
R. HALBRITTER, 38:BAND88HEFT3-416
DE FELITTA, F. OKTOBERFEST.
N. CALLENDAR, 441:25NOV73-49
DEFOE, D. A GENERAL HISTORY OF THE
PYRATES. (M. SCHONHORN, ED)
617(TLS):26JAN73-99
DEFOE, D. A JOURNAL OF THE PLAGUE YEAR.*
(L. LANDA, ED)
R.M. BAINE, 219(GAR):SPRING71-113
H.O., 430(NS):JUL70-366
173(ECS):FALL71-197
DEFOE, D. MEMOIRS OF A CAVALIER. (J.T.
BOULTON, ED)
617(TLS):5JAN73-6
DEFOE, D. MOLL FLANDERS. (J.P. HUNTER,
ED)
173(ECS):FALL71-197
DEFORD, F. CUT 'N' RUN.
M. LEVIN, 441:4MAR73-40

DEGAER, H. & OTHERS. REPERTORIUM VAN DE
PERS IN WEST-VLAANDEREN 1807-1914.
A. CORDEWIENER, 556(RLV):1970/6-678
DEGENHART, B. & A. SCHMITT. CORPUS DER
ITALIENISCHEN ZEICHNUNGEN 1300-1450.
K. CLARK, 39:APR70-260
DÉGH, L. FOLKTALES AND SOCIETY.
J.L. FISCHER, 292(JAF):JUL-SEP71-344
DEGHAYE, P. LA DOCTRINE ÉSOTÉRIQUE DE
ZINZENDORF (1700-1760).
L. CELLIER, 557(RSH):APR-JUN71-320
B. JUDEN, 402(MLR):APR72-419
DE GRÈVE, M. & F. VAN PASSEL. LINGUIS-
TIQUE ET ENSEIGNEMENT DES LANGUES
ÉTRANGÈRES.
A.W. GRUNDSTROM, 207(FR):OCT70-165
DEGUY, M. FIGURATIONS.
C. BOUCHÉ, 556(RLV):1971/6-781
P. SOMVILLE, 556(RLV):1971/3-366
D. WILHELM, 98:APR70-311
DEGUY, M. POÈMES 1960-1970.
617(TLS):3AUG73-894
DEGUY, M. TOMBEAU DE DU BELLAY.
617(TLS):14SEP73-1051
DEHENNIN, E. CÁNTICO DE JORGE GUILLÉN.
B. CIPLIJAUSKAITÉ, 240(HR):OCT71-459
L. LORENZO-RIVERO, 238:MAR71-198
DEIMLING, G. THEORIE UND PRAXIS DES
JUGENDSTRAFVOLLZUGS IN PÄDAGOGISCHER
SICHT.
W. KURTH, 182:VOL24#9/10-398
DEINHARD, H. BEDEUTUNG UND AUSDRUCK.
G. PELLES, 54:JUN71-278
DEINHARD, H. MEANING AND EXPRESSION.
B. CURTIS, 89(BJA):SPRING72-194
DEISS, J.J. THE ROMAN YEARS OF MARGARET
FULLER.*
E.B. SCHLESINGER, 432(NEQ):MAR71-147
DEISS, L. SPIRIT AND SONG OF THE NEW
LITURGY.
R. MOEVS, 363:MAY71-86
DEKKER, C. WOMAN IN MARBLE.
N. CALLENDAR, 441:11FEB73-30
DE KOCK, J. INTRODUCCIÓN AL CANCIONERO
DE MIGUEL DE UNAMUNO.
J. JOSET, 556(RLV):1971/4-502
DELACROIX, E. EUGÈNE DELACROIX: SELECTED
LETTERS 1813-1863.* (J. STEWART, ED &
TRANS)
T.J. CLARK, 592:JUL/AUG71-47
DELAISEMENT, G. LA LECTURE ET LA VIE.
M-C. WRAGE, 399(MLJ):JAN71-37
DELAISSÉ, L.M.J. A CENTURY OF DUTCH
MANUSCRIPT ILLUMINATION.*
W.O.H., 135:JAN70-48
I. TOESCA, 39:MAY71-437
DELANEY, C. - SEE CRAIGHEAD, E.S. & F.
DELANY, P. BRITISH AUTOBIOGRAPHY IN THE
SEVENTEENTH CENTURY.*
E. BOURCIER, 189(EA):APR-JUN71-198
P. SLACK, 447(N&Q):AUG71-316
G. THOMAS, 175:SPRING70-26
DELATTRE, P. COMPARING THE PHONETIC
FEATURES OF ENGLISH, GERMAN, SPANISH,
AND FRENCH.
B. MALMBERG, 596(SL):VOL25#1-63
DELATTRE, R.A. BEAUTY AND SENSIBILITY IN
THE THOUGHT OF JONATHAN EDWARDS.*
N.S. FIERING, 656(WMQ):OCT71-655
DE LAURA, D.J. HEBREW AND HELLENE IN
VICTORIAN ENGLAND.*
V.F. BLEHL, 613:AUTUMN70-457
A.O.J. COCKSHUT, 541(RES):MAY71-250
DELBANCO, N. FATHERING.
J.D. O'HARA, 441:23DEC73-12
442(NY):10DEC73-196

DELBOS, V. LA PHILOSOPHIE PRATIQUE DE
KANT. (3RD ED)
 R. MALTER, 342:BAND62HEFT1-147
DELBOUILLE, P. GENÈSE, STRUCTURE ET DES-
TIN D'ADOLPHE.
 617(TLS):12OCT73-1258
DEL BRAVO, C. SCULTURA SENESE DEL QUAT-
TROCENTO.
 J.H. BECK, 551(RENQ):AUTUMN71-358
DELCOUR, M. - SEE ERASMUS
DELCROIX, M. LE SACRÉ DANS LES TRAGÉ-
DIES PROFANES DE RACINE.
 J. DUBU, 535(RHL):JUL-AUG71-697
DELDERFIELD, E.R. WEST COUNTRY HISTORIC
HOUSES AND THEIR FAMILIES. (VOL 3)
 617(TLS):21DEC73-1574
DELDERFIELD, R.F. GIVE US THIS DAY.
 M. LEVIN, 441:18NOV73-54
DELEAR, F.J. IGOR SIKORSKY.
 J.D. WALZ, 550(RUSR):JAN71-93
DELEBECQUE, É. - SEE XENOPHON
DELEDALLE, G. L'IDÉE D'EXPÉRIENCE DANS
LA PHILOSOPHIE DE JOHN DEWEY.
 A.D.M., 543:MAR71-539
 O. REBOUL, 98:AUG-SEP70-759
DELEDALLE, G. - SEE DEWEY, J.
DELEKAT, F. IMMANUEL KANT.
 R. MALTER, 342:BAND62HEFT4-517
DELEUZE, G. DIFFÉRENCE ET RÉPÉTITION.
 M. FOUCAULT, 98:NOV70-885
DELEUZE, G. LOGIQUE DU SENS.
 M. FOUCAULT, 98:NOV70-885
 C. PANACCIO, 154:MAR71-171
DELEUZE, G. PRÉSENTATION DE SACHER-
MASOCH.
 C. RABANT, 98:FEB70-142
DELEUZE, G. PROUST ET LES SIGNES. (2ND
ED)
 J. BOREL, 98:DEC71-1060
 J.M. COCKING, 208(FS):OCT72-472
DELEUZE, G. SPINOZA ET LE PROBLÈME DE
L'EXPRESSION.
 H. DECLÈVE, 154:MAR71-164
DELEUZE, G. & F. GUATTARI. CAPITALISME
ET SCHIZOPHRÉNIE. (VOL 1)
 617(TLS):16MAR73-295
DELEYNE, J. THE CHINESE ECONOMY.
 617(TLS):13JUL73-810
DELFENDAHL, B. LE CLAIR ET L'OBSCUR.
 617(TLS):19OCT73-1274
DELGADO, A. HAVE YOU FORGOTTEN YET?
 617(TLS):23NOV73-1456
DELGADO, R. EL DESERTOR.
 I. MOLINA, 238:MAR71-220
D'ELIA, M., ED. CAPITOLI DELLA BAGLIVA
DI GALATINA.
 M.M., 228(GSLI):VOL147FASC458/459-470
DELIBES, M. LES RATAS. (L. HICKEY, ED)
 205(FMLS):OCT70-420
DELIBES, M. USA Y YO. (F.L. GORDON, ED)
 J. RIVAS, 238:DEC71-986
DELICADO, F. LA LOZANA ANDALUZA.* (B.M.
DAMIANI, ED)
 J-B. JONES, 238:DEC71-968
DELILLE, K.H. DIE GESCHICHTLICHE ENT-
WICKLUNG DES PRÄPOSITIONALEN AKKUSATIVS
IM PORTUGIESISCHEN.
 D.M. ATKINSON, 86(BHS):JUL72-315
 W. METTMANN, 72:BAND209HEFT4/6-449
DE LILLO, D. END ZONE.*
 V. CUNNINGHAM, 362:13SEP73-352
 P.M. SPACKS, 249(HUDR):AUTUMN72-502
 617(TLS):14SEP73-1045
DE LILLO, D. GREAT JONES STREET.
 S. BLACKBURN, 441:22APR73-2
 C. LEHMANN-HAUPT, 441:16APR73-41

DELIUS, H. UNTERSUCHUNGEN ZUR PROBLEM-
ATIK DER SOGENANNTEN SYNTHETISCHEN
SÄTZE APRIORI.
 G. KNAUSS, 206:MAY70-274
DELLA CORTE, F. CATONE CENSORE.* (2ND
ED)
 J-C. DUMONT, 555:VOL45FASC1-163
DELLA FAZIA, A. JEAN ANOUILH.
 B.L. KNAPP, 207(FR):OCT70-215
DELL'ARCO, M.F. - SEE UNDER FAGIOLO
DELL'ARCO, M.
DELLWING, H. STUDIEN ZUR BAUKUNST DER
BETTELORDEN IM VENETO.
 R. WAGNER-RIEGER, 683:BAND34HEFT4-296
DELMAN, D. HE WHO DIGS A GRAVE.
 N. CALLENDAR, 441:2SEP73-18
DELMAN, D. SUDDEN DEATH.*
 617(TLS):26OCT73-1324
DEL MAR, N. RICHARD STRAUSS. (VOL 3)
 J.A.W., 410(M&L):OCT72-441
 617(TLS):18MAY73-555
DELMER, S. THE COUNTERFEIT SPY.*
 617(TLS):8JUN73-648
DELOFFRE, F. LA NOUVELLE EN FRANCE À
L'ÂGE CLASSIQUE.*
 M. ROELENS, 535(RHL):JUL-AUG70-703
DELOFFRE, F. LE VERS FRANÇAIS.
 P. FORTASSIER, 557(RSH):APR-JUN71-306
DELOFFRE, F. - SEE DE MARIVAUX, P.C.D.
DELOFFRE, F. & M. GILOT - SEE DE MARI-
VAUX, P.C.D.
DE LONG, H. A PROFILE OF MATHEMATICAL
LOGIC.
 R.P.M., 543:JUN71-745
DEL PRA, M. - SEE MARTINETTI, P.
DELSEMME, P. TEODOR DE WYZEWA ET LE COS-
MOPOLITISME LITTÉRAIRE EN FRANCE À
L'ÉPOQUE DU SYMBOLISME.
 J. DE LABRIOLLE, 549(RLC):OCT-DEC70-
574
 N. SUCKLING, 182:VOL24#7/8-353
DE LUNA, B.N. THE QUEEN DECLINED.
 D. HAMER, 541(RES):AUG71-335
DELVAILLE, B. VALERY LARBAUD.
 S. FAUCHEREAU, 98:JUL71-626
DELZELL, C.F., ED. MEDITERRANEAN FASCISM,
1919-1945.
 617(TLS):2MAR73-225
DEMATS, P. - SEE HÉLISENNE DE CRENNE
DE MAURO, T. IL LINGUAGGIO DELLA CRITICA
D'ARTE.
 C. DE SIMONE, 260(IF):BAND75-229
DE MAURO, T. STORIA LINGUISTICA DELL'-
ITALIA UNITA.
 C. DE SIMONE, 260(IF):BAND75-325
DE MAURO, T. LUDWIG WITTGENSTEIN.
 S. KANNGIESSER, 260(IF):BAND75-222
DEMBO, L.S., ED. NABOKOV.*
 M. GREEN, 599:WINTER71-88
DEMBOWSKI, P.F., ED. AMI ET AMILE.*
 R. O'GORMAN, 399(MLJ):OCT71-414
DEMBOWSKI, P.F., ED. JOURDAIN DE BLAYE.
 R.F. COOK, 207(FR):FEB71-627
DEMEK, J. & OTHERS. GEOGRAPHY OF CZECHO-
SLOVAKIA.
 K.J. KANSKY, 32:JUN72-476
DEMENTIEV, A.G., L.M. POLIAK & L.I.
TIMOFEEV, EDS. ISTORIIA RUSSKOI SOV-
ETSKOI LITERATURY.
 H. ERMOLAEV, 32:MAR72-142
DEMENTIEV, A.G. & L.I. TIMOFEEV, EDS.
ISTORIIA RUSSKOI SOVETSKOI LITERATURY.
 H. ERMOLAEV, 32:MAR72-142
DEMÉNY, J. - SEE BARTÓK, B.
DEMETZ, P. POSTWAR GERMAN LITERATURE.
 H. LEHNERT, 301(JEGP):JAN72-93
 W. LEPPMAN, 131(CL):WINTER72-73
 B.J. SNYDER, 399(MLJ):OCT71-409

DEMETZ, P., T. GREENE & L. NELSON, JR.,
  EDS. THE DISCIPLINES OF CRITICISM.*
    D. DAICHES, 541(RES):FEB71-108
    L.T. LEMON, 290(JAAC):SPRING71-425
    J.K. ROBINSON, 598(SOR):SUMMER73-692
    A. RODWAY, 447(N&Q):JUL71-269
    J. VOISINE, 52:BAND5HEFT1-89
DEMIÉVILLE, P. & J. MAY - SEE "HŌBŌGIRIN"
DEMING, R.H., ED. JAMES JOYCE: THE CRIT-
  ICAL HERITAGE.*
    P. RECONDO, 202(FMOD):NOV71/FEB72-143
DEMKO, G.D. THE RUSSIAN COLONIZATION OF
  KAZAKHSTAN 1896-1916.*
    D.S.M. WILLIAMS, 575(SEER):APR72-307
DEMM, E. REFORMMÖNCHTUM UND SLAWENMIS-
  SION IM 12. JAHRHUNDERT.
    W. KAHLE, 182:VOL24#6-312
"DEMONSTRATION, VERIFICATION, JUSTIFICA-
  TION."
    R. BLANCHÉ, 542:OCT-DEC70-489
DEMPSEY, H.A. INDIAN NAMES FOR ALBERTA
  COMMUNITIES.
    M.A. MOOK, 424:DEC70-311
DEMSKE, J.M. BEING, MAN, AND DEATH.
    J.D.C., 543:MAR71-540
    J. COLLINS, 613:AUTUMN71-458
    G. WILLIAMS, 484(PPR):DEC71-287
DEMUS, O. BYZANTINE ART AND THE WEST.
    C.M. KAUFFMANN, 135:OCT71-139
    D.T. RICE, 90:SEP71-554
DEMUS, O. ROMANESQUE MURAL PAINTING.
    D.T., 135:MAY71-63
DEN BOER, J. TRYING TO COME APART.*
    D. ROSOCHACKI, 600:FALL71-138
D'ENCAUSSE, H.C. & S.R. SCHRAM.
  L'U.R.S.S. ET LA CHINE DEVANT LES
  REVOLUTIONS DANS LES SOCIETES PRE-
  INDUSTRIELLES.
    L. GOURE, 293(JAST):MAY71-670
DENEAUVE, J. LAMPES DE CARTHAGE.*
    B.H. WARMINGTON, 313:VOL61-296
DENHAM, P., ED. THE EVOLUTION OF CANAD-
  IAN LITERATURE IN ENGLISH. (VOL 4)
    J.W. LENNOX, 296:FALL73-108
DENISON, M. OVERTURE AND BEGINNERS.
    617(TLS):28DEC73-1593
DENKER, R. GRENZEN LIBERALER AUFKLÄRUNG
  BEI KANT UND ANDEREN.
    K. OEDINGEN, 342:BAND61HEFT4-532
DENKLER, H. DRAMA DES EXPRESSIONISMUS.*
    H.H.J. DE LEEUWE, 433:APR71-217
    E. MARSCH, 680(ZDP):BAND89HEFT2-297
DENNIS, J., ED. LETTERS UPON SEVERAL
  OCCASIONS.
    566:SPRING72-93
DENNIS, M. & S. FISH. PROGRAMS IN
  SEARCH OF A POLICY.
    J. PATTERSON & N.H. LITHWICK, 99:
      MAR73-20
DENNIS, N. PUBLIC PARTICIPATION AND
  PLANNERS' BLIGHT.
    617(TLS):9MAR73-271
DENNIS, R.C. THE SWEAT OF FEAR.
    N. CALLENDAR, 441:20MAY73-22
    617(TLS):26OCT73-1324
DENSEN-GERBER, J. WE MAINLINE DREAMS.
    441:2SEP73-14
DENT, A. MY COVENT GARDEN.
    617(TLS):19OCT73-1273
DENTON, D.E. THE LANGUAGE OF ORDINARY
  EXPERIENCE.
    F. KAUFFELD, 480(P&R):SUMMER71-192
DENTONE, A. IL PROBLEMA MORALE IN
  ROMAGNOSI E CATTANEO.
    E. NAMER, 542:APR-JUN70-257
DENTRY, R. ENCOUNTER AT KHARMEL.
    617(TLS):13APR73-427

DE PAULA, P. & H.S. MAGRO. LEITURAS
  BRASILEIRAS CONTEMPORÂNEAS.
    C.E. LEROY, 399(MLJ):MAR71-183
DE PETRA, Y. LA CLEF.
    G.R. DANNER, 207(FR):FEB71-591
DEPPE, W.G. HISTORY VERSUS ROMANCE.
    G. LAMBRECHTS, 189(EA):OCT-DEC70-448
DEPRUN, J., R. DESNÉ & A. SOBOUL - SEE
  MESLIER, J.
DE QUINCEY, T. DE QUINCEY AS CRITIC.
  (J.E. JORDAN, ED)
    617(TLS):19OCT73-1268
DE QUINCEY, T. RECOLLECTIONS OF THE
  LAKES AND THE LAKE POETS. (D. WRIGHT,
  ED)
    N. NICHOLSON, 565:VOL12#3-45
DERCSÉNYI, D. HISTORICAL MONUMENTS IN
  HUNGARY.
    N. PEVSNER, 46:AUG71-128
DEREGIBUS, A. LA METAFISICA CRITICA DI
  OCTAVE HAMELIN.
    E. NAMER, 542:APR-JUN70-257
DE RIJK, L.M. LOGICA MODERNORUM. (VOL
  2)
    M.T.B. BROCCHIERI, 548(RCSF):JAN-MAR
      70-100
D'ERIL, F.K.M. - SEE UNDER MELZI D'ERIL,
  F.K.
DERLETH, A. THIRTY YEARS OF ARKHAM HOUSE
  1939-1969.
    J.B. POST, 503:WINTER70-232
DERRICK, C. THE DELICATE CREATION.
    617(TLS):29JUN73-755
DERRIDA, J. DE LA GRAMMATOLOGIE.
    H. DECLÈVE, 154:DEC70-499
DERRY, J.W. CHARLES JAMES FOX.
    P. JOHNSON, 441:7JAN73-7
DERRY, T.K. A HISTORY OF MODERN NORWAY
  1814-1972.
    617(TLS):30NOV73-1482
DERUNGS, U. DER MORALTHEOLOGE J. GEI-
  SHÜTTNER (1763-1805), I. KANT UND J.G.
  FICHTE.
    W. STEINBECK, 342:BAND61HEFT4-533
DERWING, B.L. TRANSFORMATIONAL GRAMMAR
  AS A THEORY OF LANGUAGE ACQUISITION.
    617(TLS):12OCT73-1220
DESAI, A.R. RURAL SOCIOLOGY IN INDIA.
  (4TH ED)
    R.D. LAMBERT, 293(JAST):FEB71-512
DESAI, P.B., I.M. GROSSACK & K.N. SHARMA,
  EDS. REGIONAL PERSPECTIVE OF INDUSTRI-
  AL AND URBAN GROWTH.
    J.E. BRUSH, 293(JAST):MAY71-703
DE SANCTIS, F. LETTERE POLITICHE (1865-
  1880). (A. CROCE, ED)
    228(GSLI):VOL148FASC461-156
DESCH, K. CHALLENGE TO THE FUTURE. (R.
  JUNGK & H.J. MUNDT, EDS)
    G. THOMSON, 270:VOL21#4-188
DESCHARNES, R. & C. PREVOST. GAUDI THE
  VISIONARY.
    505:OCT71-145
DESCOTES, M. MOLIÈRE ET SA FORTUNE LIT-
  TÉRAIRE.
    A. EUSTIS, 188(ECR):WINTER71-67
    R. HORVILLE, 557(RSH):JUL-SEP71-472
DESCOTES, M. LE PERSONNAGE DE NAPOLÉON
  III DANS LES ROUGON-MACQUART.
    C. BECKER, 535(RHL):JUL-AUG71-715
DESCOTES, M. RACINE.*
    J. DUBU, 535(RHL):JUL-AUG71-696
DESCOTES, M.E. LA LÉGENDE DE NAPOLÉON
  ET LES ÉCRIVAINS FRANÇAIS DU XIXE
  SIÈCLE.* L'OBSESSION DE NAPOLÉON DANS
  LE "CROMWELL" DE VICTOR HUGO.
    P. BARBÉRIS, 535(RHL):MAY-JUN70-517
DESCRAINS, J. - SEE CAMUS, J-P.

DESHAYES, J. LES CIVILISATIONS DE L'ORI-
ENT ANCIEN.
D. REUILLARD, 98:OCT71-910
"DESIGN ESSENTIALS IN EARTHQUAKE RESIS-
TANT BUILDINGS."
W.J. MC GUINNESS, 44:DEC71-16
DESSAIN, C.S. & T. GORNALL - SEE NEWMAN,
J.H.
DESSEN, A.C. JONSON'S MORAL COMEDY.
W.D. KAY, 301(JEGP):JAN72-125
DESSOIR, M. AESTHETICS AND THEORY OF
ART.*
E. SCHAPER, 478:JUL71-135
DESVIGNES-PARENT, L. MARIVAUX ET L'ANGLE-
TERRE.
R. MERCIER, 557(RSH):OCT-DEC71-641
DE TROEYER, B. BIO-BIBLIOGRAPHIA FRAN-
CISCANA NEERLANDICA SAECULI XVI.
C.K. POTT, 551(RENQ):AUTUMN71-368
DETTI, E., G.F. DI PIETRO & G. FANELLI.
CITTA MURATE E SVILUPPO CONTEMPORANEO.
G. MASSON, 46:FEB71-132
DEUTSCH, E. ADVAITA VEDANTA.
B.K. MATILAL, 485(PE&W):JUL71-332
K.H. POTTER, 293(JAST):NOV70-249
R. SINARI, 484(PPR):JUN71-611
DEUTSCH, H. CONFRONTATIONS WITH MYSELF.
B.P. SOLOMON, 441:17JUN73-23
442(NY):2JUL73-76
DEUTSCH, O.E. MOZART.
M. PETERSON, 470:MAR66-27
"DEUTSCHE BEITRÄGE ZUR GEISTIGEN ÜBER-
LIEFERUNG, 1970."
E. KELLER, 67:MAY72-111
"DEUTSCHE HISTORISCHE WORTFORSCHUNG."
J. KNOBLOCH, 361:VOL26#3-294
"DIE DEUTSCHEN IM BRASILIANISCHEN SCHRIFT-
TUM."
D. CARSTENS, 430(NS):JUN71-332
DEUTSCHER, I. LENIN'S CHILDHOOD.
L. CLARK, 619(TC):VOL179#1046-54
DEUTSCHER, I. TROTSKY.
F. GUATTARI, 98:JUN71-563
DEUTSCHER, T., ED. NOT BY POLITICS
ALONE.
617(TLS):26OCT73-1297
"DEUX ANNÉES D'ÉTUDES BAUDELAIRIENNES
(JUILLET 1966 - JUIN 1968)."
205(FMLS):JUL71-295
DEVAMBEZ, P. & OTHERS. A DICTIONARY OF
ANCIENT GREEK CIVILIZATION.
É. WILL, 555:VOL45FASC2-329
DEVARAJA, N.K. THE MIND AND SPIRIT OF
INDIA.
N.L. CHOBOT, 485(PE&W):JAN70-97
DEVASURI, V. - SEE UNDER VADIN DEVASURI
"DEVELOPMENT PROBLEMS IN LATIN AMERICA."
R.T. ELY, 263:JAN-MAR72-48
DEVEREUX, E.J. A CHECKLIST OF ENGLISH
TRANSLATIONS OF ERASMUS TO 1700.*
R.R. ALLEN, 354:JUN70-164
DEVIDÉ, V. MATEMATIČKA LOGIKA. (PT 1)
I. BOH, 316:JUN70-326
DEVINE, L. THE ARROW OF APOLLYON.
W.H. NEW, 102(CANL):SUMMER72-88
DE VITO, J. THE PSYCHOLOGY OF SPEECH
AND LANGUAGE.
J.D. RAGSDALE, 583:WINTER71-210
DEVLIN, D.D. THE AUTHOR OF "WAVERLEY."
R. LAWRENCE, 175:AUTUMN71-110
"THE DEVONSHIRE ASSOCIATION: REPORT AND
TRANSACTIONS." (VOL 104)
617(TLS):14SEP73-1065
DE VORE, P.T. - SEE TATSEY, J.
DEVOTO, G. & G.C. OLI. DIZIONARIO DELLA
LINGUA ITALIANA.
D.D., 275(IQ):SPRING-SUMMER72-124
DE VRIES, D. - SEE DICKENS, C.

DE VRIES, P. FOREVER PANTING.
V. CUNNINGHAM, 362:13SEP73-352
P. GILLIATT, 442(NY):16JUL73-76
J. STURROCK, 441:13MAY73-5
617(TLS):10AUG73-921
DE VRIES, P. MRS. WALLOP.
639(VQR):WINTER71-IX
DEWEY, J. THE EARLY WORKS OF JOHN DEWEY,
1882-1898. (VOL 1)
Y.H. KRIKORIAN, 484(PPR):SEP70-140
DEWEY, J. THE EARLY WORKS OF JOHN DEWEY,
1882-1898. (VOL 3)
Y.H. KRIKORIAN, 484(PPR):SEP71-128
DEWEY, J. LOGIQUE: LA THÉORIE DE L'EN-
QUÊTE. (G. DELEDALLE, ED & TRANS)
P. DUBOIS, 542:APR-JUN70-256
DEYERMOND, A.D. EPIC POETRY AND THE
CLERGY.*
H.T. OOSTENDORP, 433:APR71-211
B. DUTTON, 400(MLN):MAR71-292
C.C. SMITH, 131(CL):WINTER72-82
DEYERMOND, A.D. A LITERARY HISTORY OF
SPAIN: THE MIDDLE AGES.
D.W. LOMAX, 402(MLR):JUL72-670
DHÔTEL, A. UN JOUR VIENDRA.
M. CAGNON, 207(FR):APR71-954
"THE DIAMOND SUTRA AND THE SUTRA OF HUI
NENG." (A.F. PRICE & WONG MOU-LAM,
TRANS)
D.J. KALUPAHANA, 485(PE&W):APR71-224
DÍAZ, G.V. - SEE UNDER VERDÍN DÍAZ, G.
DÍAZ, J.S. - SEE UNDER SIMÓN DÍAZ, J.
DÍAZ, J.W. THE MAJOR THEMES OF EXISTEN-
TIALISM IN THE WORK OF JOSÉ ORTEGA Y
GASSET.
C. MORÓN-ARROYO, 86(BHS):JUL72-309
DÍAZ, N.P. - SEE UNDER PASTOR DÍAZ, N.
DÍAZ ALEJANDRO, C.F. ESSAYS ON THE ECO-
NOMIC HISTORY OF THE ARGENTINE REPUB-
LIC.
D.E. ACEVEDO, 37:MAY71-40
DÍAZ ALEJO, A.E. & E. PRADO VELÁZQUEZ.
ÍNDICE DE LA "REVISTA AZUL" (1894-1896).
B.G. CARTER, 240(HR):OCT71-464
DÍAZ SÁNCHEZ, R. CUMBOTO.*
R. ROSALDO, 50(ARQ):SPRING70-90
DIBBEN, A.A. TITLE DEEDS.
M.P.G. DRAPER, 325:APR71-246
DI BENEDETTO, A., ED. PROSE DI GIOVANNI
DELLA CASA E ALTRI TRATTATISTI CINQUE-
CENTESCHI DEL COMPORTAMENTO.
M. POZZI, 228(GSLI):VOL148FASC464-599
DIBON, P. INVENTAIRE DE LA CORRESPON-
DANCE D'ANDRÉ RIVET (1595-1650).
G. TONELLI, 319:JAN73-119
DICEY, E. SPECTATOR OF AMERICA. (H.
MITGANG, ED)
617(TLS):19JAN73-70
DICKASON, D.H. WILLIAM WILLIAMS.
P.G. ADAMS, 27(AL):NOV72-478
A. NEUMEYER, 127:SPRING72-356
DICKENMANN, E. STUDIEN ZUR HYDRONYMIE
DES SAVESYSTEMS. (VOLS 1&2) (VOL 1 IS
2ND ED)
R. KOLARIČ, 260(IF):BAND75-365
DICKENS, A.G. THE AGE OF HUMANISM AND
REFORMATION.
617(TLS):8JUN73-651
DICKENS, C. BLEAK HOUSE. (D. DE VRIES,
ED) BLEAK HOUSE. (N. PAGE, ED)
T. BLOUNT, 155:SEP71-168
DICKENS, C. BLEAK HOUSE. (A.J. GUERARD,
ED)
T. BLOUNT, 155:SEP71-168
L. LANE, JR., 255(HAB):SUMMER70-66
DICKENS, C. "A CHRISTMAS CAROL" BY
CHARLES DICKENS. (F.B. ADAMS, JR., ED)
M.S., 155:MAY71-118

DICKENS, C. DAVID COPPERFIELD. PIP AND
THE CONVICT.
J.G., 155:SEP71-178
DICKENS, C. A DICKENS ANTHOLOGY. (H.
PLUCKROSE & F. PEACOCK, EDS)
155:MAY71-118
DICKENS, C. CHARLES DICKENS' UNCOLLECTED
WRITINGS FROM HOUSEHOLD WORDS 1850-
1859.* (H. STONE, ED)
S. MONOD, 189(EA):APR-JUN70-219
DICKENS, C. DOMBEY AND SON. (P. FAIR-
CLOUGH, ED)
P. COLLINS, 155:JAN71-47
DICKENS, C. THE LETTERS OF CHARLES
DICKENS.* (VOL 2) (M. HOUSE & G.
STOREY, EDS)
T.J. CRIBB, 541(RES):AUG71-388
S. MONOD, 189(EA):APR-JUN70-210
S. WALL, 184(EIC):JUL71-261
DICKENS, C. THE LIFE AND ADVENTURES OF
NICHOLAS NICKLEBY. NICHOLAS NICKLEBY
AT THE YORKSHIRE SCHOOL.
617(TLS):22JUN73-723
DICKENS, C. MARTIN CHUZZLEWIT.* (P.N.
FURBANK, ED)
J.C. FIELD, 556(RLV):1971/2-231
S. MONOD, 189(EA):APR-JUN70-218
DICKENS, C. OUR MUTUAL FRIEND. (S. GILL,
ED)
R. GILMOUR, 155:SEP71-173
S. WALL, 184(EIC):JUL71-261
DICKENS, C. PICTURES FROM ITALY. (D.
PAROISSIEN, ED)
617(TLS):23NOV73-1451
DICKENS, C. THE STRANGE GENTLEMAN AND
OTHER PLAYS. (J. TILLETT, ED)
617(TLS):2MAR73-235
DICKENS, C. A TALE OF TWO CITIES. (G.
WOODCOCK, ED)
S. MONOD, 155:MAY71-114
"CHARLES DICKENS." [VICTORIA AND ALBERT
MUSEUM CATALOGUE]
G. SMITH, 637(VS):JUN71-459
"DICKENS MEMORIAL LECTURES 1970."
G. SMITH, 637(VS):JUN71-459
"DICKENS STUDIES ANNUAL." (VOL 1) (R.B.
PARTLOW, JR., ED)
H.M. DALESKI, 445(NCF):MAR72-486
M.S. HELFAND, 454:WINTER72-186
S. MONOD, 189(EA):JAN-MAR71-100
M.S., 155:SEP71-177
G. SMITH, 637(VS):JUN71-459
DICKEY, J. BABEL TO BYZANTIUM.
J.K. ROBINSON, 598(SOR):SUMMER73-692
DICKEY, J. THE EYE-BEATERS, BLOOD, VIC-
TORY, MADNESS, BUCKHEAD AND MERCY.*
T. EAGLETON, 565:VOL12#3-68
S. TOULSON, 493:SUMMER71-208
639(VQR):WINTER71-XVIII
DICKEY, J. SELF-INTERVIEWS. (B. & J.
REISS, EDS)
G.D. HILDRETH, 50(ARQ):WINTER71-372
42(AR):FALL/WINTER70/71-463
639(VQR):SUMMER71-CXX
DICKEY, R.P. ACTING IMMORTAL.
J.R. REED, 491:APR73-47
DICKEY, R.P. RUNNING LUCKY.*
L.L. LEE, 649(WAL):SPRING70-79
DICKEY, W. MORE UNDER SATURN.*
J.R. REED, 491:APR73-47
DICKIE, G. AESTHETICS.
R.J. SCLAFANI, 311(JP):24MAY73-303
DICKIE, J. & A. RAKE. WHO'S WHO IN
AFRICA.
617(TLS):14DEC73-1549
DICKINSON, A.E.F. THE MUSIC OF BERLIOZ.
617(TLS):3AUG73-899

DICKINSON, G.L. THE AUTOBIOGRAPHY OF G.
LOWES DICKINSON. (D. PROCTOR, ED)
D.J. ENRIGHT, 362:5JUL73-23
617(TLS):21SEP73-1085
DICKINSON, H. MYTH ON THE MODERN STAGE.*
A. BELLI, 149:MAR72-87
J.R. BROWN, 157:SPRING70-62
R. LORRIS, 207(FR):DEC70-471
DICKINSON, H.T. WALPOLE AND THE WHIG
SUPREMACY.
617(TLS):12OCT73-1260
DICKINSON, P. THE GREEN GENE.
P. ADAMS, 61:JUN73-124
617(TLS):15JUN73-697
DICKINSON, P. MORE THAN TIME.*
T. EAGLETON, 565:VOL12#1-77
DICKINSON, P. A WINTERING TREE.
A. MAC LEAN, 362:20DEC73-859
617(TLS):17AUG73-946
DICKS, D.R. EARLY GREEK ASTRONOMY TO
ARISTOTLE.*
I. MUELLER, 122:JUL72-217
DICKSON, K.B. A HISTORICAL GEOGRAPHY OF
GHANA.
R.W. STEEL, 69:JAN71-78
DICKSON, L. H.G. WELLS.*
H. WILSON, 177(ELT):VOL13#1-85
571:SUMMER70-110
DICKSTEIN, M. KEATS AND HIS POETRY.*
T. MC FARLAND, 676(YR):WINTER72-279
J. STILLINGER, 301(JEGP):JAN72-150
"DICTIONARY OF AMERICAN BIOGRAPHY." (SUPP
3, 1941-1945) (E.T. JAMES, ED)
E.F. GOLDMAN, 441:30SEP73-14
"DICTIONARY OF CANADIAN BIOGRAPHY." (VOL
10, 1871 TO 1880)
G.W., 102(CANL):AUTUMN72-114
DI CYAN, E. & L. HESSMAN. WITHOUT PRE-
SCRIPTION.
441:25MAR73-22
DIDEROT, D. DIDEROT'S LETTERS TO SOPHIE
VOLLAND: A SELECTION.* (P. FRANCE,
TRANS)
J. STAROBINSKI, 453:22MAR73-18
DIDEROT, D. OEUVRES COMPLÈTES. (R.
LEWINTER, ED)
J. STAROBINSKI, 453:22MAR73-18
DIDEROT, D. PHILOSOPHISCHE SCHRIFTEN.
(T. LÜCKE, ED) ÄSTHETISCHE SCHRIFTEN.
(F. BASSENGE, ED)
R. WARNING, 535(RHL):MAR-APR70-314
DIDEROT, D. SALONS.* (VOL 4) (J. SEZNEC,
ED)
G. MAY, 546(RR):FEB71-60
"DIDEROT STUDIES XI ET XII."
H. MØLBJERG, 462(OL):VOL26#1-82
DIEBOLD, A.R. - SEE UNDER OSGOOD, C.E. &
T.A. SEBEOK
DIECKMANN, F. KARL VON APPENS BÜHNEN-
BILDER AM BERLINER ENSEMBLE.
617(TLS):28DEC73-1591
DIEDRICHS, U., ED. WO DER ROTE PFEFFER
WÄCHST.
U. KUTTER, 196:BAND12HEFT2/3-279
DIEDERICHS, U. - SEE FROBENIUS, L.
DIEHL, G. MAX ERNST.
J.R. MELLOW, 441:2DEC73-16
DIEKMANN, E. DIE SUBSTANTIVBILDUNG MIT
SUFFIXEN IN DEN FABLIAUX.
B. FOSTER, 208(FS):JAN72-115
DIEKSTRA, F.N.M., ED. A DIALOGUE BE-
TWEEN REASON AND ADVERSITY.*
J. DE CALUWÉ-DOR, 556(RLV):1971/5-641
S.M. KUHN, 589:JAN72-113
A. LEYLAND, 179(ES):DEC71-547
D. MC CLUSKEY, 215(GL):VOL10#1-31
J.R. SIMON, 189(EA):OCT-DEC70-436

DIENER, G. GOETHES "LILA."
F. EBNER, 182:VOL24#7/8-356
DIENER, G. PANDORA - ZU GOETHES META-
PHORIK.
G. NEUMANN, 657(WW):SEP/OCT70-355
DIENST, R-G. RICHARD LINDNER.*
S-L. SCHWARTZ, 58:SEP/OCT71-16
DIERICKX, J. GLOSSAIRE DE L'ANGLAIS DU
JOURNALISME.
I. SIMON, 556(RLV):1970/3-328
DIERICKX, J. & Y. LEBRUN, EDS. LINGUIS-
TIQUE CONTEMPORAINE: HOMMAGE À ERIC
BUYSSENS.
K. TOGEBY, 545(RPH):MAY72-472
DIERKS, M. STUDIEN ZU MYTHOS UND PSY-
CHOLOGIE BEI THOMAS MANN.
617(TLS):23NOV73-1421
DIETRICH, G. ENGLISCHE SCHULPHONETIK.
W. PRAEGER, 38:BAND88HEFT1-120
DIETRICH, G. SPRACHPHILOSOPHISCHE UND
SPRACHPSYCHOLOGISCHE GRUNDLAGEN DES
NEUSPRACHLICHEN UNTERRICHTS UNTER BE-
SONDERER BERÜCKSICHTIGUNG DER SPRACH-
THEORIE VON F. DE SAUSSURE.
H. METZGER, 38:BAND89HEFT4-474
DIETRICH, R. BE MY VICTIM. END OF A
STRIPPER. ANGEL EYES.
G. VIDAL, 453:13DEC73-6
DIETRICH, R-F. PORTRAIT OF THE ARTIST AS
A YOUNG SUPERMAN.
R-S. NELSON, 397(MD):MAY71-119
S. WEINTRAUB, 572:MAY70-86
DIETZ, K. DIE REZEPTION DES VORKONSON-
ANTISCHEN "L" IN ROMANISCHEN LEHNWÖR-
TERN DES MITTELENGLISCHEN UND SEINE
REFLEXE IM NEUENGLISCHEN STANDARD.*
M. POPP, 38:BAND88HEFT4-523
B. SUNDBY, 260(IF):BAND75-337
DIETZE, J. AUGUST SCHLEICHER ALS SLAW-
IST.
B. PANZER, 260(IF):BAND74-318
DIEZ DE MEDINA, F. OLLANTA, EL JEFE
KOLLA.*
V. DE ROZENTAL, 37:SEP71-37
DIEZCANSECO, A-P. - SEE UNDER PAREJA
DIEZCANSECO, A.
DIGGINS, J-P. MUSSOLINI AND FASCISM.*
617(TLS):2MAR73-225
DIGGLE, J. - SEE EURIPIDES
DIGGLE, J. & F-R-D. GOODYEAR - SEE COR-
IPPUS
DIGGLE, J. & F-R-D. GOODYEAR - SEE HOUS-
MAN, A-E.
"DIGNĀGA, ON PERCEPTION." (M. HATTORI,
ED & TRANS)
P-J-H., 543:JUN71-747
K-N. UPADHYAYA, 485(PE&W):APR70-195
DIHLE, A. HOMER-PROBLEME.
F-M. COMBELLACK, 122:JUL72-206
J-B. HAINSWORTH, 123:DEC72-316
M-N. NAGLER, 124:DEC71-131
DIJKSTRA, B. THE HIEROGLYPHICS OF A NEW
SPEECH.*
V-M. AMES, 290(JAAC):WINTER70-282
J-E. CHAMBERLIN, 249(HUDR):WINTER
72/73-700
C. HESS, 127:FALL71-100
P. MARIANI, 418(MR):AUTUMN72-671
G. WICKES, 131(CL):FALL72-367
DIKEMAN, M. THE DEVIL WE KNOW.
A-C-J. BERGMAN, 441:26AUG73-28
DIKSHITAR, T-A-V., ED. VEDĀNTA TATTVĀ-
LOKA OF ŚRĪ JANĀRDANA.
L. ROCHER, 318(JAOS):OCT-DEC71-548
DIL, A-S. - SEE HAUGEN, E.
DILKE, O-A-W. THE ROMAN LAND SURVEYORS.
P-N. LOCKHART, 124:MAR72-240

DILKS, D. CURZON IN INDIA.
D-C. ELLINWOOD, JR., 637(VS):DEC70-224
DILLARD, R-H-W. NEWS OF THE NILE.*
E. CUBBAGE, 398:AUTUMN73-230
639(VQR):SUMMER71-CV
DILLER, E., R-A. NICHOLLS & J-R. MC WIL-
LIAMS, EDS. MEISTERWERKE DER DEUTSCHEN
SPRACHE.
H. JAECKEL, 221(GQ):MAR71-265
DILLER, H. KLEINE SCHRIFTEN ZUR ANTIKEN
LITERATUR. (H-J. NEWIGER & H. SEYFFERT,
EDS)
F. LASSERRE, 182:VOL24#11/12-495
DILLIGAN, R-J. & T-K. BENDER, COMPS. A
CONCORDANCE TO THE ENGLISH POETRY OF
GERARD MANLEY HOPKINS.*
W-R. MUNDT, 598(SOR):AUTUMN73-1029
J. PICK, 636(VP):SUMMER70-176
DILLINGHAM, W-B. FRANK NORRIS.
D-B. GRAHAM, 594:SPRING71-122
R. LEHAN, 445(NCF):SEP70-252
A. PONCET, 189(EA):APR-JUN70-233
DILLISTONE, F-W. TRADITIONAL SYMBOLS
AND THE CONTEMPORARY WORLD.
617(TLS):7SEP73-1034
DILLON, F. A PLACE FOR HABITATION.
617(TLS):15JUN73-700
DILLON, M. THE ONE IN THE BACK IS MEDEA.
M. LEVIN, 441:20MAY73-54
DILLON, M., ED. STORIES FROM THE ACALLAM.
R-P-M. LEHMANN, 589:JAN72-116
DILMAN, I. INDUCTION AND DEDUCTION.
617(TLS):27JUL73-875
DIMA, A. PRINCIPII DE LITERATURĂ COM-
PARATĂ.
D. GRIGORESCU, 131(CL):SUMMER72-283
H. PEREZ, 52:BAND5HEFT2-199
DIMARAS, C-T. A HISTORY OF MODERN GREEK
LITERATURE.
617(TLS):9NOV73-1369
DI MONA, J. LAST MAN AT ARLINGTON.
N. CALLENDAR, 441:4NOV73-79
DINGWALL, W-O. GENERATIVE TRANSFORMA-
TIONAL GRAMMAR.
G-F. MEIER, 682(ZPSK):BAND23HEFT6-643
DINKLAGE, K., WITH E. ALBERTSEN & K.
CORINO, EDS. ROBERT MUSIL.
U. KARTHAUS, 680(ZDP):BAND90HEFT2-308
G. MULLER, 597(SN):VOL43#2-557
DINNEEN, F-P. AN INTRODUCTION TO GENERAL
LINGUISTICS.*
F-R. PALMER, 206:FEB70-150
DION, R. LES ANTHROPOPHAGES DE L'"ODYS-
SÉE."*
J-B. HAINSWORTH, 123:MAR72-100
DIONISOTTI, C. GEOGRAFIA E STORIA DELLA
LETTERATURA ITALIANA.
L-T., 275(IQ):SPRING-SUMMER72-126
DI PIETRO, R-J. LANGUAGE STRUCTURES IN
CONTRAST.
R. WARDHAUGH, 351(LL):DEC71-247
DIPPER, A. THE GOLDEN VIRGIN.
N. CALLENDAR, 441:25MAR73-49
DIRLMEIER, F. AUSGEWÄHLTE SCHRIFTEN ZUR
DICHTUNG UND PHILOSOPHIE DER GRIECHEN.
(H. GÖRGEMANNS, ED)
H. LLOYD-JONES, 123:JUN72-233
DI SALVO, T. LETTURA CRITICA DELLA
"DIVINA COMMEDIA."
J. ROSSI, 276:WINTER71-499
DISANDRO, C-A. TRÁNSITO DEL MYTHOS AL
LOGOS: HESÍODO - HERACLITO - PARMÉN-
IDES.
A. ERNOUT, 555:VOL45FASC1-160
G-B. KERFERD, 123:MAR72-117
DI SAN LAZZARO, G. COMPLETE WORKS OF
MARINO MARINI.
G. RUSSELL, 58:FEB71-10

DI SAN LAZZARO, G., ED. HOMAGE TO MAX
ERNST.
R. LEBOWITZ, 58:DEC71/JAN72-24
DI SAN LAZZARO, G., ED. HOMAGE TO HENRY
MOORE.
617(TLS):13JUL73-817
DI SAN LAZZARO, G., ED. HOMAGE TO GEORGES
ROUALT.
R. LEBOWITZ, 58:MAR72-18
DISCH, T.M., ED. THE RUINS OF EARTH.
617(TLS):20APR73-451
DISNEY, D.M. ONLY COUPLES NEED APPLY.
N. CALLENDAR, 441:22JUL73-12
DI STEFANO, G. LA DÉCOUVERTE DE PLU-
TARQUE EN OCCIDENT.
J.H. WATKINS, 208(FS):APR72-187
DITMAS, E.M.R. TRISTAN AND ISEULT IN
CORNWALL.
B.C. SPOONER, 203:AUTUMN70-233
DITTMAN, W. HARTMANNS GREGORIUS.
H. ROSENFELD, 680(ZDP):BAND89HEFT1-
115
DITTMAR, F.J. & J.J. COLLEDGE. BRITISH
WARSHIPS 1914-1919.
617(TLS):19JAN73-73
DIVINE, D. THE OPENING OF THE WORLD.
617(TLS):19OCT73-1289
DIXON, B. WHAT IS SCIENCE FOR?
617(TLS):12OCT73-1259
DIXON, H. HISTORIC BUILDINGS, GROUPS OF
BUILDINGS, AREAS OF ARCHITECTURAL IM-
PORTANCE IN THE TOWN OF ENNISKILLEN.
617(TLS):17AUG73-961
DIXON, K. SOCIOLOGICAL THEORY.
617(TLS):5OCT73-1192
DIXON, P., ED. ALEXANDER POPE.
617(TLS):30MAR73-346
DIXON, R.M.W. & J. GODRICH. RECORDING
THE BLUES.*
N.V. ROSENBERG, 650(WF):APR71-147
DJILAS, M. MEMOIR OF A REVOLUTIONARY.
W. LAQUEUR, 441:1APR73-28
E. WEEKS, 61:MAR73-105
617(TLS):28SEP73-1099
DMYTRYSHYN, B. A CONCISE HISTORY OF THE
USSR. (2ND ED)
M. MC CAULEY, 575(SEER):OCT72-619
DOBB, M. THEORIES OF VALUE AND DISTRI-
BUTION SINCE ADAM SMITH.
617(TLS):16NOV73-1406
DOBBIN, C. URBAN LEADERSHIP IN WESTERN
INDIA.
617(TLS):23FEB73-222
DOBERT, E.W. KARL GUTZKOW UND SEINE
ZEIT.
W.P. HANSON, 220(GL&L):OCT71-68
W.E. YUILL, 402(MLR):JUL72-703
DOBESCH, G. DER PANHELLENISCHE GEDANKE
IM 4. JH. V. CHR. UND DER "PHILIPPOS"
DES ISOKRATES.
É. WILL, 555:VOL45FASC2-340
DÖBLIN, A. BRIEFE. (H. GRABER, ED)
W. GROTHE, 597(SN):VOL43#2-563
DOBRAŠINOVIĆ, G. ARHIVSKA GRADA O VUKU
KARADŽIĆU, 1813-1864.
T.J. BUTLER, 32:JUN72-493
DOBRÉE, B. RUDYARD KIPLING.*
E. MERTNER, 38:BAND88HEFT1-154
DOBRIAN, W.A. & C.R. JEFFERS. SPANISH
READINGS FOR CONVERSATION.
M.E. GILES, 238:DEC71-984
J.A. TOPETE, 399(MLJ):APR71-260
DOBRIANSKY, L.E. U.S.A. AND THE SOVIET
MYTH.
R.A. SCHADLER, 396(MODA):SPRING72-209
DOBSON, E.J. ENGLISH PRONUNCIATION 1500-
1700.* (2ND ED) (VOLS 1&2)
A. RESZKIEWICZ, 353:AUG71-114

DOBSON, R.B. DURHAM PRIORY 1400-1450.
617(TLS):30NOV73-1483
DOBYNS, S. CONCURRING BEASTS.*
R. LATTIMORE, 249(HUDR):AUTUMN72-475
E. LUEDERS, 651(WHR):SUMMER72-295
R.J. MILLS, JR., 491:MAY73-105
L. RAAB, 398:SPRING73-113
DOBYNS, S. MAN OF LITTLE EVILS.
N. CALLENDAR, 441:12AUG73-12
DOBZSANSKY, T. GENETIC DIVERSITY AND
HUMAN EQUALITY.
C.P. HASKINS, 441:23DEC73-13
DOCKHORN, K. MACHT UND WIRKUNG DER
RHETORIK.
H-J. LANGE, 52:BAND5HEFT3-327
DOCKSTADER, F.J. INDIAN ART IN AMERICA.
INDIAN ART IN MIDDLE AMERICA. INDIAN
ART IN SOUTH AMERICA.
D. MARKS, 58:SUMMER71-13
DOCTOROW, E.L. THE BOOK OF DANIEL.*
J. RICHMOND, 473(PR):FALL72-627
DODD, N. & W. HICKSON, EDS. DRAMA AND
THEATRE IN EDUCATION.
617(TLS):13JUL73-817
DODDS, E.R. THE ANCIENT CONCEPT OF
PROGRESS.
W.H. AUDEN, 453:28JUN73-20
617(TLS):15JUN73-691
VON DODERER, H. DIE ERZÄHLUNGEN.
617(TLS):20APR73-449
DODGE, B. — SEE "THE FIHRIST OF AL-NADIM"
DODGE, E.S. BEYOND THE CAPES.*
W.R. KIME, 649(WAL):WINTER72-266
DODGE, E.S. THE POLAR ROSSES.
617(TLS):23MAR73-326
DODGE, F. UNDER COVER FOR WELLS FARGO.
(C. LAKE, ED)
J.G. TAYLOR, 649(WAL):SPRING71-75
DODGSHUN, A.W. FROM ZANZIBAR TO UJIJI.
(N.R. BENNETT, ED)
T.O. BEIDELMAN, 69:JAN70-88
DODGSON, J.M. THE PLACE-NAMES OF CHE-
SHIRE. (PT 1)
O. ARNGART, 597(SN):VOL43#2-571
M. GELLING, 447(N&Q):MAY71-189
DODGSON, J.M. THE PLACE-NAMES OF CHE-
SHIRE. (PT 2)
O. ARNGART, 597(SN):VOL43#2-571
B. COTTLE, 541(RES):NOV71-463
M. GELLING, 447(N&Q):MAY71-189
DODGSON, J.M. THE PLACE-NAMES OF CHE-
SHIRE. (PT 3)
B. COTTLE, 541(RES):NOV71-463
DODSON, C.J. LANGUAGE TEACHING AND THE
BILINGUAL METHOD.
A. JOHANSSON, 597(SN):VOL42#2-518
DODSWORTH, M., ED. THE SURVIVAL OF
POETRY.
J. GLOVER, 565:VOL12#4-56
W.H. PRITCHARD, 184(EIC):APR71-211
H. SERGEANT, 175:AUTUMN71-106
VAN DOESBURG, T. PRINCIPLES OF NEO-
PLASTIC ART.*
D. IRWIN, 39:AUG70-158
DOHERTY, D. THE SEXUAL DOCTRINE OF CAR-
DINAL CAJETAN.
G. MAY, 182:VOL24#6-269
DOHERTY, F. SAMUEL BECKETT.
617(TLS):12OCT73-1217
DOHERTY, F.M. BYRON.*
P. ROBERTS, 541(RES):FEB71-107
DOLAN, P.J., ED. MODES OF FICTION.
J.W. STEVENSON, 573(SSF):SUMMER71-475
DOLCE, L. ARETIN: A DIALOGUE ON PAINTING.
H. OSBORNE, 89(BJA):SPRING72-200
DOLCI, D. NON SENTITE L'ODORE DEL FUMO.
B. MERRY, 270:VOL22#2-41

DOLEŽEL, L. & R.W. BAILEY, EDS. STATIS-
TICS AND STYLE.*
    D.M. BURTON, 599:SPRING71-184
DÖLGER, F. & J. KARAYANNOPULOS. BYZAN-
TINISCHE URKUNDENLEHRE.* (PT 1)
    P.J. ALEXANDER, 589:JAN72-117
DOLGOFF, S. - SEE BAKUNIN, M.
DOLLECZEK, A. MONOGRAPHIE DER K.U.K.
ÖSTER.-UNG. BLANKEN UND HANDFEUER-
WAFFEN, KRIEGSMUSIK, FAHNEN UND STAND-
ARTEN SEIT ERRICHTUNG DES STEHENDEN
HEERES BIS ZUR GEGENWART.
    C.B., 135:FEB71-139
DOLLEY, M. MEDIEVAL ANGLO-IRISH COINS.
    617(TLS):16MAR73-305
DOLSON, H. A DYING FALL.
    N. CALLENDAR, 441:22APR73-24
DOMALAIN, J-Y. PANJAMON.
    617(TLS):12JAN73-49
DOMENICHINI-RAMIARAMANANA, B., ED & TRANS.
HAINTENY D'AUTREFOIS.
    J-L. JOUBERT, 549(RLC):OCT-DEC70-572
    M. URBAIN-FAUBLÉE, 69:APR70-186
DOMIN, H. WOZU LYRIK HEUTE?*
    K. HAMBURGER, 490:JAN/APR70-310
DOMKE, H. SPANIENS NORDEN, DER WEG NACH
SANTIAGO.
    G. HAENSCH, 430(NS):MAR71-164
DONA, M. ESPRESSIONE E SIGNIFICATO NELLA
MUSICA.
    D. STEVENS, 415:APR72-368
DONADONI, E. A HISTORY OF ITALIAN LITER-
ATURE.* (R.J. CLEMENTS, ED)
    205(FMLS):JUL71-295
DONALD, D. CHARLES SUMNER AND THE RIGHTS
OF MAN.*
    R.B. JAGER, 432(NEQ):JUN71-333
DONALDSON, E.T. SPEAKING OF CHAUCER.*
    J.A. BURROW, 541(RES):MAY71-246
    A. DAVID, 589:JUL72-509
    R.T. DAVIES, 447(N&Q):MAY71-200
    R.M. WILSON, 175:AUTUMN70-97
    J.A. YUNCK, 141:FALL71-420
DONALDSON, F. THE ACTOR-MANAGERS.
    N. MARSHALL, 157:WINTER70-67
DONALDSON, I. THE WORLD UPSIDE-DOWN.*
    D. BROOKS, 402(MLR):JAN72-167
    E.A.M. COLMAN, 67:MAY72-78
    J. DULCK, 189(EA):JUL-SEP71-335
    H. HAWKINS, 541(RES):NOV71-517
    H.E. PAGLIARO, 219(GAR):FALL71-376
    J.R. TAYLOR, 157:SPRING71-66
DONALDSON, S. POET IN AMERICA: WINFIELD
TOWNLEY SCOTT.
    617(TLS):4MAY73-497
DONALDSON-EVANS, L.K. POÉSIE ET MÉDITA-
TION CHEZ JEAN DE LA CEPPÈDE.
    R.C LA CHARITÉ, 207(FR):APR71-991
    F.L. LAWRENCE, 400(MLN):MAY71-574
"DONATELLO E IL SUO TEMPO."
    J.H. BECK, 54:MAR70-98
DONLEAVY, J.P. A FAIRY TALE OF NEW YORK.
    P. ADAMS, 61:OCT73-130
    R. BLYTHE, 362:6SEP73-320
    D.K. MANO, 441:23SEP73-6
    L.E. SISSMAN, 442(NY):8OCT73-168
    617(TLS):7SEP73-1018
DONNACHIE, I. THE INDUSTRIAL ARCHAEOLOGY
OF GALLOWAY.
    A. FENTON, 595(SCS):VOL16PT1-86
DONNARD, J-H. LE THÉÂTRE DE CARMONTELLE.
    E. GIUDICI, 535(RHL):JUL-AUG70-725
DONNE, J. DONNE'S PREBEND SERMONS. (J-M.
MUELLER, ED)
    P.G. STANWOOD, 551(RENQ):WINTER71-572
DONNE, J. FIVE SERMONS UPON SPECIAL
OCCASIONS, 1626.
    568(SCN):SUMMER72-35

DONNE, J. IGNATIUS HIS CONCLAVE.* (T.S.
HEALY, ED)
    P. LEGOUIS, 189(EA):APR-JUN71-197
    J.M.P., 568(SCN):SUMMER72-34
    A. RASPA, 541(RES):MAY71-192
    A. RASPA, 551(RENQ):SUMMER71-280
    J. SIMONS, 433:APR71-220
DONNE, J. POÈMES DE JOHN DONNE. (J.
FUZIER & Y. DENIS, TRANS) THE SONGS
AND SONNETS OF JOHN DONNE. (T. RED-
PATH, ED)
    J-M BENOIST, 98:AUG/SEP71-730
DONNE, J. THE SATIRES, EPIGRAMS AND
VERSE LETTERS OF JOHN DONNE.* (W. MIL-
GATE, ED)
    R. ELLRODT, 189(EA):JUL-SEP71-329
DONNELLY, M.C. THE NEW ENGLAND MEETING
HOUSES OF THE SEVENTEENTH CENTURY.*
    S.C. POWELL, 576:MAY70-202
DONNELLY, P.J. BLANC DE CHINE.*
    G. WILLS, 39:OCT70-316
DONNISON, D. & D. EVERSLEY, EDS. LONDON.
    G. ANNAN, 362:12JUL73-59
    617(TLS):23NOV73-1424
DONNISON, F.S.V. BURMA.
    F.N. TRAGER, 293(JAST):FEB71-502
D'ONOFRIO, C. GLI OBELISCHI DI ROMA.
(2ND ED)
    H. HIBBARD, 90:MAY71-279
D'ONOFRIO, C. IL TEVERE E ROMA.
    C.H. HEILMANN, 90:DEC71-750
DONOGHUE, D. CONNOISSEURS OF CHAOS.
    D. WEEKS, 290(JAAC):WINTER70-277
DONOGHUE, D. EMILY DICKINSON.
    R. ASSELINEAU, 189(EA):JUL-SEP70-352
DONOGHUE, D. THE ORDINARY UNIVERSE.*
    J.K. ROBINSON, 598(SOR):SUMMER73-692
DONOGHUE, D. JONATHAN SWIFT.
    V.M. HAMM, 613:SPRING70-132
    P. HARTH, 173(ECS):SUMMER71-484
    C.J. HORNE, 402(MLR):JAN72-170
    R. LAWRENCE, 175:AUTUMN70-107
DONOGHUE, D. - SEE YEATS, W.B.
DONOHUE, J.W., JR. DRAMATIC CHARACTER IN
THE ENGLISH ROMANTIC AGE.
    B. EVANS, 401(MLQ):DEC71-444
    C.B. HOGAN, 676(YR):AUTUMN71-134
    J.T. KNAPP, 191(ELN):DEC71-148
DONOHUE-GAUDET, M-L. LE VOCALISME ET LE
CONSONANTISME FRANÇAIS.
    F. CARTON, 209(FM):APR71-171
DONOSO, J. CUENTOS.
    A. ADELL, 270:VOL22#2-37
DONOSO, J. THE OBSCENE BIRD OF NIGHT.
(SPANISH TITLE: EL OBSCENO PÁJARO DE
LA NOCHE.)
    P. ADAMS, 61:JUN73-123
    R. COOVER, 441:17JUN73-1
    M. WOOD, 453:13DEC73-19
    270:VOL22#2-36
    442(NY):16JUL73-78
DONOUGHUE, B. & G. JONES. HERBERT
MORRISON.
    P. WHITEHEAD, 362:4OCT73-457
    617(TLS):19OCT73-1282
DONOVAN, B.E. EURIPIDES PAPYRI I: TEXTS
FROM OXYRHYNCHUS.
    D.F. JACKSON, 24:JUL72-497
DONOVAN, M.J. THE BRETON LAY.*
    R.W. ACKERMAN, 546(RR):FEB71-36
    D.S. BREWER, 402(MLR):JAN72-164
    M.H. MEANS, 613:SUMMER70-307
    D. MEHL, 38:BAND89HEFT4-532
    H. NIEDZIELSKI, 188(ECR):FALL70-257
    D.D.R. OWEN, 208(FS):JAN72-59

DONOVAN, M.J. & OTHERS. A MANUAL OF
THE WRITINGS IN MIDDLE ENGLISH 1050-
1500. (FASC 1)
D. MEHL, 38:BAND88HEFT4-531
DONZÉ, R. LA GRAMMAIRE GÉNÉRALE ET
RAISONNÉE DE PORT-ROYAL.*
R.H. ROBINS, 47(ARL):[N.S.]VOL1-96
DOOLEY, D.J. CONTEMPORARY SATIRE.
W. KINSLEY, 223:DEC71-348
DOPHEIDE, B. FRITZ BUSCH.
P.G., 410(M&L):APR72-196
DOR-RIVAUX, E. LES GRANDES PYRAMIDES.
N.L. GOODRICH, 207(FR):FEB71-639
DORE, R. BRITISH FACTORY - JAPANESE
FACTORY.
617(TLS):21DEC73-1571
DORENKAMP, J.A. - SEE FLETCHER, J. & P.
MASSINGER
DOREY, T.A., ED. ERASMUS.*
R.T. BRUÈRE, 122:JUL72-200
E.J. KENNEY, 123:DEC72-401
DOREY, T.A., ED. LIVY.
J.P. PACKARD, 124:JAN72-172
DOREY, T.A., ED. TACITUS.*
B. BALDWIN, 121(CJ):OCT-NOV71-75
D.A. MALCOLM, 123:MAR72-46
DOREY, T.A. & D.R. DUDLEY. ROME AGAINST
CARTHAGE.
M. IVENS, 619(TC):VOL179#1048-54
DORFLES, G. ARTIFICIO E NATURA.
R.W. KRETSCH, 290(JAAC):FALL70-138
DORFMAN, A. & A. MATTELART. PARA LEER
AL PATO DONALD.
617(TLS):23FEB73-220
DORFMAN, D. BLAKE IN THE NINETEENTH
CENTURY.*
G.E. BENTLEY, JR., 627(UTQ):FALL70-86
E.E. BOSTETTER, 405(MP):MAY71-385
M. BOTTRALL, 597(SN):VOL42#1-237
A. OSTRIKER, 637(VS):SEP70-113
G. THOMAS, 175:SUMMER70-66
DORFMAN, E. THE NARREME IN THE MEDIEVAL
ROMANCE EPIC.*
J.M. ANDERSON, 361:VOL25#2-205
G.J. BRAULT, 215(GL):VOL10#1-62
G.S. BURGESS, 402(MLR):APR72-413
L.S. CRIST, 207(FR):MAR71-812
E.R. HAYMES, 149:MAR72-92
H.G. STURM, 238:MAR71-210
F. WHITEHEAD, 208(FS):JAN72-55
DORFMÜLLER, VON DADELSEN & PETSCHULL, EDS.
QUELLENSTUDIEN ZUR MUSIK: WOLFGANG
SCHMIEDER ZUM 70. GEBURTSTAG.
S. DAW, 415:OCT72-979
DORIGO, W. LATE ROMAN PAINTING.
G.K. GALINSKY, 124:FEB72-209
DORN, F. THE FORBIDDEN CITY.
C.B. MALONE, 293(JAST):MAY71-741
DÖRRENHAUS, F. URBANITÄT UND GENTILE
LEBENSFORM.
P. VOSSELER, 182:VOL24#23/24-889
DÖRRIE, H. DER HEROISCHE BRIEF.
F. VAN INGEN, 433:OCT71-459
M.F. MOTSCH, 400(MLN):APR71-430
L. VÖLKER, 556(RLV):1971/3-357
DORSCH, T.S., ED. THE YEAR'S WORK IN
ENGLISH STUDIES. (VOLS 45 & 46)
R. HABENICHT, 570(SQ):SPRING70-183
DORSON, R.M., ED. PEASANT CUSTOMS AND
SAVAGE MYTHS.*
P.E. LEIS, 650(WF):APR70-140
VAN DORSTEN, J.A. THE RADICAL ARTS.*
L. FORSTER, 208(FS):OCT72-444
D. FREEDBERG, 447(N&Q):JUN71-234
J. GRUNDY, 541(RES):NOV71-525
J.I.J., 568(SCN):SPRING72-31

DORTU, M.G. TOULOUSE-LAUTREC ET SON
OEUVRE.
617(TLS):15JUN73-694
DOS PASSOS, J. THE FOURTEENTH CHRONICLE.
(T. LUDINGTON, ED)
R.G. DAVIS, 441:14OCT73-4
T.R. EDWARDS, 453:29NOV73-28
E. WEEKS, 61:OCT73-128
DOSTOEVSKY, F.M. THE ADOLESCENT. (A.R.
MAC ANDREW, TRANS)
G. LIVERMORE, 32:SEP72-733
DOSTOEVSKY, F.M. THE GAMBLER. (E. WASI-
OLEK, ED; V. TERRAS, TRANS)
J. UPDIKE, 442(NY):14APR73-145
617(TLS):2MAR73-235
DOSTOEVSKY, F.M. THE NOTEBOOKS FOR "THE
BROTHERS KARAMAZOV." (E. WASIOLEK, ED
& TRANS)
N. ROSEN, 32:MAR72-192
DOSTOEVSKY, F.M. THE UNPUBLISHED DOS-
TOEVSKY. (VOL 1) (C.R. PROFFER, GEN-
ERAL ED)
617(TLS):10AUG73-923
DOTTIN, G. - SEE MARGUERITE DE NAVARRE
DOUBROVSKY, S. LA DISPERSION.*
C. BACKÈS-CLÉMENT, 98:DEC70-1014
DOUCETTE, L.E. EMERY BIGOT.*
N. HEPP, 535(RHL):JUL-AUG71-694
DOUGALL, R. IN AND OUT OF THE BOX.
F. DILLON, 362:6DEC73-788
DOUGHERTY, R. GOODBYE, MR. CHRISTIAN.
M. JANEWAY, 61:OCT73-124
R.R. LINGEMAN, 441:28SEP73-37
C. LYDON, 441:14OCT73-2
442(NY):29OCT73-182
DOUGHTY, O. A VICTORIAN ROMANTIC.
M. PAGÈS, 189(EA):JUL-SEP70-311
DOUGHTY, O. & J.R. WAHL - SEE ROSSETTI,
D.G.
DOUGLAS, D.C. THE NORMAN ACHIEVEMENT,
1050-1100.
H. WIERUSZOWSKI, 589:JUL72-525
DOUGLAS, E. APOSTLES OF LIGHT.
M. LEVIN, 441:18FEB73-30
442(NY):3MAR73-113
DOUGLAS, H. BURKE AND HARE.
617(TLS):10AUG73-937
DOUGLAS, J. MANDALAS.*
D. BARBOUR, 150(DR):SPRING71-133
DOUGLAS, J.D., ED. THE RELEVANCE OF
SOCIOLOGY.
E. SUNTRUP, 258:DEC71-594
DOUGLAS, M. NATURAL SYMBOLS. (NEW ED)
617(TLS):28SEP73-1137
DOUGLAS, M., ED. RULES AND MEANINGS.
617(TLS):3AUG73-896
DOUGLAS, R. WORKING WITH R.V.W.*
H. OTTAWAY, 415:OCT72-974
DOUGLAS-HOME, C. ROMMEL.
617(TLS):9NOV73-1365
DOUGLASS, F. THE LANGUAGE OF THE CLASSI-
CAL FRENCH ORGAN.*
R. KREMER, 317:SPRING72-112
DOUGLASS, W.A. DEATH IN MURÉLAGA.*
R. BASTIDE, 182:VOL24#1/2-58
DOUMAS, C. THE N.P. GOULANDRIS COLLEC-
TION OF EARLY CYCLADIC ART.
E. VERMEULE, 121(CJ):FEB-MAR72-287
DOVER, K.J. LYSIAS AND THE "CORPUS
LYSIACUM."*
S. USHER, 303:VOL91-147
DOVER, K.J. - SEE ARISTOPHANES
DOW, G. RAILWAY HERALDRY.
617(TLS):21DEC73-1574
DOWDEN, W.S. JOSEPH CONRAD.*
W.E. DAVIS, 177(ELT):VOL14#1-53
DOWDEY, C. THE GOLDEN AGE.
639(VQR):SPRING71-LXXIV

DOWNES, K. HAWKSMOOR.
J.L-M., 135:SEP70-63
DOWNES, R.C. THE RISE OF WARREN GAMALIEL
HARDING, 1865-1920.
639(VQR):SUMMER71-CXII
DOWNEY, J. THE EIGHTEENTH-CENTURY PULPIT.
A.R. HUMPHREYS, 541(RES):FEB71-85
G. MIDGLEY, 447(N&Q):SEP71-350
G. SAMPSON, 529(QQ):SPRING71-161
J.M. WALKER, JR., 173(ECS):SPRING71-
348
DOWNEY, S.B. THE EXCAVATIONS AT DURA-
EUROPOS, FINAL REPORT III.* (PT 1,
FASC 1: THE HERACLES SCULPTURE.)
C. VERMEULE, 54:MAR71-110
DOWNIE, R.S. ROLES AND VALUES.
A. EDEL, 311(JP):22FEB73-101
N. HAINES, 518:JAN72-4
DOWNIE, R.S. & E.A. TELFER. RESPECT FOR
PERSONS.*
R.F. ATKINSON, 479(PHQ):APR71-186
T.D. CAMPBELL, 478:JUL70-184
A. EDEL, 311(JP):22FEB73-101
P. GLASSEN, 154:DEC70-465
H.D. LEWIS, 483:JUL71-282
DOWNS, I. THE STOLEN LAND.
J. GRIFFIN, 381:DEC71-454
DOWNTON, J.V., JR. REBEL LEADERSHIP.
617(TLS):16NOV73-1393
DOXAT, J. THE BOOK OF DRINKING.
617(TLS):14DEC73-1548
DOYLE, A.C. SHERLOCK HOLMES: ETUDE EN
ROUGE; LE SIGNE DES QUATRE.
F. GALICHET, 98:FEB70-115
DOYLE, C. EARTH MEDITATIONS: ONE TO
FIVE.*
L. RUSSELL, 102(CANL):SPRING72-97
DOYLE, J.F., ED. EDUCATIONAL JUDGMENTS.
617(TLS):23MAR73-330
DRABBLE, M. THE NEEDLE'S EYE.*
L. QUINN, 31(ASCH):WINTER72/73-173
R. SALE, 249(HUDR):WINTER72/73-703
DRABBLE, M. THE WATERFALL.
J.C. FIELD, 556(RLV):1971/5-627
DRACHE, D., ED. QUEBEC, ONLY THE BEGIN-
NING.
C. MILLER, 99:FEB73-37
DRACK, W., ED. UR- UND FRÜHGESCHICHT-
LICHE ARCHÄOLOGIE DER SCHWEIZ. (VOL 2)
R. PITTIONI, 182:VOL24#23/24-875
DRAGE, C.L. & W.N. VICKERY, EDS. AN
EIGHTEENTH-CENTURY RUSSIAN READER.*
M. KANTOR, 173(ECS):SUMMER72-617
205(FMLS):OCT70-421
DRAHT, V.H., ED. WIR WUNDERKINDER.
H. WEGNER, 399(MLJ):MAR71-198
DRAKE, D.B. CERVANTES: A CRITICAL BIB-
LIOGRAPHY.* (VOL 1)
J. RODRÍGUEZ-LUIS, 240(HR):APR71-216
DRAKE, M., ED. APPLIED HISTORICAL STUD-
IES.
617(TLS):16NOV73-1392
DRAKE, R. THE SINGLE HEART.
A. STONE, 396(MODA):SPRING72-220
DRAKE, S. & I.E. DRABKIN, EDS & TRANS.
MECHANICS IN SIXTEENTH-CENTURY ITALY.
E. GRANT, 551(RENQ):AUTUMN71-381
DRAKE, W.D., JR. THE CONNOISSEUR'S
HANDBOOK OF MARIJUANA.
617(TLS):10AUG73-937
"DRAMATURGIE ET SOCIÉTÉ."
V. TASCA, 549(RLC):JAN-MAR71-100
DRANGE, T. TYPE CROSSINGS.*
M. DOHERTY, 682(ZPSK):BAND24HEFT5-434
L. ZGUSTA, 353:JUN71-115
DRANSFIELD, M. THE INSPECTOR OF TIDES.
S.E. LEE, 581:DEC72-302
617(TLS):12OCT73-1216

DRANSFIELD, M. STREETS OF THE LONG
VOYAGE.*
K.L. GOODWIN, 381:SEP71-367
DRAPER, M.P.G. MARBLE HILL HOUSE AND ITS
OWNERS.
J. LEES-MILNE, 39:OCT70-318
A.A. TAIT, 90:APR71-227
DRAPER, R.P., ED. D.H. LAWRENCE: THE
CRITICAL HERITAGE.*
J.C.F. LITTLEWOOD, 184(EIC):APR71-195
S. SANDERS, 111:13NOV70-47
J. WORTHEN, 97(CQ):SPRING/SUMMER70-
104
DRAYE, H., ED. PROCEEDINGS OF THE NINTH
INTERNATIONAL CONGRESS OF ONOMASTIC
SCIENCES.
E.C. SMITH, 424:MAR70-53
DREIHELLER, F. JOHANN VON OTTHERA, DOC-
TOR JUR. UTR., DER RETTER DER THÜRING-
ISCHEN STADT MÜHLHAUSEN IM BAUERNKRIEGE.
T. KLEIN, 182:VOL24#21/22-815
DREITZEL, H.P. ELITEBEGRIFF UND SOZIAL-
STRUKTUR.
P. WEINTRAUB, 182:VOL24#3-90
DREIZEHNTER, A. - SEE ARISTOTLE
DRENNAN, R.E., ED. WIT'S END.
617(TLS):13APR73-429
DRERUP, H. GRIECHISCHE BAUKUNST IN GEO-
METRISCHER ZEIT.*
P. CHANTRAINE, 555:VOL45FASC1-145
F.M. COMBELLACK, 122:JUL72-204
DRESCHER, H.W. - SEE MACKENZIE, H.
DRESDEN, D. THE MARQUIS DE MORÈS.
J.G. TAYLOR, 649(WAL):SPRING71-76
DRETSKE, F.I. SEEING AND KNOWING.*
B. AUNE, 482(PHR):JUL71-383
L.C. HOLBOROW, 479(PHQ):JAN71-82
C.G. PRADO, 154:SEP70-261
DREW, B. THE NARRATIVES OF FUGITIVE
SLAVES IN CANADA.
C. FRASER, 296:SUMMER73-115
DREW, P. THE POETRY OF ROBERT BROWNING.*
M. HANCHER, 85:SPRING71-50
R. MAYHEAD, 175:SUMMER71-59
DREW, P. THIRD GENERATION.
617(TLS):22JUN73-708
DREXLER, H. DIE IAMBENKÜRZUNG.
J.G. GRIFFITH, 123:MAR72-70
DREXLER, R. TO SMITHEREENS.*
R. BLYTHE, 362:6SEP73-320
617(TLS):14SEP73-1045
DREYFUS, H.L. WHAT COMPUTERS CAN'T DO.*
B. WILLIAMS, 453:15NOV73-36
DRIEU LA ROCHELLE, P. SECRET JOURNAL AND
OTHER WRITINGS.
617(TLS):21SEP73-1074
DRINKOW, J. THE VINTAGE OPERETTA BOOK.
617(TLS):9FEB73-156
DRISCOLL, P. THE WILBY CONSPIRACY.*
S. HILL, 362:22FEB73-251
617(TLS):13APR73-427
DRISKELL, L.V. & J.T. BRITTAIN. THE
ETERNAL CROSSROADS.
L.Y. GOSSETT, 27(AL):NOV72-517
F.P.W. MC DOWELL, 598(SOR):AUTUMN73-
998
DRÖGEMÜLLER, H-P. SYRAKUS.*
K.J. DOVER, 487:AUTUMN71-282
DRONKE, E. POLIZEI-GESCHICHTEN.
A. BEST, 220(GL&L):OCT71-54
DRONKE, P. POETIC INDIVIDUALITY IN THE
MIDDLE AGES.*
R. AXTON, 111:29JAN71-106
J.B. FRIEDMAN, 191(ELN):MAR72-199
W.T.H. JACKSON, 589:JUL72-529
F.P. PICKERING, 220(GL&L):APR72-308
A.G. RIGG, 447(N&Q):JUN71-228
[CONTINUED]

DRONKE, P. POETIC INDIVIDUALITY IN THE
  MIDDLE AGES.* [CONTINUING]
    A.B. SCOTT, 382(MAE):1972/1-53
    205(FMLS):JUL71-295
DRONKE, U. - SEE "THE POETIC EDDA"
DROP, W. & J. HOOGTEIJLING. TOT BETER
  BEGRIP.
    S. THEISSEN, 556(RLV):1970/1-108
DROSS, F. - SEE BARLACH, E.
DROSSAART LULOFS, H.J. - SEE ARISTOTLE
VON DROSTE-HÜLSHOFF, A. DIE JUDENBUCHE.*
  (H. RÖLLEKE, ED)
    M. MARE, 220(GL&L):APR72-287
    L.W. TUSKEN, 406:SPRING72-75
VON DROSTE-HÜLSHOFF, A. DIE JUDENBUCHE.
  (K. TIFFANY, ED)
    W.L. HAHN, 399(MLJ):DEC71-528
DROUGGE, G. ORTNAMNEN I GÖTEBORGS OCH
  BOHUS LÄN. (VOL 17)
    H. HAMRE, 301(JEGP):APR72-294
DROWER, M.S. CAMBRIDGE ANCIENT HISTORY.
  (VOL 2, CHAPTER 10: SYRIA C. 1550-1400
  B.C.)
    H.W.F. SAGGS, 303:VOL91-189
DROZ, E. UN RECUEIL DE MANUSCRITS DU
  XVE SIÈCLE DE LA BIBLIOTHÈQUE DE CLAUDE-
  ENOCH VIREY.
    J. FOX, 208(FS):JAN72-65
DROZ, J., ED. HISTOIRE GÉNÉRALE DU SOC-
  IALISME. (VOL 1)
    617(TLS):12OCT73-1229
DROZ, J. L'EUROPE CENTRALE.
    M. MOLNÁR, 98:JAN70-73
DRUMMOND, C. DEATH AT THE BAR.*
    N. CALLENDAR, 441:8APR73-32
DRUMMOND, D.F. THE MOUNTAIN.
    R.P. DICKY, 649(WAL):SPRING71-65
    R. OLIVER, 598(SOR):SPRING73-492
DRUMMOND, G. ENGLISH FOR INTERNATIONAL
  BUSINESS.
    W. STUCK, 430(NS):DEC70-643
DRUMMOND, I. THE JAWS OF THE WATCHDOG.
    N. CALLENDAR, 441:1JUL73-21
    617(TLS):15JUN73-697
DRUMMOND, J. BANG! BANG! YOU'RE DEAD!
    617(TLS):17AUG73-959
DRURY, A. COME NINEVEH, COME TYRE.
    M. LEVIN, 441:9DEC73-47
DRURY, M.O. THE DANGER OF WORDS.
    617(TLS):10AUG73-935
DRUTMAN, I. - SEE FLANNER, J.
DRUZHININA, E.I. IUZHNAIA UKRAINA V
  1800-1825 GG.
    A. MC CONNELL, 32:DEC72-889
DRYANSKY, G.Y. OTHER PEOPLE.
    M. LEVIN, 441:11NOV73-51
DRYDEN, J. AURENG-ZEBE.* (F.M. LINK,
  ED)
    J.R. CLARK, 568(SCN):FALL-WINTER72-67
DRYDEN, J. THE WORKS OF JOHN DRYDEN.
  (VOL 2: POEMS 1681-1684.) (H.T. SWEDEN-
  BERG, JR., ED)
    617(TLS):14DEC73-1530
DRYDEN, J. THE WORKS OF JOHN DRYDEN.*
  (VOL 10) (M.E. NOVAK & G.R. GUFFEY,
  EDS)
    A.C. KIRSCH, 481(PQ):JUL71-426
    E. ROTHSTEIN, 173(ECS):SUMMER72-608
DU, N. THE TALE OF KIEU.
    P. ADAMS, 61:DEC73-139
DUBILLARD, R. LE JARDIN AUX BETTERAVES.
    F. TONELLI, 207(FR):OCT70-175
DUBIN, R. THEORY BUILDING.
    J.E. TOMBERLIN, 484(PPR):DEC70-309
DUBOIS, C-G. MYTHE ET LANGAGE AU SEIZ-
  IÈME SIÈCLE.
    J. CANTERA, 202(FMOD):JUN71-333

DUBOIS, C.G. PROBLÈMES DE L'UTOPIE.
    J.M. GOULEMOT, 535(RHL):JAN-FEB70-126
DUBOIS, E.T. - SEE RAPIN, R.
DUBOIS, E.T., E. RATCLIFF & P.J. YARROW,
  EDS. EIGHTEENTH CENTURY FRENCH STUDIES.
    J. UNDANK, 400(MLN):MAY71-584
DUBOIS, J. GRAMMAIRE STRUCTURALE DU
  FRANÇAIS: LA PHRASE ET LES TRANSFOR-
  MATIONS.
    K. WINN, 430(NS):NOV71-617
DUBOIS, J. - SEE ZOLA, E.
DUBOIS, J. & OTHERS. RHÉTORIQUE GÉNÉR-
  ALE.
    D. BOUVEROT, 209(FM):APR71-159
    P. FRANCE, 208(FS):JUL72-365
DUBOIS, J. & J. SUMPF, EDS. LINGUISTIQUE
  ET PÉDAGOGIE.
    D. MESSNER, 430(NS):DEC71-679
DUBOIS, P. LE PROBLÈME MORAL DANS LA
  PHILOSOPHIE ANGLAISE DE 1900 À 1950.
    C. PANACCIO, 154:SEP70-282
DU BOIS, W.E.B. A W.E.B. DU BOIS READER.
  (A.G. PASCHAL, ED)
    N. LEDERER, 584(SWR):SPRING72-165
DUBUFFET, J. PROSPECTUS ET TOUS ÉCRITS
  SUIVANTS.
    J-C. LEBENSZTEJN, 98:APR70-321
DUBY, G. GUERRIERS ET PAYSANS VII-XIIE
  SIÈCLE. HOMMES ET STRUCTURES DU MOYEN
  ÂGE.
    617(TLS):17AUG73-941
DUCASSE, C.J. TRUTH, KNOWLEDGE AND
  CAUSATION.*
    H. HEIDELBERGER, 311(JP):22NOV73-755
    R.E. SANTONI, 258:MAR71-135
DUCHACEK, O. PRÉCIS DE SÉMANTIQUE FRAN-
  ÇAISE.
    F. HELGORSKY, 209(FM):OCT71-356
    S. ULLMANN, 361:VOL25#1-70
    V. VLASÁK, 597(SN):VOL43#2-615
DUCHÊNE, F. THE CASE OF THE HELMETED
  AIRMAN.*
    S. HYNES, 659:SUMMER73-378
DUCHÊNE, R. RÉALITÉ VÉCUE ET ART ÉPIS-
  TOLAIRE. (VOL 1)
    H.T. BARNWELL, 208(FS):JUL72-327
    C. CHANTALAT, 535(RHL):MAY-JUN71-503
DUCHET, M., ED-IN-CHIEF. MANUEL D'HIS-
  TOIRE LITTÉRAIRE DE LA FRANCE. (VOL 3)
    J. PROUST, 535(RHL):MAR-APR71-300
DUCKHAM, H. & B. GREAT PIT DISASTERS.
    617(TLS):2FEB73-133
DUCKWORTH, C. ANGELS OF DARKNESS.
    617(TLS):12OCT73-1217
DUCKWORTH, G.E. VERGIL AND CLASSICAL
  HEXAMETER POETRY.*
    J. SOUBIRAN, 555:VOL45FASC2-367
DUCKWORTH, M. OVER THE FENCE IS OUT.
    P. EVANS, 368:SEP70-302
DUCLOS, C. LES CONFESSIONS DU COMTE
  DE ***. (L. VERSINI, ED)
    J. BRENGUES, 535(RHL):MAR-APR71-305
    G. MAY, 207(FR):FEB71-624
    J. MAYER, 557(RSH):JUL-SEP71-478
    V. MYLNE, 208(FS):APR72-206
DUCLOS, C. CORRESPONDANCE DE CHARLES
  DUCLOS (1704-72). (J. BRENGUES, ED)
    N. SUCKLING, 182:VOL24#5-193
DUCROS, F. TOMMASO CAMPANELLA, POÈTE.
    L. BOLZONI, 228(GSLI):VOL148FASC464-
    602
DUCROT, O. & OTHERS. QU'EST-CE QUE LE
  STRUCTURALISME?
    K. TOGEBY, 545(RPH):AUG71-97
DUCULOT, J. - SEE WARNANT, L.

DUDBRIDGE, G. THE HSI-YU CHI.
  W. EBERHARD, 196:BAND12HEFT2/3-269
  C.T. HSIA, 293(JAST):AUG71-887
  W.H. HUDSPETH, 203:WINTER70-320
DUDEK, L. COLLECTED POETRY.*
  J. DITSKY, 628:SPRING72-108
DUDLEY, D.R., ED. NERONIANS AND FLAVIANS.
  617(TLS):1JUN73-618
DUDLEY, D.R. THE ROMANS.
  R.M. OGILVIE, 123:JUN72-250
  639(VQR):SUMMER71-CXXVII
DUERDEN, D. AFRICAN ART.
  E.L.R. MEYEROWITZ, 39:JUL70-80
DUERDEN, D. & C. PIETERSE, EDS. AFRICAN
  WRITERS TALKING.*
  R.D. SMITH, 362:11JAN73-57
DUERKSEN, R.A. SHELLEYAN IDEAS IN VIC-
  TORIAN LITERATURE.
  H. BERGNER, 38:BAND88HEFT1-150
DUFF, A.B. - SEE DE GOBINEAU, J.A.
DUFF, D. ELIZABETH OF GLAMIS.
  617(TLS):27JUL73-884
DUFF, E. HOW WE ARE.
  L. MULVEY, 592:NOV71-216
DUFF, J.D. - SEE JUVENAL
DUFFEE, M.G. SKETCHES OF ALABAMA. (V.P.
  BROWN & J.P. NABERS, EDS)
  M. MC DOWELL, 9(ALAR):OCT71-289
MARCHIONESS OF DUFFERIN AND AVA. MY CAN-
  ADIAN JOURNAL 1872-78.
  G. WARKENTIN, 296:SUMMER73-107
DUFFY, C. BORODINO AND THE WAR OF 1812.
  617(TLS):16NOV73-1390
DUFFY, M. ALL HEAVEN IN A RAGE.
  A. BROYARD, 441:19APR73-47
  P. THEROUX, 441:27MAY73-16
DUFFY, M. I WANT TO GO TO MOSCOW.
  R. BRYDEN, 362:7JUN73-772
  617(TLS):8JUN73-633
DUFOUR BOZZO, C. SARCOFAGI ROMANI A
  GENOVA.
  G.M.A. HANFMANN, 54:SEP71-396
DUFOURNET, J. - SEE DE VILLEHARDOUIN, G.
DUFRENNE, M. LE POÉTIQUE.
  617(TLS):5OCT73-1191
DUFRENNE, M. POUR L'HOMME.*
  J.M. HEMS, 484(PPR):SEP71-133
DUGAN, A. COLLECTED POEMS.*
  T. EAGLETON, 565:VOL12#3-68
  A. OSTRIKER, 473(PR):SPRING72-270
  H. SERGEANT, 175:SUMMER71-65
DUGAN, J. & L. LAFORE. THE DAYS OF
  EMPEROR AND CLOWN.
  B. COLLIER, 441:30SEP73-44
DUGDALE, B. BAFFY. (N.A. ROSE, ED)
  617(TLS):30NOV73-1472
DUGGAN, A. FAMILY FAVOURITES.
  617(TLS):26OCT73-1299
DUGGAN, A. FOUNDING FATHERS. WINTER
  QUARTERS.
  617(TLS):23FEB73-219
DUGGAN, J.J. A CONCORDANCE OF THE "CHAN-
  SON DE ROLAND."
  R.T. CARGO, 207(FR):MAR71-814
  S.G. NICHOLS, JR., 589:APR72-303
  F. WHITEHEAD, 208(FS):APR72-181
DUGGAN, T. - SEE REID, T.
DUKORE, B.F. BERNARD SHAW DIRECTOR.
  F.P.W. MC DOWELL, 295:FEB73-120
  N. MARSHALL, 157:AUTUMN71-78
DUKORE, B.F. - SEE SHAW, G.B.
DULLES, J.W.F. UNREST IN BRAZIL.
  H.R. HAMMOND, 263:APR-JUN72-165
DULONG, G. BIBLIOGRAPHIE LINGUISTIQUE
  DU CANADA FRANÇAIS.
  W. SAYERS, 545(RPH):MAY72-440
  P. WUNDERLI, 260(IF):BAND74-289

DULONG, G. DICTIONNAIRE CORRECTIF DU
  FRANÇAIS AU CANADA.
  R. ARVEILLER, 209(FM):APR70-173
DULOUP, V. LA CIVILISATION FRANÇAISE.
  B.M. POHORYLES, 207(FR):MAR71-824
  M. ROSS, 399(MLJ):MAR71-189
DUMAS, A. LE DOSSIER "TUE-LA!" (A.
  LEBOIS, ED)
  J. LANDRIN, 535(RHL):JUL-AUG71-715
"DUMBARTON OAKS PAPERS, NO. 26."
  617(TLS):20JUL73-841
DUMÉZIL, G. THE DESTINY OF THE WARRIOR.
  J. FONTENROSE, 124:NOV71-98
DUMMETT, A. A PORTRAIT OF ENGLISH RAC-
  ISM.
  617(TLS):13JUL73-804
DUMMETT, M. FREGE.
  A.J. AYER, 362:13DEC73-825
  617(TLS):30NOV73-1461
DUMONT, F. LA DIALECTIQUE DE L'OBJET
  ÉCONOMIQUE.
  M. LAGUEUX, 154:MAR71-124
DUMONT, J-P., ED & TRANS. LES SCEPTIQUES
  GRECS.
  M. DAL PRA, 548(RCSF):JAN-MAR70-96
DUMONT, L. HOMO HIERARCHICUS.
  R.S. KHARE, 293(JAST):AUG71-859
DUMONT, R. CUBA EST-IL SOCIALISTE?
  W.E. RATLIFF, 396(MODA):SPRING72-211
DUMONT, R. STEFAN ZWEIG ET LA FRANCE.*
  K. BIEBER, 149:DEC72-470
DUNBAR, J. J.M. BARRIE.*
  R. MACLEAN, 157:WINTER70-66
  C.P. VALETTE, 189(EA):OCT-DEC71-440
DUNCAN, D. THOMAS RUDDIMAN.
  H.H. MEIER, 179(ES):OCT71-488
DUNCAN, D., ED. THROUGH THE YEAR WITH
  CARDINAL HEENAN.
  617(TLS):5JAN73-22
DUNCAN, D.D. PRISMATICS.
  P. ADAMS, 61:NOV73-130
  S. SCHWARTZ, 441:2DEC73-95
  617(TLS):2NOV73-1352
DUNCAN, H.D. COMMUNICATIONS AND SOCIAL
  ORDER. SYMBOLS IN SOCIETY.
  W. BURKE, 186(ETC.):JUN71-241
DUNCAN, I. THE ART OF THE DANCE. (S.
  CHENEY, ED)
  D. HERING, 151:FEB71-28
DUNCAN, J.E. MILTON'S EARTHLY PARADISE.
  617(TLS):16FEB73-187
DUNCAN, R. BENDING THE BOW.*
  J. SAUNDERS, 565:VOL12#4-63
DUNCAN, R. TRIBUNALS: PASSAGES 31-35.*
  J. GALASSI, 491:MAR73-344
DUNCAN, R. THE TRUTH & LIFE OF MYTH.
  I.L. SALOMON, 385(MQR):FALL73-389
DUNCAN, T.B. ATLANTIC ISLANDS.
  617(TLS):6JUL73-780
DUNCAN, W.R. & J.N. GOODSELL, EDS. THE
  QUEST FOR CHANGE IN LATIN AMERICA.
  A. ANGELL, 86(BHS):OCT72-413
  639(VQR):SPRING71-LXXIX
DUNLOP, I. THE SHOCK OF THE NEW.
  617(TLS):19JAN73-68
DUNMORE, J. FRENCH EXPLORERS IN THE
  PACIFIC. (VOL 2)
  H. WALLIS, 293(JAST):MAY71-652
DUNMORE, S. THE LAST HILL.
  M. LEVIN, 441:6MAY73-40
DUNN, C. & B. TORIGOE - SEE "THE ACTORS'
  ANALECTS"
DUNN, C.M. - SEE RAMUS, P.
DUNN, D. THE HAPPIER LIFE.*
  P.N. FURBANK, 362:9AUG73-190

DUNN, D. TERRY STREET.
  T. EAGLETON, 565:VOL11#2-68
  C. LEVENSON, 529(QQ):SUMMER71-309
  H. SERGEANT, 175:SUMMER71-65
DUNN, G.E., COMP. A GILBERT AND SULLIVAN
  DICTIONARY.
  A. LAMB, 415:JUN72-565
DUNN, J. THE POLITICAL THOUGHT OF JOHN
  LOCKE.*
  F.P. DE MICHELIS, 548(RCSF):JUL-SEP
    70-338
  J.A. SCHWANDT, 613:SPRING71-152
DUNN, R.S. SUGAR AND SLAVES.
  617(TLS):23MAR73-318
DUNN, T.A. - SEE MASSINGER, P. & N. FIELD
DUNNE, G.T. JUSTICE JOSEPH STORY AND THE
  RISE OF THE SUPREME COURT.
  A.S. KONEFSKY, 432(NEQ):DEC71-662
DUNNETT, D. MURDER IN FOCUS.
  N. CALLENDAR, 441:13MAY73-39
DUNNING, A. DIE STAATSMOTETTE 1480-1555.
  M. PICKER, 317:SUMMER72-258
DUNNING, J.S. PORTRAITS OF TROPICAL
  BIRDS.
  S.S. BENSON, 37:OCT71-38
DUNNING, T.P. & A.J. BLISS - SEE "THE
  WANDERER"
DUNSTAN, P. PATTERNS ON GLASS.
  B. MANHIRE, 368:MAR70-88
DUPIN, J. L'EMBRASURE.*
  P. CHAPPUIS, 98:JUN71-520
  A. MARISSEL, 207(FR):DEC70-415
DUPLAY, M. MON AMI MARCEL PROUST.
  617(TLS):13APR73-423
DU PLESSIS, I.D. NEW QUATRAINS OF OMAR
  KHAYYÁM.
  617(TLS):4MAY73-508
DUPONT, L. DE L'ANALYSE GRAMMATICALE À
  L'ANALYSE LITTÉRAIRE. (3RD ED)
  D. BOUVEROT, 209(FM):APR71-170
  A. VAN DER BIEST, 556(RLV):1971/6-783
DUPONT, L. LES PIÈGES DU VOCABULAIRE
  ITALIEN.
  W.T. ELWERT, 72:BAND209HEFT4/6-444
DUPRÉ, M. MARCEL DUPRÉ RACONTE...
  R. CRICHTON, 415:OCT72-974
  J.A.W., 410(M&L):OCT72-438
DUPRIEZ, B. L'ÉTUDE DES STYLES OU LA
  COMMUTATION EN LITTÉRATURE.*
  R. POSNER, 361:VOL26#3-325
  S. ULLMANN, 208(FS):OCT72-489
DURAFFOUR, A. GLOSSAIRE DES PATOIS
  FRANCO-PROVENÇAUX.
  W. ROTHWELL, 182:VOL24#9/10-415
DURÁN, M. & A. BARTRA. PANORAMA DE LA
  LITERATURA ESPAÑOLA.
  W.C. GOFF, 238:SEP71-619
  E. HADDAD, 238:SEP71-619
DURAND, G. LES GRANDS TEXTES DE LA
  SOCIOLOGIE MODERNE.
  205(FMLS):OCT70-421
DURAND, M.M. & N. TRAN-HUAN. INTRODUC-
  TION À LA LITTÉRATURE VIETNAMIENNE.
  A-M. MOULÈNES, 549(RLC):APR-JUN70-268
DURAS, M. ABAHN SABANA DAVID.
  J. GOLLUB, 207(FR):APR71-954
DURAS, M. DESTROY, SHE SAID.
  N.C. CARPENTER, 219(GAR):SUMMER71-252
DURAS, M. DÉTRUIRE DIT-ELLE.
  A. COHEN, 207(FR):APR71-956
DURASOFF, S. THE RUSSIAN PROTESTANTS.
  E. DUNN, 550(RUSR):JAN71-94
  B.B. SZCZESNIAK, 32:SEP72-698
DURBAND, A., ED. PLAYBILL ONE. PLAYBILL
  TWO. PLAYBILL THREE.
  A. RENDLE, 157:SPRING70-71

DÜRER, A. ALBRECHT DÜRER: DIARY OF HIS
  JOURNEY TO THE NETHERLANDS.
  R. LEBOWITZ, 58:DEC71/JAN72-24
"ALBRECHT DÜRER: MASTER PRINTMAKER."
  R. LEBOWITZ, 58:MAY72-30
DURES, A. MODERN IRELAND.
  617(TLS):12OCT73-1260
DURHAM, F. - SEE PETERKIN, J.
DURHAM, M. DUTCH UNCLE.
  M. LEVIN, 441:16SEP73-32
DURIDANOV, I. THRAKISCH-DAKISCHE STUD-
  IEN. (VOL 1)
  G.M. MESSING, 350:DEC72-960
DU RIETZ, R. BIBLIOTHECA POLYNESIANA.
  P. GATHERCOLE, 354:MAR71-77
DURNOVO, N. VVEDENIE V ISTORIJU RUSSKOGO
  JAZYKA. (VOL 1)
  R.J., 279:VOL14-210
DURNOVO, N. VVEDENIE V ISTORIJU RUSSKOGO
  JAZYKA. (L.L. KASATKIN & T.S. SUMNI-
  KOVA, EDS)
  R.J., 279:VOL14-210
DÜRR, A. DIE KANTATEN VON JOHANN SEBAS-
  TIAN BACH.
  617(TLS):27APR73-476
DURR, R.A. POETIC VISION AND THE PSYCHE-
  DELIC EXPERIENCE.*
  A.W. BRINK, 529(QQ):AUTUMN71-478
  I.H.C., 191(ELN):SEP71(SUPP)-19
DURRANT, G. WILLIAM WORDSWORTH.*
  S. GILL, 447(N&Q):OCT71-393
  H. PESCHMANN, 175:AUTUMN70-104
  J. STILLINGER, 149:SEP72-341
DURRANT, G. WORDSWORTH AND THE GREAT
  SYSTEM.*
  S.A. FARMER, 67:MAY72-91
  J.R.D. JACKSON, 529(QQ):SPRING71-155
  K.K., 191(ELN):SEP71(SUPP)-60
  F. OLSEN, 462(OL):VOL26#4-323
  H. PESCHMANN, 175:SUMMER71-57
  M. RADER, 191(ELN):DEC71-150
  J.R. WATSON, 541(RES):AUG71-354
DURRANT, M. THEOLOGY AND INTELLIGIBILITY.
  617(TLS):2NOV73-1349
DURRELL, G. BEASTS IN MY BELFRY.
  617(TLS):21SEP73-1093
DURRELL, G. A BEVY OF BEASTS.
  441:13MAY73-40
DURRELL, L. THE BLACK BOOK.
  F. RAPHAEL, 362:26APR73-558
  617(TLS):27APR73-460
DURRELL, L. TUNC.
  J.C. FIELD, 556(RLV):1971/3-340
DURRELL, L. VEGA AND OTHER POEMS.
  A. MAC LEAN, 362:20DEC73-859
  617(TLS):8JUN73-646
DURRELL, M. & OTHERS. SPRACHATLANTEN.
  E.H. YARRILL, 182:VOL24#4-148
DÜRRSON, W. - SEE GUILLAUME DE ACQUITAINE
DURZAK, M. HERMANN BROCH.*
  U. SCHELLING, 657(WW):JAN/FEB70-64
  J.J. WHITE, 220(GL&L):JAN72-199
DUSO, G.D. - SEE UNDER DE CECCHI DUSO, G.
DUSSLER, L. RAPHAEL.
  C. GOULD, 39:SEP71-246
DUSTOOR, P.E. THE WORLD OF WORDS.
  A.R. TELLIER, 189(EA):JUL-SEP71-318
DUTHIE, G.I. & J.D. WILSON - SEE SHAKE-
  SPEARE, W.
DUTTON, F.G. CHANGING SOURCES OF POWER.
  E. LATHAM, 639(VQR):AUTUMN71-597
DUTTON, G. FINDINGS AND KEEPINGS.
  K.L. GOODWIN, 381:SEP71-371
  S.E. LEE, 581:1971/3-227
DUUS, P. PARTY RIVALRY AND POLITICAL
  CHANGE IN TAISHŌ JAPAN.*
  H. FUKUI, 318(JAOS):APR-JUN71-354

DUVAL, P. CANADIAN ART: VITAL DECADES.
R.L. BLOORE, 96:APR/MAY71-82
DUVAL, P-M. LA GAULE JUSQU'AU MILIEU DU
VE SIÈCLE.
S.I. OOST, 122:JUL72-222
DUVERGER, M. THE STUDY OF POLITICS.
JANUS: LES DEUX FACES DE L'OCCIDENT.
PARTY POLITICS AND PRESSURE GROUPS.
617(TLS):19JAN73-63
DUVIVIER, R. LA GENÈSE DU "CANTIQUE
SPIRITUEL" DE SAINT JEAN DE LA CROIX.
E. SARMIENTO, 86(BHS):JAN72-69
L.J. WOODWARD, 402(MLR):OCT72-927
DVINOV, B. OT LEGAL'NOSTI K PODPOL'YU
(1921-1922).*
I. GETZLER, 575(SEER):JAN72-146
DVORNIK, F. BYZANTINE MISSIONS AMONG
THE SLAVS.*
F. GRAUS, 575(SEER):JUL72-458
W.E. KAEGI, JR., 589:APR72-304
DVORNIK, F. LES LÉGENDES DE CONSTANTIN
ET DE MÉTHODE VUES DE BYZANCE. (2ND
ED)
M. SAMILOV, 575(SEER):OCT72-639
DWYER, K.R. CHASE.
N. CALLENDAR, 441:7JAN73-35
DWYER, K.R. SHATTERED.
N. CALLENDAR, 441:30DEC73-19
DWYER-JOYCE, A. THE RAINBOW GLASS.
M. LEVIN, 441:26AUG73-31
DYCK, J.W. & W.J. SCHWARTZ. MENSCH UND
WELT.
H. JAECKEL, 221(GQ):MAR71-270
DYCK, M. DIE GEDICHTE SCHILLERS.
H.H. SCHULTE, 564:MAR70-83
DYDYMSKI, L. WPŁYW JĘZYKA ANGIELSKIEGO
NA WYMOWĘ POLSKĄ MŁODZIEŻY W LONDYNIE.
B.W. MAZUR, 575(SEER):APR72-325
DYER, A.D. THE CITY OF WORCESTER IN THE
SIXTEENTH CENTURY.
617(TLS):29JUN73-757
DYKEMAN, W. RETURN THE INNOCENT EARTH.
M. LEVIN, 441:3JUN73-32
DYLAN, B. WRITINGS AND DRAWINGS.
A. GOLDMAN, 441:30SEP73-42
DYMENT, C. COLLECTED POEMS.*
J. SAUNDERS, 565:VOL11#4-68
H. SERGEANT, 175:SUMMER71-65
DYNES, W. PALACES OF EUROPE.
J. WILTON-ELY, 39:APR70-318
DYNNIK, A. A.I. KUPRIN.*
I.I. BALOUEFF, 550(RUSR):APR71-204
DYOS, H.J. & M. WOLFF, EDS. THE VICTOR-
IAN CITY.
R. MITCHISON, 362:20SEP73-380
R. WILLIAMS, 441:4NOV73-6
617(TLS):7SEP73-1016
DYSON, A.E., ED. DICKENS: "BLEAK HOUSE."*
L. LANE, JR., 255(HAB):SUMMER70-66
DYSON, A.E. THE INIMITABLE DICKENS.*
T.J. CRIBB, 541(RES):AUG71-388
G. THOMAS, 175:SPRING71-25
S. WALL, 184(EIC):JUL71-261

EADE, S. - SEE SPENCE, C.H.
EAGLE, D., ED. THE CONCISE OXFORD DIC-
TIONARY OF ENGLISH LITERATURE. (2ND ED)
E. PUJALS, 202(FMOD):NOV71/FEB72-148
EAGLETON, T. EXILES AND ÉMIGRÉS.
J. GLOVER, 565:VOL12#4-56
B. SHARRATT, 111:13NOV70-54
EAKIN, T.C. STUDENTS AND POLITICS.
617(TLS):8JUN73-653
EALES, R.G. & A.H. WILLIAMS. ALEKHINE'S
DEFENCE.
617(TLS):15JUN73-700

EAMES, E.R. BERTRAND RUSSELL'S THEORY OF
KNOWLEDGE.*
M. KITELEY, 479(PHQ):APR71-174
E. SIMPSON, 154:JUN70-103
EAMES, H. WINNER LOSE ALL.
P. ADAMS, 61:AUG73-103
C. LEHMANN-HAUPT, 441:31JUL73-31
D. MC CULLOUGH, 441:24JUN73-6
EARHART, H.B. JAPANESE RELIGION.
W.M. FRIDELL, 318(JAOS):APR-JUN71-350
EARHART, H.B. THE NEW RELIGIONS OF JAPAN.
W.H.M. CREEMERS, 293(JAST):NOV70-195
EARLE, P. JAMES II.
617(TLS):16FEB73-189
"THE EARLIEST ENGLISH POEMS." (M. ALEX-
ANDER, TRANS)
J.M. KIRK, 191(ELN):MAR72-196
J.P., 376:JAN71-128
639(VQR):WINTER71-XXVII
EARLY, J. THE MAKING OF "GO DOWN, MOSES."
J.L. CAPPS, 578:FALL73-117
EARLY, R. THE JEALOUS EAR.
G. GODWIN, 441:30SEP73-38
M. LEVIN, 441:5AUG73-16
"EARLY AMERICAN BOOKBINDINGS FROM THE
COLLECTION OF MICHAEL PAPANTONIO."
617(TLS):9NOV73-1380
EARNEST, E. THE SINGLE VISION.
R.C. ELLSWORTH, 529(QQ):AUTUMN71-466
EASON, E.A. - SEE LOPE DE VEGA
EASSON, A. - SEE GASKELL, E.
EASSON, R.R. & R.N. ESSICK. WILLIAM
BLAKE: BOOK ILLUSTRATOR.
617(TLS):16FEB73-189
EAST, D. GOODBYE SUSAN.
A. RENDLE, 157:SPRING70-71
EASTLAKE, C. HISTORY OF THE GOTHIC RE-
VIVAL. (J.M. CROOK, ED)
R. EDWARDS, 39:JAN71-70
EASTON, M. AUBREY AND THE DYING LADY.
617(TLS):9FEB73-143
EASTON, R. MAX BRAND.
R.W. ETULAIN, 649(WAL):SPRING70-75
EATES, M. PAUL NASH.
617(TLS):27JUL73-879
EATON, L.K. AMERICAN ARCHITECTURE COMES
OF AGE.
617(TLS):9MAR73-264
EATON, L.K. TWO CHICAGO ARCHITECTS AND
THEIR CLIENTS.
H.A. BROOKS, 505:AUG70-100
J.F. O'GORMAN, 56:WINTER70-446
N.K. SMITH, 576:MAY70-205
EAVES, T.C.D. & B.D. KIMPEL. SAMUEL RICH-
ARDSON.*
F.W. HILLES, 676(YR):AUTUMN71-109
EAYRS, J. IN DEFENCE OF CANADA. (VOL 3)
R. BOTHWELL, 99:FEB73-42
EBAN, A. MY COUNTRY.
617(TLS):25MAY73-576
EBELING, G. INTRODUCTION TO A THEOLOGI-
CAL THEORY OF LANGUAGE.
617(TLS):10AUG73-933
EBER, D.H. - SEE "PITSEOLAK: PICTURES OUT
OF MY LIFE"
EBERHARD, W. SETTLEMENT AND SOCIAL CHANGE
IN ASIA. (VOL 1)
R.M. HARTWELL, 293(JAST):FEB71-421
EBERHARD, W. STUDIES IN CHINESE FOLKLORE
AND RELATED ESSAYS.
W.H. HUDSPETH, 203:AUTUMN71-252
N-T. TING, 582(SFQ):DEC71-364
EBERHARD, W. STUDIES IN TAIWANESE FOLK-
TALES.
P.D. SWART, 196:BAND12HEFT2/3-271
EBERHART, M.G. MURDER IN WAITING.
N. CALLENDAR, 441:22JUL73-12

EBERHART, R.  FIELDS OF GRACE.
617(TLS):5JAN73-10
EBERHART, R. - SEE MILTON, J.
EBERT, J.D. & OTHERS.  BIOLOGY.
C.P. HASKINS, 441:26AUG73-23
EBNER, J.  WIE SAGT MAN IN ÖSTERREICH?
E. SEIDELMANN, 439(NM):1970/4-713
E. SEIDELMANN, 657(WW):MAR/APR71-139
LORD ECCLES.  ON COLLECTING.
T. CROMBIE, 39:JAN71-74
ECCLES, M., ED.  THE MACRO PLAYS.*
A.C. CAWLEY, 447(N&Q):FEB71-70
W. HABICHT, 38:BAND89HEFT1-137
T. TURVILLE-PETRE, 597(SN):VOL42#2-
496
ECHERUO, M.  MORTALITY.
H. MAES-JELINEK, 556(RLV):1971/4-491
ECHERUO, M.J.C.  JOYCE CARY AND THE NOVEL
OF AFRICA.
617(TLS):24AUG73-972
ECHEVERRÍA, J.U. - SEE UNDER URIBE ECHE-
VERRÍA, J.U.
ECKARDT, A. & R.  ENCOUNTER WITH ISRAEL.
F.H. LITTELL, 328:WINTER71-120
"JACOB ECKHARD'S CHOIRMASTER'S BOOK OF
1809." (G.W. WILLIAMS, ED)
R. CRAWFORD, 317:SUMMER72-255
ECKMANN, J.  CHAGATAY MANUAL.
P. AALTO, 353:AUG70-114
ECKSTEIN, F. & A. LEGNER, EDS.  ANTIKE
KLEINKUNST IM LIEBIEGHAUS.
B.A. SPARKES, 303:VOL91-211
ECO, U.  IL COSTUME DI CASA.
617(TLS):5OCT73-1151
ECO, U.  LA STRUTTURA ASSENTE.
G.C. LEPSCHY, 353:OCT70-105
ECOLE, J.  LA MÉTAPHYSIQUE DE L'ÊTRE
DANS LA PHILOSOPHIE DE MAURICE BLONDEL.
A. FOREST, 542:OCT-DEC71-461
ECONOMOU, G.D.  THE GODDESS NATURA IN
MEDIEVAL LITERATURE.
617(TLS):21SEP73-1093
EDDINGS, D.  HIGH HUNT.
M. LEVIN, 441:18FEB73-30
EDDY, D.D.  A BIBLIOGRAPHY OF JOHN BROWN.
H.H. CAMPBELL, 70(ANQ):JUN73-160
EDEL, L.  HENRY JAMES.  (VOLS 1-3)
O. CARGILL, 27(AL):MAY72-330
EDEL, L.  HENRY JAMES.*  (VOL 4: THE
TREACHEROUS YEARS; 1895-1901.)
O. CARGILL, 27(AL):MAY72-330
G. CORE, 219(GAR):SUMMER70-234
K. GRAHAM, 541(RES):MAY71-235
B. NEVIUS, 445(NCF):JUN70-118
E. WAGENKNECHT, 594:SPRING70-88
EDEL, L.  HENRY JAMES.*  (VOL 5: THE
MASTER, 1901-1916.)
O. CARGILL, 27(AL):MAY72-330
G. CORE, 385(MQR):WINTER73-82
G. WOODCOCK, 102(CANL):AUTUMN72-97
EDEL, L.  HENRY D. THOREAU.
R. ASSELINEAU, 189(EA):OCT-DEC70-458
EDELEN, G. - SEE HARRISON, W.
EDELMAN, M.  THE SYMBOLIC USES OF POLI-
TICS.
A.A. BERGER, 186(ETC.):SEP71-370
EDEN, M.  CONQUEST BEFORE AUTUMN.
N. CALLENDAR, 441:26AUG73-33
EDER, W.  DAS VORSULLANISCHE REPETUNDEN-
VERFAHREN.*
U. HALL, 313:VOL61-275
R. VILLERS, 555:VOL45FASC1-190
EDGAR, F.  HAUSA READINGS, SELECTIONS
FROM EDGAR'S "TATSUNIYOYI."*  (N. SKIN-
NER, ED)
A.H.M. KIRK-GREENE, 69:JAN71-80

EDGAR, F., COMP.  HAUSA TALES AND TRADI-
TIONS.  (VOL 1) (N. SKINNER, ED & TRANS)
R. HADEL, 292(JAF):APR-JUN71-249
A.H.M. KIRK-GREENE, 69:JAN71-80
EDGAR, I.I.  SHAKESPEARE, MEDICINE AND
PSYCHIATRY.
A.L. MURPHY, 150(DR):SPRING71-116
EDGAR, W.B. - SEE PRINGLE, R.
EDGE, D.O. & J.N. WOLFE, EDS.  MEANING
AND CONTROL.
617(TLS):11MAY73-531
EDGLEY, R.  REASON IN THEORY AND PRAC-
TICE.*
M. PATERSON, 154:SEP70-253
A.D. WOOZLEY, 479(PHQ):JAN71-86
EDIE, J.M. & OTHERS, EDS.  RUSSIAN PHIL-
OSOPHY.*
A. VACHET, 154:DEC70-470
EDIGER, D.  THE WELL OF SACRIFICE.
617(TLS):14DEC73-1532
EDLER, E., ED.  ERNST DRONKE: POLIZEI-
GESCHICHTEN.
F. VAN INGEN, 433:JAN70-91
EDLER, E. - SEE PRUTZ, R.
EDLIN, H.  ATLAS OF PLANT LIFE.
617(TLS):7DEC73-1521
EDMUND OF ABINGDON.  SPECULUM RELIGIOSOR-
UM AND SPECULUM ECCLESIE.  (H.P. FOR-
SHAW, ED)
617(TLS):5OCT73-1166
"EDUCATIONAL PROBLEMS IN DEVELOPING COUN-
TRIES."
S. MILBURN, 69:OCT71-352
EDWARDES, M.  BOUND TO EXILE.
D.C. ELLINWOOD, JR., 637(VS):DEC70-224
D.M. SPENCER, 293(JAST):NOV70-198
EDWARDES, M.  RALPH FITCH, ELIZABETHAN
IN THE INDIES.
617(TLS):26JAN73-101
EDWARDES, M.  GLORIOUS SAHIBS.*
R.A. CALLAHAN, 318(JAOS):APR-JUN71-321
EDWARDES, M.  PLASSEY.
E.F. IRSCHICK, 293(JAST):FEB71-513
EDWARDES, M.  RED YEAR.
617(TLS):1JUN73-625
EDWARDES, M.  A SEASON IN HELL.
617(TLS):24AUG73-986
EDWARDS, A.  HAUNTED SUMMER.
V. CUNNINGHAM, 362:8MAR73-315
EDWARDS, A.  MIKLOS ALEXANDROVITCH IS
MISSING.
O. MAYNARD, 151:MAR71-84
EDWARDS, B. & P.R. WALKER.  SI VIS
PACEM...
617(TLS):23FEB73-200
EDWARDS, G. - SEE CALDERÓN DE LA BARCA,
P.
EDWARDS, J.  THE WORKS OF JONATHAN ED-
WARDS.*  (VOL 3) (C.A. HOLBROOK, ED)
N.S. FIERING, 656(WMQ):OCT71-655
EDWARDS, M.  LA TRAGÉDIE RACINIENNE.
617(TLS):4MAY73-507
EDWARDS, M.D.  A STAGE IN OUR PAST.*
J. HAMILTON, 157:SPRING70-66
EDWARDS, M.J., ED.  THE EVOLUTION OF CAN-
ADIAN LITERATURE IN ENGLISH.  (VOL 1)
J.W. LENNOX, 296:FALL73-108
EDWARDS, P., ED-IN-CHIEF.  THE ENCYCLO-
PEDIA OF PHILOSOPHY.*
W. CRAIG & B. MATES, 316:JUN70-295
(PLUS MANY ADDITIONAL SHORT NOTES
BY SEVERAL REVIEWERS FOLLOWING
THROUGH PAGE 310)
A.C. MICHALOS, R.E. BUTTS & M.D. RES-
NIK, 486:DEC71-612
EDWARDS, S.  THE PARIS COMMUNE.
H. BROGAN, 441:20MAY73-28

EDWARDS, S. THEODORA.
F.E. PETERS, 124:SEP71-31
EDWARDS, T.R. IMAGINATION AND POWER.*
P. CRUTTWELL, 249(HUDR):AUTUMN72-470
D.C. JUDKINS, 568(SCN):SUMMER72-40
S. MOORE, 385(MQR):SUMMER73-285
566:SPRING72-92
EFFE, B. STUDIEN ZUR KOSMOLOGIE UND
THEOLOGIE DER ARISTOTELISCHEN SCHRIFT
"ÜBER DIE PHILOSOPHIE."
P.M. HUBY, 123:JUN72-202
EFFINGER, G.A. RELATIVES.
G. WALKER, 441:23DEC73-14
EFIROV, S.A. LA FILOSOFIA BORGHESE ITALI-
ANA DEL XX SECOLO.
G. MASTROIANNI, 548(RCSF):OCT-DEC71-
466
EGAN, D. & M. HARTNETT, EDS. CHOICE.
617(TLS):27JUL73-864
EGAN, L. PAPER CHASE.*
617(TLS):18MAY73-562
EGBERT, D.D. SOCIAL RADICALISM AND THE
ARTS.
639(VQR):WINTER71-XLIII
EGEA, J.C. - SEE UNDER CORRALES EGEA, J.
EGIDI, R. ONTOLOGIA E CONOSCENZA MATE-
MATICA.
F. RIVETTI BARBÒ, 316:SEP70-446
"SIR EGLAMOUR OF ARTOIS." (F.E. RICH-
ARDSON, ED)
G.H.V. BUNT, 179(ES):FEB71-59
EGLETON, C. SEVEN DAYS TO A KILLING.
N. CALLENDAR, 441:21JAN73-26
617(TLS):16MAR73-303
EGLI-HEGGLIN, A. LA THÈME DU "TOTUM
SIMUL" DANS L'OEUVRE DE PAUL CLAUDEL.
A. BLANC, 535(RHL):JAN-FEB71-132
Y. SCALZITTI, 405(MP):AUG71-95
EGLIN, H. LIEBE UND INSPIRATION IM WERKE
VON PAUL ELUARD.
J. STAROBINSKI, 535(RHL):JAN-FEB71-
139
EGOROV, I.A. ARCHITECTURAL PLANNING OF
ST. PETERSBURG.
A.J. SCHMIDT, 576:DEC70-359
EGRET, J. LOUIS XV ET L'OPPOSITION
PARLEMENTAIRE.
J.M.J. ROGISTER, 208(FS):APR72-201
EGRI, P. SURVIE ET RÉINTERPRÉTATION DE
LA FORME PROUSTIENNE.
J-Y. TADIÉ, 535(RHL):SEP-DEC71-988
EHLE, J. THE JOURNEY OF AUGUST KING.*
42(AR):FALL71-438
EHLERS, W.W. UNTERSUCHUNGEN ZUR HAND-
SCHRIFTLICHEN ÜBERLIEFERUNG DER ARGO-
NAUTICA DES VALERIUS FLACCUS.*
E. COURTNEY, 123:JUN72-216
EHNI, R. SUPER-POSITIONS, EUGÉNIE KOPRO-
NIME (THÉÂTRE III).
D.M. CHURCH, 207(FR):APR71-958
EHRARD, J. - SEE MONTESQUIEU
EHRENBERG, V. FROM SOLON TO SOCRATES.*
P. GAUTHIER, 555:VOL45FASC1-133
M.E. WHITE, 487:SPRING71-68
EHRENFELD, D.W. CONSERVING LIFE ON
EARTH.*
617(TLS):11MAY73-537
EHRENPREIS, I., ED. WALLACE STEVENS.
617(TLS):6APR73-375
EHRENPREIS, I. JONATHAN SWIFT.
C.J. HORNE, 402(MLR):JAN72-170
EHRLICH, H-H. MONTAIGNE.
617(TLS):5OCT73-1186
EHRLICH, S., ED. POLISH ROUND TABLE:
YEARBOOK 1969.
R.F. STAAR, 32:MAR72-213

EIBL, K. DIE SPRACHSKEPSIS IM WERK GUS-
TAV SACKS.
J.M. RITCHIE, 220(GL&L):JAN72-158
VON EICHENDORFF, J. AUS DEM LEBEN EINES
TAUGENICHTS. (J.M. RITCHIE, ED)
E. STOPP, 402(MLR):JAN72-220
VON EICHENDORFF, J. DAS MARMORBILD.
(R.A. FOWKES, ED)
L.R. RADNER, 399(MLJ):OCT71-421
VON EICHENDORFF, J. SÄMTLICHE WERKE DES
FREIHERRN JOSEPH VON EICHENDORFF. (H.
KUNISCH, GENERAL ED) (VOL 8, PTS 1&2;
VOL 9, PT 3) (ALL ED BY W. MAUSER)
E. STOPP, 402(MLR):JUL72-695
EICHINGER, M. DIE VERKLÄRUNG CHRISTI BEI
ORIGENES.
H. MUSURILLO, 613:AUTUMN71-456
EICHLER, W. JAN VAN RUUSBROECS "BRU-
LOCHT" IN OBERDEUTSCHER ÜBERLIEFERUNG.*
J.E. CREAN, JR., 406:WINTER72-412
EICHNER, H. FRIEDRICH SCHLEGEL.
D.H. HAENICKE, 564:OCT71-241
E. STOPP, 402(MLR):JUL72-694
G.A. WELLS, 220(GL&L):APR72-279
EICHNER, H. - SEE SCHLEGEL, F.
EICHOFF, J. DIE SPRACHE DES NIEDERDEUT-
SCHEN REEPSCHLÄGERHANDWERKS.
K. HEEROMA, 433:JAN71-99
EICHSTÄDT, H. ŽUKOVSKIJ ALS ÜBERSETZER.*
M.V. JONES, 575(SEER):OCT72-637
EIDE, E., A. KITTANG & A. AARSETH, EDS.
TEORIER OM DIKTEKUNSTEN.
J. BANG, 172(EDDA):1971/5-310
EIFLER, G. DIE ETHISCHEN ANSCHAUUNGEN
IN "FREIDANKS BESCHEIDENHEIT."*
B. SOWINSKI, 657(WW):JUL/AUG70-280
EIGELDINGER, M. LA MYTHOLOGIE SOLAIRE
DANS L'OEUVRE DE RACINE.*
M. GUTWIRTH, 546(RR):APR71-142
VON EINEM, H. MICHELANGELO.
617(TLS):28DEC73-1585
"EINFÜHRUNG IN DIE METHODIK DER STILUN-
TERSUCHUNG."
A.B. BASILIER, 597(SN):VOL43#2-552
EINHARD. VITA KAROLI MAGNI (THE LIFE OF
CHARLEMAGNE). (E.S. FIRCHOW & E.H.
ZEYDEL, TRANS)
617(TLS):13APR73-429
EINSTEIN, A. GREATNESS IN MUSIC.
E. SAMS, 415:DEC72-1191
EINSTEIN, A. IDEAS AND OPINIONS.
617(TLS):31AUG73-1009
EIS, G. FORSCHUNGEN ZUR FACHPROSA.
E. ETTLINGER, 203:WINTER71-340
H. MARTIN, 406:SUMMER72-191
EIS, G. VOM ZAUBER DER NAMEN.
W.B., 681(ZDS):BAND27HEFT3-190
EISENMEIER, E. ADALBERT STIFTER BIBLIO-
GRAPHIE. (VOL 1)
P.H. ZOLDESTER, 301(JEGP):APR72-301
EISENSTAEDT, A. PEOPLE.
S. SCHWARTZ, 441:2DEC73-95
"SERGEI EISENSTEIN AND UPTON SINCLAIR:
THE MAKING AND UNMAKING OF 'QUE VIVA,
MEXICO!'" (H. GEDULD & R. GOTTESMAN,
EDS)
D.S. HULL, 550(RUSR):JUL71-311
EISLER, F.G. PSYCHOLINGUISTICS.
D.S. BOOMER, 361:VOL25#2-152
EISNER, F.H. & F. MENDE - SEE HEINE, H.
EISNER, F.H. & C. STOCKER - SEE HEINE, H.
EISNER, L.H. THE HAUNTED SCREEN.
R. KRAMBORG, 200:MAY70-292
EISNER, S. THE TRISTAN LEGEND.*
R.W. ACKERMAN, 50(ARQ):AUTUMN70-269
G.L. AHO, 650(WF):OCT70-294
R.J. CORMIER, 207(FR):OCT70-250
M. WILLIAMS, 203:SUMMER71-169

EISSLER, K. LEONARDO DA VINCI.
  R. COLES, 453:22FEB73-15
  R. COLES, 453:8MAR73-25
EITEL, P. DIE OBERSCHWÄBISCHEN REICHS-
  STÄDTE IM ZEITALTER DER ZUNFTHERRSCHAFT.
  H.S. OFFLER, 182:VOL24#1/2-48
EITNER, L. GÉRICAULT'S RAFT OF THE
  MEDUSA.
  H. HONOUR, 453:28JUN73-33
  617(TLS):9MAR73-265
EKELÖF, G. SELECTED POEMS.*
  V. YOUNG, 249(HUDR):WINTER72/73-671
EKLUND, S. THE PERIPHRASTIC, COMPLETIVE
  AND FINITE USES OF THE PRESENT PARTI-
  CIPLE IN LATIN.
  E. LAUGHTON, 123:JUN72-282
EKSCHMITT, W. KIE KONTROVERSE UM LINEAR
  B.* (IN PREV ALSO SEE ECKSCHMITT)
  J.T. HOOKER, 303:VOL91-164
ELBERT, J. THE THREE OF US.
  M. LEVIN, 441:8JUL73-24
ELCOCK, H. PORTRAIT OF A DECISION.
  617(TLS):12JAN73-30
ELDER, M.J. NATHANIEL HAWTHORNE.*
  E. STOCK, 445(NCF):MAR71-492
ELDERS, L. ARISTOTLE'S COSMOLOGY.
  R. BLANCHÉ, 542:OCT-DEC70-489
ELDRIDGE, C.C. ENGLAND'S MISSION.
  617(TLS):28DEC73-1580
ELERT, C-C., ED. FÖRHANDLINGAR VID SAM-
  MANKOMST FÖR ATT DRYFTA FRÅGOR RÖRANDE
  SVENSKANS BESKRIVNING. (VOL 1)
  W. THÜMMEL, 206:NOV70-574
ELERT, C-C. PHONOLOGIC STUDIES OF QUAN-
  TITY IN SWEDISH.
  W. THÜMMEL, 206:NOV70-573
ELEY, L. DIE KRISE DES APRIORI IN DER
  TRANSZENDENTALEN PHÄNOMENOLOGIE EDMUND
  HUSSERLS.
  J. GRANIER, 542:OCT-DEC71-479
ELEY, L. METAKRITIK DER FORMALEN LOGIK.
  N. FEHRINGER, 182:VOL24#7/8-325
ELIA, L. LES RATÉS DE LA DIASPORA.
  M. NAUDIN, 207(FR):OCT70-176
ELIADE, M. TWO TALES OF THE OCCULT.*
  C-S.J. WHITE, 293(JAST):MAY71-717
ELIADE, M. & M. NICULESCU. FANTASTIC
  TALES.*
  205(FMLS):APR70-205
ELIASON, N. & P. CLEMOES - SEE "AELFRIC'S
  FIRST SERIES OF CATHOLIC HOMILIES"
ELIOT, G. FELIX HOLT, THE RADICAL.
  617(TLS):20APR73-443
ELIOT, G. SCENES OF CLERICAL LIFE. (D.
  LODGE, ED)
  617(TLS):19OCT73-1289
ELIOT, T.S. THE WASTE LAND.* (V. ELIOT,
  ED)
  W.M. CHACE, 598(SOR):SPRING73-476
  R. KIRK, 569(SR):SUMMER72-470
  F. MORAMARCO, 651(WHR):SUMMER72-282
  D. MUS, 491:DEC72-156
  W.H. PRITCHARD, 249(HUDR):SPRING72-132
ELKIN, P.K. THE AUGUSTAN DEFENCE OF
  SATIRE.
  617(TLS):11MAY73-525
ELKIN, S. SEARCHES AND SEIZURES.
  T.R. EDWARDS, 441:21OCT73-3
  C. LEHMANN-HAUPT, 441:9OCT73-53
ELKINS, R.E. MANOBO-ENGLISH DICTIONARY.
  L.A. REID, 206:AUG71-449
ELLENBERGER, H.F. THE DISCOVERY OF THE
  UNCONSCIOUS.
  J. PÉPIN, 154:MAR71-177
ELLFELDT, L. & E. CARNES. DANCE PRODUC-
  TION HANDBOOK.
  B. KING, 151:SEP71-100

ELLIOT, K. & J. DUGDALE - SEE CRATHORNE,
  N.
ELLIOTT, D.W. PIECES OF NIGHT.
  G. GODWIN, 441:30SEP73-38
ELLIOTT, G.P. MURIEL.*
  J.P. DEGNAN, 249(HUDR):SUMMER72-330
ELLIOTT, G.P., ED. SYRACUSE POEMS.
  N. TALBOT, 67:NOV72-239
ELLIOTT, J.G. FIELD SPORTS IN INDIA
  1800-1947.
  617(TLS):10AUG73-937
ELLIOTT, J.H. THE OLD WORLD AND THE NEW
  1492-1650.
  J. FISHER, 86(BHS):APR72-203
  W.E. WASHBURN, 656(WMQ):OCT71-681
ELLIOTT, R.C. THE SHAPE OF UTOPIA.*
  M. BERVEILLER, 549(RLC):JUL-SEP71-403
  A. KERNAN, 191(ELN):MAR72-238
  J. RUSS, 128(CE):DEC71-368
  M. SCHLAUCH, 402(MLR):APR72-391
  42(AR):SUMMER71-288
ELLIOTT, S.L. THE MAN WHO GOT AWAY.*
  R. SALE, 249(HUDR):WINTER72/73-703
ELLIOTT, T.J. A MEDIEVAL BESTIARY.
  42(AR):SUMMER71-287
ELLIS, A.M. REBELS AND CONSERVATIVES.
  U. KELLER, 38:BAND88HEFT4-546
ELLIS, C.D. THE SECOND CRASH.
  L. WILLIAMS, 441:1JUL73-17
ELLIS, C.D. & A. SCHACHTER. ANCIENT
  GREEK.
  J.C.P. COTTER, 124:NOV71-102
ELLIS, F.H., ED. POEMS ON AFFAIRS OF
  STATE.* (VOL 6)
  J.R. MOORE, 481(PQ):JUL71-393
  C.A. ZIMANSKY, 566:AUTUMN71-23
  639(VQR):SPRING71-LXII
ELLIS, F.H. - SEE SWIFT, J.
ELLIS, H.S., ED. THE ECONOMY OF BRAZIL.
  F.J. MUNCH, 37:MAR71-37
ELLIS, J. - SEE GILBERT, W.S.
ELLIS, J.M. SCHILLER'S "KALLIASBRIEFE"
  AND THE STUDY OF HIS AESTHETIC THEORY.*
  D.E. ALLISON, 399(MLJ):FEB71-110
  V.L. RIPPERE, 222(GR):MAR71-132
  W. WHITE, 220(GL&L):JAN72-197
ELLIS, J.R. & R.D. MILNS. THE SPECTRE
  OF PHILIP.
  D.M. MAC DOWELL, 123:DEC72-425
ELLIS, M. BANNERMAN.
  617(TLS):8JUN73-633
ELLIS, R.E. THE JEFFERSONIAN CRISIS.*
  C.E. PRINCE, 656(WMQ):OCT71-671
  639(VQR):AUTUMN71-CLXXVI
ELLISON, M. SUPPORT FOR SECESSION.
  617(TLS):3AUG73-895
ELLISON, R.Y. & A. RAFFANEL. PROFIL DE
  LA FRANCE NOUVELLE.* (2ND ED)
  E. MOROT-SIR, 207(FR):DEC70-432
ELLMAN, M. PLANNING PROBLEMS IN THE
  USSR.
  617(TLS):23NOV73-1456
ELLMANN, R. EMINENT DOMAIN.*
  K.P.S. JOCHUM, 38:BAND88HEFT3-418
  P. URE, 179(ES):FEB71-84
ELLMANN, R. GOLDEN CODGERS.
  D.J. ENRIGHT, 362:4OCT73-458
  617(TLS):26OCT73-1308
ELLMANN, R. ULYSSES ON THE LIFFEY.*
  S. HAMPSHIRE, 453:18OCT73-8
  H. KENNER, 329(JJQ):WINTER73-276
  C. MAC CABE, 111:2JUN72-174
ELLMANN, R. - SEE WILDE, O.
ELLRICH, R.J. ROUSSEAU AND HIS READER.*
  R. GRIMSLEY, 402(MLR):JUL72-637
  J. SAREIL, 188(ECR):WINTER70-329

ELLRODT, R. L'INSPIRATION PERSONNELLE ET
L'ESPRIT DU TEMPS CHEZ LES POÈTES MÉTA-
PHYSIQUES ANGLAIS.
J-M. BENOIST, 98:AUG/SEP71-730
ELLSWORTH, R.H. CHINESE FURNITURE.
R. LEIBOWITZ, 58:NOV71-14
ELMAN, R. CROSSING OVER.
D.K. MANO, 441:4MAR73-41
ELMANDJRA, M. THE UNITED NATIONS SYSTEM.
617(TLS):26OCT73-1302
ELON, A. THE ISRAELIS.
H. SCHENKER, 390:AUG/SEP71-66
ELRINGTON, C.R., ED. THE VICTORIA HIS-
TORY OF THE COUNTIES OF ENGLAND: HAND-
BOOK FOR EDITORS AND AUTHORS.
J. GIBBS, 325:OCT71-344
ELSEN, A., J. KIRK & T. VARNEDOE. THE
DRAWINGS OF RODIN.
617(TLS):23MAR73-314
ELSTOB, E.C. & R. BARBER. RUSSIAN FOLK-
TALES.
J. SIMPSON, 203:SUMMER71-169
ELTON, G.R. POLICY AND POLICE.*
L. STONE, 453:22MAR73-31
P. WILLIAMS, 362:29MAR73-411
ELTON, G.R. REFORM AND RENEWAL.
617(TLS):20APR73-436
ELTON, W.R. "KING LEAR" AND THE GODS.*
C. UHLIG, 38:BAND89HEFT3-383
ELVIN, M. THE PATTERN OF THE CHINESE
PAST.
B. JENNER, 362:2AUG73-155
617(TLS):17AUG73-948
ELWARD, J. BEST OF FRIENDS.
A. RENDLE, 157:SUMMER71-82
ELWERT, W.T. & OTHERS, EDS. SERTA ROMAN-
ICA.
G. INEICHEN, 260(IF):BAND74-267
ELWIN, V., ED. THE NAGAS IN THE NINE-
TEENTH CENTURY.
A.P. MC CORMACK, 293(JAST):FEB71-480
ELWOOD, R. & V. GHIDALIA, EDS. ANDROIDS,
TIME MACHINES AND BLUE GIRAFFES.
T. STURGEON, 441:4NOV73-76
ELWORTHY, F.T. THE EVIL EYE.
T. BROWN, 203:AUTUMN71-256
EMAM, M.K. - SEE AL-ZAMAKHSHARĪ
EMANUEL, C. AUSTRALIA.
617(TLS):29JUN73-757
EMBERTON, S. SHRUB GARDENING FOR FLOWER
ARRANGEMENT.
617(TLS):8JUN73-653
EMBLEN, D.L. PETER MARK ROGET.
639(VQR):WINTER71-XXXVI
EMDEN, A.B. DONORS OF BOOKS TO S. AUG-
USTINE'S ABBEY, CANTERBURY.
W. URRY, 354:JUN70-160
EMERSON, E., ED. MAJOR WRITERS OF EARLY
AMERICAN LITERATURE.
K. KELLER, 165:SPRING73-80
EMERSON, E.H. CAPTAIN JOHN SMITH.*
P. YOUNG, 568(SCN):SUMMER72-47
EMERSON, R.W. THE JOURNALS AND MISCEL-
LANEOUS NOTEBOOKS OF RALPH WALDO EMER-
SON. (VOL 8) (W.H. GILMAN & J.E. PAR-
SONS, EDS)
J.Q. ANDERSON, 27(AL):NOV72-490
L. BUELL, 432(NEQ):DEC71-666
E.J. ROSE, 150(DR):WINTER71/72-613
639(VQR):SUMMER71-CXX
EMERSON, R.W. THE JOURNALS AND MISCEL-
LANEOUS NOTEBOOKS OF RALPH WALDO EMER-
SON.* (VOL 9) (R.H. ORTH & A.R. FER-
GUSON, EDS)
L.P. SIMPSON, 27(AL):NOV72-491
EMERSON, T.I. THE SYSTEM OF FREEDOM OF
EXPRESSION.*
R. MC GAFFEY, 583:WINTER71-211

EMERTON, J.A., J.H.C. LEBRAM & R.J. BIDA-
WID, EDS. THE OLD TESTAMENT IN SYRIAC
ACCORDING TO THE PESHITTA VERSION.
(SAMPLE ED)
J.C. GREENFIELD, 318(JAOS):APR-JUN71-
306
EMERY, A. DARTINGTON HALL.
J. HARVEY, 90:JUL71-411
EMERY, D. IN CHARACTER.
617(TLS):28DEC73-1595
EMERY, L. L'AGE CLASSIQUE.
J. BRODY, 546(RR):FEB71-50
EMERY, W.B. NATIONAL AND INTERNATIONAL
SYSTEMS OF BROADCASTING.
J.M. KUSHNER, 583:WINTER70-185
EMMA, R.D. & J.T. SHAWCROSS, EDS. LAN-
GUAGE AND STYLE IN MILTON.
H.W. DONNER, 179(ES):APR71-173
EMMANUEL, I.S. & S.A. HISTORY OF THE
JEWS OF THE NETHERLANDS ANTILLES.
S.B. LIEBMAN, 328:FALL71-498
EMMISON, F.G. ELIZABETHAN LIFE: DIS-
ORDER.
R.E. WALTON, 14:JUL71-312
EMMISON, F.G. GUIDE TO THE ESSEX RECORD
OFFICE.
F.G. BURKE, 14:JAN70-84
D.J. JOHNSON, 325:APR71-244
EMMONS, D.M. GARDEN IN THE GRASSLANDS.
R.W. MEYER, 649(WAL):WINTER72-261
EMPSON, W. & D. PIRIE - SEE COLERIDGE,
S.T.
EMRICH, D., COMP. THE NONSENSE BOOK.
D.J. WINSLOW, 292(JAF):JUL-SEP71-357
A.W. WONDERLEY, 582(SFQ):MAR71-94
EMY, H.V. LIBERALS RADICALS AND SOCIAL
POLITICS 1892-1914.
617(TLS):13APR73-416
"THE ENCHANTED APRIL."
617(TLS):28SEP73-1136
"ENCICLOPEDIA DANTESCA." (VOLS 1&2)
A. SCHIAFFINI, 228(GSLI):VOL148FASC
462/463-413
"ENCICLOPEDIA FILOSOFICA."* (2ND ED)
(VOLS 1-4)
E. CANTORE, 543:MAR71-510
A. DI LASCIA, 613:AUTUMN71-428
G. SANTINELLO, 258:MAR70-152
"ENCICLOPEDIA FILOSOFICA."* (2ND ED)
(VOLS 5 & 6)
E. CANTORE, 543:MAR71-510
"ENCYCLOPAEDIA JUDAICA." (C. ROTH & G.
WIGODER, EDS-IN-CHIEF)
617(TLS):23MAR73-309
"ENCYCLOPEDIA LITUANICA." (VOL 1)
B. JĒGERS, 215(GL):VOL11#2-138
ENDO, S. THE SEA AND POISON.* (JAPANESE
TITLE: UMI TO DOKUYAKU.)
R.L. BROWN, 270:VOL22#3-70
ENELOW, A.J. & S.N. SWISHER. INTERVIEW-
ING AND PATIENT CARE.
617(TLS):10AUG73-937
VAN DER ENG, J. & J.M. MEIJER. "THE BRO-
THERS KARAMAZOV" BY F.M. DOSTOEVSKIJ.
R. FREEBORN, 575(SEER):OCT72-638
ENGBERG, J. KILDER TIL DANSK HISTORIE I
ENGELSKE ARKIVER.
H. LARSON, 14:JAN70-85
ENGEL, M. THE HONEYMAN FESTIVAL.*
A. ROBERTSON, 648:JUN71-52
ENGELBACH, G. LASER.
617(TLS):19JAN73-69
ENGELBERT, M. - SEE CALDERÓN DE LA BARCA,
P.
ENGELER, E. FORMAL LANGUAGES.
A. BLIKLE, 316:DEC70-594

ENGELMANN, P. LUDWIG WITTGENSTEIN.
(B.F. MC GUINNESS, ED)
   A. MERCIER, 182:VOL24#11/12-449
VON ENGELN, O.D. & J.M. URQUHART. THE
STORY KEY TO GEOGRAPHIC NAMES.
   E.C. SMITH, 424:DEC71-287
ENGELS, H., ED. DAS NIBELUNGENLIED UND
DIE KLAGE.
   F. NEUMANN, 224(GRM):MAY70-221
ENGELS, H. - SEE "DAS NIBELUNGENLIED"
ENGLAND, F.E. KANT'S CONCEPTION OF GOD.
   J. KOPPER, 342:BAND62HEFT1-139
ENGLAND, M.W. & J. SPARROW. HYMNS UNBID-
DEN.
   F. LÉAUD, 189(EA):APR-JUN71-217
ENGLE, E. & L.A. PAANANEN. THE WINTER
WAR.
   441:8APR73-30
ENGLER, R. LEXIQUE DE LA TERMINOLOGIE
SAUSSURIENNE.*
   L. SÖLL, 260(IF):BAND74-182
ENGLER, R. - SEE DE SAUSSURE, F.
ENGLER, W. FRANZÖSISCHE LITERATUR IM 20.
JAHRHUNDERT.
   S. JAUERNICK, 430(NS):NOV70-584
ENGLER, W. TEXTE ZUR FRANZÖSISCHEN
ROMANTHEORIE DES 19. JAHRHUNDERTS.
   J. BROUN, 556(RLV):1971/6-780
"ENGLISCHE LEHRTEXTE: BAUWESEN."
   M. KEMTER, 682(ZPSK):BAND23HEFT2/3-
299
ENGLISH, I. LIFE AFTER ALL AND OTHER
STORIES.
   V. CUNNINGHAM, 362:8NOV73-638
   617(TLS):190CT73-1269
ENGNELL, I. A RIGID SCRUTINY. (J.T.
WILLIS, WITH H. RINGGREN, EDS & TRANS)
   M. GREENBERG, 328:SPRING71-248
ENNIS, B. PRISONERS OF PSYCHIATRY.
   P. ADAMS, 61:JAN73-100
   E. WILLIS, 441:4MAR73-6
LADY ENNISKILLEN. FLORENCE COURT, MY
IRISH HOME.
   617(TLS):7SEP73-1037
"ENQUÊTE SUR LA VIE MUSICALE AU CONGO
BELGE, 1934-1935 (QUESTIONNAIRE KNOSP)."
   A.M. JONES, 69:0CT70-403
ENRIGHT, D.J. MAN IS AN ONION.*
   J. CAREY, 362:15FEB73-218
ENRIGHT, D.J. SELECTED POEMS.
   R. FULTON, 565:VOL11#1-68
ENRIGHT, D.J. SHAKESPEARE AND THE STU-
DENTS.
   J. ELLIOTT, 619(TC):VOL178#1045-61
ENRIGHT, D.J. THE TERRIBLE SHEARS.
   R. FULLER, 362:31MAY73-727
   617(TLS):8JUN73-646
ENRIGHT, D.J. THE TYPEWRITER REVOLUTION
AND OTHER POEMS.*
   J.R. REED, 491:APR73-47
ENROTH, R.M., E.E. ERICSON, JR. & C.B.
PETERS. THE JESUS PEOPLE.*
   R.E. CROUTER, 109:FALL/WINTER72/73-
113
VON ENSE, R.V. - SEE UNDER VARNHAGEN VON
ENSE, R.
ENSLIN, T. AGREEMENT, AND BACK.
   M. CZARNECKI, 648:JUN70-37
"ENTRETIENS SUR L'ANTIQUITÉ CLASSIQUE."*
(VOL 15: LUCAIN.) (O. REVERDIN, ED)
   A. ERNOUT, 555:VOL45FASC2-293
ENZINGER, M. GESAMMELTE AUFSÄTZE ZU
ADALBERT STIFTER.
   T. ALT, 222(GR):MAR71-135
"TO EPARCHIKON BIBLION; THE BOOK OF THE
EPARCH; LE LIVRE DU PRÉFET."
   P. VANAGS, 303:VOL91-213

EPPELSHEIMER, H.W. GESCHICHTE DER EURO-
PÄISCHEN WELTLITERATUR. (VOL 1)
   M. FRANZBACH, 430(NS):MAY71-279
   H. RÜDIGER, 52:BAND6HEFT2-194
EPPES, S.B. THROUGH SOME EVENTFUL YEARS.
   E.C. WILLIAMSON, 9(ALAR):JAN70-76
EPSTEIN, E.J. NEWS FROM NOWHERE.
   H.J. GANS, 441:3JUN73-16
   J. LORD, 61:MAY73-109
   J.J. O'CONNOR, 441:5APR73-49
   R. SCHICKEL, 231:APR73-93
EPSTEIN, E.L. THE ORDEAL OF STEPHEN
DEDALUS.*
   R. BOYLE, 329(JJQ):SPRING73-354
EPTON, N. THE SPANISH MOUSETRAP.
   617(TLS):21SEP73-1081
ERASMUS. CORRESPONDANCE D'ERASME. (VOL
1) (M. DELCOUR, ED & TRANS)
   M. DE DIÉGUEZ, 98:JAN70-65
ERASMUS. THE DYALOGE CALLED "FUNUS"
(1534) & A VERY PLEASAUNT & FRUITFUL
DIOLOGE CALLED "THE EPICURE" (1545).
(R.R. ALLEN, ED)
   C.R. THOMPSON, 551(RENQ):AUTUMN71-372
ERASMUS. ERASMUS AND THE SEAMLESS COAT
OF JESUS. (R. HIMELICK, TRANS)
   P.W.B., 568(SCN):SUMMER72-54
   R.T. BRUÈRE, 122:JUL72-200
ERASMUS. OPERA OMNIA DESIDERII ERASMI
ROTERODAMI. (VOL 3) (L-E. HALKIN, F.
BIERLAIRE & R. HOVEN, EDS)
   617(TLS):2MAR73-232
ERAZMUS, E.T. & H.J. CARGAS. ENGLISH AS
A SECOND LANGUAGE: A READER.
   C.B. PAULSTON, 351(LL):JUN71-137
ERBEN, J. DEUTSCHE GRAMMATIK.
   F.G. BANTA, 221(GQ):JAN71-125
ERBSE, H., ED. SCHOLIA GRAECA IN HOMERI
ILIADEM (SCHOLIA VETERA).* (VOL 1)
   W. MC LEOD, 487:WINTER71-372
   M.M. WILLCOCK, 303:VOL91-144
ERCEG, I. TRST I BIVŠE HABSBURŠKE ZEMLJE
U MEĐUNARODNOM PROMETU (MERKANTILIZAM
U DRUGOJ POLOVICI 18. STOLJEĆA).
   T. STOIANOVICH, 32:JUN72-490
ERDÉLYI, I. SELKUPISCHES WÖRTERVER-
ZEICHNIS, TAS-DIALEKT.
   G.F. MEIER, 682(ZPSK):BAND23HEFT4-423
   E.K. RISTINEN, 350:MAR72-206
ERDMAN, D.V. BLAKE: PROPHET AGAINST
EMPIRE.* (REV)
   R.M. BAINE, 219(GAR):SUMMER71-238
   J.E. GRANT, 481(PQ):JUL71-407
   J.J. MC GANN, 405(MP):FEB72-261
ERDMAN, D.V. - SEE BLAKE, W.
ERDMAN, D.V. & J.E. GRANT, EDS. BLAKE'S
VISIONARY FORMS DRAMATIC.
   A. BLUNT, 676(YR):WINTER72-301
   D. HUGHES, 418(MR):AUTUMN72-718
   W. VAUGHAN, 592:NOV71-210
   639(VQR):SUMMER71-CX
ERDMAN, P.E. THE BILLION DOLLAR SURE
THING.
   N. CALLENDAR, 441:5AUG73-10
   C. LEHMANN-HAUPT, 441:23JUL73-29
ERDMANN, K.D. - SEE RIEZLER, K.
ERGER, J. DER KAPP-LÜTTWITZ-PUTSCH.
   F.L. CARSTEN, 575(SEER):APR72-312
ERI, V. THE CROCODILE.
   J. GRIFFIN, 381:DEC71-454
   M. WILDING, 581:SEP72-235
ERICKSON, S.A. LANGUAGE AND BEING.*
   J.P. FELL, 479(PHQ):JUL71-273
ERIKSON, E.H. GANDHI'S TRUTH.*
   R.W. NOLAND, 418(MR):AUTUMN72-726
   S.S. SANDHU, 485(PE&W):APR71-225
ERIKSON, E.H. YOUNG MAN LUTHER.
   R. COLES, 453:8MAR73-25

ERIKSON, E.H. & H.P. NEWTON. IN SEARCH
OF COMMON GROUND.
P. ROSENBERG, 441:9SEP73-48
ERIKSSON, G. ROMANTIKENS VÄRLDSBILD
SPEGLAD I 1800-TALETS SVENSKA VETENSKAP.
H. MOENKEMEYER, 563(SS):SPRING72-278
ERKEN, G. HOFMANSTHALS DRAMATISCHER
STIL.
L.M. FIEDLER, 657(WW):JUL/AUG70-286
"ERLÄUTERUNGEN ZUR DEUTSCHEN LITERATUR:
ROMANTIK."
W. EMMERICH, 221(GQ):JAN71-108
ERLAY, D. WORPSWEDE-BREMEN-MOSKAU.
617(TLS):30MAR73-344
ERLER, A. AEGIDIUS ALBORNOZ ALS GESETZ-
GEBER DES KIRCHENSTAATES.*
G. MAY, 182:VOL24#6-279
ERLER, A. & E. KAUFMANN, EDS. HANDWÖR-
TERBUCH ZUR DEUTSCHEN RECHTSGESCHICHTE.
H. WOLF, 657(WW):MAR/APR71-140
ERLICH, V. GOGOL.*
M. STEIG, 648:JUN70-34
ERNOUT, A. NOTES DE PHILOLOGIE LATINE.
A.M. DAVIES, 123:DEC72-422
ERNST, J., ED. SCHRIFTAUSLEGUNG.
F.F. BRUCE, 182:VOL24#23/24-840
ERNST, J. & T.R.S. BROUGHTON. L'ANNÉE
PHILOLOGIQUE. (VOLS 37 & 38)
A. ERNOUT, 555:VOL45FASC1-193
ERNST, P. APPROACHES PASCALIENNES.
A. BARNES, 208(FS):OCT72-450
G. DELASSAULT, 557(RSH):OCT-DEC70-639
P. SELLIER, 535(RHL):MAY-JUN71-498
ERNST, P. LA TRAJECTOIRE PASCALIENNE DE
L'"APOLOGIE."
P. SELLIER, 535(RHL):MAR-APR70-312
EROMS, H-W. VREUDE BEI HARTMANN VON AUE.
D.H. GREEN, 402(MLR):APR72-464
ERRANDONEA, I. EL CORO DE LA ELECTRA DE
SOFOCLES.
G. RONNET, 555:VOL45FASC1-149
ERRINGTON, R.M. PHILOPOEMEN.*
É. WILL, 555:VOL45FASC1-139
ERSKINE-HILL, H. POPE: THE DUNCIAD.
617(TLS):5JAN73-6
VON ERTZDORFF, X. RUDOLF VON EMS.
P. KERN, 680(ZDP):BAND89HEFT3-453
ERWIN, E. THE CONCEPT OF MEANINGLESS-
NESS.
B.S. LLAMZON, 613:AUTUMN71-460
R.P.M., 543:MAR71-540
ERWIN, W.M. A BASIC COURSE IN IRAQI
ARABIC.
E.T. ABDEL-MASSIH, 318(JAOS):OCT-DEC
71-538
ESCARPIT, R. LE FABRICANT DE NUAGES.
J. SAREIL, 207(FR):MAR71-781
ESCH, A. BONIFAZ IX. UND DER KIRCHEN-
STAAT.
W.M. BOWSKY, 589:APR72-305
"ESCHATOLOGIE ET COSMOLOGIE."
M. ADAM, 542:APR-JUN71-240
ESCHBACH, M. DIE FABEL IM MODERNEN
DEUTSCHUNTERRICHT.
W. OBERLE, 657(WW):JAN/FEB70-71
VON ESCHENBACH, W. - SEE UNDER WOLFRAM
VON ESCHENBACH, W.
ESCOFFEY, R.A. - SEE MAURIAC, F.
ESHLEMAN, C. ALTARS.*
W.H. PRITCHARD, 249(HUDR):SPRING72-119
ESHLEMAN, C. INDIANA.
J. HARRISON, 600:WINTER/SPRING70-231
ESPENSHADE, A.H. PENNSYLVANIA PLACE
NAMES.
E.P. HAMP, 269(IJAL):APR71-135
ESPESO, G.S. - SEE UNDER SÁNCHEZ ESPESO,
G.

DE ESPINOSA, F. REFRANERO (1527-1547).
(E.S. O'KANE, ED)
M.E. BARRICK, 240(HR):JUL71-322
ESPINOZA, G. HEROES, HEXES, AND HAUNTED
HALLS.
W. GARD, 584(SWR):AUTUMN72-330
ESPRIU, S. LA PEAU DE TAUREAU (LA PELL
DE BRAU).
P. ROBIN, 98:MAR71-229
DE ESPRONCEDA, J. POESÍAS LÍRICAS Y
FRAGMENTOS ÉPICOS. (R. MARRAST, ED)
M.A. REES, 86(BHS):JUL72-308
ESQUIVEL, A.M. - SEE UNDER MAGAÑA ESQUI-
VEL, A.
"ESSAYS IN FRENCH LITERATURE V."
205(FMLS):APR70-206
ESSELBORN, K.G. HOFMANNSTHAL UND DER
ANTIKE MYTHOS.*
J.H. REID, 182:VOL24#1/2-23
ESSENWEIN, A. QUELLEN ZUR GESCHICHTE DER
FEUERWAFFEN.
C.B., 135:FEB71-139
ESSLIN, M. BERTOLT BRECHT.*
K. DICKSON, 220(GL&L):JAN72-189
ESSLIN, M. BRIEF CHRONICLES.
G. MANDER, 157:WINTER70-62
ESSLIN, M. THE PEOPLED WOUND.
J. PETER, 157:SPRING71-70
S. RUSINKO, 397(MD):MAY71-114
ESSLIN, M. PINTER.
617(TLS):6JUL73-775
ESTERSON, A. THE LEAVES OF SPRING.
J.S. GORDON, 441:28JAN73-2
"ESTETIKA SEGODNIYA-AKTUALNYIE PROBLEMY-
SBORNIK STATEY."
M. RIESER, 290(JAAC):SPRING71-414
ESTIVILL, J. & OTHERS. APUNTES SOBRE EL
TRABAJO EN ESPAÑA.
617(TLS):15JUN73-696
ESTRADA, F.L. - SEE UNDER LÓPEZ ESTRADA,
F.
ETHRIDGE, W.S. SIDE BY EACH.
441:7OCT73-41
ÉTIEMBLE, J. - SEE SUPERVIELLE-ÉTIEMBLE,
J.
ÉTIENNE, R. LA VIE QUOTIDIENNE À POMPÉI.*
J.M. REYNOLDS, 123:MAR72-141
ETŌ SHINKICHI. NIHON NO SHINRO.
K. HIRANO, 293(JAST):FEB71-467
ETTER, D. STRAWBERRIES.
D. ROSOCHACKI, 600:FALL71-138
ETTINGHAUSEN, H. FRANCISCO DE QUEVEDO
AND THE NEOSTOIC MOVEMENT.
617(TLS):25MAY73-596
"ETUDES HISTORIQUES 1970 - PUBLIÉES À
L'OCCASION DU XIIIE CONGRÈS INTERNA-
TIONAL DES SCIENCES HISTORIQUES PAR LA
COMMISSION NATIONALE DES HISTORIENS
HONGROIS."
L. PÉTER, 575(SEER):JAN72-147
"ÉTUDES RABELAISIENNES."* (VOL 8)
F. CHARPENTIER, 535(RHL):JUL-AUG70-
691
"ÉTUDES RIMBALDIENNES, I."
A. ADAM, 535(RHL):MAR-APR71-323
"ÉTUDES RIMBALDIENNES II."
M. EIGELDINGER, 535(RHL):JUL-AUG71-
716
EUCLID. LES OEUVRES D'EUCLIDE. (F.
PEYRARD, TRANS)
R. BLANCHÉ, 542:OCT-DEC70-490
EUDES, D. THE KAPETANIOS.* (FRENCH
TITLE: LES KAPETANIOS.)
D. BINDER, 441:28OCT73-22
EULOGIO DE LA VIRGEN DEL CARMEN, P. EL
CÁNTICO ESPIRITTUAL.
E. SARMIENTO, 86(BHS):JAN72-69

EURIPIDES. ANDROMACHE. (P.T. STEVENS, ED)
K.J. RECKFORD, 124:FEB72-204
EURIPIDES. THE BACCHAE OF EURIPIDES. (D. SUTHERLAND, TRANS)
P. SOMVILLE, 556(RLV):1970/6-674
EURIPIDES. EURIPIDE, "MÉDÉE." (R. FLACE-LIÈRE, ED)
C. DOBIAS-LALOU, 555:VOL45FASC2-337
A.F. GARVIE, 123:JUN72-182
EURIPIDES. HELENA.* (R. KANNICHT, ED)
P.T. STEVENS, 123:DEC72-327
EURIPIDES. PHAETHON.* (J. DIGGLE, ED)
T.B.L. WEBSTER, 24:OCT72-627
"THE EUROPA YEAR BOOK 1973."
617(TLS):21SEP73-1091
EUTECNIUS. EUTECNII "PARAPHRASIS IN NICANDRI THERIACA." (I. GUALANDRI, ED)
G. GIANGRANDE, 123:MAR72-102
EUTHYMIUS. VITA EUTHYMII PATRIARCHAE CP. (P. KARLIN-HAYTER, ED & TRANS)
A. KAŽDAN, 303:VOL91-160
J. MEYENDORFF, 589:JUL72-533
EVA, MARCHIONESS OF READING. FOR THE RECORD.
617(TLS):11MAY73-514
EVANS, A.H. COLLECTED POEMS.*
639(VQR):SUMMER71-CVI
EVANS, A.R., JR., ED. ON FOUR MODERN HUMANISTS.*
F.G. CRONHEIM, 402(MLR):OCT72-950
W.A. VON SCHMIDT, 399(MLJ):OCT71-407
EVANS, C.O. THE SUBJECT OF CONSCIOUS-NESS.
D.C. DENNETT, 479(PHQ):APR71-180
EVANS, D., ED. BRITAIN IN THE EEC.
617(TLS):23NOV73-1422
EVANS, D. TOMMY JOHNSON.*
W.R. FERRIS, JR., 187:MAY73-326
EVANS, D. LANIER, HISTOIRE D'UN MOT.
A.L. COHEN, 207(FR):DEC70-468
EVANS, D., J. KERSLAKE & A. OLIVER - SEE SMIBERT, J.
EVANS, D.B. LEONTIUS OF BYZANTIUM.
J.P. CAVARNOS, 589:APR72-307
EVANS, D.D. THE LOGIC OF SELF-INVOLVE-MENT.
C.E. SHEEDY, 613:SUMMER70-311
EVANS, D.E. GAULISH PERSONAL NAMES.*
E. NEU, 260(IF):BAND74-297
R.L. THOMSON, 47(ARL):[N.S.]VOL1-99
EVANS, E.C. PHYSIOGNOMICS IN THE ANCIENT WORLD.*
E.D. PHILLIPS, 123:MAR72-148
EVANS, E.E. THE PERSONALITY OF IRELAND.
617(TLS):17AUG73-961
EVANS, E.N. THE PROVINCIALS.
L. HELLMAN, 441:11NOV73-4
EVANS, F.B., COMP. THE ADMINISTRATION OF MODERN ARCHIVES.
W.E. HEMPHILL, 14:OCT71-386
EVANS, G.E. ACKY.
617(TLS):11MAY73-517
EVANS, H. EDITING AND DESIGN. (BK 5)
617(TLS):23FEB73-220
EVANS, H. MIST ON THE RIVER.
B. MITCHELL, 296:FALL73-112
EVANS, H., ED. NEW TOWNS.
617(TLS):23FEB73-202
EVANS, H. & M. JOHN KAY OF EDINBURGH.
617(TLS):5OCT73-1168
EVANS, H. & M. THE VICTORIANS AT HOME AND AT WORK.
617(TLS):6APR73-401
EVANS, J. A HISTORY OF JEWELLERY 1100-1870. (2ND ED)
G. WILLS, 39:MAY71-436

EVANS, J.A.S. PROCOPIUS.
G.W., 102(CANL):AUTUMN72-114
EVANS, K. CREATIVE SINGING.
P. STANDFORD, 415:FEB72-158
EVANS, L. - SEE PATER, W.
EVANS, M. I AM A BLACK WOMAN.
639(VQR):WINTER71-XX
EVANS, M. SHADOW OF THUNDER.
M. BUCCO, 649(WAL):FALL70-235
EVANS, M. SPENSER'S ANATOMY OF HEROISM.*
B.E.C. DAVIS, 541(RES):NOV71-476
R.F. HILL, 402(MLR):JUL72-613
J. MAZZARO, 141:SUMMER71-312
G. THOMAS, 175:AUTUMN71-102
EVANS, M.W. MEDIEVAL DRAWINGS.
J. BECKWITH, 39:OCT71-322
EVANS, P. THE EARLY TROPE REPERTORY OF SAINT MARTIAL DE LIMOGES.*
A.E. PLANCHART, 414(MQ):JUL71-519
EVANS, R., JR. & R.D. NOVAK. NIXON IN THE WHITE HOUSE.*
617(TLS):5JAN73-11
EVANS, R.J.W. RUDOLF II AND HIS WORLD.
617(TLS):27APR73-467
EVANS, T.E. - SEE LAMPSON, M.
"WALKER EVANS."
S. SONTAG, 453:15NOV73-13
EVENSON, N. LE CORBUSIER.*
J.E. BURCHARD, 54:MAR71-133
P. SERENYI, 576:OCT71-255
EVENSON, N. TWO BRAZILIAN CAPITALS.
617(TLS):14SEP73-1047
EVERITT, B. A COLD FRONT.*
N. CALLENDAR, 441:15APR73-35
EVERS, A. THE CATSKILLS.
441:26AUG73-14
EVERSLEY, D. THE PLANNER IN SOCIETY.
617(TLS):7DEC73-1520
EVERSON, R.G. THE DARK IS NOT SO DARK.
R. GUSTAFSON, 529(QQ):SPRING71-140
L. THOMPSON, 628:FALL70-86
EVERSON, R.G. SELECTED POEMS 1920-1970.*
F. COGSWELL, 529(QQ):SUMMER71-325
EVERSON, W. THE RESIDUAL YEARS.
M. MARCUS, 502(PRS):SPRING70-79
EVERWINE, P. COLLECTING THE ANIMALS.
H. LEIBOWITZ, 441:12AUG73-5
EWAN, J. & N. JOHN BANISTER AND HIS NATURAL HISTORY OF VIRGINIA, 1678-1692.
R.M. JELLISON, 656(WMQ):OCT71-685
EWARD, S.M., COMP. A CATALOGUE OF GLOU-CESTER CATHEDRAL LIBRARY.
617(TLS):9FEB73-160
EWER, R.F. THE CARNIVORES.
617(TLS):14SEP73-1061
EWERS, J.C. - SEE CATLIN, G.
EWERT, A. - SEE BÉROUL
EWING, A.C. VALUE AND REALITY.
617(TLS):28DEC73-1594
EWTON, R.W., JR. & J. ORNSTEIN, EDS. STUDIES IN LANGUAGE AND LINGUISTICS, 1969-70.
D.M. LANCE, 215(GL):VOL11#3-175
EXLEY, C.L. A HISTORY OF THE TORKSEY AND MANSFIELD CHINA FACTORIES.
P.S-H., 135:MAY71-62
EYKMAN, C. GESCHICHTSPESSIMISMUS IN DER DEUTSCHEN LITERATUR DES ZWANZIGSTEN JAHRHUNDERTS.
A. BORGMANN, 301(JEGP):APR72-302
K. BULLIVANT, 402(MLR):OCT72-949
"EYRBYGGJA SAGA." (H. PÁLSSON & P. EDWARDS, TRANS)
617(TLS):30NOV73-1482
EYSENCK, H.J. PSYCHOLOGY IS ABOUT PEOPLE.
617(TLS):2MAR73-247

EYSENCK, H.J., W. ARNOLD & R. MEILI, EDS.
ENCYCLOPEDIA OF PSYCHOLOGY.
617(TLS):19JAN73-74


FABER, M., ED. THE DESIGN WITHIN.
R.D. CALLAHAN, 648:JUN71-54
FABER, R. PROPER STATIONS.
R. ROBINSON, 67:NOV72-231
VON FABER DU FAUR, C. GERMAN BAROQUE
LITERATURE.* (VOL 2)
J.L. FLOOD, 354:SEP70-261
H. RÜDIGER, 52:BAND6HEFT1-77
FABIAN, B., ED. EIN ANGLISTISCHER GRUND-
KURS ZUR EINFÜHRUNG IN DAS STUDIUM DER
LITERATURWISSENSCHAFT.
H. FRIEDL, 72:BAND209HEFT4/6-423
FABIO, F. GUITTONE E I GUITTONIANI.
B.L., 275(IQ):SPRING-SUMMER72-112
FABOS, J.G., G.T. MILDE & V.M. WEINMAYR.
FREDERICK LAW OLMSTED, SR.
I.R. STEWART, 576:DEC71-331
FABRE, J., ED. MANUEL D'HISTOIRE LITTÉR-
AIRE DE LA FRANCE. (VOL 3, 1715-89)
H.A. STAVAN, 207(FR):FEB71-629
FABRE, M. THE UNFINISHED QUEST OF RICH-
ARD WRIGHT.
J. WIDEMAN, 441:7OCT73-31
FÀBREGAS, X. - SEE SOLER, F.
FABRICIUS, J. THE UNCONSCIOUS AND MR.
ELIOT.
K. SMIDT, 72:BAND209HEFT4/6-419
FABRIS, A. HENRY JAMES E LA FRANCIA.
D.A. LEEMING, 131(CL):FALL72-374
FABRY, P.W. DIE SOWJETUNION UND DAS
DRITTE REICH.
G.L. WEINBERG, 32:SEP72-681
FABUN, D., ED. THREE ROADS TO AWARENESS.
R.C. HUSEMAN, 583:WINTER71-209
FACKENHEIM, E. GOD'S PRESENCE IN HIS-
TORY.
S.J.B., 543:MAR71-541
S. CAIN, 390:MAY71-73
FADIMAN, E., JR. THE PROFESSIONAL.
M. LEVIN, 441:11NOV73-51
FADIMAN, W. HOLLYWOOD NOW.
617(TLS):1JUN73-625
FADINGER, V. DIE BEGRÜNDUNG DES PRIN-
ZIPATS.*
D. FISHWICK, 24:OCT72-619
B. LEVICK, 123:MAR72-134
FAGE, J.D., ED. AFRICA DISCOVERS HER
PAST.
R. SMITH, 69:JAN71-74
DE FAGES, L. EDITH SÖDERGRAN.
G.C. SCHOOLFIELD, 563(SS):AUTUMN72-577
FAGG, W. AFRICAN TRIBAL IMAGES.
E.L.R. MEYEROWITZ, 39:JUL70-80
FAGG, W. MINIATURE WOOD CARVINGS OF
AFRICA.
D. DYCKES, 58:SUMMER71-10
W.L. HOMMEL, 127:SUMMER72-476
J. PICTON, 592:MAR71-132
FAGIOLO DELL'ARCO, M. IL PARMIGIANINO.
C. GOULD, 90:DEC71-747
FAHEY, M.A. CYPRIAN AND THE BIBLE.
W. RORDORF, 182:VOL24#19/20-708
FAHLIN, C. - SEE BENOÎT
FÄHNDERS, W., H. KARRENBROCK & M. RECTOR
- SEE JUNG, F.
FAIDIT, U. THE "DONATZ PROENSALS" OF
UC FAIDIT.* (J.H. MARSHALL, ED)
U.T. HOLMES, 589:APR72-330
P.Z., 433:JUL71-342

FAILLIE, M-H. LA FEMME ET LE CODE CIVIL
DANS LA COMÉDIE HUMAINE D'HONORÉ DE
BALZAC.
D. ADAMSON, 208(FS):JAN72-88
A. MICHEL, 535(RHL):MAY-JUN70-518
FAIN, H. BETWEEN PHILOSOPHY AND HISTORY.*
H.B., 543:DEC70-339
R. STOVER, 479(PHQ):JUL71-278
FAINLIGHT, R. THE REGION'S VIOLENCE.
617(TLS):11MAY73-516
FAINLIGHT, R. TO SEE THE MATTER CLEARLY.
J.T. IRWIN, 598(SOR):SUMMER73-720
FAIR, R. WE CAN'T BREATHE.*
M. COOKE, 676(YR):SUMMER72-599
FAIRBAIRN, D. SHOOT.
N. CALLENDAR, 441:8APR73-32
FAIRBANK, A. THE STORY OF HANDWRITING.
J. BACKHOUSE, 354:JUN71-174
R. LISTER, 503:AUTUMN70-164
FAIRBANK, J.K., E.O. REISCHAUER & A.M.
CRAIG. EAST ASIA: TRADITION AND TRANS-
FORMATION.
R. MURPHEY, 441:23SEP73-40
FAIRBANK, W. ADVENTURES IN RETRIEVAL.
617(TLS):22JUN73-722
FAIRBROTHER, N. NEW LIVES - NEW LAND-
SCAPES.
P.K. MARSTRAND, 619(TC):VOL178#1045-
46
639(VQR):WINTER71-XLIV
FAIRCHILD, H.N. RELIGIOUS TRENDS IN
ENGLISH POETRY.* (VOL 6)
R.B. WOODINGS, 597(SN):VOL42#1-245
FAIRCHILD, W. THE SWISS ARRANGEMENT.
617(TLS):16NOV73-1407
FAIRCLOUGH, P. - SEE DICKENS, C.
FAIRFAX, J. & S. COOK. OARS ACROSS THE
PACIFIC.
617(TLS):23FEB73-222
FAIRHALL, D. RUSSIAN SEA POWER.* (BRIT-
ISH TITLE: RUSSIA LOOKS TO THE SEA.)
V. PETROV, 32:MAR72-183
FAIRLIE, H. THE KENNEDY PROMISE.
C. LEHMANN-HAUPT, 441:12JAN73-35
T. WICKER, 441:21JAN73-1
442(NY):27JAN73-93
617(TLS):8JUN73-631
FAIRMAN, C. RECONSTRUCTION AND REUNION,
1864-88.
I. DILLIARD, 31(ASCH):SPRING73-347
FAIRS, G.L. A HISTORY OF THE HAY.
617(TLS):9FEB73-161
FAIRSERVIS, W.A., JR., ED. THE ROOTS
OF ANCIENT INDIA.
617(TLS):8JUN73-641
FAISS, K. "GNADE" BEI CYNEWULF UND SEIN-
ER SCHULE.
H. BECKERS, 72:BAND209HEFT4/6-398
M. LATENDORF, 38:BAND89HEFT4-513
FAITHORNE, W. THE ART OF GRAVEING AND
ETCHING.
R. EDWARDS, 39:APR71-341
FAIVRE, A. ECKARTSHAUSEN ET LA THÉOSO-
PHIE CHRÉTIENNE.
A. VIATTE, 549(RLC):JAN-MAR70-135
FAKINOS, A. THE MARKED MEN.
R. TRICKETT, 676(YR):AUTUMN71-121
FALCONI, C. THE SILENCE OF PIUS XII.
A.R. ECKARDT, 328:FALL71-502
FALDI, I. PITTORI VITERBESI DI CINQUE
SECOLI, VITERBO, CASSA DI RISPARMIO.
R.W.L., 135:APR71-291
FALK, J.S. NOMINALIZATIONS IN SPANISH.
J.N. GREEN, 545(RPH):FEB72-344
FALK, R., G. KOLKO & R.J. LIFTON, EDS.
CRIMES OF WAR.
G. BEST, 362:30AUG73-285

FALK, R.A., ED. THE VIETNAM WAR AND IN-
TERNATIONAL LAW. (VOL 2)
V.H. LI, 293(JAST):FEB71-507
FALK, S.J. QAJAR PAINTINGS.
617(TLS):6APR73-374
FALKBERGET, J. THE FOURTH NIGHT WATCH.
E.J. FRIIS, 563(SS):SPRING72-271
FALKIRK, R. BLACKSTONE.
N. CALLENDAR, 441:4MAR73-42
FALKIRK, R. BLACKSTONE'S FANCY.
N. CALLENDAR, 441:2SEP73-18
FALKUS, M.E. THE INDUSTRIALISATION OF
RUSSIA, 1700-1914.
617(TLS):9FEB73-161
FALL, F.C. ONE OF THE DAMNED.
617(TLS):23NOV73-1420
FALL, V.G. THE SEA AND THE FOREST.
617(TLS):31AUG73-1009
FALLERS, L.A. LAW WITHOUT PRECEDENT.
I. HAMNETT, 69:OCT71-328
FALSAFI, N-O-L. CHAND MAQĀLE-YE TĀRĪKHI
VA ADABI.
M.A. JAZAYERY, 318(JAOS):OCT-DEC71-536
FANE, J. GABRIEL YOUNG.
S. HILL, 362:14JUN73-808
617(TLS):14DEC73-1529
FANELLI, G. ARCHITETTURA MODERNA IN
OLANDA: 1900-1940.* (C.L. RAGGHIANTI,
ED)
T.M. BROWN, 576:OCT71-259
FANELLI, V. - SEE UBALDINI, F.
FANK, P. DIE VORAUER HANDSCHRIFT.
K.K. POLHEIM, 680(ZDP):BAND90HEFT3-
454
FANN, K.T., ED. SYMPOSIUM ON J.L. AUS-
TIN.*
J. LEIBER, 484(PPR):SEP71-118
FANN, K.T. WITTGENSTEIN'S CONCEPTION OF
PHILOSOPHY.*
D. GUSTAFSON, 484(PPR):JUN72-577
FANNIN, A. HANDSPINNING.
M. SONDAY, 139:AUG71-6
FANON, F. THE WRETCHED OF THE EARTH.
R.C. CLARK, 544:FALL71-243
FANTA, C.G. MARLOWE'S "AGONISTS."
J-B. FORT, 189(EA):OCT-DEC71-520
FANTEL, H. JOHANN STRAUSS.*
A. LAMB, 415:JAN72-45
FANTHAM, E. COMPARATIVE STUDIES IN
REPUBLICAN LATIN IMAGERY.
617(TLS):27JUL73-859
FANTI, M. IL MUSEO DI SAN PETRONIO IN
BOLOGNA: CATALOGO.
J.H. BECK, 54:JUN71-253
FAR, I. DE CHIRICO.
R. LEIBOWITZ, 58:NOV71-14
FARAGO, L. THE GAME OF THE FOXES.*
42(AR):WINTER71/72-591
FARBER, J.C. & W.D. GARRETT. THOMAS JEF-
FERSON REDIVIVUS.
639(VQR):AUTUMN71-CLXXXIV
FARBER, M. - SEE MELCHERT, N.P.
FARBER, M. - SEE RIEPE, D.
FARGEAUD, M. BALZAC ET "LA RECHERCHE DE
L'ABSOLU."*
M. REGARD, 535(RHL):MAR-APR70-319
FARGHER, R. LIFE AND LETTERS IN FRANCE:
THE EIGHTEENTH CENTURY.
J.H. BRUMFITT, 208(FS):OCT72-455
FARGUE, L-P. & V. LARBAUD. CORRESPON-
DANCE.
S. FAUCHEREAU, 98:JUL71-626
FARINATI, P. GIORNALE (1573-1606). (L.
PUPPI, ED)
D. ROSAND, 54:SEP71-407
FARINELLI, G. - SEE MARTINI, F.M.
FARLEY, J. FIGURE AND FIELD.*
639(VQR):SPRING71-LX

FARLEY-HILLS, D., ED. ROCHESTER: THE
CRITICAL HERITAGE.*
D. DILLON, 584(SWR):AUTUMN72-342
FARMER, D.H. - SEE "THE RULE OF ST. BENE-
DICT"
FARMER, F.M. THE ORIGINAL FANNIE FARMER
COOK BOOK 1896.
K. HESS, 441:14OCT73-42
FARMER, J.S. & W.E. HENLEY, EDS. SLANG
AND ITS ANALOGUES.
P.W. ROGERS, 529(QQ):SUMMER71-339
42(AR):FALL/WINTER70/71-463
FARMILOE, D. POEMS FOR APARTMENT DWEL-
LERS.
L. THOMPSON, 628:FALL70-86
FARNHAM, A.E., ED. A SOURCEBOOK IN THE
HISTORY OF ENGLISH.
A. LAUCKA, 215(GL):VOL10#1-47
FARNHAM, E. CHARLES DEMUTH.
S-L. SCHWARTZ, 58:SEP/OCT71-16
FARNHAM, W. THE SHAKESPEAREAN GROTESQUE.
H. SKULSKY, 191(ELN):JUN72-300
FARNSWORTH, P.R. THE SOCIAL PSYCHOLOGY
OF MUSIC. (2ND ED)
R.A. DALE, 290(JAAC):SUMMER71-548
FARR, F. O'HARA.
M. COWLEY, 441:18MAR73-3
FARR, J., ED. TWENTIETH CENTURY INTER-
PRETATIONS OF "SONS AND LOVERS."
K. MC SWEENEY, 529(QQ):SUMMER71-337
FARRAR, S. WHAT WITCHES DO.
C-A. BURLAND, 203:AUTUMN71-258
FARRELL, J.G. THE SIEGE OF KRISHNAPUR.
V. CUNNINGHAM, 362:30AUG73-288
617(TLS):21SEP73-1074
FARRELL, J.T. JUDITH AND OTHER STORIES.
J-C. OATES, 441:25NOV73-7
FARRELL, K. CONY-CATCHING.*
639(VQR):SUMMER71-C
FARRELL, R.B. DICTIONARY OF GERMAN SYN-
ONYMS. (2ND ED)
W.B., 681(ZDS):BAND27HEFT3-191
FARRELL, R.B., ED. POLITICAL LEADERSHIP
IN EASTERN EUROPE AND THE SOVIET UNION.
L. BLIT, 575(SEER):JUL72-484
FARRER, A. THE END OF MAN.
617(TLS):21DEC73-1571
FARRISON, W.E. WILLIAM WELLS BROWN.
R. WELBURN, 50(ARQ):AUTUMN70-275
FARUQĪ, K.A. "DASTANBU" BY MIRZA ASADUL-
LAH KHAN GHALIB.
K. SAJUNLAL, 273(IC):JUL71-216
FARUQĪ, K.A. URDU MĒN WAHHĀBI ADAB.
H.K. SHERWANI, 273(IC):JUL71-213
FARWELL, B. QUEEN VICTORIA'S LITTLE
WARS.*
617(TLS):15JUN73-659
FASSKE, H., H. JENTSCH & S. MICHALK.
SORBISCHER SPRACHATLAS. (VOL 3)
G. STONE, 575(SEER):JUL72-448
FASSKE, H. & S. MICHALK. SORBISCHE DIA-
LEKTTEXTE. (VOL 8)
G. STONE, 575(SEER):JUL72-448
FATIO, O. & O. LA BARTHE, EDS. REGISTRES
DE LA COMPAGNIE DES PASTEURS DE GENÈVE.
(VOL 3)
R.D. LINDER, 551(RENQ):SPRING71-81
FAULK, O.B. TOMBSTONE.
617(TLS):6APR73-365
FAULKNER, A.H. THE GRAND JUNCTION CANAL.
617(TLS):27JUL73-858
FAULKNER, P., ED. WILLIAM MORRIS: THE
CRITICAL HERITAGE.
617(TLS):22JUN73-712
FAULKNER, P. - SEE HOLCROFT, T.
FAULKNER, W. FLAGS IN THE DUST. (D. DAY
& A. ERSKINE, EDS)
442(NY):3SEP73-66

DU FAUR, C.V. - SEE UNDER VON FABER DU
FAUR, C.
FAURE, E.  THE HEART OF THE BATTLE.*
442(NY):24FEB73-131
FAUST, I.  FOREIGN DEVILS.
C. LEHMANN-HAUPT, 441:11JUL73-45
D.K. MANO, 441:20MAY73-7
FAUSTINELLI, M.  MAN THE ARTIST.
617(TLS):5JAN73-21
FAUSTINO SARMIENTO, D.  TRAVELS IN THE
UNITED STATES IN 1847.
37:APR71-41
639(VQR):SPRING71-LXXXII
FAVERO, G.B.  CORPUS PALLADIANUM. (VOL 5)
J. NEWMAN, 90:NOV71-675
FAVERTY, F.E., ED.  THE VICTORIAN POETS.
K. ALLOTT, 636(VP):SPRING70-82
FAVRHOLDT, D.  AN INTERPRETATION AND
CRITIQUE OF WITTGENSTEIN'S "TRACTATUS."
I.M. COPI, 482(PHR):OCT71-530
FAWCETT, T.  HEBREW MYTH AND CHRISTIAN
GOSPEL.
617(TLS):26OCT73-1319
FAY, H.C. - SEE PLAUTUS
FAYE, J-P.  L'ÉCLUSE. LE RÉCIT HUNIQUE.
LES TROYENS.
P. BOYER, 98:AUG/SEP71-770
FAZAL, M.A.  JUDICIAL CONTROL OF ADMINIS-
TRATIVE ACTION IN INDIA AND PAKISTAN.
G.H. GADBOIS, JR., 293(JAST):NOV70-248
L. STERNBACH, 318(JAOS):APR-JUN71-320
FEARNS, J. - SEE PETER THE VENERABLE
FEATHER, J.P. - SEE ARMIN, R.
FEATHERSTONE, D.  BATTLE NOTES FOR WAR-
GAMES. COLONIAL SMALL WARS, 1837-1901.
617(TLS):21DEC73-1574
FEATHERSTONE, D.F., WITH R. ALLEN.
DANCING WITHOUT DANGER.
P. RENNA, 151:FEB71-90
FECHNER, E., E. VON HIPPEL & H. FROST -
SEE HERING, C.J.
FECHNER, J-U., ED.  DAS DEUTSCHE SONETT.*
W. RUTTKOWSKI, 222(GR):MAR71-159
FEDDEN, R. & R. JOEKES, COMPS.  THE
NATIONAL TRUST GUIDE.
617(TLS):24AUG73-986
FEDER, L.  ANCIENT MYTH IN MODERN POETRY.
J.B. VICKERY, 659:SUMMER73-392
617(TLS):6APR73-396
"FEDERAL STATISTICS, A REPORT OF THE
PRESIDENT'S COMMISSION."
42(AR):WINTER71/72-596
FEDERICI, E.C.  LA STAMPA A MACERATA FINO
ALL'ANNO 1700, SEGUENDO SPECIALMENTE I
DOCUMENTI DELL'ARCHIVIO PRIORILE.
J.M. POTTER, 354:SEP70-256
FEDERMAN, R., ED.  CINQS NOUVELLES NOU-
VELLES.
M. CAGNON, 399(MLJ):MAY71-326
K.S. WHITE, 207(FR):APR71-1005
FEDERMAN, R. & J. FLETCHER.  SAMUEL
BECKETT, HIS WORKS AND HIS CRITICS.
617(TLS):12OCT73-1217
FÉDIER, F. - SEE HEIDEGGER, M.
FEDOROVA, S.G.  RUSSKOE NASELENIE ALIASKI
I KALIFORNII.
J.R. GIBSON, 32:DEC72-890
FEDOSOV, I.A. & OTHERS, EDS.  ISTOCHNIK-
OVEDENIE ISTORII SSSR XIX-NACHALA XX V.
E.C. THADEN, 32:SEP72-683
FEDYSHYN, O.S.  GERMANY'S DRIVE TO THE
EAST AND THE UKRAINIAN REVOLUTION,
1917-1918.
I. KAMENETSKY, 32:MAR72-166
FEEHAN, J.M.  TOMORROW TO BE BRAVE.
617(TLS):30MAR73-361

FEELEY, K.  FLANNERY O'CONNOR.*
L.Y. GOSSETT, 27(AL):NOV72-517
F.P.W. MC DOWELL, 598(SOR):AUTUMN73-
998
FEHDERAU, H.W.  THE ORIGIN AND DEVELOP-
MENT OF KITUBA (LINGUA FRANCA KIKONGO).
J. VOORHOEVE, 69:APR70-191
FEHÉRVÁRI, G.  ISLAMIC POTTERY.
617(TLS):28DEC73-1590
FEHLING, D.  DIE WIEDERHOLUNGSFIGUREN UND
IHR GEBRAUCH BEI DEN GRIECHEN VOR GOR-
GIAS.*
D.C. INNES, 123:DEC72-418
FEHLMANN, G.  SOMERVILLE ET ROSS TÉMOINS
DE L'IRLANDE D'HIER.
N. COGHILL, 189(EA):APR-JUN71-213
FEHRENBACHER, D.E. - SEE POTTER, D.M.
"FEI CHENG-CH'ING YÜ MAO-KUNG." (HSÜ
KAO-YÜAN, TRANS)
L.H.D. GORDON & S. CHANG, 293(JAST):
NOV70-137
FEIBLEMAN, J.K.  MORAL STRATEGY.
M. SCHUMAKER, 154:SEP71-603
FEIBLEMAN, J.K.  THE NEW MATERIALISM.
R.S. DOWNIE, 478:JUL71-131
FEIBLEMAN, P.S.  THE COLUMBUS TREE.
T. LASK, 441:20MAR73-43
D.K. MANO, 441:25FEB73-3
442(NY):24FEB73-130
617(TLS):27JUL73-851
FEIFER, G.  RUSSIA CLOSE-UP.
617(TLS):30NOV73-1481
FEIFFER, J.  A HOT PROPERTY.
A. BROYARD, 441:26MAR73-43
M. LEVIN, 441:8APR73-33
FEIN, A.  FREDERICK LAW OLMSTED AND THE
AMERICAN ENVIRONMENTAL TRADITION.*
C. WISEMAN, 231:FEB73-105
FEIN, A. - SEE OLMSTED, F.L.
FEIN, R.J.  ROBERT LOWELL.
L. PRATT, 502(PRS):WINTER71/72-361
W.B. RIDEOUT, 659:SUMMER73-384
FEINBERG, J.  DOING AND DESERVING.*
C.L. TEN, 63:MAY72-82
FEINBERG, R.E.  THE TRIUMPH OF ALLENDE.
N. GALL, 441:1JUL73-6
FEINGOLD, H.L.  THE POLITICS OF RESCUE.
F.A. LAZIN, 328:FALL71-505
FEININGER, A.  PRINCIPLES OF COMPOSITION
IN PHOTOGRAPHY.
617(TLS):8JUN73-653
FEINSTEIN, E.  THE CELEBRANTS AND OTHER
POEMS.
617(TLS):7DEC73-1513
FEINSTEIN, E.  THE CIRCLE.
E. GLOVER, 565:VOL12#3-58
FEINSTEIN, E.  THE GLASS ALEMBIC.
V. CUNNINGHAM, 362:21JUN73-837
617(TLS):29JUN73-736
FEINSTEIN, E.  THE MAGIC APPLE TREE.*
J. SAUNDERS, 565:VOL12#4-63
FEITH, H. & L. CASTLES, EDS.  INDONESIAN
POLITICAL THINKING: 1945-1965.
F.J. CORLEY, 613:SPRING71-154
S. SLOAN, 293(JAST):NOV70-234
FELD, B.T. & OTHERS, EDS.  IMPACT OF NEW
TECHNOLOGIES ON THE ARMS RACE.
V. GILINSKY, 550(RUSR):OCT71-409
FELD, H.  MARTIN LUTHERS UND WENDELIN
STEINBACHS VORLESUNGEN ÜBER DEN HEB-
RÄERBRIEF.
F.F. BRUCE, 182:VOL24#7/8-329
FELD, R.  YEARS OUT.
M. MEWSHAW, 441:4NOV73-80
FELDBAEK, O.  INDIA TRADE UNDER THE DAN-
ISH FLAG, 1772-1808.
H. FURBER, 293(JAST):NOV70-196

FELDMAN, D.M. & G.L. BOARINO. LECTURAS
CONTEMPORÁNEAS.
   J.M. YALDEN, 238:DEC71-991
FELDMAN, I. LOST ORIGINALS.
   R.W. FLINT, 441:25FEB73-41
   R. HOWARD, 491:SEP73-351
FELDMAN, I. MAGIC PAPERS AND OTHER
POEMS.*
   639(VQR):SPRING71-LX
FELDMAN, S.D. THE MORALITY-PATTERNED
COMEDY OF THE RENAISSANCE.*
   J.A.B. SOMERSET, 402(MLR):APR72-401
FELDMANN, H. DIE FIABE CARLO GOZZIS.
   D. HAAS, 72:BAND209HEFT4/6-464
FELIX, D. WALTHER RATHENAU AND THE
WEIMAR REPUBLIC.
   617(TLS):19JAN73-61
FELLINGER, I. VERZEICHNIS DER MUSIKZEIT-
SCHRIFTEN DES 19. JAHRHUNDERTS.
   A.H. KING, 354:MAR70-73
FELLOWES, E.H. ENGLISH MADRIGAL VERSE
1588-1632. (3RD ED REV & ENLARGED BY
F.W. STERNFELD & D. GREER)
   W. MAYNARD, 179(ES):FEB71-69
FELLOWS, O. FROM VOLTAIRE TO "LA NOU-
VELLE CRITIQUE."
   M. CARTWRIGHT, 207(FR):APR71-984
   A.J. KNODEL, 173(ECS):FALL71-182
   G. MAY, 546(RR):DEC71-303
   R. MERCIER, 557(RSH):JUL-SEP71-477
   R. NIKLAUS, 208(FS):OCT72-483
   R.C. ROSBOTTOM, 188(ECR):FALL71-82
FELLOWS, O. & D. GUIRAGOSSIAN, EDS. DID-
EROT STUDIES XII.*
   J.N. PAPPAS, 207(FR):OCT70-238
FELPERIN, H. SHAKESPEAREAN ROMANCE.
   617(TLS):29JUN73-752
FELSTEIN, I. LIVING TO BE A HUNDRED.
   617(TLS):13JUL73-815
FELSTINER, J. THE LIES OF ART.*
   V.S. PRITCHETT, 453:25JAN73-16
   617(TLS):23MAR73-314
FELTON, F. THOMAS LOVE PEACOCK.
   617(TLS):20APR73-443
FEN, E. REMEMBER RUSSIA.
   617(TLS):16NOV73-1391
FENDALL, C., ED. A NORFOLK ANTHOLOGY.
   617(TLS):28DEC73-1595
FÉNELON, F. LETTRE À L'ACADÉMIE. (E.
CALDARINI, ED)
   J.H. DAVIS, JR., 207(FR):APR71-988
   S. MENANT, 535(RHL):MAY-JUN71-505
FÉNÉON, F. OEUVRES PLUS QUE COMPLÈTES.
   K. CORNELL, 207(FR):MAY71-1128
FENLON, D. HERESY AND OBEDIENCE IN TRI-
DENTINE ITALY.
   617(TLS):7SEP73-1035
FENNARIO, D. WITHOUT A PARACHUTE.
   D. BARBOUR, 296:WINTER73-99
"TÖNNIES FENNE'S LOW GERMAN MANUAL OF
SPOKEN RUSSIAN, PSKOV, 1607."* (VOL 2)
(L.L. HAMMERICH & OTHERS, EDS) [SHOWN
IN PREV UNDER TÖNNIES]
   S.C. GARDINER, 402(MLR):JUL72-717
   H. LEEMING, 575(SEER):JAN72-113
FENNELL, J., ED. NINETEENTH-CENTURY
RUSSIAN LITERATURE.
   617(TLS):10AUG73-923
FENOGLIO, B. IL PARTIGIANO JOHNNY. LA
PAGA DEL SABATO.
   G. CARSANIGA, 270:VOL21#1-123
FENWICK, E. THE LAST OF LYSANDRA.
   617(TLS):16MAR73-303
FENWICK, E. ARCHITECT ROYAL.
   J.L-M., 135:FEB71-140
FERGUSON, A. JET STREAM.
   M. LEVIN, 441:23DEC73-16

FERGUSON, J. A COMPANION TO GREEK TRAG-
EDY.
   617(TLS):8JUN73-650
FERGUSON, J. THE PLACE OF SUFFERING.
   617(TLS):5OCT73-1190
FERGUSON, J. THE RELIGIONS OF THE ROMAN
EMPIRE.*
   R.M. OGILVIE, 123:DEC72-386
   V.T.T. TINH, 487:WINTER71-399
FERGUSON, J. SOCRATES: A SOURCE BOOK.
   W.E.W.S. CHARLTON, 123:JUN72-280
FERGUSON, S. A GUARD WITHIN.
   617(TLS):23NOV73-1447
FERGUSON, S. THE POETRY OF RANDALL JAR-
RELL.*
   M.B. QUINN, 27(AL):NOV72-515
   R. SQUIRES, 598(SOR):SUMMER73-745
FERGUSSON, A. THE SACK OF BATH.
   617(TLS):20JUL73-840
FERGUSSON, C.B. PLACE-NAMES AND PLACES
OF NOVA SCOTIA.
   J.A. RAYBURN, 424:MAR71-51
FERGUSSON, J. THE MAN BEHIND "MACBETH."
   R.A. FOAKES, 175:AUTUMN70-98
FERGUSSON, J. BALLOON TYTLER.
   617(TLS):5JAN73-9
FERLINGHETTI, L. THE SECRET MEANING OF
THINGS.*
   M. BENEDIKT, 491:NOV72-105
FERLOSIO, R.S. - SEE UNDER SÁNCHEZ FER-
LOSIO, R.
FERMAN, E., ED. THE BEST OF FANTASY AND
SCIENCE FICTION. (24TH SER)
   T. STURGEON, 441:4NOV73-76
FERNÁNDEZ, C.A. - SEE UNDER ARIEL FERNÁN-
DEZ, C.
FERNÁNDEZ, G. - SEE PELLICER, C.
FERNÁNDEZ, J. GUIDE TO MEXICAN ART.
   J.A. BAIRD, JR., 290(JAAC):FALL70-142
   M.S. YOUNG, 39:MAY70-404
FERNÁNDEZ, P.H. EL PROBLEMA DE LA PER-
SONALIDAD EN UNAMUNO Y EL SAN MANUEL
BUENO.
   F. FERNÁNDEZ-TURIENZO, 240(HR):APR71-
227
FERNANDEZ, T.L., ED. ORAL INTERPRETATION
AND THE TEACHING OF ENGLISH.
   B. WHITAKER, 583:SPRING71-295
FERNÁNDEZ, X.A. - SEE CALDERÓN DE LA
BARCA, P.
FERNÁNDEZ CABALLERO, C.F.S. ARANDUKA HA
KUATUANEE PARAGUAI REMBIAPOCUE.
   J.C., 37:JAN-FEB71-41
FERNÁNDEZ SHAW, G. UN POETA DE TRANSI-
CIÓN.
   I.R. GALBIS, 238:MAY71-394
FERNBACH, D. - SEE MARX, K.
FEROSSI, A. ORIGINE DEL TOMISMO PIACEN-
TINA NEL PRIMO OTTOCENTO.
   A. FOREST, 542:JAN-MAR70-98
FERRARS, E.X. FOOT IN THE GRAVE.*
   N. CALLENDAR, 441:7JAN73-35
FERRATE, J. DINÁMICA DE LA POESÍA.
   H.T. OOSTENDORP, 433:JUL71-343
FERRATER MORA, J. INDAGACIONES SOBRE EL
LENGUAJE.
   F. LACOSTA, 238:MAY71-398
   A.D.M., 543:MAR71-541
FERRATER MORA, J. ORTEGA Y GASSET.
   G. FABRE, 542:OCT-DEC71-510
FERRÉ, F. LE LANGAGE RELIGIEUX A-T-IL UN
SENS?
   J. POULAIN, 154:JUN71-401
FERRER, M. BORGES Y LA NADA.
   D.L. SHAW, 402(MLR):OCT72-933
FERRERO, E. I GERGHI DELLA MALAVITA DAL
CINQUECENTO A OGGI.
   617(TLS):6APR73-398

FERRERO, G.G. - SEE ARETINO, P.
FERRIS, P.  VERY PERSONAL PROBLEMS.
    617(TLS):22JUN73-709
FERRIS, W.R., JR.  MISSISSIPPI BLACK FOLK-
    LORE.
    F.J. GILLIS, 187:JAN73-133
FERRON, J.  LE SAINT-ELIAS.
    A. POKORNY, 296:FALL73-93
FERRY, A.D.  MILTON AND THE MILTONIC DRY-
    DEN.*
    G. BULLOUGH, 175:SPRING70-24
FERRY, W.H.  THE BUILDINGS OF DETROIT.*
    A. BURNHAM, 576:DEC70-356
    C.W. CONDIT, 56:SPRING70-76
"FESTIVE WINE." (N. BRANNEN & W. ELLIOTT,
    TRANS)
    E. MINER, 318(JAOS):OCT-DEC71-523
FESTUGIÈRE, A-J., ED & TRANS.  SAINTE
    THÈCLE, SAINTS CÔME ET DAMIEN, SAINTS
    CYR ET JEAN (EXTRAITS), SAINT GEORGES.
    A. KEMMER, 182:VOL24#13/14-526
FETHERLING, D.  OUR MAN IN UTOPIA.
    A. PURDY, 102(CANL):AUTUMN72-86
FETHERSTON, P.  NATURES OF ALL SORTS.
    617(TLS):27APR73-474
FETJÖ, F.  A HISTORY OF THE PEOPLE'S
    DEMOCRACIES.
    L. BLIT, 575(SEER):OCT72-622
    R.V. BURKS, 32:SEP72-702
FETSCHER, I. - SEE KOLLONTAI, A.
FEUER, L.S.  MARX AND THE INTELLECTUALS.
    H.B., 543:SEP70-136
FEUERLICHT, I.  THOMAS MANN.*
    H.C. SASSE, 220(GL&L):OCT71-74
FEUERSTEIN, G.  NEW DIRECTIONS IN GERMAN
    ARCHITECTURE.
    R. BANHAM, 54:SEP70-344
FEYDEAU, G.  FOUR FARCES.
    A. RENDLE, 157:SUMMER71-82
FFRENCH-BEYTAGH, G.A.  ENCOUNTERING DARK-
    NESS.
    J. BIDDULPH, 362:23AUG73-254
FIC, V.M.  PEACEFUL TRANSITION TO COMMUN-
    ISM IN INDIA.
    J.P. HAITHCOX, 293(JAST):FEB71-490
FICHTE, J.G.  ERSTE WISSENSCHAFTSLEHRE
    VON 1804.  (H. GLIWITZKY, ED)
    W. SCHWARZ, 484(PPR):SEP70-147
FICHTE, J.G.  FICHTE'S SCIENCE OF KNOW-
    LEDGE (WISSENSCHAFTSLEHRE).  (P. HEATH
    & J. LACHS, EDS & TRANS)
    J.D.C., 543:MAR71-542
FICHTE, J.G.  OEUVRES COMPLÈTES.  (R.
    LAUTH & H. JACOB, EDS)
    M. GUEROULT, 542:JAN-MAR70-89
FICHTNER, E.G. - SEE FÜETRER, U.
FICK, C.  THE DANZIGER TRANSCRIPT.*
    617(TLS):13APR73-427
FIDO, M.  CHARLES DICKENS.*
    S.C. GILL, 447(N&Q):FEB71-80
FIEDLER, L.A.  THE COLLECTED ESSAYS OF
    LESLIE FIEDLER.*
    B. WALLENSTEIN, 295:NOV72-589
FIEDLER, L.A.  THE STRANGER IN SHAKE-
    SPEARE.*
    D.J. ENRIGHT, 362:1FEB73-155
    617(TLS):30MAR73-346
FIEGUTH, G.W.  JEAN PAUL ALS APHORISTIKER.
    R.M., 191(ELN):SEP71(SUPP)-146
FIELD, G.W.  HERMAN HESSE.*
    A. HSIA, 221(GQ):JAN71-91
    J.H. REID, 402(MLR):OCT72-952
FIELD, J.  COTTAGES AND CONVERSIONS AT
    HOME AND ABROAD.
    617(TLS):3AUG73-913
FIELD, L. & J.  BERNARD MALAMUD AND THE
    CRITICS.
    G. ENGEL, 287:MAY71-27

FIELD, P.J.C.  ROMANCE AND CHRONICLE.
    E.O. BACHE, 301(JEGP):JAN72-109
FIELD, S. & M.P. LEVITT.  BLOOMSDAY.
    H. KIRKWOOD, 99:APR73-38
    S. PINSKER, 329(JJQ):SPRING73-367
FIELD, S.J.  PERSONAL REMINISCENCES OF
    EARLY DAYS IN CALIFORNIA.
    J.M. PREST, 447(N&Q):NOV71-432
FIELDEN, C.  CRYING AS SHE RAN.*
    M. BENAZON, 150(DR):SUMMER71-297
FIELDEN, J. & G. LOCKWOOD.  PLANNING AND
    MANAGEMENT IN UNIVERSITIES.
    617(TLS):7SEP73-1023
FIELDING, H.  JOSEPH ANDREWS [AND] SHAM-
    ELA.
    I. BAIN, 503:WINTER70-227
FIELDING, H.  THE CRITICISM OF HENRY
    FIELDING.  (I. WILLIAMS, ED)
    J. PRESTON, 184(EIC):JAN71-91
FIELDING, H.  THE GRUB STREET OPERA.*
    (E.V. ROBERTS, ED)
    J. MICHON, 189(EA):APR-JUN71-166
FIELDING, H.  MISCELLANIES BY HENRY
    FIELDING, ESQ.  (VOL 1) (H.K. MILLER,
    ED)
    617(TLS):29JUN73-740
FIELDING, H.  TOM THUMB AND THE TRAGEDY
    OF TRAGEDIES.  (L.J. MORISSEY, ED)
    A. RENDLE, 157:SUMMER70-75
FIELDING, J.  THE BEST OF FRIENDS.*
    P. MORLEY, 99:JAN73-34
FIELDS, A.B.  STUDENT POLITICS IN FRANCE.
    B.H. SMITH, 396(MODA):SPRING72-221
FIELDS, B.  REALITY'S DARK DREAM.*
    J.R. MAC GILLIVRAY, 627(UTQ):FALL70-73
FIELDS, K.  THE OTHER WALKER.
    F. MORAMARCO, 651(WHR):SPRING72-192
    R. OLIVER, 598(SOR):SPRING73-492
FIETZ, L.  MENSCHENBILD UND ROMANSTRUKTUR
    IN ALDOUS HUXLEYS IDEENROMANEN.
    C.W. THOMSEN, 430(NS):FEB70-102
FIFE, A. & A., EDS.  BALLADS OF THE GREAT
    WEST.
    L.W. ATTEBERY, 649(WAL):FALL70-236
FIFE, A. & A. AND H.H. GLASSIE, EDS.
    FORMS UPON THE FRONTIER.
    J.A. BURRISON, 292(JAF):OCT-DEC71-459
    F. GILLMOR, 50(ARQ):SPRING71-88
FIFE, A.E. & A.S., EDS.  COWBOY AND WEST-
    ERN SONGS.
    K.W. CLARKE, 582(SFQ):MAR71-95
FIFER, J.V.  BOLIVIA.
    617(TLS):6APR73-368
FIGGE, K.  DIE INDUSTRIEWIRTSCHAFTLICHE
    GESTALT DER FRANZÖSISCHEN ATLANTIKHÄFEN
    AN SEINE, LOIRE UND GIRONDE.
    J. COMTE, 182:VOL24#4-186
FIGUEIRA, G.  POESÍA BRASILEÑA CONTEMPOR-
    ÁNEA (1920-68).
    D.S. KELLER, 238:MAY71-400
FIGUERAS, J.R. - SEE UNDER ROMEU FIGUERAS,
    J.
FIGUEROA, J., ED.  CARRIBEAN VOICES.*
    (VOL 2)
    A. CLUYSENAAR, 565:VOL12#3-72
FIGUREL, J.A., ED.  READING GOALS FOR THE
    DISADVANTAGED.
    G. LEICHTMAN, 351(LL):JUN71-143
"THE FIHRIST OF AL-NADIM."* (B. DODGE,
    ED & TRANS)
    F. ROSENTHAL, 318(JAOS):OCT-DEC71-531
FILENE, P.G., ED.  AMERICAN VIEWS OF
    SOVIET RUSSIA, 1917-1965.
    H.H. FISHER, 32:MAR72-169
FILENE, P.G.  AMERICANS AND THE SOVIET
    EXPERIMENT, 1917-1933.
    H.H. FISHER, 32:MAR72-169

FILESI, T. L'ISTITUTO DELLA FAMIGLIA
NELLE COSTITUZIONI DEGLI STATI AFRI-
CANI.
B. BERNARDI, 69:OCT70-394
FILIN, F.P., ED. TEORETIČESKIE PROBLEMY
SOVETSKOGO JAZYKOZNANIJA.
H.D. POHL, 353:JUN71-110
"FINAL REPORT OF THE JOINT AHA-OAH AD HOC
COMMITTEE TO INVESTIGATE THE CHARGES
AGAINST THE FRANKLIN D. ROOSEVELT
LIBRARY AND RELATED MATTERS."
R. POLENBERG, 14:JUL71-277
FINBERG, H.P.R., ED. THE AGRARIAN HIS-
TORY OF ENGLAND AND WALES. (VOL 1, PT
2)
617(TLS):25MAY73-592
FINCH, C. THE ART OF WALT DISNEY.
R.O. BLECHMAN, 441:2DEC73-55
C. LEHMANN-HAUPT, 441:29OCT73-39
FINCH, C. PATRICK CAULFIELD.
T. HILTON, 592:MAR71-129
FINCH, H.L. - SEE WOODBURY, C.J.
FINCH, R. A LITTLE LEARNING.
617(TLS):4MAY73-489
FINDLATER, R. THE PLAYER KINGS.
N. MARSHALL, 157:SUMMER71-80
FINDLAY, J.N. ASCENT TO THE ABSOLUTE.
J. KING-FARLOW, 154:SEP71-572
FINDLAY, J.N. AXIOLOGICAL ETHICS.*
C.J.F. WILLIAMS, 393(MIND):OCT71-633
FINDLAY, J.N. MEINONG'S THEORY OF OB-
JECTS AND VALUES.
M. CHASTAING, 542:OCT-DEC71-497
FINDLAY, J.N. THE TRANSCENDENCE OF THE
CAVE.
G.P. HENDERSON, 393(MIND):JUL71-453
DE FINE LICHT, K. THE ROTUNDA IN ROME.
J.B. WARD-PERKINS, 313:VOL61-289
FINESTRES, J. EPISTOLARI: SUPLEMENT. (M.
BATLLORI, ED)
J-L. MARFANY, 86(BHS):JUL72-322
FINGARETTE, H. SELF-DECEPTION.*
R.B. DE SOUSA, 262:AUTUMN70-308
FINK, R.O. ROMAN MILITARY RECORDS ON
PAPYRUS.
G.M. BROWNE, 124:DEC71-132
C.G. STARR, 122:JUL72-227
FINKEL, D. ADEQUATE EARTH.
R. HOWARD, 491:SEP73-351
FINKELPEARL, P.J. JOHN MARSTON OF THE
MIDDLE TEMPLE.*
R.E. BRETTLE, 541(RES):MAY71-196
D.C. GUNBY, 67:NOV72-223
J. LEVENSON, 405(MP):NOV70-199
FINKELSTEIN, L. NEW LIGHT FROM THE PRO-
PHETS.
J. NEUSNER, 318(JAOS):APR-JUN71-303
FINKELSTEIN, S. MC LUHAN, PROPHÈTE OU
IMPOSTEUR?
M-C. DELVAUX, 154:DEC71-855
FINKENSTAEDT, T. YOU AND THOU.
H. UTZ, 343:BAND13HEFT1-75
FINLAY, I. CELTIC ART.
617(TLS):21DEC73-1568
FINLAY, I.H. THE DANCERS INHERIT THE
PARTY.*
T. EAGLETON, 565:VOL11#2-68
FINLAY, I.H. POEMS TO HEAR AND SEE.
M. BENEDIKT, 491:NOV72-105
FINLAY, J.F. TRANSLATING.
R. HAESERYN, 75:4/1971-50
FINLAY, M. THE HARPO SCROLLS.
J. DITSKY, 628:SPRING72-108
FINLEY, J.E. THE CORRUPT KINGDOM.
C. LEHMANN-HAUPT, 441:27FEB73-31
442(NY):7APR73-151

FINLEY, M.I. ASPECTS OF ANTIQUITY.
R. BROWNING, 313:VOL61-268
P. GAUTHIER, 555:VOL45FASC1-136
FINLEY, M.I. DEMOCRACY ANCIENT AND MOD-
ERN.
J. DUNN, 362:23AUG73-252
FINLEY, M.I. EARLY GREECE.*
J.H. YOUNG, 24:JUL72-507
FINLEY, M.I. A HISTORY OF SICILY.*
(VOL 1)
P. GAUTHIER, 555:VOL45FASC1-137
FINLEY, M.I. - SEE THUCYDIDES
FINN, R.W. THE NORMAN CONQUEST AND ITS
EFFECTS ON THE ECONOMY: 1066-86.
J. BEELER, 589:APR72-308
FINNERAN, R.J. - SEE YEATS, W.B.
FINNEY, B.H. "SINCE HOW IT IS."
617(TLS):12OCT73-1217
FINNEY, J. MARION'S WALL.
M. LEVIN, 441:15APR73-34
FINNIGAN, J. IT WAS WARM AND SUNNY WHEN
WE SET OUT.*
M. FIAMENGO, 102(CANL):SUMMER72-104
R. GUSTAFSON, 529(QQ):SPRING71-140
FINZI, C. - SEE MOROSINI, D.
FINZI, G. - SEE CAMERANA, G.
FINZI, J. A POINT OF DEPARTURE.
L. BONNEROT, 189(EA):OCT-DEC70-452
FIORI, G. ANTONIO GRAMSCI.*
42(AR):WINTER71/72-594
FIORI, T., ED. ARCHIVI DEL DIVISIONISMO.
M.W. MARTIN, 54:DEC71-547
FIRE, J. & R. ERDOES. LAME DEER.*
617(TLS):6JUL73-780
FIRESIDE, H. ICON AND SWASTIKA.
M. BOURDEAUX, 32:MAR72-175
J.S. CURTISS, 550(RUSR):OCT71-410
FIRMICUS MATERNUS. THE ERROR OF THE PAGAN
RELIGIONS. (C.A. FORBES, TRANS)
R.J. WURTZ, 122:JUL72-221
FIRPO, L. - SEE VERGIL
FIRTH, F. - SEE PIRANDELLO, L.
FIRTH, J.R. SELECTED PAPERS OF J.R.
FIRTH, 1952-59.* (F.L. PALMER, ED)
P.B. PANDIT, 297(JL):SEP70-280
FISCHEL, W.J. JEWS IN THE ECONOMIC AND
POLITICAL LIFE OF MEDIEVAL ISLAM.
J. LASSNER, 318(JAOS):OCT-DEC71-539
FISCHER, A. DIE PHILOSOPHISCHE GRUND-
LAGEN DER WISSENSCHAFTLICHEN ERKENNT-
NIS. (2ND ED)
R. BLANCHÉ, 542:OCT-DEC70-490
FISCHER, B., S. MARGULIES & D. MOSENFEL-
DER. BOBBY FISCHER TEACHES CHESS.
617(TLS):30MAR73-362
FISCHER, D.H. HISTORIANS' FALLACIES.
K.J. HANSEN, 529(QQ):AUTUMN71-471
R.A. SKOTHEIM, 656(WMQ):APR71-318
FISCHER, E. ART AGAINST IDEOLOGY.
W.H. TRUITT, 290(JAAC):SPRING71-417
FISCHER, F.W. MAX BECKMANN.
617(TLS):24AUG73-980
FISCHER, H., ED. ENGLISH SATIRICAL
POETRY FROM JOSEPH HALL TO PERCY B.
SHELLEY.
B-F., 566:AUTUMN71-5
FISCHER, H. STUDIEN ZUR DEUTSCHEN MÄREN-
DICHTUNG DES 15. JAHRHUNDERTS.*
J.L. FLOOD, 220(GL&L):APR72-320
D. HUSCHENBETT, 224(GRM):MAY70-222
H-R., 657(WW):MAR/APR70-135
FISCHER, H. - SEE KRAUS, K.
FISCHER, H.C. & E. KOCK. LUDWIG VAN
BEETHOVEN.
617(TLS):16FEB73-170

FISCHER, I., ED. DIE HANDSCHRIFTEN DER
NIEDERSACHSISCHEN STAATS- UND UNIVERSI-
TÄTSBIBLIOTHEK GÖTTINGEN.
M. WIERSCHIN, 182:VOL24#7/8-321
FISCHER, J.L. THE CASE OF SOCRATES.*
N. GULLEY, 123:MAR72-118
FISCHER, L. GEBUNDENE REDE.*
W. DIMTER, 490:JUL/OCT70-638
FISCHER, P. & A. WOLFENSTEIN. DER EXPRES-
SIONISMUS UND DIE VERENDENDE KUNST.
T. MEYER, 657(WW):JUL/AUG71-285
FISCHER, T. UNTERSUCHUNGEN ZUM PARTHER-
KRIEG ANTIOCHOS' VII. IM RAHMEN DER
SELEUKIDENGESCHICHTE.
M.A.R. COLLEDGE, 123:DEC72-426
S.I. OOST, 122:JUL72-225
FISH, R.L., WITH H. ROTHBLATT. A HANDY
DEATH.
N. CALLENDAR, 441:28OCT73-49
FISH, S.E. SELF-CONSUMING ARTIFACTS.
617(TLS):7SEP73-1025
FISH, S.E. SURPRISED BY SIN.*
P. GRANT, 376:OCT71-129
FISHER, A.G.B. & H.J. SLAVERY AND MUSLIM
SOCIETY IN AFRICA.
H. DESCHAMPS, 69:JUL71-260
FISHER, A.L. & G.B. MURRAY, EDS. PHILOSO-
PHY AND SCIENCE AS MODES OF KNOWING.
L.G., 543:JUN71-764
FISHER, A.W. THE RUSSIAN ANNEXATION OF
THE CRIMEA, 1772-1783.*
A.S. DONNELLY, 550(RUSR):JAN71-88
J.E. MANDAVILLE, 318(JAOS):OCT-DEC71-
541
R.A. PIERCE, 529(QQ):SUMMER71-329
FISHER, D. COMMERCIAL ENGLISH COMPRE-
HENSION PASSAGES.
A. MOULIN, 556(RLV):1970/3-329
FISHER, E.M. & M.C. BASSIOUNI. STORM OVER
THE ARAB WORLD.*
P. GROSE, 441:21JAN73-4
FISHER, J. FUNNY WAY TO BE A HERO.
617(TLS):24AUG73-986
FISHER, J.E. SYLLOGE NUMMORUM GRAECORUM:
THE COLLECTION OF THE AMERICAN NUMIS-
MATIC SOCIETY. (PT 1)
C.M. KRAAY, 123:MAR72-141
FISHER, J.H., GENERAL ED. THE MEDIEVAL
LITERATURE OF WESTERN EUROPE.
J.A.W.B., 382(MAE):1972/3-240
H. GNEUSS, 38:BAND88HEFT1-99
FISHER, N. THE LAST ASSIGNMENT.
N. CALLENDAR, 441:5AUG73-10
FISHER, N. IAIN MACLEOD.
R. CROSSMAN, 362:17MAY73-657
617(TLS):11MAY73-515
FISHER, R. COLLECTED POEMS 1968.
R. FULTON, 565:VOL11#1-68
C. LEVENSON, 529(QQ):SUMMER71-309
E. MOTTRAM, 565:VOL11#1-9
FISHER, R. DEAR ISRAELIS, DEAR ARABS.*
P. GROSE, 441:21JAN73-4
FISHER, R. THE SHIP'S ORCHESTRA.
E. MOTTRAM, 565:VOL11#1-9
FISHER, R. TWILIGHT TALES OF THE BLACK
BAGANDA. (M. POSNANSKY, ED)
J. BEATTIE, 69:JUL71-251
FISHER, S. THE FEMALE ORGASM.*
A. COMFORT, 362:26APR73-549
FISHMAN, J.A., ED. ADVANCES IN THE
SOCIOLOGY OF LANGUAGES.
617(TLS):3AUG73-909
FISHMAN, J.A. LANGUAGE IN SOCIOCULTURAL
CHANGE.
617(TLS):3AUG73-909
FISHMAN, J.A. SOCIOLINGUISTICS.
R. BURLING, 350:MAR72-233
E. TARONE, 399(MLJ):FEB71-116

FISIAK, J. A SHORT GRAMMAR OF MIDDLE
ENGLISH. (PT 1)
L.W. COLLIER, 382(MAE):1972/2-177
R.D. STEVICK, 589:JAN72-119
R.M. WILSON, 402(MLR):JAN72-163
FISTIÉ, P. SOUS-DÉVELOPPEMENT ET UTOPIE
AU SIAM.
N. SNIDVONGS, 293(JAST):NOV70-238
FITCH, B.T. DIMENSIONS ET STRUCTURES
CHEZ BERNANOS.
E. BEAUMONT, 208(FS):APR72-223
M. ESTÈVE, 98:DEC70-1023
E.M. O'SHARKEY, 402(MLR):JUL72-657
FITCH, B.T. NARRATEUR ET NARRATION DANS
"L'ÉTRANGER" D'ALBERT CAMUS. (2ND ED)
R. BALIBAR, 535(RHL):JUL-AUG70-736
I.H. WALKER, 208(FS):JUL72-360
FITCH, B.T. & OTHERS. ALBERT CAMUS:
AUTOUR DE "L'ETRANGER."
W.W. HOLDHEIM, 188(ECR):SPRING70-90
W.D. REDFERN, 546(RR):APR71-160
FITCHEN, J. THE NEW WORLD DUTCH BARN.*
F.W.B. CHARLES, 46:APR70-316
FITTING, M.C. INTUITIONISTIC LOGIC
MODEL THEORY AND FORCING.
F.R. DRAKE, 316:MAR71-166
FITZ, J. DIE LAUFBAHN DER STATTHALTER IN
DER RÖMISCHEN PROVINZ MOESIA INFERIOR.
E. BIRLEY, 313:VOL61-274
FITZ-GERALD, D., ED. GEORGIAN FURNITURE.
N. GOODISON, 90:FEB71-101
G. WILLS, 39:NOV71-421
FITZ-GERALD, D. THE NORFOLK HOUSE MUSIC
ROOM.
617(TLS):22JUN73-708
FITZ GERALD, F. FIRE IN THE LAKE.*
M. BELL, 362:11JAN73-55
617(TLS):12JAN73-27
FITZGERALD, F.S. THE BASIL AND JOSEPHINE
STORIES. (J. KUEHL & J. BRYER, EDS)
N. BALAKIAN, 441:20CT73-47
FITZGERALD, F.S. & M. PERKINS. DEAR
SCOTT/DEAR MAX.* (J. KUEHL & J.R.
BRYER, EDS)
617(TLS):18MAY73-546
FITZ GERALD, G. TOWARDS A NEW IRELAND.*
C.C. O'BRIEN, 453:25JAN73-36
FITZGERALD, R. SPRING SHADE.*
R. OLIVER, 598(SOR):SPRING73-492
FITZ GERALD, R.D. - SEE MC CRAE, H.
FITZGERALD, S. & R. - SEE O'CONNOR, F.
FITZ GIBBON, C. A CONCISE HISTORY OF
GERMANY.
442(NY):16JUL73-79
617(TLS):5JAN73-21
FITZ GIBBON, C. IN THE BUNKER.
S. HILL, 362:22MAR73-390
M. LEVIN, 441:17JUN73-28
442(NY):6AUG73-87
617(TLS):23MAR73-313
FITZ GIBBON, C. THE LIFE AND TIMES OF
EAMON DE VALERA.
617(TLS):14SEP73-1043
FITZGIBBON, L. THE KATYN COVER-UP.
617(TLS):2FEB73-133
"GEORGE FITZMAURICE: FOLK PLAYS."
A. RENDLE, 157:SUMMER70-75
FITZPATRICK, S. THE COMMISSARIAT OF
ENLIGHTENMENT.*
D.A. LAW, 550(RUSR):OCT71-405
J.J. TOMIAK, 575(SEER):JUL72-472
FITZSIMONS, R. BARNUM IN LONDON.
B. GUINNESS, 39:APR70-322
FITZSIMONS, R. THE CHARLES DICKENS SHOW.
J.G., 155:JAN71-54
"FIVE NEW GUINEA PLAYS."
M. WILDING, 581:SEP72-235
FLACELIÈRE, R. - SEE EURIPIDES

114

FLACELIÈRE, R. & É. CHAMBRY - SEE PLU-
TARCH
FLAGG, J.B. THE LIFE AND LETTERS OF
WASHINGTON ALLSTON.
M. FRIEDLAENDER, 432(NEQ):SEP71-523
FLAHERTY, J. FOGARTY & CO.
S. BLACKBURN, 441:28JAN73-6
C. LEHMANN-HAUPT, 441:4JAN73-39
FLAKER, A. & K. PRANJIĆ, EDS. HRVATSKA
KNJIŽEVNOST PREMA EVROPSKIM KNJIŽEV-
NOSTIMA OD NARODNOG PREPORODA K NAŠIM
DANIMA.
A. KADIĆ, 32:SEP72-722
FLAMAND, J. L'IDÉE DE MÉDIATION CHEZ
MAURICE BLONDEL.
M. RENAULT, 154:DEC70-415
FLANAGAN, R. THE HUNTING VARIETY.
N. CALLENDAR, 441:23SEP73-48
FLANNER, J. PARIS WAS YESTERDAY: 1925-
1939.* (I. DRUTMAN, ED)
617(TLS):7SEP73-1019
FLASCHE, H., ED. AUFSÄTZE ZUR PORTUGIES-
ISCHEN KULTURGESCHICHTE. (VOL 8)
N.J. LAMB, 86(BHS):JUL72-316
FLASCHE, H., ED. LITTERAE HISPANAE ET
LUSITANAE.*
G. SOBEJANO, 240(HR):JAN71-76
FLASCHE, H. DIE STRUKTUR DES AUTO SAC-
RAMENTAL "LOS ENCANTOS DE LA CULPA" VON
CALDERÓN.
A.L. MACKENZIE, 86(BHS):JAN72-79
FLATHMAN, R.E. POLITICAL OBLIGATION.
617(TLS):25MAY73-580
FLAUBERT, G. CORRESPONDANCE. (VOL 1)
(J. BRUNEAU, ED)
617(TLS):3AUG73-904
FLAUBERT, G. FLAUBERT IN EGYPT.* (F.
STEEGMULLER, ED & TRANS)
W.H. AUDEN, 442(NY):2JUL73-72
G. BRÉE, 441:29APR73-3
A. BROYARD, 441:22MAR73-47
FLAUBERT, G. MADAME BOVARY. (C. GOTHOT-
MERSCH, ED)
A. FAIRLIE, 208(FS):OCT72-464
FLECHTHEIM, O.K. STORIA E FUTUROLOGIA.
M. DEL VECCHIO, 548(RCSF):JAN-MAR70-
106
FLEET, B. BULLETS AND CATHEDRALS.*
C.X. RINGROSE, 102(CANL):SPRING72-87
FLEETWOOD, H. FOREIGN AFFAIRS.
R. BLYTHE, 362:29NOV73-752
617(TLS):7DEC73-1495
FLEETWOOD, H. THE GIRL WHO PASSED FOR
NORMAL.
N. CALLENDAR, 441:22JUL73-14
FLEISCHER, N. JACK DEMPSEY.
441:25FEB73-22
FLEISCHMANN, C. MARK IN TIME. (N. HAR-
VEY, ED)
42(AR):SUMMER71-285
FLEISCHMANN, W.B., GENERAL ED. ENCYCLO-
PEDIA OF WORLD LITERATURE IN THE 20TH
CENTURY.* (VOLS 1&2)
F. STOCK, 52:BAND6HEFT2-192
FLEISHER, M., ED. MACHIAVELLI AND THE
NATURE OF POLITICAL THOUGHT.
617(TLS):4MAY73-502
FLEISHMAN, A. THE ENGLISH HISTORICAL
NOVEL: WALTER SCOTT TO VIRGINIA WOOLF.
R. LEHAN, 445(NCF):DEC71-366
K.J. LONG, 648:APR72-21
J.H. RALEIGH, 191(ELN):JUN72-326
H. SMITH, 376:OCT71-127
FLEISSER, M. GESAMMELTE WERKE. (G.
RÜHLE, ED)
617(TLS):12OCT73-1218

FLEMING, A. A PIECE OF TRUTH.
S. SCHLESINGER, 441:8APR73-12
442(NY):21APR73-135
453:5APR73-37
617(TLS):19JAN73-58
FLEMING, G.H. ROSSETTI AND THE PRE-
RAPHAELITE BROTHERHOOD.
J-J. MAYOUX, 98:MAR70-210
FLEMING, J. ALAS POOR FATHER.
N. CALLENDAR, 441:11FEB73-30
FLEMING, J. YOU WON'T LET ME FINISH.
617(TLS):26OCT73-1324
FLEMING, J.V. THE "ROMAN DE LA ROSE."
J.A.W. BENNETT, 447(N&Q):MAY71-187
W. CALIN, 589:APR72-311
C.R. DAHLBERG, 149:MAR72-95
A. DAVID, 191(ELN):DEC71-134
A.M.F. GUNN, 405(MP):AUG71-57
W.L. HENDRICKSON, 207(FR):OCT70-248
FLEMING, T. THE FORGOTTEN VICTORY.
G.F. SCHEER, 441:16DEC73-12
FLEMING, T. - SEE FRANKLIN, B.
FLEMMING, W. ANDREAS GRYPHIUS.*
A.G. DE CAPUA, 133:1970/2&3-298
FLESSAU, K-I. DER MORALISCHE ROMAN.
H-J. ILSMANN, 654(WB):7/1971-174
FLETCHER, A. THE PROPHETIC MOMENT.
J. APTEKAR, 551(RENQ):WINTER71-560
H. BLOOM, 639(VQR):SUMMER71-477
A.C. HAMILTON, 529(QQ):AUTUMN71-480
H. MACLEAN, 301(JEGP):APR72-243
FLETCHER, A. THE TRANSCENDENTAL MASQUE.
C.J. SUMMERS, 651(WHR):SUMMER72-284
FLETCHER, C.M. COMMUNICATION IN MEDICINE.
617(TLS):13JUL73-815
FLETCHER, G. THE ENGLISH WORKS OF GILES
FLETCHER THE ELDER. (L.E. BERRY, ED)
W. BLISSETT, 179(ES):FEB71-66
FLETCHER, J. THE PAINTED CHURCHES OF
ROMANIA.
617(TLS):23FEB73-215
FLETCHER, J. PETER PAUL RUBENS.
G. MARTIN, 39:MAY71-437
FLETCHER, J. & B.S. - SEE BECKETT, S.
FLETCHER, J. & P. MASSINGER. BEGGARS
BUSH. (J.A. DORENKAMP, ED)
H. GRABES, 38:BAND88HEFT2-263
FLETCHER, J. & J. SPURLING. BECKETT.
617(TLS):12OCT73-1217
FLETCHER, L. SILVER.
617(TLS):27JUL73-884
FLETCHER, W.C. RELIGION AND SOVIET FOR-
EIGN POLICY 1945-1970.
617(TLS):27APR73-459
FLETCHER-COOKE, J. THE EMPEROR'S GUEST
1942-45.
617(TLS):19JAN73-74
FLEW, A. CRIME OR DISEASE?
M. WARNOCK, 362:12APR73-488
617(TLS):2MAR73-242
FLEW, A. AN INTRODUCTION TO WESTERN
PHILOSOPHY.*
C. WRIGHT, 518:MAY72-16
42(AR):SUMMER71-289
FLEXNER, J.T. GEORGE WASHINGTON. (VOL 3)
D. JACKSON, 639(VQR):SPRING71-299
R.H. KOHN, 656(WMQ):OCT71-667
FLEXNER, J.T. GEORGE WASHINGTON.* (VOL
4)
B. BLIVEN, JR., 442(NY):10MAR73-131
FLINT, F.C. AMY LOWELL.
R. ASSELINEAU, 189(EA):JUL-SEP71-348
FLINT, R.W. - SEE MARINETTI, F.T.
FLINT, W.R. IN PURSUIT.
F.G.R., 135:MAY71-62
FLORENCE, R. FRITZ.
C.A. MACARTNEY, 32:MAR72-211

FLORES, J.M.  POETRY IN EAST GERMANY.*
P. HUTCHINSON, 220(GL&L):APR72-297
A. HUYSSEN, 406:SPRING72-94
H. WINTER, 32:JUN72-515
639(VQR):SUMMER71-CXII
FLORES, S.R. - SEE UNDER RECIO FLORES, S.
"FLORIS AND BLAUNCHEFLUR." (F.C. DE
VRIES, ED)
A. ZETTERSTEN, 179(ES):AUG71-359
FLOROS, C.  UNIVERSALE NEUMENKUNDE.
M. VELIMIROVIĆ, 317:FALL72-479
E.J.W., 410(M&L):JAN72-79
FLOTO, I.  COLONEL HOUSE IN PARIS.
617(TLS):10AUG73-929
FLOTTES, P.  VIGNY ET SA FORTUNE LITTÉR-
AIRE.
205(FMLS):OCT71-413
FLOWER, J.E.  "LES ANGES NOIRS" DE FRAN-
ÇOIS MAURIAC.
J. ONIMUS, 535(RHL):MAR-APR71-330
FLOWER, J.E.  INTENTION AND ACHIEVEMENT.*
J.C. MC LAREN, 207(FR):MAY71-1127
R.J. NORTH, 208(FS):APR72-222
FLOWER, S.J.  BULWER-LYTTON.
617(TLS):15JUN73-699
FLYNN, G.C. - SEE BAROJA, P.
FLYNN, J.R.  HUMANISM AND IDEOLOGY.
617(TLS):1JUN73-612
FLYS, M.J.  LA POESÍA EXISTENCIAL DE
DÁMASO ALONSO.*
J. GONZÁLEZ MUELA, 202(FMOD):NOV70/
FEB71-164
FOAKES, R.A.  SHAKESPEARE: THE DARK COME-
DIES TO THE LAST PLAYS.*
G. THOMAS, 175:AUTUMN71-102
FODOR, I.  THE RATE OF LINGUISTIC CHANGE.
I. DYEN, 269(IJAL):APR71-130
FODOR, J.A.  PSYCHOLOGICAL EXPLANATION.
C. TAYLOR, 482(PHR):JAN71-108
FOERSTER, O.H.  EUROPAEISCHE KUNST.
A. WERNER, 127:WINTER71/72-230
FOERSTER, W., ED.  GNOSIS.  (VOL 1)
617(TLS):19JAN73-74
FOERSTER, W.  WÖRTERBUCH ZU KRISTIAN VON
TROYES' SÄMTLICHEN WERKEN.  (3RD ED REV
BY H. BREUER)
T.B.W. REID, 47(ARL):VOL17FASC1-62
FOGELIN, R.J.  EVIDENCE AND MEANING.*
K. BAIER, 321:SPRING70-77
FOGELQUIST, D.  ESPAÑOLES DE AMÉRICA Y
AMERICANOS DE ESPAÑA.
M. D'AMBROSIO DE SERVODIDIO, 546(RR):
APR71-151
FOGLE, R.H.  HAWTHORNE'S IMAGERY.
W.J. FREE, 219(GAR):FALL70-364
E. STOCK, 445(NCF):MAR71-485
FOHNAL, B.  PŘEKLADATEL A BÁSNIK PETR
KŘIČKA A ČEZKÉ I CIZÍ PŘEKLADY Z PUŠ-
KINA.
75:2/1971-42
FOHRER, G.  HISTORY OF ISRAELITE RELI-
GION.
617(TLS):19OCT73-1285
FOLEY, M., ED.  THE BEST AMERICAN SHORT
STORIES 1973.
A. BROYARD, 441:12SEP73-51
FOLEY, M. & D. BURNETT, EDS.  THE BEST
AMERICAN SHORT STORIES 1970.
J.B. MOORE, 573(SSF):SUMMER71-478
639(VQR):SPRING71-LVI
FOLEY, M. & D. BURNETT, EDS.  THE BEST
AMERICAN SHORT STORIES: 1971.
S-F. PICKERING, 569(SR):SUMMER72-499
"FOLGER SHAKESPEARE LIBRARY: CATALOG OF
THE SHAKESPEARE COLLECTION."
617(TLS):16NOV73-1408
"FOLKLORE, MYTHS AND LEGENDS OF BRITAIN."
617(TLS):20JUL73-841

FOLLAIN, J.  TRANSPARENCE OF THE WORLD.
R.S., 376:APR71-127
FOLSOM, M.H.  THE SYNTAX OF SUBSTANTIVE
AND NON-FINITE SATELLITES TO THE FINITE
VERB IN GERMAN.
K. BRINKER, 361:VOL25#4-432
FOLTIN, L.B. & H. HEINEN, EDS.  PATHS TO
GERMAN POETRY.*
R.H. WOOLLEY, 220(GL&L):JAN72-185
FOLTINEK, H.  VORSTUFEN ZUM VIKTORIAN-
ISCHEN REALISMUS.*
J. DELBAERE-GARANT, 179(ES):JUN71-276
H. OPPEL, 430(NS):MAR70-155
FONER, E.  FREE SOIL, FREE LABOR, FREE
MEN.*
F.J. MILLER, 432(NEQ):SEP71-505
DA FONSECA, C., ED.  PORTUGIESISCHE
LYRIK DER RENAISSANCE.
J. HORRENT, 556(RLV):1971/4-500
FONTANE, T.  SÄMTLICHE WERKE.  (VOL 1 ED
BY J. KOLBE; VOL 2 ED BY S. GERNDT)
F.R. SCHRÖDER, 224(GRM):AUG70-359
FONTEIN, J. & M.L. HICKMAN.  ZEN PAINTING
AND CALLIGRAPHY.
R. LEIBOWITZ, 58:NOV71-14
FONTINELL, E.  TOWARD A RECONSTRUCTION OF
RELIGION.
G.A. MC COOL, 613:SPRING71-145
FONVIEILLE-ALQUIER, F.  THE FRENCH AND
THE PHONEY WAR 1939-40.
617(TLS):17AUG73-957
FOOT, M.  ANEURIN BEVAN.  (VOL 2)
E. POWELL, 362:11OCT73-489
617(TLS):12OCT73-1233
FOOT, M.R.D., ED.  WAR AND SOCIETY.
617(TLS):7DEC73-1503
FOOTE, P. & D.M. WILSON.  THE VIKING
ACHIEVEMENT.*
R.I. PAGE, 382(MAE):1972/1-89
FORBES, C.  TARGET FIVE.
N. CALLENDAR, 441:9SEP73-40
FORBES, I.  SQUAD MAN.
617(TLS):17AUG73-961
FORBES, T.R.  CHRONICLE FROM ALDGATE.
568(SCN):SPRING72-13
639(VQR):AUTUMN71-CLXXXIV
FORCIONE, A.K.  CERVANTES, ARISTOTLE AND
THE "PERSILES."*
S. ZIMIC, 399(MLJ):OCT71-412
639(VQR):SPRING71-LXVI
FORD, A.  THE LIFE BEYOND DEATH.
617(TLS):16FEB73-190
FORD, B.J.  THE EARTH WATCHERS.
617(TLS):1JUN73-625
FORD, F.M.  CRITICAL WRITINGS OF FORD
MADOX FORD.  (F. MAC SHANE, ED)
R.A. CASSELL, 136:VOL3#1-115
FORD, F.M.  RETURN TO YESTERDAY.*
J.J. KIRSCHKE, 31(ASCH):AUTUMN73-702
FORD, F.M.  SELECTED POEMS.  (B. BUNTING,
ED)
J. ATLAS, 491:JAN73-229
FORD, F.M.  YOUR MIRROR TO MY TIMES.*
(M. KILLIGREW, ED)
C-X. RINGROSE, 150(DR):WINTER71/72-615
FORD, G.  THIS TIME.
M. CZARNECKI, 648:JUN70-37
FORD, G.B., JR. - SEE ST. ISIDORE OF
SEVILLE
FORD, G.B., JR. - SEE MAŽVYDAS, M.
FORD, H. - SEE CUNARD, N.
FORD, P.L., ED.  PAMPHLETS ON THE CONSTI-
TUTION OF THE UNITED STATES.
S.M. COOPER, 447(N&Q):SEP71-349
FORDERER, M.  ANFANG UND ENDE DER ABEND-
LÄNDISCHEN LYRIK.
F. LASSERRE, 182:VOL24#3-103

FORDHAM, P. THE VILLAINS.
441:2SEP73-14
"FOREIGN POLICY FOR CANADIANS."
I.M. ABELLA, 529(QQ):SPRING71-143
FORESTIER, L. CHARLES CROS, L'HOMME ET
L'OEUVRE.
S.I. LOCKERBIE, 208(FS):JUL72-347
M. SCHAETTEL, 557(RSH):OCT-DEC70-647
FOREY, A.J. THE TEMPLARS IN THE "CORONA
DE ARAGON."
617(TLS):5OCT73-1171
FORGE, A. ROBERT RAUSCHENBERG.
T. HILTON, 592:NOV70-207
FORGUE, G.J. H.L. MENCKEN.
M. CUNLIFFE, 189(EA):APR-JUN70-231
FORMA, W. THE FALLING MAN.
M. LEVIN, 441:14OCT73-48
FORMAN, D. MOZART'S CONCERTO FORM.*
J.B., 412:FEB72-71
A.H., 410(M&L):JUL72-329
A. HUTCHINGS, 415:FEB72-151
FORMENTI, A.G. MEXICO, COUNTRY OF LIGHT.
A.G.F., 135:OCT70-138
FORMIGARI, L. LINGUISTICA ED EMPIRISMO
NEL SEICENTO INGLESE.
J.L. DELAPLAIN, 481(PQ):JUL71-354
FORNARA, C.W. HERODOTUS.
F.R. BLISS, 124:FEB72-205
F.J. FROST, 122:JUL72-220
FORNARI, H. MUSSOLINI'S GADFLY.
617(TLS):2MAR73-225
FORNER Y SEGARRA, J.P. LOS GRAMATICOS.
(J. JURADO, ED)
R.G. KEIGHTLEY, 86(BHS):JUL72-305
FORNER Y SEGARRA, J.P. LOS GRAMATICOS,
HISTORIA CHINESCA. (J.H.R. POLT, ED)
R.G. KEIGHTLEY, 86(BHS):JUL72-305
I.L. MC CLELLAND, 402(MLR):JAN72-199
FORNI, G. IL SOGNO FINITO.
M. RIESER, 319:JUL73-430
FORREST, D. TEA FOR THE BRITISH.
E.S. TURNER, 362:26APR73-552
617(TLS):20APR73-447
FORREST, E.R. WITH A CAMERA IN OLD
NAVAHOLAND.
B. TOELKEN, 650(WF):OCT70-268
FORREST, L. THERE IS A TREE MORE ANCIENT
THAN EDEN.
A. BROYARD, 441:8JUN73-43
L.J. DAVIS, 441:21OCT73-48
"FORSCHUNGEN ZUR OSTEUROPAISCHEN GESCHICH-
TE."* (VOL 15) (M. BERNATH, H. JABLON-
OVSKI & W. PHILIPP, EDS)
J. KEEP, 575(SEER):APR72-303
J. RABA, 104:WINTER72-646
FORSHAW, H.P. - SEE EDMUND OF ABINGDON
FORSTER, E.M. ALBERGO EMPEDOCLE AND
OTHER WRITINGS.
M. MUDRICK, 249(HUDR):SPRING72-142
FORSTER, E.M. GOLDSWORTHY LOWES DICKIN-
SON AND RELATED WRITINGS.
617(TLS):21SEP73-1085
FORSTER, E.M. THE LIFE TO COME AND OTHER
STORIES.*
A. BROYARD, 441:4JUN73-33
K. MILLER, 453:28JUN73-9
E. WELTY, 441:13MAY73-27
F. WYNDHAM, 362:22MAR73-378
FORSTER, E.M. MAURICE.*
M. MUDRICK, 249(HUDR):SPRING72-142
S. SPENDER, 473(PR):1/1972-113
42(AR):FALL71-439
FORSTER, E.M. TWO CHEERS FOR DEMOCRACY.
(NEW ED) (O. STALLYBRASS, ED)
617(TLS):16FEB73-177

FORSTER, L. JANUS GRUTER'S ENGLISH
YEARS.*
G.C. SCHOOLFIELD, 568(SCN):SUMMER72-
41
FORSTER, L. THE ICY FIRE.*
A. CIORANESCU, 549(RLC):OCT-DEC70-550
A. GERARD, 556(RLV):1971/3-348
D.L. GUSS, 149:MAR72-100
H-J. LOPE, 52:BAND6HEFT3-329
H. MELLER, 72:BAND209HEFT4/6-391
F.J. WARNKE, 401(MLQ):MAR71-107
M. WHITE, 208(FS):OCT72-443
205(FMLS):OCT70-421
FORSTER, L. DIE NIEDERLANDE UND DIE
ANFANGE DER BAROCKLYRIK IN DEUTSCHLAND.
J. BARTHELS, 556(RLV):1970/2-218
FORSTER, L. THE POET'S TONGUES.*
G.C. SCHOOLFIELD, 563(SS):WINTER72-153
G. STEINER, 111:19FEB71-149
FORSTER, M.H., ED. LA MUERTE EN LA
POESIA MEXICANA.
S. KARSEN, 238:MAY71-402
FORSTER, R. & J.P. GREENE, EDS. PRECON-
DITIONS OF REVOLUTION IN EARLY MODERN
EUROPE.
639(VQR):SUMMER71-CXXIII
FORSYTH, G.H. & K. WEITZMANN. THE MON-
ASTERY OF SAINT CATHERINE AT MOUNT
SINAI.
J. CANADAY, 441:2DEC73-89
FORSYTH, J. A GRAMMAR OF ASPECT.*
A.V. ISACENKO, 350:SEP72-715
T-F. MAGNER, 32:MAR72-202
205(FMLS):JAN71-94
FORSYTH, J. - SEE VINOKUR, G.O.
FORSYTH, W.H. THE ENTOMBMENT OF CHRIST.
J. SEZNEC, 208(FS):JAN72-67
FORTINI, F. QUESTO MURO 1962-1972.
617(TLS):5OCT73-1176
"THE FORTY-SECOND VOLUME OF THE WALPOLE
SOCIETY 1968-1970."
R. EDWARDS, 39:JAN71-68
FOSCOLO, U. ESPERIMENTI DI TRADUZIONE
DELL'ILIADE. (G. BARBARISI, ED)
G. FISCHETTI, 228(GSLI):VOL147FASC
460-558
FOSS, M. TUDOR PORTRAITS.
617(TLS):20JUL73-841
FOSSIER, R. HISTOIRE SOCIALE DE L'OCCI-
DENT MEDIEVAL.
R.D. FACE, 589:JAN72-122
FOSSOUL-RISSELIN, A-M. LE VOCABULAIRE DE
LA VIE FAMILIALE A SAINT-VAAST (1890-
1914).
B. FOSTER, 208(FS):JUL72-367
FOSTER, A.S. GOOD-BYE BOBBY THOMSON!
GOOD-BYE JOHN WAYNE!
J. YARDLEY, 441:13MAY73-37
442(NY):10MAR73-134
FOSTER, B. THE CHANGING ENGLISH LANGUAGE.
W. BRONZWAER, 179(ES):OCT71-471
FOSTER, D.W. & V.R. RESEARCH GUIDE TO
ARGENTINE LITERATURE.
W.L. MEINHARDT, 399(MLJ):MAR71-189
FOSTER, J. CHURCH HISTORY 1.
617(TLS):19JAN73-74
FOSTER, L., ED. BIBLIOGRAPHY OF RUSSIAN
EMIGRE LITERATURE, 1918-1968.
M. SLONIM, 550(RUSR):OCT71-400
FOSTER, M. JOYCE CARY.*
R. LAWRENCE, 175:AUTUMN70-107
FOSTER, M.H. & M.L. MARTIN, EDS. PROBA-
BILITY, CONFIRMATION, AND SIMPLICITY.
D. MILLER, 316:SEP70-451
FOSTER, P. HEIMSKRINGLA OR THE STONED
ANGELS.
A. RENDLE, 157:AUTUMN71-82

117

FOTHERGILL, B. SIR WILLIAM HAMILTON.*
J.L-M., 135:JAN70-48
FOTHERGILL, J. CHAIN OF FRIENDSHIP.
(B.C. CORNER & C.C. BOOTH, EDS)
E.B. BRONNER, 656(WMQ):OCT71-688
F.W. HILLES, 676(YR):AUTUMN71-109
FOTION, N. MORAL SITUATIONS.
R. ABELSON, 482(PHR):JAN71-122
FOUCAULT, M. THE ARCHAEOLOGY OF KNOW-
LEDGE.* (FRENCH TITLE: L'ARCHÉOLOGIE
DU SAVOIR.)
I. HACKING, 111:2JUN72-166
F. KERMODE, 453:17MAY73-37
FOUCAULT, M. MADNESS AND CIVILIZATION.
G.S. ROUSSEAU, 173(ECS):FALL70-90
FOUCAULT, M. THE ORDER OF THINGS.
J. CULLER, 111:29JAN71-104
FOUGERET DE MONBRON. LE COSMOPOLITE OU
LE CITOYEN DU MONDE, SUIVI DE LA CAPI-
TALE DES GAULES OU LA NOUVELLE BABY-
LONE. (R. TROUSSON, ED)
J.H. BROOME, 402(MLR):OCT72-892
FOUGEYROLLAS, P. LA RÉVOLUTION FREUD-
IENNE.
Y. BRÈS, 542:APR-JUN71-189
R. JACCARD, 98:FEB71-190
FOURCADE, D. - SEE MATISSE, H.
FOURIER, C. OEUVRES COMPLÈTES.
R. BARTHES, 98:OCT70-789
FOURQUET, J. PROLEGOMENA ZU EINER DEUT-
SCHEN GRAMMATIK.
A. ALTMANN, 682(ZPSK):BAND23HEFT6-616
FOURQUET, J. WOLFRAM D'ESCHENBACH ET LE
CONTE DEL GRAL.
G. MEISSBURGER, 657(WW):MAY/JUN70-209
FOWKES, R.A. - SEE VON EICHENDORFF, J.
FOWLER, A., ED. SILENT POETRY.
T.A. SHIPPEY, 402(MLR):JAN72-161
639(VQR):WINTER71-XXVI
FOWLER, A. TRIUMPHAL FORMS.*
A.K. HIEATT, 551(RENQ):WINTER71-557
N.L. RUDENSTINE, 191(ELN):JUN72-295
G. THOMAS, 175:AUTUMN71-102
FOWLER, D.C. A LITERARY HISTORY OF THE
POPULAR BALLAD.*
W.E. RICHMOND, 223:JUN70-198
FOWLER, F.M. - SEE SCHILLER, F.
FOWLER, R., ED. OLD ENGLISH PROSE AND
VERSE.
P.W., 206:NOV70-595
FOWLER, R. & OTHERS. THE LANGUAGES OF
LITERATURE.
M.H. SHORT, 402(MLR):OCT72-866
G. STEINER, 111:5MAY72-143
FOWLER, W. STENDHAL.
J.S.P., 191(ELN):SEP71(SUPP)-109
FOWLES, A. DOUBLE FEATURE.
N. CALLENDAR, 441:27MAY73-19
FOWLES, J. THE FRENCH LIEUTENANT'S
WOMAN.*
J. DITSKY, 628:FALL70-91
R.B. EATON, JR., 636(VP):SPRING70-79
J.B. GORDON, 598(SOR):WINTER73-217
J.P., 376:JUL70-114
FOWLIE, W. THE FRENCH CRITIC: 1549-1967.*
A. GLAUSER, 546(RR):FEB71-81
FOX, C. THE JOURNALS OF CAROLINE FOX
(1835-1871). (W. MONK, ED)
617(TLS):7SEP73-1022
FOX, D. - SEE HENRYSON, R.
FOX, E.I. - SEE MARTÍNEZ RUIZ, J.
FOX, E.S. & E.H. CHRIST IS GOD'S MIDDLE
NAME.
M. LAVANOUX, 363:MAY71-84
FOX, G. BRITAIN AND JAPAN 1858-1883.
G. DANIELS, 293(JAST):NOV70-191
R. DINGMAN, 244(HJAS):VOL31-300

FOX, J. THE LYRIC POETRY OF CHARLES
D'ORLÉANS.*
J.C. LAIDLAW, 208(FS):JAN72-66
205(FMLS):APR70-206
FOX, J. & R. WOOD. A CONCISE HISTORY OF
THE FRENCH LANGUAGE.
P.A. GAENG, 207(FR):FEB71-599
FOX, L. EL ROSTRO DE LA PATRIA EN LA
LITERATURA PERUANA.
D.A. YATES, 263:JAN-MAR72-58
FOX, P. DESPERATE CHARACTERS.
C.L. CHUA, 573(SSF):SUMMER71-489
FOX, P. THE WESTERN COAST.*
S. HILL, 362:25JAN73-124
R. SALE, 249(HUDR):WINTER72/73-703
617(TLS):9FEB73-140
FOX, W.L. THE IRON WIND.
J. DITSKY, 628:SPRING72-108
FOXX, J. THE JADE FIGURINE.
N. CALLENDAR, 441:25MAR73-49
VAN FRAASSEN, B.C. AN INTRODUCTION TO
THE PHILOSOPHY OF TIME AND SPACE.
J. EARMAN, 482(PHR):OCT71-516
Y. GAUTHIER, 154:MAR71-199
FRACHON, B. AU RYTHME DES JOURS. (VOL
2)
I.M. WALL, 207(FR):DEC70-398
FRAENKEL, B. - SEE TROTSKY, L.
FRAISSE, R. COURS DE LOGIQUE MATHEMAT-
IQUE. (VOL 1)
D. PONASSE, 316:DEC70-580
FRAKES, G.E. LABORATORY FOR LIBERTY.
L. GRIFFITH, 656(WMQ):OCT71-675
639(VQR):AUTUMN71-CLXXVI
FRAME, D.M. MONTAIGNE'S ESSAIS.*
F. GRAY, 188(ECR):SUMMER70-158
FRAME, J. DAUGHTER BUFFALO.*
617(TLS):26JAN73-85
FRAME, J. INTENSIVE CARE.
A. EDELSTEIN, 598(SOR):SUMMER73-736
FRAMERY, N.E. & OTHERS. ENCYCLOPÉDIE
MÉTHODIQUE [MUSIQUE].
J. RUSHTON, 415:SEP72-868
FRAN, A.P. KENNETH BURKE.
A. HELLER, 430(NS):MAY71-287
FRANCESC DE LA VIA. OBRES II. (A.
PACHECO, ED)
R.G. KEIGHTLEY, 86(BHS):JAN72-102
J.M. SOLÀ-SOLÉ, 240(HR):APR71-234
FRANCESCO DI GIORGIO MARTINI. TRATTATI
DI ARCHITETTURA INGEGNERIA E ARTE MILI-
TARE. (C. MALTESE, ED)
G. SCAGLIA, 54:DEC70-439
P.V., 228(GSLI):VOL147FASC458/459-469
FRANCIONI, M. - SEE MINKOWSKI, E.
FRANCIS, D. SMOKESCREEN.*
P. ADAMS, 61:MAR73-107
N. CALLENDAR, 441:25FEB73-50
442(NY):10MAR73-136
FRANCIS, E. UN AUTRE CLAUDEL.
617(TLS):25MAY73-573
FRANCIS, F., ED. TREASURES OF THE BRIT-
ISH MUSEUM.
H. OSBORNE, 89(BJA):SPRING72-204
FRANCIS, P. - SEE PALMA, R.
FRANCIS, R. THE TROUBLE WITH FRANCIS.*
R.B. SHAW, 491:NOV72-102
FRANCIS, R. - SEE FROST, R.
FRANCISCONO, M. WALTER GROPIUS AND THE
CREATION OF THE BAUHAUS IN WEIMAR.
H. VON ERFFA, 127:SUMMER72-480
R.V. WIEDENHOEFT, 56:WINTER71-487
FRANCK, T.M. & E. WEISBAND. WORD POLI-
TICS.
617(TLS):5JAN73-3

FRANCO, J. AN INTRODUCTION TO SPANISH-
AMERICAN LITERATURE.*
  M.H. FORSTER, 238:MAR71-231
  M.E. VENIER, 400(MLN):MAR71-315
  205(FMLS):JUL70-312
FRANCO, J. SPANISH AMERICAN LITERATURE
SINCE INDEPENDENCE.
  617(TLS):15JUN73-697
FRANDA, M.F. RADICAL POLITICS IN WEST
BENGAL.
  42(AR):WINTER71/72-599
FRANK, C. LA NUIT AMÉRICAINE.
  617(TLS):16FEB73-169
FRANK, H.G. KYBERNETIK UND PHILOSOPHIE.
  H.W. BRANN, 258:MAR71-137
FRANK, J-M. MA FENÊTRE SUR LA FOLIE.
  R.B. JOHNSON, 207(FR):APR71-966
FRANK, M. DIE FARB- UND LICHTSYMBOLIK IM
PROSAWERK HERMAN MELVILLES.
  M. HOENISCH, 38:BAND88HEFT3-407
FRANK, N. LE BRUIT PARMI LE VENT.
  S. FAUCHEREAU, 98:JUL71-626
FRANK, R.I. SCHOLAE PALATINAE.*
  J-P. CALLU, 555:VOL45FASC2-385
  A. CAMERON, 123:MAR72-136
FRANK, W. MEMOIRS OF WALDO FRANK. (A.
TRACHTENBERG, ED)
  H. CLURMAN, 441:23SEP73-42
  442(NY):8OCT73-170
FRANKE, W. AN INTRODUCTION TO THE
SOURCES OF MING HISTORY.*
  C.O. HUCKER, 244(HJAS):VOL30-256
  C. MAC SHERRY, 318(JAOS):OCT-DEC71-519
FRANKEL, H. NOTEN ZU DEN "ARGONAUTIKA"
DES APOLLONIOS.*
  G. LAWALL, 121(CJ):OCT-NOV71-81
FRANKEL, J. CONTEMPORARY INTERNATIONAL
THEORY AND THE BEHAVIOUR OF STATES.
  617(TLS):11MAY73-520
FRANKEL, M.E. CRIMINAL SENTENCES.
  L. OELSNER, 441:13MAY73-4
FRANKFORT, E. VAGINAL POLITICS.
  F. HOWE, 31(ASCH):AUTUMN73-676
FRANKFURT, H.G. DEMONS, DREAMERS, AND
MADMEN.*
  R.N. BECK, 321:SUMMER71-226
  L.G. MILLER, 154:DEC71-839
FRANKL, P. PRINCIPLES OF ARCHITECTURAL
HISTORY. (J.F. O'GORMAN, ED & TRANS)
  S. KOSTOF, 576:DEC71-334
  P. ZUCKER, 290(JAAC):FALL70-139
FRANKLIN, B. BENJAMIN FRANKLIN: A BIOG-
RAPHY IN HIS OWN WORDS.* (T. FLEMING,
ED) THE AUTOBIOGRAPHY OF BENJAMIN
FRANKLIN. (L.W. LABAREE & OTHERS, EDS)
  J.H. PLUMB, 453:19APR73-4
FRANKLIN, B. THE PAPERS OF BENJAMIN
FRANKLIN.* (VOL 14) (L.W. LABAREE, ED)
  639(VQR):WINTER71-XXXII
FRANKLIN, B. THE PAPERS OF BENJAMIN
FRANKLIN. (VOL 16) (W.B. WILLCOX, ED)
  617(TLS):12OCT73-1215
FRANKLIN, B. - SEE STALIN, I.V.
FRANKLIN, H.B. FUTURE PERFECT.
  P. MICHEL, 556(RLV):1971/5-649
FRANKLIN, H.B. THE WAKE OF THE GODS.
  J.G. RIEWALD, 179(ES):APR71-181
FRANKLIN, J. NARRATIVE OF A JOURNEY TO
THE SHORES OF THE POLAR SEA.
  A.W. PURDY, 102(CANL):WINTER72-92
FRANKLIN, R.L. FREEWILL AND DETERMINISM.
  R.C. BUCK, 482(PHR):JAN71-113
  G. NERLICH, 63:MAY72-76
FRANKLIN, S.H. THE EUROPEAN PEASANTRY.
  D. MITRANY, 32:JUN72-417

FRANZ, H. DAS BILD GRIECHENLANDS UND
ITALIENS IN DEN MITTELHOCHDEUTSCHEN
EPISCHEN ERZÄHLUNGEN VOR 1250.
  H. ADOLF, 182:VOL24#6-292
FRANZ, H.G. NIEDERLÄNDISCHE LANDSCHAFTS-
MALEREI IM ZEITALTER DES MANIERISMUS.
  H. MIELKE, 683:BAND34HEFT4-303
FRANZBACH, M. ABRISS DER SPANISCHEN UND
PORTUGIESISCHEN LITERATURGESCHICHTE IN
TABELLEN.
  F. NIEDERMAYER, 430(NS):SEP71-501
FRANZÉN, G. PROSE AND POETRY OF MODERN
SWEDEN.
  R-M. OSTER, 563(SS):SPRING72-284
FRASER, A. CROMWELL.
  C. LEHMANN-HAUPT, 441:23OCT73-51
  K. THOMAS, 362:7JUN73-760
  C.V. WEDGWOOD, 441:28OCT73-7
  B. WORDEN, 453:15NOV73-24
  617(TLS):20JUL73-823
FRASER, A.S. THE HILLS OF HOME.
  617(TLS):22JUN73-717
FRASER, B. - SEE GOWERS, E.
"BLAIR FRASER REPORTS." (J. & G. FRASER,
EDS)
  F. SUTHERLAND, 102(CANL):WINTER72-101
FRASER, C. HARRY FERGUSON.
  617(TLS):16FEB73-176
FRASER, C.M. & K. EMSLEY. TYNESIDE.
  617(TLS):9MAR73-277
FRASER, D. THE EVOLUTION OF THE BRITISH
WELFARE STATE.
  617(TLS):14SEP73-1052
FRASER, G.M. FLASHMAN AT THE CHARGE.
  P. ANDREWS, 441:11NOV73-6
  R. GARFITT, 362:20SEP73-384
  617(TLS):21DEC73-1557
FRASER, G.M. THE GENERAL DANCED AT DAWN.
  M. LEVIN, 441:20MAY73-54
FRASER, M. CHILDREN IN CONFLICT.
  C.M. PARKES, 362:21JUN73-838
  617(TLS):27JUL73-870
FRASER, P.M. PTOLEMAIC ALEXANDRIA.
  617(TLS):9NOV73-1357
FRASER, R. THE BLACK HORSE TAVERN.
  C. MAC CULLOCH, 296:FALL73-106
FRASER, R. I'VE LAUGHED AND SUNG THROUGH
THE WHOLE NIGHT LONG.
  L. THOMPSON, 628:FALL70-86
FRASER, R. TAJOS.
  A. BROYARD, 441:11DEC73-49
  N. TARN, 441:18NOV73-45
  442(NY):10DEC73-198
FRASER, R. THE WAR AGAINST POETRY.*
  H. SMITH, 401(MLQ):MAR72-72
FRASER, S. PANDORA.*
  R-P. BRICKNER, 441:11FEB73-28
FRATER, D.G. AERE PERENNIUS.
  R. GLEN, 123:MAR72-96
FRAUWALLNER, E. MATERIALEN ZUR ÄLTESTEN
ERKENNTNISLEHRE DER KARMAMIMAMSA.
  H. SCHARFE, 318(JAOS):APR-JUN71-316
FRAYN, M. SWEET DREAMS.
  A. BROYARD, 441:31DEC73-15
  D. MAY, 362:16AUG73-224
  617(TLS):10AUG73-921
FRAYNE, J.P. - SEE YEATS, W.B.
FRAZIER, N. & M. SADKER. SEXISM IN
SCHOOL AND SOCIETY.
  F. HOWE, 31(ASCH):AUTUMN73-676
FRÉCHET, R. - SEE BOREL, E.
FRECOT, J., J.F. GEIST & D. KERBS.
FIDUS 1868-1948.
  617(TLS):30MAR73-344
FREDE, D. ARISTOTELES UND DIE "SEESCH-
LACHT."*
  P.M. HUBY, 123:JUN72-272

FREDEMAN, W.E.  PRE-RAPHAELITISM.
P. ROETZEL, 54:DEC70-465
FREDERICK, J.T.  THE DARKENED SKY.*
J.J. MC ALEER, 613:SPRING70-125
FREDERICKS, P.G.  THE SEPOY AND THE
COSSACK.
42(AR):WINTER71/72-592
617(TLS):23FEB73-207
FREDMAN, J.  EPITAPH TO A DEAD COP.
N. CALLENDAR, 441:12AUG73-10
FREE, W.J.  "THE COLUMBIAN MAGAZINE" AND
AMERICAN LITERARY NATIONALISM.*
W.S. KABLE, 219(GAR):SUMMER70-246
R.E. STREETER, 405(MP):NOV71-180
FREEBORN, R.  THE RISE OF THE RUSSIAN
NOVEL.
617(TLS):9MAR73-272
FREED, D.  AGONY IN NEW HAVEN.
C. LEHMANN-HAUPT, 441:5MAR73-27
FREEDBERG, S.J.  ANDREA DEL SARTO.
I.H. CHENEY, 54:DEC71-532
FREEDLAND, M.  JOLSON.
441:18MAR73-32
FREEDMAN, M., ED.  FAMILY AND KINSHIP IN
CHINESE SOCIETY.
B. PASTERNAK, 293(JAST):FEB71-426
FREEDMAN, R.O.  ECONOMIC WARFARE IN THE
COMMUNIST BLOC.
M. BORNSTEIN, 550(RUSR):OCT71-402
P. MARER, 32:JUN72-464
FREELAND, J.M.  ARCHITECTURE IN AUSTRALIA.
D.L. JOHNSON, 576:MAY70-200
FREEMAN, A.  THOMAS KYD.*
J. SCHÄFER, 38:BAND88HEFT3-382
FREEMAN, B.C. & A. BATSON.  CONCORDANCE
DU THÉÂTRE ET DES POÉSIES DE JEAN
RACINE.
J. MOREL, 535(RHL):SEP-DEC70-1072
FREEMAN, D., ED.  BOSTON ARCHITECTURE.
J.J. BISHOP, 576:DEC71-339
D.J. COOLIDGE, 432(NEQ):JUN71-312
FREEMAN, E.  THE THEATRE OF ALBERT CAMUS.
R. HAYMAN, 157:AUTUMN71-79
A.P. HINCHLIFFE, 148:WINTER71-381
FREEMAN, J.W.  DISCOVERING SURNAMES.
M.A. MOOK, 424:JUN70-118
FREEMAN, R.  "THE FAERIE QUEENE," A COM-
PANION FOR READERS.
A.K. HIEATT, 551(RENQ):WINTER71-557
C.V. KASKE, 301(JEGP):JAN72-121
FREEMAN, R.A.  AMERICAN BOMBERS OF
WORLD WAR TWO.  (VOL 1)
617(TLS):16MAR73-305
FREEMANTLE, B.  GOODBYE TO AN OLD FRIEND.
M. LEVIN, 441:25FEB73-49
442(NY):21APR73-136
617(TLS):16MAR73-303
FREETH, Z. & H.V.F. WINSTONE.  KUWAIT.
617(TLS):19JAN73-60
FREGE, G.  CONCEPTUAL NOTATION AND RE-
LATED ARTICLES.  (T.W. BYNUM, ED &
TRANS)
617(TLS):2FEB73-130
FREGE, G.  NACHGELASSENE SCHRIFTEN.
(H. HERMES, F. KAMBARTEL & F. KAULBACH,
EDS)
V.H. DUDMAN, 63:MAY72-67
R.H. STOOTHOFF, 479(PHQ):JAN71-77
FREGE, G.  ON THE FOUNDATIONS OF GEOMETRY
AND FORMAL THEORIES OF ARITHMETIC.
J.E. LLEWELYN, 518:OCT72-21
FREIBERG, M., ED.  JOURNALS OF THE HOUSE
OF REPRESENTATIVES OF MASSACHUSETTS.
(VOLS 38-40)
J. CARY, 656(WMQ):JUL71-515

FREIDEL, F.  FRANKLIN D. ROOSEVELT:
LAUNCHING THE NEW DEAL.
O.L. GRAHAM, JR., 441:23SEP73-5
442(NY):15OCT73-186
FREILIGRATH, F., K. MARX & F. ENGELS.
FREILIGRATHS BRIEFWECHSEL MIT MARX UND
ENGELS.  (M. HÄCKEL, ED)
H. RIDLEY, 220(GL&L):OCT71-29
FREIMARCK, V. & B. ROSENTHAL, EDS.  RACE
AND THE AMERICAN ROMANTICS.
K. JEFFREY, 109:FALL/WINTER72/73-93
FRÉNAUD, A.  LA SORCIÈRE DE ROME.
617(TLS):12OCT73-1244
FRENCH, H.  "I SWORE I NEVER WOULD."
N. MARSHALL, 157:AUTUMN70-72
FRENCH, H.  I THOUGHT I NEVER COULD.
617(TLS):20APR73-439
FRENCH, P.J.  JOHN DEE.*
M.C. BRADBROOK, 362:18JAN73-88
F. YATES, 453:25JAN73-39
"THE FRENCH RENAISSANCE AND ITS HERITAGE."
E. BALMAS, 535(RHL):JUL-AUG71-692
FREND, W.H.C.  THE RISE OF THE MONOPHYS-
ITE MOVEMENT.
617(TLS):19JAN73-72
FRENTZ, H.  DER UNBEKANNTE LUDENDORFF.
617(TLS):17AUG73-947
FRÈRE, E. & R. LABORDE.  QUELQUES JOUR-
NÉES FRANÇAISES.*
H. JAECKEL, 207(FR):FEB71-590
FREUD, A.  PROBLEMS OF PSYCHOANALYTIC
TECHNIQUE AND THERAPY, 1966-1970.
617(TLS):9MAR73-277
FREUD, A. & OTHERS, EDS.  THE PSYCHOAN-
ALYTIC STUDY OF THE CHILD.  (VOL 26)
617(TLS):5JAN73-22
FREUD, S.  LEONARDO DA VINCI AND A MEMORY
OF HIS CHILDHOOD.  (J. STRACHEY &
OTHERS, EDS)
R. COLES, 453:22FEB73-15
FREUD, S.  NEW INTRODUCTORY LECTURES ON
PSYCHOANALYSIS.  (J. STRACHEY & A.
RICHARDS, EDS)  INTRODUCTORY LECTURES
ON PSYCHOANALYSIS.
617(TLS):2NOV73-1340
FREUD, S.  LA VIE SEXUELLE.  MALAISE DANS
LA CIVILISATION.
Y. BRÈS, 542:APR-JUN71-189
FREUD, S. & L. ANDREAS-SALOMÉ.  SIGMUND
FREUD AND LOU ANDREAS-SALOMÉ LETTERS.
(E. PFEIFFER, ED)
F. BROWN, 231:FEB73-100
P.A. ROBINSON, 441:11MAR73-22
617(TLS):26JAN73-81
FREUD, S. & W.C. BULLITT.  THOMAS WOODROW
WILSON.
R. COLES, 453:22FEB73-15
FREUDENBERGER, R.  DAS VERHALTEN DER
RÖMISCHEN BEHÖRDEN GEGEN DIE CHRISTEN
IM 2. JAHRHUNDERT, DARGESTELLT AM
BRIEF DES PLINIUS AN TRAJAN UND DEN
RESKRIPTEN TRAJANS UND HADRIANS.  (2ND
ED)
T.D. BARNES, 313:VOL61-311
L.H. FELDMAN, 318(JAOS):OCT-DEC71-531
FREUDENTHAL, H.  EINFÜHRUNG IN DIE
SPRACHE DER LOGIK.  (2ND ED)
E. VOLKMANN, 682(ZPSK):BAND24HEFT1/2-
165
FREUDENTHAL, H.  THE LANGUAGE OF LOGIC.
H.B. CURRY, 206:MAY70-279
FREY, B.J.  BASIC HELPS FOR TEACHING
ENGLISH AS A SECOND LANGUAGE.
L. MC INTOSH, 399(MLJ):MAR71-185
FREY, G.  THE MODERN CHAIR.
R. BLETTER, 576:DEC71-340
FREYRE, G.  NOVO MUNDO NOS TRÓPICOS.
G. SOBRAL, 263:JUL-SEP72-304

FRIAR, K., ED & TRANS. MODERN GREEK POETRY.
  J. ARTHOS, 441:4NOV73-10
FRICK, F.C. GAMES, ASTERISKS, AND PEOPLE.
  R. SMITH, 441:20MAY73-42
FRICKE, D. DIE FRANZÖSISCHEN FASSUNGEN DER "INSTITUTIO PRINCIPIS CHRISTIANI" DES ERASMUS VON ROTTERDAM.
  W. BOERNER & J.Y. POUILLOUX, 545(RPH): FEB72-367
FRICKE, H.W. THE CORAL SEAS.
  W.H. HONAN, 441:2DEC73-97
FRIDAY, N., COMP. MY SECRET GARDEN.
  C. SEEBOHM, 441:7OCT73-20
FRIDENSON, P. HISTOIRE DES USINES RENAULT. (VOL 1)
  617(TLS):5JAN73-21
FRIEBEL, I. & H. HÄNDEL, EDS. BRITAIN - USA.
  L. BORINSKI, 38:BAND88HEFT3-425
FRIED, C. AN ANATOMY OF VALUES.
  A. BERLEANT, 484(PPR):MAR72-416
FRIED, E. DIE FREIHEIT DEN MUND AUFZUMACHEN.
  617(TLS):23MAR73-319
FRIED, E. ON PAIN OF SEEING.
  L. SHAYKIN, 114(CHIR):WINTER72-114
FRIED, J.J. LIFE ALONG THE SAN ANDREAS FAULT.
  441:14OCT73-49
FRIED, M. MORRIS LOUIS.
  T. HILTON, 592:NOV71-210
FRIED, M. POWERS.
  A. MACLEAN, 362:25OCT73-565
  617(TLS):3AUG73-894
FRIED, R.C. PLANNING THE ETERNAL CITY.
  617(TLS):7DEC73-1520
FRIEDBERG, M. - SEE TROTSKY, L.
FRIEDENTHAL, R. ENTDECKER DES ICH.
  K. BAHNERS, 430(NS):JUN71-329
FRIEDENTHAL, R. KETZER UND REBELL.
  617(TLS):2FEB73-127
FRIEDENTHAL, R. LUTHER.
  I.D.K. SIGGINS, 639(VQR):SPRING71-303
FRIEDLANDER, A.H. LEO BAECK.*
  617(TLS):16NOV73-1403
FRIEDMAN, A.W. LAWRENCE DURRELL AND "THE ALEXANDRIA QUARTET."
  A. GOULDEN, 648:OCT70-83
  639(VQR):SPRING71-LXIV
FRIEDMAN, B.H. JACKSON POLLOCK.*
  S. SPENDER, 362:15FEB73-216
  617(TLS):9NOV73-1362
FRIEDMAN, D.M. MARVELL'S PASTORAL ART.*
  A.E. BERTHOFF, 401(MLQ):MAR71-110
  M.C. BRADBROOK, 551(RENQ):WINTER71-584
  J. CAREY, 541(RES):NOV71-496
  R.A. FOAKES, 175:SPRING71-23
  P. LEGOUIS, 189(EA):JAN-MAR71-94
  M. MC CANLES, 141:SPRING71-201
  639(VQR):SUMMER71-CIX
FRIEDMAN, E. & M. SELDEN, EDS. AMERICA'S ASIA.
  42(AR):WINTER71/72-600
FRIEDMAN, I. THE QUESTION OF PALESTINE, 1914-1918.
  617(TLS):2NOV73-1343
FRIEDMAN, J.B. ORPHEUS IN THE MIDDLE AGES.
  J.B. ALLEN, 301(JEGP):APR72-241
  D.A. WRIGHT, 382(MAE):1972/3-268
  639(VQR):SUMMER71-CVIII
FRIEDMAN, L., ED. ARGUMENT.
  R. STRICKLAND, 583:SPRING71-288
FRIEDMAN, L. THE WISE MINORITY.
  I. DILLIARD, 31(ASCH):SPRING73-347

FRIEDMAN, M. BURIED ALIVE.
  A. BROYARD, 441:15AUG73-43
  M. DECTER, 441:12AUG73-1
  D. WAKEFIELD, 61:SEP73-108
FRIEDMAN, M. PROBLEMATIC REBEL.
  E. PARKER, 188(ECR):WINTER71-70
FRIEDMAN, M.J., ED. SAMUEL BECKETT NOW.*
  H.P. ABBOTT, 399(MLJ):OCT71-405
  J.V. ALTER, 207(FR):MAR71-793
  F.G. BLAHA, 502(PRS):SUMMER71-180
  J. FLETCHER, 188(ECR):FALL71-67
FRIEDMAN, M.J., ED. THE VISION OBSCURED.
  V.F. BLEHL, 613:WINTER71-618
FRIEDMAN, M.J. & J.B. VICKERY, EDS. THE SHAKEN REALIST.*
  R. BENOIT, 613:SUMMER71-306
  J. OLLIER, 189(EA):APR-JUN71-218
  639(VQR):WINTER71-XXIV
FRIEDMANN, A., J.F. PILE & F. WILSON. INTERIOR DESIGN.
  505:JUN71-118
FRIEDRICH, J. HETHITISCHES ELEMENTARBUCH. (PT 2)
  E. NEU, 260(IF):BAND74-209
FRIEDRICHS, R.W. A SOCIOLOGY OF SOCIOLOGY.
  H. CARSCH, 154:JUN71-369
  D.C. HODGES, 484(PPR):SEP71-120
FRIEL, B. CRYSTAL AND FOX.
  A. RENDLE, 157:SUMMER71-82
FRIEND, C. - SEE YASHPAL
FRIEND, D. SAVE ME FROM THE SHARK.
  S. HILL, 362:17MAY73-658
"DONALD FRIEND IN BALI."
  617(TLS):20JUL73-827
FRIES, U. ZUR SYNTAX DER CHESTER PLAYS.
  B. CARSTENSEN, 38:BAND89HEFT4-538
FRIESE, W. NORDISCHE BAROCKDICHTUNG.*
  B.J. NOLIN, 405(MP):AUG70-107
  H. RITTE, 224(GRM):MAY70-229
FRINTA, M.S. THE GENIUS OF ROBERT CAMPIN.*
  S.N. BLUM, 54:DEC70-434
FRISCH, M. TAGEBUCH 1966-1971.*
  H.F. GARTEN, 270:VOL22#4-91
FRISCH, M. A WILDERNESS OF MIRRORS.
  D.S. LOW, 220(GL&L):OCT71-55
FRISCHAUER, W. MILLIONAIRES' ISLANDS.
  617(TLS):23FEB73-206
FRISK, H. GRIECHISCHES ETYMOLOGISCHES WÖRTERBUCH. [PTS UNKNOWN]
  F.R. SCHRÖDER, 224(GRM):JAN70-105
FRISK, H. GRIECHISCHES ETYMOLOGISCHES WÖRTERBUCH. (VOL 2; WHICH IS PTS 11-22)
  J. HASENOHR, 182:VOL24#5-229
FRISK, H. GRIECHISCHES ETYMOLOGISCHES WÖRTERBUCH.* (PT 18)
  W. DRESSLER, 260(IF):BAND74-229
FRISK, H. GRIECHISCHES ETYMOLOGISCHES WÖRTERBUCH.* (PTS 19 & 20)
  W. DRESSLER, 260(IF):BAND75-306
FRITH, D. THE PLASTIC UNDERGROUND.
  J. DITSKY, 628:SPRING72-108
FRITZ, F.P. - SEE THEOCRITUS
VON FRITZ, K. GRUNDPROBLEME DER GESCHICHTE DER ANTIKEN WISSENSCHAFT.
  C. CALAME, 182:VOL24#21/22-806
FROBENIUS, L. DAS SCHWARZE DEKAMERON, GESCHICHTEN AUS AFRIKA, AUF DER TEXTGRUNDLAGE DER SAMMLUNG ATLANTIS. (U. DIEDERICHS, ED)
  F. HARKORT, 196:BAND12HEFT2/3-274
FRODSHAM, J.D. THE POEMS OF LI HO 791-817.
  C. CHOW, 293(JAST):FEB71-431

FROHOCK, W.M., ED. IMAGE AND THEME.*
    S.M. BELL, 208(FS):JUL72-358
    E.H. FALK, 546(RR):APR71-158
FROHOCK, W.M. RIMBAUD'S POETIC PRACTICE.
    E.J. AHEARN, 599:WINTER70-59
FROMILHAGUE, R. & R. LEBÈGUE - SEE DE
  MALHERBE, F.
FROMM, E. THE ANATOMY OF HUMAN DESTRUC-
  TIVENESS.
    S. SANBORN, 441:18NOV73-3
FROMM, E. & M. MACCOBY. SOCIAL CHARACTER
  IN A MEXICAN VILLAGE.
    A.M. PADILLA & D. MACIEL, 263:OCT-
    DEC72-414
FROMMEL, C.L. BALDASSARE PERUZZI ALS
  MALER UND ZEICHNER.
    N. DACOS, 54:DEC70-442
FROMMER, H. DAS IDEAL DER FRANZÖSISCHEN
  MONARCHIE BEI MONTESQUIEU.
    J. MAYER, 557(RSH):APR-JUN70-322
FRONCEK, T., ED. THE HORIZON BOOK OF THE
  ARTS OF RUSSIA.
    S. FRANK, 58:NOV70-16
FRONSPERGER, L. VON KAYSERLICHEM KRIEGS-
  SRECHTEN.
    C.B., 135:FEB71-139
FROST, R. ROBERT FROST: A TIME TO TALK.*
  (R. FRANCIS, ED)
    617(TLS):23NOV73-1416
FROST, R. ROBERT FROST ON WRITING. (E.
  BARRY, ED)
    A. BROYARD, 441:29NOV73-47
FROST, R. SELECTED POEMS. (I. HAMILTON,
  ED)
    617(TLS):19OCT73-1276
FROST, R. & E. FAMILY LETTERS OF ROBERT
  AND ELINOR FROST.* (A. GRADE, ED)
    442(NY):27JAN73-95
    617(TLS):26JAN73-86
FROST, R.H. THE MOONEY CASE.
    C.J. BAYARD, 649(WAL):WINTER72-265
FROTHINGHAM, A.W. TILE PANELS OF SPAIN
  1500-1650.*
    M.A., 135:MAY70-48
    E. YOUNG, 39:MAY70-403
FROUDE, J.A. THE TWO CHIEFS OF DUNBOY.
  (A.L. ROWSE, ED)
    P. GROSSKURTH, 627(UTQ):SPRING71-266
FRUCHON, P. CRÉATION OU CONSENTEMENT.
    F. HEIDSIECK, 542:OCT-DEC70-477
FRUITHOF, A. DE DOOD AAN DE TELEFON.
    J. GOFFART, 556(RLV):1971/6-786
FRUMAN, N. COLERIDGE, THE DAMAGED ARCH-
  ANGEL.*
    G. STEINER, 442(NY):27AUG73-77
FRUTON, J.S. MOLECULES AND LIFE.
    617(TLS):9MAR73-262
FRY, A. THE REVENGE OF ANNIE CHARLIE.
    R.M. BROWN, 296:FALL73-92
FRY, C. A YARD OF SUN.
    H-F. SALERNO, 160:WINTER70/71-134
FRY, E.M. ART IN A MACHINE AGE.
    J. PRITCHARD, 46:MAR70-234
FRY, R. LETTERS OF ROGER FRY.* (D. SUT-
  TON, ED)
    R. DOWNES, 441:11MAR73-6
    H. KRAMER, 441:27APR73-41
    442(NY):17MAR73-130
FRYDE, E.B. & E. MILLER, EDS. HISTORICAL
  STUDIES OF THE ENGLISH PARLIAMENT.
  (VOLS 1&2)
    G. NIEDHART, 182:VOL24#5-242
FRYE, N. THE CRITICAL PATH.*
    H.L., 131(CL):WINTER72-72
FRYE, N. FOOLS OF TIME.*
    C. UHLIG, 38:BAND89HEFT3-385
FRYE, N. A NATURAL PERSPECTIVE.
    C.L. BARBER, 570(SQ):WINTER71-68

FRYE, N. THE STUBBORN STRUCTURE.*
    A. CAPELLÁN GONZALO, 202(FMOD):NOV71/
    FEB72-132
    D. DAICHES, 541(RES):NOV71-522
    A.J. FRY, 433:OCT71-466
    R.C. LEWIS, 150(DR):SPRING71-109
    S. SANDERS, 111:7MAY71-177
    G. THOMAS, 175:SUMMER71-62
    639(VQR):SUMMER71-CXII
FRYE, N. A STUDY OF ENGLISH ROMANTICISM.*
    J. LUNDIN, 597(SN):VOL43#2-590
FU TSUNG-MAO. CH'ING-TAI CHUN-CHI CH'U
  TSU-CHIH CHI CHIH-CHANG CHIH YEN-CHIU.
    PEI HUANG, 244(HJAS):VOL30-248
FU-KIAU KIA BUNSEKI-LUMANISA, A. N'KONGO
  YE NZA YAKUN'ZUNGIDILA.
    A. DOUTRELOUX, 69:APR71-172
FUCHS, A. GOETHE STUDIEN.
    H-J. GEERDTS, 654(WB):7/1970-220
    H. NIELSEN, 462(OL):VOL26#2-168
FUCHS, E. & J. ANTLER. YEAR ONE OF THE
  EMPIRE.
    I.R. DEE, 441:16DEC73-5
FUCKS, W. NACH ALLEN REGELN DER KUNST.
    J.M. COETZEE, 599:WINTER71-92
FUEGI, J. THE ESSENTIAL BRECHT.
    617(TLS):28DEC73-1591
FUENTES, C. CUMPLEAÑOS.
    R.M. REEVE, 238:MAR71-212
FUENTES, C., J. DONOSO & S. SARDUY.
  TRIPLE CROSS.*
    M. WOOD, 453:19APR73-35
FÜETRER, U. DER TROJANERKRIEG.* (E.G.
  FICHTNER, ED)
    G.P. KNAPP, 657(WW):SEP/OCT70-349
    D.R. MC LINTOCK, 220(GL&L):OCT71-22
FUGARD, A. PEOPLE ARE LIVING THERE.
    A. RENDLE, 157:AUTUMN70-77
FUHRMANN, J.T. THE ORIGINS OF CAPITALISM
  IN RUSSIA.
    S.H. BARON, 104:WINTER72-651
    K. VON LOEWE, 32:DEC72-885
FUHRMANN, J.T., E.C. BOCK & L.I. TWAROG.
  ESSAYS ON RUSSIAN INTELLECTUAL HISTORY.
    J.M. EDIE, 319:OCT73-563
FUHRMANN, M. DIE ANTIKE UND IHRE VER-
  MITTLER.*
    P. LOUIS, 555:VOL45FASC1-128
FUHRMANS, H. - SEE SCHELLING, F.W.J.
FUKS, A. THE ATHENIAN COMMONWEALTH. [IN
  HEBREW]
    J. GLUCKER, 303:VOL91-194
FUKS, L., ED. DAS ALTJIDDISCHE EPOS
  MELOKĪM-BŪK. (VOL 1)
    C. MINIS, 433:APR70-196
FUKUI, H. PARTY IN POWER.
    F.C. LANGDON, 293(JAST):MAY71-685
FUKUZAWA YUKICHI. AN ENCOURAGEMENT OF
  LEARNING.* (D.A. DILWORTH & UMEYO
  HIRANO, TRANS)
    T.R.H. HAVENS, 244(HJAS):VOL31-320
FULBRIGHT, J.W. THE CRIPPLED GIANT.
    D.P. CALLEO, 441:25FEB73-44
    H.S. COMMAGER, 453:19JUL73-10
FULCHIGNONI, E. LA CIVILISATION DE
  L'IMAGE.
    J-M. PIEMME, 556(RLV):1971/5-635
FULD, J.J. THE BOOK OF WORLD-FAMOUS
  MUSIC. (REV)
    A.H. KING, 415:JUN72-563
FÜLLEBORN, U. DAS DEUTSCHE PROSAGEDICHT.
    G. JÄGER, 224(GRM):BAND21HEFT4-479
FULLER, B. WEST OF THE BIGHT.
    617(TLS):6APR73-401
FULLER, E. PRUDENCE CRANDALL.
    B. CLAYTON, 432(NEQ):DEC71-668

FULLER, J. A READER'S GUIDE TO W.H.
AUDEN.*
   D. BURKE, 613:SUMMER71-305
FULLER, J.O. CONVERSATIONS WITH A CAP-
TOR.
   617(TLS):21DEC73-1560
FULLER, J.O. SWINBURNE.*
   F.A.C. WILSON, 648:OCT70-76
FULLER, R. PROFESSORS AND GODS.
   617(TLS):14DEC73-1530
FULLER, R. TINY TEARS.
   617(TLS):7DEC73-1513
FULLER, R.B. OPERATING MANUAL FOR SPACE-
SHIP EARTH.
   W.C. MILLER, 50(ARQ):AUTUMN71-283
"FUND OG FORSKNING." (VOL 17)
   B.G.F. HOLT, 78(BC):SPRING71-117
"LOS 'FUNDADORES' EN LA FILOSOFÍA DE
AMÉRICA LATINA."
   M. GARCÍA TUDURÍ, 263:JUL-SEP72-301
   J.C. TORCHIA-ESTRADA, 37:APR71-38
FUNDERBURK, L. ERLEBNIS, VERSTEHEN, ER-
KENNTNIS.
   S. DECLOUX, 182:VOL24#23/24-837
FUNKE, P. OSCAR WILDE IN SELBSTZEUGNIS-
SEN UND BILDDOKUMENTEN.
   P.G., 430(NS):JUL70-366
FURBANK, P.N. - SEE DICKENS, C.
FURET, F. & D. RICHET. THE FRENCH REVO-
LUTION.
   N. HAMPSON, 208(FS):JAN72-82
FURLEY, D.J. TWO STUDIES IN THE GREEK
ATOMISTS.*
   K.P. FREEMAN, 321:SUMMER70-153
FURLEY, D.J. & R.E. ALLEN, EDS. STUDIES
IN PRESOCRATIC PHILOSOPHY.* (VOL 1)
   D.W. HAMLYN, 483:OCT71-354
   J.J.R., 543:JUN71-745
   R.K. SPRAGUE, 122:OCT72-298
FURLONG, W.B. SHAW AND CHESTERTON.
   J.C. MAXWELL, 447(N&Q):JUL71-280
   A. SEABROOK, 572:SEP70-132
FURNEAUX, R. THE SEVEN YEARS WAR.
   617(TLS):17AUG73-957
FURRER, D. MODUSPROBLEME BEI NOTKER.
   H. TIEFENBACH, 182:VOL24#17/18-665
FURST, L.R. ROMANTICISM.
   E. ECHEVARRÍA, 149:SEP72-340
   R. TAYLOR, 220(GL&L):OCT71-62
   205(FMLS):OCT70-419
FURST, L.R. ROMANTICISM IN PERSPECTIVE.*
   F.P. BOWMAN, 188(ECR):SPRING71-94
   F. GARBER, 131(CL):SPRING72-185
   J. VOISINE, 549(RLC):APR-JUN71-280
FURTH, C. TING WEN-CHIANG.*
   HO PENG YOKE, 302:JUL71-369
   P.K.T. SIH, 293(JAST):FEB71-442
FUSERO, C. THE BORGIAS.*
   442(NY):28APR73-148
FUSS, P. & H. SHAPIRO - SEE NIETZSCHE,
F.W.
FUSSELL, G.E. JETHRO TULL.
   617(TLS):11MAY73-533
FUSSELL, P. SAMUEL JOHNSON AND THE LIFE
OF WRITING.*
   J.J. GOLD, 301(JEGP):OCT72-548
   P.E. MEDINE, 50(ARQ):WINTER71-376
FUSSELL, P., JR. POETIC METER AND POETIC
FORM.
   R. OVERSTREET, 583:SUMMER71-407
FUSSNER, F.S. TUDOR HISTORY AND THE HIS-
TORIANS.
   A.B. FERGUSON, 551(RENQ):WINTER71-550
FUSTIER, P. LA ROUTE.
   A.R. NEUMANN, 182:VOL24#15/16-626

FUTABATEI SHIMEI. JAPAN'S FIRST MODERN
NOVEL: UKIGUMO OF FUTABATEI SHIMEI.
(M.G. RYAN, ED & TRANS)
   J.R. MORITA, 244(HJAS):VOL30-274
FUTRELLE, J. BEST "THINKING MACHINE"
DETECTIVE STORIES.
   N. CALLENDAR, 441:30DEC73-19
FUZÜLÏ. LEYLÄ AND MEJNÜN.* (S. HURI,
TRANS; A. BOMBACI, ED)
   J.W. SPELLMAN, 628:SPRING72-118
FYZEE, A.A.A. COMPENDIUM OF FATIMID LAW.
   J.A. BELLAMY, 318(JAOS):OCT-DEC71-532

GAÁL, K. DIE VOLKSMÄRCHEN DER MAGYAREN
IM SÜDLICHEN BURGENLAND.
   E.H. REHERMANN, 196:BAND12HEFT2/3-275
GABAUDE, J-M. LE JEUNE MARX ET LE
MATÉRIALISME ANTIQUE.
   K. HARTMANN, 53(AGP):BAND53HEFT3-318
GABBA, E. - SEE APPIAN
GABE, D. MOTHER PARASHKEVA.
   270:VOL22#2-34
GABLIK, S. MAGRITTE.
   M.V. ALPER, 58:FEB71-12
   F. DUTTON, 90:OCT71-616
   A. FORGE, 592:NOV70-218
   A. POWELL, 39:JUN71-525
   R.S., 376:APR71-124
GABOR, M. THE PIN-UP.*
   617(TLS):30NOV73-1473
GABORIT-CHOPIN, D. LA DÉCORATION DES
MANUSCRITS À SAINT-MARTIAL DE LIMOGES
ET EN LIMOUSIN DU IXE AU XIIE SIÈCLE.*
   W. CAHN, 54:DEC71-518
GABRIEL, J. THINKING ABOUT TELEVISION.
   617(TLS):14DEC73-1542
GAD, F. THE HISTORY OF GREENLAND. (VOL
1)
   D. SWAINSON, 529(QQ):WINTER71-628
GAD, F. THE HISTORY OF GREENLAND. (VOL
2)
   617(TLS):30NOV73-1482
GADAMER, H-G. PLATOS DIALEKTISCHE ETHIK
UND ANDERE STUDIEN ZUR PLATONISCHEN
PHILOSOPHIE.
   P.M. HUBY, 123:MAR72-103
GADDA, C.E. LA MECCANICA.
   G-P. BIASIN, 275(IQ):WINTER71-123
   J. RISSET, 98:NOV70-944
GADDA, C.E. NOVELLA SECONDA.
   617(TLS):27APR73-461
GADDA, C.E. I VIAGGI LA MORTE. QUER
PASTICCIACCIO BRUTTO DE VIA MERULANA.
LA COGNIZIONE DEL DOLORE.
   J. RISSET, 98:NOV70-944
GADDA CONTI, G. WILLIAM DEAN HOWELLS.
   J. WOODRESS, 27(AL):JAN73-686
GADDIS, J.L. THE UNITED STATES AND THE
ORIGINS OF THE COLD WAR 1941-1947.*
   R. STEEL, 453:14JUN73-33
GADENNE, P. LES HAUTS-QUARTIERS.
   617(TLS):2NOV73-1334
GADOL, J. LEON BATTISTA ALBERTI.*
   I. GALANTIC, 56:WINTER71-482
   C. GRAYSON, 551(RENQ):SPRING71-51
   C. PEDRETTI, 275(IQ):SPRING-SUMMER72-
   103
   C.W. WESTFALL, 54:DEC71-526
   P. ZUCKER, 290(JAAC):FALL70-140
GADOLIN, A. A THEORY OF HISTORY AND
SOCIETY WITH SPECIAL REFERENCE TO THE
"CHRONOGRAPHIA" OF MICHAEL PSELLUS.
   K. GIOCARINIS, 589:APR72-313
GAENG, P.A. AN INQUIRY INTO LOCAL VARIA-
TIONS IN VULGAR LATIN.*
   B. FOSTER, 208(FS):JAN72-114
                              [CONTINUED]

GAENG, P.A. AN INQUIRY INTO LOCAL VARIA-
TIONS IN VULGAR LATIN.* [CONTINUING]
    C.S. LEONARD, JR., 207(FR)OCT70-262
    R.L. POLITZER, 350:SEP72-702
    W. ROTHWELL, 402(MLR):JUL72-604
GAGE, J. COLOR IN TURNER.*
    G.E. FINLEY, 529(QQ):AUTUMN71-469
    L.H., 135:DEC70-290
    H.E. ROBERTS, 637(VS):SEP70-102
    J. ZIFF, 54:MAR71-125
GAGE, J. TURNER: RAIN, STEAM AND SPEED.*
    R. DOWNES, 441:2DEC73-93
GAGE, N. MAFIA!
    617(TLS):6JUL73-789
GAGEY, J. ANALYSE SPECTRALE DE LA PSY-
CHOLOGIE.
    N.L., 154:JUN71-427
GAGEY, J. GASTON BACHELARD OU LA CONVER-
SION À L'IMAGINAIRE.
    M. PRÉCLAIRE, 154:DEC70-487
GAGG, J. THE CANALLERS' BEDSIDE BOOK.
    617(TLS):2NOV73-1352
GAGG, J. 5000 MILES 3000 LOCKS.
    617(TLS):27JUL73-858
GAGNEBIN, B. & M. RAYMOND - SEE ROUS-
SEAU, J-J.
GAIKWAD, V.R. PANCHAYATI RAJ AND BUR-
EAUCRACY.
    M.G. MARSH, 293(JAST):FEB71-486
GAIL, A. BHAKTI IM BHĀGAVATAPURĀNA.*
    L. STERNBACH, 318(JAOS):OCT-DEC71-543
GAILEY, A. IRISH FOLK DRAMA.*
    A. HELM, 203:SPRING70-65
GAILEY, A. & A. FENTON, EDS. THE SPADE
IN NORTHERN AND ATLANTIC EUROPE.*
    F.L. KRAMER, 292(JAF):OCT-DEC71-465
GAILLARD, J. COMMUNES DE PROVINCE, COM-
MUNE DE PARIS.
    M. REBÉRIOUX, 98:NOV71-979
GAINES, C. STAY HUNGRY.*
    D. MAHON, 362:21JUN73-840
    617(TLS):15JUN73-661
GAINES, E.J. THE AUTOBIOGRAPHY OF MISS
JANE PITTMAN.
    V. CUNNINGHAM, 362:8FEB73-189
    617(TLS):16MAR73-303
GAINHAM, S. MACULAN'S DAUGHTER.
    R. GARFITT, 362:13DEC73-828
    617(TLS):23NOV73-1417
GAINZA, M.C.G. - SEE UNDER GARCÍA GAINZA,
M.C.
GAIR, J.W. COLLOQUIAL SINHALESE CLAUSE
STRUCTURES.
    W.A. COATES, 350:JUN72-463
GAISER, G. AM PASS NASCONDO UND ANDERE
ERZÄHLUNGEN. (K. BULLIVANT, ED)
    205(FMLS):APR70-206
GALAI, S. THE LIBERATION MOVEMENT IN
RUSSIA 1900-1905.
    617(TLS):9MAR73-260
GALAKTIONOV, I.V. - SEE ORDIN-NASHCHOKIN,
A.L.
GALAMINI, L. ESISTENZA E COESISTENZA.
    E. NAMER, 542:JAN-MAR70-99
GALAND, R. BAUDELAIRE - POÉTIQUES ET
POÉSIE.
    W.T. BANDY, 207(FR):OCT70-228
GALANTE, P. MADEMOISELLE CHANEL.
    442(NY):10SEP73-134
GALATAPOULOS, S. ITALIAN OPERA.
    C. GRAHAM, 415:JAN72-45
GALAVARIS, G. THE ILLUSTRATIONS OF THE
LITURGICAL HOMILIES OF GREGORY NAZI-
ANZENUS.
    J. BECKWITH, 39:JUL70-79
    W.O.H., 135:APR71-291
    M.B. MC NAMEE, 377:MAR72-55
GALBRAITH, G. - SEE STEVENS, W.B.

GALBRAITH, J.K. A CHINA PASSAGE.
    P. ADAMS, 61:APR73-128
    M. BERNAL, 453:9AUG73-21
    H.L. BOORMAN, 441:22APR73-5
    442(NY):5MAY73-151
    617(TLS):3AUG73-897
GALBRAITH, J.K. ECONOMICS AND THE PUBLIC
PURPOSE.
    R.J. BARNET, 441:16SEP73-1
    N. BLIVEN, 442(NY):31DEC73-57
    L. SILK, 441:18SEP73-47
    P.M. SWEEZY, 453:15NOV73-3
GALBRAITH, J.K. THE NEW INDUSTRIAL
STATE.* (2ND ED)
    617(TLS):9FEB73-148
GALDÓS, B.P. - SEE UNDER PÉREZ GALDÓS, B.
GALEN. ON THE USEFULLNESS OF THE PARTS
OF THE BODY.* (M.T. MAY, ED & TRANS)
    C. MUGLER, 555:VOL45FASC1-156
GALET, Y. L'ÉVOLUTION DE L'ORDRE DES
MOTS DANS LA PHRASE FRANÇAISE DE 1600
À 1700.
    H. MEIER, 72:BAND209HEFT1/3-200
GALIANI, F. DIALOGUES ENTRE M. MARQUIS
DE ROQUEMAURE ET M. LE CHEVALIER ZAN-
OBI.* (P. KOCH, ED)
    A. MAFFEY, 546(RR):OCT71-237
GALINDO, S. THE PRECIPICE.
    J.D. MC KEE, 649(WAL):SPRING70-65
GALINSKY, G.K. AENEAS, SICILY, AND
ROME.*
    H.W. BENARIO, 121(CJ):OCT-NOV71-70
    R. BRILLIANT, 54:MAR71-110
    R.B. LLOYD, 24:OCT72-616
GALINSKY, H. AMERIKA UND EUROPA.
    F.H. LINK, 38:BAND88HEFT1-156
GALINSKY, H. WEGBEREITER MODERNER AMERI-
KANISCHER LYRIK.
    H. PRIESSNITZ, 430(NS):JAN71-47
GALISSON, R. INVENTAIRE THÉMATIQUE ET
SYNTAGMATIQUE DU FRANÇAIS FONDAMENTAL.
    J. CANTERA, 202(FMOD):NOV71-FEB72-146
GALISSON, R. L'APPRENTISSAGE SYSTÉMA-
TIQUE DU VOCABULAIRE.
    J. CANTERA, 202(FMOD):NOV71/FEB72-147
GALLAGHER, D.P. MODERN LATIN AMERICAN
LITERATURE.
    617(TLS):5OCT73-1185
GALLAGHER, J., G. JOHNSON & A. SEAL, EDS.
LOCALITY, PROVINCE AND NATIONS.
    617(TLS):7SEP73-1037
GALLAGHER, P. THE LIFE AND WORKS OF
GARCI SÁNCHEZ DE BADAJOZ.*
    F. MÁRQUEZ VILLANUEVA, 240(HR):OCT71-
445
    H.T. OOSTENDORP, 433:APR71-212
    R. POPE, 546(RR):APR71-134
    N.G. ROUND, 205(FMLS):APR70-178
GALLAHUE, J. THE JESUIT.
    W. SCHOTT, 441:27MAY73-6
GALLANT, M. A FAIRLY GOOD TIME.
    A. EDELSTEIN, 598(SOR):SUMMER73-736
GALLANT, M. THE PEGNITZ JUNCTION.
    W.H. PRITCHARD, 441:24JUN73-4
GALLATI, E. JEREMIAS GOTTHELFS GESELL-
SCHAFTSKRITIK.
    H.M. WAIDSON, 301(JEGP):OCT72-589
    F. WASSERMANN, 406:SUMMER72-201
GÁLLEGO, C.P. - SEE UNDER PÉREZ GÁLLEGO,
C.
GÁLLEGO, J. VISION ET SYMBOLES DANS LA
PEINTURE ESPAGNOLE DU SIÈCLE D'OR.
    D. FITZ DARBY, 54:SEP71-416
GALLEN, J., ED. EUCHARISTIC LITURGIES.
    C.J. MC NASPY, 363:MAY71-84
GALLER, M. & H.E. MARQUESS. SOVIET PRISON
CAMP SPEECH.*
    A. ROTHBERG, 584(SWR):AUTUMN72-338

GALLET, M. PARIS DOMESTIC ARCHITECTURE
OF THE 18TH CENTURY.*
H. ROSENAU, 89(BJA):SUMMER72-311
GALLI DE' PARATESI, N. SEMANTICA DELL'
EUFEMISMO.
G. LEPSCHY, 47(ARL):VOL17FASC1-44
GALLO, I. LA CIVILTÀ MICENEA.
K. BRANIGAN, 303:VOL91-190
GALLO, M. THE NIGHT OF LONG KNIVES.*
617(TLS):13JUL73-817
GALLO, M. SPAIN UNDER FRANCO.
617(TLS):2NOV73-1336
GALLO, R. IL TESORO DI SAN MARCO E LA
SUA STORIA.
O. DEMUS, 54:SEP70-309
GALLOWAY, D., ED. THE ELIZABETHAN THE-
ATRE. (VOL 1)
M. TAYLOR, 255(HAB):WINTER71-59
GALLOWAY, D., ED. THE ELIZABETHAN THE-
ATRE. (VOL 2)
J.R. TAYLOR, 157:SPRING71-66
M. TAYLOR, 255(HAB):WINTER71-59
GALLOWAY, D., ED. THE ELIZABETHAN THE-
ATRE. (VOL 3)
617(TLS):14SEP73-1063
GALLOWAY, D. & J. WHITLEY, EDS. TEN
MODERN AMERICAN SHORT STORIES.*
M. BRADBURY, 148:SUMMER71-185
H.O., 430(NS):MAR71-168
GALLOWAY, K.B. & R.B. JOHNSON, JR. WEST
POINT.
G. VIDAL, 453:18OCT73-21
441:26AUG73-8
GALLUP, D. ON CONTEMPORARY BIBLIOGRAPHY.
E.S. FOX, 354:DEC71-361
GALPIN, F.W. THE MUSIC OF THE SUMERIANS
AND THEIR IMMEDIATE SUCCESSORS, THE
BABYLONIANS AND ASSYRIANS.*
412:MAY72-151
GALSTER, G. SYLLOGE OF COINS OF THE
BRITISH ISLES. (VOLS 13-15)
J.D. BRADY, 589:JAN72-125
GALT, J. ANNALS OF THE PARISH. (J. KINS-
LEY, ED) THE ENTAIL.* (J.A. GORDON,
ED)
H. GIBAULT, 189(EA):APR-JUN71-162
GALTON, D. SURVEY OF A THOUSAND YEARS OF
BEEKEEPING IN RUSSIA.
E.R. LENG, 32:JUN72-445
W. RYAN, 575(SEER):JAN72-140
GAMBARIN, G. - SEE CARRER, L.
GAMBARIN, G. - SEE TOMMASEO, N.
GAMBER, K. DOMUS ECCLESIAE.
H-G. THÜMMEL, 182:VOL24#6-274
GAMBER, K. - SEE NICETA VON REMESIANA
GAMBERINI, S. LO STUDIO DELL'ITALIANO IN
INGHILTERRA NEL '500 E NEL '600.
B. RICHARDSON, 402(MLR):JUL72-663
DE GÁMEZ, T. ALICIA ALONSO AT HOME AND
ABROAD.
O. MAYNARD, 151:JUL71-90
GAMMAGE, R.G. THE HISTORY OF THE CHART-
IST MOVEMENT.
J.E. WILLIAMS, 637(VS):SEP70-94
GAMMOND, P., ED. BEST MUSIC HALL AND
VARIETY SONGS.*
A. LAMB, 415:DEC72-1188
GAMMOND, P. ONE MAN'S MUSIC.
K. SPENCE, 415:JAN72-50
GAMSON, W.A. & A. MODIGLIANI. UNTANGLING
THE COLD WAR.
J.F. TRISKA, 32:JUN72-436
GAṆAPATI ŚĀSTRI, M.T., ED. SAMARĀṄGAṆA
SŪTRADHĀRA. (REV BY V.S. AGRAWALA)
E. BENDER, 318(JAOS):OCT-DEC71-567

DE GANDILLAC, M. & E. JEAUNEAU, EDS.
ENTRETIENS SUR LE RENAISSANCE DU 12E
SIÈCLE.
P.Z., 433:JAN70-84
GANDZ, S. STUDIES IN HEBREW ASTRONOMY
AND MATHEMATICS. (S. STERNBERG, ED)
B.R. GOLDSTEIN, 589:JAN72-124
GANIVET, A. LOS TRABAJOS DEL INFATIGABLE
CREADOR PÍO CID.
A. NOUGUÉ, 182:VOL24#4-159
GANS, E.L. THE DISCOVERY OF ILLUSION.
A. FAIRLIE, 208(FS):APR72-216
GANSS, G.E. - SEE SAINT IGNATIUS OF
LOYOLA
GANZ, A., ED. PINTER.
617(TLS):6JUL73-775
GANZ, M. ELIZABETH GASKELL.
J. ESPEY, 445(NCF):JUN70-123
E. WRIGHT, 637(VS):SEP70-97
GANZ, P.F., ED. THE DISCONTINUOUS TRA-
DITION.
205(FMLS):APR71-192
GANZ, P.F. & W. SCHRÖDER, EDS. PROBLEME
MITTELALTERLICHER ÜBERLIEFERUNG UND
TEXTKRITIK.*
H. BLOSEN, 680(ZDP):BAND90HEFT1-109
A. VAN DER LEE, 433:JUL71-345
D.G. MOWATT, 220(GL&L):APR72-321
657(WW):NOV/DEC70-432
GANZEL, D. MARK TWAIN ABROAD.*
L.T. DICKINSON, 405(MP):AUG70-117
GANZL, S. ENCOMBREMENT.
L. RIESE, 207(FR):MAR71-781
GARAB, A.M. BEYOND BYZANTIUM.*
W.M. CARPENTER, 405(MP):MAY71-398
H. SERGEANT, 175:SPRING71-26
648:JAN71-66
GARAGORRI, P. EJERCICIOS INTELECTUALES.
ESPAÑOLES RAZONANTES.
V. RÜFNER, 182:VOL24#9/10-385
GARAGORRI, P. INTRODUCCIÓN A ORTEGA.
J.L. BENBOW, 399(MLJ):MAY71-336
GARASA, D.L. LOS GÉNEROS LITERARIOS.
D. JAÉN, 238:MAY71-398
GARAUDY, R. MARXISM IN THE TWENTIETH
CENTURY.*
K.F. KOECHER, 550(RUSR):OCT71-388
GARAVINI, F. L'EMPÈRI DOU SOULÈU, LA
RAGIONE DIALETTALE NELLA FRANCIA D'OC.
LA LETTERATURA OCCITANICA MODERNA.
P. GARDY, 98:JUN71-508
GARBER, K. - SEE HARSDÖRFFER, G.P., S.
VON BIRKEN & J. KLAJ
GARBER, L. CIRCUIT.
S. SCOBIE, 102(CANL):SPRING72-105
GARBER, L. GARBER'S TALES FROM THE
QUARTER.*
M. CZARNECKI, 648:OCT71-54
GARCÍA GAINZA, M.C. LA ESCULTURA ROMAN-
ISTA EN NAVARRA.
B.G. PROSKE, 54:DEC71-535
GARCÍA MÁRQUEZ, G. LEAF STORM AND OTHER
STORIES.*
M. DEAS, 362:1FEB73-157
GARCÍA MÁRQUEZ, G. ONE HUNDRED YEARS OF
SOLITUDE.* (SPANISH TITLE: CIEN AÑOS
DE SOLEDAD.)
G. DARÍO CARRILLO, 263:JUL-SEP72-257
G.R. MC MURRAY, 649(WAL):WINTER71-308
42(AR):SPRING70-129
GARCÍA PAVÓN, F. LAS HERMANAS COLORADAS.
L. GUINAZZO, 238:MAY71-394
GARCÍA PAVÓN, F. EL RAPTO DE LA SABINAS.
M. JATO MACÍAS, 238:MAY71-395
GARCÍA Y BELLIDO, A. ARTE ROMANO.
617(TLS):7SEP73-1036
GARD, R.E. JOHNNY CHINOOK.
L.R. RICOU, 296:SPRING73-83

GARD, R.E. & L.G. SORDEN. THE ROMANCE OF
WISCONSIN PLACE NAMES.
F.G. CASSIDY, 424:SEP70-231
J.B. MC MILLAN, 650(WF):APR70-137
GARDAVSKY, V. GOD IS NOT YET DEAD.
617(TLS):26OCT73-1319
GARDEL, L. BRAZIL.
F.L.P., 37:SEP70-43
GARDEN, E. TCHAIKOVSKY.
617(TLS):24AUG73-974
GARDIES, A. ALAIN ROBBE-GRILLET.
617(TLS):12JAN73-33
GARDINER, C.H. WILLIAM HICKLING PRES-
COTT.*
W.R. LUX, 37:FEB70-42
GARDINER, C.H. - SEE WARREN, J. & E.
GERRY
GARDINER, K.J.H. THE EARLY HISTORY OF
KOREA.
W.E. HENTHORN, 293(JAST):NOV70-150
GARDNER, E.S. THE CASE OF THE POSTPONED
MURDER.
N. CALLENDAR, 441:4FEB73-16
GARDNER, H., ED. THE NEW OXFORD BOOK OF
ENGLISH VERSE 1250-1950.*
D. DONOGHUE, 453:19APR73-26
F. KERMODE, 61:JAN73-88
617(TLS):16FEB73-179
GARDNER, H. THE QUEST FOR MIND.
C. LEHMANN-HAUPT, 441:16JAN73-41
442(NY):3FEB73-100
GARDNER, H. RELIGION AND LITERATURE.
R.L. BRETT, 148:AUTUMN71-281
D. BUSH, 191(ELN):JUN72-323
676(YR):AUTUMN71-VI
GARDNER, H. - SEE WILSON, F.P.
GARDNER, J., ED. THE COMPLETE WORKS OF
THE GAWAIN-POET.
R.M. WILSON, 402(MLR):JAN72-163
GARDNER, J. JASON AND MEDEIA.
P. ADAMS, 61:SEP73-118
D.S. CARNE-ROSS, 453:4OCT73-35
M. DICKSTEIN, 441:1JUL73-4
E. SHORRIS, 231:AUG73-90
GARDNER, J. NICKEL MOUNTAIN.
C. LEHMANN-HAUPT, 441:20DEC73-37
G. STADE, 441:9DEC73-5
GARDNER, J. THE RESURRECTION. THE
WRECKAGE OF AGATHON.* GRENDEL.*
E. SHORRIS, 231:AUG73-90
GARDNER, J. THE SUNLIGHT DIALOGUES.*
P. ADAMS, 61:JAN73-100
M. MADDOCKS, 61:MAR73-98
E. SHORRIS, 231:AUG73-90
442(NY):13JAN73-92
617(TLS):23NOV73-1455
GARDNER, J.L. DEPARTING GLORY.
E. WEEKS, 61:SEP73-117
GARDNER, M. THE FLIGHT OF PETER FROMM.
M. LEVIN, 441:23DEC73-16
GARDNER, P., ED. E.M. FORSTER: THE
CRITICAL HERITAGE.
617(TLS):26OCT73-1316
GARDNER, W.H. & N.H. MAC KENZIE - SEE
HOPKINS, G.M.
GARFIELD, B. TRIPWIRE.
N. CALLENDAR, 441:29APR73-29
GARIAN, P.B. SPANIEN HEUTE.
C. SÁNCHEZ, 430(NS):DEC70-642
GARIN, E. L'ETÀ NUOVA.
E. NAMER, 542:APR-JUN70-262
GARIN, E. - SEE PICO DELLA MIRANDOLA, G.
GARLAND, H. HAMLIN GARLAND'S DIARIES.
(D. PIZER, ED)
W.I. TITUS, 577(SHR):SUMMER71-292

GARLAND, H.B. A CONCISE SURVEY OF GERMAN
LITERATURE.
J.M. RITCHIE, 402(MLR):JAN72-212
J.L. SAMMONS, 301(JEGP):JAN72-95
GARLAND, H.B. SCHILLER: THE DRAMATIC
WRITER.*
C.E. SCHWEITZER, 222(GR):MAR71-153
GARLAND, M. THE CHANGING FORM OF FASHION.
G. SQUIRE, 157:SPRING71-76
GARLAND, P. THE SOUND OF SOUL.
M. PETERSON, 470:JAN71-44
GARNER, A. RED SHIFT.
M. LEVIN, 441:28OCT73-48
GARNER, H. VIOLATION OF THE VIRGINS.*
D. STEPHENS, 102(CANL):AUTUMN72-84
GARNER, R.T. & B. ROSEN. A SYSTEMATIC
INTRODUCTION TO NORMATIVE ETHICS AND
META-ETHICS.
K. SEGERBERG, 316:SEP70-459
GARNER, S. HAROLD FREDERIC.
R. ASSELINEAU, 189(EA):JUL-SEP71-348
GARNETT, D. PLOUGH OVER THE BONES.
R. GARFITT, 362:18OCT73-528
GARNETT, D. PURL AND PLAIN.
617(TLS):30MAR73-340
GARNETT, D. - SEE "CARRINGTON: LETTERS
AND EXTRACTS FROM HER DIARIES"
GARNSEY, P. SOCIAL STATUS AND LEGAL
PRIVILEGE IN THE ROMAN EMPIRE.*
F.C. BOURNE, 24:OCT72-605
J. CROOK, 123:JUN72-238
GARRARD, J.G. MIXAIL ČULKOV.*
M. BERMAN, 550(RUSR):OCT71-410
A.G. CROSS, 575(SEER):APR72-295
GARRETT, G. DEATH OF THE FOX.
M.C. BATTESTIN, 219(GAR):WINTER71-511
R.W. FRENCH, 568(SCN):SPRING72-16
GARRETT, G. THE MAGIC STRIPTEASE.
M. LEVIN, 441:16DEC73-18
GARRETT, J. ROGER WILLIAMS.
639(VQR):SPRING71-LXXII
GARRETT, P.K. SCENE AND SYMBOL FROM
GEORGE ELIOT TO JAMES JOYCE.*
P. JENKINS, 541(RES):AUG71-390
R. LAWRENCE, 175:SUMMER71-70
J. LEJE, 597(SN):VOL43#1-323
M. STEIG, 648:OCT70-73
GARRETT, R.E.F. CHANCERY AND OTHER LEGAL
PROCEEDINGS.
W.J. JONES, 325:APR71-246
GARRIDO PALLARDÓ, F. LOS ORIGENES DEL
ROMANTICISMO.
B.J.D., 191(ELN):SEP71(SUPP)-11
GARRIGUE, J. STUDIES FOR AN ACTRESS AND
OTHER POEMS.
A. OSTRIKER, 441:11NOV73-42
H. SHAPIRO, 441:22JUN73-41
R. TONKS, 453:4OCT73-8
GARRISON, W.L. THE LETTERS OF WILLIAM
LLOYD GARRISON. (VOL 1) (W.M. MERRILL
& L. RUCHAMES, EDS)
D.B. DAVIS, 676(YR):AUTUMN71-117
M.D. PETERSON, 639(VQR):AUTUMN71-622
A. ZILVERSMIT, 432(NEQ):DEC71-677
GARRISON, W.L. THE LETTERS OF WILLIAM
LLOYD GARRISON. (VOL 2) (L. RUCHAMES,
ED)
M.D. PETERSON, 639(VQR):AUTUMN71-622
617(TLS):19JAN73-70
GARRO, E. RECOLLECTIONS OF THINGS TO
COME.
J.D. MC KEE, 649(WAL):SPRING70-65
GARTEN, H.F. - SEE HAUPTMANN, G.
GARTON, C. PERSONAL ASPECTS OF THE ROMAN
THEATRE.
617(TLS):22JUN73-710

GARVEY, E.M. & P.A. WICK. THE ARTS OF
THE FRENCH BOOK 1900-1965.
P.H., 503:SUMMER68-82
GARVIE, A.F. AESCHYLUS' "SUPPLICES."*
J. PERADOTTO, 121(CJ):OCT-NOV71-85
A.J. PODLECKI, 487:WINTER71-377
GARVIN, P.L., ED. COMPUTATION IN LIN-
GUISTICS.
I.A. MEL'ČUK, 353:MAR71-97
GARY, D.H. & R. PAYNE. THE SPLENDORS OF
ASIA.
G. TARR, 318(JAOS):JAN-MAR71-156
GARY, R. LES ENCHANTEURS.
617(TLS):29JUN73-737
GARY, R. THE GASP.
A. BROYARD, 441:2MAR73-29
M. LEVIN, 441:25MAR73-48
E. WEEKS, 61:MAR73-105
442(NY):31MAR73-118
617(TLS):29JUN73-737
DE LA GARZA, M.G. - SEE UNDER GONZÁLEZ DE
LA GARZA, M.
GASCOIGNE, B. THE HEYDAY.
E. FEINSTEIN, 362:25OCT73-572
617(TLS):19OCT73-1270
GASCOIGNE, B. THE TREASURES AND DYNAS-
TIES OF CHINA.
617(TLS):28DEC73-1579
GASCOYNE, D. COLLECTED VERSE TRANSLA-
TIONS.
A. CLUYSENAAR, 565:VOL12#2-63
GASKELL, E. NORTH AND SOUTH. (A. EAS-
SON, ED)
617(TLS):17AUG73-950
GASKELL, P. & P. BRADFORD - SEE HORN-
SCHUCH, J.
GASPARINI, L. CUTTY SARK.*
D. BARBOUR, 150(DR):SPRING71-133
R. GUSTAFSON, 529(QQ):SPRING71-140
GASPARINI, L. TUNNEL BUS TO DETROIT.
C.X. RINGROSE, 102(CANL):SPRING72-87
P. STEVENS, 529(QQ):WINTER71-627
GASPARINI, L. - SEE WARR, B.
GASSET, J.O. - SEE UNDER ORTEGA Y GASSET,
J.
GASSIER, P. FRANCISCO GOYA DRAWINGS.
J. CANADAY, 441:2DEC73-88
GASSNER, J. & E. QUINN, EDS. THE READ-
ER'S ENCYCLOPEDIA OF WORLD DRAMA.
J.C. TREWIN, 157:WINTER70-64
GASSTER, M. CHINESE INTELLECTUALS AND
THE REVOLUTION OF 1911.*
C. TUNG, 318(JAOS):APR-JUN71-362
GASTALDELLI, F. - SEE GEOFFREY OF AUXERRE
GASTER, T.H. MYTH, LEGEND AND CUSTOM IN
THE OLD TESTAMENT.
E.O. JAMES, 203:SPRING71-74
GASTON, P.M. THE NEW SOUTH CREED.*
R.B. EVERETT, 219(GAR):SPRING71-102
GATCH, M.M. LOYALTIES AND TRADITIONS.
A. CRÉPIN, 189(EA):OCT-DEC71-518
GATELL, A. NERUDA.
617(TLS):11MAY73-532
GATENBY, R. HANGED FOR A SHEEP.
N. CALLENDAR, 441:18MAR73-41
GATES, R.J., ED. THE AWNTYRS OFF ARTHURE
AT THE TERNE WATHELYNE.*
A. HEISERMAN, 405(MP):AUG71-60
J. WEISS, 382(MAE):1972/1-74
GATHORNE-HARDY, J. THE UNNATURAL HISTORY
OF THE NANNY.* (BRITISH TITLE: THE
RISE AND FALL OF THE BRITISH NANNY.)
J. WILSON, 441:1JUL73-3
442(NY):13AUG73-88
GATTI PERER, M.L., ED. IL DUOMO DI
MILANO.
A. BLUNT, 90:JUL71-406

GAUBIL, P.A. CORRESPONDANCE DE PEKIN
1722-1759. (R. SIMON, ED)
J.S. SEBES, 293(JAST):MAY71-661
GAUDON, J. LE TEMPS DE LA CONTEMPLA-
TION.*
J-B. BARRÈRE, 205(FMLS):JUL71-237
R.B. GRANT, 207(FR):OCT70-230
J. SEEBACHER, 535(RHL):MAY-JUN71-520
GAUGER, H-M. WORT UND SPRACHE.
E. SCHEPPER, 224(GRM):BAND21HEFT1-121
GAULDIE, W.S. THE APPRECIATION OF THE
ARTS: ARCHITECTURE.*
S. ROSENTHAL, 58:MAR71-15
GAULMIER, J. - SEE DE GOBINEAU, J.A.
GAULUPEAU, S. ANDRÉ MALRAUX ET LA MORT.
J. CARDUNER, 207(FR):FEB71-602
P. GAILLARD, 535(RHL):MAR-APR71-331
GAUNT, D.M. SURGE AND THUNDER.
H. CLARKE, 124:MAR72-239
GAUNT, W. THE GREAT CENTURY OF BRITISH
PAINTING.
R. EDWARDS, 39:DEC71-519
GAUNT, W. THE IMPRESSIONISTS.
R.S., 376:APR71-125
GAUNT, W. & M.D.E. CLAYTON-STAMM. WILLIAM
DE MORGAN.
A. FORGE, 592:NOV71-215
GAURICUS, P. DE SCULPTURA (1504). (A.
CHASTEL & R. KLEIN, EDS & TRANS)
M.L. D'ANCONA, 551(RENQ):SPRING71-69
GAUS, H. & A.J. VERMEERSCH. RÉPERTOIRE
DE LA PRESSE BRUXELLOISE (1789-1914)/
REPERTORIUM VAN DE BRUSSELSE PERS
(1789-1914). (L-Z & INDEX A-Z)
A. CORDEWIENER, 556(RLV):1970/6-678
GAUTHIER, D.P. THE LOGIC OF "LEVIATHAN."*
H.J. JOHNSON, 185:OCT71-83
GAUTHIER, M-M. EMAUX DU MOYEN ÂGE
OCCIDENTAL.
617(TLS):6APR73-374
GAUTHIER, R-A. & J-Y. JOLIF - SEE ARIS-
TOTLE
GAUTHIER, Y. L'ARC ET LE CERCLE.
J. TAMINIAUX, 154:MAR71-146
GAUTIER, J-M. - SEE DE CHATEAUBRIAND, F-R.
GAUTIER, T. ÉMAUX ET CAMÉES.* (M. COT-
TIN, ED)
C. BOOK-SENNINGER, 535(RHL):JAN-FEB
70-142
A-C. DOBBS, 290(JAAC):WINTER70-279
GAUTIER, T. GISELLE OR THE WILIS.
(ADAPTED BY V. VERDY)
M. MARKS, 151:NOV70-23
GAVIDIA, J.M. - SEE UNDER MATA GAVIDIA, J.
GAY, J. THE BEGGAR'S OPERA. (V. DUPONT,
TRANS)
J. MICHON, 189(EA):APR-JUN71-201
GAY, J. THE BEGGAR'S OPERA.* (E.V.
ROBERTS, ED)
J. MICHON, 189(EA):APR-JUN71-166
GAY, J. THE LETTERS OF JOHN GAY. (C.F.
BURGESS, ED)
H.W. DRESCHER, 38:BAND88HEFT1-145
GAY, P. THE BRIDGE OF CRITICISM.
R. FADEM, 319:APR73-267
J.A. LEITH, 173(ECS):FALL71-157
GAY, P. THE ENLIGHTENMENT. (VOL 1)
H. KOHN, 322(JHI):JUL-SEP70-465
GAY, P. THE ENLIGHTENMENT.* (VOL 2)
A.J. BINGHAM, 399(MLJ):JAN71-30
H. KOHN, 322(JHI):JUL-SEP70-465
J.A. LEITH, 173(ECS):FALL71-157
GAYFORD, E. THE AMATEUR BOATWOMAN.
617(TLS):27JUL73-884
GAYLE, A., JR., ED. THE BLACK AESTHETIC.
B. BELL, 418(MR):AUTUMN72-715

GAZDARU, D. CONTROVERSIAS Y DOCUMENTOS
LINGÜÍSTICOS.
T.A. SEWARD, 215(GL):VOL10#3-220
GAZLEY, J.G. THE LIFE OF ARTHUR YOUNG
1741-1820.
617(TLS):28DEC73-1587
GEACH, P.T. GOD AND THE SOUL.*
J. DONNELLY, 258:JUN71-268
GEACH, P.T. LOGIC MATTERS.
617(TLS):2FEB73-130
GEAREY, J. HEINRICH VON KLEIST.*
R. SAMUEL, 564:JUN70-177
GEBHARDT, P. A.W. SCHLEGELS SHAKESPEARE-
ÜBERSETZUNG.*
R. BORGMEIER, 490:APR71-277
GEDDES, P. THE OTTAWA ALLEGATION.
N. CALLENDAR, 441:8JUL73-26
GEDULD, C. FILMGUIDE TO "2001: A SPACE
ODYSSEY."
617(TLS):9NOV73-1378
GEDULD, H. & R. GOTTESMAN - SEE "SERGEI
EISENSTEIN AND UPTON SINCLAIR: THE MAK-
ING AND UNMAKING OF 'QUE VIVA, MEXICO!'"
GEDULD, H.M. PRINCE OF PUBLISHERS.*
T. BELANGER, 354:JUN70-166
P.J. KORSHIN, 173(ECS):FALL71-180
O.F. SIGWORTH, 50(ARQ):SPRING70-88
GEEN, R. - SEE ROUSSEAU, J-J.
GEERING, A. & H. TRÜMPY - SEE HEER, J.
GEERING, R.G. CHRISTINA STEAD.
D. GREEN, 381:JUN71-251
GEIGER, D. THE DRAMATIC IMPULSE IN
MODERN POETICS.
P.H. GRAY, 583:FALL70-93
GEIPEL, J. THE VIKING LEGACY.
R.M. WILSON, 175:AUTUMN71-96
GEIRINGER, K. HAYDN.
412:MAY72-149
GEISER, C. NATURALISMUS UND SYMBOLISMUS
IM FRÜHWERK THOMAS MANNS.
H.W. REICHERT, 406:FALL72-298
GEISMAR, M. MARK TWAIN.*
C.L. GRIMM, JR., 594:SPRING71-118
GEISS, I. STUDIEN ÜBER GESCHICHTE UND
GESCHICHTS-WISSENSCHAFT.
617(TLS):31AUG73-1006
GEISS, I. & B.J. WENDT, EDS. DEUTSCHLAND
IN DER WELTPOLITIK DES 19. UND 20.
JAHRHUNDERTS.
617(TLS):31AUG73-1006
GEISSEN, A. DER SEPTUAGINTA-TEXT DES
BUCHES DANIEL, 5-12, SOWIE ESTHER, 1-2,
15, NACH DEM KÖLNER TEIL DES P. 967.
A. PELLETIER, 555:VOL45FASC2-351
GEISSLER, R. & P. HASUBEK. DER ROMAN IM
UNTERRICHT.
W. OBERLE, 657(WW):JAN/FEB70-70
GEISSNER, H. SPRECHKUNDE UND SPRECHER-
ZIEHUNG.
H. ULBRICH, 682(ZPSK):BAND23HEFT1-103
GEIST, J.F. PASSAGEN.*
V. GRUEN, 441:MAY70-84
S. MUTHESIUS, 46:NOV70-328
GELB, B. SO SHORT A TIME.
P. ADAMS, 61:OCT73-130
S. BROWNMILLER, 441:30SEP73-4
C. LEHMANN-HAUPT, 441:27SEP73-43
GELDZAHLER, H. NEW YORK PAINTING AND
SCULPTURE: 1940-1970.
D. IRWIN, 39:APR71-342
GELFAND, M. THE GENUINE SHONA.
617(TLS):31AUG73-995
GELLENS, J., ED. TWENTIETH CENTURY IN-
TERPRETATIONS OF "A FAREWELL TO ARMS."
K. MC SWEENEY, 529(QQ):SUMMER71-337

GELLINEK, C., ED. FESTSCHRIFT FÜR KON-
STANTIN REICHARDT.
C.E. REED, 221(GQ):JAN71-93
M.O. WALSHE, 220(GL&L):OCT71-18
GELLINEK, C. "KÖNIG ROTHER."*
M. CALIEBE, 657(WW):JAN/FEB71-68
GELLING, M., W.F.H. NICOLAISEN & M.
RICHARDS, COMPS. THE NAMES OF TOWNS
AND CITIES IN BRITAIN.* (W.F.H. NIC-
OLAISEN, ED)
M.A. MOOK, 424:JUN71-147
GELLNER, E. CAUSE AND MEANING IN THE
SOCIAL SCIENCES. (I.C. JARVIE & J.
AGASSI, EDS)
617(TLS):21SEP73-1079
GELLNER, E. THOUGHT AND CHANGE.
L. ADDIS, 486:MAR70-159
617(TLS):16FEB73-171
GELLNER, E. & C. MICAUD, EDS. ARABS AND
BERBERS.
617(TLS):15JUN73-696
GELMIS, J. THE FILM DIRECTOR AS SUPER-
STAR.
P. GIDAL, 592:JUL/AUG71-42
GELTMAN, M. THE CONFRONTATION.
T.W. ROGERS, 396(MODA):WINTER72-107
GELVEN, M. A COMMENTARY ON HEIDEGGER'S
"BEING AND TIME."
J.D.C., 543:JUN71-746
GELY, C. VICTOR HUGO POÈTE DE L'INTIM-
ITÉ.
P. MOREAU, 557(RSH):APR-JUN70-325
GEN, T., ED. DERTZEILUNGEN FUN IDDISHE
SOVETISHE SHRAIBER.
S. LEHRMAN, 287:OCT70-24
GENDERS, R. BULBS.
617(TLS):20APR73-454
GENDRE, A. RONSARD, POÈTE DE LA CONQUÊTE
AMOUREUSE.
M.C. SMITH, 208(FS):JUL72-321
GENDRON, J-D. & G. STRAKA, EDS. ÉTUDES
DE LINGUISTIQUE FRANCO-CANADIENNE.
A. HULL, 207(FR):OCT70-263
W. SAYERS, 545(RPH):MAY72-440
GENDZIER, I.L. FRANTZ FANON.
D. CAUTE, 362:6SEP73-318
P. GREEN, 441:25FEB73-1
E.J. HOBSBAWM, 453:22FEB73-6
T. LASK, 441:13JAN73-33
617(TLS):25MAY73-580
"THE GENEVA BIBLE."
J.G.M., 570(SQ):SPRING71-177
GENNARO, C. FRIDUGISO DI TOURS E IL
"DE SUBSTANTIA NIHILI ET TENEBRARUM."
A. FOREST, 542:APR-JUN70-231
GENOVESE, E.D. IN RED AND BLACK.*
W.T. LHAMON, JR., 651(WHR):SPRING72-
169
GENT, P. NORTH DALLAS FORTY.
D. SCHAAP, 441:28OCT73-44
GENTILE, G. GENESIS AND STRUCTURE OF
SOCIETY.*
L.M. PALMER, 154:DEC70-439
GENTILE, G. STUDI VICHIANI.
E. NAMER, 542:APR-JUN70-240
GENTILE, G. & D. JAJA. CARTEGGIO GENTILE-
JAJA. (M. SANDIROCCO, ED)
P. PICCONE, 484(PPR):SEP71-139
GENTILHOMME, Y. RUSSIAN FOR SCIENTISTS.
N.D. GERSHEVSKY, 32:DEC72-948
GENTRY, C. FRAME-UP.
C.J. BAYARD, 649(WAL):WINTER72-265
GEOFFREY OF AUXERRE. GOFFREDO DI AUXERRE:
SUPER APOCALYPSIM. RICERCHE SU GOFFREDO
D'AUXERRE: IL COMPENDIO ANONIMO DEL
"SUPER APOCALYPSIM." (BOTH ED BY F.
GASTALDELLI)
W. SAUER, 382(MAE):1972/2-151

GEOGHEGAN, A.R. BIBLIOGRAFÍA DE BIBLIO-
GRAFÍAS ARGENTINAS 1807-1970. (PRELIMI-
NARY ED)
  J.B. CHILDS, 263:OCT-DEC72-417
  H.C. WOODBRIDGE, 517(PBSA):JAN-MAR72-
  82
GEORGACAS, D.J. & W.A. MC DONALD. PLACE
NAMES OF SOUTHWEST PELOPONNESUS: REGIS-
TER AND INDEXES.
  L. ZGUSTA, 424:JUN70-131
GEORGE IV. THE CORRESPONDENCE OF GEORGE,
PRINCE OF WALES, 1770-1812. (VOLS 6&7)
(A. ASPINALL, ED)
  D.V.E., 191(ELN):SEP71(SUPP)-13
GEORGE, A. & J. WILSON AND COLONEL HOUSE.
  R. COLES, 453:22FEB73-15
GEORGE, D.L. - SEE UNDER LLOYD GEORGE, D.
GEORGE, E. THE LIFE AND DEATH OF BENJA-
MIN ROBERT HAYDON. (2ND ED REV BY D.
GEORGE)
  K. GARLICK, 39:FEB70-168
GEORGE, F.H. AUTOMATION CYBERNETICS AND
SOCIETY.
  H.B. ENDERTON, 316:SEP71-544
GEORGE, F.H. SEMANTICS.
  L. ZGUSTA, 353:FEB71-119
GEORGE, M. ONE WOMAN'S "SITUATION."
  W. CHRISTIAN, 173(ECS):SUMMER72-627
GEORGE, R.E. A LEADER AND A LAGGARD.
  Z. LINKLATTER, 150(DR):SPRING71-105
GEORGE, T.J.S. LEE KUAN YEW'S SINGAPORE.
  D.J. ENRIGHT, 362:6DEC73-786
  617(TLS):14DEC73-1527
GEORGEL, J. LE FRANQUISME.
  J. BÉCARUD, 98:MAR71-288
GEORGEL, P. L'ALBUM DE LÉOPOLDINE HUGO.
LÉOPOLDINE HUGO, UNE JEUNE FILLE ROMAN-
TIQUE. (2ND ED)
  J. SEEBACHER, 535(RHL):JUL-AUG70-726
GEORGES, E.S. STUDIES IN ROMANCE NOUNS
EXTRACTED FROM PAST PARTICIPLES. (REV
BY J.R. CRADDOCK & Y. MALKIEL)
  W.H. HAVERKATE, 182:VOL24#15/16-588
  R.G. KEIGHTLEY, 86(BHS):JUL72-289
GEORGESCU, V.A. & E. POPESCU, EDS & TRANS.
LEGISLAŢIA AGRARĂ A ŢĂRII ROMÂNEŞTI
(1775-82).
  V.G. CADERE, 182:VOL24#17/18-659
GEORGI, A. DAS LATEINISCHE UND DEUTSCHE
PREISGEDICHT DES MITTELALTERS IN DER
NACHFOLGE DES "GENUS DEMONSTRATIVUM."*
  R.W. FISHER, 67:NOV72-245
  W.T.H. JACKSON, 221(GQ):NOV71-564
  B. MURDOCH, 220(GL&L):JUL72-383
  O. SAYCE, 402(MLR):JUL72-686
"GEORGIAN FURNITURE: VICTORIA AND ALBERT
MUSEUM."
  R.E., 135:AUG70-290
GEORGIEV, V. DIE DEUTUNG DER ALTERTÜM-
LICHEN THRAKISCHEN INSCHRIFT AUS
KJOLMEN.
  A. HUS, 343:BAND13HEFT2-192
GEORGIEV, V.I. INTRODUZIONE ALLA STORIA
DELLE LINGUE IND-EUROPEE.*
  R. SCHMITT, 343:BAND13HEFT1-35
GEORGIEV, V.I. OSNOVNI PROBLEMI NA SLAV-
YANSKATA DIAKHRONNA MORFOLOGIYA.*
  M. SAMILOV, 575(SEER):OCT72-635
GEORGIN, R. GUIDE DE LA LANGUE FRAN-
ÇAISE. COMMENT S'EXPRIMER EN FRANÇAIS.
  G. GOUGENHEIM, 209(FM):APR70-157
VON GERAMB, V. KINDER- UND HAUSMÄRCHEN
AUS DER STEIERMARK. (4TH ED) (K. HAID-
ING, ED)
  F. HARKORT, 196:BAND12HEFT2/3-276
GÉRARD, A. LES TAMBOURS DU NÉANT.*
  P.R. PLANTE, 454:WINTER72-180

GÉRARD, A.S. ENGLISH ROMANTIC POETRY.*
  J. DELBAERE-GARANT, 556(RLV):1971/1-
  111
GERASIMOV, I.P., D.L. ARMAND & K.M. YEF-
RON, EDS. NATURAL RESOURCES OF THE
SOVIET UNION.
  R.N. TAAFFE, 32:SEP72-695
GERBER, D. AMERICAN ATLAS.
  J.R. FRAKES, 441:16SEP73-4
GERBER, D.E., ED. EUTERPE.
  D.A. CAMPBELL, 123:DEC72-321
  E.D. FLOYD, 124:SEP71-23
GERBER, H.E. - SEE MOORE, G.
GERBOTH, W. AN INDEX TO MUSICAL FEST-
SCHRIFTEN AND SIMILAR PUBLICATIONS.*
  M. PETERSON, 470:NOV70-43
GERDTS, W.H. & R. BURKE. AMERICAN STILL
LIFE PAINTING.
  R. LEIBOWITZ, 58:NOV71-14
GERE, J.A. TADDEO ZUCCARO.
  J. BEAN, 90:NOV71-675
  J.D., 135:JUN71-150
  C. PEDRETTI, 275(IQ):SPRING-SUMMER72-
  103
GERETSEGGER, H. & M. PEINTNER. OTTO
WAGNER 1841-1918.
  E. KAUFMANN, JR., 44:JUN71-12
  N. PEVSNER, 46:FEB71-132
  45:MAR71-50
GERHARD, H.P. THE WORLD OF ICONS.*
  D.T. RICE, 89(BJA):SPRING72-201
GERHARDIE, W. FUTILITY. PENDING HEAVEN.
  N. BRAYBROOKE, 619(TC):VOL179#1047-48
GERHARDT, D. GOGOL' UND DOSTOJEVSKIJ IN
IHREM KÜNSTLERISCHEN VERHÄLTNIS.*
  D. BORKER, 32:MAR72-193
GERHARDT, M.I. THE ART OF STORY TELLING.
  N. SALEM, 196:BAND11HEFT1/2-161
GÉRIN, W. EMILY BRONTË.*
  P. DANE, 67:NOV72-229
  M. ELLMANN, 31(ASCH):WINTER72/73-170
  F.A.C. WILSON, 648:APR72-14
GÉRIN, W. HORATIA NELSON.
  639(VQR):WINTER71-XXXII
GERKE, E-O. DER ESSAY ALS KUNSTFORM BEI
HUGO VON HOFMANNSTHAL.*
  R. EXNER, 222(GR):NOV71-313
  E. KRISPYN, 221(GQ):JAN71-70
  J.H. REID, 182:VOL24#1/2-23
GERLACH, A.C., ED. THE NATIONAL ATLAS OF
THE UNITED STATES OF AMERICA.
  M.P. CLAUSSEN, 141:APR71-194
GERLACH, H. DER ENGLISCHE BAUERNAUFSTAND
VON 1381 UND DER DEUTSCHE BAUERNKRIEG.
  R.B. DOBSON, 182:VOL24#4-176
GERLACH, R. GLANZ ÜBER DEM BODENSEE.
  617(TLS):12OCT73-1244
GERLO, A. ERASME ET SES PORTRAITISTES.
(2ND ED)
  S. MANDEVILLE, 551(RENQ):SPRING71-77
GERMAIN, F. L'IMAGINATION D'ALFRED DE
VIGNY.
  J-P. RICHARD, 98:FEB70-99
GERMAIN, S. LES MOSAÏQUES DE TIMGAD.
  D.J. SMITH, 313:VOL61-291
GERMANN, D. & E. HAUFE - SEE SCHILLER, F.
GERMANN, G. GOTHIC REVIVAL IN EUROPE
AND BRITAIN.
  617(TLS):23FEB73-203
GERMASHEVA, F.V. KATALOG INKUNABULOV
NAUCHNOĬ BIBLIOTEKI SARATOVSKOGO UNI-
VERSITETA.
  J.S.G. SIMMONS, 78(BC):WINTER71-548
GERMER, H. THE GERMAN NOVEL OF EDUCA-
TION, 1792-1805.*
  J. MOUNIER, 549(RLC):JUL-SEP70-424
  B. PESCHKEN, 564:OCT70-237
GERNDT, S. - SEE FONTANE, T.

129

GERNET, J. DAILY LIFE IN CHINA (ON THE
EVE OF THE MONGOL INVASION 1250-1276).
E.H. KAPLAN, 293(JAST):NOV70-174
GERRATANA, V. & A. GUERRA - SEE LABRIOLA,
A.
GERRESSEN, W. TIBULLS ELEGIE 2, 5 UND
VERGILS AENEIS.
E.J. KENNEY, 123:JUN72-277
GERSBACH-BÄSCHLIN, A. REFLEKTORISCHER
STIL UND ERZÄHLSTRUKTUR.
P. POLLARD, 208(FS):APR72-221
GERSHMAN, H. A BIBLIOGRAPHY OF THE SUR-
REALIST REVOLUTION IN FRANCE.*
M.A. CAWS, 188(ECR):SUMMER70-150
GERSHMAN, H. THE SURREALIST REVOLUTION
IN FRANCE.*
F.J. CARMODY, 546(RR):FEB71-73
M.A. CAWS, 188(ECR):SUMMER70-150
M.A. CAWS, 207(FR):OCT70-255
GERSHWIN, I. LYRICS ON SEVERAL OCCASIONS.
W. CLEMONS, 441:23SEP73-3
GERSON, N.B. DAUGHTER OF EARTH AND
WATER.
S. BROWNMILLER, 441:11FEB73-10
GERSON, S. A GLOSSARY OF GRAMMATICAL
TERMS.
P. SALMON, 220(GL&L):APR72-305
N.C.W. SPENCE, 208(FS):APR72-241
GERSON, S. SOUND AND SYMBOL IN THE DIA-
LOGUE OF THE WORKS OF CHARLES DICKENS.*
G. BAUER, 179(ES):JUN71-284
A. WOLLMANN, 38:BAND89HEFT1-150
GERSON, W. PATTERNS OF URBAN LIVING.
S.D. LASH, 529(QQ):WINTER71-636
GERSTEIN, L. NIKOLAI STRAKHOV.*
R.L. STRONG, JR., 32:MAR72-194
GERSTENMAIER, C. THE VOICES OF THE SI-
LENT.
442(NY):3MAR73-115
GERSTER, G. CHURCHES IN ROCK.
M.M. SHEEHAN, 363:MAY71-80
GERTEL, Z. BORGES Y SU RETORNO A LA
POESÍA.*
D.A. YATES, 238:MAR71-203
GERTEL, Z. LA NOVELA HISPANOAMERICANA
CONTEMPORÁNEA.
H. CASTILLO, 238:SEP71-601
J. HIGGINS, 86(BHS):APR72-205
GERTZ, E. FOR THE FIRST HOURS OF TOMOR-
ROW.
I. DILLIARD, 31(ASCH):SPRING73-348
GERZ-VON BÜREN, V. GESCHICHTE DES CLARIS-
SENKLOSTERS ST. CLARA IN KLEINBASEL,
1266-1529.
G. ZIMMERMANN, 182:VOL24#21/22-818
GESKE, R. GÓNGORAS WARNREDE IM ZEICHEN
DER HEKATE.
M. BARRIO, 430(NS):OCT70-533
GESNER, C. SHAKESPEARE AND THE GREEK
ROMANCE.*
G. LAMBIN, 189(EA):JUL-SEP71-325
M.A. SHAABER, 551(RENQ):WINTER71-568
639(VQR):AUTUMN71-CLXXII
GETTENS, R.J. THE FREER CHINESE BRONZES.
(VOL 2)
W. FAIRBANK, 244(HJAS):VOL30-240
I. MC LACHLAN, 302:JAN71-173
L.J. MAJEWSKI, 54:JUN71-239
C.S. SMITH, 293(JAST):NOV70-170
A. SOPER, 57:VOL33#1/2-154
GETTLEMAN, M.E. THE DORR REBELLION.
441:16SEP73-16
GETTO, G. BAROCCO IN PROSA E IN POESIA.
D. CONRIERI, 228(GSLI):VOL148FASC461-
120
D.D., 275(IQ):SPRING-SUMMER72-119
GEYER, D. DIE RUSSISCHE REVOLUTION.
H.J. ELLISON, 32:JUN72-426

GEYTENBEEK, B. & H. GIDABAL GRAMMAR AND
DICTIONARY.
D.T. TRYON, 67:NOV72-265
GHALIB. THE GHAZALS OF GHALIB. (A. AH-
MAD, ED)
Z. GHOSE, 249(HUDR):SUMMER72-309
GHISELIN, B. COUNTRY OF THE MINOTAUR.*
R. SQUIRES, 134(CP):FALL70-77
GHISELIN, M.T. THE TRIUMPH OF THE DAR-
WINIAN METHOD.
B.J. LOEWENBERG, 637(VS):MAR71-343
GHOSE, S. THE RENAISSANCE TO MILITANT
NATIONALISM IN INDIA.
J.R. MC LANE, 293(JAST):FEB71-482
GHOSE, S. SOCIALISM, DEMOCRACY AND
NATIONALISM IN INDIA.
617(TLS):31AUG73-1009
GHOSH, A. THE CITY IN EARLY HISTORICAL
INDIA.
617(TLS):26OCT73-1325
GHOUSE, M. SECULARISM, SOCIETY AND LAW
IN INDIA.
617(TLS):31AUG73-1009
GHYKA, M.G. LE NOMBRE D'OR.
J. ROUDAUT, 98:JAN71-26
GIANAKARIS, C.J. PLUTARCH.
H. MARTIN, JR., 399(MLJ):DEC71-532
P.A. STADTER, 24:SEP71-23
GIANCOTTI, F. MIMO ET GNOME.
A. HUS, 555:VOL45FASC1-164
GIANNANTONIO, P. DANTE E L'ALLEGORISMO.
F.F., 228(GSLI):VOL148FASC461-152
GIANNARIS, G. MIKIS THEODORAKIS.
617(TLS):17AUG73-951
GIANTURCO, E. A SELECTIVE BIBLIOGRAPHY
OF VICO SCHOLARSHIP (1948-1968).*
G. TAGLIACOZZO, 276:SPRING71-100
GIAVERI, M.T. L'ALBUM DE VERS ANCIENS
DI PAUL VALÉRY.*
I. GHEORGHE, 557(RSH):OCT-DEC71-673
GIBBON, E. THE ENGLISH ESSAYS OF EDWARD
GIBBON. (P.B. CRADDOCK, ED)
H.R. TREVOR-ROPER, 453:18OCT73-29
617(TLS):1JUN73-613
GIBBON, M. THE BRAHMS WALTZ.
J. RYAN, 159(DM):SPRING73-108
GIBBONS, E. STALKING THE GOOD LIFE.
639(VQR):AUTUMN71-CLXXXVIII
GIBBONS, F. DOSSO AND BATTISTA DOSSI,
COURT PAINTERS AT FERRARA.
C. GILBERT, 290(JAAC):FALL70-140
F.L. RICHARDSON, 56:AUTUMN70-309
"STANLEY GIBBONS ELIZABETHAN POSTAGE
STAMP CATALOGUE." (9TH ED)
617(TLS):2MAR73-250
"STANLEY GIBBONS EUROPE 3 FOREIGN STAMP
CATALOGUE Q-Z."
617(TLS):23FEB73-221
GIBBS, A.M. SHAW.
W.A. ARMSTRONG, 571:SUMMER70-104
GIBBS, R. EARTH CHARMS HEARD SO EARLY.
D. BARBOUR, 150(DR):SPRING71-133
GIBBS-SMITH, C.H. THE BAYEUX TAPESTRY.
617(TLS):21SEP73-1093
GIBIAN, G. - SEE KHARMS, D. & A. VVEDEN-
SKY
GIBLIN, C.H. IN HOPE OF GOD'S GLORY.
S.E. DONLON, 613:SUMMER71-287
GIBSON, A. THE SILENCE OF GOD.
J.B.L., 543:DEC70-339
GIBSON, A.B. MUSE AND THINKER.*
B.T., 543:MAR71-542
GIBSON, A.B. THE RELIGION OF DOSTOEVSKY.
617(TLS):12OCT73-1239
GIBSON, A.B. THEISM AND EMPIRICISM.*
J. HICK, 483:OCT71-365
GIBSON, A.M. THE CHICKASAWS.*
G.A. BAILEY, 377:NOV72-188

GIBSON, D.B. THE FICTION OF STEPHEN
CRANE.
J.W. GARGANO, 594:FALL70-368
GIBSON, G. COMMUNION.
W.H. NEW, 102(CANL):SUMMER72-88
GIBSON, G. ELEVEN CANADIAN NOVELISTS.
J.G. MOSS, 296:FALL73-115
GIBSON, G. FIVE LEGS.*
J. MILLS, 648:JUN70-35
GIBSON, I. THE DEATH OF LORCA.
V.S. PRITCHETT, 453:29NOV73-18
S. SPENDER, 441:9SEP73-43
A. TERRY, 362:7JUN73-767
GIBSON, I. LA REPRESIÓN NACIONALISTA DE
GRANADA EN 1936 Y LA MUERTE DE FEDERICO
GARCÍA LORCA.*
G. CONNELL, 402(MLR):OCT72-931
GIBSON, J., ED. LET THE POET CHOOSE.
617(TLS):8JUN73-646
GIBSON, J. A SMALL AND CHARMING WORLD.
617(TLS):13JUL73-811
GIBSON, J.R. FEEDING THE RUSSIAN FUR
TRADE.*
R.H. FISHER, 550(RUSR):JUL71-303
GIBSON, R. DEJA-VU.
S. SCHWARTZ, 441:2DEC73-95
GIBSON, R. NEMERTEANS.
617(TLS):9MAR73-262
GIBSON, T. TEACHERS TALKING.
617(TLS):21SEP73-1089
GIBSON, W.M. - SEE TWAIN, M.
GIBSON, W.S. HIERONYMUS BOSCH.
617(TLS):9NOV73-1363
GICOVATE, B. SAN JUAN DE LA CRUZ (SAINT
JOHN OF THE CROSS).
E. SARMIENTO, 86(BHS):JAN72-69
GICOVATE, B. & A. - SEE MALLEA, E.
GIDDENS, A. CAPITALISM AND MODERN SOCIAL
THEORY.
G. POGGI, 111:2JUN72-157
N. SPULBER, 32:SEP72-687
GIDDINGS, R.W., COMP. YAQUI MYTHS AND
LEGENDS.* (H. BEHN, ED)
B. TOELKEN, 650(WF):OCT70-268
GIDION, H. ZUR DARSTELLUNGSWEISE VON
GOETHES "WILHELM MEISTERS WANDERJAHRE."*
H. REISS, 220(GL&L):JAN72-176
GIEDION, S. ARCHITECTURE AND THE PHENO-
MENA OF TRANSITION.
E. SCHAPER, 89(BJA):WINTER72-102
GIERGIELEWICZ, M. INTRODUCTION TO POLISH
VERSIFICATION.*
W.K. KONDY, 497(POLR):AUTUMN70-116
GIESELMANN, R. CONTEMPORARY CHURCH ARCH-
ITECTURE.
617(TLS):27APR73-464
GIESEY, R.A. IF NOT, NOT.
G. TILANDER, 240(HR):OCT71-439
GIFFEN, J.H. THE LEGAL AND PRACTICAL
ASPECTS OF TRADE WITH THE SOVIET UNION.
P.B. MAGGS, 550(RUSR):JAN71-89
GIFFORD, D. - SEE HOGG, J.
GIL, A.M. - SEE BUERO VALLEJO, A.
GILBERT, B. CHULO.
P. ADAMS, 61:DEC73-138
GILBERT, C. CHANGE IN PIERO DELLA FRAN-
CESCA.*
G. ROBERTSON, 56:AUTUMN71-356
GILBERT, G.G., ED. THE GERMAN LANGUAGE
IN AMERICA.
H.A. POCHMANN, 301(JEGP):OCT72-558
GILBERT, G.G., ED. TEXAS STUDIES IN
BILINGUALISM.
J. EICHHOFF, 406:WINTER72-400
K. WHINNOM, 86(BHS):JUL72-293
GILBERT, H. HOTELS WITH EMPTY ROOMS.
N. CALLENDAR, 441:20MAY73-22

GILBERT, M. WINSTON S. CHURCHILL. (COM-
PANION VOL 3)
J. GRIGG, 362:18JAN73-90
617(TLS):9MAR73-256
GILBERT, M. THE 92ND TIGER.
P. ADAMS, 61:SEP73-118
N. CALLENDAR, 441:19AUG73-13
GILBERT, M. SIR HORACE RUMBOLD.
R. CROSSMAN, 362:27DEC73-889
GILBERT, V. COVENTRY AS IT WAS.
617(TLS):31AUG73-1009
GILBERT, W.S. THE BAB BALLADS BY W.S.
GILBERT. (J. ELLIS, ED)
J.B. JONES, 636(VP):AUTUMN71-359
GILBEY, Q. QUEEN OF THE TURF.
617(TLS):14DEC73-1533
GILBOA, Y.A. THE BLACK YEARS OF SOVIET
JEWRY, 1939-1953.*
L. KOCHAN, 32:JUN72-447
GILDEA, J. - SEE "PARTONOPEU DE BLOIS"
GILDER, G.F. SEXUAL SUICIDE.
A. BROYARD, 441:13NOV73-49
J.A. HENNESSEE, 441:9DEC73-36
442(NY):17DEC73-154
GILDNER, G. DIGGING FOR INDIANS.
J. GALASSI, 491:MAR73-343
W.H. PRITCHARD, 249(HUDR):SPRING72-120
42(AR):WINTER71/72-588
GILDNER, G. FIRST PRACTICE.
D. ACKERSON, 448:SPRING71-94
GILES, J.H. SIX-HORSE HITCH.
R.A. RORIPAUGH, 649(WAL):SUMMER70-159
GILES, K. A FILE ON DEATH.
A. BROYARD, 441:1AUG73-31
N. CALLENDAR, 441:1JUL73-21
617(TLS):13APR73-427
GILFORD, C. ACOUSTICS FOR RADIO AND
TELEVISION STUDIOS.
R. LEWCOCK, 415:NOV72-1092
GILKEY, L. RELIGION AND SCIENTIFIC FU-
TURE.
J.J.E., 543:MAR71-543
GILL, A. MALLARMÉ'S POEM "LA CHEVELURE
VOL D'UNE FLAMME..."
A.R. CHISHOLM, 67:NOV72-245
D.J. MOSSOP, 208(FS):OCT72-468
GILL, B. TALLULAH.*
E. WEEKS, 61:JAN73-98
617(TLS):21SEP73-1093
GILL, B. - SEE ZERBE, J.
GILL, M.S. HIMALAYAN WONDERLAND.
617(TLS):23MAR73-333
GILL, R. HAPPY RURAL SEAT.
617(TLS):16MAR73-289
GILL, R. - SEE MARLOWE, C.
GILL, S. - SEE DICKENS, C.
GILL, S.M. SIX SYMBOLIST PLAYS OF YEATS.
R.J. FINNERAN, 295:FEB73-129
GILLEN, M. ASSASSINATION OF THE PRIME
MINISTER.
617(TLS):9FEB73-147
GILLESPIE, G. GERMAN BAROQUE POETRY.
J.M. WOODS, 131(CL):FALL72-377
GILLESSEN, H. THEMEN, BILDER UND MOTIVE
IM WERK EDUARDO MALLEAS.
M. BARRIO, 430(NS):NOV70-581
GILLETT, C. THE SOUND OF THE CITY.*
M. PETERSON, 470:JAN71-45
GILLHAM, D.G. WILLIAM BLAKE.
617(TLS):18MAY73-564
GILLIATT, M. A HOUSE IN THE COUNTRY.
617(TLS):14DEC73-1549
GILLIATT, P. UNHOLY FOOLS.
D. BROMWICH, 441:20MAY73-5
617(TLS):7SEP73-1020
GILLIE, C. LONGMAN COMPANION TO ENGLISH
LITERATURE.
617(TLS):6APR73-396

131

GILLIES, A. A HEBRIDEAN IN GOETHE'S
WEIMAR.*
G.F. PROBST, 399(MLJ):DEC71-528
GILLIES, A. - SEE VON HERDER, J.G.
GILLIES, D.A. AN OBJECTIVE THEORY OF
PROBABILITY.
617(TLS):10AUG73-935
GILLON, A., ED & TRANS. POEMS OF THE
GHETTO.*
M. STEIN, 497(POLR):SUMMER70-81
GILLOTT, J. SALVAGE.
L.T. LEMON, 502(PRS):FALL71-270
GILMAN, D. A PALM FOR MRS. POLLIFAX.
N. CALLENDAR, 441:1APR73-34
GILMAN, R. THE CONFUSION OF REALMS.
J. BAYLEY, 473(PR):SUMMER72-398
GILMAN, W.H. & J.E. PARSONS - SEE EMER-
SON, R.W.
GILMORE, T.B., JR. THE EIGHTEENTH-CENTURY
CONTROVERSY OVER RIDICULE AS A TEST OF
TRUTH.*
A.J. SPINA, 481(PQ):JUL71-355
GILSON, É. LINGUISTIQUE ET PHILOSOPHIE.
R. BLANCHÉ, 542:OCT-DEC70-491
A. ERNOUT, 555:VOL45FASC1-192
GIMBUTAS, M. THE SLAVS.
A. FARKAS, 32:DEC72-877
GIMPEL, J. THE CULT OF ART.
T. CROMBIE, 39:JUL70-82
A. LOVELL, 592:MAR70-131
GIMSON, A.C. AN INTRODUCTION TO THE PRO-
NUNCIATION OF ENGLISH. (2ND ED)
N.E. ENKVIST, 597(SN):VOL43#2-581
P.J. ROACH, 297(JL):OCT71-307
A. WARD, 447(N&Q):JUL71-266
GINDIN, J. HARVEST OF A QUIET EYE.
J.M. FLORA, 385(MQR):WINTER73-90
GINESTIER, P. JEAN ANOUILH.
S.J. COLLIER, 208(FS):APR72-226
GINESTIER, P. POUR CONNAÎTRE LA PENSÉE
DE BACHELARD.
N. BAILEY, 402(MLR):OCT72-915
GINGER, J. NOTHING AND A SHADE.
R. GARFITT, 362:18OCT73-528
617(TLS):26OCT73-1324
GINSBERG, A. THE FALL OF AMERICA.
H. VENDLER, 441:15APR73-1
617(TLS):27APR73-474
GINSBERG, R., ED. THE CRITIQUE OF WAR.*
G. WILLIAMS, 484(PPR):MAR71-455
GINSBURG, C.D. INTRODUCTION TO THE MASSO-
RETICO-CRITICAL EDITION OF THE HEBREW
BIBLE.
B.A. LEVINE, 318(JAOS):APR-JUN71-307
GINSBURG, M. - SEE ZAMYATIN, Y.
GINSCHEL, G. DER JUNGE JACOB GRIMM
1805-1819.
R. HIERSCHE, 260(IF):BAND75-341
GINZBURG, N. CARO MICHELE.
617(TLS):15JUN73-661
GIONO, J. LE DÉSERTEUR ET AUTRES RÉCITS.
617(TLS):28DEC73-1581
GIONO, J. L'IRIS DE SUSE.
D. TAILLEUX, 207(FR):MAR71-783
GIORDAN, H. - SEE ROLLAND, R.
DI GIORGIO MARTINI, F. - SEE UNDER FRAN-
CESCO DI GIORGIO MARTINI
"GIORNALE ITALIANO DI FILOLOGIA." (VOL 1)
A. ERNOUT, 555:VOL45FASC1-195
GIOVANETTI, L. THE MAN WHO WON THE MEDAL
OF HONOR.
M. LEVIN, 441:4NOV73-81
DE GIOVANNI, E. FILOSOFIA E DIRITTO
IN FRANCESCO D'ANDREA.
E. NAMER, 542:JAN-MAR70-100

GIOVANNI, N. BLACK FEELING, BLACK TALK,
BLACK JUDGMENT.
N.A. BRITTIN, 577(SHR):SPRING71-207
A. OSTRIKER, 473(PR):SPRING72-270
DI GIOVANNI, N.T. - SEE BORGES, J.L.
DI GIOVANNI, N.T., WITH J.L. BORGES -
SEE BORGES, J.L.
GIOVANNINI, A. ETUDE HISTORIQUE SUR LES
ORIGINES DU CATALOGUE DES VAISSEAUX.*
E. WILL, 555:VOL45FASC1-137
GIOVENE, A. THE DILEMMA OF LOVE.
R. BRYDEN, 362:18JAN73-90
M. LEVIN, 441:20MAY73-54
617(TLS):26JAN73-84
GIPPER, H. SPRACHLICHE UND GEISTIGE
METAMORPHOSEN BEI GEDICHTÜBERSETZUNGEN.
G. KOLDE, 260(IF):BAND74-185
GIPSON, L.H. A BIBLIOGRAPHICAL GUIDE TO
THE HISTORY OF THE BRITISH EMPIRE,
1748-1776.
M. KAMMEN, 432(NEQ):JUN71-335
GIPSON, L.H. A GUIDE TO MANUSCRIPTS RE-
LATING TO THE HISTORY OF THE BRITISH
EMPIRE, 1748-1776.
M. KAMMEN, 432(NEQ):JUN71-335
639(VQR):SUMMER71-CXXII
GIRALDI, G. LA FILOSOFIA DEL SENTIMENTO
DI A. CONSENTINO.
E. NAMER, 542:OCT-DEC71-463
GIRARD, J. GENÈSE DU POUVOIR CHARISMA-
TIQUE EN BASSE CASAMANCE (SÉNÉGAL).
R. BRAIN, 69:JAN71-69
GIRARD, R. LENZ, 1751-1792.*
R. LEROY, 556(RLV):1970/5-552
GIRARD, R. LA VIOLENCE ET LE SACRÉ.
617(TLS):5OCT73-1192
GIRAUD, H. LA MORALE D'ALAIN.
O. REBOUL, 154:JUN71-417
GIRAUD, J. MANUEL DE BIBLIOGRAPHIE LIT-
TÉRAIRE POUR LES XVIE, XVIIE ET XVIIIE
SIÈCLES FRANÇAIS, 1946-1955.
R. MERCIER, 557(RSH):JUL-SEP71-467
GIRAUD, Y. - SEE DASSOUCY, C.
GIRAUD, Y.F-A. LA FABLE DE DAPHNÉ.
J. MOREL, 535(RHL):MAR-APR70-310
P. NEWMAN-GORDON, 207(FR):OCT70-260
GIRAUDOUX, J. AMPHITRYON 38. (R.K.
TOTTON, ED)
E. RATCLIFF, 208(FS):JAN72-93
GIRAUDOUX, J. CARNET DES DARDANELLES.
J. ONIMUS, 557(RSH):OCT-DEC70-651
GIRAUDOUX, J. LA MENTEUSE.
R. WEIL-MALHERBE, 207(FR):OCT70-176
GIRAUDY, D. CAMOIN.
617(TLS):19OCT73-1277
GIRDLESTONE, C. POÉSIE, POLITIQUE,
PYRÉNÉES.*
P. MOREAU, 535(RHL):JAN-FEB71-107
J.S.P., 191(ELN):SEP71(SUPP)-98
GIRDLESTONE, C. LA TRAGÉDIE EN MUSIQUE
(1673-1750).
617(TLS):30MAR73-345
GIRKE, W. STUDIEN ZUR SPRACHE N.S.
LESKOVS.*
D. TSCHIŽEWSKIJ, 72:BAND209HEFT4/6-
476
GIRMOUNSKI, V. DRAMA ALEKSANDRA BLOKA
"ROSA I KREST."
J-L. BACKÈS, 549(RLC):JUL-SEP71-435
GIROD, R. & F. GRAND-CLÉMENT. COMMENT
VIVANT LES FRANÇAIS.
G. SCHWEIG, 430(NS):AUG71-443
DI GIROLAMO, N. CULTURA ET COSCIENZA
CRITICA NELL'HERODIADE DI MALLARMÉ.
D.J. MOSSOP, 208(FS):APR72-217
J. ONIMUS, 557(RSH):JUL-SEP71-487

DI GIROLAMO, N. MITE E SIMBOLI NAPOLE-
TANI NELL'OPERA DI NERVAL.
F. CONSTANS, 557(RSH):JAN-MAR70-169
DI GIROLAMO, N. TEODOR DE WYZEWA, DAL
SIMBOLISMO AL TRADIZIONALISMO (1885-
1887).
L. GUICHARD, 535(RHL):MAR-APR71-324
D.J. MOSSOP, 208(FS):APR72-218
J. ONIMUS, 557(RSH):JUL-SEP71-486
GIRRI, A. EN LA LETRA, AMBIGUA SELVA.
617(TLS):18MAY73-548
GIRVAN, R. BEOWULF AND THE SEVENTH CEN-
TURY.
R.D., 179(ES):FEB71-96
R.T. FARRELL, 382(MAE):1972/3-292
GISH, L. DOROTHY AND LILLIAN GISH.
P. ADAMS, 61:DEC73-139
W. MARKFIELD, 441:2DEC73-96
GISHFORD, A., ED. GRAND OPERA.
442(NY):21APR73-135
617(TLS):5JAN73-14
GISSING, G. LES CARNETS D'HENRY RYE-
CROFT.
J. CAZEMAJOU, 549(RLC):JAN-MAR70-139
GISSING, G. ESSAYS AND FICTION.* (P.
COUSTILLAS, ED)
W.D. SCHAEFER, 445(NCF):DEC70-380
GISSING, G. GEORGE GISSING'S LETTERS TO
EDWARD CLODD. (P. COUSTILLAS, ED)
617(TLS):12OCT73-1212
GITELMAN, Z.Y. JEWISH NATIONALITY AND
SOVIET POLITICS.
L. SCHAPIRO, 453:19JUL73-3
617(TLS):3AUG73-910
GITTINGS, J. A CHINESE VIEW OF CHINA.
J.K. FAIRBANK, 453:1NOV73-3
617(TLS):29JUN73-754
GITTINGS, R. - SEE KEATS, J.
GITTINGS, R. - SEE SOUTHEY, R. & S.T.
COLERIDGE
GITTLEMAN, A.I. LE STYLE ÉPIQUE DANS
GARIN LE LOHERAIN.
P.J. ARCHAMBAULT, 593:SUMMER72-190
GITTLEMAN, S. FRANK WEDEKIND.*
E.A. ALBRECHT, 397(MD):DEC70-344
GIUDICI, E. SPIRITUALISMO E CARNASCIAL-
ISMO NELLA FRANCIA DEL CINQUECENTO.
J-C. MARGOLIN, 535(RHL):MAR-APR70-305
GIUDICI, P. I ROMANZI DI ANTONIO FOGAZ-
ZARO E ALTRI SAGGI.
L. PORTIER, 182:VOL24#21/22-785
GIULIANI, A. CHI L'AVREBBE DETTO.
617(TLS):5OCT73-1176
GIURESCU, C.C. TRANSYLVANIA IN THE HIS-
TORY OF ROMANIA.
W.O. OLDSON, 32:JUN72-484
GJELSNESS, B. ON THE RAFT.
R. SHELTON, 600:SPRING71-179
GLADIATOR, K. UNTERSUCHUNGEN ZUR STRUK-
TUR DER MITTELBAIRISCHEN MUNDART VON
GROSSBERGHOFEN.
E.H. YARRILL, 182:VOL24#15/16-591
GLADISH, D.F. - SEE DAVENANT, W.
GLADT, K. DIE HANDSCHRIFTEN JOHANN NES-
TROYS.
P. BRANSCOMBE, 220(GL&L):JAN72-157
GLADWIN, D.D. THE CANALS OF BRITAIN.
617(TLS):19OCT73-1287
LORD GLADWYN. THE MEMOIRS OF LORD GLAD-
WYN.*
P. JOHNSON, 441:7JAN73-6
GLANVILLE, B. MONEY IS LOVE.
M. LEVIN, 441:14JAN73-25
GLANVILLE, B. THE THING HE LOVES.
V. CUNNINGHAM, 362:30AUG73-288
617(TLS):14SEP73-1045

GLÄSER, K.G. DER FREMDENVERKEHR IN DER
NORDWESTEIFEL UND SEINE KULTURGEOGRAPH-
ISCHEN AUSWIRKUNGEN.
C. LIENAU, 182:VOL24#13/14-572
GLASER, M. GRAPHIC DESIGN.
C. LEHMANN-HAUPT, 441:14DEC73-51
L. NOCHLIN, 441:2DEC73-40
GLASS, D.V. NUMBERING THE PEOPLE.
617(TLS):12OCT73-1226
GLASSER, R.J. 365 DAYS.*
42(AR):FALL71-443
GLASSER, R.J. WARD 402.
P. ADAMS, 61:SEP73-118
T. BUCKLEY, 441:8SEP73-29
M. SCARF, 441:12AUG73-4
GLASSER, W. THE IDENTITY SOCIETY.
J.S. GORDON, 441:28JAN73-2
GLASSIE, H. PATTERNS IN THE MATERIAL
FOLK CULTURE OF THE EASTERN UNITED
STATES.*
R.M. CANDEE, 576:DEC71-337
A.A. HART, 650(WF):JAN71-61
GLASSL, H. DIE SLOVAKISCHE GESCHICHTS-
WISSENSCHAFT NACH 1945.
S.Z. PECH, 32:MAR72-223
GLAZEBROOK, G.P.D. THE STORY OF TORONTO.
G.W., 102(CANL):AUTUMN72-115
GLEASON, A. EUROPEAN AND MUSCOVITE.
617(TLS):16FEB73-174
GLEASON, H.A., JR. LINGUISTISCHE ASPEKTE
DER ENGLISCHEN GRAMMATIK. (K. WÄCHT-
LER, ED)
R. EMONS, 38:BAND89HEFT4-494
GLEASON, J., WITH A. AWORINDE & J.O.
OGUNDIPE. A RECITATION OF IFA, ORACLE
OF THE YORUBA.
P. ADAMS, 61:OCT73-130
GLEN, D., ED. AKROS ANTHOLOGY OF SCOT-
TISH POETRY.
A. CLUYSENAAR, 565:VOL12#2-63
GLEN, D. IN APPEARANCES.
A. CLUYSENAAR, 565:VOL12#4-68
H. SERGEANT, 175:AUTUMN71-106
GLEN, D., ED. HUGH MAC DIARMID.
617(TLS):5JAN73-10
GLENDINNING, N. THE EIGHTEENTH CENTURY.
617(TLS):23MAR73-331
GLENN, J. - SEE "LESSING YEARBOOK I"
GLESSING, R.J. THE UNDERGROUND PRESS IN
AMERICA.
42(AR):SPRING71-138
GLETTLER, M. SOKOL UND ARBEITERTURNVER-
EINE (D.T.J.) DER WIENER TSCHECHEN BIS
1914.
S.B. WINTERS, 32:JUN72-473
GLICK, T.F. IRRIGATION AND SOCIETY IN
MEDIEVAL VALENCIA.
639(VQR):WINTER71-XL
GLICK, W., ED. THE RECOGNITION OF HENRY
DAVID THOREAU.*
L. BUELL, 432(NEQ):JUN71-323
GLIER, I. ARTES AMANDI.
P. SCHÄFFER, 182:VOL24#6-286
GLIMCHER, A.B. LOUISE NEVELSON.*
617(TLS):9NOV73-1362
GLINZ, H. GRUNDBEGRIFFE UND METHODEN
INHALTSBEZOGENER TEXT- UND SPRACHANAL-
YSE.
M. BIERWISCH, 206:MAY70-284
L. ZGUSTA, 353:OCT71-104
GLIWITZKY, H. - SEE FICHTE, J.G.
GLOAG, J. A WOMAN OF CHARACTER.
P. THEROUX, 441:27MAY73-17
GLOB, P.V. THE BOG PEOPLE.
D.M. DIXON, 447(N&Q):FEB71-69
GLOB, P.V. DANISH PREHISTORIC MONUMENTS.
R.N. BAILEY, 447(N&Q):SEP71-346

"GLOSSAR ZU DEN ERLÄUTERUNGEN ZUM ZOLL-
TARIF DER EUROPÄISCHEN GEMEINSCHAFTEN."
75:4/1971-51
"GLOSSARIUM MEDIAE LATINITATIS SUECIAE."
(VOL 1, FASC 2)
J. ANDRÉ, 555:VOL45FASC1-194
GLOTZ, P. BUCHKRITIK IN DEUTSCHEN ZEIT-
UNGEN.
P.U. HOHENDAHL, 221(GQ):MAY71-441
H. SINGER, 490:JAN/APR70-332
GLOVER, J. THE GRASS'S TIME.
A. CLUYSENAAR, 565:VOL12#2-63
GLOVER, J. RESPONSIBILITY.
B. BEROFSKY, 311(JP):7JUN73-331
T.L.S. SPRIGGE, 262:WINTER71-464
GLOVER, M. LEGACY OF GLORY.*
617(TLS):21SEP73-1081
GLOVER, R. BRITAIN AT BAY.
617(TLS):13JUL73-817
GŁOWIŃSKI, M. POWIEŚĆ MŁODOPOLSKA.
J.T. BAER, 497(POLR):WINTER71-124
GNÄDINGER, L. HIUDAN UND PETITCREIU.
F.H. BÄUML, 406:WINTER72-384
GNEUSS, H. HYMNAR UND HYMNEN IM ENG-
LISCHEN MITTELALTER.
R.H. ROBBINS, 589:OCT72-759
C. SISAM, 38:BAND89HEFT4-523
GOBAL, S. - SEE NEHRU, J.
GÖBEL, H. BILD UND SPRACHE BEI LESSING.
J.A. KRUSE, 182:VOL24#11/12-479
DE GOBINEAU, J.A. CE QUI EST ARRIVÉ À LA
FRANCE EN 1870. (A.B. DUFF, ED)
J. BOISSEL, 535(RHL):MAY-JUN71-526
DE GOBINEAU, J.A. LE MOUCHOIR ROUGE ET
AUTRES NOUVELLES. (J. GAULMIER, ED)
J. BOISSEL, 535(RHL):JAN-FEB70-149
GÖBL, R. DOKUMENTE ZUR GESCHICHTE DER
IRANISCHEN HUNNEN IN BAKTRIEN UND IN-
DIEN.
C.M. KIEFFER, 343:BAND13HEFT1-56
GODBOLD, E.S., JR. ELLEN GLASGOW AND THE
WOMAN WITHIN.
F.P.W. MC DOWELL, 27(AL):NOV72-500
GODDARD, D., ED. A BUDDHIST BIBLE.
A. BLOOM, 485(PE&W):JUL71-347
GÖDDE-BAUMANNS, B. DEUTSCHE GESCHICHTE
IN FRANZÖSISCHER SICHT.
A. WAHL, 182:VOL24#3-110
GODDEN, G.A. CAUGHLEY AND WORCESTER POR-
CELAINS 1775-1800.
A.W.J.H., 135:NOV70-215
GODDEN, G.A. COALPORT AND COALBROOKDALE
PORCELAINS.
J. DE GORIS, 90:OCT71-613
A.W.J.H., 135:FEB71-139
GODDEN, G.A. THE ILLUSTRATED GUIDE TO
LOWESTOFT PORCELAIN.
A.W.J.H., 135:DEC70-292
GODE, P.K. P.K. GODE STUDIES. (VOL 6)
L. STERNBACH, 318(JAOS):OCT-DEC71-544
GODECHOT, J. TAKING OF THE BASTILLE.
C. DOTSON, 529(QQ):AUTUMN71-470
GODENNE, R. HISTOIRE DE LA NOUVELLE
FRANÇAISE AUX XVIIE ET XVIIIE SIÈCLES.
R. DEMORIS, 557(RSH):JUL-SEP71-473
V. MYLNE, 208(FS):JAN72-75
M. ROELENS, 535(RHL):JAN-FEB71-90
E. SHOWALTER, JR., 173(ECS):SPRING72-
467
GODEY, J. THE CRIME OF THE CENTURY AND
OTHER MISDEMEANORS.
G. BURNSIDE, 441:18NOV73-46
GODEY, J. THE TAKING OF PELHAM ONE TWO
THREE.
N. CALLENDAR, 441:4MAR73-42
C. LEHMANN-HAUPT, 441:7FEB73-41
442(NY):17MAR73-131

GODIN, A. L'HOMÉLIAIRE DE JEAN VITRIER.
A. RAYEZ, 182:VOL24#21/22-773
GODIN, J-C. HENRI BOSCO.*
J.R. CARDUNER, 401(MLQ):SEP71-334
J. ONIMUS, 535(RHL):JUL-AUG70-735
GODLOVITCH, S. & R. AND J. HARRIS, EDS.
ANIMALS, MEN AND MORALS.*
P. SINGER, 453:5APR73-17
GODSON, J. RUNWAY.
617(TLS):6APR73-401
GODWIN, W. CALEB WILLIAMS. (D. MC CRAC-
KEN, ED)
R.M. BAINE, 219(GAR):SPRING71-113
GODWIN, W. & M. WOLLSTONECRAFT. GODWIN
& MARY. (R.M. WARDLE, ED)
W. CHRISTIAN, 173(ECS):SUMMER72-627
GOEBEL, J., JR. ANTECEDENTS AND BEGIN-
NINGS TO 1801.
I. DILLIARD, 31(ASCH):SPRING73-347
GOEBEL, J., JR. - SEE HAMILTON, A.
GOEDERTIER, J. A DICTIONARY OF JAPANESE
HISTORY.
J.W. HALL, 293(JAST):NOV70-155
DE GOER DE HERVE, J. MÉCANISME ET INTEL-
LIGENCE.
R. BLANCHÉ, 542:OCT-DEC70-487
VON GOETHE, J.W. EGMONT. (U. COLBY, ED)
T. ALT, 221(GQ):MAY71-431
VON GOETHE, J.W. EPEN. (VOLS 1&2) (S.
SCHEIBE, ED)
F.R. SCHRÖDER, 224(GRM):JAN70-113
VON GOETHE, J.W. GESAMTAUSGABE DER WERKE
UND SCHRIFTEN IN 22 BANDEN.
N.H. SMITH, 182:VOL24#15/16-598
VON GOETHE, J.W. GOETHE'S COLOUR THEORY.
(R. MATTHAEI, ED; ENGLISH ED TRANS &
ED BY H. AACH)
J. GAGE, 592:NOV71-207
H.J. SANBORN, 127:SUMMER72-480
VON GOETHE, J.W. GOETHE'S "FAUST." (B.
FAIRLEY, TRANS)
A.D. LATTA, 150(DR):SUMMER71-273
A.W. RILEY, 589:SUMMER71-333
VON GOETHE, J.W. GOETHES GESPRÄCHE.
(VOL 3, PT 1) (W. HERWIG, ED)
S. ATKINS, 406:WINTER72-393
VON GOETHE, J.W. TORQUATO TASSO. (C.P.
MAGILL, ED)
J. ANNABLE, 402(MLR):APR72-467
205(FMLS):APR70-206
VON GOETHE, J.W. WINCKELMANN UND SEIN
JAHRHUNDERT IN BRIEFEN UND AUFSÄTZEN.
V.L., 131(CL):SPRING72-182
M.K. TORBRUEGGE, 406:SPRING72-79
"JOHANN WOLFGANG GOETHE: GEDENKAUSGABE DER
WERKE, BRIEFE UND GESPRÄCHE." (REGIS-
TERBAND)
S. ATKINS, 406:FALL72-306
"GOETHE-WÖRTERBUCH." (VOL 1, PT 2)
L. VÖLKER, 556(RLV):1971/3-358
GOETSCH, P. DIE ROMANKONZEPTION IN
ENGLAND 1880-1910.
L. BORINSKI, 38:BAND89HEFT4-545
GOETZ, C. KOMÖDIEN. (W. NEUSE, ED)
E.J. LEO, 221(GQ):JAN71-71
GOETZ, H-G. GESCHICHTE DES WORTES "RŪN
(RUNE)" UND SEINER ABLEITUNGEN IM
ENGLISCHEN.
H. BECKERS, 72:BAND209HEFT4/6-397
GOFF, P., COMP. WILLIAM BLAKE, CATALOGUE
OF THE PRESTON BLAKE LIBRARY.
K. GARLICK, 39:NOV70-398
GOFFMAN, E. ASYLUMS.
R. SENNETT, 453:1NOV73-29
GOFFMAN, E. ENCOUNTERS.
R. SENNETT, 453:1NOV73-29
617(TLS):2MAR73-247

GOFFMAN, E. THE PRESENTATION OF SELF IN
EVERYDAY LIFE.
R. SENNETT, 453:1NOV73-29
R. TODD, 61:NOV73-111
GOFFMAN, E. RELATIONS IN PUBLIC.*
R. JOBLING, 111:2JUN72-160
R. SENNETT, 453:1NOV73-29
GOFMAN, J.W. & A.R. TAMPLIN. POISONED
POWER.
42(AR):FALL71-445
617(TLS):7SEP73-1030
VAN GOGH, V. CORRESPONDANCE COMPLÈTE.
R. LAPORTE, 98:FEB70-124
VAN GOGH, V. VAN GOGH'S "DIARY." (J.
HULSKER, ED)
R. LEIBOWITZ, 58:NOV71-14
GOGOL, N.V. MARRIAGE. (B. COSTELLO,
TRANS)
205(FMLS):JUL70-313
GOHDES, C. BIBLIOGRAPHICAL GUIDE TO THE
STUDY OF THE LITERATURE OF THE U.S.A.
(3RD ED)
R. ASSELINEAU, 189(EA):APR-JUN71-220
GOHDES, C., ED. ESSAYS ON AMERICAN LIT-
ERATURE IN HONOR OF JAY B. HUBBELL.
H-J. LANG, 38:BAND89HEFT4-540
GOHDES, C. - SEE LIBMAN, V.A.
GOHEEN, J.D. & J.L. MOTHERSHEAD, JR. -
SEE LEWIS, C.I.
GOHIN, Y. SUR L'EMPLOI DES MOTS "IMMA-
NENT" ET "IMMANENCE" CHEZ VICTOR HUGO.
J. SEEBACHER, 535(RHL):SEP-DEC70-1085
GOICHON, A.M. THE PHILOSOPHY OF AVICENNA
AND ITS INFLUENCE ON MEDIEVAL EUROPE.
G.F. HOURANI, 318(JAOS):OCT-DEC71-533
S. VAHIDUDDIN, 273(IC):JUL70-191
GOKAK, V.K. INDIA AND WORLD CULTURE.
617(TLS):2MAR73-250
GOKHALE, G.K. SPEECHES AND WRITINGS OF
GOPAL KRISHNA GOKHALE. (VOL 3) (D.G.
KARVE & D.V. AMBEKAR, EDS)
E.E. MC DONALD, 293(JAST):NOV70-211
GOLAN, G. REFORM RULE IN CZECHOSLOVAKIA.
N. ASCHERSON, 453:5APR73-34
617(TLS):16FEB73-177
GOLAY, F.H. & OTHERS. UNDERDEVELOPMENT
AND ECONOMIC NATIONALISM IN SOUTHEAST
ASIA.
J. BADGLEY, 293(JAST):MAY71-724
GOLD, H. MY LAST TWO THOUSAND YEARS.*
V. CUNNINGHAM, 362:30AUG73-288
617(TLS):7SEP73-1018
GOLDBECK, N. & D. THE SUPERMARKET HAND-
BOOK.
J.L. HESS, 441:23DEC73-9
GOLDBERG, E.M. & J.E. NEILL. SOCIAL WORK
IN GENERAL PRACTICE.
617(TLS):6APR73-372
GOLDBERG, H. THE ART OF "JOSEPH AN-
DREWS."*
J.H. ADLER, 594:FALL70-371
G.B., 502(PRS):FALL70-275
M. IRWIN, 541(RES):FEB71-89
R. LAWRENCE, 175:AUTUMN70-107
J. PRESTON, 184(EIC):JAN71-91
GOLDBERG, L. & J. SAKOL. PURR, BABY,
PURR.
P.M. SPACKS, 249(HUDR):SPRING72-160
GOLDBERG, M. CARLYLE AND DICKENS.
617(TLS):27APR73-478
GOLDBERG, M.A. THE POETICS OF ROMANTI-
CISM.*
J.R. MAC GILLIVRAY, 627(UTQ):FALL70-73
GOLDBERG, S. THE INEVITABILITY OF PATRI-
ARCHY.
M. ELLMANN, 453:1NOV73-18
GOLDBERG, S. PROBABILITY.
S. BAUER-MENGELBERG, 316:SEP71-543

GOLDEN, H. & R. GOLDHURST. TRAVELS
THROUGH JEWISH AMERICA.
H. GOLD, 441:11NOV73-4
GOLDEN, H.H., ED. STUDIES IN HONOR OF
SAMUEL MONTEFIORE WAXMAN.
U.J. DE WINTER, 240(HR):JAN71-82
GOLDEN, J.L. & E.P.J. CORBETT, EDS. THE
RHETORIC OF BLAIR, CAMPBELL, AND
WHATELY.
C.R. SMITH, 480(P&R):SPRING70-129
"THE GOLDEN HAGGADAH."
W.O. HASSALL, 135:OCT70-94
GOLDFARB, R.L. & L. SINGER. AFTER CON-
VICTION.
D.J. ROTHMAN, 441:27MAY73-4
GOLDFARB, S. SPEECH, FOR INSTANCE.
W. CORBETT, 600:WINTER/SPRING70-233
GOLDFINGER, M. VILLAGES IN THE SUN.
C. HEINSATH, 363:NOV70-26
D. WATSON, 44:JUN70-76
GOLDIN, M.G. SPANISH CASE AND FUNCTION.*
H. CONTRERAS, 361:VOL25#1-12
GOLDING, J. BOCCIONI'S UNIQUE FORMS OF
CONTINUITY IN SPACE.
617(TLS):30MAR73-344
GOLDING, J. DUCHAMP: THE BRIDE STRIPPED
BARE BY HER BACHELORS, EVEN.
R. DOWNES, 441:2DEC73-93
GOLDKNOPF, D. THE LIFE OF THE NOVEL.
617(TLS):9MAR73-272
GOLDMAN, I. ANCIENT POLYNESIAN SOCIETY.
C. ROBINEAU, 182:VOL24#17/18-697
GOLDMAN, M. SHAKESPEARE AND THE ENERGIES
OF DRAMA.
617(TLS):2FEB73-126
GOLDMAN, P. THE DEATH AND LIFE OF MAL-
COLM X.
O. COOMBS, 441:28JAN73-40
C. LEHMANN-HAUPT, 441:8JAN73-37
442(NY):13JAN73-92
GOLDMAN, W. THE PRINCESS BRIDE.
G. WALKER, 441:23DEC73-14
442(NY):12NOV73-217
GOLDMAN, W. THE SEASON.
J.R. TAYLOR, 157:AUTUMN71-76
GOLDMANN, KANT. IMMANUEL KANT.*
B. WILLIAMS, 111:2JUN72-163
GOLDMANN, L. THE PHILOSOPHY OF THE EN-
LIGHTENMENT.
617(TLS):7DEC73-1498
GOLDMANN, L. RACINE.
617(TLS):23FEB73-218
GOLDONI, C. THE COMIC THEATRE.
E. KERN, 276:WINTER71-503
GOLDSCHMIDT, E.M. - SEE MAC LEISH, A.
GOLDSCHMIDT, L. - SEE MELLIN, G.S.A.
GOLDSCHMIDT, L. & H. SCHIMMEL - SEE DE
TOULOUSE-LAUTREC, H.
GOLDSMITH, E. & OTHERS. A BLUEPRINT FOR
SURVIVAL.
617(TLS):12JAN73-46
GOLDSMITH, M.E. THE MODE AND MEANING OF
"BEOWULF."*
W.F. BOLTON, 541(RES):AUG71-317
J.A. BURROW, 184(EIC):JUL71-280
R.M. WILSON, 175:SPRING71-22
GOLDSMITH, V.F. A SHORT TITLE CATALOGUE
OF FRENCH BOOKS 1601-1700 IN THE LIB-
RARY OF THE BRITISH MUSEUM. (FASC 7)
617(TLS):16FEB73-188
GOLDSTEIN, D., ED & TRANS. HEBREW POEMS
FROM SPAIN.
K.R. SCHOLBERG, 328:WINTER70-121
GOLDSTEIN, J.H. COMPETITION FOR WETLANDS
IN THE MIDWEST.
42(AR):WINTER71/72-598

GOLDSTEIN, K.S. & D. BEN-AMOS, EDS.
THRICE TOLD TALES.
R. BAUMAN, 582(SFQ):DEC71-362
K.M. BRIGGS, 203:WINTER71-337
GOLDSTEIN, R. THE POETRY OF ROCK.
A. HENRI, 493:SPRING71-63
GOLDSTEIN, R.L., ED. BLACK LIFE AND CUL-
TURE IN THE UNITED STATES.
N. LEDERER, 584(SWR):WINTER72-86
GOLDSTEIN, S. & S. SHINODA - SEE "TANGLED
HAIR"
GOLDSTROM, J.M. THE SOCIAL CONTENT OF
EDUCATION 1808-1870.
617(TLS):5JAN73-19
GOLDTHWAITE, R.A. PRIVATE WEALTH IN
RENAISSANCE FLORENCE.
D.M. BUENO DE MESQUITA, 447(N&Q):
JUN71-239
GOLDZIHER, I. MUSLIM STUDIES.* (VOL 1)
(S.M. STERN, ED)
G.F. HOURANI, 318(JAOS):JAN-MAR71-145
GOLINO, C.L. & F. FRANCK. TUTTE LE
STRADE PORTANO A ROMA.*
R.J. TRIVELLI, 276:SUMMER71-273
GOLL, Y. LACKAWANNA ELEGY.
R.J. MILLS, JR., 491:MAY73-105
GOLL, Y. POEMS. (P. ZWEIG, ED)
E. FEINSOD, 114(CHIR):JAN-FEB71-156
GOLOMBEK, H. FISCHER V. SPASSKY.
617(TLS):18MAY73-550
GOMBRICH, E.H. IN SEARCH OF CULTURAL
HISTORY.
D. SUTTON, 39:APR70-320
GOMBRICH, E.H., J. HOCHBERG & M. BLACK.
ART, PERCEPTION AND REALITY.
617(TLS):13JUL73-814
GOMBROWICZ, W. COSMOS.
502(PRS):SPRING71-92
GOMBROWICZ, W. JOURNAL PARIS BERLIN.
R. MICHA, 98:DEC71-1050
GÓMEZ, C.B. - SEE UNDER BANDERA GÓMEZ, C.
GÓMEZ, J. HOW NOT TO DIE YOUNG.
617(TLS):11MAY73-537
GÓMEZ DE LA SERNA, R. NUEVAS PÁGINAS DE
MI VIDA.
E.L. PLACER, 238:DEC71-971
GÓMEZ IGLESIAS, A., ED. LIBROS DE ACUER-
DOS DEL CONCEJO MADRILEÑO, 1464-1600.
(VOL 2)
A.I.K. MAC KAY, 86(BHS):APR72-182
GOMME, A.H., ED. JACOBEAN TRAGEDIES.*
F. LAGARDE, 189(EA):OCT-DEC70-442
GOMME, A.W., A. ANDREWES & K.J. DOVER.
A HISTORICAL COMMENTARY ON THUCYDIDES.
(VOL 4)
H.D. WESTLAKE, 123:JUN72-188
GOMME, A.W. & F.H. SANDBACH. MENANDER.
617(TLS):22JUN73-728
GÖMÖRI, G. & J. ATLAS - SEE JÓZSEF, A.
GOMRINGER, E. JOSEF ALPERS.*
M. BRUMER, 58:SEP/OCT70-20
GONÇALVES DA COSTA, M., C.F. BECKINGHAM
& D.M. LOCKHART - SEE LOBO, J.
GONDA, J. A CONCISE ELEMENTARY GRAMMAR
OF THE SANSKRIT LANGUAGE.*
R.A. FOWKES, 215(GL):VOL11#2-127
V. MILTNER, 353:JUN70-125
H. QUELLET, 343:BAND13HEFT2-187
GONDA, J. THE VISION OF THE VEDIC POETS.
R. SCHMITT, 343:BAND13HEFT2-185
GONDOS, V., JR., ED. READER FOR ARCHIVES
AND RECORDS CENTER BUILDINGS.
J.R. EDE, 325:OCT71-345
GONZÁLEZ, E., S. LIPP & H. PIÑERA. SPAN-
ISH CULTURAL READER.
M-L. GAZARIAN, 238:MAY71-410
GONZÁLEZ DE LA GARZA, M. WALT WHITMAN.
H.C. WOODBRIDGE, 646(WWR):DEC71-142

GONZÁLEZ LÓPEZ, E. EL ARTE DRAMÁTICO DE
VALLE-INCLÁN (DEL DECADENTISMO AL
EXPRESIONISMO).
R. WHITTREDGE, 240(HR):JAN71-118
GONZÁLEZ MAS, E. HISTORIA DE LA LITERA-
TURA ESPAÑOLA. (VOL 1)
J. ROCA-PONS, 238:MAY71-392
GONZÁLEZ MUELA, J. - SEE MARTÍNEZ DE
TOLEDO, A.
GOOCH, A. DIMINUTIVE, AUGMENTATIVE AND
PEJORATIVE SUFFIXES IN MODERN SPANISH.*
Y. MALKIEL, 361:VOL26#2-205
GOOCH, R.K. THE FRENCH PARLIAMENTARY
COMMITTEE SYSTEM.
M. ANDERSON, 208(FS):APR72-238
GOOD, H.E. BLACK SWAMP FARM.
H.H. LEE, 650(WF):JAN70-58
GOODE, H.D. LA PROSA RETÓRICA DE FRAY
LUIS DE LEÓN EN "LOS NOMBRES DE CRISTO."
G.A. DAVIES, 86(BHS):JAN72-73
H.T. OOSTENDORP, 433:JUL71-343
205(FMLS):APR70-207
GOODE, J., ED. THE AIR OF REALITY.
617(TLS):30NOV73-1467
GOODELL, C. POLITICAL PRISONERS IN
AMERICA.
H.S. COMMAGER, 453:19JUL73-10
GOODFIELD, J. COURIER TO PEKING.
N. CALLENDAR, 441:18FEB73-29
D. MAHON, 362:24MAY73-696
617(TLS):3AUG73-911
GOODHART, P., WITH U. BRANSTON. THE 1922.
E. BOYLE, 362:9AUG73-188
617(TLS):27JUL73-849
GOODHEART, E. CULTURE AND THE RADICAL
CONSCIENCE.
617(TLS):3AUG73-904
GOODMAN, A.E. POLITICS IN WAR.
617(TLS):23NOV73-1423
GOODMAN, E.J. THE EXPLORERS OF SOUTH
AMERICA.
617(TLS):11MAY73-533
GOODMAN, G.K., COMP. THE AMERICAN OCCUPA-
TION OF JAPAN.
B.H. HAZARD, 318(JAOS):OCT-DEC71-522
GOODMAN, J., ED. TRIAL OF IAN BRADY AND
MYRA HINDLEY.
617(TLS):13APR73-427
GOODMAN, L.E. - SEE IBN TUFAYL AL QAYSI
GOODMAN, N. LANGUAGES OF ART.*
M.C. BEARDSLEY, 486:SEP70-458
B.C. O'NEILL, 479(PHQ):OCT71-361
D.B. VAN DOMMELEN, 480(P&R):WINTER70-
62
P. ZIFF, 482(PHR):OCT71-509
W.M. ZUCKER, 54:JUN70-223
GOODMAN, P. SPEAKING AND LANGUAGE.*
617(TLS):21JUL73-874
GOODMAN, R. AFTER THE PLANNERS.*
617(TLS):23FEB73-204
GOODMAN, W. A PERCENTAGE OF THE TAKE.
639(VQR):SUMMER71-CXXXII
GOODRICH, F. & A. HACKETT. THE DIARY OF
ANNE FRANK.
A. RENDLE, 157:WINTER70-70
GOODRICH, L. EDWARD HOPPER.*
G. WEALES, 249(HUDR):SPRING72-111
GOODRICH, N.L. GIONO, MASTER OF FICTION-
AL MODES.
617(TLS):21DEC73-1574
GOODSTADT, L. MAO TSE TUNG.
617(TLS):13APR73-407
GOODWIN, A., ED. THE NEW CAMBRIDGE MOD-
ERN HISTORY. (VOL 8)
R. MARX, 189(EA):APR-JUN71-215
GOODWIN, G. A HISTORY OF OTTOMAN ARCHI-
TECTURE.
P.A. MACKAY, 32:JUN72-505

GOODWYN, E.A., COMP. SELECTIONS FROM
NORWICH NEWSPAPERS 1760-1790.
617(TLS):23FEB73-220
GOODY, J. COMPARATIVE STUDIES IN KIN-
SHIP.
R. HARRIS, 69:APR71-164
GOODY, J. TECHNOLOGY, TRADITION AND THE
STATE IN AFRICA.
C. MEILLASSOUX, 69:OCT71-331
GOODY, M.E. & R.P. WALSH, EDS. BOSTON
SOCIETY OF ARCHITECTS, THE FIRST HUN-
DRED YEARS, 1867-1967.
B. BUNTING, 576:DEC70-354
GOOSSEN, E.C. HELEN FRANKENTHALER.
D. IRWIN, 39:APR71-342
GOOSSEN, E.C. ELLSWORTH KELLY.
L. NOCHLIN, 441:2DEC73-36
GOOSSENS, J. STRUKTURELLE SPRACHGEO-
GRAPHIE.*
D. STELLMACHER, 439(NM):1971/1-184
NA GOPALEEN, M. [F. O'BRIEN], ED. THE
POOR MOUTH.
617(TLS):7DEC73-1495
GÖPFERT, H.G. & OTHERS - SEE LESSING,
G.E.
GOPNIK, I. A THEORY OF STYLE AND RICH-
ARDSON'S "CLARISSA."
S. VAN MARTER, 405(MP):MAY72-352
481(PQ):JUL71-475
GORDIS, R. POETS, PROPHETS AND SAGES.
R.B.Y. SCOTT, 328:FALL71-494
GORDON, A.L. THE LAST LETTERS 1868-1870.
(H. ANDERSON, ED)
T.I. MOORE, 381:SEP71-353
GORDON, A.L. RONSARD ET LA RHÉTORIQUE.
E. ARMSTRONG, 402(MLR):OCT72-885
W.L. WILEY, 551(RENQ):WINTER71-546
GORDON, C. THE GLORY OF HERA.
D.E. STANFORD, 385(MQR):WINTER73-89
GORDON, D.C. THE MOMENT OF POWER.
R. KUBICEK, 637(VS):DEC70-209
D.M. SCHURMAN, 529(QQ):WINTER71-624
GORDON, D.C. SELF-DETERMINATION AND HIS-
TORY IN THE THIRD WORLD.
639(VQR):AUTUMN71-CLXXXI
GORDON, D.E. ERNST LUDWIG KIRCHNER.*
P. VERGO, 90:OCT71-616
GORDON, E. THE CHAPERONE.
N. CALLENDAR, 441:28JAN73-20
GORDON, F.L. - SEE DELIBES, M.
GORDON, G. PICTURES FROM AN EXHIBITION.
R. PYBUS, 565:VOL12#1-68
GORDON, H.J., JR. HITLER AND THE BEER
HALL PUTSCH.*
617(TLS):30NOV73-1470
GORDON, I.A. JOHN GALT.
617(TLS):16FEB73-176
GORDON, I.A. THE MOVEMENT OF ENGLISH
PROSE.*
I. GOPNIK, 599:WINTER70-89
GORDON, I.L. THE DOUBLE SORROW OF TROI-
LUS.*
R.T. DAVIES, 541(RES):NOV71-468
J.E. GALLAGHER, 382(MAE):1972/1-39
S.S. HUSSEY, 447(N&Q):FEB71-73
C.A. OWEN, JR., 405(MP):AUG71-63
R.M. WILSON, 175:AUTUMN70-97
GORDON, J.A. - SEE GALT, J.
GORDON, L.G. STRATAGEMS TO UNCOVER
NAKEDNESS.*
A.P. HINCHLIFFE, 397(MD):FEB71-449
GORDON, L.H.D., ED. TAIWAN: STUDIES IN
CHINESE LOCAL HISTORY.
R.H. MYERS, 293(JAST):FEB71-453
GORDON, R., ED. THE AUSTRALIAN NEW LEFT.
D. AITKIN, 381:MAR71-118
GORDON, R. MYSELF AMONG OTHERS.
P.M. SPACKS, 249(HUDR):SPRING72-157

GORDON, R.C. UNDER WHICH KING?*
T. CRAWFORD, 541(RES):MAY71-223
J. ESPEY, 445(NCF):JUN70-121
G.A.M. WOOD, 175:SPRING70-27
GORDON, W.A. THE MIND AND ART OF HENRY
MILLER.
G.M. PERKINS, 599:WINTER70-85
GORE, I. AGE AND VITALITY.
617(TLS):7SEP73-1037
GORES, J. FINAL NOTICE.
N. CALLENDAR, 441:9SEP73-40
GORFUNKEL', A.K. KATALOG KNIG KIRILLOV-
SKOĬ PECHATI 16-17 VEKOV.
J.S.G. SIMMONS, 78(BC):SUMMER71-257
GÖRGEMANNS, H. UNTERSUCHUNGEN ZU PLU-
TARCHS DIALOG, DE FACIE IN ORBE LUNAE.
H. MARTIN, JR., 124:OCT71-65
GÖRGEMANNS, H. - SEE DIRLMEIER, F.
GORHAM, M., ED. DUBLIN FROM OLD PHOTO-
GRAPHS.
617(TLS):9FEB73-161
GORMAN, J. BANNER BRIGHT.
617(TLS):6JUL73-767
GORMAN, T.P., ED. LANGUAGE IN EDUCATION
IN EASTERN AFRICA.
J.D. BOWEN, 350:DEC72-976
GORNICK, V. IN SEARCH OF ALI MAHMOUD.
E. JANEWAY, 441:21OCT73-31
GOROVITZ, S. PHILOSOPHICAL ANALYSIS.
P.W., 206:NOV70-595
GORTAN, V. & V. VRATOVIĆ, EDS. HRVATSKI
LATINISTI.
A. KADIĆ, 32:MAR72-228
GOSE, E.B., JR. IMAGINATION INDULGED.
G. WOODCOCK, 102(CANL):AUTUMN72-97
GOSLING, J.C.B. PLEASURE AND DESIRE.*
J. TEICHMANN, 393(MIND):APR71-306
GOSSEN, C.T. FRANZÖSISCHE SKRIPTASTUD-
IEN.
G. INEICHEN, 260(IF):BAND74-271
GOSSEN, C.T. GRAMMAIRE DE L'ANCIEN
PICARD.
F. KOENIG, 545(RPH):MAY72-473
R. ROHR, 72:BAND209HEFT1/3-191
GOSSMAN, L. MEDIEVALISM AND THE IDEOLO-
GIES OF THE ENLIGHTENMENT.*
A. AGES, 188(ECR):FALL71-79
B. BEIT-ISHOO, 173(ECS):FALL70-107
J. DAGEN, 535(RHL):JAN-FEB71-95
H. DURANTON, 557(RSH):JUL-SEP70-476
H. KELLENBERGER, 207(FR):FEB71-621
H. MONOD-CASSIDY, 546(RR):FEB71-62
GOSWAMI, S. - SEE ŚRĪJĪVA, G.
GOSWAMY, B.N. & J.S. GREWAL. THE MUGHAL
AND SIKH RULERS AND THE VAISHNAVAS OF
PINDORI.
M.N. PEARSON, 318(JAOS):OCT-DEC71-559
GOSWAMY, B.N. & J.S. GREWAL. THE MUGHALS
AND THE JOGIS OF JAKHBAR.
M. HABIB, 273(IC):JAN71-72
GOTH, J. NIETZSCHE UND DIE RHETORIK.
H. BLUHM, 221(GQ):MAY71-410
R. BUCHBINDER, 680(ZDP):BAND90HEFT2-
299
GOTHOT-MERSCH, C. - SEE FLAUBERT, G.
GOTLIEB, S. THE GOURMET'S CANADA.
A. APPENZELL, 102(CANL):AUTUMN72-104
GOTTESMAN, R. & S. BENNETT, EDS. ART AND
ERROR.*
W.R. LE FANU, 541(RES):NOV71-488
GÖTTING, M. HYPSIPYLE IN DER THEBAIS
DES STATIUS.
A.J. GOSSAGE, 123:MAR72-111
GOTTSCHED, J.C. AUSGEWÄHLTE WERKE. (VOL
4) (J. BIRKE, ED)
H. MEYER, 400(MLN):OCT71-734

"GOTTSCHEER VOLKSLIEDER."
J. MÜLLER-BLATTAU, 680(ZDP):BAND89
HEFT3-473
GOUBERT, P. L'ANCIEN RÉGIME.* (VOL 1)
K. BAHNERS, 430(NS):JUN71-328
GOUBERT, P. LOUIS XIV AND TWENTY MILLION
FRENCHMEN.
J. LOUGH, 208(FS):JUL72-331
GOUGENHEIM, G. ÉTUDES DE GRAMMAIRE ET DE
VOCABULAIRE FRANÇAIS.
J. DARBELNET, 320(CJL):FALL70-61
GOUGLIANE, C-I. HEGEL OU LA PHILOSOPHIE
DE LA CRISE.
A. BARAQUIN, 557(RSH):OCT-DEC71-657
GOUHIER, H. BERGSON ET LE CHRIST DES
EVANGILES.
M. BARTHÉLEMY-MADAULE, 542:OCT-DEC71-
448
GOUHIER, H. LES MÉDITATIONS MÉTAPHYS-
IQUES DE JEAN-JACQUES ROUSSEAU.
P. BURGELIN, 535(RHL):JUL-AUG71-704
GOULD, J. & L. HICKOK. WALTER REUTHER.*
B.J. WIDICK, 441:21JAN73-7
GOULD, J.B. THE PHILOSOPHY OF CHRYSIP-
PUS.
J. PHILIP, 154:DEC71-802
J.M. RIST, 487:WINTER71-386
GOULD, J.D. ECONOMIC GROWTH IN HISTORY.
617(TLS):6APR73-399
GOULDEN, J.C. MEANY.*
M. KEMPTON, 231:MAY73-96
442(NY):3MAR73-115
GOULDNER, A. THE COMING CRISIS OF
WESTERN SOCIOLOGY.
D. ATKINSON, 111:19FEB71-150
GOULEMOT, J-M. - SEE MARQUIS DE SADE
GOULIANE, C.I. LE MARXISME DEVANT
L'HOMME.
E. NAMER, 542:APR-JUN70-263
GOURÉVITCH, D-J. & E.M. STADLER. PREM-
IERS TEXTES LITTÉRAIRES.
V.W., 206:NOV70-596
GOURLAY, L., ED. OLIVIER.
617(TLS):28DEC73-1593
DE GOURMONT, R. POUR COMMENTER KANT.
R. MALTER, 342:BAND61HEFT1-145
GOWANS, A. KING CARTER'S CHURCH.
M. WHIFFEN, 576:MAY70-202
GOWDA, H.H.A. DRAMATIC POETRY.
617(TLS):2MAR73-246
GOWDA, K.K. GOWDA KANNADA.
K. RAJA, 318(JAOS):OCT-DEC71-557
GOWER, J. JOHN GOWER: "CONFESSIO AMAN-
TIS." (R.A. PECK, ED)
P.F. THEINER, 179(ES):JUN71-261
GOWER, J. SELECTIONS FROM JOHN GOWER.
(J.A.W. BENNETT, ED)
W.F. SCHIRMER, 38:BAND88HEFT4-539
P.F. THEINER, 179(ES):JUN71-261
GOWERS, E. THE COMPLETE PLAIN WORDS.
(B. FRASER, ED)
617(TLS):22JUN73-719
GOWING, L. VERMEER.
E. LARSEN, 127:WINTER71/72-214
GOWRIE, G. A POSTCARD FROM DON GIOVANNI.
617(TLS):16FEB73-183
GOYANES, M.B. - SEE UNDER BAQUERO GOY-
ANES, M.
GOYEN, W. A BOOK OF JESUS.
R. PHILLIPS, 441:6MAY73-30
GOYTISOLO, J. REIVINDICACIÓN DEL CONDE
DON JULIÁN.
K. SCHWARTZ, 238:DEC71-960
GOZZANO, G. LA MONETA SEMINATA E ALTRI
SCRITTI.
A.S., 228(GSLI):VOL147FASC458/459-475
GOZZANO, G. LE POESIE.
M. PUCCINI, 270:VOL22#3-65

DE GRAAF, H.J. THE SPREAD OF PRINTING:
INDONESIA.
B.C. BLOOMFIELD, 354:MAR71-70
R. CAVE, 503:SUMMER70-99
"REGNIER DE GRAAF ON THE HUMAN REPRODUC-
TIVE ORGANS." (H.D. JOCELYN & B.P.
SETCHELL, EDS & TRANS)
617(TLS):13APR73-425
GRAB, W. & U. FRIESEL. NOCH IST DEUTSCH-
LAND NICHT VERLOREN.
G. FRIESEN, 400(MLN):APR71-435
O.W. JOHNSTON, 221(GQ):NOV71-583
GRABAR, A. CHRISTIAN ICONOGRAPHY.*
J. BECKWITH, 39:JUL70-79
A. NEUMEYER, 290(JAAC):FALL70-139
GRABAR, O. THE FORMATION OF ISLAMIC ART.
617(TLS):28DEC73-1590
GRABBE, C.D. SCHERZ, SATIRE, IRONIE UND
TIEFERE BEDEUTUNG. (R.C. COWEN, ED)
G.E. BIRRELL, 399(MLJ):FEB71-132
205(FMLS):JAN71-94
GRABER, H. - SEE DÖBLIN, A.
GRACIÁN, B. OBRAS COMPLETAS. (VOL 1)
(M. BATLLORI & C. PERALTA, EDS)
G.A. DAVIES, 86(BHS):JAN72-81
GRACIÁN DANTISCO, L. GALATEO ESPAÑOL.*
(M. MORREALE, ED)
S. GAROFALO, 276:AUTUMN71-394
E. GLASER, 405(MP):MAY72-341
GRACQ, J. LA PRESQU'ÎLE.
A-C. DOBBS, 207(FR):APR71-959
GRADE, A. - SEE FROST, R. & E.
GRAESER, A. PROBLEME DER PLATONISCHEN
SEELENTEILUNGSLEHRE.*
P. LOUIS, 555:VOL45FASC2-342
GRAF, D. MASTER DRAWINGS OF THE ROMAN
BAROQUE FROM THE KUNSTMUSEUM, DÜSSEL-
DORF.
617(TLS):3AUG73-900
GRAF, H., ED. DER KLEINE SALON.
H. MODLMAYR-HEIMATH, 402(MLR):JAN72-
226
GRAF, O.A. DIE VERGESSENE WAGNERSCHULE.
E. KAUFMANN, JR., 576:MAR70-71
GRAFF, G. POETIC STATEMENT AND CRITICAL
DOGMA.
M. HANCHER, 400(MLN):DEC71-948
V.A. KRAMER, 290(JAAC):SPRING71-427
M. RUDICK, 651(WHR):SPRING72-176
DE GRAFT, J.C. THROUGH A FILM DARKLY.
A. RENDLE, 157:AUTUMN70-77
GRAHAM, C.P. IME.
42(AR):SUMMER70-268
GRAHAM, F.L. HECTOR GUIMARD.
F. HABER, 576:DEC70-354
GRAHAM, J., ED. GREAT AMERICAN SPEECHES
1898-1963.
J. TARVER, 583:FALL71-106
GRAHAM, J.A. BABE RUTH CAUGHT IN A
SNOWSTORM.
M. LEVIN, 441:17JUN73-28
"JOHN GRAHAM'S SYSTEM AND DIALECTICS OF
ART."
C. NEMSER, 58:APR72-26
GRAHAM, L.R. SCIENCE AND PHILOSOPHY IN
THE SOVIET UNION.*
A. ASTRACHAN, 442(NY):24SEP73-119
GRAHAM, M. THE NOTEBOOKS OF MARTHA
GRAHAM.
A. KISSELGOFF, 441:10NOV73-29
M.B. SIEGEL, 441:16DEC73-2
GRAHAM, S. A STATE OF HEAT.*
617(TLS):4MAY73-509
GRAHAM, V.E. THE IMAGERY OF PROUST.
L.B. PRICE, 207(FR):OCT70-226

GRAHAM, W.S.  MALCOLM MOONEY'S LAND.*
  R.S., 376:JUL70-123
  J. SAUNDERS, 565:VOL11#4-68
  H. SERGEANT, 175:SUMMER71-65
GRAHAMS, J.  THE KHUFRA RUN.
  N. CALLENDAR, 441:12AUG73-12
GRAM, M.S.  KANT, ONTOLOGY, AND THE A
  PRIORI.
  S. KÖRNER, 482(PHR):JAN71-129
GRAML, H. & OTHERS.  THE GERMAN RESIS-
  TANCE TO HITLER.
  J. STEINBERG, 220(GL&L):JUL72-393
GRAÑA, C.  FACT AND SYMBOL.
  J.E. CHAMBERLIN, 249(HUDR):WINTER
  72/73-701
GRANAROLO, J.  D'ENNIUS À CATULLE.
  J-D. MINYARD, 124:MAR72-235
GRANAT, R.  REGENESIS.*
  A. BROYARD, 441:1JAN73-11
GRANATSTEIN, J.L. & P. STEVENS, EDS.
  FORUM: CANADIAN LIFE AND LETTERS 1920-
  1970.
  E.Z. FRIEDENBERG, 453:17MAY73-29
  G. WOODCOCK, 99:MAR73-43
"THE GRANDES HEURES OF JEAN, DUKE OF
  BERRY."* (BRITISH TITLE: LES GRANDES
  HEURES DE JEAN DUC DE BERRY.) (M.
  THOMAS, ED)
  R. LEIBOWITZ, 58:NOV71-14
GRANDGENT, C.H. - SEE DANTE ALIGHIERI
GRANDJEAN, B.O.  THE PHYSIOLOGICAL BASIS
  OF THE FINE ARTS.  ART AND ANATOMY OF
  ARCHAIC EGYPT.  A CONCISE HISTORY OF THE
  STEREOMETRY AND THE BODY MEASURES, AC-
  CORDING TO THE CONTEMPORARY SOURCES,
  FROM ARCHAIC EGYPT TO THE VIKING AGE.
  I. TATTERSALL & K.R. WEEKS, 318(JAOS):
  APR-JUN71-294
GRANDPIERRE, E.K.  DRÁMA FELVÁLLRÓL.
  K. PÁLMAI, 270:VOL21#3-172
GRANESE, A.  G.E. MOORE E LA FILOSOFIA
  ANALITICA INGLESE.
  E. NAMER, 542:APR-JUN70-263
GRANGER, G.  ESSAI D'UNE PHILOSOPHIE DU
  STYLE.
  V. THERRIEN, 154:JUN71-389
GRANIER, J.  LE PROBLÈME DE LA VÉRITÉ
  DANS LA PHILOSOPHIE DE NIETZSCHE.
  S. KOFMAN, 98:APR70-359
GRANLID, H.  HENRY MILLERS MOTSÄGELSER.
  O. ØVERLAND, 172(EDDA):1970/4-249
GRANSDEN, K.W., ED.  TUDOR VERSE SATIRE.*
  K.W. CAMERON, 551(RENQ):WINTER71-555
  J. CHALKER, 597(SN):VOL43#2-581
  T.W. CRAIK, 447(N&Q):JUN71-237
GRANT, B.  THE CRISIS OF LOYALTY.
  617(TLS):29JUN73-754
GRANT, B.D.  CHILDREN, YOU ARE VERY LIT-
  TLE.
  P.M. SPACKS, 249(HUDR):SPRING72-166
GRANT, D.  YOUR DAILY FOOD.
  617(TLS):28DEC73-1583
GRANT, D. - SEE SMOLLETT, T.
GRANT, E.M.  VICTOR HUGO.
  J. GAUDON, 535(RHL):MAY-JUN70-519
GRANT, J.C.  THE PREACHER ON THE MOOR.
  A. CLUYSENAAR, 565:VOL12#4-68
GRANT, M.  THE ANCIENT HISTORIANS.*
  C.T. MURPHY, 651(WHR):WINTER72-88
GRANT, M.  THE ANCIENT MEDITERRANEAN.*
  T.W. AFRICA, 121(CJ):OCT-NOV71-74
GRANT, M.  CLEOPATRA.
  617(TLS):30NOV73-1471
GRANT, M., ED.  GREEK LITERATURE IN
  TRANSLATION.
  617(TLS):9MAR73-277

GRANT, M.  NERO.*
  R. HIGGINS, 39:AUG71-162
  G.B. TOWNEND, 31·3:VOL61-311
GRANT, M.  THE ROMAN FORUM.
  R.L. VANN, 576:DEC71-339
GRANT, M.  ROMAN IMPERIAL MONEY.
  617(TLS):16MAR73-305
GRANT, M.A.  FOLKTALE AND HERO-TALE
  MOTIFS IN THE ODES OF PINDAR.*
  G.K. GRESSETH, 650(WF):JUL70-212
GRANT, N.  SOCIETY, SCHOOLS AND PROGRESS
  IN EASTERN EUROPE.
  G. PROCUTA, 32:MAR72-210
GRANT, R.M.  AUGUSTUS TO CONSTANTINE.*
  W.H.C. FREND, 453:8FEB73-32
GRANT, R.M. - SEE THEOPHILUS
GRANT, U.S.  THE PAPERS OF ULYSSES S.
  GRANT.  (VOL 2) (J.Y. SIMON, ED)
  F.C. GALE, 14:OCT70-413
GRANT, W. & D.D. MURISON, EDS.  THE
  SCOTTISH NATIONAL DICTIONARY.  (VOL 7,
  PT 4)
  K. WITTIG, 38:BAND89HEFT2-248
GRAPPIN, P. - SEE HESSE, H. & R. ROLLAND
GRASS, G.  FROM THE DIARY OF A SNAIL.
  P. ADAMS, 61:OCT73-130
  N. ASCHERSON, 453:1NOV73-10
  M. GALLANT, 441:30SEP73-4
  J. UPDIKE, 442(NY):15OCT73-182
GRATE, P., ED.  TREASURES OF SWEDISH
  ART.*
  J.F.M., 135:FEB70-126
GRATTAN-GUINNESS, I., WITH J.R. RAVETZ.
  JOSEPH FOURIER, 1768-1830.
  617(TLS):11MAY73-531
GRAU, S.A.  THE WIND SHIFTING WEST.
  A. BROYARD, 441:1NOV73-47
  J. YARDLEY, 441:23DEC73-11
GRAUBARD, A.  FREE THE CHILDREN.
  R. GROSS, 441:25MAR73-40
  H. KOHL, 453:13DEC73-48
GRAUBARD, S.R.  KISSINGER.
  F. FITZ GERALD, 441:15JUL73-3
  C. LEHMANN-HAUPT, 441:29JUN73-41
  E. WEEKS, 61:JUL73-101
GRAUS, F. & OTHERS.  EASTERN AND WESTERN
  EUROPE IN THE MIDDLE AGES.  (G. BARRA-
  CLOUGH, ED)
  H. KAMINSKY, 589:APR72-315
GRAUSTEIN, J.E.  THOMAS NUTTALL, NATURAL-
  IST.
  P. BRYANT, 649(WAL):SPRING70-73
GRAVA, A.  A STRUCTURAL INQUIRY INTO THE
  SYMBOLIC REPRESENTATION OF IDEAS.
  P. LACKOWSKI, 361:VOL25#3-330
GRAVER, B.D. & K.J.T. HOILE, EDS.  MILI-
  TARY TEXTS.
  P. MICHEL, 556(RLV):1971/5-649
GRAVER, L.  CONRAD'S SHORT FICTION.*
  B.R. MC ELDERRY, JR., 573(SSF):SUM-
  MER71-480
  I. VIDAN, 177(ELT):VOL13#1-79
GRAVER, L.  CARSON MC CULLERS.
  R. ASSELINEAU, 189(EA):JUL-SEP71-349
GRAVES, J.C.  THE CONCEPTUAL FOUNDATIONS
  OF CONTEMPORARY RELATIVITY THEORY.*
  G. NERLICH, 63:MAY72-84
GRAVES, R.  DEYÁ.
  617(TLS):15JUN73-693
GRAVES, R.  DIFFICULT QUESTIONS, EASY
  ANSWERS.
  617(TLS):19JAN73-69
GRAVES, R.  POEMS: 1965-1968.*  POEMS
  ABOUT LOVE.*
  P.J. CALLAHAN, 502(PRS):SUMMER70-173
GRAVES, R.  POEMS 1968-1970.
  W.H. PRITCHARD, 249(HUDR):SPRING72-127

GRAVES, R.  POEMS 1970-1972.
    A. MACLEAN, 362:22MAR73-389
    S. SPENDER, 441:11MAR73-7
    617(TLS):19JAN73-69
GRAVES, R.  TIMELESS MEETING.
    617(TLS):19OCT73-1276
GRAVES, R.L.  THE BLACK GOLD OF MALAVERDE.
    N. CALLENDAR, 441:30DEC73-18
GRAY, B.  STYLE.*
    R.W. BAILEY, 599:SPRING71-177
GRAY, C.  THE RUSSIAN EXPERIMENT IN ART
    1863-1922.
    A. BIRD, 90:NOV71-676
GRAY, C. - SEE "JOHN MARIN BY JOHN
    MARIN"
GRAY, D.  THE ONE AND THE MANY.
    E. BINNS, 613:SUMMER71-300
GRAY, H. - SEE BAZIN, A.
GRAY, I., ED.  CHELTENHAM SETTLEMENT
    EXAMINATIONS, 1815-1826.
    B.S. SMITH, 325:APR71-248
GRAY, J., ED.  MODERN CHINA'S SEARCH FOR
    A POLITICAL FORM.*
    J.K. KALLGREN, 318(JAOS):JAN-MAR71-148
GRAY, J.  JOHN STEINBECK.
    R. ASSELINEAU, 189(EA):OCT-DEC71-548
GRAY, J.G.  ON UNDERSTANDING VIOLENCE
    PHILOSOPHICALLY, AND OTHER ESSAYS.*
    R.E. SANTONI, 484(PPR):SEP71-126
GRAY, J.G. - SEE HEGEL, G.W.F.
GRAY, J.H.  BOOZE.
    J.L. GRANATSTEIN, 99:MAR73-47
GRAY, J.S.  VICTORIAN AND EDWARDIAN
    SUSSEX FROM OLD PHOTOGRAPHS.
    617(TLS):21DEC73-1573
GRAY, M., WITH M. GALLO.  FOR THOSE I
    LOVED.*
    J. LIND, 362:3MAY73-590
    E. WEEKS, 61:JAN73-99
    617(TLS):13APR73-417
GRAY, N.S.  GAWAIN AND THE GREEN KNIGHT.
    A. RENDLE, 157:SUMMER70-75
GRAY, R.P.  SONGS AND BALLADS OF THE
    MAINE LUMBERJACKS WITH OTHER SONGS
    FROM MAINE.
    J.L. CUTLER, 582(SFQ):DEC70-375
GRAY, T.  THE COMPLETE POEMS OF THOMAS
    GRAY.  (H.W. STARR & J.R. HENDRICKSON,
    EDS)
    J. KINSLEY, 179(ES):APR71-180
GRAYSON, C. - SEE ALBERTI, L.B.
GRAYSON, M.J. & T.R. SHEPARD, JR.  THE
    DISASTER LOBBY.
    441:2SEP73-10
GRAYSON, R.  STAND FAST, THE HOLY GHOST.
    617(TLS):20JUL73-827
GRAZIA PROFETI, M.  MONTALBÁN.
    V. DIXON, 86(BHS):APR72-186
GRAZZINI, G.  SOLZHENITSYN.
    D. CAUTE, 362:8FEB73-188
GREAVES, J., COMP.  WHO'S WHO IN DICKENS.
    617(TLS):2MAR73-235
GREAVES, R.L.  JOHN BUNYAN.
    J. DELAPLAIN, 481(PQ):JUL71-412
GREBANIER, B.  THE UNINHIBITED BYRON.*
    E.E.B., 191(ELN):SEP71(SUPP)-36
GREBE, P. & OTHERS.  WAS BEDEUTET DAS?
    M.H. FOLSOM, 221(GQ):MAR71-272
    205(FMLS):JAN71-93
"GREEK HANDICRAFT."
    Y.J. MILSPAW, 292(JAF):OCT-DEC71-466
GREELEY, A.M.  THE NEW AGENDA.
    J-B. BRESLIN, 441:11NOV73-14
    E.B. FISKE, 441:30NOV73-41
GREELEY, A.M.  UNSECULAR MAN.  (BRITISH
    TITLE: THE PERSISTENCE OF RELIGION.)
    442(NY):3MAR73-114
    617(TLS):19OCT73-1285

GREELEY, D.M.  25 BEACON STREET AND OTHER
    RECOLLECTIONS.
    C.A. HOLBROOK, 432(NEQ):DEC71-670
GREEN, A.  LE DISCOURS VIVANT.
    617(TLS):12OCT73-1248
GREEN, A.  ONLY A MINER.
    F. HOWES, 415:DEC72-1189
GREEN, A., COMP.  OUR HAUNTED KINGDOM.
    617(TLS):24AUG73-986
GREEN, A.  LA PORTE DES SONGES.
    W.V. GUGLI, 207(FR):DEC70-416
GREEN, A.W.  SIR FRANCIS BACON.
    H-J. MÜLLENBROCK, 72:BAND209HEFT4/6-
    403
GREEN, B.K.  WILD COW TALES.
    L. ATTEBERY, 650(WF):JAN71-64
GREEN, D.  ULYSSES BOUND.
    617(TLS):23NOV73-1454
GREEN, F.M.  DEMOCRACY IN THE OLD SOUTH
    AND OTHER ESSAYS.  (J.I. COPELAND, ED)
    H.C. BAILEY, 9(ALAR):JUL71-221
GREEN, G.  THE STONES OF ZION.
    A. COOPER, 287:SEP71-27
GREEN, G.  TOURIST.
    A. BROYARD, 441:23NOV73-39
    M. LEVIN, 441:25NOV73-48
GREEN, H.  THE DEAD OF THE HOUSE.*
    D. MARKOS, 598(SOR):SUMMER73-713
    P.M. SPACKS, 249(HUDR):AUTUMN72-497
GREEN, J.  L'AUTRE.
    M.G. ROSE, 454:WINTER72-177
GREEN, J.  OEUVRES COMPLÈTES.  (VOL 2)
    (J. PETIT, ED)
    617(TLS):8JUN73-633
GREEN, J.  THE OTHER ONE.
    G. GODWIN, 441:1JUL73-5
    E. WEEKS, 61:JUN73-120
    442(NY):2JUN73-122
    617(TLS):8JUN73-633
GREEN, J.R.  A GESTURE INVENTORY FOR THE
    TEACHING OF SPANISH.
    F.C. HAYES, 399(MLJ):OCT71-411
GREEN, J.R.  SPANISH PHONOLOGY FOR
    TEACHERS.
    R.L. HADLICH, 238:MAY71-408
GREEN, L.  CHRONICLE INTO HISTORY.
    617(TLS):26JAN73-95
GREEN, L.G.  WHEN THE JOURNEY'S OVER.
    617(TLS):18MAY73-565
GREEN, M.  CITIES OF LIGHT AND SONS OF
    THE MORNING.*
    N. BLIVEN, 442(NY):13JAN73-89
    W.H. PRITCHARD, 249(HUDR):WINTER72/73-
    685
GREEN, M.  TELEVISION NEWS.
    G.E. MILLS, 583:WINTER71-213
GREEN, M.J., ED.  THE MONOPOLY MAKERS.
    S. LAZARUS & L. ROSS, 453:28JUN73-31
GREEN, O.H.  THE LITERARY MIND OF MEDIEVAL
    AND RENAISSANCE SPAIN.*  (J.E. KELLER,
    ED)
    B. GICOVATE, 238:DEC71-967
    E.C. RILEY, 402(MLR):JUL72-672
    E.L. RIVERS, 400(MLN):MAR71-300
GREEN, P.  ALEXANDER THE GREAT.*
    J. BRISCOE, 123:DEC72-423
    A.R. BURN, 303:VOL91-195
    C.L. MURISON, 487:SUMMER71-194
GREEN, P.  ARMADA FROM ATHENS.
    G.L. CAWKWELL, 123:JUN72-245
GREEN, P.  A CONCISE HISTORY OF ANCIENT
    GREECE.
    617(TLS):30NOV73-1471
GREEN, P.  THE SHADOW OF THE PARTHENON.
    617(TLS):12JAN73-28
GREEN, P.  THE YEAR OF SALAMIS 480-479
    B.C.*
    J. BRISCOE, 123:DEC72-423
    C.W.J. ELIOT, 487:SPRING71-86

GREEN, P. - SEE "LOOKING AT PARIS"
GREEN, P.S., ED. PLANTS: WILD AND CULTI-
VATED.
    617(TLS):12OCT73-1260
GREEN, S.E. SELECTED LEGENDS OF LEICES-
TERSHIRE.
    T. BROWN, 203:AUTUMN71-257
GREEN, W., COMP. THE OBSERVER'S BOOK OF
AIRCRAFT. (22ND ED)
    617(TLS):11MAY73-537
GREENAN, R.H. THE SECRET LIFE OF ALGER-
NON PENDLETON.
    C. LEHMANN-HAUPT, 441:4MAY73-41
    M. LEVIN, 441:1APR73-33
VAN GREENAWAY, P. THE MEDUSA TOUCH.
    N. CALLENDAR, 441:11NOV73-50
GREENBAUM, S. STUDIES IN ENGLISH ADVER-
BIAL USAGE.
    H. HARTVIGSON, 179(ES):APR71-189
    S. JACOBSON, 597(SN):VOL42#2-510
    E. KOTTKE, 320(CJL):FALL71-65
GREENBAUM, S. VERB-INTENSIFIER COLLOCA-
TIONS IN ENGLISH.*
    A.R. TELLIER, 189(EA):JUL-SEP71-319
GREENBERG, A. GOING NOWHERE.
    J.C. OATES, 473(PR):SUMMER72-462
    42(AR):FALL71-437
GREENBERG, A. & H., WITH L. HULACK.
SOUTH AMERICA ON $5 AND $10 A DAY.
(REV 1971-72 ED)
    S.S. BENSON, 37:OCT71-42
GREENBERG, C. ART AND CULTURE.
    617(TLS):14SEP73-1062
GREENBERG, H. QUEST FOR THE NECESSARY.
    D.S. JOHNSON, 191(ELN):DEC71-157
    J.K. ROBINSON, 598(SOR):SUMMER73-692
    H. SERGEANT, 175:SUMMER70-68
GREENBERG, J. RITES OF PASSAGE.*
    V. CUNNINGHAM, 362:11JAN73-56
    617(TLS):16MAR73-303
GREENBERG, L.M. SISTERS OF LIBERTY.
    639(VQR):AUTUMN71-CLXXVII
GREENBERG, M. THE TERROR OF ART.*
    D.S. LOW, 220(GL&L):JAN72-187
GREENBERGER, E.B. ARTHUR HUGH CLOUGH.*
    F.L. MULHAUSER, 636(VP):AUTUMN71-356
    P.G. SCOTT, 637(VS):JUN71-465
GREENE, A.C. THE LAST CAPTIVE.*
    W. GARD, 584(SWR):SUMMER72-V
GREENE, A.C. THE SANTA CLAUS BANK ROB-
BERY.*
    W. GARD, 584(SWR):AUTUMN72-330
GREENE, B. RUNNING.
    L.C. LEWIN, 441:20MAY73-16
GREENE, D. THE AGE OF EXUBERANCE.*
    481(PQ):JUL71-383
GREENE, D. SAMUEL JOHNSON.
    H.D. WEINBROT, 481(PQ):JUL71-446
GREENE, D. & F. KELLY, EDS & TRANS.
IRISH BARDIC POETRY.
    P.K. FORD, 589:OCT72-761
GREENE, G. COLLECTED STORIES.*
    C.C. O'BRIEN, 453:18OCT73-56
    R. PRICE, 441:9SEP73-1
GREENE, G. A GUN FOR SALE. MINISTRY OF
FEAR.
    617(TLS):20APR73-437
GREENE, G. THE HEART OF THE MATTER. (P.
TAYLOR, ED)
    J.C. FIELD, 556(RLV):1971/3-361
GREENE, G. THE HONORARY CONSUL.
    W. ABRAHAMS, 61:NOV73-114
    A. BROYARD, 441:6SEP73-39
    C.C. O'BRIEN, 453:18OCT73-56
    R. PRICE, 441:9SEP73-1
    R.W., 606(TAMR):#61-73
    F. WYNDHAM, 362:13SEP73-350
    617(TLS):14SEP73-1055

GREENE, G. THE PLEASURE DOME. (J.R.
TAYLOR, ED)
    617(TLS):2MAR73-228
GREENE, G. THE QUIET AMERICAN.
    D.J. ENRIGHT, 362:12APR73-486
    617(TLS):20APR73-437
GREENE, G. A SORT OF LIFE.*
    F.A.C. WILSON, 648:JAN72-76
GREENE, G. TRAVELS WITH MY AUNT.*
    J.C. FIELD, 556(RLV):1971/6-766
    R. LÓPEZ ORTEGA, 202(FMOD):JUN71-329
    S. MONOD, 189(EA):OCT-DEC70-453
GREENE, H. CANCELED ACCOUNTS.
    N. CALLENDAR, 441:8APR73-32
GREENE, H. THE CROOKED COUNTIES.
    E.S. TURNER, 362:22NOV73-720
GREENE, J. PSYCHOLINGUISTICS.
    617(TLS):11MAY73-518
GREENE, P. THE JANE CASTLE MANUSCRIPT.
    J.C. OATES, 473(PR):SUMMER72-462
GREENE, R. JAMES THE FOURTH. FRIAR
BACON AND FRIAR BUNGAY. (J.A. LAVIN,
ED OF BOTH)
    J.C. MAXWELL, 447(N&Q):MAY71-198
GREENE, R.A. & H. MAC CALLUM - SEE CULVER-
WELL, N.
GREENE, T.M. RABELAIS.*
    G.J. BRAULT, 141:SPRING71-207
    F.S. BROWN, 207(FR):MAY71-1133
    R.D. COTTRELL, 399(MLJ):FEB71-113
GREENE, T.P. AMERICA'S HEROES.*
    M.R. STERN, 141:FALL71-422
GREENE, W.C. THE CHOICES OF CRITICISM.
    J.M., 206:NOV70-596
GREENFIELD, E. JOAN SUTHERLAND.*
    K. SPENCE, 415:DEC72-1191
GREENFIELD, E. & I. MARCH. THE THIRD
PENGUIN GUIDE TO BARGAIN RECORDS.
    M. GOFF, 415:OCT72-980
GREENFIELD, J. NO PEACE, NO PLACE.
    C. WOODS, 441:13MAY73-18
    442(NY):9JUN73-116
GREENHOUSE, H.B. PREMONITIONS.
    617(TLS):12JAN73-48
GREENSLADE, S.L., ED. THE CAMBRIDGE
HISTORY OF THE BIBLE. (VOL 3)
    J.F. KELLY, 613:WINTER70-630
GREENWAY, J. THE LAST FRONTIER.
    617(TLS):18MAY73-553
GREENWOOD, D. WILLIAM KING.
    G.H. JONES, 173(ECS):SUMMER71-487
    R. LAWRENCE, 175:SUMMER70-69
GREENWOOD, J. & H. BARROW. THE WRITINGS
OF JOHN GREENWOOD AND HENRY BARROW
1591-1593.* (L.H. CARLSON, ED)
    B.W. BECKINGSALE, 447(N&Q):JUN71-240
GREER, C. THE GREAT SCHOOL LEGEND.*
    C. LASCH, 453:17MAY73-19
GREER, G. THE FEMALE EUNUCH.
    A. DIAMOND, 418(MR):WINTER-SPRING72-
275
    P.M. SPACKS, 249(HUDR):SPRING72-160
GREG, W.W. & C. HINMAN - SEE SHAKESPEARE,
W.
GREGG, J. BABY BOY.
    M. LEVIN, 441:19AUG73-12
GREGG, R.B. WHAT'S IT ALL ABOUT AND
WHAT AM I?
    L.B. CEBIK, 219(GAR):SPRING70-85
GREGOR, A. A BED BY THE SEA.
    H.T. KIRBY-SMITH, JR., 569(SR):SUM-
MER72-483
GREGOR, A. SELECTED POEMS.*
    R. OLIVER, 598(SOR):SPRING73-492
    F.D. REEVE, 491:JAN73-234
GREGOR, A.J. CONTEMPORARY RADICAL
IDEOLOGIES. THE IDEOLOGY OF FASCISM.
    H.L. PARSONS, 484(PPR):DEC70-306

GREGORES, E. & J.A. SUÁREZ. A DESCRIP-
TION OF COLLOQUIAL GUARANÍ.
   M.D. KINKADE, 353:NOV71-123
GREGORIAN, V. THE EMERGENCE OF MODERN
AFGHANISTAN.
   R.S. NEWELL, 293(JAST):NOV70-224
GREGORIETTI, G. JEWELLERY THROUGH THE
AGES.
   G. WILLS, 39:MAY71-436
GREGOROVIUS, F. ROMAN AND MEDIEVAL CUL-
TURE. (K.F. MORRISON, ED)
   B. BRESLOW, 651(WHR):AUTUMN72-383
LADY GREGORY. CUCHULAIN OF MUIRTHEMNE.
GODS AND FIGHTING MEN. VISIONS AND
BELIEFS IN THE WEST OF IRELAND.
   R.S., 376:OCT70-94
LADY GREGORY. SIR HUGH LANE.
   617(TLS):22JUN73-726
LADY GREGORY. OUR IRISH THEATRE.
   617(TLS):30MAR73-354
POPE GREGORY VII. THE EPISTOLAE VAGANTES
OF POPE GREGORY VII. (H.E.J. COWDREY,
ED & TRANS)
   617(TLS):5JAN73-18
SAINT GREGORY. GRÉGOIRE LE THAUMATURGE,
"REMERCIEMENT À ORIGÈNE," SUIVI DE LA
"LETTRE D'ORIGÈNE À GRÉGOIRE." (H.
CROUZEL, ED & TRANS)
   É. DES PLACES, 555:VOL45FASC1-159
GREGORY, A. THE CRY OF A GULL. (M.
ADAM, ED)
   617(TLS):14SEP73-1053
GREGORY, D. DICK GREGORY'S NATURAL DIET
FOR FOLKS WHO EAT: COOKIN' WITH MOTHER
NATURE.
   441:13MAY73-40
GREGORY, H. SPIRIT OF TIME AND PLACE.
   E. JOHNSON, 441:25MAR73-7
GREGORY, L. CRYING DRUMS.
   617(TLS):23MAR73-318
GREGORY, R.L. THE INTELLIGENT EYE.
   A. FORGE, 592:JUL-AUG70-61
GREGOTTI, V. NEW DIRECTIONS IN ITALIAN
ARCHITECTURE.
   R. BANHAM, 54:SEP70-344
   G. FANELLI, 576:DEC70-360
GREIFENHAGEN, A. DAS VESTARELIEF AUS
WILTON HOUSE.*
   A. HUS, 555:VOL45FASC1-190
GREIFF, C.M., ED. LOST AMERICA.
   R. JELLINEK, 441:26AUG73-4
GREIG, I. SUBVERSION.
   617(TLS):26OCT73-1302
GREIMAS, A.J. DICTIONNAIRE DE L'ANCIEN
FRANÇAIS JUSQU'AU MILIEU DU XIVE
SIÈCLE.*
   C. RÉGNIER, 209(FM):OCT70-458
GREINER, B. FRIEDRICH NIETZSCHE, VERSUCH
UND VERSUCHUNG IN SEINEN APHORISMEN.
   H. MEYER, 182:VOL24#23/24-864
GREINER, W.F. STUDIEN ZUR ENTSTEHUNG
DER ENGLISCHEN ROMANTHEORIE AN DER
WENDE ZUM 18. JAHRHUNDERT.
   P. GOETSCH, 430(NS):NOV71-614
   D. MEHL, 182:VOL24#9/10-419
GREIVE, A. ETYMOLOGISCHE UNTERSUCHUNGEN
ZUM FRANZÖSISCHEN "H" ASPIRÉ.*
   B. FOSTER, 208(FS):OCT72-500
GRENANDER, M.E. AMBROSE BIERCE.
   J.D. HART, 27(AL):MAR72-163
   J.G. TAYLOR, 649(WAL):SPRING71-76
GRENDLER, P.F. CRITICS OF THE ITALIAN
WORLD, 1530-1560.
   F. CERRETA, 546(RR):OCT71-233
   D.S. CHAMBERS, 551(RENQ):SPRING71-67
   R.J. CLEMENTS, 401(MLQ):JUN71-218
GRENE, D. REALITY AND THE HEROIC PATTERN.
   K. RICHARDS, 597(SN):VOL42#1-230

GRENE, M. APPROACHES TO A PHILOSOPHICAL
BIOLOGY.
   R. ROSTHAL, 484(PPR):JUN71-608
GRENE, M. - SEE POLANYI, M.
GRENIER, F. JOURNAL DE LA DRÔLE DE GUERRE
(SEPTEMBRE 1939 - JUILLET 1940).
   I.M. WALL, 207(FR):APR71-941
GRENIER, J. LES PLUS BELLES PAGES DE
SENANCOUR.
   B. DIDIER, 535(RHL):JAN-FEB70-143
GRENIER, R. CINÉ-ROMAN.
   617(TLS):9MAR73-257
GRESSWELL, P. ENVIRONMENT.
   M. MIDDLETON, 46:JUL71-64
GRÉTRY, A.E.M. MÉMOIRES, OU ESSAIS SUR
LA MUSIQUE.
   J. RUSHTON, 415:OCT72-980
   J.A.W., 410(M&L):OCT72-448
DE GRÈVE, M. & F. VAN PASSEL. LINGUIS-
TIQUE ET ENSEIGNEMENT DES LANGUES
ÉTRANGÈRES.
   B. MALMBERG, 596(SL):VOL25#1-61
GRÉVISSE, M. LE BON USAGE. (NEW ED)
   M. GOUGENHEIM, 209(FM):JUL70-359
   P. RICKARD, 208(FS):JAN72-109
GRÉVISSE, M. PROBLÈMES DE LANGAGE.*
(VOL 4)
   L. CHALON, 556(RLV):1971/5-639
   N.C.W. SPENCE, 208(FS):OCT72-494
GRÉVISSE, M. PROBLÈMES DE LANGAGE. (VOL
5)
   G. SCHWEIG, 430(NS):FEB71-103
   N.C.W. SPENCE, 208(FS):OCT72-494
GREVLUND, M. PAYSAGE INTÉRIEUR ET PAY-
SAGE EXTÉRIEUR DANS LES "MÉMOIRES
D'OUTRE-TOMBE."
   M. GUGGENHEIM, 207(FR):DEC70-456
GREY, I. BORIS GODUNOV.
   617(TLS):3AUG73-910
GREY, I. THE HORIZON HISTORY OF RUSSIA.
   D. VON MOHRENSCHILDT, 550(RUSR):APR
   71-205
GREY, I. THE ROMANOVS.
   A.E. ADAMS, 550(RUSR):JUL71-306
GREYSMITH, D. RICHARD DADD.
   617(TLS):31AUG73-998
GRIBBIN, W. THE CHURCHES MILITANT.
   617(TLS):13JUL73-811
GRIBBLE, C.E., ED. STUDIES PRESENTED TO
PROFESSOR ROMAN JAKOBSON BY HIS STU-
DENTS.
   M. SAMILOV, 575(SEER):OCT72-636
GRIEDER, J.B. HU SHIH AND THE CHINESE
RENAISSANCE.
   D.T. ROY, 293(JAST):FEB71-440
GRIERSON, H.J.C., ED. METAPHYSICAL LYR-
ICS AND POETS OF THE SEVENTEENTH CEN-
TURY.
   J-M. BENOIST, 98:AUG/SEP71-730
GRIEST, G.L. MUDIE'S CIRCULATING LIBRARY
AND THE VICTORIAN NOVEL.*
   V. COLBY, 637(VS):MAR71-349
   J. ESPEY, 445(NCF):JUN71-126
   G.P. LANDOW, 405(MP):MAY72-367
GRIEVE, A.I. THE PRE-RAPHAELITE PERIOD
1848-50.
   617(TLS):28SEP73-1102
GRIFFIN, C.W., JR. SYSTEMS.
   505:SEP71-196
GRIFFIN, E.M. JONATHAN EDWARDS.
   R. ASSELINEAU, 189(EA):OCT-DEC71-547
GRIFFIN, J.H. A HIDDEN WHOLENESS.
   T. CONNER, 613:WINTER71-623
GRIFFIN, R. CORONATION OF THE POET.
   C. NELSON, 551(RENQ):SUMMER71-257
   P. SHARRATT, 402(MLR):OCT72-883
   D. STONE, JR., 405(MP):MAY71-382
   205(FMLS):OCT71-413

GRIFFITH, L. THE VIRGINIA HOUSE OF BUR-
GESSES, 1750-1774.
G.M. CURTIS 3D, 656(WMQ):JUL71-510
GRIFFITH, P. MY STILLNESS.*
M. LEVIN, 441:7JAN73-34
GRIFFITH, R. THE MOVIE STARS.
A.H. WITHAM, 200:JAN71-30
GRIFFITHS, B. BEASTHOODS.
617(TLS):9MAR73-270
GRIFFITHS, B. SCARS.
H. SERGEANT, 175:SPRING70-29
GRIFFITHS, G. REPRESENTATIVE GOVERNMENT
IN WESTERN EUROPE IN THE SIXTEENTH
CENTURY.
R. VIRGOE, 325:APR71-253
GRIFFITHS, J.G. - SEE PLUTARCH
GRIFFITHS, N. & R. BALLANTINE. SILENT
SLAUGHTER.
441:11MAR73-46
GRIFFITHS, R., ED. CLAUDEL.*
W.H. MATHESON, 207(FR):FEB71-607
GRIFFITHS, R. THE DRAMATIC TECHNIQUE OF
ANTOINE DE MONTCHRESTIEN.*
J. MOREL, 535(RHL):JUL-AUG71-691
N.B. SPECTOR, 551(RENQ):WINTER71-543
205(FMLS):JAN71-95
GRIGG, J. THE YOUNG LLOYD GEORGE.
R. CROSSMAN, 362:21JUN73-836
617(TLS):10AUG73-930
GRIGGS, S.E. IMPERIUM IN IMPERIO. OVER-
SHADOWED. UNFETTERED. THE HINDERED
HAND. POINTING THE WAY.
J.W. BYRD, 584(SWR):SUMMER72-262
"APOLLON GRIGOR'EV: SOCHINENIIA."* (VOL
1) (V.S. KRUPITSCH, ED)
I.I. BALOUEFF, 550(RUSR):JAN71-83
GRIGSBY, J.S., ED & TRANS. THE ORCHID
DOOR.
E.D. ROCKSTEIN, 318(JAOS):OCT-DEC71-
523
GRIGSON, G., ED. THE FABER BOOK OF LOVE
POEMS.
617(TLS):16NOV73-1405
GRIGSON, G. POEMS AND POETS.
R. LAWRENCE, 175:SPRING71-28
GRIGSON, G. SAD GRAVE OF AN IMPERIAL
MONGOOSE.
A. MACLEAN, 362:25OCT73-565
617(TLS):1JUN73-610
GRIGSON, J. THE INTERNATIONAL WINE AND
FOOD SOCIETY'S GUIDE TO FISH COOKERY.
617(TLS):14DEC73-1548
GRILLPARZER, F. DES MEERES UND DER LIEBE
WELLEN. (R.C. COWEN, ED)
205(FMLS):JAN71-95
GRILLPARZER, F. DER TRAUM EIN LEBEN.*
(W.E. YATES, ED)
A. BURKHARD, 400(MLN):APR71-436
"FRANZ GRILLPARZER."* (K. PÖRNBACHER,
ED)
F. STOCK, 52:BAND6HEFT1-106
GRIMAL, P. ÉTUDES DE CHRONOLOGIE CICÉR-
ONIENNE.
J-C. DUMONT, 555:VOL45FASC1-166
GRIMAL, P. - SEE SENECA
GRIMALDI, U.A. & G. BOZZETTI. FARINACCI.
617(TLS):2MAR73-225
GRIMES, W.F. THE EXCAVATION OF ROMAN AND
MEDIAEVAL LONDON.
R. HIGGINS, 39:AUG71-162
GRIMM, J. DIE EINHEIT DER ARIOST'SCHEN
SATIRE.
D. HAAS, 72:BAND209HEFT1/3-209
GRIMM, J. DIE LITERARISCHE DARSTELLUNG
DER PEST IN DER ANTIKE UND IN DER
ROMANIA.
W. ENGLER, 430(NS):MAY71-285

GRIMM, J. & W. DEUTSCHES WÖRTERBUCH.
(VOL 1, PTS 1-3)
R. RIS, 343:BAND13HEFT2-195
K. SPALDING, 47(ARL):[N.S.]VOL2-154
GRIMM, J. & W. THE JUNIPER TREE AND
OTHER TALES FROM GRIMM. (L. SEGAL &
M. SENDAK, EDS)
C. LEHMANN-HAUPT, 441:6DEC73-51
GRIMM, R. BERTOLT BRECHT. (3RD ED)
U.K. GOLDSMITH, 406:SUMMER72-179
GRIMM, R., ED. DEUTSCHE ROMANTHEORIEN.*
H. EICHNER, 224(GRM):MAY70-232
S.P. SCHER, 680(ZDP):BAND89HEFT2-302
GRIMM, R. & J. HERMAND, EDS. DIE KLASSIK-
LEGENDE/SECOND WISCONSIN WORKSHOP.
E.M. OPPENHEIMER, 406:WINTER72-418
GRIMM, R. & J. HERMAND, EDS. DIE SOGE-
NANNTEN ZWANZIGER JAHRE.
K. SCHRÖTER, 406:SPRING72-64
GRIMM, R. & H.J. SCHMIDT, EDS. BRECHT
FIBEL.
B.A. WOODS, 221(GQ):MAR71-269
GRIMM, R. & C. WIEDEMANN, EDS. LITERATUR
UND GEISTESGESCHICHTE.*
E. RIBBAT, 657(WW):NOV/DEC70-429
M. STEINS, 433:APR71-215
VON GRIMMELSHAUSEN, H.J.C. DER ABEN-
THEURLICHE SIMPLICISSIMUS TEUTSCH UND
CONTINUATIO DES ABENTHEURLICHEN SIMPLI-
CISSIMI.* (R. TAROT, ED) LEBENSBE-
SCHREIBUNG DER ERTZBETRÜGERIN UND LAND-
STÖRTZERIN COURASCHE.* (W. BENDER, ED)
DIETWALTS UND AMELINDEN ANMUTHIGE LIEB-
UND LEIDS-BESCHREIBUNG.* (R. TAROT,
ED)
H. RÜDIGER, 52:BAND6HEFT1-77
VON GRIMMELSHAUSEN, H.J.C. DES DURCH-
LEUCHTIGSTEN PRINTZEN PROXIMI UND
SEINER OHNVERGLEICHLICHEN LYMPIDAE
LIEBS-GESCHICHT-ERZEHLUNG.* (F.G.
SIEVEKE, ED) SIMPLICIANISCHER ZWEYKÖP-
FFIGER RATIO STATUS.* (R. TAROT, ED)
DES VORTREFFLICH KEUSCHEN JOSEPHS IN
EGYPTEN LEBENSBESCHREIBUNG SAMT DES
MUSAI LEBENS-LAUFF.* (W. BENDER, ED)
C.J. WAGENKNECHT, 657(WW):NOV/DEC70-
431
VON GRIMMELSHAUSEN, H.J.C. DER SELTZSAME
SPRINGINSFELD. (F.G. SIEVEKE, ED) DAS
WUNDERBARLICHE VOGELNEST. (R. TAROT,
ED) SATYRISCHER PILGRAM. (W. BENDER,
ED)
C.J. WAGENKNECHT, 657(WW):JUL/AUG71-
287
GRIMMINGER, R. POETIK DES FRÜHEN MINNE-
SANGS.*
M.E. GIBBS, 220(GL&L):JUL72-384
GRIMSLEY, R. SØREN KIERKEGAARD.
617(TLS):7SEP73-1034
GRIMSLEY, R. THE PHILOSOPHY OF ROUSSEAU.
617(TLS):4MAY73-502
GRIMSLEY, R. - SEE ROUSSEAU, J-J.
GRINSELL, L.V. THE ARCHAEOLOGY OF EXMOOR.
T. BROWN, 203:SPRING71-81
GRISAY, A., G. LAVIS & M. DUBOIS-STASSE.
LES DÉNOMINATIONS DE LA FEMME DANS LES
ANCIENS TEXTES LITTÉRAIRES FRANÇAIS.
J. ANDRÉ, 555:VOL45FASC2-377
M.D. LEGGE, 208(FS):JAN72-56
GRISCHIN, N., G. HAENSCH & R. RENNER.
DEUTSCH-RUSSISCHE WIRTSCHAFTSSPRACHE,
NEMECKO-RUSSKIJ ÈKONOMIČESKIJ SLOVAR'.
S. MAWRITZKI, 75:4/1970-232
W. SCHAMSCHULA, 430(NS):APR71-223

GRISET, I. LA PARLATA PROVENZALEGGIANTE
DI INVERSO PINASCA (TORINO) E LA PENE-
TRAZIONE DEL PIEMONTESE IN VAL PEROSA
E IN VAL SAN MARTINO.
G.P. CLIVIO, 545(RPH):AUG71-123
GRISEZ, G.G. ABORTION.
R.J. GERBER, 185:JAN72-137
GRIVELET, M. - SEE SHAKESPEARE, W.
GROBOVSKY, A.N. THE "CHOSEN COUNCIL" OF
IVANOIV.*
J. RABA, 104:FALL72-496
GRODECKI, R. POLSKA PIASTOWSKA. (J.
WYROZUMSKI, ED)
P.W. KNOLL, 32:JUN72-466
GROENNINGS, S. SCANDINAVIA IN SOCIAL
SCIENCE LITERATURE.*
H.P. KROSBY, 563(SS):WINTER72-135
GROGAN, E. RINGOLEVIO.*
617(TLS):26JAN73-91
GROH, D. NEGATIVE INTEGRATION UND REV-
OLUTIONÄRER ATTENTISMUS.
617(TLS):12OCT73-1230
GRONOWICZ, A. AN ORANGE FULL OF DREAMS.*
E.S. RABKIN, 385(MQR):SUMMER73-291
GROOM, B. THE BLUES REVIVAL.
W.R. FERRIS, JR., 187:MAY73-327
DE GROOT, A.W. BETEKENIS EN BETEKENIS-
STRUKTUUR. (G.F. BOS & H. ROOSE, EDS)
P.A.M. SEUREN, 206:MAY70-282
GROPP, A.E., COMP. A BIBLIOGRAPHY OF
LATIN AMERICAN BIBLIOGRAPHIES. (SUPP)
D.S. ZUBATSKY, 263:OCT-DEC72-419
GROS, F. & R. NAGASWAMY. UTTARAMERUR.
O. VON HINÜBER, 182:VOL24#13/14-556
GROS-GALLINER, G. GLASS.
G. WILLS, 39:NOV70-400
GROSS, A. ETCHING, ENGRAVING AND INTAG-
LIO PRINTING.
J. BURR, 39:OCT71-324
639(VQR):SPRING71-LXXXIV
GROSS, H. THE CONTRIVED CORRIDOR.*
S. MOORE, 385(MQR):SUMMER73-285
GROSS, H., ED. THE STRUCTURE OF VERSE.
F.L. UTLEY, 545(RPH):FEB72-352
GROSS, J., ED. THE AGE OF KIPLING.*
N. ANNAN, 453:8MAR73-13
GROSS, J. JAMES JOYCE.
P. RECONDO, 202(FMOD):JUN71-331
S.M. ROBERTS, 648:OCT71-59
GROSS, J. THE RISE AND FALL OF THE MAN
OF LETTERS.*
R.D. ALTICK, 637(VS):SEP70-93
GROSS, J.G., R.D. DIKKERS & J.C. GROGAN.
RECOMMENDED PRACTICE FOR ENGINEERED
BRICK MASONRY. (2ND ED)
W.J. MC GUINNESS, 505:MAR71-120
GROSS, M. GRAMMAIRE TRANSFORMATIONNELLE
DU FRANÇAIS, SYNTAXE DU VERBE.
R.W. LANGACKER, 361:VOL26#3-315
GROSS, M. & A. LENTIN. INTRODUCTION TO
FORMAL GRAMMARS.
B. BRAINERD, 320(CJL):FALL70-66
A.S. FEREBEE, 316:JUN71-346
GROSS, R. & B., EDS. RADICAL SCHOOL
REFORM.
639(VQR):SPRING71-LXXX
GROSS, T.L. THE HEROIC IDEAL IN AMERICAN
LITERATURE.
T.F. GOSSETT, 27(AL):MAY72-339
GROSS, V. NIJINSKY ON STAGE.
J. PERCIVAL, 415:FEB72-158
"DER GROSSE DUDEN, GRAMMATIK DER DEUT-
SCHEN GEGENWARTSSPRACHE."
M. REGULA, 343:BAND13HEFT1-103
GROSSER, A. GERMANY IN OUR TIME.*
(FRENCH TITLE: L'ALLEMAGNE DE NOTRE
TEMPS.)
617(TLS):26JAN73-91

GROSSETESTE, R. THE MIDDLE ENGLISH
TRANSLATIONS OF ROBERT GROSSETESTE'S
"CHÂTEAU D'AMOUR."* (K. SAJAVAARA, ED)
B. CARSTENSEN, 430(NS):APR71-226
F.C. DE VRIES, 179(ES):JUN71-259
GROSSHANS, H., ED. TO FIND SOMETHING
NEW.
D.A. GRAHAM, 50(ARQ):AUTUMN70-285
GROSSMAN, A.R. POETIC KNOWLEDGE IN THE
EARLY YEATS.*
G. GUNN, 405(MP):AUG71-87
GROSSMAN, V. FOREVER FLOWING.* (RUSSIAN
TITLE: VSE TECHET...)
P.M. SPACKS, 249(HUDR):AUTUMN72-505
G. STRUVE, 32:DEC72-943
617(TLS):23FEB73-197
GROSSMANN, F. PIETER BRUEGEL. (3RD ED)
617(TLS):16NOV73-1394
GROSSMANN, G. PROMETHIE UND ORESTIE.
H. LLOYD-JONES, 123:JUN72-178
GROSSMANN, R. GESCHICHTE UND PROBLEME
DER LATEINAMERIKANISCHEN LITERATUR.*
F. NIEDERMAYER, 430(NS):JUL70-360
D. REICHARDT, 490:JAN71-105
J.E. TOMLINS, 546(RR):APR71-136
GROSSMANN, R. REFLECTIONS ON FREGE'S
PHILOSOPHY.
E.W. KLUGE, 154:DEC70-401
K.N. MONTAGUE, 483:JUL71-283
R.H. STOOTHOFF, 311(JP):8FEB73-77
GROSSVOGEL, D.I. LIMITS OF THE NOVEL.*
C.L. CHUA, 651(WHR):SPRING72-185
J. MILLS, 648:OCT71-55
GROSVENOR, P. & J. MC MILLAN. THE
BRITISH GENIUS.
C. DRIVER, 362:22FEB73-249
617(TLS):23MAR73-321
GROTOWSKI, J. TOWARDS A POOR THEATRE.
C. AUBERT, 98:NOV70-952
E.J. CZERWINSKI, 397(MD):MAY70-106
R. SENNETT, 453:1NOV73-29
GROUSSET, R. THE EMPIRE OF THE STEPPES.
D. SINOR, 293(JAST):MAY71-633
639(VQR):SUMMER71-CXXX
GROVE, F.P. TALES FROM THE MARGIN. (D.
PACEY, ED)
R. DANIELLS, 102(CANL):WINTER72-84
GRUBMÜLLER, K. VOCABULARIUS EX QUO.
R.M. KULLY, 657(WW):SEP/OCT71-352
H. STOPP, 680(ZDP):BAND90HEFT3-466
GRUEN, J. THE PARTY'S OVER NOW.*
42(AR):WINTER71/72-590
GRUENTER, R. - SEE VON KEYSERLING, E.
GRUMACH, E. & R. GOETHE, BEGEGNUNGEN UND
GESPRÄCHE.
A. KELLETAT, 564:OCT70-244
GRUN, B. - SEE BERG, A.
VON DER GRUN, M. MENSCHEN IN DEUTSCHLAND
(BRD).
617(TLS):20JUL73-836
GRÜNBAUM, A. GEOMETRY AND CHRONOMETRY IN
PHILOSOPHICAL PERSPECTIVE.*
J. MERLEAU-PONTY, 542:OCT-DEC70-471
GRUNBERGER, R. RED RISING IN BAVARIA.
617(TLS):3AUG73-891
GRUNBERGER, R. THE TWELVE-YEAR REICH.*
(BRITISH TITLE: A SOCIAL HISTORY OF THE
THIRD REICH.)
L. CLARK, 619(TC):VOL179#1049-51
GRUNDY, J. THE SPENSERIAN POETS.
K. DUNCAN-JONES, 541(RES):MAY71-248
S. FRIEDMAN, 551(RENQ):SPRING71-94
R. LAWRENCE, 175:AUTUMN70-107
568(SCN):FALL-WINTER72-64
GRUNER, E. & OTHERS. DIE SCHWEIZERISCHE
BUNDESVERSAMMLUNG 1920-68.
A. LASSERRE, 182:VOL24#4-180

GRUNWALD, J. & P. MUSGROVE. NATURAL
RESOURCES IN LATIN AMERICAN DEVELOP-
MENT.
M. BUCHINGER, 37:JAN-FEB71-40
GRUPPE, H. THE TRUXTON CIPHER.
N. CALLENDAR, 441:23SEP73-48
GRUSON, F. LA CLÔTURE.
J. LECOCQ-LEINER, 207(FR):OCT70-177
GRÜTTER, T. JOHANNES VON MÜLLERS BEGEG-
NUNG MIT ENGLAND.
H.S. OFFLER, 182:VOL24#7/8-370
GRYAZNOV, M. SOUTH SIBERIA.* (FRENCH
TITLE: SIBÉRIE DU SUD.)
P. GUERRE, 98:DEC71-1093
GRYPHIUS, A. GESAMTAUSGABE DER DEUTSCH-
SPRACHIGEN WERKE. (VOL 7) (H. POWELL,
ED)
F. VAN INGEN, 433:OCT71-460
GRZEGORCZYK, A. & H. RASIOWA - SEE
MAZUR, S.
GSTEIGER, M. FRANZÖSISCHE SYMBOLISTEN IN
DER DEUTSCHEN LITERATUR DER JAHRHUNDERT-
WENDE (1869-1914).
H.F. GARTEN, 270:VOL22#2-48
GUAGLIANONE, A. - SEE PHAEDRUS
GUALANDRI, I. - SEE EUTECNIUS
GUARDUCCI, P. COLLODI E IL MELODRAMMA
OTTOCENTESCO.
B. CORRIGAN, 276:SPRING71-102
GUARINI, G. ARCHITETTURA CIVILE. (NOTES
BY B.T. LA GRECA)
A. BLUNT, 46:FEB70-164
"GUARINO GUARINI E L'INTERNAZIONALITA DEL
BAROCCO."
A. BLUNT, 46:OCT71-259
GUATTARI, F. PSYCHANALYSE ET TRANSVER-
SALITÉ.
617(TLS):16MAR73-295
GUCHMAN, M.M. & OTHERS. SRAVNITEL'NAJA
GRAMMATIKA GERMANSKICH JAZYKOV V PJATI
TOMACH. (VOL 4)
R. RIS, 343:BAND13HEFT2-197
GUDIOL, J. EL GRECO, 1541-1614.
J. CANADAY, 441:2DEC73-90
GUENÉE, B. L'OCCIDENT AUX XIVE ET XVE
SIÈCLES: LES ÉTATS.
A.R. LEWIS, 589:OCT72-765
GUENTHER, H.V., ED & TRANS. THE ROYAL
SONG OF SARAHA.*
A. BHARATI, 293(JAST):NOV70-216
GUERARD, A.J. ANDRÉ GIDE. (2ND ED)
J.C. MC LAREN, 207(FR):DEC70-444
P. POLLARD, 208(FS):APR72-220
GUERARD, A.J. - SEE DICKENS, C.
GUERINOT, J.V. PAMPHLET ATTACKS ON ALEX-
ANDER POPE 1711-1744.*
I. GRUNDY, 541(RES):FEB71-83
C. PULLEN, 529(QQ):SPRING71-151
O.F. SIGWORTH, 50(ARQ):SPRING71-91
J. SUTHERLAND, 354:MAR71-81
GUÉROULT, M. SPINOZA. (VOL 1)
J-P. BRODEUR, 154:MAR71-162
J-L. BRUCH, 542:APR-JUN70-207
GUERRA, A. STUDI SULLA VITA E IL PEN-
SIERO DI ANTONIO LABRIOLA.
E. NAMER, 542:JAN-MAR70-100
GUERRAZZI, F.D. PAGINE AUTOBIOGRAFICHE.
(G. RAGONESE, ED)
P.A. TRIVERO, 228(GSLI):VOL148FASC
464-619
"LA GUERRE ET SES THÉORIES."
J. RUEST, 154:JUN71-412
GUERREIRO, M.V. BOCHIMANES /KHU DE
ANGOLA.
A.C. EDWARDS, 69:OCT71-344
GUERS-VILLATE, Y. CHARLES-FERDINAND
RAMUZ.
C.R. PARSONS, 207(FR):OCT70-223

GUEST, H. & L. AND K. SHOZO, EDS & TRANS.
POST-WAR JAPANESE POETRY.
617(TLS):13APR73-424
GUETTI, J. ACTION.
R. SALE, 249(HUDR):WINTER72/73-703
DE GUEVARA, J.V. - SEE UNDER VÉLEZ DE
GUEVARA, J.
DE GUEVARA, L.V. - SEE UNDER VÉLEZ DE
GUEVARA, L.
GUFFEY, G.R., ED. AFTER "THE TEMPEST."*
M.T. JONES-DAVIES, 189(EA):OCT-DEC70-
441
GUHIN, M.A. JOHN FOSTER DULLES.
617(TLS):6APR73-367
ABBOT GUIBERT OF NOGENT. SELF AND SOCI-
ETY IN MEDIEVAL FRANCE. (J.F. BENTON,
ED)
F.J. WARNE, 208(FS):APR72-178
GUIBERT, A-J. BIBLIOGRAPHIE DES OEUVRES
DE JEAN RACINE PUBLIÉES AU XVIIE SIÈCLE
ET OEUVRES POSTHUMES.
R. PICARD, 535(RHL):MAY-JUN71-500
E. ZIMMERMANN, 182:VOL24#3-104
GUIBERT, R. SEVEN VOICES.
M. WOOD, 453:19APR73-35
442(NY):13JAN73-92
GUICCIARDINI, F. HISTORY OF ITALY. (S.
ALEXANDER, TRANS)
M. MILLER, 275(IQ):SUMMER71-108
GUICHARD, L. - SEE BERLIOZ, H.
GUICHARNAUD, J., ED. LA MODIFICATION DE
MICHEL BUTOR.
A. ABEL, 399(MLJ):MAY71-328
GUICHEMERRE, R. LA COMÉDIE AVANT MOLIÈRE
1640-1660.
617(TLS):25MAY73-588
"GUIDE DU SLAVISTE."
J.S.G. SIMMONS, 575(SEER):APR72-327
"GUIDE TO CIVIL WAR RECORDS IN THE NORTH
CAROLINA STATE ARCHIVES."
C.S. RYAN, 14:JAN70-87
"GUIDE TO LEGISLATIVE RECORDS IN THE
OREGON STATE ARCHIVES."
L.C. WAFFEN, 14:APR71-197
"GUIDE TO THE CONTENTS OF THE PUBLIC
RECORD OFFICE." (VOL 3)
J. MC DONOUGH, 14:OCT70-405
GUIDO, M. SOUTHERN ITALY: AN ARCHAEO-
LOGICAL GUIDE.
617(TLS):8JUN73-648
GUIDO DE COLONNA. LA CORONICA TROYANA.
(F.P. NORRIS 2D, ED)
R.B. TATE, 86(BHS):APR72-176
GUIETTE, R. POÉSIE 1922-1967.
G. BRÉE, 207(FR):DEC70-404
GUIGUET, J. ASPECTS DE LA CIVILISATION
AMÉRICAINE.
P. MICHEL, 556(RLV):1971/3-362
GUILCHER, J.M. LA CONTREDANSE ET LES
RENOUVELLEMENTS DE LA DANSE FRANÇAISE.
V. ALFORD, 203:SPRING70-77
GUILES, F.L. MARION DAVIES.*
617(TLS):18MAY73-563
GUILLAIN, R. THE JAPANESE CHALLENGE.
R.A. MILLER, 639(VQR):SPRING71-286
GUILLAUME DE ACQUITAINE. WILHELM VON
AQUITANIEN, GESAMMELTE LIEDER. (W.
DÜRRSON, ED)
O. SAYCE, 220(GL&L):APR72-319
GUILLAUME DE LORRIS. DER ROSENROMAN.
(G. INEICHEN, ED)
J. WAHL, 680(ZDP):BAND89HEFT1-155
GUILLAUME DE LORRIS & JEAN DE MEUN. THE
ROMANCE OF THE ROSE. (C. DAHLBERG,
TRANS)
639(VQR):SPRING71-LXVI

GUILLAUME LE VINIER. LES POÉSIES DE
GUILLAUME LE VINIER. (P. MÉNARD, ED)
    W.M. HACKETT, 382(MAE):1972/1-64
    N. WILKINS, 208(FS):JUL72-317
GUILLAUME, J. - SEE DE NERVAL, G.
GUILLAUME, J-M. MARIA TERESA.
    M. SAKHAROFF, 207(FR):FEB71-640
GUILLAUMIN, É. CENT DIX-NEUF LETTRES
D'ÉMILE GUILLAUMIN (1894-1951). (R.
MATHÉ, ED)
    P. VERNOIS, 535(RHL):MAY-JUN70-537
GUILLEMIN, H. JOAN, MAID OF ORLÉANS.
    441:2SEP73-14
    442(NY):12MAY73-147
GUILLEMIN, H. LA LIAISON MUSSET-SAND.
    617(TLS):30NOV73-1478
GUILLEMIN, H. NAPOLÉON TEL QUEL.
    H.W. BRANN, 207(FR):OCT70-202
GUILLÉN, C. LITERATURE AS SYSTEM.
    R. LÓPEZ LANDEIRA, 579(SAQ):SUMMER
    72-459
    R. WELLEK, 676(YR):WINTER72-254
GUILLERMAZ, J. A HISTORY OF THE CHINESE
COMMUNIST PARTY 1921-1949.
    J. ISRAEL, 441:20MAY73-52
    617(TLS):23FEB73-198
GUILLERMAZ, J. LE PARTI COMMUNISTE
CHINOIS AU POUVOIR.
    617(TLS):23FEB73-198
GUILLEVIC. SELECTED POEMS.
    R. FEDERMAN, 207(FR):OCT70-178
GUILLEVIC. VILLE.*
    J. SOJCHER, 98:FEB71-149
"GUILLEVIC." (T. SAVORY, TRANS)
    J. HART, 661:SUMMER70-113
GUINEY, M. - SEE BERNANOS, G.
GUINNESS, D. & W. RYAN. IRISH HOUSES AND
CASTLES.*
    A. CLIFTON-TAYLOR, 135:DEC71-289
GUINNESS, D. & J.T. SADLER, JR. MR.
JEFFERSON ARCHITECT.
    R. JELLINEK, 441:26AUG73-5
GUINNESS, O. THE DUST OF DEATH.
    617(TLS):7SEP73-1034
GUIOMAR, M. PRINCIPES D'UNE ESTHÉTIQUE
DE LA MORT.
    R. TROUSSON, 535(RHL):SEP-DEC70-1092
GUIRAUD, P. LE JARGON DE VILLON OU LE
GAI SAVOIR DE LA COQUILLE. LE TESTA-
MENT DE VILLON OU LE GAI SAVOIR DE LA
BASOCHE.
    A. REY, 98:AUG/SEP71-688
GUIRAUD, P. LES MOTS SAVANTS.
    N. GUEUNIER, 209(FM):OCT70-457
GUIRAUD, P. PATOIS ET DIALECTES FRANÇAIS.
    J-C. BOUVIER, 209(FM):JUL70-369
GUIRAUD, P. STRUCTURES ÉTYMOLOGIQUES DU
LEXIQUE FRANÇAIS.
    B. MALMBERG, 596(SL):VOL24#1-64
GUIRAUD, P. LA VERSIFICATION.
    J. FOX, 208(FS):APR72-240
GUISAN, G., ED. C-F. RAMUZ, SES AMIS ET
SON TEMPS. (VOLS 1-3)
    A. BARNES, 208(FS):JAN72-105
GUISAN, G., ED. C-F. RAMUZ, SES AMIS ET
SON TEMPS. (VOL 4)
    A. BARNES, 208(FS):JAN72-105
    C. GUYOT, 535(RHL):JAN-FEB70-155
GUISAN, G., ED. C-F. RAMUZ, SES AMIS ET
SON TEMPS. (VOL 5)
    A. BARNES, 208(FS):JAN72-105
    C. GUYOT, 535(RHL):MAY-JUN70-532
GUITTON, J. REGARDS SUR LA PENSÉE FRAN-
ÇAISE, 1870-1940.
    R.L., 154:JUN70-127
GULDAN, E. WOLFGANG ANDREAS HEINDL.
    H. AURENHAMMER, 683:BAND34HEFT2-156

VAN GULIK, R.H., ED & TRANS. HSI K'ANG
AND HIS POETICAL ESSAY ON THE LUTE.*
(2ND ED)
    J.L.B., 244(HJAS):VOL30-278
VAN GULIK, R.H. THE LORE OF THE CHINESE
LUTE.
    J.L.B., 244(HJAS):VOL30-278
GULLACE, G. GABRIELE D'ANNUNZIO AND
FRANCE.
    H.E. STEWART, 207(FR):FEB71-611
GULLANS, C.B., WITH J.J. ESPEY. A CHECK-
LIST OF TRADE BINDINGS DESIGNED BY
MARGARET ARMSTRONG.*
    G. BARBER, 354:DEC70-367
GULLBERG, E. & P. ÅSTRÖM. THE THREAD OF
ARIADNE.
    J.M. COOK, 123:JUN72-293
GULLEY, N. THE PHILOSOPHY OF SOCRATES.*
    J. HOWIE, 321:WINTER70[VOL5#1]-73
GULLÓN, R. LA INVENCIÓN DEL 98 Y OTROS
ENSAYOS.*
    M-C. PEÑUELAS, 240(HR):JUL71-334
GULVIN, C. THE TWEEDMAKERS.
    617(TLS):12OCT73-1224
GUNDERT, H. DIALOG UND DIALEKTIK.
    H.W. SCHNEIDER, 319:OCT73-540
GUNDREY, E., ED. THEN 1815.
    617(TLS):2MAR73-249
GUNN, J. THE LISTENERS.
    T. STURGEON, 441:22APR73-16
GUNN, T. MOLY.*
    A. CLUYSENAAR, 565:VOL12#4-68
    H. SERGEANT, 175:AUTUMN71-106
    S. TOULSON, 493:SUMMER71-208
GUNN, T. MOLY AND MY SAD CAPTAINS.
    S. SPENDER, 453:20SEP73-8
GUNN, T. POEMS 1950-1966, A SELECTION.
    E.N. CHUILLEANÁIN, 159(DM):SPRING70-
    111
GUNSTON, B. BOMBERS OF THE WEST.
    617(TLS):30NOV73-1485
GUNTER, A.Y. THE BIG THICKET.
    C. WHALEY, 584(SWR):SUMMER72-256
GUNTER, P.A.Y., ED & TRANS. BERGSON AND
THE EVOLUTION OF PHYSICS.
    W.H. DAVIS, 577(SHR):WINTER71-88
GUNTON, L. ROME'S HISTORIC CHURCHES.
    J. LEES-MILNE, 39:JUN70-490
GUPTA, A.S. CLASSICAL SAMKHYA.
    K.N. UPADHYAYA, 485(PE&W):JUL71-341
GUPTA, L.C. THE CHANGING STRUCTURE OF
INDUSTRIAL FINANCE IN INDIA.
    G.P. PAPANEK, 293(JAST):NOV70-205
GUPTA, M. HISTORY OF THE INDIAN REVOLU-
TIONARY MOVEMENT.
    617(TLS):27APR73-482
GUPTA, S.M. FROM DAITYAS TO DEVATAS
IN HINDU MYTHOLOGY.
    617(TLS):27JUL73-884
GURNEY, I. POEMS OF IVOR GURNEY 1890-
1937.
    617(TLS):31AUG73-996
GURR, A. THE SHAKESPEAREAN STAGE 1574-
1642.*
    I. BROWN, 157:SPRING71-65
    R.A. FOAKES, 175:AUTUMN71-98
    M. JONES, 541(RES):NOV71-485
    M.L. VAWTER, 301(JEGP):APR72-249
GURR, A. - SEE BEAUMONT, F.
GURR, A. - SEE BEAUMONT, F. & J. FLETCHER
GURTOV, M. SOUTHEAST ASIA TOMORROW.
    C.E. MORRISON, 293(JAST):NOV70-227
GUSDORF, G. LA RÉVOLUTION GALILÉENNE.
    C. LIMOGES, 154:MAR71-116
GUSDORF, G. LES SCIENCES HUMAINES ET LA
PENSÉE OCCIDENTALE. (VOL 4)
    S. DANGELMAYR, 182:VOL24#3-65

GUSMANI, R. IL LESSICO ITTITO.
    A. HEUBECK, 260(IF):BAND75-297
GUSSOW, M. DON'T SAY YES UNTIL I FINISH
TALKING.
    C. DAVIDSON, 200:AUG-SEP71-435
GUSTAFSON, R. SELECTED POEMS.
    M.T. LANE, 198:WINTER73-106
GUSTAFSON, R. THEME AND VARIATIONS FOR
SOUNDING BRASS.
    M.T. LANE, 198:WINTER73-106
GUSTAFSSON, L. SELECTED POEMS.
    V. YOUNG, 249(HUDR):WINTER72/73-673
GUTHKE, K.S. WEGE ZUR LITERATUR.*
    J. BIRKE, 564:MAR70-81
GUTHRIE, A.B., JR. ARFIVE.*
    M.S. TRIMBLE, 649(WAL):SUMMER71-158
GUTHRIE, A.B., JR. WILD PITCH.
    N. CALLENDAR, 441:11FEB73-30
    E. WEEKS, 61:MAR73-106
    442(NY):24FEB73-130
GUTHRIE, R. MAXIMUM SECURITY WARD.*
    A. OBERG, 598(SOR):WINTER73-243
GUTHRIE, W.K.C. A HISTORY OF GREEK PHIL-
OSOPHY.* (VOL 3)
    G.B. KERFERD, 123:MAR72-52
    C. MUGLER, 555:VOL45FASC1-151
    J.B. SKEMP, 303:VOL91-178
GUTIERREZ, G. A THEOLOGY OF LIBERATION.
    J.M. CAMERON, 453:31MAY73-19
GUTMANN, J., ED. BEAUTY IN HOLINESS.
    R. WISCHNITZER, 328:WINTER71-127
GUTNOV, A. & OTHERS. THE IDEAL COMMUNIST
CITY.*
    F. ALBERT, 45:OCT71-111
GUTSCHOW, H. LEISTUNGSDIFFERENZIERUNG
IM ENGLISCHUNTERRICHT DER HAUPTSCHULE.
    W. STUCK, 430(NS):MAY70-260
GUTTMACHER, A.F. PREGNANCY, BIRTH &
FAMILY PLANNING.
    J.E. BRODY, 441:2FEB73-33
GUTTMANN, A. THE CONSERVATIVE TRADITION
IN AMERICA.*
    U. BRUMM, 38:BAND89HEFT3-411
    R. DECANCQ, 556(RLV):1970/1-105
    J.T. FLANAGAN, 179(ES):OCT71-464
GUTTMANN, A. THE JEWISH WRITER IN
AMERICA.
    E. ROVIT, 27(AL):MAY72-340
GUY, A. ORTEGA Y GASSET OU LA RAISON
VITALE ET HISTORIQUE.
    P. BAUMANNS, 53(AGP):BAND53HEFT3-325
GUYOT, C. DE ROUSSEAU À MARCEL PROUST.*
    J. ONIMUS, 557(RSH):OCT-DEC70-652
GUYOTAT, P. EDEN, EDEN, EDEN.
    P. SOLLERS, 98:JUL71-607
GWALTNEY, F.I. DESTINY'S CHICKENS.
    M. LEVIN, 441:26AUG73-31
GWYNN, A. & R.N. HADCOCK. MEDIEVAL RELI-
GIOUS HOUSES, IRELAND.
    E. JOHN, 589:JAN72-127
GYARMATHI, S. AFFINITAS LINGUAE HUNGAR-
ICAE CUM LINGUIS FENNICAE ORIGINIS GRAM-
MATICE DEMONSTRATA.
    H.M. HOENIGSWALD, 318(JAOS):OCT-DEC71-
    564
GYBBON-MONYPENNY, G.B., ED. "LIBRO DE
BUEN AMOR" STUDIES.*
    H.U. GUMBRECHT, 72:BAND209HEFT4/6-452
    D.W. LOMAX, 86(BHS):JAN72-67
GYGLI-WYSS, B. DAS NOMINALE POLYPTOTON
IM ÄLTEREN GRIECHISCH.
    A.P. DORJAHN, 122:JUL72-226
GYURKÓ, L. AZ EGÉSZ ÉLET.
    T. KOLTAI, 270:VOL21#4-192

H.D. TRIBUTE TO FREUD.
    617(TLS):23MAR73-317
HAAS, A.M. NIM DIN SELBES WAR.
    R. RUDOLF, 182:VOL24#4-162
HAAS, B. DAISY CANFIELD.
    N. CALLENDAR, 441:29APR73-28
HAAS, C. D'AUTRES MONDES.
    G.J. HASENAUER, 207(FR):OCT70-153
HAAS, M. HULDRYCH ZWINGLI UND SEINE
ZEIT.
    E-W. KOHLS, 182:VOL24#4-137
HAAS, M.R. THE PREHISTORY OF LANGUAGES.
    M. KOMÁREK, 353:NOV71-97
    S. NEWMAN, 361:VOL27#1-97
HÁBA, A. MEIN WEG ZUR VIERTEL- UND SECH-
STELTONMUSIK.
    M.C., 410(M&L):OCT72-436
HABE, H. THE MISSION.
    M. MASHBERG, 390:NOV70-74
HABERLAND, E. UNTERSUCHUNGEN ZUM ÄTHIOP-
ISCHEN KÖNIGTUM.
    L. VAJDA, 182:VOL24#17/18-699
HABERMAN, M. & T. MEISEL. DANCE - AN ART
IN ACADEME.
    P. RENNA, 151:OCT70-86
HABERMAS, J. ERKENNTNIS UND INTERESSE.
    G. FLØISTAD, 262:SUMMER70-175
HABERMAS, J. TOWARD A RATIONAL SOCIETY.
    D.A. KELLY, 484(PPR):DEC71-281
    B. SCHEFOLD, 111:7MAY71-178
HABIBULLAH, A.B.M. DESCRIPTIVE CATALOGUE
OF THE PERSIAN, URDU AND ARABIC MANU-
SCRIPTS IN THE DACCA UNIVERSITY LIBRARY.
(VOL 2)
    A. AHMAD, 318(JAOS):OCT-DEC71-535
HABICHT, C. GOTTMENSCHENTUM UND GRIECH-
ISCHE STÄDTE. (2ND ED)
    O. MURRAY, 123:DEC72-427
HABICHT, W., ED. ENGLISH AND AMERICAN
STUDIES IN GERMAN (1968 & 1969).*
    R.D., 179(ES):APR71-194
HABICHT, W. STUDIEN ZUR DRAMENFORM VOR
SHAKESPEARE.*
    G. LAMBRECHTS, 189(EA):APR-JUN71-195
    M. MINCOFF, 447(N&Q):DEC71-469
    H. OPPEL, 430(NS):JUL71-392
    J. WESTLAKE, 402(MLR):JAN72-165
VON HABSBURG, O. CHARLES V.*
    J.W. O'MALLEY, 613:SPRING71-150
HACHMANN, R. DIE GOTEN UND SKANDINAVIEN.*
    J. FLECK, 563(SS):AUTUMN72-548
HACK, B. & M. KLEISS - SEE "HERMANN
BROCH - DANIEL BRODY: BRIEFWECHSEL
1930-1951"
HÄCKEL, M. - SEE FREILIGRATH, F., K.
MARX & F. ENGELS
HACKETT, C.A. AUTOUR DE RIMBAUD.*
    J.U. HALPERIN, 402(MLR):JUL72-642
HACKETT, C.A., ED. NEW FRENCH POETRY.
    617(TLS):29JUN73-750
HACKETT, E. BLOOD.
    617(TLS):8JUN73-649
HACKETT, M.B. THE ORIGINAL STATUTES OF
CAMBRIDGE UNIVERSITY.*
    P. KIBRE, 377:MAR72-52
HADDON, J. BATH.
    617(TLS):13JUL73-817
HADDOX, J.H. ANTONIO CASA, PHILOSOPHER
OF MEXICO.
    J. HIMELBLAU, 263:OCT-DEC72-435
    H.D. SIMS, 37:SEP71-37
HADEN-GUEST, A. THE PARADISE PROGRAM.
    D. GODDARD, 441:30DEC73-16
HADFIELD, C. INTRODUCING INLAND WATER-
WAYS.
    617(TLS):2NOV73-1352

HADFIELD, J., ED. THE SATURDAY BOOK.
(NO. 33)
  617(TLS):14DEC73-1549
HADLEY, G. CENTO - THE FORGOTTEN ALLI-
ANCE.
  617(TLS):20APR73-434
HADLICH, R.L. A TRANSFORMATIONAL GRAMMAR
OF SPANISH.
  A. BELL, 67:NOV72-257
HADOT, I. SENECA UND DIE GRIECHISCH-
RÖMISCHE TRADITION DER SEELENLEITUNG.
  A.A. IMHOLTZ, JR., 24:JUL72-505
HADOT, P. MARIUS VICTORINUS.
  W. BEIERWALTES, 182:VOL24#19/20-753
HADOT, P. PORPHYRE ET VICTORINUS.*
  M.T. CLARK, 258:JUN70-322
HAEBLER, C. GRAMMATIK DER ALBANISCHEN
MUNDART VON SALAMIS.
  S.E. MANN, 575(SEER):JUL72-450
DE HAES, F. IMAGES DE LAUTRÉAMONT.*
  S.I. LOCKERBIE, 208(FS):OCT72-469
  M. SCHAETTEL, 557(RSH):APR-JUN71-327
HAFTMANN, W. EMIL NOLDE, UNPAINTED PIC-
TURES. (REV)
  R. LEBOWITZ, 58:MAR72-18
HAGEDORN, G., ED. ERLÄUTERUNGEN UND DOKU-
MENTE: HEINRICH VON KLEIST; "MICHAEL
KOHLHAAS."
  I.F., 191(ELN):SEP71(SUPP)-150
HAGELMAN, C.W., JR. & R.J. BARNES, EDS.
A CONCORDANCE TO BYRON'S "DON JUAN."*
  J. SCHÄFER, 38:BAND88HEFT4-548
HAGEN, C. SUNSHINE.
  639(VQR):SUMMER71-C
HÄGG, T. NARRATIVE TECHNIQUE IN ANCIENT
GREEK ROMANCES.
  F. LASSERRE, 182:VOL24#5-233
HAGGARD, W. THE NOTCH ON THE KNIFE.
  N. CALLENDAR, 441:16SEP73-30
HAGGARD, W. THE OLD MASTERS.
  617(TLS):26OCT73-1324
HAGGART, R. & A. GOLDEN. RUMOURS OF WAR.
  D. DUFFY, 331:AUG71-57
  G. WOODCOCK, 102(CANL):WINTER72-73
HAGGERTY, J. DAUGHTERS OF THE MOON.
  W.H. NEW, 102(CANL):SUMMER72-88
  P.M. SPACKS, 249(HUDR):SPRING72-163
HAGGIN, B.H. BALLET CHRONICLE.
  J. GALE, 151:DEC71-89
  S. RUDIN, 418(MR):SUMMER72-487
HAGGIS, D.R. C-F. RAMUZ, OUVRIER DU
LANGAGE.*
  A.P. HARTMAN, 207(FR):OCT70-224
  D.D. RONCO, 208(FS):JAN72-103
  P. VERNOIS, 535(RHL):JAN-FEB71-137
  205(FMLS):APR70-207
HAGGLOF, G. DIPLOMAT.
  617(TLS):19JAN73-58
HAGSPIEL, R. - SEE DE MONTHERLANT, H.
HAGSTRUM, J.H. SAMUEL JOHNSON'S LITERARY
CRITICISM.* (2ND ED)
  J.T. BOULTON, 179(ES):JUN71-274
HAHLWEG, W., ED. DER FRIEDE VON BREST-
LITOWSK.*
  F.L. CARSTEN, 575(SEER):JUL72-473
HAHN, E. RAFFLES OF SINGAPORE.
  T.R. FENNELL, 293(JAST):NOV70-231
HAHN, E.A. NAMING-CONSTRUCTIONS IN SOME
INDO-EUROPEAN LANGUAGES.
  G.S. LANE, 487:WINTER71-388
  G.M. MESSING, 122:OCT72-296
  W.F. WYATT, JR., 24:APR72-354
  L. ZGUSTA, 350:SEP72-695
  R.A. ZIRIN, 124:SEP71-22
HAHN, M. BÜRGERLICHER OPTIMISMUS IM
NIEDERGANG.
  D. HOWARD, 182:VOL24#13/14-522

HAHN, R. THE ANATOMY OF A SCIENTIFIC
INSTITUTION.
  L.M. MARSAK, 173(ECS):SPRING72-488
HAHN, W.G. THE POLITICS OF SOVIET AGRI-
CULTURE, 1960-1970.
  617(TLS):21DEC73-1572
HAHNLOSER-INGOLD, M. DAS ENGLISCHE THE-
ATER UND BERT BRECHT.
  R. COHN, 397(MD):DEC71-357
  K.P. STEIGER, 402(MLR):APR72-409
HAIDING, K. MÄRCHEN UND SCHWÄNKE AUS
OBERÖSTERREICH.
  E. MOSER-RATH, 196:BAND12HEFT2/3-277
HAIDING, K. - SEE VON GERAMB, V.
HAIDU, P. AESTHETIC DISTANCE IN CHRÉTIEN
DE TROYES.
  D.C. FOWLER, 546(RR):DEC71-291
  G.J. HALLIGAN, 402(MLR):JUL72-626
HAIGHT, G.S. GEORGE ELIOT.*
  R. BENVENUTO, 594:FALL70-355
  J. GILSDORF, 502(PRS):SPRING71-85
  M. HARRIS, 648:OCT70-74
HAILEY, A. & J. CASTLE. RUNWAY ZERO-
EIGHT.
  M. LEVIN, 441:24JUN73-12
HAINES, J. TWENTY POEMS.*
  W. DICKEY, 249(HUDR):SUMMER72-303
  R. SCHRAMM, 651(WHR):AUTUMN72-389
HAIR, P., ED. BEFORE THE BAWDY COURT.
  617(TLS):5JAN73-22
HAIR, W.I. BOURBONISM AND AGRARIAN PRO-
TEST.
  W.W. ROGERS, 9(ALAR):APR71-151
HAISLIP, J. NOT EVERY YEAR.
  W. HEYEN, 398:AUTUMN73-233
HAITHCOX, J.P. COMMUNISM AND NATIONALISM
IN INDIA.
  639(VQR):AUTUMN71-CLXXXI
HAJJAR, G. - SEE KHALED, L.
ḤĀJJĪ AD-DABĪR, A.M-A.A-A. ZAFAR UL WĀLIH
BI MUZAFFAR WA ĀLIHI. (VOL 1)
  M.N. PEARSON, 318(JAOS):OCT-DEC71-559
HAKANCHULU, H., COMP. A CHINESE-MONGOL-
IAN DICTIONARY.
  J.G. HANGIN, 293(JAST):FEB71-428
HÅKANSON, L. STATIUS' "SILVAE."*
  G. LUCK, 24:JUL72-493
HAKEDA, Y.S. KUKAI: MAJOR WORKS.
  617(TLS):2MAR73-237
HAKKARAINEN, H.J. SENTENCE ANALYSIS IN
MODERN ENGLISH.
  R.M. HOGG, 433:JAN71-107
HAKKARAINEN, H.J. STUDIEN ZUM CAMBRIDGER
CODEX T-S.10.K.22. (VOL 1)
  M. CALIEBE, 657(WW):MAR/APR70-139
HALBAUER, S. RUSSISCH FÜR NATURWISSEN-
SCHAFTLER UND INGENIEURE.
  W. SCHAMSCHULA, 430(NS):APR71-223
HALBERSTAM, D. THE BEST AND THE BRIGHT-
EST.*
  R. CROSSMAN, 362:24MAY73-693
  M. MC CARTHY, 453:25JAN73-3
  617(TLS):18MAY73-543
HALDANE, A.R.B. NEW WAYS THROUGH THE
GLENS.
  617(TLS):31AUG73-1001
HALDANE, A.R.B. THREE CENTURIES OF SCOT-
TISH POSTS.*
  E.R. CREGEEN, 595(SCS):VOL16PT2-181
HALDANE, S. THE FRIGHT OF TIME.
  G. WICKES, 27(AL):MAR72-156
HALE, J. THE FORT.
  617(TLS):23NOV73-1455
HALE, J.R., ED. RENAISSANCE VENICE.
  617(TLS):12OCT73-1223
HALE, N. SECRETS.
  639(VQR):SUMMER71-XCVII
HALE, N.A. - SEE SCHATOFF, M.

HALE, O.J. THE GREAT ILLUSION, 1900-1914.
C.F. DELZELL, 639(VQR):SPRING71-282
HALES, J.W. & F.J. FURNIVALL. BISHOP
PERCY'S FOLIO MANUSCRIPT.
L. LANE, JR., 255(HAB):FALL69-83
HALEWOOD, W.H. THE POETRY OF GRACE.*
J.H. SUMMERS, 401(MLQ):JUN72-195
J. WEBBER, 301(JEGP):JAN72-128
HALEY, J. UNCOMMON THERAPY.
E. FIRST, 441:23SEP73-20
HALEY, K.H.D., ED. THE STUARTS.
617(TLS):10AUG73-927
HALFMANN, U. DER AMERIKANISCHE "NEW
CRITICISM."
R.E. PALMER, 72:BAND209HEFT1/3-172
HALIBURTON, T.C. THE CLOCKMAKER. THE
SAM SLICK ANTHOLOGY. THE OLD JUDGE.
T.H. RADDALL, 296:SUMMER73-105
HALIFAX, B. SMALL LATIN.
R. GLEN, 123:MAR72-97
HALKETT, J.G. MILTON AND THE IDEA OF
MATRIMONY.*
R. LEJOSNE, 189(EA):JUL-SEP71-331
HALKIN, L-E. ÉRASMUS ET L'HUMANISME
CHRÉTIEN.
J-P. MASSAUT, 556(RLV):1971/3-349
C.R. THOMPSON, 551(RENQ):AUTUMN71-372
HALKIN, L-E., F. BIERLAIRE & R. HOVEN -
SEE ERASMUS
HALL, A. THE TANGO BRIEFING.
N. CALLENDAR, 441:23SEP73-48
617(TLS):26OCT73-1324
HALL, D. THE ALLIGATOR BRIDE.*
S. PLUMLY, 600:SPRING71-170
HALL, D. MARIANNE MOORE.
H. MORRIS, 569(SR):AUTUMN72-627
HALL, D.G.E. A HISTORY OF SOUTH-EAST
ASIA. (3RD ED)
L.R. WRIGHT, 302:JUL71-380
HALL, D.K. & S.C. CLARK. ROCK - A WORLD
BOLD AS LOVE.*
M. PETERSON, 470:JAN71-45
HALL, E.C. PRINTED BOOKS 1481-1900 IN
THE HORTICULTURAL SOCIETY OF NEW YORK.
D.D. VOGT, 517(PBSA):JAN-MAR72-82
HALL, E.T. THE HIDDEN DIMENSION.*
(FRENCH TITLE: LA DIMENSION CACHÉE.)
J. PIEL, 98:AUG/SEP71-830
HALL, H.A. A PARTIAL VOCABULARY OF THE
NGALOOMA ABORIGINAL TRIBE.
D.T. TRYON, 67:NOV72-266
HALL, I. & E. HISTORIC BEVERLEY.
617(TLS):20JUL73-841
HALL, J. THE LUNATIC GIANT IN THE DRAW-
ING ROOM.*
R.K. MORRIS, 594:SPRING71-123
HALL, J.B. - SEE CLAUDIAN
HALL, J.C. A HOUSE OF VOICES.
A. MACLEAN, 362:25OCT73-565
617(TLS):17AUG73-946
HALL, J.C. ROUSSEAU.
617(TLS):13APR73-426
HALL, R. HEAVEN, IN A WAY.*
K.L. GOODWIN, 381:SEP71-371
HALL, R.A., JR. AN ESSAY ON LANGUAGE.*
R.M. HOGG, 433:JAN70-94
J. LEVITT, 353:JAN71-102
HALL, R.A., JR. ESSENTIALS OF ENGLISH
PHRASE- AND CLAUSE-STRUCTURE IN DIA-
GRAMS, WITH COMMENTARY.
G.P. FAUST, 215(GL):VOL11#2-112
HALL, R.A., JR. IDEALISM IN ROMANCE
LINGUISTICS.
J. FOX, 47(ARL):VOL17FASC1-40
HALL, R.D. - SEE UNDER DE ZOUCHE HALL, R.
HALL, R.J. THE MAIN TRAIL.
W. GARD, 584(SWR):SPRING72-V

HALL, T. CARL FRIEDRICH GAUSS.
639(VQR):WINTER71-XXXIII
HALL, T.H. MATHEMATICALL RECREATIONS.
R. STOKES, 503:WINTER71-196
P. WALLIS, 354:MAR71-66
HALL, T.H. OLD CONJURING BOOKS.
617(TLS):30MAR73-360
HALLAHAN, W.H. THE DEAD OF WINTER.
N. CALLENDAR, 441:4FEB73-16
HALLAM, A. A REVOLUTION IN THE EARTH
SCIENCES.
617(TLS):14SEP73-1061
HALLE, L.J. THE SEA AND THE ICE.
P. ADAMS, 61:OCT73-130
441:21OCT73-20
HALLETT, G. THE SOCIAL ECONOMY OF WEST
GERMANY.
617(TLS):12OCT73-1259
HALLIBURTON, D. EDGAR ALLAN POE.
P.F. QUINN, 578:FALL73-81
617(TLS):13JUL73-800
HALLIDAY, D. DOLLY AND THE STARRY BIRD.
617(TLS):17AUG73-959
HALLIDAY, J. & G. MC CORMAK. JAPANESE
IMPERIALISM TODAY.
G. BARRACLOUGH, 453:14JUN73-27
617(TLS):3AUG73-897
HALLIE, P.P. THE SCAR OF MONTAIGNE.
G. NUCHELMANS, 206:NOV70-589
HALLIWELL, L. THE FILMGOER'S COMPANION.
(3RD ED)
200:OCT70-499
HALLOWS, J. THE DREAMTIME SOCIETY.
D. AITKIN, 381:MAR71-118
HALLS, Z. MEN'S COSTUME 1750-1800.
617(TLS):2NOV73-1352
HALPERIN, D.A. THE ANCIENT SYNAGOGUES OF
THE IBERIAN PENINSULA.
R. WISCHNITZER, 576:OCT70-279
HALPERT, H. & G.M. STORY, EDS. CHRISTMAS
MUMMING IN NEWFOUNDLAND.*
E. ETTLINGER, 203:SUMMER70-149
W.E. RICHMOND, 292(JAF):APR-JUN71-255
HALPERT, S. & B. - SEE RADWAY, G.F.
HALSBAND, R. LORD HERVEY, EIGHTEENTH-
CENTURY COURTIER.
A. BELL, 362:20DEC73-860
617(TLS):2NOV73-1329
HALSBAND, R. - SEE MONTAGU, M.W.
HALSEY, A.H., ED. EDUCATIONAL PRIORITY.
(VOL 1)
J. VAIZEY, 362:15FEB73-215
HÄLSIG, M. GRAMMATISCHER LEITFADEN DES
HINDI.
A. DEBRECZENI, 353:APR71-113
HALTER, T. VERGIL UND HORAZ.
F. LASSERRE, 182:VOL24#4-173
HAMANN, M. MECKLENBURGISCHE GESCHICHTE.
K. KRÜGER, 182:VOL24#11/12-501
HAMANN, R. & J. HERMAND. GRÜNDERZEIT.
R.H. THOMAS, 220(GL&L):APR72-289
HAMBLET, E.C. MARCEL DUBÉ AND FRENCH
CANADIAN DRAMA.*
W. ANGUS, 529(QQ):SUMMER71-329
B-Z. SHEK, 207(FR):APR71-992
HAMBLIN, C.L. FALLACIES.*
R. BLANCHÉ, 542:OCT-DEC70-492
M. KNEALE, 479(PHQ):APR71-183
HAMBLY, G., ED. CENTRAL ASIA.*
G.L. PENROSE, 293(JAST):MAY71-693
HAMBURGER, K. DIE LOGIK DER DICHTUNG.*
(2ND ED)
E. RIBBAT, 657(WW):NOV/DEC70-429
HAMBURGER, M. OWNERLESS EARTH.
617(TLS):20APR73-442
HAMBURGER, M. REASON AND ENERGY. (2ND
ED)
M.B. BENN, 402(MLR):JUL72-702

HAMBURGER, M.   TRAVELLING.*
  J. GLOVER, 565:VOL11#4-52
HAMBURGER, M.   TRAVELLING I-V.
  617(TLS):19JAN73-69
HAMBURGER, M.   THE TRUTH OF POETRY.*
  S. FAUCHEREAU, 98:APR70-382
  D.D. GALLOWAY, 659:SUMMER73-398
  J. GLOVER, 565:VOL11#4-52
HAMBURGER, M. - SEE BÜCHNER, G.
HAMER, R., ED & TRANS.   A CHOICE OF
  ANGLO-SAXON VERSE.*
  J.P., 376:JAN71-128
HAMILL, P.   THE GIFT.
  C. LEHMANN-HAUPT, 441:28NOV73-49
  M. MEWSHAW, 441:11NOV73-24
HAMILTON, A.   THE LAW PRACTICE OF ALEXAN-
  DER HAMILTON.*  (VOL 2) (J. GOEBEL, JR.,
  ED)
  E.C. SURRENCY, 656(WMQ):JAN71-152
  L.K. WROTH, 432(NEQ):SEP71-514
HAMILTON, A.   THE PAPERS OF ALEXANDER
  HAMILTON.  (VOLS 16 & 17) (H.C. SYRETT,
  ED)
  617(TLS):13APR73-414
HAMILTON, A., ED.   TRIANGLES.
  V. CUNNINGHAM, 362:8NOV73-638
HAMILTON, A.   THE WORKS OF ALEXANDER
  HAMILTON.
  M. JEFFERSON, 480(P&R):SUMMER71-178
HAMILTON, A. & K.   THE ELEMENTS OF JOHN
  UPDIKE.*
  L. CASPER, 613:WINTER70-615
  W.T. STAFFORD, 295:NOV72-569
HAMILTON, A.C.   THE EARLY SHAKESPEARE.*
  G.K. HUNTER, 570(SQ):SPRING70-182
HAMILTON, D.   TECHNOLOGY, MAN AND THE
  ENVIRONMENT.
  617(TLS):12OCT73-1259
HAMILTON, F.   RIZZO.
  441:2SEP73-8
HAMILTON, H.W.   DOCTOR SYNTAX.*
  G.S. ROUSSEAU, 173(ECS):WINTER71/72-
  353
HAMILTON, I.   A POETRY CHRONICLE.
  A. MACLEAN, 362:25JAN73-121
  617(TLS):23MAR73-319
HAMILTON, I.   THE VISIT.*
  A. CLUYSENAAR, 565:VOL11#4-74
  H. SERGEANT, 175:SUMMER71-65
HAMILTON, I. - SEE FROST, R.
HAMILTON, K.G.   THE TWO HARMONIES.*
  R. ELLRODT, 189(EA):JUL-SEP70-339
HAMILTON, L.   GOLIAD SURVIVOR.
  W. GARD, 584(SWR):WINTER72-76
HAMILTON, N.Q.   JESUS FOR A NO-GOD WORLD.
  S.O.H., 543:SEP70-137
HAMILTON, P.N.   ALBERT EINSTEIN.
  617(TLS):8JUN73-649
HAMILTON, R.N.   MARQUETTE'S EXPLORATIONS.
  C. NISH, 656(WMQ):OCT71-684
  W. RUNDELL, JR., 14:JUL71-313
HAMILTON, S.   EARLY AMERICAN BOOK ILLUS-
  TRATORS AND WOOD ENGRAVERS 1670-1870.
  (VOL 1)
  A.H. MAYOR, 90:JUN71-342
HAMILTON, S.   EARLY AMERICAN BOOK ILLUS-
  TRATORS AND WOOD ENGRAVERS 1670-1870.*
  (VOL 2)
  J.A.L. LEMAY, 165:SPRING73-66
  A.H. MAYOR, 90:JUN71-342
HAMILTON-HILL, D.   SOE ASSIGNMENT.
  617(TLS):12OCT73-1240
HAMLYN, D.W.   THE THEORY OF KNOWLEDGE.
  D. MC QUEEN, 518:JAN72-6
HAMM, W.   DER SEPTUAGINTA-TEXT DES BUCHES
  DANIEL, 1-2, NACH DEM KÖLNER TEIL DES
  P. 967.
  A. PELLETIER, 555:VOL45FASC2-351

HAMMACHER, A.M.   LE MONDE DE HENRY VAN
  DE VELDE.*
  L. CHATELET-LANGE, 576:MAY71-181
HAMMACHER, K.   DIE PHILOSOPHIE FRIEDRICH
  HEINRICH JACOBIS.
  S. DECLOUX, 182:VOL24#4-131
HAMMARSTRÖM, G.   LINGUISTISCHE EINHEITEN
  IM RAHMEN DER MODERNEN SPRACHWISSEN-
  SCHAFT.*
  R.R.K. HARTMANN, 206:FEB70-146
  H. WODE, 260(IF):BAND75-242
HAMMERICH, L.L. & OTHERS - SEE "TÖNNIES
  FENNE'S LOW GERMAN MANUAL OF SPOKEN
  RUSSIAN, PSKOV, 1607"
HAMMOND, A.L.   IDEAS ABOUT SUBSTANCE.*
  R. REIN'L, 319:OCT73-570
HAMMOND, B.   SOVEREIGNTY AND AN EMPTY
  PURSE.*
  639(VQR):SPRING71-LXXV
HAMMOND, N.G.L.   EPIRUS.
  H-G. BUCHHOLZ, 182:VOL24#17/18-686
HAMMOND, N.G.L. & H.H. SCULLARD, EDS.
  THE OXFORD CLASSICAL DICTIONARY.*  (2ND
  ED)
  W. DEN BOER, 313:VOL61-269
HAMMOND, R. & L. BARROW.   CREATIVE FRENCH.
  A. HULL, 207(FR):DEC70-434
HAMPE, R. & H. GROPENGIESSER.   AUS DER
  SAMMLUNG DES ARCHÄOLOGISCHEN INSTITUTES
  DER UNIVERSITÄT HEIDELBERG.
  R.A. HIGGINS, 182:VOL24#23/24-877
HAMPSHIRE, S.   FREEDOM OF MIND AND OTHER
  ESSAYS.
  H.G. FRANKFURT, 311(JP):19JUL73-418
HAMPSON, N.   STORIA E CULTURA DELL'IL-
  LUMINISMO.
  R. PARENTI, 548(RCSF):JAN-MAR71-107
HAMPTON, C.   AN EXILE'S ITALY.
  617(TLS):19JAN73-69
HAMSUN, K.   MYSTERIES.*
  42(AR):FALL71-438
  617(TLS):14DEC73-1547
HAN SUYIN.   THE MORNING DELUGE.*
  R. TERRILL, 441:14JAN73-5
HAN, W-K.   THE HISTORY OF KOREA.  (G.K.
  MINTZ, ED)
  H.F. COOK, 293(JAST):MAY71-689
HAN-SHAN.   COLD MOUNTAIN.  (B. WATSON,
  TRANS)
  639(VQR):SPRING71-LXI
HANBURY-TENISON, R.   A QUESTION OF SUR-
  VIVAL.
  617(TLS):25MAY73-583
HANCOCKS, D.   ANIMALS AND ARCHITECTURE.
  J.B., 45:OCT71-214
"HANDELINGEN VAN HET DERTIGSTE NEDER-
  LANDS FILOLOGENCONGRES, GEHOUDEN TE
  LEIDEN OP WOENSDAG 10 EN DONDERDAG 11
  APRIL 1968."
  M. ESCH-PELGROMS, 556(RLV):1971/5-655
HANDKE, P.   THE GOALIE'S ANXIETY AT THE
  PENALTY KICK.*
  P.M. SPACKS, 249(HUDR):AUTUMN72-508
HANDKE, P.   OFFENDING THE AUDIENCE [AND]
  SELF ACCUSATION.
  A. RENDLE, 157:SUMMER71-82
HANDL, I.   THE GOLD TIP PFITZER.
  617(TLS):4MAY73-489
HANDY, R.   THE MEASUREMENT OF VALUES.
  A. BERLEANT, 484(PPR):JUN72-573
HANDY, R.   VALUE THEORY AND THE BEHAVIOR-
  AL SCIENCES.*
  R.F. ATKINSON, 479(PHQ):JAN71-89
HANFMANN, G.M.A.   LETTERS FROM SARDIS.
  P. ADAMS, 61:AUG73-103

HANGIN, J.G. BASIC COURSE IN MONGOLIAN.
P. AALTO, 353:AUG70-114
T. RICCARDI, JR., 318(JAOS):JAN-MAR71-
158
HANGIN, J.G. A CONCISE ENGLISH-MONGOLIAN
DICTIONARY.
H. SERRUYS, 32:SEP72-741
HANH, E.V.D. - SEE UNDER VO DUC HANH, E.
HANHAM, A., ED. CHURCHWARDENS' ACCOUNTS
OF ASHBURTON, 1479-1580.
B.R. MASTERS, 325:OCT71-343
HANKINS, T.L. JEAN D'ALEMBERT.
R. GRIMSLEY, 208(FS):OCT72-458
A. THOMSON, 479(PHQ):JUL71-268
H. WAGNER, 53(AGP):BAND53HEFT3-317
HANLEY, J. A WOMAN IN THE SKY.
E. FEINSTEIN, 362:27SEP73-426
617(TLS):5OCT73-1157
HANLEY, T.O. CHARLES CARROLL OF CARROLL-
TON.
A.C. LAND, 656(WMQ):OCT71-673
HANLY, C. & M. LAZEROWITZ, EDS. PSYCHO-
ANALYSIS AND PHILOSOPHY.
E. WILSON, JR., 311(JP):8MAR73-128
HANNAH, B. NIGHTWATCHMEN.
J. YARDLEY, 441:18NOV73-34
HANNAH, B. STRIVING TOWARDS WHOLENESS.
617(TLS):8JUN73-638
HANNAH, W.H. BOBS: KIPLING'S GENERAL.
617(TLS):11MAY73-534
HANNEMA, S. FADS, FAKES AND FANTASIES.
A.G., 135:JAN71-55
HANNEMAN, A. ERNEST HEMINGWAY.
D. MEINDL, 38:BAND89HEFT2-276
E. MOTTRAM, 354:MAR70-78
HANNIBAL, E. DANCING MAN.
B. HAYES, 441:18NOV73-52
HANNIGAN, P. LAUGHING.*
J.D. REED, 600:WINTER71-154
HANRAHAN, B. THE SCENT OF EUCALYPTUS.
617(TLS):22JUN73-728
HANSEL, J. BÜCHERKUNDE FÜR GERMANISTEN:
STUDIENAUSGABE.* (5TH ED)
P. OCHSENBEIN, 657(WW):NOV/DEC70-427
HANSEN, I.V. THE CAPTAIN AND THE BIRDS.
S.E. LEE, 581:DEC72-302
HANSEN, J. DEATH CLAIMS.
N. CALLENDAR, 441:21JAN73-26
442(NY):17MAR73-132
HANSEN, S. & J. JENSEN, WITH W. ROBERTS.
THE LITTLE RED SCHOOLBOOK.
R. FREEMAN, 111:7MAY71-165
HANSFORD, S.H. JADE.
M. MOORE, 139:DEC70-9
HANSON, W.P. - SEE RAABE, W.
HANSSON, G. FÖRFATTAREN DIKTEN LÄSAREN.
B. TYSDAHL, 172(EDDA):1970/6-363
HANSSON, P. HVEM VAR HENRY RINNAN?
270:VOL22#4-85
HANZELI, V.E. MISSIONARY LINGUISTICS IN
NEW FRANCE.
H. LANDAR, 353:NOV71-100
J.H. ROGERS, 320(CJL):FALL70-68
HANZLICEK, C.G. LIVING IN IT.
W. DICKEY, 249(HUDR):SUMMER72-307
HAO, Y-P. THE COMPRADOR IN NINETEENTH
CENTURY CHINA.
S.C. CHU, 293(JAST):MAY71-663
HAO-JO, H. - SEE UNDER HO HAO-JO
HAPGOOD, H. THE SPIRIT OF THE GHETTO.
(NEW ED)
M. MUDRICK, 249(HUDR):SUMMER72-339
HARASZTI, G., G. HERCZEGH & K. NAGY.
NEMZETKÖZI JOG.
B.A. RACZ, 32:DEC72-925
HARASZTI-TAKÁCS, M. RUBENS AND HIS AGE.
617(TLS):19JAN73-68

HARBAGE, A. SHAKESPEARE WITHOUT WORDS
AND OTHER ESSAYS.
617(TLS):19OCT73-1272
HARBAGE, A. - SEE SHAKESPEARE, W.
HARBAUGH, W.H. LAWYER'S LAWYER.
R. KLUGER, 441:30DEC73-5
442(NY):24DEC73-80
HARD, F. - SEE WOTTON, H.
HARDEE, A.M. JEAN DE LANNEL AND THE PRE-
CLASSICAL FRENCH NOVEL.
M. DASSONVILLE, 207(FR):OCT70-246
HARDER, H-B. SCHILLER IN RUSSLAND.*
H. ROTHE, 52:BAND6HEFT3-339
HARDGRAVE, R.L., JR. INDIA.
R.W. JONES, 293(JAST):FEB71-478
HARDIE, M. WATERCOLOUR PAINTING IN
BRITAIN.* (VOL 3) (D. SNELGROVE, WITH
J. MAYNE & B. TAYLOR, EDS)
W.J. HIPPLE, JR., 290(JAAC):WINTER70-
280
H.E. ROBERTS, 637(VS):SEP70-102
HARDIE, W.F.R. ARISTOTLE'S ETHICAL
THEORY.*
W. LESZL, 548(RCSF):APR-JUN71-217
HARDING, A. THE LAW COURTS OF MEDIEVAL
ENGLAND.
617(TLS):15JUN73-668
HARDING, C. & C. ROPER - SEE "LATIN AMER-
ICA REVIEW OF BOOKS" (VOL 1)
HARDING, J. GOUNOD.
617(TLS):30NOV73-1480
HARDING, J. THE OX ON THE ROOF.*
R. CRICHTON, 415:OCT72-974
HARDING, J. ROSSINI.
W. DEAN, 415:MAR72-269
HARDING, R.E.M. A THEMATIC CATALOGUE OF
THE WORKS OF MATTHEW LOCKE.*
M. TILMOUTH, 415:JUN72-561
J.A.W., 410(M&L):OCT72-442
HARDISON, O.B., JR. TOWARD FREEDOM &
DIGNITY.
W.F. CLAIRE, 31(ASCH):AUTUMN73-700
HARDISON, O.B., JR. - SEE ARISTOTLE
HARDMAN, M.J. JAQARU.
D.F. SOLÁ, 269(IJAL):JUL71-208
HARDOY, J. URBAN PLANNING IN PRE-COLUM-
BIAN AMERICA.
J.E. SIMPSON, 576:DEC70-358
HARDOY, J.E. PRE-COLUMBIAN CITIES.
617(TLS):14DEC73-1532
HARDWICK, M. A LITERARY ATLAS & GAZET-
TEER OF THE BRITISH ISLES.
617(TLS):26OCT73-1325
HARDWICK, M. THE OSPREY GUIDE TO OSCAR
WILDE. THE OSPREY GUIDE TO JANE AUS-
TEN.
617(TLS):31AUG73-1005
HARDWICK, M. & M., EDS. THE CHARLES
DICKENS ENCYCLOPEDIA.
617(TLS):2MAR73-235
HARDWICK, M. & M. THE GAME'S AFOOT.
A. RENDLE, 157:SPRING70-71
HARDWICK, M. & M. THE BERNARD SHAW COM-
PANION.
617(TLS):10AUG73-937
HARDY, A., ED. WHERE TO EAT IN CANADA,
1972-73.
A. APPENZELL, 102(CANL):AUTUMN72-104
HARDY, B., ED. CRITICAL ESSAYS ON GEORGE
ELIOT.
I. SIMON, 541(RES):MAY71-231
G. THOMAS, 175:SUMMER71-62
HARDY, B. CHARLES DICKENS: THE LATER
NOVELS.*
J.C. FIELD, 556(RLV):1971/2-231

HARDY, B. THE MORAL ART OF DICKENS.*
S. GILL, 447(N&Q):NOV71-425
E.D.H. JOHNSON, 445(NCF):DEC71-349
K. MUIR, 402(MLR):APR72-405
M. PRICE, 676(YR):WINTER72-271
G. THOMAS, 175:SPRING71-25
S. WALL, 184(EIC):JUL71-261
A. WILSON, 155:JAN71-45
639(VQR):SUMMER71-CXI
HARDY, B. THE NOVELS OF GEORGE ELIOT.
J. DELBAERE-GARANT, 556(RLV):1970/1-
103
HARDY, E. THE NATURALIST IN LAKELAND.
617(TLS):20JUL73-842
HARDY, G. LA VOCATION DE LA LIBERTÉ CHEZ
LOUIS LAVELLE.
G. CROMP, 154:JUN70-110
HARDY, J., S. LANDI & C.D. WRIGHT. A
STATE BED FROM ERTHIG.
617(TLS):22JUN73-708
HARDY, P. THE MUSLIMS OF BRITISH INDIA.
617(TLS):23MAR73-318
HARDY, P. PARTNERS IN FREEDOM - AND TRUE
MUSLIMS.
B. TYABJI, 273(IC):OCT71-302
HARDY, R. THE FACE OF JALANATH.
M. LEVIN, 441:1APR73-33
HARE, R.M. ESSAYS ON THE MORAL CONCEPTS.
APPLICATIONS OF MORAL PHILOSOPHY.
617(TLS):19JAN73-65
HARE, R.M. FREEDOM AND REASON.*
J. MARGOLIS, 321:WINTER70[VOL5#1]-57
HARE, R.M. THE LANGUAGE OF MORALS.
B.F. CHELLAS, 316:MAR71-180
HARE, R.M. PRACTICAL INFERENCES. ESSAYS
ON PHILOSOPHICAL METHOD.
A. FLEW, 518:MAY72-19
HARGREAVES-MAWDSLEY, W.N. THE ENGLISH
DELLA CRUSCANS AND THEIR TIME, 1783-
1828.*
M. PRAZ, 179(ES):JUN71-280
HARGREAVES-MAWDSLEY, W.N. OXFORD IN THE
AGE OF JOHN LOCKE.
617(TLS):13JUL73-817
HARGREAVES-MAWDSLEY, W.N., ED & TRANS.
SPAIN UNDER THE BOURBONS, 1700-1833.
617(TLS):25MAY73-597
HARICH-SCHNEIDER, E. A HISTORY OF JAPAN-
ESE MUSIC.
617(TLS):3AUG73-899
HARING, F. A PERFECT STRANGER.
M. ENGEL, 441:20MAY73-24
HARINGTON, D. SOME OTHER PLACE, THE
RIGHT PLACE.*
617(TLS):31AUG73-993
HARIYANNA, M. REVIEWS.
L. STERNBACH, 318(JAOS):OCT-DEC71-546
HARJAN, G. JAN PARANDOWSKI.
H.B. SEGEL, 32:MAR72-216
HARJULA, R. GOD AND THE SUN IN MERU
THOUGHT.
B. BERNARDI, 69:JUL71-256
HARKABI, Y. ARAB ATTITUDES TO ISRAEL.*
617(TLS):23FEB73-205
HARKER, J.S. WELL DONE LEANDER.
617(TLS):7SEP73-1037
HARKESS, S. & F. SCHMIDT. A WORKBOOK OF
ENGLISH PRONUNCIATION.
G.F. MEIER, 682(ZPSK):BAND23HEFT4-425
HARKORT, F., K.C. PEETERS & R. WILDHABER,
EDS. VOLKSÜBERLIEFERUNG.
M. DE MEYER, 196:BAND11HEFT1/2-203
HARLAN, L.R. BOOKER T. WASHINGTON.
J. ANDERSON, 453:9AUG73-34
J.H. BRACEY, JR., 441:4MAR73-34
617(TLS):13APR73-414
HARLAN, L.R. - SEE WASHINGTON, B.T.

HARLEY, J. MUSIC IN PURCELL'S LONDON.
D.G., 173(ECS):FALL70-115
HARLEY, J.B., ED. THE FIRST EDITION OF
THE ONE-INCH ORDNANCE SURVEY.
J.L. HOWGEGO, 325:APR71-247
HARLEY, N. RUSSIAN TALES.*
R. BARTHÉLEMY, 556(RLV):1971/4-512
HARLOW, R. SCANN.
J.G. MOSS, 198:WINTER73-114
HARMAN, G. THOUGHT.
617(TLS):28DEC73-1594
HARMENING, D. & OTHERS, EDS. VOLKSKULTUR
UND GESCHICHTE.
E. ETTLINGER, 203:AUTUMN71-259
HARMON, M., ED. THE CELTIC MASTER.
A. GOLDMAN, 541(RES):MAY71-237
HARMON, W. TREASURY HOLIDAY.*
A. OSTRIKER, 473(PR):SUMMER72-464
42(AR):FALL/WINTER70/71-465
639(VQR):SUMMER71-CVI
HARMONIUS. IOANNIS HARMONII MARSI: "COM-
OEDIA STEPHANIUM." (W. LUDWIG, ED)
L.V.R., 568(SCN):SUMMER72-55
HARMS, R.T. INTRODUCTION TO PHONOLOGICAL
THEORY.
B.F.O. HILDEBRANDT, 221(GQ):MAY71-421
P.H. MATTHEWS, 297(JL):SEP70-306
HARMS, W. HOMO VIATOR IN BIVIO.
D.H. GREEN, 402(MLR):JAN72-207
J.G. KUNSTMANN, 182:VOL24#15/16-615
TEN HARMSEL, H. JACOBUS REVIUS.
G.C. SCHOOLFIELD, 568(SCN):SPRING72-10
HARNACK, C. WE HAVE ALL GONE AWAY.
A. BROYARD, 441:16MAR73-43
G. HICKS, 441:15APR73-31
442(NY):17MAR73-131
HARNER, M.J. THE JÍVARO.
617(TLS):24AUG73-985
HAROOTUNIAN, H.D. TOWARD RESTORATION.
C. TOTMAN, 293(JAST):FEB71-459
HARPER, D. THE GREEN AIR.
M. LEVIN, 441:28OCT73-48
HARPER, J.R., ED. PAUL KANE'S FRONTIER.
H.P. GUNDY, 529(QQ):AUTUMN71-484
HARPER, M.S. DEAR JOHN, DEAR COLTRANE.*
L. HART, 661:SUMMER/FALL71-85
C. PEEK, 502(PRS):SPRING71-84
HARPER, M.S. HISTORY IS YOUR OWN HEART-
BEAT.
L. MUELLER, 491:AUG73-293
HARPPRECHT, K. WILLY BRANDT.
617(TLS):5JAN73-21
HARR, B. THE MORTGAGED WIFE.
M.G. PERLOFF, 659:WINTER73-97
S.G. RADHUBER, 448:SPRING71-84
HARRÉ, R. THE PRINCIPLES OF SCIENTIFIC
THINKING.*
C.A. HOOKER, 154:DEC71-825
E.H. MADDEN, 486:JUN71-321
HARRÉ, R. - SEE WAISMANN, F.
HARRELL, J. & C. BARRETT - SEE TATARKIE-
WICZ, W.
HARRIMAN, W.A. AMERICA AND RUSSIA IN A
CHANGING WORLD.
H. FEIS, 550(RUSR):OCT71-392
HARRINGTON, W. MISTER TARGET.
N. CALLENDAR, 441:5AUG73-10
HARRIS, C.B. CONTEMPORARY AMERICAN
NOVELISTS OF THE ABSURD.
W. FRENCH, 27(AL):NOV72-520
HARRIS, C.R.S. THE HEART AND THE VASCU-
LAR SYSTEM IN ANCIENT GREEK MEDICINE.
617(TLS):4MAY73-506
HARRIS, E.E. FUNDAMENTALS OF PHILOSOPHY.*
M. FOX, 255(HAB):SUMMER71-64
L.G., 543:JUN71-746
HARRIS, E.E. HYPOTHESIS AND PERCEPTION.
R. PALTER, 311(JP):12APR73-202

HARRIS, F.R. THE NEW POPULISM.
442(NY):13AUG73-87
HARRIS, H. INDUSTRIAL ARCHAEOLOGY OF
DARTMOOR.
617(TLS):31AUG73-999
HARRIS, H.A. SPORT IN GREECE AND ROME.*
E. SEGAL, 441:15APR73-30
HARRIS, H.S. HEGEL'S DEVELOPMENT.*
W.H. WERKMEISTER, 319:JUL73-416
HARRIS, H.S. THE SOCIAL PHILOSOPHY OF
GIOVANNI GENTILE.
L.M. PALMER, 154:DEC70-439
HARRIS, J. SIR WILLIAM CHAMBERS.*
M. HECKSCHER, 576:OCT71-252
D. HINTON, 135:OCT71-139
J. LEES-MILNE, 39:JAN71-71
J. SUMMERSON, 46:JAN71-66
HARRIS, J. UNEMPLOYMENT AND POLITICS.
617(TLS):9MAR73-267
HARRIS, J. - SEE RICHARDSON, S.
HARRIS, J. - SEE WILLIAMSON, H.N.H.
HARRIS, J.C. ÉDOUARD MANET, GRAPHIC
WORKS.
A. DE LEIRIS, 127:WINTER71/72-216
G.P. WEISBERG, 135:NOV71-216
HARRIS, J.E. & K.R. WEEKS. X-RAYING THE
PHARAOHS.
617(TLS):21DEC73-1561
HARRIS, J.W. SPANISH PHONOLOGY.
W.W. CRESSEY, 215(GL):VOL11#1-63
O.T. MYERS, 545(RPH):MAY72-412
HARRIS, L. THE RUSSIAN BALLET SCHOOL.
P. RENNA, 151:JAN71-80
HARRIS, M. BULL FIRE.
J. YARDLEY, 441:13MAY73-37
HARRIS, M. THE GOY.
G. WEALES, 390:DEC70-71
HARRIS, M. GRESLEY'S COACHES.
617(TLS):21SEP73-1093
HARRIS, M. KILLING EVERYBODY.
R.A. SOKOLOV, 441:1JUL73-23
HARRIS, M. TEXT FOR NAUSIKAA.*
D. BARBOUR, 150(DR):SPRING71-133
P. STEVENS, 628:SPRING72-103
HARRIS, N. HUMBUG.
J. CHILDS, 441:21OCT73-4
HARRIS, N. PICTURE HISTORY OF WORLD
ART.
617(TLS):21SEP73-1078
HARRIS, P.B. STUDIES IN AFRICAN POLI-
TICS.
L. MAIR, 69:OCT71-330
HARRIS, R. CANALS AND THEIR ARCHITEC-
TURE.
46:JUN70-456
HARRIS, R. DECISION.
C.H. PRITCHETT, 639(VQR):AUTUMN71-611
HARRIS, R. SYNONYMY AND LINGUISTIC ANAL-
YSIS.
617(TLS):25MAY73-591
HARRIS, R.M. & R.N. SHARMA. A BASIC
HINDI READER.
V. MILTNER, 353:AUG70-111
B.R. PRAY, 293(JAST):NOV70-220
T. RICCARDI, JR., 318(JAOS):JAN-MAR71-
158
HARRIS, S. THE SISTERS.
M.A. KRAL, 363:AUG71-116
HARRIS, T.A. I'M OK - YOU'RE OK.
R. TODD, 61:NOV73-108
HARRIS, W. THE MISTRESS OF DOWNING
STREET.
617(TLS):2FEB73-129
HARRIS, W.V. ARTHUR HUGH CLOUGH.
P.G. SCOTT, 637(VS):JUN71-465
HARRIS, Z.S. PAPERS IN STRUCTURAL AND
TRANSFORMATIONAL LINGUISTICS.
G.D. PRIDEAUX, 399(MLJ):DEC71-535

HARRISON, A.R.W. THE LAW OF ATHENS: PRO-
CEDURE.* (D.M. MAC DOWELL, ED)
M. CHAMBERS, 124:JAN72-169
HARRISON, B. DRINK AND THE VICTORIANS.
M. COOKE, 676(YR):SPRING72-433
HARRISON, B.G. UNLEARNING THE LIE.
F. HOWE, 31(ASCH):AUTUMN73-676
HARRISON, H. THE STAINLESS STEEL RAT
SAVES THE WORLD.
617(TLS):9NOV73-1377
HARRISON, H. A TRANSATLANTIC TUNNEL,
HURRAH!
617(TLS):2FEB73-129
HARRISON, H. & B.W. ALDISS, EDS. THE
ASTOUNDING-ANALOG READER.
T. STURGEON, 441:28JAN73-10
HARRISON, H.W., COMP. AN ANALYTICAL
INDEX OF THE COMPLETE POETICAL WORKS
OF RUBÉN DARIO.
B.G. CARTER, 263:OCT-DEC72-428
HARRISON, J. A GOOD DAY TO DIE.
S. BLACKBURN, 441:9SEP73-4
C. LEHMANN-HAUPT, 441:13SEP73-51
442(NY):5NOV73-185
HARRISON, J. OUR KNOWLEDGE OF RIGHT AND
WRONG.
J. HOWIE, 518:MAY72-21
HARRISON, J. OUTLYER AND GHAZALS.*
F. MORAMARCO, 651(WHR):SPRING72-193
HARRISON, J. WOLF.
J.C. OATES, 473(PR):SUMMER72-462
HARRISON, J.A. THE FOUNDING OF THE RUS-
SIAN EMPIRE IN ASIA AND AMERICA.
G.A. LENSEN, 32:DEC72-892
HARRISON, J.P. THE LONG MARCH TO POWER.
J. ISRAEL, 441:20MAY73-52
617(TLS):21SEP73-1076
HARRISON, M. THE LIEDER OF BRAHMS.*
J.A.W., 410(M&L):OCT72-458
HARRISON, M. THE LONDON OF SHERLOCK
HOLMES.* IN THE FOOTSTEPS OF SHERLOCK
HOLMES.
N. CALLENDAR, 441:4FEB73-14
HARRISON, M. & B. WATERS. BURNE-JONES.
617(TLS):12OCT73-1206
HARRISON, T. THE LOINERS.*
A. CLUYSENAAR, 565:VOL12#1-72
D. TIPTON, 619(TC):VOL179#1047-46
HARRISON, W. THE DESCRIPTION OF ENGLAND.
(G. EDELEN, ED)
M.E. JAMES, 447(N&Q):JUN71-236
HARRISON, W., Y. CLARKSON & S. LE FLEM-
ING. COLLOQUIAL RUSSIAN.
617(TLS):29JUN73-745
HARRISON, W. & S. LE FLEMING. RUSSIAN-
ENGLISH AND ENGLISH-RUSSIAN DICTIONARY.
617(TLS):29JUN73-745
HARRISON-ROSS, P. & B. WYDEN. THE BLACK
CHILD.
J. HASKINS, 441:18NOV73-44
HARROD, R. ECONOMIC DYNAMICS.
617(TLS):27JUL73-880
HARSDÖRFFER, G.P., S. VON BIRKEN & J.
KLAJ. PEGNESISCHES SCHÄFERGEDICHT
1644-1645. (K. GARBER, ED)
H. RÜDIGER, 52:BAND6HEFT1-77
HARSENT, D. A VIOLENT COUNTRY.*
R.S., 376:JAN70-111
HART, C., ED. JAMES JOYCE'S "DUBLINERS."*
P. REDONDO, 202(FMOD):JUN70-346
HART, E.L. - SEE NICHOLS, J.
HART, F.R. LOCKHART AS ROMANTIC BIOG-
RAPHER.
A. WELSH, 579(SAQ):SUMMER72-456
HART, F.R. SCOTT'S NOVELS.
H. SCHMIDT, 38:BAND89HEFT4-543

HART, G.W. RIGHT FROM THE START.
   E. DREW, 441:15JUL73-6
   M. JANEWAY, 61:OCT73-124
   G. WILLS, 453:40CT73-3
HART, J.A. THE DEVELOPING VIEWS ON THE
NEWS.*
   E. WOLF 2D, 432(NEQ):SEP71-511
HART, J.D. - SEE NORRIS, F.
HART, P. ORPHEUS IN THE NEW WORLD.
   D. HENAHAN, 441:28JUL73-21
   A. RICH, 441:5AUG73-7
   442(NY):12NOV73-218
HART, S. LISTEN TO THE WILD.
   617(TLS):2FEB73-131
HART, T. A WALK WITH ALAN.
   617(TLS):21DEC73-1563
HART-DAVIS, R. A CATALOGUE OF THE CARI-
CATURES OF MAX BEERBOHM.*
   V.S. PRITCHETT, 453:25JAN73-16
HART-DAVIS, R. - SEE BEERBOHM, M.
HARTH, D. PHILOLOGIE UND PRAKTISCHE
PHILOSOPHIE.
   R.H. BAINTON, 182:VOL24#17/18-644
HARTH, E. CYRANO DE BERGERAC AND THE
POLEMICS OF MODERNITY.
   H. BROWN, 401(MLQ):DEC71-433
   T.J. REISS, 188(ECR):WINTER70-340
HARTH, K.L. ÜBER AUTOGENES SIGMATIKER-
TRAINING.
   F. GRÜNWALD, 682(ZPSK):BAND24HEFT1/2-
130
HARTH, P. CONTEXTS OF DRYDEN'S THOUGHT.*
   P. LEGOUIS, 189(EA):OCT-DEC71-533
   E. SPÄTH, 38:BAND89HEFT3-395
HARTH, P. - SEE MANDEVILLE, B.
HARTIG, P., ED. AMERIKAKUNDE. (4TH ED)
   H. OPPEL, 430(NS):MAR70-154
HARTLEY, A. GAULLISM.*
   B.H. SMITH, 396(MODA):SUMMER72-329
HARTLEY, A.J. - SEE MAURICE, F.D.
HARTLEY, L. & G. CORE, EDS. KATHERINE
ANNE PORTER.*
   E.C. BUFKIN, 219(GAR):SUMMER71-247
HARTLEY, L.P. THE WILL AND THE WAY.
   R. BRYDEN, 362:12APR73-489
   617(TLS):13APR73-408
HARTLEY, M. & J. INGILBY. LIFE IN THE
MOORLANDS OF NORTH-EAST YORKSHIRE.
   617(TLS):2FEB73-133
HARTLEY, R.D. ARTISTS' PIGMENTS C. 1600-
1835.
   D.T., 135:NOV70-215
HARTMAN, G.G. EMPHASIZING AND CONNECTING
PARTICLES IN THE THIRTEEN PRINCIPAL
UPANISHADS.
   H. BERGER, 343:BAND13HEFT2-187
   M. VAN STRIEN-GERRITSEN, 353:APR71-
109
HARTMAN, G.H. BEYOND FORMALISM.*
   G. BORNSTEIN, 385(MQR):SUMMER73-278
   G. GILLESPIE, 149:DEC72-455
HARTMAN, J.M. CHINESE JADE OF FIVE CEN-
TURIES.
   H. TRUBNER, 318(JAOS):APR-JUN71-361
HARTMANN VON AUE. IWEIN, EINE ERZÄHLUNG
VON HARTMANN VON AUE. (G.F. BENECKE &
K. LACHMANN, EDS; 7TH ED REV BY L.
WOLFF)
   T.E. HART, 405(MP):MAY72-330
HARTMANN VON AUE. DIE KLAGE. (H. ZUTT,
ED)
   J.L. FLOOD, 220(GL&L):OCT71-23
   P. OCHSENBEIN, 657(WW):SEP/OCT70-348
HARTMANN, H. WALLENSTEIN.
   H.S. DAEMMRICH, 564:JUN71-161
HARTMANN, J. - SEE TŐKEI, F.
HARTMANN, N. L'ESTETICA.
   E. NAMER, 542:APR-JUN70-253

HARTNACK, J. KANT'S THEORY OF KNOWLEDGE.
   K. OEDINGEN, 342:BAND61HEFT3-419
HARTNOLL, P. A CONCISE HISTORY OF THE
THEATRE.*
   B. WÖLFL, 430(NS):MAY71-286
HARTSHORNE, C. CREATIVE SYNTHESIS AND
PHILOSOPHIC METHOD.
   J.A. BENARDETE, 311(JP):12APR73-210
HARTT, F. A HISTORY OF RENAISSANCE ART.
   J. DANIELS, 135:OCT71-140
HARTT, F. LOVE IN BAROQUE ART.
   F. HASKELL, 54:MAR70-104
HARTT, F. MICHELANGELO, THE COMPLETE
SCULPTURE.
   J. DANIELS, 135:OCT71-140
   R.W. LIGHTBOWN, 39:JUN71-529
   90:MAR71-172
HARTT, F., G. CORTI & C. KENNEDY. THE
CHAPEL OF THE CARDINAL OF PORTUGAL AT
SAN MINIATO IN FLORENCE.*
   C. SEYMOUR, JR., 54:JUN70-212
HARTT, F. & D. FINN. DONATELLO.
   J. CANADAY, 441:2DEC73-88
HARTVIGSON, H.H. ON THE INTONATION AND
POSITION OF THE SO-CALLED SENTENCE MODI-
FIERS IN PRESENT-DAY ENGLISH.
   D. BOLINGER, 350:JUN72-454
   J.D. O'CONNOR, 597(SN):VOL42#2-507
HARTWELL, R.M. & OTHERS. THE LONG DE-
BATE ON POVERTY.
   617(TLS):16MAR73-291
HARTWIG, R.B. FIBERGLASS BUILDINGS.
   45:OCT71-218
HARVESTER, S. A CORNER OF THE PLAY-
GROUND.
   617(TLS):17AUG73-959
HARVEY, J.H. - SEE WORCESTRE, W.
HARVEY, J.R. VICTORIAN NOVELISTS AND
THEIR ILLUSTRATORS.
   A.B., 155:MAY71-105
   T.J. CRIBB, 111:13NOV70-53
   C.B. GULLANS, 445(NCF):DEC71-363
   A. SALE, 97(CQ):SPRING71-278
   S. WALL, 184(EIC):JUL71-261
HARVEY, L.E. SAMUEL BECKETT.*
   J. FLETCHER, 188(ECR):FALL71-67
   D. HAYMAN, 454:WINTER72-183
HARVEY, N. - SEE FLEISCHMANN, C.
HARWOOD, A. WITCHCRAFT, SORCERY, AND
SOCIAL CATEGORIES AMONG THE SAFWA.
   J. BEATTIE, 69:OCT70-391
HARWOOD, R. ARTICLES OF FAITH.
   617(TLS):16NOV73-1407
HARWOOD, R. & H. JOHNSON. LYNDON.
   442(NY):29OCT73-183
"HARY'S 'WALLACE'."* (VOL 1) (M.P.
MC DIARMID, ED)
   J.R. SIMON, 189(EA):APR-JUN71-194
"HARY'S 'WALLACE'."* (VOL 2) (M.P.
MC DIARMID, ED)
   K. WITTIG, 38:BAND89HEFT2-261
HAŠEK, J. THE GOOD SOLDIER SVEJK.
   D.J. ENRIGHT, 362:30AUG73-284
   617(TLS):21SEP73-1083
HASENJAEGER, G. INTRODUCTION TO THE
BASIC CONCEPTS AND PROBLEMS OF MODERN
LOGIC.
   J. VAN HEIJENOORT, 311(JP):8FEB73-86
HASLUCK, P. AUSTRALIA IN THE WAR OF 1939-
1945. (SER 4, VOL 2)
   A.A. CALWELL, 381:DEC71-465
HASLUCK, P. COLLECTED VERSE.
   K.L. GOODWIN, 381:SEP71-371
HASLUND, E. SYNDEBUKKENS KRETS.
   M.K. THOMASSEN, 270:VOL21#2-153
HASS, H. TO UNPLUMBED DEPTHS.
   617(TLS):10AUG73-936
HASS, H-E. - SEE HAUPTMANN, G.

HASS-VON REITZENSTEIN, U. BEITRÄGE ZUR
GATTUNGSGESCHICHTLICHEN INTERPRETATION
DES DIALOGUS "DE ORATORIBUS."
R.H. MARTIN, 123:DEC72-356
HASSAN, I. THE DISMEMBERMENT OF ORPHEUS.*
M.J. FRIEDMAN, 396(MODA):SPRING72-215
D.D. GALLOWAY, 659:SUMMER73-398
639(VQR):AUTUMN71-CLXVIII
HASSELL, J.W., JR. SOURCES AND ANALOGUES
OF THE "NOUVELLES RÉCRÉATIONS ET JOYEUX
DEVIS" OF BONAVENTURE DES PÉRIERS.
(VOL 2)
N. CAZAURAN, 535(RHL):MAY-JUN71-495
A. TAYLOR, 650(WF):JAN71-62
D. WILSON, 208(FS):JUL72-318
HASTINGS, M. TUSSY IS ME.
571:SPRING71-147
HASTINGS, P., ED. PAPUA/NEW GUINEA.*
M. WILDING, 581:SEP72-235
HASWELL, J. BRITISH MILITARY INTELLI-
GENCE.
617(TLS):20APR73-453
HATADA, T. - SEE UNDER TAKASHI HATADA
HATCH, J. THE HISTORY OF BRITAIN IN
AFRICA.
H. DESCHAMPS, 69:JAN71-72
HATCH, J. TANZANIA.
617(TLS):26JAN73-82
HATCHER, J. RURAL ECONOMY AND SOCIETY IN
THE DUCHY OF CORNWALL, 1300-1500.
J.M.W. BEAN, 589:OCT72-766
HATFIELD, G.W. HENRY FIELDING AND THE
LANGUAGE OF IRONY.*
H.K. MILLER, 594:SUMMER70-230
I. RIVERS, 148:AUTUMN71-282
HATFIELD, H. MODERN GERMAN LITERATURE.
F.H. WOOD, 593:SPRING72-91
HATHERILL, G. A DETECTIVE'S STORY.
442(NY):7APR73-151
HATHORN, R., W.H. GENNE & M. BRILL, EDS.
MARRIAGE.
E.T. SANDROW, 328:SUMMER71-380
HATT, J-J. THE ANCIENT CIVILIZATION OF
CELTS AND GALLO-ROMANS.
S. HAYNES, 39:DEC71-524
M.R., 135:APR71-290
HATTON, R. LOUIS XIV AND HIS WORLD.
617(TLS):8JUN73-651
HATTORI, M. - SEE "DIGNĀGA, ON PERCEP-
TION"
HATTORI, S. - SEE UNDER SHIRÔ HATTORI
HATZFELD, H. TRENDS AND STYLES IN TWEN-
TIETH CENTURY FRENCH LITERATURE. (2ND
ED)
W.W. KIBLER, 599:SPRING70-155
HATZFELD, H.A. SANTA TERESA DE AVILA.
P. DESCOUZIS, 238:MAR71-195
205(FMLS):JAN71-95
HAUBRICHS, W. ORDO ALS FORM.
D.H. GREEN, 402(MLR):JUL72-681
HAUCK, D. DAS KAUFMANNSBUCH DES JOHANN
BLASI (1329-1337).
Å. GRAFSTRÖM, 597(SN):VOL42#1-274
HAUCK, K. GOLDBRAKTEATEN AUS SIEVERN.
R. HAUSSHERR, 683:BAND34HEFT3-250
HAUCK, R.B. A CHEERFUL NIHILISM.*
J. BAIRD, 401(MLQ):JUN72-206
R. LEHAN, 445(NCF):SEP71-245
HAUFE, E. - SEE RÜCKERT, J.
HAUG, H. "ERKENNTNISEKEL."*
C.A.M. NOBLE, 221(GQ):JAN71-95
J. ROTHENBERG, 680(ZDP):BAND90HEFT4-
545
H.C. SASSE, 220(GL&L):JAN72-184
HAUGE, I. JONAS LIES DIKTNING.
S.A. AARNES, 172(EDDA):1971/3-189

HAUGEN, E. THE ECOLOGY OF LANGUAGE.
(A.S. DIL, ED)
617(TLS):16FEB73-175
HAUGEN, E. & A.E. SANTANIELLO - SEE KOHT,
H.
HAUPTMANN, G. DIE RATTEN. (H.F. GARTEN,
ED)
E. MC INNES, 220(GL&L):JAN72-153
HAUPTMANN, G. SÄMTLICHE WERKE. (VOLS
1&2) (H-E. HASS, ED)
E. MC INNES, 220(GL&L):JAN72-154
HAUPTMANN, G. SÄMTLICHE WERKE. (VOL 9)
(H-E. HASS, ED)
E. MC INNES, 220(GL&L):JAN72-154
F.R. SCHRÖDER, 224(GRM):BAND21HEFT1-
117
HAURY, A. - SEE CICERO
HAUSER, W.L. AMERICA'S ARMY IN CRISIS.
D. SCHOENBAUM, 441:28OCT73-18
HAUSSIG, H.W. A HISTORY OF BYZANTINE
CIVILIZATION.
D.D. ABRAHAMSE, 32:JUN72-412
J. BECKWITH, 39:OCT71-322
HAUSSIG, H.W. WÖRTERBUCH DER MYTHOLOGIE.
(1ST SECTION, PT 9)
F. VIAN, 555:VOL45FASC2-328
HAVELOCK, C.M. HELLENISTIC ART.
M.A. DEL CHIARO, 124:NOV71-105
HAVEMANN, R. AN ALIENATED MAN.
617(TLS):21SEP73-1093
HAVEN, R. PATTERNS OF CONSCIOUSNESS.*
J.A. APPLEYARD, 401(MLQ):JUN71-206
J.R. MAC GILLIVRAY, 627(UTQ):FALL70-73
D.R. MURDOCH, 597(SN):VOL43#1-321
M.F. SCHULZ, 405(MP):NOV71-142
HAVENS, T.R.H. NISHI AMANE AND MODERN
JAPANESE THOUGHT.
R.T. CHANG, 293(JAST):NOV70-189
HAVERSCHMIDT, F. BIRDS OF SURINAM.
S.S. BENSON, 37:OCT71-38
HAVIV, Y., COMP. NEVER DESPAIR. (E.
CHEICHEL, ED)
B. KIRSHENBLATT-GIMBLETT, 582(SFQ):
DEC70-371
HAVRAN, M.J. CAROLINE COURTIER.
617(TLS):18MAY73-561
HAWES, J.M. CHILDREN IN URBAN SOCIETY.
N. MILLS, 676(YR):WINTER72-306
HAWKES, J. CASSANDRA.
N. KATTAN, 98:JUL71-666
HAWKES, J. THE FIRST GREAT CIVILIZATIONS.
P. ADAMS, 61:OCT73-130
M.I. FINLEY, 441:4NOV73-4
HAWKES, T. COLERIDGE ON SHAKESPEARE.
L. DESVIGNES, 549(RLC):JAN-MAR71-120
"THE W. WRIGHT HAWKES COLLECTION OF
REVOLUTIONARY WAR DOCUMENTS, A CATA-
LOGUE."
R.E. WALTON, 14:JAN70-90
HAWKINS, D. AVALON AND SEDGEMOOR.
617(TLS):17AUG73-961
HAWKINS, G.S. BEYOND STONEHENGE.
E. JANEWAY, 441:29JUL73-17
HAWKINS, H. BETWEEN HARVARD AND AMERICA.*
617(TLS):7DEC73-1521
HAWKINS, H. LIKENESSES OF TRUTH IN
ELIZABETHAN AND RESTORATION DRAMA.
617(TLS):29JUN73-752
HAWKINS, J. ANYTHING FOR A QUIET LIFE.
617(TLS):16NOV73-1391
HAWKINS, W.F. & R. MACKIN, EDS. PHYSICS,
MATHEMATICS, BIOLOGY, APPLIED SCIENCE.
LIBERAL STUDIES.
P. MICHEL, 556(RLV):1971/5-649
HAWLEY, E. & C. ROSSI. BERTIE.
617(TLS):13JUL73-817

HAWORTH, D. WE ALL COME TO IT IN THE
END.
F. DILLON, 362:15FEB73-221
HAWTHORN, J. IDENTITY AND RELATIONSHIP.
617(TLS):8JUN73-636
HAWTHORN, J.R. - SEE SALLUST
VON HAXTHAUSEN, A. STUDIES ON THE IN-
TERIOR OF RUSSIA. (S.F. STARR, ED)
617(TLS):26JAN73-95
HAY, D. ITALIAN CLERGY AND ITALIAN CUL-
TURE IN THE FIFTEENTH CENTURY.
617(TLS):7SEP73-1035
HAY, G. ARCHITECTURE OF SCOTLAND.
46:JAN70-84
HAY, G. DARSTELLUNG DES MENSCHENHASSES
IN DER DEUTSCHEN LITERATUR DES 18. UND
19. JAHRHUNDERTS.
M.B. BENN, 402(MLR):OCT72-940
HAY, J. & R. KAUFFMAN. THE PRIMAL ALLI-
ANCE. (K. BROWER, ED)
617(TLS):23MAR73-333
HAY, P. BRUNEL.
617(TLS):13APR73-429
HAY, S. - SEE MORRISON, G.
HAY, S.N. ASIAN IDEAS OF EAST AND WEST.
D. DALTON, 293(JAST):NOV70-209
R.A. MC DERMOTT, 485(PE&W):JUL71-332
HAYASHI, T. ARTHUR MILLER CRITICISM
(1930-1967).
R.A. MARTIN, 397(MD):FEB71-448
HAYDEN, J.O. THE ROMANTIC REVIEWERS,
1802-1824.*
J.R. MAC GILLIVRAY, 627(UTQ):FALL70-73
D. ROPER, 541(RES):AUG71-362
HAYDEN, J.O., ED. SCOTT: THE CRITICAL
HERITAGE.*
K.C., 191(ELN):SEP71(SUPP)-51
F.R. HART, 445(NCF):JUN71-115
HAYDEN, R. WORDS IN THE MOURNING TIME.
W. WALLIS, 502(PRS):FALL71-278
HAYDEN, T. THE LOVE OF POSSESSION IS A
DISEASE WITH THEM.
K.P. SHOREY, 396(MODA):FALL72-435
HAYES, A. THE STOCKBROKER, THE BITTER
YOUNG MAN, AND THE BEAUTIFUL GIRL.
R. BRYDEN, 362:15MAR73-348
617(TLS):23MAR73-312
HAYES, A.S. LANGUAGE LABORATORY FACILI-
TIES.
J. LÉTARGEZ, 556(RLV):1971/2-238
HAYES, C. - SEE STIFTER, A.
HAYES, D. QUITE A GOOD ADDRESS.
617(TLS):23NOV73-1455
HAYES, G.P. WORLD WAR 1.
617(TLS):2MAR73-231
HAYES, G.R. THE VIOLS AND OTHER BOWED
INSTRUMENTS.
H.M. BROWN, 415:DEC72-1191
HAYES, J. CATALOGUE OF THE OIL PAINTINGS
IN THE LONDON MUSEUM.
R. EDWARDS, 39:JAN71-69
D.T., 135:JUN71-152
HAYES, J. THE DRAWINGS OF THOMAS GAINS-
BOROUGH.
R. EDWARDS, 135:AUG71-302
E. WATERHOUSE, 39:AUG71-158
HAYES, J.H. INTRODUCTION TO THE BIBLE.
617(TLS):17AUG73-961
HAYES, R. THE HUNGARIAN GAME.
N. CALLENDAR, 441:24JUN73-32
617(TLS):26OCT73-1324
HAYFORD, H., H. PARKER & G.T. TANSELLE -
SEE MELVILLE, H.
HAYMAN, R. JOHN GIELGUD.
I. BROWN, 157:AUTUMN71-75
HAYMAN, R. ARTHUR MILLER.
J.R. TAYLOR, 157:AUTUMN70-69

HAYMAN, R. HAROLD PINTER.
S.H. GALE, 397(MD):FEB72-478
HAYMAN, R. TECHNIQUES OF ACTING.
A. CAIRNS, 157:SPRING71-72
HAYMAN, R. TOLSTOY.
L.G. LEIGHTON, 550(RUSR):APR71-204
HAYNE, D.M. & M. TIROL. BIBLIOGRAPHIE
CRITIQUE DU ROMAN CANADIEN-FRANÇAIS,
1837-1900.
R. ROBIDOUX, 208(FS):JAN72-107
HAYNES, D. FIFTY MASTERPIECES OF CLASSI-
CAL ART IN THE BRITISH MUSEUM.
H. HOFFMANN, 39:DEC71-522
HAYNES, D.K. HASTE YE BACK.
617(TLS):11MAY73-537
HAYS, H.R. BIRDS, BEASTS, AND MEN.
617(TLS):14SEP73-1061
HAYS, H.R. POEMS 1933-67.
E. FEINSOD, 114(CHIR):JAN-FEB71-156
HAYTER, A. OPIUM AND THE ROMANTIC IMAGI-
NATION.*
I.H.C., 191(ELN):SEP71(SUPP)-20
HAYTER, A. A VOYAGE IN VAIN.
R. FULLER, 362:27SEP73-419
617(TLS):2NOV73-1351
HAYTER, W. WILLIAM OF WYKEHAM.
S. WHITTINGHAM, 90:AUG71-478
HAYWARD, J. THE ONE AND INDIVISIBLE
FRENCH REPUBLIC.
617(TLS):21DEC73-1560
HAYWOOD, C., ED. 1972 YEARBOOK OF THE
INTERNATIONAL FOLK MUSIC COUNCIL.
617(TLS):12OCT73-1247
HAYWOOD, J., COMP. VICTORIA AND ALBERT
MUSEUM ENGLISH CABINETS.
617(TLS):22JUN73-708
HAZEN, A.T. A BIBLIOGRAPHY OF THE
STRAWBERRY HILL PRESS.
617(TLS):16NOV73-1408
HAZEN, A.T. A CATALOGUE OF HORACE WAL-
POLE'S LIBRARY.*
R.J. ROBERTS, 354:SEP71-280
HAZEN, E.P., G. MILNE & P.H. HEMINGSON -
SEE "AMERICAN BOOK-PRICES CURRENT, 1968"
HAZEN, E.P., G. MILNE & W.J. SMITH - SEE
"AMERICAN BOOK-PRICES CURRENT, 1967"
HAZLEHURST, F.H. JACQUES BOYCEAU AND THE
FRENCH FORMAL GARDEN.
R. STRANDBERG, 576:OCT70-280
HAZO, S. BLOOD RIGHTS.
L. HART, 661:SUMMER/FALL71-85
HAZO, S. ONCE FOR THE LAST BANDIT.
R. LATTIMORE, 249(HUDR):AUTUMN72-480
R. PINSKY, 491:JUN73-168
HAZZARD, S. DEFEAT OF AN IDEAL.
G. IGNATIEFF, 99:NOV-DEC73-52
K. KYLE, 362:26APR73-556
C. LEHMANN-HAUPT, 441:1MAR73-45
617(TLS):20APR73-433
HEAD, B. A QUESTION OF POWER.
E. FEINSTEIN, 362:22NOV73-721
HEAD, M. THE DEVIL IN THE BUSH.
P. ADAMS, 61:MAY73-123
HEADLEY, J.M. - SEE MORE, T.
HEALD, T. UNBECOMING HABITS.
N. CALLENDAR, 441:25NOV73-49
617(TLS):16NOV73-1407
HEALEY, B. THE STONE BABY.
P. ADAMS, 61:AUG73-103
N. CALLENDAR, 441:12AUG73-12
442(NY):23JUL73-80
HEALEY, F.G. FOREIGN LANGUAGE TEACHING
IN THE UNIVERSITIES.
M.W. SUGATHAPALA DE SILVA, 353:OCT71-
115
HEALEY, G.H. - SEE JOYCE, S.
"HEALTH HAZARDS OF THE HUMAN ENVIRONMENT."
617(TLS):6APR73-401

HEALY, T.S. - SEE DONNE, J.
HEANEY, S.  DOOR INTO THE DARK.*
    T. BROWN, 159(DM):SPRING70-107
    S. FAUCHEREAU, 98:MAY70-438
    H. SERGEANT, 175:SPRING70-29
    W. WALLIS, 502(PRS):FALL71-278
HEANEY, S.  WINTERING OUT.*
    S. SPENDER, 453:20SEP73-8
HEARNE, S.  A JOURNEY FROM PRINCE OF
    WALES'S FORT IN HUDSON'S BAY TO THE
    NORTHERN OCEAN.
    R. GIBBS, 296:SUMMER73-104
HEARON, S.  THE SECOND DUNE.
    M. LEVIN, 441:7OCT73-47
HEARTZ, D.  PIERRE ATTAINGNANT, ROYAL
    PRINTER OF MUSIC.*
    N. BARKER, 78(BC):SUMMER71-261
    L.F. BERNSTEIN, 551(RENQ):SUMMER71-
    248
    H. CARTER, 354:JUN71-176
    P.H.L., 414(MQ):JAN71-155
HEATH, C.  STONE WALLS.
    S. HILL, 362:19JUL73-92
    617(TLS):17AUG73-945
HEATH, E.  OLD WORLD, NEW HORIZONS.
    C. MELCHIOR DE MOLÈNES, 189(EA):OCT-
    DEC71-449
HEATH, P. & J. LACHS - SEE FICHTE, J.G.
HEATH, S.  THE NOUVEAU ROMAN.
    617(TLS):12JAN73-33
HEATH, S., C. MAC CABE & C. PRENDERGAST.
    SIGNS OF THE TIMES.
    J. CULLER, 111:28MAY71-225
HEATH, W.  WORDSWORTH AND COLERIDGE.
    S.A. FARMER, 67:MAY72-91
    H. PESCHMANN, 175:SUMMER71-57
HEATH-STUBBS, J.  ARTORIUS.
    617(TLS):5OCT73-1154
HEATH-STUBBS, J. & M. GREEN, EDS.  HOMAGE
    TO GEORGE BARKER ON HIS SIXTIETH BIRTH-
    DAY.
    G. BARKER, 362:8MAR73-315
    617(TLS):13APR73-413
HEAVEN, C.  THE ASTROV INHERITANCE.
    617(TLS):2MAR73-229
HEBEL, J.P.  SÄMTLICHE WERKE.  BRIEFE.
    (BOTH ED BY W. ZENTNER)
    F. CRONHEIM, 402(MLR):JUL72-699
HÉBERT, A.  KAMOURASKA.
    L. JONES, 207(FR):APR71-961
    C.H. ROBERTS-VAN OORDT, 99:NOV-DEC73-
    32
HECHT, W., ED.  BRECHT-DIALOG 1968.
    J. FUEGI, 397(MD):SEP70-229
HECHT, W.  SIEBEN STUDIEN ÜBER BRECHT.
    617(TLS):28DEC73-1591
HECHT, W. - SEE BRECHT, B.
HECHT, W. - SEE SCHOTTELIUS, J.G.
HEDBERG, H.  JAPAN'S REVENGE.
    617(TLS):3AUG73-897
HEDEVIND, B.  THE DIALECT OF DENTDALE IN
    THE WEST RIDING OF YORKSHIRE.
    G. KRISTENSSON, 179(ES):APR71-186
HEDGEPETH, W. & D. STOCK.  THE ALTERNA-
    TIVE.
    42(AR):SPRING71-135
HEENEY, A.  THE THINGS THAT ARE CAESAR'S.
    J.L. GRANATSTEIN, 99:FEB73-36
HEER, F.  THE INTELLECTUAL HISTORY OF
    EUROPE.
    L. KRIEGER, 322(JHI):APR-JUN70-305
HEER, J.  DAS LIEDERBUCH DES JOHANNES
    HEER VON GLARUS.  (A. GEERING & H.
    TRÜMPY, EDS)
    L. LITTERICK, 317:SPRING72-108

HEER, N.W.  POLITICS AND HISTORY IN THE
    SOVIET UNION.*
    S. FITZPATRICK, 575(SEER):APR72-323
    J.S. ROUCEK, 550(RUSR):OCT71-411
HEEROMA, K. & A. KYLSTRA - SEE DE VRIES,
    J.
HEESE, G. & H. WEGENER, EDS.  ENZYKLOPÄ-
    DISCHES HANDBUCH DER SONDERPÄDAGOGIK
    UND IHRER GRENZGEBIETE.  (3RD ED)
    G. LINDNER, 682(ZPSK):BAND23HEFT2/3-
    313
HEFFER, E.S.  THE CLASS STRUGGLE IN PAR-
    LIAMENT.
    R. CROSSMAN, 362:22MAR73-384
    617(TLS):30MAR73-342
HEFFERNAN, J.A.W.  WORDSWORTH'S THEORY OF
    POETRY.*
    C. CLARKE, 148:SPRING71-88
    J.J. DUFFY, 399(MLJ):MAR71-199
    J.R. MAC GILLIVRAY, 627(UTQ):FALL70-73
HEFNER-ALTENECK, J.H.  WAFFEN.
    C.B., 135:FEB71-139
HEFTER, J.  THE ARMY OF THE REPUBLIC OF
    TEXAS.
    W. GARD, 584(SWR):SPRING72-V
HEFTING, V.  JONKIND D'APRÈS SA CORRES-
    PONDANCE.*
    C. GOTTLIEB, 90:MAR71-160
HEFTRICH, E.  STEFAN GEORGE.
    F. CRONHEIM, 402(MLR):JUL72-706
    H. KNUST, 131(CL):SPRING72-184
HEGARTY, W.  THE PRICE OF CHIPS.
    617(TLS):19OCT73-1270
HEGEL, G.W.F.  GESAMMELTE WERKE.  (VOL 7)
    (R-P. HORSTMANN & J.H. TREDE, EDS)
    H.W. BRANN, 319:JUL73-417
HEGEL, G.W.F.  HEGEL'S PHILOSOPHY OF
    NATURE.*  (A.V. MILLER, TRANS)  HEGEL'S
    PHILOSOPHY OF NATURE.  (M.J. PETRY, ED
    & TRANS)
    T.M. KNOX, 483:OCT71-355
HEGEL, G.W.F.  ON ART, RELIGION, PHILOS-
    OPHY.  (J.G. GRAY, ED)
    J.T. GOLDTHWAIT, 290(JAAC):SUMMER71-
    538
HEGEL, G.W.F.  LA PREMIÈRE PHILOSOPHIE DE
    L'ESPRIT (IÉNA, 1803-1804).  (G.
    PLANTY-BONJOUR, ED & TRANS)
    J. BERNHARDT, 542:APR-JUN70-248
HEGEL, G.W.F.  VORLESUNGEN ÜBER RECHTS-
    PHILOSOPHIE.  (VOL 1)  (K-H. ILTING, ED)
    617(TLS):12OCT73-1237
HEGELE, W.  GRABBES DRAMENFORM.*
    D. HEALD, 220(GL&L):JAN72-164
    R.A. NICHOLLS, 405(MP):MAY72-363
HEGENBERG, L.  EXPLICAÇÕES CIENTÍFICAS,
    INTRODUÇÃO A FILOSOFIA DA CIÊNCIA.
    A.M., 543:JUN71-747
HEGER, K.  DIE BEZEICHNUNG TEMPORAL-
    DEIKTISCHER BEGRIFFSKATEGORIEN IM
    FRANZÖSISCHEN UND SPANISCHEN KONJU-
    GATIONSSYSTEM.
    T.B.W. REID, 47(ARL):VOL17FASC1-63
HEIBER, H.  JOSEPH GOEBBELS.*
    617(TLS):7DEC73-1509
HEIBERG, H.  IBSEN.
    J. COAKLEY, 385(MQR):FALL73-386
    E. DURBACH, 563(SS):WINTER72-140
    O. REINERT, 397(MD):FEB72-481
HEIDEGGER, M.  CHEMINS QUI NE MÈNENT
    NULLE PART.  (F. FÉDIER, ED)
    P. AUBENQUE, 542:OCT-DEC71-470
HEIDEGGER, M.  HEGEL'S CONCEPT OF EXPERI-
    ENCE.
    R.J.B., 543:DEC70-340
HEIDEGGER, M.  LE PRINCIPE DE RAISON.
    P. AUBENQUE, 542:OCT-DEC71-471

HEIDEGGER, M. ZUR SACHE DES DENKENS.*
  P. EMAD, 484(PPR):JUN71-617
HEIDENREICH, H. THE LIBRARIES OF DANIEL
DEFOE AND PHILLIPS FAREWELL.*
  W.L. BRAEKMAN, 182:VOL24#21/22-789
  J.R. MOORE, 481(PQ):JUL71-326
HEIDENREICH, H., ED. PIKARISCHE WELT.
  U. WICKS, 454:FALL71-71
HEIDENREICH, R. & H. JOHANNES, EDS. DAS
GRABMAL THEODERICHS ZU RAVENNA.
  K. WESSEL, 182:VOL24#11/12-489
HEIDSIECK, A. DAS GROTESKE UND DAS
ABSURDE IM MODERNEN DRAMA.*
  397(MD):DEC70-342
HEIDUK, F. - SEE HÖLMANN, C.
VAN HEIJENOORT, J. - SEE HERBRAND, J.
HEIKAL, M.H. THE CAIRO DOCUMENTS.
  E. PACE, 441:21JAN73-5
HEIKE, G. SPRACHLICHE KOMMUNIKATION UND
LINGUISTISCHE ANALYSE.
  S.G. NOOTEBOOM, 361:VOL27#2/3-282
HEIKE, G. ZUR PHONOLOGIE DER STADTKÖLNER
MUNDART.
  C. MINIS, 361:VOL26#2-221
HEILBRONNER, W.L. PRINTING AND THE BOOK
IN FIFTEENTH-CENTURY ENGLAND.
  A.I. DOYLE, 38:BAND88HEFT3-380
HEILBRUN, C.G. TOWARD A RECOGNITION OF
ANDROGYNY. (BRITISH TITLE: TOWARDS
ANDROGYNY.)
  A. BROYARD, 441:24MAR73-31
  M. DRABBLE, 362:27SEP73-416
  J.C. OATES, 441:15APR73-7
  617(TLS):12OCT73-1239
HEILMAN, R.B. TRAGEDY AND MELODRAMA.*
  W.A. ELWOOD, 219(GAR):FALL70-366
  J.K. ROBINSON, 598(SOR):SUMMER71-692
HEIMBACH, E.E., COMP. WHITE MEO-ENGLISH
DICTIONARY.
  K. CHANG, 293(JAST):FEB71-503
HEIMBECK, R.S. THEOLOGY AND MEANING.*
  B.E. GRONBECK, 480(P&R):SUMMER71-187
  J. KING-FARLOW, 479(PHQ):JAN71-92
HEIMERT, A. & P. MILLER, EDS. THE GREAT
AWAKENING: DOCUMENTS ILLUSTRATING THE
CRISIS AND ITS CONSEQUENCES.
  E.S. GAUSTAD, 656(WMQ):APR71-314
HEIMPEL, H. & H. GEUSS - SEE DAHLMANN,
F.C. & G. WAITZ
HEIMSOETH, H. STUDIEN ZUR PHILOSOPHIE
IMMANUEL KANTS II.
  M. KLEINSCHNIEDER, 342:BAND62HEFT4-
503
HEIN, H.S. ON THE NATURE AND ORIGIN OF
LIFE.
  M. MC VAUGH, 385(MQR):SUMMER73-294
HEINE, B. AFRIKANISCHE VERKEHRSSPRACHEN.*
  I. HERMS, 682(ZPSK):BAND24HEFT5-439
  R. OHLY, 353:JAN71-120
HEINE, B. DIE VERBREITUNG UND GLIEDERUNG
DER TOGORESTSPRACHEN.
  W.A.A. WILSON, 69:JAN70-95
HEINE, H. HEINRICH HEINE: SÄMTLICHE
SCHRIFTEN. (VOL 2) (K. BRIEGLEB, ED)
  J.L.S., 191(ELN):SEP71(SUPP)-129
HEINE, H. HEINRICH HEINE: SELECTED
WORKS. (H.M. MUSTARD, ED & TRANS)
  E. PAWEL, 441:23DEC73-8
HEINE, H. REISEBILDER I: 1824-1828.
(K.W. BECKER & F. MENDE, EDS) BRIEFE
1815-1831. (F.H. EISNER & F. MENDE,
EDS) BRIEFE 1831-1841. (F.H. EISNER
& C. STOCKER, EDS)
  J.L.S., 191(ELN):SEP71(SUPP)-135
HEINE, H. ÜBER FRANKREICH 1831-1837.*
(F. MENDE & K.H. HAHN, EDS)
  J.L.S., 191(ELN):SEP71(SUPP)-135
  P.F. VEIT, 221(GQ):MAY71-426

"HEINRICH HEINE." (N. ALTENHOFER, ED)
  R. GRIMM, 406:SUMMER72-172
  J.L. SAMMONS, 301(JEGP):OCT72-580
"HEINE-JAHRBUCH 1966."
  P. LAUXTERMANN, 433:JUL70-315
HEINER, H-J. DAS GANZHEITSDENKEN FRIED-
RICH SCHLEGELS.
  N.H. SMITH, 182:VOL24#21/22-791
HEINESEN, W. PANORAMA MED REGNBUE.
  617(TLS):2MAR73-245
HEINLEIN, R.A. TIME ENOUGH FOR LOVE.
  J. LEONARD, 441:22AUG73-29
  T. STURGEON, 441:23SEP73-38
HEINO, A. DIE BEIDEN FASSUNGEN VON GOTT-
FRIED KELLERS "GRÜNEM HEINRICH."
  R. KOSKIMIES, 439(NM):1970/3-522
HEINRICHS, J. DAS PROBLEM DER ZEIT IN
DER PRAKTISCHEN PHILOSOPHIE KANTS.
  W. STEINBECK, 342:BAND61HEFT2-269
HEINSIUS, D. ON PLOT IN TRAGEDY. (P.R.
SELLIN & J.J. MC MANMON, TRANS)
  P.W.B., 568(SCN):SUMMER72-55
  L.V.R., 568(SCN):SPRING72-30
HEINTEL, P. DIE BEDEUTUNG DER KRITIK DER
ÄSTHETISCHEN URTEILSKRAFT FÜR DIE TRANS-
ZENDENTALE SYSTEMATIK.
  W. STEINBECK, 342:BAND61HEFT4-525
HEINTZE, B. BESESSENHEITS-PHÄNOMENE IM
MITTLEREN BANTU-GEBIET.
  P. ERNY, 182:VOL24#21/22-827
VON HEINTZE, H. ROMAN ART.* (GERMAN
TITLE: RÖMISCHE KUNST.)
  M.A.R. COLLEDGE, 313:VOL61-288
  617(TLS):30MAR73-356
HEINZ, G. KUNSTHISTORISCHES MUSEUM:
VIENNA.
  58:SEP/OCT70-18
HEISE, E.T. FRENCH FOR REVIEW. (2ND ED)
  G.J. HASENAUER, 399(MLJ):APR71-254
HEISE, H-J. BESITZUNGEN IN UNTERSEE.
  617(TLS):12OCT73-1244
HEISENBERG, W. PHYSICS AND BEYOND.
  R. PEARCE, 418(MR):AUTUMN72-709
HEISKANEN-MÄKELÄ, S. IN QUEST OF TRUTH.
  A. OJALA, 439(NM):1971/2-375
HEISKE, W., E. SEEMANN & R. WILH, EDS.
DEUTSCHE VOLKSLIEDER MIT IHREN MELODIEN-
BALLADEN. (VOL 5, PT 2)
  T.J. GARBÁTY, 650(WF):APR70-133
HEISSENBÜTTEL, H. GELEGENHEITSGEDICHTE
UND KLAPPENTEXTE.
  617(TLS):17AUG73-946
HEIST, W.W. "SERMON JOYEUX" AND "POLEM-
IC."*
  H.F. WILLIAMS, 593:FALL72-285
HEITMAN, S., ED. NIKOLAI I. BUKHARIN.*
  W. LERNER, 550(RUSR):APR71-202
HEITNER, R.R., ED. THE CONTEMPORARY
NOVEL IN GERMAN.
  P. PROCHNIK, 220(GL&L):OCT71-52
HEITSCH, E. EPISCHE KUNSTSPRACHE UND
HOMERISCHE CHRONOLOGIE.*
  P. CHANTRAINE, 555:VOL45FASC1-143
HEIZER, R.F. LANGUAGES, TERRITORIES, AND
NAMES OF CALIFORNIA INDIAN TRIBES.
  M.R. KEY, 353:AUG70-118
HELBIG, G. & W. SCHENKEL. WÖRTERBUCH ZUR
VALENZ UND DISTRIBUTION DEUTSCHER VER-
BEN.
  M. KAEMPFERT, 680(ZDP):BAND90HEFT3-
467
  W.D. KLIMONOW, 682(ZPSK):BAND23HEFT
2/3-300
HELD, J.S. REMBRANDT'S ARISTOTLE AND
OTHER REMBRANDT STUDIES.*
  C. FOX, 592:JUL-AUG70-62
  F.W. ROBINSON, 56:AUTUMN71-358
                  [CONTINUED]

HELD, J.S. REMBRANDT'S ARISTOTLE AND
OTHER REMBRANDT STUDIES.* [CONTINUING]
E. SCHEYER, 290(JAAC):SUMMER71-559
C. WHITE, 39:MAR71-229
HELGESEN, A.M. LA LITTÉRATURE FRANÇAISE
CONTEMPORAINE.
G.J. HASENAUER, 399(MLJ):FEB71-122
HELICK, R.M. VARIETIES OF HUMAN HABITA-
TION.
45:MAR71-50
HÉLISENNE DE CRENNE. LES ANGOISSES DOU-
LOUREUSES QUI PROCÈDENT D'AMOURS.
(PT 1) (J. VERCRUYSSE, ED)
Y. GIRAUD, 535(RHL):MAY-JUN70-500
HÉLISENNE DE CRENNE. LES ANGOYSSES
DOULOUREUSES QUI PROCÈDENT D'AMOURS,
ROMAN (1538). (PT 1) (P. DEMATS, ED)
J. FRAPPIER, 535(RHL):MAR-APR71-291
HELLER, E. & J. BEUG - SEE "FRANZ KAFKA"
HELLER, E. & J. BORN - SEE KAFKA, F.
HELLER, L.G. & J. MACRIS. PARAMETRIC
LINGUISTICS.*
B. BRAINERD, 206:FEB70-114
HELLER, P., J. SCHAEFER & E. EHRLICH,
EDS. GERMAN ESSAYS AND EXPOSITORY
PROSE.
H. BROCKHAUS, 221(GQ):JAN71-124
HELLER, R. MUNCH: THE SCREAM.
R. DOWNES, 441:2DEC73-93
HELLIE, R. ENSERFMENT AND MILITARY CHANGE
IN MUSCOVY.*
J.D. CLARKSON, 32:SEP72-658
S.L. PARSONS, 104:FALL72-478
HELLINGA, W. & L. - SEE BRADSHAW, H.
HELLMAN, L. PENTIMENTO.
C. LEHMANN-HAUPT, 441:17SEP73-31
M. SCHORER, 441:23SEP73-1
HELLMANN, D.C. JAPANESE DOMESTIC POLITICS
AND FOREIGN POLICY.*
T. MC NELLY, 293(JAST):FEB71-470
HELM, A. THE CHAPBOOK MUMMERS' PLAYS.
CHESHIRE FOLK DRAMA.
A. BRODY, 292(JAF):APR-JUN71-256
HELM, E. BÉLA BARTÓK.*
412:MAY72-147
HELM, P. THE VARIETIES OF BELIEF.
617(TLS):10AUG73-933
HELMERS, H. WILHELM RAABE.*
W.P. HANSON, 220(GL&L):OCT71-75
F.W. KORFF, 657(WW):SEP/OCT71-356
V. SANDER, 222(GR):MAY71-229
HELMERS, H., ED. RAABE IN NEUER SICHT.
V. SANDER, 222(GR):MAY71-229
HELMS, H.G. - SEE WALSER, R.
HELWIG, D. THE DAY BEFORE TOMORROW.*
W.H. NEW, 102(CANL):SUMMER72-88
A. ROBERTSON, 648:APR72-18
HELWIG, D., ED. 72: NEW CANADIAN STORIES.
R. GIBBS, 296:WINTER73-93
HELWIG, D. THE STREETS OF SUMMER.*
J. MILLS, 648:JAN71-59
L. ROOKE, 376:OCT71-140
HELWIG, D. & J. HARCOURT, EDS. NEW
CANADIAN STORIES.
617(TLS):13JUL73-797
HELWIG, D. & T. MARSHALL, EDS. FOURTEEN
STORIES HIGH.*
A. ROBERTSON, 648:APR72-18
D. STEPHENS, 102(CANL):AUTUMN72-84
HEMINGWAY, E. ISLANDS IN THE STREAM.*
J.L. HALIO, 598(SOR):SPRING73-455
M. WESTBROOK, 649(WAL):FALL70-234
639(VQR):WINTER71-VIII
HEMINGWAY, E. THE NICK ADAMS STORIES.*
(P. YOUNG, ED)
F.C. WATKINS, 598(SOR):SPRING73-481
HEMLOW, J. - SEE BURNEY, F.

HEMLOW, J., WITH P. BOUTILIER & A. DOUG-
LAS - SEE BURNEY, F.
HEMMER, B. KEJSER ELLER GALILAEER.
E. BEYER, 172(EDDA):1971/4-251
HEMMINGS, F.W.J. BALZAC: AN INTERPRETA-
TION OF "LA COMÉDIE HUMAINE."
C.F. COATES, 593:FALL72-280
HEMMINGS, F.W.J. EMILE ZOLA. (2ND ED)
B. BRAY, 433:APR70-193
HEMPEL, C. FILOSOFIA DELLE SCIENZE
NATURALI. (A. PASQUINELLI, ED)
M. DAL PRA, 548(RCSF):OCT-DEC71-472
HEMPEL, C.G. ASPECTS OF SCIENTIFIC
EXPLANATION AND OTHER ESSAYS IN THE
PHILOSOPHY OF SCIENCE.
H. VEATCH, 486:JUN70-312
HEMPEL, E. BAROQUE ART AND ARCHITECTURE
IN CENTRAL EUROPE.
S.L. FAISON, JR., 576:MAY70-195
HEMPEL, H. GOTISCHES ELEMENTARBUCH.
G. WIENOLD, 343:BAND13HEFT1-78
HEMPEL, W. ÜBERMUOT DIU ALTE...DER
SUPERBIA-GEDANKE UND SEINE ROLLE IN DER
DEUTSCHEN LITERATUR DES MITTELALTERS.
D.H. GREEN, 402(MLR):APR72-461
V. GÜNTHER, 182:VOL24#23/24-850
H. HOMANN, 400(MLN):OCT71-717
HEMPHILL, P. THE NASHVILLE SOUND.
M. PETERSON, 470:JAN71-44
HENDERSON, B., ED. THE PUBLISH-IT-YOUR-
SELF HANDBOOK.
J. SEELYE, 441:21OCT73-44
HENDERSON, D. DE MAYOR OF HARLEM.
639(VQR):SPRING71-LXI
HENDERSON, G. CHARTRES.
R. BRANNER, 54:MAR70-94
HENDERSON, G.P. THE REVIVAL OF GREEK
THOUGHT 1620-1830.
W. KNEALE, 479(PHQ):JUL71-262
HENDERSON, J.S. VOLTAIRE'S "TANCRÈDE."
A. JOVICEVICH, 546(RR):FEB71-56
HENDERSON, M. DANTE GABRIEL ROSSETTI.
617(TLS):21SEP73-1093
HENDERSON, R.M. D.W. GRIFFITH.*
T. SOBCHACK, 651(WHR):AUTUMN72-380
A.H. WITHAM, 200:OCT70-499
HENDERSON, R.N. THE KING IN EVERY MAN.
617(TLS):9MAR73-258
HENDERSON, S. UNDERSTANDING THE NEW
BLACK POETRY.
B. BECKHAM, 441:1APR73-32
T. LASK, 441:17JAN73-41
HENDIN, D. DEATH AS A FACT OF LIFE.
A. BROYARD, 441:25JAN73-37
D. SANFORD, 441:25FEB73-16
HENDIN, J. THE WORLD OF FLANNERY O'CON-
NOR.*
P.M. BROWNING, JR., 573(SSF):FALL71-
653
M.J. FRIEDMAN, 578:SPRING73-116
F.P.W. MC DOWELL, 598(SOR):AUTUMN73-
998
HENDRIX, W.S. & W. MEIDEN. BEGINNING
FRENCH.* (4TH ED)
P.H. KENNEDY, 207(FR):MAR71-817
HENDRY, J.F. A DEFINITIVE STUDY OF YOUR
FUTURE IN TRANSLATING AND INTERPRETING.
(REV)
F. BÄSE, 75:3/1971-44
J.J. NAGLE, 399(MLJ):DEC71-536
HENDY, P. PIERO DELLA FRANCESCA AND THE
EARLY RENAISSANCE.*
G. ROBERTSON, 56:AUTUMN71-356
HENIGE, D.P. COLONIAL GOVERNORS FROM THE
FIFTEENTH CENTURY TO THE PRESENT.
W.J. FISCHEL, 318(JAOS):OCT-DEC71-562
M. FREIBERG, 432(NEQ):MAR71-165

HENISSART, P. WOLVES IN THE CITY.
639(VQR):SPRING71-LXXIX
HENKEL, A. & A. SCHÖNE, EDS. EMBLEMATA.*
H.M. VON ERFFA, 54:SEP71-412
B. GAJEK, 224(GRM):BAND21HEFT2-247
HENKIN, L. FOREIGN AFFAIRS AND THE CON-
STITUTION.
N.D. KATZENBACH, 441:18FEB73-12
HENN, T.R. THE BIBLE AS LITERATURE.
H. FISCH, 191(ELN):SEP71-61
SISTER M. THERESA, 613:SUMMER71-303
HENNESSY, J.P. - SEE UNDER POPE HENNESSY,
J.
HENNIG, C. LANDMARKS OF AMERICAN WRIT-
ING.
A. WILLOT, 556(RLV):1971/5-650
HENRETTA, J.A. "SALUTARY NEGLECT."
617(TLS):6APR73-373
HENRICH, D., ED. KANT, GENTZ, REHBERG -
ÜBER THEORIE UND PRAXIS.
E.W. ORTH, 342:BAND62HEFT4-523
HENRIKSON, T. ROMANTIK OCH MARXISM.
W.A. BERENDSOHN, 182:VOL24#17/18-672
HENRIOT, J. LE JEU.
J.D.C., 543:DEC70-340
HENRY, D.P. THE "DE GRAMMATICO" OF ST.
ANSELM.
E.C. LUSCHEI, 316:SEP71-509
HENRY, F. IRISH ART IN THE ROMANESQUE
PERIOD 1020-1170 A.D.
J. BECKWITH, 39:OCT70-314
HENRY, F. & S. SABERWAL, EDS. STRESS AND
RESPONSE IN FIELDWORK.
P. ALEXANDRE, 69:OCT70-390
HENRY, P.L. THE EARLY ENGLISH AND CELTIC
LYRIC.
M.N. NAGLER, 179(ES):JUN71-255
HENRY, W. THE BEAR PAW HORSES.
M. LEVIN, 441:15APR73-33
HENRYSON, R. THE TESTAMENT OF CRESSEID.*
(D. FOX, ED)
W. WEISS, 38:BAND88HEFT1-129
HENZEN, W. DIE BEZIECHUNG VON RICHTUNG
UND GEGENRICHTUNG IM DEUTSCHEN.
H. WELLMANN, 657(WW):JUL/AUG70-274
HENZO D'ALESSIO, R. LOGÍA DE LA SOLEDAD.
E.B. LABRADA, 37:OCT70-40
HEPBURN, A. RAND MC NALLY GUIDE TO
MEXICO.
S.S. BENSON, 37:OCT71-42
HEPBURN, J. - SEE BENNETT, A.
HEPPENSTALL, R. THE SEX WAR AND OTHERS.
617(TLS):13APR73-427
HERBERT, A.B., WITH J.T. WOOTEN. SOLDIER.
P. ADAMS, 61:FEB73-103
J.G. GRAY, 441:18FEB73-2
C. LEHMANN-HAUPT, 441:30JAN73-39
442(NY):17MAR73-130
HERBERT, K. GREEK AND LATIN INSCRIPTIONS
IN THE BROOKLYN MUSEUM.
J. LECLANT, 182:VOL24#19/20-749
HERBERT, R.L. DAVID: BRUTUS.*
R. DOWNES, 441:2DEC73-92
HERBERT, R.L. SEURAT'S DRAWINGS.
H. DORRA, 54:JUN71-271
HERBRAND, J. ECRITS LOGIQUES.* (J. VAN
HEIJENOORT, ED)
R. BLANCHÉ, 542:OCT-DEC70-492
HERBURGER, G. DIE AMERIKANISCHE TOCHTER.
617(TLS):28DEC73-1593
HERBURGER, G. A MONOTONOUS LANDSCAPE.
J.J. WHITE, 220(GL&L):OCT71-41
HERCULANO DE CARVALHO, J.G. ESTUDIOS
LINGÜÍSTICOS.
A.J. NARO, 206:FEB71-148
HERD, D., ED. ANCIENT AND MODERN SCOT-
TISH SONGS.
617(TLS):21SEP73-1074

VON HERDER, J.G. J.G. HERDER ON SOCIAL
AND POLITICAL CULTURE.* (F.M. BARNARD,
ED & TRANS)
H.B. NISBET, 220(GL&L):OCT71-65
VON HERDER, J.G. ÜBER DIE NEUERE DEUTSCHE
LITERATUR. (ABRIDGED & ED BY A. GIL-
LIES)
H.B. NISBET, 220(GL&L):JAN72-166
HEREN, L. GROWING UP POOR IN LONDON.
D.J. ENRIGHT, 362:18OCT73-527
617(TLS):19OCT73-1273
HEREN, L. NO HAIL, NO FAREWELL.
639(VQR):WINTER71-XLII
HEREN, L. & OTHERS. CHINA'S THREE THOU-
SAND YEARS.
617(TLS):28DEC73-1579
HERGÉ. LES BIJOUX DE LA CASTAFIORE.
M. SERRES, 98:JUN70-485
HERGENHAN, L.T. - SEE CLARKE, M.
HERING, C.J. AEQUITAS UND TOLERANZ. (E.
FECHNER, E. VON HIPPEL & H. FROST, EDS)
G. MAY, 182:VOL24/24-845
HERINGER, H.J. DIE OPPOSITION VON "KOM-
MEN" UND "BRINGEN" ALS FUNKTIONSVERBEN.
B. SOWINSKI, 657(WW):JUL/AUG70-275
A.W. STANFORTH, 220(GL&L):APR72-295
HERMAND, J. POP INTERNATIONAL.
E. SCHWARZ, 406:SPRING72-92
HERMAND, J. UNBEQUEME LITERATUR.
J.D. ZIPES, 406:SPRING72-90
HERMAND, J. VON MAINZ NACH WEIMAR (1793-
1919).*
H. MEYER, 400(MLN):APR71-436
P. PROCHNIK, 222(GR):MAR71-161
H. STEINECKE, 52:BAND6HEFT2-220
HERMANN, H.P. NATURNACHAHMUNG UND EIN-
BILDUNGSKRAFT.
J. BRUCK, E. FELDMEIER, H. HIEBEL &
K.H. STAHL, 680(ZDP):BAND90HEFT4-
563
HERMANSEN, J. THE WAXMAN PRODUCTION.
M. LEVIN, 441:18NOV73-55
HERMERÉN, G. REPRESENTATION AND MEANING
IN THE VISUAL ARTS.
M.C. BEARDSLEY, 322(JHI):JAN-MAR71-
143
HERMES, E. DIE DREI RINGE.
E. DUBRUCK, 400(MLN):APR71-420
HERMES, H. EINE TERMLOGIK MIT AUSWAHL-
OPERATOR.
G.H. MÜLLER, 316:SEP70-440
HERMES, H. EINFÜHRUNG IN DIE VERBANDS-
THEORIE. (2ND ED)
P. JORDAN, 316:DEC71-677
HERMES, H., F. KAMBARTEL & F. KAULBACH -
SEE FREGE, G.
HERMSDORF, K. THOMAS MANNS SCHELME.
F. DIECKMANN, 654(WB):7/1970-200
HERNÁNDEZ, F.J. EL TEATRO DE MONTHER-
LANT.
R. VIDÁN, 202(FMOD):NOV71/FEB72-151
HERNDL, G.C. THE HIGH DESIGN.*
I. RIBNER, 402(MLR):JUL72-616
J.R. TAYLOR, 157:SPRING71-66
HERNDON, J. HOW TO SURVIVE IN YOUR
NATIVE LAND.*
H. KOHL, 453:13DEC73-48
42(AR):SPRING71-135
HERODAS. MIMIAMBI.* (I.C. CUNNINGHAM,
ED)
F. LASSERRE, 182:VOL24#7/8-365
HERODIAN. HISTORY.* (LOEB, VOL 1, BKS
1-4) (C.R. WHITTAKER, ED & TRANS)
G. DOWNEY, 121(CJ):DEC71/JAN72-182
F. MILLAR, 303:VOL91-156
HERODIAN. HISTORY. (LOEB, VOL 2, BKS
5-8) (C.R. WHITTAKER, ED & TRANS)
F. MILLAR, 303:VOL91-156

HEROLD, C.P. THE MORPHOLOGY OF KING
ALFRED'S TRANSLATION OF THE "OROSIUS."*
J.M. BATELY, 38:BAND89HEFT4-516
HERRE, G. - SEE "LUDWIG VAN BEETHOVEN:
NEUN AUSGEWÄHLTE BRIEFE AN ANTON SCHIND-
LER"
VON HERRENBERG, J.W. - SEE UNDER WENCK
VON HERRENBERG, J.
HERRING, P.F. - SEE JOYCE, J.
HERRIOT, J. ALL CREATURES GREAT AND
SMALL.*
N. BRYANT, 441:18FEB73-10
HERRIOT, P. AN INTRODUCTION TO THE PSY-
CHOLOGY OF LANGUAGE.
J. LINDENFELD, 350:MAR72-238
HERRMANN, L. BRITISH LANDSCAPE PAINTING
OF THE EIGHTEENTH CENTURY.
617(TLS):14DEC73-1528
HERRMANN, M. DAS GESELLSCHAFTSTHEATER
DES LOUIS CARROGIS DE CARMONTELLE
(1717-1802).
H. SCKOMMODAU, 535(RHL):JAN-FEB71-97
HERRMANN, W. THE THEORY OF CLAUDE PER-
RAULT.
617(TLS):12OCT73-1203
HERRNSTADT, R.L. - SEE ALCOTT, A.B.
HERRON, J. FIFTY YEARS ON THE OWL HOOT
TRAIL. (H.E. CHRISMAN, ED)
L. ATTEBERY, 650(WF):JAN71-65
HERRON, S. THROUGH THE DARK AND HAIRY
WOOD.*
617(TLS):13APR73-427
HERRON, S. THE WHORE-MOTHER.
A.C.J. BERGMAN, 441:26AUG73-28
A. BROYARD, 441:12MAR73-35
617(TLS):24AUG73-969
HERSEY, G.L. ALFONSO II AND THE ARTISTIC
RENEWAL OF NAPLES 1485-1495.
A. BLUNT, 90:JUL71-409
R.W. LIGHTBOWN, 39:DEC70-498
HERSEY, G.L. THE ARAGONESE ARCH AT
NAPLES 1443-1475.
617(TLS):9NOV73-1366
HERSHKOWITZ, L. & I.J. MEYER, EDS. THE
LEE MAX FRIEDMAN COLLECTION OF AMERICAN
JEWISH COLONIAL CORRESPONDENCE: LETTERS
OF THE FRANKS FAMILY (1733-1748).
R. SHOSTECK, 14:JAN70-94
HERTZBERG, A. THE FRENCH ENLIGHTENMENT
AND THE JEWS.
K. BIEBER, 207(FR):DEC70-402
HERTZBERG, H.W. THE SEARCH FOR AN AMERI-
CAN INDIAN IDENTITY.
V. SIGNORILE, 628:FALL71-89
DE HERVE, J.D. - SEE UNDER DE GOER DE
HERVE, J.
HERWIG, W. - SEE VON GOETHE, J.W.
HERZEN, A. MY PAST AND THOUGHTS. (ED &
ABRIDGED BY D. MACDONALD)
P. ROSENBERG, 441:21OCT73-6
442(NY):19NOV73-246
HERZKA, H.S. DIE SPRACHE DES SÄUGLINGS.
W. KAPER, 206:FEB70-112
HERZOG, A. THE B.S. FACTOR.
R. LASSON, 441:3JUN73-22
HERZOG, V. IRONISCHE ERZÄHLFORMEN BEI
CONRAD FERDINAND MEYER DARGESTELLT AM
"JÜRG JENATSCH."
M. BURKHARD, 301(JEGP):JAN72-83
HESELTINE, J.E., ED. THE OXFORD BOOK OF
FRENCH PROSE.
B. DANSON, 402(MLR):JAN72-179
HESIOD. HESIODI THEOGONIA, OPERA ET
DIES, SCUTUM. (F. SOLMSEN, ED)
J.E. REXINE, 124:JAN72-169
HESIOD. SÄMTLICHE GEDICHTE: THEOGONIE,
ERGA, FRAUENKATALOGE. (W. MARG, TRANS)
D.J. STEWART, 124:SEP71-24

HESIOD. THEOGONY. WORKS AND DAYS. [TO-
GETHER WITH] THEOGNIS. ELEGIES. (D.
WENDER, TRANS OF BOTH)
617(TLS):16MAR73-305
HESKY, O. LIFE SENTENCE.
N. CALLENDAR, 441:7JAN73-35
HESLA, D.H. THE SHAPE OF CHAOS.*
J.D. O'HARA, 651(WHR):SUMMER72-289
D. SCHIER, 109:FALL/WINTER72/73-108
617(TLS):12OCT73-1217
HESS, G. DEUTSCH-LATEINISCHE NARREN-
ZUNFT.
568(SCN):FALL-WINTER72-82
HESS, H. MAFIA.
H. WIENOLD, 182:VOL24#4-145
HESS, H. MAFIA AND MAFIOSI.
617(TLS):5OCT73-1182
HESS, R. DAS ETRUSKISCHE ITALIEN.
617(TLS):25MAY73-583
HESS, T.B. WILLEM DE KOONING DRAWINGS.
442(NY):31MAR73-119
617(TLS):9NOV73-1362
HESS, T.B. & E.C. BAKER, EDS. ART AND
SEXUAL POLITICS.
A. BROYARD, 441:28JUN73-51
HESS, T.B. & L. NOCHLIN, EDS. ART NEWS
ANNUAL XXXVIII: WOMAN AS SEX OBJECT.
C. ROBINS, 441:25MAR73-18
HESSE, E., ED. NEW APPROACHES TO EZRA
POUND.*
M.E. BROWN, 290(JAAC):SPRING71-412
A.J. PALANDRI, 648:OCT70-77
HESSE, E. DER SOWJETRUSSISCHE PARTISAN-
ENKRIEG 1941-44 IM SPIEGEL DEUTSCHER
KAMPFANWEISUNGEN UND BEFEHLE.
E. KESSEL, 182:VOL24#5-244
HESSE, H. AUTOBIOGRAPHICAL WRITINGS.*
(T. ZIOLKOWSKI, ED)
617(TLS):4MAY73-497
HESSE, H. DIE KUNST DES MÜSSIGGANGS.
(V. MICHELS, ED) DIE ERZÄHLUNGEN.
KNULP. STRANGE NEWS FROM ANOTHER STAR
AND OTHER TALES. GESAMMELTE BRIEFE.
(VOL 1) (U. & V. MICHELS, WITH H.
HESSE, EDS) WANDERING. IF THE WAR
GOES ON.
617(TLS):31AUG73-989
HESSE, H. POEMS OF HERMANN HESSE. (J.
WRIGHT, ED & TRANS)
A. HOLLIS, 565:VOL12#4-62
639(VQR):WINTER71-XXIV
HESSE, H. STORIES OF FIVE DECADES. (T.
ZIOLKOWSKI, ED)
E. PAWEL, 441:11FEB73-7
HESSE, H. & K. KERÉNYI. HERMANN HESSE -
KARL KERÉNYI: BRIEFWECHSEL AUS DER
NÄHE. (M. KERÉNYI, ED)
617(TLS):31AUG73-989
HESSE, H. & R. ROLLAND. D'UNE RIVE À
L'AUTRE. (P. GRAPPIN, ED)
617(TLS):31AUG73-989
HESSE, J. - SEE DE TORRES VILLARROEL, D.
HESSE, M.B. MODELS AND ANALOGIES IN
SCIENCE.
T.G. GROVE, 480(P&R):SUMMER70-190
HESTER, M.B. THE MEANING OF POETIC META-
PHOR.*
E.P. NOLAN, 353:JUN70-92
HESTER, R.M., ED. TEACHING A LIVING LAN-
GUAGE.*
M.R. DONOGHUE, 238:DEC71-981
B. EBLING, 207(FR):APR71-1008
HETZRON, R. THE VERBAL SYSTEM OF SOUTH-
ERN AGAW.
P.H. MATTHEWS, 297(JL):APR71-145
A.N. TUCKER, 361:VOL26#2-223
HEUER, F. DARSTELLUNG DER FREIHEIT.
N.H. SMITH, 182:VOL24#4-165

HEUER, H., WITH E.T. SEHRT & R. STAMM.
SHAKESPEARE JAHRBUCH. (VOL UNKNOWN)
K. OTTEN, 430(NS):SEP70-479
HEURGON, J. THE RISE OF ROME TO 264 B.C.
617(TLS):13JUL73-812
HEWARD, E. MATTHEW HALE.
617(TLS):16FEB73-189
HEWIG, A. PHANTASTISCHE WIRKLICHKEIT.
I. HILTON, 220(GL&L):OCT71-70
HEWISH, J. EMILY BRONTË.
P. THOMSON, 541(RES):MAY71-228
HEWISON, W. MINDFIRE.
617(TLS):31AUG73-1007
HEWITT, B. HISTORY OF THE THEATRE FROM
1800 TO THE PRESENT.
J.C. TREWIN, 157:SPRING71-69
HEWITT, D. CONRAD: A REASSESSMENT.
N. SHERRY, 402(MLR):OCT72-876
HEWITT, G., ED. QUICKLY AGING HERE.
M. CZARNECKI, 648:JUN70-37
HEWITT, H. - SEE PETRUCCI, O.
HEWLETT, D. A LIFE OF JOHN KEATS.* (3RD
ED)
J.D. JUMP, 148:SPRING71-87
HEWLINGS, M. THE RELEASE.
617(TLS):12JAN73-36
HEXTER, J.H. THE VISION OF POLITICS ON
THE EVE OF THE REFORMATION.
617(TLS):26OCT73-1304
VON HEYDEBRAND, R. & K.G. JUST, EDS.
WISSENSCHAFT ALS DIALOG.*
N.A. FURNESS, 220(GL&L):JUL72-407
R. LORBE, 149:SEP72-349
HEYEN, W. DEPTH OF FIELD.
B.J. ELKINS, 577(SHR):SUMMER71-293
J. MAZZARO, 628:FALL70-102
A. OBERG, 598(SOR):WINTER73-243
S.G. RADHUBER, 448:SPRING71-84
639(VQR):SPRING71-LX
HEYM, G. GEORG HEYM: DICHTUNGEN UND
SCHRIFTEN. (VOL 6) (K.L. SCHNEIDER &
G. BURCKHARDT, EDS)
E. KRISPYN, 401(MLQ):SEP71-331
R.R. READ, 221(GQ):NOV71-603
HEYM, S. THE KING DAVID REPORT.
R. BRYDEN, 362:2AUG73-155
617(TLS):3AUG73-893
HEYWOOD, T. A WOMAN KILLED WITH KIND-
NESS. (R.W. VAN FOSSEN, ED)
205(FMLS):JUL71-296
HEYWORTH, P., ED. CONVERSATIONS WITH
KLEMPERER.
617(TLS):2NOV73-1339
HEYWORTH, P. - SEE NEWMAN, E.
HEYWORTH, P.L., ED. "JACK UPLAND,"
"FRIAR DAW'S REPLY" AND "UPLAND'S
REJOINDER."*
W. WEISS, 38:BAND89HEFT4-537
HEZLET, A. THE "B" SPECIALS.
617(TLS):12JAN73-50
HIATT, D.F. & E.H. CADY - SEE HOWELLS,
W.D.
HIBBARD, H. CARLO MADERNO AND ROMAN
ARCHITECTURE 1580-1630.
617(TLS):6APR73-374
HIBBERD, D. - SEE OWEN, W.
HIBBERT, C. THE DRAGON WAKES.
Y.C. WANG, 293(JAST):AUG71-877
639(VQR):SUMMER71-CXXVII
HIBBERT, C. GEORGE IV: REGENT AND KING.
617(TLS):30NOV73-1464
HICK, H. HENRY HICK'S RECOLLECTIONS OF
GEORGE GISSING. (P. COUSTILLAS, ED)
617(TLS):12OCT73-1212
HICK, J. ARGUMENTS FOR THE EXISTENCE OF
GOD.
I.M. CROMBIE, 518:JAN72-8
HICKEY, L. - SEE DELIBES, M.

HICKS, J. CAPITAL AND TIME.
617(TLS):27JUL73-880
HICKS, J. A THEORY OF ECONOMIC HISTORY.*
P. VANAGS, 303:VOL91-197
HIDDEN, N. DR. KINK AND HIS OLD-STYLE
BOARDING SCHOOL.
617(TLS):22JUN73-728
HIEATT, C.B. THE REALISM OF DREAM
VISIONS.
W. WEISS, 38:BAND88HEFT4-537
HIETSCH, O., ED. ÖSTERREICH UND DIE
ANGELSÄCHSISCHE WELT. (VOL 2)
W. HÉRAUCOURT, 430(NS):MAR70-153
C.E. WILLIAMS, 220(GL&L):OCT71-82
HIGGIN, G. SYMPTOMS OF TOMORROW.
617(TLS):24AUG73-970
HIGGINBOTHAM, J., ED. GREEK AND LATIN
LITERATURE.*
R. BROWNING, 313:VOL61-299
HIGGINS, A. THE BALCONY OF EUROPE.*
P. ADAMS, 61:FEB73-103
T. LASK, 441:27JAN73-29
P. SOURIAN, 441:28JAN73-43
HIGGINS, G.V. THE DIGGER'S GAME.
P. ADAMS, 61:APR73-128
C. LEHMANN-HAUPT, 441:23MAR73-43
J. MILLS, 441:25MAR73-2
442(NY):7APR73-150
HIGGINS, I., ED. LITERATURE AND THE
PLASTIC ARTS, 1880-1930.
617(TLS):2NOV73-1335
HIGGINS, J. VISIÓN DEL HOMBRE Y DE LA
VIDA EN LAS ÚLTIMAS OBRAS DE CÉSAR
VALLEJO.
D.L. SHAW, 86(BHS):JAN72-104
HIGGINS, J. - SEE VALLEJO, C.
HIGGINS, R. UNITED NATIONS PEACEKEEPING,
1946-1967. (VOL 2)
C.V. CRABB, JR., 293(JAST):NOV70-243
HIGGINS, R.A. GREEK TERRACOTTAS.*
H. HOFFMANN, 39:JAN70-87
HIGGS, E.S., ED. PAPERS IN ECONOMIC
PREHISTORY.
617(TLS):3AUG73-908
HIGHAM, C. THE ART OF THE AMERICAN FILM.
W. MARKFIELD, 441:2DEC73-96
HIGHAM, C. CECIL B. DE MILLE.
G. WALKER, 441:17NOV73-29
HIGHAM, C. THE VOYAGE TO BRINDISI.
K.L. GOODWIN, 381:SEP71-367
HIGHAM, C. ZIEGFELD.*
441:18MAR73-32
HIGHET, G. EXPLORATIONS.
H. BEVINGTON, 579(SAQ):SUMMER72-436
HIGHET, G. THE SPEECHES IN VERGIL'S
"AENEID."
617(TLS):10AUG73-932
HIGHTOWER, J.R. - SEE T'AO CH'IEN
HIGMAN, F.M. - SEE CALVIN, J.
HIGONNET, P.L-R. PONT-DE-MONTVERT.
639(VQR):SUMMER71-CXXVI
HIGSON, M.F. LONDON MIDLAND FIREMAN.
617(TLS):12JAN73-50
HIKMET, N. THE MOSCOW SYMPHONY.
A. CLUYSENAAR, 565:VOL12#3-72
L. SHAYKIN, 114(CHIR):WINTER72-114
HILDEBERT OF LAVARDIN. HILDEBERTUS: CAR-
MINA MINORA. (A.B. SCOTT, ED)
P.G. WALSH, 382(MAE):1972/3-244
HILDEBRANDT, D., ED. HERMAN BROCH.
P.M. LÜTZELER, 406:SPRING72-70
HILDESHEIMER, W. MASANTE.
617(TLS):18MAY73-545
HILEN, A. - SEE LONGFELLOW, H.W.
HILL, A.A., ED. LINGUISTICS TODAY.
C. DUNCAN, 350:SEP72-677
HILL, B. JULIA MARGARET CAMERON.
617(TLS):31AUG73-992

HILL, B.H. CORINTH. (VOL 1, PT 6)
D.G. MITTEN, 576:OCT71-261
HILL, B.H. THE TEMPLE OF ZEUS AT NEMEA.
(REV BY C.K. WILLIAMS, JR.)
S.A. IMMERWAHR, 54:JUN71-242
HILL, C. ANTICHRIST IN SEVENTEENTH-CEN-
TURY ENGLAND.*
T.W. HAYES, 568(SCN):SPRING72-12
HILL, C. GOD'S ENGLISHMAN.*
G.W. GRAY, 656(WMQ):OCT71-682
HILL, C. JEREMIAH 8:20.
E. GOODHEART, 390:OCT70-73
HILL, C. SUBSISTENCE U.S.A.
E. HOAGLAND, 441:21OCT73-22
HILL, C. THE WORLD TURNED UPSIDE DOWN.*
P. ROSENBERG, 441:28JAN73-38
HILL, C. - SEE WINSTANLEY, G.
HILL, E. THE TRINIDAD CARNIVAL.
A.R. SCHRAMM, 187:SEP73-547
HILL, G. KING LOG.*
J.C. FIELD, 556(RLV):1971/1-98
HILL, H. MARK TWAIN.
E. WEEKS, 61:AUG73-102
HILL, H. - SEE TWAIN, M.
HILL, L.A. PREPOSITIONS AND ADVERBIAL
PARTICLES.
A. BRISAU, 556(RLV):1970/6-682
A.R. TELLIER, 189(EA):JUL-SEP71-317
HILL, M., ED. A SOCIOLOGICAL YEARBOOK
OF RELIGION IN BRITAIN 6.
617(TLS):20JUL73-842
HILL, P. THE DEVIL OF ASKE.
M. LEVIN, 441:15JUL73-16
HILL, P. STUDIES IN RURAL CAPITALISM IN
WEST AFRICA.
K. HART, 69:APR71-170
HILL, R. RULING PASSION.
617(TLS):13APR73-427
HILL, R.M.T. THE LABOURER IN THE VINE-
YARD.
E. WELCH, 325:APR71-249
HILL, S. THE BIRD OF NIGHT.*
P. THEROUX, 441:27MAY73-16
442(NY):17FEB73-110
HILL, S. A BIT OF SINGING AND DANCING.
J. HUNTER, 362:29MAR73-423
617(TLS):30MAR73-341
HILL, W.S. RICHARD HOOKER.
P.G. STANWOOD, 551(RENQ):WINTER71-572
HILLACH, A. DIE DRAMATISIERUNG DES KOM-
ISCHEN DIALOGS.
P. BRANSCOMBE, 220(GL&L):JAN72-157
HILLER, K. LEBEN GEGEN DIE ZEIT.
617(TLS):27JUL73-872
HILLERMAN, T. DANCE HALL OF THE DEAD.
N. CALLENDAR, 441:25NOV73-49
442(NY):31DEC73-60
HILLIER, B. 100 YEARS OF POSTERS.
617(TLS):23FEB73-220
HILLIER, B. THE WORLD OF ART DECO.
P. WOLLEN, 592:NOV71-213
HILLS, H.C. LIVING DANGEROUSLY.
617(TLS):24AUG73-986
HILLS, L.R. HOW TO RETIRE AT 41.
C. LEHMANN-HAUPT, 441:15JUN73-39
441:26AUG73-10
HILSCHER, E. GERHART HAUPTMANN.
G. ERDMANN, 654(WB):6/1971-186
HILSCHER, E. THOMAS MANN.
N. OELLERS, 680(ZDP):BAND89HEFT4-628
HILTON, R. LA AMÉRICA LATINA DE AYER Y
DE HOY.
M.E. RUIZ, 238:MAR71-229
HILTON, T. KEATS AND HIS WORLD.
T. MC FARLAND, 676(YR):WINTER72-279

HILTON, T. THE PRE-RAPHAELITES.
R.E., 135:MAY71-63
J. MAAS, 592:NOV70-220
R. MANDER, 39:FEB71-148
"WALTER HILTON'S EIGHT CHAPTERS ON PER-
FECTION." (F. KURIYAGAWA, ED)
F.G.A.M. AARTS, 179(ES):APR71-162
W. RIEHLE, 38:BAND88HEFT3-376
P. THEINER, 72:BAND209HEFT4/6-401
HINCHLIFFE, A.P. THE ABSURD.
205(FMLS):OCT70-420
HINCK, W. DIE DEUTSCHE BALLADE VON BÜR-
GER BIS BRECHT.
C. PIETZCKER, 657(WW):SEP/OCT70-356
HINDE, W. GEORGE CANNING.
K. KYLE, 362:27DEC73-890
617(TLS):30NOV73-1464
"HINDEMITH-JAHRBUCH: ANNALES HINDEMITH
1971/I."
617(TLS):16MAR73-298
HINDERLING, R. STUDIEN ZU DEN STARKEN
VERBALABSTRAKTA DES GERMANISCHEN.
A. BAMMESBERGER, 343:BAND13HEFT2-198
E. DITTMER, 680(ZDP):BAND89HEFT3-463
HINDLEY, C. A HISTORY OF THE CRIES OF
LONDON.
J.L. CUTLER, 582(SFQ):DEC70-375
HINDLEY, G. CASTLES OF EUROPE.
J. WILTON-ELY, 39:APR70-318
HINDLEY, G. - SEE "THE LAROUSSE ENCYCLO-
PEDIA OF MUSIC"
HINDUS, M. THE KREMLIN'S HUMAN DILEMMA.
H.J. ELLISON, 32:JUN72-426
HINE, R.V. & S. LOTTINVILLE - SEE TALBOT,
T.
HINGLEY, R. THE RUSSIAN SECRET POLICE.
R.H. MC NEAL, 32:MAR72-152
HINMAN, C. - SEE SHAKESPEARE, W.
HINSKE, N. KANTS WEG ZUR TRANSZENDENTAL-
PHILOSOPHIE.
G. TONELLI, 342:BAND62HEFT4-509
HINSKE, N. & W. WEISCHEDEL. KANT-SEITEN-
KONKORDANZ.
R. MALTER, 342:BAND62HEFT2-258
HINSLEY, F.H. NATIONALISM AND THE INTER-
NATIONAL SYSTEM.
617(TLS):29JUN73-754
HINTERHÄUSER, H. - SEE SCANFERLATO, A.
HINTIKKA, J. LOGIC, LANGUAGE-GAMES AND
INFORMATION.
617(TLS):20JUL73-838
HINTON, A.G. SHELLS OF NEW GUINEA AND
THE CENTRAL INDO-PACIFIC.
617(TLS):22JUN73-728
HINTON, H.C. CHINA'S TURBULENT QUEST.
Y.J. CHIH, 318(JAOS):OCT-DEC71-520
S-Y. DAI, 550(RUSR):JAN71-91
M. PILLSBURY, 293(JAST):NOV70-183
HINTON, J.M. EXPERIENCES.
617(TLS):10AUG73-935
HINTON, P., ED. TRIBESMEN AND PEASANTS
IN NORTH THAILAND.
A.Y. DESSAINT, 293(JAST):MAY71-726
HINTON, W. HUNDRED DAY WAR.
H.E. SALISBURY, 441:14JAN73-4
R. TERRILL, 453:19APR73-32
617(TLS):29JUN73-738
HINTON, W. TURNING POINT IN CHINA.
H.E. SALISBURY, 441:14JAN73-4
R. TERRILL, 453:19APR73-32
HINZ, W. THE LOST WORLD OF ELAM.
617(TLS):16MAR73-293
HIPPIUS, Z. SELECTED WORKS OF ZINAIDA
HIPPIUS. (T. PACHMUSS, ED & TRANS)
617(TLS):22JUN73-728
HIPPOCRATES. HIPPOCRATE. (VOL 11) (R.
JOLY, ED & TRANS)
P. DE LACY, 124:SEP71-23

HIRN, S. TEATER I VIBORG 1743-1870.
J.S. MARTIN, 67:NOV72-260
HIRSCH, D.H. REALITY AND IDEA IN THE
EARLY AMERICAN NOVEL.
R.R. MALE, 27(AL):NOV72-483
HIRSCH, E.D., JR. VALIDITY IN INTERPRE-
TATION.
R. BLANCHE, 542:OCT-DEC70-493
R.D. HUME, 556(RLV):1970/3-326
J.J.A. MOOIJ, 206:NOV71-602
G. REBING, 52:BAND6HEFT2-230
E.N. TIGERSTEDT, 597(SN):VOL42#2-483
HIRSCHMAN, A.O. EXIT, VOICE, AND LOYALTY.
639(VQR):WINTER71-XLIII
HIRSCHMANN, I. RED STAR OVER BETHLEHEM.
J. GREENFIELD, 287:OCT71-24
L. KOCHAN, 32:JUN72-447
HIRSHFIELD, D.S. THE LOST REFORM.
639(VQR):SUMMER71-CXXXII
HIRSHSON, S.P. THE LION OF THE LORD.
K. YOUNG, 649(WAL):SUMMER70-156
HIRST, P.H. & R.S. PETERS. THE LOGIC OF
EDUCATION.
I. GREGORY, 518:JAN72-9
HIRTSIEFER, G. ORDNUNG UND RECHT IN DER
DICHTUNG JOHANN PETER HEBELS.
G. RODGER, 220(GL&L):OCT71-38
HISLOP, C. ELIPHALET NOTT.
H.W. SCHNEIDER, 319:APR73-274
HISLOP, J. THE BRIGADIER.
617(TLS):23NOV73-1425
"HISTORIA TOY HELLĒNIKOY, ETHNOYS."
(VOL 1)
A.R. BURN, 303:VOL91-189
"THE HISTORY OF REYNARD THE FOX."* (W.
CAXTON, TRANS; N.F. BLAKE, ED)
A.A. PRINS, 597(SN):VOL43#1-305
"A HISTORY OF THE HIGHWAYS AND BYWAYS OF
ESSEX."
W.B. STEPHENS, 325:APR71-249
HITCHCOCK, G., ED. LOSERS WEEPERS.
R.S., 376:JAN70-111
HITCHCOCK, G. A SHIP OF BELLS.
E. FEINSOD, 114(CHIR):JAN-FEB71-156
HITCHCOCK, H-R. GERMAN ROCOCO: THE ZIM-
MERMANN BROTHERS.*
M.J. SOLIMENA, 505:JAN70-140
HITCHCOCK, H-R. ROCOCO ARCHITECTURE IN
SOUTHERN GERMANY.*
S.L. FAISON, JR., 576:MAY70-195
J.R.F.T., 135:JUL70-213
HITCHCOCK, H-R. & OTHERS. THE RISE OF AN
AMERICAN ARCHITECTURE.* (E. KAUFMANN,
JR., ED)
W.S. RUSK, 127:FALL71-106
L. WODEHOUSE, 576:DEC71-333
HITCHCOCK, H.W. - SEE CACCINI, G.
HITCHCOCK, J. THE DECLINE AND FALL OF
RADICAL CATHOLICISM.
F.X. CURRAN, 613:WINTER71-622
HITCHINGS, S. BOSTON IMPRESSIONS.
639(VQR):SPRING71-LXXXIII
HITLER, A. MEIN KAMPF. (R. MANHEIM,
TRANS)
H. TREVOR-ROPER, 362:25JAN73-101
HITNER, J.M. BROWNING ANALYSIS OF A
MURDER.
C. DAHL, 85:FALL70-32
HITTI, P.K. CAPITAL CITIES OF ARAB
ISLAM.
617(TLS):30NOV73-1483
HIXSON, W.B., JR. MOORFIELD STOREY AND
THE ABOLITIONIST TRADITION.*
K. JEFFREY, 109:FALL/WINTER72/73-93
HJELMSLEV, L. LANGUAGE.*
P.W. ROGERS, 529(QQ):AUTUMN71-474

HJELMSLEV, L. PROLEGOMENA OF A THEORY
OF LANGUAGE. (DANISH TITLE: OMKRING
SPROGTEORIENS GRUNDLAEGGELSE.)
B-O. QVARNSTRÖM, 316:MAR71-153
HJORTH, A. LA PARTIE CAMBRÉSIENNE DU
POLYPTYQUE DIT "TERRIER L'EVÊQUE" DE
CAMBRAI, LE MANUSCRIT ET LA LANGUE.
S. ANDOLF, 597(SN):VOL43#2-608
HJORTSBERG, W. GRAY MATTERS.
617(TLS):18MAY73-562
HJORTSBERG, W. SYMBIOGRAPHY.
B. HAYES, 441:18NOV73-53
C. LEHMANN-HAUPT, 441:28NOV73-49
HLAWITSCHKA, E., K. SCHMID & G. TELLEN-
BACH, EDS. LIBER MEMORIALIS VON REMIRE-
MONT.
G. CONSTABLE, 589:APR72-261
HNILICKA, K. DAS ENDE AUF DEM BALKAN
1944/45.
J.M. BRIDGMAN, 32:MAR72-225
HO HAO-JO. MEI-KUO KU-HSI FEN-TZU YU
T'AI-WAN TU-LI YÜN-TUNG.
L.H.D. GORDON & S. CHANG, 293(JAST):
NOV70-137
HO PING-TI. HUANG-T'U YÜ CHUNG-KUO NUNG-
YEH TI CH'I-YÜAN.
J.B.R. WHITNEY, 302:JAN71-174
HOAGLAND, E. WALKING THE DEAD DIAMOND
RIVER.
A. KAZIN, 441:25MAR73-31
C. LEHMANN-HAUPT, 441:12APR73-49
HOAR, V. - SEE LIVERSEDGE, R.
HOBAN, R. THE LION OF BOAZ-JACHIN AND
JACHIN-BOAZ.
R. BLYTHE, 362:8MAR73-312
617(TLS):16MAR73-285
HOBBES, T. THE ELEMENTS OF LAW NATURAL
AND POLITIC. (2ND ED) BEHEMOTH OR THE
LONG PARLIAMENT. (2ND ED) (BOTH ED BY
F. TÖNNIES)
J.M.P., 568(SCN):SPRING72-4
HOBBS, J.L. LOCAL HISTORY AND THE LIB-
RARY. (REV BY G.A. CARTER)
617(TLS):20APR73-454
HOBBS, M. BORN TO STRUGGLE.
S. CLAPP, 362:26JUL73-124
617(TLS):31AUG73-992
HOBERT, E. DIE FRANZÖSISCHE FRAUENSATIRE
(1600-1800), UNTER BERÜCKSICHTIGUNG
DER ANTIKEN TRADITION.
P. HOFFMANN, 535(RHL):JAN-FEB71-106
HOBHOUSE, C. A WELL-TOLD LIE.*
M. LEVIN, 441:11MAR73-49
442(NY):21APR73-134
"HŌBŌGIRIN." (FASC 4) (P. DEMIÉVILLE &
J. MAY, EDS)
A.E. LINK, 318(JAOS):OCT-DEC71-526
VAN HOBOKEN, A., COMP. JOSEPH HAYDN:
THEMATISCH-BIBLIOGRAPHISCHES WERKVER-
ZEICHNIS. (VOL 2)
K. GEIRINGER, 317:FALL72-471
HOBSBAUM, P. COME OUT FIGHTING.
H. SERGEANT, 175:SPRING70-29
HOBSBAUM, P. A READER'S GUIDE TO
CHARLES DICKENS.
617(TLS):27APR73-478
HOBSBAUM, P. THEORY OF CRITICISM.
P. CRUTTWELL, 249(HUDR):SUMMER72-323
HOBSBAWM, E.J. REVOLUTIONARIES.
R. MITCHISON, 362:2AUG73-153
S-S. WOLIN, 441:25NOV73-4
617(TLS):17AUG73-949
HOBSBAWM, E.J. & G. RUDE. CAPTAIN SWING.*
M. NEUMAN, 637(VS):SEP70-105
HOBSON, A. GREAT LIBRARIES.
R.D. PRATT, 503:SUMMER71-98
HOC, M. HISTOIRE MONÉTAIRE DE TOURNAI.
B. LYON, 589:OCT72-769

HOCART, A.M. KINGS AND COUNCILLORS.
(R. NEEDHAM, ED)
R. BASTIDE, 182:VOL24#1/2-61
J. HITCHCOCK, 293(JAST):FEB71-419
HOCH, E.D. THE FELLOWSHIP OF THE HAND.
N. CALLENDAR, 441:11MAR73-50
HOCHHUTH, R. GUERILLAS.
E. LARSON, 270:VOL22#2-38
HOCHMAN, B. ANOTHER EGO.*
K. CUSHMAN, 405(MP):NOV71-152
J. ZASLOVE, 648:OCT71-60
HOCHMAN, S. EARTHWORKS.*
A. OSTRIKER, 473(PR):SPRING72-270
HOCHMAN, S. WALKING PAPERS.
P.M. SPACKS, 249(HUDR):SPRING72-163
42(AR):SUMMER71-283
HOCKETT, C.F. LANGUAGE, MATHEMATICS,
AND LINGUISTICS.
I. REVZIN, 353:JUN71-117
HOCKETT, C.F. MAN'S PLACE IN NATURE.
617(TLS):14DEC73-1548
HOCKETT, C.F. THE STATE OF THE ART.*
F.W. HOUSEHOLDER, 297(JL):FEB70-129
P.H. MATTHEWS, 269(IJAL):JAN71-49
L.R. MICKLESEN, 215(GL):VOL11#1-28
HOCKETT, C.F. - SEE BLOOMFIELD, L.
HOCKEY, S.F. QUARR ABBEY AND ITS LANDS,
1132-1631.
C.V. GRAVES, 589:JAN72-127
HODDER-WILLIAMS, C. PANIC O'CLOCK.
617(TLS):9NOV73-1378
VAN HODDIS, J. "WELTENDE." (P. PÖRT-
NER, ED)
R. MAJUT, 220(GL&L):APR72-270
HODES, A. ENCOUNTER WITH MARTIN BUBER.
617(TLS):28DEC73-1577
HODGART, M. SATIRE.*
W. KINSLEY, 223:DEC71-348
HODGETT, G.A.J. A SOCIAL AND ECONOMIC
HISTORY OF MEDIEVAL EUROPE.
617(TLS):6APR73-401
HODGE, J.A. STRANGERS IN COMPANY.
N. CALLENDAR, 441:28JAN73-20
HODGINS, A.F.W., GENERAL ED. LE FRANÇAIS
PARTOUT.
M. WALTER, 399(MLJ):MAR71-184
HODGINS, E. TROLLEY TO THE MOON.
E. WEEKS, 61:MAY73-120
HODGKINSON, T. THE JAMES A. DE ROTH-
SCHILD COLLECTION AT WADDESDON MANOR:
THE SCULPTURE.
M. LEVEY, 90:MAR71-162
F.J.B. WATSON, 39:MAY71-434
HODGSON, P.C. - SEE STRAUSS, D.F.
HODGSON, S. UNHISTORIC ACTS.
V. CUNNINGHAM, 362:3MAY73-591
617(TLS):11MAY73-535
HODNETT, G. & P.J. POTICHNYJ. THE UKRAINE
AND THE CZECHOSLOVAK CRISIS.
H. HANAK, 575(SEER):APR72-320
HOEBEKE, M. DE MIDDELEEUWSE OORKONDEN-
TAAL TE OUDENAARDE.
J.P. WILLEMS, 556(RLV):1971/5-654
HOF, W. PESSIMISTISCH-NIHILISTISCHE
STRÖMUNGEN IN DER DEUTSCHEN LITERATUR
VOM STURM UND DRANG BIS ZUM JUNGEN
DEUTSCHLAND.*
W.L. HAHN, 221(GQ):NOV71-592
HOFER, H. - SEE BARBEY D'AUREVILLY, J.
HOFF, A. AIRGUNS AND OTHER PNEUMATIC
ARMS.
617(TLS):14DEC73-1545
HOFF, A. FEUERWAFFEN.
S.J.F., 135:JAN71-54
HOFF, B.J. THE CARIB LANGUAGE.*
G.L. HUTTAR, 269(IJAL):OCT70-298
HOFFER, C.R. THE UNDERSTANDING OF MUSIC.
P.J.P., 412:MAY72-149

HOFFMAN, D. BARBAROUS KNOWLEDGE.*
J.K. ROBINSON, 598(SOR):SUMMER73-692
HOFFMAN, D. BROKEN LAWS.*
N.A. BRITTIN, 577(SHR):SPRING71-207
H.T. KIRBY-SMITH, JR., 569(SR):SUM-
MER72-483
H. SERGEANT, 175:SUMMER71-65
HOFFMAN, D. POE POE POE POE POE POE POE.*
H. LEVIN, 27(AL):NOV72-488
HOFFMAN, H., WITH H.A. CAHN. COLLECTING
GREEK ANTIQUITIES.
J.V. NOBLE, 124:OCT71-66
HOFFMAN, P. LIONS IN THE STREET.
J.C. GOULDEN, 441:8JUL73-10
HOFFMAN, R.L. REVOLUTIONARY JUSTICE.
617(TLS):19OCT73-1284
HOFFMAN, S.D. COMEDY AND FORM IN THE
FICTION OF JOSEPH CONRAD.*
J. ESPEY, 445(NCF):JUN70-125
HOFFMAN, W. A WALK TO THE RIVER.
R. BUFFINGTON, 396(MODA):WINTER72-109
HOFFMANN, B., WITH H. DUKAS. ALBERT EIN-
STEIN.*
617(TLS):8JUN73-649
HOFFMANN, E.T.A. MEISTER FLOH. (W.
SEGEBRECHT, ED)
R.M., 191(ELN):SEP71(SUPP)-144
HOFFMANN, E.T.A. SELECTED WRITINGS OF
E.T.A. HOFFMANN. (L.J. KENT & E.C.
KNIGHT, EDS & TRANS)
R.M., 191(ELN):SEP71(SUPP)-143
W.W., 502(PRS):FALL70-274
HOFFMANN, E.T.A. TAGEBÜCHER. (F.
SCHNAPP, ED)
H. STEINECKE, 680(ZDP):BAND90HEFT4-
601
HOFFMANN, E.T.A. THREE MÄRCHEN OF E.T.A.
HOFFMANN. (C.E. PASSAGE, TRANS)
J.L. GREENWAY, 406:WINTER72-382
HOFFMANN, F. GESCHICHTE DER LUXEMBURGER
MUNDARTDICHTUNG.
M. ZENDER, 680(ZDP):BAND90HEFT4-623
HOFFMANN, K-D. DAS MENSCHENBILD BEI
AGNES MIEGEL.
I. MEIDINGER-GEISE, 680(ZDP):BAND90
HEFT2-316
HOFFMANN, L-F. RÉPERTOIRE GÉOGRAPHIQUE
DE LA "COMÉDIE HUMAINE." (VOL 2)
C.F. COATES, 207(FR):OCT70-231
HOFFMANN, L-F. TRAVAUX PRATIQUES.
G. SCHWEIG, 430(NS):FEB71-103
HOFFMANN, O. GESCHICHTE DER GRIECHISCHEN
SPRACHE. (A. DEBRUNNER, ED; 2ND ED REV
BY A. SCHERER)
A.M. DAVIES, 123:MAR72-72
HOFFMANN, W. ALTDEUTSCHE METRIK.
H.V.D. KOLK, 433:APR70-199
P. OCHSENBEIN, 657(WW):JAN/FEB71-63
H. TERVOOREN, 680(ZDP):BAND90HEFT1-
102
HOFFMANN-CURTIUS, K. DAS PROGRAMM DER
FONTANA MAGGIORE IN PERUGIA.
J. WHITE, 54:DEC70-437
HOFIUS, O. KATAPAUSIS.
F. BOVON, 182:VOL24#3-84
HÖFLER, M. UNTERSUCHUNGEN ZUR TUCH- UND
STOFFBENENNUNG IN DER FRANZÖSISCHEN
URKUNDENSPRACHE.
T. BERCHEM, 209(FM):OCT70-452
J.R. CRADDOCK, 545(RPH):FEB72-363
G. INEICHEN, 260(IF):BAND74-287
HOFMANN, C. SOUNDS FOR SILENTS.
P. COOK, 200:JAN71-30
HOFMANN, D. - SEE RANKE, F.
HOFMANN, H. SEARCH FOR THE REAL.
R.D. ABBEY, 127:FALL71-110

165

HOFMANN, K.   DAS BILD IN ANDREW MARVELLS
  LYRISCHEN GEDICHTEN.
    C.W. THOMSEN, 430(NS):NOV70-580
HOFMO, G.   GJEST PÅ JORDEN.
    E. HASLUND, 270:VOL22#4-87
HOFSTADTER, A.   AGONY AND EPITAPH.
    W.N. CLARKE, 258:JUN71-276
    C. WELCH, 321:SUMMER71-231
HOFSTADTER, R. & M. WALLACE, EDS.   AMERI-
  CAN VIOLENCE.
    C.P. IVES, 396(MODA):WINTER72-94
    639(VQR):SUMMER71-CXXXIII
HOFTUN, S. & R. TOBIASSEN, EDS.   MÅL OG
  METODER I LITTERATURFORSKNINGEN.
    A. LIEN, 563(SS):SPRING72-272
HOGAN, C.B., ED.   THE LONDON STAGE, 1660-
  1800.   (PT 5: 1776-1800)
    R.D. HUME, 481(PQ):JUL71-389
    J.G.M., 570(SQ):AUTUMN71-410
    C. PRICE, 570(SQ):WINTER71-67
HOGARTH, W.   THE ANALYSIS OF BEAUTY.
    H. OSBORNE, 89(BJA):SPRING72-200
HOGG, G.W. & J.C. TYSON, COMPS.   POPULAR
  EDUCATION, 1700-1870.
    W.B. STEPHENS, 325:APR71-249
HOGG, J.   MEMOIRS OF THE AUTHOR'S LIFE
  AND FAMILIAR ANECDOTES OF SIR WALTER
  SCOTT.   (D.S. MACK, ED)
    J. CAREY, 362:15MAR73-346
    617(TLS):2FEB73-112
HOGG, J.   THE PRIVATE MEMOIRS AND CONFES-
  SIONS OF A JUSTIFIED SINNER.   (J.
  CAREY, ED)
    W. PACHE, 430(NS):SEP71-498
HOGG, J.   THE THREE PERILS OF MAN.   (D.
  GIFFORD, ED)
    J. CAREY, 362:15MAR73-346
HOGGART, R.   ON CULTURE AND COMMUNICATION.
    N. BLIVEN, 442(NY):28APR73-143
HOGGE, T.   EXPOSTULATIONS [TOGETHER WITH]
  POPE, A.   THE WOODEN MUSE.
    W.G. SHEPHERD, 493:SUMMER71-204
HOHENBALKEN, P. - SEE VON LÜTZOW, H.
HOHENDAHL, P.U.   DAS BILD DER BÜRGERLICHEN
  WELT IM EXPRESSIONISTISCHEN DRAMA.
    B. MOGRIDGE, 220(GL&L):JAN72-161
HOHNISCH, E.   DAS GEFANGENE ICH.
    J. ONIMUS, 557(RSH):JAN-MAR70-178
HOLADAY, A. - SEE CHAPMAN, G.
HOLBROOK, C.A. - SEE EDWARDS, J.
HOLBROOK, D.   ENGLISH IN AUSTRALIA NOW.
    617(TLS):13APR73-412
HOLCROFT, T.   THE ADVENTURES OF HUGH
  TREVOR.   (S. DEANE, ED)
    617(TLS):13JUL73-800
HOLCROFT, T.   ANNA ST. IVES.   (P. FAULK-
  NER, ED)
    R.M. BAINE, 219(GAR):SPRING71-113
    W. CHRISTIAN, 173(ECS):SPRING72-493
HOLDEN, A.   THE GIRL ON THE BEACH.
    617(TLS):18MAY73-562
HOLDEN, D.   GREECE WITHOUT COLUMNS.*
    R. CLOGG, 453:19JUL73-28
HOLDEN, D.   WHISTLER; LANDSCAPES AND SEA-
  SCAPES.*
    H.E. ROBERTS, 637(VS):SEP70-102
HÖLDERLIN, F.   POEMS AND FRAGMENTS.   (M.
  HAMBURGER, TRANS)
    I. SEIDLER, 133:1970/2&3-324
HÖLDERLIN, F.   DER TOD DES EMPEDOKLES.
  (M.B. BENN, ED)
    L. RYAN, 221(GQ):JAN71-104
HÖLDERLIN, F. & E. MÖRIKE.   SELECTED
  POEMS.   (C. MIDDLETON, TRANS)
    617(TLS):11MAY73-516

HOLDHEIM, W.W.   DER JUSTIZIRRTUM ALS
  LITERARISCHE PROBLEMATIK.
    E. MARSCH, 52:BAND6HEFT2-225
    J. PURVER, 402(MLR):JAN72-222
HOLDHEIM, W.W.   THEORY AND PRACTICE OF
  THE NOVEL.*
    B. BRAY, 433:OCT71-467
HOLIDAY, F.W.   THE DRAGON AND THE DISC.
    617(TLS):27JUL73-871
"THE HOLIDAY MAGAZINE GUIDE TO MEXICO."
    S.S. BENSON, 37:OCT71-43
HOLL, A.   JESUS IN BAD COMPANY.
    617(TLS):16FEB73-185
HOLLAND, N.   THE MILITANTS.
    A. RENDLE, 157:SUMMER70-75
HOLLAND, N.N.   THE DYNAMICS OF LITERARY
  RESPONSE.*
    E. DELAVENAY, 189(EA):APR-JUN71-216
    D. HALLIBURTON, 290(JAAC):WINTER70-275
HOLLAND, N.N.   POEMS IN PERSONS.
    P. DELANY, 441:28OCT73-38
HOLLANDER, J.   SELECTED POEMS.
    617(TLS):11MAY73-516
HOLLANDER, J.   TYPES OF SHAPE.*
    D.H. SULLIVAN, 648:OCT70-69
HOLLANDER, P.   SOVIET AND AMERICAN SOCI-
  ETY.
    H. SCHWARTZ, 441:4JUL73-13
HOLLANDER, R.   ALLEGORY IN DANTE'S "COM-
  MEDIA."*
    P. CHERCHI, 405(MP):FEB72-252
    B. CORRIGAN, 149:MAR72-101
HOLLANDER, S.   THE ECONOMICS OF ADAM
  SMITH.
    617(TLS):27JUL73-880
HOLLINGDALE, R.J.   THOMAS MANN.
    H.W. REICHERT, 406:FALL72-288
HOLLIS, A.S. - SEE OVID
HOLLIS, C.   THE MIND OF CHESTERTON.
    L. CUNNINGHAM, 613:SPRING71-137
HOLLIS, C.   PARLIAMENT AND ITS SOVER-
  EIGNTY.
    617(TLS):3AUG73-906
HOLLIS, J.R.   HAROLD PINTER.*
    J. PETER, 157:SPRING71-70
    J.M. WARE, 141:SPRING71-216
HOLLISTER-SHORT, G.J.   DISCOVERING
  WROUGHT IRON.
    A.C-T., 135:JAN71-55
HOLLO, A.   ALEMBIC.
    617(TLS):23NOV73-1452
HOLLOWAY, G.   TO HAVE EYES.
    617(TLS):12JAN73-36
HOLLOWAY, J.   BLAKE: THE LYRIC POETRY.*
    G.E. BENTLEY, JR., 627(UTQ):FALL70-86
HOLLOWAY, R.R.   SATRIANUM.
    R.M. OGILVIE, 123:JUN72-265
HOLLOWAY, R.R.   A VIEW OF GREEK ART.
    617(TLS):1JUN73-625
HOLLYMAN, K.J.   A SHORT DESCRIPTIVE GRAM-
  MAR OF OLD FRENCH.
    N.H.J. VAN DEN BOOGAARD, 433:OCT71-
    451
HOLM, G., ED.   EN DISKUSSION OM STA-
  NAMNEN.
    H. KUHN, 260(IF):BAND75-346
HOLMAN, A.   A SHADOW AND A WISH.
    S.E. LEE, 581:DEC72-302
HOLMAN, C.H. - SEE THRALL, W.F. & A. HIB-
  BARD
HOLMAN, C.H. & L.D. RUBIN, JR. - SEE
  HOOPER, J.J.
HOLMAN, R.   TRADING IN CHILDREN.
    617(TLS):10AUG73-934
HOLMAN-HUNT, D.   MY GRANDFATHER, HIS
  WIVES AND LOVES.*
    R. MANDER, 39:FEB71-148

HÖLMANN, C. GALANTE GEDICHTE. (F. HEIDUK, ED)
B.L. SPAHR, 133:1971/1&2-196
HOLMBERG, M.Å. EXZIPIEREND-EINSCHRÄN-KENDE AUSDRUCKSWEISEN.
F. TSCHIRCH, 433:JAN71-102
HØLMEBAKK, S. JENTESPRANGET.
M. NAG, 270:VOL21#2-142
HOLMER, N.M. NOTES ON THE BANDJALANG DIALECT.
D.T. TRYON, 67:NOV72-265
HOLMES, C.M. ALDOUS HUXLEY AND THE WAY TO REALITY.
A.M. DUCKWORTH, 191(ELN):JUN72-320
HOLMES, C.S. THE CLOCKS OF COLUMBUS.*
A. MIZENER, 441:25MAR73-32
617(TLS):1JUN73-608
HOLMES, D. - SEE MORECAMBE, E. & E. WISE
HOLMES, D.M. THE ART OF THOMAS MIDDLE-TON.*
M. LAWLIS, 551(RENQ):WINTER71-574
S.G. PUTT, 175:AUTUMN71-101
H.U. SEEBER, 182:VOL24#7/8-358
HOLMES, G. THE FLORENTINE ENLIGHTENMENT 1400-50.
C.H. CLOUGH, 39:JAN70-88
HOLMES, G. THE TRIAL OF DOCTOR SACHEV-ERELL.
M. HODGART, 362:22MAR73-381
617(TLS):6APR73-373
HOLMES, J.S., F. DE HAAN & A. POPOVIČ, EDS. ESSAYS ON THE THEORY AND PRACTICE OF LITERARY TRANSLATION.
D. GUILD, 402(MLR):OCT72-861
HOLMES, M. SHAKESPEARE AND HIS PLAYERS.
617(TLS):12JAN73-44
HOLMES, O.W. RALPH WALDO EMERSON.
L. LANE, JR., 255(HAB):SPRING70-60
HOLMES, S.L. YIRRAWALA, ARTIST AND MAN.
617(TLS):12OCT73-1206
HOLMES, U.T. CHRÉTIEN DE TROYES.
C.A. KNUDSON, 589:OCT72-770
HOLMES, U.T., JR. DAILY LIVING IN THE TWELFTH CENTURY.
A.W. GODFREY, 363:MAY71-78
HOLROYD, M. LYTTON STRACHEY.* (VOLS 1&2)
M. THORPE, 179(ES):AUG71-375
HOLROYD, M. UNRECEIVED OPINIONS.
617(TLS):7SEP73-1025
HOLROYDE, P. INDIAN MUSIC.*
L. DURÁN, 415:DEC72-1187
HÖLSCHER, T. IDEAL UND WIRKLICHKEIT IN DEN BILDNISSEN ALEXANDERS DES GROSSEN.
E.C. BANKS, 124:MAR72-237
HOLST, I. BYRD.
P. BRETT, 415:AUG72-773
HOLST, I. HOLST.
H. OTTAWAY, 415:JUN72-566
HOLST, S. THE LANGUAGE OF CATS AND OTHER STORIES.
K. CONGDON, 37:MAY71-40
HOLT, A.H. AMERICAN PLACE NAMES.
E.P. HAMP, 269(IJAL):APR71-136
HOLT, E. PLON-PLON.
617(TLS):8JUN73-637
HOLT, J. BEITRÄGE ZUR SPRACHLICHEN IN-HALTSANALYSE.
U. EGLI, 343:BAND13HEFT2-175
HOLT, J. HOW CHILDREN FAIL. HOW CHILD-REN LEARN. THE UNDERACHIEVING SCHOOL.
N. CROOK, 97(CQ):SPRING71-266
HOLT, K. KONGEN. FREDLØSE MENN. HERSKER OG TRELL.
O. SOLUMSMOEN, 270:VOL21#2-143
HOLT, K. OPPSTANDELSEN.
270:VOL22#1-22

HOLT, M. & D.T.E. MARJORAM. MATHEMATICS IN A CHANGING WORLD.
617(TLS):23MAR73-333
HOLT, M.P. - SEE RUIZ IRIARTE, V.
HOLT, M.P. & G.W. WOODYARD - SEE RUIZ IRIARTE, V.
HOLT, P.M. STUDIES IN THE HISTORY OF THE NEAR EAST.
617(TLS):1JUN73-609
HOLT, P.M., A.K.S. LAMBTON & B. LEWIS, EDS. THE CAMBRIDGE HISTORY OF ISLAM.*
A.A.A. FYZEE, 273(IC):OCT71-295
HOLT, V. THE CURSE OF THE KINGS.
M. LEVIN, 441:9SEP73-42
HOLTAN, O.I. MYTHIC PATTERNS IN IBSEN'S LAST PLAYS.
R. FJELDE, 563(SS):AUTUMN72-566
HOLTER, K. MEURSAULT - EN FREMMED?
E. EIDE, 172(EDDA):1970/3-190
HOLTON, M. CYLINDER OF VISION.
D.D. ANDERSON, 27(AL):JAN73-689
HOLTZ, W.V. IMAGE AND IMMORTALITY.*
B.D. JAMESON, 651(WHR):WINTER72-89
R. PAULSON, 481(PQ):JUL71-484
J. STEDMOND, 173(ECS):SPRING72-489
M. WAINGROW, 401(MLQ):MAR72-81
HOLUB, M. ALTHOUGH.*
A. CLUYSENAAR, 565:VOL12#3-72
HOLZHEID, S. DIE NOMINALKOMPOSITA IN DER ILIASÜBERSETZUNG VON N.I. GNEDIČ.*
H. KEIPERT, 72:BAND209HEFT4/6-474
HOLZHEY, H. KANTS ERFAHRUNGSBEGRIFF.*
R.W.K. PATERSON, 479(PHQ):JUL71-271
W. SCHWARZ, 484(PPR):DEC71-289
W. STEINBECK, 342:BAND62HEFT2-249
HÖLZL, N. THEATERGESCHICHTE DES ÖST-LICHEN TIROL: VOM MITTELALTER BIS ZUR GEGENWART.* (PT 2)
R.M. KULLY, 657(WW):MAY/JUN70-216
HOMANN-WEDEKING, E. THE ART OF ARCHAIC GREECE.*
G.M.A. RICHTER, 54:JUN70-195
HOMBERGER, E., ED. EZRA POUND: THE CRITICAL HERITAGE.
617(TLS):16MAR73-292
HOME, H. ELEMENTS OF CRITICISM.
V.M. BEVILACQUA, 480(P&R):WINTER71-55
"HOME COMFORT."
R. TODD, 61:APR73-115
442(NY):10MAR73-134
HOMER. THE ILIAD OF HOMER.* THE ODYSSEY OF HOMER.* (BOTH TRANS BY A. POPE & ED BY M. MACK)
I. SIMON, 179(ES):DEC71-557
HOMER, W.I., WITH V. ORGAN. ROBERT HENRI AND HIS CIRCLE.*
N.A. GESKE, 54:DEC71-549
"THE HOMERIC HYMNS."* (C. BOER, TRANS)
A. ALLEN, 124:NOV71-95
D.S. CARNE-ROSS, 5:WINTER70-421
HOMEYER, H. - SEE HROTSVITHA OF GANDER-SHEIM
HOMMEL, R.P. CHINA AT WORK.
R.H. MYERS, 293(JAST):NOV70-186
HONDERICH, T., ED. ESSAYS ON FREEDOM OF ACTION.
617(TLS):1JUN73-612
HONDERICH, T. PUNISHMENT.*
P.S. ÅRDAL, 154:DEC70-468
J. GLOVER, 262:AUTUMN71-347
HONEYCOMBE, G. DRAGON UNDER THE HILL.*
M. LEVIN, 441:30SEP73-20
HONOUR, H. CABINET MAKERS AND FURNITURE DESIGNERS.
R. EDWARDS, 39:OCT70-318
N. GOODISON, 90:JAN71-52

HONOUR, H. NEO-CLASSICISM.*
   T. PELZEL, 56:WINTER70-443
   P. WALCH, 54:JUN70-216
HONOUR, H. & J. FLEMING - SEE SAXL, F.
HONRI, P. WORKING THE HALLS.
   617(TLS):2NOV73-1352
HOOD, H. AROUND THE MOUNTAIN.
   A. ROBERTSON, 648:JUN71-52
HOOD, H. THE FRUIT MAN, THE MEATMAN &
  THE MANAGER.*
   A. ROBERTSON, 648:APR72-18
   D. STEPHENS, 102(CANL):AUTUMN72-84
HOOD, H. THE GOVERNOR'S BRIDGE IS CLOSED.
   I.M.O., 606(TAMR):#61-75
HOOD, H. YOU CAN'T GET THERE FROM HERE.
   617(TLS):30MAR73-340
HOOD, M. THE ETHNOMUSICOLOGIST.
   A. BOYD, 415:SEP72-863
HOOD, T. SELECTED POEMS OF THOMAS HOOD.
  (J. CLUBBE, ED)
   J.R. CURTIS, 50(ARQ):AUTUMN71-285
   J.E.J., 191(ELN):SEP71(SUPP)-45
VAN HOOF, H. DE VERTAALMARKT IN BELGIË -
  LE MARCHÉ DE LA TRADUCTION EN BELGIQUE.
   R. HAESERYN, 75:3/1971-43
'T HOOFT, W.A.V. MEMOIRS.
   E.B. FISKE, 441:16JUN73-25
HOOGTEYLING, J. TAALKUNDE IN ARTIKELEN.
   J.P. WILLEMS, 556(RLV):1970/3-332
HOOK, J. THE SACK OF ROME, 1527.
   617(TLS):27APR73-468
HOOK, S., ED. LANGUAGE AND PHILOSOPHY.*
   L.J. COHEN, 297(JL):FEB70-134
   G.B. OLIVER, 321:FALL70-235
   205(FMLS):OCT71-413
HOOKER, A.C. LA NOVELA DE FEDERICO GAM-
  BOA.
   D.L. SHAW, 402(MLR):APR72-448
HOOLE, K. FORGOTTEN RAILWAYS: NORTH-EAST
  ENGLAND.
   617(TLS):23MAR73-333
HOOLE, W.S., ED. AND STILL WE CONQUER!
   R. PARTIN, 9(ALAR):APR70-154
HOOPER, J.J. ADVENTURES OF CAPTAIN SIMON
  SUGGS, LATE OF THE TALLAPOOSA VOLUN-
  TEERS. (C.H. HOLMAN & L.D. RUBIN, JR.,
  EDS)
   F.N. BONEY, 219(GAR):SUMMER71-246
HOOPER, W. - SEE LEWIS, C.S.
HOOPES, T. THE DEVIL AND JOHN FOSTER
  DULLES.
   A. KAZIN, 441:9DEC73-6
   C. LEHMANN-HAUPT, 441:19NOV73-39
   442(NY):19NOV73-246
HOOVER, H. THE YEARS OF THE FOREST.
   G. CARSON, 441:20MAY73-51
HOOYKAAS, R. THE PRINCIPLE OF UNIFORMITY
  IN GEOLOGY, BIOLOGY, AND THEOLOGY.
   R.A. WATSON, 486:JUN70-316
HOPE, A.D. DUNCIAD MINOR.*
   K.L. GOODWIN, 381:SEP71-375
   A.J. HASSALL, 566:AUTUMN71-5
   S.E. LEE, 581:1971/3-227
HOPE, A.D. A MIDSUMMER EVE'S DREAM.*
   J. WORDSWORTH, 541(RES):NOV71-475
   205(FMLS):JUL71-296
HOPE, A.D. NEW POEMS: 1965-1969.
   K.L. GOODWIN, 381:SEP71-375
HOPE, D.M. THE LEONINE SACRAMENTARY.
   J.H. CREHAN, 382(MAE):1972/3-241
HOPE, Q.M. SPOKEN FRENCH IN REVIEW.
   B.M. POHORYLES, 207(FR):DEC70-433
HOPE, T.E. LEXICAL BORROWINGS IN THE
  ROMANCE LANGUAGES.
   T.G. GRIFFITH, 208(FS):APR72-234
   A.C. KEYS, 67:NOV72-272

HOPKINS, A. TALKING ABOUT SONATAS.*
   K. SPENCE, 415:JUN72-567
HOPKINS, A.G. AN ECONOMIC HISTORY OF WEST
  AFRICA.
   617(TLS):30NOV73-1479
HOPKINS, B. - SEE WÖRNER, K.H.
HOPKINS, E.J. & E.F. RIMBAULT. THE ORGAN.
   617(TLS):4MAY73-509
HOPKINS, G.M. THE POEMS OF GERARD MANLEY
  HOPKINS. (4TH ED) (W.H. GARDNER & N.H.
  MAC KENZIE, EDS)
   G. KLÖHN, 38:BAND89HEFT2-271
HOPKINS, J. A COMPANION TO THE STUDY OF
  ST. ANSELM.
   617(TLS):5OCT73-1196
HOPKINS, R. THE RAID ON THE VILLA JOY-
  OSA.
   N. CALLENDAR, 441:1JUL73-21
HOPKINS, R.H. THE TRUE GENIUS OF OLIVER
  GOLDSMITH.*
   J. PRESTON, 541(RES):MAY71-216
HOPKINSON, J. MEMOIRS OF A VICTORIAN
  CABINET MAKER.
   A.C. PERCIVAL, 203:AUTUMN70-236
HOPKINSON, T., ED. PICTURE POST 1938-
  1950.
   S. HALL, 111:19FEB71-140
   571:SPRING71-146
HOPPE, A. MISS LOLLIPOP AND THE DOOM
  MACHINE.
   M. LEVIN, 441:7OCT73-47
HOPPE, H. KANTS THEORIE DER PHYSIK.*
   A. HÄUSSLING, 342:BAND61HEFT2-271
HOPPE, K. WILHELM RAABE.
   W.P. HANSON, 220(GL&L):OCT71-75
HOPPEN, K.T. THE COMMON SCIENTIST IN THE
  SEVENTEENTH CENTURY.*
   J.M.P., 568(SCN):SUMMER72-44
"HORA DE ESPAÑA." (VOLS 1-5)
   617(TLS):28SEP73-1134
HORACE - SEE UNDER CATULLUS & HORACE
HORACE & PERSIUS. THE SATIRES OF HORACE
  AND PERSIUS. (N. RUDD, ED & TRANS)
   617(TLS):7DEC73-1521
HORACEK, B. KUNSTPRINZIPIEN DER SATZ-
  UND VERSGESTALTUNG.
   K-E. GEITH, 657(WW):SEP/OCT70-358
   O. LUDWIG, 343:BAND13HEFT1-84
HORAN, W.D. - SEE CALVO, B.
HORGAN, P. APPROACHES TO WRITING.
   442(NY):17SEP73-155
HORGAN, P. ENCOUNTERS WITH STRAVINSKY.*
   R. EVETT, 61:JAN73-91
   L.C. MILAZZO, 584(SWR):SUMMER72-258
HORGAN, P. WHITEWATER.*
   M. WESTBROOK, 649(WAL):WINTER71-306
   639(VQR):WINTER71-IX
"THE HORIZON BOOK OF THE ARTS OF RUSSIA."
   D. VON MOHRENSCHILDT, 550(RUSR):APR
   71-205
HORL, S. LEIDENSCHAFTEN UND AFFEKTE IM
  DRAMATISCHEN WERK TIRSO DE MOLINAS.
   A.L. MACKENZIE, 86(BHS):JAN72-76
HÖRMANN, H. PSYCHOLINGUISTICS.
   H.D. BROWN, 351(LL):DEC71-253
HÖRMANN, H. PSYCHOLOGIE DER SPRACHE.
   B. FECHNER-GUTJAHR, 682(ZPSK):BAND23
   HEFT6-625
HORN, A. KUNST UND FREIHEIT.
   J.T. GOLDTHWAIT, 290(JAAC):SUMMER71-
   538
HORN, D., ED. THE LITERATURE OF AMERICAN
  MUSIC.
   617(TLS):7SEP73-1024
HORN, D. MUTINY ON THE HIGH SEAS.
   617(TLS):5OCT73-1195

HORNBACK, B.G. THE METAPHOR OF CHANCE.
D. EDWARDS, 177(ELT):VOL14#4-257
R. LEHAN, 445(NCF):DEC71-369
HORNBACK, B.G. "NOAH'S ARKITECTURE."
617(TLS):27APR73-478
HORNE, A. SMALL EARTHQUAKE IN CHILE.*
N. GALL, 441:1JUL73-6
HORNE, D. THE AUSTRALIAN PEOPLE.
617(TLS):6JUL73-789
HORNE, D. THE NEXT AUSTRALIA.
D. AITKIN, 381:MAR71-118
J.H. DAVIDSON, 381:DEC71-440
HORNER, A.M. MOVEMENT, VOICE AND SPEECH.
C. LAMBERT, 157:SUMMER70-73
HORNSBY, A., JR., ED. IN THE CAGE.
639(VQR):SUMMER71-CXXXIII
HORNSBY, R.A. PATTERNS OF ACTION IN THE
"AENEID."*
J.P. BEWS, 487:WINTER71-407
F.A. SULLIVAN, 122:JUL72-209
G.W. WILLIAMS, 123:JUN72-276
HORNSCHUCH, J. HORNSCHUCH'S "ORTHOTYPO-
GRAPHIA." (P. GASKELL & P. BRADFORD,
EDS & TRANS)
617(TLS):26JAN73-100
HORNSEY, A.W. - SEE MANN, T.
HOROSZ, W. THE PROMISE AND PERIL OF
HUMAN PURPOSE.
J.G. GILL, 480(P&R):SUMMER71-182
HOROVITZ, I. CAPPELLA.
D.K. MANO, 441:25FEB73-2
HOROWITZ, I.L., ED. MASSES IN LATIN
AMERICA.
R.V. KEMPER, 263:JAN-MAR72-64
HORRUT, C. FRÉDÉRIC LUGARD ET LA PENSÉE
COLONIALE BRITANNIQUE DE SON TEMPS.
H. DESCHAMPS, 69:OCT71-339
HORSLEY, P.M. EIGHTEENTH-CENTURY NEW-
CASTLE.
M.R., 135:JUN71-150
HORST, U. UMSTRITTENE FRAGEN DER EKKLE-
SIOLOGIE.
J-D. BURGER, 182:VOL24#11/12-458
HORSTMANN, R-P. & J.H. TREDE - SEE HEGEL,
G.W.F.
HORTON, C. CLEANING AND PRESERVING BIND-
INGS AND RELATED MATERIALS.
G.W., 503:SUMMER68-81
HORTON, E. THE AGE OF THE AIRSHIP.
617(TLS):24AUG73-986
HORTON, J. MENDELSSOHN CHAMBER MUSIC.*
H. KELLER, 415:SEP72-868
HORTON, R. & R. FINNEGAN, EDS. MODES OF
THOUGHT.
617(TLS):14SEP73-1044
HORVAT-PINTARIĆ, V. VJENCESLAV RICHTER.
J. BENTHALL, 592:MAR71-136
HORVATH, V.M. ANDRÉ MALRAUX.*
P-A. FORTIER, 188(ECR):WINTER70-345
N.L. GOODRICH, 549(RLC):JAN-MAR71-136
E. MOROT-SIR, 50(ARQ):SPRING71-87
HORWITZ, H. - SEE LUTTRELL, N.
HORWITZ, J. THE MARRIED LOVERS.
A. BROYARD, 441:24SEP73-31
J.R. FRAKES, 441:16SEP73-4
442(NY):27AUG73-90
HORWOOD, H. WHITE ESKIMO.*
B. GODARD, 296:WINTER73-98
HOSHI AYAO. THE MING TRIBUTE GRAIN SYS-
TEM.
R. HUANG, 293(JAST):NOV70-176
HOSKING, E. & J. GOODERS. WILDLIFE
PHOTOGRAPHY.
617(TLS):23NOV73-1456
HOSKING, G.A. THE RUSSIAN CONSTITUTIONAL
EXPERIMENT.
617(TLS):3AUG73-910

HOSKINS, P. THE SOUND OF MURDER.
617(TLS):31AUG73-1009
HOSKINS, W.G. ENGLISH LANDSCAPES.
617(TLS):12OCT73-1260
HOSKINS, W.G. LEICESTERSHIRE.
S.T. SCOTT, 46:OCT70-266
HÖSLE, J. PIETRO ARETINOS WERK.
W. DROST, 52:BAND5HEFT3-317
R.F. ROEMING, 399(MLJ):MAY71-333
HÖSLE, J., ED. TEXTE ZUM ANTIPETRARKIS-
MUS.
L. FORSTER, 208(FS):APR72-190
HOSLEY, R., A. KIRSCH & J.W. VELZ - SEE
MC MANAWAY, J.G.
HOTHAM, D. THE TURKS.
617(TLS):19JAN73-60
HOTZ, K. BEDEUTUNG UND FUNKTION DES
RAUMES IM WERK WILHELM RAABES.
L.H.C. THOMAS, 402(MLR):OCT72-947
HOTZENKÖCHERLE, R., ED. SPRACHATLAS DER
DEUTSCHEN SCHWEIZ.* (VOL 4)
H. KURATH, 350:MAR72-195
HOU LI-CH'AO. HSIEN-TAI CHUNG-KUO SHIH
TE CHEN-HSIANG.
L.H-D. GORDON & S. CHANG, 293(JAST):
NOV70-137
HOUGH, J., JR. A TWO-CAR FUNERAL.
N. CALLENDAR, 441:23SEP73-48
442(NY):29OCT73-180
HOUGH, J.F. THE SOVIET PREFECTS.*
H.W. MORTON, 550(RUSR):APR71-207
HOUGH, R. ADMIRAL OF THE FLEET.
C.J. BARTLETT, 637(VS):MAR71-347
HOUGH, R. CAPTAIN BLIGH AND MR. CHRIS-
TIAN.
A. VILLIERS, 441:23SEP73-26
442(NY):10FEB73-115
617(TLS):26JAN73-101
HOUGHTON, R. TALES FROM ETERNITY.
617(TLS):15JUN73-663
HOUGHTON, R.E.C. - SEE SHAKESPEARE, W.
HOUGHTON, W.E., ED. THE WELLESLEY INDEX
TO VICTORIAN PERIODICALS 1824-1900.
(VOL 2)
617(TLS):9FEB73-160
HOUPPERT, J.W. - SEE LODGE, T.
HOURANI, G.F. ISLAMIC RATIONALISM.
R.J. MC CARTHY, 382(MAE):1972/3-249
HOUSE, M. & G. STOREY - SEE DICKENS, C.
HOUSEHOLD, G. THE LIVES AND TIMES OF
BERNARDO BROWN.
V. CUNNINGHAM, 362:6DEC73-793
617(TLS):14DEC73-1547
HOUSEHOLDER, F. & S. SAPORTA, EDS. PROB-
LEMS IN LEXICOGRAPHY.
A. REY, 98:FEB70-163
HOUSEHOLDER, F.W., JR., WITH M. LOTFI.
BASIC COURSE IN AZERBAIJANI.
L. HŘEBÍČEK, 353:APR71-114
HOUSEMAN, J. RUN-THROUGH.*
D. AARON, 473(PR):FALL72-615
617(TLS):2MAR73-228
HOUSEPIAN, M. SMYRNA 1922.
617(TLS):12JAN73-32
HOUSMAN, A.E. THE CLASSICAL PAPERS OF
A.E. HOUSMAN. (J. DIGGLE & F.R.D.
GOODYEAR, EDS)
617(TLS):9FEB73-137
HOUSMAN, A.E. THE LETTERS OF A.E. HOUS-
MAN.* (H. MAAS, ED)
B.P. REARDON, 124:JAN72-168
676(YR):SPRING72-IX
HOUSMAN, A.E. - SEE MANILIUS, M.
HOUSTON, J. THE WHITE DAWN.
H.P. GUNDY, 529(QQ):WINTER71-640
HOUSTON, J.P. THE DEMONIC IMAGINATION.*
C.C., 191(ELN):SEP71(SUPP)-69

HOUSTON, J.W. & J.D.  FAREWELL TO MAN-
ZANAR.
442(NY):5NOV73-186
HOUSTON, L.  PLAIN CLOTHES.
A. CLUYSENAAR, 565:VOL12#4-68
HOVANNISIAN, R.G.  THE REPUBLIC OF ARMEN-
IA. (VOL 1)
M.K. MATOSSIAN, 32:SEP72-731
HOWAR, B.  LAUGHING ALL THE WAY.
C. CURTIS, 441:20MAY73-4
442(NY):16JUL73-80
HOWARD, B.  THE MANIPULATOR.
K. THOMPSON, 198:SPRING73-112
E. ZIMMER, 296:SPRING73-91
HOWARD, C.  THE KILLINGS.
N. CALLENDAR, 441:7OCT73-44
HOWARD, D.  THE DEVELOPMENT OF THE MARX-
IAN DIALECTIC.
617(TLS):9FEB73-142
HOWARD, D.  LONDON THEATRES AND MUSIC
HALLS, 1850-1950.
W. KENDALL, 157:SPRING70-67
HOWARD, F.  CHARLIE FLOWERS AND THE
MELODY GARDENS.
M. LEVIN, 441:28JAN73-34
HOWARD, J.  A DIFFERENT WOMAN.
C. LEHMANN-HAUPT, 441:6NOV73-31
J. WILSON, 441:18NOV73-6
442(NY):10DEC73-198
HOWARD, M.  STUDIES IN WAR AND PEACE.
L. CLARK, 619(TC):VOL179#1046-54
HOWARD, M.W.  THE INFLUENCE OF PLUTARCH
IN THE MAJOR EUROPEAN LITERATURES OF
THE EIGHTEENTH CENTURY.
O.F. SIGWORTH, 50(ARQ):WINTER71-374
HOWARD, R.  ALONE WITH AMERICA.*
L.T. LEMON, 502(PRS):SPRING71-89
HOWARD, R.  FINDINGS.*
L. LIEBERMAN, 676(YR):AUTUMN71-82
639(VQR):AUTUMN71-CLXIV
HOWARD, R.  UNTITLED SUBJECTS.*
R. LANGBAUM, 636(VP):WINTER71-467
HOWARD-HILL, T.H., ED.  OXFORD SHAKESPEARE
CONCORDANCES. (ALL 37 VOLS)
D.F. MC KENZIE, 67:NOV72-277
HOWARD-HILL, T.H., ED.  OXFORD SHAKESPEARE
CONCORDANCES: ALL'S WELL THAT ENDS WELL;
AS YOU LIKE IT; THE MERCHANT OF VENICE;
THE TAMING OF THE SHREW; TWELFTH NIGHT;
THE WINTER'S TALE.
C. SPENCER, 570(SQ):AUTUMN70-501
HOWARD-HILL, T.H., ED.  OXFORD SHAKESPEARE
CONCORDANCES: CYMBELINE [AND] HAMLET.
617(TLS):21SEP73-1090
HOWARD-HILL, T.H., ED.  OXFORD SHAKESPEARE
CONCORDANCES: THE TEMPEST;* TWO GENTLE-
MEN OF VERONA;* THE MERRY WIVES OF WIND-
SOR; MEASURE FOR MEASURE; THE COMEDY OF
ERRORS.
G.W. WILLIAMS, 551(RENQ):SPRING71-90
HOWARD-JOHNSTON, X. & M. BOURDEAUX, EDS.
AIDA OF LENINGRAD.
617(TLS):2MAR73-234
HOWARTH, H.  THE TIGER'S HEART.
S.R. MAVEETY, 648:JAN72-72
D.J. PALMER, 541(RES):NOV71-480
HOWARTH, P.  PLAY UP AND PLAY THE GAME.
617(TLS):24AUG73-972
HOWARTH, T.G.  COLOUR IDENTIFICATION
GUIDE TO BRITISH BUTTERFLIES.
617(TLS):3AUG73-913
HOWARTH, T.G.  SOUTH'S BRITISH BUTTER-
FLIES.
617(TLS):4MAY73-509
HOWARTH, W.L., ED.  TWENTIETH CENTURY
INTERPRETATIONS OF POE'S TALES.
J. PINKERTON, 573(SSF):FALL71-641
639(VQR):SUMMER71-CXI

HOWARTH, W.L. - SEE STOWELL, R.F.
HOWATCH, S.  CALL IN THE NIGHT.
N. CALLENDAR, 441:30SEP73-18
HOWE, C.  WAGE PATTERNS AND WAGE POLICY
IN MODERN CHINA, 1919-1972.
617(TLS):13JUL73-810
HOWE, D.W.  THE UNITARIAN CONSCIENCE.
B. CLAYTON, 432(NEQ):JUN71-341
HOWE, E. - SEE SMITH, C.M.
HOWE, G.M.  MAN, ENVIRONMENT AND DISEASE
IN BRITAIN.
617(TLS):12JAN73-46
HOWE, I.  THE CRITICAL POINT.
A. BROYARD, 441:20NOV73-43
HOWE, I.  DECLINE OF THE NEW.*
P. PARRINDER, 111:7MAY71-163
HOWE, I.  STEADY WORK.
J.L. SHOVER, 186(ETC.):SEP71-367
HOWE, I. & E. GREENBERG, EDS.  A TREASURY
OF YIDDISH POETRY.
S. BERCOVITCH, 328:SPRING71-236
V. YOUNG, 249(HUDR):WINTER72/73-661
HOWELL, A.  IMRUIL.*
A. CLUYSENAAR, 565:VOL12#3-72
HOWELL, B.  THE RED FOX.
A. PURDY, 102(CANL):AUTUMN72-86
HOWELL, J.T.  HARD LIVING ON CLAY STREET.
G. BURNSIDE, 441:30SEP73-6
HOWELLS, W.D.  A CHANCE ACQUAINTANCE.*
(J. THOMAS & D.J. NORDLOH, EDS)  THE
RISE OF SILAS LAPHAM.* (W.J. MESERVE,
ED)
C.L. ANDERSON, 579(SAQ):SUMMER72-445
T. WORTHAM, 445(NCF):SEP71-234
HOWELLS, W.D.  W.D. HOWELLS AS CRITIC.
(E.H. CADY, ED)
617(TLS):21DEC73-1555
HOWELLS, W.D.  THEIR WEDDING JOURNEY.*
(J.K. REEVES, ED)  LITERARY FRIENDS AND
ACQUAINTANCE. (D.F. HIATT & E.H. CADY,
EDS)  THE ALTRURIAN ROMANCES. (C. & R.
KIRK, EDS)  THE SON OF ROYAL LANG-
BRITH.* (D. BURROWS, WITH R. GOTTESMAN
& D.J. NORDLOH, EDS)  THE SHADOW OF A
DREAM [AND] AN IMPERATIVE DUTY.* (M.
BANTA, WITH R. GOTTESMAN & D.J. NORD-
LOH, EDS)
T. WORTHAM, 445(NCF):SEP71-234
HOWES, B.  THE BLUE GARDEN.
R.B. SHAW, 491:SEP73-344
HOWES, R.C., ED & TRANS.  THE TESTAMENTS
OF THE GRAND PRINCES OF MOSCOW.*
J. PELENSKI, 32:DEC72-878
HOWIE, G. - SEE ST. AUGUSTINE
HOWSON, G.  THE MACARONI PARSON.
617(TLS):21SEP73-1085
HOWSON, G.  THIEF-TAKER GENERAL.*
639(VQR):AUTUMN71-CLXXVI
HOYER, L.G.  ENCHANTMENT.*
P.M. SPACKS, 249(HUDR):SPRING72-166
HOYLE, F.  NICOLAUS COPERNICUS.
617(TLS):29JUN73-744
HOYLES, J.  THE WANING OF THE RENAIS-
SANCE, 1640-1740.*
L. DOBREZ, 67:MAY72-81
"HRAFNKEL'S SAGA AND OTHER ICELANDIC
STORIES." (H. PÁLSSON, TRANS)
W.F. BOLTON, 563(SS):WINTER72-131
HROCH, M.  DIE VORKÄMPFER DER NATIONALEN
BEWEGUNG BEI DEN KLEINEN VÖLKERN EURO-
PAS.
S.B. KIMBALL, 32:JUN72-478
HROTSVITHA OF GANDERSHEIM.  HROTSVITHAE
OPERA.* (H. HOMEYER, ED)
R. DÜCHTING, 190:BAND65HEFT4-433
"HRVATSKI KNJIŽEVNI JEZIK I PITANJE
VARIJANATA."
L. MATEJKA, 32:JUN72-494

170

HUGHES, J.B. ARTE Y SENTIDO DE "MARTÍN
FIERRO."
P.R. BEARDSELL, 402(MLR):JAN72-201
J. HIGGINS, 86(BHS):JAN72-103
HUGHES, J.Q. LIVERPOOL.
T. WRIGHT, 46:FEB70-166
HUGHES, L. THE DRAMA'S PATRONS.
566:SPRING72-94
HUGHES, P. SHELL GUIDE TO KENT.
46:AUG70-131
HUGHES, R. THE WOODEN SHEPHERDESS.
E. JANEWAY, 441:19AUG73-1
R. JELLINEK, 441:31AUG73-23
D. MAY, 362:5APR73-451
617(TLS):6APR73-369
HUGHES, S. THE TOSCANINI LEGACY.
M. PETERSON, 470:MAY71-35
HUGHES, T. CROW.*
A. CLUYSENAAR, 565:VOL12#2-63
J.M. NEWTON, 97(CQ):SUMMER/AUTUMN71-
376
M.G. PERLOFF, 659:WINTER73-97
R.S., 376:APR71-128
H. SERGEANT, 175:SUMMER71-65
HUGO, R. THE LADY IN KICKING HORSE
RESERVOIR.
S. FRIEDMAN, 398:WINTER73-344
HUGO, R.F. GOOD LUCK IN CRACKED ITALIAN.*
J.D. REED, 600:WINTER71-154
HUGO, V. LES CONTEMPLATIONS. (L.
CELLIER, ED)
E. BARINEAU, 405(MP):NOV71-184
M. SCHAETTEL, 557(RSH):APR-JUN70-327
HUGO, V. DIEU (FRAGMENTS). (R. JOURNET
& G. ROBERT, EDS)
J. SEEBACHER, 208(FS):APR72-213
HUGO, V. L'ANE. (P. ALBOUY, ED)
A. UBERSFELD, 535(RHL):SEP-DEC70-1086
HUGO, V. MANGERONT-ILS? (R. JOURNET &
G. ROBERT, EDS)
J. SEEBACHER, 208(FS):JUL72-337
HUGO, V. LES ORIENTALES. (É. BARINEAU,
ED)
C. AFFRON, 207(FR):DEC70-453
HUISMAN, P. FRENCH WATERCOLOURS OF THE
18TH CENTURY.
D.T., 135:FEB70-125
HUIZER, G. PEASANT REBELLION IN LATIN
AMERICA.
617(TLS):1JUN73-606
HULL, D.L. DARWIN AND HIS CRITICS.
P.B. MEDAWAR, 453:15NOV73-12
617(TLS):9NOV73-1360
HULL, D.S. FILM IN THE THIRD REICH.
E.H. NASH, 200:MAY70-291
HULSKER, J. - SEE VAN GOGH, V.
HULTBERG, H. HEINE.
B. PEDERSEN, 462(OL):VOL26#2-165
J.L.S., 191(ELN):SEP71(SUPP)-132
HULTBERG, P. STYL WCZESNEJ PROZY FABU-
LARNEJ WACŁAWA BERENTA.
J. BAER, 497(POLR):AUTUMN70-112
HULTÉN, K.G.P. THE MACHINE AS SEEN AT
THE END OF THE MECHANICAL AGE.
W.A. CAMFIELD, 54:JUN71-275
"THE HUMAN AGENT."*
K. LEHRER, 482(PHR):JAN71-100
"HUMANIZM SOCJALISTYCZNY."
A. GELLA, 32:DEC72-920
DE HUMBOLDT, G. DE L'ORIGINE DES FORMES
GRAMMATICALES, SUIVI DE LETTRE À M.
ABEL RÉMUSAT.*
J. BERNHARDT, 542:APR-JUN70-264
VON HUMBOLDT, W. THE LIMITS OF STATE
ACTION. (J.W. BURROW, ED)
W.H. BRUFORD, 220(GL&L):JUL72-406
W. CHRISTIAN, 173(ECS):SUMMER71-481

HUME, I.N. GLASS IN COLONIAL WILLIAMS-
BURG'S ARCHAEOLOGICAL COLLECTIONS.
R.J.C., 135:JUN71-151
HUME, R.D. DRYDEN'S CRITICISM.*
E.D. CUFFE, 613:WINTER71-612
P. HARTH, 481(PQ):JUL71-427
E. MINER, 401(MLQ):DEC71-439
A. ROPER, 301(JEGP):JUL72-448
"DORIS HUMPHREY: AN ARTIST FIRST."*
(ED & COMPLETED BY S.J. COHEN)
D. JOWITT, 441:18FEB73-24
HUMPHREY, G.R. L'ESTHÉTIQUE DE LA
POÉSIE DE GÉRARD DE NERVAL.
A.E. CARTER, 207(FR):FEB71-616
HUMPHREY, W. PROUD FLESH.
R.P. BRICKNER, 441:29APR73-26
C. LEHMANN-HAUPT, 441:4APR73-47
617(TLS):3AUG73-893
HUMPHREYS, A.R. - SEE SHAKESPEARE, W.
HUMPHREYS, W.C. ANOMALIES AND SCIENTIFIC
THEORIES.
M. RUSE, 486:DEC71-614
HUMPHRIES, S.V. THE LIFE OF HAMILTON
BAILEY.
617(TLS):23NOV73-1456
HUNN, D. EPSOM RACECOURSE.
617(TLS):23NOV73-1425
HUNNIUS, G., G.D. GARSON & J. CASE, EDS.
WORKERS' CONTROL.
B. RAMIREZ, 99:SEP73-37
HUNOLD, C.F. DIE LIEBENSWÜRDIGE ADALIE.
A. MENHENNET, 220(GL&L):OCT71-32
HUNT, E.H. REGIONAL WAGE VARIATIONS IN
BRITAIN 1850-1914.
617(TLS):2NOV73-1350
HUNT, E.H., JR. THE BERLIN ENDING.
N. CALLENDAR, 441:26AUG73-32
G. VIDAL, 453:13DEC73-6
HUNT, E.H., JR. EAST OF FAREWELL. LIMIT
OF DARKNESS. STRANGER IN TOWN. MAEL-
STROM. BIMINI RUN.
G. VIDAL, 453:13DEC73-6
HUNT, E.H., JR. GIVE US THIS DAY.
T. HIGGINS, 441:30SEP73-7
G. VIDAL, 453:13DEC73-6
HUNT, G., COMP. PENNYWORTHS.
617(TLS):1JUN73-624
HUNT, H. - SEE UNDER HUNT, E.H., JR.
HUNT, J.D. THE PRE-RAPHAELITE IMAGINA-
TION, 1848-1900.*
J-J. MAYOUX, 98:MAR70-210
W.D. SCHAEFER, 636(VP):SPRING70-67
HUNT, M. THE MUGGING.*
617(TLS):16FEB73-173
HUNT, S. FROM BOTTLE CREEK.
B. MANHIRE, 368:MAR70-88
HUNTER, A.C. LEXIQUE DE LA LANGUE DE
JEAN CHAPELAIN.*
B. BRAY, 535(RHL):MAY-JUN70-510
HUNTER, E. CHRISTABEL.
617(TLS):12OCT73-1251
HUNTER, E. COME WINTER.
617(TLS):13JUL73-797
HUNTER, G. THE ADMINISTRATION OF AGRI-
CULTURAL DEVELOPMENT.
U.J. LELE, 293(JAST):AUG71-909
HUNTER, G. METALOGIC.
H.A. LEWIS, 518:JAN72-12
HUNTER, G.K. - SEE WILSON, F.P.
HUNTER, G.K. & S.K. - SEE "JOHN WEBSTER"
HUNTER, J. KINSHIP.
V. CUNNINGHAM, 362:26JUL73-125
617(TLS):28SEP73-1100
HUNTER, J., ED. THE MODERN NOVEL IN
ENGLISH (STUDIES IN EXTRACTS).
W. STUCK, 430(NS):JAN71-51
HUNTER, J.P. - SEE DEFOE, D.

HUNTER, R. & I. MACALPINE - SEE CONOLLY, J.

HUNTER, R.G. SHAKESPEARE AND THE COMEDY OF FORGIVENESS.*
   J.B. FORT, 189(EA):JUL-SEP70-337

HUNTER, S. AMERICAN ART OF THE 20TH CENTURY.
   441:2SEP73-10
   617(TLS):9NOV73-1362

HUNTER, S. LARRY RIVERS.
   T. HILTON, 592:JUL/AUG71-42

HUNTER, W.B., C.A. PATRIDES & J.H. ADAMSON. BRIGHT ESSENCE.*
   S. MUSGROVE, 67:MAY72-85

HUNTER BLAIR, P. THE WORLD OF BEDE.
   W.H.C. FREND, 123:JUN72-286
   C.W. JONES, 589:APR72-285

HUNTLEY, H.R. THE ALIEN PROTAGONIST OF FORD MADOX FORD.*
   R.W. LID, 639(VQR):SPRING71-317
   A. MIZENER, 454:FALL71-79

HUNVALD, H. THE MASTERPIECE OF NICE MR. BREEN.
   N. CALLENDAR, 441:14JAN73-30

HUPPÉ, B.F. THE WEB OF WORDS.*
   J.E. CROSS, 382(MAE):1972/1-47
   E.G. SCHREIBER, 301(JEGP):JAN72-106

HUPPERT, G. THE IDEA OF PERFECT HISTORY.
   W.J. BAKER, 577(SHR):FALL71-411
   639(VQR):WINTER71-XXXIX

HURLEY, N.P. THEOLOGY THROUGH FILM.
   J.F. KELLY, 613:AUTUMN71-455

HURNARD, N.D. THE KING'S PARDON FOR HOMOCIDE BEFORE A.D. 1307.
   T.A. GREEN, 589:OCT72-774

HURNE, R. THE YELLOW JERSEY.
   M. LEVIN, 441:27MAY73-19

HURST, M. MARIA EDGEWORTH AND THE PUBLIC SCENE.
   J. ESPEY, 445(NCF):JUN70-121
   R. LAWRENCE, 175:SPRING70-33
   A.T. MC KENZIE, 594:FALL70-373

HURST, M. PARNELL AND IRISH NATIONALITY.
   F.S.L. LYONS, 637(VS):SEP70-114

HURSTFIELD, J. FREEDOM, CORRUPTION AND GOVERNMENT IN ELIZABETHAN ENGLAND.
   617(TLS):5OCT73-1171

HURSTFIELD, J., ED. THE TUDORS.
   617(TLS):10AUG73-927

HURT, J. CATILINE'S DREAM.
   R. STODDARD, 70(ANQ):JAN73-77

HUS, J. THE LETTERS OF JOHN HUS. (M. SPINKA, TRANS)
   617(TLS):2FEB73-127

HUSA, V., J. PETRÁN & A. SUBRTOVÁ. TRADITIONAL CRAFTS AND SKILLS.
   C.H. CLOUGH, 39:FEB70-167
   J.F.M., 135:MAY70-50

HUSÁK, G. PROJEVY A STATI. VYBRANÉ PROJEVY.
   617(TLS):4MAY73-492

HUSS, R.E. THE DEVELOPMENT OF PRINTERS' MECHANICAL TYPESETTING METHODS 1822-1925.
   617(TLS):7DEC73-1519

HUSSELMAN, E.M., ED. PAPYRI FROM KARANIS. (3RD SER)
   F.T. GIGNAC, 124:NOV71-102

HUSSERL, E. BRIEFE AN ROMAN INGARDEN. (R. INGARDEN, ED)
   S.L. HART, 484(PPR):SEP70-145

HUSSERL, E. THE CRISIS OF EUROPEAN SCIENCES AND TRANSCENDENTAL PHENOMENOLOGY. (D. CARR, ED & TRANS)
   185:OCT70-86

HUSSERL, E. FORMAL AND TRANSCENDENTAL LOGIC.
   A.W. WOOD, 482(PHR):APR71-267

HUSSERL, E. LOGICAL INVESTIGATIONS.*
   W. MAYS, 111:13NOV70-58
   W. MAYS, 483:JUL71-262
   E. PIVČEVIĆ, 393(MIND):JUL71-462
   R. SOKOLOWSKI, 262:AUTUMN71-318

HUSSERL, G. PERSON, SACHE, VERHALTEN.
   S.L. HART, 484(PPR):DEC70-314

HUSSEY, C. ENGLISH GARDENS AND LANDSCAPES 1700-1750.*
   M.D. ROSS, 576:MAR70-67
   A.J. SAMBROOK, 173(ECS):FALL70-100

HUSSEY, E. THE PRESOCRATICS.
   617(TLS):9FEB73-157

HUSSEY, M., A.C. SPEARING & J. WINNY. AN INTRODUCTION TO CHAUCER.
   L. MATEOS, 202(FMOD):FEB70-225

HUSSEY, S.S., ED. "PIERS PLOWMAN:" CRITICAL APPROACHES.*
   R.M. WILSON, 175:SPRING71-22
   A.D. WOOD, 541(RES):MAY71-182

HUSSON, G. - SEE LUCIAN

HUSTON, F. THE RICH GET IT ALL.
   N. CALLENDAR, 441:5AUG73-10

HUTCHENS, J.K. & G. OPPENHEIMER, EDS. THE BEST IN THE WORLD.
   A. WHITMAN, 441:8DEC73-39

HUTCHINGS, A. (4TH ED)
   617(TLS):9MAR73-277

HUTCHINGS, P.A. KANT ON ABSOLUTE VALUE.
   617(TLS):4MAY73-502

HUTCHINGS, R. SEASONAL INFLUENCES IN SOVIET INDUSTRY.
   D. GRANICK, 32:JUN72-443
   A. MC AULEY, 575(SEER):OCT72-631
   617(TLS):16FEB73-174

HUTCHINGS, R. SOVIET ECONOMIC DEVELOPMENT.
   R.W. CAMPBELL, 32:MAR72-186
   J.S. PRYBYLA, 550(RUSR):OCT71-412
   617(TLS):2FEB73-116

HUTCHINSON, P. WATCHING THE MORNING GROW.
   617(TLS):27JUL73-864

HUTCHISON, T.W. & OTHERS, EDS. AFRICA AND LAW.
   N. RUBIN, 69:OCT70-382

HUTH, A. VIRGINIA FLY IS DROWNING.*
   C. SEEBOHM, 441:27MAY73-19
   442(NY):9JUN73-114

HUTH, H. LACQUER IN THE WEST.
   E.T. JOY, 135:SEP71-62

HUTT, A. THE CHANGING NEWSPAPER.
   617(TLS):26OCT73-1322

HUTTER, I. EARLY CHRISTIAN AND BYZANTINE ART.*
   R. LEBOWITZ, 58:MAR72-18

HUWS, D. NOTH.
   617(TLS):11MAY73-516

HUXLEY, A. LETTERS OF ALDOUS HUXLEY. (G. SMITH, ED)
   42(AR):SPRING70-131

HUXLEY, E., COMP. THE KINGSLEYS.
   617(TLS):31AUG73-1005

HUXLEY, G.L. GREEK EPIC POETRY FROM EUMELOS TO PANYASSIS.*
   N. AUSTIN, 121(CJ):APR-MAY72-375
   F.M. COMBELLACK, 122:JUL72-205
   J. RUSSO, 24:OCT72-621

HUXLEY, H.H., ED. COROLLA CAMENAE.*
   I.A.F. BRUCE, 255(HAB):SPRING70-62
   L.R. LIND, 121(CJ):OCT-NOV71-83
   D.F.S. THOMSON, 487:SPRING71-90

HUXLEY, J. MEMORIES II.
   617(TLS):5OCT73-1189

HUYGHE, R., GENERAL ED. LAROUSSE ENCYCLOPEDIA OF BYZANTINE AND MEDIEVAL ART.
   J. BECKWITH, 39:JAN70-84

HUYSSEN, A. DIE FRÜHROMANTISCHE KONZEP-
TION VON ÜBERSETZUNG UND ANEIGNUNG.*
C. KOELB, 405(MP):MAY72-360
H. PAUCKER, 406:SUMMER72-173
HVIŠČ, J. EPICKÉ LITERÁRNE DRUHY V SLOV-
ENSKOM A POL'SKOM ROMANTIZME.
B.R. BRADBROOK, 575(SEER):JUL72-453
HYAM, R. THE FAILURE OF SOUTH AFRICAN
EXPANSION, 1908-1948.
617(TLS):1JUN73-625
HYAMS, E. A DICTIONARY OF MODERN REVO-
LUTION.
617(TLS):23NOV73-1422
HYAMS, E. THE FINAL AGENDA.
V. CUNNINGHAM, 362:30AUG73-288
HYATT, H.M. HOODOO - CONJURATION - WITCH-
CRAFT - ROOTWORK.
J.E. KELLER, 582(SFQ):JUN71-169
HYATT, J. PACIFISM.
617(TLS):16MAR73-288
HYDE, D. A LITERARY HISTORY OF IRELAND.
(NEW ED)
R. FRÉCHET, 189(EA):OCT-DEC70-456
HYDE, F.E. FAR EASTERN TRADE 1860-1914.
617(TLS):11MAY73-533
HYDE, H.M. BALDWIN.
617(TLS):7DEC73-1509
HYDE, H.M. HENRY JAMES AT HOME.*
D.R. BISHOP, 613:SUMMER70-298
HYDE, H.M. STALIN.*
R.H. MC NEAL, 32:DEC72-901
42(AR):WINTER71/72-593
HYDE, J.K. SOCIETY AND POLITICS IN
MEDIEVAL ITALY.
617(TLS):28SEP73-1107
HYDE, M. THE IMPOSSIBLE FRIENDSHIP.
F. STEEGMULLER, 441:15APR73-24
J. WAIN, 453:19JUL73-21
442(NY):5MAY73-150
HYDER, C.K., ED. SWINBURNE: THE CRITICAL
HERITAGE.
J.Y. LE BOURGEOIS, 447(N&Q):NOV71-429
HYLAND, J.S. READING PROFICIENCY IN
FRENCH.
G.R. DANNER, 207(FR):MAY71-1137
HYMAN, H.M. A MORE PERFECT UNION.
441:2SEP73-14
HYMAN, L. THE JEWS OF IRELAND.*
B. BENSTOCK, 329(JJQ):SPRING73-356
HYMES, D., ED. PIDGINISATION AND CREOLI-
SATION OF LANGUAGES.
D.T. TRYON, 67:NOV72-270
HYMES, D.H., WITH W.E. BITTLE, EDS.
STUDIES IN SOUTHWESTERN ETHNOLINGUIS-
TICS.*
M.R. KEY, 353:AUG70-121
HYNES, S. EDWARDIAN OCCASIONS.*
442(NY):20JAN73-104
HYNES, S. THE EDWARDIAN TURN OF MIND.*
R. LAWRENCE, 175:SUMMER70-69
HYNES, S. - SEE CAUDWELL, C.
HYPPOLITE, J. STUDIES ON MARX AND HEGEL.
(J. O'NEILL, ED & TRANS)
H. LAYCOCK, 154:SEP70-248
HYSLOP, L.B., ED. BAUDELAIRE AS A LOVE
POET AND OTHER ESSAYS.*
M. ZIMMERMAN, 546(RR):DEC71-307


IANNI, F.A.J., WITH E. REUSS-IANNI. A
FAMILY BUSINESS.*
617(TLS):26JAN73-91
IANORA, C. SINT STEPHEN CANADA, POLYME-
PHUS' CAVE AND THE BOOBIELAND EXPRESS.
J. MILLS, 648:JAN71-59

IANSEN, S.A.P.J.H. VERKENNINGEN IN
MATTHIJS CASTELEINS CONST VAN RHETORI-
KEN.
C.F.P. STUTTERHEIM, 204(FDL):1971/
3&4-245
IBN KAMMŪNA, S.M. SA'D B. MANŞŪR IBN
KAMMŪNA'S EXAMINATION OF THE INQUIRIES
INTO THE THREE FAITHS. (M. PERLMANN,
ED)
L.V. BERMAN, 318(JAOS):APR-JUN71-333
IBSEN, H. THE OXFORD IBSEN. (VOL 1)
(J.W. MC FARLANE & G. ORTON, EDS &
TRANS)
B.W. DOWNS, 402(MLR):JAN72-235
J. HURT, 160:FALL71-57
W. JOHNSON, 397(MD):DEC71-360
A. RENDLE, 157:SPRING71-77
205(FMLS):JUL71-297
IDUARTE, A. NIÑO, CHILD OF THE MEXICAN
REVOLUTION.
G. DE BEER, 263:OCT-DEC72-411
IGGERS, W.A. KARL KRAUS.
E. HELLER, 453:3MAY73-21
DE LA IGLESIA, M.E. THE CATALOGUE OF
AMERICAN CATALOGUES.
C. LEHMANN-HAUPT, 441:6DEC73-51
IGLESIAS, A. ERCILLA Y LA ARAUCANA.
M.T. RUDD, 37:AUG71-42
IGLESIAS, A.G. - SEE UNDER GÓMEZ IGLESIAS,
A.
SAINT IGNATIUS OF LOYOLA. THE CONSTITU-
TIONS OF THE SOCIETY OF JESUS. (G.E.
GANSS, ED & TRANS)
W.V. BANGERT, 613:AUTUMN71-475
IGNATOW, D. POEMS 1934-1969.*
J.T. IRWIN, 598(SOR):SUMMER73-720
IGOV, S. KOLYO SEVOV.
270:VOL22#3-61
IHIMAERA, W. POUNAMU, POUNAMU.
617(TLS):9FEB73-141
IJSEWIJN, J., ED. HUMANISTICA LOVANIEN-
SIA.* (VOL 17)
G. LUCK, 52:BAND5HEFT3-320
IJSSELING, S. HEIDEGGER, DENKEN ET DAN-
KEN, GEVEN EN ZIJN.
P. SOMVILLE, 542:OCT-DEC71-475
IKELER, A.A. PURITAN TEMPER AND TRANS-
CENDENTAL FAITH.
617(TLS):1JUN73-620
IKLE, F.C. EVERY WAR MUST END.
639(VQR):AUTUMN71-CLXXXVII
ILIE, P., ED. DOCUMENTS OF THE SPANISH
VANGUARD.*
M. DURÁN, 546(RR):APR71-102
R.M. JACKSON, 131(CL):SUMMER72-271
C.B. MORRIS, 402(MLR):APR72-442
ILIE, P. THE SURREALIST MODE IN SPANISH
LITERATURE.*
M.A. CAWS, 188(ECR):SUMMER70-150
J.F. CIRRE, 240(HR):OCT71-456
R.M. JACKSON, 131(CL):SUMMER72-271
ILIFFE, J. TANGANYIKA UNDER GERMAN RULE
1902-1912.
R.G. ABRAHAMS, 69:APR71-169
ILLICH, I.D. DESCHOOLING SOCIETY.*
R. FREEMAN, 111:19NOV71-47
ILLICH, I.D. TOOLS FOR CONVIVIALITY.
S. HAMPSHIRE, 362:22NOV73-711
M.G. MICHAELSON, 441:16SEP73-26
ILTING, K-H. - SEE HEGEL, G.W.F.
IM BANG & YI RYUK. KOREAN FOLK TALES.
(J.S. GALE, TRANS)
G. LEDYARD, 352(LE&W):VOL15#2-324
DE IMAZ, J.L. LOS QUE MANDAN (THOSE WHO
RULE).
R.A. POTASH, 263:JAN-MAR72-62

IMBERT, H-F. LES MÉTAMORPHOSES DE LA
    LIBERTÉ.*
    G. STRICKLAND, 402(MLR):JUL72-638
    E.J. TALBOT, 188(ECR):FALL70-259
IMBERT, H-F. STENDHAL ET LA TENTATION
    JANSÉNISTE.
    L. LE GUILLOU, 535(RHL):JUL-AUG71-711
    G. STRICKLAND, 402(MLR):JUL72-638
IMBODEN, M. DIE SURREALE KOMPONENTE IM
    ERZÄHLENDEN WERK ARTHUR SCHNITZLERS.
    J.D. WORKMAN, 406:SUMMER72-165
IMBS, P. - SEE "TRÉSOR DE LA LANGUE FRAN-
    ÇAISE"
IMERSLUND, K., ED. NORSK LITTERATUR-
    KRITIKK 1914-1945.
    A. TVINNEREIM, 172(EDDA):1971/1-59
"IMPRESSIONISM."
    442(NY):12NOV73-220
"IMPRIMEURS ET LIBRAIRES PARISIENS DU
    XVIE SIÈCLE." (VOL 2)
    N. BARKER, 78(BC):SUMMER71-261
    H. CARTER, 354:SEP71-272
INADA, K.K. - SEE "NĀGĀRJUNA, A TRANSLA-
    TION OF HIS MŪLAMADHYAMAKAKĀRIKĀ"
INADA, L.F. BEFORE THE WAR.
    S.G. RADHUBER, 448:SPRING71-84
INALCIK, H. THE OTTOMAN EMPIRE.
    617(TLS):13APR73-422
"INDIAN AESTHETICS AND ART ACTIVITY."*
    E.H. DUNCAN, 290(JAAC):FALL70-132
"ÍNDICES DA REVISTA LUSITANA, VOLS. I-
    XXXVIII, 1887-1943."
    H. MEIER, 72:BAND209HEFT1/3-174
"ÍNDICES DE VOCES Y MORFEMAS DE LA
    REVISTA DE FILOLOGÍA ESPAÑOLA, TOMOS
    I-XLV."
    H. MEIER, 72:BAND209HEFT1/3-174
INDICOPLEUSTÈS, C. - SEE UNDER COSMAS
    INDICOPLEUSTÈS
INEICHEN, G. - SEE GUILLAUME DE LORRIS
INGAMELLS, J. CATALOGUE OF PORTRAITS AT
    BISHOPTHORPE PALACE.
    617(TLS):16MAR73-305
INGARDEN, R. ERLEBNIS, KUNSTWERK UND
    WERT.*
    J. STRELKA, 221(GQ):MAR71-242
INGARDEN, R. UNTERSUCHUNGEN ZUR ONTOLO-
    GIE DER KUNST.
    P. CHARLSON, 484(PPR):DEC71-269
INGARDEN, R. VOM ERKENNEN DES LITERAR-
    ISCHEN KUNSTWERKS.*
    R. WEISBACH, 654(WB):1/1970-217
INGARDEN, R. Z BADAŃ NAD FILOZOFIĄ
    WSPÓŁCZESNĄ.
    I. DAMBSKA, 542:OCT-DEC71-436
INGARDEN, R. - SEE HUSSERL, E.
INGLE, C.R. FROM VILLAGE TO STATE IN
    TANZANIA.
    617(TLS):26OCT73-1302
INGLIS, B. ROGER CASEMENT.
    M. DEAS, 362:10MAY73-621
    617(TLS):11MAY73-513
INGRAM, G. RED ADAM'S LADY.
    P. ADAMS, 61:SEP73-119
IÑIGUEZ, D.A. & A.E. PÉREZ SANCHEZ - SEE
    UNDER ANGULO IÑIGUEZ, D. & A.E. PÉREZ
    SANCHEZ
INNES, G. A MENDE-ENGLISH DICTIONARY.
    R.A. SPEARS, 399(MLJ):APR71-262
INNES, H. GOLDEN SOAK.
    S. HILL, 362:22FEB73-251
INNES, M. APPLEBY'S ANSWER.
    N. CALLENDAR, 441:27MAY73-18
    617(TLS):23FEB73-219
INOUE, K. A STUDY OF JAPANESE SYNTAX.
    R.A. MILLER, 350:MAR72-214

INOUE KIYOSHI, ED. TAISHŌKI NO SEIJI TO
    SHAKAI.
    E.G. GRIFFIN, 293(JAST):MAY71-683
INSALL, D.W. THE CARE OF OLD BUILDINGS
    TODAY.
    617(TLS):30MAR73-361
INSINGEL, M. REFLECTIONS.
    E. GLOVER, 565:VOL12#4-53
    M. LEVIN, 441:7OCT73-47
INSTINSKY, H.U. FORMALIEN IM BRIEFWECH-
    SEL DEL PLINIUS MIT KAISER TRAJAN.
    J. CROOK, 123:JUN72-222
"INTERNATIONALE BIBLIOGRAPHIE ZUR GE-
    SCHICHTE DER DEUTSCHEN LITERATUR."
    (PT 1)
    E. KUNZE, 439(NM):1970/3-518
"AN INVENTORY OF HISTORICAL MONUMENTS IN
    THE COUNTY OF CAMBRIDGE."* (VOL 1:
    WEST CAMBRIDGESHIRE.)
    D. STILLMAN, 576:OCT70-284
"INVENTORY OF RESEARCH IN PROGRESS IN THE
    HUMANITIES."
    K.V. SINCLAIR, 67:NOV72-279
"AN INVENTORY OF THE HISTORICAL MONUMENTS
    IN THE CITY OF YORK." (VOL 2: THE DE-
    FENCES.)
    617(TLS):20JUL73-840
"AN INVENTORY OF THE HISTORICAL MONUMENTS
    IN THE COUNTY OF DORSET." (VOL 2)
    J. LEES-MILNE, 39:APR71-343
"INVESTMENT IN OPPRESSION."
    M. MASON, 99:OCT73-37
IONESCO, E. FRAGMENTS OF A JOURNAL.
    S.O.H., 543:SEP70-137
    L.C. PRONKO, 397(MD):DEC70-340
IONESCO, E. JEUX DE MASSACRE.
    B.L. KNAPP, 207(FR):FEB71-641
IONESCO, E. LE SOLITAIRE.
    617(TLS):5OCT73-1158
IORDAN, I. TOPONIMIA ROMÎNEASCĂ.
    E.P. HAMP, 215(GL):VOL11#2-133
IORDAN, I. & J. ORR. AN INTRODUCTION TO
    ROMANCE LINGUISTICS.* (REV BY R. POS-
    NER)
    C. BLAYLOCK, 215(GL):VOL11#2-140
    S. GREGORY, 402(MLR):JAN72-181
    M. HARRIS, 297(JL):OCT71-301
    J-M. KLINKENBERG, 209(FM):OCT71-358
IREDALE, D. ENJOYING ARCHIVES.
    617(TLS):9FEB73-161
IRELAND, G.W. ANDRÉ GIDE.*
    205(FMLS):JUL71-296
IRESON, J.C. LAMARTINE.
    M. SCHAETTEL, 557(RSH):OCT-DEC70-640
    C.W. THOMPSON, 402(MLR):OCT72-914
    205(FMLS):JAN71-96
IRIARTE, V.R. - SEE UNDER RUIZ IRIARTE, V.
IRIMIE, C. & M. FOCŞA. ROMANIAN ICONS
    PAINTED ON GLASS.
    K. HITCHINS, 32:JUN72-489
IRONSIDE, J. JANEY.
    E. TENNANT, 362:2AUG73-154
    617(TLS):29JUN73-741
IRSCHICK, E.F. POLITICS AND SOCIAL CON-
    FLICT IN SOUTH INDIA.*
    M. DEMBO, 318(JAOS):APR-JUN71-324
IRVING, C. FAKE!
    B. DENVIR, 592:JUL-AUG70-57
IRVING, E.B., JR. INTRODUCTION TO "BEO-
    WULF."
    T.P. LOGAN, 399(MLJ):FEB71-120
IRVING, E.B., JR. A READING OF "BEO-
    WULF."*
    M. GREEN, 599:SPRING71-206
    205(FMLS):JAN71-96
IRVING, M., WITH C. SOPKIN. THE BANK
    BOOK.
    441:21OCT73-18

175

IRVING, W. JOURNALS AND NOTEBOOKS.*
(VOL 1) (N. WRIGHT, ED).
M. ROTH, 405(MP):NOV71-178
IRWIN, J. & K.B. BRETT. ORIGINS OF
CHINTZ.
F. IRWIN, 90:MAY71-280
S. ROBINSON, 39:AUG70-156
ISAAC, P.C.G. THE BURMAN ALNWICK COL-
LECTION.
617(TLS):24AUG73-984
ISAAC, P.C.G. WILLIAM DAVISON OF ALN-
WICK.
G.W., 503:AUTUMN68-123
ISAACS, J. MARÍA. (D. MC GRADY, ED)
J.M. FLINT, 86(BHS):APR72-204
ISAACS, N.D. STRUCTURAL PRINCIPLES IN
OLD ENGLISH POETRY.*
D.C. GREEN, 405(MP):NOV70-192
M. MASON, 648:JUN70-43
G. WIENOLD, 490:JUL/OCT70-629
ISAACS, N.D. & R.A. ZIMBARDO, EDS. TOL-
KIEN AND THE CRITICS.*
R. KIELY, 613:SPRING70-134
J.R. WATSON, 175:AUTUMN71-252
ISAACSON, I., COMP. UNIVERSITY OF WIT-
WATERSRAND LIBRARY: GUIDE TO THE AR-
CHIVES AND PAPERS. (2ND ED) [1ST ED
SHOWN IN PREV UNDER TITLE]
J.P. HEARD, 14:APR71-199
ISAACSON, J. MONET: LE DÉJEUNER SUR
L'HERBE.*
R. DOWNES, 441:2DEC73-93
ISAČENKO, A.V. DIE RUSSISCHE SPRACHE DER
GEGENWART. (PT 1)
W. SCHAMSCHULA, 430(NS):JUN70-306
ISAČENKO, A.V. SPRACHWISSENSCHAFT UND
AKUSTIK.
I. LEHISTE, 206:AUG71-437
ISBÂSESCU, C. EL ESPAÑOL EN CUBA.
J. JOSET, 556(RLV):1971/5-658
ISCHBOLDIN, B. HISTORY OF THE RUSSIAN
NON-MARXIAN SOCIAL-ECONOMIC THOUGHT.
N. SPULBER, 32:SEP72-688
ISEKI, K. KIGÔ RONRIGAKU (MEIDAI RONRI).
A. NAKAMURA, 316:DEC70-580
ISELLA, D. - SEE PARINI, G.
ISER, W. DIE APPELLSTRUKTUR DER TEXTE.
G. KAISER, 490:APR71-267
ISER, W., ED. IMMANENTE ÄSTHETIK - ÄS-
THETISCHE REFLEXION.
R. PALMER, 141:WINTER71-95
ISHERWOOD, R.M. MUSIC IN THE SERVICE OF
THE KING.
617(TLS):28SEP73-1139
ISHIGURO, H. LEIBNIZ'S PHILOSOPHY OF
LOGIC AND LANGUAGE.
617(TLS):20JUL73-838
ISHWARAN, K., ED. CHANGE AND CONTINUITY
IN INDIA'S VILLAGES.
R.G. FOX, 293(JAST):AUG71-911
ISICHEI, E. THE IBO PEOPLE AND THE EURO-
PEANS.
617(TLS):30NOV73-1479
ISICHEI, E. VICTORIAN QUAKERS.
L.F. BARMANN, 613:WINTER71-625
ST. ISIDORE OF SEVILLE. THE LETTERS OF
ST. ISIDORE OF SEVILLE.* (2ND ED)
(G.B. FORD, JR., ED & TRANS)
P.G. WALSH, 123:JUN72-279
ISIDRO, A. MUSLIM-CHRISTIAN INTEGRATION
AT THE MINDANAO STATE UNIVERSITY. THE
MORO PROBLEM.
M. MEDNICK, 293(JAST):NOV70-241
ISIDRO, A. & M. SABER, EDS. MUSLIM PHIL-
IPPINES.
M. MEDNICK, 293(JAST):NOV70-241
ISLAM, R. INDO-PERSIAN RELATIONS.
617(TLS):8JUN73-641

ISLER, G. DIE SENNENPUPPE.
H. GERNDT, 182:VOL24#7/8-377
ISLER, H.P. ACHELOOS.*
N.G.L. HAMMOND, 303:VOL91-177
ISON, L. & W. ENGLISH CHURCH ARCHITEC-
TURE THROUGH THE AGES.
617(TLS):2FEB73-133
ISSACHAROFF, M. J-K. HUYSMANS DEVANT LA
CRITIQUE EN FRANCE (1874-1960).
P. BRADY, 207(FR):MAR71-801
A. KIES, 549(RLC):JUL-SEP71-428
205(FMLS):JUL71-297
"ISTORIA LIMBII ROMÂNE." (VOL 2)
J. ANDRÉ, 555:VOL45FASC2-355
"ISTORIA TOU ELLINIKOU ETHNOUS." (VOL 3)
617(TLS):8JUN73-650
"ISTORIIA SIBIRI S DREVNEISHIKH VREMEN
DO NASHIKH DNEI."
293(JAST):NOV70-246
ITARD, J. THE WILD BOY OF AVEYRON.
617(TLS):9FEB73-145
ITO, T. THE JAPANESE GARDEN.
617(TLS):13APR73-410
ITOH, T. TRADITIONAL DOMESTIC ARCHITEC-
TURE OF JAPAN. THE CLASSIC TRADITION
IN JAPANESE ARCHITECTURE.
617(TLS):9FEB73-149
VAN ITTERBEEK, E. TEKENS VAN LEVEN.
J. TANS, 535(RHL):MAY-JUN70-539
ITZKOFF, S.W. ERNST CASSIRER.
W.H. WERKMEISTER, 319:JAN73-139
IVANOV, A.I. LITERATURNOE NASLEDIE MAK-
SIMA GREKA.
V. VODOFF, 549(RLC):JUL-SEP71-408
IVANOV, V.V. ISTORIČESKAJA FONOLOGIJA
RUSSKOGO JAZYKA.*
A.J. PRZEKOP, 215(GL):VOL11#1-38
IVANOVA, A. THE DANCE IN SPAIN.
F. JACKSON, 37:APR71-38
IVASK, I. & J. MARICHAL, EDS. LUMINOUS
REALITY.*
P. SILVER, 400(MLN):MAR71-311
IVENS, M. PRIVATE AND PUBLIC.*
H. SERGEANT, 175:SPRING70-29
IVERSEN, E. OBELISKS IN EXILE. (VOL 1)
H. HIBBARD, 90:MAY71-279
IVES, C.E. MEMOS. (J. KIRKPATRICK, ED)
617(TLS):7SEP73-1024
IVES, E.D. LAWRENCE DOYLE, THE FARMER
POET OF PRINCE EDWARD ISLAND.
W.H. NEW, 102(CANL):WINTER72-99
IVIĆ, M. TRENDS IN LINGUISTICS.
G.C. LEPSCHY, 353:MAY70-100
G.F. MEIER & B. FLEGEL, 682(ZPSK):
BAND23HEFT1-96
IVINS, W.M., JR. PRINTS AND VISUAL COM-
MUNICATION.* PRINTS AND BOOKS.
E. YOUNG, 39:FEB70-168
IYENGAR, D.K. NEW MODEL SANSKRIT GRAM-
MAR.
R. ROCHER, 318(JAOS):OCT-DEC71-554
IYER, S.V., ED. DHĀTUKĀVYA OF NĀRĀYAŅA-
BHAṬṬA, WITH THE COMMENTARIES KŖṢṆĀR-
PAŅA AND RĀMAPĀŅIVĀDA'S VIVARAŅA.
R. ROCHER, 318(JAOS):OCT-DEC71-553
"IZ ISTORII MEŽDUNARODNOGO OB-EDINENIJA
REVOLJUCIONNICH PISATELEJ (MORP)."
S. BARCK, 654(WB):5/1971-214
"THE IZUMI SHIKIBU DIARY."* (E.A. CRAN-
STON, TRANS)
H. MC CULLOUGH, 244(HJAS):VOL30-268
E. MINER, 318(JAOS):APR-JUN71-347
IZZO, C. LA LETTERATURA NORD-AMERICANA.
R. ASSELINEAU, 189(EA):OCT-DEC70-456

JABLONICKÝ, J. Z ILEGALITY DO POVSTANIA.
V.S. MAMATEY, 32:DEC72-923

JABLONSKI, E. & L.D. STEWART. THE GERSH-
WIN YEARS.
W. CLEMONS, 441:23SEP73-3
JACHNOW, H. DIE SLAVISCHEN PERSONEN-
NAMEN IN BERLIN BIS ZUR TSCHECHISCHEN
EINWANDERUNG IM 18. JAHRHUNDERT.
R. AUTY, 575(SEER):APR72-288
JACK, D. THAT'S ME IN THE MIDDLE.
M. LEVIN, 441:20MAY73-54
JACK, I. - SEE BROWNING, R.
JACK, J. & M. SMITH - SEE BRONTË, C.
JACKENDOFF, R.S. SEMANTIC INTERPRETA-
TION IN GENERATIVE GRAMMAR.
617(TLS):5OCT73-1181
JACKSON, A. THE POLITICS OF ARCHITEC-
TURE.
R.F. JORDAN, 46:SEP70-199
JACKSON, B., ED. WAKE UP DEAD MAN.*
W. RHODES, 187:SEP73-548
617(TLS):27JUL73-852
JACKSON, C.J.L. KICKED TO DEATH BY A
CAMEL.
N. CALLENDAR, 441:16SEP73-30
JACKSON, C.O. FOOD AND DRUG LEGISLATION
IN THE NEW DEAL.
639(VQR):WINTER71-XLII
JACKSON, G. PEOPLE'S PRISON.
617(TLS):9NOV73-1368
JACKSON, G.B. - SEE JONSON, B.
JACKSON, J.N. THE URBAN FUTURE.
617(TLS):23FEB73-204
JACKSON, J.R.D., ED. COLERIDGE: THE
CRITICAL HERITAGE.*
D.V.E., 191(ELN):SEP71(SUPP)-40
JACKSON, J.R.D. METHOD AND IMAGINATION
IN COLERIDGE'S CRITICISM.*
I.A. RICHARDS, 627(UTQ):FALL70-102
M.F. SCHULZ, 405(MP):NOV71-142
JACKSON, L. THE TELLING.
617(TLS):9FEB73-151
JACKSON, M.P. LABOUR RELATIONS ON THE
DOCKS.
617(TLS):27JUL73-884
JACKSON, R. AIR WAR OVER KOREA.
617(TLS):30NOV73-1485
JACKSON, R. AT WAR WITH THE BOLSHEVIKS.
617(TLS):5JAN73-22
JACKSON, S. CARUSO.*
617(TLS):23FEB73-217
JACKSON, T.H. THE EARLY POETRY OF EZRA
POUND.*
W. MARTIN, 72:BAND209HEFT1/3-166
P. RUSSELL, 598(SOR):WINTER73-257
JACKSON, W.A.D., ED. AGRARIAN POLICIES
AND PROBLEMS IN COMMUNIST AND NON-
COMMUNIST COUNTRIES.*
M. MC CAULEY, 32:JUN72-463
JACKSON, W.T.H. THE ANATOMY OF LOVE.*
P.W. TAX, 301(JEGP):OCT72-565
F. WASSERMANN, 406:WINTER72-378
JACKSON, W.T.H. DIE LITERATUREN DES
MITTELALTERS.
M. FELDGES, 657(WW):JAN/FEB71-65
JACOB, A., ED. POINTS DE VUE SUR LE LAN-
GAGE.
J. CHAURAND, 209(FM):OCT71-365
D. JANICAUD, 557(RSH):APR-JUN71-304
B. POTTIER, 353:AUG71-113
JACOB, A. TEMPS ET LANGAGE.* LES EXI-
GENCES THÉORIQUES DE LA LINGUISTIQUE
SELON GUSTAVE GUILLAUME.
D. JANICAUD, 557(RSH):APR-JUN71-304
JACOB, F. LA LOGIQUE DU VIVANT.
M. SERRES, 98:JUN71-483
JACOB, L.A. & OTHERS, COMPS. SOUTH ASIA:
A BIBLIOGRAPHY FOR UNDERGRADUATE LIB-
RARIES.
R.I. CRANE, 293(JAST):MAY71-649

JACOB, M. BALLADES.
S. LÉVY, 207(FR):APR71-962
JACOB, M. POP GOES JESUS.
617(TLS):23FEB73-221
JACOBEIT, W. & P. NEDO, EDS. PROBLEME
UND METHODEN VOLKSKUNDLICHER GEGENWARTS-
FORSCHUNG.
R.L. WELSCH, 292(JAF):JUL-SEP71-354
JACOBI, E.R. - SEE "JEAN-PHILIPPE RAMEAU:
COMPLETE THEORETICAL WRITINGS"
JACOBI, E.R. - SEE TÜRCK, D.G.
JACOBI, H. KLEINE SCHRIFTEN. (B. KÖLVER,
ED)
O. VON HINÜBER, 182:VOL24#1/2-15
JACOBI, J. & R.F.C. HULL - SEE JUNG, C.G.
JACOBS, A., ED. THE MUSIC YEARBOOK.
(1971)
N. GOODWIN, 415:SEP72-867
JACOBS, A. A SHORT HISTORY OF WESTERN
MUSIC.
H.M. BROWN, 415:DEC72-1183
617(TLS):23FEB73-217
JACOBS, A. & S. SADIE. OPERA.
C. GRAHAM, 415:JAN72-45
JACOBS, C. - SEE DE MILÁN, L.
JACOBS, C. & B. SOUTH AMERICAN TRAVEL
DIGEST. (7TH ED)
S.S. BENSON, 37:OCT71-43
JACOBS, F. THE MAD WORLD OF WILLIAM M.
GAINES.
441:25FEB73-22
JACOBS, F.R. EVERY WOMAN IS A VIRGIN
SOMEWHERE.
A. RENDLE, 157:SPRING71-77
JACOBS, J. WIELANDS ROMANE.*
A. PHELAN, 220(GL&L):JAN72-152
JACOBS, L. HASIDIC PRAYER.
617(TLS):15JUN73-700
JACOBS, N.J. NAMING DAY IN EDEN.
R.W. CONDEE, 215(GL):VOL11#1-59
JACOBS, R.A. & P.S. ROSENBAUM. ENGLISH
TRANSFORMATIONAL GRAMMAR.*
D.L.F. NILSEN, 353:JUL70-113
W.C. WATT, 297(JL):APR71-101
JACOBS, R.D. POE: JOURNALIST AND CRITIC.*
H. BRADDY, 648:OCT70-73
J.R. MC ELRATH, JR., 577(SHR):SUMMER
71-289
R. REGAN, 445(NCF):JUN70-112
F. STOVALL, 219(GAR):SUMMER70-239
S.L. VARNADO, 613:SUMMER70-297
JACOBS, W.G. TRIEB ALS SITTLICHES PHÄNO-
MEN.
W. STEINBECK, 342:BAND61HEFT2-277
JACOBSEN, C.W. CHECK POINTS ON HOW TO
BUY ORIENTAL RUGS.
M.H. BEATTIE, 39:MAY71-438
JACOBSEN, Q. SOLITARY IN JOHANNESBURG.
617(TLS):27JUL73-850
JACOBSON, D. INKLINGS.
F. WYNDHAM, 362:22MAR73-378
617(TLS):16MAR73-285
JACOBSON, D. THE RAPE OF TAMAR.*
E.M. BRONER, 390:MAR71-75
JACOBSON, D. THE WONDER-WORKER.
R. BLYTHE, 362:1NOV73-605
617(TLS):2NOV73-1333
JACOBSON, J. LOCARNO DIPLOMACY.
P.S. WANDYCZ, 32:DEC72-915
617(TLS):29JUN73-739
JACOBSON, N.P. BUDDHISM.
K.K. INADA, 484(PPR):SEP71-132
A. WAYMAN, 293(JAST):AUG71-905
JACOBSSON, R. L'EXPRESSION IMAGÉE DANS
"LES THIBAULT" DE ROGER MARTIN DU GARD.
M. LEHTONEN, 439(NM):1970/1-168
J. MILLY, 209(FM):JAN70-75
[CONTINUED]

177

JACOBSSON, H. L'EXPRESSION IMAGÉE DANS "LES THIBAULT" DE ROGER MARTIN DU GARD. [CONTINUING]
    M-T. VEYRENC, 535(RHL):JAN-FEB71-136
    J.S. WOOD, 546(RR):FEB71-71
JACOBSTAHL, P. EARLY CELTIC ART.
    R. BRUCE-MITFORD, 90:AUG71-478
DI JACOPO, M. [TACCOLA] LIBER TERTIUS DE INGENEIS AC EDIFITIIS NON USITATIS. (J.H. BECK, ED)
    B. DIBNER, 551(RENQ):SPRING71-62
JACOT, M. THE LAST BUTTERFLY.
    J.R., 606(TAMR):#61-77
JACQUES, J-M. - SEE MENANDER
JACQUIOT, J. MÉDAILLES ET JETONS DE LOUIS XIV D'APRÈS LE MANUSCRIT DE LONDRES ADD. 31.908.
    R. LEBÈGUE, 535(RHL):MAY-JUN71-501
JACQUOT, J. & D. BABLET, EDS. LES VOIES DE LA CRÉATION THÉÂTRALE.
    G. BRÉE, 397(MD):DEC71-355
JAEGER, P.L. - SEE SCHRÖER, M.M.A.
JAEGGI, U. KAPITAL UND ARBEIT IN DER BUNDESREPUBLIK.
    617(TLS):28DEC73-1592
JAEHRLING, J. DIE PHILOSOPHISCHE TERMINOLOGIE NOTKERS DES DEUTSCHEN IN SEINER ÜBERSETZUNG DER ARISTOTELISCHEN "KATEGORIEN."*
    J.C. KING, 564:MAR71-70
    B. SOWINSKI, 657(WW):JAN/FEB71-68
JAFFA, H.C. KENNETH SLESSOR.*
    T-I. MOORE, 381:DEC71-471
JAFFE, A.H. & V. SCOTT, EDS. STUDIES IN THE SHORT STORY. (3RD ED)
    J.W. STEVENSON, 573(SSF):SUMMER71-475
JAFFE, I.B. JOSEPH STELLA.
    D. IRWIN, 39:APR71-342
    M. POPS, 141:SUMMER71-317
JÄGER, G. EMPFINDSAMKEIT UND ROMAN.
    A. MARTINO, 680(ZDP):BAND90HEFT2-281
    L. PIKULIK, 490:JUL71-417
JAGER, R. THE DEVELOPMENT OF BERTRAND RUSSELL'S PHILOSOPHY.
    617(TLS):23MAR73-330
JAGGER, C. CLOCKS.
    617(TLS):27JUL73-884
JAHN, E.A., ED. LATIN AMERICAN TRAVEL AND PAN AMERICAN HIGHWAY GUIDE.
    S.S. BENSON, 37:OCT71-41
JAHN, E.K. DIE DEUTSCHEN IN DER SLOWAKEI IN DEN JAHREN 1918-1929.
    S.B. WINTERS, 32:JUN72-473
JAHN, J. INTERREGNUM UND WAHLDIKTATUR.
    J. LINDERSKI, 487:WINTER71-394
JAHN, J. & C.P. DRESSLER. BIBLIOGRAPHY OF CREATIVE AFRICAN WRITING.
    W. GOLDWATER, 517(PBSA):APR-JUN72-223
JAHN, M. ROCK FROM ELVIS PRESLEY TO THE ROLLING STONES.
    J. ROCKWELL, 441:26DEC73-43
"JAHRBUCH DES VEREINS FÜR NIEDERDEUTSCHE SPRACHFORSCHUNG." (VOL 91)
    B. KRATZ, 133:1970/2&3-343
"JAHRBUCH FÜR AMERIKASTUDIEN." (VOLS 12-14)
    H. HELMCKE, 430(NS):MAY71-281
"JAHRBUCH FÜR VOLKSLIEDFORSCHUNG." (VOLS 13-16) (R. WILH, ED)
    D. STOCKMANN, 187:MAY73-328
JAHSMANN, A.H. POWER BEYOND WORDS.
    E.W. HARRIS, 186(ETC.):MAR71-120
JAIN, M.S. EMERGENCE OF A NEW ARISTOCRACY IN NEPAL (1837-58).
    617(TLS):18MAY73-565
JAIRAZBHOY, N.A. THE RĀGS OF NORTH INDIAN MUSIC.*
    B.C. WADE, 187:MAY73-331

JAIS, P. & H. LAHANA. BRIDGE SIMPLE ET MODERNE.
    F. GALICHET, 98:JAN71-70
JAKI, S.L. THE MILKY WAY.
    617(TLS):31AUG73-994
JAKOBOVITS, L.A. FOREIGN LANGUAGE LEARNING.*
    D.K. SHAKESPEARE, 238:SEP71-607
    D.C. SHEPPARD, 399(MLJ):FEB71-107
JAKOBSON, R. CHILD LANGUAGE, APHASIA AND PHONOLOGICAL UNIVERSALS.
    M. ZAREBINA, 353:JAN71-115
JAKOBSON, R. LINGÜÍSTICA E COMUNICAÇÃO.
    B. MALMBERG, 596(SL):VOL24#1-69
JAKOBSON, R. MAIN TRENDS IN THE SCIENCE OF LANGUAGE.
    617(TLS):23NOV73-1456
JAKOBSON, R. QUESTIONS DE POÉTIQUE. (T. TODOROV, ED)
    617(TLS):25MAY73-591
JAKOBSON, R. SLOVESNÉ UMĚNÍ A UMĚLECKÉ SLOVO.
    M. HALLE, 279:VOL14-211
JAMES, B. BRAHMS.*
    M.M., 410(M&L):OCT72-439
    412:NOV72-330
JAMES, D.G. THE DREAM OF PROSPERO.
    C. UHLIG, 38:BAND89HEFT2-263
JAMES, E.T. - SEE "DICTIONARY OF AMERICAN BIOGRAPHY"
JAMES, G.F. - SEE JOYCE, A.
JAMES, H. WILLIAM WETMORE STORY AND HIS FRIENDS FROM LETTERS, DIARIES, AND RECOLLECTIONS.
    M. FRIEDLAENDER, 432(NEQ):SEP71-523
JAMES, L. THE PUSH-BUTTON SPY.
    J.L. HALIO, 598(SOR):SPRING73-455
JAMES, L. TRIPLE MIRROR.
    N. CALLENDAR, 441:14OCT73-47
JAMES, P.D. AN UNSUITABLE JOB FOR A WOMAN.*
    N. CALLENDAR, 441:22APR73-24
    442(NY):23JUL73-80
JAMES, R.L. JANUS.
    M. LEVIN, 441:6MAY73-40
JAMES, R.R. - SEE UNDER RHODES JAMES, R.
JAMESON, A. WINTER STUDIES AND SUMMER RAMBLES IN CANADA.
    G. WARKENTIN, 296:SUMMER73-107
JAMESON, F. MARXISM AND FORM.
    617(TLS):27APR73-462
JAMESON, F. THE PRISON-HOUSE OF LANGUAGE.
    617(TLS):8JUN73-636
JAMESON, S. PARTHIAN WORDS.
    R. LAWRENCE, 175:AUTUMN71-110
JAMESON, S. THERE WILL BE A SHORT INTERVAL.
    V. CUNNINGHAM, 362:11JAN73-56
    E. JANEWAY, 441:20MAY73-56
    442(NY):26MAY73-135
    617(TLS):5JAN73-5
JAMIESON, E. ENGLISH EMBOSSED BINDINGS 1825-1850.
    617(TLS):11MAY73-536
JAMIESON, G. CHINESE FAMILY AND COMMERCIAL LAW.
    D.C. BUXBAUM, 293(JAST):FEB71-424
    A.R. DICKS, 302:JAN71-178
"JAMMES." (T. SAVORY, TRANS)
    J. HART, 661:SUMMER70-113
JANÁČEK, J. ČESKÉ DĚJINY: DOBA PŘEDBĚLOHORSKÁ, 1526-1547. (VOL 1, PT 1)
    O. ODLOZILIK, 551(RENQ):WINTER71-534
JANERT, K.L. AN ANNOTATED BIBLIOGRAPHY OF THE CATALOGUES OF INDIAN MANUSCRIPTS. (VOL 1)
    L. ROCHER, 343:BAND13HEFT2-188

JANEWAY, E. MAN'S WORLD, WOMAN'S PLACE.*
A. DIAMOND, 418(MR):WINTER-SPRING72-
275
P.M. SPACKS, 249(HUDR):SPRING72-160
JANEWAY, E. WHAT SHALL I DO WITH MY
MONEY?
639(VQR):SPRING71-LXXX
JANICAUD, D. UNE GÉNÉALOGIE DU SPIRITU-
ALISME FRANÇAIS.
M. PICLIN, 542:OCT-DEC71-451
JANIK, A. & S. TOULMIN. WITTGENSTEIN'S
VIENNA.
C. LEHMANN-HAUPT, 441:19MAR73-39
A. RYAN, 362:9AUG73-191
G. STEINER, 442(NY):23JUL73-73
441:2SEP73-14
617(TLS):17AUG73-953
JANIK, D. GESCHICHTE DER ODE UND DER
"STANCES" VON RONSARD BIS BOILEAU.*
H. WEBER, 535(RHL):JUL-AUG70-695
JANIS, I.L. VICTIMS OF GROUPTHINK.
S. ALSOP, 441:28JAN73-36
JANKÉLÉVITCH, V. LA MORT.
B. BERLOWITZ, 98:JUL70-640
JANNACO, C., ED. ALESSANDRO TASSONI.
A. MANCINI, 275(IQ):FALL70-113
JANNACO, C. & U. LIMENTANI, EDS. STUDI
SECENTESCHI. (VOL 10)
R. ALONGE, 228(GSLI):VOL148FASC462/
463-443
JANOS, A.C. & W.B. SLOTTMAN, EDS. REVO-
LUTION IN PERSPECTIVE.
R.L. TŐKÉS, 32:DEC72-924
JÁNOSSY, F. THE END OF THE ECONOMIC
MIRACLE.
G.M. WALTON, 32:DEC72-907
JANOUCH, G. CONVERSATIONS WITH KAFKA.
J.C. OATES, 473(PR):SPRING72-266
JANSEN, E., ED. ERNST BARLACH: WERK
UND WIRKUNG.
617(TLS):5OCT73-1168
JANSEN, F.J.B. & P.M. MITCHELL, EDS.
ANTHOLOGY OF DANISH LITERATURE.*
J.S. MARTIN, 67:NOV72-258
JANSOHN, H. KANTS LEHRE VON DER SUBJEK-
TIVITÄT.
W. TEICHNER, 342:BAND61HEFT2-258
JANSSEN, E.M. JACOB BURCKHARDT UND DIE
RENAISSANCE.
V-L. TAPIÉ, 182:VOL24#3-112
JANSSEN, P. GESCHICHTE UND LEBENSWELT.
W.H. WERKMEISTER, 319:JUL73-427
JANSSENS, E. TRÉBIZONDE EN COLCHIDE.
M.J. ANGOLD, 303:VOL91-213
C. CAHEN, 182:VOL24#9/10-435
JANSSENS, G.A.M. THE AMERICAN LITERARY
REVIEW.
K.L. ANDERSON, 598(SOR):SPRING73-449
J.T. FLANAGAN, 179(ES):APR71-184
B. POLI, 189(EA):APR-JUN71-221
JANSSON, S-B. MEDELTIDENS RIMKRÖNIKOR.
T.M. ANDERSSON, 589:APR72-316
JANTZ, H. THE MOTHERS IN "FAUST."*
H. HENEL, 405(MP):NOV71-175
J.A. PFEFFER & D. HANKS, 149:SEP72-
341
JANTZ, H. THE SOOTHSAYINGS OF BAKIS.
H. NIELSEN, 462(OL):VOL26#2-170
JANVIER, L. BECKETT PAR LUI-MÊME.
J. FLETCHER, 188(ECR):FALL71-67
P. RECONDO, 202(FMOD):NOV70/FEB71-166
JARAUSCH, K.H. THE ENIGMATIC CHANCELLOR.
617(TLS):31AUG73-1006
JARRY, M. THE CARPETS OF AUBUSSON.*
F.J.B. WATSON, 39:JAN70-85
JARVIE, I.C. & J. AGASSI - SEE GELLNER,
E.

JÄSCHKE, K-U. DIE ÄLTESTE HALBERSTÄDTER
BISCHOFSCHRONIK.
E. DEMM, 589:JUL72-532
JASEN, D.A. A BIBLIOGRAPHY AND READER'S
GUIDE TO THE FIRST EDITIONS OF P.G.
WODEHOUSE.
B.W. ALDISS, 503:WINTER71-190
JASIMUDDIN. GIPSY WHARF. (B. PAINTER &
Y. LOVELOCK, TRANS)
M.S. KHAN, 273(IC):JAN71-70
JASINSKI, B.W. L'ENGAGEMENT DE BENJAMIN
CONSTANT.*
A. FAIRLIE, 208(FS):JAN72-83
JASINSKI, R. MOLIÈRE.
G. MONGREDIEN, 535(RHL):MAR-APR70-313
JASON, P.K. - SEE NIN, A.
JASPERS, K. PHILOSOPHY. (VOL 1)
J.D.C., 543:SEP70-138
E. SCHAPER, 478:JAN71-69
JASPERT, B. - SEE BARTH, K. & R. BULTMANN
JÁSZI, O. THE DISSOLUTION OF THE HABS-
BURG MONARCHY.
M. MOLNÁR, 98:JAN70-72
DE JÁUREGUI, J. AMINTA. (J. ARCE, ED)
R.O. JONES, 86(BHS):JUL72-302
JAUSS, H.R. LITERATURGESCHICHTE ALS
PROVOKATION DER LITERATURWISSENSCHAFT.*
I. BROSE, 657(WW):MAR/APR70-136
H. DYSERINCK, 433:OCT70-434
JAUSS, H.R., ED. DIE NICHT MEHR SCHÖNEN
KÜNSTE.*
R. PALMER, 141:WINTER71-95
JAUSS, H.R., J. BEYER & F. KOPPE, EDS.
LA LITTÉRATURE DIDACTIQUE, ALLÉGORIQUE
ET SATIRIQUE (PARTIE DOCUMENTAIRE).
D. KELLY, 589:OCT72-777
JAVITS, J.K., WITH D. KELLERMANN. WHO
MAKES WAR.
H.S. COMMAGER, 453:18OCT73-49
P.B. KURLAND, 441:14OCT73-34
JAWORSKA, W. GAUGUIN AND THE PONT-AVEN
SCHOOL.
617(TLS):25MAY73-585
JAY, B. VICTORIAN CAMERAMAN.
617(TLS):11MAY73-530
JAY, B. VICTORIAN CANDID CAMERA.
617(TLS):21DEC73-1573
JAY, M. THE DIALECTICAL IMAGINATION.
G. LENZER, 441:28OCT73-31
JAY, P., ED. THE GREEK ANTHOLOGY AND
OTHER ANCIENT GREEK EPIGRAMS.
617(TLS):29JUN73-750
JEAL, T. LIVINGSTONE.
F.M. BRODIE, 441:7OCT73-1
P. WHITEHEAD, 362:30AUG73-287
A. WHITMAN, 441:4OCT73-49
617(TLS):27JUL73-858
JEAN DU PRIER. JEHAN DU PRIER, DIT LE
PRIEUR, "LE MYSTÈRE DU ROY ADVENIR."
(A. MEILLER, ED)
J.H. CAULKINS, 207(FR):DEC70-467
C.J. THIRY, 556(RLV):1971/3-351
C.C. WILLARD, 545(RPH):NOV71-260
JEAN, M. - SEE ARP, J.
JEAN, R. NERVAL PAR LUI-MÊME.
J. BELLEMIN-NOËL, 535(RHL):MAY-JUN70-
523
JEAN-FRANCIS. L'ETERNEL AUJOURD'HUI DE
MICHEL DE GHELDERODE.
M. PIEMME, 556(RLV):1971/4-499
JEANNERET, M. POÉSIE ET TRADITION BIB-
LIQUE AU XVIE SIÈCLE.
I.D. MC FARLANE, 208(FS):JAN72-69
J. PINEAUX, 535(RHL):MAR-APR71-296
JEAUNEAU, E. - SEE SCOT, J.
JĘDRZEJEWICZ, W. - SEE ŁUKASIEWICZ, J.

JEFFARES, A.N. THE CIRCUS ANIMALS.*
    F. LENTRICCHIA, 659:SPRING73-247
    N.H. MAC KENZIE, 529(QQ):AUTUMN71-462
    H. SERGEANT, 175:SPRING71-26
JEFFARES, A.N., ED. A COMMENTARY ON THE
  COLLECTED POEMS OF W.B. YEATS.*
    E. ENGELBERG, 636(VP):WINTER70-354
    H. KOSOK, 430(NS):MAR71-167
    H. PESCHMANN, 175:SPRING70-28
JEFFERS, R. CAWDOR/MEDEA.
    R.I. SCOTT, 648:JAN71-60
JEFFERSON, A. DELIUS.*
    C. PALMER, 415:MAY72-460
JEFFERSON, A. THE LIEDER OF STRAUSS.
    E. SAMS, 415:JAN72-44
JEFFERSON, D.W., ED. THE MORALITY OF ART.
    S.G. PUTT, 175:SUMMER70-64
JEFFERY, B. FRENCH RENAISSANCE COMEDY
  1552-1630.*
    E. JACOBS, 157:SUMMER70-71
    R. LEBÈGUE, 551(RENQ):SUMMER71-259
    C.N. SMITH, 208(FS):APR72-188
JEFFERY, G. THE BARNABAS BIBLE.
    617(TLS):27JUL73-884
JEFFNER, A. THE STUDY OF RELIGIOUS LAN-
  GUAGE.
    617(TLS):10AUG73-933
JEFFREYS, J.G. A WICKED WAY TO DIE.
    N. CALLENDAR, 441:23DEC73-16
JEFFRIES, C. WHITEHALL AND THE COLONIAL
  SERVICE.
    617(TLS):24AUG73-968
JENA, R.M. THE BROTHERS GRIMM.
    D.L., 191(ELN):SEP71(SUPP)-127
JENCKS, C. ARCHITECTURE 2000.
    R.J., 45:OCT71-112
    505:OCT71-160
JENCKS, C. LE CORBUSIER AND THE TRAGIC
  VIEW OF ARCHITECTURE.
    617(TLS):9NOV73-1381
JENCKS, C. MODERN MOVEMENTS IN ARCHITEC-
  TURE.
    617(TLS):26OCT73-1298
JENCKS, C. & OTHERS. INEQUALITY.*
    H. FLUXGOLD, 99:NOV-DEC73-53
    C. LASCH, 453:17MAY73-19
    A. RYAN, 362:18OCT73-526
JENCKS, C. & G. BAIRD, EDS. MEANING IN
  ARCHITECTURE.*
    R. BLETTER, 576:MAY71-178
    P.D. EISENMAN, 44:JUL/AUG70-88
    G.L. HERSEY, 56:SPRING71-116
JENKINS, A. LONDON'S CITY.
    617(TLS):21DEC73-1574
JENKINS, D. JOB POWER.
    R. SHERRILL, 441:8JUL73-2
    L. SILK, 441:12JUL73-43
JENKINS, D. SEMI-TOUGH.*
    R. SALE, 453:25JAN73-42
JENKINS, G.K. ANCIENT GREEK COINS.
    617(TLS):20APR73-452
JENKINS, M. SCHOOL WITHOUT TEARS.
    617(TLS):25MAY73-597
JENKINS, R. A FAR CRY FROM BOWMORE.
    E. MORGAN, 362:12JUL73-58
    617(TLS):6JUL73-769
JENKINS, W.H. & J. KNOX. THE STORY OF
  DECATUR, ALABAMA.
    R.L. PARTIN, 9(ALAR):APR71-150
JENKINSON, D. RAILS IN THE FELLS.
    617(TLS):13JUL73-817
JENNER, W.J.F., ED. MODERN CHINESE STOR-
  IES.
    P.G. PICKOWICZ, 293(JAST):AUG71-888
JENNETT, S. PARIS.
    617(TLS):24AUG73-975
JENNINGS, E. LUCIDITIES.
    A. CLUYSENAAR, 565:VOL12#3-72

JENNINGS, E. RELATIONSHIPS.
    A. MACLEAN, 362:22MAR73-389
JENNINGS, J.M. THE LIBRARY OF THE COLLEGE
  OF WILLIAM AND MARY IN VIRGINIA, 1693-
  1793.*
    R.W. KENNY, 354:JUN70-168
JENNINGS, J.N. - SEE LASERON, C.F.
JENNINGS, L.C. FRANCE AND EUROPE IN
  1848.
    617(TLS):17AUG73-957
JENNY, M. DIE EINHEIT DES ABENDMAHLS-
  GOTTESDIENSTES BEI DEN ELSÄSSISCHEN UND
  SCHWEIZERISCHEN REFORMATOREN.
    F. KRÜGER, 182:VOL24#13/14-527
JENOFF, M. NO LINGERING PEACE.
    B. FLEET, 198:SPRING73-121
JENS, I. DICHTER ZWISCHEN RECHTS UND
  LINKS.
    617(TLS):22JUN73-705
JENSEN, A.R. GENETICS AND EDUCATION.
  EDUCABILITY AND GROUP DIFFERENCES.
    617(TLS):3AUG73-889
JENSEN, F.E. DA FORNUFTEN SEJREDE.
    617(TLS):9FEB73-154
JENSEN, G.F. SCANDINAVIAN PERSONAL NAMES
  IN LINCOLNSHIRE AND YORKSHIRE.
    G. FRANZÉN, 424:JUN70-128
JENSEN, H. MOTIVATION AND THE MORAL
  SENSE IN FRANCIS HUTCHESON'S ETHICAL
  THEORY.
    H.W. SCHNEIDER, 311(JP):22FEB73-106
JENSEN, H. SIGN, SYMBOL, AND SCRIPT.*
  (3RD ED)
    R.D., 179(ES):DEC71-591
    S. POTTER, 402(MLR):JAN72-151
JENSEN, H.J. A GLOSSARY OF JOHN DRYDEN'S
  CRITICAL TERMS.*
    E. MACKENZIE, 541(RES):MAY71-212
JENSEN, H.J. & M.R. ZIRKER, JR., EDS.
  THE SATIRIST'S ART.
    617(TLS):5JAN73-6
JENSEN, J.V. PERSPECTIVES ON ORAL COM-
  MUNICATION.
    J.T. YAUGER, 583:FALL71-111
JENSMA, W. SING FOR OUR EXECUTION.
    S. TOULSON, 493:SUMMER71-208
JENTZSCH, P., M. BRAUNECK & E.E. STARKE.
  DAS 17. JAHRHUNDERT IN NEUER SICHT.*
    R.T. LLEWELLYN, 220(GL&L):JAN72-146
    F.G. SIEVEKE, 224(GRM):BAND21HEFT4-
    476
JENYNS, S. JAPANESE POTTERY.
    M. MEDLEY, 39:NOV71-418
JEPHCOTT, E.F.N. PROUST AND RILKE.
    617(TLS):9NOV73-1369
JEREMIAS, J. NEW TESTAMENT THEOLOGY.
  (VOL 1)
    E. ANDREWS, 529(QQ):AUTUMN71-482
JÉRÔME, G. LA PHILOSOPHIE, SA VOCATION
  CRÉATRICE, SA POSITION DEVANT LES
  SCIENCES, SES RAPPORTS AVEC L'HOMME
  ET LA SOCIÉTÉ D'AUJOURD'HUI.
    M. CARIGNAN, 154:DEC70-477
JERPHAGNON, L. DE LA BANALITÉ.
    C. PRUDI, 542:OCT-DEC70-481
JERPHAGNON, L. INTRODUCTION À LA PHIL-
  OSOPHIE GÉNÉRALE.
    M.C., 154:JUN71-428
JERSTAD, L.G. MANI-RIMDU.*
    H.W. WELLS, 397(MD):FEB71-452
JESPERSEN, O. ANALYTIC SYNTAX.
    R.A. BOGGS, 215(GL):VOL11#1-32
JEUNE, S. MUSSET ET SA FORTUNE LITTÉR-
  AIRE.
    M. SCHAETTEL, 557(RSH):JUL-SEP71-483
JEUNE, S. POÉSIE ET SYSTÈME.*
    P. MOREAU, 557(RSH):JUL-SEP70-488

JEVONS, W.S. PAPERS AND CORRESPONDENCE
OF WILLIAM STANLEY JEVONS. (VOL 2)
(R.D.C. BLACK, ED)
617(TLS):3AUG73-898
JEWELL, D. SELLOUT.
617(TLS):7SEP73-1018
JEWELL, H.M. ENGLISH LOCAL ADMINISTRATION
IN THE MIDDLE AGES.
617(TLS):19JAN73-62
JEWETT, R. THE CAPTAIN AMERICA COMPLEX.
E.F. GOLDMAN, 441:21OCT73-38
JEZIORKOWSKI, K. RHYTHMUS UND FIGUR.
E. FRIEDRICHSMEYER, 221(GQ):JAN71-79
JEZIORKOWSKI, K. - SEE KELLER, G.
JEZIORKOWSKI, K. - SEE "GOTTFRIED KELLER"
JHABVALA, R.P. A NEW DOMINION.
R. BRYDEN, 362:15FEB73-219
617(TLS):16FEB73-169
JHABVALA, R.P. TRAVELERS.
P. ADAMS, 61:JUL73-104
J. CANADAY, 441:30AUG73-37
V.S. PRITCHETT, 442(NY):16JUN73-106
D. RABINOWITZ, 441:8JUL73-6
JIMÉNEZ, J.O., ED. ANTOLOGÍA DE LA
POESÍA HISPANOAMERICANA CONTEMPORÁNEA,
1914-1970.
O. FERNÁNDEZ DE LA VEGA, 263:OCT-
DEC72-429
JITSUZO, T., IMANISHI SHUNJŪ & SATŌ HI-
SASHI - SEE UNDER TAMURA JITSUZO,
IMANISHI SHUNJŪ & SATŌ HISASHI
JOAQUIN, N. TROPICAL GOTHIC.
617(TLS):11MAY73-535
JOBES, K.T., ED. TWENTIETH CENTURY IN-
TERPRETATIONS OF "THE OLD MAN AND THE
SEA."
K. MOORE, 219(GAR):SPRING70-87
JOBSON, A. VICTORIAN SUFFOLK.
617(TLS):9MAR73-277
JOBST, W. DIE HÖHLE IM GRIECHISCHEN
THEATER DES 5. UND 4. JAHRHUNDERTS V.
CHR.
T.B.L. WEBSTER, 303:VOL91-209
JOCELYN, H.D. & B.P. SETCHELL - SEE "REG-
NIER DE GRAAF ON THE HUMAN REPRODUCTIVE
ORGANS"
JOCHMANN, C.G. ÜBER DIE SPRACH. (C.J.
WAGENKNECHT, ED)
O. REICHMANN, 433:JAN70-90
A.W. STANFORTH, 220(GL&L):JUL72-389
JODELLE, É. OEUVRES COMPLÈTES. (E.
BALMAS, ED)
Y. GIRAUD, 535(RHL):MAY-JUN70-501
JOEDICKE, J. ARCHITECTURE SINCE 1945.
S. MOHOLY-NAGY, 576:DEC70-360
O. NEWMAN, 505:SEP70-132
JOEL, C.E., ED. THE NEW DIFFUSIONIST.
E.O. JAMES, 203:WINTER70-318
JOEL, D. BRITISH FURNITURE DESIGN SET
FREE.
B.G.B., 135:JUN70-134
"JOEY," WITH D. FISHER. KILLER.
617(TLS):9NOV73-1381
JOFFROY, P. A SPY FOR GOD.
K. GERSHON, 390:AUG/SEP71-73
JOHANN, E. & J. JUNKER. DEUTSCHE KULTUR-
GESCHICHTE DER LETZTEN HUNDERT JAHRE.
J.A.A. TER HAAR, 221(GQ):MAR71-251
JOHANNESEN, R.L., R. STRICKLAND & R.T.
EUBANKS, EDS. LANGUAGE IS SERMONIC.
J.L. GOLDEN, 583:SUMMER71-404
JOHANNESSON, E.O. THE NOVELS OF AUGUST
STRINDBERG.*
H.H. BORLAND, 402(MLR):APR72-474
E. POULENARD, 189(EA):APR-JUN70-233

JOHANNSEN, R.W. STEPHEN A. DOUGLAS.
R.N. CURRENT, 441:22APR73-6
H. MITGANG, 441:25APR73-35
442(NY):28APR73-146
JOHANSEN, J.D. NOVELLETEORI EFTER 1945.
H.B. JOHANSEN, 172(EDDA):1971/5-311
POPE JOHN XXIII. LETTERS TO HIS FAMILY.
(L.F. CAPOVILLA, ED)
H. MAGARET, 613:AUTUMN71-450
ST. JOHN OF THE CROSS. THE POEMS OF ST.
JOHN OF THE CROSS. (J.F. NIMS, TRANS)
L.R.P., 502(PRS):FALL70-274
JOHN, O. SABOTAGE.
N. CALLENDAR, 441:24JUN73-34
JOHNPOLL, B.K. PACIFIST'S PROGRESS.
639(VQR):SUMMER71-CXVI
JOHNS, F.A. A BIBLIOGRAPHY OF ARTHUR
WALEY.
B.C. BLOOMFIELD, 354:JUN70-172
JOHNS, L. GARDEN TREES.
617(TLS):29JUN73-757
JOHNSON, A. & B. DRAMA FOR CLASSROOM
AND STAGE.
G. TYLER, 157:WINTER70-69
JOHNSON, A.F. SELECTED ESSAYS ON BOOKS
AND PRINTING. (P.H. MUIR, ED)
D. CHAMBERS, 503:WINTER71-192
JOHNSON, A.H. EXPERIENTIAL REALISM.
617(TLS):20JUL73-838
JOHNSON, B. CONRAD'S MODELS OF MIND.*
S. PINSKER, 136:VOL3#2-99
617(TLS):15JUN73-664
JOHNSON, B., ED. NEW WRITING IN YUGO-
SLAVIA.*
S. FAUCHEREAU, 98:DEC71-1114
JOHNSON, B. THE POLITICS OF MONEY.
E. HOLLOWAY, 619(TC):VOL179#1046-51
JOHNSON, B. THE UNITED NATIONS SYSTEM
AND THE HUMAN ENVIRONMENT.
617(TLS):20APR73-434
JOHNSON, B.S., ED. ALL BULL.
D.A.N. JONES, 362:10MAY73-622
JOHNSON, B.S. AREN'T YOU RATHER YOUNG TO
BE WRITING YOUR MEMOIRS?
617(TLS):9NOV73-1361
JOHNSON, B.S. CHRISTIE MALRY'S OWN
DOUBLE-ENTRY.
V. CUNNINGHAM, 362:8FEB73-189
D.K. MANO, 441:23SEP73-6
617(TLS):9FEB73-141
JOHNSON, C., ED. BEST LITTLE MAGAZINE
FICTION, 1970.
N.A. BRITTIN, 577(SHR):FALL71-418
JOHNSON, C., ED. CHANGE IN COMMUNIST
SYSTEMS.*
L. BLIT, 575(SEER):JUL72-484
R.F. STAAR, 550(RUSR):APR71-206
JOHNSON, C. COMMUNIST CHINA AND LATIN
AMERICA, 1959-1967.
J. SUCHLICKI, 293(JAST):AUG71-885
JOHNSON, C. & L. SLEIGH. BOYS' AND
GIRLS' NAMES.
617(TLS):17AUG73-961
JOHNSON, D. LESSER LIVES.*
M. DRABBLE, 362:19JUL73-91
H. KRAMER, 441:23JAN73-41
JOHNSON, D. THE MAN AMONG THE SEALS.
639(VQR):WINTER71-XX
JOHNSON, D.C. & OTHERS. SOUTHEAST ASIA:
A BIBLIOGRAPHY FOR UNDERGRADUATE LIB-
RARIES.
R.I. CRANE, 293(JAST):MAY71-649
JOHNSON, D.G. WORLD AGRICULTURE IN DIS-
ARRAY.
617(TLS):30MAR73-361
JOHNSON, D.L., ED. THE CHILEAN ROAD TO
SOCIALISM.
N. GALL, 441:1JUL73-6

JOHNSON, E.  SIR WALTER SCOTT.*
  M.E. BRADFORD, 569(SR):SUMMER72-478
  K.C., 191(ELN):SEP71(SUPP)-52
  J.H. MADDOX, JR., 301(JEGP):JAN72-146
  B. TYSDAHL, 172(EDDA):1971/5-313
  E. WAGENKNECHT, 594:SPRING71-103
JOHNSON, F.R.  LEGENDS AND MYTHS OF NORTH
  CAROLINA'S ROANOKE-CHOWAN AREA.  TALES
  FROM OLD CAROLINA.
  C.G. ZUG, 292(JAF):OCT-DEC71-462
JOHNSON, F.R.  THE NAT TURNER STORY.
  W.R. FERRIS, JR., 292(JAF):JUL-SEP71-
  353
JOHNSON, F.R.  WITCHES AND DEMONS IN HIS-
  TORY AND FOLKLORE.
  M. HAGLER, 292(JAF):APR-JUN71-259
  C.G. ZUG, 292(JAF):OCT-DEC71-462
JOHNSON, I.D.  GLENWAY WESCOTT.
  W. WASSERSTROM, 27(AL):MAR72-167
JOHNSON, J.J. & OTHERS, EDS.  THE MEXICAN-
  AMERICAN.
  F. GILLMOR, 292(JAF):APR-JUN71-260
JOHNSON, J.S.  THE NAGARS OF RUNSWICK
  BAY.
  617(TLS):23NOV73-1456
JOHNSON, J.W.  THE FORMATION OF ENGLISH
  NEO-CLASSICAL THOUGHT.
  F. KREY, 38:BAND88HEFT3-395
JOHNSON, J.W.  SEVEN HOUSES.
  P. MERAS, 441:13MAY73-14
  442(NY):5MAY73-150
JOHNSON, L.  LAND LIKE A LIZARD.
  S.E. LEE, 581:1971/3-227
JOHNSON, O.A.  THE MORAL LIFE.*
  R.F. ATKINSON, 393(MIND):OCT71-630
JOHNSON, P.  FORM AND TRANSFORMATION IN
  MUSIC AND POETRY OF THE ENGLISH RENAIS-
  SANCE.
  617(TLS):1JUN73-611
JOHNSON, P.  THE OFFSHORE ISLANDERS.*
  A. BURGESS, 441:28JAN73-4
JOHNSON, P. & G. GALE.  THE HIGHLAND
  JAUNT.
  617(TLS):11MAY73-534
JOHNSON, P.H.  THE HOLIDAY FRIEND.*
  442(NY):28APR73-145
JOHNSON, P.H.  THE HONOURS BOARD.*
  J.L. HALIO, 598(SOR):SPRING73-455
JOHNSON, R.  MAN'S PLACE.
  D. DONOGHUE, 453:19JUL73-17
  617(TLS):3AUG73-894
JOHNSON, R.B.  HENRY DE MONTHERLANT.*
  F. VIAL, 546(RR):APR71-156
JOHNSON, R.C.  JOHN HEYWOOD.
  K.W. CAMERON, 551(RENQ):WINTER71-555
JOHNSON, R.S.  MORE'S "UTOPIA."*
  B.W. BECKINGSALE, 447(N&Q):JUN71-232
  H.W. DONNER, 597(SN):VOL42#1-226
JOHNSON, R.V.  AESTHETICISM.
  205(FMLS):OCT70-419
JOHNSON, S.  JOHNSON ON SHAKESPEARE.*
  (A. SHERBO, ED)
  J.T. BOULTON, 179(ES):DEC71-560
  F.W. HILLES, 570(SQ):SPRING71-169
JOHNSON, S.  LIFE OF SAVAGE.*  (C. TRACY,
  ED)
  F.W. HILLES, 676(YR):AUTUMN71-109
  P. O'FLAHERTY, 150(DR):WINTER71/72-
  609
  566:AUTUMN71-27
JOHNSON, S.  THE POPULATION PROBLEM.
  617(TLS):1NOV73-1450
JOHNSON, S.  THE RAMBLER.*  (W.J. BATE &
  A.B. STRAUSS, EDS)
  R.G. DUBUQUE, 613:AUTUMN70-455
  J.D. FLEEMAN, 541(RES):AUG71-348
  A. FURTWANGLER, 405(MP):FEB72-256
                              [CONTINUED]

[CONTINUING]
  J.H. HAGSTRUM, 597(SN):VOL43#1-318
  C. TRACY, 173(ECS):WINTER71-231
JOHNSON, T.  THOMAS HARDY.
  P. ROBERTS, 541(RES):FEB71-107
JOHNSON, W., WITH C. EVANS - SEE STEVEN-
  SON, A.E.
JOHNSON, W.B. - SEE CARRINGTON, J.
JOHNSON, W.R.  LUXURIANCE AND ECONOMY.
  W.L. WATSON, 124:DEC71-134
JOHNSON, W.S.  GERARD MANLEY HOPKINS.*
  W.R. MUNDT, 598(SOR):AUTUMN73-1029
JOHNSTON, E.  FORMAL PENMANSHIP AND OTHER
  PAPERS.*  (H. CHILD, ED)
  N. BARKER, 78(BC):WINTER71-535
JOHNSTON, F.S., JR.  THE LOGIC OF RELA-
  TIONSHIP.
  J.J. JENKINS, 478:JUL71-132
JOHNSTON, G.  ANNALS OF AUSTRALIAN LIT-
  ERATURE.*
  581:MAR72-77
JOHNSTON, G.  CLEAN STRAW FOR NOTHING.
  L. CANTRELL, 381:MAR71-125
JOHNSTON, J.  THE GATES.
  R. BRYDEN, 362:18JAN73-90
  617(TLS):26JAN73-85
JOHNSTON, J.  LESBIAN NATION.
  M. ELLMANN, 453:1NOV73-18
JOHNSTON, J.  MARMALADE ME.
  T. BOREK, 151:OCT71-97
JOHNSTON, R.C. & D.D.R. OWEN, EDS.  TWO
  OLD FRENCH GAUVAIN ROMANCES.
  617(TLS):20APR73-440
JOHNSTON, W.  THE STILL POINT.*
  A. BATTEEN, 485(PE&W):JUL71-343
  R.E. KENNEDY, 613:AUTUMN71-452
JOHNSTONE, P.  A GUIDE TO GREEK ISLAND
  EMBROIDERY.
  617(TLS):6APR73-401
JOLL, J.  EUROPE SINCE 1870.
  617(TLS):24AUG73-968
JOLLES, F. - SEE SCHLEGEL, A.W.
JOLLY, R.  PLANNING FOR AFRICAN DEVELOP-
  MENT.
  S. MILBURN, 69:JAN71-77
JOLLY, W.P.  MARCONI.
  617(TLS):23FEB73-206
JOLOWICZ, H.F. & B. NICHOLAS.  HISTORICAL
  INTRODUCTION TO THE STUDY OF ROMAN LAW.
  617(TLS):30MAR73-356
JOLY, A. - SEE THUROT, F.
JOLY, R.  DEUX ÉTUDES SUR LA PRÉHISTOIRE
  DU RÉALISME.
  J.V. ALTER, 207(FR):MAR71-806
  J. MAYER, 557(RSH):JUL-SEP70-475
  V. MYLNE, 208(FS):JAN72-80
  M. ROELENS, 535(RHL):JAN-FEB71-99
JOLY, R. - SEE HIPPOCRATES
JONARD, N.  ITALO SVEVO ET LA CRISE DE LA
  BOURGEOISIE EUROPÉENNE.
  R.O.J. VAN NUFFEL, 549(RLC):OCT-DEC
  70-577
JONAS, C.  THE SPUTNIK RAPIST.
  D.K. MANO, 441:25FEB73-2
JONAS, D. & D. KLEIN.  MAN-CHILD.
  R. DUNSTAN, 619(TC):VOL179#1048-56
JONAS, G.  VISCERAL LEARNING.
  C. LEHMANN-HAUPT, 441:25JUL73-35
  441:16SEP73-14
JONAS, H.  THE PHENOMENON OF LIFE.
  R. BLANCHÉ, 542:OCT-DEC70-494
JONAS, I.B.  THOMAS MANN UND ITALIEN.*
  H. HATFIELD, 221(GQ):MAY71-412
JONDORF, G.  ROBERT GARNIER AND THE
  THEMES OF POLITICAL TRAGEDY IN THE SIX-
  TEENTH CENTURY.*
  J.C. LAPP, 551(RENQ):AUTUMN71-383
                              [CONTINUED]

JONDORF, G. ROBERT GARNIER AND THE
THEMES OF POLITICAL TRAGEDY IN THE SIX-
TEENTH CENTURY.*  [CONTINUING]
  R. LEBÈGUE, 549(RLC):OCT-DEC70-553
  J. PINEAUX, 557(RSH):JAN-MAR70-156
  C.N. SMITH, 205(FMLS):APR70-188
JONES, A. FIGURES.
  R.S., 376:OCT70-92
JONES, A. THE NEW INFLATION.
  617(TLS):13JUL73-807
JONES, A. UNCLE TOM'S CAMPUS.
  F.M. HECHINGER, 441:30MAR73-43
JONES, A.G. THE GERMANS.
  C. BAIER, 220(GL&L):OCT71-46
JONES, A.H.M. THE CITIES OF THE EASTERN
ROMAN PROVINCES. (2ND ED) (REV BY M.
AVI-YONAH & OTHERS)
  T.E. GREGORY, 124:APR-MAY72-279
  F. LASSERRE, 182:VOL24#1/2-40
JONES, A.H.M., J.R. MARTINDALE & J. MOR-
RIS. THE PROSOPOGRAPHY OF THE LATER
ROMAN EMPIRE. (VOL 1)
  C.P. JONES, 124:FEB72-207
JONES, A.R. & G. THOMAS, EDS. PRESENTING
SAUNDERS LEWIS.
  617(TLS):25MAY73-590
JONES, A.R. & W. TYDEMAN - SEE COLERIDGE,
S.T.
JONES, B. & B.L. HAWES. STEP IT DOWN.
  W. RHODES, 187:SEP73-549
JONES, C. AN INTRODUCTION TO MIDDLE
ENGLISH.
  E.J. CROOK, 301(JEGP):JUL72-439
JONES, C.E., JR. NEGRO MYTHS FROM THE
GEORGIA COAST.
  M.A. TWINING, 292(JAF):OCT-DEC71-464
JONES, D. THE TRIBUNE'S VISITATION.*
  J. SAUNDERS, 565:VOL11#4-68
JONES, D. - SEE THOMAS, D.
JONES, D. & D. WARD. THE PHONETICS OF
RUSSIAN.*
  O. AKHMANOVA, 297(JL):OCT71-298
  C.L. DRAGE, 402(MLR):APR72-475
JONES, D.G. BUTTERFLY ON ROCK.*
  K.L. GOODWIN, 67:NOV72-240
  D.O. SPETTIGUE, 529(QQ):SPRING71-154
  P. STEVENS, 141:WINTER71-108
  P. STEVENS, 628:SPRING71-84
  G. WOODCOCK, 648:JAN71-70
JONES, D.J.V. BEFORE REBECCA.
  617(TLS):19OCT73-1275
JONES, D.M. & N.G. WILSON, EDS. SCHOLIA
IN ARISTOPHANEM. (PT 1, FASC 2)
  K.J. DOVER, 123:MAR72-21
  W. MORRIS, 24:JUL72-481
JONES, D.P. AFTER LIVINGSTONE.
  G. SHEPPERSON, 69:JAN70-89
JONES, E. SCENIC FORM IN SHAKESPEARE.*
  S. WELLS, 402(MLR):OCT72-871
JONES, E. LA VIE ET L'OEUVRE DE SIGMUND
FREUD. (VOL 3)
  Y. BRÈS, 542:APR-JUN71-189
JONES, E.H. MRS. HUMPHRY WARD.
  617(TLS):7SEP73-1022
JONES, E.Y. FATHER OF ART PHOTOGRAPHY.
  617(TLS):21DEC73-1573
JONES, G. THE DRAGON HAS TWO TONGUES.
  R. LAWRENCE, 175:SUMMER70-69
  F. LEFRANC, 189(EA):JUL-SEP70-346
JONES, G. A HISTORY OF THE VIKINGS.*
  R.I. PAGE, 382(MAE):1972/1-89
JONES, G. KING, BEASTS, AND HEROES.*
  F. BRAENDEL, 109:SPRING/SUMMER73-168
JONES, G. UNDER THREE FLAGS.
  617(TLS):28DEC73-1595

JONES, G.C. L'IRONIE DANS LES ROMANS DE
STENDHAL.
  V. BROMBERT, 535(RHL):MAR-APR70-318
  R.M. CHADBOURNE, 207(FR):OCT70-232
JONES, G.F. WALTHER VON DER VOGELWEIDE.*
  G.P. KNAPP, 657(WW):JUL/AUG71-284
  O. SAYCE, 220(GL&L):APR72-314
  V. ZIMMERMANN, 224(GRM):JAN70-110
JONES, G.W. - SEE MATHER, C.
JONES, H. LE SURRÉALISME IGNORÉ [AVEC UN
TÉMOIGNAGE DE] PASTOUREAU, H. LE SUR-
RÉALISME DE L'APRÈS-GUERRE (1946-1950).
  R. MERCIER, 557(RSH):OCT-DEC70-665
JONES, H.G. THE RECORDS OF A NATION.
  P. WALNE, 325:OCT71-340
JONES, H.L. ROBERT LAWSON.
  M. CIMINO, 441:18MAR73-10
JONES, H.M. THE AGE OF ENERGY.
  L.C. MILAZZO, 584(SWR):WINTER72-85
JONES, H.M. BELIEF AND DISBELIEF IN
AMERICAN LITERATURE.*
  U. BRUMM, 38:BAND88HEFT3-405
JONES, I. INIGO JONES ON PALLADIO. (B.
ALLSOPP, ED)
  J.-L-M., 135:MAY71-62
JONES, I. THE MOST NOTABLE ANTIQUITY OF
GREAT BRITAIN VULGARLY CALLED STONE-
HENGE 1655.
  617(TLS):23FEB73-214
JONES, J. THE GYPSIES OF GRANADA.
  P.W., 135:APR70-276
JONES, J. JOHN KEATS'S DREAM OF TRUTH.*
  J.R. MAC GILLIVRAY, 627(UTQ):FALL70-73
JONES, J. THE MERRY MONTH OF MAY.*
  639(VQR):SUMMER71-C
JONES, J. A TOUCH OF DANGER.
  A. BROYARD, 441:21MAY73-37
  N. CALLENDAR, 441:13MAY73-38
  442(NY):26MAY73-136
JONES, J. & J. AUTHORS AND AREAS OF
AUSTRALIA.*
  581:MAR72-77
JONES, J.A. POPE'S COUPLET ART.*
  W. BLISSETT, 627(UTQ):WINTER71-183
JONES, J.P. GAMBLING YESTERDAY AND
TODAY.
  617(TLS):15JUN73-700
JONES, J.R. THE REVOLUTION OF 1688 IN
ENGLAND.
  617(TLS):19OCT73-1279
JONES, J.R. & J.E. KELLER - SEE ALFONSO,
P.
JONES, K. A HISTORY OF THE MENTAL HEALTH
SERVICES.
  617(TLS):23FEB73-200
JONES, L. BLACK MAGIC POETRY.
  P. GOW, 648:OCT71-59
JONES, L.M. CUSTOMS AND FOLKLORE OF
WORCESTERSHIRE.
  T. BROWN, 203:SUMMER70-153
JONES, L.M. - SEE REYNOLDS, J.H.
JONES, L.T. SO SAY THE INDIANS.
  B. TOELKEN, 650(WF):OCT70-268
JONES, M. A CRY OF ABSENCE.*
  M.K. SPEARS, 569(SR):WINTER72-168
  639(VQR):AUTUMN71-CLX
JONES, M. HOLDING ON.
  R. BRYDEN, 362:2AUG73-155
  617(TLS):29JUN73-736
JONES, M. THE REVOLVING DOOR.
  R. BRYDEN, 362:2AUG73-155
  617(TLS):17AUG73-945
JONES, P., ED. IMAGIST POETRY.
  617(TLS):2FEB73-109
JONES, P.E., ED. THE FIRE COURT. (VOL 2)
  R.E. WALTON, 14:JUL71-317
JONES, R.D. FRANCESCO VETTORI.
  617(TLS):23MAR73-326

JONES, R.E. THE EMANCIPATION OF THE
RUSSIAN NOBILITY 1762-1785.
617(TLS):14DEC73-1546
JONES, R.O. A LITERARY HISTORY OF SPAIN:
THE GOLDEN AGE.*
P.N. DUNN, 402(MLR):OCT72-925
JONES, W. THE LETTERS OF SIR WILLIAM
JONES.* (G. CANNON, ED)
P.M. GRIFFITH, 173(ECS):SUMMER71-478
W.P. JONES, 481(PQ):JUL71-449
JONES, W.R.D. THE TUDOR COMMONWEALTH,
1529-1559.
S.E. LEHMBERG, 551(RENQ):SUMMER71-270
JONG, E. FEAR OF FLYING.
B. DE MOTT, 61:DEC73-125
C. LEHMANN-HAUPT, 441:6NOV73-31
T. STOKES, 441:11NOV73-40
J. UPDIKE, 442(NY):17DEC73-149
JONG, E. FRUIT & VEGETABLES.*
617(TLS):27APR73-474
JONG, E. HALF LIVES.
H. SHAPIRO, 441:25AUG73-21
H. VENDLER, 441:12AUG73-6
DE JONG, G., JR. FOUR HUNDRED YEARS OF
BRAZILIAN LITERATURE.
O. FERNÁNDEZ, 399(MLJ):MAR71-190
DE JONGE, C.H. DELFT CERAMICS.
J.V.G. MALLET, 90:AUG71-479
DE JONGH, J.F. & OTHERS. PRIMARY EDUCA-
TION IN SUKUMALAND (TANZANIA).
S. MILBURN, 69:JUL71-257
JONSON, B. THE ALCHEMIST. (F.H. MARES,
ED)
E. LEHMANN, 38:BAND89HEFT3-391
JONSON, B. EVERY MAN IN HIS HUMOR.*
(G.B. JACKSON, ED)
W.D. KAY, 405(MP):MAY72-339
B. SÖDERBERG, 597(SN):VOL43#2-585
JONSON, B. BEN JONSON: THE COMPLETE
MASQUES.* (S. ORGEL, ED)
L.A. BEAURLINE, 219(GAR):SPRING71-103
P. D'ANDREA, 405(MP):AUG71-68
J.A. VAN DORSTEN, 179(ES):APR71-168
B. SÖDERBERG, 597(SN):VOL42#2-465
JONSON, B. SELECTED MASQUES.* (S. ORGEL,
ED)
J.P. CUTTS, 551(RENQ):AUTUMN71-404
JOOST, N. & A. SULLIVAN. D.H. LAWRENCE
AND THE "DIAL."*
K. CUSHMAN, 405(MP):NOV71-152
JORAVSKY, D. THE LYSENKO AFFAIR.*
M. MC CAULEY, 575(SEER):APR72-313
JORAVSKY, D. & G. HAUPT - SEE MEDVEDEV,
R.A.
JORDAN, A.T. - SEE BARTOSZEWSKI, W. & Z.
LEWIN
JORDAN, B. PAUPERS.
617(TLS):4MAY73-487
JORDAN, D. NILE GREEN.
617(TLS):18MAY73-562
JORDAN, D.K. GODS, GHOSTS, AND ANCES-
TORS.
617(TLS):24AUG73-985
JORDAN, D.P. GIBBON AND HIS ROMAN EM-
PIRE.*
D.M. OLIVER, 301(JEGP):APR72-252
639(VQR):AUTUMN71-CLXXVI
JORDAN, J. SOME CHANGES.
J. KESSLER, 491:FEB73-292
JORDAN, J., ED. SOULSCRIPT.
639(VQR):WINTER71-XX
JORDAN, J.E. - SEE DE QUINCEY, T.
JORDAN, R.F. A CONCISE HISTORY OF WEST-
ERN ARCHITECTURE.
S.W. LITTLE, 50(ARQ):SUMMER71-177
JORDAN, R.M. CHAUCER AND THE SHAPE OF
CREATION.*
C. BROOKHOUSE, 599:SPRING71-203

JORDAN, W.K. EDWARD VI: THE THRESHOLD OF
POWER.
J. HITCHCOCK, 377:JUL72-121
JØRGENSEN, A. H.C. ANDERSEN-LITTERATUREN
1875-1968.*
R. KLEIN, 78(BC):AUTUMN71-407
JORGENSEN, J.G. THE SUN DANCE RELIGION.
W.C. STURTEVANT, 441:18MAR73-36
JORGENSEN, P.A. OUR NAKED FRAILTIES.
E.M. WAITH, 676(YR):SPRING72-441
JORRÍN, M. & J.D. MARTZ. LATIN AMERICAN
POLITICAL THOUGHT AND IDEOLOGY.
A. ANGELL, 86(BHS):OCT72-413
639(VQR):SUMMER71-CXXVI
JOSEPH OF EXETER. THE ILIAD OF DARES
PHRYGIUS. (G. ROBERTS, ED & TRANS)
A.K. BATE, 382(MAE):1972/1-61
JOSEPH, G. JOHN BARTH.
R. ASSELINEAU, 189(EA):JUL-SEP71-350
JOSEPH, G. TENNYSONIAN LOVE.*
G.O. MARSHALL, JR., 219(GAR):SUMMER
70-261
JOSEPHS, H. DIDEROT'S DIALOGUE OF GES-
TURE AND LANGUAGE.*
V. BOWEN, 149:MAR72-118
R.J. ELLRICH, 207(FR):FEB71-620
R. NIKLAUS, 208(FS):JAN72-80
JOSHI, L. STUDIES IN THE BUDDHIST
CULTURE OF INDIA.
D.W. MITCHELL, 485(PE&W):JUL71-338
JOSHI, S.D. - SEE "PATAÑJALI'S 'VYĀKARAṆA-
MAHĀBHĀṢYA'"
JOSIPOVICI, G. THE WORLD AND THE BOOK.*
P.P. CLARK, 149:DEC72-473
JOSKI, D. ARTAUD.
F.A., 154:JUN71-426
JOSPE, A., ED. TRADITION AND CONTEM-
PORARY EXPERIENCE.
T. DIVINE, 328:SUMMER71-378
JOSSELSON, H.H., ED. RUSSIAN-ENGLISH
PLASTICS DICTIONARY.
J. STEWARD & H. FISCHBACH, 75:4/1970-
217
JOST, F. ESSAIS DE LITTÉRATURE COM-
PARÉE.* (VOL 2)
A.G. ENGSTROM, 207(FR):FEB71-630
V. HELL, 52:BAND6HEFT3-302
H.H.H. REMAK, 149:SEP72-328
JOUANNY, R.A. JEAN MORÉAS, ÉCRIVAIN
FRANÇAIS.*
M. SCHAETTEL, 557(RSH):OCT-DEC70-648
JOUANNY, R.A. - SEE MORÉAS, J.
JOUHANDEAU, M. BON AN, MAL AN, 1908-
1928.
617(TLS):8JUN73-647
JOUHANDEAU, M. PAULO MINUS AB ANGELIS.
617(TLS):12OCT73-1253
JOUHAUD, M. LE PROBLÈME DE L'ÊTRE ET
L'EXPÉRIENCE MORALE CHEZ MAURICE BLON-
DEL.
A. FOREST, 542:OCT-DEC71-454
M. RENAULT, 154:DEC71-770
JOUHER. PRIVATE MEMOIRS OF THE MUGHAL
EMPEROR HUMĀYŪN. (C. STEWART, TRANS)
A. AHMAD, 318(JAOS):OCT-DEC71-534
JOUKOVSKY, F. LA GLOIRE DANS LA POÉSIE
FRANÇAISE ET NÉOLATINE DU XVIE SIÈCLE.*
R.M. BURGESS, 551(RENQ):SUMMER71-255
J. PINEAUX, 557(RSH):APR-JUN71-314
C.J. THIRY, 556(RLV):1971/3-353
JOUKOVSKY, F. ORPHÉE ET SES DISCIPLES
DANS LA POÉSIE FRANÇAISE ET NÉO-LATINE
DU XVIE SIÈCLE.*
G. DOTTIN, 535(RHL):MAY-JUN71-494
J. PINEAUX, 557(RSH):APR-JUN71-315
A. SCAGLIONE, 545(RPH):AUG71-143
M. THIRY-STASSIN, 556(RLV):1971/5-632

"JOURNAL OF THE SOCIETY FOR ARMY HISTORI-
CAL RESEARCH." (VOL 1)
  617(TLS):28SEP73-1134
JOURNET, R., J. PETIT & G. ROBERT. MOTS
ET DICTIONNAIRES (1798-1878) II (CAN-
CRE-DÉVOUEMENT).
  J. DUBOIS, 535(RHL):JAN-FEB70-152
JOURNET, R., J. PETIT & G. ROBERT. MOTS
ET DICTIONNAIRES (1798-1878), III
(DEXTREMENT-HAGARD).
  R. ARVEILLER, 209(FM):JAN70-70
JOURNET, R., J. PETIT & G. ROBERT. MOTS
ET DICTIONNAIRES (1798-1878). (VOLS
4&5)
  J. DUBOIS, 535(RHL):MAY-JUN71-519
JOURNET, R. & G. ROBERT - SEE HUGO, V.
JOVÉ, J.F.V. - SEE UNDER VIDAL JOVÉ, J.F.
JOVINO, M.B. & R. DONCEEL - SEE UNDER
BONGHI JOVINO, M. & R. DONCEEL
JOYAUX, G.J. & A. TUKEY, EDS. SI NOUS
COMMENCIONS À LIRE...*
  D. NOAKES, 207(FR):DEC70-429
JOYAUX, J. LE LANGAGE, CET INCONNU.
  A. REY, 209(FM):JAN71-75
JOYCE, A. A HOMESTEAD HISTORY. (G.F.
JAMES, ED)
  F.H.A. MICKLEWRIGHT, 447(N&Q):JUL71-
273
JOYCE, J. JOYCE'S "ULYSSES" NOTESHEETS
IN THE BRITISH MUSEUM. (P.F. HERRING,
ED)
  A.W. LITZ, 329(JJQ):SPRING73-349
JOYCE, S. THE COMPLETE DUBLIN DIARY OF
STANISLAUS JOYCE. (G.H. HEALEY, ED)
  639(VQR):AUTUMN71-CLXXIV
JÓZSEF, A. SELECTED POEMS AND TEXTS.
(G. GÖMÖRI AND J. ATLAS, EDS)
  617(TLS):5OCT73-1184
JUCHEM, H-G. DIE ENTWICKLUNG DES BE-
GRIFFS DES SCHÖNEN BEI KANT UNTER
BESONDERER BERÜCKSICHTIGUNG DES BE-
GRIFFS DER VERWORRENEN ERKENNTNIS.
  W. STEINBECK, 342:BAND62HEFT4-513
"JUDAICA." [WIDENER LIBRARY SHELFLIST,
39]
  617(TLS):16FEB73-188
JUDD, D. THE LIFE AND TIMES OF GEORGE V.
  617(TLS):2NOV73-1331
JUDD, F.C. ELECTRONICS IN MUSIC.
  617(TLS):27APR73-481
JUDSON, M.A. THE POLITICAL THOUGHT OF
SIR HENRY VANE THE YOUNGER.
  G.W. GRAY, 656(WMQ):OCT71-682
JUDSON, W. ALICE AND ME.
  P. ADAMS, 61:JUN73-123
  N. CALLENDAR, 441:17JUN73-32
  617(TLS):23NOV73-1455
JUHÁSZ, F. THE BOY CHANGED INTO A STAG.*
  M.G. PERLOFF, 659:WINTER73-97
JUILLAND, A., ED. LINGUISTIC STUDIES
PRESENTED TO ANDRÉ MARTINET.
  R.A. BOGGS, 215(GL):VOL11#2-142
JUILLAND, A., ED. LINGUISTIC STUDIES
PRESENTED TO ANDRÉ MARTINET ON THE
OCCASION OF HIS SIXTIETH BIRTHDAY.
(VOL 1)
  M.D. MOODY, 207(FR):FEB71-585
JUILLAND, I. DICTIONNAIRE DES IDÉES
DANS L'OEUVRE DE ANDRÉ MALRAUX.
  R. GOLDTHORPE, 208(FS):JAN72-99
  W.G. LANGLOIS, 207(FR):OCT70-219
JUKES, G. THE SOVIET UNION IN ASIA.
  617(TLS):16NOV73-1397
JULIARD, P. PHILOSOPHIES OF LANGUAGE IN
EIGHTEENTH-CENTURY FRANCE.
  W.R. ALBURY, 173(ECS):WINTER71/72-344

JULIUS AFRICANUS. LES "CESTES" DE JULIUS
AFRICANUS. (J-R. VIEILLEFOND, ED &
TRANS)
  W.R. CHALMERS, 123:JUN72-210
JULLIAN, P. D'ANNUNZIO.
  L. BARZINI, 453:4OCT73-15
  A. BROYARD, 441:11JAN73-41
  G. GERSH, 99:SEP73-40
  C.D. HEYMANN, 441:25FEB73-5
  617(TLS):23FEB73-199
JULLIAN, P. DREAMERS OF DECADENCE.*
  D.R. FAULKNER, 676(YR):SUMMER72-615
  A. FORGE, 592:NOV71-215
JULLIAN, P. OSCAR WILDE.
  W.N. KING, 397(MD):FEB71-453
  J.T. MC CARTIN, 50(ARQ):AUTUMN70-283
JULY, R.W. A HISTORY OF THE AFRICAN
PEOPLE.
  R. SMITH, 69:JAN71-71
JUMP, J.D. BURLESQUE.
  566:SPRING72-95
JUMP, J.D. BYRON.*
  F.W. BATESON, 453:22FEB73-32
JUNG, C.G. EXPERIMENTAL RESEARCHES. (L.
STEIN, WITH D. RIVIERE, TRANS)
  617(TLS):21SEP73-1080
JUNG, C.G. LETTERS. (VOL 1) (G. ADLER,
WITH A. JAFFÉ, EDS)
  R. DAVIES, 441:25FEB73-31
  617(TLS):19OCT73-1271
JUNG, C.G. PSYCHOLOGICAL REFLECTIONS.
(J. JACOBI & R.F.C. HULL, EDS)
  639(VQR):AUTUMN71-CLXXXVII
JUNG, F. JOE FRANK ILLUSTRIERT DIE
WELT. (W. FÄHNDERS, H. KARRENBROCK &
M. RECTOR, EDS) DIE EROBERUNG DER
MASCHINEN.
  617(TLS):5OCT73-1185
JUNG, H. DIE ARDENNEN-OFFENSIVE 1944/45.
  H.R. KURZ, 52:VOL24#23/24-881
JUNG, M-R. ÉTUDES SUR LE POÈME ALLÉGOR-
IQUE EN FRANCE AU MOYEN ÂGE.
  L.J. FRIEDMAN, 589:APR72-316
JUNGBLUTH, G. - SEE VON SAAZ, J.
JÜNGER, H., ED. THE LITERATURES OF THE
SOVIET PEOPLES.
  R.C. CLARK, 544:SPRING72-244
JÜNGER, H. ALEXEJ TOLSTOI.
  H. HERTING, 654(WB):4/1971-222
JUNGK, R. & H.J. MUNDT - SEE DESCH, K.
JUNGRAITHMAYR, H. DIE RON-SPRACHEN,
TSCHADOHAMITISCHE STUDIEN IN NORDNI-
GERIEN.
  A.N. TUCKER, 315(JAL):VOL10PT2-60
JURADO, J. - SEE FORNER Y SEGARRA, J.P.
JUST, G. IRONIE UND SENTIMENTALITÄT IN
DEN ERZÄHLENDEN DICHTUNGEN ARTHUR
SCHNITZLERS.
  R. MAJUT, 224(GRM):JAN70-114
JUST, W. THE CONGRESSMAN WHO LOVED
FLAUBERT.
  P. ANDERSON, 441:26AUG73-22
  C. LEHMANN-HAUPT, 441:27JUL73-35
JUST, W. MILITARY MEN.*
  639(VQR):SUMMER71-CXXXII
JUSTICE, D. DEPARTURES.
  H. SHAPIRO, 441:22SEP73-29
JUVENAL. D. IVNII IVVENALIS "SATVRAE"
XIV. (J.D. DUFF, ED)
  W.S. ANDERSON, 124:SEP71-28
JUVENAL. THE "SATIRES" OF JUVENAL. (C.
PLUMB, TRANS)
  M.L. CLARKE, 123:DEC72-414

KABIR, H. THE BENGALI NOVEL.
 T. RICCARDI, JR., 318(JAOS):JAN-MAR71-
 158
KAC, M. & S.M. ULAM. MATHEMATICS AND
 LOGIC.
 D. BOOTH, 316:DEC71-677
KACHRU, Y. AN INTRODUCTION TO HINDI
 SYNTAX.
 W.E. JONES, 297(JL):FEB70-151
KACZEROWSKY, K. BÜRGERLICHE ROMANKUNST
 IM ZEITALTER DES BAROCK.*
 F.G. SIEVEKE, 680(ZDP):BAND90HEFT4-
 579
KACZMAREK, L., Z. DOBRZAŃSKI & J. KANIA,
 EDS. POLSKA BIBLIOGRAFIA LOGOPEDYCZNA.
 G.F. MEIER, 682(ZPSK):BAND24HEFT5-445
KADLER, E.H. LINGUISTICS AND TEACHING
 FOREIGN LANGUAGES.
 P.A. GAENG, 207(FR):FEB71-598
KADLER, E.H. LITERARY FIGURES IN FRENCH
 DRAMA (1784-1834).
 C.G.S. WILLIAMS, 399(MLJ):FEB71-123
KAEL, P. THE CITIZEN KANE BOOK.*
 M. WOOD, 453:29NOV73-6
KAEL, P. DEEPER INTO MOVIES.
 A. BROYARD, 441:22FEB73-41
 I. HOWE, 441:18FEB73-1
 M. WOOD, 453:8MAR73-3
KAEL, P. GOING STEADY.
 J.P., 376:APR71-126
 J. SHADOIAN, 418(MR):SUMMER72-490
KAEUPER, R.W. BANKERS TO THE CROWN.
 617(TLS):21SEP73-1071
KAFENGAUZ, B.B. DREVNII PSKOV.
 J. RABA, 104:WINTER72-650
KAFITZ, D. LOHENSTEINS ARMINIUS.
 E. SAGARRA & P. SKRINE, 402(MLR):
 JUL72-689
KAFKA, F. LETTERS TO FELICE.* (GERMAN
 TITLE: BRIEFE AN FELICE.) (E. HELLER &
 J. BORN, EDS)
 P. ADAMS, 61:OCT73-130
 M. DICKSTEIN, 441:30SEP73-1
 C. LEHMANN-HAUPT, 441:25SEP73-47
 U. WEISSTEIN, 133:1971/3-321
 442(NY):5NOV73-187
KAFKA, F. DER PROZESS. (H.F. BROOKES &
 C.E. GAWNE-CAINE, EDS)
 H. REISS, 220(GL&L):JAN72-188
"FRANZ KAFKA."* (E. HELLER & J. BEUG,
 EDS)
 F. STOCK, 52:BAND6HEFT1-106
 P.K. WHITAKER, 133:1971/3-329
KAGAME, A. INTRODUCTION AUX GRANDS
 GENRES LYRIQUES DE L'ANCIEN RWANDA.
 M. D'HERTEFELT, 69:OCT70-386
KAGAN, D. THE OUTBREAK OF THE PELOPON-
 NESIAN WAR.*
 R.S. STROUD, 121(CJ):OCT-NOV71-87
 M.E. WHITE, 487:WINTER71-380
KAGAN, Z., ED. A TALE FOR EACH MONTH
 1964.
 B. KIRSHENBLATT-GIMBLETT, 582(SFQ):
 DEC70-371
KAGANOVICH, A.L. ARTS OF RUSSIA: 17TH
 AND 18TH CENTURIES.
 A. BRYER, 39:NOV70-397
 G.H. HAMILTON, 32:MAR72-203
KAGANOVICH, A.L. SPLENDOURS OF LENINGRAD.
 G. DONCHIN, 575(SEER):APR72-330
KAHLER, E. THE ORBIT OF THOMAS MANN.*
 W.N. HUGHES, 399(MLJ):MAR71-199
 R. LEROY, 556(RLV):1971/6-778
 R.A. NICHOLLS, 405(MP):FEB71-310
 E.A. WIRTZ, 220(GL&L):JAN72-180
 205(FMLS):APR70-208
KAHN, E.J., JR. FRAUD.
 P. ADAMS, 61:NOV73-129

KAHN, F. INTRODUCTION À L'ÉTUDE DE LA
 MÉLODIE DE L'ÉNONCÉ FRANÇAIS CHEZ UN
 JEUNE PARISIEN CULTIVÉ DU 16E ARRONDIS-
 SEMENT.
 G.F. MEIER, 682(ZPSK):BAND23HEFT4-424
KAHN, H. THE EMERGING JAPANESE SUPER-
 STATE.
 R.A. MILLER, 639(VQR):SPRING71-286
KAHN, J., ED. TRIAL AND TERROR.
 442(NY):29OCT73-184
KAHN, L. MIRRORS OF THE JEWISH MIND.
 S.D. BRAUN, 207(FR):OCT70-208
KAHN, R. THE BOYS OF SUMMER.*
 G. ISEMINGER, 109:FALL/WINTER72/73-90
KAHN, T.C. AN INTRODUCTION TO HOMINOLOGY.
 H.J. BIRX, 484(PPR):MAR72-432
KAHNWEILER, D-H., WITH F. CREMIEUX. MY
 GALLERIES AND PAINTERS.*
 R. LEIBOWITZ, 58:NOV71-14
KAILASAPATHY, K. TAMIL HEROIC POETRY.*
 A.T. HATTO, 303:VOL91-163
 S. VAIDYANATHAN, 318(JAOS):OCT-DEC71-
 556
KAIMIO, M. THE CHORUS OF GREEK DRAMA
 WITHIN THE LIGHT OF THE PERSON AND
 NUMBER USED.*
 G. RONNET, 555:VOL45FASC2-331
 T.B.L. WEBSTER, 303:VOL91-147
 E.W. WHITTLE, 123:DEC72-361
KAINZ, F. PHILOSOPHISCHE ETYMOLOGIE UND
 HISTORISCHE SEMANTIK.
 A.M. DAVIES, 123:MAR72-74
KAISER, G. BEITRÄGE ZU DEN LIEDERN DES
 MINNESÄNGERS RUBIN.*
 M.E. GIBBS, 220(GL&L):APR72-318
KAISER, G., ED. DIE DRAMEN DES ANDREAS
 GRYPHIUS.*
 E.A. PHILIPPSON, 222(GR):MAR71-148
KAISER, G. DIE KORALLE, GAS - ERSTER
 TEIL, GAS - ZWEITER TEIL.* (B.J. KEN-
 WORTHY, ED)
 B. MOGRIDGE, 220(GL&L):JAN72-160
KAISER, G. WERKE. (VOLS 1-4) (W. HUDER,
 ED)
 W. PAULSEN, 301(JEGP):OCT72-593
 617(TLS):1JUN73-621
KAISER, G. WERKE. (VOLS 5&6) (W. HUDER,
 ED)
 617(TLS):1JUN73-621
KAJANTO, I. THE LATIN COGNOMINA.*
 M. GLÜCK, 343:BAND13HEFT2-127
KAJIMA, M. MODERN JAPAN'S FOREIGN POL-
 ICY.
 A. WATANABE, 302:JUL71-378
KALBFLEISCH, H.K. THE HISTORY OF THE
 PIONEER GERMAN LANGUAGE PRESS OF
 ONTARIO, 1835-1918.
 W. BAUSENHART, 564:JUN70-182
KALDER, E.H. LITERARY FIGURES IN FRENCH
 DRAMA (1784-1834).
 P. DEGUISE, 207(FR):MAR71-805
 M. DESCOTES, 535(RHL):MAR-APR71-306
KALDOR, M. EUROPEAN DEFENCE INDUSTRIES -
 NATIONAL AND INTERNATIONAL IMPLICATIONS.
 617(TLS):20APR73-434
KALECKI, M. SELECTED ESSAYS ON THE
 ECONOMIC GROWTH OF THE SOCIALIST AND
 THE MIXED ECONOMY.
 617(TLS):27APR73-481
KALHAN, P. KAMALA NEHRU.
 617(TLS):2NOV73-1352
KALLAS, M. KONSTYTUCJA KSIĘSTWA WARSZAW-
 SKIEGO.
 W.J. WAGNER, 32:DEC72-919
KALLEN, H.M. LIBERTY, LAUGHTER, AND
 TEARS.*
 G. DICKER, 321:WINTER71-315

KALLEN, H.M. WHAT I BELIEVE AND WHY -
MAYBE. (A.J. MARROW, ED)
Y.H. KRIKORIAN, 484(PPR):JUN72-574
KALLICH, M. THE ASSOCIATION OF IDEAS AND
CRITICAL THEORY IN EIGHTEENTH-CENTURY
ENGLAND.
R.L. BRETT, 402(MLR):JAN72-172
T.O. OLSHIN, 566:AUTUMN71-27
I. ROSS, 481(PQ):JUL71-385
KALLICH, M. THE OTHER END OF THE EGG.*
P. HARTH, 405(MP):NOV71-165
M. JOHNSON, 481(PQ):JUL71-489
KALLICH, M.I. HEAV'N'S FIRST LAW.*
I. SIMON, 179(ES):APR71-174
KALLIR, A. SIGN AND DESIGN.
G.F. MEIER, 682(ZPSK):BAND24HEFT1/2-
136
KALLIR, O. GRANDMA MOSES.
A. BROYARD, 441:7DEC73-45
L. NOCHLIN, 441:2DEC73-44
KALLIR, O. EGON SCHIELE.*
D.T., 135:JAN70-49
KALMYKOW, A.D. MEMOIRS OF A RUSSIAN DIP-
LOMAT.* (A. KALMYKOW, ED)
E.C. THADEN, 32:SEP72-670
KALNEIN, W.G. & M. LEVEY. ART AND ARCHI-
TECTURE OF THE EIGHTEENTH CENTURY IN
FRANCE. (PT 2)
617(TLS):11MAY73-527
KÁLNOKY, L. LÁNGOK ÁRNYÉKÁBAN.
G. RABA, 270:VOL21#3-174
KAMANIN, N.P. - SEE RIABCHIKOV, E.
KAMAT, A.R. PROGRESS OF EDUCATION IN
RURAL MAHARASHTRA.
E.M. GUMPERZ, 293(JAST):FEB71-487
KAMBARTEL, F. ERFAHRUNG UND STRUKTUR.
J. GLÖCKL, 53(AGP):BAND53HEFT2-219
KAMEN, H. THE WAR OF SUCCESSION IN SPAIN
1700-1715.*
O. RANUM, 173(ECS):WINTER71/72-348
KAMENKA, E. MARXISM AND ETHICS.*
D.R. BELL, 479(PHQ):JAN71-88
T.J. BLAKELEY, 321:FALL70-240
KAMENKA, E. THE PHILOSOPHY OF LUDWIG
FEUERBACH.
Z.A. JORDAN, 479(PHQ):APR71-173
KAMENOV, E., T. VŬLCHEV & E. MALKHASIAN.
IKONOMICHESKITE VRŬZKI NA BŬLGARIIA S
RAZVIVASHTITE SE STRANI.
L.A.D. DELLIN, 32:SEP72-731
KAMINSKY, J. LANGUAGE AND ONTOLOGY.
M. FRYE, 482(PHR):JUL71-394
KAMINSKY, P. REFLECTIONS IN THE EYE OF
GOD.
J. LURIA, 287:MAY70-37
KAMMEN, M. EMPIRE AND INTEREST.*
I.K. STEELE, 656(WMQ):JUL71-496
KAMMEN, M. - SEE SMITH, W., JR.
KAMMENHUBER, A. DIE ARIER IM VORDEREN
ORIENT.
H.M. KÜMMEL, 260(IF):BAND75-286
KÄMMERER, E.W. DAS LEIB-SEELE-GEIST-
PROBLEM BEI PARACELSUS UND EINIGEN
AUTOREN DES 17. JAHRHUNDERTS.
X. TILLIETTE, 182:VOL24#17/18-645
KAMPF, L. & P. LAUTER, EDS. THE POLITICS
OF LITERATURE.*
P. LANGE, 584(SWR):AUTUMN72-344
W.H. PRITCHARD, 249(HUDR):WINTER72/73-
685
KÄMPFERT, M. SÄKULARISATION UND NEUE
HEILIGKEIT.
H. BLUHM, 406:WINTER72-402
KANDAOUROFF, D. COLLECTING POSTAL HIS-
TORY.
617(TLS):2NOV73-1352

KANDUTH, E. CESARE PAVESE IM RAHMEN DER
PESSIMISTISCHEN ITALIENISCHEN LITERATUR.
D. SCHLUMBOHM, 72:BAND209HEFT4/6-467
KANE, H. DECISION.
N. CALLENDAR, 441:4NOV73-79
KANE, J. & M. KIRKLAND. CONTEMPORARY
SPOKEN ENGLISH. (VOL 1)
J.E. PIERCE, 353:JUL70-122
KANE, J.N. & G.L. ALEXANDER. NICKNAMES
AND SOBRIQUETS OF U.S. CITIES AND
STATES. (2ND ED)
K.B. HARDER, 424:DEC70-321
KANE, P. WANDERINGS OF AN ARTIST.*
S. ATHERTON, 296:SUMMER73-110
KANFER, S. A JOURNAL OF THE PLAGUE YEARS.
M. GUSSOW, 441:11JUN73-39
R. TODD, 61:JUL73-99
D. TRILLING, 441:8JUL73-4
442(NY):26MAY73-135
KANIN, G. A THOUSAND SUMMERS.
E. WEEKS, 61:NOV73-127
KANNICHT, R. - SEE EURIPIDES
KANOF, A. JEWISH CEREMONIAL ART & RE-
LIGIOUS OBSERVANCE.
P. GOODMAN, 363:AUG71-117
KANT, I. AUSGEWÄHLTE KLEINE SCHRIFTEN.
R. MALTER, 342:BAND62HEFT4-521
KANT, I. BRIEFE. (J. ZEHBE, ED)
R. MALTER, 342:BAND62HEFT4-518
KANT, I. CRITICA DELLA RAGION PURA.
(P. CHIODI, ED)
K. OEDINGEN, 342:BAND61HEFT3-411
KANT, I. ERSTE EINLEITUNG IN DIE KRITIK
DER URTEILSKRAFT. (2ND ED) (G. LEH-
MANN, ED)
R. MALTER, 342:BAND61HEFT4-520
KANT, I. GEDANKEN VON DER WAHREN SCHÄTZ-
UNG DER LEBENDIGEN KRÄFTE.
R. MALTER, 342:BAND61HEFT2-252
KANT, I. KANT'S POLITICAL WRITINGS.*
(H. REISS, ED)
R.J.B., 543:SEP70-146
KANT, I. KRITIK DER REINEN VERNUNFT.
(R. SCHMIDT, ED)
R. MALTER, 342:BAND62HEFT4-520
KANT, I. KRITIKA NA ČISTIJA RASUM. (Z.
TORBOV, ED)
G. SCHISCHKOFF, 342:BAND62HEFT3-397
KANT, I. LETTRE À MARCUS HERZ DU 21
FÉVRIER 1772. (R. VERNEAUX, ED & TRANS)
J. KOPPER, 342:BAND61HEFT1-143
KANT, I. MÉTAPHYSIQUE DES MOEURS. (A.
PHILONENKO, ED & TRANS)
J. KOPPER, 342:BAND61HEFT1-144
KANT, I. PREMIÈRE INTRODUCTION À LA
CRITIQUE DE LA FACULTÉ DE JUGER, D'UN
TON GRAND SEIGNEUR ADOPTÉ NAGUÈRE EN
PHILOSOPHIE, ANNONCE DE LA PROCHE CON-
CLUSION D'UN TRAITÉ DE PAIX PERPÉTUELLE
EN PHILOSOPHIE. (L. GUILLERMIT, TRANS)
J. KOPPER, 342:BAND61HEFT1-145
KANT, I. LE PROGRÈS DE LA MÉTAPHYSIQUE
EN ALLEMAGNE DEPUIS LEIBNIZ ET WOLF.
(L. GUILLERMIT, TRANS)
J. KOPPER, 342:BAND61HEFT1-144
KANT, I. PROLOGOMENI KŬM VSJAKA BUDEŠTA
METAFISKA, KOJATO ŠTE MOŽE DA SE PRED-
STAVI KATO NAUKA. (V. TOPUSOVA, ED)
G. SCHISCHKOFF, 342:BAND62HEFT3-397
KANT, I. LA RELIGIÓN DENTRO DE LOS LÍM-
ITES DE LA MERÁ RAZÓN. (F. MARTINEZ
MARZOA, ED & TRANS)
F. MONTERO MOLINER, 342:BAND62HEFT3-
402
KANT, I. SELECTED PRE-CRITICAL WRITINGS
AND CORRESPONDENCE WITH BECK. (G.B.
KERFERD & D.E. WALFORD, TRANS)
R. MALTER, 342:BAND61HEFT3-411

187

KANT, I. THÉORIE ET PRATIQUE, DROIT DE
MENTIR. (L. GUILLERMIT, TRANS)
  J. KOPPER, 342:BAND61HEFT1-145
KANT, I. WAS IST AUFKLÄRUNG? (J. ZEHBE,
ED)
  K. OEDINGEN, 342:BAND61HEFT2-252
KANT, I. ZUM EWIGEN FRIEDEN. (T. VALEN-
TINER, ED)
  R. MALTER, 342:BAND62HEFT4-521
"IMMANUELIS KANTII OPERA AD PHILOSOPHIAM
CRITICAM." (F. BORN, TRANS)
  R. MALTER, 342:BAND61HEFT3-412
"IMMANUEL KANTS GEDÄCHTNISFEYER ZU KÖNIGS-
BERG AM 22STEN APRIL 1810."
  R. MALTER, 342:BAND61HEFT2-253
KANTOR, A. THE BOOK OF ALFRED KANTOR.
  A. WERNER, 287:NOV71-26
KANTOR, M. THE CHILDREN SING.
  M. LEVIN, 441:11NOV73-51
KANTOR, M. & T. HAMILTON COUNTY.
  639(VQR):SPRING72-LXXXII
KAPLAN, A. PAPER AIRPLANE.*
  M.G. PERLOFF, 659:WINTER73-97
KAPLAN, B., ED. THE INNER WORLD OF MEN-
TAL ILLNESS.
  D. LESSING, 441:23SEP73-16
KAPLAN, B. PRISONERS OF THIS WORLD.
  42(AR):SPRING70-130
KAPLAN, C., ED. THE OVERWROUGHT URN.
  L.T.T., 502(PRS):FALL70-270
KAPLAN, H. DEMOCRATIC HUMANISM AND
AMERICAN LITERATURE.
  J. LYDENBERG, 27(AL):JAN73-703
  K.T. REED, 70(ANQ):OCT72-29
KAPLEAU, P., WITH P. SIMONS, EDS. THE
WHEEL OF DEATH.
  617(TLS):18MAY73-559
KAPOOR, A. INTERNATIONAL BUSINESS NEGO-
TIATIONS.
  V.D. KENNEDY, 293(JAST):MAY71-708
KAPS, H.K. MORAL PERSPECTIVE IN "LA
PRINCESSE DE CLÈVES."*
  D.R. HALL, 207(FR):OCT70-245
  F.L. LAWRENCE, 546(RR):DEC71-296
  W. LEINER, 401(MLQ):MAR72-80
  C.G.S. WILLIAMS, 399(MLJ):JAN71-42
KAPUR, H. THE EMBATTLED TRIANGLE.
  617(TLS):4MAY73-509
KARADY, V. - SEE MAUSS, M.
KARALICHEV, A. MEMOIRS.
  S. IGOV, 270:VOL22#3-61
KARANFILOV, E. SAVREMENNOST I BELETRIS-
TICA.
  N. DONTCHEV, 270:VOL21#3-169
KARÁTSON, A. LE SYMBOLISME EN HONGRIE.*
  A. DEMAITRE, 149:SEP72-357
  A. MERCIER, 557(RSH):JAN-MAR70-179
KARDOS, T. AZ ÁRGIRUS-SZÉPHISTÓRIA.
  T. DÖMÖTÖR, 196:BAND11HEFT1/2-165
KAREEM, A. MURSHID QULI KHAN AND HIS
TIMES.
  K.S. LAL, 273(IC):OCT70-254
KARLEN, A. SEXUALITY AND HOMOSEXUALITY.
  42(AR):SUMMER71-285
KARLIN, W., B.T. PAQUET & L. ROTTMANN,
EDS. FREE FIRE ZONE.
  G. EMERSON, 231:JUL73-98
  J.G. GRAY, 453:28JUN73-22
KARLIN-HAYTER, P. - SEE EUTHYMIUS
KARLINGER, F. EINFÜHRUNG IN DIE ROMAN-
ISCHE VOLKSLITERATUR. (VOL 1)
  J. GULSOY, 545(RPH):NOV71-255
KARLINSKY, S. - SEE CHEKHOV, A.
KARMEL, I. AN ESTATE OF MEMORY.
  J. GREENFIELD, 287:APR70-23
KARMEL-WOLFE, H. THE BADERS OF JACOB
STREET.
  H. GERSH, 328:FALL70-500

KÄRNELL, K-A. STRINDBERGSLEXIKON.
  S. SWAHN, 172(EDDA):1970/2-122
KARNICK, M. "WILHELM MEISTERS WANDER-
JAHRE" ODER DIE KUNST DES MITTELBAREN.*
  H. REISS, 220(GL&L):OCT71-40
KARNOW, S. MAO AND CHINA.*
  617(TLS):13APR73-407
KAROL, K.S. GUERILLAS IN POWER.
  W.E. RATLIFF, 396(MODA):SPRING72-211
  42(AR):SUMMER71-286
KAROLI, C. IDEAL UND KRISE ENTHUSIASTIS-
CHEN KÜNSTLERTUMS IN DER DEUTSCHEN
ROMANTIK.
  D.H. HAENICKE, 133:1971/3-330
KARP, A.J., ED. THE JEWISH EXPERIENCE IN
AMERICA.*
  J.A. BOROME, 328:SPRING71-250
  S.M. DUBOW, 14:JAN71-68
KARP, W. INDISPENSABLE ENEMIES.
  C. LEHMANN-HAUPT, 441:30MAY73-43
  G. WILLS, 441:15JUL73-6
KARPELES, M., ED. EIGHTY ENGLISH FOLK
SONGS FROM THE SOUTHERN APPALACHIANS.
  D.J. MC MILLAN, 599:WINTER71-98
KARPELES, M. FOLK SONGS FROM NEWFOUND-
LAND.* (NEW ED)
  S. DJWA, 102(CANL):SUMMER72-97
  H. GLASSIE, 292(JAF):OCT-DEC71-467
KARPINSKI, C., ED. ITALIAN CHIAROSCURO
WOODCUTS.
  A. FERN, 127:SPRING72-354
KARST, R. THOMAS MANN ODER DER DEUTSCHE
ZWIESPALT.
  439(NM):1971/4-763
KARVE, D.G. & D.V. AMBEKAR - SEE GOKHALE,
G.K.
KASATKIN, L.L. & T.S. SUMNIKOVA - SEE
DURNOVO, N.
KÄSEMANN, E. PAULINISCHE PERSPEKTIVEN.
  S.G. WILSON, 182:VOL24#1/2-4
KASER, M. SOVIET ECONOMICS.*
  A. ZAUBERMAN, 575(SEER):JAN72-138
KASER, M. & J. ZIELINSKI. PLANNING IN
EAST EUROPE.
  J.M. MONTIAS, 32:MAR72-238
  A. ZAUBERMAN, 575(SEER):JAN72-138
KASHIKAR, C.G. A SURVEY OF THE ŚRAUTA-
SŪTRAS.
  L. ROCHER, 318(JAOS):JAN-MAR71-153
KASSÁK, L., ED. MA (1916-1925).
  592:JUL/AUG71-51
KASTNER, W. DIE GRIECHISCHEN ADJEKTIVE
ZWEIER ENDUNGEN AUF -ΟΣ.
  E. NEU, 260(IF):BAND74-235
KASTOVSKY, D. OLD ENGLISH DEVERBAL SUB-
STANTIVES DERIVED BY MEANS OF A ZERO
MORPHEME.
  E. STANDOP, 260(IF):BAND75-356
KATAOKA, J. AN ANALYTICAL APPROACH TO
COMPARATIVE LITERATURE.
  A.O.A., 149:DEC72-478
KATARA, P. DAS FRANZÖSISCHE LEHNGUT IN
MITTELNIEDERDEUTSCHEN DENKMÄLERN VON
1300 BIS 1600.
  C. MINIS, 361:VOL26#1-105
KATARSKIJ, I. DIKKENS V ROSSII.
  J-L. BACKÈS, 549(RLC):APR-JUN71-287
KATKOV, G. & OTHERS, EDS. RUSSIA ENTERS
THE TWENTIETH CENTURY. (GERMAN TITLE:
RUSSLANDS AUFBRUCH INS 20. JAHRHUNDERT.)
  L. KOEHLER, 550(RUSR):JUL71-308
  W.E. MOSSE, 575(SEER):JAN72-130
  H. SETON-WATSON, 32:JUN72-421
KATO, S. FORM STYLE TRADITION.
  M. HILLIER, 89(BJA):AUTUMN72-406
KATRE, S.M. DICTIONARY OF PANINI.
  J. GONDA, 361:VOL26#3-334
  R. ROCHER, 318(JAOS):OCT-DEC71-552

KATRE, S.M. PROBLEMS OF RECONSTRUCTION IN
INDO-ARYAN.
R. ROCHER, 318(JAOS):JAN-MAR71-155
KATSH, A.I. GINZEI MISHNA.
I.T. NAAMANI, 399(MLJ):DEC71-540
KATSNELSON, S.D. SRAVNITEL'NAYA AKTSEN-
TOLOGIYA GERMANSKIX YAZYKOV.
A.S. LIBERMAN, 1(ALH):VOL12#1-121
KATZ, A. POLAND'S GHETTOS AT WAR.
L. KOCHAN, 32:JUN72-447
KATZ, E. & D.R. HALL. EXPLICATING FRENCH
TEXTS.
M-C. WRAGE, 399(MLJ):FEB71-124
KATZ, J. OUT OF THE GHETTO.
617(TLS):7DEC73-1501
KATZ, J., ED. PROOF. (VOL 2)
617(TLS):3AUG73-912
KATZ, J.J. LINGUISTIC PHILOSOPHY.
617(TLS):9FEB73-157
KATZ, J.J. THE PROBLEM OF INDUCTION AND
ITS SOLUTION.
A. CHURCH, 316:JUN71-320
KATZ, M. ROCKROSE.
P.C., 502(PRS):SUMMER71-184
502(PRS):SPRING71-92
KATZ, M.B. CLASS, BUREAUCRACY, AND
SCHOOLS.*
C. LASCH, 453:17MAY73-19
KATZ, R. THE FALL OF THE HOUSE OF SAVOY.
617(TLS):8MAR73-225
KATZENELSON, Y. KTAVIM ACHRONIM, 1939-
43.
T.N. LEWIS, 287:JUL/AUG71-27
KATZMAN, A. THE IMMACULATE.
J.D. REED, 600:SPRING71-177
KATZNELSON, I. BLACK MEN, WHITE CITIES.
617(TLS):11MAY73-524
KAU, W. & I. KUHN. DIE KURZFRISTIGEN
KREDITE DER GESCHÄFTSBANKEN IN DEN
LÄNDERN DER EUROPÄISCHEN WIRTSCHAFTS-
GEMEINSCHAFT UND DIE KREDITPOLITISCHEN
PROBLEME IHRER KONTROLLE.
H.C. BINSWANGER, 182:VOL24#6-283
KAUF, R. & D.C. MC CLUNEY, JR., EDS.
PROBEN DEUTSCHER PROSA.
I.D. HALPERT, 221(GQ):NOV71-626
KAUFELT, D.A. SIX MONTHS WITH AN OLDER
WOMAN.
A. BROYARD, 441:29AUG73-41
M. LEVIN, 441:30SEP73-20
KAUFFMANN, S. FIGURES OF LIGHT.
J. DIDION, 453:22MAR73-15
KAUFMAN, G. TO BUILD THE PROMISED LAND.
617(TLS):25MAY73-576
KAUFMAN, G.D. GOD THE PROBLEM.
617(TLS):15JUN73-695
KAUFMAN, M.T. IN THEIR OWN GOOD TIME.
441:24JUN73-10
KAUFMAN, P. LIBRARIES AND THEIR USERS.
P. MORGAN, 354:DEC70-361
KAUFMAN, R. INSIDE SCIENTOLOGY.
C. DRIVER, 362:26JUL73-122
617(TLS):1JUN73-619
KAUFMAN, R.R. THE POLITICS OF LAND
REFORM IN CHILE.
N. GALL, 441:1JUL73-6
KAUFMAN, S. THE FLOOR KEEPS TURNING.
L. HART, 661:SUMMER/FALL71-85
M. MARCUS, 502(PRS):FALL71-275
KAUFMAN, W.I. CHAMPAGNE.
R.A. SOKOLOV, 441:2DEC73-84
KAUFMANN, E., JR. - SEE HITCHCOCK, H-R.
& OTHERS
KAUFMANN, H. ERNST FÖRSTEMANN, ALT-
DEUTSCHE PERSONENNAMEN; ERGÄNZUNGS-
BAND.*
A.G. JANZÉN, 405(MP):AUG71-80
H. KRATZ, 133:1970/2&3-341

KAUFMANN, H. HEINRICH HEINE.*
F. MENDLE, 654(WB):7/1971-185
KAUFMANN, L. THE VILLAIN OF THE PIECE.
617(TLS):16NOV73-1407
KAUFMANN, N.Y. BULGARSKATA MNOGOGLASNA
NARODNA PESEN.
B. KREMENLIEV, 187:SEP73-551
KAUFMANN, P. KURT LEWIN, UNE THÉORIE DU
CHAMP DANS LES SCIENCES DE L'HOMME.
B. SAINT-GIRONS, 542:APR-JUN71-183
KAUFMANN, W., ED. HEGEL'S POLITICAL
PHILOSOPHY.
R.J.B., 543:DEC70-351
KAUFMANN, W. TRAGEDY AND PHILOSOPHY.*
L.B. CEBIK, 219(GAR):SPRING71-66
D. SCHÄFER-WEISS, 131(CL):SUMMER72-281
KAUFMANN, W. WITHOUT GUILT AND JUSTICE.
A. BROYARD, 441:7APR73-37
KAUFMANN, W. - SEE NIETZSCHE, F.W.
KAUL, A.N. THE ACTION OF ENGLISH COMEDY.*
B. CORMAN, 405(MP):FEB72-277
H. HAWKINS, 541(RES):NOV71-517
R. LAWRENCE, 175:SUMMER71-70
K. MUIR, 402(MLR):JAN72-166
KAULBACH, F. IMMANUEL KANT.
W. STEINBECK, 342:BAND61HEFT4-521
KAUTSKY, K., JR. - SEE BEBEL, A.
KAVAN, A. SLEEP HAS HIS HOUSE.
617(TLS):20APR73-439
KAVANAGH, T.M. THE VACANT MIRROR.
617(TLS):13JUL73-816
KAVERINE, V. PEINTRE INCONNU.
R. MICHA, 98:JUL70-581
KAVIC, L. CANADA AND THE PACIFIC.
C.S. BURCHILL, 529(QQ):SPRING71-159
KAVOLIS, V. ARTISTIC EXPRESSION.
R.N. WILSON, 290(JAAC):WINTER70-273
KAWABATA, Y. THE HOUSE OF THE SLEEPING
BEAUTIES.*
R.H. BAYES, 50(ARQ):AUTUMN71-287
M. BROCK, 285(JAPQ):JUL-SEP71-351
KAWABATA, Y. THE MASTER OF GO.*
V. CUNNINGHAM, 362:8MAR73-315
G. STEINER, 442(NY):27JAN73-89
617(TLS):16MAR73-303
KAWABATA, Y. THE SOUND OF THE MOUNTAIN.*
(JAPANESE TITLE: YAMA NO OTO.)
R.L. BROWN, 270:VOL22#2-45
KAY, M. - SEE RIGAUT, J.
KAY, N. SHOSTAKOVICH.*
D. BROWN, 415:FEB72-153
KAYE, M. A LIVELY GAME OF DEATH.
N. CALLENDAR, 441:21JAN73-26
KAYE, M. MORALS AND COMMITMENT.
617(TLS):17AUG73-959
KAYE, M. THE STEIN AND DAY HANDBOOK OF
MAGIC.
W. ARNOLD, 441:16DEC73-7
KAZIN, A. BRIGHT BOOK OF LIFE.
A. BROYARD, 441:29MAY73-33
V.S. PRITCHETT, 441:20MAY73-3
KAZUE, M. - SEE UNDER MIYAZAKI KAZUE
KEARNEY, H.F. SCHOLARS AND GENTLEMEN.*
G.A. SMITH, 568(SCN):SUMMER72-40
KEARNS, F.E. THE BLACK EXPERIENCE.
N. SCHRAUFNAGEL, 502(PRS):FALL70-265
KEARNS, J.L. STRESS IN INDUSTRY.
617(TLS):4MAY73-509
KEATING, H.R.F. INSPECTOR GHOTE TRUSTS
THE HEART.*
N. CALLENDAR, 441:20MAY73-22
442(NY):20AUG73-92
KEATING, P.J. THE WORKING CLASSES IN VIC-
TORIAN FICTION.
M. COOKE, 676(YR):SPRING72-433

KEATS, J. THE ODES OF KEATS AND THEIR
EARLIEST KNOWN MANUSCRIPTS. (R. GIT-
TINGS, ED)
D.V.E., 191(ELN):SEP71(SUPP)-46
J. STILLINGER, 301(JEGP):APR72-263
KEATS, J. THE POEMS OF JOHN KEATS.* (M.
ALLOTT, ED)
R.W. KING, 541(RES):NOV71-504
KEAY, J. INTO INDIA.
617(TLS):7DEC73-1510
KEE, R. THE GREEN FLAG.*
O.D. EDWARDS, 441:11FEB73-6
C.C. O'BRIEN, 453:25JAN73-36
KEEBLE, T.W. COMMERCIAL RELATIONS BETWEEN
BRITISH OVERSEAS TERRITORIES AND SOUTH
AMERICA, 1806-1914.
M.H.J. FINCH, 86(BHS):OCT72-416
KEELER, W. WALKING ON THE GREENHOUSE
ROOF.*
D. BARBOUR, 150(DR):SPRING71-133
P. STEVENS, 628:SPRING72-103
KEELEY, E. & P. BIEN, EDS. MODERN
GREEK WRITERS.
617(TLS):23MAR73-320
KEEN, B. THE AZTEC IMAGE IN WESTERN
THOUGHT.
617(TLS):9NOV73-1374
KEEN, G. THE SALE OF WORKS OF ART.
T. CROMBIE, 39:JUL71-78
R. SINNOTT, 135:NOV71-215
KEEN, G. & M. LA RUE, EDS. UNDERGROUND
GRAPHICS.
E. LUCIE-SMITH, 592:NOV70-221
KEEN, M.H. ENGLAND IN THE LATER MIDDLE
AGES.
617(TLS):20APR73-436
KEENAN, E.L. THE KURBSKII-GROZNYI APOC-
RYPHA.
S.G. MACZKO, 104:FALL72-490
M. SZEFTEL, 32:DEC72-882
KEENE, D. LANDSCAPES AND PORTRAITS.
M. BROCK, 285(JAPQ):OCT-DEC71-481
E. WEBB, 648:JAN72-78
KEENE, D., ED. TWENTY PLAYS OF THE NŌ
THEATRE.
639(VQR):SPRING71-LXII
KEENE, G.B. ABSTRACT SETS AND FINITE
ORDINALS.
A.S. FEREBEE, 316:SEP71-543
KEENE, G.B. FIRST-ORDER FUNCTIONAL CAL-
CULUS.
W.E. GOULD, 316:MAR71-167
KEENE, G.B. THE RELATIONAL SYLLOGISM.
G.J. MASSEY, 316:SEP70-448
KEENE, R.D. & G.S. BOTTERILL. THE
MODERN DEFENCE.
617(TLS):1JUN73-625
KEER, D. MAHATMA GANDHI.
617(TLS):7DEC73-1510
KEIL, G. & OTHERS, EDS. FACHLITERATUR
DES MITTELALTERS.*
B. HAAGE, 597(SN):VOL42#1-284
KEITH, A.N. BELOVED EXILES.*
617(TLS):8JUN73-633
KEITH-SMITH, B. JOHANNES BOBROWSKI.
K. BULLIVANT, 402(MLR):JUL72-711
KEITHLEY, G. THE DONNER PARTY.*
D. ALLEN, 491:JUN73-173
E. LUEDERS, 651(WHR):SUMMER72-298
KELEMEN, P. ART OF THE AMERICAS.*
F.L. PHELPS, 37:AUG70-40
KELEMEN, P. BAROQUE AND ROCOCO IN LATIN
AMERICA.*
T. CROMBIE, 39:APR71-344
KELLAS, J.G. THE SCOTTISH POLITICAL
SYSTEM.
617(TLS):13APR73-416

KELLENS, J. & M. DEFOURNY, EDS & TRANS.
SĀVITRYUPĀKHYĀNAM OU CÉLÉBRATION DE LA
FIDÉLITÉ.
J. DE CALUWÉ, 556(RLV):1971/3-367
KELLER, A.C. - SEE RABELAIS, F.
KELLER, B. THE BAGHDAD DEFECTIONS.
N. CALLENDAR, 441:19AUG73-13
KELLER, G. AUFSÄTZE ZUR LITERATUR. (K.
JEZIORKOWSKI, ED)
F. WASSERMANN, 406:SPRING72-78
"GOTTFRIED KELLER."* (K. JEZIORKOWSKI,
ED)
H. LAUFHÜTTE, 680(ZDP):BAND90HEFT2-
285
F. STOCK, 52:BAND6HEFT1-106
KELLER, J.E. - SEE GREEN, O.H.
KELLER, J.E. & R.W. LINKER, EDS. EL
LIBRO DE CALILA E DIGNA.*
C. LÓPEZ-MORILLAS, 545(RPH):AUG71-85
KELLER, M. JOHANN KLAJS WEIHNACHTSDICH-
TUNG.
R. RUDOLF, 182:VOL24#23/24-867
KELLER, W.P. HAWAIIAN INTERLUDE.
617(TLS):29JUN73-757
KELLETT, A. - SEE DE MAUPASSANT, G.
KELLEY, D.R. FOUNDATIONS OF MODERN HIS-
TORICAL SCHOLARSHIP.
185:OCT70-87
KELLEY, E.S. WEEDS.*
A. WHITMAN, 441:11MAR73-48
KELLEY, P. & R. HUDSON - SEE BROWNING,
E.B.
KELLEY, R.E. & O.M. BRACK, JR. SAMUEL
JOHNSON'S EARLY BIOGRAPHERS.
R.B. SCHWARTZ, 301(JEGP):JUL72-452
KELLOGG, G. THE VITAL TRADITION.
K.J. ATCHITY, 613:AUTUMN71-471
KELLOGG, M. LIKE THE LION'S TOOTH.*
617(TLS):11MAY73-535
KELLS, J.H. - SEE SOPHOCLES
KELLY, D. INSTRUCTIONS FOR VIEWING A
SOLAR ECLIPSE.
R. PINSKY, 491:JUN73-168
KELLY, F.D. "SENS" AND "CONJOINTURE" IN
THE "CHEVALIER DE LA CHARRETTE."*
J. DEROY, 433:JAN70-85
KELLY, F.J. & OTHERS. RESEARCH DESIGN IN
THE BEHAVIORAL SCIENCES.
M. HICKSON 3D, 583:WINTER70-190
KELLY, F.M. SHAKESPEARE COSTUME FOR
STAGE AND SCREEN. (REV BY A. MANS-
FIELD)
J. LAVER, 39:NOV70-398
G. SQUIRE, 157:AUTUMN70-74
KELLY, H.A. DIVINE PROVIDENCE IN THE
ENGLAND OF SHAKESPEARE'S HISTORIES.*
C.A. PATRIDES, 191(ELN):DEC71-139
W.G. ZEEVELD, 570(SQ):AUTUMN71-406
KELLY, K. GARBAGE.
441:7OCT73-41
442(NY):20AUG73-91
KELLY, L.G., ED. THE DESCRIPTION AND
MEASUREMENT OF BILINGUALISM.
R.B. LE PAGE, 361:VOL26#4-427
KELLY, L.G. 25 CENTURIES OF LANGUAGE
TEACHING.
H.J. FREY, 238:MAY71-406
R.W. NEWMAN, 207(FR):FEB71-600
KELLY, L.L. LA CLÉ DU FRANÇAIS.
E.H. KADLER, 399(MLJ):FEB71-119
KELLY, M. SOLO RECITAL. (H. VAN THAL,
ED)
A.H. KING, 415:DEC72-1187
KELLY, R. THE COMMON SHORE.*
M. BENEDIKT, 491:NOV72-105
KELLY, R. FLESH:DREAM:BOOK.* KALI YUGA.
L. MUELLER, 491:AUG73-293

KELLY, R. THE NIGHT OF NOAH.
   J. TIPTON, 577(SHR):SPRING71-196
KELMAN, S. BEHIND THE BERLIN WALL.
   N. ASCHERSON, 453:8MAR73-31
   441:18MAR73-32
KELTON, E. THE DAY THE COWBOYS QUIT.
   W. GARD, 584(SWR):WINTER72-76
KEMAL, Y. ANATOLIAN TALES.
   T.S. HALMAN, 352(LE&W):VOL15#1-175
KEMAL, Y. THEY BURN THE THISTLES.
   617(TLS):25MAY73-575
KEMAL, Y. THE WIND FROM THE PLAIN.
   R.B. WINDER, 352(LE&W):VOL15#1-173
KEMP, F. - SEE VARNHAGEN VON ENSE, R.
KEMP, J. THE PHILOSOPHY OF KANT.
   K. OEDINGEN, 342(BAND61HEFT3-419
KEMPF, J-P. & J. PETTIT. ÉTUDES SUR LA
TRILOGIE DE CLAUDEL. (VOL 3)
   J-N. SEGRESTAA, 535(RHL):JUL-AUG70-
   735
KEMPNER, M.J. INVITATION TO PORTUGAL.
   J.F. THORNING, 613:AUTUMN70-478
KEMPTON, M. THE BRIAR PATCH.
   A. HACKER, 453:1NOV73-36
   C. NEWMAN, 231:NOV73-116
   G. WILLS, 441:26AUG73-1
KENAN, L.R. GALERIE DE PORTRAITS CON-
TEMPORAINS.
   R.C. KELLY, 207(FR):OCT70-155
KENDALL, A. EVERYDAY LIFE OF THE INCAS.
   617(TLS):9NOV73-1374
KENDALL, K.E. LEIGH HUNT'S REFLECTOR.
   L. LANDRÉ, 189(EA):JUL-SEP71-340
KENDALL, P.M. & V. ILARDI, EDS. DISPAT-
CHES WITH RELATED DOCUMENTS OF MILANESE
AMBASSADORS IN FRANCE AND BURGUNDY.
(VOL 1)
   L. MARTINES, 589:JAN72-129
KENDRICK, D. & G. PUXON. THE DESTINY OF
EUROPE'S GYPSIES.
   N. ASCHERSON, 453:14JUN73-3
   441:13MAY73-40
KENEALLY, T. BRING LARKS AND HEROES.
   617(TLS):26OCT73-1299
KENEALLY, T. THE SURVIVOR.
   L. CANTRELL, 381:MAR71-125
KENEZ, P. CIVIL WAR IN SOUTH RUSSIA,
1918.
   J.M. THOMPSON, 32:DEC72-897
   639(VQR):AUTUMN71-CLXXX
KEN'ICHI, M. - SEE UNDER MIZUSAWA KEN'ICHI
KENISTON, K. YOUTH AND DISSENT.*
   E. ASHBY, 676(YR):SUMMER72-633
KENNA, V.E.G. THE CRETAN TALISMANIC
STONE IN THE LATE MINOAN AGE.*
   J. BOARDMAN, 123:MAR72-139
KENNAN, G.F. THE MARQUIS DE CUSTINE AND
HIS "RUSSIA IN 1839."*
   F.C. BARGHOORN, 639(VQR):SUMMER71-464
KENNAN, G.F. MEMOIRS: 1950-1963.*
   A. RYAN, 362:1FEB73-153
   617(TLS):2FEB73-111
KENNAWAY, J. SILENCE.*
   S. CLAPP, 362:1MAR73-281
KENNEBECK, E. JUROR NUMBER FOUR.
   C. LEHMANN-HAUPT, 441:5MAR73-27
   442(NY):17MAR73-130
KENNEDY, E.C. - SEE CAESAR
KENNEDY, G. THE ART OF RHETORIC IN THE
ROMAN WORLD. 300 B.C.-A.D. 300.
   617(TLS):16FEB73-184
KENNEDY, J. A HISTORY OF MALAYA. (2ND
ED)
   A. JONES, 293(JAST):MAY71-736
KENNEDY, J.M. & J.A. REITHER, EDS. A
THEATRE FOR SPENSERIANS.
   617(TLS):5OCT73-1178

KENNEDY, M. BARBIROLLI.*
   R. ANDERSON, 415:MAR72-271
KENNEDY, M. THE HISTORY OF THE ROYAL
MANCHESTER COLLEGE OF MUSIC 1893-1972.*
   J.A.W., 410(M&L):APR72-220
KENNEDY, M. THE WORKS OF RALPH VAUGHAN
WILLIAMS.
   H. OTTAWAY, 415:FEB72-154
KENNEDY, R.S. & P. REEVES - SEE WOLFE, T.
KENNEDY, R.W. A CLASSICAL EDUCATION.
   M. LEVIN, 441:28OCT73-48
KENNEDY, X.J. GROWING INTO LOVE.*
   502(PRS):SPRING70-89
KENNELLY, B., ED. THE PENGUIN BOOK OF
IRISH VERSE.
   H. MURPHY, 159(DM):WINTER70/71-112
   R.S., 376:OCT70-91
KENNELLY, B. SALVATION, THE STRANGER.
   617(TLS):16FEB73-183
KENNER, H. BUCKY.
   C. LEHMANN-HAUPT, 441:19FEB73-21
   E.E. MORISON, 441:11MAR73-5
   442(NY):24FEB73-130
KENNER, H. THE COUNTERFEITERS.
   W. KINSLEY, 173(ECS):SUMMER71-494
KENNER, H. THE POUND ERA.*
   N. BLIVEN, 442(NY):13JAN73-90
   A. GELPI, 27(AL):NOV72-502
   C.M. MAHON, 651(WHR):SUMMER72-275
   D. O'BRIEN, 329(JJQ):WINTER73-271
   W.H. PRITCHARD, 249(HUDR):SUMMER72-316
   H. WITEMEYER, 659:SPRING73-240
   M. WOOD, 453:8FEB73-7
   G. WOODCOCK, 102(CANL):AUTUMN72-97
KENNER, H. A READER'S GUIDE TO SAMUEL
BECKETT.
   J. EPSTEIN, 441:25NOV73-6
   617(TLS):12OCT73-1217
KENNETT, J. SELLING WATER BY THE RIVER.
   617(TLS):21SEP73-1080
KENNEY, E.J. - SEE LUCRETIUS
KENNEY, L.B. MBOKA.
   441:15APR73-32
KENNEY, R.W. ELIZABETH'S ADMIRAL.
   W.T. MAC CAFFREY, 551(RENQ):SUMMER71-
   272
KENNINGTON, D. THE LITERATURE OF JAZZ.*
   J. BURNS, 503:AUTUMN71-148
KENNY, A. THE FIVE WAYS.*
   A. FLEW, 482(PHR):JUL71-411
   J.W., 154:JUN70-130
KENNY, A. WITTGENSTEIN.
   617(TLS):1JUN73-612
KENNY, A.J.P. & OTHERS. THE NATURE OF
MIND.
   617(TLS):22JUN73-711
KENNY, B. & T. WHITEHEAD. INSIGHT.
   617(TLS):17AUG73-961
KENNY, R.W. ELIZABETH'S ADMIRAL.
   W.W. MAC DONALD, 613:AUTUMN71-476
KENNY, S.S. - SEE STEELE, R.
KENRICK, D. THE BOOK OF SUMO.
   R.L. BACKUS, 318(JAOS):OCT-DEC71-526
KENT, H.S.K. WAR AND TRADE IN NORTHERN
SEAS.
   617(TLS):11MAY73-533
KENT, J. THE SOLOMON ISLANDS.
   617(TLS):17AUG73-956
KENT, L.J. & E.C. KNIGHT - SEE HOFFMANN,
E.T.A.
KENWORTHY, B.J. - SEE KAISER, G.
KENYON, K.M. PALESTINE IN THE MIDDLE
BRONZE AGE.
   G.E. WRIGHT, 318(JAOS):APR-JUN71-276
KEOGH, J. PRESIDENT NIXON AND THE PRESS.*
   C.P. IVES, 396(MODA):FALL72-426

KEPES, G. LA STRUCTURE DANS LES ARTS ET DANS LES SCIENCES.
  P. DUFOUR, 98:AUG/SEP71-805
KER, N.R. MEDIEVAL MANUSCRIPTS IN BRITISH LIBRARIES. (VOL 1)
  J. BACKHOUSE, 354:SEP70-253
  D. GRAY, 541(RES):AUG71-387
  P.D.A. HARVEY, 325:APR71-242
KERBER, L.K. FEDERALISTS IN DISSENT.
  D-W. HOWE, 432(NEQ):JUN71-329
  B.W. SHEEHAN, 656(WMQ):JAN71-134
KERENSKY, O. ANNA PAVLOVA.
  H. KELLER, 362:6DEC73-790
  617(TLS):23NOV73-1418
KERÉNYI, M. - SEE HESSE, H. & K. KERÉNYI
KERESZTES, K. MORPHEMIC AND SEMANTIC ANALYSIS OF THE WORD FAMILIES FINNISH ETE- AND HUNGARIAN EL- "FORE-."
  R. HETZRON, 353:JAN70-123
KERESZTURY, D. ÖRÖKSÉG.
  A. BEKE, 270:VOL21#4-189
KERESZTY, R.A. GOD SEEKERS FOR A NEW AGE.
  B.S. LLAMZON, 613:AUTUMN71-460
KERMAN, J. - SEE "LUDWIG VAN BEETHOVEN: AUTOGRAPH MISCELLANY FROM CIRCA 1786 TO 1799"
KERMODE, F. CONTINUITIES.*
  E. DELAVENAY, 189(EA):JAN-MAR70-103
  J.K. ROBINSON, 598(SOR):SUMMER73-692
  A. RODWAY, 447(N&Q):JUL71-269
KERMODE, F. PUZZLES AND EPIPHANIES.
  L.C. BONNEROT, 189(EA):JAN-MAR70-102
KERMODE, F. THE SENSE OF AN ENDING.*
  C.F. SCHRODER, 290(JAAC):WINTER70-268
KERMODE, F. SHAKESPEARE, SPENSER, DONNE.*
  R.A. FOAKES, 175:AUTUMN71-98
  A.B. GIAMATTI, 676(YR):WINTER72-298
KERMODE, F. - SEE BERNSTEIN, J.
KERMODE, F. & J. HOLLANDER, GENERAL EDS. THE OXFORD ANTHOLOGY OF ENGLISH LITERATURE.
  H. KENNER, 441:30DEC73-6
  617(TLS):2NOV73-1337
KERN, E. EXISTENTIAL THOUGHT AND FICTIONAL TECHNIQUE.*
  M.J. FRIEDMAN, 401(MLQ):MAR71-119
  J.M. MORSE, 149:DEC72-468
  W. REED, 454:SPRING72-254
KERN, P. TRINITÄT, MARIA, INKARNATION.*
  H. ADOLF, 301(JEGP):JAN72-57
KERN, P.C. ZUR GEDANKENWELT DES SPÄTEN HOFMANNSTHAL.
  E.A. METZGER, 399(MLJ):APR71-257
  W.E. YATES, 402(MLR):JUL72-705
KEROUAC, J. PIC [AND] THE SUBTERRANEANS.
  617(TLS):6APR73-369
KEROUAC, J. VISIONS OF CODY.
  A. BROYARD, 441:9JAN73-39
  A. LATHAM, 441:28JAN73-42
  442(NY):17FEB73-110
  617(TLS):2NOV73-1333
KERR, A. THE FAMILY COOKBOOK: FRENCH.
  P. ADAMS, 61:MAR73-107
KERR, E.M. YOKNAPATAWPHA.
  J.R. BARTH, 613:SPRING70-128
  D. MEINDL, 38:BAND89HEFT4-554
KERR, H. MEDIUMS, AND SPIRIT-RAPPERS, AND ROARING RADICALS.
  M.B. STERN, 27(AL):JAN73-700
KERRIDGE, E. AGRARIAN PROBLEMS IN THE SIXTEENTH CENTURY AND AFTER.
  J.M.W. BEAN, 551(RENQ):AUTUMN71-389
KERSH, C. THE DIABOLICAL LIBERTIES OF UNCLE MAX.
  617(TLS):6APR73-369
KERSHAW, A. - SEE ALDINGTON, R.

KESEY, K. KESEY'S GARAGE SALE.
  M. RICHLER, 441:7OCT73-6
KESSEL, E. - SEE MEINECKE, F.
KESSELRING, W. DIE FRANZÖSISCHE SPRACHE IM 20. JAHRHUNDERT, CHARAKTERISTIKA - TENDENZEN - PROBLEME.
  G. SCHWEIG, 430(NS):AUG71-445
KESSLER, C.S. MAX BECKMANN'S TRIPTYCHS.*
  C. AMYX, 54:SEP71-426
  R.A. HELLER, 56:AUTUMN71-365
  M.S. YOUNG, 39:NOV71-421
KESSLER, E. IMAGES OF WALLACE STEVENS.*
  J. PINKERTON, 27(AL):NOV72-510
KESSLER, H.L. - SEE WEITZMANN, K.
KETCHAM, C.H. - SEE WORDSWORTH, J.
KETCHUM, A.A. COLETTE, OU LA NAISSANCE DU JOUR.*
  E. MARKS, 546(RR):APR71-154
KETCHUM, R.M. WILL ROGERS.
  R.R. LINGEMAN, 441:11NOV73-46
  E. WEEKS, 61:NOV73-122
KETCHUM, R.M. THE WINTER SOLDIERS.
  442(NY):9JUN73-115
  617(TLS):12OCT73-1215
KETTLE, J. - SEE SAFDIE, M.
KEY, H.H. MORPHOLOGY OF CAYUVAVA.
  H.W. LAW, 353:NOV71-115
KEY, M.R. COMPARATIVE TACANAN PHONOLOGY.
  V. GIRARD, 269(IJAL):JAN70-73
  M.D. KINKADE, 353:NOV71-120
KEYES, R.S. & K. MIZUSHIMA. THE THEATRICAL WORLD OF OSAKA PRINTS.
  J. CANADAY, 441:2DEC73-90
KEYNES, G. A BIBLIOGRAPHY OF DR. JOHN DONNE, DEAN OF SAINT PAUL'S.
  617(TLS):1JUN73-624
KEYNES, G. JOHN EVELYN. (2ND ED)
  J. HORDEN, 354:MAR70-64
KEYNES, G. WILLIAM PICKERING, PUBLISHER.* (REV)
  J. CARTER, 39:JUN70-487
  J. COTTON, 503:AUTUMN70-158
KEYNES, J.M. THE COLLECTED WRITINGS OF JOHN MAYNARD KEYNES. (VOLS 7; 8; 13, PT 1; 14, PT 2) (D. MOGGRIDGE, ED)
  617(TLS):27JUL73-880
KEYNES, J.M. THE COLLECTED WRITINGS OF JOHN MAYNARD KEYNES.* (VOL 9)
  L. SILK, 441:3JAN73-39
KEYNES, J.M. THE COLLECTED WRITINGS OF JOHN MAYNARD KEYNES.* (VOL 10)
  L. SILK, 441:2JAN73-37
VON KEYSERLING, E. WERKE. (R. GRUENTER, ED)
  617(TLS):12OCT73-1257
KEYSSAR, A. MELVILLE'S "ISRAEL POTTER."*
  C. NICHOLS, 454:WINTER72-181
KHADDURI, M. ARAB CONTEMPORARIES.
  617(TLS):16NOV73-1393
KHAKETLA, B.M. LESOTHO 1970.
  617(TLS):26JAN73-82
KHALED, L. MY PEOPLE SHALL LIVE. (G. HAJJAR, ED)
  617(TLS):13JUL73-799
KHAN, M.A., ED. INTERNATIONAL ISLAMIC CONFERENCE, FEBRUARY, 1968. (VOL 1)
  J. VAN ESS, 182:VOL24#13/14-515
KHARMS, D. & A. VVEDENSKY. RUSSIA'S LOST LITERATURE OF THE ABSURD. (G. GIBIAN, ED & TRANS)
  B. SCHERR, 32:JUN72-513
KHAYYÁM, O. - SEE UNDER OMAR KHAYYÁM
KHRUSHCHEV, N.S. KHRUSHCHEV REMEMBERS. (S. TALBOTT, ED & TRANS)
  J.A. FAHEY, 550(RUSR):JUL71-287
  S.I. PLOSS, 32:MAR72-178
  L.D. STOKES, 150(DR):SPRING71-130

KIBLER, R.J., L.L. BARKER & D.T. MILES.
BEHAVIORAL OBJECTIVES AND INSTRUCTION.
C.R. GRUNER, 583:SUMMER72-451
KICKNOSWAY, F. O. YOU CAN WALK ON THE
SKY? GOOD.
E.M. BRONER, 398:SPRING73-125
KIDD, B. & J. MACFARLANE. THE DEATH OF
HOCKEY.
H. SCOTT, 99:JAN73-28
KIEFER, F. MATHEMATICAL LINGUISTICS IN
EASTERN EUROPE.*
G. ALTMANN, 353:JUN71-120
KIEFER, F. ON EMPHASIS AND WORD ORDER
IN HUNGARIAN.*
K. WODARZ-MAGDICS, 353:DEC70-124
KIEFER, F., ED. STUDIES IN SYNTAX AND
SEMANTICS.
R. BUGARSKI, 215(GL):VOL11#3-179
G.M. GREEN, 350:SEP72-667
F.J. NEWMEYER, 361:VOL27#1-93
KIEFER, F. SWEDISH MORPHOLOGY.
J. MEY, 350:DEC72-947
KIEFER, H.E. & M.K. MUNITZ, EDS. ETHICS
AND SOCIAL JUSTICE.
R.S. DOWNIE, 478:JUL71-131
KIEFER, T.M. TAUSUG ARMED CONFLICT.
M. MEDNICK, 293(JAST):AUG71-926
KIELHORN, F. KLEINE SCHRIFTEN MIT EINER
AUSWAHL DER EPIGRAPHISCHEN AUFSÄTZE.
(PTS 1 & 2) (W. RAU, ED)
M.J. DRESDEN, 318(JAOS):OCT-DEC71-549
KIELY, B. A BALL OF MALT AND MADAME
BUTTERFLY.
D. MAHON, 362:21JUN73-840
617(TLS):13JUL73-797
KIELY, R. THE ROMANTIC NOVEL IN ENGLAND.
L. BRAUDY, 441:1APR73-30
617(TLS):4MAY73-494
KIENIEWICZ, S. HISTORIA POLSKI, 1795-
1918.
P.S. WANDYCZ, 32:MAR72-211
"KIERKEGAARD VIVANT."
J-N. VUARNET, 98:JUN71-542
KIERNAN, C. SCIENCE AND THE ENLIGHTEN-
MENT IN EIGHTEENTH-CENTURY FRANCE.
J. MAYER, 535(RHL):JAN-FEB70-127
V.W. TOPAZIO, 546(RR):FEB71-54
KIERNAN, T. JANE.
A. GOTTLIEB, 441:18NOV73-31
KIEV, A. TRANSCULTURAL PSYCHIATRY.
617(TLS):6APR73-372
KIEVE, J. THE ELECTRIC TELEGRAPH.
617(TLS):6APR73-399
KILEY, F. & J.M. SHUTTLEWORTH, EDS.
SATIRE FROM AESOP TO BUCHWALD.
W. KINSLEY, 223:DEC71-348
KILGARRIFF, M., ED. THREE MELODRAMAS.
A. RENDLE, 157:AUTUMN70-77
LORD KILLEARN - SEE UNDER LAMPSON, M.
KILLICK, B. THE HERALDS.
R. BLYTHE, 362:1NOV73-605
KILLIGREW, M. - SEE FORD, F.M.
KILLY, W. & H. SZKLENAR - SEE TRAKL, G.
KILPI, E. TAMARA.
617(TLS):5JAN73-5
KILROY, T. THE DEATH AND RESURRECTION OF
MR. ROCHE.
F.G.B., 502(PRS):SUMMER71-185
A. RENDLE, 157:SPRING70-71
KILROY-SILK, R. SOCIALISM SINCE MARX.
617(TLS):16MAR73-288
KILSON, M. KPELE LALA.
B.L. HAMPTON, 187:JAN73-134
KIM, R.E. LOST NAMES.*
E. MC CUNE, 293(JAST):FEB71-472
KIMBALL, F., ED. THOMAS JEFFERSON, ARCH-
ITECT.*
P.F. NORTON, 45:APR70-129

KIMBALL, R. & A. SIMON. THE GERSHWINS.
W. CLEMONS, 441:23SEP73-3
KIMBELL, E.E. THE COMPLEAT TRACTION
ENGINEMAN.
617(TLS):21SEP73-1093
KIMCHE, J. THERE COULD HAVE BEEN PEACE.
D. HOLDEN, 441:28OCT73-8
KIMPEL, D. & C. WIEDEMANN, EDS. THEORIE
UND TECHNIK DES ROMANS IM 17. UND 18.
JAHRHUNDERT.
L.E. KURTH, 221(GQ):MAR71-236
KINCAID, D. BRITISH SOCIAL LIFE IN INDIA
1608-1937.
617(TLS):22JUN73-722
KINCH, S., JR. & B. PROCTER. TEXAS UNDER
A CLOUD.
W. GARD, 584(SWR):SUMMER72-V
KIND, H. DAS ZEITALTER DER REFORMATION
IM HISTORISCHEN ROMAN DER JUNGDEUTSCHEN.
P. SKRINE, 402(MLR):OCT72-946
KINDER, C. SNAKEHUNTER.
M. LEVIN, 441:18NOV73-55
KINDLEBERGER, C.P. THE WORLD IN DEPRES-
SION 1929-1939.
617(TLS):1JUN73-607
"KINDLERS LITERATUR-LEXIKON." (VOLS 3&4)
H. RÜDIGER, 52:BAND5HEFT1-84
KING, A.L. LOUIS T. WIFGALL.
639(VQR):SPRING71-LXXIII
KING, C. ON IRELAND.
617(TLS):16NOV73-1399
KING, C., ED. TWELVE MODERN SCOTTISH
POETS.
R.D.S. JACK, 595(SCS):VOL16PT1-82
KING, F. FLIGHTS.
R. GARFITT, 362:18OCT73-528
617(TLS):19OCT73-1269
KING, F.H.H., ED. THE DEVELOPMENT OF
JAPANESE STUDIES IN SOUTHEAST ASIA.
L. OLSON, 293(JAST):NOV70-226
KING, F.P. THE NEW INTERNATIONALISM.
617(TLS):14SEP73-1050
KING, G.E., ED. CONFLICT AND HARMONY.
617(TLS):11MAY73-537
KING, J.C., ED. THE FIRST WORLD WAR.
617(TLS):3AUG73-913
KING, P.D. LAW AND SOCIETY IN THE VISI-
GOTHIC KINGDOM.
617(TLS):2FEB73-133
KING, R.A., JR. THE FOCUSING ARTIFICE.*
I. ARMSTRONG, 637(VS):DEC70-207
KING, R.A., JR., ED. THE RING AND THE
BOOK.
R.O. PREYER, 637(VS):SEP70-98
KING, R.A., JR. & OTHERS - SEE BROWNING,
R.
KING, R-D. HISTORICAL LINGUISTICS AND
GENERATIVE GRAMMAR.*
N.E. COLLINGE, 297(JL):OCT71-253
J.H. JASANOFF, 545(RPH):AUG71-74
KING, T.J. SHAKESPEAREAN STAGING, 1599-
1642.
R.A. FOAKES, 175:AUTUMN71-98
L.R. STAR, 150(DR):AUTUMN71-436
M.L. VAWTER, 301(JEGP):APR72-249
KING, W.L.M. THE MACKENZIE KING RECORD.*
(VOLS 3 & 4) (J.W. PICKERSGILL & D.F.
FORSTER, EDS)
R.A. MAC KAY, 150(DR):SUMMER71-257
KING-HELE, D. SHELLEY.
N. ROGERS, 402(MLR):JUL72-622
KINGHORN, A.M. MEDIAEVAL DRAMA.
D. GRAY, 447(N&Q):JAN71-38
KINGHORN, A.M. & A. LAW - SEE RAMSAY, A.
KINGSBURY, R.C. AN ATLAS OF INDIANA.
K.B. HARDER, 424:MAR71-62

KINKADE, K. A WALDEN TWO EXPERIMENT.
  P. DELANY, 441:18FEB73-3
  A. BROYARD, 441:29JAN73-31
KINKADE, R.P., ED. LOS "LUCIDARIOS"
ESPAÑOLES.
  J.E. KELLER, 405(MP):MAY71-375
  V.R.B. OELSCHLÄGER, 589:JUL72-535
  H.T. OOSTENDORP, 433:APR71-211
  R.M. WALKER, 400(MLN):MAR71-294
  H.F. WILLIAMS, 240(HR):JAN71-86
KINKEAD-WEEKES, M., ED. TWENTIETH CENTURY
INTERPRETATIONS OF "THE RAINBOW."
  K. MC SWEENEY, 529(QQ):SUMMER71-337
KINNAMON, K. THE EMERGENCE OF RICHARD
WRIGHT.
  A-T. GILMORE, 31(ASCH):SUMMER73-531
KINNEAR, M. THE FALL OF LLOYD GEORGE.
  R. CROSSMAN, 362:21JUN73-836
KINNELL, G. BODY RAGS.*
  M. BROWN, 565:VOL11#2-57
KINNELL, G. THE BOOK OF NIGHTMARES.*
  M. BENEDIKT, 491:NOV72-105
  B.G. HORNBACK, 600:FALL71-130
  F. MORAMARCO, 651(WHR):SPRING72-189
  E. OCHESTER, 398:VOL3#5-230
  M.G. PERLOFF, 659:WINTER73-97
KINROSS, J. DISCOVERING CASTLES IN ENG-
LAND AND WALES.
  617(TLS):23NOV73-1456
KINSELLA, T. NEW POEMS 1973.
  A. MAC LEAN, 362:20DEC73-859
  617(TLS):17AUG73-946
  617(TLS):23NOV73-1452
KINSELLA, T. NIGHTWALKER AND OTHER
POEMS.*
  S. FAUCHEREAU, 98:MAY70-438
KINSELLA, T. SELECTED POEMS.
  617(TLS):23NOV73-1452
KINSELLA, T. - SEE "THE TAIN"
KINSEY, T.E. - SEE CICERO
KINSLEY, J., ED. THE OXFORD BOOK OF
BALLADS.*
  D.C. FOWLER, 405(MP):MAY71-405
  D. FOX, 447(N&Q):JUN71-230
KINSLEY, J. - SEE BURNS, R.
KINSLEY, J. - SEE GALT, J.
KINSLEY, J. & J.T. BOULTON, EDS. ENGLISH
SATIRIC POETRY.
  566:SPRING72-90
KINSMAN, R.S. - SEE SKELTON, J.
KINSMAN, R.S. & T. YOUNG. JOHN SKELTON.
  J.A.W. BENNETT, 354:SEP71-271
KINTNER, E. - SEE BROWNING, R. & E.B.
BARRETT
KINTNER, W.R. & R.L. PFALTZGRAFF. SOVIET
MILITARY TRENDS.
  R.A. SCHADLER, 396(MODA):WINTER72-103
KIPLING, R. THE COMPLETE BARRACK-ROOM
BALLADS OF RUDYARD KIPLING. (C. CAR-
RINGTON, ED)
  617(TLS):14DEC73-1530
KIRÁLY, B.K. HUNGARY IN THE LATE EIGHT-
EENTH CENTURY.
  J. HELD, 497(POLR):AUTUMN70-118
KIRÁLY, I. ADY ENDRE.
  A.N. NYERGES, 32:JUN72-482
KIRBY, J.L., ED. ANNUAL BULLETIN OF
HISTORICAL LITERATURE. (VOL 56)
  617(TLS):5OCT73-1193
KIRBY, J.L. HENRY IV OF ENGLAND.
  M. HASTINGS, 589:OCT72-777
KIRBY, M. FUTURIST PERFORMANCE.
  R. LEIBOWITZ, 58:NOV71-14
KIRBY, T.A. & W.J. OLIVE, EDS. ESSAYS
IN HONOR OF ESMOND LINWORTH MARILLA.
  T.W. HERBERT, 570(SQ):SPRING71-175

KIRCHNER, G. FORTUNA IN DICHTUNG UND
EMBLEMATIK DES BAROCK.
  P. SKRINE, 402(MLR):JAN72-210
KIRCHNER, G. DIE SYNTAKTISCHEN EIGENTÜM-
LICHKEITEN DES AMERIKANISCHEN ENGLISCH.
(VOL 1)
  R.W. ZANDVOORT, 179(ES):AUG71-379
KIRCHNER, J. AUSGEWÄHLTE AUFSÄTZE AUS
PALÄOGRAPHIE, HANDSCHRIFTENKUNDE, ZEIT-
SCHRIFTENWESEN UND GEISTESGESCHICHTE.
  F.A. SCHMIDT-KÜNSEMÜLLER, 182:VOL24#5-
  195
KIRCHNER, J. BIBLIOGRAPHIE DER ZEIT-
SCHRIFTEN DES DEUTSCHEN SPRACHGEBIETES
BIS 1900. (VOL 1)
  J.L. FLOOD, 354:DEC70-363
KIRK, C. & R. - SEE HOWELLS, W.D.
KIRK, G.S. MYTH.*
  J.G. GRIFFITHS, 123:JUN72-235
KIRK, R. ELIOT AND HIS AGE.*
  J.D. MARGOLIS, 651(WHR):SUMMER72-279
  W.H. PRITCHARD, 249(HUDR):SUMMER72-321
  M.L. RAINA, 295:FEB73-134
  H. REGNERY, 396(MODA):SUMMER72-315
  G. SCOTT-MONCRIEFF, 569(SR):AUTUMN72-
  632
KIRKENDALE, U. ANTONIO CALDARA.*
  D.J. GROUT, 317:FALL72-474
KIRKER, H. THE ARCHITECTURE OF CHARLES
BULFINCH.*
  S.M. BOYD, 576:OCT71-253
  D. STILLMAN, 56:SUMMER71-242
  J. SUMMERSON, 46:OCT70-264
KIRKER, J. ADVENTURES TO CHINA.
  R.G. KNAPP, 293(JAST):MAY71-662
KIRKHAM, M. THE POETRY OF ROBERT GRAVES.*
  P.J. CALLAHAN, 502(PRS):SUMMER70-173
  J.K. ROBINSON, 598(SOR):SUMMER73-692
KIRKPATRICK, D. PAOLOZZI.
  A. HIGGINS, 592:MAR71-131
KIRKPATRICK, J. - SEE IVES, C.E.
KIRSCHENMANN, P.P. INFORMATION AND RE-
FLECTION.*
  A. VUCINICH, 550(RUSR):APR71-187
KIRSHNER, S. - SEE SCHILLER, F.
KIRSOP, W., ED. STUDIES IN HONOUR OF
A.R. CHISHOLM.
  J. CRUICKSHANK, 208(FS):JAN72-102
KIRST, H.H. DAMNED TO SUCCESS.
  N. CALLENDAR, 441:3JUN73-34
KIRSTEIN, L. MOVEMENT AND METAPHOR.*
  J.B. MYERS, 139:AUG71-6
  639(VQR):SPRING71-LXXXIV
KIRSTEIN, L. ELIE NADELMAN.
  H. KRAMER, 441:11NOV73-1
KIRSTEIN, L. THE NEW YORK CITY BALLET.
  C. BARNES, 441:11NOV73-1
  A. KISSELGOFF, 441:22DEC73-23
KISCH, G. CONSILIA.
  W. ULLMANN, 551(RENQ):WINTER71-530
KISCH, G. ERASMUS' STELLUNG ZU JUDEN
UND JUDENTUM.
  W. SCHWARZ, 220(GL&L):APR72-277
KISLING, J., ED. KISLING.
  J.R. MELLOW, 441:2DEC73-12
KISSEN, I.A. KURS SOPOSTAVITEL'NOJ
GRAMMATIKI RUSSKOGO I UZBEKSKOGO JAZY-
KOV.
  L. HŘEBÍČEK, 353:DEC70-122
KISTLER, M.O. DRAMA OF THE STORM AND
STRESS.
  F.R. LOVE, 221(GQ):NOV71-589
KITSON CLARK, G. CHURCHMEN AND THE CON-
DITION OF ENGLAND 1832-1885.
  617(TLS):5OCT73-1165
KITTANG, A. D'AMOUR DE POÉSIE.
  R. CARDINAL, 208(FS):JUL72-355

KITZINGER, U. DIPLOMACY AND PERSUASION.
R. MAYNE, 362:1FEB73-140
KIVIMAA, K. ÞE AND ÞAT AS CLAUSE CONNEC-
TIVES IN EARLY MIDDLE ENGLISH WITH
ESPECIAL CONSIDERATION OF THE EMER-
GENCE OF THE PLEONASTIC ÞAT.
K.C. PHILLIPPS, 179(ES):APR71-160
KIYOSHI, I. - SEE UNDER INOUE KIYOSHI
KIZER, C. MIDNIGHT WAS MY CRY.*
F. MORAMARCO, 651(WHR):SPRING72-191
W.H. PRITCHARD, 249(HUDR):SPRING72-124
G. WHITESIDE, 398:SPRING73-116
KJELLBERG, E. & G. SÄFLUND. GREEK AND
ROMAN ART.
J.F.H., 135:MAY70-49
KLAKOWICZ, B. LA COLLEZIONE DEI CONTI
FAINA IN ORVIETO.
A. NEUMANN, 182:VOL24#13/14-558
KLAMKIN, L. HELLO, GOOD-BYE.
M. LEVIN, 441:9SEP73-42
KLAPPERT, P. LUGGING VEGETABLES TO NAN-
TUCKET.*
P. COOLEY, 398:WINTER73-349
M.G. PERLOFF, 659:WINTER73-97
R.B. SHAW, 491:SEP73-344
KLEBER, K-H. DE PARVITATE MATERIAE IN
SEXTO.
J.G. ZIEGLER, 182:VOL24#13/14-530
KLEENE, S.C. MATHEMATICAL LOGIC.
M. YASUGI, 316:SEP70-438
KLEIBER, W. OTFRID VON WEISSENBURG.
R. RUDOLF, 182:VOL24#21/22-778
KLEIN, A., ED. AKTIONEN, BEKENNTNISSE,
PERSPEKTIVEN.
H-N. SMITH, 182:VOL24#19/20-730
KLEIN, C. THE SINGLE PARENT EXPERIENCE.
A. BROYARD, 441:8MAR73-43
KLEIN, D. THE LIVING SHAKESPEARE.
R.C. CLARK, 544:FALL72-185
KLEIN, D.W. & A.B. CLARK. BIOGRAPHIC
DICTIONARY OF CHINESE COMMUNISM, 1921-
1965.*
639(VQR):SUMMER71-CXVII
KLEIN, E., ED. A COMPREHENSIVE ETYMOLO-
GICAL DICTIONARY OF THE ENGLISH LAN-
GUAGE.*
C.J.E. BALL, 361:VOL25#1-64
H. SCHABRAM, 260(IF):BAND75-332
P-M. VERMEER, 182:VOL24#17/18-668
W. WINTER, 353:JUL71-108
KLEIN, E.C. SOZIALER WANDEL IN KITEEZI/
BUGANDA.
D. PARKIN, 69:JAN71-65
KLEIN, H. THERE IS NO DISPUTING ABOUT
TASTE.
N. WÜRZBACH, 38:BAND89HEFT1-146
KLEIN, H-W. SCHWIERIGKEITEN DES DEUTSCH-
FRANZÖSISCHEN WORTSCHATZES.
J. LEJEUNE, 556(RLV):1970/3-330
KLEIN, R. SYMMACHUS.
F. LASSERRE, 182:VOL24#19/20-756
KLEIN, R., ED. DAS WEISSE, DAS SCHWARZE
UND DAS FEUERROTE MEER.
I. SCHELLBACH, 196:BAND11HEFT1/2-170
KLEIN, Z. LA NOTION DE DIGNITÉ HUMAINE
DANS LA PENSÉE DE KANT ET DE PASCAL.
R. MALTER, 342:BAND61HEFT1-137
"KLEINES LITERARISCHES LEXIKON." (VOL 1,
PT 1) (4TH ED) (H. RÜDIGER & E. KOPPEN,
EDS)
G. RAUSCHER, 406:SUMMER72-175
F-R. SCHRÖDER, 224(GRM):AUG70-356
KLEINEWEFERS, H. THEORIE UND POLITIK DER
ABWERTUNG.
A. OCKER, 182:VOL24#11/12-469
KLEINSTÜCK, J. WIRKLICHKEIT UND REALI-
TÄT.
R. SCHOLL, 301(JEGP):JAN72-98

VON KLEIST, H. DER FINDLING, DIE HEILIGE
CÄCILIE, ANEKDOTEN. (D.H. CROSBY &
A.F. GOESSL, EDS)
A. CLAESGES, 399(MLJ):FEB71-116
"HEINRICH VON KLEIST."* (H. SEMBDNER,
ED)
F. STOCK, 52:BAND6HEFT1-106
KLEMKE, E.D. THE EPISTEMOLOGY OF G.E.
MOORE.*
A. AMBROSE, 482(PHR):APR71-257
M. KITELEY, 479(PHQ):APR71-174
R.A. KOEHL, 484(PPR):DEC70-310
H. WAGNER, 53(AGP):BAND53HEFT1-110
KLEMKE, E.D., ED. ESSAYS ON FREGE.*
D.A. ROHATYN, 258:MAR70-161
KLEMKE, E.D., ED. ESSAYS ON BERTRAND
RUSSELL.
M. RADNER, 154:SEP71-594
KLEMKE, E.D., ED. ESSAYS ON WITTGEN-
STEIN.
J. BURNHEIM, 63:MAY72-81
KLEMKE, E.D., ED. STUDIES IN THE PHILOS-
OPHY OF G.E. MOORE.
D.A. ROHATYN, 258:SEP70-489
VON KLEMPERER, K. IGNAZ SEIPEL.
617(TLS):24AUG73-981
KLESCZEWSKI, R. DIE FRANZÖSISCHEN ÜBER-
SETZUNGEN DES CORTEGIANO VON BALDASSARE
CASTIGLIONE.
U. MÖLK, 224(GRM):MAY70-225
KLESSE, B. SEIDENSTOFFE IN DER ITALIEN-
ISCHEN MALEREI DES VIERZEHNTEN JAHR-
HUNDERTS.
J. MAILEY, 54:DEC71-523
KLESSMANN, E. DIE WELT DER ROMANTIK.
F. WHITFORD, 592:MAR71-132
KLIBANSKY, R., ED. CONTEMPORARY PHILOSO-
PHY. (VOL 3)
A. MANSER, 479(PHQ):APR71-177
KLIMOV, G.V. DIE KAUKASISCHEN SPRACHEN.*
M.J. DRESDEN, 318(JAOS):JAN-MAR71-154
KLIMOWSKY, E.W. DAS MANN-WEIBLICHE LEIT-
BILD IN DER ANTIKE.
617(TLS):16FEB73-184
KLIMPE, P. DIE "ELECTRA" DES SOPHOKLES
UND EURIPIDES' "IPHIGENIE BEI DEN
TAURERN."
G. RONNET, 555:VOL45FASC2-335
E.W. WHITTLE, 123:JUN72-180
KLINCK, C.F. & R.E. WATTERS, EDS. CANAD-
IAN ANTHOLOGY.
W. STUCK, 430(NS):JAN70-51
KLINCK, R. DIE LATEINISCHE ETYMOLOGIE DES
MITTELALTERS.*
D.H. GREEN, 402(MLR):JUL72-606
KLINE, M. MATHEMATICAL THOUGHT FROM
ANCIENT TO MODERN TIMES.
617(TLS):15JUN73-657
KLINE, M. WHY JOHNNY CAN'T ADD.
H. SCHWARTZ, 441:20JUL73-29
KLINEBERG, O. & M. ZAVALLONI. NATIONAL-
ISM AND TRIBALISM AMONG AFRICAN STU-
DENTS.
S. MILBURN, 69:OCT70-399
KLINKOWITZ, J. & J. SOMER, EDS. THE
VONNEGUT STATEMENT.
M. WOOD, 453:31MAY73-23
KLOOSTER, W.G. & A. KRAAK. SYNTAXIS.
R.P.G. DE RIJK, 433:APR70-207
KLOPFENSTEIN, E. ERZÄHLER UND LESER BEI
WILHELM RAABE.*
F.W. KORFF, 657(WW):JUL/AUG70-282
KLOSSOWSKI, P. NIETZSCHE ET LE CERCLE
VICIEUX.
R. HÉBERT, 154:JUN71-407
KLUG, U. JURISTISCHE LOGIK. (3RD ED)
G.H. MÜLLER, 316:SEP71-545

KLUXEN, K. GESCHICHTE ENGLANDS, VON DEN
ANFÄNGEN BIS ZUR GEGENWART.
G. HAEFNER, 430(NS):JUL71-389
KLYMASZ, R.B., COMP. A BIBLIOGRAPHY OF
UKRAINIAN FOLKLORE IN CANADA, 1902-64.*
B. KIRSHENBLATT-GIMBLETT, 203:SPRING
70-67
KNAPP, B. JEAN RACINE.
R.L. FARMER, 160:FALL71-59
KNAPP, B.L. ANTONIN ARTAUD.*
G. BRÉE, 397(MD):SEP70-231
G.E. WELLWARTH, 546(RR):APR71-155
KNAPP, B.L. JEAN COCTEAU.
A. AMOIA, 207(FR):FEB71-604
L. LE SAGE, 397(MD):MAY71-120
KNAPP, B.L. JEAN GENET.*
M. DE ROUGEMONT, 535(RHL):JAN-FEB70-
161
KNAPP, B.L. & A. DELLA FAZIA - SEE
ANOUILH, J.
KNAPP, G.C. STANGLEHOLD.
N. CALLENDAR, 441:9SEP73-40
KNAPP, L.M. - SEE SMOLLETT, T.
KNAPP, W. FRANCE: PARTIAL ECLIPSE.
617(TLS):27APR73-465
KNAPP-TEPPERBERG, E-M. ROBERT CHALLES
"ILLUSTRES FRANÇOISES."
I. STEMPEL, 72:BAND209HEFT4/6-460
KNAUB, R.K. - SEE REYNOLDS, G.F.
KNEBEL, F. DARK HORSE.*
R. BRYDEN, 362:5JUL73-25
KNEF, H. THE GIFT HORSE.
P.M. SPACKS, 249(HUDR):SPRING72-157
KNEIF, T. MUSIKSOZIOLOGIE.
K-P. ETZKORN, 187:MAY73-335
KNETSCHKE, E. & M. SPERLBAUM. ANLEITUNG
FÜR DIE HERSTELLUNG DER MONOGRAPHIEN
DER LAUTBIBLIOTHEK.
I. KOSSEL, 682(ZPSK):BAND23HEFT2/3-
308
KNIES, E.A. THE ART OF CHARLOTTE BRONTË.
L.A. RUFF, 613:SPRING71-136
W.D. SCHAEFER, 445(NCF):DEC70-379
"KNIGA I PROGRESS."
J.S.G. SIMMONS, 78(BC):WINTER71-548
"KNIGA: ISSLEDOVANIYA I MATERIALY." (VOL
21)
J.S.G. SIMMONS, 78(BC):AUTUMN71-399
KNIGGE, A.F. DER TRAUM DES HERRN BRICK.
(H. VOEGT, ED)
C. TRÄGER, 654(WB):4/1970-217
KNIGHT, D. FARQUHARSON'S PHYSIQUE: AND
WHAT IT DID TO HIS MIND.*
A. BOXILL, 198:SPRING73-116
M. WOLFE, 102(CANL):SUMMER72-105
KNIGHT, D., ED. A SCIENCE FICTION AR-
GOSY.
617(TLS):9NOV73-1378
KNIGHT, D.M. NATURAL SCIENCE BOOKS IN
ENGLISH, 1600-1900.
617(TLS):2MAR73-250
KNIGHT, E. A THEORY OF THE CLASSICAL
NOVEL.
A. KETTLE, 541(RES):NOV71-520
KNIGHT, F. BEETHOVEN AND THE AGE OF
REVOLUTION.
617(TLS):1JUN73-611
KNIGHT, G.W. BYRON AND SHAKESPEARE.
SHAKESPEARE AND RELIGION.
T.B. STROUP, 570(SQ):SPRING70-188
KNIGHT, G.W. NEGLECTED POWERS.*
I. JONES, 619(TC):VOL179#1049-57
G. THOMAS, 175:SUMMER71-62
KNIGHT, K.G., ED. DEUTSCHE ROMANE DER
BAROCKZEIT.*
A. MENHENNET, 220(GL&L):JAN72-147

KNIGHT, W.F.J. MANY-MINDED HOMER.*
(J.D. CHRISTIE, ED)
J. CROSSETT, 121(CJ):APR-MAY72-368
KNILLI, F. & U. MÜNCHOW. FRÜHES DEUT-
SCHES ARBEITERTHEATER, 1847-1918.
R. WEISBACH, 654(WB):6/1971-175
KNIPPING, F., ED. AKTEN ZUR DEUTSCHEN
AUSWÄRTIGEN POLITIK 1918-1945. (SER
C, VOL 1)
F.L. CARSTEN, 575(SEER):OCT72-620
KNOBLOCH, J., ED. SPRACHWISSENSCHAFT-
LICHES WÖRTERBUCH. (PTS 2&3)
W.B., 681(ZDS):BAND27HEFT3-190
KNOEPFLMACHER, U.C. GEORGE ELIOT'S EARLY
NOVELS.*
R. BENVENUTO, 594:FALL70-355
R. BÖHM, 430(NS):JUL71-390
D.P. DENEAU, 577(SHR):SPRING71-198
S.J. SPANBERG, 541(RES):AUG71-367
KNOEPFLMACHER, U.C. LAUGHTER & DESPAIR.
M. COOKE, 676(YR):SPRING72-433
G.J. WORTH, 301(JEGP):JUL72-454
KNOEPFLMACHER, U.C. RELIGIOUS HUMANISM
AND THE VICTORIAN NOVEL.
B. WILLEY, 148:SPRING71-94
KNOKE, U. DIE SPANISCHE MAURENROMANZE,
DER WANDEL IHRER INHALTE, GEHALTE UND
AUSDRUCKSFORMEN ZWISCHEN DEM SPÄTMIT-
TELALTER UND DEM BEGINN DES BAROCK.
D. MESSNER, 430(NS):APR71-227
H.T. OOSTENDORP, 433:APR71-212
KNOTT, B. AUTO-NECROPHILIA.
W. HUNT, 491:MAY73-103
KNOTT, J.R., JR. MILTON'S PASTORAL
VISION.*
W.G. RICE, 385(MQR):SPRING73-202
J.G. TAAFFE, 301(JEGP):JAN72-130
J.C. ULREICH, JR., 50(ARQ):WINTER71-
370
"KNOWLEDGE AND NECESSITY."
R.W. NEWELL, 479(PHQ):JUL71-275
KNOWLES, A. LAKELAND TODAY.
617(TLS):30NOV73-1485
KNOWLES, C.C. & P.H. PITT. THE HISTORY
OF BUILDING REGULATIONS IN LONDON 1189-
1972.
617(TLS):3AUG73-900
KNOWLES, D. THOMAS BECKET.
C.R. YOUNG, 589:OCT72-779
KNOWLES, D. ENGLISCHE MYSTIK.
W. RIEHLE, 38:BAND88HEFT4-541
KNOWLES, J. THE PARAGON.
42(AR):SPRING71-131
KNOWLSON, J. SAMUEL BECKETT.
E. WEBB, 648:APR72-20
KNOWLTON, D. THE NATURALIST IN CENTRAL
SOUTHERN ENGLAND.
617(TLS):10AUG73-936
KNOX, A. NIGHT OF THE WHITE BEAR.*
R.M. BROWN, 102(CANL):AUTUMN72-93
KNOX, A. TOTEM DREAM.
M. LEVIN, 441:3JUN73-32
KNOX, B. THE ARCHITECTURE OF POLAND.
J.I. DANIEC, 497(POLR):AUTUMN71-77
J.L.S. LOZINSKI, 32:SEP72-715
KNOX, B. DRAW BATONS!
N. CALLENDAR, 441:14OCT73-47
KNOX, B. STORMTIDE.
N. CALLENDAR, 441:18FEB73-29
KNOX, D. THE MAGIC FACTORY.
M. WOOD, 453:29NOV73-6
KNOX, M. ACTION.*
F.I. DRETSKE, 482(PHR):APR71-251
KNOX, M. A LAYMAN'S QUEST.*
D.C. HICKS, 483:JAN71-71
KNUDSEN, G. THE PHILOSOPHY OF FORM.
C. PRÉVOST, 542:OCT-DEC71-491

KOBEL, E. HUGO VON HOFMANNSTHAL.*
E. WEBER, 399(MLJ):APR71-261
KOBLER, J. CAPONE.*
D.R. NOLAN, 396(MODA):WINTER72-99
KOBS, J. KAFKA. (U. BRECH, ED)
J.C. BRUCE, 406:WINTER72-418
KOCH, H. CASABLANCA.
P. ADAMS, 61:AUG73-103
M. WOOD, 453:29NOV73-6
KOCH, H. & H. BAUER, EDS. DEUTSCH-
SPANISCHES WÖRTERBUCH.
L. TARÍN TORRECILLA, 556(RLV):1971/5-
659
KOCH, H.W., ED. THE ORIGINS OF THE FIRST
WORLD WAR.
617(TLS):31AUG73-1006
KOCH, K. A CHANGE OF HEARTS.
S. SPENDER, 453:20SEP73-8
KOCH, K. THE PLEASURES OF PEACE.*
G. KUZMA, 502(PRS):SPRING70-84
KOCH, K. ROSE, WHERE DID YOU GET THAT
RED?
J. GARDNER, 441:23DEC73-1
C. LEHMANN-HAUPT, 441:3OCT73-49
442(NY):19NOV73-246
KOCH, K. & OTHERS. WISHES, LIES, AND
DREAMS.
J. GARDNER, 441:23DEC73-1
639(VQR):SPRING71-LXXX
KOCH, P. - SEE GALIANI, F.
KOCH, S. STARGAZER.
L. BRAUDY, 441:7OCT73-7
KOCH, W.A. VOM MORPHEM ZUM TEXTEM.*
L. MOESSNER, 38:BAND89HEFT4-476
KOCHAN, L. ED. THE JEWS IN SOVIET RUS-
SIA SINCE 1917.
J. GOODMAN, 550(RUSR):APR71-196
KOCHER, P.H. MASTER OF MIDDLE-EARTH.*
617(TLS):8JUN73-629
KOCHNO, B. DIAGHILEV AND THE BALLETS
RUSSES.*
O. MAYNARD, 151:MAR71-50
KODÁLY, Z. FOLK MUSIC OF HUNGARY.* (2ND
ED REV BY L. VARGYAS)
F. HOWES, 415:AUG72-775
KOEHLER, L. ANTON ANTONOVIČ DEL'VIG.*
R-A. GREGG, 32:MAR72-189
R.F. GUSTAFSON, 550(RUSR):JUL71-312
KOEHLER, W. THE TASK OF GESTALT PSYCHOL-
OGY.
R. ARNHEIM, 290(JAAC):SPRING71-423
KOENIG, L.W. BRYAN.
H.M. ADAMS, 396(MODA):SPRING72-204
KOENIG, T. THE PHILOSOPHY OF GEORGES
BASTIDE.
E. MOROT-SIR, 319:JUL73-430
KOENIGSBERGER, H.G. THE HABSBURGS AND
EUROPE, 1516-1660.
R-A. KANN, 32:MAR72-205
KOEPCKE, M. THE BIRDS OF THE DEPARTMENT
OF LIMA, PERU. (REV)
S.S. BENSON, 37:OCT71-38
KOEPF, H. DIE GOTISCHEN PLANRISSE DER
WIENER SAMMLUNGEN.
F. BUCHER, 54:MAR71-113
KOEPPEN, W. ROMANISCHES CAFÉ.
617(TLS):7SEP73-1017
KOESTLER, A. THE CALL GIRLS.*
A. BROYARD, 441:3APR73-47
E. WEEKS, 61:MAY73-116
442(NY):21APR73-134
KOESTLER, A. THE GHOST IN THE MACHINE.
W.T. JONES, 321:SPRING71-148
KOHL, H. READING, HOW TO.
453:3MAY73-35
KOHL-LARSEN, L. DER PERLENBAUM.
H. VON SICARD, 196:BAND11HEFT1/2-173

KÖHLER, E. "CONSEIL DES BARONS" UND
"JUGEMENT DES BARONS."*
J. SCHULZE, 490:JUL/OCT70-632
KOHLER, F.D. UNDERSTANDING THE RUSSIANS.*
T.P. WHITNEY, 550(RUSR):APR71-189
639(VQR):WINTER71-XLII
KOHLHAUSSEN, H. NÜRNBERGER GOLDSCHMIEDE-
KUNST DES MITTELALTERS UND DER DÜRER-
ZEIT, 1240 BIS 1540.*
J.F.H., 135:FEB70-124
KOHLMEIER, L.M., JR. "GOD SAVE THIS
HONOURABLE COURT!"
442(NY):3FEB73-100
KOHLSCHMIDT, W. & P. ZINSLI, EDS. PHIL-
OLOGIA DEUTSCH.
C-D. COSSAR, 47(ARL):VOL17FASC1-68
H. WELLMANN, 680(ZDP):BAND89HEFT1-141
KOHN, P. THE CRADLE.
F.L. OWSLEY, JR., 9(ALAR):APR70-152
KOHT, H. LIFE OF IBSEN. (E. HAUGEN &
A.E. SANTANIELLO, EDS & TRANS)
E. DURBACH, 563(SS):WINTER72-140
J. MC FARLANE, 301(JEGP):OCT72-597
H.S. NAESS, 406:SUMMER72-185
KOJECKY, R. T.S. ELIOT'S SOCIAL CRITI-
CISM.*
J.D. MARGOLIS, 385(MQR):FALL73-381
M.L. RAINA, 295:FEB73-134
KOJÈVE, A. ESSAI D'UNE HISTOIRE RAISON-
NÉE DE LA PHILOSOPHIE PAÏENNE. [VOL
UNKNOWN]
E. GANS, 98:NOV71-1009
"KOJIKI."* (D.L. PHILIPPI, TRANS)
R.L. BACKUS, 318(JAOS):OCT-DEC71-525
"KOKUHŌ, NATIONAL TREASURES OF JAPAN."
A. SOPER, 57:VOL32#2/3-237
KOLAKOWSKI, L. CHRÉTIENS SANS ÉGLISE.
F.P. DE MICHELIS, 548(RCSF):JAN-MAR
71-97
KOLASKY, J. TWO YEARS IN SOVIET UKRAINE.
J.S. RESHETAR, JR., 32:MAR72-172
KOLATCH, J. SPORTS, POLITICS AND IDEOL-
OGY IN CHINA.
J. SPENCE, 441:14JAN73-4
KOLB, E. PHONOLOGICAL ATLAS OF THE
NORTHERN REGION.
M-F. WAKELIN, 47(ARL):[N.S.]VOL1-94
KOLB, H.H., JR. THE ILLUSION OF LIFE.*
R. LEHAN, 445(NCF):SEP71-245
D. PIZER, 223:DEC70-376
KOLB, P. - SEE PROUST, M.
KOLB, P. & L.B. PRICE - SEE PROUST, M.
KOLBE, J., ED. ANSICHTEN EINER KÜNFTI-
GEN GERMANISTIK.* (2ND ED)
R. GRUENTER, 190:BAND65HEFT1-97
L. HERMODSSON, 597(SN):VOL42#1-298
L. PIKULIK, 190:BAND65HEFT1-84
KOLBE, J. GOETHES "WAHLVERWANDTSCHAFTEN"
UND DER ROMAN DES 19. JAHRHUNDERTS.*
H. OHL, 657(WW):SEP/OCT71-352
H-R. VAGET, 222(GR):MAR71-157
KOLBE, J. - SEE FONTANE, T.
VAN DER KOLK, H. DAS HILDEBRANDLIED.*
C. MINIS, 680(ZDP):BAND89HEFT3-447
H. PÖRNBACHER, 433:APR70-196
KOLKO, J. & G. THE LIMITS OF POWER.*
R. STEEL, 453:31MAY73-29
KOLKOWICZ, R. & OTHERS. THE SOVIET
UNION AND ARMS CONTROL.
Y-L. WU, 550(RUSR):OCT71-393
KOLLER, J.M. ORIENTAL PHILOSOPHIES.
N.L. CHOBOT, 485(PE&W):JAN71-93
A.W. MUNK, 484(PPR):MAR72-433
K-M. WU, 258:SEP71-443
KOLLMAN, E.C. THEODOR KÖRNER.
617(TLS):24AUG73-981

KOLLONTAI, A. THE AUTOBIOGRAPHY OF A
SEXUALLY EMANCIPATED COMMUNIST WOMAN.*
(I. FETSCHER, ED)
J. LABER, 32:SEP72-678
KOLODIN, I. THE CONTINUITY OF MUSIC.*
M. PETERSON, 470:MAR71-35
KOLPACOFF, V. THE RAID.
M. COOKE, 676(YR):SUMMER72-599
KOLVE, V.A. THE PLAY CALLED CORPUS
CHRISTI.
H-J. DILLER, 179(ES):OCT71-446
KÖLVER, B. - SEE JACOBI, H.
KOLYCHEVA, E.I. KHOLOPSTVO I KREPOST-
NICHESTVO (KONETS XV-XVI V.).
R. HELLIE, 32:SEP72-659
KOMAR, A. SCHUMANN: DICHTERLIEBE.
E. SAMS, 415:SEP72-869
KOMINES, A.D. FACSIMILES OF DATED PAT-
MIAN CODICES.
R. BROWNING, 303:VOL91-215
A. DILLER, 377:MAR72-49
KONCHALOVSKY, D.P. OT GUMANIZMA K KHRIS-
TU.
S. PUSHKAREV, 32:JUN72-425
KONCZEWSKI, C. LA PSYCHOLOGIE DYNAMIQUE
ET LA PENSÉE VÉCUE.
G. CANGUILHEM, 542:JAN-MAR71-119
KÖNIG, I. DIE MEILENSTEINE DER GALLIA
NARBONENSIS.
R.P. WRIGHT, 313:VOL61-286
KÖNIG, R., ED. HANDBUCH DER EMPIRISCHEN
SOZIALFORSCHUNG. (2ND ED) (VOLS 1&2)
E.M. WALLNER, 182:VOL24#9/10-412
KONING, H. THE ALMOST WORLD.
R.P. BRICKNER, 441:25MAR73-20
"KONTAKTE UND GRENZEN."
E. ETTLINGER, 203:AUTUMN71-254
KONWICKI, T. A DREAMBOOK FOR OUR TIME.
J.R. KRZYŻANOWSKI, 497(POLR):AUTUMN
70-110
KOOL, F. & W. KRAUSE, EDS. DIE FRÜHEN
SOZIALISTEN.
A. LASSERRE, 182:VOL24#23/24-884
KOPECKY, M., ED. OBAROKNÍ KULTURE.
D. TSCHIZEWSKIJ, 72:BAND209HEFT1/3-
230
KOPIT, A. CHAMBER MUSIC AND OTHER PLAYS.
A. RENDLE, 157:SPRING70-71
KOPIT, A. INDIANS.
A. RENDLE, 157:SPRING71-77
KOPP, A. TOWN AND REVOLUTION. (FRENCH
TITLE: VILLE ET RÉVOLUTION.)
S. CANTACUZINO, 46:MAR71-195
K. FRAMPTON, 44:MAR71-76
S.F. STARR, 576:MAY71-171
J. WOLIN, 45:JAN71-48
KOPP, R. - SEE BAUDELAIRE, C.
KOPPITZ, H-J. - SEE PFEIFFER, F. & K.
BARTSCH
KOPS, B. FOR THE RECORD.*
J. SAUNDERS, 565:VOL12#4-63
KOPS, B. SETTLE DOWN SIMON KATZ.
617(TLS):18MAY73-545
KORBEL, J. DÉTENTE IN EUROPE.
617(TLS):30NOV73-1470
KORDA, M. MALE CHAUVINISM!
P. ADAMS, 61:JUL73-103
A. BROYARD, 441:14JUN73-45
M. ELLMANN, 453:1NOV73-18
KORETSKY, V.I. ZAKREPOSHCHENIE KREST'IAN
I KLASSOVAIA BOR'BA V ROSSII VO VTOROI
POLOVINE XVI V.
R. HELLIE, 32:SEP72-659
KOREY, W. THE SOVIET CAGE.
L. SCHAPIRO, 453:19JUL73-3
KORFF, F.W. DIASTOLE UND SYSTOLE.*
J.W. SMEED, 220(GL&L):JAN72-145
B. THUM, 190:BAND65HEFT3-339

KORFHAGE, R.R. LOGIC AND ALGORITHMS
WITH APPLICATIONS TO THE COMPUTER AND
INFORMATION SCIENCES.
J. BECVÁR, 316:JUN71-344
KORG, J., ED. TWENTIETH CENTURY INTER-
PRETATIONS OF "BLEAK HOUSE."*
S. MONOD, 189(EA):APR-JUN70-218
KORHONEN, M. DIE KONJUGATION IM LAPPIS-
CHEN.
A. RAUN, 361:VOL26#1-108
KORMAN, G., ED. HUNTER AND HUNTED.
N. ASCHERSON, 453:14JUN73-3
KÖRNER, K-H. DIE "AKTIONSGEMEINSCHAFT
FINITES VERB + INFINITIV" IM SPANISCHEN
FORMENSYSTEM.*
H. MENDELOFF, 240(HR):JAN71-98
J.D.W. SCHROTEN, 433:APR70-192
KÖRNER, S. CATEGORIAL FRAMEWORKS.
D.W. HAMLYN, 483:JUL71-276
KÖRNER, S. KANT'S CONCEPTION OF FREEDOM.
E.A.R., 543:DEC70-340
KÖRNER, S. WHAT IS PHILOSOPHY?*
M. HOLLIS, 483:JAN71-73
G.L. VANDER VEER, 479(PHQ):JAN71-78
KORNILOVICH, K. ARTS OF RUSSIA: FROM
THE ORIGINS TO THE END OF THE 16TH
CENTURY.
A. BRYER, 39:NOV70-397
KOROPECKYJ, I.S. LOCATION PROBLEMS IN
SOVIET INDUSTRY BEFORE WORLD WAR II.
H. HUNTER, 32:DEC72-909
"KORRESPONDENZBLATT DES VEREINS FÜR NIE-
DERDEUTSCHE SPRACHFORSCHUNG." (NO. 75)
B. KRATZ, 133:1970/2&3-343
KORSHIN, P.J., PROCEEDINGS OF THE
MODERN LANGUAGE ASSOCIATION NEOCLASSI-
CISM CONFERENCES 1967-1968.*
481(PQ):JUL71-386
KORSHIN, P.J., ED. STUDIES IN CHANGE AND
REVOLUTION.
617(TLS):11MAY73-525
KORTE, D.M. AN ANNOTATED BIBLIOGRAPHY OF
SMOLLETT SCHOLARSHIP 1946-68.
P-G. BOUCÉ, 189(EA):JUL-SEP70-343
G.S. ROUSSEAU, 173(ECS):SPRING71-336
T. WRIGHT, 447(N&Q):OCT71-398
KORTEPETER, C.M. OTTOMAN IMPERIALISM
DURING THE REFORMATION.
617(TLS):16NOV73-1404
KORTUM, H. CHARLES PERRAULT UND NICOLAS
BOILEAU.
S. MENANT, 535(RHL):MAR-APR70-311
KOS-RABCEWICZ-ZUBKOWSKI, L. EAST EURO-
PEAN RULES ON THE VALIDITY OF INTER-
NATIONAL COMMERCIAL ARBITRATION AGREE-
MENTS.
Z.L. ZILE, 32:MAR72-239
KOSÁRY, D. BEVEZETÉS MAGYARORSZÁG TÖR-
TÉNETÉNEK FORRÁSAIBA ÉS IRODALMÁBA.
(VOL 1)
G. BARANY, 32:SEP72-718
KOSCH, W., COMP. DEUTSCHES LITERATUR-
LEXIKON.* (VOL 1) (3RD ED) (B. BERGER
& H. RUPP, EDS)
K. TOBER, 133:1970/1-122
KOSCH, W., COMP. DEUTSCHES LITERATUR-
LEXIKON. (VOL 3) (3RD ED) (H. RUPP, ED)
P.M. MITCHELL, 301(JEGP):JUL72-406
KOSCHATZKY, W. ALBRECHT DÜRER.
J. CANADAY, 441:2DEC73-90
KOSCHATZKY, W. & A. STROBL. DÜRER DRAW-
INGS IN THE ALBERTINA.
617(TLS):27APR73-464
KOSCHMIEDER, E. BEITRÄGE ZUR ALLGEMEINEN
SYNTAX.
K.E. NAYLOR, 215(GL):VOL11#2-117

KOSINSKI, J. BEING THERE.*
  M. COOKE, 676(YR):SUMMER72-599
  L.T.L., 502(PRS):WINTER71/72-369
KOSINSKI, J. THE DEVIL TREE.
  P. ADAMS, 61:MAR73-107
  R. ALTER, 441:11FEB73-2
  V. CUNNINGHAM, 362:28JUN73-873
  T.R. EDWARDS, 453:22MAR73-29
  C. LEHMANN-HAUPT, 441:13FEB73-39
  G. STADE, 231:MAY73-86
  617(TLS):6JUL73-783
KOSKENNIEMI, I. REPETITIVE WORD PAIRS IN
  OLD AND EARLY MIDDLE ENGLISH PROSE.
  M. KILPIÖ, 439(NM):1971/2-373
KOSKENNIEMI, I. JOHN WEBSTER'S "THE
  WHITE DEVIL" AND LUDWIG TIECK'S "VIT-
  TORIA ACCOROMBONA."
  F. LAGARDE, 189(EA):JUL-SEP70-338
KOSKIMIES, R. DER NORDISCHE DEKADENT.*
  J.A. DALE, 172(EDDA):1970/1-57
KOSKO, M. LE FILS ASSASSINÉ (AT 939 A).
  M. FRAUENRATH, 535(RHL):MAY-JUN70-541
KOSS, S. FLEET STREET RADICAL.
  A. BOYLE, 362:26APR73-554
  617(TLS):4MAY73-492
KOSS, S. JOHN MORLEY AT THE INDIA OFFICE:
  1905-1910.
  M. ISRAEL, 293(JAST):NOV70-199
KOSSMANN, O. POLEN IM MITTELALTER.
  F. GRAUS, 575(SEER):OCT72-639
KOSTARAS, G.P. DER BEGRIFF DES LEBENS
  BEI PLOTIN.*
  R. STAVRIDES, 319:JAN73-116
  R.T. WALLIS, 123:DEC72-412
KOSTELANETZ, R., ED. BREAKTHROUGH FIC-
  TIONEERS.
  L.J. DAVIS, 441:21OCT73-48
  617(TLS):18MAY73-557
KOSTELANETZ, R. IN THE BEGINNING.
  L.J. DAVIS, 441:21OCT73-48
KOSTELANETZ, R., ED. MOHOLY-NAGY.
  G. RUSSELL, 58:DEC70/JAN71-10
KOSTOROSKI, E.P. THE EAGLE AND THE DOVE.
  617(TLS):19JAN73-59
KOTHARI, R. POLITICS IN INDIA.
  N.D. PALMER, 293(JAST):MAY71-698
KOTLOWITZ, R. SOMEWHERE ELSE.*
  617(TLS):21DEC73-1557
KOTT, J. THE EATING OF THE GODS.
  D.S. CARNE-ROSS, 453:19JUL73-8
KOUMAKIS, G. PLATONS PARMENIDES.
  F. LASSERRE, 182:VOL24#21/22-809
KOURILSKY, F. LE THÉÂTRE AUX ETATS-UNIS.
  G. DEBUSSCHER, 556(RLV):1970/4-444
KOUROUMA, A. LES SOLEILS DES INDÉPEN-
  DANCES.
  E. SELLIN, 207(FR):FEB71-641
KOUTSOUDAS, A. WRITING TRANSFORMATIONAL
  GRAMMARS.*
  E.C. TRAUGOTT, 206:NOV70-565
KOVÁCS, E. LIMOGES CHAMPLEVÉ ENAMELS IN
  HUNGARY.
  J. BECKWITH, 39:JAN70-84
KOVÁCS, S.V., ED. MAGYAR HUMANISTÁK
  LEVELEI.
  J.M. BAK, 32:JUN72-478
KOVALENKO, D.A. OBORONNAIA PROMYSHLEN-
  NOST' SOVETSKOI ROSSII V 1918-1920 GG.
  J.P. MC KAY, 32:SEP72-675
KOVALEVSKY, P.E. ZARUBEZHNAIA ROSSIIA.
  L.A. FOSTER, 32:MAR72-204
KOVÁLY, H. & E. KOHÁK. THE VICTORS AND
  THE VANQUISHED.
  A. KAZIN, 441:19AUG73-5
KOWAL, D. & D. MEILACH. SCULPTURE CAST-
  ING, MOULD TECHNIQUES AND MATERIALS.
  617(TLS):17AUG73-961

KOWZAN, T. LITTÉRATURE ET SPECTACLE DANS
  LEURS RAPPORTS ESTHÉTIQUES, THÉMAT-
  IQUES ET SÉMIOLOGIQUES.*
  Z. MARKIEWICZ, 549(RLC):OCT-DEC71-613
  R. MERCIER, 557(RSH):APR-JUN71-310
KOYRÉ, A. ÉTUDES D'HISTOIRE DE LA PENSÉE
  PHILOSOPHIQUE. ÉTUDES D'HISTOIRE DE LA
  PENSÉE SCIENTIFIQUE. THE ASTRONOMICAL
  REVOLUTION.
  617(TLS):31AUG73-994
KOZAKIEWICZ, S. BERNARDO BELLOTTO.
  617(TLS):5JAN73-1
KOZIOL, H. GRUNDZÜGE DER ENGLISCHEN
  SEMANTIK.*
  B. CARSTENSEN, 430(NS):OCT70-534
KOZLOFF, M. CUBISM/FUTURISM.
  J.R. MELLOW, 441:2DEC73-10
KRAAK, A. & W.G. KLOOSTER. SYNTAXIS.*
  P.A.M. SEUREN, 206:AUG71-441
KRAAY, C.M. GREEK COINS AND HISTORY.
  J. SCARBOROUGH, 121(CJ):FEB-MAR72-288
KRAEMER, J. SPLENDEUR ET MISÈRE DE
  MINETTE LA BONNE LORRAINE.
  D.M. CHURCH, 207(FR):FEB71-643
KRAFT, H., ED. SCHILLERS KABALE UND
  LIEBE.
  H.C. SEEBA, 221(GQ):JAN71-112
KRAFT, H. - SEE SCHILLER, F.
KRAFT, J. THE CHINESE DIFFERENCE.
  M. BERNAL, 453:9AUG73-21
KRAFT, J. THE EARLY TALES OF HENRY
  JAMES.*
  W.R. PATRICK, 573(SSF):SPRING71-338
  W.T. STAFFORD, 445(NCF):SEP70-237
KRAFT, M. STUDIEN ZUR THEMATIK VON MAX
  FRISCHS ROMAN "MEIN NAME SEI GANTEN-
  BEIN."*
  G. HILLEN, 400(MLN):OCT71-746
  J.J. WHITE, 220(GL&L):JUL72-396
KRAFT, W. REBELLEN DES GEISTES.
  E.F. TIMMS, 402(MLR):APR72-472
KRAHE, H. HISTORISCHE LAUT- UND FORMEN-
  LEHRE DES GOTISCHEN. (2ND ED) (E.
  SEEBOLD, ED)
  H-R., 657(WW):MAR/APR71-144
KRAMER, D. BOB DYLAN.
  M. PETERSON, 470:JAN71-44
KRAMER, E. ART AS THERAPY WITH CHILDREN.
  617(TLS):16NOV73-1409
KRAMER, J. GARDENING AND HOME LAND-
  SCAPING.
  617(TLS):5JAN73-21
KRAMER, J. ALLEN GINSBERG IN AMERICA.
  L. CASPER, 613:SUMMER70-302
KRAMER, J., ED. PFÄLZISCHES WÖRTERBUCH.*
  (VOL 1)
  J-P. PONTEN, 433:JAN71-100
KRAMER, K.D. THE CHAMELEON AND THE DREAM.
  A.B. MC MILLIN, 575(SEER):JAN72-142
KRAMER, M. MOTHER WALTER AND THE PIG
  TRAGEDY.
  T. LASK, 441:6JAN73-27
  R. TODD, 61:APR73-116
KRÁMSKÝ, J. THE WORD AS A LINGUISTIC
  UNIT.
  U.L. FIGGE, 490:JUL71-409
KRANE, B. SIGRID UNDSET.
  S. JOHANSEN, 172(EDDA):1971/6-377
KRANIDAS, T., ED. NEW ESSAYS ON "PARA-
  DISE LOST."
  M. HUGHES, 549(RLC):APR-JUN71-267
  R. LEJOSNE, 189(EA):JUL-SEP71-332
  M-S. RØSTVIG, 179(ES):OCT71-457
KRANOWSKI, N. LE THÈME DE PARIS DANS LES
  ROMANS D'EMILE ZOLA.*
  M. KANES, 546(RR):APR71-150
KRANTZLER, M. CREATIVE DIVORCE.
  B. DE MOTT, 61:DEC73-127

KRASLOW, D. & S.H. LOORY. THE SECRET
  SEARCH FOR PEACE IN VIETNAM.
    L-S. TAO, 293(JAST):AUG71-923
KRASNOSHCHEKOVA, E. "OBLOMOV" I.A. GON-
  CHAROVA.
    M. EHRE, 32:MAR72-189
KRASSÓ, N., ED. TROTSKY, THE GREAT
  DEBATE RENEWED.
    L. KOLAKOWSKI, 473(PR):FALL72-589
KRATOCHVÍL, P. THE CHINESE LANGUAGE
  TODAY.
    M. CHEN, 361:VOL25#1-82
    R.L. CHENG, 297(JL):FEB70-152
KRATZ, B. ZUR BEZEICHNUNG VON PFLUGMES-
  SER UND MESSERPFLUG IN GERMANIA UND
  ROMANIA.
    R. RIS, 343:BAND13HEFT2-200
KRATZ, H. FRÜHES MITTELALTER.*
    S. BERR, 221(GQ):MAY71-422
    D.H. GREEN, 402(MLR):JAN72-202
KRAUS, H.P. SIR FRANCIS DRAKE.
    D.B. QUINN, 551(RENQ):AUTUMN71-392
KRAUS, J.L. JOHN LOCKE.
    J.J. JENKINS, 478:JUL71-135
KRAUS, K. DIE DRITTE WALPURGISNACHT.
  (H. FISCHER, ED)
    D.S. LOW, 220(GL&L):OCT71-56
KRAUS, K. WERKE. (H. FISCHER, ED)
    E. HELLER, 453:3MAY73-21
KRAUSS, H. DIE PRAXIS DER "LITTÉRATURE
  ENGAGÉE" IM WERK JEAN-PAUL SARTRES
  1938-1948.
    U. SCHULZ-BUSCHHAUS, 72:BAND209HEFT
    4/6-470
KRAUSS, W. & M. FONTIUS, EDS. FRANZÖ-
  SISCHE DRUCKE DES 18. JAHRHUNDERTS IN
  DEN BIBLIOTHEKEN DER DEUTSCHEN DEMO-
  KRATISCHEN REPUBLIK.
    R. SHACKLETON, 208(FS):JAN72-76
KRAUSZ, M., ED. CRITICAL ESSAYS ON THE
  PHILOSOPHY OF R.G. COLLINGWOOD.
    617(TLS):30MAR73-337
KRAUTH, L. DIE PHILOSOPHIE CARNAPS.*
    R. BLANCHÉ, 542:OCT-DEC71-462
    Y. GAUTHIER, 154:JUN71-357
KRECH, E-M. SPRECHWISSENSCHAFTLICH-PHON-
  ETISCHE UNTERSUCHUNGEN ZUM GEBRAUCH DES
  GLOTTISSCHLAGEINSATZES IN DER ALLGEMEIN-
  EN DEUTSCHEN HOCHLAUTUNG.
    G. HEIKE, 260(IF):BAND75-361
    H. ULBRICH, 682(ZPSK):BAND23HEFT1-105
KREISEL, H. DIE KUNST DES DEUTSCHEN
  MÖBELS. (VOL 2)
    H. HUTH, 54:SEP71-420
    P. THORNTON, 90:DEC71-745
KREISSLER, F. DAS FRANZÖSISCHE BEI RAI-
  MUND UND NESTROY.
    S. JAUERNICK, 430(NS):JAN71-50
KREJCÍ, K. HEROIKOMIKA V BÁSNICTVÍ
  SLOVANU.
    H. JECHOVA', 549(RLC):APR-JUN71-259
KRENN, H. DIE SPRACHWISSENSCHAFTLICHE
  FRAGE DER SEMANTIK UND FUNKTION, ERÖR-
  TERT AN DEN GEGEBENHEITEN DER "CONSECU-
  TIO TEMPORUM" IM ITALIENISCHEN.
    R. STEFANINI, 545(RPH):AUG71-101
KRETSCH, W. IMAGES ET REFLETS LITTER-
  AIRES.
    H. JAECKEL, 207(FR):FEB71-589
KRETSCHMER, P. EINLEITUNG IN DIE GESCHI-
  CHTE DER GRIECHISCHEN SPRACHE. (2ND ED)
    A.M. DAVIES, 123:DEC72-420
KRETSCHMER, P. WORTGEOGRAPHIE DER HOCH-
  DEUTSCHEN UMGANGSSPRACHE. (2ND ED)
    J.L. FLOOD, 220(GL&L):APR72-296
KRETZMANN, N. - SEE WILLIAM OF SHERWOOD

KREUTER-EGGEMANN, H. DAS SKIZZENBUCH DES
  "JACQUES DALIWE."
    M.S. FRINTA, 54:MAR70-100
KREUTZER, H.J. DIE DICHTERISCHE ENTWICK-
  LUNG HEINRICHS VON KLEIST.
    R. SAMUEL, 564:JUN70-177
KREUZER, H., ED. LITERARISCHE UND NATUR-
  WISSENSCHAFTLICHE INTELLIGENZ.
    H. PIETSCH, 654(WB):6/1971-178
KREUZER, K.F. - SEE BOEHMER, G.
KREUZER, L. ALFRED DÖBLIN.
    W. GROTHE, 597(SN):VOL43#2-563
KRIEG, W., ED. BIBLIOTHEKSWISSENSCHAFT.
    R. CAZDEN, 182:VOL24#17/18-641
KRIEGEL, A. THE FRENCH COMMUNISTS.*
    617(TLS):21DEC73-1560
KRIEGEL, A. AUX ORIGINES DU COMMUNISME
  FRANÇAIS. LES COMMUNISTES FRANÇAIS,
  ESSAI D'ETHNOGRAPHIE POLITIQUE.
    I.M. WALL, 207(FR):MAY71-1119
KRIEGEL, L. EDMUND WILSON.*
    S. PAUL, 579(SAQ):SUMMER72-450
KRIEGER, M., ED. NORTHROP FRYE IN
  MODERN CRITICISM.*
    F.D. HOENIGER, 52:BAND5HEFT1-94
KRIEGLER, H. UNTERSUCHUNGEN ZU DEN OPTIS-
  CHEN UND AKUSTISCHEN DATEN DER BACCHY-
  LIDEISCHEN DICHTUNG.
    D.C. INNES, 123:MAR72-15
VON KRIES, F.W. TEXTKRITISCHE STUDIEN
  ZUM WELSCHEN GAST THOMASINS VON ZER-
  CLAERE.
    W. SCHRÖDER, 680(ZDP):BAND90HEFT1-119
KRIPALANI, K. MODERN INDIAN LITERATURE.*
    S. CHANDOLA, 352(LE&W):VOL15#2-325
KRIS, E. PSYCHOANALYTIC EXPLORATIONS IN
  ART.
    R. COLES, 453:22FEB73-15
KRISHNA, D. SOCIAL PHILOSOPHY.
    R.M. MOORE, 485(PE&W):JUL70-323
KRISHNAMACHARYA, V., ED. SANATKUMĀRA-
  SAMHITĀ OF THE PAÑCARĀTRĀGAMA.
    L. ROCHER, 318(JAOS):OCT-DEC71-548
KRISHNAMURTI, J. BEYOND VIOLENCE.
    617(TLS):2MAR73-249
KRISTELLER, P.O. RENAISSANCE CONCEPTS OF
  MAN AND OTHER ESSAYS.
    617(TLS):27APR73-467
KRISTELLER, P.O. - SEE CASSIRER, E.
KRISTELLER, P.O. & F.E. CRANZ, EDS. CAT-
  ALOGUS TRANSLATIONUM ET COMMENTARIORUM.
  (VOL 2)
    F. LASSERRE, 182:VOL24#1/2-42
KRISTENSSON, G. STUDIES ON MIDDLE
  ENGLISH TOPOGRAPHICAL TERMS.*
    K. CAMERON, 382(MAE):1972/2-161
    E.G. STANLEY, 447(N&Q):MAY71-188
KRISTEVA, J. SĒMEIŌTIAĒ: RECHERCHES POUR
  UNE SÉMANALYSE.
    J-L. HOUDEBINE, 98:APR71-318
KRIVINE, J-L. THÉORIE AXIOMATIQUE DES
  ENSEMBLES.
    Y. GAUTHIER, 154:DEC70-496
KROCK, A. CONSENT OF THE GOVERNED, AND
  OTHER DECEITS.
    C.P. IVES, 396(MODA):SPRING72-202
KROCK, A. MEMOIRS.
    J.E. TALMADGE, 219(GAR):SPRING70-73
KROCK, A. MYSELF WHEN YOUNG.
    441:20MAY73-20
KROEBER, K. STYLES IN FICTIONAL STRUC-
  TURE.*
    M. ELLMANN, 676(YR):AUTUMN71-132
    D. LODGE, 454:SPRING72-260
    639(VQR):SUMMER71-CXII
KROEBER, T. ALFRED KROEBER, A PERSONAL
  CONFIGURATION.
    Y. MALKIEL, 545(RPH):FEB72-370

KROETSCH, R., ED. CREATION.
A. ROBERTSON, 648:JUN71-52
KROLOW, K. ZEITVERGEHEN.
617(TLS):12JAN73-36
KRÖMER, C. DIE VEREINIGTEN STAATEN VON
AMERIKA UND DIE FRAGE KÄRNTEN 1918-
1920.
K.R. STADLER, 575(SEER):JAN72-145
KRÖMER, W. ZUR WELTANSCHAUUNG, ÄSTHETIK
UND POETIK DES NEOKLASSIZISMUS UND DER
ROMANTIK IN SPANIEN.*
E. GRAMBERG, 546(RR):APR71-144
KROOK, D. ELEMENTS OF TRAGEDY.*
A.D. NUTTALL, 541(RES):AUG71-382
S.G. PUTT, 175:AUTUMN71-101
KRUEGER, J.R., WITH E.D. FRANCIS, EDS.
CHEREMIS-CHUVASH LEXICAL RELATIONSHIPS.
P. AALTO, 353:AUG70-116
KRÜGER, H. ZUR GESCHICHTE VON DANGER IM
FRANZÖSISCHEN.
P. ZUMTHOR, 433:OCT70-427
KRUGLIKOVA, I.T. BOSPOR V POZDNEANTICH-
NOE VREMYA.
D.J. BLACKMAN, 303:VOL91-198
KRUK, Z. THE TASTE OF FEAR.
617(TLS):19OCT73-1289
KRUPITSCH, V.S. - SEE "APOLLON GRIGOR'EV:
SOCHINENIIA"
KRYZYTSKI, S. THE WORKS OF IVAN BUNIN.
617(TLS):24AUG73-972
KUBE, J. "TECHNĒ" UND "ARETĒ."*
P. LOUIS, 555:VOL45FASC2-341
KUBIJOVYČ, V., ED. UKRAINE, A CONCISE
ENCYCLOPEDIA. (VOL 2)
R.A. PIERCE, 529(QQ):WINTER71-638
L. TILLETT, 32:JUN72-456
KUBINSZKY, M. BAHNHÖFE EUROPAS.
N.P., 46:MAY70-388
KUČERA, H. & W.N. FRANCIS. COMPUTATIONAL
ANALYSIS OF PRESENT-DAY AMERICAN ENG-
LISH.*
S.R. ANDERSON, 206:AUG71-453
R. LAMÉRAND, 343:BAND13HEFT2-175
G.F. MEIER, 682(ZPSK):BAND23HEFT1-91
L. ORSZÁGH, 179(ES):AUG71-381
KUCK, L. THE WORLD OF THE JAPANESE
GARDEN.
W.S. BALDINGER, 127:SUMMER72-468
KUCKUK, P., ED. REVOLUTION UND RÄTERE-
PUBLIK IN BREMEN.
H.H. HERWIG, 32:SEP72-713
KUCZYNSKI, J. GESTALTEN UND WERKE.
D. SOMMER, 654(WB):8/1971-184
KUDIELKA, R. ROBYN DENNY.
617(TLS):14SEP73-1062
KUDSI-ZADEH, A.A. SAYYID JAMĀL AL DĪN
AL-AFGHĀNĪ: AN ANNOTATED BIBLIOGRAPHY.
J.A. BELLAMY, 318(JAOS):OCT-DEC71-532
KUDSZUS, W. SPRACHVERLUST UND SINNWAN-
DEL.*
G.L. JONES, 220(GL&L):OCT71-69
L. RYAN, 221(GQ):JAN71-100
KUEHL, J. & J. BRYER - SEE FITZGERALD,
F.S.
KUEHL, J. & J.R. BRYER - SEE FITZGERALD,
F.S. & M. PERKINS
KUGEL, J.L. THE TECHNIQUES OF STRANGE-
NESS IN SYMBOLIST POETRY.
639(VQR):AUTUMN71-CLXIX
KÜGLER, H. LITERATUR UND KOMMUNIKATION.
Z. TAKACS, 182:VOL24#17/18-674
KÜHLWEIN, W. DIE VERWENDUNG DER FEIND-
SELIGKEITSBEZEICHNUNGEN IN DER ALTENG-
LISCHEN DICHTERSPRACHE.*
K. FAISS, 353:JUL70-108
E.G. STANLEY, 260(IF):BAND75-352

KUHN, C.L. GERMAN AND NETHERLANDISH
SCULPTURE, 1280-1800; THE HARVARD COL-
LECTIONS.
D.L. EHRESMANN, 54:DEC70-449
KUHN, D. EMPIRISCHE UND IDEELLE WIRK-
LICHKEIT.
L. LÖB, 220(GL&L):OCT71-78
KUHN, H. DAS ALTE ISLAND.
M. STEBLIN-KAMENSKIJ, 301(JEGP):APR
72-309
KUHN, H. MINNESANGS WENDE. (2ND ED)
H.R., 657(WW):MAR/APR70-138
KUHN, H. TEXT UND THEORIE.
D.R. MC LINTOCK, 220(GL&L):JUL72-385
KUHN, H., K. STACKMANN & D. WUTTKE, EDS.
KOLLOQUIUM ÜBER PROBLEME ALTGERMANIST-
ISCHER EDITIONEN.
U. MÜLLER, 680(ZDP):BAND90HEFT1-112
KUHN, P.A. REBELLION AND ITS ENEMIES IN
LATE IMPERIAL CHINA.
M-C. BERGERE, 293(JAST):MAY71-664
KÜHNE, J. DAS GLEICHNIS.
E. BOA, 402(MLR):JAN72-226
KÜHNE, P. ARBEITERKLASSE UND LITERATUR.
617(TLS):20JUL73-836
KÜHNEL, E. ISLAMIC ARTS.
D.T. RICE, 135:DEC71-289
KÜHNEL, W-D. FERDINAND KÜRNBERGER ALS
LITERATURTHEORETIKER IM ZEITALTER DES
REALISMUS.
L.H.C. THOMAS, 402(MLR):OCT72-947
KUHNS, R. LITERATURE AND PHILOSOPHY.
S.R. SUTHERLAND, 89(BJA):WINTER72-82
KUHNS, W. THE REUNION.
M. LEVIN, 441:8APR73-33
KUIPERS, A.H. THE SQUAMISH LANGUAGE.
(PT 2)
M.D. KINKADE, 361:VOL26#4-433
KUKENHEIM, L. GRAMMAIRE HISTORIQUE DE LA
LANGUE FRANÇAISE.*
R. ARVEILLER, 209(FM):JUL70-366
J. PURCZINSKY, 545(RPH):AUG71-145
KUKENHEIM, L. & H. ROUSSEL. FÜHRER
DURCH DIE FRANZÖSISCHE LITERATUR DES
MITTELALTERS.
J. FELIXBERGER, 430(NS):MAY70-257
M. KRÜGER, 224(GRM):AUG70-363
KUKUŁKA, J. FRANCJA A POLSKA PO TRAK-
TACIE WERSALSKIM, 1919-1922.
P.S. WANDYCZ, 32:JUN72-470
KULLI, R.M. DIE STÄNDESATIRE IN DEN
DEUTSCHEN GEISTLICHEN SCHAUSPIELEN
DES AUSGEHENDEN MITTELALTERS.
G.F. JONES, 133:1970/2&3-289
KULLY, R.M. JOHANN PETER HEBEL.
W. POPP, 657(WW):JUL/AUG70-281
KULP, K.K. MANNER AND MOOD IN ROSALÍA DE
CASTRO.
191(ELN):SEP71(SUPP)-177
KULTERMANN, U., ED. KENZO TANGE, 1946-
1969.
R. BOYD, 44:OCT71-8
J.T. BURNS, JR., 505:APR71-112
T. CROSBY, 46:JAN71-64
W.J. MALARCHER, 363:MAY71-84
"KULTUREEL JAARBOEK VOOR DE PROVINCIE
OOSTVLAANDEREN, TWINTIGSTE JAAR, 1966."
J. BARTHELS, 556(RLV):1971/6-785
KULUNDŽIĆ, Z. TRAGEDIJA HRVATSKE HIS-
TORIOGRAFIJE. (2ND ED)
M.M. MEŠTROVIĆ, 32:MAR72-226
KUMIN, M. THE ABDUCTION.
P.M. SPACKS, 249(HUDR):SPRING72-166
KUMIN, M. THE NIGHTMARE FACTORY.
639(VQR):SPRING71-LX

KÜMMEL, H.M. ERSATZRITUALE FÜR DEN
HETHITISCHEN KÖNIG.
E. NEU, 343:BAND13HEFT1-67
G. NEUMANN, 260(IF):BAND75-294
KUNENE, M. ZULU POEMS.
A. CLUYSENAAR, 565:VOL12#3-72
KÜNG, H. INFALLIBLE?*
J.F. MITROS, 613:SUMMER71-289
KÜNG, H. WHY PRIESTS?*
617(TLS):16FEB73-185
KUNISCH, H. - SEE VON EICHENDORFF, J.
KUNITZ, S. THE TESTING TREE.
R.H. BAYES, 50(ARQ):WINTER71-375
L. LIEBERMAN, 676(YR):AUTUMN71-82
R.S., 376:JUL71-115
KUNITZ, S. & M. HAYWARD - SEE AKHMATOVA,
A.
KUNNES, R. THE AMERICAN HEROIN EMPIRE.
P. STEINFELS & R.M. VEATCH, 441:
4FEB73-6
KUNTZ, P.G., ED. THE CONCEPT OF ORDER.*
R.M. MOORE, 485(PE&W):JAN70-95
KUNTZ, P.G. - SEE SANTAYANA, G.
KUNZ, H. BILDERSPRACHE ALS DASEINSER-
SCHLIESSUNG.
F. WASSERMANN, 406:SUMMER72-201
KUNZ, J. DIE DEUTSCHE NOVELLE IM 19.
JAHRHUNDERT.*
H.A. HESSE, 67:MAY72-113
KUNZ, J., ED. NOVELLE.*
D. LO CICERO, 221(GQ):MAY71-389
KUNZE, R. WITH THE VOLUME TURNED DOWN.
617(TLS):17AUG73-946
KUNZE, R. ZIMMERLAUTSTÄRKE.
617(TLS):12JAN73-36
KÜNZIG, J. SCHWARZWALD-SAGEN. (2ND ED)
F. HARKORT, 196:BAND11HEFT1/2-177
KÜNZLE, P. - SEE BERNARDUS DE TRILIA
"KUO-MIN HSÜEH-HSIAO CH'ANG-YUNG TZE-HUI
YEN-CHIU."
D. BARNES, 293(JAST):AUG71-889
KUPER, A. ANTHROPOLOGISTS AND ANTHRO-
POLOGY.
617(TLS):6JUL73-773
KUPER, H. A WITCH IN MY HEART.
T.O. BEIDELMAN, 69:JUL71-251
KUPPERMAN, J.J. ETHICAL KNOWLEDGE.
K. WARD, 518:JAN72-14
KURAN, A. THE MOSQUE IN EARLY OTTOMAN
ARCHITECTURE.
H. CRANE, 576:DEC71-336
KURATOWSKI, K. & A. MOSTOWSKI. SET
THEORY.
J. WOODS, 486:JUN71-314
KURIYAGAWA, F. - SEE "WALTER HILTON'S
EIGHT CHAPTERS ON PERFECTION"
DE KURLAT, F.W. - SEE SÁNCHEZ DE BADAJOZ,
D.
KURODA, S-Y. YAWELMANI PHONOLOGY.*
M.R. KEY, 353:APR71-122
KURSCHAT, A. LITAUISCH-DEUTSCHES WÖRTER-
BUCH.* (VOL 1) (W. WISSMANN & E. HOF-
MANN, EDS)
W.R. SCHMALSTIEG, 215(GL):VOL10#1-33
KURTÉN, B. THE ICE AGE.
617(TLS):16MAR73-293
KURTH, L.E. DIE ZWEITE WIRKLICHKEIT.
R.L. JOHNSON, 399(MLJ):JAN71-32
M. VON POSER, 52:BAND6HEFT1-97
G. STERN, 400(MLN):APR71-427
KURTI, A. PERSIAN FOLKTALES.
J. SIMPSON, 203:SUMMER71-169
KURTZ, P., ED. AMERICAN PHILOSOPHY IN
THE TWENTIETH CENTURY.
A. CHURCH, 316:JUN70-312
KURTZ, P., ED. SIDNEY HOOK AND THE CON-
TEMPORARY WORLD.*
C. EVANS, 321:SPRING71-156

KURTZ, P., ED. LANGUAGE AND HUMAN NATURE.
A. MONTEFIORE, 311(JP):22MAR73-166
KURVINEN, A., ED. THE SIEGE OF JERUSALEM
IN PROSE.*
B. CARSTENSEN, 430(NS):SEP71-506
N. JACOBS, 597(SN):VOL42#2-494
M. MILLS, 541(RES):MAY71-247
KURYŁOWICZ, J. INDOGERMANISCHE GRAMMATIK.
(VOL 2)
F. BADER, 555:VOL45FASC2-325
KURYŁOWICZ, J. - SEE WATKINS, C.
KURZ, H.R., ED. DOKUMENTE DES AKTIV-
DIENSTES.
A. WAHL, 182:VOL24#15/16-628
KURZ, P.K. ON MODERN GERMAN LITERATURE.
E. BOA, 402(MLR):JAN72-226
R. SPAETHLING, 141:SUMMER71-321
KURZMAN, D. GENESIS 1948.*
639(VQR):WINTER71-XXXVIII
KUSIN, V.V. POLITICAL GROUPING IN THE
CZECHOSLOVAK REFORM MOVEMENT.
N. ASCHERSON, 453:5APR73-34
KUSPIT, D.B. THE PHILOSOPHICAL LIFE OF
THE SENSES.*
W.J. GAVIN, 258:JUN71-277
KUTCHER, A. THE NEW JERUSALEM.
617(TLS):2NOV73-1344
KÜTHER, W. VACHA UND SEIN SERVITENKLOSTER
IM MITTELALTER.
I. MÜLLER, 182:VOL24#15/16-627
KUTTNER, H. FURY.
T. STURGEON, 441:22APR73-16
KUUSI, M. OVAMBO PROVERBS WITH AFRICAN
PARALLELS.
B. GUNDA, 203:AUTUMN71-251
KUXDORF, M. DIE SUCHE NACH DEM MENSCHEN
IM DRAMA GEORG KAISERS.
E. KRISPYN, 406:SUMMER72-203
KUZMA, G. SITTING AROUND.*
H.J.L., 502(PRS):SUMMER70-185
KUZNETSOV, A. [A. ANATOLI] BABI YAR.*
(RUSSIAN TITLE: BABIJ JAR.)
M. FRIEDBERG, 390:FEB71-75
639(VQR):AUTUMN71-CLXI
KWAVNICK, D. ORGANIZED LABOUR AND PRES-
SURE POLITICS.
P. PHILLIPS, 99:MAY73-38
KYBURG, H. PROBABILITY AND INDUCTIVE
LOGIC.
R.H.K., 543:JUN71-748
KYBURG, H.E., JR. PROBABILITY AND THE
LOGIC OF RATIONAL BELIEF.
P. KRAUSS, 316:MAR70-127
KYD, T. THE SPANISH TRAGEDY. (T.W. ROSS,
ED)
J.C. MAXWELL, 184(EIC):OCT71-382
KYGER, J. PLACES TO GO.
A. OSTRIKER, 473(PR):SPRING72-270
KYRIAKIDES, S.P. TWO STUDIES ON MODERN
GREEK FOLKLORE.
M.L. ARNOTT, 650(WF):JUL70-216
KYTZLER, B. - SEE CICERO


LAADE, W., ED. ORAL TRADITIONS AND WRIT-
TEN DOCUMENTS ON THE HISTORY AND ETH-
NOGRAPHY OF THE NORTHERN TORRES STRAIT
ISLANDS, SAIBAI - DAUAN - BOIGU. (VOL
1)
R. BASTIDE, 182:VOL24#13/14-573
LAAGE, K.E., ED. SCHRIFTEN DER THEODOR-
STORM-GESELLSCHAFT.* (SCHRIFT 17)
J.W. SMEED, 220(GL&L):JAN72-144
LAAGE, K.E., ED. SCHRIFTEN DER THEODOR-
STORM-GESELLSCHAFT. (SCHRIFT 18)
J.U. TERPSTRA, 433:OCT70-431

LAAGE, K.E. THEODOR STORM UND IWAN TUR-
GENJEW.
F.R. SAMMERN-FRANKENEGG, 597(SN):
VOL42#1-305
D. STATKOV, 52:BAND5HEFT3-332
LAAGE, K.E., ED. WEGE ZUM NEUEN VER-
STÄNDNIS THEODOR STORMS.
J.U. TERPSTRA, 433:OCT70-430
VAN DE LAAR, E.T.M. THE INNER STRUCTURE
OF "WUTHERING HEIGHTS."
J. ESPEY, 445(NCF):JUN70-122
LABALME, P.H. BERNARDO GIUSTINIANI.*
F. CHEYETTE, 589:JUL72-535
LABAREE, L.W. - SEE FRANKLIN, B.
LABAREE, L.W. & OTHERS - SEE FRANKLIN, B.
LABARRE, A. HISTOIRE DU LIVRE.
E. ARMSTRONG, 208(FS):APR72-247
LA BARRE, W. THE GHOST DANCE.*
M. MARCUS, 502(PRS):SUMMER71-182
LABEDZ, L., ED. SOLZHENITSYN.
D. BROWN, 32:DEC72-942
LA BERN, A. HAIGH.
617(TLS):31AUG73-1007
LABORDE, A.M. L'ESTHÉTIQUE CIRCÉENNE.
B. BEIT-ISHOO, 173(ECS):SPRING71-351
P. ROBINSON, 208(FS):APR72-195
E. SHOWALTER, JR., 207(FR):DEC70-477
J. UNDANK, 400(MLN):MAY71-578
LABOUCHEIX, H. RICHARD PRICE, THÉORICIEN
DE LA RÉVOLUTION AMÉRICAINE.
W. CHRISTIAN, 173(ECS):WINTER71/72-
341
DE LA BRETONNE, R. - SEE UNDER RESTIF DE
LA BRETONNE
LABRIOLA, A. SAGGI SUL MATERIALISMO
STORICO. (V. GERRATANA & A. GUERRA,
EDS)
E. NAMER, 542:OCT-DEC71-491
LABROUSSE, A. THE TUPAMAROS.* (FRENCH
TITLE: LES TUPAMAROS.)
617(TLS):30NOV73-1481
LA CAPRA, D. ÉMILE DURKHEIM.*
P. ROSENBERG, 441:15JUL73-21
LACEY, W.K. & B.W.J.G. WILSON - SEE
CICERO
LACH, D.F. ASIA IN THE MAKING OF EUROPE.
(VOL 2, BK 1)
A. MARCH, 293(JAST):AUG71-869
LACH, F. - SEE SCHWITTERS, K.
LACHANCE, L. L'HUMANISME POLITIQUE DE
SAINT THOMAS D'AQUIN.
A. FOREST, 542:APR-JUN70-233
LA CHARITÉ, V.A. THE POETICS AND THE
POETRY OF RENÉ CHAR.*
M-A. CAWS, 188(ECR):SUMMER70-150
C.J. VAN REES, 433:JUL70-313
LACHELIER, J. LA NATURE; L'ESPRIT; DIEU.
(L. MILLET, ED)
R. BALMÈS, 542:OCT-DEC71-492
LACHENSCHMID, R. LOUIS DE THOMASSINS
INKARNATIONSLEHRE.
J-R. ARMOGATHE, 182:VOL24#17/18-653
LACHS, J. THE TIES OF TIME.*
D. BARBOUR, 150(DR):SPRING71-133
P. STEVENS, 628:SPRING72-103
LACHS, J. & S. - SEE SANTAYANA, G.
LACKEY, D. - SEE RUSSELL, B.
LACOMBA, J.A. LA CRISIS ESPAÑOLA DE
1917.
F. CAUDET, 86(BHS):APR72-194
LACOSTA, F. LECTURAS DE COSAS I.
R. ANDERSON, 399(MLJ):NOV71-482
I. MOLINA, 238:MAR71-220
LACOSTE, C. TRADUCTION DES "LÉGENDES ET
CONTES MERVEILLEUX DE LA GRANDE KABY-
LIE" RECUEILLIS PAR AUGUSTE MOULIÉRAS.
G. MASSIGNON, 196:BAND11HEFT1/2-178

LACOSTE-DUJARDIN, C. LE CONTE KABYLE.
M. URBAIN-FAUBLÉE, 69:OCT71-351
LACOUTURE, J. ANDRÉ MALRAUX.
617(TLS):7DEC73-1504
LACOUTURE, J. NASSER.
R.H. NOLTE, 441:19AUG73-17
442(NY):3SEP73-68
LACROIX, J. LA CRISE INTELLECTUELLE DU
CATHOLICISME FRANÇAIS. LE SENS DE
L'ATHÉISME MODERNE. (6TH ED) SPINOZA
ET LE PROBLÈME DU SALUT.
E. LEVINAS, 98:JUN71-532
LACTANTII, L.C.F. DE MORTIBUS PERSECU-
TORUM. (F. CORSARO, ED)
J. ANDRÉ, 555:VOL45FASC2-370
LADER, L. ABORTION II.
J.E. BRODY, 441:8AUG73-29
LADOO, H.S. NO PAIN LIKE THIS BODY.
B.F. BAILEY, 99:MAR73-48
LADRIÈRE, J. LANGUAGE AND BELIEF.
617(TLS):10AUG73-933
LADRIÈRE, J. L'ARTICULATION DU SENS.
Y. GAUTHIER, 154:SEP71-625
"THE LADY'S REALM."
617(TLS):30MAR73-358
VAN LAERE, F. UNE LECTURE DU TEMPS DANS
"LA NOUVELLE HÉLOÏSE."
R. GRIMSLEY, 402(MLR):JUL72-636
LAERMANN, K. EIGENSCHAFTSLOSIGKEIT.
U. KARTHAUS, 680(ZDP):BAND90HEFT4-616
MADAME DE LA FAYETTE. ROMANS ET NOU-
VELLES. (E. MAGNE & A. NIDERST, EDS)
H.G. HALL, 208(FS):JUL72-329
S. LOTRINGER, 98:JUN70-498
LAFFAN, K.B. ZOO ZOO WIDDERSHINS ZOO.
A. RENDLE, 157:SPRING70-71
LAFFIN, J., ED. LETTERS FROM THE FRONT
1914-1918.
617(TLS):15JUN73-659
LAFFOUCREIÈRE, O. LE DESTIN DE LA PENSÉE
ET "LA MORT DE DIEU" SELON HEIDEGGER.*
P-M. LEMAIRE, 154:JUN71-399
LAFONT, R. LA PHRASE OCCITANE.
G. PRICE, 47(ARL):N.S.JVOL1-100
LAFONT, R. RENAISSANCE DU SUD.
P. GARDY, 98:JUN71-508
LAFORGUE, J. LES PAGES DE "LA GUÊPE."
(J.L. DEBAUVE, ED) POÉSIES COMPLÈTES.
(P. PIA, ED)
D. GROJNOWSKI, 98:JAN71-94
LAFORGUE, J. POÉSIES COMPLÈTES. (P.
PIA, ED)
617(TLS):27JUL73-864
LA FRANCE, A. & G. MARSOLAIS, EDS. CINE-
MA D'ICI.
P. HARCOURT, 99:NOV-DEC73-37
LA FRANCE, M. A READING OF STEPHEN
CRANE.
J.B. COLVERT, 27(AL):NOV72-497
W. RANDEL, 579(SAQ):SUMMER72-448
LAGARDE, F. JOHN WEBSTER.*
R.W. DENT, 405(MP):AUG71-70
DE LAGARDE, G. LA NAISSANCE DE L'ESPRIT
LAÏQUE AU DÉCLIN DU MOYEN-ÂGE. (VOL 3)
D. ANGERS, 154:DEC70-445
LAGERCRANTZ, E. LAPPISCHE VOLKSDICHTUNG
VII.
A. RAUN, 361:VOL26#1-107
LAGERCRANTZ, O. VERSUCH ÜBER DIE LYRIK
DER NELLY SACHS.*
G. STERN, 133:1970/2&3-339
DE LA GRANGE, H-L. MAHLER. (VOL 1)
R. CRAFT, 453:29NOV73-10
D. HENAHAN, 441:26OCT73-47
C.E. SCHORSKE, 441:7OCT73-3
442(NY):19NOV73-248

LAGRAVE, H. MARIVAUX ET SA FORTUNE LIT-
TÉRAIRE.
R. MERCIER, 557(RSH):JUL-SEP71-474
LA GRECA, B.T. - SEE GUARINI, G.
LA GRONE, G. & P. O'CONNOR. EN LAS AMÉRI-
CAS. (REV)
J.G. MIRSKY, 399(MLJ):NOV71-481
LAGRONE, G.G., A.A. MILDENBERGER & P.
O'CONNOR. PRIMEROS PASOS AND SEGUNDOS
PASOS.
C.W. STANSFIELD, 399(MLJ):FEB71-128
DE LA HARPE, J.F. JEAN FRANÇOIS DE LA
HARPE: LETTERS TO THE SHUVALOVS. (C.
TODD, ED)
617(TLS):21SEP73-1090
LAHEY, G.F. GERARD MANLEY HOPKINS.
W.R. MUNDT, 598(SOR):AUTUMN73-1029
LAHR, J. THE AUTOGRAPH HOUND.
V. CUNNINGHAM, 362:13SEP73-352
T.R. EDWARDS, 453:22MAR73-29
C. LEHMANN-HAUPT, 441:7MAR73-35
C. WOODS, 441:4MAR73-4
442(NY):17MAR73-129
617(TLS):9NOV73-1361
LAHR, J., ED. A CASEBOOK ON HAROLD PIN-
TER'S "THE HOMECOMING."
S.H. GALE, 397(MD):FEB72-478
LAHRKAMP, H., ED. KRIEGSABENTEUER DES
RITTMEISTERS HIERONYMUS CHRISTIAN VON
HOLSTEN, 1655-1666.
W. KIRCHNER, 32:MAR72-206
LAHUE, K.C. COLLECTING CLASSIC FILMS.
S.A. PEEPLES, 200:OCT70-501
LAIDLAW, G.N. ELYSIAN ENCOUNTER.
G.I. BRACHFELD, 207(FR):OCT70-239
LAING, R.D. THE POLITICS OF THE FAMILY
AND OTHER ESSAYS.
M. LEBOWITZ, 676(YR):SPRING72-448
LAISTNER, M.L.W. CHRISTIANITY AND PAGAN
CULTURE IN THE LATER ROMAN EMPIRE, TO-
GETHER WITH AN ENGLISH TRANSLATION OF
JOHN CHRYSOSTOM'S ADDRESS ON VAINGLORY
AND THE RIGHT WAY FOR PARENTS TO BRING
UP THEIR CHILDREN.
L.J. FRIEDMAN, 545(RPH):NOV71-256
LAKATOS, I. & A. MUSGRAVE, EDS. CRITI-
CISM AND THE GROWTH OF KNOWLEDGE.
J. AGASSI, 262:SUMMER71-152
R.J.B., 543:DEC70-349
K.K. LEE, 483:OCT71-368
F. WILSON, 154:DEC71-829
LAKE, C. - SEE DODGE, F.
LAKOFF, G. IRREGULARITY IN SYNTAX.
E.P. HAMP, 269(IJAL):JUL71-210
LAKOFF, R.T. ABSTRACT SYNTAX AND LATIN
COMPLEMENTATION.
H. PINKSTER, 361:VOL26#4-383
W.E. SWEET, 24:JUL72-468
LAL, K.S., ED. STUDIES IN ASIAN HISTORY.
R.A. HUTTENBACK, 293(JAST):NOV70-243
LAL, P., ED. MODERN INDIAN POETRY IN
ENGLISH.
Y.J. DAYANANDA, 352(LE&W):VOL15#1-165
LALANDE, L. & E., EDS. INVITATION À LIRE.
R-M. DAELE-GUINAN, 207(FR):MAR71-820
LAMANNA, E.P. INTRODUZIONE ALLA LETTURA
DI CROCE.
E. NAMER, 542:APR-JUN70-252
LAMANNA, E.P. STUDI SUL PENSIERO MORALE
E POLITICO DI KANT. (D. PESCE, ED)
K. OEDINGEN, 342:BAND62HEFT3-408
DE LAMARTINE, A.M.L.D. MÉDITATIONS.*
(F. LETESSIER, ED)
M-F. GUYARD, 535(RHL):JAN-FEB70-138
LAMB, H.B. VIETNAM'S WILL TO LIVE.
617(TLS):12OCT73-1235
LAMB, W.K. - SEE MACKENZIE, A.
LAMBERT, B.G. - SEE MORE, P.E.

LAMBERT, G. GWTW: THE MAKING OF GONE
WITH THE WIND.
G. WALKER, 441:17NOV73-29
M. WOOD, 453:29NOV73-6
LAMBERT, G. ON CUKOR.*
617(TLS):7SEP73-1020
LAMBERT, K., ED. THE LOGICAL WAY OF
DOING THINGS.*
R. BLANCHÉ, 542:OCT-DEC70-494
LAMBERT, K., ED. PHILOSOPHICAL PROBLEMS
IN LOGIC.
R.P.M., 543:MAR71-556
LAMBERT, K. & G.G. BRITTAN, JR. AN
INTRODUCTION TO THE PHILOSOPHY OF SCI-
ENCE.
A. MUSGRAVE, 63:MAY72-89
LAMBERT, S. BILLS AND ACTS.
J.B. CHILDS, 517(PBSA):OCT-DEC72-443
LAMBERT, W.G. & A.R. MILLARD. CATALOGUE
OF THE CUNEIFORM TABLETS IN THE KOUYUN-
JIK COLLECTION OF THE BRITISH MUSEUM.
(2ND SUPP)
E. LEICHTY, 318(JAOS):OCT-DEC71-529
LAME DEER, J., WITH R. ERDOES. LAME
DEER, SEEKER OF VISIONS.
W.C. STURTEVANT, 441:18MAR73-37
LAMÉRAND, R. SYNTAXE TRANSFORMATIONNELLE
DES PROPOSITIONS HYPOTHÉTIQUES DU FRAN-
ÇAIS PARLÉ.*
J. CASAGRANDE, 207(FR):MAR71-788
W.D. DONALDSON, JR., 399(MLJ):DEC71-
539
LAMÉRAND, R. THÉORIES D'ENSEIGNEMENT
PROGRAMMÉ ET LABORATOIRES DE LANGUES.
J. GREENLEE, 207(FR):MAR71-790
LA MESLÉE, E.M. THE NEW AUSTRALIA 1883.
(R. WARD, ED & TRANS)
617(TLS):18MAY73-553
LAMM, M. AUGUST STRINDBERG. (H.G. CARL-
SON, ED & TRANS)
W. JOHNSON, 301(JEGP):JAN72-104
Y.L. SANDSTROEM, 563(SS):WINTER72-147
LÄMMERT, E. & OTHERS. GERMANISTIK - EINE
DEUTSCHE WISSENSCHAFT.
L. HERMODSSON, 597(SN):VOL42#1-298
LAMONT, C. FREEDOM OF CHOICE AFFIRMED.
J. SOMERVILLE, 484(PPR):SEP70-131
LAMONT-BROWN, R. ROBERT BURNS'S TOUR OF
THE BORDERS.
617(TLS):9MAR73-277
LAMOTHE, C. ESQUISSE DU SYSTÈME GRAMMAT-
ICAL LOBI.
W.A.A. WILSON, 69:JAN70-96
LAMOUCHE, A. LA DESTINÉE HUMAINE.
R. BLANCHÉ, 542:OCT-DEC70-495
LAMPE, G.W.H., ED. THE CAMBRIDGE HISTORY
OF THE BIBLE. (VOL 2)
J.F. KELLY, 613:WINTER70-630
LAMPE, G.W.H. A PATRISTIC GREEK LEXICON.
(FASC 5)
P. CHANTRAINE, 555:VOL45FASC1-157
LAMPSON, M. (LORD KILLEARN) THE KILLEARN
DIARIES 1934-1946. (T.E. EVANS, ED)
R. CROSSMAN, 362:11JAN73-54
617(TLS):9FEB73-139
"L'ANALYSE DU LANGAGE THÉOLOGIQUE."
M.J.V., 543:JUN71-761
LANAVERE, A., ED. PASCAL: MIROIR DE LA
CRITIQUE.
C. ABRAHAM, 399(MLJ):NOV71-485
J.H. BROOME, 208(FS):JUL72-325
LANCASTER, O. THE LITTLEHAMPTON BEQUEST.
617(TLS):28DEC73-1589
LANCASTER, O. SAILING TO BYZANTIUM.
J. BECKWITH, 39:JUL70-80
S. PEROWNE, 46:OCT70-264
LAND, H.C. BIRDS OF GUATEMALA.
S.S. BENSON, 37:OCT71-38

LANDA, L. - SEE DEFOE, D.
LANDAU, R.  NEW DIRECTIONS IN BRITISH
ARCHITECTURE.
R. BANHAM, 54:SEP70-344
LANDE, L.  THE LAWRENCE LANDE COLLECTION
OF CANADIANA IN THE REDPATH LIBRARY OF
MC GILL UNIVERSITY.
S.B. LILJEGREN, 439(NM):1970/2-328
LANDEN, R.G.  OMAN SINCE 1856.*
K.S. LAL, 273(IC):JAN71-69
LANDER, E.M., JR.  THE TEXTILE INDUSTRY
IN ANTEBELLUM SOUTH CAROLINA.
J. FULLER, 9(ALAR):APR71-152
LANDMANN, M.  DAS ENDE DES INDIVIDUUMS.
M. ROCK, 182:VOL24#15/16-577
LANDON, H.C.R., ED.  BEETHOVEN.*
J.P., 376:JAN71-135
639(VQR):SPRING71-LXX
LANDON, H.C.R.  ESSAYS ON THE VIENNESE
CLASSICAL STYLE.*
639(VQR):SPRING71-LXXXIV
LANDON, M.  THE TRIUMPH OF THE LAWYERS.*
G.H. JONES, 173(ECS):SUMMER72-615
LANDOR, W.S.  SELECTED IMAGINARY CONVER-
SATIONS OF LITERARY MEN AND STATESMEN.*
(C.L. PROUDFIT, ED)
P. TURNER, 447(N&Q):OCT71-395
502(PRS):SPRING70-88
LANDOW, G.P.  THE AESTHETIC AND CRITICAL
THEORIES OF JOHN RUSKIN.
M. BEATTY, 150(DR):AUTUMN71-449
J.L. BRADLEY, 401(MLQ):JUN71-231
J. CLUBBE, 579(SAQ):SUMMER72-458
P. FONTANEY, 189(EA):JUL-SEP71-344
E.K. HELSINGER, 301(JEGP):APR72-274
LANDRESS, M.M., WITH B. DOBLER.  I MADE
IT MYSELF.
D.E. WESTLAKE, 441:29APR73-20
LANDSBERG, M.  DOS PASSOS' PATH TO
"U.S.A."
R.G. DAVIS, 441:14OCT73-4
T.R. EDWARDS, 453:29NOV73-28
LANDSBERGER, H.A., ED.  THE CHURCH AND
SOCIAL CHANGE IN LATIN AMERICA.
J.F. THORNING, 613:WINTER71-626
LANDSHUT, S.  KRITIK DER SOZIOLOGIE UND
ANDERE SCHRIFTEN ZUR POLITIK.
H. HESS, 182:VOL24#1/2-11
LANDWEHR, J.  ROMEYN DE HOOGHE (1645 TO
1708) AS BOOK ILLUSTRATOR.
E. ZIMMERMANN, 182:VOL24#1/2-35
LANDWEHR, J.  ROMEYN DE HOOGHE THE ETCHER.
617(TLS):20APR73-438
LANDY, J.  THE ARCHITECTURE OF MINARD
LAFEVER.
H. MORRISON, 54:JUN71-266
LANE, A.  GREEK POTTERY.  (3RD ED)
R. HIGGINS, 39:AUG71-161
LANE, B.M.  ARCHITECTURE AND POLITICS IN
GERMANY, 1918-1945.*
R.V. WIEDENHOEFT, 56:WINTER71-487
LANE, D. & G. KOLANKIEWICZ, EDS.  SOCIAL
GROUPS IN POLISH SOCIETY.
617(TLS):20JUL73-824
LANE, G.  ETRE ET LANGAGE.
M-C. DELVAUX, 154:SEP71-631
LANE, G.  L'AVENIR D'UNE PRÉDICTION.
Y. GAUTHIER, 154:JUN71-420
LANG, D.M. - SEE "THE BALAVARIANI"
LANG, M.L.  THE PALACE OF NESTOR AT PYLOS
IN WESTERN MESSENIA.*  (VOL 2)
E. VERMEULE, 54:DEC70-428
LANG, P.H.  THE EXPERIENCE OF OPERA.
617(TLS):23MAR73-333
LANG, R.  BELIEBIGE PERSONEN.
G. FISCHER, 270:VOL21#3-170
LANG-SIMS, L.  FLOWER IN A TEACUP.
617(TLS):5OCT73-1163

LANGACKER, R.W.  LANGUAGE AND ITS STRUC-
TURE.
J.J. CHRISTIE, 297(JL):FEB70-154
M.P. HAGIWARA, 399(MLJ):MAY71-323
L. ZAWADOWSKI, 353:MAR71-91
LANGBAINE, G.  AN ACCOUNT OF THE ENGLISH
DRAMATICK POETS.
G. MARSHALL, 568(SCN):FALL-WINTER72-
68
LANGBAUM, R.  THE MODERN SPIRIT.*
G. BORNSTEIN, 385(MQR):SUMMER73-278
P. HONAN, 402(MLR):OCT72-874
R.J. THOMPSON, 613:WINTER71-616
639(VQR):WINTER71-XXIV
LANGBEHN-ROHLAND, R.  ZUR INTERPRETATION
DER ROMANE DES DIEGO DE SAN PEDRO.
K. WHINNOM, 86(BHS):APR72-179
LANGE, D. & M.K. MITCHELL.  TO A CABIN.
S. SCHWARTZ, 441:2DEC73-95
LANGE, D.L., ED.  BRITANNICA REVIEW OF
FOREIGN LANGUAGE EDUCATION.  (VOL 2)
J.G. MIRSKY, 238:DEC71-978
LANGE, H.  THEATERSTÜCKE 1960-72.
617(TLS):25MAY73-588
LANGE, J.  THE COGNITIVITY PARADOX.
M. DEUTSCHER, 63:DEC72-293
LANGE, J. - SEE LEWIS, C.I.
LANGE, K. & M. HIRMER.  EGYPT: ARCHITEC-
TURE - SCULPTURE - PAINTING.
J.D., 135:NOV70-215
LANGE, K-P.  THEORETIKER DES LITERARIS-
CHEN MANIERISMUS.*
R. FERNANDEZ, 405(MP):FEB72-254
H-J. LANGE, 52:BAND5HEFT3-329
LANGE, M.  A LITTLE GIRL UNDER A MOSQUITO
NET.
M. LEVIN, 441:28OCT73-48
442(NY):31DEC73-59
LANGE, O.  INCIDENT AT LA JUNTA.
A. BROYARD, 441:17AUG73-35
M. LEVIN, 441:12AUG73-20
LANGE, O.  VANDENBERG.
L.L. LEE, 649(WAL):WINTER72-268
LANGE, V., ED.  GOETHE: A COLLECTION OF
CRITICAL ESSAYS.*
R. GRAY, 220(GL&L):APR72-280
LANGE, V., ED.  HUMANISTIC SCHOLARSHIP
IN AMERICA.  (VOL 2)
J. GONZÁLEZ MUELA, 240(HR):OCT71-468
LANGE, W-D. & H-J. WOLF, EDS.  PHILOLO-
GISCHE STUDIEN FÜR JOSEPH M. PIEL.
B. FOSTER, 208(FS):JAN72-116
K.D. SCHNEIDER, 72:BAND209HEFT4/6-432
LANGENDOEN, D.T.  ESSENTIALS OF ENGLISH
GRAMMAR.
F.W. HOUSEHOLDER, 350:MAR72-184
LANGENDOEN, D.T.  THE LONDON SCHOOL OF
LINGUISTICS.
W.P. LEHMANN, 545(RPH):MAY72-421
LANGENDOEN, D.T.  THE STUDY OF SYNTAX.*
R.W. LANGACKER, 215(GL):VOL10#3-175
G. SAMPSON, 297(JL):SEP70-267
"LANGENSCHEIDT STANDARD DICTIONARY OF THE
FRENCH AND ENGLISH LANGUAGES."*  (K.
URWIN, ED)
F.W. VOGLER, 399(MLJ):MAY71-326
"LANGENSCHEIDTS HANDWÖRTERBUCH SPANISCH."
(H. MÜLLER, G. HAENSCH & E. ALVAREZ-
PRADA, EDS)
E. LORENZO, 202(FMOD):NOV71/FEB72-137
VON LANGENSTEIN, H.  ERCHANTNUZZ DER
SUND.*  (P.R. RUDOLF, ED)
A. MASSER, 182:VOL24#11/12-475
LANGER, S.K.  MIND.*  (VOL 1)
E.E. HARRIS, 321:WINTER70[VOL4#4]-308
R.M. LIDDY, 258:SEP70-481
LANGER, S.K.  MIND.  (VOL 2)
M. ROSENBERG, 31(ASCH):SUMMER73-522

205

LANGER, W.C. THE MIND OF ADOLF HITLER.*
R. COLES, 453:8MAR73-25
D.W. HARDING, 362:22FEB73-247
LANGFORD, C. THE WINTER OF THE FISHER.
P. BARCLAY, 102(CANL):SUMMER72-110
LANGFORD, G. FAULKNER'S REVISION OF
"ABSALOM, ABSALOM!"
J.L. CAPPS, 578:FALL73-117
J.B. MERIWETHER, 27(AL):JAN73-693
LANGFORD, G. FAULKNER'S REVISION OF
"SANCTUARY."
J.L. CAPPS, 578:FALL73-117
LANGFORD, G. & D.J. O'CONNOR, EDS. NEW
ESSAYS IN THE PHILOSOPHY OF EDUCATION.
617(TLS):28DEC73-1594
LANGFORD, P. THE FIRST ROCKINGHAM AD-
MINISTRATION 1765-66.
617(TLS):20JUL73-833
LANGHAM, R. THE MODERN SPIRIT.
M. PECKHAM, 85:FALL71-52
LANGIULLI, N. - SEE ABBAGNANO, N.
LANGLEY, J.L., JR. THE TRAGIC MASK.
M. BRADBURY, 148:SUMMER71-185
LANGLOIS, W.G., ED. THE PERSISTENT VOICE.
J. SEZNEC, 208(FS):OCT72-482
LANGOSCH, K., ED. MITTELLATEINISCHES
JAHRBUCH. (VOLS 2-4)
R. DÜCHTING, 680(ZDP):BAND89HEFT1-111
"A LANGUAGE-TEACHING BIBLIOGRAPHY."*
A. WOLLMANN, 38:BAND89HEFT4-470
LANGWILL, L.G. AN INDEX OF MUSICAL WIND-
INSTRUMENT MAKERS. (3RD ED)
G. OLDHAM, 415:AUG72-776
LANHAM, R.A. A HANDLIST OF RHETORICAL
TERMS.
D. NEWTON-DE MOLINA, 148:SUMMER71-189
LANHAM, R.A. TRISTRAM SHANDY.
617(TLS):24AUG73-972
LANIUS, E.W. CYRANO DE BERGERAC AND THE
THE UNIVERSE OF THE IMAGINATION.
T.J. REISS, 188(ECR):WINTER70-340
LANKESTER, R.F. CHINA 1927-1949.
617(TLS):27APR73-481
LANLY, A. - SEE "LE COURONNEMENT DE
LOUIS"
LANLY, A. - SEE VILLON, F.
"L'ANNÉE BALZACIENNE 1968."
A. LACAUX, 535(RHL):MAR-APR70-319
"L'ANNÉE BALZACIENNE 1970."
B. VANNIER, 400(MLN):MAY71-592
LANNOY, R. THE SPEAKING TREE.*
R.J. VARNEY, 89(BJA):WINTER72-95
42(AR):WINTER71/72-599
LANSING, J.B., R.W. MARANS & R.B. ZEHNER.
PLANNED RESIDENTIAL ENVIRONMENTS.
505:OCT71-145
LANTERI-LAURA, G. HISTOIRE DE LA PHRÉ-
NOLOGIE.
S. MORAVIA, 548(RCSF):JAN-MAR71-108
LAO SHE. CAT COUNTRY.*
P.C-T. WANG, 352(LE&W):VOL15#1-155
LAPLANCHE, J. VIE ET MORT EN PSYCHANA-
LYSE.
Y. BRÈS, 542:APR-JUN71-189
LAPORTE, R. UNE VOIX DE FIN SILENCE.
PORQUOI?
C. BACKÈS-CLÉMENT, 98:MAY70-412
LAPP, J.C. THE ESTHETICS OF NEGLIGENCE.
R.W. FRENCH, 568(SCN):FALL-WINTER72-
70
LAPP, P.W. BIBLICAL ARCHAEOLOGY AND
HISTORY.
K.S. FREEDY, 318(JAOS):APR-JUN71-302
LAPP, R.E. THE LOGARITHMIC CENTURY.
441:7OCT73-41
LAQUEUR, W. A HISTORY OF ZIONISM.*
617(TLS):12JAN73-32

DE LARA, M.T. - SEE UNDER TUÑÓN DE LARA,
M.
LARBAUD, V. & G. JEAN-AUBRY. CORRESPON-
DANCE.
S. FAUCHEREAU, 98:JUL71-626
LARGEAULT, J. LOGIQUE ET PHILOSOPHIE
CHEZ FREGE.
M-A. SINACEUR, 98:JAN71-58
LARKIN, D., ED. FANTASTIC ART.
617(TLS):2NOV73-1335
LARKIN, P., ED. THE OXFORD BOOK OF
TWENTIETH-CENTURY ENGLISH VERSE.
C. BEDIENT, 441:17JUN73-4
D. DAVIE, 362:29MAR73-420
D. DONOGHUE, 453:19APR73-26
L.E. SISSMAN, 442(NY):9JUN73-110
617(TLS):13APR73-405
LAROCHE, M. MARCEL DUBÉ.
G. TARRAB, 102(CANL):WINTER72-97
DE LA ROCHEFOUCAULD, F. MAXIMES. (M.
ARNAOUDOV, TRANS)
N. DONTCHEV, 535(RHL):JAN-FEB70-122
LA ROCHELLE, P.D. - SEE UNDER DRIEU LA
ROCHELLE, P.
LA ROCQUE, G. APRÈS LA BOUE.
A.E. POKORNY, 296:SPRING73-89
"THE LAROUSSE ENCYCLOPEDIA OF MUSIC."*
(G. HINDLEY, ED)
L. SALTER, 415:MAY72-458
LARROWE, C.P. HARRY BRIDGES.
M. KEMPTON, 231:MAY73-96
C. SIGAL, 441:7JAN73-3
LARSEN, E. JAMES AGEE.
R. ASSELINEAU, 189(EA):OCT-DEC71-547
LARSON, C. SOMEONE'S DEATH.
N. CALLENDAR, 441:1JUL73-21
LARSON, C.R., ED. AFRICAN SHORT STORIES.
R.K. SINGH, 573(SSF):SPRING71-344
LARSON, G.J. CLASSICAL SĀMKHYA.*
L. ROCHER, 318(JAOS):OCT-DEC71-547
LARSON, J.L. REASON AND EXPERIENCE.*
P.R. SLOAN, 319:APR73-265
LARTIGUE, J.H. DIARY OF A CENTURY. (R.
AVEDON, ED)
J.B. MYERS, 139:AUG71-6
LARY, N.M. DOSTOEVSKY AND DICKENS.
617(TLS):10AUG73-923
LASCELLES, M. NOTIONS AND FACTS.
617(TLS):26JAN73-89
LASCH, C. THE WORLD OF NATIONS.
S.S. WOLIN, 441:30SEP73-31
LASCHEN, G. LYRIK IN DER DDR.
P. HUTCHINSON, 220(GL&L):APR72-297
LASERON, C.F. THE FACE OF AUSTRALIA.
(REV BY J.N. JENNINGS)
617(TLS):13APR73-429
LASH, J.P. ELEANOR: THE YEARS ALONE.*
P. WHITEHEAD, 362:19APR73-519
617(TLS):8JUN73-632
LASH, J.P. ELEANOR AND FRANKLIN.*
J.M. BLUM, 676(YR):SPRING72-422
M. HEATH, 418(MR):WINTER-SPRING72-281
LASK, T., ED. THE NEW YORK TIMES BOOK OF
VERSE.
K. CONGDON, 37:SEP71-39
LASKER, E. CHESS.
617(TLS):8JUN73-653
LASKI, M. GEORGE ELIOT AND HER WORLD.
617(TLS):29JUN73-740
LASKO, P. ARS SACRA 800-1200.
617(TLS):14DEC73-1528
LASLETT, P., ED. HOUSEHOLD AND FAMILY
IN PAST TIME.
617(TLS):4MAY73-485
LASS, R., ED. APPROACHES TO ENGLISH
HISTORICAL LINGUISTICS.
W.F. BOLTON, 297(JL):OCT71-293
LASSERRE, F. - SEE STRABO

206

LASSNER, J. THE TOPOGRAPHY OF BAGHDAD IN THE EARLY MIDDLE AGES.
    M.L. SWARTZ, 589:APR72-320
LAST, J. THE YOUNG PIANIST.
    F. DAWES, 415:SEP72-871
LAST, R.W. HANS ARP.
    M. SANOUILLET, 220(GL&L):JAN72-141
"THE LAST JAPANESE SOLDIER."
    617(TLS):9FEB73-161
"THE LAST TWO MILLION YEARS."
    617(TLS):14DEC73-1548
LASTRA, Y. COCHABAMBA QUECHUA SYNTAX.
    X. ALBÓ, 269(IJAL):JAN71-55
    B. POTTIER, 353:NOV71-122
LASZLO, E. INTRODUCTION TO SYSTEMS PHILOSOPHY.
    S.C. PEPPER, 484(PPR):JUN72-548
LASZLO, E. SYSTEM, STRUCTURE, AND EXPER-IENCE.
    R. BLANCHÉ, 542:OCT-DEC70-488
    M. CLARK, 479(PHQ):APR71-183
LÁSZLÓ, F. DIE PARALLELVERSION DER MANUSMṚTI IM BHAVIṢYAPURĀṆA.
    O. VON HINÜBER, 182:VOL24#23/24-853
LA TERREUR, M., ED. DICTIONARY OF CAN-ADIAN BIOGRAPHY. (VOL 10: 1871-1880)
    617(TLS):19JAN73-56
LATHAM, R. & W. MATTHEWS - SEE PEPYS, S.
LATHEM, E.C. - SEE COOLIDGE, C.
LATHEN, E. MURDER WITHOUT ICING.*
    617(TLS):18MAY73-562
LATIMER, J. BORDER OF DARKNESS.
    N. CALLENDAR, 441:7JAN73-35
"LATIN AMERICA REVIEW OF BOOKS." (VOL 1) (C. HARDING & C. ROPER, EDS)
    617(TLS):6JUL73-778
"LATIN AMERICA: STUDY, TRAVEL, AND WORK OPPORTUNITIES."
    S.S. BENSON, 37:OCT71-43
LATOUR, C.F. & T. VOGELSANG. OKKUPATION UND WIEDERAUFBAU.
    617(TLS):31AUG73-1006
LATTANZI, A.D. & M. DEBAE. LA MINIATURE ITALIENNE DU XE AU XVIE SIÈCLE.
    M.L. D'ANCONA, 54:DEC71-520
LATTIMORE, R. POEMS FROM THREE DECADES.*
    W. HEYEN, 491:JUL73-237
LAU, D.C. - SEE "MENCIUS"
LAU, J.S.M. TS'AO YÜ.
    D.S-P. YANG, 293(JAST):MAY71-674
"L'AUBRAC." (VOL 1)
    P. VOSSELER, 182:VOL24#3-123
LAUDE, J. THE ARTS OF BLACK AFRICA.
    D.F. DYCKES, 58:APR72-26
LAUENER, H. HUME UND KANT.
    W. STEINBECK, 342:BAND62HEFT2-252
LAUFHÜTTE, H. WIRKLICHKEIT UND KUNST IN GOTTFRIED KELLERS ROMAN "DER GRÜNE HEINRICH."*
    A. HEINO, 439(NM):1971/3-574
LAUNAY, M. ROUSSEAU.
    J-L. LECERCLE, 535(RHL):JAN-FEB70-132
LAUNAY, M. & OTHERS. JEAN-JACQUES ROUS-SEAU ET SON TEMPS.
    R. MERCIER, 557(RSH):APR-JUN70-321
LAUNAY, M. & G. MAILHOS. INTRODUCTION À LA VIE LITTÉRAIRE DU XVIIIE SIÈCLE.
    205(FMLS):APR70-208
LAURENCE, D.H. - SEE SHAW, G.B.
LAURENCE, M. A BIRD IN THE HOUSE.
    G.R. ELLIOTT, 648:OCT70-68
    J-P., 376:JUL70-113
LAURENCE, M. THE FIRE-DWELLERS.*
    B. MITCHELL, 296:FALL73-112
LAURENS, A. L'EUROPE AVEC LES ANGLAIS.
    617(TLS):5JAN73-11

LAURENTI, J.L. ESTUDIOS SOBRE LA NOVELA PICARESCA ESPAÑOLA.
    A. NOUGUÉ, 182:VOL24#6-296
LAURENTI, R. STUDI SULL' ECONOMICO ATTRI-BUITO AD ARISTOTELE.
    F. ADORNO, 548(RCSF):APR-JUN70-197
LAURENTIUS GUILELMUS OF SAONA. THE "EPI-TOME MARGARITAE ELOQUENTIAE" OF LAUR-ENTIUS GUILELMUS DE SAONA. (R.H. MARTIN WITH J.E. MORTIMER, EDS)
    J.J. MURPHY, 589:OCT72-783
LAUSBERG, M. UNTERSUCHUNGEN ZU SENECAS FRAGMENTEN.*
    M. WINTERBOTTOM, 123:JUN72-226
LAUTH, R. & H. JACOB - SEE FICHTE, J.G.
COMTE DE LAUTRÉAMONT. OEUVRES COMPLÈTES. (P-O. WALZER, ED)
    M. SCHAETTEL, 557(RSH):APR-JUN71-326
LAVAGNINO, A. THE LIZARDS.
    P.M. SPACKS, 249(HUDR):AUTUMN72-497
LAVALLEYE, J. BRUEGEL AND LUCAS VAN LEYDEN.*
    J.F.M., 135:MAR70-202
LAVENDER, D. CALIFORNIA.
    J. SEELYE, 441:5AUG73-4
LAVERS, A. - SEE BARTHES, R.
LAVIN, I. BERNINI AND THE CROSSING OF SAINT PETER'S.*
    J. MONTAGU, 56:WINTER71-490
    M.S. WEIL, 90:FEB71-98
LAVIN, J.A. - SEE GREENE, R.
LAVIN, M. COLLECTED STORIES.* HAPPINESS AND OTHER STORIES.
    J.H. WILDMAN, 598(SOR):WINTER73-233
LAVIN, M. A MEMORY.*
    J.C. OATES, 441:25NOV73-7
    E. WEEKS, 61:OCT73-129
LAVIN, M.A. PIERO DELLA FRANCESCA: THE FLAGELLATION.*
    R. DOWNES, 441:2DEC73-92
LAVRIN, J. A PANORAMA OF RUSSIAN LITERA-TURE.
    617(TLS):22JUN73-713
VAN LAWICK, H. SOLO.
    617(TLS):9NOV73-1381
LAWLER, J.R. THE LANGUAGE OF FRENCH SYM-BOLISM.*
    V.M. AMES, 290(JAAC):WINTER70-278
    J.F. ERWIN, JR., 207(FR):DEC70-476
    A. FONGARO, 535(RHL):MAR-APR71-319
    P.A. FORTIER, 149:DEC72-478
    E.R. JACKSON, 188(ECR):FALL70-261
    205(FMLS):JAN71-97
LAWLOR, J., ED. HIGHER EDUCATION.
    617(TLS):5JAN73-4
LAWRENCE, A. FOREIGN CORRESPONDENT.
    617(TLS):9FEB73-139
LAWRENCE, A.W. GREEK AND ROMAN SCULP-TURE.
    617(TLS):2MAR73-249
LAWRENCE, B. COLERIDGE AND WORDSWORTH IN SOMERSET.
    H. PESCHMANN, 175:SUMMER71-57
LAWRENCE, B. SOMERSET LEGENDS.
    617(TLS):21DEC73-1574
LAWRENCE, D.H. THE FIRST LADY CHATTER-LEY.*
    617(TLS):27APR73-471
LAWRENCE, D.H. JOHN THOMAS AND LADY JANE.*
    L.E. SISSMAN, 442(NY):6JAN73-73
    617(TLS):27APR73-471
LAWRENCE, D.H. THE QUEST FOR RANANIM.* (G.J. ZYTARUK, ED)
    E. DELAVENAY, 189(EA):APR-JUN71-206
    K. MC LEOD, 541(RES):AUG71-378
    R.B. WOODINGS, 597(SN):VOL43#2-596

LAWRENCE, F.L. MOLIÈRE.*
  R. GUICHEMERRE, 535(RHL):JAN-FEB71-89
  R.N. NICOLICH, 207(FR):DEC70-461
LAWRENCE, I. & P. MONTGOMERY. AN INTRO-
DUCTION TO WORDS AND MUSIC.
  P. STANDFORD, 415:NOV72-1091
LAWRENCE, J. RETREAT WITH HONOR.
  M. LEVIN, 441:19AUG73-12
LAWRENCE, P. & C. TRENGOVE. IT'S YOUR
MONEY IN MY POCKET, DEAR, NOT MINE IN
YOURS.
  617(TLS):17AUG73-959
LAWRENCE, T.E. SEVEN PILLARS OF WISDOM.
  617(TLS):10AUG73-925
LAWRENCE, V. AN END TO FLIGHT.
  617(TLS):5OCT73-1158
LAWRENSON, T.E. - SEE LESAGE, A-R.
LAWRY, J.S. THE SHADOW OF HEAVEN.*
  F.T. PRINCE, 541(RES):MAY71-206
LAWRY, J.S. SIDNEY'S TWO "ARCADIAS."
  617(TLS):14SEP73-1063
LAWSON, H. HENRY LAWSON: AUTOBIOGRAPHI-
CAL AND OTHER WRITINGS 1887-1922. (C.
RODERICK, ED)
  S. MURRAY-SMITH, 71(ALS):MAY73-104
LAWSON, H. HENRY LAWSON LETTERS 1890-
1922. (C. RODERICK, ED)
  T.I. MOORE, 381:SEP71-353
LAWSON, H. HENRY LAWSON: SHORT STORIES
AND SKETCHES 1888-1922. (C. RODERICK,
ED)
  L. CANTRELL, 71(ALS):MAY73-99
LAWSON, L.A. KIERKEGAARD'S PRESENCE IN
CONTEMPORARY AMERICAN LIFE.
  J. THOMPSON, 563(SS):SPRING72-270
LAWTON, R. & H. LECKEY. GRAND ILLUSIONS.
  W. MARKFIELD, 441:2DEC73-96
LAYTON, I. THE COLLECTED POEMS OF IRVING
LAYTON.*
  M. WILSON, 606(TAMR):#61-56
LAYTON, I. ENGAGEMENTS. (S. MAYNE, ED)
  R. ADAMS, 296:WINTER73-96
LAYTON, I. LOVERS AND LESSER MEN.
  S. DRAGLAND, 198:FALL73-99
LAYTON, I. NAIL POLISH.
  F. COGSWELL, 529(QQ):SUMMER71-325
  D. LOCHHEAD, 150(DR):SUMMER71-280
  E. WATERSTON, 102(CANL):SPRING72-102
LAZAREV, V.N. MOSCOW SCHOOL OF ICON-
PAINTING.
  617(TLS):12JAN73-47
LAZAREV, V.N. STORIA DELLA PITTURA
BIZANTINA.*
  H. BELTING, 683:BAND34HEFT4-330
  R.W.L., 135:OCT70-139
LAZITCH, B. & M.M. DRACHKOVITCH. LENIN
AND THE COMINTERN. (VOL 1)
  617(TLS):4MAY73-492
LAZZARINI, L., ED. DANTE E LA CULTURA
TEDESCA.
  G.P. NORTON, 276:SPRING71-93
LAZZARINI, R. ANALISI FENOMENOLOGICA
DEL TEMPO IN RAPPORTO ALLA DECISIONE.
  E. NAMER, 542:JAN-MAR70-101
LEA, R. COUNTRY CURIOSITIES.
  617(TLS):10AUG73-937
LEACH, C. THE SEND-OFF.
  D. MAHON, 362:24MAY73-696
LEACH, E. GENESIS AS MYTH AND OTHER
ESSAYS.
  W.P. ZENNER, 390:APR71-69
LEACH, J. BRIGHT PARTICULAR STAR.*
  J. HAMILTON, 157:SPRING71-74
  639(VQR):WINTER71-XXXVII
LEACOCK, S. FEAST OF STEPHEN.* (R.
DAVIES, ED)
  E. CAMERON, 529(QQ):SPRING71-139

LEADER, M. TRIAD.
  M. LEVIN, 441:11MAR73-49
LEADER, N.A.M. HUNGARIAN CLASSICAL BAL-
LADS AND THEIR FOLKLORE.*
  E. SZINYEI-MERSE, 650(WF):JUL70-209
LEAKEY, F.W. BAUDELAIRE AND NATURE.
  M. SCHAETTEL, 557(RSH):APR-JUN70-331
  205(FMLS):JAN71-97
LEAL, L. - SEE RULFO, J.
LEAN, E.T. THE NAPOLEONISTS.
  D.V.E., 191(ELN):SEP71(SUPP)-15
  639(VQR):SUMMER71-CXXVI
LEARMONTH, N. THE AUSTRALIANS.
  617(TLS):18MAY73-565
LEARY, F. & J. COLONIAL HERITAGE.
  617(TLS):20JUL73-840
LEARY, L. - SEE TWAIN, M. & H.H. ROGERS
LEARY, T. CONFESSIONS OF A HOPE FIEND.
  C. WOODS, 441:22JUL73-22
LEASE, B. THAT WILD FELLOW JOHN NEAL AND
THE AMERICAN LITERARY REVOLUTION.
  617(TLS):8JUN73-638
LEASKA, M.A. VIRGINIA WOOLF'S "LIGHT-
HOUSE."*
  M. DONALD, 184(EIC):JUL71-311
  D.L. HIGDON, 594:SPRING71-108
  D.M. MONAGHAN, 150(DR):SPRING71-126
  C. OHMANN, 659:SPRING73-260
  S. PROUDFIT, 191(ELN):SEP71-71
  502(PRS):WINTER71/72-370
LEASOR, J. FOLLOW THE DRUM.
  N. BLIVEN, 442(NY):17MAR73-128
  M. LEVIN, 441:18FEB73-30
LEASOR, J. HOST OF EXTRAS.
  617(TLS):15JUN73-697
LEAVIS, F.R. "ANNA KARENINA" AND OTHER
ESSAYS.*
  D. HALLIBURTON, 290(JAAC):WINTER70-
  267
LEAVIS, F.R. & Q.D. DICKENS THE NOVEL-
IST.*
  C. BRISTOW, 111:13NOV70-52
  G.H. FORD, 445(NCF):JUN71-95
  S. MONOD, 189(EA):JAN-MAR71-59
  M. PRICE, 676(YR):WINTER72-271
  W.W. ROBSON, 155:MAY71-99
  D.R.G. SHAYER, 565:VOL12#2-74
  A. SHELSTON, 148:SPRING71-89
  S. WALL, 184(EIC):JUL71-261
  571:SPRING71-152
LEAVIS, F.R. & Q.D. LECTURES IN AMERICA.
  H. GIFFORD, 541(RES):FEB71-113
  L.T. LEMON, 502(PRS):FALL70-263
LEBEK, W.D. VERBA PRISCA.
  J.M. HUNT, 124:SEP71-31
  M. WINTERBOTTOM, 123:DEC72-353
LEBLON, J. - SEE PEREC, G.
LEBOIS, A. - SEE DUMAS, A.
LE BONNIEC, H. - SEE OVID
LEBOWITZ, A. PROGRESS INTO SILENCE.*
  J.G., 502(PRS):WINTER71/72-369
  H. PARKER, 401(MLQ):MAR72-54
LE BRAS-BARRET, J. MARTIN ANDERSEN NEXÖ.
  L.P. RØMHILD, 172(EDDA):1971/4-253
LEBREC, J. JOSEPH MALÈGUE ROMANCIER ET
PENSEUR.
  P. MOREAU, 535(RHL):MAR-APR71-327
LE BROCQUY, S. SWIFT'S MOST VALUABLE
FRIEND.
  P. DANCHIN, 179(ES):DEC71-559
  C.J. HORNE, 402(MLR):JAN72-170
LEBRUN, F. LES HOMMES ET LA MORT EN
ANJOU AUX 17E ET 18E SIÈCLES.
  R. DARNTON, 453:5APR73-25
LE BRUN, J. LES OPUSCULES SPIRITUELS DE
BOSSUET.
  T. GOYET, 535(RHL):JUL-AUG71-699
  A. LEVI, 208(FS):JUL72-328

LEBRUN, Y. ANATOMIE ET PHYSIOLOGIE DE
L'APPAREIL PHONATOIRE.*
  A. BOILEAU, 556(RLV):1971/4-504
  G.F. MEIER, 682(ZPSK):BAND24HEFT5-442
LEBRUN, Y., ED. LINGUISTIC RESEARCH IN
BELGIUM.
  K.H. SCHMIDT, 260(IF):BAND74-174
LECERCLE, J-L. ROUSSEAU ET L'ART DU
ROMAN.
  R.L. FRAUTSCHI, 207(FR):FEB71-617
  M. LAUNAY, 535(RHL):JAN-FEB71-100
LECKE, B. - SEE "FRIEDRICH SCHILLER"
LECKY, W.E.H. A HISTORY OF IRELAND IN
THE EIGHTEENTH CENTURY. (L.P. CURTIS,
JR., ED)
  617(TLS):5JAN73-19
LECLERC, I. THE NATURE OF PHYSICAL EXIS-
TENCE.
  617(TLS):23FEB73-218
LE CLÉZIO, J.M.G. THE BOOK OF FLIGHTS.*
(FRENCH TITLE: LE LIVRE DES FUITES.)
  M. CAGNON, 207(FR):FEB71-644
  J.P. DEGNAN, 249(HUDR):SUMMER72-330
LE CLÉZIO, J.M.G. LES GÉANTS.
  617(TLS):5OCT73-1156
LE CLÉZIO, J.M.G. LA GUERRE.
  M. CAGNON, 207(FR):MAY71-1122
LE CLÉZIO, J.M.G. WAR.
  V. CUNNINGHAM, 362:28JUN73-873
  B.P. SOLOMON, 441:15JUL73-4
  617(TLS):21SEP73-1074
LECOCQ, L. LA SATIRE EN ANGLETERRE DE
1588 À 1603.
  W. KINSLEY, 223:DEC71-348
  B.A. MILLIGAN, 551(RENQ):AUTUMN71-395
  K. MUIR, 189(EA):OCT-DEC70-395
LE CORBUSIER. THE NURSERY SCHOOLS.
  R.W. HAASE, 505:MAY70-128
LEDEEN, M.A. UNIVERSAL FASCISM.
  H.W. SCHNEIDER, 319:OCT73-565
  617(TLS):2MAR73-225
LEDER, I. RUSSISCHE FISCHNAMEN.
  E. DICKENMANN, 343:BAND13HEFT2-160
LEDERER, H. REFERENCE GRAMMAR OF THE
GERMAN LANGUAGE.*
  G. KOLISKO, 220(GL&L):APR72-291
LEDERER, H. - SEE SCHNITZLER, A.
LEDERMANN, E.K. EXISTENTIAL NEUROSIS.
  617(TLS):18MAY73-550
LEDERMANN, E.K. PHILOSOPHY AND MEDICINE.
  C. SMITH, 483:APR71-181
LEDÉSERT, R.P.L. & M. - SEE MANSION, J.E.
DE LEDESMA, A. CONCEPTOS ESPIRITUALES Y
MORALES. (E.J. MARTÍNEZ, ED)
  F. SMIEJA, 86(BHS):OCT72-404
LEDESMA, F.N. CERVANTES.
  T.G. BERGIN, 441:18FEB73-20
LEDUC, V. MAD IN PURSUIT.* (FRENCH
TITLE: LA FOLIE EN TÊTE.)
  M. BROC-LAPEYRE, 98:NOV70-935
  P.M. SPACKS, 249(HUDR):SPRING72-157
LEDUC, V. THE TAXI.* (FRENCH TITLE: LE
TAXI.)
  617(TLS):2MAR73-229
LEE, B.A. BRITAIN AND THE SINO-JAPANESE
WAR, 1937-1939.
  G. BARRACLOUGH, 453:31MAY73-9
LEE, C. MO TZU, THE GREAT EDUCATOR.
  B. SCHATTLE, 258:MAR71-141
LEE, C.N. THE NOVELS OF MARK ALEKSAN-
DROVIČ ALDANOV.*
  L.I. TWAROG, 550(RUSR):JAN71-77
LEE, D.L. DIRECTIONSCORE.
  J. KESSLER, 491:FEB73-292
LEE, D.N. & H.G. WOODHOUSE. ART ON THE
ROCKS OF SOUTHERN AFRICA.
  D. SAMACHSON, 363:AUG71-122

LEE, J. THE MODERNISATION OF IRISH
SOCIETY 1848-1918.
  617(TLS):16NOV73-1399
LEE, J.N. SWIFT AND SCATALOGICAL SATIRE.
  J. TRAUGOTT, 566:AUTUMN71-22
LEE, M. & H. CYPRUS.
  617(TLS):19OCT73-1287
LEE, M.O. WORD, SOUND, AND IMAGE IN THE
ODES OF HORACE.*
  C.L. BABCOCK, 24:JUL72-501
LEE, R. & M. CASEBIER. THE SPOUSE GAP.
  617(TLS):24AUG73-986
LEE, R.A. ORWELL'S FICTION.*
  K.J. ATCHITY, 613:SUMMER70-304
  R. MITCHELL, 399(MLJ):NOV71-484
LEE, R.F. CONRAD'S COLONIALISM.*
  J. ESPEY, 445(NCF):JUN70-125
  I. VIDAN, 136:VOL3#1-119
LEE, R.H.G. THE MANCHURIAN FRONTIER IN
CH'ING HISTORY.
  CHAO CHUNG-FU, 293(JAST):FEB71-437
LEE, S.E. ANCIENT CAMBODIAN SCULPTURE.
  A. LE BONHEUR, 57:VOL33#3-235
  W. WATSON, 90:APR71-223
LEE, S.E. JAPANESE DECORATIVE STYLE.
  R.L.B., 135:AUG70-289
LEE, V. THE HANDLING OF WORDS AND OTHER
STUDIES IN LITERARY PSYCHOLOGY.
  P. MICHEL-MICHOT, 556(RLV):1971/6-776
LEE, V.G. & J.D. GAUTIER, EDS. LA VIE DES
LETTRES.
  M.M. CELLER, 207(FR):APR71-1001
LEE, W.S. COLORADO.
  M.S. TRIMBLE, 649(WAL):SPRING71-70
LEE, Y-B. DIPLOMATIC RELATIONS BETWEEN
THE UNITED STATES AND KOREA 1866-1887.
  S.J. PALMER, 293(JAST):MAY71-691
LEECH, C., ED. SHAKESPEARE: THE TRAGE-
DIES.
  J.B. FORT, 189(EA):OCT-DEC70-439
LEECH, C. TRAGEDY.
  M. BERVEILLER, 549(RLC):JUL-SEP70-417
  205(FMLS):OCT70-419
LEECH, G.N. A LINGUISTIC GUIDE TO ENG-
LISH POETRY.
  W.O. HENDRICKS, 361:VOL25#2-165
  J.P. THORNE, 541(RES):FEB71-114
LEECH, G.N. TOWARDS A SEMANTIC DESCRIP-
TION OF ENGLISH.
  J.M.E. MORAVCSIK, 350:JUN72-445
  J. PELLOWE, 597(SN):VOL42#2-513
LEECH, K. YOUTHQUAKE.
  617(TLS):16NOV73-1392
LEEDS, C. TILLIE'S PUNCTURED ROMANCE.
  A. ROBERTSON, 648:JUN71-52
LEEK, F.F. THE HUMAN REMAINS FROM THE
TOMB OF TUT'ANKHAMUN.
  617(TLS):8JUN73-648
LEEMING, O. VENUS IS SETTING.
  617(TLS):27APR73-474
LEES, D. RAPE OF A QUIET TOWN.
  N. CALLENDAR, 441:26AUG73-33
LEES, D. ZODIAC.*
  N. CALLENDAR, 441:8APR73-32
LEES, H. & M. LOVELL - SEE SYRETT, I.
LEES-MILNE, J. ENGLISH COUNTRY HOUSES:
BAROQUE 1685-1715.
  A.C-T., 135:JAN71-54
  R. EDWARDS, 39:JAN71-67
LEES-MILNE, J. HERETICS IN LOVE.
  617(TLS):2MAR73-229
LEESON, R. VOYAGE À PARIS.
  D. SCHLESINGER, 207(FR):DEC70-432
LEESON, R.A. STRIKE.
  617(TLS):6JUL73-767
LEETE, H.M., ED. THE BEST OF BICYCLING!*
  H. HUYCK, 109:SPRING/SUMMER73-175

LEFEBVRE, G. THE GREAT FEAR OF 1789.
R.M. ANDREWS, 441:2SEP73-7
J. DUNN, 362:22MAR73-380
442(NY):17SEP73-155
LEFÈVRE, E. DIE EXPOSITIONSTECHNIK IN
DEN KOMODIEN DES TERENZ.*
A.S. GRATWICK, 123:MAR72-29
LEFF, G. TYRANNY OF CONCEPTS.
L.B. CEBIK, 219(GAR):FALL71-382
LEFKOWITZ, M., ED. TROIS MASQUES À LA
COUR DE CHARLES IER D'ANGLETERRE.
A.H. KING, 182:VOL24#4-171
LE FORESTIER, R. LA FRANC-MAÇONNERIE
OCCULTISTE AU XVIIIe SIÈCLE ET L'ORDRE
DES ELUS COËNS.
J. ROUDAUT, 98:JAN71-26
LE FORESTIER, R. LA FRANC-MAÇONNERIE
TEMPLIÈRE ET OCCULTISTE AUX XVIIIE ET
XIXE SIÈCLES.
N.L., 154:JUN71-426
LEFORT, C. LE TRAVAIL DE L'OEUVRE:
MACHIAVEL.
617(TLS):8JUN73-640
LEFORT, C. - SEE MERLEAU-PONTY, M.
LEFRANC, G. LE MOUVEMENT SYNDICAL SOUS
LA TROISIÈME RÉPUBLIQUE.
M. BRAUN, 207(FR):OCT70-199
LE FRANC, M. MARTIN LE FRANC: LE CHAM-
PION DES DAMES. (PT 1) (A. PIAGET, ED)
K. CHESNEY, 382(MAE):1972/2-168
LEFRANC, P. SIR WALTER RALEGH ÉCRIVAIN.*
P. MICHEL-MICHOT, 179(ES):AUG71-363
LE GALL, B. L'IMAGINAIRE CHEZ SENANCOUR.
A. CAPRIO, 546(RR):DEC71-306
LEGARÉ, H.S. WRITINGS OF HUGH SWINTON
LEGARÉ, LATE ATTORNEY GENERAL AND ACT-
ING SECRETARY OF STATE OF THE UNITED
STATES. (M. LEGARE, ED)
J.H. HARRISON, JR., 9(ALAR):JUL71-217
LE GENTIL, P. THE "CHANSON DE ROLAND."
J.A. NELSON, 188(ECR):SUMMER70-157
LEGERS, H. - SEE MACHIAVELLI, N.
LEGEZA, I.L. A DESCRIPTIVE AND ILLUS-
TRATED CATALOGUE OF THE MALCOLM MAC DON-
ALD CHINESE CERAMICS IN THE GULBENKIAN
MUSEUM OF ART AND ARCHAEOLOGY, SCHOOL
OF ORIENTAL STUDIES, UNIVERSITY OF DUR-
HAM.
617(TLS):5OCT73-1168
LEGGET, R.F. RAILWAYS OF CANADA.
617(TLS):5OCT73-1196
LEGGETT, B.J. HOUSMAN'S LAND OF LOST
CONTENT.
W.R. BRASHEAR, 636(VP):WINTER71-458
J.W. STEVENSON, 577(SHR):FALL71-413
LE GUILLOU, L. LAMENNAIS.
J. GAULMIER, 535(RHL):MAR-APR71-307
J.S.P., 191(ELN):SEP71(SUPP)-91
LEGUM, C., ED. AFRICA CONTEMPORARY
RECORD. (1972-1973)
617(TLS):14SEP73-1042
LEGUM, C. THE UNITED NATIONS AND SOUTH-
ERN AFRICA.
617(TLS):20APR73-434
LEGVOLD, R. SOVIET POLICY IN WEST AF-
RICA.*
R.E. KANET, 550(RUSR):APR71-207
LEHAN, R. THEODORE DREISER.
W.M. FROHOCK, 454:FALL71-82
J.J. MC ALEER, 613:SPRING71-130
LEHANE, B. THE COMPANION GUIDE TO IRE-
LAND.
617(TLS):17AUG73-956
LEHISTE, I., ED. READINGS IN ACOUSTIC
PHONETICS.
C-W. KIM, 399(MLJ):DEC71-533

LEHMAN, W.C. HENRY HOME, LORD KAMES AND
THE SCOTTISH ENLIGHTENMENT.
D.F. NORTON, 319:OCT71-547
LEHMANN, G. BEITRÄGE ZUR GESCHICHTE UND
INTERPRETATION DER PHILOSOPHIE KANTS.
R. MALTER, 342:BAND62HEFT4-516
LEHMANN, G. - SEE KANT, I.
LEHMANN, J. IN MY OWN TIME.*
T.F. STALEY, 295:NOV72-576
LEHMANN, L. EIGHTEEN SONG CYCLES.*
A.D., 410(M&L):APR72-217
LEHMANN, W.P. EINFÜHRUNG IN DIE HISTOR-
ISCHE LINGUISTIK.
H. BECKERS, 72:BAND209HEFT4/6-396
LEHMANN, W.P., ED & TRANS. A READER IN
NINETEENTH-CENTURY HISTORICAL INDO-
EUROPEAN LINGUISTICS.
D. CRYSTAL, 297(JL):FEB70-156
H.M. HOENIGSWALD, 361:VOL26#4-423
W.K. PERCIVAL, 269(IJAL):JUL70-228
LEHMANN, W.P. & Y. MALKIEL, EDS. DIREC-
TIONS FOR HISTORICAL LINGUISTICS.*
G.C. LEPSCHY, 297(JL):FEB70-136
O. SZEMERÉNYI, 215(GL):VOL10#2-121
LEHMANN-HAUPT, H., ED. BOOKBINDING IN
AMERICA.
G. BARBER, 354:SEP70-274
LEHMBERG, S.E. THE REFORMATION PARLIA-
MENT 1529-36.
G. NIEDHART, 182:VOL24#5-242
LEHNER, E. & J. FOLKLORE AND ODYSSEYS
OF FOOD AND MEDICINAL PLANTS.
617(TLS):30NOV73-1485
LEHNERT, H. THOMAS MANN.
R. MAJUT, 224(GRM):AUG70-362
LEHNING, A. - SEE BAKUNIN, M.
LEHRER, A. & K., EDS. THEORY OF MEANING.
R.P.M., 543:MAR71-556
LEHTINEN, M. BASIC COURSE IN FINNISH.
(T.A. SEBEOK, ED)
G.F. MEIER, 682(ZPSK):BAND23HEFT2/3-
315
LEHTO, L. ENGLISH STRESS AND ITS MODIFI-
CATION BY INTONATION.
I. LEHISTE, 350:MAR72-190
LEIBFRIED, E. FABEL.
M. FELDGES, 657(WW):MAR/APR71-141
LEIBFRIED, E. KRITISCHE WISSENSCHAFT VOM
TEXT.
D. HARTH, 224(GRM):BAND21HEFT2-248
LEIBNIZ, G.W. COMPLETE WRITINGS AND LET-
TERS.* (GERMAN TITLE: SÄMTLICHE SCHRIF-
TEN UND BRIEFE.) (1ST SER, VOL 8) (K.
MÜLLER, G. SCHEEL & G. GERBER, EDS)
D. TURCK, 322(JHI):OCT-DEC71-627
LEIBNIZ, G.W. CONFESSIO PHILOSOPHI.
(O. SAAME, ED)
H. POSER, 53(AGP):BAND53HEFT1-105
LEIBNIZ, G.W. THE POLITICAL WRITINGS OF
LEIBNIZ.* (P. RILEY, ED & TRANS)
G.H.R. PARKINSON, 518:OCT72-27
LEIDERER, R., ED. WILHALM VON ORLENS.*
V. GÜNTHER, 182:VOL24#7/8-350
D. HEALD, 220(GL&L):APR72-324
LEIGH, R.A. - SEE ROUSSEAU, J-J.
LEIGHTON, A.H. COME NEAR.
R. TRICKETT, 676(YR):AUTUMN71-121
LEIMBERG, I. SHAKESPEARE'S "ROMEO UND
JULIA."
G. LAMBRECHTS, 189(EA):JAN-MAR71-90
R.P. LESSENICH, 597(SN):VOL42#1-228
H. OPPEL, 430(NS):JUL71-393
LEIRIES, M. & J. DELANGE. AFRICAN ART.
E.L.R. MEYEROWITZ, 39:JUL70-80
DE LEIRIS, A. THE DRAWINGS OF EDOUARD
MANET.
A.C. HANSON, 54:DEC71-542
[CONTINUED]

DE LEIRIS, A. THE DRAWINGS OF EDOUARD
MANET. [CONTINUING]
    R.S., 376:JUL70-120
    G.P. WEISBERG, 127:WINTER71/72-224
LEISHMAN, J.B. THE ART OF MARVELL'S
POETRY.
    M.W., 502(PRS):FALL70-276
LEISHMAN, J.B. MILTON'S MINOR POEMS.*
(G. TILLOTSON, ED)
    J.M. ALLEN, 67:MAY72-86
    G. BULLOUGH, 175:AUTUMN70-101
    F.T. PRINCE, 541(RES):MAY71-206
LEISINGER, A.H., JR. MICROPHOTOGRAPHY
FOR ARCHIVES.
    C.W. NELSON, 14:APR71-201
LEISNER, W. MONARCHISCHES HAUSRECHT IN
DEMOKRATISCHER GLEICHHEITSORDNUNG.
    H-W. STRÄTZ, 182:VOL24#9/10-403
LEITCH, D. GOD STAND UP FOR BASTARDS.
    442(NY):21APR73-134
    617(TLS):2MAR73-234
LEITES, N. THE RULES OF THE GAME IN
PARIS.*
    M. ANDERSON, 208(FS):APR72-238
LEJEUNE, P. L'OMBRE ET LA LUMIÈRE DANS
"LES CONTEMPLATIONS" DE VICTOR HUGO.
    L. CELLIER, 535(RHL):JUL-AUG71-714
LEJEUNE, R. & J. STIENNON. THE LEGEND
OF ROLAND IN THE MIDDLE AGES.*
    W.O. HASSALL, 135:DEC71-290
LELAND, J. LIRRI.
    617(TLS):6JUL73-769
LELAND, J. A RIVER DECREES.
    R. CAREW, 159(DM):SPRING70-113
LELCHUK, A. AMERICAN MISCHIEF.
    P. ADAMS, 61:MAR73-107
    L.E. SISSMAN, 442(NY):7APR73-147
    A. KAZIN, 441:11FEB73-2
    C. LEHMANN-HAUPT, 441:24JAN73-43
    D. MAHON, 362:21JUN73-840
    R. SALE, 453:8FEB73-21
    G. STADE, 231:MAY73-86
    617(TLS):1JUN73-605
LEM, S. THE INVINCIBLE.
    T. STURGEON, 441:23SEP73-39
    617(TLS):9NOV73-1377
LEM, S. MEMOIRS FOUND IN A BATHTUB.
    T. STURGEON, 441:23SEP73-39
LEMARCHAND, E. CYANIDE WITH COMPLIMENTS.*
    N. CALLENDAR, 441:29JUL73-13
LEMARCHAND, E. LET OR HINDRANCE.
    617(TLS):3AUG73-911
LEMARCHAND, R. RWANDA AND BURUNDI.
    L. MAIR, 69:APR71-167
LEMARIÉ, J. - SEE CHROMATIUS
LEMAY, J.A.L. MEN OF LETTERS IN COLONIAL
MARYLAND.
    R. BAIN, 578:SPRING73-124
    J.B. BOLES, 70(ANQ):MAY73-141
LE MAY, P. PICOUNOC LE MAUDIT.
    A. POKORNY, 296:SUMMER73-117
LEMBACH, K. DIE PFLANZEN BEI THEOKRIT.
    N. AUSTIN, 124:MAR72-240
LE MIRE, E.D. - SEE MORRIS, W.
LEMMER, M. - SEE SCHERNBERG, D.
LENAGHAN, J.O. A COMMENTARY ON CICERO'S
ORATION "DE HARUSPICUM RESPONSO."*
    E.S. RAMAGE, 24:APR72-371
    B. RAWSON, 122:APR72-141
LENARD, Y. JEUNES VOIX, JEUNES VISAGES.
    P. SILBERMAN, 207(FR):APR71-996
LENAU, N. FAUST. (H. STEINECKE, ED)
    H. SLESSAREV, 406:SPRING73-87
LENČEK, R.L. THE VERB PATTERN OF CONTEM-
PORARY STANDARD SLOVENE.
    G.K. BEYNEN, 206:FEB70-144

LENDERS, W. DIE ANALYTISCHE BEGRIFFS-
UND URTEILSTHEORIE VON G.W. LEIBNIZ
UND CHR. WOLFF.
    C.A. CORR, 319:OCT73-545
"LENGUAJE Y FILOSOFÍA."
    R.G. KEIGHTLEY, 402(MLR):OCT72-860
LENGYEL, J. CONFRONTATION.* (HUNGARIAN
TITLE: SZEMBESÍTÉS.)
    R. GARFITT, 362:13DEC73-828
    617(TLS):21DEC73-1557
LENIN, V.I. OPERE COMPLETE. (VOL 38)
(I. AMBROGIO, ED)
    G. MASTROIANNI, 548(RCSF):APR-JUN71-
229
"VLADIMIR IL'ICH LENIN: BIOGRAFICHESKAIA
KHRONIKA, 1870-1924." (VOL 1)
    B.D. WOLFE, 32:SEP72-676
LENK, W. DIE REFORMATION IM ZEITGENÖS-
SISCHEN DIALOG.
    H. HARTMANN, 654(WB):7/1970-212
LENNIG, R. TRAUM UND SINNESTÄUSCHUNG
BEI AISCHYLOS, SOPHOKLES, EURIPIDES.
    W.C. SCOTT, 24:APR72-369
LENNOX-SHORT, A. EFFECTIVE EXPRESSION.
    J. ROME, 180(ESA):MAR72-63
LENSELINK, S.J. - SEE MAROT, C.
LENSEN, G.A. APRIL IN RUSSIA.
    D. VON MOHRENSCHILDT, 550(RUSR):OCT71-
412
LENSEN, G.A. JAPANESE RECOGNITION OF THE
USSR.*
    J.K. EMMERSON, 550(RUSR):APR71-193
    D.B. RAMSDELL, 293(JAST):FEB71-469
LENSEN, G.A. - SEE WILL, B.
LENSU, M.I. & E.S. PROKOSHINA, EDS.
BAPTIZM I BAPTISTY (SOTSIOLOGICHESKII
OCHERK).
    P.D. STEEVES, 32:SEP72-699
LENTZEN, M. CARLOS ARNICHES (VOM "GENERO
CHICO" ZUR "TRAGEDIA GROTESKA").
    M. BARRIO, 430(NS):NOV70-578
LENTZEN, M. STUDIEN ZUR DANTE-EXEGESE
CRISTOFORO LANDINOS.
    G. TOURNOY, 568(SCN):SUMMER72-54
    G. TOURNOY, 568(SCN):FALL-WINTER72-84
LENZ, J.M.R. THE TUTOR. THE SOLDIERS.
(W.E. YUILL, ED & TRANS OF BOTH)
    617(TLS):5OCT73-1185
LENZ, S. THE GERMAN LESSON.* (GERMAN
TITLE: DEUTSCHSTUNDE.)
    P.M. SPACKS, 249(HUDR):AUTUMN72-505
LENZ, S. DAS VORBILD.
    617(TLS):14DEC73-1547
LENZ, S. DAS WRACK AND OTHER STORIES.
(C.A.H. RUSS, ED)
    D.S. LOW, 220(GL&L):OCT71-57
VON LENZ, W. GREAT PIANO VIRTUOSOS OF
OUR TIME. (REV BY P. REDER)
    F. DAWES, 415:OCT72-977
LEON, P.L. & P. MARTIN. PROLÉGOMÈNES À
L'ÉTUDE DES STRUCTURELLES INTONATIVES.
    F. CARTON, 209(FM):OCT71-362
    A.W. GRUNDSTROM, 207(FR):DEC70-439
LÉON, P.R., ED. RECHERCHES SUR LA STRUC-
TURE PHONIQUE DU FRANÇAIS CANADIEN.
    R. ARVEILLER, 209(FM):OCT71-363
    M. CAGNON, 399(MLJ):FEB71-127
LEÓN-PORTILLA, M. PRE-COLUMBIAN LITERA-
TURES OF MEXICO.
    B. TOELKEN, 650(WF):OCT70-268
LEONARD, J. BLACK CONCEIT.
    P. ADAMS, 61:DEC73-139
    S. BLACKBURN, 441:28OCT73-46
    C. LEHMANN-HAUPT, 441:31OCT73-37
    442(NY):10DEC73-196
LEONARD, R.A. THE STREAM OF MUSIC.
    P.J.P., 412:MAY72-149

LEONARD, T. POEMS.
617(TLS):2NOV73-1348
LEONARDO DA VINCI. THE LITERARY WORKS
OF LEONARDO DA VINCI. (2ND ED) (J.P.
RICHTER, ED)
J. WASSERMAN, 90:MAR71-162
LEONHARDI, A. & B.W.W. WELSH. GRAMMATI-
CAAL WOORENBOEK ENGELS.
P. MICHEL-MICHOT, 556(RLV):1971/5-648
LEONTIEV, K. AGAINST THE CURRENT. THE
EGYPTIAN DOVE. (G. IVASK, ED OF BOTH)
S.A. ZENKOVSKY, 550(RUSR):JAN71-81
LEOPARDI, G. SCRITTI FILOLOGICI (1817-
1832).* (G. PACELLA & S. TIMPANARO,
EDS)
V. DI BENEDETTO, 228(GSLI):VOL148FASC
464-618
LEOPARDI, G. TUTTE LE OPERE. (W. BINNI,
WITH E. GHIDETTI, EDS)
G. SAVARESE, 228(GSLI):VOL148FASC461-
137
LEOPARDI, G. TUTTI GLI SCRITTI INEDITI,
RARI E EDITI 1809-1810 DI GIACOMO LEO-
PARDI. (M. CORTI, ED)
617(TLS):11MAY73-516
LEOPOLD, R. EGON SCHIELE.
A. BROYARD, 441:8OCT73-31
J.R. MELLOW, 441:2DEC73-12
617(TLS):28SEP73-1102
LEOPOLD, W.F. ENGLISH INFLUENCE ON POST-
WAR GERMAN.
H. GALINSKY, 38:BAND89HEFT3-359
LE PAN, D. THE DESERTER.
B. MITCHELL, 296:FALL73-112
"L'ÉPIGRAMME GRECQUE" - SEE UNDER RAUBIT-
SCHEK, A.E. & OTHERS
LEPING, E.I & OTHERS. DAS GROSSE
DEUTSCH-RUSSISCHE WÖRTERBUCH. (O.I.
MOSKALSKAJA, ED)
E. KRACK, 430(NS):APR71-227
LEPPMANN, W. WINCKELMANN.
H. HATFIELD, 222(GR):MAR71-139
V.L., 131(CL):SPRING72-182
M.K. TORBRUEGGE, 406:SPRING72-79
LEPROHON, P. THE ITALIAN CINEMA.
617(TLS):28SEP73-1109
LEPROHON, R. ANTOINETTE DE MIRECOURT.
L. SHOHET, 296:SUMMER73-101
LEPSCHY, A.L.M. - SEE UNDER MOMIGLIANO
LEPSCHY, A.L.
LEPSCHY, G.C. A SURVEY OF STRUCTURAL LIN-
GUISTICS.
F.P. DINNEEN, 297(JL):OCT71-287
R.M. WILSON, 175:SPRING71-22
DE LERMA, D-R., ED. BLACK MUSIC IN OUR
CULTURE.
H. GLASSIE, 292(JAF):JUL-SEP71-357
LERMAN, R. CALL ME ISHTAR.
H. ROSENSTEIN, 441:25NOV73-46
LERNER, A. PSYCHOANALYTICALLY ORIENTED
CRITICISM OF THREE AMERICAN POETS.
A. BLINDERMAN, 646(WWR):JUN71-66
J.S. BOIS, 186(ETC.):SEP71-373
LERNER, M.P. THE NEW SOCIALIST REVOLU-
TION.
M. HARRINGTON, 441:11MAR73-42
LERNER, M-P. LA NOTION DE FINALITÉ CHEZ
ARISTOTE.*
D.W. HAMLYN, 303:VOL91-186
LERNER, W. KARL RADEK.*
L.H. LEGTERS, 550(RUSR):JUL71-298
DE LÉRY, J. INDIENS DE LA RENAISSANCE.
(A-M. CHARTIER, ED)
617(TLS):9MAR73-258
LESAGE, A-R. LE DIABLE BOITEUX.
Y. COIRAULT, 535(RHL):MAY-JUN71-510
D. SHAW, 208(FS):JUL72-332

LESAGE, A-R. TURCARET.* (T.E. LAWREN-
SON, ED)
205(FMLS):APR70-208
LE SAGE, L. & A. YON. DICTIONNAIRE DES
CRITIQUES LITTÉRAIRES.*
R.E. JONES, 207(FR):DEC70-472
LESAGE, M. LES RÉGIMES POLITIQUES DE
L'U.R.S.S. ET DE L'EUROPE DE L'EST.
J.N. HAZARD, 32:JUN72-452
LESCURE, P. LES RIVES DE L'HUDSON.
J. LECOCQ-LEINER, 207(FR):OCT70-180
LESLAU, W. HEBREW COGNATES IN AMHARIC.
J.C. GREENFIELD, 318(JAOS):OCT-DEC71-
528
LESLEY, P. RENAISSANCE JEWELS AND
JEWELLED OBJECTS FROM THE MELVIN GUT-
MAN COLLECTION.
J.F. HAYWARD, 54:SEP70-318
LESLIE, A. THE MARLBOROUGH HOUSE SET.
A. FREMANTLE, 441:6MAY73-4
LESLIE, R.F. - SEE "THE WANDERER"
LESSING, D. BRIEFING FOR A DESCENT INTO
HELL.*
M.B., 502(PRS):WINTER71/72-368
E. GLOVER, 565:VOL12#4-53
LESSING, D. THE FOUR-GATED CITY.
J.B. GORDON, 598(SOR):WINTER73-217
LESSING, D. THE SUMMER BEFORE THE DARK.
A. BROYARD, 441:7MAY73-43
R. BRYDEN, 362:10MAY73-623
E. HARDWICK, 441:13MAY73-1
J. HENDIN, 231:JUN73-82
A. LURIE, 453:14JUN73-18
M. MANNING, 61:JUN73-116
R.L. WIDMANN, 659:AUTUMN73-582
442(NY):9JUN73-113
617(TLS):4MAY73-489
LESSING, D. THE TEMPTATION OF JACK ORK-
NEY AND OTHER STORIES.*
R. SALE, 453:25JAN73-42
LESSING, E. THE BIBLE.
J.G. PLANTE, 363:AUG71-116
LESSING, G.E. MINNA VON BARNHELM.
(K.J. NORTHCOTT, ED & TRANS)
617(TLS):5OCT73-1185
LESSING, G.E. NATHAN DER WEISE. (C.
SCHWEITZER, ED)
T. ALT, 221(GQ):MAY71-431
LESSING, G.E. WERKE. (H.G. GÖPFERT &
OTHERS, EDS)
617(TLS):6JUL73-777
LESSING, G.E. WERKE. (O. MANN, ED)
617(TLS):6JUL73-777
LESSING, G.E., M. MENDELSSOHN & F. NICO-
LAI. BRIEFWECHSEL ÜBER DAS TRAUER-
SPIEL. (J. SCHULTE-SASSE, ED)
617(TLS):6JUL73-777
"LESSING UND DIE ZEIT DER AUFKLÄRUNG."
H.B. GARLAND, 220(GL&L):OCT71-30
"LESSING YEARBOOK I, 1969." (J. GLENN,
ED)
E. DVORETZKY, 221(GQ):NOV71-570
"LESSING YEARBOOK II, 1970."
M. STOLJAR, 67:MAY72-108
LESTER, J.A., JR. JOURNEY THROUGH
DESPAIR, 1880-1914.*
P. GOETSCH, 430(NS):JUL71-387
LESTER, M., ED. READINGS IN APPLIED
TRANSFORMATIONAL GRAMMAR.*
R.M. HOGG, 433:JUL71-348
LESTOCQUOY, J. HISTOIRE DU PATRIOTISME
EN FRANCE.
J-A. BOUR, 207(FR):OCT70-209
LESURE, F. BIBLIOGRAPHIE DES ÉDITIONS
MUSICALES PUBLIÉES PAR ESTIENNE ROGER
ET MICHEL-CHARLES LE CÈNE (AMSTERDAM,
1696-1743).
A.H. KING, 354:SEP70-265

LESURE, M. LES SOURCES DE L'HISTOIRE DE
RUSSIE AUX ARCHIVES NATIONALES.
J.M.P. MC ERLEAN, 32:SEP72-665
LESY, M. WISCONSIN DEATH TRIP.
P. ADAMS, 61:JUN73-123
W.H. GASS, 441:24JUN73-7
C. LEHMANN-HAUPT, 441:1JUN73-39
LESZL, W. LOGIC AND METAPHYSICS IN
ARISTOTLE.
W. CHARLTON, 518:JAN72-16
LETESSIER, F. - SEE DE LAMARTINE, A.M.L.D.
LETHÈVE, J. DAILY LIFE OF FRENCH ARTISTS
IN THE NINETEENTH CENTURY.
617(TLS):26JAN73-96
LEUBE, E. FORTUNA IN KARTHAGO.*
A. BUCK, 52:BAND6HEFT1-92
J.B. HALL, 123:MAR72-62
LEUILLOT, B. VICTOR HUGO PUBLIE "LES
MISÉRABLES" (CORRESPONDANCE AVEC ALBERT
LACROIX, AOÛT 1861-JUILLET 1862).
H.J. HUNT, 208(FS):JUL72-339
LEVACK, B.P. THE CIVIL LAWYERS IN ENG-
LAND 1603-1641.
617(TLS):10AUG73-927
LEVARIE, N. THE ART & HISTORY OF BOOKS.
R. MC LEAN, 135:JAN70-50
LEVAS, S. SIBELIUS.*
R. LAYTON, 415:SEP72-869
J.A.W., 410(M&L):OCT72-438
LEVENDOSKY, C. PERIMETERS.
J.D. REED, 600:WINTER71-153
LEVENSON, C. CAIRNS.
T. EAGLETON, 565:VOL11#2-68
LEVENSON, E.A. THE FALLACY OF UNDER-
STANDING.
J.S. GORDON, 441:28JAN73-2
LEVENSON, S. JAMES CONNOLLY.
R. KEE, 362:7JUN73-761
617(TLS):27JUL73-857
LEVENTHAL, A.R. WAR.
A. BROYARD, 441:3DEC73-43
LEVER, J. & P. SCHWARTZ. WOMEN AT YALE.
P.M. SPACKS, 249(HUDR):SPRING72-160
LEVER, J.W. THE TRAGEDY OF STATE.
G.R. HIBBARD, 402(MLR):JUL72-618
J.D. JUMP, 447(N&Q):DEC71-478
LEVERIDGE, A. YOUR LOVING ANNA. (L.
TIVY, ED)
617(TLS):26OCT73-1321
LEVERT, P. L'ÊTRE ET LE RÉEL SELON
LOUIS LAVELLE.
M. BARTHÉLEMY-MADAULE, 542:OCT-DEC71-
493
LEVERTOV, D. FOOTPRINTS.
J.C. OATES, 598(SOR):AUTUMN73-1014
C. RICKS, 441:7JAN73-5
LEVERTOV, D. RELEARNING THE ALPHABET.*
E.M. BRONER, 390:JAN71-73
V. CONTOSKI, 600:SPRING71-175
T. EAGLETON, 565:VOL12#1-77
G. FOX, 529(QQ):SPRING71-160
LEVERTOV, D. TO STAY ALIVE.
G. BURNS, 584(SWR):SPRING72-162
M.G. PERLOFF, 659:WINTER73-97
W.H. PRITCHARD, 249(HUDR):SPRING72-124
D.H. ZUCKER, 398:AUTUMN73-235
LEVEY, M. THE LIFE AND DEATH OF MOZART.*
S. SADIE, 415:MAR72-270
LEVEY, M. NATIONAL GALLERY CATALOGUES:
THE SEVENTEENTH AND EIGHTEENTH CENTURY
ITALIAN SCHOOLS.
J. DANIELS, 135:DEC71-290
LEVEY, M. PAINTING AT COURT.
T.J. CLARK, 592:JUL/AUG71-47
LEVI, A. IL PROBLEMA DELL'ERRORE NELLA
METAFISICA E NELLA GNOSEOLOGIA DI
PLATONE.* (G. REALE, ED)
P.M. HUBY, 123:DEC72-334

LÉVI, E. ELIPHAS LÉVI, VISIONNAIRE ROMAN-
TIQUE.* (F.P. BOWMAN, ED)
M. EIGELDINGER, 557(RSH):OCT-DEC70-
645
LEVI, I. GAMBLING WITH TRUTH.
D. MILLER, 316:JUN71-318
LEVI, P. THE LIGHT GARDEN OF THE ANGEL
KING.*
A. BROYARD, 441:6FEB73-39
442(NY):17FEB73-111
LEVI, P. RUINED ABBEYS. PANCAKES FOR
THE QUEEN OF BABYLON.
J. TIPTON, 661:SPRING71-64
LÉVI-STRAUSS, C. FROM HONEY TO ASHES.
J. BAMBERGER, 441:3JUN73-23
R. JELLINEK, 441:12MAY73-37
442(NY):23JUN73-92
617(TLS):9FEB73-157
LÉVI-STRAUSS, C. TRISTES TROPIQUES.
M. DEAS, 362:20DEC73-857
LEVIANT, C., ED & TRANS. KING ARTUS.*
E. RODITI, 328:SUMMER71-371
LEVIN, D.M. REASON AND EVIDENCE IN
HUSSERL'S PHENOMENOLOGY.*
D.W. SMITH, 311(JP):21JUN73-356
LEVIN, H. GROUNDS FOR COMPARISON.
H. LEIBOWITZ, 441:29JUL73-6
617(TLS):25MAY73-579
LEVIN, H. THE MYTH OF THE GOLDEN AGE IN
THE RENAISSANCE.*
R.R. BOLGAR, 111:13NOV70-68
R.F. HILL, 402(MLR):JAN72-159
M. HUGHES, 549(RLC):JUL-SEP71-412
P. MERIVALE, 131(CL):WINTER72-88
G. THOMAS, 175:AUTUMN71-102
E.N. TIGERSTEDT, 149:MAR72-102
R. VIDÁN, 202(FMOD):NOV70/FEB71-171
LEVIN, R. THE MULTIPLE PLOT IN ENGLISH
RENAISSANCE DRAMA.*
B. COCHRANE, 67:MAY72-79
LEVINE, B. THE DISSOLVING IMAGE.*
G. GUNN, 405(MP):AUG71-87
N.H. MAC KENZIE, 529(QQ):AUTUMN71-462
H. SERGEANT, 175:SPRING71-26
LEVINE, D.H. CONFLICT AND POLITICAL
CHANGE IN VENEZUELA.
N. GALL, 453:15NOV73-29
LEVINE, E.B. HIPPOCRATES.
J.S. KIEFFER, 124:DEC71-137
LEVINE, G. THE BOUNDARIES OF FICTION.*
D.A. DOWNES, 636(VP):SPRING70-70
LEVINE, G. & W. MADDEN, EDS. THE ART OF
VICTORIAN PROSE.*
J.R. BENNFTT, 599:SPRING70-177
LEVINE, J.P. CREATION AND CRITICISM.*
K. ALLDRITT, 301(JEGP):OCT72-554
LEVINE, M. TUDOR DYNASTIC PROBLEMS
1460-1571.
617(TLS):26OCT73-1325
LEVINE, N. I DON'T WANT TO KNOW ANYONE
TOO WELL.*
D. STEPHENS, 102(CANL):AUTUMN72-84
LEVINE, P. PILI'S WALL.* RED DUST.
R. SCHRAMM, 651(WHR):AUTUMN72-389
LEVINE, P. THEY FEED THEY LION.*
R. LATTIMORE, 249(HUDR):AUTUMN72-475
J.C. OATES, 598(SOR):AUTUMN73-1014
R. SCHRAMM, 651(WHR):AUTUMN72-389
S. SPENDER, 453:20SEP73-8
LEVINE, R.A. BENJAMIN DISRAELI.*
J. ESPEY, 445(NCF):JUN70-122
LEVINSON, J. & J. DE ONÍS. THE ALLIANCE
THAT LOST ITS WAY.
639(VQR):SPRING71-LXXVIII
LEVINSON, M. THE TAXI GAME.
617(TLS):8JUN73-653
LEVIS, L. WRECKING CREW.
J. KESSLER, 491:FEB73-292

213

LIFTON, R.J. HOME FROM THE WAR.
   J.G. GRAY, 453:28JUN73-22
   C. LEHMANN-HAUPT, 441:6AUG73-29
   R. LOCKE, 441:24JUN73-23
   F. WEINSTEIN, 31(ASCH):AUTUMN73-696
   442(NY):20AUG73-90
LIKHACHEV, D.S., & OTHERS, EDS. RUSSKIE
PISATELI: BIOBIBLIOGRAFICHESKII SLO-
VAR'.
   V. SETCHKAREV, 32:DEC72-941
LILIENTHAL, D.E. THE JOURNALS OF DAVID
E. LILIENTHAL.* (VOL 5)
   J.M. BURNS, 639(VQR):AUTUMN71-629
LILIUS, H. DER PEKKATORI IN RAAHE.
   P. ZUCKER, 576:MAR70-68
LILLARD, C. CULTUS COULEE.
   J. DITSKY, 628:SPRING72-108
LILLIE, B., WITH J. PHILIP & J. BROUGH.
EVERY OTHER INCH A LADY.
   617(TLS):2FEB73-114
LILLY, J.C. THE CENTER OF THE CYCLONE.*
   617(TLS):9MAR73-277
LILLY, M. SICKERT.*
   P. ADAMS, 61:FEB73-103
LIMBOUR, G. CONTES ET RÉCITS.
   617(TLS):12OCT73-1243
LIMENTANI, A. - SEE VÄÄNÄNEN, V.
LIMMER, R. - SEE BOGAN, L.
LIN, J.C. MODERN CHINESE POETRY.
   617(TLS):9MAR73-270
LINCK, C.E., JR. EDGAR RYE, NORTH CEN-
TRAL TEXAS CARTOONIST AND JOURNALIST.
   W. GARD, 584(SWR):SUMMER72-V
LINCOLN, H.B., ED. THE COMPUTER AND
MUSIC.*
   R.F. ERICKSON, 317:SPRING72-102
LIND, G.R. WELTSPRACHE PORTUGIESISCH.
(2ND ED)
   J. PINTO NOVAIS, 430(NS):SEP71-503
LIND, J. ERGO.
   D.S. LOW, 220(GL&L):OCT71-55
LIND, J. NUMBERS.*
   D. MAHON, 362:15FEB73-217
   617(TLS):9MAR73-261
LIND, J. THE SILVER FOXES ARE DEAD AND
OTHER PLAYS.
   J.J. WHITE, 220(GL&L):OCT71-47
LINDBERG, C., ED. MS BODLEY 959.* (VOL
5)
   B. DANIELSSON, 597(SN):VOL42#2-498
   A. HUDSON, 541(RES):MAY71-178
LINDBERG, D.C., ED & TRANS. JOHN PECHAM
AND THE SCIENCE OF OPTICS.
   B.S. EASTWOOD, 589:APR72-322
LINDBERG, J.D. - SEE WEISE, C.
LINDBERG-SEYERSTED, B. THE VOICE OF THE
POET.
   D. DUNCAN, 179(ES):DEC71-562
   J.B. MEROD, 290(JAAC):SUMMER71-557
   J.E. TODD, 599:FALL71-319
LINDBERGH, A.M. HOUR OF GOLD, HOUR OF
LEAD.
   M. HENTOFF, 453:19APR73-3
   A. KAZIN, 441:4MAR73-1
   E. TENNANT, 362:24MAY73-694
   E. WEEKS, 61:APR73-124
   442(NY):14APR73-156
   617(TLS):29JUN73-735
LINDBERGH, C.A. THE WARTIME JOURNALS OF
CHARLES A. LINDBERGH.*
   H.E. BATEMAN, 50(ARQ):SUMMER71-174
   M. SYRKIN, 390:DEC70-50
   639(VQR):WINTER71-XXX
LINDEBOOM, G.A. HERMAN BOERHAAVE.
   R. JARVIS, 325:APR71-255
LINDEMANN, G. A HISTORY OF GERMAN ART.
   F. WHITFORD, 592:NOV71-216

LINDEMANN, G. PRINTS AND DRAWINGS.
   A. WERNER, 127:SPRING72-352
LINDEMANN, J.W.R. OLD ENGLISH PREVERBAL
"GE-."
   M.L. SAMUELS, 382(MAE):1972/3-289
   Z., 179(ES):JUN71-302
LINDEN, A.M., ED. LIVING IN THE SEVEN-
TIES.
   D.J. BELLAMY, 529(QQ):WINTER71-635
LINDO, H. LA INTEGRACIÓN CENTROAMERICANA
ANTE EL DERECHO INTERNACIONAL. (VOL 1)
   A. NARANJO VILLEGAS, 263:JUL-SEP72-287
LINDOP, A.E. JOURNEY INTO STONE.*
   617(TLS):13APR73-427
LINDSAY, I. & M. COSH. INVERARAY AND THE
DUKES OF ARGYLL.
   R. MITCHISON, 362:25OCT73-568
LINDSAY, I.G. GEORGIAN EDINBURGH. (2ND
ED REV BY D. WALKER)
   617(TLS):30NOV73-1485
LINDSAY, J. CLEOPATRA.
   J.M. BENARIO, 124:NOV71-98
   J.M. CARTER, 123:JUN72-249
   617(TLS):30NOV73-1471
LINDSAY, J. THE ORIGINS OF ALCHEMY IN
GRAECO-ROMAN EGYPT.*
   D. BARGRAVE-WEAVER, 313:VOL61-281
LINDSAY, J.M. GOTTFRIED KELLER.
   S. POWELL, 402(MLR):JAN72-224
   W.E. YUILL, 205(FMLS):OCT70-413
LINDSAY, M. ROBERT BURNS. (2ND ED)
   I. ROSS, 173(ECS):WINTER71/72-350
LINDSAY, M. LE TEMPS JAUNE.
   617(TLS):27JUL73-864
LINDSAY, R.O. & J. NEU, COMPS. FRENCH
POLITICAL PAMPHLETS 1547-1648.
   L. GERSHOY, 551(RENQ):SUMMER71-247
   B.L.O. RICHTER, 207(FR):APR71-947
LINDSAY, V. THE ART OF THE MOVING PIC-
TURE.
   D.W. COPE, 200:MAY70-292
LINEHAN, P. THE SPANISH CHURCH AND THE
PAPACY IN THE THIRTEENTH CENTURY.
   A. LUTTRELL, 382(MAE):1972/3-285
LINFERT, C. HIERONYMUS BOSCH.
   617(TLS):12JAN73-47
LING, K. THE REVENGE OF HEAVEN.* (I. &
M. LONDON, EDS)
   J.M. LALLEY, 396(MODA):SPRING72-194
LININGTON, E. CRIME BY CHANCE.
   N. CALLENDAR, 441:6MAY73-41
LINK, A.S. & OTHERS - SEE WILSON, W.
LINK, F.H., ED. AMERIKA - VISION UND
WIRKLICHKEIT.
   T. SENN, 447(N&Q):OCT71-391
LINK, F.H. AMERIKANISCHE LITERATURGE-
SCHICHTESSCHREIBUNG.
   R. ASSELINEAU, 189(EA):JAN-MAR71-105
LINK, F.H. EDGAR ALLAN POE.
   A. HELLER, 430(NS):JUN71-327
LINK, F.M. - SEE DRYDEN, J.
LINK, J. ARTISTISCHE FORM UND ÄSTHETIS-
CHER SINN IN PLATENS LYRIK.
   J.L. SAMMONS, 406:SUMMER72-189
LINK, W. DIE AMERIKANISCHE STABILISIER-
UNGSPOLITIK IN DEUTSCHLAND 1921-32.
   A. WAHL, 182:VOL24#1/2-50
LINKE, H. EPISCHE STRUKTUREN IN DER
DICHTUNG HARTMANNS VON AUE.*
   T. CRAMER, 190:BAND64HEFT1-115
   W. SCHULTE, 680(ZDP):BAND90HEFT1-115
LINKE, P-F. NIEDERGANGSERSCHEINUNGEN IN
DER PHILOSOPHIE DER GEGENWART.
   J. GRANIER, 542:OCT-DEC71-437
LINKLATER, E. THE VOYAGE OF THE CHALLEN-
GER.
   617(TLS):12JAN73-46

LINKUGEL, W.A. & D.M. BERG. A TIME TO
SPEAK, OR HOW TO PREPARE AND PRESENT
A SPEECH.
R. BREWER, 583:SPRING71-291
LINN, R.N. HEINRICH MANN.
K. SCHRÖTER, 222(GR):JAN71-83
LINSTRUM, D. SIR JEFFRY WYATVILLE.
617(TLS):23FEB73-203
LIONBERGER, H.F. & H.C. CHANG. FARM IN-
FORMATION FOR MODERNIZING AGRICULTURE.
Y-M. HO, 293(JAST):NOV70-187
LIOU, B. PRAETORES ETRURIAE XV POPU-
LORUM.*
A. ERNOUT, 555:VOL45FASC1-184
J-M. REYNOLDS, 123:MAR72-142
LIPKING, L. THE ORDERING OF THE ARTS IN
EIGHTEENTH-CENTURY ENGLAND.*
B.H. BRONSON, 401(MLQ):DEC71-440
D.V.E., 191(ELN):SEP71(SUPP)-15
E.R. MARKS, 141:SUMMER71-314
R. PAULSON, 191(ELN):MAR72-207
H. TROWBRIDGE, 173(ECS):WINTER71/72-
331
481(PQ):JUL71-388
639(VQR):AUTUMN71-CLXXXIV
LIPMAN, J. & OTHERS, COMPS. THE COLLEC-
TOR IN AMERICA.
E. LUCIE-SMITH, 592:JUL/AUG71-44
D. THOMAS, 135:NOV71-214
LIPMAN, M. DISCOVERING PHILOSOPHY.
L.G., 543:MAR71-544
LIPP, S. THREE ARGENTINE THINKERS.*
A. DONOSO, 258:DEC71-597
LIPPARD, L.R. CHANGING.
S.L. SCHWARTZ, 58:SEP/OCT71-16
LIPPMANN, H. HONECKER AND THE NEW
POLITICS OF EUROPE.
N. ASCHERSON, 453:8MAR73-31
617(TLS):18MAY73-549
LIPPOLD, E. ZUR FRAGE DER ÄSTHETISCHEN
INHALT-FORM-RELATIONEN IN DER MUSIK.
E. SAMS, 415:JUN72-566
LIPSCHITZ, J., WITH H.H. ARNASON. MY
LIFE IN SCULPTURE.*
617(TLS):9FEB73-149
LIPSCHUTZ, I.H. SPANISH PAINTING AND THE
FRENCH ROMANTICS.
617(TLS):29JUN73-742
LIPSMEIER, A. TECHNIK UND SCHULE.
W. GEORG, 182:VOL24#15/16-584
LIPSYTE, R. & S. CADY. SOMETHING GOING.
M. LEVIN, 441:20MAY73-54
LIPTZIN, S. THE MATURING OF YIDDISH LIT-
ERATURE.*
M. FRIEDBERG, 32:JUN72-514
LISCANO, J. EDAD OBSCURA.
A. PLANELLS, 37:OCT70-42
LISH, G., ED. THE SECRET OF OUR TIMES.
A. BROYARD, 441:10OCT73-39
LISHEV, S.N. BŬLGARSKIIAT SREDNOVEKOVEN
GRAD.
T. STOIANOVICH, 32:JUN72-500
DE L'ISLE-ADAM, P.A.M.D. - SEE UNDER DE
VILLIERS DE L'ISLE-ADAM, P.A.M.
LISNER, M. HOLZKRUZIFIXE IN FLORENZ UND
IN DER TOSKANA.
J. BALOGH, 683:BAND34HEFT4-300
LISSAGARAY, P-O. HISTOIRE DE LA COMMUNE
DE 1871.
P. AUBERY, 207(FR):FEB71-581
LISSITZKY, L. RUSSIA: AN ARCHITECTURE
FOR WORLD REVOLUTION.
45:MAR71-45
LISSITZKY-KÜPPERS, S. EL LISSITZKY.*
A.C. BIRNHOLZ, 56:SUMMER70-182

LISTER, R. ANTIQUE MAPS AND THEIR CAR-
TOGRAPHERS.
H.R. FRIIS, 14:JAN71-66
G. WILLS, 39:JUL71-79
LISTER, R. BRITISH ROMANTIC ART.
617(TLS):4MAY73-499
LISTER, R. SAMUEL PALMER AND HIS ETCH-
INGS.*
A.L. GRIFFIN, 637(VS):DEC70-213
A.S. ROE, 54:SEP71-421
LISTOWEL, J. AMIN.
617(TLS):26JAN73-82
"L'ITALIANISME EN FRANCE AU XVIIE
SIÈCLE."*
D. DALLA VALLE, 549(RLC):OCT-DEC70-
559
"L'ITALIANO SECONDO IL 'METODO NATURA'."
P. BORRANI CASTIGLIONE, 276:SUMMER71-
271
LITT, E. THE PUBLIC VOCATIONAL UNIVER-
SITY.
R.C. ELLSWORTH, 529(QQ):SUMMER71-340
LITTELL, B. THE DOLOROSA DEAL.
N. CALLENDAR, 441:26AUG73-33
617(TLS):9MAR73-257
LITTELL, R. THE DEFECTION OF A.J. LEWIN-
TER.
N. CALLENDAR, 441:4MAR73-42
C. LEHMANN-HAUPT, 441:15FEB73-45
"LITTÉRATURE ET SOCIÉTÉ."
J. DUBOIS, 556(RLV):1971/4-497
"LA LITTÉRATURE POTENTIELLE."
617(TLS):12OCT73-1256
LITTLE, R. SAINT-JOHN PERSE.
617(TLS):21DEC73-1562
LITTLE, R. - SEE PERSE, S-J.
LITTLE, S.W. & A. CANTOR. THE PLAY-
MAKERS.
J.R. TAYLOR, 157:AUTUMN71-76
LITTLEJOHN, J. SOCIAL STRATIFICATION.
617(TLS):9MAR73-271
LITTLEWOOD, C. THE WORLD'S VANISHING
BIRDS.
617(TLS):9FEB73-161
LITTRELL, D. A PERFECTLY NATURAL ACT.
M. LEVIN, 441:16SEP73-32
LITVINOFF, E. A DEATH OUT OF SEASON.
V. CUNNINGHAM, 362:31MAY73-728
617(TLS):29JUN73-736
LITVINOV, I. HIS MASTER'S VOICE.
617(TLS):16NOV73-1407
LITWAK, L. WAITING FOR THE NEWS.
B. ROSENBERG, 390:MAY70-78
LITZ, A.W. JANE AUSTEN.
J. DELBAERE-GARANT, 556(RLV):1970/1-
103
LITZ, A.W., ED. ELIOT IN HIS TIME.
441:7OCT73-20
LITZ, A.W. INTROSPECTIVE VOYAGER.
F. LENTRICCHIA, 659:SPRING73-247
LITZINGER, B. & D. SMALLEY, EDS. BROWN-
ING: THE CRITICAL HERITAGE.
K.L. KNICKERBOCKER, 85:SPRING71-46
LIU SHIH-HONG. CHINESE CHARACTERS AND
THEIR IMPACT ON OTHER LANGUAGES OF
EAST ASIA.
W.S-Y. WANG, 399(MLJ):MAR71-187
LIUDVIG, G.M., ED. OCHERKI ISTORII
STROITELNOI TEKHNIKI ROSSI XIX-NACHALA
XX VV.
S.F. STARR, 576:MAY71-172
LIVEANU, V. & OTHERS. RELAȚII AGRARE ȘI
MIȘCĂRI ȚĂRĂNEȘTI ÎN ROMÂNIA, 1908-1921.
P. EIDELBERG, 32:JUN72-487
LIVERMORE, A. A SHORT HISTORY OF SPANISH
MUSIC.
L. SALTER, 415:DEC72-1185

LIVERMORE, H.V. PORTUGAL.
617(TLS):27JUL73-867
"LIVERPUDLIAN OR WHAT IS WHO CALLED
WHERE?!"
E.C. SMITH, 424:SEP71-218
LIVERSEDGE, R. RECOLLECTIONS OF THE ON
TO OTTAWA TREK. (V. HOAR, ED)
D. ORLIKOW, 99:NOV-DEC73-22
LIVERSIDGE, J. BRITAIN IN THE ROMAN
EMPIRE.
R. HIGGINS, 39:AUG71-162
LIVESAY, D. COLLECTED POEMS - THE TWO
SEASONS. NINE POEMS OF FAREWELL -
1972-1973.
B. MITCHELL, 198:FALL73-96
LIVESAY, D. A WINNIPEG CHILDHOOD.
J.R., 606(TAMR):#61-76
LIVINGS, H. PONGO PLAYS 1-6.
A. RENDLE, 157:SUMMER71-82
LIVINGSTON, B. THEIR TURF.
G.F.T. RYALL, 441:2DEC73-91
LIVINGSTON, G. EXILE'S END.
617(TLS):7SEP73-1018
LIVINGSTONE, D. EYES CLOSED AGAINST THE
SUN.
E. NÍ CHUILLEANÁIN, 159(DM):WINTER
70/71-124
R.S., 376:JUL70-125
LIVINGSTONE, I. & OTHERS, EDS. THE
TEACHING OF ECONOMICS IN AFRICA.
617(TLS):16MAR73-291
LIVINGSTONE, R. - SEE LUKÁCS, G.
LIVNEH, E. AHARON ARONSOHN.
S.Z. ABRAMOV, 390:JAN70-72
LIVOCK, G.E. TO THE ENDS OF THE AIR.
617(TLS):31AUG73-1009
LIVY. TITUS LIVIUS, "AB URBE CONDITA."
(VOL 1) (C.J. WITTLIN, ED)
W. ROTHWELL, 208(FS):APR72-248
M. SANDMANN, 545(RPH):NOV71-257
LIZZANI, G. IL MOBILE ROMANO.
P. THORNTON, 39:OCT71-320
LLEÓ, C. PROBLEMS OF CATALAN PHONOLOGY.
P. RUSSELL-GEBBETT, 86(BHS):JUL72-320
LLEWELLYN, P. ROME IN THE DARK AGES.
R. SCHUMANN, 589:APR72-326
LLOSA, M.V. - SEE UNDER VARGAS LLOSA, M.
LLOYD, A. KING JOHN.
617(TLS):15JUN73-699
LLOYD, A. THE ZULU WAR, 1879.
617(TLS):26OCT73-1325
LLOYD, A.L., ED. DER MÜNCHENER PSALTER
DES 14. JAHRHUNDERTS.*
D.E. LE SAGE, 402(MLR):JUL72-687
LLOYD, C. MR. BARROW OF THE ADMIRALTY.
C.J. BARTLETT, 637(VS):MAR71-347
LLOYD, C. FOLIAGE PLANTS.
617(TLS):6APR73-401
LLOYD, C. NELSON AND SEA POWER.
617(TLS):8JUN73-653
LLOYD, C. THE NILE CAMPAIGN.
617(TLS):17AUG73-961
LLOYD, C. THE SEARCH FOR THE NIGER.
617(TLS):4MAY73-493
LLOYD, G.E.R. ARISTOTLE: THE GROWTH AND
STRUCTURE OF HIS THOUGHT.*
R.J. CHAMBERLAIN, 480(P&R):SUMMER71-
195
LLOYD, G.E.R. GREEK SCIENCE AFTER ARIS-
TOTLE.
617(TLS):13JUL73-815
LLOYD, M. THE BORZOI BOOK OF MODERN
DANCE.
A. PAGE, 290(JAAC):SUMMER71-552
LLOYD, P.M. VERB-COMPLEMENT COMPOUNDS IN
SPANISH.
J.R. CRADDOCK, 545(RPH):MAY72-437
J.D.W. SCHROTEN, 433:JUL70-311

LLOYD, T.H. THE MOVEMENT OF WOOL PRICES
IN MEDIEVAL ENGLAND.
617(TLS):18MAY73-561
LLOYD-JONES, H. THE JUSTICE OF ZEUS.*
W.R. CONNOR, 124:MAR72-233
F. LASSERRE, 182:VOL24#23/24-878
LLOYD-JONES, H. - SEE AESCHYLUS
LLOYD GEORGE, D. FAMILY LETTERS 1885-
1936. (K.O. MORGAN, ED)
J. GRIGG, 362:8MAR73-314
617(TLS):6APR73-367
LOBEL, E., ED. THE OXYRHYNCHUS PAPYRI.
(VOL 35)
L.W. DALY, 24:APR72-374
LOBELL, J. & M. JOHN & MIMI.
B. DE MOTT, 61:DEC73-125
LOBET, M. LE FEU DU CIEL.
S. MAX, 207:OCT70-254
LOBO, J. ITINERÁRIO E OUTROS ESCRITOS
INÉDITOS. (M. GONÇALVES DA COSTA, C.F.
BECKINGHAM & D.M. LOCKHART)
617(TLS):12JAN73-48
LO CASTRO, A. DANTE E LA SOCIETÀ.
M. HERNÁNDEZ ESTEBAN, 202(FMOD):JUN
70-346
LOCHER, G.W. HULDRYCH ZWINGLI IN NEUER
SICHT.
E-W. KOHLS, 182:VOL24#4-137
LOCHER, K.T. GOTTFRIED KELLER.*
E.A. MC CORMICK, 221(GQ):MAY71-387
S. POWELL, 402(MLR):JUL72-704
B.G. THOMAS, 400(MLN):OCT71-738
LOCHHEAD, D., COMP. BIBLIOGRAPHY OF CAN-
ADIAN BIBLIOGRAPHIES/BIBLIOGRAPHIE DES
BIBLIOGRAPHIES CANADIENNES. (2ND ED)
J.R. SORFLEET, 296:SPRING73-94
LOCKE, D. MEMORY.
E.J. FURLONG, 518:JAN72-19
LOCKE, D. PERCEPTION AND OUR KNOWLEDGE
OF THE EXTERNAL WORLD.*
D.D. TODD, 154:JUN71-353
LOCKE, J. SOME THOUGHTS CONCERNING EDU-
CATION 1693.
J.R. CLARK, 568(SCN):SPRING72-4
LOCKHART, H. ON MY WAVELENGTH.
617(TLS):18MAY73-565
LOCKHART, R.B. THE DIARIES OF SIR ROBERT
BRUCE LOCKHART. (VOL 1) (K. YOUNG, ED)
J. VINCENT, 362:22NOV73-708
617(TLS):7DEC73-1509
LOCKRIDGE, R. WRITE MURDER DOWN.*
N. CALLENDAR, 441:7JAN73-35
LOCKSPEISER, E. MUSIC AND PAINTING.
617(TLS):4MAY73-505
LOCKWOOD, W.B. HISTORICAL GERMAN SYNTAX.*
H. KUHN, 402(MLR):APR72-450
LOCKWOOD, W.B. INDO-EUROPEAN PHILOLOGY.*
V. MAŽIULIS, 215(GL):VOL10#3-193
LODGE, D. THE NOVELIST AT THE CROSS-
ROADS.*
A.J. HANSEN, 454:SPRING72-263
P. PARRINDER, 402(MLR):OCT72-878
LODGE, D. THE PICTUREGOERS. THE BRITISH
MUSEUM IS FALLING DOWN. OUT OF THE
SHELTER. GINGER, YOU'RE BARMY.
P. HONAN, 454:WINTER72-167
LODGE, D. - SEE ELIOT, G.
LODGE, H.C. THE STORM HAS MANY EYES.
M.F. NOLAN, 441:13MAY73-19
LODGE, T. THE WOUNDS OF THE CIVIL WAR.
(J.W. HOUPPERT, ED)
E. CUVELIER, 189(EA):JUL-SEP71-324
LOEWENBERG, B.J. AMERICAN HISTORY IN
AMERICAN THOUGHT.*
R.B. NYE, 27(AL):NOV72-523
LOEWINSOHN, R. MEAT AIR.*
W. HENKIN, 600:FALL70-123

LOPEZ, R.S. THE THREE AGES OF THE ITAL-
IAN RENAISSANCE.
T.G. BERGIN, 551(RENQ):SUMMER71-232
639(VQR):WINTER71-XXXIX
LÓPEZ ESTRADA, F. RUBÉN DARÍO Y LA EDAD
MEDIA.
A.S. TRUEBLOOD, 402(MLR):OCT72-929
L'ORANGE, H.P. LIKENESS AND ICON.
617(TLS):21SEP73-1077
LORD, E. & C. BAILEY, EDS. A READER IN
RELIGIOUS AND MORAL EDUCATION.
617(TLS):13JUL73-814
LORD, G. A ROOF UNDER YOUR FEET.
617(TLS):26OCT73-1324
LORD, P.S. & D.J. FOLEY. EASTER THE
WORLD OVER.
M.A. KRAL, 363:AUG71-120
LORD, R.T. DOSTOEVSKY.*
R.A. GREGG, 550(RUSR):JAN71-78
LORD, W. THE DAWN'S EARLY LIGHT.*
617(TLS):19JAN73-70
"CLAUDIO LORENESE: DISEGNI, SCELTI E
ANNOTATI DA MARCO CHIARINI."
M. RÖTHLISBERGER, 54:MAR70-105
LORENTZ, H.A. A VIEW OF CHINESE RUGS
FROM THE SEVENTEENTH TO THE TWENTIETH
CENTURY.
617(TLS):2MAR73-237
LORENZ, G.W. MIGUEL ÁNGEL ASTURIAS.
M. FRANZBACH, 430(NS):SEP71-502
LORENZ, R. MAX HERRMANN-NEISSE.
B. MOGRIDGE, 220(GL&L):JAN72-162
LORENZ, R., ED. PROLETARISCHE KULTUR-
REVOLUTION IN SOWJETRUSSLAND (1917-
1921).
A.C. BIRNHOLZ, 127:SUMMER72-478
DE LORENZI, A. FONTI DI OMERO.
F.M. COMBELLACK, 122:JAN72-73
LORENZO, C.M. LES ANARCHISTES ESPAGNOLS
ET LE POUVOIR.
J. GEORGEL, 98:MAY71-460
LORIAUX, R., ED & TRANS. LE "PHÉDON" DE
PLATON.* (VOL 1)
P. LOUIS, 555:VOL45FASC1-153
LORIMER, J. & M. PHILLIPS. WORKING PEO-
PLE.
H. GARNER, 606(TAMR):#58-72
LORIOT, R. LA FRONTIÈRE DIALECTALE
MODERNE EN HAUTE-NORMANDIE.
J. CHAURAND, 209(FM):JAN70-66
"LA LORRAINE DANS L'EUROPE DES LUMIÈRES."
D-H. PAGEAUX, 549(RLC):JAN-MAR70-132
L. VERSINI, 535(RHL):JAN-FEB70-129
DE LORRIS, G. - SEE UNDER GUILLAUME DE
LORRIS
DE LORRIS, G. & JEAN DE MEUN - SEE UNDER
GUILLAUME DE LORRIS & JEAN DE MEUN
LOSEE, J. A HISTORICAL INTRODUCTION TO
THE PHILOSOPHY OF SCIENCE.
617(TLS):27APR73-482
LÖSEL, F. A SHORT OLD HIGH GERMAN GRAM-
MAR AND READER WITH GLOSSARY.
K. DENNER, 220(GL&L):OCT71-16
D.E. LE SAGE, 402(MLR):JUL72-680
205(FMLS):OCT70-421
LOTHIAN, J.M. - SEE SMITH, A.
LOTMAN, I.M. STRUKTURA KHUDOZHESTVENNOGO
TEKSTA.
A. SHUKMAN, 402(MLR):JUL72-713
R.L. BELKNAP, 32:DEC72-946
LOTT, R.E. LANGUAGE AND PSYCHOLOGY IN
"PEPITA JIMÉNEZ."
R.F. BROWN, 402(MLR):JUL72-678
LOTTIN, A. VIE ET MENTALITÉ D'UN LILLOIS
SOUS LOUIS XIV.
M. SORIANO, 557(RSH):JUL-SEP71-471

"LORENZO LOTTO: IL 'LIBRO DI SPESE DI-
VERSE' (1538-1556)."* (P. ZAMPETTI,
ED)
C.E. GILBERT, 551(RENQ):SPRING71-71
D. ROSAND, 54:SEP71-407
LOUGH, J. THE CONTRIBUTORS TO THE "EN-
CYCLOPÉDIE."
617(TLS):6JUL73-789
LOUGH, J. "ENCYCLOPÉDIE" IN EIGHT-
EENTH CENTURY ENGLAND AND OTHER STUD-
IES.
A.W. FAIRBAIRN, 402(MLR):APR72-417
J. GURY, 549(RLC):JUL-SEP71-423
J. MAYER, 557(RSH):JUL-SEP71-480
G.A. PERLA, 173(ECS):SUMMER72-619
LOUGH, J. ESSAYS ON THE "ENCYCLOPÉDIE"
OF DIDEROT AND D'ALEMBERT.*
H. DIECKMANN, 405(MP):NOV70-206
S.S.B. TAYLOR, 205(FMLS):OCT70-346
LOUIS XIV. MÉMOIRES FOR THE INSTRUCTION
OF THE DAUPHIN. (P. SONNINO, ED &
TRANS)
J. LOUGH, 208(FS):JUL72-332
LOUKOTKA, Č. CLASSIFICATION OF SOUTH
AMERICAN INDIAN LANGUAGES. (J. WILBERT,
ED)
Z. SALZMANN, 269(IJAL):JAN70-70
L.M. WISTRAND, 353:NOV71-106
LOURIA, Y. LA CONVERGENCE STYLISTIQUE
CHEZ PROUST.
617(TLS):13APR73-423
LOVE, E.G. A SMALL BEQUEST.
G. BURNSIDE, 441:18NOV73-46
LOVE, J.L. RIO GRANDE DO SUL AND BRAZIL-
IAN REGIONALISM, 1882-1930.
D. CARNEIRO, 263:JUL-SEP72-285
LOVE, J.O. WORLDS IN CONSCIOUSNESS.*
D.L. HIGDON, 594:SPRING71-108
C. OHMANN, 659:SPRING73-260
LOVEJOY, D.S., ED. RELIGIOUS ENTHUSIASM
AND THE GREAT AWAKENING.*
H.R. CEDERBERG, 481(PQ):JUL71-359
E.S. GAUSTAD, 656(WMQ):APR71-315
LOVELL, E.J., JR. - SEE LADY BLESSINGTON
LOVELOCK, Y. THE VEGETABLE BOOK.
617(TLS):5JAN73-22
LOVELUCK, J., ED. LA NOVELA HISPANOAMERI-
CANA.
H.F. GIACOMAN, 238:MAR71-201
LOVESEY, P. MAD HATTER'S HOLIDAY.
N. CALLENDAR, 441:30SEP73-18
617(TLS):15JUN73-697
LOVINS, A.B. OPENPIT MINING.
617(TLS):19OCT73-1287
LOVY, C.W. SILHOUETTE DE LA FRANCE.
R-M. DAELE-GUINAN, 207(FR):FEB71-588
LOW, A. AUGUSTINE BAKER.*
P. THEINER, 72:BAND209HEFT4/6-402
LOW, D. "WITH ALL FAULTS."
617(TLS):30MAR73-360
LOW, D.A., J.C. ILTIS & M.D. WAINWRIGHT,
EDS. GOVERNMENT ARCHIVES IN SOUTH
ASIA.*
E. BENDER, 318(JAOS):JAN-MAR71-162
D.N. MARSHALL, 182:VOL24#13/14-517
B.R. MASTERS, 325:APR71-250
LOWBURY, E., T. SALTER & A. YOUNG. THOMAS
CAMPION.*
J.P. CUTTS, 551(RENQ):AUTUMN71-404
LOWDEN, D. THE BOONDOCKS.
N. CALLENDAR, 441:29APR73-28
LOWELL, R. THE DOLPHIN. FOR LIZZIE AND
HARRIET. HISTORY.
C. BEDIENT, 441:29JUL73-15
A. BROYARD, 441:18JUN73-27
C. RICKS, 362:21JUN73-830
617(TLS):10AUG73-917

LOWELL, R. NOTEBOOK.* (NEW ED)
A. CLUYSENAAR, 565:VOL12#3-72
H. SERGEANT, 175:SUMMER71-65
G. WILLIS, 493:SUMMER71-196
LOWELL, R. NOTEBOOK 1967-68.*
G. WILLIS, 493:SUMMER71-196
LOWELL, R. PROMETHEUS BOUND.
A. RENDLE, 157:SUMMER70-75
LOWENFELS, W., ED. THE WRITING ON THE
WALL.*
K. CONGDON, 37:OCT70-41
LOWENFELS, W. - SEE WHITMAN, W.
LOWENS, I. MUSIC AND MUSICIANS IN EARLY
AMERICA.
M. PETERSON, 470:JAN66-44
LÖWENSTEIN, K. DAS LYRISCHE WERK. (J.
WAGNER, ED)
F. USINGER, 182:VOL24#21/22-793
LOWRY, J. TIBETAN ART.
617(TLS):8JUN73-653
LOWRY, M. OCTOBER FERRY TO GABRIOLA.*
(M. LOWRY, ED)
P. DELANEY, 648:JUN71-51
639(VQR):SPRING71-LVI
LOY, J.R. MONTESQUIEU.*
G. BENREKASSA, 535(RHL):JAN-FEB70-128
LOYEN, A. - SEE SIDONIUS
LOYER, O. LES CHRÉTIENTÉS CELTIQUES.
H. NEWSTEAD, 545(RPH):AUG71-126
LOYOLA, H. - SEE NERUDA, P.
LOZADA, A. EL MONISMO AGÓNICO DE PABLO
NERUDA.
617(TLS):11MAY73-532
LU, F-P. T.S. ELIOT.
K. SMIDT, 72:BAND209HEFT4/6-419
LUBBERS, K. EMILY DICKINSON.*
M. HOLTON, 399(MLJ):OCT71-414
LUBBERS, K. EINFÜHRUNG IN DAS STUDIUM
DER AMERIKANISTIK.
M. SCHULZE, 72:BAND209HEFT4/6-429
LUBIN, C.K. LANGUAGE DISTURBANCE AND
INTELLECTUAL FUNCTIONING.
E.H. LENNEBERG, 353:MAR71-113
B.T. TERVOORT, 361:VOL26#1-111
LUBIN, G., ED. ALBUM SAND.
617(TLS):30NOV73-1478
LUBIN, G. - SEE SAND, G.
LUCAS, A., ED. GREAT CANADIAN SHORT
STORIES.
G. STOW, 296:WINTER73-102
LUCAS, A. HUGH MAC LENNAN.*
B. NESBITT, 648:JAN71-68
LUCAS, C. THE STRUCTURE OF THE TERROR.
617(TLS):26OCT73-1320
LUCAS, J., ED. LITERATURE AND POLITICS
IN THE NINETEENTH CENTURY.*
J. SEARLE, 111:19NOV71-54
LUCAS, J. THE MELANCHOLY MAN.
K.J. FIELDING, 155:MAY71-115
S. MONOD, 189(EA):JAN-MAR71-97
K. MUIR, 402(MLR):APR72-405
G. THOMAS, 175:SPRING71-25
S. WALL, 184(EIC):JUL71-261
LUCAS, J. & N. DUPLAIX-HALL, WITH R.
BIÉGLER, EDS. INTERNATIONAL ZOO YEAR-
BOOK. (VOL 12)
617(TLS):9MAR73-262
LUCAS, J.R. THE FREEDOM OF THE WILL.*
A. FLEW, 479(PHQ):OCT71-378
M.D.P., 543:JUN71-748
LUCAS, J.R. A TREATISE ON TIME AND
SPACE.
617(TLS):29JUN73-753
LUCAS, R. FRIEDA LAWRENCE.
P. ADAMS, 61:SEP73-118
J. CAREY, 362:7JUN73-759
441:16SEP73-14
617(TLS):15JUN73-660

LUCAS PHILLIPS, C.E. VICTORIA CROSS
BATTLES OF THE SECOND WORLD WAR.
617(TLS):23NOV73-1423
LUCE, G.H. OLD BURMA - EARLY PAGÁN.
J.T. BAILEY, 57:VOL33#3-233
LUCIAN. LUCIEN, "LE NAVIRE OU LES SOU-
HAITS."* (G. HUSSON, ED & TRANS)
M.D. MACLEOD, 123:DEC72-411
LUCID, R.F., ED. NORMAN MAILER.*
J.E. MULLIN, 385(MQR):FALL73-370
LUCID, R.F. - SEE MAILER, N.
LUCIE-SMITH, E., ED. BRITISH POETRY
SINCE 1945.
T. EAGLETON, 565:VOL12#2-59
G. MELLY, 493:SPRING71-77
LUCIE-SMITH, E. MOVEMENTS IN ART SINCE
1945.*
D. IRWIN, 39:MAR70-248
LUCIE-SMITH, E., ED. PRIMER OF EXPERI-
MENTAL POETRY 1, 1870-1922.
A. CLUYSENAAR, 565:VOL12#4-68
LUCIE-SMITH, E. & P. WHITE. ART IN
BRITAIN 1969-70.*
T. HILTON, 592:JUL-AUG70-58
DE LUCIO-MEYER, J.J. VISUAL AESTHETICS.
617(TLS):7DEC73-1502
LUCK, G. UNTERSUCHUNGEN ZUR TEXTGE-
SCHICHTE OVIDS.*
R.P. OLIVER, 121(CJ):APR-MAY72-372
LUCK, R. GOTTFRIED KELLER ALS LITERATUR-
KRITIKER.
H. LAUFHÜTTE, 680(ZDP):BAND90HEFT4-
608
V. LEMKE, 406:SPRING72-89
S. MEWS, 301(JEGP):JAN72-81
LÜCKE, T. - SEE DIDEROT, D.
LUCKETT, R. THE WHITE GENERALS.*
J.F.N. BRADLEY, 575(SEER):JUL72-469
P. KENEZ, 32:JUN72-424
LUCRETIUS. DE RERUM NATURA. (BK 3)
(E.J. KENNEY, ED)
V.J. CLEARY, 124:MAR72-235
LUCRETIUS. ON THE NATURE OF THINGS.*
(M.F. SMITH, TRANS)
P.M. BROWN, 123:MAR72-32
LUCRETIUS. THE WAY THINGS ARE.* (R.
HUMPHRIES, TRANS; NOTES BY G.K. STRO-
DACH)
D.L. SIGSBEE, 121(CJ):DEC71/JAN72-181
LUDAT, H. AN ELBE UND ODER UM DAS JAHR
1000.
F.L. CARSTEN, 575(SEER):JUL72-459
R. FOLZ, 182:VOL24#9/10-436
LÜDERS, D., ED. JAHRBUCH DES FREIEN
DEUTSCHEN HOCHSTIFTS 1969.
H.S. DAEMMRICH, 222(GR):MAY71-234
I.F., 191(ELN):SEP71(SUPP)-125
LUDEWIG, W. LEXIKON DER DEUTSCHEN SPRACH-
LEHRE.
H. WELLMANN, 657(WW):JUL/AUG70-271
LUDINGTON, T. - SEE DOS PASSOS, J.
LUDLUM, R. THE MATLOCK PAPER.
N. CALLENDAR, 441:6MAY73-41
617(TLS):3AUG73-911
LÜDTKE, G., ED. THE ERL OF TOLOUS AND
THE EMPERES OF ALMAYN.
E.G. STANLEY, 72:BAND209HEFT4/6-399
LUDWIG, C. MAXFIELD PARRISH.
P. ADAMS, 61:DEC73-138
L. NOCHLIN, 441:2DEC73-50
LUDWIG, J. A WOMAN OF HER AGE.
I.M.O., 606(TAMR):#61-76
LUDWIG, W. - SEE HARMONIUS
LUDZ, P.C. THE CHANGING PARTY ELITE IN
EAST GERMANY.
N. ASCHERSON, 453:8MAR73-31
617(TLS):28DEC73-1592

LUGNANI, L. PIRANDELLO.
   O. RAGUSA, 276:WINTER71-505
DE LUIS, L., ED. POESÍA RELIGIOSA.
   A. TERRY, 86(BHS):JAN72-96
LUKÁCS, G. HISTORY AND CLASS CONSCIOUS-
   NESS.*
   42(AR):FALL71-443
LUKÁCS, G. POLITICAL WRITINGS 1919-
   1929. (R. LIVINGSTONE, ED)
   617(TLS):5OCT73-1183
LUKÁCS, G. LA THÉORIE DU ROMAN.
   S. LOTRINGER, 98:JUN70-498
LUKAS, J. STUDIEN ZUR SPRACHE DER GISIGA
   (NORDKAMERUN).
   A.N. TUCKER, 315(JAL):VOL10PT2-60
LUKASHEVICH, S. KONSTANTIN LEONTEV
   (1831-1891).
   A. KLIMOV, 154:JUN71-410
ŁUKASIEWICZ, J. DIPLOMAT IN PARIS, 1936-
   1939.* (W. JEDRZEJEWICZ, ED)
   L. BUSHKOFF, 497(POLR):WINTER71-118
ŁUKASIEWICZ, J. SELECTED WORKS. (L.
   BORKOWSKI, ED)
   C. LEJEWSKI, 311(JP):8FEB73-81
LUKE, M.M. GLORIANA.
   P. ADAMS, 61:DEC73-138
LUKES, S. ÉMILE DURKHEIM.
   P. ROSENBERG, 441:15JUL73-21
   A. RYAN, 362:22MAR73-383
   617(TLS):16MAR73-281
LUKES, S. INDIVIDUALISM.
   J. DUNN, 362:20DEC73-860
   617(TLS):13JUL73-804
LULOFS, H.J.D. - SEE UNDER DROSSAART
   LULOFS, H.J.
LULLUS, R. QUATTUOR LIBRI PRINCIPIORUM.
   J.N. HILLGARTH, 86(BHS):JAN72-100
LUMIANSKY, R.M. & H. BAKER, EDS. CRITI-
   CAL APPROACHES TO SIX MAJOR ENGLISH
   WORKS.*
   P.A. JORGENSEN, 570(SQ):SPRING71-174
LUMLEY, R. WHITE-COLLAR UNIONISM IN
   BRITAIN.
   617(TLS):18MAY73-565
LUMPP, H-M. PHILOLOGIA CRUCIS.
   J.C. O'FLAHERTY, 182:VOL24#17/18-676
LUMUMBA, P. LUMUMBA SPEAKS. (J. VAN
   LIERDE, ED)
   C. HOSKYNS, 453:5APR73-8
DE LUNA, B.N. THE QUEEN DECLINED.*
   J. APTEKAR, 551(RENQ):WINTER71-560
   R.M. CUMMINGS, 447(N&Q):AUG71-319
LUNN, J.E. & U. VAUGHAN WILLIAMS. RALPH
   VAUGHAN WILLIAMS.*
   H. OTTAWAY, 415:FEB72-154
   J-A.W., 410(M&L):JUL72-337
LUNT, H.G., ED. HARVARD SLAVIC STUDIES.*
   (VOL 5)
   C. BRYNER, 550(RUSR):JAN71-95
DE LUPPÉ, R. - SEE "MADAME DE STAËL ET
   J-B-A. SUARD, CORRESPONDANCE INÉDITE
   (1786-1817)"
LUPSA, M., ED & TRANS. CHANTS À KĀLĪ DE
   RĀMPRASĀD.
   O. VON HINÜBER, 182:VOL24#23/24-870
LURIA, A.R. THE MAN WITH A SHATTERED
   WORLD.
   O. SACKS, 362:28JUN73-870
LURIA, A.R. TRAUMATIC APHASIA.
   N. GESCHWIND, 350:SEP72-755
LUSTIG, A. A PRAYER FOR KATERINA HORO-
   VITZOVA.
   M. LEVIN, 441:21OCT73-51
LÜTCKE, K-H. "AUCTORITAS" BEI AUGUSTIN,
   MIT EINER EINLEITUNG ZUR RÖMISCHEN
   VORGESCHICHTE DES BEGRIFFS.
   H. CHADWICK, 123:MAR72-116

LÜTHI, H.J. HERMANN HESSE.
   A. HSIA, 221(GQ):MAR71-250
LÜTOLF, M. DIE MEHRSTIMMIGEN ORDINARIUM
   MISSAE-SÄTZE VOM AUSGEHENDEN 11. BIS
   ZUR WENDE DES 13. ZUM 14. JAHRHUNDERT.
   G.A. ANDERSON, 414(MQ):OCT71-665
LÜTT, J. HINDU-NATIONALISMUS IN UTTAR
   PRADÉS, 1867-1900.
   W. MAAS, 182:VOL24#5-249
LUTTRELL, N. THE PARLIAMENTARY DIARY OF
   NARCISSUS LUTTRELL, 1691-1693. (H.
   HORWITZ, ED)
   617(TLS):18MAY73-561
LUTYENS, E. A GOLDFISH BOWL.
   617(TLS):2FEB73-114
LUTYENS, M. CLEO.
   617(TLS):23NOV73-1455
LUTZ, F.A. ZINSTHEORIE. (2ND ED)
   A. HÜFNER, 182:VOL24#11/12-470
LÜTZELER, P.M. - SEE BROCH, H.
VON LÜTZOW, H. IM DIPLOMATISCHEN DIENST
   DER K.U.K. MONARCHIE.* (P. HOHENBALKEN,
   ED)
   F.R. BRIDGE, 575(SEER):JUL72-488
LUXEMBURG, R. & N. BUKHARIN. IMPERIALISM
   AND THE ACCUMULATION OF CAPITAL. (K.J.
   TARBUCK, ED; R. WICHMANN, TRANS)
   617(TLS):12JAN73-45
LUXENBURG, N. - SEE SKRJABINA, E.
LWOFF, A. L'ORDRE BIOLOGIQUE.
   M. SERRES, 98:JUN71-483
LYALL, A. THE COMPANION GUIDE TO TUS-
   CANY.
   617(TLS):25MAY73-583
LYALL, G. BLAME THE DEAD.*
   P. ADAMS, 61:JUN73-123
   N. CALLENDAR, 441:24JUN73-32
"LYBEAUS DESCONUS."* (M. MILLS, ED)
   A.J. BLISS, 597(SN):VOL42#2-491
   D. MEHL, 38:BAND89HEFT4-534
   F.C. DE VRIES, 541(RES):FEB71-67
LYCAN, G.L. ALEXANDER HAMILTON & AMERI-
   CAN FOREIGN POLICY.
   J.A. COMBS, 656(WMQ):JUL71-513
LYDGATE, J. JOHN LYDGATE: POEMS. (J.
   NORTON-SMITH, ED)
   H. QUISTORP, 38:BAND88HEFT2-258
LYDON, J. & M. MAC CURTAIN, EDS. THE
   GILL HISTORY OF IRELAND.
   J. VINCENT, 362:6SEP73-315
LYNAM, E.W. THE IRISH CHARACTER IN
   PRINT 1571-1923.
   R. CAVE, 503:SPRING70-40
LYNAM, R., ED. COUTURE.* (BRITISH
   TITLE: PARIS FASHION.)
   P. ADAMS, 61:FEB73-103
LYNCH, K. WHAT TIME IS THIS PLACE?
   R-F. LUCID, 31(ASCH):SPRING73-336
LYNCH, K.M. JACOB TONSON.
   F.B. WILLIAMS, JR., 517(PBSA):JUL-SEP
   72-337
   C. WINTON, 579(SAQ):SUMMER72-453
   639(VQR):AUTUMN71-CLXXIV
LYNEN, J.F. THE DESIGN OF THE PRESENT.
   R.H. FOGLE, 445(NCF):JUN70-109
   J.K. ROBINSON, 598(SOR):SUMMER73-692
   B. ST. ARMAND, 454:WINTER72-162
LYNES, R. GOOD OLD MODERN.
   G. GLUECK, 441:24JUN73-1
   H. KRAMER, 441:2JUL73-25
   442(NY):30JUL73-72
LYNGSTAD, A. & S. IVAN GONCHAROV.
   M. EHRE, 32:DEC72-937
LYNN, K.S. WILLIAM DEAN HOWELLS.*
   E.H. CADY, 639(VQR):SUMMER71-474
   M. FELLMAN, 651(WHR):SUMMER72-287
   F. TURAJ, 579(SAQ):SUMMER72-446

LYNN, R. PERSONALITY AND NATIONAL CHAR-
ACTER.
H.J. EYSENCK, 619(TC):VOL179#1049-55
LYON, J.K. & C. INGLIS. KONKORDANZ ZUR
LYRIK GOTTFRIED BENNS.
R.E. LORBE, 301(JEGP):OCT72-596
LYON, M. SYMBOL AND IDEA IN HENRY ADAMS.*
R. LEHAN, 445(NCF):SEP71-245
LYONS, C.R. BERTOLT BRECHT.
L. DESVIGNES, 549(RLC):OCT-DEC70-584
C. HILL, 397(MD):MAY70-103
U. WEISSTEIN, 400(MLN):APR71-440
LYONS, D. FORMS AND LIMITS OF UTILITAR-
IANISM.
R.P. BLUM, 321:SUMMER70-140
LYONS, E. PORTRAIT OF A SUMMER VIRGIN.
J.R. FRAKES, 441:16SEP73-5
LYONS, J. NOAM CHOMSKY.*
H.M. BRACKEN, 154:DEC71-808
D. HYMES, 350:NOV71-416
G. SCHELSTRAETE, 75:3/1971-45
LYONS, J. INTRODUCTION TO THEORETICAL
LINGUISTICS.*
O. AKHMANOVA, 353:NOV71-93
C.E. BAZELL, 47(ARL):[N.S.]VOL2-151
H. GECKELER, 490:JUL/OCT70-594
H.M. HOENIGSWALD, 318(JAOS):OCT-DEC71-
564
D.T. LANGENDOEN, 269(IJAL):JAN70-80
LYONS, J. STRUCTURAL SEMANTICS.
N.E. COLLINGE, 47(ARL):VOL17FASC1-53
W. DRESSLER, 343:BAND13HEFT1-101
LYONS, R., ED. POETRY NORTH.
M. BUCCO, 649(WAL):SUMMER71-155
LYOTARD, J-F. DISCOURS, FIGURE.
V. FORREST-THOMSON, 89(BJA):WINTER72-
92
LYSAUGHT, J.P. & C.M. WILLIAMS. EINFÜH-
RUNG IN DIE UNTERRICHTSPROGRAMMIERUNG.
P. QUINCHE, 657(WW):MAR/APR70-143
LYSIAS. SELECTED SPEECHES. (C.D. ADAMS,
ED)
T.B. CURTIS, 124:OCT71-62

MAAS, H. - SEE HOUSMAN, A.E.
MAAS, H., J.L. DUNCAN & W.G. GOOD - SEE
BEARDSLEY, A.
MAAS, J. VICTORIAN PAINTERS.*
J.D. MACMILLAN, 637(VS):DEC70-217
G. REYNOLDS, 39:MAR70-246
MAAS, P. SERPICO.
A. HACKER, 453:19APR73-9
R.R. LINGEMAN, 441:26MAY73-29
M.P. NICHOLS, 441:27MAY73-3
442(NY):2JUL73-76
617(TLS):14DEC73-1541
MAAS, P. & C.A. TRYPANIS, EDS. SANCTI
ROMANI MELODI CANTICA: CANTICA DUBIA.
R.C. MC CAIL, VOL91-159
D.M. NICOL, 123:JUN72-269
MAATJE, F.C. DER DOPPELROMAN. (2ND ED)
J.J. WHITE, 220(GL&L):OCT71-77
MABBETT, I.W. A SHORT HISTORY OF INDIA.
O.P. SHARMA, 293(JAST):FEB71-477
MABBOTT, J.D. JOHN LOCKE.
617(TLS):13JUL73-814
MABBOTT, T.O. - SEE POE, E.A.
MACADAM, I., ED. THE ANNUAL REGISTER:
WORLD EVENTS IN 1972.
617(TLS):21SEP73-1091
MAC ADAMS, L., JR. THE POETRY ROOM.*
M.G. PERLOFF, 659:WINTER73-97
MACALPINE, I. & R. HUNTER. GEORGE III AND
THE MAD-BUSINESS.
W.B. WILLCOX, 656(WMQ):JUL71-489

MACAULAY, T.B. THOMAS BABINGTON MACAULAY:
SELECTED WRITINGS.* (J. CLIVE & T. PIN-
NEY, EDS)
O.D. EDWARDS, 441:1APR73-1
H.R. TREVOR-ROPER, 453:3MAY73-3
MC AULEY, J. SURPRISES OF THE SUN.
K.L. GOODWIN, 381:SEP71-377
MC AULEY, J.J. DRAFT BALANCE SHEET.
R.S., 376:JUL70-124
MC AVOY, T.T. A HISTORY OF THE CATHOLIC
CHURCH IN THE UNITED STATES.
J. HENNESEY, 613:WINTER70-632
MC BAIN, E. HAIL TO THE CHIEF.
N. CALLENDAR, 441:21OCT73-49
MC BAIN, E. LET'S HEAR IT FOR THE DEAF
MAN.
N. CALLENDAR, 441:1APR73-34
617(TLS):17AUG73-959
MAC BETH, G. THE BURNING CONE.*
A. CLUYSENAAR, 565:VOL11#4-74
MAC BETH, G. COLLECTED POEMS 1958-1970.*
R. LATTIMORE, 249(HUDR):AUTUMN72-479
E. LUEDERS, 651(WHR):SUMMER72-294
MAC BETH, G. MY SCOTLAND.
A. MACLEAN, 362:16AUG73-223
617(TLS):10AUG73-920
MAC BETH, G. A POET'S YEAR.
617(TLS):19OCT73-1276
MAC BETH, G. PRAYERS.
617(TLS):31AUG73-996
MAC BETH, G. SHRAPNEL.
A. MACLEAN, 362:16AUG73-223
617(TLS):9MAR73-270
MC BRIDE, A.B. THE GROWTH AND DEVELOP-
MENT OF MOTHERS.
L.C. POGREBIN, 441:17JUN73-2
MC CABE, J. GEORGE M. COHAN.
442(NY):31MAR73-119
MC CAFFERTY, L.M. RIVER OF LIGHT.
A.W. ANDERSON, 485(PE&W):APR71-222
MC CAFFREY, A. DRAGONQUEST.
617(TLS):9NOV73-1377
MAC CAIG, N. RINGS ON A TREE.
C. LEVENSON, 529(QQ):SUMMER71-309
MAC CAIG, N. THE WHITE BIRD.
A. MACLEAN, 362:16AUG73-223
617(TLS):11MAY73-516
MC CALL, D. THE EXAMPLE OF RICHARD
WRIGHT.*
R. WELBURN, 50(ARQ):SPRING71-81
MC CALL, D.K. THE THEATRE OF JEAN-PAUL
SARTRE.*
R.N. COE, 535(RHL):MAY-JUN71-531
J.N.J. PALMER, 208(FS):JAN72-98
MC CALL, G.J.H. METEORITES AND THEIR
ORIGINS.
617(TLS):18MAY73-565
MC CALL, M.H., JR. ANCIENT RHETORICAL
THEORIES OF SIMILE AND COMPARISON.*
M.L. CLARKE, 123:MAR72-66
MC CALL, S., ED. POLISH LOGIC 1920-1939.
R. BLANCHÉ, 542:OCT-DEC70-495
W.A. POGORZELSKI, 316:SEP70-442
MAC CALLUM, H. - SEE WOODHOUSE, A.S.P.
MC CANN, A.M. THE PORTRAITS OF SEPTIMIUS
SEVERUS (A.D. 193-211).*
P.P. BOBER, 54:JUN71-242
MC CARRY, C. CITIZEN NADER.*
C. DRIVER, 362:22MAR73-379
617(TLS):27APR73-463
MC CARRY, C. THE MIERNIK DOSSIER.
N. CALLENDAR, 441:8JUL73-26
442(NY):13AUG73-88
MC CARTHY, C. CHILD OF GOD.
A. BROYARD, 441:5DEC73-51

MC CARTHY, E.  OTHER THINGS AND THE AARD-
VARK.*
    C. RAKOSI, 600:SPRING71-182
    42(AR):FALL/WINTER70/71-464
    502(PRS):FALL71-280
MC CARTHY, M.  BIRDS OF AMERICA.*
    J.L. HALIO, 598(SOR):SPRING73-455
    J. RAPOPORT, 606(TAMR):#58-83
    P.M. SPACKS, 249(HUDR):SPRING72-166
    639(VQR):AUTUMN71-CLX
MC CARTHY, M.  MEDINA.*
    R. FULLER, 362:22FEB73-248
    617(TLS):16MAR73-283
MC CARTHY, M.  THE WRITING ON THE WALL.
    J. BAYLEY, 473(PR):SUMMER72-398
MC CARTHY, W.E.J. & N.D. ELLIS.  MANAGE-
MENT BY AGREEMENT.
    617(TLS):17AUG73-958
MC CARTY, C.  PUBLISHED SCREENPLAYS.
    C.N., 200:AUG-SEP71-434
MC CASLAND, S.V., G.E. CAIRNS & D.C. YU.
RELIGIONS OF THE WORLD.
    L. ROTHENHEBER, 318(JAOS):APR-JUN71-
    330
MC CAUGHEY, G. & M. LEGRIS, EDS.  OF
SEVERAL BRANCHES.*
    R. DANIELLS, 255(HAB):WINTER70-45
MC CAY, W.  LITTLE NEMO.
    M. SENDAK, 441:25NOV73-3
MC CHESNEY, D.  A HOPKINS COMMENTARY.*
    W.R. MUNDT, 598(SOR):AUTUMN73-1029
MACCHI, V., GENERAL ED.  THE SANSONI-
HARRAP STANDARD ITALIAN AND ENGLISH
DICTIONARY.*  (PT 1, VOL 1) (I. MC GILV-
RAY & OTHERS, COMPS)
    D.J.B. ROBEY, 402(MLR):APR72-428
MACCIOCCHI, M.A.  DAILY LIFE IN REVOLU-
TIONARY CHINA.
    H.E. SALISBURY, 441:14JAN73-4
MC CLARY, B.H.  WASHINGTON IRVING AND THE
HOUSE OF MURRAY.
    E. CURRENT-GARCIA, 577(SHR):SUMMER71-
    299
    A.B. MYERS, 613:SPRING71-126
MC CLELLAN, E.  TWO JAPANESE NOVELISTS.*
    J. ASHMEAD, 293(JAST):NOV70-195
    M. MATSUTORI, 502(PRS):WINTER71/72-
    363
MC CLELLAN, J.  JOSEPH STORY AND THE
AMERICAN CONSTITUTION.
    F.G. WILSON, 396(MODA):SUMMER72-326
MC CLELLAND, I.L.  BENITO JERÓNIMO FEI-
JÓO.*
    A.O. ALDRIDGE, 402(MLR):JUL72-676
    J. ASENSIO, 546(RR):APR71-143
    D-H. PAGEAUX, 549(RLC):OCT-DEC70-563
MC CLELLAND, J.S., ED.  THE FRENCH RIGHT
(FROM DE MAISTRE TO MAURRAS).*
    N. HAMPSON, 208(FS):JAN72-112
MC CLELLAND, V.A.  ENGLISH ROMAN CATHO-
LICS AND HIGHER EDUCATION, 1830-1903.
    617(TLS):16MAR73-299
MC CLOSKEY, H.J.  META-ETHICS AND NORMA-
TIVE ETHICS.*
    T. REGAN, 154:MAR71-154
    J.T. WILCOX, 321:WINTER70[VOL4#4]-321
MC CLOSKEY, H.J.  JOHN STUART MILL.
    R.J. HALLIDAY, 518:JAN72-21
    H. JACK, 154:SEP71-601
MC CLOY, H.  A CHANGE OF HEART.
    N. CALLENDAR, 441:25FEB73-50
MC CLUNG, N.  IN TIMES LIKE THESE.
    G.W., 102(CANL):AUTUMN72-113
MC CLURE, J.  THE CATERPILLAR COP.*
    N. CALLENDAR, 441:1JUL73-21
MC CLURE, J.  FOUR AND TWENTY VIRGINS.
    617(TLS):26OCT73-1324

MC CLUSKEY, N.G., ED.  THE CATHOLIC UNI-
VERSITY.
    J. BARZUN, 613:SPRING71-119
    A.W. GODFREY, 363:AUG71-121
MC COLLOM, W.G.  THE DIVINE AVERAGE.
    S.F. RENDALL, 131(CL):FALL72-364
MC CONICA, J.K.  ENGLISH HUMANISTS AND
REFORMATION POLITICS UNDER HENRY VIII
AND EDWARD VI.*
    G.K. HUNTER, 179(ES):FEB71-65
MC CORD, H.  LONGJAUNES HIS PERIPLUS.
    E. FEINSOD, 114(CHIR):JAN-FEB71-156
MC CORMACK, J.R., ED.  GUI DE NANTEUIL:
CHANSON DE GESTE.
    W.G. VAN EMDEN, 208(FS):JUL72-316
    M-H. TWEEDY, 382(MAE):1972/2-145
MC COY, G., ED.  DAVID SMITH.
    617(TLS):9NOV73-1362
MC CRACKEN, D. - SEE GODWIN, W.
MC CRAE, H.  THE LETTERS OF HUGH MC CREA.
(R.D. FITZ GERALD, ED)
    T.I. MOORE, 381:SEP71-353
MC CREERY, C.  PSYCHICAL PHENOMENA AND
THE PHYSICAL WORLD.
    617(TLS):23FEB73-221
MC CULLA, D.  VICTORIAN AND EDWARDIAN
BIRMINGHAM FROM OLD PHOTOGRAPHS.
    617(TLS):21DEC73-1573
MC CULLIN, D.  IS ANYONE TAKING ANY
NOTICE?
    G. EMERSON, 441:23DEC73-4
MC CULLOUGH, C.  STRANGER IN CHINA.
    441:11MAR73-46
MAC CURDY, R.R. - SEE DE ROJAS ZORRILLA,
F.
MC CUTCHION, D.  INDIAN WRITING IN ENG-
LISH.
    M.E. DERRETT, 293(JAST):FEB71-498
MC DERMOTT, J.F., ED.  FRENCHMEN AND
FRENCH WAYS IN THE MISSISSIPPI VALLEY.
    C. NISH, 656(WMQ):JAN71-149
MC DERMOTT, J.J. - SEE ROYCE, J.
MAC DIARMID, H.  MORE COLLECTED POEMS.
    R.P. DICKEY, 649(WAL):SUMMER71-151
MAC DIARMID, H.  SELECTED POEMS.  (D.
CRAIG & J. MANSON, EDS)
    R. FULTON, 565:VOL12#2-12
MAC DIARMID, H. & D. GLEN.  A CONVERSA-
TION.
    R. FULTON, 565:VOL12#2-12
MC DIARMID, M.P., ED.  THE KINGIS QUAIR
OF JAMES STEWART.
    617(TLS):20JUL73-842
MC DIARMID, M.P. - SEE "HARY'S 'WALLACE'"
MC DONAGH, D.  MARTHA GRAHAM.
    A. BROYARD, 441:25DEC73-19
    M.B. SIEGEL, 441:16DEC73-2
MC DONAGH, D.  THE RISE AND FALL AND RISE
OF MODERN DANCE.
    T. BOREK, 151:MAY71-47
MAC DONALD, A.  BETWEEN SOMETHING AND
SOMETHING.
    R. GUSTAFSON, 529(QQ):SPRING71-140
MC DONALD, A. & S.J. MILLER.  GREEK
UNPREPARED TRANSLATION.
    R. GLEN, 123:MAR72-97
MACDONALD, C. - SEE CICERO
MACDONALD, D. - SEE HERZEN, A.
MAC DONALD, J.  A COMPLEAT THEORY OF THE
SCOTS HIGHLAND BAGPIPE.
    P. COOKE, 595(SCS):VOL16PT1-84
MAC DONALD, M.  HAVERGAL BRIAN.
    H. COLE, 415:MAY72-459
MACDONALD, R.  THE SLEEPING BEAUTY.
    A. BROYARD, 441:21MAY73-37
    C. WOODS, 441:20MAY73-55

MACDONALD, S. THE HISTORY AND PHILOSOPHY
OF ART EDUCATION.*
Q. BELL, 39:JAN71-74
MAC DONNELL, K. EADWEARD MUYBRIDGE.
617(TLS):9MAR73-275
MAC DOUGALL, R.D. THE CHEERLEADER.
C. LEHMANN-HAUPT, 441:1FEB73-37
M. LEVIN, 441:4FEB73-27
MAC DOWELL, D.M. - SEE ARISTOPHANES
MAC DOWELL, D.M. - SEE HARRISON, A.R.W.
MC DOWELL, F.P.W. E.M. FORSTER.
G.H. THOMSON, 177(ELT):VOL13#1-81
MC DOWELL, R.B. - SEE BURKE, E.
MC DOWELL, W.L., JR., ED. THE COLONIAL
RECORDS OF SOUTH CAROLINA: DOCUMENTS
RELATING TO INDIAN AFFAIRS, 1754-1765.*
W.N. FENTON, 656(WMQ):APR71-344
E.E. HILL, 14:OCT71-384
MACE, C.A. SELECTED PAPERS. (M. MACE,
ED)
617(TLS):11MAY73-518
MC ELROY, J. ANCIENT HISTORY.
639(VQR):AUTUMN71-CLX
MAC EWEN, G. KING OF EGYPT, KING OF
DREAMS.*
C.X. RINGROSE, 102(CANL):SUMMER72-102
MAC EWEN, G. NOMAN.
R. GIBBS, 296:WINTER73-93
MC FADDEN, D. LETTERS FROM THE EARTH
TO THE EARTH.*
D.H. SULLIVAN, 648:OCT70-69
MC FARLAND, J.D. KANT'S CONCEPT OF TELE-
OLOGY.
T.P.A., 543:JUN71-750
L. FUNDERBURK, 342:BAND62HEFT1-137
A.C. GENOVA, 185:JAN71-186
MC FARLAND, T. COLERIDGE AND THE PAN-
THEIST TRADITION.*
J.A. APPLEYARD, 401(MLQ):JUN71-206
J. BEER, 191(ELN):SEP71-66
M.F. SCHULZ, 405(MP):NOV71-142
G. THOMAS, 175:AUTUMN70-105
MC FARLAND, T. SHAKESPEARE'S PASTORAL
COMEDY.
617(TLS):24AUG73-982
MACFARLANE, A. THE FAMILY LIFE OF RALPH
JOSSELIN, A SEVENTEENTH-CENTURY CLERGY-
MAN.*
C. HILL, 551(RENQ):AUTUMN71-410
MACFARLANE, A. WITCHCRAFT IN TUDOR AND
STUART ENGLAND.
D.C. GUNBY, 67:MAY72-87
MC FARLANE, I.D. - SEE AGRIPPA D'AUBIGNÉ
MC FARLANE, J., ED. HENRIK IBSEN.
R. DUMONT, 549(RLC):APR-JUN71-290
MC FARLANE, J.W. & G. ORTON - SEE IBSEN,
H.
MC FARLANE, K.B. HANS MEMLING.* (E.
WIND, WITH G.L. HARRISS, EDS)
F. AMES-LEWIS, 89(BJA):SUMMER72-308
MC GANN, J.J. FIERY DUST.*
G. THOMAS, 175:AUTUMN70-105
MC GANN, J.J. SWINBURNE.
617(TLS):23NOV73-1454
MC GANN, M.J. STUDIES IN HORACE'S FIRST
BOOK OF EPISTLES.*
A. ERNOUT, 555:VOL45FASC1-172
MC GARRITY, M. LITTLE AUGIE'S LAMENT.
M. LEVIN, 441:8APR73-33
MC GARRY, M., COMP. BEST SONGS AND
BALLADS OF OLD IRELAND.
F. HOWES, 415:AUG72-775
MC GARVEY, P.J. C.I.A.: THE MYTH AND THE
MADNESS.
441:25MAR73-26
MC GILVRAY, I. & OTHERS - SEE MACCHI, V.
MC GINLEY, P. SAINT-WATCHING.
J. GILSDORF, 502(PRS):WINTER70/71-360

MC GINNIS, J. THE DREAM TEAM.*
617(TLS):25MAY73-575
MC GIVERN, W. REPRISAL.
N. CALLENDAR, 441:25MAR73-49
MC GIVERN, W.P. CAPRIFOIL.*
617(TLS):31AUG73-1007
MC GOUGH, R. GIG.
617(TLS):19OCT73-1276
MC GOVERN J.W. PLAYS TO PONDER.
A. RENDLE, 157:SPRING71-77
MC GOWAN, A.P., ED. THE JACOBEAN COMMIS-
SIONS OF ENQUIRY 1608 AND 1618.
617(TLS):14DEC73-1546
MC GRADY, D. MATEO ALEMÁN.*
J.V. RICAPITO, 546(RR):APR71-134
MC GRADY, D. - SEE ISAACS, J.
MC GRATH, D.F. BOOKMAN'S PRICE INDEX.
(VOL 4)
M. PAPANTONIO, 517(PBSA):JAN-MAR72-79
MC GRATH, P. THE NATURE OF MORAL JUDG-
MENT.
J. MOLINE, 480(P&R):WINTER71-61
MC GRATH, T. LETTER TO AN IMAGINARY
FRIEND, PARTS I AND II.*
R.P. DICKY, 649(WAL):SPRING71-65
42(AR):FALL/WINTER70/71-465
"MC GRAW-HILL DICTIONARY OF ART."* (B.S.
MYERS, ED)
R. SQUIRRU, 37:OCT70-42
MAC GREGOR, J. TIBET.
E.D. THORP, 293(JAST):AUG71-903
MAC GREGOR, J.G. A HISTORY OF ALBERTA.
H. BOWSFIELD, 99:APR73-36
MC GREGOR, M.G., COMP. GUIDE TO THE
MANUSCRIPT COLLECTIONS OF COLONIAL
WILLIAMSBURG. (2ND ED)
R.E. WALTON, 14:JAN70-88
MC GREGOR, R.S. EXERCISES IN SPOKEN
HINDI.
I.K. WATSON, 302:JUL71-382
MAC GREGOR, S. THE SINNER.
617(TLS):17AUG73-959
MC GUANE, T. THE BUSHWHACKED PIANO.*
J. RICHMOND, 473(PR):FALL72-627
MC GUANE, T. NINETY-TWO IN THE SHADE.
A. BROYARD, 441:26JUL73-41
T.R. EDWARDS, 441:29JUL73-1
L.E. SISSMAN, 442(NY):23JUN73-88
R. TODD, 61:SEP73-104
M. WOOD, 453:13DEC73-19
MC GUFFIN, J. INTERNMENT.
617(TLS):31AUG73-997
MC GUINNESS, A.E. HENRY HOME, LORD
KAMES.*
W. JACKSON, 481(PQ):JUL71-450
D.F. NORTON, 319:OCT73-547
MC GUINNESS, B.F. - SEE ENGELMANN, P.
MC GUINNESS, B.F., T. NYBERG & G.H. VON
WRIGHT - SEE WITTGENSTEIN, L.
MC GUINNESS, R. ENGLISH COURT ODES 1660-
1820.*
P.J.D., 410(M&L):APR72-204
M. TILMOUTH, 415:FEB72-155
MC GUINNESS, W.J. & B. STEIN. MECHANICAL
AND ELECTRICAL EQUIPMENT FOR BUILDINGS.
(5TH ED)
R.H. EMERICK, 505:JUN71-108
MC GUIRE, E.B. IRISH WHISKEY.
617(TLS):20APR73-441
MC GUIRE, M. TO TAKE ARMS.
G. FITZGERALD, 362:1MAR73-282
MACHADO DE ASSIS, J.M. COUNSELOR AYRES'
MEMORIAL.
S. HILL, 362:22FEB73-251
A. WEST, 442(NY):31MAR73-117
M. WOOD, 453:19APR73-35
MC HALE, T. FARRAGAN'S RETREAT.*
639(VQR):SUMMER71-C

MAC HALE, T.P. & J. DEL VALLE, COMPS.
ESTUDIOS EN HONOR DE PEDRO LIRA URQUI-
ETA.
J. LOVELUCK, 263:JUL-SEP72-276
MC HARG, I. DESIGN WITH NATURE.
M.B. WELLS, 505:DEC71-80
DE MACHAUT, G. LA LOUANGE DES DAMES.
(N. WILKINS, ED)
617(TLS):23FEB73-217
MACHEREY, P. POUR UNE THÉORIE DE LA
PRODUCTION LITTÉRAIRE. (2ND ED)
E. WALTER, 535(RHL):JAN-FEB71-144
MACHIAVELLI, N. DAS LEBEN DES CASTRUCCIO
CASTRACANI VON LUCCA. (H. LEGERS, ED)
H-J. LOPE, 52:BAND5HEFT3-316
MACHIAVELLI, N. OPERE POLITICHE. (M.
PUPPO, ED)
P. ZOCCOLA, 228(GSLI):VOL148FASC461-
116
MACHIAVELLI, N. IL PRINCIPE. (J.H.
WHITFIELD, ED)
C.H. CLOUGH, 551(RENQ):WINTER71-527
MACHILEK, F. LUDOLF VON SAGAN UND SEINE
STELLUNG IN DER AUSEINANDERSETZUNG UM
KONZILIARISMUS UND HUSSITISMUS.
F.G. HEYMANN, 32:JUN72-457
MACHOVEC, M. TOMÁŠ G. MASARYK. (2ND ED)
S.B. WINTERS, 497(POLR):SUMMER70-94
MC INERNY, R.M. & A.R. CAPONIGRI. A HIS-
TORY OF WESTERN CIVILIZATION.
H.W. SCHNEIDER, 319:JAN73-107
MC INNES, A. ROBERT HARLEY, PURITAN
POLITICIAN.
R. WALCOTT, 566:AUTUMN71-21
MAC INNES, C. LOVING THEM BOTH.
M. DRABBLE, 362:27SEP73-416
MAC INNES, H. CALL-OUT.
617(TLS):2NOV73-1347
MAC INNIS, D.E. RELIGIOUS POLICY AND
PRACTICE IN COMMUNIST CHINA.
617(TLS):5JAN73-16
MC INTOSH, A. & M.A.K. HALLIDAY. PAT-
TERNS OF LANGUAGE.* (2ND ED)
G.F. MEIER, 682(ZPSK):BAND24HEFT5-442
J.S. PETÖFI, 215(GL):VOL10#2-138
MAC INTOSH, J.J. & S.C. COVAL, EDS. THE
BUSINESS OF REASON.*
A.W. CRAGG, 154:JUN70-124
R.A. SHARPE, 262:WINTER70-468
MACINTYRE, A. AGAINST THE SELF-IMAGES OF
THE AGE.*
M. LEBOWITZ, 676(YR):SPRING72-448
G. WERSON, 619(TC):VOL179#1049-53
MAC INTYRE, A. HERBERT MARCUSE.*
R.J.B., 543:SEP70-138
L. EVANS, 154:MAR71-184
P. JOHNSON, 185:JUL71-350
W.H. TRUITT, 290(JAAC):SUMMER71-569
MAC INTYRE, A. & P. RICOEUR. THE RELIG-
IOUS SIGNIFICANCE OF ATHEISM.
D.Z. PHILLIPS, 479(PHQ):JAN71-93
MAC INTYRE, D. SEA POWER IN THE PACIFIC.
617(TLS):2FEB73-133
MAC INTYRE, T. THE CHAROLLAIS.
R. CAREW, 159(DM):SUMMER/AUTUMN70-126
MAC INTYRE, T. DANCE THE DANCE.
J.P., 376:OCT70-95
MACK, D.S. - SEE HOGG, J.
MACK, M. THE GARDEN AND THE CITY.*
F. BRACHER, 405(MP):AUG71-74
N.B. HANSEN, 462(OL):VOL26#4-321
R. LAWRENCE, 175:AUTUMN70-107
R. PARKIN, 173(ECS):FALL70-97
C. PULLEN, 529(QQ):SPRING71-151
C.J. RAWSON, 447(N&Q):SEP71-351
MACK, M. - SEE HOMER

MACK, M. & I. GREGOR, EDS. IMAGINED
WORLDS.*
S. SACKS, 173(ECS):SUMMER71-488
M. WILDI, 179(ES):FEB71-87
MACK SMITH, D., ED. GARIBALDI.
J.W. BUSH, 276:AUTUMN71-399
MC KAY, A.G. VERGIL'S ITALY.
J. RUSSELL, 487:WINTER71-402
MC KAY, A.G. & D.M. SHEPHERD - SEE CATUL-
LUS & HORACE
MAC KAY, D.M. INFORMATION, MECHANISM
AND MEANING.
G.A. BORDEN, 215(GL):VOL11#1-53
MACKAY, J. THE ANIMALIERS.
617(TLS):12OCT73-1259
MACKAY, J. AN INTRODUCTION TO SMALL
ANTIQUES.
G. WILLS, 39:NOV70-400
MC KAY, R. JOHN LEONARD WILSON, CONFES-
SOR FOR THE FAITH.
617(TLS):19OCT73-1273
MC KELVEY, J.L. GEORGE III AND LORD
BUTE.
617(TLS):20JUL73-833
MAC KENDRICK, P. THE ATHENIAN ARISTOC-
RACY, 399 TO 31 B.C.*
P.S. DEROW, 487:WINTER71-383
MAC KENDRICK, P. THE IBERIAN STONES
SPEAK.*
A.W. GODFREY, 363:MAY71-85
MAC KENDRICK, P. ROMAN FRANCE.
617(TLS):20APR73-452
MAC KENDRICK, P. ROMANS ON THE RHINE.*
R.L. VANN, 576:DEC71-339
MACKENNA, F.S. 18TH-CENTURY ENGLISH
PORCELAIN.
P.S-H, 135:JUN71-152
MC KENNEY, K. THE ORDERLY.
D. MC ELDOWNEY, 368:MAR71-103
MAC KENZIE, A. A GALLERY OF GHOSTS.
617(TLS):12JAN73-48
MACKENZIE, A. THE JOURNALS AND LETTERS
OF SIR ALEXANDER MACKENZIE. (W.K.
LAMB, ED)
R. DANIELLS, 150(DR):WINTER71/72-590
MACKENZIE, A. VOYAGES FROM MONTREAL ON
THE RIVER ST. LAWRENCE, THROUGH THE CON-
TINENT OF NORTH AMERICA TO THE FROZEN
AND PACIFIC OCEANS IN THE YEARS 1789
AND 1793.
R. GIBBS, 296:SUMMER73-104
MAC KENZIE, D. POSTSCRIPT TO A DEAD
LETTER.
N. CALLENDAR, 441:25MAR73-49
MC KENZIE, D.F. & J.C. ROSS, EDS. A LED-
GER OF CHARLES ACKERS, PRINTER OF "THE
LONDON MAGAZINE."
P. DIXON, 447(N&Q):FEB71-75
D.F. FOXON, 354:MAR70-65
MAC KENZIE, D.N., ED. THE "SŪTRA OF THE
CAUSES AND EFFECTS OF ACTIONS" IN SOG-
DIAN.
I. GERSHEVITCH, 260(IF):BAND75-303
MACKENZIE, H. LETTERS TO ELIZABETH ROSE
OF KILRAVOCK. (H.W. DRESCHER, ED)
M. GASSENMEIER, 38:BAND88HEFT3-398
J. KINSLEY, 179(ES):OCT71-461
MC KENZIE, J.L. DID I SAY THAT?
R. MATZEK, 441:7OCT73-38
MAC KENZIE, N. & J. H.G. WELLS.
N. ANNAN, 453:15NOV73-33
M. HOLROYD, 441:2SEP73-3
J. KAPLAN, 61:OCT73-112
C. LEHMANN-HAUPT, 441:11SEP73-49
MAC KENZIE, N. & J. THE TIME TRAVELLER.
F. KERMODE, 362:14JUN73-806
617(TLS):29JUN73-735

MAC KENZIE, N.H. HOPKINS.
W.R. MUNDT, 598(SOR):AUTUMN73-1029
MC KERSIE, R.B. & L.C. HUNTER. PAY,
PRODUCTIVITY AND COLLECTIVE BARGAINING.
617(TLS):17AUG73-958
MACKEY, L. KIERKEGAARD.
G.L. STENGREN, 319:JUL73-421
MACKEY, W.F. BILINGUALISM AS A WORLD
PROBLEM.
A. BOILEAU, 556(RLV):1971/5-641
MACKEY, W.F. LE BILINGUISME.
G.F. MEIER, 682(ZPSK):BAND24HEFT1/2-
140
MC KIE, D. A SADLY MISMANAGED AFFAIR.
617(TLS):9NOV73-1381
MC KIE, D. & C. COOK, EDS. THE DECADE OF
DISILLUSION.
617(TLS):23FEB73-196
MACKIE, J.L. TRUTH, PROBABILITY AND
PARADOX.
617(TLS):24AUG73-971
MACKIN, J.H. CLASSICAL RHETORIC FOR
MODERN DISCOURSE.
V.R. KENNEDY, 583:FALL70-98
B.R. RUCKER, 480(P&R):SUMMER71-190
MACKIN, R. & D. CARVER. A HIGHER COURSE
OF ENGLISH STUDY 1.
R. GALDEROUX, 556(RLV):1970/6-686
MC KINNON, A. FALSIFICATION AND BELIEF.*
M.D.P., 543:MAR71-544
C.G. PRADO, 154:MAR71-186
MC KINNON, B. THE CARCASSES OF SPRING.
D. BARBOUR, 102(CANL):SPRING72-77
MAC KINNON, F. POSTURES AND POLITICS.
G. WOODCOCK, 99:OCT73-35
MAC KINNON, R. GAELIC.
M. MAC LEOD, 595(SCS):VOL16PT1-83
MC KINNON, W.T. APOLLO'S BLENDED DREAM.*
M. RICHARDS, 67:MAY72-94
R. SKELTON, 376:OCT71-130
MACKINTOSH, W.H. DISESTABLISHMENT AND
LIBERATION.
617(TLS):16MAR73-299
MC KISACK, M. MEDIEVAL HISTORY IN THE
TUDOR AGE.
S.A. GLASS, 568(SCN):SPRING72-14
MC KNIGHT, G. COMPUTER CRIME.
617(TLS):26OCT73-1307
MACKSEY, R. & E. DONATO, EDS. THE LAN-
GUAGES OF CRITICISM AND THE SCIENCES OF
MAN.
R. MARSH, 149:DEC72-458
L.S. ROUDIEZ, 546(RR):DEC71-310
MACKWORTH-PRAED, C.W. & C.H.B. GRANT.
BIRDS OF WEST CENTRAL AND WESTERN
AFRICA.
617(TLS):11MAY73-537
MC LANATHAN, R. ART IN AMERICA.
617(TLS):9NOV73-1362
MC LAREN, M. BONNIE PRINCE CHARLIE.*
P. JOHNSON, 441:7JAN73-7
MC LAUGHLIN, B.L. DIDEROT ET L'AMITIÉ.
617(TLS):4MAY73-507
MC LAUGHLIN, J.C. ASPECTS OF THE HISTORY
OF ENGLISH.*
A. CAMERON, 320(CJL):FALL70-55
C. CARLTON, 215(GL):VOL11#2-119
MC LAURIN, A. VIRGINIA WOOLF.
617(TLS):20JUL73-831
MACLEAN, A. FROM THE WILDERNESS.
P. BEER, 362:20DEC73-858
617(TLS):7DEC73-1513
MAC LEAN, A. THE WAY TO DUSTY DEATH.
N. CALLENDAR, 441:9SEP73-40
V. CUNNINGHAM, 362:13SEP73-352
617(TLS):14SEP73-1045
MACLEAN, A.D., ED. WINTER'S TALES 18.*
A. BROYARD, 441:26FEB73-29

MACLEAN, A.D., ED. WINTER'S TALES 19.
V. CUNNINGHAM, 362:8NOV73-638
MC LEAN, G.F. & P.J. ASPELL, EDS. READ-
INGS IN ANCIENT WESTERN PHILOSOPHY.
E.A.R., 543:DEC70-352
MC LEAN, J. THE INDIANS.
K. O'DONNELL, 296:SUMMER73-120
MC LEAN, R. PICTORIAL ALPHABETS.
R. CAVE, 503:SPRING70-40
MC LEAN, R. VICTORIAN BOOK DESIGN AND
COLOUR PRINTING.* (2ND ED)
S. ALLEN, 70(ANQ):MAR73-108
MC LEAN, S.K. THE BÄNKELSANG AND THE
WORK OF BERTOLT BRECHT.
617(TLS):28DEC73-1591
MACLEAN, V. MUCH ENTERTAINMENT.
617(TLS):31AUG73-1003
MC LEAVE, H. THE DAMNED DIE HARD.
441:2SEP73-10
MC LEAVE, H. A QUESTION OF NEGLIGENCE.
617(TLS):16NOV73-1407
MAC LEISH, A. CHAMPION OF A CAUSE. (E.M.
GOLDSCHMIDT, COMP)
L.S. THOMPSON, 263:JUL-SEP72-289
MC LELLAN, D. KARL MARX.
A. GAMBLE, 362:25OCT73-562
617(TLS):19OCT73-1283
MC LELLAN, D. THE YOUNG HEGELIANS AND
KARL MARX.*
L.D. EASTON, 321:WINTER70[VOL4#4]-320
H. RIDLEY, 220(GL&L):OCT71-28
MC LELLAN, D. - SEE MARX, K.
MC LELLAN, R. THE HYPOCRITE.
P. ROBERTS, 565:VOL12#2-72
MAC LENNAN, D.A. PREACHING THE GOOD NEWS
FOR MODERN MAN.
617(TLS):23MAR73-333
MC LEOD, A.L., ED. THE PATTERN OF NEW
ZEALAND CULTURE.
D. ANIDO, 368:JUN71-192
MC LEOD, A.L. - SEE SMUTS, J.C.
MC LEOD, W. COMPOSITE BOWS FROM THE
TOMB OF TUT'ANKHAMUN.
617(TLS):8JUN73-648
MC LOUGHLIN, J. THE LAW RELATING TO POL-
LUTION.
617(TLS):2FEB73-131
MC LOUGHLIN, W.G. NEW ENGLAND DISSENT,
1630-1833.*
E.S. GAUSTAD, 432(NEQ):SEP71-483
C.C. GOEN, 656(WMQ):OCT71-664
MC LUHAN, M. THE INTERIOR LANDSCAPE.*
(E. MC NAMARA, ED)
K.J. ATCHITY, 529(QQ):SUMMER71-321
A.E. MALLOCH, 627(UTQ):FALL70-103
P. POLSON, 648:JUN70-38
MC LUHAN, M. MUTATIONS 1990.
J-M. PIEMME, 556(RLV):1971/5-636
MC LUHAN, M. WAR AND PEACE IN THE GLOBAL
VILLAGE.
A.E. MALLOCH, 627(UTQ):FALL70-103
MC LUHAN, M., WITH H. PARKER. COUNTER-
BLAST.*
A.E. MALLOCH, 627(UTQ):FALL70-103
P. POLSON, 648:JUN70-38
MC LUHAN, M., WITH H. PARKER. THROUGH
THE VANISHING POINT.*
A.E. MALLOCH, 627(UTQ):FALL70-103
MAC LYSAGHT, E. THE SURNAMES OF IRELAND.
L.R.N. ASHLEY, 424:DEC70-313
MC MAHON, T.P. THE HUBSCHMANN EFFECT.
N. CALLENDAR, 441:22APR73-24
MC MAHON, T.P. THE ISSUE OF THE BISHOP'S
BLOOD.
617(TLS):18MAY73-562

MC MANAWAY, J.G. STUDIES IN SHAKESPEARE,
BIBLIOGRAPHY AND THEATER.* (R. HOSLEY,
A.C. KIRSCH & J.W. VELZ, EDS)
  M. GRIVELET, 189(EA):JAN-MAR71-89
  E.A.J. HONIGMANN, 354:SEP70-259
  C. LEECH, 570(SQ):AUTUMN70-502
MC MANNERS, J. THE SOCIAL CONTRACT AND
ROUSSEAU'S REVOLT AGAINST SOCIETY.
  J-L. LECERCLE, 535(RHL):JAN-FEB70-134
MC MASTER, G., ED. WILLIAM WORDSWORTH:
A CRITICAL ANTHOLOGY.
  617(TLS):2FEB73-117
MC MASTER, R. THE BRINESHRIMP.
  S.E. LEE, 581:DEC72-302
  617(TLS):12OCT73-1216
MC MICHAEL, J. AGAINST THE FALLING EVIL.
  R.J. MILLS, JR., 491:MAY73-105
MC MICHAEL, J. & D. SALEH, EDS. JUST
WHAT THE COUNTRY NEEDS, ANOTHER POETRY
ANTHOLOGY.
  F. MORAMARCO, 651(WHR):SPRING72-195
MAC MILLAN, F. THE SPREAD OF PRINTING:
NEW ZEALAND.
  R. CAVE, 503:SUMMER70-99
  K.I.D. MASLEN, 354:MAR71-75
MACMILLAN, H. AT THE END OF THE DAY,
1961-1963.
  R. CROSSMAN, 362:27SEP73-422
  617(TLS):28SEP73-1097
MACMILLAN, H. RIDING THE STORM.
  L. CLARK, 619(TC):VOL179#1047-47
MAC MULLEN, R. CONSTANTINE.*
  F.M. CLOVER, 121(CJ):DEC71/JAN72-179
MC MULLEN, R. VICTORIAN OUTSIDER.
  A. BROYARD, 441:30OCT73-47
  442(NY):10DEC73-199
MACMURRAY, J. THE FORM OF THE PERSONAL.
  A. KJAERGAARD, 262:SUMMER70-160
MC MURTRY, L. ALL MY FRIENDS ARE GOING
TO BE STRANGERS.*
  H.L. VAN BRUNT, 584(SWR):AUTUMN72-340
  617(TLS):23MAR73-313
MACNAB, P.A. THE ISLE OF MULL.
  I. FRASER, 595(SCS):VOL16PT2-189
MC NALLY, K. ACHILL.
  617(TLS):7SEP73-1037
MC NALLY, K. THE NARROW STREETS.
  617(TLS):23MAR73-333
MC NALLY, R.T. CHAADAYEV AND HIS FRIENDS.
  617(TLS):16FEB73-174
MC NALLY, R.T. & R. FLORESCU. IN SEARCH
OF DRACULA.*
  S. KANFER, 231:APR73-98
  G. STADE, 441:14JAN73-2
MC NAMARA, B. THE AMERICAN PLAYHOUSE IN
THE EIGHTEENTH CENTURY.*
  R. EDWARDS, 135:OCT71-140
  J. HAMILTON, 157:SPRING70-66
MC NAMARA, E. OUTERINGS.*
  D. BARBOUR, 150(DR):SPRING71-133
MC NAMARA, E. PASSAGES AND OTHER POEMS.
  J. DITSKY, 99:AUG73-35
MC NAMARA, E. - SEE MC LUHAN, M.
MC NASPY, C.J. WORSHIP AND WITNESS.
  M. LAVANOUX, 363:MAY71-84
MC NAUGHTON, A., COMP. THE BOOK OF KINGS.
  E. POWELL, 362:6DEC73-783
MC NAUGHTON, W. THE TAOIST VISION.
  639(VQR):AUTUMN71-CLXXXVII
MC NEAL, R.H. BRIDE OF THE REVOLUTION.*
  617(TLS):9FEB73-144
MAC NEIL, D. THE LIEUTENANT OF THE LINE.
  M. LEVIN, 441:15JUL73-16
MAC NEIL, D. SAHDU ON THE MOUNTAIN PEAK.
  M. LEVIN, 441:23DEC73-16
MC NEIL, I. JOSEPH BRAMAH.
  E.A. BATTISON, 637(VS):SEP70-112

MC NEIL, I. HYDRAULIC POWER.
  617(TLS):13APR73-425
MC NEILL, D. THE ACQUISITION OF LAN-
GUAGE.
  A.I. MOSKOWITZ, 350:SEP72-747
MC NEILL, M.R. GUIDELINES TO PROBLEMS OF
EDUCATION IN BRAZIL.
  A.E. TOWARD, 37:SEP71-38
MC NEILL, W.H. & J.W. SEDLAR, EDS. THE
CLASSICAL MEDITERRANEAN WORLD.
  M. GREEN, 123:MAR72-138
MC NEIR, W.F. & T.N. GREENFIELD, EDS.
PACIFIC COAST STUDIES IN SHAKESPEARE.*
  J. SHAW, 570(SQ):WINTER70-91
MC NEISH, J. MACKENZIE.
  L. JONES, 368:MAR71-93
MC NERNEY, R.F., JR. - SEE O'LEARY, D.F.
MC NICHOL, S. - SEE WOOLF, V.
MC NICKLE, D. INDIAN MAN.
  M. WESTBROOK, 27(AL):MAR72-170
MC NIECE, G. SHELLEY AND THE REVOLUTION-
ARY IDEA.*
  G. ENSCOE, 191(ELN):MAR72-216
  J. REES, 541(RES):AUG71-360
  M.T. SOLVE, 50(ARQ):SUMMER70-189
  G. THOMAS, 175:AUTUMN70-105
  D.G. WILLIAMS, 405(MP):MAY72-358
MACPHAIL, I., COMP. ALCHEMY AND THE
OCCULT.*
  H. BOBER, 551(RENQ):SUMMER71-241
MC PHEE, J. THE DELTOID PUMPKIN SEED.
  R. FREDE, 441:29JUL73-11
  C. LEHMANN-HAUPT, 441:13JUL73-39
MC PHEETERS, D.W. CAMILO JOSÉ CELA.*
  J-L. MARFANY, 86(BHS):JAN72-97
  J.K. WOODS, 400(MLN):MAR71-313
MACPHERSON, C.B. DEMOCRATIC THEORY.
  A. RYAN, 362:15MAR73-345
  617(TLS):25MAY73-580
MC PHERSON, H. HAWTHORNE AS MYTH-MAKER.
  E. STOCK, 445(NCF):MAR71-487
MC PHERSON, S. ELEGIES FOR THE HOT
SEASON.
  M. DE FREES, 448:SPRING71-80
  M.G. PERLOFF, 659:WINTER73-97
MC PHERSON, T. THE ARGUMENT FROM DESIGN.*
  A. FLEW, 518:OCT72-22
MACQUARRIE, J. THREE ISSUES IN ETHICS.
  D.F.D., 543:SEP70-139
MAC QUEEN, J. ALLEGORY.
  205(FMLS):OCT70-420
MAC QUEEN, J., ED. BALLATIS OF LUVE.*
  H.M. SHIRE, 382(MAE):1972/2-180
  205(FMLS):JUL71-294
MAC QUEEN, J. ROBERT HENRYSON.
  W. WEISS, 38:BAND89HEFT2-259
MACREA, D. STUDII DE ISTORIE A LIMBII ŞI
A LINGVISTICII ROMÂNE.
  G. PRICE, 47(ARL):VOL17FASC1-66
MC RITCHIE, K. THE BANDÍT.
  D. BARBOUR, 150(DR):SPRING71-133
MACROBIUS. THE SATURNALIA.* (P.V.
DAVIES, TRANS)
  A. CAMERON, 123:MAR72-44
  P.F. WIDDOWS, 122:JUL72-213
MACROBIUS. I SATURNALIA DI MACROBIO TEO-
DOSIO. (N. MARINONE, ED & TRANS)
  A. CAMERON, 123:MAR72-44
MAC SHANE, F. THE LIFE AND WORK OF FORD
MADOX FORD.
  R.A. CASSELL, 136:VOL3#1-115
MAC SHANE, F. - SEE FORD, F.M.
MC SHERRY, J.E. STALIN, HITLER, AND
EUROPE.* (VOL 2)
  R.G. WESSON, 550(RUSR):OCT71-413
MAC SKIMMING, R. FORMENTERA.
  J.G. MOSS, 296:WINTER73-101

MAC SWEENEY, B. THE BOY FROM THE GREEN
CABARET TELLS OF HIS MOTHER.
R. FULTON, 565:VOL11#1-68
MAC SWEENEY, B. BROTHER WOLF.
617(TLS):9MAR73-270
MACURA, P. RUSSIAN-ENGLISH DICTIONARY OF
ELECTROTECHNOLOGY AND ALLIED SCIENCES.
M. ALFORD, 32:DEC72-949
MC WATTERS, K.G. STENDHAL LECTEUR DES
ROMANCIERS ANGLAIS.
R.M. CHADBOURNE, 207(FR):OCT70-232
205(FMLS):APR70-208
MC WEISS, C. & F.A. POTTLE - SEE BOSWELL,
J.
MC WHINEY, G. SOUTHERNERS AND OTHER
AMERICANS.
442(NY):20AUG73-91
MC WHIRTER, N. & R. GUINNESS BOOK OF
WORLD RECORDS. (REV)
R. LASSON, 441:29APR73-22
MC WILLIAMS, W.C. THE IDEA OF FRATERNITY
IN AMERICA.
W.F. BUCKLEY, JR., 441:5AUG73-17
MADAULE, J. CLAUDEL ET LE LANGAGE.*
A. BLANC, 535(RHL):MAR-APR70-341
MADDALENA, A. FILONE ALESSANDRINO.
R.T. WALLIS, 123:DEC72-341
MADDEN, D. THE SHADOW KNOWS.
H.V. CALLISON, 573(SSF):FALL71-651
A. EDELSTEIN, 598(SOR):SUMMER73-736
MADDEN, E.H. CIVIL DISOBEDIENCE AND
MORAL LAW IN NINETEENTH-CENTURY AMERI-
CAN PHILOSOPHY.*
W. HARDING, 321:WINTER70[VOL5#1]-72
MADDEN, E.H., R. HANDY & M. FARBER, EDS.
THE IDEA OF GOD.
W. HOROSZ, 484(PPR):DEC71-273
G.V. JONES, 478:JAN70-94
MADDEN, E.H. & P.H. HARE. EVIL AND THE
CONCEPT OF GOD.
W.E. MC MAHON, 321:WINTER70[VOL5#1]-
70
MADDEX, J.P., JR. THE VIRGINIA CONSERVA-
TIVES, 1867-1879.
B. CLAYTON, 579(SAQ):SUMMER72-434
MADDICOTT, J.R. THOMAS OF LANCASTER,
1307-1322.
G.L. HARRISS, 382(MAE):1972/3-286
B. WILKINSON, 589:OCT72-781
MADDOX, R.J. THE NEW LEFT AND THE ORI-
GINS OF THE COLD WAR.
R. BOTHWELL, 99:NOV-DEC73-50
F. LOEWENHEIM, 441:17JUN73-6
R. STEEL, 453:14JUN73-33
MADDUX, R., S. SILLIPHANT & N.D. ISAACS.
FICTION INTO FILM.*
W.J. FREE, 219(GAR):WINTER71-513
MADGE, C. & B. WEINBERGER. ART STUDENTS
OBSERVED.
617(TLS):21SEP73-1078
MADGWICK, P.J. THE POLITICS OF RURAL
WALES.
617(TLS):21DEC73-1572
MADINIER, G. CONSCIENCE ET AMOUR.
C. PRÉVOST, 542:OCT-DEC71-494
MADISON, V. THE BIG BEND COUNTRY OF
TEXAS. (REV)
J.L. FORSYTHE, 650(WF):JAN70-61
MADISON, V. & H. STILLWELL. HOW COME
IT'S CALLED THAT?
J.B. MC MILLAN, 650(WF):APR70-137
MADSEN, W.G. FROM SHADOWY TYPES TO
TRUTH.*
R. LENGELER, 72:BAND209HEFT4/6-407
MAEHLER, H. ÄGYPTISCHE URKUNDEN AUS
DEN STAATLICHEN MUSEEN BERLIN.*
É. WILL, 555:VOL45FASC2-329

MAEHLER, H., ED. URKUNDEN RÖMISCHER
ZEIT.
S.I. OOST, 122:JUL72-224
MAERTH, O.K. THE BEGINNING WAS THE END.
617(TLS):20JUL73-841
DE LA MAESTRE, A.E. CLAUDEL ET LE MONDE
GERMANIQUE.
A. VIATTE, 549(RLC):JAN-MAR70-138
DE LA MAESTRE, A.E. DAS GÖTTLICHE ABEN-
TEUER, PAUL CLAUDEL UND SEIN WERK.
J. WILHELM, 535(RHL):JAN-FEB71-131
MAFFEI, D., ED. ENEA SILVIO PICCOLOMINI
PAPA PIO II.
W.J. BOUWSMA, 589:JUL72-537
MAFFEY, A. IL PENSIERO POLITICO DEL
MABLY.
J-L. LECERCLE, 535(RHL):JAN-FEB71-95
F. VIAL, 546(RR):FEB71-63
MAGALOTTI, L. RELAZIONI DI VIAGGIO IN
INGHILTERRA, FRANCIA E SVEZIA. (W.
MORETTI, ED)
R.A., 228(GSLI):VOL148FASC462/463-463
P. ZAMBELLI, 548(RCSF):JAN-MAR71-102
MAGAÑA ESQUIVEL, A., ED. TEATRO MEXICANO
DEL SIGLO XX.
G. WOODYARD, 238:MAY71-403
MAGARSHACK, D. PUSHKIN.
L.T. LEMON, 502(PRS):FALL71-277
MAGEE, B. POPPER.
A. RYAN, 362:14JUN73-808
MAGEE, D. INFINITE RICHES.
442(NY):16JUN73-112
617(TLS):17AUG73-960
MAGEE, W. URBAN GORILLA.
617(TLS):1JUN73-610
MAGENAU, D. DIE BESONDERHEITEN DER
DEUTSCHEN SCHRIFTSPRACHE IN LUXEMBURG
UND IN DEN DEUTSCHSPRACHIGEN TEILEN
BELGIENS.
G. LERCHNER, 682(ZPSK):BAND23HEFT4-
417
MAGIDOFF, R. YEHUDI MENUHIN. (2ND ED)
617(TLS):12OCT73-1247
MAGILL, C.P. - SEE VON GOETHE, J.W.
MAGIS, C.H. LA LÍRICA POPULAR CONTEM-
PORÁNEA.*
D. JAÉN, 238:MAY71-399
E.L. RIVERS, 400(MLN):MAR71-302
MAGNANI, L. IL NIPOTE DI BEETHOVEN.
617(TLS):2NOV73-1334
MAGNE, É. & A. NIDERST - SEE MADAME DE
LA FAYETTE
MAGNER, T.F. & W.R. SCHMALSTIEG. BALTIC
LINGUISTICS.
F. SCHOLZ, 215(GL):VOL11#3-171
MAGNUS, B. HEIDEGGER'S METAHISTORY OF
PHILOSOPHY.
E.F. HIRSCH, 319:OCT73-567
DE MAGNY, O. LES CENT DEUX SONNETS DES
"AMOURS" DE 1553. (M.S. WHITNEY, ED)
R. KLESCZEWSKI, 72:BAND209HEFT1/3-211
J. PINEAUX, 557(RSH):APR-JUN71-313
D.B. WILSON, 208(FS):OCT72-446
MAGON, L. & OTHERS, EDS. STUDIEN ZUR
GESCHICHTE DER DEUTSCH-UNGARISCHEN LIT-
ERARISCHEN BEZIEHUNGEN.
M.A. GREEN, 131(CL):SUMMER72-273
MAGUIRE, J. MARX'S PARIS WRITINGS.
617(TLS):9FEB73-142
MAGUIRE, W.A. THE DOWNSHIRE ESTATES IN
IRELAND 1801-1845.
617(TLS):5JAN73-19
"A MAGYAR TÖRTÉNETTUDOMÁNY VÁLOGATOTT
BIBLIOGRÁFIAJA, 1945-1968."
F.S. WAGNER, 32:SEP72-720
MAHADEVAN, T.M.P., ED. INDIAN PHILO-
SOPHICAL ANNUAL. (VOL 3)
E.J. QUIGLEY, 485(PE&W):OCT70-436

MAHADEVAN, T.M.P., ED. THE RELEVANCE OF
MAHATMA GANDHI TO THE WORLD OF THOUGHT.
E.J. QUIGLEY, 485(PE&W):APR71-223
MAHDI, M. - SEE "AL-FĀRĀBĪ'S BOOK OF LET-
TERS"
MAHER, J.T. - SEE WILDER, A.
MAHGOUB, F.M. A LINGUISTIC STUDY OF
CAIRENE PROVERBS.
W.B. BISHAI, 318(JAOS):OCT-DEC71-537
MAHMOOD, S. A POLITICAL STUDY OF PAKIS-
TAN.
617(TLS):8JUN73-653
MAHON, J.K. THE WAR OF 1812.
617(TLS):6APR73-401
MAHOOD, M.M. SHAKESPEARE'S WORDPLAY.
R.V. ADKINSON, 556(RLV):1970/1-101
MAHR, J. ÜBERGANG ZUM ENDLICHEN.*
N.H. SMITH, 182:VOL24#5-217
R.J. TAYLOR, 220(GL&L):APR72-283
MAHULKAR, D.D. THE GROUNDWORK OF MODERN
LOGIC.
P. SMITH, 316:SEP71-545
MAI, D.T. - SEE UNDER DANG THAI MAI
MAIA, P.A. - SEE UNDER AMÉRICO MAIA, P.
DA MAIANO, D. RIME. (R. BETTARINI, ED)
M.P., 228(GSLI):VOL148FASC464-625
MAIER, G. MENSCH UND FREIER WILLE NACH
DEN JÜDISCHEN RELIGIONSPARTEIEN ZWIS-
CHEN BEN SIRA UND PAULUS.
C.K. BARRETT, 182:VOL24#11/12-460
MAIER, P. FROM RESISTANCE TO REVOLUTION.*
E. FONER, 453:22FEB73-35
617(TLS):4MAY73-493
MAIER, P.L. FIRST EASTER.
N.K. BURGER, 441:1APR73-14
MAIER, W. LEBEN, TAT UND REFLEXION.*
M.J. GONZÁLEZ, 202(FMOD):JUN70-360
MAILER, N. THE LONG PATROL.* (R.F.
LUCID, ED)
J.E. MULLIN, 385(MQR):FALL73-370
MAILER, N. MARILYN.
G.P. ELLIOTT, 231:OCT73-106
P. KAEL, 441:22JUL73-1
C. LEHMANN-HAUPT, 441:16JUL73-33 [&
CONT IN] 441:17JUL73-43
P. WHITEHEAD, 362:8NOV73-636
M. WOOD, 453:20SEP73-22
442(NY):6AUG73-87
617(TLS):30NOV73-1477
MAILER, N. OF A FIRE ON THE MOON.
E. BURDICK, 159(DM):SPRING71-112
J.P., 376:JUL71-117
MAILER, N. THE PRISONER OF SEX.*
A. BARNES, 418(MR):WINTER-SPRING72-269
MAILER, N. WHY ARE WE IN VIETNAM?
J.C. FIELD, 556(RLV):1971/6-769
MAILHOS, G. - SEE DE VOLTAIRE, F.M.A.
MAILLOT, J. LA TRADUCTION SCIENTIFIQUE
ET TECHNIQUE.
75:1/1971-53
MAIN, J.T. THE SOVEREIGN STATES, 1775-
1783.
I.R. DEE, 441:16DEC73-5
MAINLAND, W.F. - SEE VON SCHILLER, J.C.F.
MAINS, G. THE OXYGEN REVOLUTION.
617(TLS):9FEB73-158
MAINWARING, M., ED. THE PORTRAIT GAME.
617(TLS):20JUL73-841
MAIR, C. A TIME IN TURKEY.
617(TLS):20APR73-450
MAITRON, J., GENERAL ED. DICTIONNAIRE
BIOGRAPHIQUE DU MOUVEMENT OUVRIER
FRANÇAIS. (PT 2, VOLS 4-7)
V.R. LORWIN, 207(FR):APR71-943
MAIWORM, H. NEUE DEUTSCHE EPIK.
H.J. SCHUELER, 564:OCT70-243
J.J. WHITE, 220(GL&L):OCT71-37

MAJOR, C. NO.
G. DAVIS, 441:1JUL73-22
MAJOR, C. SWALLOW THE LAKE.
639(VQR):WINTER71-XX
MAJUMDAR, B. KRSNA IN HISTORY AND LEGEND.
L. STERNBACH, 318(JAOS):OCT-DEC71-543
MAKAEV, É.A. JAZYK DREVNEJŠICH RUNIČES-
KICH NADPISEJ.
R. RIS, 343:BAND13HEFT2-145
MAKDISI, G. IBN 'AQIL ET LA RÉSURGENCE
DE L'ISLAM TRADITIONALISTE AU XIE
SIÈCLE (VE SIÈCLE DE L'HÉGIRE).
N.L. HEER, 318(JAOS):APR-JUN71-331
MAKEPEACE, C. MANCHESTER AS IT WAS.
(VOL 1)
617(TLS):12JAN73-49
MALAGOLI, L. SEICENTO ITALIANO E MODERN-
ITÀ.
A. ILLIANO, 131(CL):FALL72-369
MALAGÓN, J. O FUTURO DA UNIVERSIDADE.
J.V., 37:JAN-FEB71-39
MALAGÓN, J. & S. ZAVALA. RAFAEL ALTAMIRA
Y CREVEA.
J.L. HELGUERA, 263:OCT-DEC72-422
MALAMUD, B. PICTURES OF FIDELMAN.*
C. STETLER, 573(SSF):SPRING71-341
MALAMUD, B. REMBRANDT'S HAT.
A. BROYARD, 441:17MAY73-47
V. CUNNINGHAM, 362:11OCT73-491
R. KIELY, 441:3JUN73-7
J. LEONARD, 61:JUN73-116
L. MICHAELS, 453:20SEP73-37
617(TLS):5OCT73-1158
MALAMUD, B. THE TENANTS.*
J. LUDWIG, 473(PR):FALL72-596
M. SYRKIN, 390:NOV71-64
42(AR):FALL71-438
MALANGA, G. 10 POEMS FOR 10 POETS.
639(VQR):SPRING71-LXI
MALAPARTE, C. IL BALLO AL CREMLINO E
ALTRI INEDITI DI ROMANZO.
617(TLS):12JAN73-39
MALAUSSENA, P-L. LA VIE EN PROVENCE ORI-
ENTALE AUX XIVE ET XVE SIÈCLES.
R.W. EMERY, 589:APR72-329
MALCOLMSON, R.W. POPULAR RECREATIONS IN
ENGLISH SOCIETY 1700-1850.
617(TLS):16NOV73-1388
MALEFAKIS, E.E. AGRARIAN REFORM AND
PEASANT REVOLUTION IN SPAIN.
617(TLS):16MAR73-290
MALET, H. IN THE WAKE OF THE GODS.
L. DALY, 159(DM):SUMMER/AUTUMN70-123
DE MALHERBE, F. OEUVRES POÉTIQUES. (R.
FROMILHAGUE & R. LEBEGUE, EDS)
J. PINEAUX, 535(RHL):MAY-JUN70-509
P-A. WADSWORTH, 546(RR):FEB71-51
MALIN, I. SAUL BELLOW'S FICTION.*
R.H. FOSSUM, 594:SPRING70-99
MALING, A. THE SNOWMAN.
N. CALLENDAR, 441:15APR73-35
MALINS, E. SAMUEL PALMER'S ITALIAN
HONEYMOON.*
A.L. GRIFFIN, 637(VS):DEC70-213
A.S. ROE, 54:SEP71-421
MALKIEL, Y. ESSAYS ON LINGUISTIC THEMES.*
M.P.A.M. KERKHOF, 433:OCT71-452
MALKIEL, Y. LINGUISTICA GENERALE, FILO-
LOGIA ROMANZA, ETIMOLOGIA.
R. POSNER, 361:VOL27#2/3-293
MALLARMÉ, S. CORRESPONDANCE III, 1886-
1889. (H. MONDOR & L.J. AUSTIN, EDS)
A. GILL, 402(MLR):JUL72-647
G. ZAYED, 535(RHL):JAN-FEB71-124
MALLARMÉ, S. CORRESPONDANCE IV, 1890-
1891. (H. MONDOR & L.J. AUSTIN, EDS)
617(TLS):28DEC73-1582

MALLEA, E. CHAVES. (B. & A. GICOVATE, EDS)
    E.M. ALDRICH, JR., 238:DEC71-988
MALLEA, E. LA PENÚLTIMA PUERTA.
    M.I. LICHTBLAU, 238:MAR71-204
MALLESON, A. NEED YOUR DOCTOR BE SO USE-
LESS?
    617(TLS):23NOV73-1450
MALLET, M. THE BORGIAS.
    C.C. BAYLEY, 551(RENQ):SPRING71-63
MALLET-JORIS, F. LE JEU DU SOUTERRAIN.
    617(TLS):4MAY73-489
MALLET-JORIS, F. LA MAISON DE PAPIER.
    M. NAUDIN, 207(FR):OCT70-181
MALLIN, T. CURTAINS.
    A. RENDLE, 157:AUTUMN71-82
MALMBERG, B. NEW TRENDS IN LINGUISTICS.
(FRENCH TITLE: LES NOUVELLES TENDANCES
DE LA LINGUISTIQUE.)
    R.H. ROBINS, 206:AUG71-431
    L. ZGUSTA, 353:JUN71-106
MALMSTRÖM, G. MENNESKEHJERTETS VERDEN.
    S. LINNÉR, 172(EDDA):1971/3-191
MALOFF, S. HEARTLAND.
    A. BROYARD, 441:20SEP73-51
    J.R. FRAKES, 441:16SEP73-5
    442(NY):5NOV73-185
MALONE, D. JEFFERSON THE PRESIDENT:
FIRST TERM, 1801-1805.*
    K. BERWICK, 656(WMQ):OCT71-653
MALONE, J. THE CORRUPTION OF HAROLD
HOSKINS.
    M. LEVIN, 441:3JUN73-33
MALONE, M. THE PLAYS OF SEAN O'CASEY.
    D. KRAUSE, 397(MD):DEC70-336
MALORY, T. LE MORTE DARTHUR. (ILLUS-
TRATED BY A. BEARDSLEY)
    617(TLS):9FEB73-143
MALORY, T. THE WORKS OF SIR THOMAS
MALORY.* (2ND ED) (E. VINAVER, ED)
    P.H. SALUS, 179(ES):OCT71-455
MALOUF, D. BICYCLE AND OTHER POEMS.
    K.L. GOODWIN, 381:SEP71-375
MAŁOWIST, M. EUROPA A AFRYKA ZACHODNIA
W DOBIE EKSPANSJI KOLONIALNEJ.
    R. SMITH, 69:JUL71-259
MALRAUX, A. LE TRIANGLE NOIR.
    N. KATTAN, 98:FEB71-155
MALRAUX, A. & A. PARROT - SEE HUBERT, J.,
J. PORCHER & W.F. VOLBACH
MALRAUX, C. VOICI QUE VIENT L'ÉTÉ.
    617(TLS):28DEC73-1582
MALSON, L. WOLF CHILDREN.*
    617(TLS):9FEB73-145
MALSTROM, R. & M. ORCEYRE. JUG NIGHT.
    N. CALLENDAR, 441:9SEP73-40
MALTA, D.A. - SEE UNDER AGUILERA MALTA, D.
MALTESE, C. - SEE FRANCESCO DI GIORGIO
MARTINI
MALVASIA, C.C. LE PITTURE DI BOLOGNA
1686.
    D. POSNER, 54:MAR71-123
MAMATEY, V.S. RISE OF THE HABSBURG EM-
PIRE 1526-1815.
    P.P. BERNARD, 32:SEP72-705
    L. PÉTER, 575(SEER):JUL72-487
MAMATEY, V.S. THE UNITED STATES AND EAST
CENTRAL EUROPE 1914-1918.
    M. MOLNÁR, 98:JAN70-72
MAMDANI, M. THE MYTH OF POPULATION CON-
TROL.
    617(TLS):24AUG73-985
MAN, F.H. ARTISTS' LITHOGRAPHS.
    D.T., 135:FEB71-140
DE MAN, P. BLINDNESS AND INSIGHT.*
    J. CULLER, 676(YR):WINTER72-259
"MAN IN THE LIVING ENVIRONMENT."
    617(TLS):9FEB73-158

MANACORDA, G. - SEE BUTTI, E.A.
MANADA, Y. & I.A. URQUHART. ACUPUNCTURE.
    617(TLS):23FEB73-221
MAÑALICH, R. HISPANOAMÉRICA.
    M.J. DOUDOROFF, 238:MAR71-230
MANCALL, M. RUSSIA AND CHINA.
    A. PARRY, 32:SEP72-662
MANCEAUX, M. LES POLICIERS PARLENT.
    P. AUBERY, 207(FR):MAR71-773
MANCINI, F. FESTE E APPARATI CIVILI E
RELIGIOSI IN NAPOLI DAL VICEREGNO
ALLA CAPITALE.
    M.V. FERRERO, 90:JUN71-341
MANCINI, I., ED. THE FIFTH GOSPEL.
    P.L. MAIER, 441:22APR73-10
MAŃCZAK, W. LE DÉVELOPPEMENT PHONÉTIQUE
DES LANGUES ROMANES ET LA FRÉQUENCE.
    J.L. BUTLER, 545(RPH):FEB72-331
    R. POSNER, 361:VOL25#4-440
MANDEL, B. LITERATURE AND THE ENGLISH
DEPARTMENT.
    J.F. HUNTLEY, 128(CE):DEC71-362
MANDEL, E., ED. CONTEXTS OF CANADIAN
CRITICISM.*
    S. DJWA, 296:WINTER73-77
    W.H. NEW, 102(CANL):SUMMER72-101
MANDEL, E. CRUSOE. STONY PLAIN.
    A.B. CAMERON, 99:NOV-DEC73-34
MANDEL, O. COLLECTED PLAYS. (VOL 1)
    J.K. CLARK, 160:FALL71-57
MANDELSTAM, N. HOPE AGAINST HOPE.*
    M. FRIEDBERG, 390:FEB71-75
    R.P. HUGHES, 550(RUSR):APR71-184
    639(VQR):SPRING71-LXX
MANDELSTAM, O. SELECTED POEMS. (C.
BROWN & W.S. MERWIN, TRANS) SELECTED
POEMS. (D. MC DUFF, TRANS)
    J. BAYLEY, 362:6DEC73-781
MANDER-JONES, P., ED. MANUSCRIPTS IN
THE BRITISH ISLES RELATING TO AUSTRAL-
IA, NEW ZEALAND, AND THE PACIFIC.
    617(TLS):20APR73-454
MANDEVILLE, B. THE FABLE OF THE BEES.
(P. HARTH, ED)
    D.D. EDDY, 481(PQ):JUL71-461
    566:SPRING72-93
MANDIĆ, O.D. HRVATI I SRBI.
    M. MEŠTROVIĆ, 32:DEC72-930
MANDROU, R. LOUIS XIV EN SON TEMPS.
    617(TLS):8JUN73-651
MANDROU, R. MAGISTRATS ET SORCIERS EN
FRANCE AU XVIIE SIÈCLE.
    J. FAVRET, 98:APR71-351
    J-Y. POUILLOUX, 535(RHL):SEP-DEC70-
1070
MANE, R. HENRY ADAMS ON THE ROAD TO
CHARTRES.
    R.E. SPILLER, 27(AL):NOV72-496
MANFORD, F. A GOLDENROD WILL GROW.
    M. WESTBROOK, 649(WAL):SUMMER71-154
MANGANELLI, G. AGLI DÈI ULTERIORI.
    B. MERRY, 270:VOL22#4-81
    617(TLS):30MAR73-341
MANGIONE, J. THE DREAM AND THE DEAL.*
    H. KRAMER, 441:28JAN73-1
    H. ROSENBERG, 442(NY):20JAN73-99
MANGO, A. LA COMMEDIA IN LINGUA NEL CIN-
QUECENTO.
    R. ALONGE, 228(GSLI):VOL147FASC457-
137
MANGUM, D. THE FARGUS TECHNIQUE.
    J. YARDLEY, 441:13MAY73-36
MANHIRE, B. MALADY.
    G. COLLIER, 368:DEC70-418
MANIERI, M.R. UMANESIMO E CIVILTÀ NEO-
TECNICA.
    E. NAMER, 542:APR-JUN70-264

MANIFOLD, J.S.  OP. 8 POEMS 1961-69.
  S.E. LEE, 581:1971/3-227
MANILIUS, M.  ASTRONOMICON.  (A.E. HOUS-
  MAN, ED)
  W. WHITE, 70(ANQ):MAY73-143
MANKIEWICZ, F.  PERFECTLY CLEAR.
  S.R. WEISMAN, 441:23DEC73-4
  442(NY):24DEC73-80
MANKIEWICZ, J.L.  MORE ABOUT "ALL ABOUT
  EVE."*
  M. WOOD, 453:29NOV73-6
MANKOVITZ, W.  THE BLUE ARABIAN NIGHTS.
  617(TLS):31AUG73-993
MANLEY, M.D.  THE NOVELS OF MARY DELARI-
  VIERE MANLEY.
  566:SPRING72-94
MANN, A.  TIARA.
  617(TLS):16NOV73-1407
MANN, J.  THE ONLY SECURITY.
  617(TLS):16MAR73-303
MANN, J.  TROUBLE-CROSS.
  N. CALLENDAR, 441:26AUG73-33
MANN, M.  CONSCIOUSNESS AND ACTION
  AMONG THE WESTERN WORKING CLASS.
  617(TLS):15JUN73-667
MANN, M.  WORKERS ON THE MOVE.
  617(TLS):25MAY73-597
MANN, O., ED.  CHRISTLICHE DICHTER IM 20.
  JAHRHUNDERT.*  (2ND ED)
  H. HATZFELD, 133:1970/2&3-337
  K.S. WEIMAR, 221(GQ):JAN71-89
MANN, O. - SEE LESSING, G.E.
MANN, O. & W. ROTHE, EDS.  DEUTSCHE LIT-
  ERATUR IM 20. JAHRHUNDERT.  (5TH ED)
  V. ŽMEGAČ, 657(WW):JUL/AUG70-287
MANN, O. & R. STRAUBEMANN.  LESSING-KOM-
  MENTAR.
  617(TLS):6JUL73-777
MANN, P.  THE VACANCY.
  N. CALLENDAR, 441:14OCT73-47
MANN, R.  FOREIGN BODY.
  617(TLS):7DEC73-1495
MANN, R.  RIVERS IN THE CITY.
  P. GOLDBERGER, 441:21OCT73-39
MANN, T.  THE LETTERS OF THOMAS MANN,
  1889-1955.*  (R. & C. WINSTON, EDS &
  TRANS)
  42(AR):SPRING71-133
  639(VQR):SUMMER71-CXVII
MANN, T.  DER TOD IN VENEDIG.  (A.W.
  HORNSEY, ED)
  H.C. SASSE, 220(GL&L):JAN72-184
MANN, T. & G.B. FISCHER.  THOMAS MANN:
  BRIEFWECHSEL MIT SEINEM VERLEGER GOTT-
  FRIED BERMANN FISCHER 1932-1955.  (P.
  DE MENDELSSOHN, ED)
  617(TLS):17AUG73-943
MANNACK, E., ED.  DIE PEGNITZ-SCHÄFER -
  NÜRNBERGER BAROCKDICHTUNG.
  H. RÜDIGER, 52:BAND6HEFT1-77
MANNACK, E. - SEE RIST, J.
MANNERS, A.  POOR COUSINS.*
  M. MUDRICK, 249(HUDR):SUMMER72-338
MANNES, M.  OUT OF MY TIME.*
  P.M. SPACKS, 249(HUDR):SPRING72-157
MANNI, E., ED.  TREBELLIO POLLIONE, "LE
  VITE DI VALERIANO E DI GALLIENO."
  A. CAMERON, 123:MAR72-115
MANNIN, E.  STORIES FROM MY LIFE.
  617(TLS):12OCT73-1259
MANNING, J.C.  BLUE INVECTIVE.
  N. CALLENDAR, 441:30DEC73-18
MANNING, S.B.  DICKENS AS SATIRIST.
  M.S. HELFAND, 454:WINTER72-186
  K. MUIR, 402(MLR):APR72-405
  M. PRICE, 676(YR):WINTER72-271

MANNONI, M.  THE BACKWARD CHILD AND HIS
  MOTHER.
  J.S. GORDON, 441:28JAN73-2
MANNONI, O.  FREUD: THE THEORY OF THE
  UNCONSCIOUS.
  617(TLS):23MAR73-317
MANNSPERGER, D.  PHYSIS BEI PLATON.
  J. SPRUTE, 53(AGP):BAND53HEFT1-112
MANO, D.K.  THE BRIDGE.
  S. BLACKBURN, 441:9SEP73-4
MANO, D.K.  THE PROSELYTIZER.*
  P.M. SPACKS, 249(HUDR):AUTUMN72-502
MANSBERGH, N. & E.W.R. LUMBY, EDS.  CON-
  STITUTIONAL RELATIONS BETWEEN BRITAIN
  AND INDIA: THE TRANSFER OF POWER 1942-
  1947.  (VOL 2)
  L. CLARK, 619(TC):VOL179#1049-51
MANSELL, D.  THE NOVELS OF JANE AUSTEN.
  617(TLS):17AUG73-950
MANSFIELD, A. - SEE KELLY, F.M.
MANSFIELD, A. & P. CUNNINGTON.  HANDBOOK
  OF ENGLISH COSTUMES IN THE 20TH CEN-
  TURY, 1900-1950.
  617(TLS):19OCT73-1289
MANSFIELD, J.  THE PSEUDO-HIPPOCRATIC
  TRACT "PERI HEBDOMADŌN," CH. 1-11 AND
  GREEK PHILOSOPHY.
  J. SCARBOROUGH, 319:OCT73-541
MANSFIELD, P., ED.  THE MIDDLE EAST.
  617(TLS):18MAY73-544
MANSION, J.E., COMP.  HARRAP'S NEW
  STANDARD FRENCH AND ENGLISH DICTIONARY.
  (PT 1: FRENCH-ENGLISH) (REV & ED BY
  R.P.L. & M. LEDÉSERT)
  617(TLS):6APR73-398
MANSKE, E.  DIE ZEITGENÖSSISCHE LITERA-
  TURWISSENSCHAFT IN DEN USA.
  E. MANSKE, 654(WB):12/1970-218
MANSON, H.W.D.  THE COUNSELLORS.  THE FES-
  TIVAL.  POTLUCK.  MAGNUS.
  T.J. COUZENS, 180(ESA):SEP72-117
MANSON, R.  THE THEORY OF KNOWLEDGE OF
  GIAMBATTISTA VICO.
  H.B., 543:DEC70-341
MANSUY, M.  GASTON BACHELARD ET LES
  ÉLÉMENTS.*
  J. BELLEMIN-NOËL, 535(RHL):SEP-DEC70-
  1091
MANSUY, M.  ÉTUDES SUR L'IMAGINATION DE
  LA VIE.
  N. BAILEY, 402(MLR):APR72-410
  M. BOWIE, 208(FS):APR72-229
  J. ONIMUS, 535(RHL):MAY-JUN71-533
MANTEUFFEL, T.  NAISSANCE D'UNE HÉRÉSIE.
  L.K. LITTLE, 589:JUL72-537
MANTRAN, R.  L'EXPANSION MUSULMANE (VIIE-
  XIE SIÈCLES).
  W. MADELUNG, 318(JAOS):JAN-MAR71-146
MANUEL, F.E.  A PORTRAIT OF ISAAC NEWTON.
  A. THACKRAY, 173(ECS):SUMMER71-485
  617(TLS):1JUN73-615
MANUPPELLA, G.  BIBLIOGRAFIA DEGLI
  SCRITTI DI MAX LEOPOLD WAGNER.
  H. MEIER, 72:BAND209HEFT1/3-174
MANVELL, R., ED.  THE INTERNATIONAL ENCY-
  CLOPEDIA OF FILM.
  617(TLS):2MAR73-228
MANVELL, R.  SARAH SIDDONS.
  N. MARSHALL, 157:SPRING71-73
MANZ-KUNZ, M-A.  EUDORA WELTY.
  L.D. RUBIN, JR., 27(AL):NOV72-516
MAO TSE-TUNG.  MAO PAPERS.  (J. CH'EN, ED)
  Y.J. CHIH, 318(JAOS):OCT-DEC71-521
  S. MERRILL, 293(JAST):MAY71-673
  639(VQR):AUTUMN71-CLXXXI
MAO TSE-TUNG.  THE POEMS OF MAO TSE-TUNG.*
  (W. BARNSTONE, ED & TRANS)
  R. LATTIMORE, 249(HUDR):AUTUMN72-482

MAQUET, J. AFRICANITY.
617(TLS):27APR73-480
MARA, M.G. CONTRIBUTO ALLO STUDIO DELLA
"PASSIO ANTHIMI."
P. COURCELLE, 555:VOL45FASC2-375
MARABOTTINI, A. POLIDORO DA CARAVAGGIO.*
C. GOULD, 39:OCT70-315
MARAN, R. BATOUALA.
M. OLMERT, 441:28JAN73-43
MARANA, G.P. LETTERS WRIT BY A TURKISH
SPY.* (A.J. WEITZMAN, ED)
M.R. BROWNELL, 481(PQ):JUL71-461
J. DULCK, 189(EA):JUL-SEP71-337
MARANDA, P. & K., EDS. STRUCTURAL ANALY-
SIS OF ORAL TRADITION.
E.O. JAMES, 203:WINTER71-341
MARANINI, L. IL THEATRO FRANCESE. (VOL
1)
J. ONIMUS, 557(RSH):OCT-DEC70-638
MARASCO, R. BURNT OFFERINGS.
C. LEHMANN-HAUPT, 441:7FEB73-41
M. LEVIN, 441:4MAR73-40
MARAVALL, J.M. EL DESARROLLO ECONÓMICO
Y LA CLASE OBRERA.
617(TLS):15JUN73-696
MARCH, M.E. FORMA E IDEA DE LOS ESPER-
PENTOS DE VALLE-INCLÁN.*
J.E. LYON, 402(MLR):APR72-444
MARC'HADOUR, G. THOMAS MORE ET LA BIBLE.*
R.S. SYLVESTER, 189(EA):JUL-SEP70-336
MARCHAND, H. THE CATEGORIES AND TYPES OF
PRESENT-DAY ENGLISH WORD-FORMATION.*
(2ND ED)
V. ADAMS, 297(JL):APR71-125
A. BRISAU, 556(RLV):1971/5-645
L. PEDERSON, 215(GL):VOL10#2-132
E. STANDOP, 38:BAND88HEFT3-347
A.R. TELLIER, 189(EA):JUL-SEP71-317
S.A. THOMPSON, 361:VOL27#1-82
MARCHAND, L.A. BYRON.
E.E.B., 191(ELN):SEP71(SUPP)-36
MARCHAND, L.A. - SEE LORD BYRON
"DAS MÄRCHENBUCH DER WELT."
F. HARKORT, 196:BAND12HEFT2/3-280
MARCHEV, Y. - SEE TSCHENKÉLI, K.
MARCHL, H., ED. BEITRÄGE ZUR LINGUISTIK
UND INFORMATIONSVERARBEITUNG.
G. SCHELSTRAETE, 75:4/1970-231
MARCILLET-JAUBERT, J. LES INSCRIPTIONS
D'ALTAVA.
A. CHASTAGNOL, 555:VOL45FASC1-187
MARCKWARDT, A.H. & R. QUIRK. A COMMON
LANGUAGE.
A. WILLOT, 556(RLV):1971/5-651
MARCORELLES, L. LIVING CINEMA.
617(TLS):21SEP73-1093
MARCOS, M.B. - SEE UNDER BERMEJO MARCOS,
M.
MARCOVICH, M. HERACLITUS.*
H. VON STADEN, 24:OCT72-608
MARCUCCI, S. HENRY L. MANSEL.
F. RESTAINO, 548(RCSF):APR-JUN71-225
MARCUS, E., ED. MIN HA-MABUA (FROM THE
FOUNTAINHEAD).
B. KIRSHENBLATT-GIMBLETT, 582(SFQ):
DEC70-371
MARCUS, P.L. YEATS AND THE BEGINNING OF
THE IRISH RENAISSANCE.
J.P. FRAYNE, 301(JEGP):APR72-280
MARCUS, R.D. GRAND OLD PARTY.*
639(VQR):SUMMER71-CXXII
MARCUS, S. FATHER COUGHLIN.
W.V. SHANNON, 441:9SEP73-22
MARCUS, S. INTRODUCTION MATHÉMATIQUE À
LA LINGUISTIQUE STRUCTURALE.
I.I. REVZIN, 361:VOL27#2/3-277

MARCUSE, H. AN ESSAY ON LIBERATION.*
N. ROTENSTREICH, 321:WINTER70[VOL5#1]-
44
MARCUSE, H. FIVE LECTURES.*
P. JOHNSON, 185:JUL71-350
MARCUSE, H. L'ONTOLOGIA DI HEGEL E LA
FONDAZIONE DI UNA TEORIA DELLA STORI-
CITÀ. (M. DAL PRA, ED)
M. DEL VECCHIO, 548(RCSF):JUL-SEP71-
350
MARCUSE, L. HEINE.
J.L.S., 191(ELN):SEP71(SUPP)-133
J.L. SAMMONS, 221(GQ):NOV71-591
MARCZALI, P. APÁM PÁLYÁJA, BARÁTAI.
617(TLS):23NOV73-1420
MARDER, H. FEMINISM AND ART.*
D.L. HIGDON, 594:SPRING71-108
D. ZIMMERMAN, 502(PRS):SUMMER71-173
MARDON, E.G. THE NARRATIVE UNITY OF THE
"CURSOR MUNDI."
P.E. BEICHNER, 589:JUL72-539
DE LA MARE, A.C. THE HANDWRITING OF
ITALIAN HUMANISTS. (VOL 1, FASC 1)
617(TLS):19OCT73-1288
DE MARÉ, E. THE LONDON DORÉ SAW.
617(TLS):16FEB73-183
DE LA MARE, W. THE COMPLETE POEMS OF
WALTER DE LA MARE.*
J. SAUNDERS, 565:VOL11#3-75
N. TALBOT, 67:NOV72-236
MAREK, G.R. BEETHOVEN.
M. HALGARD, 502(PRS):WINTER70/71-366
MAREK, G.R. GENTLE GENIUS.
617(TLS):3AUG73-899
MAREŞ, A., ED. LITURGHIERUL LUI CORESI.
E.M. WALLNER, 182:VOL24#9/10-399
MAREŞ, F.H. - SEE JONSON, B.
MARESCA, T.E. POPE'S HORATIAN POEMS.
H. GRABES, 38:BAND88HEFT1-146
MARETZEK, M. REVELATIONS OF AN OPERA
MANAGER IN 19TH-CENTURY AMERICA.*
M. PETERSON, 470:MAY71-36
MAREVNA. LIFE WITH THE PAINTERS OF LA
RUCHE.
617(TLS):17AUG73-944
MARGETTS, J. DIE SATZSTRUKTUR BEI MEISTER
ECKHART.
D. BLAMIRES, 402(MLR):JUL72-687
MARGOLIES, E. THE ART OF RICHARD WRIGHT.
N.M. TISCHLER, 594:FALL70-365
R. WELBURN, 50(ARQ):SPRING71-81
MARGOLIN, J-C. L'IDÉE DE NATURE DANS LA
PENSÉE D'ERASME.
H. VÉDRINE, 542:APR-JUN71-241
MARGOLIN, J-C. QUATORZE ANNÉES DE BIBLI-
OGRAPHIE ÉRASMIENNE (1936-1949).
J. PINEAUX, 557(RSH):APR-JUN70-317
C.R. THOMPSON, 551(RENQ):AUTUMN71-372
MARGOLIN, J-C. RECHERCHES ÉRASMIENNES.*
J. CHOMARAT, 535(RHL):JAN-FEB71-67
J. PINEAUX, 557(RSH):OCT-DEC70-637
MARGOLIS, J., ED. FACT AND EXISTENCE.*
185:OCT70-87
MARGOLIS, J. KNOWLEDGE AND EXISTENCE.
617(TLS):27JUL73-875
MARGOLIS, J.D. T.S. ELIOT'S INTELLECTUAL
DEVELOPMENT, 1922-1939.*
M.L. RAINA, 295:FEB73-134
S. STEPANCHEV, 27(AL):NOV72-505
MARGOLIUS, S. HEALTH FOODS.
G. GOLD, 441:19JUL73-39
MARGUERITE DE NAVARRE. CHANSONS SPIRIT-
UELLES. (G. DOTTIN, ED)
J. PINEAUX, 557(RSH):APR-JUN71-316
MARGUERITE DE NAVARRE. TALES FROM THE
HEPTAMÉRON. (H.P. CLIVE, ED)
R. LEBÈGUE, 549(RLC):JUL-SEP71-416
D.B. WILSON, 208(FS):OCT72-445

MARGULIES, S.R. THE PILGRIMAGE TO RUS-
SIA.*
H.H. FISHER, 32:MAR72-169
MARIANI, P.L. A COMMENTARY ON THE COM-
PLETE POEMS OF GERARD MANLEY HOPKINS.
W.R. MUNDT, 598(SOR):AUTUMN73-1029
MARÍAS, J. IDÉE DE LA MÉTAPHYSIQUE.
A. BLANC, 542:JAN-MAR70-94
MARÍAS, J. JOSÉ ORTEGA Y GASSET.
A. DONOSO, 258:DEC71-599
DE MARICHAL, S.S. - SEE UNDER SALINAS DE
MARICHAL, S.
MARIE, A. NAISSANCE DE VERSAILLES, LE
CHÂTEAU, LES JARDINS.
G. WALTON, 54:SEP71-418
SISTER MARIE-CÉLESTE. BERNANOS ET SON
OPTIQUE DE LA VIE CHRÉTIENNE.
D.W. STEEDMAN, 207(FR):DEC70-445
"JOHN MARIN BY JOHN MARIN." (C. GRAY,
ED)
R. LEBOWITZ, 58:MAR71-12
MARINACCI, B. O WONDROUS SINGER!
H. ASPIZ, 646(WWR):SEP70-92
MARINE, G. A MALE GUIDE TO WOMEN'S LIB-
ERATION.
C. DREIFUS, 441:11MAR73-26
MARINETTI, F.T. MARINETTI: SELECTED
WRITINGS.* (R.W. FLINT, ED)
442(NY):3MAR73-116
MARINI, V. ARRIGO BOITO TRA SCAPIGLIA-
TURA E CLASSICISMO.
P.Z., 228(GSLI):VOL148FASC462/463-468
DE MARINIS, T. & A. PEROSA, EDS. NUOVI
DOCUMENTI PER LA STORIA DEL RINASCI-
MENTO.
G. TOURNOY, 568(SCN):SUMMER72-54
MARIÑO, M.B. - SEE UNDER BREY MARIÑO, M.
MARINONE, N. - SEE MACROBIUS
MARISSEL, A. SAMUEL BECKETT.
J. FLETCHER, 188(ECR):FALL71-67
MARISTANY, L. - SEE CERNUDA, L.
DE MARIVAUX, P.C.D. JOURNAUX ET OEUVRES
DIVERSES.* (F. DELOFFRE & M. GILOT,
EDS)
O.A. HAAC, 546(RR):FEB71-57
R. MERCIER, 557(RSH):JAN-MAR70-157
J. SGARD, 535(RHL):JAN-FEB71-92
DE MARIVAUX, P.C.D. DAS LEBEN DER MARI-
ANNE/DER BAUER IM GLÜCK. (N. MILLER,
ED)
S. JAUERNICK, 224(GRM):MAY70-231
DE MARIVAUX, P.C.D. THÉÂTRE COMPLET.*
(F. DELOFFRE, ED)
O.A. HAAC, 546(RR):FEB71-57
R. MERCIER, 557(RSH):JAN-MAR70-157
MARKALE, J. LA FEMME CELTE.
617(TLS):14SEP73-1048
MARKANDAYA, K. THE NOWHERE MAN.
R. BRYDEN, 362:12APR73-489
M. LEVIN, 441:14JAN73-24
617(TLS):20APR73-437
MARKANDAYA, K. TWO VIRGINS.
442(NY):22OCT73-174
MARKESINIS, B.S. THE THEORY AND PRACTICE
OF DISSOLUTION OF PARLIAMENT.
617(TLS):19JAN73-56
"MARKET TOWNS AND SPATIAL DEVELOPMENT IN
INDIA."
J.E. BRUSH, 293(JAST):MAY71-703
MARKO, K. DOGMATISMUS UND EMANZIPATION
IN DER SOWJETUNION.
T.J. BLAKELEY, 32:DEC72-903
MARKOOSIE. HARPOON OF THE HUNTER.*
H.P. GUNDY, 529(QQ):WINTER71-641
H. STEWART, 255(HAB):WINTER71-56
MARKOV, V. RUSSIAN FUTURISM.
F. SCHOLZ, 490:JAN/APR70-329
E. WASIOLEK, 405(MP):MAY72-369

MARKOVIĆ, V.E. THE CHANGING FACE.
A. KETTLE, 541(RES):NOV71-520
A. MESSENGER, 648:JUN71-57
MARKS, E. SIMONE DE BEAUVOIR.
441:6MAY73-42
MARKS, E.R. - SEE SAINTE-BEUVE, C-A.
MARKS, J. HARRAP'S FRENCH/ENGLISH DIC-
TIONARY OF SLANG AND COLLOQUIALISMS.
J.A. DUNCAN, 402(MLR):JAN72-180
MARKS, P. HANG-UPS.
M. LEVIN, 441:6MAY73-40
MARKS, R.W. THE MEANING OF MARCUSE.*
P. JOHNSON, 185:JUL71-350
MARKUS, G. ÜBER DIE ERKENNTNISSTHEORET-
ISCHEN ANSICHTEN DES JUNGEN MARX.
J. GOLDMAN, 542:APR-JUN71-242
MARLIER, G. LA RENAISSANCE FLAMANDE,
PIERRE COECK D'ALOST.
C.D. CUTTLER, 54:SEP71-409
MARLITT, R. NINETEENTH STREET.
M.D. ROSS, 576:MAY70-205
MARLOW, J. CAPTAIN BOYCOTT AND THE IRISH.
617(TLS):27JUL73-857
MARLOW, J. THE LIFE AND TIMES OF GEORGE
I.
617(TLS):30NOV73-1464
MARLOWE, C. CHRISTOPHER MARLOWE: THE
COMPLETE POEMS AND TRANSLATIONS. (S.
ORGEL, ED)
H. RUSCHE, 568(SCN):FALL-WINTER72-63
MARLOWE, C. THE PLAYS OF CHRISTOPHER
MARLOWE. (R. GILL, ED)
J-B. FORT, 189(EA):OCT-DEC71-520
MARLOWE, J. CECIL RHODES.
617(TLS):12JAN73-48
MARLOWE, S. COLOSSUS.
617(TLS):23MAR73-316
MARMETTE, J. LE CHEVALIER DE MORNAC.
A. POKORNY, 296:SUMMER73-117
MARONITIS, D.N. ANAZĒTĒSE KAI NOSTOS TOY
ODYSSEA.
J.B. HAINSWORTH, 123:MAR72-100
MAROT, C. LES ÉPIGRAMMES.* (C.A. MAYER,
ED)
F. JOUKOVSKY, 545(RPH):MAY72-477
K-H. MEHNERT, 72:BAND209HEFT1/3-205
J. VOISINE, 549(RLC):JUL-SEP71-414
MAROT, C. LES PSAUMES. (S.J. LENSE-
LINK, ED)
R. LEBÈGUE, 549(RLC):OCT-DEC70-551
J. PINEAUX, 535(RHL):JAN-FEB71-68
C. THIRY, 556(RLV):1971/4-484
MARÓTI, L. A KOLOSTOR. HIPPI AKVÁRIUM.
270:VOL22#3-62
MAROTTI, F. - SEE DE' SOMMI, L.
MAROWITZ, C. A MACBETH.
P. ROBERTS, 565:VOL12#4-60
MARQUES, A.H.D. - SEE UNDER DE OLIVEIRA
MARQUES, A.H.
MÁRQUEZ, G.G. - SEE UNDER GARCÍA MÁRQUEZ,
G.
MARRAST, R. - SEE CALDERÓN DE LA BARCA,
P.
MARRAST, R. - SEE DE ESPRONCEDA, J.
MARRIOTT, A. & C.K. RACHLIN. PEYOTE.*
P. PAVICH, 649(WAL):SPRING71-72
MARROU, H-I. - SEE CLEMENT OF ALEXANDER
MARROW, A.J. - SEE KALLEN, H.M.
MARSDEN, E.W. GREEK AND ROMAN ARTILLERY:
TECHNICAL TREATISES.
J.K. ANDERSON, 124:DEC71-133
C.G. STARR, 122:JUL72-227
MARSDEN, G.M. THE EVANGELICAL MIND AND
THE NEW SCHOOL PRESBYTERIAN EXPERIENCE.
H.Y. VANDERPOOL, 432(NEQ):MAR71-166

MARSDEN, K. THE POEMS OF THOMAS HARDY.*
  R. BENVENUTO, 637(VS):DEC70-220
  R. LAWRENCE, 175:SPRING71-28
  W.W. MORGAN, 177(ELT):VOL13#3-250
  H.O., 430(NS):SEP70-474
  M. WILLIAMS, 541(RES):FEB71-112
  W. WRIGHT, 502(PRS):SUMMER71-176
MARSH, H. DARK AGE BRITAIN.
  J.S. BEDDIE, 589(JAN72-133
MARSH, P.T. THE VICTORIAN CHURCH IN
  DECLINE.
  K.S. INGLIS, 637(VS):MAR71-340
MARSH, W. BEACHHEAD IN BOHEMIA.
  J.H. WILDMAN, 598(SOR):WINTER73-233
MARSHACK, A. THE ROOTS OF CIVILIZATION.*
  C.B.M. MC BURNEY, 453:20SEP73-35
  617(TLS):12JAN73-34
MARSHALL, A., ED. THE 1971 SOUTH AMERI-
  CAN HANDBOOK.
  S.S. BENSON, 37:OCT71-42
MARSHALL, A., ED. PIONEERS AND PAINTERS.
  W. BATE, 381:SEP71-359
MARSHALL, B. URBAN THE NINTH.
  617(TLS):2MAR73-229
MARSHALL, D. INDUSTRIAL ENGLAND 1776-
  1851.
  617(TLS):22JUN73-714
MARSHALL, D.W., ED. BEDFORD HISTORICAL
  RECORDS. (VOL 4)
  J. GREGORY, 70(ANQ):JAN73-78
MARSHALL, J. THE CONSTITUTIONAL DECISIONS
  OF JOHN MARSHALL. (J.P. COTTON, JR.,
  ED)
  D.N. MAC CORMICK, 447(N&Q):OCT71-394
MARSHALL, J.D. THE OLD POOR LAW, 1795-
  1834.
  G. HIMMELFARB, 637(VS):DEC70-203
MARSHALL, J.H. - SEE FAIDIT, U.
MARSHALL, J.V. THE WIND AT MORNING.
  M. LEVIN, 441:9SEP73-42
MARSHALL, R. ALASKA WILDERNESS. (G.
  MARSHALL, ED)
  J. BONI, 649(WAL):WINTER71-315
MARSHALL, R.H., JR., T.E. BIRD & A.Q.
  BLANE, EDS. ASPECTS OF RELIGION IN
  THE SOVIET UNION, 1917-1967.
  J.P. SCANLAN, 32:MAR72-175
MARSHALL, R.L. THE COMPOSITIONAL PROCESS
  OF J.S. BACH.
  617(TLS):16MAR73-298
MARSHALL, S.L.A. CRIMSONED PRAIRIE.
  D. BROWN, 441:22APR73-20
  617(TLS):21SEP73-1093
MARSHALL, T. MAGIC WATER.*
  P. STEVENS, 529(QQ):WINTER71-627
MARSHALL, T. THE PSYCHIC MARINER.*
  J. ZASLOVE, 648:OCT71-60
MARSHALL, W. THE FIRE CIRCLE. THE AGE
  OF DEATH.
  L. CANTRELL, 381:MAR71-125
MARSHALL, W.H. WILKIE COLLINS.
  W.D. SCHAEFER, 445(NCF):DEC70-379
MARSHALL, W.H. THE WORLD OF THE VICTOR-
  IAN NOVEL.*
  R.D. HUME, 556(RLV):1970/2-216
MARSHFIELD, A. DRAGONFLY.
  617(TLS):19JAN73-69
MARSZALEK, J.F., JR. COURT MARTIAL.
  441:11MAR73-46
MARTENS, G. & H. ZELLER, EDS. TEXTE UND
  VARIANTEN.
  E.A. PHILIPPSON, 406:WINTER72-380
MARTENS, W. DIE BOTSCHAFT DER TUGEND.*
  L. VÖLKER, 556(RLV):1971/4-492
MARTENS, W. - SEE "DER PATRIOT"
MARTÍ, J. PÁGINAS LITERARIAS. (A.A.
  CASTRO & D.V. BENSON, EDS)
  S.R. MAC LEOD, 238:MAR71-233

MARTÍ, J. VERSOS LIBRES. (I.A. SCHULMAN,
  ED)
  J.C. KINNEAR, 86(BHS):JUL72-324
MARTÍ, K. ZUM BEISPIEL: BERN 1972.
  617(TLS):12OCT73-1218
MARTÍ, M., ED. POETI DEL DOLCE STIL
  NUOVO.
  D. VALLI, 228(GSLI):VOL148FASC461-98
MARTÍ, M. - SEE BOCCACCIO, G.
MARTIAL. THE EPIGRAMS OF MARTIAL. (J.
  MICHIE, ED & TRANS)
  617(TLS):4MAY73-491
MARTIMORT, A.-G., ED. THE CHURCH AT
  PRAYER. (VOL 2)
  617(TLS):1JUN73-625
MARTIN, A., ED. WINTER'S TALES FROM
  IRELAND.
  T. CROWE, 159(DM):WINTER70/71-121
MARTIN, B., ED. GREAT 20TH CENTURY
  JEWISH PHILOSOPHERS.
  S. FELDMAN, 328:SUMMER70-380
MARTIN, B. FRANK MARTIN.
  617(TLS):5OCT73-1167
MARTIN, B. & SHUI CHIEN-TUNG. MAKERS
  OF CHINA.
  617(TLS):2MAR73-249
MARTIN, B.K. & S.T. KNIGHT. ASPECTS OF
  CELTIC LITERATURE.
  R. BROMWICH, 382(MAE):1972/1-78
MARTIN, C. IN AN IRON GLOVE.
  G. DAVIES, 255(HAB):SPRING70-61
MARTIN, D. THE RELIGIOUS AND THE SECU-
  LAR.
  J.B.L., 543:SEP70-139
MARTIN, D. TRACTS AGAINST THE TIMES.
  A. RYAN, 362:27DEC73-891
MARTIN, F.X. & F.J. BYRNE, EDS. THE
  SCHOLAR REVOLUTIONARY.
  617(TLS):16NOV73-1399
MARTIN, G., ED. ALLGEMEINER KANTINDEX ZU
  KANTS GESAMMELTEN SCHRIFTEN. (VOL 20)
  R. MALTER, 342:BAND61HEFT4-520
MARTIN, G., ED. ELIOT IN PERSPECTIVE.
  G. DONALDSON, 184(EIC):JUL71-308
  J.P., 376:APR71-131
  A. RIDLER, 541(RES):AUG71-380
  H.H. WAGGONER, 149:JUN72-240
MARTIN, G. IMMANUEL KANT. (4TH ED)
  L.W. BECK, 342:BAND61HEFT2-273
MARTIN, G. NATIONAL GALLERY CATALOGUES:
  THE FLEMISH SCHOOL C.`1600-C. 1900.
  C. WHITE, 39:JUN71-527
MARTIN, G. ROMA SANCTA (1581).* (G.B.
  PARKS, ED)
  R.E. MC NALLY, 551(RENQ):AUTUMN71-370
MARTIN, G.H. & S. MC INTYRE. A BIBLIO-
  GRAPHY OF BRITISH AND IRISH MUNICIPAL
  HISTORY. (VOL 1)
  617(TLS):9FEB73-161
MARTIN, H.H. RALPH MC GILL, REPORTER.
  T. LIPPMAN, JR., 441:22JUL73-19
  H.E. SALISBURY, 441:18JUL73-41
MARTIN, H-J. LIVRE, POUVOIRS ET SOCIÉTÉ
  À PARIS AU XVIIe SIÈCLE (1598-1701).*
  C. CRISTIN, 557(RSH):JAN-MAR71-127
  R. MANDROU, 535(RHL):SEP-DEC70-1066
  R.A. SAYCE, 354:SEP71-275
MARTIN, J. ROBERT LOWELL.
  R. ASSELINEAU, 189(EA):JUL-SEP71-350
  H. LINK, 502(PRS):SUMMER70-183
MARTIN, J. THE 95 FILE.
  N. CALLENDAR, 441:18MAR73-41
MARTIN, J.L., B. NICHOLSON & N. GABO -
  SEE "CIRCLE"
MARTIN, J.R. THE CEILING PAINTINGS FOR
  THE JESUIT CHURCH IN ANTWERP.
  C. WHITE, 39:JUN71-527

MARTIN, J.R. THE DECORATIONS FOR THE
POMPA INTROITUS FERDINANDI.
617(TLS):19JAN73-68
MARTIN, J.R. EXPLAINING, UNDERSTANDING,
AND TEACHING.
G. LANGFORD, 483:APR71-182
MARTIN, J.R., ED. RUBENS BEFORE 1620.
617(TLS):6JUL73-766
MARTIN, J.R. RUBENS: THE ANTWERP ALTAR-
PIECES.
G. MARTIN, 39:FEB70-168
MARTIN, J-Y. LES MATAKAM DU CAMEROUN.
F. REHFISCH, 69:JUL71-253
MARTIN, L.A. EDUCATION IN KENYA BEFORE
INDEPENDENCE.
M. COUCH, 69:OCT70-401
MARTIN, M. A HALF-CENTURY OF ELIOT
CRITICISM.
617(TLS):6APR73-401
MARTIN, M. THREE POPES AND A CARDINAL.*
617(TLS):19OCT73-1285
MARTIN, M.W. FUTURIST ART AND THEORY
1909-15.*
R. ALLEY, 39:MAR70-247
MARTIN, P. VOICE UNACCOMPANIED.
F.D. REEVE, 491:MAR73-348
MARTIN, R. INTERNATIONAL DICTIONARY OF
FOOD AND COOKING.
617(TLS):21DEC73-1574
MARTIN, R. - SEE WAIN, J.
MARTIN, R. & R.H. FRYER. REDUNDANCY AND
PATERNALIST CAPITALISM.
617(TLS):18MAY73-565
MARTIN, R.G. JENNIE.* (BRITISH TITLE:
LADY RANDOLPH CHURCHILL.) (VOLS 1&2)
617(TLS):5JAN73-9
MARTIN, R.H., WITH J.E. MORTIMER - SEE
LAURENTIUS GUILELMUS OF SAONA
MARTIN, R.L., ED. THE PARADOX OF THE
LIAR.*
A.I.F. URQUHART, 154:DEC71-823
MARTIN, R.M. BELIEF, EXISTENCE, AND
MEANING.
K.T., 543:JUN71-749
MARTIN, S.E. & Y-S.C. LEE. BEGINNING
KOREAN.*
P.H. LEE, 318(JAOS):JAN-MAR71-150
MARTIN, S.E., Y.H. LEE & S-U. CHANG. A
KOREAN-ENGLISH DICTIONARY.*
H.B. LEE, 47(ARL):[N.S.]VOL1-112
MARTÍN SANTOS, L. APÓLOGOS.
J.W. DÍAZ, 238:MAY71-396
MARTINA, A., ED. SOLON, TESTIMONIA VET-
ERUM.*
J-D. SMART, 487:SPRING71-86
MARTINES, L., ED. VIOLENCE AND CIVIL
DISORDER IN ITALIAN CITIES 1200-1500.
617(TLS):2FEB73-120
MARTINET, A. LANGUE ET FONCTION.
H. BONNARD, 209(FM):APR71-161
MARTINET, A., ED. LA LINGUISTIQUE.
E.F.K. KOERNER, 353:SEP70-103
V. VÄÄNÄNEN, 439(NM):1971/4-766
MARTINETTI, P. KANT. (NEW ED) (M. DEL
PRA, ED)
K. OEDINGEN, 342:BAND62HEFT3-407
MARTÍNEZ, E.J. - SEE DE LEDESMA, A.
MARTÍNEZ, T.E. SAGRADO.
G.R. MC MURRAY, 238:MAR71-205
MARTÍNEZ DE TOLEDO, A. ARCIPRESTE DE
TALAVERA O CORBACHO. (J. GONZÁLEZ
MUELA, ED)
D.W. LOMAX, 86(BHS):APR72-177
MARTÍNEZ MARZOA, F. - SEE KANT, I.
MARTÍNEZ NADAL, R. "EL PÚBLICO."
I. GIBSON, 86(BHS):JUL72-311

MARTÍNEZ RUIZ, J. ANTONIO AZORÍN. (E.I.
FOX, ED)
C.A. LONGHURST, 86(BHS):APR72-193
MARTÍNEZ TORNER, E. LÍRICA HISPÁNICA.
R. PAOLI, 545(RPH):NOV71-247
MARTINI, F. & W. MÜLLER-SEIDEL, EDS.
KLASSISCHE DEUTSCHE DICHTUNG. (VOL 18)
C.P. MAGILL, 220(GL&L):JAN72-156
MARTINI, F.D. - SEE UNDER FRANCESCO DI
GIORGIO MARTINI
MARTINI, F.M. TUTTE LE OPERE. (G. FARI-
NELLI, ED)
S.O., 228(GSLI):VOL148FASC462/463-469
MARTINO, A. STORIA DELLE TEORIE DRAMMA-
TICHE NELLA GERMANIA DEL SETTECENTO
(1730-1780).* (VOL 1)
W. HIRDT, 52:BAND5HEFT3-313
MARTINS, E. STUDIEN ZUR FRAGE DER LIN-
GUISTISCHEN INTERFERENZ.*
J. HORNE, 220(GL&L):JUL72-390
MARTON, G. & C. FELIX. THREE-CORNERED
COVER.
N. CALLENDAR, 441:14JAN73-30
MARTY, M.A. LUTHERANS AND ROMAN CATHOLI-
CISM.
J-D. BURGER, 182:VOL24#7/8-332
MARTY, M.E. THE FIRE WE CAN LIGHT.
J.B. BRESLIN, 441:11NOV73-14
E.B. FISKE, 441:30NOV73-41
MARTY, M.E. PROTESTANTISM.*
617(TLS):2MAR73-243
MARTZ, L.L. THE WIT OF LOVE.*
R.A. FOAKES, 175:SPRING71-23
J.H. MC CABE, 613:SPRING71-135
P.K. SUNDARARAJAN, 648:JAN71-66
J.M. WALLACE, 551(RENQ):SUMMER71-282
MARTZ, L.L. & R.S. SYLVESTER - SEE
"THOMAS MORE'S PRAYER BOOK"
MARTZ, W.J. JOHN BERRYMAN.
R. ASSELINEAU, 189(EA):JUL-SEP71-349
MARUO, S. & OTHERS. ZŌZŌ MEIKI.
A. SOPER, 57:VOL32#2/3-238
MARVELL, A. THE GARDEN. (T.O. CALHOUN
& J.M. POTTER, EDS)
P. LEGOUIS, 189(EA):JAN-MAR71-93
MARVELL, A. THE REHEARSAL TRANSPROS'D
[AND] THE REHEARSAL TRANSPROS'D THE
SECOND PART. (D.I.B. SMITH, ED)
T. HAYES, 568(SCN):SUMMER72-38
MARWICK, A. THE NATURE OF HISTORY.
K.J. HANSEN, 529(QQ):AUTUMN71-471
MARWICK, H. THE PLACE-NAMES OF BIRSAY.
(W.F.H. NICOLAISEN, ED)
F.L. UTLEY, 424:MAR71-47
MARX, A. SON OF GROUCHO.
R.R. LINGEMAN, 441:5JAN73-33
F. MUIR, 362:7JUN73-769
617(TLS):18MAY73-563
MARX, G. & R.J. ANOBILE. THE MARX
BROTHERS SCRAPBOOK.
W. MARKFIELD, 441:2DEC73-96
MARX, K. LE CAPITAL.
J. BERNHARDT, 542:APR-JUN71-249
MARX, K. EARLY TEXTS.* (D. MC LELLAN,
ED & TRANS)
A. WALKER, 575(SEER):JAN72-144
MARX, K. THE GRUNDRISSE. (D. MC LELLAN,
ED & TRANS)
H.B. ACTON, 32:SEP72-687
639(VQR):AUTUMN71-CLXXXVI
MARX, K. GRUNDRISSE. (M. NICOLAUS, ED &
TRANS)
A. GAMBLE, 362:25OCT73-562
617(TLS):19OCT73-1284
MARX, K. POLITICAL WRITINGS. (VOLS 1&2)
(D. FERNBACH, ED)
617(TLS):19OCT73-1284

MARX, P., ED. 12 SHORT STORY WRITERS.
  J.W. STEVENSON, 573(SSF):SUMMER71-475
"MARX AND CONTEMPORARY SCIENTIFIC
  THOUGHT."
  K.F. KOECHER, 550(RUSR):OCT71-388
SISTER MARY AGNES. NO ORDINARY LOVER.
  617(TLS):16NOV73-1405
"MARYLAND, HALL OF RECORDS: THIRTY-FOURTH
  ANNUAL REPORT OF THE ARCHIVIST...FOR
  THE FISCAL YEAR JULY 1, 1968 TO JUNE
  30, 1969."
  C.F.W. COKER, 14:JUL71-323
MARZIO, P.C. RUBE GOLDBERG.
  R. LYNES, 441:16DEC73-6
MARZOA, F.M. - SEE UNDER MARTINEZ MARZOA,
  F.
MAS, E.G. - SEE UNDER GONZÁLEZ MAS, E.
MASAJI, C. - SEE UNDER CHIBA MASAJI
MASEFIELD, J. THE TWENTY-FIVE DAYS.
  617(TLS):19JAN73-71
MASER, E.A. - SEE "CESARE RIPA"
MA'SHAR, A. - SEE UNDER ABŪ MA'SHAR
MASLEN, K.I.D. THE BOWYER ORNAMENT
  STOCK.
  617(TLS):3AUG73-912
MASON, A.T. & W.M. BEANEY. AMERICAN
  CONSTITUTIONAL LAW.
  I. DILLIARD, 31(ASCH):SPRING73-348
MASON, C. HOSTAGE.
  N. CALLENDAR, 441:30DEC73-18
  617(TLS):3AUG73-911
MASON, C. & J. DIXON. THE JOURNAL OF
  CHARLES MASON AND JEREMIAH DIXON.
  (TRANSCRIBED BY A.H. MASON)
  N. REINGOLD, 14:JAN71-64
MASON, E.S. & R.E. ASHER. THE WORLD
  BANK SINCE BRETTON WOODS.
  J.K. GALBRAITH, 441:7OCT73-4
MASON, F.V. LOG CABIN NOBLE.
  M. LEVIN, 441:30SEP73-20
MASON, G. THE PAPERS OF GEORGE MASON.
  (R.A. RUTLAND, ED)
  R. FRIEDENBERG, 583:SPRING72-326
  J.C. ROBERT, 639(VQR):WINTER71-133
  G.C. ROGERS, JR., 656(WMQ):OCT71-676
MASON, H. GILGAMESH.
  639(VQR):SPRING71-LXII
MASON, H.A. EDITING WYATT.
  617(TLS):6JUL73-768
MASON, H.A. SHAKESPEARE'S TRAGEDIES OF
  LOVE.
  A.L. FRENCH, 97(CQ):SUMMER/AUTUMN71-
  393
  E. QUINN, 551(RENQ):WINTER71-571
MASON, H.A. TO HOMER THROUGH POPE.
  617(TLS):5JAN73-8
MASON, K.L.J. & J.C. SAGER. SPANISH
  ORAL DRILL BOOK.
  M. BARRIO, 430(NS):MAR70-153
  F.J. SHAMBERG, 399(MLJ):OCT71-413
MASON, O. THE GAZETTEER OF ENGLAND.
  617(TLS):20APR73-450
MASON, P. PATTERNS OF DOMINANCE.*
  B. RYAN, 293(JAST):MAY71-651
MASS, E. - SEE MARQUIS D'ADHEMAR
MASSENZIO, M. CULTURA E CRISI PERMA-
  NENTE.
  R.E. WITT, 123:JUN72-287
MASSER, A. BIBEL, APOKRYPHEN UND LEGEN-
  DEN.*
  P. SALMON, 220(GL&L):APR72-306
LORD MASSEREENE AND FERRARD. THE LORDS.
  617(TLS):3AUG73-906
MASSET, P. LA PENSÉE DE HERBERT MARCUSE.
  R. NADEAU, 154:SEP71-639
MASSEY, G.J. UNDERSTANDING SYMBOLIC
  LOGIC.
  G. MATTHEWS, 316:DEC71-678

MASSEY, I. THE UNCREATING WORD.
  G.L. BRUNS, 481(PQ):JAN71-150
MASSEY, I. - SEE SHELLEY, P.B.
MASSEY, L.R., COMP. "MAN WORKING," 1919-
  1962.*
  E. MOTTRAM, 354:MAR70-78
MASSIN. LA LETTRE ET L'IMAGE.
  G. LASCAULT, 98:FEB71-160
MASSINGER, P. & N. FIELD. THE FATAL
  DOWRY. (T.A. DUNN, ED)
  J.C. MAXWELL, 184(EIC):OCT71-382
MASSIP, R. LA VIE ABSENTE.
  617(TLS):12OCT73-1210
MASSOLO, A. PRIME RICERCHE DI HEGEL.
  B. TEYSSÈDRE, 542:JAN-MAR70-101
"ANDRÉ MASSON: DRAWINGS."
  617(TLS):19JAN73-73
MASSON, É. RECHERCHES SUR LES PLUS AN-
  CIENS EMPRUNTS SÉMITIQUES EN GREC.*
  D.M. JONES, 123:DEC72-369
MASSON, G. A CONCISE HISTORY OF REPUB-
  LICAN ROME.
  617(TLS):30NOV73-1471
MASSON, J.L. & M.V. PATWARDHAN. ŚĀNTARASA
  AND ABHINAVAGUPTA'S PHILOSOPHY OF AES-
  THETICS.
  E. DEUTSCH, 293(JAST):NOV70-215
MASTER, A. A GRAMMAR OF OLD MARATHI.
  H. BERGER, 343:BAND13HEFT1-99
"THE MASTER OF MARY OF BURGUNDY."
  ATIRNOMIS, 58:NOV70-13
  J.G. PLANTE, 363:AUG71-119
"MASTERPIECES OF FIFTY CENTURIES: THE
  METROPOLITAN MUSEUM OF ART."
  T.A. HEINRICH, 96:OCT/NOV71-73
  S. ROSENTHAL, 58:SUMMER71-13
  639(VQR):SUMMER71-CXXXIV
MASTERS, A. THE SUMMER THAT BLED.
  617(TLS):19JAN73-58
MASTERS, E.L. WHITMAN.
  C.E. BURGESS, 646(WWR):MAR71-25
MASTERS, G.M. RABELAISIAN DIALECTIC AND
  THE PLATONIC-HERMETIC TRADITION.*
  J-M. KLINKENBERG, 556(RLV):1971/5-633
  J-Y. POUILLOUX, 535(RHL):SEP-DEC70-
  1064
MASTERSON, P. ATHEISM AND ALIENATION.
  C. LYAS, 518:JAN72-23
MASTERSON, W. THE UNDERTAKER WIND.
  N. CALLENDAR, 441:17JUN73-32
MASTNY, V. THE CZECHS UNDER NAZI RULE.
  F.L. CARSTEN, 575(SEER):APR72-314
MASULLO, A. METAFISICA ED EMPIRISMO NEL
  PENSIERO DI B. CROCE.
  E. NAMER, 542:OCT-DEC71-464
MA'ŞŪMĪ, M.Ş.H. - SEE AL-RĀZĪ, F.A.
MASUR, G. IMPERIAL BERLIN.
  A. WALDENRATH, 221(GQ):NOV71-610
MASUR, H.Q. THE ATTORNEY.
  N. CALLENDAR, 441:6MAY73-41
MATA GAVIDIA, J. MAGNIFICENCIA ESPIRI-
  TUAL DE FRANCISCO GAVIDIA.
  E.U. IRVING, 238:MAY71-404
MATCZAK, S.A. PHILOSOPHY.
  W.A. SMITH, 258:DEC71-603
MATCZAK, S.A. RESEARCH AND COMPOSITION
  IN PHILOSOPHY.
  E.R.K., 477:AUTUMN70-546
MATEJKA, L. & K. POMORSKA, EDS. READ-
  INGS IN RUSSIAN POETICS.
  J. FIZER, 32:SEP72-735
MATER, E. DEUTSCHE VERBEN. (PTS 1, 2,
  5 & 7)
  D. NERIUS, 682(ZPSK):BAND23HEFT6-636
MATER, E. DEUTSCHE VERBEN. (PTS 3&4)
  M.H. FOLSOM, 353:DEC70-113
  D. NERIUS, 682(ZPSK):BAND23HEFT6-636

237

MATERNUS, F. - SEE UNDER FIRMICUS MATER-
NUS
MATHAUSER, Z. NEPOPULÁRNÍ STUDIE.
K. POMORSKA, 279:VOL14-212
MATHÉ, R. - SEE GUILLAUMIN, É.
MATHER, B. SNOWLINE.
N. CALLENDAR, 441:8JUL73-26
617(TLS):17AUG73-959
MATHER, C. THE ANGEL OF BETHESDA. (G.W.
JONES, ED)
V. BULLOUGH, 165:FALL73-205
MATHERS, M. RIDING THE RAILS.
W.H. HONAN, 441:2DEC73-97
442(NY):31DEC73-60
MATHESON, S.A. PERSIA: AN ARCHAEOLOGICAL
GUIDE.
617(TLS):12JAN73-42
MATHEW, D. LORD ACTON AND HIS TIMES.
R.J. SCHOECK, 637(VS):DEC70-212
MATHEWS, A.S. LAW, ORDER AND LIBERTY IN
SOUTH AFRICA.
617(TLS):26JAN73-82
MATHEWS, J. - SEE VALÉRY, P.
MATHEWS, M.M. HENRY OSSAWA TANNER,
AMERICAN ARTIST.*
R. PINCUS-WITTEN, 54:SEP70-336
R. WELBURN, 50(ARQ):AUTUMN70-275
MATHEWS, O. EARLY PHOTOGRAPHS AND EARLY
PHOTOGRAPHERS.
617(TLS):11MAY73-530
MATHEWS, T.F. THE EARLY CHURCHES OF
CONSTANTINOPLE.
617(TLS):9MAR73-264
MATHIAS, P. THE FIRST INDUSTRIAL NATION.
E.W. COONEY, 637(VS):DEC70-223
MATHUR, D.C. NATURALISTIC PHILOSOPHIES
OF EXPERIENCE.
H.J. BIRX, 484(PPR):JUN72-581
MATHY, H., ED. DIE GESCHICHTE DES MAIN-
ZER ERZKANZLERARCHIVS 1782-1815.
U. HELFENSTEIN, 182:VOL24#11/12-504
MATILLA, A. & I. SILÉN, EDS. THE PUERTO
RICAN POETS.
W. BARNSTONE, 441:4MAR73-18
MATISOFF, J.A. - SEE UNDER BURLING, R.
MATISSE, H. ECRITS ET PROPOS SUR L'ART.
(D. FOURCADE, ED)
A. BLUNT, 453:14JUN73-31
617(TLS):16FEB73-170
MATORÉ, G. HISTOIRE DES DICTIONNAIRES
FRANÇAIS.
R.W. LANGACKER, 206:AUG71-434
K. OHNESORG, 353:APR71-103
A. REY, 98:FEB70-163
MATORELL, J. & M. JOAN DE GALBA. TIRANT
LO BLANC. (M. DE RIQUER, ED)
J-L. MARFANY, 86(BHS):APR72-198
MATORELL, J. & M. JOAN DE GALBA. TIRANT
LO BLANC. (J.F. VIDAL JOVÉ, ED & TRANS)
J-L. MARFANY, 86(BHS):APR72-198
205(FMLS):APR70-209
MATSUBARA, N. & S. HITCHINGS. BOSTON
IMPRESSIONS.
D.J. COOLIDGE, 432(NEQ):JUN71-312
MATSUI, T. & TOSHIO YAMAZAKI - SEE UNDER
TÕRU MATSUI & TOSHIO YAMAZAKI
MATSUMOTO, K. ON THE VOWEL SYSTEM OF
IONIC-ATTIC.*
R. SCHMITT, 260(IF):BAND74-232
MATSUMOTO, S. MOTOORI NORINAGA, 1730-
1801.
D.M. EARL, 293(JAST):FEB71-458
MATSUNAGA, A. THE BUDDHIST PHILOSOPHY OF
ASSIMILATION.
L. HURVITZ, 293(JAST):NOV70-244
VON MATT, P. DIE AUGEN DER AUTOMATEN.
J.M. MC GLATHERY, 301(JEGP):OCT72-583

MATTAUCH, H. DIE LITERARISCHE KRITIK DER
FRÜHEN FRANZÖSISCHEN ZEITSCHRIFTEN
(1665-1748).
W. ENGLER, 430(NS):MAY71-284
M-F. MORRIS, 546(RR):FEB71-53
F. RAU, 224(GRM):BAND21HEFT1-111
MATTENKLOTT, G. MELANCHOLIE IN DER
DRAMATIK DES STURM UND DRANG.*
H.B. GARLAND, 220(GL&L):JAN72-165
H-J. SCHINGS, 52:BAND6HEFT2-215
MATTES, J. DER WAHNSINN IM GRIECHISCHEN
MYTHOS UND IN DER DICHTUNG BIS ZUM
DRAMA DES FÜNFTEN JAHRHUNDERTS.
N. ROBERTSON, 124:APR-MAY72-274
MATTFELD, J. VARIETY MUSIC CAVALCADE,
1620-1969.
E.N. WATERS, 415:JAN72-47
MATTHAEI, R. - SEE VON GOETHE, J.W.
MATTHEW, H.C.G. THE LIBERAL IMPERIALISTS.
617(TLS):13APR73-416
MATTHEW, R., J. REID & M. LINDSAY, EDS.
THE CONSERVATION OF GEORGIAN EDINBURGH.
A. MANNING, 362:15MAR73-347
MATTHEWS, B. THE RECEDING WAVE.
L. CANTRELL, 71(ALS):MAY73-99
MATTHEWS, D., ED. KEYBOARD MUSIC.*
F. DAWES, 415:JUN72-560
MATTHEWS, D. SUE THE B*ST*RDS.
G. GOLD, 441:16AUG73-39
MATTHEWS, H.L. HALF OF SPAIN DIED.
442(NY):31MAR73-118
MATTHEWS, H.M.V. CHARACTER AND SYMBOL IN
SHAKESPEARE'S PLAYS.
J. BRITTON, 613:SPRING70-131
J.B. FORT, 189(EA):JAN-MAR71-88
MATTHEWS, J. BEYOND THE BRIDGE.*
J.L. HALIO, 598(SOR):SPRING73-455
MATTHEWS, J. PICTURES OF THE JOURNEY
BACK.
D.K. MANO, 441:11MAR73-48
MATTHEWS, J. THE TALE OF ASA BEAN.
639(VQR):SUMMER71-XCVII
MATTHEWS, J.H. SURREALIST POETRY IN
FRANCE.*
A. BALAKIAN, 401(MLQ):JUN72-208
H.S. GERSHMAN, 207(FR):FEB71-605
S.I. LOCKERBIE, 208(FS):JAN72-92
MATTHEWS, N. MATERIALS FOR WEST AFRICAN
HISTORY IN THE ARCHIVES OF THE UNITED
KINGDOM.
617(TLS):2NOV73-1352
MATTHEWS, R.A. THE MULTINATIONAL CORPORA-
TION AND THE WORLD OF TOMORROW.
C.S. BURCHILL, 529(QQ):SPRING71-159
MATTHEWS, W. OLD AND MIDDLE ENGLISH LIT-
ERATURE.
H. GNEUSS, 38:BAND88HEFT1-99
MATTHEWS, W. SLEEK FOR THE LONG FLIGHT.
V. YOUNG, 249(HUDR):WINTER72/73-668
MATTHIAS, J. BUCYRUS.*
J.R. REED, 491:APR73-47
MATTHIESSEN, P. & E. PORTER. THE TREE
WHERE MAN WAS BORN.*
C. CONNOLLY, 453:25JAN73-19
617(TLS):19JAN73-73
MATURE, A. WENCESLAO FERNÁNDEZ FLÓREZ
Y SU NOVELA.
R. ZAETTA, 238:MAR71-197
MATUTE, A.M. FIESTA AL NOROESTE. (L.
ALPERA, ED)
E.M. DIAL, 238:DEC71-988
M.M. DÍAZ, 399(MLJ):DEC71-543
MATZ, F. DIE DIONYSISCHEN SARKOPHAGE.
G.M.A. HANFMANN, 54:SEP71-397
MATZEL, K. EINFÜHRUNG IN DIE SINGHALES-
ISCHE SPRACHE.
R.E. ASHER, 260(IF):BAND74-226

MÄTZLER, M.C. ROMANISCHES WORTGUT IN DEN
MUNDARTEN VORARLBERGS.
G. FRANCESCATO, 433:APR71-209
MAUCH, C. THE JOURNALS OF CARL MAUCH,
1869-1872. (E.E. BURKE, ED)
A.D. ROBERTS, 69:OCT70-385
MAUCH, U. GESCHEHEN "AN SICH" UND VOR-
GANG OHNE URHEBERZUG IM MODERNEN
FRANZÖSISCH.*
B. FOSTER, 208(FS):JUL72-367
MAUD, R. - SEE THOMAS, D.
MAUGENDRE, L.A. LA RENAISSANCE CATHO-
LIQUE AU DÉBUT DU XXE SIÈCLE. (VOLS
4&5)
J. ONIMUS, 557(RSH):JAN-MAR70-177
MAUGENDRE, L.A. - SEE DE BRÉMOND D'ARS, E.
MAUGER, G. GRAMMAIRE PRATIQUE DU FRAN-
ÇAIS D'AUJOURD'HUI.*
J. LANHER, 209(FM):OCT70-453
MAUGER, G. & M. BRUÉZIÈRE. LA FRANÇAIS
ET LA VIE 1.
J. CANTERA, 202(FMOD):JUN71-333
MAUGHAM, R. THE BARRIER.
S. HILL, 362:19APR73-520
617(TLS):20APR73-451
MAUGHAM, R. ESCAPE FROM THE SHADOWS.*
P. ADAMS, 61:APR73-128
MAUGHAM, R. THE LAST ENCOUNTER.*
M. LEVIN, 441:21OCT73-51
DE MAUPASSANT, G. CONTES DU SURNATUREL.*
(A. KELLETT, ED)
P-J. WHYTE, 208(FS):JAN72-90
MAURACH, G. DER BAU VON SENECAS EPISTULAE
MORALES.
M. WINTERBOTTOM, 123:JUN72-224
MAURENS, J. LA TRAGÉDIE SANS TRAGIQUE.
R. GARAPON, 535(RHL):JUL-AUG70-701
MAURER, F. ABRAHAM A SANCTA CLARAS "HUY!
UND PFUY! DER WELT."
G.P. KNAPP, 657(WW):NOV/DEC70-432
MAURER, F., ED. DIE RELIGIÖSEN DICHTUN-
GEN DES 11. UND 12. JAHRHUNDERTS.
(VOL 3)
D.H. GREEN, 402(MLR):JUL72-684
B. NAUMANN, 382(MAE):1972/2-154
MAURER, F. - SEE BESCH, W. & OTHERS
MAURER, R.K. HEGEL UND DAS ENDE DER
GESCHICHTE.*
K. HARTMANN, 53(AGP):BAND53HEFT1-107
A. LICHTIGFELD, 182:VOL24#6-257
MAURIAC, C. THE OTHER DE GAULLE.
617(TLS):16NOV73-1393
MAURIAC, F. "LE BAISER AU LÉPREUX" AND
"GÉNITRIX." (R.A. ESCOFFEY, ED)
R.J. NORTH, 208(FS):JUL72-355
MAURICE. MAURICIUS, "ARTA MILITARĂ."
(H. MIHĂESCU, ED & TRANS)
R. BROWNING, 123:JUN72-285
MAURICE, F.D. SKETCHES OF CONTEMPORARY
AUTHORS, 1828. (A.J. HARTLEY, ED)
G.N. SHARMA, 150(DR):SUMMER71-301
DU MAURIER, D. RULE BRITANNIA.*
M. LEVIN, 441:21JAN73-24
E. WEEKS, 61:FEB73-101
442(NY):17FEB73-110
MAUROIS, A. MEMOIRS 1885-1967.
639(VQR):WINTER71-XXXII
MAUROIS, M. CONTES DE MICHELLE MAUROIS.
(W. MEIDEN, ED)
R-M. DAELE-GUINAN, 207(FR):OCT70-156
MAURON, C. PHÈDRE.
B. CHÉDOZEAU, 535(RHL):SEP-DEC70-1072
MAURRAS, C. DE LA POLITIQUE NATURELLE
AU NATIONALISME INTÉGRAL. (F. NATTER
& C. ROUSSEAU, EDS)
617(TLS):5OCT73-1186
MAURY, C. FOLK ORIGINS OF INDIAN ART.
S. KRAMRISCH, 293(JAST):NOV70-217

MAUSER, U. GOTTESBILD UND MENSCHWERDUNG.
F.F. BRUCE, 182:VOL24#11/12-462
MAUSER, W. - SEE VON EICHENDORFF, J.
MAUSS, M. OEUVRES DE MARCEL MAUSS. (V.
KARADY, ED)
R. LENOIR, 542:APR-JUN71-244
MAUTNER, F.H. LICHTENBERG, GESCHICHTE
SEINES GEISTES.*
H. MEYER, 133:1970/2&3-300
P. PÜTZ, 680(ZDP):BAND89HEFT2-315
MAUTNER, F.H. - SEE NESTROY, J.
MAVOR, E. A GREEN EQUINOX.
R. GARFITT, 362:15NOV72-674
617(TLS):7DEC73-1512
MAVROCORDATO, A. - SEE WYCHERLEY, W.
MAVRODES, G.I. BELIEF IN GOD.
R.A. OAKES, 477:WINTER71-135
R.A. OAKES, 484(PPR):JUN71-616
R.E. SANTONI, 258:SEP71-440
MAVRODIN, V.V. & OTHERS. KREST'IANSKAIA
VOINA V ROSSII V 1773-1775 GODAKH: VOS-
STANIE PUGACHEVA. (VOL 3)
J.T. ALEXANDER, 32:JUN72-419
MAW, J. SENTENCES IN SWAHILI.
L. HARRIES, 69:APR70-189
MAX, S. CAHIER DE TRAVAUX PRATIQUES.
B. EBLING, 207(FR):APR71-1003
MAX, S. DIALOGUES ET SITUATIONS.
B. EBLING, 207(FR):APR71-1003
G.J. HASENAUER, 399(MLJ):MAR71-193
MAXELON, M-O. STRESEMANN UND FRANKREICH
1914-1929.
617(TLS):29JUN73-739
MAXTONE-GRAHAM, J. THE ONLY WAY TO
CROSS.*
442(NY):6JAN73-76
MAXWELL, D.E.S. POETS OF THE THIRTIES.*
J. REPLOGLE, 191(ELN):DEC71-155
MAY, D. THE LAUGHTER IN DJAKARTA.
617(TLS):7SEP73-1017
MAY, E.R. & J. FRASER, EDS. CAMPAIGN
'72.
G. WILLS, 453:4OCT73-3
MAY, G. MADAME ROLAND AND THE AGE OF
REVOLUTION.*
H. PEYRE, 546(RR):APR71-148
MAY, J. & J. COMMEMORATIVE POTTERY 1780-
1900.
617(TLS):2FEB73-133
MAY, J.A. KANT'S CONCEPT OF GEOGRAPHY.
T.P.A., 543:MAR71-545
MAY, M.T. - SEE GALEN
MAY, R. PAULUS.
H. COX, 441:14OCT73-31
E.B. FISKE, 441:27OCT73-35
MAY, R. WHO'S WHO IN SHAKESPEARE.
617(TLS):5JAN73-21
MAY, W. A BAD GIRL'S BOOK OF ANIMALS.
502(PRS):FALL71-281
MAY, W.E. A HISTORY OF MARINE NAVIGA-
TION.
617(TLS):31AUG73-1009
MAY, W.E. & P.G.W. ANNIS. SWORDS FOR
SEA SERVICE.
C. BLAIR, 135:OCT71-140
MAYER, A.J. POLITICAL ORIGINS OF THE NEW
DIPLOMACY, 1917-1918. POLITICS AND
DIPLOMACY OF PEACEMAKING.
M. MOLNÁR, 98:JAN70-73
MAYER, C.A. - SEE MAROT, C.
MAYER, C.C. MASTERPIECES OF WESTERN
TEXTILES FROM THE ART INSTITUTE OF
CHICAGO.
D. KING, 39:JAN70-88
MAYER, D. 3D. HARLEQUIN IN HIS ELEMENT.
R.C. SCHWEIK, 160:VOL8#1-81
MAYER, E.N. STRUCTURE OF FRENCH.
R.W. NEWMAN, 207(FR):OCT70-164

MAYER, G-R. DIE FUNKTION MYTHOLOGISCHER
NAMEN UND ANSPIELUNGEN IN LA FONTAINES
FABELN.
  A. BILLAZ, 535(RHL):JUL-AUG70-703
  P. POLLARD, 208(FS):OCT72-454
MAYER, H.E. THE CRUSADES.
  617(TLS):30MAR73-355
MAYER, R. A DICTIONARY OF ART TERMS AND
TECHNIQUES.
  D.T., 135:NOV70-215
MAYERHÖFER, J. & W. RITZER, WITH M. RAZU-
MOVSKY, EDS. FESTSCHRIFT JOSEF STUMM-
VOLL.*
  R.E. CAZDEN, 517(PBSA):JAN-MAR72-86
MAYERS, M.K., ED. LANGUAGES OF GUATEMALA.
  G. SIMEON, 353:APR71-119
MAYERSON, P. CLASSICAL MYTHOLOGY IN LIT-
ERATURE, ART, AND MUSIC.
  R.T. BRUÈRE, 122:APR72-151
  D.P. HARMON, 124:FEB72-205
MAYEUR, J-M. UN PRÊTRE DÉMOCRATE.
  H. PEYRE, 207(FR):OCT70-195
MAYFIELD, S. EXILES FROM PARADISE.*
  M. HEATH, 418(MR):WINTER-SPRING72-281
  H.D. PIPER, 27(AL):NOV72-512
MAYHEAD, R. WALTER SCOTT.
  617(TLS):4MAY73-494
MAYHEW, H. THE UNKNOWN MAYHEW. (E.P.
THOMPSON & E. YEO, EDS)
  G. CROSSICK, 111:7MAY71-168
MAYNARD, J. LOOKING BACK.
  A. GOTTLIEB, 441:22APR73-26
MAYNE, A. BRITISH PROFILE MINIATURISTS.
  P.H., 135:OCT70-139
MAYNE, R.H. OLD CHANNEL ISLANDS SILVER,
ITS MAKERS AND MARKS.
  C.O., 135:MAR70-202
MAYNE, S. MOUTH.
  D. BARBOUR, 150(DR):SPRING71-133
  J. PIVATO, 102(CANL):SPRING72-106
MAYNE, S. MUTETATIONS.
  D.H. SULLIVAN, 648:OCT70-69
MAYNE, S. - SEE LAYTON, I.
MAYO, R.S. HERDER AND THE BEGINNINGS OF
COMPARATIVE LITERATURE.*
  H.S. DAEMMRICH, 564:MAR71-74
  L.R. FURST, 220(GL&L):OCT71-66
  J. RIESZ, 52:BAND6HEFT3-308
  M. STOLJAR, 67:MAY72-107
MAYOR, A.H. PRINTS AND PEOPLE.
  W.D. CASE, 58:FEB72-21
MAYOUX, J-J. LA PEINTURE ANGLAISE.
  G-A. ASTRE, 98:OCT70-881
MAYRHOFER, M. DIE INDO-ARIER IM ALTEN
VORDERASIEN.
  H.J. VERMEER, 343:BAND13HEFT1-52
MAYRHOFER, M. KURZGEFASSTES ETYMOLO-
GISCHES WÖRTERBUCH DES ALTINDISCHEN.
  C. MALAMOUD, 182:VOL24#15/16-592
MAYRHOFER, M., WITH F. LOCHNER-HÜTTENBACH
& H. SCHMEJA, EDS. STUDIEN ZUR SPRACH-
WISSENSCHAFT UND KULTURKUNDE.*
  W.P. LEHMANN, 350:MAR72-161
  W. THOMAS, 260(IF):BAND75-265
MAYUYAMA, J., ED. JAPANESE ART IN THE
WEST.
  A. SOPER, 57:VOL32#2/3-238
MAZET, H.S. WILD IVORY.
  617(TLS):13APR73-429
MAZIÈRES, J. ARSÈNE VERMENOUZE (1850-
1910) ET LA HAUTE-AUVERGNE DE SON
TEMPS.
  C. ANATOLE, 535(RHL):JAN-FEB70-151
MAZLAKH, S. & V. SHAKHRAI. ON THE CUR-
RENT SITUATION IN THE UKRAINE.* (P.J.
POTICHNYJ, ED & TRANS)
  B. DMYTRYSHYN, 550(RUSR):OCT71-413
  J.S. RESHETAR, JR., 32:MAR72-172

MAZLICH, B., ED. PSYCHOANALYSIS AND
HISTORY.
  R. COLES, 453:22FEB73-15
MAZLISH, B. IN SEARCH OF NIXON.*
  R. COLES, 453:8MAR73-25
MAZMANIAN, A.B. THE STRUCTURE OF PRAISE.*
  J.J. BISHOP, 576:MAY71-183
  M. LAVANOUX, 363:AUG71-120
  45:SEP70-142
MAZOUR, A.G. THE WRITING OF HISTORY IN
THE SOVIET UNION.*
  J. KEEP, 32:SEP72-684
MAZRUI, A.A. THE TRIAL OF CHRISTOPHER
OKIGBO.*
  P.M. SPACKS, 249(HUDR):AUTUMN72-505
MAZUR, S. COMPUTABLE ANALYSIS. (A.
GRZEGORCZYK & H. RASIOWA, EDS)
  R.L. GOODSTEIN, 316:MAR71-148
MAŽVYDAS, M. THE OLD LITHUANIAN CATE-
CHISM OF MARTYNAS MAŽVYDAS (1547).*
(G.B. FORD, JR., ED & TRANS)
  H. LEEMING, 575(SEER):JAN72-115
MAZZARO, J., ED. MODERN AMERICAN POETRY.
  M.E. BROWN, 141:SPRING71-218
MAZZARO, J. TRANSFORMATIONS IN THE
RENAISSANCE ENGLISH LYRIC.
  G. THOMAS, 175:AUTUMN71-102
  639(VQR):SUMMER71-CIX
MAZZOLANI, L.S. THE IDEA OF THE CITY IN
ROMAN THOUGHT.
  R.M. OGILVIE, 123:JUN72-252
MAZZOTTI, A., ED. CANTARI DEL TRECENTO.
  M.M., 228(GSLI):VOL148FASC462/463-461
MBITI, J.S. AFRICAN RELIGIONS AND PHIL-
OSOPHY.
  N.S. BOOTH, JR., 258:JUN71-266
MEACHER, M. TAKEN FOR A RIDE.
  617(TLS):5JAN73-22
MEAD, M. IN THE EYES OF THE PEOPLE.
  617(TLS):16NOV73-1405
MEAD, M. TWENTIETH CENTURY FAITH.
  W. DAVISON, 441:7JAN73-37
MEAD, M. & J. BALDWIN. A RAP ON RACE.
  D. DONALD, 639(VQR):AUTUMN71-619
MEAD, R. & M. - SEE UNDER "BIENEK" AND
"BORCHERS"
MEAD, S. FREE THE MALE MAN!*
  617(TLS):23FEB73-222
MEADE, M. BITCHING.
  617(TLS):30NOV73-1473
MEANY, E.S. ORIGIN OF WASHINGTON GEO-
GRAPHIC NAMES.
  E.P. HAMP, 269(IJAL):APR71-135
MEARES, A. DIALOGUE WITH YOUTH.
  617(TLS):20APR73-454
MEAUZÉ, P. AFRICAN ART, SCULPTURE.
  E.L.R. MEYEROWITZ, 39:JUL70-80
VON MECK, G. AS I REMEMBER THEM.
  617(TLS):29JUN73-735
MECKIER, J. ALDOUS HUXLEY.
  R. HOPE, 541(RES):FEB71-112
  K. WIEGNER, 399(MLJ):MAY71-330
MEDEIROS, W.D. HIPPONACTEA.*
  P. CHANTRAINE, 555:VOL45FASC2-329
  D.E. GERBER, 487:SUMMER71-166
MEDHURST, K. GOVERNMENT IN SPAIN.
  617(TLS):2NOV73-1336
"MEDIEVAL FRENCH PLAYS." (R. AXTON & J.
STEVENS, TRANS)
  I.D. BENT, 415:JUN72-562
"MEDIEVAL LATIN LYRICS."* (B. STOCK,
TRANS)
  R.D. SIDER, 124:APR-MAY72-276
DE MEDINA, F.D. - SEE UNDER DIEZ DE
MEDINA, F.
DE MEDINA, P. A NAVIGATOR'S UNIVERSE.
(U. LAMB, TRANS)
  617(TLS):12JAN73-49

THE DUCHESS OF MEDINA SIDONIA.  MY
PRISON.*
   J. BLACK, 453:5APR73-36
MEDJDOUB.  LES QUATRAINS DE MEDJDOUB LE
SARCASTIQUE.  (J. SCELLES-MILLIE, ED &
TRANS)
   J.A. BELLAMY, 318(JAOS):OCT-DEC71-532
MEDLICOTT, W.N., D. DAKIN & M.E. LAMBERT,
EDS.  DOCUMENTS ON BRITISH FOREIGN
POLICY 1919-1939.  (SER 1A, VOL 5)
   617(TLS):29JUN73-739
MEDLIN, D.M.  THE VERBAL ART OF JEAN-
FRANÇOIS REGNARD.*
   B. BRAY, 433:JUL70-311
   E. KERN, 207(FR):FEB71-624
MEDLIN, W.K., W.M. CAVE & I. CARPENTER.
EDUCATION AND DEVELOPMENT IN CENTRAL
ASIA.
   D.S.M. WILLIAMS, 575(SEER):APR72-329
MEDLIN, W.K. & C.G. PATRINELIS.  REN-
AISSANCE INFLUENCES AND RELIGIOUS
REFORMS IN RUSSIA.
   G.P. MAJESKA, 32:MAR72-150
MEDVEDEV, R.A.  LET HISTORY JUDGE.*  (D.
JORAVSKY & G. HAUPT, EDS)
   G.P. HOLMAN, JR., 396(MODA):FALL72-438
MEDVEDEV, Z.A.  THE MEDVEDEV PAPERS.*
   A. ASTRACHAN, 442(NY):24SEP73-130
   B.M. COHEN, 32:SEP72-697
MEDVEDEV, Z.A.  TEN YEARS AFTER IVAN
DENISOVICH.
   R. WILLIAMS, 362:29NOV73-750
MEE, C.L., JR.  WHITE ROBE, BLACK ROBE.*
   441:25MAR73-22
MEEK, C.R.  BEYOND INDIVIDUALITY.
   M.F. CHRISTOPHERSON, 480(P&R):SUMMER
   71-183
MEEK, R.L. - SEE TURGOT, A.R.J.
MEEKS, C.L.V.  ITALIAN ARCHITECTURE 1750-
1914.
   A. ROWAN, 90:NOV71-679
MEETHAM, A.R., ED-IN-CHIEF.  ENCYCLOPAED-
IA OF LINGUISTICS, INFORMATION AND CON-
TROL.
   E.P. HAMP, 269(IJAL):JUL71-210
MEGARRY, R.  INNS ANCIENT AND MODERN.
   617(TLS):11MAY73-537
MEGAS, A.C. - SEE MUSSATO, A.
MEGGERS, B.J.  ECUADOR.
   S·S·, 37:MAR71-42
MEHENDALE, M.A.  SOME ASPECTS OF INDO-
ARYAN LINGUISTICS.
   G. CARDONA, 350:MAR72-171
   R. SCHMITT, 182:VOL24#4-152
MÉHEUST, J. - SEE STATIUS
MEHNERT, K-H.  SAL ROMANUS UND ESPRIT
FRANÇAIS.
   F.R. HAUSMANN, 72:BAND209HEFT4/6-455
MEHTA, J.L., WITH A.K. CHATTERJEE & S.
KUMAR, EDS.  LANGUAGE AND REALITY.
   R. SINARI, 485(PE&W):JAN71-89
MEID, V. - SEE VON ZESEN, P.
MEID, W., ED.  BEITRÄGE ZUR INDOGERMAN-
ISTIK UND KELTOLOGIE.
   K.H. SCHMIDT, 260(IF):BAND75-276
MEIDEN, W. - SEE MAUROIS, M.
MEIER, C.  ENTSTEHUNG DES BEGRIFFS "DEMO-
KRATIE."
   J·P·V·D· BALSDON, 123:DEC72-429
MEIER, H.  DEUTSCHE SPRACHSTATISTIK.
(2ND ED)
   B. BOCK, 657(WW):MAR/APR70-133
MEIER, M.S. & F. RIVERA.  THE CHICANOS.*
   W. GARD, 584(SWR):AUTUMN72-330
MEIGGS, R.  THE ATHENIAN EMPIRE.*
   617(TLS):18MAY73-541

MEIGGS, R. & D. LEWIS.  A SELECTION OF
GREEK HISTORICAL INSCRIPTIONS TO THE
END OF THE FIFTH CENTURY B.C.*
   M.H. JAMESON, 24:JUL72-474
   H.B. MATTINGLY, 123:MAR72-75
MEILACH, D.Z.  CONTEMPORARY STONE SCULP-
TURE.
   M. EASTHAM, 89(BJA):WINTER72-110
MEILACH, D.Z.  MACRAMÉ.
   S. MAREIN, 139:JUN71-8
MEILAND, J.W.  THE NATURE OF INTENTION.*
   C·G· PRADO, 529(QQ):SPRING71-157
MEILAND, J.W.  TALKING ABOUT PARTICULARS.*
   D. SIEVERT, 399(MLJ):NOV71-486
   P.F. STRAWSON, 479(PHQ):JUL71-276
MEILCOUR, N.  ROSE ET CARMA.
   M. NAUDIN, 207(FR):DEC70-417
MEILLER, A. - SEE JEAN DU PRIER
MEILLET, A.  THE COMPARATIVE METHOD IN
HISTORICAL LINGUISTICS.
   H.E. KIJLSTRA, 353:JAN70-109
   G. STORMS, 433:JAN70-86
MEINECKE, F.  WERKE.  (VOL 8)  (E. KESSEL,
ED)
   K. VON KLEMPERER, 182:VOL24#4-182
MEINERS, I.  SCHELM UND DÜMMLING IN
ERZÄHLUNGEN DES DEUTSCHEN MITTELALTERS.*
   M. FELDGES, 657(WW):MAR/APR71-142
   A. VAN OOIJ, 433:JAN71-105
MEINERS, R.K.  EVERYTHING TO BE ENDURED.
   L. PRATT, 502(PRS):WINTER71-361
MEISEL, M.  SHAW AND THE NINETEENTH CEN-
TURY THEATRE.
   A·P· HINCHLIFFE, 148:AUTUMN71-283
MEISS, M.  FRENCH PAINTING IN THE TIME OF
JEAN DE BERRY.*  (PT 1)
   L.M.J. DELAISSÉ, 54:JUN70-206
MEISS, M.  THE GREAT AGE OF FRESCO.
   B. BETTINSON, 363:FEB71-59
   M·E·, 135:MAR71-214
   R. LEBOWITZ, 58:NOV70-I2
MEISS, M. & E.W. KIRSCH - SEE "THE VIS-
CONTI HOURS"
MEISSBURGER, G.  GRUNDLAGEN ZUM VERSTÄND-
NIS DER DEUTSCHEN MÖNCHSDICHTUNG IM 11.
UND 12. JAHRHUNDERT.
   I. GLIER, 382(MAE):1972/3-255
   D.H. GREEN, 402(MLR):OCT72-936
MEISSNER, K.  JAPANESE WOODBLOCK PRINTS
IN MINIATURE: THE GENRE OF SURIMONO.
   B.W. ROBINSON, 39:AUG70-158
MELADA, I.  THE CAPTAIN OF INDUSTRY IN
ENGLISH FICTION, 1821-1871.*
   K.J. FIELDING, 445(NCF):MAR72-485
"MÉLANGES DE PHILOLOGIE ET DE LINGUIS-
TIQUE OFFERTS À TAUNO NURMELA."*
   P.F. DEMBOWSKI, 545(RPH):NOV71-253
"MÉLANGES D'HISTOIRE LITTÉRAIRE (XVIE-
XVIIE SIÈCLES)."
   J-P. CHAUVEAU, 535(RHL):MAY-JUN70-504
"MÉLANGES D'INDIANISME À LA MÉMOIRE DE
LOUIS RENOU."
   R. SCHMITT, 343:BAND13HEFT2-113
"MÉLANGES MARCEL COHEN."
   R. HETZRON, 350:SEP72-719
MELAS, E., ED.  TEMPLES AND SANCTUARIES
OF ANCIENT GREECE.
   617(TLS):24AUG73-975
MELCHERT, N.P.  REALISM, MATERIALISM,
AND THE MIND.*  (M. FARBER, ED)
   S.E. GLUCK, 483:JUL71-281
   A.W.M., 477:AUTUMN70-547
MELCHINGER, C.  ILLUSION UND WIRKLICHKEIT
IM DRAMATISCHEN WERK ARTHUR SCHNITZLERS.
   C.E. WILLIAMS, 220(GL&L):JAN72-171
MELCHIORI, B.  BROWNING'S POETRY OF
RETICENCE.*
   G. PITTS, 636(VP):SUMMER70-180

MELDEN, A.I., ED. HUMAN RIGHTS.
M.D.P., 543:MAR71-554
MELE, F. POLPETTO.
M. LEVIN, 441:24JUN73-12
MELEGARI, V. THE GREAT MILITARY SIEGES.
617(TLS):20APR73-453
MELLEN, P. THE GROUP OF SEVEN.*
R.L. BLOORE, 96:APR/MAY71-82
MELLERS, W. MUSIC IN A NEW FOUND LAND.
M. PETERSON, 470:JAN66-43
MELLERSH, M.E.L. THE DESTRUCTION OF
KNOSSOS.
K. BRANIGAN, 123:DEC72-381
MELLIN, G.S.A. MARGINALIEN UND REGISTER
ZU KANTS KRITIK DER ERKENNTNISVERMÖGEN.
(PTS 1&2) (L. GOLDSCHMIDT, ED)
R. MALTER, 342:BAND62HEFT2-259
MELLINKOFF, R. THE HORNED MOSES IN
MEDIEVAL ART AND THOUGHT.
W.O. HASSALL, 382(MAE):1972/2-178
F. MC CULLOCH, 589:JAN72-134
639(VQR):AUTUMN71-CLXXXV
MELLISH, M. THE DOCKS AFTER DEVLIN.
617(TLS):16MAR73-300
MELLONI, R.C. - SEE UNDER CUCCIOLI MEL-
LONI, R.
MELLOWN, E.W. BIBLIOGRAPHY OF THE WRIT-
INGS OF EDWIN MUIR.
P.H., 503:SUMMER68-84
MELLY, G. & J.R. GLAVES-SMITH. A CHILD
OF SIX COULD DO IT!
617(TLS):20JUL73-828
MELMOTH. BEING.
S. MAX, 207(FR):APR71-963
DE MELO, V. XARIAS E CANGULEIROS.
G. MONTEIRO, 650(WF):APR71-143
MELODY, W. CHILDREN'S TELEVISION.
S. HARRINGTON, 441:25NOV73-39
617(TLS):14DEC73-1542
MELOGRANI, P. GLI INDUSTRIALI E MUSSO-
LINI.
617(TLS):2MAR73-225
MELTZER, B. & D. MICHIE, EDS. MACHINE
INTELLIGENCE 7.
617(TLS):9FEB73-158
MELTZER, D. LUNA.
L. MUELLER, 491:AUG73-293
MELVIL, Y.K. CHARLES PEIRCE AND PRAGMA-
TISM. [IN RUSSIAN]
P.K. CROSSER, 484(PPR):DEC71-271
MELVILLE, G. GANSEVOORT MELVILLE'S 1846
LONDON JOURNAL AND LETTERS FROM ENG-
LAND, 1845. (H. PARKER, ED)
J.G. RIEWALD, 179(ES):AUG71-375
MELVILLE, H. THE WRITINGS OF HERMAN MEL-
VILLE. (VOL 6: PIERRE: OR THE AMBI-
GUITIES.) (H. HAYFORD, H. PARKER & G.T.
TANSELLE, EDS)
C.N. WATSON, JR., 27(AL):JAN73-684
MELVILLE, R. EROTIC ART OF THE WEST.
J. UPDIKE, 441:28OCT73-4
MELVILLE, R. HENRY MOORE.
J.P., 376:JUL71-120
MELZI D'ERIL, F.K. - SEE MONTALEMBERT,
C.F. & C. CANTÙ
MEMMI, A. LE SCORPION OU LA CONFESSION
IMAGINAIRE.
J. LEINER, 207(FR):DEC70-417
MENANDER. MÉNANDRE: "LA SAMIENNE."
(J-M. JACQUES, ED & TRANS)
B.F. DICK, 124:JAN72-170
MENANDER. MENANDRI RELIQVIAE SELECTAE.
(F.H. SANDBACH, ED)
617(TLS):5JAN73-21
MÉNARD, P. MANUEL D'ANCIEN FRANÇAIS.*
(FASC 3)
C. RÉGNIER, 209(FM):APR70-172
MÉNARD, P. - SEE GUILLAUME LE VINIER

MÉNARD, R. ARCHITECTE DE LA SOLITUDE.
M. CRANSTON, 207(FR):APR71-964
R. MUNIER, 98:APR71-303
MENASHE, S. FRINGE OF FIRE.
A. MACLEAN, 362:25OCT73-565
MENASHE, S. NO JERUSALEM BUT THIS.
C. BEDIENT, 441:18FEB73-26
J. KESSLER, 491:FEB73-292
W.W., 502(PRS):WINTER71/72-368
"MENCIUS." (D.C. LAU, TRANS)
WONG SIU-KIT, 302:JUL71-368
MENCKEN, H.L. THE YOUNG MENCKEN. (C.
BODE, ED)
H. KRAMER, 441:19AUG73-4
MENDE, F. HEINRICH HEINE: CHRONIK SEINES
LEBENS UND WERKES.*
R.C. FIGGE, 301(JEGP):JAN72-80
J.L.S., 191(ELN):SEP71(SUPP)-134
J.L. SAMMONS, 221(GQ):JAN71-82
R.E. STIEFEL, 406:SUMMER72-188
MENDE, F. & K.H. HAHN - SEE HEINE, H.
MENDE, T. FROM AID TO RE-COLONIALIZATION.
J. STERBA, 441:30SEP73-26
MENDELL, C.W. TACITUS, THE MAN AND HIS
WORK.
J. CROOK, 123:JUN72-221
MENDELOFF, H. A MANUAL OF COMPARATIVE
ROMANCE LINGUISTICS.
J. KLAUSENBURGER, 399(MLJ):FEB71-131
MENDELSOHN, E. CLASS STRUGGLE IN THE
PALE.
H.J. TOBIAS, 550(RUSR):OCT71-403
A.K. WILDMAN, 32:MAR72-163
MENDELSON, D. LE VERRE ET LES OBJETS DE
VERRE DANS L'UNIVERS IMAGINAIRE DE
MARCEL PROUST.*
B. VERCIER, 535(RHL):SEP-DEC71-998
MENDELSON, E. - SEE AUDEN, W.H.
DE MENDELSSOHN, P. VON DEUTSCHER REPRÄS-
ENTANZ.
617(TLS):6APR73-396
DE MENDELSSOHN, P. S. FISCHER UND SEIN
VERLAG.
H.F. GARTEN, 270:VOL21#1-119
DE MENDELSSOHN, P. - SEE MANN, T. & G.B.
FISCHER
MENDONÇA TELES, G. LA POESÍA BRASILEÑA
EN LA ACTUALIDAD.
G.M. MOSER, 240(HR):JUL71-344
MENEGHELLO-DINCIC, K. LES EXPÉRIENCES
YOUGOSLAVES D'INDUSTRIALISATION ET DE
PLANIFICATION.
D.D. MILENKOVITCH, 32:SEP72-726
F. SINGLETON, 575(SEER):APR72-317
MENEN, A. CITIES IN THE SAND.
442(NY):15OCT73-187
617(TLS):16MAR73-293
MENGALDO, P.V. - SEE DANTE ALIGHIERI
DE MENIL, A. & W. READ. OUT OF SILENCE.
102(CANL):WINTER72-103
MENNINGER, K. A CULTURAL HISTORY OF NUM-
BERS.
W.H. HELD, 215(GL):VOL11#2-124
MENNINGER, K. NUMBER WORDS AND NUMBER
SYMBOLS.*
I.M. COPI, 485(PE&W):JAN71-97
MENNINGER, K. WHATEVER BECAME OF SIN?
442(NY):22OCT73-175
MENUHIN, Y. THEME AND VARIATIONS.*
K. SPENCE, 415:AUG72-775
MENUT, A.D. & A.J. DENOMY - SEE ORESME,
N.
MENYUK, P. SENTENCES CHILDREN USE.
D.S. PALERMO, 215(GL):VOL10#3-173
MENZEL, H. ANTIKE LAMPEN IM RÖMISCH-
GERMANISCHEN ZENTRALMUSEUM ZU MAINZ.
D.E. STRONG, 123:MAR72-144

MENZIES, R. THE MEASURE OF THE YEARS.
  D. AITKIN, 381:MAR71-118
MERCADIER, G. - SEE DE TORRES VILLARROEL,
  D.
MERCER, D. FLINT.
  P. ROBERTS, 565:VOL12#2-72
MERCER, D. ON THE EVE OF PUBLICATION AND
  OTHER PLAYS.
  S. DAY-LEWIS, 157:SUMMER70-74
MERCER, E. FURNITURE 700-1700.
  R. EDWARDS, 39:FEB70-167
MERCER, P. SYMPATHY AND ETHICS.*
  E.M. LOUDFOOT, 518:OCT72-24
MERCHANT, L. THE NATIONAL FOOTBALL
  LOTTERY.
  J. FLAHERTY, 441:7OCT73-21
  C. LEHMANN-HAUPT, 441:1OCT73-39
MERCIÉ, J-L. VICTOR HUGO ET JULIE
  CHENAY.*
  P. GEORGEL, 535(RHL):MAY-JUN70-520
MERCIER, A. LES SOURCES ÉSOTÉRIQUES ET
  OCCULTES DE LA POÉSIE SYMBOLISTE (1870-
  1914).
  J. BELLEMIN-NOËL, 535(RHL):MAY-JUN70-
  529
  J. DECOTTIGNIES, 557(RSH):APR-JUN71-
  329
MERCIER, V. THE IRISH COMIC TRADITION.
  W. KLUGE, 72:BAND209HEFT4/6-420
MERCIER, V. THE NEW NOVEL FROM QUENEAU
  TO PINGET.
  L. LE SAGE, 188(ECR):WINTER71-72
  A. WEINSTEIN, 454:SPRING72-272
MEREAU, S. KALATHISKOS.
  B. GAJEK, 657(WW):JUL/AUG70-280
MEREDITH, G. THE LETTERS OF GEORGE MERE-
  DITH.* (C.L. CLINE, ED)
  M. HARRIS, 72:BAND209HEFT4/6-416
  A.G. HILL, 541(RES):NOV71-512
  L. STEVENSON, 445(NCF):MAR71-479
  639(VQR):SPRING71-LXVIII
MEREDITH, G. POÈMES CHOISIS. (L. & M.
  CAZAMIAN, EDS & TRANS)
  F. LÉAUD, 189(EA):OCT-DEC70-451
  M. MORAUD, 207(FR):MAY71-1130
MEREDITH, P. DYSLEXIA AND THE INDIVIDU-
  AL.
  617(TLS):9FEB73-161
MEREDITH, W. EARTH WALK AND SELECTED
  POEMS.*
  42(AR):SPRING70-134
MÉREI, G. FÖDERÁCIÓS TERVEK DÉLKELET-
  EURÓPÁBAN ÉS A HABSBURG MONARCHIA,
  1840-1918.
  M. MOLNÁR, 98:JAN70-72
MÉRIMÉE, P. 1572. (R.J.B. CLARK, ED)
  T.G.S. COMBE, 208(FS):JUL72-340
  205(FMLS):OCT70-421
MÉRIMÉE, P. ROMANS ET NOUVELLES.* (M.
  PATURIER, ED)
  H. REDMAN, JR., 207(FR):FEB71-615
MERIVALE, P. PAN THE GOAT-GOD.*
  H.W. FULWEILER, 636(VP):SUMMER70-172
  M.N. NAGLER, 650(WF):OCT70-297
MERK, F. SLAVERY AND THE ANNEXATION OF
  TEXAS.
  617(TLS):2MAR73-230
MERKER, E., WITH OTHERS, EDS. WÖRTERBUCH
  ZU GOETHES "WERTHER."
  W.H. BRUFORD, 182:VOL24#5-208
MERLEAU-PONTY, M. HUMANISM AND TERROR.*
  (J. O'NEILL, ED & TRANS)
  J-M. EDIE, 321:WINTER70[VOL4#4]-314
  J. SOMERVILLE, 484(PPR):DEC71-241
  185:OCT70-88
MERLEAU-PONTY, M. LA PROSE DU MONDE.
  R. MONTPETIT, 154:DEC70-502

MERLEAU-PONTY, M. THEMES FROM THE LEC-
  TURES AT THE COLLÈGE DE FRANCE, 1952-
  1960.
  185:OCT70-88
MERLEAU-PONTY, M. THE VISIBLE AND THE
  INVISIBLE.* (FRENCH TITLE: LE VISIBLE
  ET L'INVISIBLE.) (C. LEFORT, ED)
  F. KAPLAN, 542:OCT-DEC71-497
MERLINGEN, W. EINE ÄLTERE LEHNWÖRTER-
  SCHICHT IM GRIECHISCHEN.
  K. STRUNK, 343:BAND13HEFT2-120
MERLOTTI, E. L'INTENTION SPÉCULATIVE DE
  BENEDETTO CROCE.
  E. NAMER, 542:OCT-DEC71-465
MERMOD, M. THE VOYAGE OF THE GENÈVE.
  617(TLS):22JUN73-728
MERRIAM, A.P. AFRICAN MUSIC ON LP.
  H. TRACEY, 187:MAY73-337
MERRIAM, E., ED. GROWING UP FEMALE IN
  AMERICA.
  P.M. SPACKS, 249(HUDR):SPRING72-157
MERRIAM, H.G., ED. WAY OUT WEST.
  L. ATTEBERY, 650(WF):JAN71-65
MERRIFIELD, D.F. DAS BILD DER FRAU BEI
  MAX FRISCH.
  H.F. PFANNER, 406:FALL72-313
MERRILEES, B.S. - SEE "LE PETIT PLET"
MERRILL, J. BRAVING THE ELEMENTS.*
  X.J. KENNEDY, 61:MAR73-101
  D. KENWORTHY, 31(ASCH):SUMMER73-514
  S. SPENDER, 453:20SEP73-8
  S. YENSER, 491:JUN73-163
  617(TLS):20APR73-442
MERRILL, J. THE FIRE SCREEN.*
  R.H. BAYES, 50(ARQ):SUMMER70-183
MERRILL, W.M. & L. RUCHAMES - SEE GARRI-
  SON, W.L.
MERRY, H.J. MONTESQUIEU'S SYSTEM OF
  NATURAL GOVERNMENT.
  185:OCT70-88
MERSENNE, M. CORRESPONDANCE DU PÈRE
  MARIN MERSENNE. (VOL 10)
  G. RODIS-LEWIS, 542:JAN-MAR70-90
MERSENNE, M. CORRESPONDANCE DU PÈRE
  MARIN MERSENNE, RELIGIEUX MINIME. (VOL
  11) (C. DE WAARD, ED)
  A. MERCIER, 182:VOL24#3-75
MERTENS, J., ED. ALBA FUCENS.
  A. HUS, 555:VOL45FASC2-379
MERTENS, J. DE LAAT-MIDDELEEUWSE LAND-
  BOUWECONOMIE IN ENKELE GEMEENTEN VAN
  HET BRUGSE PLATTELAND.
  D. NICHOLAS, 589:APR72-331
MERTNER, E. & H. MAINUSCH. PORNOTOPIA.*
  H-J. MODLMAYR, 402(MLR):JAN72-233
MERTON, R.K. SOCIAL THEORY AND SOCIAL
  STRUCTURE. (REV)
  P. HELM, 479(PHQ):JAN71-51
MERTON, R.K. THE SOCIOLOGY OF SCIENCE.
  (N.W. STORER, ED)
  J. BEN-DAVID, 441:11NOV73-31
MERTON, T. THE ASIAN JOURNAL OF THOMAS
  MERTON. (N. BURTON & OTHERS, EDS)
  E. RICE, 441:8JUL73-13
MERTON, T. CABLES TO THE ACE.
  L. FLAHERTY, 539(REN):AUTUMN71-3
  W. SUTTON, 659:WINTER73-49
MERTON, T. CONTEMPLATION IN A WORLD OF
  ACTION.*
  A.W. GODFREY, 363:AUG71-113
MERTON, T. THE GEOGRAPHY OF LOGRAIRE.
  W. SUTTON, 659:WINTER73-49
MERTON, T. & J.H. GRIFFIN. A HIDDEN
  WHOLENESS.*
  A.W. GODFREY, 363:AUG71-113
MERWIN, H.C. THE LIFE OF BRET HARTE.
  R. LEHAN, 445(NCF):SEP70-249

MERWIN, W.S. ASIAN FIGURES.
   H. SHAPIRO, 441:22JUN73-41
   617(TLS):8JUN73-646
MERWIN, W.S. THE CARRIER OF LADDERS.*
   H.T. KIRBY-SMITH, JR., 569(SR):SUM-
   MER72-483
   639(VQR):WINTER71-XVIII
MERWIN, W.S. THE MINER'S PALE CHILDREN.*
   J.L. HALIO, 598(SOR):SPRING73-455
   502(PRS):WINTER71/72-370
MERWIN, W.S. WRITINGS TO AN UNFINISHED
 ACCOMPANIMENT.
   H. SHAPIRO, 441:22JUN73-41
   S. SPENDER, 453:20SEP73-8
MESCHONNIC, H. POUR LA POÉTIQUE. (VOLS
 1-3)
   617(TLS):5OCT73-1170
MESERVE, W.J. ROBERT E. SHERWOOD.*
   C.G. MASINTON, 397(MD):MAY71-123
MESERVE, W.J. - SEE HOWELLS, W.D.
MESERVE, W.J. & R.I., EDS. MODERN DRAMA
 FROM COMMUNIST CHINA.
   C. TUNG, 293(JAST):MAY71-675
   WONG SHIU HON, 302:JUL71-370
MESHAW, M. WAKING SLOW.
   617(TLS):6JUL73-769
MESHCHERIUK, I.I. SOTSIAL'NO-EKONOMICH-
 ESKOE RAZVITIE BOLGARSKIKH I GAGAUZ-
 SKIKH SEL V IUZHNOI BESSARABII (1808-
 1856 GG.).
   B. CVETKOVA, 32:SEP72-728
MESLIER, J. OEUVRES COMPLÈTES. (VOL 1)
 (J. DEPRUN, R. DESNÉ & A. SOBOUL, EDS)
   R. MERCIER, 557(RSH):APR-JUN71-318
   617(TLS):5JAN73-13
MESLIER, J. OEUVRES COMPLÈTES. (VOLS
 2&3) (J. DEPRUN, R. DESNÉ & A. SOBOUL,
 EDS)
   617(TLS):5JAN73-13
MESLIN, M. LA FÊTE DES KALENDES DE
 JANVIER DANS L'EMPIRE ROMAIN.
   M.J. BOYD, 123:JUN72-289
MESMER, F-A. LE MAGNÉTISME ANIMAL. (R.
 AMADOU, ED)
   L. CELLIER, 557(RSH):OCT-DEC71-670
MESSENGER, J.C. INIS BEAG, ISLE OF
 IRELAND.
   E. ETTLINGER, 203:SUMMER70-150
MESSER, T.M. MUNCH.
   J. CANADAY, 441:23JUN73-29
MESSINGER, H. LANGENSCHEIDTS GROSSWÖR-
 TERBUCH ENGLISCH-DEUTSCH.
   J. EICHHOFF, 406:WINTER72-388
MESSMER, W. FRANZÖSISCHER SPRACHHUMOR.
   G. SCHWEIG, 430(NS):FEB71-104
MÉSZÁROS, I. MARX'S THEORY OF ALIENA-
 TION.*
   H.B., 543:JUN71-750
METCALF, J. GOING DOWN SLOW.
   K. GIBSON, 99:SEP73-41
   D. JEWISON, 296:WINTER73-91
   J. SHERMAN, 198:WINTER73-116
METCALF, J. THE LADY WHO SOLD FURNITURE.*
   J. MILLS, 648:JAN71-59
METCALF, P. GENOA.
   R. BANKS, 600:WINTER/SPRING70-236
METEYARD, E. THE LIFE OF JOSIAH WEDG-
 WOOD.
   J.V.G. MALLET, 90:SEP71-555
"MET'Q'VELEBIS ANALIZIS, SINTEZISA DA
 ST'AT'IST'IK'IS SAK'ITHEBI."
   G.F. MEIER, 682(ZPSK):BAND23HEFT1-95
"MET'Q'VELEBIS ANALIZISA DA SINTEZISA
 SAK'ITHEBI."
   G.F. MEIER, 682(ZPSK):BAND23HEFT1-93
METSCHER, T. SEAN O'CASEY'S DRAMATISCHER
 STIL.
   H-J. KANN, 599:SPRING70-187

METZ, J.B. THEOLOGY OF THE WORLD.
   C.M. GOING, 613:SPRING71-139
METZKER, I., ED. A BINTEL BRIEF.
   K. SEIGEL, 390:AUG/SEP71-69
MEUSS, R.E.K. BRETON FOLKTALES.
   J. SIMPSON, 203:SUMMER71-169
MEWS, H. FRAIL VESSELS.
   R. LAWRENCE, 175:SUMMER70-69
   S. MONOD, 189(EA):JUL-SEP70-345
   639(VQR):WINTER71-XXVI
MEWSHAW, M. MAN IN MOTION.
   639(VQR):WINTER71-VIII
MEWSHAW, M. WAKING SLOW.*
   R. BRYDEN, 362:7JUN73-772
MEYER, E. REALISM AND REALITY.
   A.C. SPRAGUE, 179(ES):OCT71-463
MEYER, E. VOM BEKANNTEN UND UNBEKANNTEN
 KANT.
   R. MALTER, 342:BAND61HEFT4-524
MEYER, G. SCHLESWIG-HOLSTEINER SAGEN.
 (NEW ED)
   F. HARKORT, 196:BAND12HEFT2/3-284
MEYER, H. GOETHE.
   A.O. JASZI, 400(MLN):APR71-434
MEYER, H. THE POETICS OF QUOTATION IN
 THE EUROPEAN NOVEL.
   H.C. SASSE, 220(GL&L):OCT71-33
   J. WEISGERBER, 149:JUN72-237
MEYER, K.E. THE PLEASURES OF ARCHAEOL-
 OGY.
   D. MARKS, 58:DEC70/JAN71-10
MEYER, K.E. THE PLUNDERED PAST.
   C. LEHMANN-HAUPT, 441:26NOV73-29
   S.D. RIPLEY, 441:9DEC73-10
   E. WEEKS, 61:DEC73-136
MEYER, M. IBSEN.*
   J. COAKLEY, 385(MQR):FALL73-386
   O. REINERT, 397(MD):FEB72-481
MEYER, R. ZUR MORPHOLOGIE UND SPRACH-
 GEOGRAPHIE DES ARTIKELS IN SCHWEIZER-
 DEUTSCHEN.*
   E. BAUER, 597(SN):VOL42#2-529
   W. MARTI, 343:BAND13HEFT1-86
MEYER, U. CONCEPTUAL ART.
   R. LEBOWITZ, 58:MAY72-30
MEYER-BAER, K. MUSIC OF THE SPHERES AND
 THE DANCE OF DEATH.*
   D.C-B., 412:FEB72-65
   J. HOLLANDER, 551(RENQ):SUMMER71-239
MEYER-EPPLER, W. GRUNDLAGEN UND ANWEN-
 DUNGEN DER INFORMATIONSTHEORIE. (2ND
 ED)
   I. CURIO, 682(ZPSK):BAND23HEFT4-411
MEYER-MYKLESTADT, J. AN ADVANCED ENGLISH
 GRAMMAR FOR STUDENTS AND TEACHERS.
   B. CARSTENSEN, 38:BAND89HEFT4-497
   J. SÖDERLIND, 597(SN):VOL42#2-509
MEYEROWITZ, P. JEWELRY AND SCULPTURE
 THROUGH UNIT CONSTRUCTION.
   E. PARDON, 139:JAN-FEB70-11
MEYERS, B. THE DARK BIRDS.
   S. BERCOVITCH, 390:APR70-73
MEYERS, G.E. SELF.
   J.A-W., 543:MAR71-546
MEYERS, J. THE WOUNDED SPIRIT.
   617(TLS):10AUG73-925
MEYLAN, J-P. LA REVUE DE GENÈVE.*
   J-D. CANDAUX, 557(RSH):APR-JUN70-337
MEYNELL, F. MY LIVES.*
   J. COTTON, 503:AUTUMN71-147
   42(AR):FALL71-442
MEYRIAT, J., WITH M. BEAUCHET. GUIDE FOR
 THE ESTABLISHMENT OF NATIONAL SOCIAL
 SCIENCES DOCUMENTATION CENTERS IN
 DEVELOPING COUNTRIES.
   M.H. FISHBEIN, 14:JAN71-58
MEZEY, R. A BOOK OF DYING.
   639(VQR):SPRING71-LVII

MEZU, S.O. THE POETRY OF LÉOPOLD SÉDAR
SENGHOR.
617(TLS):13JUL73-794
MIALL, A. - SEE TURNER, M.R.
MICHAEL, I. THE TREATMENT OF CLASSICAL
MATERIAL IN THE "LIBRO DE ALEXANDRE."*
K.R. SCHOLBERG, 238:DEC71-967
MICHAEL, W.F. DAS DEUTSCHE DRAMA DES
MITTELALTERS.
J.E. ENGEL, 301(JEGP):OCT72-571
MICHAELIS-JENA, R. THE BROTHERS GRIMM.
K.M. BRIGGS, 203:WINTER70-319
MICHAELS, B. THE DARK ON THE OTHER SIDE.
617(TLS):3AUG73-911
MICHAELS, L. GOING PLACES.*
E. BALDESHWILER, 573(SSF):FALL71-643
MICHAELSON, L.W. SONGS OF MY DIVIDED
SELF.
L.L. LEE, 649(WAL):SPRING70-79
MICHAELSON, L.W. & G.B. MORGAN, EDS.
MOUNTAINS IN THE WIND.
M. BUCCO, 649(WAL):SUMMER71-155
MICHALOWSKI, K. THE ART OF ANCIENT
EGYPT.
H.A. FRANKFORT, 54:MAR71-109
T.G.H. JAMES, 39:FEB71-147
MICHAUD, G. LA MENTALITÉ FRANÇAISE.
A-M. BRYAN, 207(FR):DEC70-396
MICHAUD, G. RÉVOLUTION DANS L'UNIVERSITÉ.
W.W. THOMAS, 207(FR):OCT70-191
MICHAUD-QUANTIN, P. ÉTUDES SUR LE VOCAB-
ULAIRE PHILOSOPHIQUE DU MOYEN ÂGE.
G. PECK, 589:OCT72-784
MICHAUX, H. EMERGENCES-RÉSURGENCES.
617(TLS):4MAY73-491
MICHEL, C. ERLÄUTERUNGEN ZUM "N" DER
ILIAS.
J. CLAY, 124:APR-MAY72-278
MICHEL, G. LES BANCS.
B.L. KNAPP, 207(FR):MAR71-784
MICHEL, H. THE SHADOW WAR.
442(NY):10FEB73-116
MICHEL, H. WORLD WAR II.* (FRENCH TITLE:
LA SECONDE GUERRE MONDIALE.)
617(TLS):21SEP73-1093
MICHEL, J. - SEE DEL VALLE-INCLÁN, R.
MICHEL, L. THE THING CONTAINED.*
C. SPENCER, 570(SQ):SPRING71-176
MICHEL, P. MONTAIGNE.*
R.D. COTTRELL, 207(FR):MAR71-810
MICHEL, W. - SEE "WYNDHAM LEWIS: PAINT-
INGS AND DRAWINGS"
MICHEL, W. & C.J. FOX - SEE "WYNDHAM
LEWIS ON ART"
"MICHELANGELO: A SELF-PORTRAIT." (REV)
(R.J. CLEMENTS, ED & TRANS)
R.W. LIGHTBOWN, 39:JUN71-529
D. NOLAN, 276:SPRING71-96
DE MICHELE, V. THE WORLD OF MINERALS.
617(TLS):16MAR73-305
MICHELET, J. LA SORCIÈRE.
J. FAVRET, 98:APR71-351
DE MICHELIS, E. LA VERGINE E IL DRAGO.
V.S., 275(IQ):SPRING-SUMMER72-121
MICHELS, A.K. THE CALENDAR OF THE ROMAN
REPUBLIC.*
A. DRUMMOND, 313:VOL61-282
MICHELS, U. & V., WITH H. HESSE - SEE
HESSE, H.
MICHELS, V., ED. MATERIALEN ZU HERMANN
HESSES "DER STEPPENWOLF."
617(TLS):31AUG73-989
MICHELS, V. - SEE HESSE, H.
MICHELSON, P. THE AESTHETICS OF PORNOG-
RAPHY.
E. SEGAL, 131(CL):SUMMER72-264
MICHENER, J., ED. FIRSTFRUITS.
A.A. COHEN, 441:30SEP73-46

MICHIE, J. - SEE MARTIAL
MICHLER, M. DAS SPEZIALISIERUNGSPROBLEM
UND DIE ANTIKE CHIRURGIE.
E.D. PHILLIPS, 123:MAR72-146
MICHON, J. LA MUSIQUE ANGLAISE.*
H.R. COHEN, 189(EA):JUL-SEP71-347
MICKEL, E.J., JR. THE ARTIFICIAL PARA-
DISES IN FRENCH LITERATURE.
M. DAVIES, 402(MLR):OCT72-881
MICU, D. & N. MANOLESCU. RUMÄNISCHE LIT-
ERATUR DER GEGENWART (1944-1966).
M. LENTZEN, 72:BAND209HEFT1/3-220
MIDDENDORF, J.H., ED. ENGLISH WRITERS OF
THE EIGHTEENTH CENTURY.
J.T. LAVIA, 579(SAQ):SUMMER72-454
MIDDLEKAUFF, R. THE MATHERS.*
D.D. HALL, 432(NEQ):DEC71-659
T. HORNBERGER, 27(AL):NOV72-477
M.I. LOWANCE, JR., 165:FALL73-209
639(VQR):AUTUMN71-CLXXIII
MIDDLETON, L. PLACE NAMES OF THE PACIFIC
NORTHWEST COAST.
B.H. GRANGER, 424:SEP71-215
MIDDLETON, N. - SEE STONE, I.F.
MIDDLETON, R. POP MUSIC AND THE BLUES.
617(TLS):23FEB73-217
MIDDLETON, S. A MAN MADE OF SMOKE.
V. CUNNINGHAM, 362:31MAY73-728
617(TLS):1JUN73-604
MIDDLETON, T. A CHASTE MAIDE IN CHEAP-
SIDE. (R.B. PARKER, ED)
A. BRISSENDEN, 541(RES):MAY71-199
MIDDLETON, T. WOMEN BEWARE WOMEN. A
CHASTE MAID IN CHEAPSIDE. (BOTH ED BY
C. BARBER)
J.C. MAXWELL, 184(EIC):OCT71-382
MIDELFORT, H.C.E. WITCH HUNTING IN SOUTH-
WESTERN GERMANY, 1562-1684.
617(TLS):7SEP73-1035
MIDGLEY, G. THE LIFE OF ORATOR HENLEY.
617(TLS):15JUN73-666
MIEL, J. PASCAL AND THEOLOGY.*
M. BISHOP, 401(MLQ):MAR71-109
J.H. BROOME, 208(FS):APR72-192
C.F. MOONEY, 546(RR):FEB71-52
P. SELLIER, 535(RHL):MAY-JUN71-499
J. WEBER, 207(FR):APR71-989
MIELZINER, J. THE SHAPES OF OUR THEATRES.
H. WEESE, 505:DEC70-86
MIERTSCHING, J. FROZEN SHIPS. (L.H.
NEATBY, ED & TRANS)
D.W. SWAINSON, 529(QQ):SUMMER71-323
MIETH, D. DIE EINHEIT VON VITA ACTIVA
UND VITA CONTEMPLATIVA IN DEN DEUTSCHEN
PREDIGTEN UND TRAKTATEN MEISTER ECK-
HARTS UND BEI JOHANNES TAULER.
J. SUDBRACK, 182:VOL24#7/8-333
MIGLIORINI, B. DAL NOME PROPRIO AL NOME
COMUNE. (2ND ED)
Y. MALKIEL, 545(RPH):AUG71-155
MIGNUCCI, M. IL SIGNIFICATO DELLA LOGICA
STOICA.
L.M.P., 543:MAR71-545
MIHÄESCU, H. - SEE MAURICE
MIHALIC, F. THE JACARANDA DICTIONARY AND
GRAMMAR OF MELANESIAN PIDGIN.
D. LAYCOCK, 67:NOV72-266
MIHARDJA, A.K. ATHEIS.
617(TLS):11MAY73-535
MIHINNICK, J. AT HOME IN UPPER CANADA.
102(CANL):WINTER72-104
MIKES, G. THE SPY WHO DIED OF BOREDOM.
V. CUNNINGHAM, 362:13SEP73-352
617(TLS):7SEP73-1017
MIKHOV, N.V. CONTRIBUTION À L'HISTOIRE
DU COMMERCE DE LA TURQUIE ET DE LA
BULGARIE. (VOL 6)
T. STOIANOVICH, 32:DEC72-934

MIKKOLA, E. DIE ABSTRAKTION.*
  K.H. SCHMIDT, 260(IF):BAND74-242
MIKKOLA, E. DAS KOMPOSITUM.
  A. RAUN, 361:VOL26#1-110
MIKKOLA, E. DIE KONZESSIVITÄT DES ALT-
  LATEINS IM BEREICH DES SATZGANZEN.*
  K.H. SCHMIDT, 260(IF):BAND74-244
MIKO, S.J., ED. TWENTIETH CENTURY INTER-
  PRETATIONS OF "WOMEN IN LOVE."
  K. MC SWEENEY, 529(QQ):SUMMER71-337
MIKROGIANNAKIS, E.I. AI METAXY ALEXANDROY
  G KAI DAREIOY G DIPLŌMATIKAI EPAPHAI.
  J. BRISCOE, 123:MAR72-82
DE MILÁN, L. EL MAESTRO. (C. JACOBS,
  ED & TRANS)
  T.F. HECK, 317:FALL72-487
MILANI, L. LETTERE ALLA MAMMA 1943-1967.
  617(TLS):6JUL73-784
MILDE, W. DER BIBLIOTHEKSKATALOG DES
  KLOSTERS MURBACH AUS DEM 9. JAHRHUN-
  DERT.
  P. OCHSENBEIN, 657(WW):SEP/OCT70-350
MILENKOVITCH, D. PLAN AND MARKET IN
  YUGOSLAV ECONOMIC THOUGHT.
  S. MARKOWSKI, 575(SEER):OCT72-630
MILES, J. THE NIGHT HUNTERS.
  N. CALLENDAR, 441:5AUG73-10
MILES, J. STYLE AND PROPORTION.
  M.F. WAKELIN, 541(RES):MAY71-243
MILES, T.R. RELIGIOUS EXPERIENCE.*
  A. FLEW, 518:OCT72-25
MILET, J. GABRIEL TARDE ET LA PHILOSO-
  PHIE DE L'HISTOIRE.
  C. SCHUWER, 542:OCT-DEC71-516
MILFORD, N. ZELDA.* (BRITISH TITLE:
  ZELDA FITZGERALD.)
  J.W. BYRD, 584(SWR):SPRING72-167
MILGATE, W. - SEE BALD, R.C.
MILGATE, W. - SEE DONNE, J.
MILHAVEN, J.G. TOWARD A NEW CATHOLIC
  MORALITY.*
  G. BAUM, 363:FEB71-55
  R.J. TAPIA, 613:AUTUMN71-448
MILIC, L.T. A QUANTITATIVE APPROACH TO
  THE STYLE OF JONATHAN SWIFT.
  I. POMMERENING, 38:BAND88HEFT2-271
MILIC, L.T., ED. STUDIES IN EIGHTEENTH-
  CENTURY CULTURE.
  566:SPRING72-90
MILIC, L.T. STYLE AND STYLISTICS.
  D.C. FREEMAN, 206:NOV70-590
MILICHIUS, L. ZAUBERTEUFEL, SCHRAPTEUFEL.
  (R. STAMBAUGH, ED)
  E.H. ZEYDEL, 221(GQ):MAR71-253
"THE MILITARY UNBALANCE."
  R.A. SCHADLER, 396(MODA):WINTER72-103
MILIVOJEVIĆ, D.D. CURRENT RUSSIAN PHON-
  EMIC THEORY 1952-1962.
  D. WARD, 575(SEER):JAN72-112
MILJUS, B. LES HABSBOURG, L'ÉGLISE, ET
  LES SLAVES DU SUD.
  F.R. BRIDGE, 575(SEER):JAN72-143
MILL, J.S. COLLECTED WORKS OF JOHN
  STUART MILL.* (VOL 10: ESSAYS ON
  ETHICS, RELIGION AND SOCIETY.) (J.M.
  ROBSON, ED) [SHOWN IN PREV UNDER BOTH
  SERIES TITLE & SUBTITLE]
  J. NARVESON, 154:SEP70-264
MILL, J.S. THE LATER LETTERS OF JOHN
  STUART MILL 1849-1873. (VOLS 14-17)
  (F.E. MINEKA & D.N. LINDLEY, EDS)
  617(TLS):14SEP73-1058
"THE ERIC GEORGE MILLAR BEQUEST OF MANU-
  SCRIPTS AND DRAWINGS, 1967."*
  J.J.G. ALEXANDER, 354:MAR70-61
MILLAR, F., ED. THE ROMAN EMPIRE AND
  ITS NEIGHBOURS.*
  C.M. WELLS, 487:WINTER71-395

MILLAR, J.F. THE ARCHITECTS OF THE
  AMERICAN COLONIES.
  M.C. DONNELLY, 576:MAY70-204
MILLAR, J.R., ED. THE SOVIET RURAL COM-
  MUNITY.
  M. MC CAULEY, 575(SEER):APR72-319
  A. NOVE, 32:SEP72-693
  S.I. PLOSS, 550(RUSR):OCT71-401
MILLAR, O. THE AGE OF CHARLES I.
  617(TLS):12JAN73-47
MILLAR, O. THE LATER GEORGIAN PICTURES
  IN THE COLLECTION OF HER MAJESTY THE
  QUEEN.
  R.E., 135:JUL70-212
  K. GARLICK, 39:APR70-321
  M. WEBSTER, 90:APR71-220
MILLARES CARLO, A. ENSAYO DE UNA BIBLIO-
  GRAFÍA DE LA IMPRENTA Y EL PERIODISMO
  EN VENEZUELA.
  L.A. MUSSO, 263:OCT-DEC72-420
DE MILLE, A. SPEAK TO ME, DANCE WITH ME.
  A. KISSELGOFF, 441:6JUL73-21
  L. NICHOLS, 441:6MAY73-4
"MILLE." [CIRCOLO LINGUISTICO FLOREN-
  TINO]
  R.J. DI PIETRO, 350:SEP72-685
MILLER, A., WITH N.L. BROWNING. MILLER'S
  HIGH LIFE.*
  441:25MAR73-22
MILLER, B. ROBERT BROWNING.
  442(NY):12MAY73-148
MILLER, B.D.H. - SEE ONIONS, C.T.
MILLER, E.H., ED. THE ARTISTIC LEGACY OF
  WALT WHITMAN.
  R. ASSELINEAU, 189(EA):OCT-DEC70-457
MILLER, E.H., ED. A CENTURY OF WHITMAN
  CRITICISM.*
  R. ASSELINEAU, 189(EA):OCT-DEC70-457
  S.A. BLACK, 648:JUN70-40
  T.L. BRASHER, 646(WWR):JUN70-60
MILLER, E.H. - SEE WHITMAN, W.
MILLER, F.P. MAN FROM THE VALLEY.*
  A.K. DAVIS, JR., 639(VQR):AUTUMN71-632
MILLER, G.A. THE PSYCHOLOGY OF COMMUNI-
  CATION.
  C.N. COFER, 215(GL):VOL11#2-109
MILLER, G.M., ED. BBC PRONOUNCING DIC-
  TIONARY OF BRITISH NAMES.
  B.M.H. STRANG, 447(N&Q):SEP71-347
MILLER, H & J.R. CHILDS. COLLECTOR'S
  QUEST. (R.C. WOOD, ED)
  J. COTTON, 503:WINTER69-190
MILLER, H.K. - SEE FIELDING, H.
MILLER, H.K., E. ROTHSTEIN & G.S. ROUS-
  SEAU, EDS. THE AUGUSTAN MILIEU.*
  P.K. ELKIN, 67:MAY72-89
  R. LAWRENCE, 175:AUTUMN71-110
  639(VQR):SUMMER71-CX
MILLER, J., ED. FREUD.*
  617(TLS):23MAR73-317
MILLER, J. MC LUHAN.
  J. BENTHALL, 592:MAR71-135
MILLER, J. POPERY AND POLITICS IN ENG-
  LAND 1660-1688.
  617(TLS):26OCT73-1304
MILLER, J.E., JR., ED. THEORY OF FICTION.
  G. CORE, 385(MQR):WINTER73-82
MILLER, J.H. CHARLES DICKENS.
  S. MONOD, 189(EA):APR-JUN70-219
MILLER, J.H. THOMAS HARDY.*
  R.C. CARPENTER, 191(ELN):DEC71-153
  R.G. COX, 148:SPRING71-91
  H. KENNER, 445(NCF):SEP71-230
  M.L. SEITZ, 636(VP):WINTER70-359
  M. STEIG, 648:OCT70-76
  M. WILLIAMS, 541(RES):AUG71-369
  P. ZIETLOW, 637(VS):MAR71-351

246

MILLER, J.I. THE SPICE TRADE OF THE
ROMAN EMPIRE, 29 B.C. TO A.D. 641.*
J. ANDRÉ, 555:VOL45FASC1-184
MILLER, K., ED. A SECOND LISTENER AN-
THOLOGY.
617(TLS):13APR73-411
MILLER, L., ED. THE DOLMEN PRESS YEATS
CENTENARY PAPERS MCMLXV.
R. FRÉCHET, 189(EA):APR-JUN71-211
MILLER, L. THE DUN EMER PRESS, LATER THE
CUALA PRESS.
617(TLS):29JUN73-749
MILLER, L., ED. IN RETROSPECT.
617(TLS):2NOV73-1351
MILLER, N. DER EMPFINDSAME ERZÄHLER.
A. ANGER, 221(GQ):MAY71-413
MILLER, N. - SEE DE MARIVAUX, P.C.D.
MILLER, R. .THE POETRY OF EMILY DICKIN-
SON.*
J.B. MEROD, 290(JAAC):SUMMER71-557
MILLER, R.A. THE JAPANESE LANGUAGE.
E.A. CRANSTON, 244(HJAS):VOL30-232
I.A. MAC DOUGALL, 47(ARL):[N.S.]VOL1-
109
G.B. MATHIAS, 318(JAOS):APR-JUN71-348
SAYO YOTSUKURA, 353:DEC71-103
MILLER, R.A. - SEE "BERNARD BLOCH ON
JAPANESE"
MILLER, R.D. SCHILLER AND THE IDEAL OF
FREEDOM.
E.J. ENGEL, 402(MLR):OCT72-943
MILLER, R.F. ONE HUNDRED THOUSAND TRAC-
TORS.*
H. HUNTER, 550(RUSR):JUL71-312
MILLER, R.L. THE LINGUISTIC RELATIVITY
PRINCIPLE AND HUMBOLDTIAN ETHNOLINGUIS-
TICS.
J.D. HALL, 221(GQ):MAY71-416
V. SKALIČKA, 353:JAN71-114
MILLER, S.C. THE UNWELCOME IMMIGRANT.*
D.W. GOODRICH, 318(JAOS):OCT-DEC71-520
MILLER, W. WHO ARE THE RUSSIANS?
617(TLS):27JUL73-865
MILLET, L. - SEE LACHELIER, J.
MILLETT, K. SEXUAL POLITICS.*
G. SPEIRS, 67:MAY72-123
MILLGATE, J. MACAULAY.
617(TLS):7DEC73-1501
MILLGATE, M. THOMAS HARDY.*
D. BARON, 150(DR):WINTER71/72-596
R.G. COX, 148:WINTER71-379
MILLHAUSER, S. EDWIN MULLHOUSE.*
R. SALE, 453:25JAN73-42
MILLIGAN, S. THE GOON SHOW SCRIPTS.*
J. LENNON, 441:30SEP73-6
L.E. SISSMAN, 442(NY):24DEC73-77
MILLS, E. & T.C. MURPHY, EDS. THE SUZUKI
CONCEPT.
D. SCHOENBAUM, 441:2SEP73-15
MILLS, H. PEACOCK.*
G.E. ENSCOE, 401(MLQ):JUN71-226
MILLS, H. - SEE PEACOCK, T.L.
MILLS, J. THE LAND OF IS.
J.R. SORFLEET, 198:SPRING73-120
617(TLS):11MAY73-535
MILLS, J.A. LANGUAGE AND LAUGHTER.*
W.N. KING, 599:FALL71-309
W. KLUGE, 38:BAND89HEFT4-548
E.H. MIKHAIL, 397(MD):SEP70-236
S. WEINTRAUB, 405(MP):NOV70-215
MILLS, L.R., ED. LE MYSTÈRE DE SAINT
SÉBASTIEN.
M. ROUSSE, 545(RPH):MAY72-460
MILLS, M. - SEE "LYBEAUS DESCONUS"
MILLS, R.J., JR. - SEE ROETHKE, T.
"MILLSTÄTTER GENESIS UND PHYSIOLOGUS
HANDSCHRIFT."
H. STEGER, 657(WW):JUL/AUG70-279

MILLY, J., ED. LES PASTICHES DE PROUST.
J.M. COCKING, 208(FS):JUL72-352
L. MOULINE, 557(RSH):JUL-SEP71-487
J-Y. TADIÉ, 535(RHL):SEP-DEC71-989
617(TLS):13APR73-423
MILLY, J. PROUST ET LE STYLE.
J-Y. TADIÉ, 535(RHL):SEP-DEC71-988
S. ULLMANN, 208(FS):JUL72-353
MILLY, J. - SEE PROUST, M.
MILNE, A.J.M. FREEDOM AND RIGHTS.*
D.R. BELL, 479(PHQ):JAN71-87
MILNE, A.T., ED. LIBRARIANSHIP AND LIT-
ERATURE.
A.I. DOYLE, 354:DEC71-363
MILNE, MRS. L. & W.W. COCHRANE. SHANS
AT HOME.
W. EBERHARD, 318(JAOS):OCT-DEC71-527
MILNE, L. & M. THE ARENA OF LIFE.
617(TLS):12JAN73-46
MILNER, I. THE STRUCTURE OF VALUES IN
GEORGE ELIOT.*
C. BEDIENT, 445(NCF):SEP70-235
D. OLDFIELD, 637(VS):SEP70-115
R. ROBINSON, 368:JUN70-199
S.J. SPANBERG, 541(RES):AUG71-367
MILNER, J. SYMBOLISTS AND DECADENTS.
A. FORGE, 592:NOV71-215
R. LEBOWITZ, 58:DEC71/JAN72-24
MILNER, M. BAUDELAIRE, ENFER OU CIEL,
QU'IMPORTE.
A. FAIRLIE, 535(RHL):SEP-DEC70-1090
MILOŠEVIĆ, N. ROMAN MILOŠA CRNJANSKOG.
M. MATEJIĆ, 32:MAR72-227
DE L-MILOSZ, O.V. SOIXANTE-QUINZE LET-
TRES INÉDITES.
J. BELLEMIN-NOËL, 535(RHL):MAY-JUN70-
532
MILSOM, J. RUSSIAN TANKS, 1900-1970.
E. O'BALLANCE, 32:SEP72-680
MILTON, J. PARADISE LOST. (BKS 1&2)
(J. BROADBENT, ED)
568(SCN):FALL-WINTER72-65
MILTON, J. PARADISE LOST, PARADISE RE-
GAINED, SAMSON AGONISTES. (R. EBERHART,
ED)
J.A. MC SHANE, 502(PRS):WINTER70/71-
368
MILTON, J. THE POEMS OF JOHN MILTON.*
(J. CAREY & A. FOWLER, EDS)
E. SAILLENS, 189(EA):OCT-DEC70-444
MILWARD, P.C. A COMMENTARY ON G.M. HOP-
KINS' "THE WRECK OF THE DEUTSCHLAND."*
A COMMENTARY ON THE SONNETS OF G.M.
HOPKINS.*
W.R. MUNDT, 598(SOR):AUTUMN73-1029
MINADEO, R. THE LYRE OF SCIENCE.*
D. HENRY, 122:OCT72-301
C.W. MACLEOD, 447(N&Q):DEC71-480
MINÁŘ, J. LE ROMAN FRANÇAIS DU CLASSI-
CISME AUX LUMIÈRES.
A. ZATLOUKAL, 535(RHL):MAY-JUN70-513
MINEAR, R.H. JAPANESE TRADITION AND
WESTERN LAW.
H.D. HAROOTUNIAN, 293(JAST):AUG71-895
B. TETERS, 244(HJAS):VOL31-346
MINEAR, R.H. VICTOR'S JUSTICE.*
42(AR):WINTER71/72-590
MINEKA, F.E. & D.N. LINDLEY - SEE MILL,
J.S.
MINER, E. THE CAVALIER MODE FROM JONSON
TO COTTON.*
V.R. MOLLENKOTT, 568(SCN):SUMMER72-36
MINER, E., ED. JOHN DRYDEN.
617(TLS):30MAR73-346
MINER, E. THE METAPHYSICAL MODE FROM
DONNE TO COWLEY.*
R. ELLRODT, 189(EA):JUL-SEP71-327
R.A. FOAKES, 175:SPRING71-23 [CONT]

247

MINER, E. THE METAPHYSICAL MODE FROM
DONNE TO COWLEY.* [CONTINUING]
H. TOLIVER, 551(RENQ):SPRING71-97
F.J. WARNKE, 191(ELN):JUN72-303
MINER, E., ED. SEVENTEENTH-CENTURY
IMAGERY.
R.L. COLIE, 676(YR):SUMMER72-591
MINETREE, H. COOLEY.
M.G. MICHAELSON, 441:1APR73-23
MINIO-PALUELLO, L. & B.G. DOD, EDS.
ARISTOTELES LATINUS.* (VOL 4, PTS 1-4)
G. POTVIN, 154:SEP71-614
MINK, L.O. MIND, HISTORY, AND DIALECTIC.
T.M. KNOX, 393(MIND):JAN71-150
M. KRAUSZ, 154:MAR71-151
MINKOFF, G.R. A BIBLIOGRAPHY OF THE
BLACK SUN PRESS.
J. COTTON, 503:WINTER70-230
MINKOWSKI, E. FILOSOFIA, SEMANTICA,
PSICOPATOLOGIA. (M. FRANCIONI, ED &
TRANS)
E. NAMER, 542:APR-JUN71-246
MǏNN LATT YĔKHĀUN. MODERNIZATION OF
BURMESE.
E. RICHTER, 682(ZPSK):BAND24HEFT1/2-
158
MINNEY, R.J. "PUFFIN" ASQUITH.
F. WYNDHAM, 362:7JUN73-767
617(TLS):29JUN73-757
MINNEY, R.J. RASPUTIN.
617(TLS):9FEB73-144
MINNEY, R.J. RECOLLECTIONS OF GEORGE
BERNARD SHAW. (BRITISH TITLE: THE
BOGUS IMAGE OF BERNARD SHAW.)
D.J. MURPHY, 397(MD):SEP70-234
R.S. NELSON, 50(ARQ):WINTER70-371
F.L. RADFORD, 572:JAN70-37
MINNIS, N., ED. LINGUISTICS AT LARGE.
S.G. PUTT, 175:AUTUMN71-84
MINOGUE, K.R. THE CONCEPT OF A UNIVER-
SITY.
617(TLS):29JUN73-738
MINOR, W.S., ED. PHILOSOPHY OF CREATIV-
ITY. (VOL 1)
A.W. MUNK, 484(PPR):DEC70-311
MINOW, N.N., J.B. MARTIN & L.M. MITCHELL.
PRESIDENTIAL TELEVISION.
G.E. REEDY, 441:25NOV73-38
MINSKY, M., ED. SEMANTIC INFORMATION
PROCESSING.
M.B.M., 543:DEC70-353
MINTO, C.S. VICTORIAN AND EDWARDIAN
EDINBURGH FROM OLD PHOTOGRAPHS.
617(TLS):21DEC73-1573
MINTS, I.I. ISTORIIA VELIKOGO OKTIABRIA
V TREKH TOMAKH. (VOLS 1&2)
J.D. CLARKSON, 550(RUSR):APR71-179
MINTZ, G.K. - SEE HAN, W-K.
MINTZ, M. & J.S. COHEN. AMERICA, INC.
617(TLS):16MAR73-283
MINTZ, M.M. GOUVERNEUR MORRIS AND THE
AMERICAN REVOLUTION.
W.H. VALIS, 396(MODA):FALL72-430
MIRA DE AMESCUA, A. NO HAY DICHA NI
DESDICHA HASTA LA MUERTE. (V.G. WIL-
LIAMSEN, ED)
D. ROGERS, 86(BHS):JAN72-75
J. VINCI, 238:DEC71-969
"LES MIRABEAU ET LEUR TEMPS."
J-M. GOULEMOT, 535(RHL):JUL-AUG71-706
R. MERCIER, 557(RSH):JAN-MAR70-162
DELLA MIRANDOLA, G.P. - SEE UNDER PICO
DELLA MIRANDOLA, G.
DE MIRAVAL, R. - SEE UNDER RAIMON DE
MIRAVAL
MIRRI, P.S. RICHARD SIMON E IL METODO
STORICO-CRITICO DI B. SPINOZA.
H.W.S., 319:JUL73-433

MIRSKY, D.S. A HISTORY OF RUSSIAN LIT-
ERATURE. (F.J. WHITFIELD, ED)
R.C. CLARK, 544:SPRING72-248
MISCHEL, T., ED. HUMAN ACTION.*
V.J. MC GILL, 484(PPR):JUN71-606
MISH, C.C., ED. RESTORATION PROSE FIC-
TION, 1666-1700.*
P.T. NOLAN, 573(SSF):SPRING71-335
R.O.S., 502(PRS):SUMMER71-185
MISHAN, E.J. MAKING THE WORLD SAFE FOR
PORNOGRAPHY.
A. RYAN, 362:27DEC73-891
617(TLS):16NOV73-1392
MISHIMA, Y. RUNAWAY HORSES.
E. WHITE, 441:24JUN73-3
442(NY):23JUN73-89
617(TLS):30NOV73-1466
MISHIMA, Y. SPRING SNOW.*
R. SALE, 249(HUDR):WINTER72/73-703
MISHIMA, Y. THE TEMPLE OF DAWN.
P. THEROUX, 441:14OCT73-6
MISHIMA, Y. & G. BOWNAS, EDS. NEW WRIT-
ING IN JAPAN.
617(TLS):13APR73-424
MISKIMIN, A. - SEE "SUSANNAH"
MISRA, G.S.P. THE AGE OF THE VINAYA.
617(TLS):31AUG73-1009
MISRA, K.P. THE ROLE OF THE UNITED
NATIONS IN THE INDO-PAKISTANI CON-
FLICT, 1971.
617(TLS):30NOV73-1485
MISRA, K.P., ED. STUDIES IN INDIAN FOR-
EIGN POLICY.
N.P. PALMER, 293(JAST):NOV70-202
MISRA, S.C. MUSLIM COMMUNITIES IN GUJ-
ARAT.
K.S. LAL, 273(IC):OCT71-298
MISRA, V.N. THE DESCRIPTIVE TECHNIQUE OF
PĀNINI.*
V. MILTNER, 353:MAY70-103
S. SEN GUPTA, 682(ZPSK):BAND24HEFT5-
450
MISRAHI, R. SPINOZA.
S. ZAC, 542:JUL-SEP70-358
"MISS READ." TYLER'S ROW.
M. LEVIN, 441:11FEB73-31
MISTRAL, F. LIS ISCLO D'OR. (J. BOU-
TIÈRE, ED)
C. ROSTAING, 535(RHL):JUL-AUG71-718
H.L. SPANJAARD, 433:APR71-213
MISTRAL, F. MÉMOIRES ET RÉCITS, CORRES-
PONDANCE. (P. ROLLET, ED)
C. ROSTAING, 535(RHL):MAR-APR71-317
MITAMURA, T. CHINESE EUNUCHS.
C.S. GOODRICH, 318(JAOS):OCT-DEC71-514
M. ROSSABI, 293(JAST):FEB71-432
MITAMURA, T. KANGAN.
R.L. BROWN, 270:VOL21#1-125
MITCHELL, A. CATHEDRALS OF EUROPE.
J. WILTON-ELY, 39:APR70-318
MITCHELL, A. WARTIME.
R. BLYTHE, 362:29NOV73-752
617(TLS):30NOV73-1466
MITCHELL, B. ALEXANDER HAMILTON: THE
REVOLUTIONARY YEARS.
H.F. RANKIN, 656(WMQ):JAN71-159
MITCHELL, B. LAW, MORALITY & RELIGION IN
A SECULAR SOCIETY.
W.D. GLASGOW, 393(MIND):JUL71-475
MITCHELL, B. FREDERICK LAW OLMSTED.
I.R. STEWART, 576:DEC71-331
MITCHELL, B. THE RISE OF THE COTTON
MILLS IN THE SOUTH.
J.F. DOSTER, 9(ALAR):APR71-154
MITCHELL, C. - SEE OPPÉ, A.P.
MITCHELL, D. 1919.
R.V. DANIELS, 32:MAR72-167

MITCHELL, J.  THOMAS HOCCLEVE.*
  A.S.G. EDWARDS, 439(NM):1971/1-186
  S.W. HOLTON, 597(SN):VOL43#1-303
  M. POLLET, 189(EA):OCT-DEC71-519
  R. PRYOR, 38:BAND88HEFT3-378
MITCHELL, J.  RUSSIAN ROULETTE.
  N. CALLENDAR, 441:23DEC73-16
MITCHELL, J.  WOMAN'S ESTATE.*
  E.G. ROSTOW, 676(YR):SUMMER72-628
MITCHELL, L.G., ED.  THE PUREFOY LETTERS
  1735-1753.
  R. MITCHISON, 362:7JUN73-764
  617(TLS):1JUN73-613
MITCHELL, P.  THE COVENANT.
  W. SCHOTT, 441:27MAY73-6
MITCHELL, P.  EUROPEAN FLOWER PAINTERS.
  617(TLS):2NOV73-1335
MITCHELL, P.  AN INTRODUCTION TO PICTURE
  COLLECTING.
  T. CROMBIE, 39:JAN71-74
MITCHELL, P.M.  A BIBLIOGRAPHY OF 17TH
  CENTURY GERMAN IMPRINTS IN DENMARK
  AND THE DUCHIES OF SCHLESWIG-HOLSTEIN,
  I-II.
  J.L. FLOOD, 354:SEP71-278
  G.C. SCHOOLFIELD, 563(SS):AUTUMN72-573
MITCHELL, W.R.  HIGHLAND WINTER.
  617(TLS):21SEP73-1093
MITCHELL, W.S.  CATALOGUE OF THE INCUNABU-
  ULA IN ABERDEEN UNIVERSITY LIBRARY.*
  D.E. RHODES, 354:MAR70-62
"THE MITCHELL TRIO SONG BOOK."  (MUSIC
  ED BY W. RAIM)
  J.O. WEST, 650(WF):JAN70-62
MITCHISON, N.  A LIFE FOR AFRICA.
  617(TLS):17AUG73-949
MITCHISON, N.  SMALL TALK...
  E.S. TURNER, 362:7JUN73-764
  617(TLS):29JUN73-757
MITFORD, J.  KIND AND UNUSUAL PUNISHMENT.
  C. LEHMANN-HAUPT, 441:19SEP73-53
  D.J. ROTHMAN, 441:9SEP73-2
MITFORD, T.B.  THE INSCRIPTIONS OF KOUR-
  ION.
  D.W. BRADEEN, 124:JAN72-169
MITGANG, H. - SEE DICEY, E.
MITTENZWEI, I.  DIE SPRACHE ALS THEMA.
  R.K. ANGRESS, 406:SUMMER72-190
MITTENZWEI, W., ED.  POSITIONEN.
  K. JARMATZ, 654(WB):6/1970-211
MITTERAND, F.  LA ROSE AU POING.
  617(TLS):16FEB73-177
MITTINS, W.H. & OTHERS.  ATTITUDES TO
  ENGLISH USAGE.
  J.F. POVEY, 399(MLJ):APR71-253
MITTMANN, S.  BEITRÄGE ZUR SIEDLUNGS- UND
  TERRITORIALGESCHICHTE DES NÖRDLICHEN
  OSTJORDANLANDES.
  E. KUTSCH, 182:VOL24#17/18-656
MITTON, C.L., ED.  THE SOCIAL SCIENCES
  AND THE CHURCHES.
  617(TLS):16FEB73-190
MITZKA, W.  KLEINE SCHRIFTEN ZUR SPRACH-
  GESCHICHTE UND SPRACHGEOGRAPHIE.  (L.E.
  SCHMITT, ED)
  J. ALDENHOFF, 556(RLV):1970/2-222
  H. STOPP, 680(ZDP):BAND90HEFT1-134
MITZKA, W., ED.  WORTGEOGRAPHIE UND
  GESELLSCHAFT.
  H.R., 657(WW):MAR/APR70-134
MIX, E.R.  MARCUS ATILIUS REGULUS, EXEM-
  PLUM HISTORICUM.
  A.H. MC DONALD, 123:DEC72-428
  A.M. WARD, 124:SEP71-30
MIYAZAKI KAZUE, ED.  KUNISAKI HANTŌ NO
  MUKASHIBANASHI.
  F.H. MAYER, 244(HJAS):VOL30-263

MIYOSHI, M.  THE DIVIDED SELF.
  A. FLEISHMAN, 636(VP):SPRING70-76
  B.A. INMAN, 50(ARQ):AUTUMN71-273
  R.W. KING, 541(RES):AUG71-373
  R. MAYHEAD, 175:SUMMER71-59
  B. WILLEY, 148:SPRING71-94
MIZENER, A.  THE SADDEST STORY.*
  R.W. LID, 639(VQR):SPRING71-317
  676(YR):AUTUMN71-XX
MIZUSAWA KEN'ICHI.  AKAI KIKIMIMI ZUKIN.
  F.H. MAYER, 244(HJAS):VOL30-263
MJÖBERG, J.  DRÖMMEN OM SAGATIDEN.
  J.L. GREENWAY, 563(SS):SPRING72-265
MOAT, J.  THE TUGEN AND THE TOOT.
  R. GARFITT, 362:20SEP73-384
  617(TLS):19OCT73-1270
MOBERG, V.  A HISTORY OF THE SWEDISH
  PEOPLE.  (VOLS 1&2)
  617(TLS):21SEP73-1075
MOBLEY, H.W.  THE GHANAIAN'S IMAGE OF THE
  MISSIONARY.
  G. JAHODA, 69:OCT71-345
MOCH, J.  RENCONTRES AVEC...LÉON BLUM.
  W. LOGUE, 207(FR):MAY71-1118
MOCKEL, A.  ESTHÉTIQUE DU SYMBOLISME,
  PROPOS DE LITTÉRATURE (1898), STÉPHANE
  MALLARMÉ, UN HÉROS (1899), TEXTES
  DIVERS.
  A. GILL, 535(RHL):MAR-APR70-333
"LA MODALITÉ DU JUGEMENT CHEZ ARISTOTE
  ET DANS LA LOGIQUE CONTEMPORAINE."
  R. BLANCHÉ, 542:APR-JUN71-227
"MODERN POETRY IN TRANSLATION."  (NO. 16)
  (A. RUDOLPH, ED)
  617(TLS):1JUN73-610
"MODERNITY AND CONTEMPORARY INDIAN LIT-
  ERATURE."
  R. LAWRENCE, 175:SPRING70-33
MODLMAYR, H-J.  KÖNIG LEAR AUF PATMOS.
  617(TLS):12OCT73-1244
MODLYN, M.  PARDON MY CHEEK.
  617(TLS):7DEC73-1521
MOFFAT, G.  LADY WITH A COOL EYE.
  617(TLS):17AUG73-959
MOFFETT, J. & K.R. MC ELHENEY, EDS.
  POINTS OF VIEW.
  D. BARNHILL, 186(ETC.):MAR70-107
MOFFITT, J.F.  SPANISH PAINTING.
  617(TLS):14SEP73-1065
MOGGRIDGE, D. - SEE KEYNES, J.M.
MOHAN, G.B.  THE RESPONSE TO POETRY.*
  W. MOSHER, 318(JAOS):JAN-MAR71-159
MOHAN, R.P.  PHILOSOPHY OF HISTORY.
  H.B., 543:SEP70-140
MOHANTI, P.  MY VILLAGE, MY LIFE.
  617(TLS):7DEC73-1510
MOHANTY, J.  GANGEŚA'S "THEORY OF TRUTH."*
  A. WAYMAN, 318(JAOS):OCT-DEC71-550
MOHL, R.  JOHN MILTON AND HIS "COMMON-
  PLACE BOOK."*
  D.D.C. CHAMBERS, 541(RES):MAY71-208
MOHL, R.A.  POVERTY IN NEW YORK, 1783-
  1825.
  639(VQR):SUMMER71-CXXIII
MÖHLIG, W.J.G.  DIE SPRACHE DER DCIRIKU.
  E. WESTPHAL, 69:JUL70-291
MOHOLY-NAGY, L.  PAINTING, PHOTOGRAPHY,
  FILM.
  C. MILES, 290(JAAC):SUMMER71-560
MOHOLY-NAGY, S.  MOHOLY-NAGY, EXPERIMENT
  IN TOTALITY.  (2ND ED)
  C. MILES, 290(JAAC):SUMMER71-560
VON MOHRENSCHILDT, D., ED.  THE RUSSIAN
  REVOLUTION OF 1917: CONTEMPORARY AC-
  COUNTS.
  R.V. DANIELS, 550(RUSR):JUL71-316
  W.E. MOSSE, 575(SEER):JUL72-470
MOIGNET, G. - SEE "LA CHANSON DE ROLAND"

LE MOINE, R., ED. L'AMÉRIQUE ET LES
POÈTES FRANÇAIS DE LA RENAISSANCE.
617(TLS):23MAR73-320
LE MOINE, R. JOSEPH MARMETTE, SA VIE,
SON OEUVRE [SUIVI DE] A TRAVERS LA VIE.
R. MERCIER, 557(RSH):OCT-DEC70-663
MOIR, A. THE ITALIAN FOLLOWERS OF CARA-
VAGGIO.
C. DEMPSEY, 54:SEP70-324
MOIR, J.S., ED. CHARACTER AND CIRCUM-
STANCE.
G.A. RAWLYK, 150(DR):SUMMER71-276
MOISAN, C. HENRI BREMOND ET LA POÉSIE
PURE.
K. DUTTON, 535(RHL):MAY-JUN70-536
MOIX, T. OLAS SOBRE UNA ROCA DESIERTA.
R.L. SHEEHAN, 238:SEP71-600
MOK, Q.I.M. CONTRIBUTION À L'ÉTUDE DES
CATÉGORIES MORPHOLOGIQUES DU GENRE ET
DU NOMBRE DANS LE FRANÇAIS PARLÉ
ACTUEL.*
H. BONNARD, 209(FM):JAN70-63
R. POSNER, 545(RPH):AUG71-108
MOL, H., ED. WESTERN RELIGION.
617(TLS):5JAN73-18
MOLAGER, J. - SEE CICERO
MOLDENHAUER, J.J. - SEE THOREAU, H.D.
MOLER, K.L. JANE AUSTEN'S ART OF ALLU-
SION.*
J. DELBAERE-GARANT, 556(RLV):1970/2-
217
A.M. DUCKWORTH, 405(MP):AUG70-112
P. GOETSCH, 430(NS):NOV70-582
MOLES, A. INFORMATION THEORY AND
ESTHETIC PERCEPTION.* (J.S. COHEN, ED
& TRANS)
F. RASTIER, 215(GL):VOL10#3-214
MOLESWORTH, H.D. THE PRINCES.
A. VON SCHUCKMANN, 39:DEC70-497
MOLHO, M. INTRODUCTION À LA PENSÉE
PICARESQUE.
C. CAVILLAC, 549(RLC):OCT-DEC70-554
MOLHO, M. LINGUISTIQUES ET LANGAGE.*
J. CHAURAND, 209(FM):JAN71-79
MOLHO, M. SÉMANTIQUE ET POÉTIQUE, À
PROPOS DES SOLITUDES DE GÓNGORA.
C. SMITH, 86(BHS):JAN72-80
P. SOMVILLE, 556(RLV):1971/5-656
205(FMLS):OCT70-422
MOLHO, R. - SEE SAINTE-BEUVE, C.A.
MOLIÈRE, J.B.P. LE TARTUFFE. (H. WALKER,
ED)
B.E. HICKS, 399(MLJ):FEB71-121
DE MOLINA, T. - SEE UNDER TIRSO DE MOLINA
MOLINARO, J.A., COMP. A BIBLIOGRAPHY OF
SIXTEENTH-CENTURY ITALIAN VERSE COLLEC-
TIONS IN THE UNIVERSITY OF TORONTO LIB-
RARY.
E.B., 228(GSLI):VOL147FASC458/459-472
A. BULLOCK, 402(MLR):APR72-433
J.G. FUCILLA, 276:WINTER71-501
MÖLK, U. FRANZÖSISCHE LITERARÄSTHETIK
DES 12. UND 13. JAHRHUNDERTS.
W.G. VAN EMDEN, 208(FS):JAN72-58
MØLLER, S.J. BIDRAG TIL H.C. ANDERSENS
BIBLIOGRAFI. (VOL 3)
R. KLEIN, 78(BC):WINTER71-540
VON MOLNÁR, G. NOVALIS'S "FICHTE STUD-
IES."
C. HERING, 406:SPRING72-81
E. STOPP, 402(MLR):JAN72-217
MOLNAR, J.W., ED. SONGS FROM THE WIL-
LIAMSBURG THEATRE.
617(TLS):30NOV73-1480
MOLONEY, B. FLORENCE AND ENGLAND.
205(FMLS):OCT70-422

MOLONY, C.J.C., WITH OTHERS. HISTORY OF
THE SECOND WORLD WAR. (VOL 5)
617(TLS):14DEC73-1543
MOLS, M.H. ALLGEMEINE STAATSLEHRE ODER
POLITISCHE THEORIE?
H. DOMBOIS, 182:VOL24#17/18-661
MOLTHAGEN, J. DER RÖMISCHE STAAT UND DIE
CHRISTEN IM ZWEITEN UND DRITTEN JAHRHUN-
DERT.
W.H.C. FREND, 123:DEC72-392
MOMADAY, N.S. HOUSE MADE OF DAWN.
J.Z. BENNETT, 649(WAL):SPRING70-69
MOMADAY, N.S. THE WAY TO RAINY MOUNTAIN.*
B. TOELKEN, 650(WF):OCT70-268
MOMBELLO, G. LA TRADIZIONE MANOSCRITTA
DELL'"EPISTRE OTHEA" DI CHRISTINE DE
PIZAN.*
C.C. WILLARD, 545(RPH):MAY72-467
MOMIGLIANO LEPSCHY, A.L., ED. VIAGGIO
IN TERRASANTA DI SANTO BRASCA 1480 CON
L'ITINERARIO DI GABRIELE CAPODILISTA
1458.
M. WIS, 439(NM):1970/3-522
"MON-KHMER STUDIES III."
G.F. MEIER, 682(ZPSK):BAND23HEFT6-634
MONACO, G. - SEE PLAUTUS
MONAN, J.D. MORAL KNOWLEDGE AND ITS
METHODOLOGY IN ARISTOTLE.*
W. LESZL, 548(RCSF):JUL-SEP71-343
DE MONBRON, F. - SEE UNDER FOUGERET DE
MONBRON
MONCK, F.E.O.C. MONCK LETTERS AND JOUR-
NALS, 1863-1868. (W.L. MORTON, ED)
P.B. WAITE, 150(DR):AUTUMN71-435
MONDEN, L. FAITH.
R.J. TAPIA, 613:WINTER70-625
MONDOR, H. & L.J. AUSTIN - SEE MALLARMÉ,
S.
MONECKE, W. STUDIEN ZUR EPISCHEN TECHNIK
KONRADS VON WÜRZBURG.
W. SCHRÖDER, 680(ZDP):BAND90HEFT3-459
MONET, D. SQUANDERING.
P.M. SPACKS, 249(HUDR):SPRING72-163
MONEY, J. & A.A. EHRHARDT. MAN AND WOMAN
BOY AND GIRL.
J.L. COLLIER, 441:25FEB73-6
MONGLOND, A. LA FRANCE RÉVOLUTIONNAIRE
ET IMPÉRIALE. (VOL 9) LE PRÉROMAN-
TISME FRANÇAIS. (VOLS 1&2) (NEW ED)
PÈLERINAGES ROMANTIQUES.
P. VIALLANEIX, 98:NOV71-933
MONGRÉDIEN, G. DAILY LIFE IN THE FRENCH
THEATRE AT THE TIME OF MOLIÈRE.
E. JACOBS, 157:SUMMER70-71
MONK, S. - SEE FOX, C.
MONNEROT, J. LES LOIS DU TRAGIQUE.
J. GRENIER, 542:APR-JUN71-248
MONOD, J. CHANCE AND NECESSITY.* (FRENCH
TITLE: LE HASARD ET LA NÉCESSITÉ.)
R. BLANCHÉ, 542:JUL-SEP71-389
C.M. CROW, 402(MLR):JAN72-153
M. SERRES, 98:JUN71-483 [& CONT IN]
98:JUL71-579
42(AR):WINTER71/72-595
MONOD, J. LEÇON INAUGURALE.
M. SERRES, 98:JUL71-579
MONOD, S. DICKENS THE NOVELIST.*
M. SLATER, 189(EA):APR-JUN70-212
MONROE, E. THE CHANGING BALANCE OF POWER
IN THE PERSIAN GULF.
617(TLS):19JAN73-60
MONROE, E. PHILBY OF ARABIA.
R. CROSSMAN, 362:15NOV73-672
617(TLS):7DEC73-1494
MONSANTO, C.H. LA PROTESTA SOCIAL EN LA
DRAMATURGIA DE ACEVEDO HERNÁNDEZ.
H. CASTILLO, 263:JUL-SEP72-293

MONSARRAT, N. THE KAPPILLAN OF MALTA.
617(TLS):19OCT73-1270
MONSARRAT, N. RICHER THAN ALL HIS TRIBE.
J.C. FIELD, 556(RLV):1971/1-97
MONTAGNE, R. THE BERBERS.
617(TLS):15JUN73-696
MONTAGU, A. IMMORTALITY, RELIGION AND
MORALS.
L.A. OLAN, 328:FALL71-495
MONTAGU, M.W. THE COMPLETE LETTERS OF
LADY MARY WORTLEY MONTAGU. (VOLS 1-3)
(R. HALSBAND, ED)
A.J. SAMBROOK, 179(ES):FEB71-77
MONTAGU, M.W. THE SELECTED LETTERS OF
LADY MARY WORTLEY MONTAGU. (R. HALS-
BAND, ED)
566:AUTUMN71-25
MONTAGUE, J. THE BREAD GOD. HYMN TO THE
NEW OMAGH ROAD.
S. FAUCHEREAU, 98:MAY70-438
MONTAGUE, J. A CHOSEN LIGHT.
W. WALLIS, 502(PRS):FALL71-278
MONTAGUE, J. THE ROUGH FIELD.
S. HEANEY, 362:26APR73-550
617(TLS):16FEB73-183
MONTAGUE, J. TIDES.*
A. CLUYSENAAR, 565:VOL12#2-63
T.D. REDSHAW, 159(DM):SPRING71-109
H. SERGEANT, 175:SUMMER71-65
W. WALLIS, 502(PRS):FALL71-278
DE MONTAIGNE, M. ESSAIS.
J. BERNHARDT, 542:APR-JUN71-249
MONTALBÁN, M.V. - SEE UNDER VÁZQUEZ MON-
TALBÁN, M.
MONTALE, E. & V. BRANCA - SEE CECCHI, E.
MONTALEMBERT, C.F. & C. CANTÙ. CARTEGGIO
MONTALEMBERT - CANTÙ, 1842-1868. (F.K.
MELZI D'ERIL, ED)
J. ONIMUS, 557(RSH):JUL-SEP71-485
MONTANO, R. LO SPIRITO E LE LETTERE.
G. DI PINO, 149:MAR72-103
DE MONTCLOS, J-M.P. - SEE UNDER PÉROUSE
DE MONTCLOS, J-M.
DO MONTE, G. SUBSÍDIOS PARA A HISTÓRIA
DA TIPOGRAFIA EM ÉVORA NOS SÉCULOS
XVI A XVIII.
H-G. WHITEHEAD, 354:DEC70-364
MONTEL, J-C. LE CARNAVAL.
N. GREENE, 207(FR):DEC70-418
MONTELL, W.L. THE SAGA OF COE RIDGE.
R.A. REUSS, 292(JAF):JUL-SEP71-351
MONTELLO, J. UN MAÎTRE OUBLIÉ DE STEN-
DHAL.
J.S.P., 191(ELN):SEP71(SUPP)-111
MONTER, B.H. KOZ'MA PRUTKOV.
617(TLS):25MAY73-595
MONTER, E.W. EUROPEAN WITCHCRAFT.
C.A. BURLAND, 203:WINTER70-321
MONTESINOS, J.F. GALDÓS. (VOL 3)
617(TLS):12OCT73-1227
MONTESQUIEU. CONSIDÉRATIONS SUR LES
CAUSES DE LA GRANDEUR DES ROMAINS ET
DE LEUR DÉCADENCE.* (J. EHRARD, ED)
J-M. GOULEMOT, 535(RHL):JUL-AUG70-711
MONTGOMERY, B. A FIELD-MARSHAL IN THE
FAMILY.
617(TLS):26OCT73-1309
MONTGOMERY, C.F. A HISTORY OF AMERICAN
PEWTER.
R. REIF, 441:24NOV73-29
MONTGOMERY, E.D., ED. LE CHASTOIEMENT
D'UN PÈRE A SON FILS.
J. CANTERA, 202(FMOD):NOV71/FEB72-150
MONTGOMERY, F. PRINTED TEXTILES.*
M. LYON, 139:FEB71-8
J.L. NEVINSON, 135:DEC71-290
MONTGOMERY, J.A. THE SAMARITANS.
W.A. MEEKS, 318(JAOS):OCT-DEC71-529

MONTGOMERY, L.M. THE BLUE CASTLE. A TAN-
GLED WEB.
H. PORTER, 296:FALL73-102
MONTGOMERY, M. THE GULL AND OTHER GEORGIA
SCENES.*
J.T. IRWIN, 598(SOR):SUMMER73-720
MONTGOMERY, S. CIRCE.*
G.R. STRICKLAND, 97(CQ):SPRING/SUM-
MER70-99
MONTGOMERY-MASSINGBERD, H. - SEE "BURKE'S
LANDED GENTRY"
DE MONTHERLANT, H. LES GARÇONS.
H. KOPS, 573(SSF):FALL71-642
DE MONTHERLANT, H. PORT-ROYAL. (R. HAGS-
PIEL, ED)
J. DECOCK, 207(FR):OCT70-159
DE MONTHERLANT, H. LA TRAGÉDIE SANS
MASQUE. LA MARÉE DU SOIR. MAIS AIMONS-
NOUS CEUX QUE NOUS AIMONS?
617(TLS):25MAY73-571
DE MONTHERLANT, H. LE TREIZIÈME CÉSAR.
J. CRUICKSHANK, 208(FS):JUL72-356
MONTI, V. POESIE. (G. BEZZOLA, ED)
A.M.M., 228(GSLI):VOL147FASC460-634
MONTY, J. LES ROMANS DE L'ABBÉ PRÉVOST.
D.W. WELCH, 402(MLR):OCT72-894
MOODY, R. LILLIAN HELLMAN.*
J.H. ADLER, 578:SPRING73-131
MOON, P. - SEE LORD WAVELL
MOONEY, H.J., JR. & T.F. STALEY, EDS.
THE SHAPELESS GOD.*
L.T.L., 502(PRS):SPRING70-86
MOONEY, S. SELVES.
J. TIPTON, 577(SHR):SPRING71-196
MOONMAN, E. RELUCTANT PARTNERSHIP.
V.E. LINE, 619(TC):VOL179#1046-49
MOORAT, S.A.J. CATALOGUE OF WESTERN
MANUSCRIPTS ON MEDICINE AND SCIENCE IN
THE WELLCOME HISTORICAL LIBRARY. (VOL
2)
617(TLS):7DEC73-1493
MOORCOCK, M. THE OAK AND THE RAM.
617(TLS):9NOV73-1377
MOORCRAFT, C. MUST THE SEAS DIE?*
441:25MAR73-24
MOORE, B. CATHOLICS.*
A. BROYARD, 441:17APR73-45
P. THEROUX, 441:18MAR73-39
G. NOONAN, 99:APR73-40
442(NY):5MAY73-149
MOORE, B. I AM MARY DUNNE.*
J.C. FIELD, 556(RLV):1971/3-332
MOORE, B. REFLECTIONS ON THE CAUSES OF
HUMAN MISERY AND UPON CERTAIN PROPOSALS
TO ELIMINATE THEM.*
R. COLES, 442(NY):3MAR73-106
MOORE, B. THE REVOLUTION SCRIPT.*
J. GOODE, 473(PR):SPRING72-276
A.N. RASPA, 150(DR):WINTER71/72-584
G. WOODCOCK, 102(CANL):WINTER72-73
MOORE, C.A., WITH A.V. MORRIS, EDS. THE
INDIAN MIND.
R.H. ROBINSON, 485(PE&W):APR70-183
MOORE, C.A., WITH A.V. MORRIS, EDS. THE
JAPANESE MIND.*
M. KIYOTA, 485(PE&W):APR70-175
MOORE, C.C. THE NIGHT BEFORE CHRISTMAS
(A VISIT FROM ST. NICHOLAS)
S.S.B., 37:NOV-DEC71-37
MOORE, D. & J. THE FIRST 150 YEARS OF
SINGAPORE.
R. VAN NIEL, 293(JAST):NOV70-249
MOORE, D.B. THE POETRY OF LOUIS
MAC NEICE.*
S. HYNES, 659:SUMMER73-378

MOORE, F.C.T. THE PSYCHOLOGY OF MAINE
DE BIRAN.*
    I.W. ALEXANDER, 483:JUL71-269
    D. JANICAUD, 542:JUL-SEP71-390
MOORE, G. THE CHOSEN TONGUE.*
    R. LAWRENCE, 175:SUMMER70-69
MOORE, G. GEORGE MOORE IN TRANSITION.*
    (H.E. GERBER, ED)
    P. GOETSCH, 430(NS):DEC70-639
    G. LINDOP, 447(N&Q):NOV71-431
MOORE, G. WOLE SOYINKA.*
    617(TLS):27JUL73-876
MOORE, G.T., ED. EMERGING METHODS IN
ENVIRONMENTAL DESIGN AND PLANNING.
    J-M. ADDISS, 505:MAY71-126
MOORE, H.T. TWENTIETH CENTURY GERMAN
LITERATURE.
    F.H. WOOD, 593:SPRING72-91
MOORE, J.E., ED. JANE'S POCKET BOOK OF
MAJOR WARSHIPS.
    617(TLS):15JUN73-700
MOORE, J.R. MASKS OF LOVE AND DEATH.
    G.M. HARPER, 191(ELN):JUN72-316
    D.E.S. MAXWELL, 150(DR):SUMMER71-290
    676(YR):AUTUMN71-XII
MOORE, P., ED. ASTRONOMICAL TELESCOPES
AND OBSERVATORIES FOR AMATEURS.
    617(TLS):13JUL73-817
MOORE, P., ED. ASTRONOMY AND SPACE.
(VOL 2)
    617(TLS):7SEP73-1037
MOORE, P. THE COMETS.
    617(TLS):30NOV73-1485
MOORE, P., ED. 1974 YEARBOOK OF ASTRON-
OMY.
    617(TLS):19OCT73-1289
MOORE, R. THE FIFTH ESTATE.
    M. LEVIN, 441:24JUN73-14
MOORE, R. TIME'S WEB.
    J. KESSLER, 491:FEB73-292
MOORE, R. WORD FROM THE HILLS.
    J.H. WILDMAN, 598(SOR):SUMMER73-748
MOORE, R.S. PAUL HAMILTON HAYNE.
    T.D. YOUNG, 578:FALL73-101
MOORE, T. & T. DAWE. CONNECTIONS.
    A. NOWLAN, 198:SPRING73-119
MOORE, T.I. SOCIAL PATTERNS IN AUSTRAL-
IAN LITERATURE.*
    A.A. PHILLIPS, 381:DEC71-469
    M. WILDING, 581:MAR72-68
MOORE, W.G. THE CLASSICAL DRAMA OF
FRANCE.
    R. HAYMAN, 157:AUTUMN71-79
    R.C. KNIGHT, 208(FS):APR72-193
MOORE, W.G. LA ROCHEFOUCAULD.*
    J. LAFOND, 535(RHL):JAN-FEB71-83
    205(FMLS):APR70-209
MOORE, W.G. - SEE DE BALZAC, H.
MOORE, W.J. DOWN EASTER CAPTAIN.
    S.E. MORISON, 432(NEQ):MAR71-155
MOORHOUSE, F. FUTILITY AND OTHER ANI-
MALS.
    M. WILDING, 381:JUN71-265
MOORHOUSE, G. THE MISSIONARIES.
    P. WHITEHEAD, 362:30AUG73-287
MOORMAN, M. - SEE WORDSWORTH, W. & D.
MOORMAN, M. & A.G. HILL - SEE WORDSWORTH,
W. & D.
VON MOOS, S. LE CORBUSIER, ELEMENTE
EINER SYNTHESE.
    P. SERENYI, 576:OCT71-255
MOOTE, A.L. THE REVOLT OF THE JUDGES.
    617(TLS):27APR73-468
MOR, A. & J. WEISGERBER. LE LETTERATURE
DEL BELGIO. (NEW ED)
    H-J. LOPE, 52:BAND5HEFT3-306
MORA, J.F. - SEE UNDER FERRATER MORA, J.

MORAES, F. WITNESS TO AN ERA.
    617(TLS):13JUL73-795
MORALES-PINO, A. RÉQUIEM POR UN CORAZÓN.
    G.E. WADE, 238:DEC71-974
MORAN, H.A. & D.H. KELLEY. THE ALPHABET
AND THE ANCIENT CALENDAR SIGNS.
    C.S. GOODRICH, 318(JAOS):OCT-DEC71-516
MORAN, J. PRINTING PRESSES.
    617(TLS):7DEC73-1500
DE MORATÍN, L.F. DIARIO (MAYO 1780-MARZO
1808). (R. & M. ANDIOC, EDS)
    R.P. SEBOLD, 240(HR):JAN71-106
MORAUX, P. & D. HARLFINGER, EDS. UNTER-
SUCHUNGEN ZUR EUDEMISCHEN ETHIK.
    J. JOPE, 124:NOV71-96
MORAVIA, A. BOUGHT AND SOLD.
    A. BROYARD, 441:6MAR73-45
MORAVIA, A. COMMAND, AND I WILL OBEY
YOU.
    C. FANTAZZI, 573(SSF):FALL71-646
MORAVIA, A. TWO.*
    P.M. SPACKS, 249(HUDR):AUTUMN72-497
MORAVIA, A. UN'ALTRA VITA.
    617(TLS):21DEC73-1557
MORBY, E.S. - SEE LOPE DE VEGA
MORE, P.E. THE ESSENTIAL PAUL ELMER
MORE. (B.G. LAMBERT, ED)
    T.W. ROGERS, 396(MODA):FALL72-436
MORE, T. RESPONSIO AD LUTHERUM. (J.M.
HEADLEY, ED; S. MANDEVILLE, TRANS)
    H.W. DONNER, 597(SN):VOL42#2-459
    R. PINEAS, 551(RENQ):SPRING71-85
"THOMAS MORE'S PRAYER BOOK."* (L.L.
MARTZ & R.S. SYLVESTER, EDS)
    H.W. DONNER, 597(SN):VOL42#1-225
MORÉAS, J. CENT SOIXANTE-TREIZE LETTRES
DE JEAN MORÉAS.* (R.A. JOUANNY, ED)
    M.C. PAKENHAM, 535(RHL):JAN-FEB71-127
MOREAU, J. ARISTOTE ET SON ÉCOLE.
    H. DUMÉRY, 542:JAN-MAR70-79
MOREAU, J. DICTIONNAIRE DE GÉOGRAPHIE
HISTORIQUE DE LA GAULE ET DE LA FRANCE.
    I. MÜLLER, 182:VOL24#17/18-692
MOREAU, J. LE DIEU DES PHILOSOPHES.
    J. KOPPER, 342:BAND62HEFT1-145
MOREAU, J. POUR OU CONTRE L'INSENSÉ?
    A. FOREST, 542:APR-JUN70-232
MOREAU, P. BARRÈS.
    E. CARASSUS, 535(RHL):JUL-AUG71-717
    G. VANWELKENHUYZEN, 549(RLC):JUL-SEP
    71-430
MOREAU, P. L'OFFRANDE LYRIQUE DE PAUL
CLAUDEL.
    J-N. SEGRESTAA, 535(RHL):MAR-APR71-
    326
MORECAMBE, E. & E. WISE. ERIC AND ERNIE.
(D. HOLMES, ED)
    F. DILLON, 362:6DEC73-788
    617(TLS):26OCT73-1325
MOREL, G. NIETZSCHE.
    C. MURIN, 154:DEC71-866
MORENZ, S. DIE BEGEGNUNG EUROPAS MIT
ÄGYPTEN.
    M. DAVID, 542:APR-JUN71-250
MORETTI, W. - SEE MAGALOTTI, L.
MORFORD, M.P.O. & R.J. LENARDON. CLASSI-
CAL MYTHOLOGY.
    R.T. BRUÈRE, 122:APR72-151
MORGAN, A.E. DAMS AND OTHER DISASTERS.
    42(AR):WINTER71/72-597
MORGAN, B. & B. MEYRICK. BEHIND THE
STEAM.
    617(TLS):14DEC73-1549
MORGAN, C. SELECTED LETTERS OF CHARLES
MORGAN. (E. LEWIS, ED)
    R. WIEDER, 189(EA):JAN-MAR70-19

MORGAN, E. FROM GLASGOW TO SATURN.
A. MACLEAN, 362:25OCT73-565
617(TLS):20JUL73-826
MORGAN, E. GLASGOW SONNETS.
617(TLS):19JAN73-69
MORGAN, E. INSTAMATIC POEMS.
A. MACLEAN, 362:16AUG73-223
617(TLS):9MAR73-270
MORGAN, E. THE WHITTRICK.
617(TLS):18MAY73-548
MORGAN, F. A BOOK OF CHANGE.
G. DAVENPORT, 441:1APR73-26
W. HEYEN, 491:JUL73-237
J.C. OATES, 598(SOR):AUTUMN73-1014
MORGAN, K.O. - SEE LLOYD GEORGE, D.
MORGAN, M.M. THE SHAVIAN PLAYGROUND.*
F.A.C. WILSON, 648:APR72-16
MORGAN, P., COMP. OXFORD LIBRARIES OUT-
SIDE THE BODLEIAN.
617(TLS):20JUL73-840
MORGAN, P. WARWICKSHIRE PRINTERS' NOT-
ICES 1799-1866.
G. WAKEMAN, 354:DEC71-362
MORGAN, R., ED. SISTERHOOD IS POWERFUL.
639(VQR):SPRING71-LXXX
MORGAN-GRENVILLE, G. HOLIDAY CRUISING
IN FRANCE. BARGING INTO SOUTHERN
FRANCE.
617(TLS):27JUL73-858
MORGENBESSER, S., P. SUPPES & M. WHITE,
EDS. PHILOSOPHY, SCIENCE, AND METHOD.*
M. RUSE, 154:SEP71-581
MORGENTHAU, H.J. TRUTH AND POWER.
639(VQR):SPRING71-LXXVIII
MORHANGE-BEGUE, C. "LA CHANSON DU MAL-
AIMÉ" D'APOLLINAIRE.
M-N. GARY-PRIEUR, 557(RSH):OCT-DEC71-
680
MORHOF, D.G. UNTERRICHT VON DER TEUT-
SCHEN SPRACHE UND POESIE. (H. BOETIUS,
ED)
H. RÜDIGER, 52:BAND6HEFT1-77
MÖRIKE, E. MOZART AUF DER REISE NACH
PRAG. (M.B. BENN, ED)
E. STOPP, 402(MLR):JAN72-220
MORIN, E. THE RED AND THE WHITE.
L.S. LEWIS, 207(FR):MAR71-775
639(VQR):SUMMER71-CXXXVI
MORISON, S. A TALLY OF TYPES. (B.
CRUTCHLEY, ED)
617(TLS):15JUN73-698
MORISON, S.E. THE EUROPEAN DISCOVERY OF
AMERICA: THE NORTHERN VOYAGES.
S.G. MORSE, 432(NEQ):DEC71-657
N.J.W. THROWER, 377:JUL72-122
W.E. WASHBURN, 639(VQR):SUMMER71-469
MORISSEY, L.J. - SEE FIELDING, H.
MORITZ, K.P. ANDREAS HARTKNOPF. (H.J.
SCHRIMPF, ED)
J.U. TERPSTRA, 433:OCT70-429
MORITZ, K.P. ANTON REISER. (K-D. MÜL-
LER, ED)
M.K. TORBRUEGGE, 406:WINTER72-407
MORLAND, D. HEART CLOCK.
617(TLS):15JUN73-697
MORLET, M-T. LE VOCABULAIRE DE LA CHAM-
PAGNE SEPTENTRIONALE AU MOYEN AGE.
G. HOLMÉR, 597(SN):VOL43#1-267
MORLEY, J. DEATH, HEAVEN AND THE VIC-
TORIANS.*
D.R. FAULKNER, 676(YR):SUMMER72-615
MORLEY, P.A. THE IMMORAL MORALISTS.
J. ORANGE, 296:SPRING73-86
MORLEY, P.A. THE MYSTERY OF UNITY.
J. COLMER, 71(ALS):MAY73-95
617(TLS):6APR73-401

MORLEY, S.G. & C. BRUERTON. CRONOLOGÍA
DE LAS COMEDIAS DE LOPE DE VEGA.
J.A. CASTAÑEDA, 546(RR):APR71-135
A.G. REICHENBERGER, 240(HR):JAN71-95
MÖRNER, M., ED. RACE AND CLASS IN LATIN
AMERICA.
R.J. ALEXANDER, 263:JAN-MAR72-66
MOROSINI, D. DE BENE INSTITUTA RE PUB-
LICA. (C. FINZI, ED)
W.J. BOUWSMA, 589:JUL72-540
MOROT-SIR, E. LA MÉTAPHYSIQUE DE PASCAL.
617(TLS):12OCT73-1258
MORPHETT, T. THORSKALD.
L. CANTRELL, 381:MAR71-125
MORPURGO-TAGLIABUE, G. LINGUISTICA E
STILISTICA DI ARISTOTELE.
M. RIESER, 290(JAAC):FALL70-129
MORREALE, B. A FEW VIRTUOUS MEN.
442(NY):31DEC73-59
MORREALE, M. - SEE GRACIÁN DANTISCO, L.
MORRELL, W.P. BRITISH COLONIAL POLICY
IN THE MID-VICTORIAN AGE.
P. BURROUGHS, 637(VS):SEP70-109
MORRILL, J.R. THE PRACTICE AND POLITICS
OF FIAT FINANCE.
M.L.M. KAY, 656(WMQ):JAN71-155
MORRIS, B., ED. CHRISTOPHER MARLOWE.*
R. BÖHM, 430(NS):MAY70-258
MORRIS, B., ED. JOHN WEBSTER.
J.D. JUMP, 447(N&Q):JAN71-39
F. LAGARDE, 189(EA):OCT-DEC70-443
M. MINCOFF, 179(ES):AUG71-366
E.M. YEARLING, 541(RES):MAY71-202
MORRIS, B. & E. WITHINGTON - SEE CLEVE-
LAND, J.
MORRIS, C. THE DISCOVERY OF THE INDI-
VIDUAL, 1050-1200.
617(TLS):6APR73-397
MORRIS, C. HISTORY OF THE HANTS & DORSET
MOTOR SERVICES LIMITED.
617(TLS):21SEP73-1093
MORRIS, C. THE PRAGMATIC MOVEMENT IN
AMERICAN PHILOSOPHY.*
Y.H. KRIKORIAN, 484(PPR):MAR72-419
MORRIS, C.B. A GENERATION OF SPANISH
POETS, 1920-1936.*
J. CRISPÍN, 202(FMOD):FEB70-226
J. GONZÁLEZ MUELA, 400(MLN):MAR71-309
C. HUGHES, 149:SEP72-360
P.R. OLSON, 131(CL):WINTER72-76
H.T. YOUNG, 238:MAR71-228
205(FMLS):APR71-192
MORRIS, D.J. WE MUST MAKE HASTE - SLOWLY.
N. GALL, 441:1JUL73-6
MORRIS, E. BLOCKADE.
617(TLS):13JUL73-799
MORRIS, E.E. DICTIONARY OF AUSTRAL ENG-
LISH.
J.S. RYAN, 67:NOV72-261
MORRIS, H.F. & J.S. READ. INDIRECT
RULE AND THE SEARCH FOR JUSTICE.
617(TLS):19JAN73-74
MORRIS, I., ED. MADLY SINGING IN THE
MOUNTAINS.
M. BROCK, 285(JAPQ):JAN-MAR71-106
E. SEIDENSTICKER, 293(JAST):MAY71-638
MORRIS, I. - SEE "AS I CROSSED A BRIDGE
OF DREAMS"
MORRIS, I. - SEE SHŌNAGON, S.
MORRIS, J. THE AGE OF ARTHUR.
P. ADAMS, 61:AUG73-103
442(NY):27AUG73-91
617(TLS):21SEP73-1071
MORRIS, J. CORRESPONDENCE OF JOHN MORRIS
WITH JOHANNES DE LAET (1634-1649).*
(J.A.F. BEKKERS, ED)
A.G. WATSON, 78(BC):WINTER71-551

MORRIS, J. HEAVEN'S COMMAND.
  R. MITCHISON, 362:20DEC73-857
MORRIS, J. THE NUDE IN CANADIAN PAINTING.
  V. D'OR, 99:NOV-DEC73-42
MORRIS, J. PLACES.*
  A. BURGESS, 441:8APR73-28
MORRIS, J. THE PREACHERS.
  E.B. FISKE, 441:14AUG73-27
  L.L. KING, 441:5AUG73-4
  442(NY):3SEP73-67
MORRIS, J.W. - SEE UNDER WALKER MORRIS, J.
MORRIS, M. THE BRITISH GENERAL STRIKE,
  1926.
  617(TLS):26OCT73-1325
MORRIS, M. MY LIFE IN MOVEMENT.
  P. ARNOLD, 157:SPRING70-69
MORRIS, R.B. THE EMERGING NATIONS AND
  THE AMERICAN REVOLUTION.*
  P.A. VARG, 656(WMQ):JAN71-136
MORRIS, R.B. SEVEN WHO SHAPED OUR DES-
  TINY.
  G.F. SCHEER, 441:25NOV73-22
MORRIS, S. A PROGRAMMED LATIN COURSE.
  (PT 2)
  R. GLEN, 123:MAR72-97
MORRIS, W. THE HOME PLACE.
  P. MICHEL, 556(RLV):1971/5-650
MORRIS, W. THE LAST OF THE SOUTHERN
  GIRLS.
  D.K. MANO, 441:20MAY73-7
  442(NY):2JUN73-123
MORRIS, W. A LIFE.
  A. BROYARD, 441:23AUG73-41
  N. KOLTZ, 441:26AUG73-6
  E. WEEKS, 61:SEP73-116
MORRIS, W. A NOTE ON HIS AIMS IN
  FOUNDING THE KELMSCOTT PRESS.
  R. CAVE, 503:SPRING70-40
MORRIS, W. THE UNPUBLISHED LECTURES OF
  WILLIAM MORRIS.* (E.D. LE MIRE, ED)
  E. ENGELBERG, 637(VS):DEC70-205
  K.L. GOODWIN, 447(N&Q):NOV71-437
  N. KELVIN, 405(MP):FEB72-273
MORRISON, G., COMP. A GUIDE TO BOOKS ON
  SOUTHEAST ASIAN HISTORY (1961-1966).
  (S. HAY, ED)
  D.R. SAR DESAI, 318(JAOS):JAN-MAR71-
  151
MORRISON, G.E. AN AUSTRALIAN IN CHINA.
  617(TLS):22JUN73-722
MORRISON, J. TREEHOUSE.*
  S. HILL, 362:25JAN73-124
  617(TLS):9FEB73-140
MORRISON, J.C. MEANING AND TRUTH IN
  WITTGENSTEIN'S "TRACTATUS."*
  D.L. COUPRIE, 206:NOV70-562
MORRISON, K.F. TRADITION & AUTHORITY IN
  THE WESTERN CHURCH, 300-1140.
  H.A. OBERMAN, 589:JUL72-541
  J.J. RYAN, 377:MAR72-48
MORRISON, K.F. - SEE GREGOROVIUS, F.
MORRISON, R.H. OPUS 4.
  S.E. LEE, 581:DEC72-302
MORRISON, T. SULA.
  S. BLACKBURN, 441:30DEC73-3
MORRISSETT, I. & W.W. STEVENS, EDS.
  SOCIAL SCIENCE IN THE SCHOOLS.
  J.P. LOVEKIN, 529(QQ):SUMMER71-331
MORSE, J.M. THE IRRELEVANT ENGLISH
  TEACHER.*
  W.H. PRITCHARD, 249(HUDR):WINTER72/73-
  685
  J.P. ROSENBLATT, 31(ASCH):SPRING73-338
MORSE, P. JOHN SLOAN'S PRINTS.
  D.T., 135:MAR71-216
MORSE, S.F. WALLACE STEVENS.*
  639(VQR):SPRING71-LXIV

MORTIER, R. CLARTÉS ET OMBRES DU SIÈCLE
  DES LUMIÈRES.*
  H. DIECKMANN, 52:BAND6HEFT2-209
  R. MERCIER, 557(RSH):APR-JUN70-320
MORTIER, R. DIDEROT IN DEUTSCHLAND 1750-
  1850.
  D. GUTZEN, 52:BAND5HEFT1-102
  R. WARNING, 190:BAND64HEFT2-231
MORTIMER, E. FRANCE AND THE AFRICANS,
  1944-1960.
  H. DESCHAMPS, 69:JAN70-83
MORTIMER, R. THE HISTORY OF THE DERBY
  STAKES. (2ND ED)
  617(TLS):21DEC73-1574
MORTON, B.N. - SEE DE BEAUMARCHAIS, P.A.C.
MORTON, D. MINISTERS AND GENERALS.
  D.M. SCHURMAN, 529(QQ):WINTER71-626
MORTON, D. & R.H. ROY, EDS. TELEGRAMS OF
  THE NORTH-WEST CAMPAIGN 1885.
  617(TLS):2NOV73-1332
MORTON, R., COMP. COME DAY, GO DAY, GOD
  SEND SUNDAY.
  617(TLS):12OCT73-1247
MORTON, W.L. - SEE MONCK, F.E.O.C.
MORTON, W.S. JAPAN.
  617(TLS):2MAR73-237
MORWOOD, W. TRAVELLER IN A VANISHED
  LANDSCAPE.
  617(TLS):19OCT73-1287
MOSER, G.M. PENN STATE STUDIES: ESSAYS
  IN PORTUGUESE-AFRICAN LITERATURE.
  N. ARAUJO, 238:MAR71-200
MOSER, H., ED. SPRACHE DER GEGENWART.*
  (VOLS 1&2)
  W.G. ADMONI, 680(ZDP):BAND89HEFT3-436
MOSER, H. SPRACHE - FREIHEIT ODER LEN-
  KUNG?
  H. ZIMMERMANN, 657(WW):NOV/DEC70-420
MOSER, H. & OTHERS, EDS. SPRACHNORM,
  SPRACHPFLEGE, SPRACHKRITIK.*
  D. NERIUS, 682(ZPSK):BAND23HEFT2/3-
  319
MOSER, H. & J. MÜLLER-BLATTAU, EDS.
  DEUTSCHE LIEDER DES MITTELALTERS.
  D-R. MOSER, 680(ZDP):BAND90HEFT1-104
  R. TAYLOR, 220(GL&L):OCT71-19
MOSER, H. & I. SCHRÖBLER - SEE PAUL, H.
MOSER, L.E. HOME CELEBRATIONS.
  C.J. MC NASPY, 363:MAY71-84
MOSER, S. ABSOLUTISM AND RELATIVISM IN
  ETHICS.
  L.M. PALMER, 319:JAN73-133
MOSER-RATH, E. PREDIGTMÄRLEIN DER
  BAROCKZEIT.
  K. HORÁLEK, 196:BAND11HEFT1/2-179
MOSKALSKAJA, O.I. - SEE LEPING, E.I. &
  OTHERS
MOSKOWITZ, H. LECTURAS MADRILEÑAS.
  I. MOLINA, 238:MAR71-220
MOSLEY, L. POWER PLAY.
  C. LEHMANN-HAUPT, 441:10JUL73-45
MOSS, H. SELECTED POEMS.*
  R-C. ACKART, 398:AUTUMN73-225
  L. LIEBERMAN, 676(YR):AUTUMN71-82
  R. MAZZOCCO, 453:13DEC73-45
  R. SCHRAMM, 651(WHR):AUTUMN72-389
  639(VQR):AUTUMN71-CLXIV
MOSS, S.P. POE'S MAJOR CRISIS.*
  H. BUS, 182:VOL24#11/12-481
  A. HAMMOND, 445(NCF):MAR71-493
MOSSÉ, C. THE ANCIENT WORLD AT WORK.*
  C.G. STARR, 24:OCT72-642
MOSSÉ, F. A HANDBOOK OF MIDDLE ENGLISH.
  (REV)
  J. SIMON, 189(EA):JUL-SEP70-335
MOSSÉ, F. HANDBUCH DES MITTELENGLISCHEN.
  (H. PILCH & U. STEWART, EDS)
  J. SIMON, 189(EA):JUL-SEP70-335

MOSSE, G.L. THE CRISIS OF GERMAN IDEOL-
OGY.
S.M. POPPEL, 390:JAN70-67
MOSSÉ-BASTIDE, R-M. BERGSON ÉDUCATEUR.
E. AMADO LÉVY-VALENSI, 542:OCT-DEC71-
446
MOSSÉ-BASTIDE, R-M. - SEE BERGSON, H.
MOSSOP, D.J. PURE POETRY.
617(TLS):12OCT73-1248
MOSSUZ, J. ANDRÉ MALRAUX ET LE GAUL-
LISME.
M. ANDERSON, 208(FS):OCT72-480
MOSTELLER, F. & D.P. MOYNIHAN, EDS. ON
EQUALITY OF EDUCATIONAL OPPORTUNITY.
M.P. ZUCKERT, 109:SPRING/SUMMER73-130
MOSZKOWSKI, A. CONVERSATIONS WITH EIN-
STEIN.
617(TLS):8JUN73-649
"MOTÁKY Z RUZYNĚ."
617(TLS):20JUL73-824
"MOTION PICTURES 1960-1969: CATALOG OF
COPYRIGHT ENTRIES."
B. LACY, 200:AUG-SEP71-431
MOTROSHILOVA, N.V. PRINCIPLES AND CON-
TRADICTIONS OF PHENOMENOLOGICAL PHIL-
OSOPHY. [IN RUSSIAN]
P.K. CROSSER, 484(PPR):MAR72-436
MOTTER, C.K. THEATRE IN HIGH SCHOOL.
C.W. BRADFORD, 583:FALL71-109
MOTTO, A.L. SENECA SOURCEBOOK.
J.F. BRADY, JR., 124:MAR72-236
MOU TSUNG-SAN. HSIN-T'I YÜ HSING-T'I.
S-H. LIU, 485(PE&W):OCT70-419
W-M. TU, 293(JAST):MAY71-642
MOULD, C. THE MUSICAL MANUSCRIPTS OF
ST. GEORGE'S CHAPEL WINDSOR CASTLE.
617(TLS):1JUN73-624
MOULOUD, N. LANGAGE ET STRUCTURES.
C. FAVRE, 542:JUL-SEP71-391
MOULOUD, N. LA PSYCHOLOGIE ET LES
STRUCTURES.
R. BLANCHE, 542:APR-JUN71-253
MOULT, T. DOWN TO EARTH.
F. DILLON, 362:6DEC73-788
MOULTON, P.P. - SEE WOOLMAN, J.
MOUNI, S. MEDITATION.
J.B.L., 543:SEP70-140
MOUNIN, G. HISTOIRE DE LA LINGUISTIQUE
DES ORIGINES AU XXE SIÈCLE.*
L. ZAWADOWSKI, 353:MAR71-95
MOUNIN, G. SAUSSURE OU LE STRUCTURALISTE
SANS LE SAVOIR.* (SPANISH TITLE: SAUS-
SURE: PRESENTACIÓN Y TEXTOS.)
E.F.K. KOERNER, 545(RPH):NOV71-254
MOURALIS, B. INDIVIDU ET COLLECTIVITÉ
DANS LE ROMAN NÉGRO-AFRICAIN D'EXPRES-
SION FRANÇAISE.
R. MERCIER, 535(RHL):JAN-FEB71-147
MOURELATOS, A.P.D. THE ROUTE OF PAR-
MENIDES.*
M.E. REESOR, 154:MAR71-161
MOURELLE-LEMA, M. LA TEORÍA LINGÜÍSTICA
EN LA ESPAÑA DEL SIGLO XIX.
C.J. POUNTAIN, 86(BHS):JAN72-87
MOURÉLOS, G. BERGSON ET LES NIVEAUX DE
RÉALITÉ.
F. HEIDSIECK, 542:OCT-DEC71-447
DE MOURGUES, O. RACINE OR THE TRIUMPH
OF RELEVANCE.
P. DELBOUILLE, 556(RLV):1970/3-327
MOURIER, M. LE MIROIR MITÉ.
617(TLS):26JAN73-85
MOUSNIER, R. THE ASSASSINATION OF HENRY
IV.
N. BLIVEN, 442(NY):26NOV73-194

MOUSNIER, R. PEASANT UPRISINGS IN SEVEN-
TEENTH-CENTURY FRANCE, RUSSIA, AND
CHINA.
D. MITRANY, 32:JUN72-417
MOUSNIER, R. LA VÉNALITÉ DES OFFICES
SOUS HENRI IV ET LOUIS XIII.
617(TLS):6JUL73-780
MOUTON, J. LES INTERMITTENCES DU REGARD
CHEZ L'ÉCRIVAIN.
617(TLS):25MAY73-595
MOUTOTE, D. LES IMAGES VÉGÉTALES DANS
L'OEUVRE L'ANDRÉ GIDE.
R. STORRIE, 208(FS):OCT72-471
MOUTOTE, D. LE JOURNAL DE GIDE ET LES
PROBLÈMES DU MOI (1889-1925).*
P. MOREAU, 535(RHL):MAR-APR70-338
MOVIA, G. ALESSANDRO DI AFRODISIA.
P. DONINI, 548(RCSF):APR-JUN71-221
P. LOUIS, 555:VOL45FASC2-348
MOVIA, G. ANIMA E INTELLETTO.*
P. DONINI, 548(RCSF):APR-JUN71-221
P. LOUIS, 555:VOL45FASC1-154
MOWAT, F. THE SIBERIANS.
J.R. GIBSON, 32:JUN72-446
MOWAT, F. A WHALE FOR THE KILLING.*
617(TLS):16FEB73-182
MOWATT, D.G. FRIDERICH VON HÛSEN.
S.M. JOHNSON, 406:SUMMER72-162
MOWATT, D.G. & H. SACKER. THE NIBELUN-
GENLIED.*
W. HEMPEL, 564:MAR70-77
MOWATT, I. JUST SHEAFFER OR STORMS IN
THE TROUBLED HEIR.
N. CALLENDAR, 441:29APR73-28
MOWBRAY, A.Q. THE OPERATION.
617(TLS):31AUG73-1009
MOXON, J. MECHANICK EXERCISES OR THE
DOCTRINE OF HANDY-WORKS.
R. EDWARDS, 39:JUL71-75
MOYA, M. LE POESIE. (L. STEGAGNO PIC-
CHIO, ED)
T.R. HART, 400(MLN):MAR71-289
MOYERS, B. LISTENING TO AMERICA.
42(AR):SPRING71-134
639(VQR):SUMMER71-CXXX
MOYES, P. THE CURIOUS AFFAIR OF THE
THIRD DOG.
N. CALLENDAR, 441:11NOV73-50
617(TLS):26OCT73-1324
MOYLES, L. I PROPHESY SURVIVORS.
R. MOORE, 661:SUMMER/FALL71-92
MOYNAHAN, J. GARDEN STATE.
M. ENGEL, 441:2SEP73-4
MOYNAHAN, J. VLADIMIR NABOKOV.
R. ASSELINEAU, 189(EA):OCT-DEC71-547
MOYNIHAN, D.P. THE POLITICS OF A GUARAN-
TEED INCOME.
P. PASSELL & L. ROSS, 441:14JAN73-1
A.L. SCHORR, 231:JUN73-86
T. WICKER, 453:22MAR73-9
MOYNIHAN, M., ED. PEOPLE AT WAR 1914-
1918.
617(TLS):16NOV73-1409
MOYNIHAN, W.T. THE CRAFT AND ART OF
DYLAN THOMAS.
A.R. TELLIER, 189(EA):JAN-MAR70-95
MOZART, W.A. DON GIOVANNI.* IDOMENEO.*
LE NOZZE DI FIGARO.* COSÌ FAN TUTTE.*
DIE ZAUBERFLÖTE.* (ALL TRANS BY L. SAL-
TER)
S. SADIE, 415:FEB72-152
412:MAY72-147
MOZART, W.A. THE SERAGLIO. (A. WOOD &
E. TRACY, TRANS)
412:MAY72-147
MRAS, G.P. EUGÈNE DELACROIX'S THEORY OF
ART.
T.E. KLITZKE, 54:JUN71-269

MROCZKOWSKI, P. CONRADIAN COMMENTARIES.
T.S. WILLIAM, 136:VOL3#1-127
MUCHA, J. ALPHONSE MUCHA, HIS LIFE AND
ART.
A. FERN, 54:JUN70-221
MUCHNIC, H. RUSSIAN WRITERS.*
G. STRUVE, 550(RUSR):OCT71-397
MUECKE, D.C. THE COMPASS OF IRONY.*
R. LAWRENCE, 175:SPRING71-28
205(FMLS):APR70-209
MUECKE, D.C. IRONY.
205(FMLS):OCT70-420
MUELA, J.G. - SEE UNDER GONZÁLEZ MUELA, J.
MUELLER, J.M. - SEE DONNE, J.
MUELLER, T. & H. NIEDZIELSKI. BASIC
FRENCH.
A.E. DASH, 399(MLJ):MAR71-185
MUENCH, D. UTAH.
P. ADAMS, 61:SEP73-119
MUENSTERBERGER, W. & S. AXELRAD, EDS.
PSYCHOANALYSIS AND THE SOCIAL SCIENCES.
(VOL 4)
R. COLES, 453:22FEB73-15
MUGGERIDGE, M. CHRONICLES OF WASTED
TIME.* (VOL 1)
P. JOHNSON, 441:30SEP73-3
MUGGERIDGE, M. CHRONICLES OF WASTED
TIME. (VOL 2)
R. CROSSMAN, 362:20SEP73-381
617(TLS):28SEP73-1103
"THE MUGHAL AND SIKH RULERS AND THE
VAISHNAVAS OF PINDORI."
M. HABIB, 273(IC):JAN71-72
MUGLER, C. - SEE ARCHIMEDES
MUIR, F. & D. NORDEN. YOU CAN'T HAVE
YOUR KAYAK AND HEAT IT.
617(TLS):9NOV73-1381
MUIR, K. THE COMEDY OF MANNERS.
M-L. FLUCHÈRE, 189(EA):JUL-SEP70-340
MUIR, K., ED. SHAKESPEARE SURVEY 20.*
W.O. SCOTT, 570(SQ):WINTER70-88
MUIR, K., ED. SHAKESPEARE SURVEY 21.*
R.A. FOAKES, 175:SPRING70-22
MUIR, K., ED. SHAKESPEARE SURVEY 22.*
M. BLUESTONE, 551(RENQ):AUTUMN71-398
I. BROWN, 157:SPRING70-61
M.W. BUNDY, 570(SQ):SPRING71-171
R.A. FOAKES, 175:AUTUMN70-98
J-B. FORT, 189(EA):APR-JUN70-224
K.M. LEA, 541(RES):FEB71-73
T.P. LOGAN, 399(MLJ):OCT71-418
J. WILDERS, 447(N&Q):DEC71-473
MUIR, K., ED. SHAKESPEARE SURVEY 23.*
R.A. FOAKES, 175:AUTUMN71-98
M.A. SHAABER, 551(RENQ):WINTER71-568
MUIR, K. SHAKESPEARE THE PROFESSIONAL.
617(TLS):19OCT73-1272
MUIR, K. SHAKESPEARE'S TRAGIC SEQUENCE.
617(TLS):12JAN73-44
MUIR, K. - SEE SHAKESPEARE, W.
MUIR, K. & S. SCHOENBAUM, EDS. A NEW
COMPANION TO SHAKESPEARE STUDIES.
R.A. FOAKES, 175:AUTUMN71-98
MUIR, K. & P. THOMSON - SEE WYATT, T.
MUIR, L.R. - SEE "ADAM"
MUIR, P.H. - SEE JOHNSON, A.F.
MUKHERJEE, B. THE TIGER'S DAUGHTER.*
617(TLS):29JUN73-736
MUKHERJEE, B.N. THE KUSHANA GENEALOGY.
R.M. SMITH, 318(JAOS):APR-JUN71-318
MULCAHY, B. TO SPEAK TRUE.
C. LAMBERT, 157:SUMMER70-73
MULDER, J.R. THE TEMPLE OF THE MIND.
E.F. DANIELS, 551(RENQ):SUMMER71-278
MULDER, J.W.F. SETS AND RELATIONS IN
PHONOLOGY.
R.L. CHENG, 361:VOL25#1-47

MULDOON, P. NEW WEATHER.
A. MACLEAN, 362:16AUG73-223
617(TLS):20APR73-442
MULHAUSER, R., M. KUPERSMITH & J. LUSSEY-
RAN - SEE CAMUS, A.
MULHAUSER, R.E. SAINTE-BEUVE AND GRECO-
ROMAN ANTIQUITY.*
B.F. BART, 401(MLQ):JUN71-229
MULJAČIC, Ž. FONOLOGIA GENERALE E FONO-
LOGIA DELLA LINGUA ITALIANA.
R.J. DI PIETRO, 276:SUMMER71-266
C. SCHWARZE, 72:BAND209HEFT1/3-179
MULKEEN, T.P. HONOR THY GODFATHER.
N. CALLENDAR, 441:4FEB73-41
MULKEEN, T.P. MY KILLER DOESN'T UNDER-
STAND ME.
N. CALLENDAR, 441:21OCT73-49
MULLARD, C. BLACK BRITAIN.
617(TLS):11MAY73-524
MÜLLENBROCK, H-J. LITERATUR UND ZEITGE-
SCHICHTE IN ENGLAND ZWISCHEN DEM ENDE
DES 19. JAHRHUNDERTS UND DEM AUSBRUCH
DES ERSTEN WELTKRIEGES.*
J. BOURKE, 38:BAND88HEFT3-415
MÜLLER, A. DAS PROBLEM VON BEFEHL UND
GEHORSAM IM LEBEN DER KIRCHE.
M. VIDAL, 182:VOL24#5-197
MÜLLER, A. THE SEVEN WONDERS OF THE
WORLD.
R. HIGGINS, 39:AUG71-159
MULLER, A.V., ED & TRANS. THE SPIRITUAL
REGULATION OF PETER THE GREAT.
617(TLS):9MAR73-260
MÜLLER, C. OBERST I.G. STAUFFENBERG.
I. JONES, 619(TC):VOL179#1048-55
MULLER, G.H. NIGHTMARES AND VISIONS.*
L.Y. GOSSETT, 27(AL):JAN73-697
MÜLLER, H., J. HAENSCH & E. ALVAREZ-
PRADA - SEE "LANGENSCHEIDTS HANDWÖRTER-
BUCH SPANISCH"
MULLER, H.J. THE CHILDREN OF FRANKEN-
STEIN.
C-M. CIPOLLA, 639(VQR):WINTER71-156
E.T. DELANEY, 363:FEB71-58
MULLER, J. DICTIONNAIRE ABRÉGÉ DES
IMPRIMEURS/ÉDITEURS FRANÇAIS DU XVIe
SIÈCLE.
E. ZIMMERMANN, 182:VOL24#19/20-705
MÜLLER, J. LITERARISCHE ANALOGIEN IN
HEINRICH VON KLEISTS NOVELLE "DER
ZWEIKAMPF."
E. MARSCH, 52:BAND6HEFT3-337
MÜLLER, J-D. WIELANDS SPÄTE ROMANE.
L. BORNSCHEUER, 406:FALL72-310
A.R. SCHMITT, 301(JEGP):APR72-299
MÜLLER, K., G. SCHEEL & G. GERBER - SEE
LEIBNIZ, G.W.
MÜLLER, K-D. DIE FUNKTION DER GESCHICHTE
IM WERK BERTOLT BRECHTS.*
K. DICKSON, 220(GL&L):OCT71-71
MÜLLER, K-D. - SEE MORITZ, K.P.
MÜLLER, L., ED & TRANS. DIE WERKE DES
METROPOLITEN ILARION.
D. TSCHIŽEWSKIJ, 72:BAND209HEFT1/3-
225
MÜLLER, O.W. INTELLIGENCIJA.
H. SETON-WATSON, 575(SEER):OCT72-614
MÜLLER, P., ED. DER JUNGE GOETHE IM
ZEITGENÖSSISCHEN URTEIL.
E. BOA, 182:VOL24#21/22-795
MÜLLER, P. ZEITKRITIK UND UTOPIE IN
GOETHES "WERTHER."
H-G. WERNER, 654(WB):7/1970-193
MÜLLER, U., ED. KREUZZUGSDICHTUNG.*
G.F. JONES, 400(MLN):APR71-422
M. WIS, 439(NM):1970/3-520
MÜLLER-LAUTER, W. NIETZSCHE.*
H.W. REICHERT, 406:SUMMER72-181

MÜLLER-SCHOTTE, H. DER MARITIME SONDER-
CHARAKTER DES BRITISCHEN VOLKES IM
SPIEGEL DER ENGLISCHEN SPRACHE.
205(FMLS):OCT71-414
MULLIN, D.C. THE DEVELOPMENT OF THE
PLAYHOUSE.
S.T.S., 46:APR71-260
G.W. STONE, 173(ECS):FALL71-185
MULLIN, G.W. FLIGHT AND REBELLION.
617(TLS):9FEB73-159
MULRYNE, J.R. - SEE WEBSTER, J.
MULVIHILL, E.R. & R. SÁNCHEZ - SEE PÉREZ
GALDOS, B.
MUMFORD, L. INTERPRETATIONS AND FORE-
CASTS: 1922-1972.
G. LEVINE, 441:22APR73-21
MUMFORD, L. THE MYTH OF THE MACHINE.*
W.H. MC NEILL, 639(VQR):SPRING71-296
MUNARI, F. - SEE VALERIUS, M.
MUNCH, P.A. THE SONG TRADITION OF TRIS-
TAN DA CUNHA.
M. KARPELES, 203:AUTUMN70-231
B. NETTL, 292(JAF):JUL-SEP71-348
MÜNCHOW, U. DEUTSCHER NATURALISMUS.
E. MC INNES, 220(GL&L):JAN72-155
MUNCY, R.L. SEX AND MARRIAGE IN UTOPIAN
SOCIETIES.
M. DUBERMAN, 441:12AUG73-17
617(TLS):14SEP73-1057
MUNDT, T. DIE KUNST DER DEUTSCHEN PROSA.
N.A. FURNESS, 220(GL&L):APR72-285
MUNDY, J.H. EUROPE IN THE HIGH MIDDLE
AGES 1150-1309.
617(TLS):11MAY73-523
MUNGO, R. TOTAL LOSS FARM.*
639(VQR):SPRING71-LXX
MUNHALL, E. MASTERPIECES OF THE FRICK
COLLECTION.*
C.J. MC NASPY, 363:NOV70-24
MUNIER, R. L'INSTANT.
617(TLS):31AUG73-1004
MUNIER, R. LE SEUL [TOGETHER WITH] D'UN
SEUL TENANT COMMENTAIRE.
H. RAYNAL, 98:AUG/SEP71-704
MUNITZ, M.K. THE MYSTERY OF EXISTENCE.
L.B. CEBIK, 219(GAR):SPRING70-81
MUNKSGAARD, E. DENMARK.
R.N. BAILEY, 447(N&Q):FEB71-69
MUNRO, A. DANCE OF THE HAPPY SHADES.*
M. LEVIN, 441:23SEP73-48
442(NY):5NOV73-186
MUNRO, A. LIVES OF GIRLS AND WOMEN.*
R. BLYTHE, 362:29NOV73-752
J. POLK, 102(CANL):AUTUMN72-102
442(NY):6JAN73-75
MUNRO, D.J. THE CONCEPT OF MAN IN EARLY
CHINA.*
H. ROSEMONT, JR., 485(PE&W):APR71-203
A.C. YU, 613:SUMMER70-313
MUNRO, J.M. THE DECADENT POETRY OF THE
EIGHTEEN-NINETIES.
D.J. WATT, 177(ELT):VOL14#2-152
MUNRO, T. EVOLUTION IN THE ARTS.
V.A. SORRELL, 127:FALL71-98
P. WELSH, 54:SEP70-354
MUNROE, T. FORM AND STYLE IN THE ARTS.
E. SCHAPER, 89(BJA):WINTER72-87
H.M. SCHUELLER, 290(JAAC):SPRING71-
410
MUNZ, H. DIE DARSTELLUNG DER KRANKHEIT
BEI GIOVANNI VERGA UND ROGER MARTIN DU
GARD.
R.O.J. VAN NUFFEL, 549(RLC):JAN-MAR71-
124
MURARI, T. THE MARRIAGE.
617(TLS):30NOV73-1465

MURARO, M. PAOLO DA VENEZIA.
H. BUCHTHAL, 54:SEP71-400
M. DAVIES, 90:AUG71-479
MURASE, M. BYOBU.
S. ROSENTHAL, 58:APR72-27
MURATA, K. JAPAN'S NEW BUDDHISM.
E.J. SUTFIN, 363:MAY71-88
K. TANAKA, 318(JAOS):OCT-DEC71-524
MURCHLAND, B. THE AGE OF ALIENATION.
C.R. THOMAS, 484(PPR):MAR72-429
MURDOCH, I. AN ACCIDENTAL MAN.*
M. COOKE, 676(YR):SUMMER72-599
J.P. DEGNAN, 249(HUDR):SUMMER72-330
MURDOCH, I. THE BLACK PRINCE.
G. ANNAN, 362:22FEB73-249
A. BROYARD, 441:6JUN73-39
K. FRASER, 442(NY):30JUL73-69
L. GRAVER, 441:3JUN73-1
A. LURIE, 453:14JUN73-18
E. WEEKS, 61:JUL73-101
617(TLS):23FEB73-197
MURDOCH, I. BRUNO'S DREAM.*
J.C. FIELD, 556(RLV):1971/5-621
MURDOCH, I. A FAIRLY HONOURABLE DEFEAT.*
J.L. HALIO, 598(SOR):SPRING73-455
MURDOCH, I. THE SOVEREIGNTY OF GOOD.*
A. KENNY, 447(N&Q):OCT71-389
MURDOCH, I. THE THREE ARROWS AND THE
SERVANTS AND THE SNOW.
617(TLS):23NOV73-1418
MURPHY, D.J., R.B. JOYCE & C.A. HUGHES,
EDS. PRELUDE TO POWER.
R. WARD, 381:SEP71-357
MURPHY, F., ED. EDWIN ARLINGTON ROBIN-
SON: A COLLECTION OF CRITICAL ESSAYS.
I.D. MAC KILLOP, 184(EIC):JUL71-297
MURPHY, G., WITH V. LASKY. SAY...DIDN'T
YOU USED TO BE GEORGE MURPHY?
E.H. NASH, 200:OCT70-501
MURPHY, J.D. & H. GOFF, COMPS. A BIBLI-
OGRAPHY OF AFRICAN LANGUAGES AND LIN-
GUISTICS.
R.J., 69:APR70-192
MURPHY, J.G. KANT: THE PHILOSOPHY OF
RIGHT.
K. OEDINGEN, 342:BAND62HEFT3-411
M.D.P., 543:JUN71-751
K. WARD, 479(PHQ):JUL71-272
MURPHY, L.R. PHILMONT.
W. GARD, 584(SWR):AUTUMN72-330
MURPHY, P.L. THE CONSTITUTION IN CRISIS
TIMES: 1918-1969.*
I. DILLIARD, 31(ASCH):SPRING73-347
MURPHY, R. THE BATTLE OF AUGHRIM.*
S. FAUCHEREAU, 98:MAY70-438
MURPHY, R. THE STREAM.
42(AR):SPRING71-136
MURPHY, R. & H. GULLIVER. THE SOUTHERN
STRATEGY.
639(VQR):SUMMER71-CXXXII
MURPHY, R.F. ROBERT H. LOWIE.
617(TLS):11MAY73-537
MURPHY, W.P.D., ED. THE EARL OF HERT-
FORD'S LIEUTENANCY PAPERS, 1603-1612.*
E. KERRIDGE, 447(N&Q):AUG71-314
MURRAY, A. THE HERO AND THE BLUES.
442(NY):6AUG73-88
MURRAY, A. & R. THOMAS, EDS. THE SCHOL-
ASTIC BLACK LITERATURE SERIES.
C.A. PEEK, 502(PRS):SUMMER71-183
MURRAY, A.W. - SEE POE, E.A.
MURRAY, D. THE YORK BUILDINGS COMPANY.
617(TLS):19OCT73-1289
MURRAY, D.S. BLUEPRINT FOR HEALTH.
617(TLS):3AUG73-896
MURRAY, E.P. KULUBI.
I. REED, 441:7OCT73-46

MURRAY, F. THE DEAR COLLEAGUE.
  M. LEVIN, 441:8JUL73-24
MURRAY, G. VOLTAIRE'S "CANDIDE."
  J.H. BRUMFITT, 208(FS):JAN72-78
  H.T. MASON, 400(MLN):MAY71-590
MURRAY, J.G. HENRY DAVID THOREAU.
  G.B.S.C., 543:DEC70-342
MURRAY, L.A. THE WEATHERBOARD CATHEDRAL.
  K.L. GOODWIN, 381:SEP71-373
MURRAY, P. THE SHAKESPEARIAN SCENE.*
  R.A. FOAKES, 175:SPRING70-22
  M.A. SHAABER, 551(RENQ):AUTUMN71-402
MURRAY, P.B. A STUDY OF JOHN WEBSTER.*
  C.R. FORKER, 401(MLQ):JUN72-191
  F. LAGARDE, 189(EA):JUL-SEP71-326
  M. MINCOFF, 179(ES):AUG71-366
MURRAY, R. THE SPLIT.
  D. AITKIN, 381:MAR71-118
MURRAY-BROWN, J. KENYATTA.*
  442(NY):20AUG73-90
MURRIN, M. THE VEIL OF ALLEGORY.*
  A.C. HAMILTON, 401(MLQ):JUN72-190
  R.O. IREDALE, 541(RES):MAY71-248
  R. LAWRENCE, 175:AUTUMN70-107
  502(PRS):FALL70-277
MURSIA, U. - SEE CONRAD, J.
MURTI, T.R.V., ED. THE CONCEPT OF PHIL-
OSOPHY.
  R. SINARI, 485(PE&W):JAN71-89
DE MURVILLE, M.C. - SEE UNDER COUVE DE
MURVILLE, M.
MUS, P. & J. MC ALISTER, JR. LES VIÊT-
NAMIENS ET LEUR RÉVOLUTION. (S. THION,
ED)
  617(TLS):12JAN73-27
MUSA, M. DANTE'S VITA NUOVA.
  617(TLS):12OCT73-1260
MUSGRAVE, C. REGENCY FURNITURE. (2ND
ED)
  R. EDWARDS, 39:JUL71-75
MUSGRAVE, S. ENTRANCE OF THE CELEBRANT.
  G. FOX, 99:SEP73-43
  617(TLS):5JAN73-10
MUSGRAVE, S. SONGS OF THE SEA-WITCH.*
  M. FIAMENGO, 102(CANL):SUMMER72-104
MUSGROVE, F. & P.H. TAYLOR. SOCIETY AND
THE TEACHER'S ROLE.
  N. CROOK, 97(CQ):SPRING71-266
MUSICK, R.A. GREEN HILLS OF MAGIC.
  K.M. BRIGGS, 203:SPRING71-81
  L. MONTELL, 292(JAF):JUL-SEP71-356
MUSICK, R.A. THE TELLTALE LILAC BUSH
AND OTHER WEST VIRGINIA GHOST TALES.
  H. LIXFELD, 196:BAND11HEFT1/2-180
MUSIKER, R. GUIDE TO SOUTH AFRICAN REF-
ERENCE BOOKS. (5TH ED)
  J.B. CHILDS, 517(PBSA):OCT-DEC72-446
MUSSATO, A. ALBERTINOU MOUSSATOU HOI
HYPOTHESEIS TŌN TRAGŌDIŌN TOU SENEKA.
(A.C. MEGAS, ED)
  E.J. KENNEY, 123:MAR72-114
  A. MAC GREGOR, 122:JAN72-64
MUSSET, L. INTRODUCTION À LA RUNOLOGIE.*
  G. WIENOLD, 38:BAND88HEFT2-243
MUSSULMAN, J.A. MUSIC IN THE CULTURED
GENERATION.
  F.H., 410(M&L):JUL72-321
MUSTARD, H.M. - SEE HEINE, H.
MUSTO, D.F. THE AMERICAN DISEASE.
  J.M. MARKHAM, 441:29APR73-1
  617(TLS):20JUL73-837
MUTHESIUS, S. THE HIGH VICTORIAN MOVE-
MENT IN ARCHITECTURE 1850-1870.
  617(TLS):17AUG73-944
MYERS, B.S. - SEE "MC GRAW-HILL DICTION-
ARY OF ART"
MYERS, M. THE ASSIGNMENT.
  D. DUFFY, 102(CANL):AUTUMN72-107

MYERS, N. THE LONG AFRICAN DAY.*
  F.D. GRAY, 453:28JUN73-25
MYERS, R. THE BRITISH BOOK TRADE.
  617(TLS):5OCT73-1193
MYERS, R. MODERN FRENCH MUSIC.*
  G.W. HOPKINS, 415:JUL72-671
  R.D.E.N., 410(M&L):APR72-211
MYERS, R., ED. RICHARD STRAUSS AND
ROMAIN ROLLAND.
  M.L. COTTAM, 402(MLR):JUL72-655
MYERS, R.H. THE CHINESE PEASANT ECONOMY.
  N-R. CHEN, 293(JAST):MAY71-666
MYERS, R.L. RÉMOND DE SAINT-MARD.
  V. MYLNE, 402(MLR):OCT72-893
MYERS, R.M., ED. THE CHILDREN OF PRIDE.*
  W.W. ABBOT, 31(ASCH):WINTER72/73-168
MYLLENT, P. THE IDEAL WORLD.
  617(TLS):9FEB73-161
MYLONAS, G.E. MYCENAE'S LAST CENTURY OF
GREATNESS.*
  É. WILL, 555:VOL45FASC1-129
MYRDAL, G. AGAINST THE STREAM.
  N. BLIVEN, 442(NY):31DEC73-58
  J. ROBINSON, 441:23SEP73-31
MYRDAL, J. CHINA: THE REVOLUTION CON-
TINUED.
  J. GRAY, 111:19NOV71-52
MYRER, A. THE TIGER WAITS.
  M. LEVIN, 441:8APR73-33
MYRES, S.D. - SEE SONNICHSEN, C.L.


NABARRO, G. EXPLOITS OF A POLITICIAN.
  R. CROSSMAN, 362:11OCT73-490
NABERT, J. ESSAI SUR LE MAL.
  D. JANICAUD, 542:OCT-DEC71-508
NABOKOV, V. ADA.*
  J.C. FIELD, 556(RLV):1971/5-629
NABOKOV, V. THE ANNOTATED "LOLITA."*
  (A. APPEL, JR., ED)
  D. FLOWER, 418(MR):SUMMER72-498
NABOKOV, V. MARY.*
  M.K. HULTQUIST, 502(PRS):FALL71-276
  639(VQR):WINTER71-XII
NABOKOV, V. A RUSSIAN BEAUTY.
  P. ADAMS, 61:MAY73-123
  A. BROYARD, 441:11MAY73-43
  V. CUNNINGHAM, 362:11OCT73-491
  L. MICHAELS, 453:20SEP73-37
  P. ZWEIG, 441:29APR73-21
  617(TLS):12OCT73-1210
NABOKOV, V. STRONG OPINIONS.
  R.P. BRICKNER, 441:11NOV73-36
  442(NY):24DEC73-80
NABOKOV, V. TRANSPARENT THINGS.*
  J. MITCHELL, 362:24MAY73-695
  617(TLS):4MAY73-488
NACHTMANN, F.W. EXERCISES IN FRENCH
PHONICS.
  J.L. SHEPHERD 3D, 399(MLJ):MAY71-327
  A. VALDMAN, 207(FR):FEB71-596
NADAL, R.M. - SEE UNDER MARTÍNEZ NADAL,
R.
NADARAJAH, D. WOMEN IN TAMIL SOCIETY
(THE CLASSICAL PERIOD).
  S. AGESTHIALINGOM, 293(JAST):AUG71-907
  D.M. SPENCER, 318(JAOS):OCT-DEC71-557
NADDEI, M.C. - SEE UNDER CARBONARA NAD-
DEI, M.
NADEAU, M. GUSTAVE FLAUBERT ÉCRIVAIN.*
  M. BUTOR, 98:MAY70-387
NADEL, H.M. & C.G., EDS. THE DANCE
EXPERIENCE.
  M. MARKS, 151:MAR71-85
NADER, R. & K. BLACKWELL. YOU AND YOUR
PENSION.
  T. LASK, 441:20JAN73-33
  R. SHERRILL, 441:4MAR73-3

NADER, R. & M.J. GREEN, EDS. CORPORATE
POWER IN AMERICA.
    R. SHERRILL, 441:4MAR73-3
NAESS, A. FOUR MODERN PHILOSOPHERS.
    A. MANSER, 393(MIND):OCT71-623
NAESS, A. THE PLURALIST AND POSSIBILIST
ASPECT OF THE SCIENTIFIC ENTERPRISE.
    617(TLS):4MAY73-502
NAESS, A. SCEPTICISM.*
    B. STROUD, 482(PHR):APR71-253
"NĀGĀRJUNA, A TRANSLATION OF HIS MŪLAMAD-
HYAMAKAKĀRIKĀ." (K.K. INADA, TRANS)
    D. RIEPE, 484(PPR):SEP71-124
NAGATSUKA, R. I WAS A KAMIKAZE.
    617(TLS):3AUG73-913
NAGEL, E., S. BROMBERGER & A. GRÜNBAUM.
OBSERVATION AND THEORY IN SCIENCE.
    A. MATTHEW, 518:MAY72-23
    42(AR):SUMMER71-290
NAGEL, O. KATHE KOLLWITZ.*
    P. RUTA, 58:FEB72-21
NAGUIB, N. ROBERT WALSER.
    G.C. AVERY, 182:VOL24#4-168
    H.M. WAIDSON, 220(GL&L):OCT71-42
    J.J. WHITE, 402(MLR):JUL72-708
NAGY, G. GREEK DIALECTS AND THE TRANS-
FORMATION OF AN INDO-EUROPEAN PROCESS.*
    F. BADER, 555:VOL45FASC1-124
    A.M. DAVIES, 123:DEC72-371
    W.R. SCHMALSTIEG, 215(GL):VOL10#3-195
    J.F. VIGORITA, 399(MLJ):DEC71-531
    W.F. WYATT, JR. 121(CJ):APR-MAY72-365
DE NAGY, N.C. THE POETRY OF EZRA POUND.
(2ND ED)
    W. MARTIN, 72:BAND209HEFT1/3-166
DE NAGY, N.C. EZRA POUND'S POETICS AND
LITERARY TRADITION.
    W. MARTIN, 179(ES):FEB71-85
NAHAL, C. THE NARRATIVE PATTERN IN
ERNEST HEMINGWAY'S FICTION.
    L. GURKO, 27(AL):MAR72-165
NAIPAUL, S. THE CHIP-CHIP GATHERERS.
    R. BRYDEN, 362:12APR73-489
    442(NY):6AUG73-87
    617(TLS):13APR73-409
NAIPAUL, S. FIREFLIES.*
    42(AR):SPRING71-132
NAIPAUL, V.S. THE OVERCROWDED BARRACOON.*
    441:16SEP73-18
NAIR, B.N. SYSTEMATIC APPROACHES TO
INDIAN SOCIO-ECONOMIC DEVELOPMENT.
    617(TLS):3AUG73-913
NAIR, K. THE LONELY FURROW.
    W.C. NEALE, 293(JAST):AUG71-873
NAKAMURA YASUO. NOH, THE CLASSICAL THEA-
TER.
    M. PRESS, 285(JAPQ):OCT-DEC71-479
    M. URY, 318(JAOS):OCT-DEC71-524
NAKANE, C. JAPANESE SOCIETY.
    R.E. COLE, 293(JAST):MAY71-678
NAKANE, C. TATESHAKAI NO NINGEN-KANKEI -
TANITSU-SHAKAI NO RIRON CHUO KORON SHA.
    R.L. BROWN, 270:VOL21#1-126
NAKAYAMA, S. A HISTORY OF JAPANESE
ASTRONOMY.
    I. DOSZPOLY, 293(JAST):NOV70-188
NALBACH, D. THE KING'S THEATRE 1704-
1867.
    617(TLS):28SEP73-1139
NAMER, E. LA PHILOSOPHIE ITALIENNE.
    G. OLDRINI, 548(RCSF):OCT-DEC71-462
NAMMACK, G.C. FRAUD, POLITICS, AND THE
DISPOSSESSION OF THE INDIANS.
    D.A. ARMOUR, 656(WMQ):JUL71-506
NANCE, W.L. THE WORLDS OF TRUMAN CAPOTE.*
    617(TLS):27JUL73-856

NANDRIS, G. CHRISTIAN HUMANISM IN THE
NEO-BYZANTINE MURAL PAINTING OF EASTERN
EUROPE.
    G. MATHEW, 575(SEER):JAN72-136
NANSEN, O. LANGS VEIEN.
    E. HASLUND, 270:VOL21#3-178
NANTET, J. TOCQUEVILLE.
    J. PETIT, 98:AUG/SEP71-831
NAPIER, J. BIGFOOT.
    P. ADAMS, 61:MAY73-122
    617(TLS):20APR73-452
NARANG, G.C., ED. URDU: READINGS IN
LITERARY URDU PROSE.
    J. QAZI, 352(LE&W):VOL15#2-327
NARAYAN, S. INDIA AND NEPAL.
    L.E. ROSE, 293(JAST):MAY71-720
NARAYAN, S. LETTERS FROM GANDHI, NEHRU,
VINOBA.
    B. POUDEL, 293(JAST):MAY71-716
NARCY, M. SIMONE WEIL, MALHEUR ET BEAUTÉ
DU MONDE.
    M. ADAM, 542:OCT-DEC71-521
NAREMORE, J. THE WORLD WITHOUT A SELF.
    617(TLS):13APR73-413
NARKIEWICZ, O.A. THE MAKING OF THE
SOVIET STATE APPARATUS.*
    P. AVRICH, 32:MAR72-168
NARKISS, B. HEBREW ILLUMINATED MANU-
SCRIPTS.
    J.G. PLANTE, 363:FEB71-56
    R. WISCHNITZER, 328:WINTER71-126
NASH, H.P., JR. A NAVAL HISTORY OF THE
CIVIL WAR.
    617(TLS):23MAR73-329
NASH, J.M. THE AGE OF REMBRANDT AND
VERMEER.
    617(TLS):23MAR73-314
NASH, J.R. BLOODLETTERS AND BADMEN.
    H.C. GARDNER, 441:29JUL73-4
"PAUL NASH'S PHOTOGRAPHS." (A. CAUSEY,
ED)
    617(TLS):27JUL73-879
NASH, R. AMERICAN PENMANSHIP 1800-1850.
    617(TLS):15JUN73-698
NASH, R.H., ED. IDEAS OF HISTORY.
    H.B., 543:SEP70-146
NASILOV, V.M., ED. VOPROSY TJURKSKOJ
FILOLOGII.
    L. HŘEBÍČEK, 353:MAR71-117
NASR, R.T. THE STRUCTURE OF ARABIC.
    C.G. KILLEAN, 318(JAOS):OCT-DEC71-536
NASR, S.H. SUFI ESSAYS.
    617(TLS):2FEB73-127
NASSAUER, R. THE EXAMINATION.
    617(TLS):12OCT73-1210
NATAN, A., ED. GERMAN MEN OF LETTERS.
(VOL 5)
    E. BOA, 402(MLR):JUL72-701
    J.M. ELLIS, 221(GQ):JAN71-72
    E.F. GEORGE, 220(GL&L):JAN72-170
NATAN, A., ED. SWISS MEN OF LETTERS.
    L. LÖB, 220(GL&L):JAN72-169
    J.H. REID, 402(MLR):OCT72-957
NATANSON, M. THE JOURNEYING SELF.
    F. KERSTEN, 484(PPR):MAR72-423
NATEW, A. DAS DRAMATISCHE UND DAS DRAMA.
    G.L. TRACY, 406:FALL72-302
NATHAN, M. & D. ROCHE - SEE THOMAS, D.
NATHAN, N.M.L. THE CONCEPT OF JUSTICE.
    M.T. DALGARNO, 518:MAY72-24
NATHAN, R. THE SUMMER MEADOWS.
    M. LEVIN, 441:21OCT73-51
NATHANSON, M. - SEE STRAUS, E.W., M.
NATHANSON & H. EY
"THE NATIONAL GALLERY: ILLUSTRATED GENERAL
CATALOGUE."
    617(TLS):23NOV73-1456

"THE NATIONAL UNION CATALOG OF MANUSCRIPT
COLLECTIONS, 1968 AND INDEX 1967-1968."
 J.R.K. KANTOR, 14:JUL70-334
 W.W. PARKER, 517(PBSA):JAN-MAR72-81
"THE NATIONAL UNION CATALOG OF MANUSCRIPT
COLLECTIONS, 1969 AND INDEX 1967-1969."
 R.D. ARMSTRONG, 14:OCT71-389
NATTER, F. & C. ROUSSEAU - SEE MAURRAS,
C.
NAU, H-W. DIE SYSTEMATISCHE STRUKTUR
VON ERICH ROTHACKERS KULTURBEGRIFF.
 H. ZANDER, 53(AGP):BAND53HEFT2-203
NAUD, J. STRUCTURE ET SENS DU SYMBOLE.
 V. THERRIEN, 154:DEC71-859
NAUEN, F.G. REVOLUTION, IDEALISM AND
HUMAN FREEDOM.
 W.H. WERKMEISTER, 319:JUL73-416
NAUMAN, S., JR. THE NEW DICTIONARY OF
EXISTENTIALISM.
 H.M. ESTALL, 154:SEP71-610
NAUMANN, B. DICHTER UND PUBLIKUM IN
DEUTSCHER UND LATEINISCHER BIBELEPIK
DES FRÜHEN XII. JAHRHUNDERTS.
 C. MINIS, 52:BAND6HEFT2-197
DE NAVARRE, M. - SEE UNDER MARGUERITE DE
NAVARRE
NAVARRETE, R. LUZ QUE SE DUERME.
 C.A. HOLDSWORTH, 238:MAR71-209
DE NAVARRO, J.M. THE FINDS FROM THE SITE
OF LA TÈNE. (VOL 1)
 617(TLS):6APR73-370
NAVAS-RUIZ, R. EL ROMANTICISMO ESPAÑOL.
 191(ELN):SEP71(SUPP)-174
NAVILLE, P. & OTHERS. L'ETAT ENTREPRE-
NEUR.
 617(TLS):5JAN73-21
"NAWAB MEHDI NAWAZ JUNG MEMORIAL VOLUME/
YÄDGÄR-I-MEHDÏ."
 H.K. SHERWANI, 273(IC):APR71-139
NAWRATIL, K. ROBERT REININGER.
 A. STERN, 477:AUTUMN70-551
NAYAR, B.R. NATIONAL COMMUNICATION AND
LANGUAGE POLICY IN INDIA.
 M.L. APTE, 293(JAST):MAY71-700
NAYEEM, M.A. HISTORY OF POSTAL ADMINIS-
TRATION IN HYDERABAD.
 K. SAJUNLAL, 273(IC):JUL71-214
NAYLOR, G. THE ARTS AND CRAFTS MOVEMENT.
 A. FORGE, 592:NOV71-215
N'DIAYE, G. STRUCTURE DU DIALECTE BASQUE
DE MAYA.
 T.H. WILBUR, 350:DEC72-963
NEAL, W.K. & D.H.L. BACK. FORSYTH & CO.
 J.F. HAYWARD, 90:JAN71-52
NEALE, R.E. IN PRAISE OF PLAY.
 J.D.C., 543:SEP70-141
NEALE, R.S. CLASS AND IDEOLOGY IN THE
NINETEENTH CENTURY.
 617(TLS):25MAY73-592
NEATBY, L.H. CONQUEST OF THE LAST FRON-
TIER.
 D.W. SWAINSON, 529(QQ):SUMMER71-323
NEATBY, L.H. THE SEARCH FOR FRANKLIN.
 G.W., 102(CANL):AUTUMN72-115
NEATBY, L.H. - SEE MIERTSCHING, J.
NEBEHAY, C.M. GUSTAV KLIMT.
 F. WHITFORD, 592:MAR70-135
NEBOLSINE, G. JOURNEY INTO ROMANESQUE.
 C.J. MC NASPY, 363:NOV70-24
NEDELJKOVIĆ, D. ROMAIN ROLLAND ET STEFAN
ZWEIG.
 A. MONCHOUX, 549(RLC):APR-JUN71-294
NEDEV, N. ASEN ZLATAROV.
 M. PUNDEFF, 32:JUN72-501
NÉDONCELLE, M. LE CHRÉTIEN APPARTIENT À
DEUX MONDES.
 M. ADAM, 542:OCT-DEC71-508

NÉDONCELLE, M. EXPLORATIONS PERSONNAL-
ISTES.
 M. ADAM, 542:OCT-DEC71-509
NEDREAAS, T. VED NESTE NYMÅNE.
 E. HASLUND, 270:VOL22#1-22
 270:VOL22#2-46
NEE, V.G. & B.D. LONGTIME CALIFORN'.
 H. GOLD, 441:19AUG73-6
 442(NY):10SEP73-134
NEEDHAM, J. CLERKS AND CRAFTSMEN IN
CHINA AND THE WEST.
 E-T.Z. SUN, 293(JAST):FEB71-423
NEEDHAM, J. THE GRAND TITRATION.
 E.J. COLEMAN, 485(PE&W):JUL71-331
 N. SIVIN, 293(JAST):AUG71-870
 M. TOPLEY, 302:JUL71-371
NEEDHAM, J. WITHIN THE FOUR SEAS.
 A. ABRAHAM, 619(TC):VOL179#1049-56
 S-H. LIU, 485(PE&W):JUL70-331
NEEDHAM, L.W. FIFTY YEARS OF FLEET
STREET.
 617(TLS):7SEP73-1037
NEEDHAM, R. BELIEF, LANGUAGE, AND EX-
PERIENCE.
 617(TLS):2FEB73-130
NEEDHAM, R. - SEE HOCART, A.M.
NEEDLEMAN, J. THE NEW RELIGIONS.*
 R.E. CROUTER, 109:FALL/WINTER72/73-
113
NEELKANT, K. PARTNERS IN PEACE.
 617(TLS):1JUN73-606
NEELY, R. THE SEXTON WOMEN.
 N. CALLENDAR, 441:28JAN73-20
NEF, E. DER ZUFALL IN DER ERZÄHLKUNST.*
 R.K. ANGRESS, 221(GQ):MAR71-239
 G. HAAS, 52:BAND6HEFT3-327
 J. PURVER, 402(MLR):JAN72-222
NEGBI, O. THE HOARDS OF GOLDWORK FROM
TELL EL-'AJJUL.
 R.A. HIGGINS, 303:VOL91-200
NEGRI, A. LA COMUNITÀ ESTETICA IN
KANT.
 E. NAMER, 542:APR-JUN70-246
NEGRI, A. SAGGI SULLO STORICISMO TEDESCO,
DILTHEY E MEINECKE.
 E. NAMER, 542:JAN-MAR70-102
NEGRI, P. MEMOIRS OF A STAR.
 J. CHANDLER, 200:OCT70-500
NEGRI, R. ITALIANISTICA.
 M-P., 228(GSLI):VOL147FASC458/459-480
NEGRI, R. LEOPARDI NELLA POESIA ITALIANA.
 O-R., 191(ELN):SEP71(SUPP)-168
NEGROPONTE, N. THE ARCHITECTURE MACHINE.
 M. MILNE, 505:JUL71-98
NEHMAD, M. THE NEW GARMENT. (O. SCHNITZ-
LER, ED)
 B. KIRSHENBLATT-GIMBLETT, 582(SFQ):
DEC70-371
NEHRU, J. SELECTED WORKS OF JAWAHARLAL
NEHRU. (VOLS 1&2)
 617(TLS):21SEP73-1093
NEHRU, J. SELECTED WORKS OF JAWAHARLAL
NEHRU. (VOLS 3&4) (S. GOBAL, ED)
 617(TLS):16NOV73-1409
NEIHARDT, J.G. BLACK ELK SPEAKS.
 617(TLS):6JUL73-780
NEIL, W. THE ACTS OF THE APOSTLES.
 617(TLS):5OCT73-1190
NEILL, A.S. "NEILL! NEILL! ORANGE
PEEL!"*
 E.S. TURNER, 362:7JUN73-764
 617(TLS):27JUL73-855
NEILL, R. A NEW THEORY OF VALUE.
 I. PARKER, 99:MAY73-35
NEILL, T.P. MODERN EUROPE.
 R.J. MARAS, 613:SPRING71-151
NELLI, H.S. THE ITALIANS IN CHICAGO.
 639(VQR):SPRING71-LXXVI

NELLIST, J.B. BRITISH ARCHITECTURE AND
ITS BACKGROUND.*
S.C., 46:AUG70-131
NÉLOD, G. PANORAMA DU ROMAN HISTORIQUE.
G. VANWELKENHUYSEN, 549(RLC):JUL-SEP
71-425
NELSON, B. ARTHUR MILLER.*
J.R. TAYLOR, 157:AUTUMN70-69
502(PRS):FALL71-280
NELSON, G. CHANGES OF HEART.*
D.S. JOHNSON, 191(ELN):DEC71-157
P. THOMAS, 648:JUN70-33
NELSON, J.A. FORM AND IMAGE IN THE FIC-
TION OF HENRY MILLER.
K.J. ATCHITY, 149:JUN72-239
NELSON, J.G. THE EARLY NINETIES.
676(YR):SUMMER72-VI
NELSON, L. CRITIQUE OF PRACTICAL REASON.
R.M. CHISHOLM, 311(JP):22NOV73-772
NELSON, L., JR., ED. CERVANTES: A COL-
LECTION OF CRITICAL ESSAYS.*
D.B. DRAKE, 399(MLJ):MAR71-199
NELSON, M. CAPTAIN BLOSSOM.
617(TLS):9MAR73-277
NELSON, N. DENMARK.
617(TLS):20JUL73-842
NELSON, O.W. & D.A. LA RUSSO. ORAL COM-
MUNICATION IN THE SECONDARY SCHOOL
CLASSROOM.
G.R. CAPP, 583:SUMMER72-447
NELSON, R.J. IMMANENCE AND TRANSCEN-
DENCE.
F.K. DAWSON, 208(FS):APR72-191
M. GUTWIRTH, 207(FR):DEC70-462
W.L. WILEY, 551(RENQ):SPRING71-101
NELSON, R.J. INTRODUCTION TO AUTOMATA.
R. MC NAUGHTON, 316:MAR71-151
NELSON, S.M. THE VIOLIN AND VIOLA.*
H.M. BROWN, 415:NOV72-1089
NELSON, T. THE OLD MAN.
W.M. MERRILL, 441:25MAR73-16
NEMCEK, P. THE FILMS OF NANCY CARROLL.
J.R. CHESTER, 200:OCT70-502
NĚMCOVÁ, J.W., ED & TRANS. CZECH AND
SLOVAK SHORT STORIES.
R.V. ADKINSON, 556(RLV):1970/1-107
NEMENZO, C.A., COMP. THE FLORA AND FAUNA
OF THE PHILIPPINES, 1851-1966. (VOL 1)
D.V. HART, 293(JAST):MAY71-741
NENCI, G., ED. ANTOLOGIA DI PROSA STOR-
ICA GRECA.
R. DREWS, 124:MAR72-239
NERO (H. BLACKER). WITH LAUGH AND AFFEC-
TION.
617(TLS):27JUL73-884
DER NERSESSIAN, S. L'ILLUSTRATION DES
PSAUTIERS GRECS DU MOYEN ÂGE. (VOL 2)
G. GALAVARIS, 589:JUL72-523
NERSOYAN, H.J. ANDRÉ GIDE.*
J. DE LABRIOLLE, 549(RLC):JAN-MAR70-
140
NERUDA, P. ANTOLOGÍA ESENCIAL. (H.
LOYOLA, ED) GEOGRAFÍA INFRUCTUOSA.
INCITACIÓN AL NIXONICIDIO Y ALABANZA
DE LA REVOLUCIÓN CHILENA.
617(TLS):11MAY73-532
NERUDA, P. SELECTED POEMS.* (N. TARN,
ED)
R. LATTIMORE, 249(HUDR):AUTUMN72-482
P.R. YANNELLA, 598(SOR):SPRING73-445
DE NERVAL, G. LES CHIMÈRES. (N. RINS-
LER, ED)
617(TLS):21DEC73-1562
DE NERVAL, G. "ERREUR DE NOM" OU "LE
CAFÉ DU THÉÂTRE." (J. SENELIER, ED)
M. DESCOTES, 535(RHL):MAR-APR71-312

DE NERVAL, G. PANDORA.* (J. GUILLAUME,
ED)
F. CONSTANS, 557(RSH):JAN-MAR70-171
DE NERVAL, G. SYLVIE. (P-G. CASTEX, ED)
R. CHAMBERS, 208(FS):APR72-215
F. CONSTANS, 557(RSH):APR-JUN71-324
DE NERVAL, G. THÉÂTRE: PIQUILLO, LES
MONTÉNÉGRINS, EBAUCHES. (J. RICHER,
ED)
F. BASSAN, 207(FR):DEC70-454
"GÉRARD DE NERVAL, PROSA E POESIA." (M.L.
BELLELI, ED)
F. CONSTANS, 557(RSH):JUL-SEP70-485
NESBITT-DUFORT, J. BLACK LYSANDER.
617(TLS):29JUN73-757
NESSELROTH, P.W. LAUTRÉAMONT'S IMAGERY.*
W. BEAUCHAMP, 546(RR):FEB71-68
NESTROY, J. KOMÖDIEN.* (F.H. MAUTNER,
ED)
J.D. BARLOW, 406:SPRING72-76
H. ZOHN, 221(GQ):NOV71-605
NETHERSOLE-THOMPSON, D. THE DOTTEREL.
617(TLS):7SEP73-1030
NETTEL, R. A SOCIAL HISTORY OF TRADI-
TIONAL SONG.
L. ARMSTRONG, 203:SPRING70-73
NETZBAND, K-B. & H.P. WIDMAIER. WÄHRUNGS-
UND FINANZPOLITIK DER ÄRA LUTHER, 1923-
25.
E. CARELL, 182:VOL24#7/8-342
NETZER, K. DER LESER DES NOUVEAU ROMAN.
F. WOLFZETTEL, 72:BAND209HEFT1/3-218
NEUBAUER, J. BIFOCAL VISION.
J.M. MC GLATHERY, 301(JEGP):JUL72-429
NEUBERG, V.E. THE PENNY HISTORIES.
G.W., 503:SUMMER68-81
NEUBERG, V.E. POPULAR EDUCATION IN
EIGHTEENTH CENTURY ENGLAND.
617(TLS):5JAN73-19
NEUBURG, P. THE HERO'S CHILDREN.*
Z.A.B. ZEMAN, 441:13MAY73-32
NEUFERT, E. ERNST NEUFERT ARCHITECTS'
DATA.
505:DEC71-100
NEUGEBOREN, J. CORKY'S BROTHER.
C. MORAN, 573(SSF):FALL71-644
NEUHAUS, H. THE ART OF PIANO PLAYING.
617(TLS):29JUN73-751
"BENJAMIN NEUKIRCHS ANTHOLOGIE." (VOL 2)
(A.G. DE CAPUA & E.A. PHILIPPSON, EDS)
K.G. KNIGHT, 220(GL&L):JAN72-150
NEUMANN, F. DAS NIBELUNGENLIED IN SEINER
ZEIT.
B. NAGEL, 680(ZDP):BAND89HEFT1-111
NEUMANN, F. STUDIEN ZUR GESCHICHTE DER
DEUTSCHEN PHILOLOGIE.
E.A. PHILIPPSON, 301(JEGP):OCT72-559
NEUMANN, G. INDOGERMANISCHE SPRACHWIS-
SENSCHAFT 1816 UND 1966.
E. NEU, 260(IF):BAND75-271
R. SCHMITT, 343:BAND13HEFT2-180
NEUMANN, H.L. SPRACHLICHE EINSCHLÄGE IN
SOGENANNTEN SPRACHFREIEN TESTS. GE-
SCHICHTSPUNKTE ZUR UNTERSUCHUNG TAUB-
STUMMER.
J. TIGGES, 657(WW):JUL/AUG71-286
NEUMANN, P.H. WORT-KONKORDANZ ZUR LYRIK
PAUL CELANS BIS 1967.
M. GUMMERT, 190:BAND64HEFT3/4-441
NEUMANN, S. EIN MECKLENBURGISCHER VOLK-
SERZÄHLER. (2ND ED)
E. MOSER-RATH, 196:BAND12HEFT2/3-282
R.L. WELSCH, 650(WF):APR71-144
NEUMANN, S. PLATTDEUTSCHE SCHWÄNKE.
E-H. REHERMANN, 196:BAND12HEFT2/3-280
NEUMEISTER, S. DAS SPIEL MIT DER HÖF-
ISCHEN LIEBE.
F. WOLFZETTEL, 430(NS):AUG70-421

NEUSE, W. - SEE GOETZ, C.
NEVEU, B.   SÉBASTIEN JOSEPH DU CAMBOUT
  DE PONTCHÂTEAU (1634-1690) ET SES
  MISSIONS À ROME.*
    J. LE BRUN, 535(RHL):JAN-FEB71-83
NEVINS, A.   THE ORDEAL OF THE UNION.
  (VOLS 7&8)
    R.F. DURDEN, 579(SAQ):SUMMER72-435
NEW, M.   LAURENCE STERNE AS SATIRIST.*
    M.V. DE PORTE, 405(MP):FEB72-258
    T.A. OLSHIN, 556(RLV):1971/4-488
    R.W. UPHAUS, 290(JAAC):WINTER70-283
NEW, W.H.   ARTICULATING WEST.
    D. ARNASON, 296:SPRING73-96
    F. DAVEY, 99:MAY73-42
NEW, W.H., ED.   DRAMATISTS IN CANADA.
    E. WATERSTON, 296:FALL73-118
NEW, W.H., ED.   FOUR HEMISPHERES.
    D. PACEY, 102(CANL):SUMMER72-109
"NEW CHILE."
    N. GALL, 441:1JUL73-6
"THE NEW ENGLISH BIBLE, WITH THE APOCRY-
  PHA."*
    C.H. GIBLIN, 613:WINTER70-629
    R. LAWRENCE, 175:AUTUMN70-107
"THE NEW SCHÖFFLER-WEIS COMPACT GERMAN
  AND ENGLISH DICTIONARY." (REV BY E. &
  E. WEIS)
    205(FMLS):JUL70-313
"THE NEW YORK TIMES GERSHWIN YEARS IN
  SONG."
    W. CLEMONS, 441:23SEP73-3
"NEW ZEALAND UNIVERSITIES' ARTS FESTIVAL
  YEARBOOK: 1968, 1969, 1970."
    D. ANIDO, 368:DEC70-423
NEWALL, V.   AN EGG AT EASTER.
    K.M. BRIGGS, 203:SPRING71-73
NEWBY, P.H.   A LOT TO ASK.
    D.J. ENRIGHT, 362:3MAY73-591
    617(TLS):11MAY73-517
NEWCOMER, J.   MARIA EDGEWORTH THE NOVEL-
  IST.
    A.T. MC KENZIE, 594:FALL70-373
NEWELL, K.B.   STRUCTURE IN FOUR NOVELS BY
  H.G. WELLS.
    J.B. BATCHELOR, 402(MLR):APR72-407
NEWELL, L.E.   A BATAD IFUGAO VOCABULARY.
    L.A. REID, 206:AUG71-451
NEWFIELD, J.   ROBERT KENNEDY.
    C.R. SMITH, 583:WINTER71-215
NEWHALL, B.   THE HISTORY OF PHOTOGRAPHY
  FROM 1839 TO THE PRESENT DAY.
    617(TLS):29JUN73-757
NEWIGER, H-J., ED.   ANTIKE KOMÖDIEN -
  ARISTOPHANES.  (REV TRANS BY L.
  SEEGER & ANNOTATED BY H-J. NEWIGER &
  P. RAU)
    M. LANDFESTER, 52:BAND5HEFT2-205
NEWIGER, H-J. & H. SEYFFERT - SEE DILLER,
  H.
NEWLOVE, D.   LEO AND THEODORE.
    R.P. BRICKNER, 441:11FEB73-28
    442(NY):27JAN73-93
NEWLOVE, J.   THE CAVE.*
    B. CHILDS, 50(ARQ):SPRING71-83
    R. GUSTAFSON, 529(QQ):SPRING71-140
NEWMAN, A., ED.   THE PARLIAMENTARY LISTS
  OF THE EARLY EIGHTEENTH CENTURY.
    617(TLS):27APR73-482
NEWMAN, C.   A CHILD'S HISTORY OF AMERICA.
    J. MC ELROY, 441:14OCT73-7
NEWMAN, C.   THE PROMISEKEEPER.*
    J.C. OATES, 473(PR):1/1972-118
NEWMAN, C.J.   A RUSSIAN NOVEL.
    V. CUNNINGHAM, 362:11JAN73-56
    A. DONALDSON, 198:SUMMER73-121
    617(TLS):2FEB73-113

NEWMAN, E.   BERLIOZ, ROMANTIC AND CLAS-
  SIC.* (P. HEYWORTH, ED)
    H. MAC DONALD, 415:MAR72-269
NEWMAN, F.W.   PHASES OF FAITH.
    J.L. BRADLEY, 402(MLR):JAN72-176
NEWMAN, F.X., ED.   THE MEANING OF COURTLY
  LOVE.*
    J.V. FLEMING, 149:MAR72-93
    W. VON KOPPENFELS, 72:BAND209HEFT1/3-
    138
    C.S. WRIGHT, 191(ELN):MAR72-203
NEWMAN, J.   THE BUILDINGS OF ENGLAND:
  WEST KENT AND THE WEALD.   THE BUILDINGS
  OF ENGLAND: NORTH-EAST AND EAST KENT.
    A.C-T., 135:DEC70-291
    P. METCALF, 46:JAN71-66
NEWMAN, J.H.   THE LETTERS AND DIARIES OF
  JOHN HENRY NEWMAN.  (VOLS 23 & 24)
  (C.S. DESSAIN & T. GORNALL, EDS)
    617(TLS):27JUL73-882
NEWMAN, L.M.   LIBRARIES IN PARIS.
    D.M. SUTHERLAND, 208(FS):OCT72-486
NEWMAN, M. & B. BERKOWITZ, WITH J. OWEN.
  HOW TO BE YOUR OWN BEST FRIEND.
    H. SCHWARTZ, 441:13OCT73-33
    R. TODD, 61:NOV73-109
NEWMAN, O.   DEFENSIBLE SPACE.
    S. KAPLAN, 441:29APR73-16
    617(TLS):14SEP73-1047
NEWMAN, P.   A GRAMMAR OF TERA.
    J.T. RITTER, 350:MAR72-200
    N.V. SMITH, 315(JAL):VOL10PT2-54
NEWMAN, W.S.   PERFORMANCE PRACTICES IN
  BEETHOVEN'S PIANO SONATAS.*
    H.F., 410(M&L):OCT72-459
NEWMAN, W.S.   THE SONATA SINCE BEETHOVEN.*
    639(VQR):WINTER71-XLIV
NEWMAN-GORDON, P.   DICTIONNAIRE DES
  IDÉES DANS L'OEUVRE DE MARCEL PROUST.
    R. GOLDTHORPE, 208(FS):JAN72-99
NEWTON, H.P.   TO DIE FOR THE PEOPLE.*
    C. NEWMAN, 231:NOV73-116
NEWTON, H.P., WITH J.H. BLAKE.   REVOLU-
  TIONARY SUICIDE.
    M. KEMPTON, 441:20MAY73-35
    C. LEHMANN-HAUPT, 441:6APR73-45
    C. NEWMAN, 231:NOV73-116
NEWTON, I.   FINCHES.
    617(TLS):7SEP73-1030
NEWTON, P.   SHEEP THIEF.
    617(TLS):23FEB73-219
NEWTON, S.C., ED.   THE LONDONDERRY PAPERS.
    C.R.H. COOPER, 325:OCT71-346
NGANGGOUM, F.B.   LE BAMILÉKÉ DES FE?FE?
    J. VOORHOEVE, 315(JAL):VOL10PT2-54
NIALL, I.   AROUND MY HOUSE.
    617(TLS):14DEC73-1549
"DAS NIBELUNGENLIED." (H. ENGELS, ED)
    M.S. BATTS, 405(MP):FEB71-301
NIBLETT, W.R., ED.   HIGHER EDUCATION.
    R.C. ELLSWORTH, 529(QQ):SUMMER71-340
NIBLETT, W.R. & R.F. BUTTS, EDS.   UNIVER-
  SITIES FACING THE FUTURE.
    617(TLS):16FEB73-189
NICETA VON REMESIANA.   DE LAPSU SUSANNAE.
  (K. GAMBER, ED)
    E. KÄHLER, 182:VOL24#21/22-776
NIČEV, A.   L'ÉNIGME DE LA CATHARSIS TRAG-
  IQUE DANS ARISTOTE.*
    D.W. LUCAS, 123:JUN72-204
NICHOL, B.P.   TWO NOVELS.*
    J. MILLS, 648:JUN70-35
    R. WILLMOT, 296:FALL73-98
NICHOLLS, R.A.   THE DRAMAS OF CHRISTIAN
  DIETRICH GRABBE.*
    P.K. JANSEN, 405(MP):NOV71-181
    E. MC INNES, 220(GL&L):JUL72-402
    P.C. THORNTON, 402(MLR):APR72-470

NICHOLS, J. EMBLEMS OF PASSAGE.
  M. MARCUS, 502(PRS):FALL71-275
NICHOLS, J. MINOR LIVES.* (E.L. HART,
  ED)
  F.W. HILLES, 676(YR):AUTUMN71-109
  H. PETTIT, 191(ELN):JUN72-310
  566:AUTUMN71-28
NICHOLS, J.B. ANECDOTES OF WILLIAM
  HOGARTH.
  R. EDWARDS, 39:APR71-341
NICHOLS, J.G. THE POETRY OF BEN JONSON.*
  M. EVANS, 551(RENQ):SUMMER71-277
  C.F. WILLIAMSON, 541(RES):MAY71-194
NICHOLS, J.P. SKYLINE QUEEN AND THE
  MERCHANT PRINCE.
  L. SLOANE, 441:1JUL73-16
NICHOLSON, H. ELLA.
  S. HILL, 362:22FEB73-251
  617(TLS):2MAR73-229
NICHOLSON, N. CHAMELEON'S DISH.
  617(TLS):28DEC73-1593
"NICHOLSON'S GUIDES TO THE WATERWAYS."
  (VOL 3)
  617(TLS):27JUL73-884
NICKEL, G. DIE EXPANDED FORM IM ALTENG-
  LISCHEN.*
  C.J.E. BALL, 297(JL):FEB70-157
  T. GARDNER, 38:BAND89HEFT1-121
NICKEL, G., ED. PAPERS IN CONTRASTIVE
  LINGUISTICS.
  R. WARDHAUGH, 351(LL):DEC71-245
NICKISCH, R.M.G. DIE STILPRINZIPIEN IN
  DEN DEUTSCHEN BRIEFSTELLERN DES 17. UND
  18. JAHRHUNDERTS.*
  F. VAN INGEN, 433:JAN70-88
  W. VOSSKAMP, 224(GRM):BAND21HEFT1-113
NICKL, T. & H. SCHNITZLER - SEE SCHNITZ-
  LER, A.
NICOD, J. GEOMETRY AND INDUCTION.
  L.J. COHEN, 479(PHQ):OCT71-376
NICOÏDSKI, C. LA MORT DE GILLES.
  J-P. CAUVIN, 207(FR):MAY71-1124
NICOLAIEVSKY, B. & O. MAENCHEN-HELFEN.
  KARL MARX.
  617(TLS):15JUN73-667
NICOLAISEN, P. DIE BILDLICHKEIT IN DER
  DICHTUNG EDWARD TAYLORS.
  F.W. SCHULZE, 72:BAND209HEFT4/6-410
NICOLAISEN, W.F.H. - SEE GELLING, M.,
  W.F.H. NICOLAISEN & M. RICHARDS
NICOLAISEN, W.F.H. - SEE MARWICK, H.
NICOLAS, J-H. DIEU CONNU COMME INCONNU.
  G. LANGEVIN, 154:JUN70-108
NICOLAUS, M. - SEE MARX, K.
NICOLE, C. THE EXPURGATOR.
  N. CALLENDAR, 441:18FEB73-29
NICOLET, H. DIE "VERLORENE" ZEIT.
  B.N. JOHN, 67:MAY72-114
  S. PRAWER, 220(GL&L):JAN72-175
NICOLIN, G., ED. HEGEL IN BERICHTEN
  SEINER ZEITGENOSSEN.
  H.B., 543:JUN71-762
  H.W. BRANN, 258:DEC71-585
  T.M. KNOX, 479(PHQ):JAN71-76
  X. TILLIETTE, 182:VOL24#3-72
  E. WEIL, 98:MAY71-477
NICOLL, A. ENGLISH DRAMA 1900-1930.
  617(TLS):29JUN73-747
NICOLL, J. THE PRE-RAPHAELITES.
  R. MANDER, 39:FEB71-148
NICOLSON, B. COURBET: THE STUDIO OF THE
  PAINTER.
  R. DOWNES, 441:2DEC73-92
  617(TLS):6JUL73-766
NICOLSON, B. JOSEPH WRIGHT OF DERBY.*
  R.R. WARK, 56:SPRING70-71

NICOLSON, M. & G.S. ROUSSEAU. "THIS LONG
  DISEASE, MY LIFE."*
  I. SIMON, 179(ES):AUG71-370
NICOLSON, N. ALEX.
  R.H.S. CROSSMAN, 362:5APR73-455
  617(TLS):30MAR73-351
NICOLSON, N. PORTRAIT OF A MARRIAGE.
  W. ABRAHAMS, 61:DEC73-128
  S. BEDFORD, 362:25OCT73-556
  B. GILL, 442(NY):29OCT73-173
  C. LEHMANN-HAUPT, 441:5OCT73-35
  J. RICHARDSON, 453:15NOV73-20
  N. SAYRE, 441:28OCT73-2
  617(TLS):2NOV73-1331
NIDA, E.A. A SYNOPSIS OF ENGLISH SYNTAX.
  A.P. NILSEN, 353:JUL71-118
NIEDECKER, L. COLLECTED POEMS, 1968: MY
  LIFE BY WATER.*
  W.G. SHEPHERD, 493:SUMMER71-204
NIEDERGANG, M. THE TWENTY LATIN AMERI-
  CAS.
  E.J. HOBSBAWM, 111:5MAY72-113
NIEL, H. L'ANALYSE DU DESTIN.
  M. CHASTAING, 542:OCT-DEC70-483
NIELD, B. FAREWELL TO THE ASSIZES.
  617(TLS):16FEB73-190
NIELSEN, C. MY CHILDHOOD.
  J.A.W., 410(M&L):OCT72-438
NIELSEN, W.A. THE GREAT POWERS AND
  AFRICA.
  468:VOL23#4-425
NIERAAD, J. STANDPUNKTBEWUSSTEIN UND
  WELTZUSAMMENHANG.
  J. DELAPLAIN, 481(PQ):JUL71-455
NIESEWAND, P. IN CAMERA.
  J. BIDDULPH, 362:27SEP73-421
  617(TLS):26OCT73-1315
NIESS, R.J. ZOLA, CÉZANNE, AND MANET.*
  A. EHRARD, 535(RHL):MAY-JUN70-530
  M. KANES, 405(MP):NOV70-209
  P. WALKER, 188(ECR):WINTER70-344
NIETHAMMER, L. ENTNAZIFIZIERUNG IN
  BAYERN.
  617(TLS):9FEB73-154
NIETO ALCAIDE, V.M. DIBUJOS DE LA R.
  ACADEMIA DE SAN FERNANDO: CARLO MARATTI,
  43 DIBUJOS DE TEMA RELIGIOSO.
  F.H. DOWLEY, 54:DEC70-456
NIETZSCHE, F.W. LE LIVRE DU PHILOSOPHE.
  LA NAISSANCE DE LA TRAGÉDIE. LA NAIS-
  SANCE DE LA PHILOSOPHIE À L'ÉPOQUE DE
  LA TRAGÉDIE GRECQUE.
  S. KOFMAN, 98:AUG/SEP71-783
NIETZSCHE, F.W. NIETZSCHE: A SELF-POR-
  TRAIT FROM HIS LETTERS. (P. FUSS & H.
  SHAPIRO, EDS & TRANS)
  C.J. TERRY, 150(DR):AUTUMN71-438
NIETZSCHE, F.W. NIETZSCHE: WERKE. (PT
  3, VOL 1; PT 8, VOL 3) (G. COLLI & M.
  MONTINARI, EDS)
  617(TLS):2MAR73-233
NIETZSCHE, F.W. NIETZSCHE: WERKE. (PT 4,
  VOLS 1-3; PT 6, VOLS 1-3) (G. COLLI &
  M. MONTINARI, EDS)
  H.W. REICHERT, 319:JAN73-128
NIETZSCHE, F.W. NIETZSCHE: WERKE. (PT 4,
  VOL 4 & PT 8, VOL 2) (G. COLLI & M.
  MONTINARI, EDS)
  H.W. REICHERT, 319:JAN73-128
  H.W. REICHERT, 406:SUMMER72-183
NIETZSCHE, F.W. NIETZSCHE: WERKE. (PT
  5, VOL 1) (G. COLLI & M. MONTINARI, EDS)
  H.W. REICHERT, 319:JAN73-128
  617(TLS):2MAR73-233
NIETZSCHE, F.W. THE WILL TO POWER. (W.
  KAUFMANN, ED)
  J.E. LLEWELYN, 478:JAN70-91

263

NIEVA, C.S. THIS TRANSCENDING GOD.
S. BROOK, 402(MLR):APR72-395
NIGHTINGALE, B. CHARITIES.
A. FAIRLEY, 362:21JUN73-838
LADY NIJŌ. THE CONFESSIONS OF LADY NIJŌ.
(K. BRAZELL, TRANS)
P. ADAMS, 61:SEP73-119
D. CHANG, 441:21OCT73-24
442(NY):31DEC73-60
NIKAM, N.A. SOME CONCEPTS OF INDIAN CUL-
TURE.
J.B.L., 543:DEC70-342
NIKIPROWETZKY, V. LA TROISIÈME SIBYLLE.
E.M. SMALLWOOD, 303:VOL91-158
NIKITIN, S.A. OCHERKI PO ISTORII IUZHN-
YKH SLAVIAN I RUSSKO-BALKANSKIKH SVIA-
ZEI V 50-70-E GODY XIX V.
D. MAC KENZIE, 32:SEP72-668
NIKLAUS, R. A LITERARY HISTORY OF FRANCE:
THE EIGHTEENTH CENTURY 1715-1789.*
639(VQR):WINTER71-XXX
NILSSON, E. LES TERMES RELATIFS ET LES
PROPOSITIONS RELATIVES EN ROUMAIN MOD-
ERNE.*
R. HOLTZMAN, 545(RPH):FEB72-347
NILSSON, S. EUROPEAN ARCHITECTURE IN
INDIA 1750-1850.*
M. ARCHER, 54:JUN70-218
D. FITZ-GERALD, 39:AUG70-152
NIMETZ, M. HUMOR IN GALDÓS.*
H.B. HALL, 86(BHS):OCT72-410
D. LIDA, 240(HR):JAN71-112
NIN, A. ANAÏS NIN READER. (P.K. JASON,
ED)
W. FOWLIE, 441:9SEP73-26
"NIPPON TO AMERIKA."
270:VOL22#2-43
NISBET, A. & B. NEVIUS, EDS. DICKENS
CENTENNIAL ESSAYS.
R.D. MC MASTER, 445(NCF):SEP71-219
617(TLS):27APR73-478
NISBET, H.B. HERDER AND THE PHILOSOPHY
AND HISTORY OF SCIENCE.*
E.B. SCHICK, 301(JEGP):JAN72-67
NISBET, R.G.M. & M. HUBBARD. A COMMEN-
TARY ON HORACE: "ODES," BOOK I.*
F. CAIRNS, 313:VOL61-305
A. ERNOUT, 555:VOL45FASC1-99
NISH, I.H. ALLIANCE IN DECLINE.
617(TLS):5JAN73-16
NISSEN, C. DIE ZOOLOGISCHE BUCHILLUSTRA-
TION.
H. LEHMANN-HAUPT, 517(PBSA):JUL-SEP72-
338
NISSILÄ, V. DIE DORFNAMEN DES ALTEN
LÜDISCHEN GEBIETES.
A. RAUN, 361:VOL26#1-108
NITCHIE, G.W. MARIANNE MOORE.*
C.M. TAYLOR, 597(SN):VOL43#1-325
NITISASTRO, W. - SEE UNDER WIDJOJO NITI-
SASTRO
NITSCHKE, U. STUDIEN ZUM SCHICKSALSGE-
DANKEN UND SEINER DICHTERISCHEN GES-
TALTUNG BEI ALFRED DE VIGNY.
A. BILLAZ, 535(RHL):JUL-AUG71-712
NIVELLE, A. KUNST- UND DICHTUNGSTHEORIEN
ZWISCHEN AUFKLÄRUNG UND KLASSIK. (2ND
ED)
E. SCHAPER, 89(BJA):SPRING72-197
NIVEN, J. GIDEON WELLES.
A. WHITMAN, 441:21NOV73-41
NIVEN, L. INCONSTANT MOON.
617(TLS):20APR73-451
NIVER, K. MARY PICKFORD, COMEDIENNE.
(B. BERGSTEN, ED)
R. GIROUX, 200:MAY70-287

NIVER, K.R., COMP. BIOGRAPH BULLETINS
1896-1908. (B. BERGSTEN, ED)
H.H., 200:AUG-SEP71-431
NIVETTE, J. PRINCIPES DE GRAMMAIRE
GÉNÉRATIVE.
R.M. HOGG, 433:APR71-218
NIXON, H.M. SIXTEENTH-CENTURY GOLD-TOOLED
BOOKBINDINGS IN THE PIERPONT MORGAN
LIBRARY.
M-M. ROMME, 78(BC):WINTER71-539
NIXON, M. THE OXFORD BOOK OF VERTEBRATES.
617(TLS):12JAN73-46
NIZAMI, K.A., ED. MEDIEVAL INDIA. (VOL
1)
A. AHMAD, 318(JAOS):OCT-DEC71-534
NIZAN, P. ANTOINE BLOYÉ.
K. MILLER, 453:15NOV73-26
B.P. SOLOMON, 441:24JUN73-4
442(NY):30JUL73-71
617(TLS):24AUG73-969
NIZER, L. THE IMPLOSION CONSPIRACY.
R. COOVER, 441:11FEB73-4
C. LEHMANN-HAUPT, 441:5FEB73-27
NOBELSINE, G. JOURNEY INTO ROMANESQUE.
J. BECKWITH, 39:OCT70-314
NOBLE, J.R., ED. RECOLLECTIONS OF VIR-
GINIA WOOLF BY HER CONTEMPORARIES.*
W. MAXWELL, 442(NY):3FEB73-96
NOBLE, R.W. JOYCE CARY.
617(TLS):24AUG73-972
NOCK, O.S. THE GOLDEN AGE OF STEAM.
617(TLS):28DEC73-1595
NOCK, O.S. RAILWAYS OF CANADA.
617(TLS):16NOV73-1409
NOCK, O.S. UNDERGROUND RAILWAYS OF THE
WORLD.
617(TLS):6JUL73-789
NOEHLES, K. LA CHIESA DEI SS. LUCA E
MARTINA NELL'OPERA DI PIETRO DA COR-
TONA.
A. BLUNT, 90:NOV71-672
NOER, D. THE MODERNIST MUSLIM MOVEMENT
IN INDONESIA 1900-1942.
617(TLS):21SEP73-1076
NOFERI, A. POÉTIQUES CRITIQUES DU XXE
SIÈCLE.
J-M. GARDAIR, 98:DEC70-1067
NOGALES, L.G., ED. THE MEXICAN AMERICAN.
(2ND ED)
J. SOMMERS, 238:SEP71-610
DALLE NOGARE, P. CORPS IMAGINAIRE.
R.B. JOHNSON, 207(FR):DEC70-419
NOGEE, J.L., ED. MAN, STATE, AND SOCIETY
IN THE SOVIET UNION.
617(TLS):24AUG73-983
NOLAN, R. FOUNDATIONS FOR AN ADEQUATE
CRITERION OF PARAPHRASE.
L.J. COHEN, 297(JL):OCT71-296
NOLTE, H-H. RELIGIÖSE TOLERANZ IN RUSS-
LAND 1600-1725.
Z-R. DITTRICH, 575(SEER):APR72-305
NOLTING-HAUFF, I. VISION, SATIRE AND
POINTE IN QUEVEDOS "SUEÑOS."
H.T. OOSTENDORP, 433:JUL71-344
NOONAN, J.T., JR., ED. THE MORALITY OF
ABORTION.
J.V. DOLAN, 613:SUMMER71-294
R.J. GERBER, 185:JAN72-137
VAN NOORD, A. RUDIMENTS DE LA SYNTAXE
FRANÇAISE. (3RD ED)
M-L. MOREAU, 556(RLV):1970/3-334
NORBECK, E. RELIGION AND SOCIETY IN
MODERN JAPAN.
A. BLOOM, 293(JAST):MAY71-679
NORDAHL, H. LES SYSTÈMES DU SUBJONCTIF
CORRÉLATIF.
J. CHAURAND, 209(FM):JUL71-261
[CONTINUED]

264

NORDAHL, H. LES SYSTEMES DU SUBJONCTIF
CORRELATIF. [CONTINUING]
K. TOGEBY, 597(SN):VOL42#1-279
205(FMLS):JAN71-98
NORDEGG, M. THE POSSIBILITIES OF CANADA
ARE TRULY GREAT. (T.D. REGEHR, ED)
D. SWAINSON, 529(QQ):AUTUMN71-467
NORDENSTAM, T. SUDANESE ETHICS.*
T. ASAD, 69:JAN70-85
NORDENTOFT, S. HEIDEGGERS OPGOR MED DEN
FILOSOFISKE TRADITION KRITISK BELYST.
P. KEMP, 542:OCT-DEC71-472
NORDLAND, O. BREWING AND BEER TRADITIONS
IN NORWAY.
R.L. WELSCH, 292(JAF):OCT-DEC71-465
NORDOFF, P. & C. ROBBINS. MUSIC THERAPY
FOR HANDICAPPED CHILDREN.
M. SEARS, 470:MAY66-25
P. STANDFORD, 415:FEB72-158
NORDRÅ, O. RÖD HÖST.
I.T. STENNING, 270:VOL21#2-144
NORDWALL, O. GYORGY LIGETI.
R. SMALLEY, 415:SEP72-870
NORMAN, B. SECRET WARFARE.
617(TLS):7DEC73-1503
NORMAN, F. ONE OF OUR OWN.
617(TLS):23FEB73-219
NORMAN, M. OKLAHOMA CRUDE.
M. LEVIN, 441:25FEB73-49
NORMAN, R. REASONS FOR ACTIONS.
G. MARSHALL, 63:AUG72-192
J. WILLIAMSON, 518:JAN72-26
NORMAN-BUTLER, B. VICTORIAN ASPIRATIONS.
617(TLS):26JAN73-81
NORMAND, J. NATHANIEL HAWTHORNE.*
J.D. CROWLEY, 445(NCF):JUN71-121
K. MC SWEENEY, 529(QQ):SPRING71-150
B. ST. ARMAND, 454:WINTER72-162
NORQUEST, C. RIO GRANDE WETBACKS.
W. GARD, 584(SWR):SUMMER72-V
NØRRETRANDERS, B. THE SHAPING OF CZARDOM
UNDER IVAN GROZNYJ.
S.L. PARSONS, 104:FALL72-493
NORRIS, F. A NOVELIST IN THE MAKING.
(J.D. HART, ED)
W.M. FROHOCK, 454:FALL71-82
M. WESTBROOK, 649(WAL):WINTER71-310
639(VQR):SPRING71-LXIV
NORRIS, F.P. 2D - SEE GUIDO DE COLONNA
NORRIS, K. FALLING OFF.
W.H. PRITCHARD, 249(HUDR):SPRING72-123
NORRIS, L., ED. VERNON WATKINS 1905-
1967.
F. LEFRANC, 189(EA):JUL-SEP70-348
NORTH, H. EXPRESSWAY.
617(TLS):27APR73-460
NORTH, M. THE SECULAR PRIESTS.
617(TLS):9FEB73-145
NORTHAM, J. IBSEN.
617(TLS):11MAY73-521
NORTHCOTT, K.J. - SEE LESSING, G.E.
NORTON, C.E. - SEE CARLYLE, T.
NORTON, F.J. & E.M. WILSON. TWO SPANISH
VERSE CHAP-BOOKS.*
D.C. CLARKE, 405(MP):MAY71-378
E. LUCIE-SMITH, 503:WINTER69-192
NORTON, L. - SEE DUC DE SAINT-SIMON
NORTON, M.B. THE BRITISH-AMERICANS.*
E. FONER, 453:22FEB73-35
NORTON-SMITH, J. - SEE LYDGATE, J.
NORWICH, J.J. THE KINGDOM IN THE SUN.*
J. BECKWITH, 39:OCT71-322
NORWOOD, J. VICTORIAN AND EDWARDIAN
HAMPSHIRE AND THE ISLE OF WIGHT FROM
OLD PHOTOGRAPHS.
617(TLS):21DEC73-1573
NORWOOD, W.D., JR. THE JUDOKA.
441:2SEP73-8

NOSKE, G. QUAESTIONES PSEUDACRONEAE.
M.J. MC GANN, 123:MAR72-110
NOTTRIDGE, H.E. THE SOCIOLOGY OF URBAN
LIVING.
617(TLS):9MAR73-277
NOULET, E. ALPHABET CRITIQUE 1924-1964.
J. DE CALUWÉ, 556(RLV):1970/2-214
NOURISSIER, F. ALLEMANDE.
617(TLS):17AUG73-945
NOUSIAINEN, J. THE FINNISH POLITICAL
SYSTEM.
D. KIRBY, 575(SEER):APR72-324
"NOUVEAU CHOIX D'INSCRIPTIONS GRECQUES."
J.A.O. LARSEN, 122:OCT72-311
NOVAK, B. AMERICAN PAINTING OF THE NINE-
TEENTH CENTURY.*
R. LANIER, 56:SPRING71-118
R. REES, 592:JUL-AUG70-62
R. SQUIRRU, 37:JAN-FEB71-40
NOVAK, M. THE RISE OF THE UNMELTABLE
ETHNICS.*
K.B. CLARK, 31(ASCH):WINTER72/73-156
NOVAK, M.E. WILLIAM CONGREVE.
R.D. HUME, 173(ECS):SUMMER72-622
566:SPRING72-89
NOVAK, M.E. & G.R. GUFFEY - SEE DRYDEN,
J.
NOVALIS. IN SELBSTZEUGNISSEN UND BILD-
DOKUMENTEN. (G. SCHULZ, ED)
R. SCHLICHTING, 654(WB):8/1971-178
E. STOPP, 220(GL&L):JAN72-183
NOVALIS. NOVALIS SCHRIFTEN.* (VOL 3)
(R. SAMUEL, WITH H-J. MÄHL & G. SCHULZ,
EDS)
L.F. HELBIG, 564:OCT70-239
NOVALIS. WERKE.* (G. SCHULZ, ED)
R. LITTLEJOHNS, 220(GL&L):JAN72-196
B-M., 191(ELN):SEP71(SUPP)-159
NOVÁS CALVO, L. MANERAS DE CONTAR.
J.A. HERNÁNDEZ, 263:OCT-DEC72-432
"NOVELLA DEL GRASSO LEGNAIUOLO, NELLA
REDAZIONE DEL CODICE PALATINO 200."
P. CHERCHI, 405(MP):NOV71-159
NOVIELLI, V. WITTGENSTEIN E LA FILOSOFIA.
E. NAMER, 542:APR-JUN70-256
L.M.P., 543:JUN71-751
L. THIRY, 154:MAR71-207
NOVOTNY, F. TOULOUSE-LAUTREC.
D. FARR, 90:OCT71-614
NOVOTNY, F. & J. DOBAI. GUSTAV KLIMT.
J.P. HODIN, 290(JAAG):FALL70-143
NOWAK, J., COMP. THE JOSEPH CONRAD COL-
LECTION IN THE POLISH LIBRARY IN LONDON.
T.S. WILLIAM, 136:VOL3#1-127
NOWELL, C.E. PORTUGAL.
617(TLS):27JUL73-867
NOWELL-SMITH, S. INTERNATIONAL COPYRIGHT
LAW AND THE PUBLISHER IN THE REIGN OF
QUEEN VICTORIA.*
N. BARKER, 354:MAR70-76
NOWLAN, A. VARIOUS PERSONS NAMED KEVIN
O'BRIEN.
D. CAVANAGH, 296:FALL73-111
NOWLAN, K.B., ED. TRAVEL AND TRANSPORT
IN IRELAND.
617(TLS):1JUN73-625
NOXON, J. HUME'S PHILOSOPHICAL DEVELOP-
MENT.
617(TLS):31AUG73-1004
NOY, D. JEFET SCHWILI ERZÄHLT, HUNDERT-
UNDNEUNUNDSECHZIG JEMENITISCHE VOLK-
SERZÄHLUNGEN.
F. HARKORT, 196:BAND12HEFT2/3-284
NOZZOLI, G. I RAS DEL REGIME.
617(TLS):2MAR73-225
NÜBEL, O. MITTELALTERLICHE BEGINEN- UND
SOZIALSIEDLUNGEN IN DEN NIEDERLANDEN.
H.S. OFFLER, 182:VOL24#3-115

NÚÑEZ, A.R., ED. POESÍA EN ÉXODO.
  J.H. WARD, 238:MAY71-402
"NUOVE LETTURE DANTESCHE."
  M. POZZI, 228(GSLI):VOL147FASC458/
  459-447
NURSE, P.H., ED. THE ART OF CRITICISM.*
  H. DE LEY, 207(FR):DEC70-479
  205(FMLS):JUL70-312
NUSSER, P. MUSILS ROMANTHEORIE.
  R. VON HEYDEBRAND, 657(WW):SEP/OCT71-
  358
NUTTALL, A.D. TWO CONCEPTS OF ALLEGORY.*
  D. EBNER, 570(SQ):SPRING70-178
NUTTALL, D. A HISTORY OF PRINTING IN
  CHESTER FROM 1688 TO 1965.
  P.C.G. ISAAC, 354:DEC70-366
NUTTALL, J. POEMS: 1962-69.*
  A. CLUYSENAAR, 565:VOL12#4-68
NUTTGENS, P. YORK.
  D. LLOYD, 46:SEP71-194
NWANKWO, A.A. NIGERIA.
  617(TLS):21DEC73-1556
NWOGA, D.I., ED. WEST AFRICAN VERSE.
  H. MAES-JELINEK, 556(RLV):1971/4-491
NYBØ, G. KNUT HAMSUNS MYSTERIER.
  E. EGGEN, 172(EDDA):1970/5-315
NYE, R. THE UNEMBARRASSED MUSE.
  W. RANDEL, 27(AL):NOV72-523
NYE, R. - SEE SWINBURNE, A.C.
NYGARD, J. & R.R. DIKT OG FORM.
  A.H. LERVIK, 172(EDDA):1970/5-313
NYNYCH, S.J. ...AND LIKE I SEE IT.
  F. COGSWELL, 296:SPRING73-88


OAKES, P. EXPERIMENT AT PROTO.
  N. CALLENDAR, 441:29APR73-29
  S. HILL, 362:14JUN73-808
  617(TLS):20JUL73-825
OAKLEY, B. A SALUTE TO THE GREAT MC CAR-
  THY. LET'S HEAR IT FOR PRENDERGAST.
  L. CANTRELL, 381:MAR71-125
OATES, J.C. ANGEL FIRE.
  J. MAZZARO, 398:AUTUMN73-228
  H. VENDLER, 441:1APR73-7
OATES, J.C. ANONYMOUS SINS AND OTHER
  POEMS.*
  R.W. FRENCH, 502(PRS):SUMMER70-177
  G. MIRANDA, 648:OCT71-57
  D. ROGERS, 613:AUTUMN70-453
  R.S., 376:JAN70-110
OATES, J.C. DO WITH ME WHAT YOU WILL.
  C. BEDIENT, 441:14OCT73-1
  B. DE MOTT, 61:DEC73-127
  C. LEHMANN-HAUPT, 441:15OCT73-41
  442(NY):15OCT73-185
OATES, J.C. LOVE AND ITS DERANGEMENTS.
  S. ANDERSEN, 590:FALL72-24
  H. GREGORY, 502(PRS):SPRING71-78
  A. OBERG, 598(SOR):WINTER73-243
  639(VQR):SUMMER71-CVIII
OATES, J.C., ED. SCENES FROM AMERICAN
  LIFE.
  441:7OCT73-42
OATES, J.C. UPON THE SWEEPING FLOOD AND
  OTHER STORIES.
  J. HUNTER, 362:1MAR73-284
  617(TLS):9MAR73-257
OATES, J.C. THE WHEEL OF LOVE AND OTHER
  STORIES.
  J.H. WILDMAN, 598(SOR):WINTER73-233
  639(VQR):WINTER71-XV
OATES, J.C. WITH SHUDDERING FALL. A GAR-
  DEN OF EARTHLY DELIGHTS. EXPENSIVE
  PEOPLE.* THEM.*
  M. MUDRICK, 249(HUDR):SPRING72-142

OATES, J.C. WONDERLAND.*
  C. BEDIENT, 473(PR):1/1972-124
  M. MUDRICK, 249(HUDR):SPRING72-142
  P.M. SPACKS, 249(HUDR):SPRING72-166
OATES, S.B. TO PURGE THIS LAND WITH
  BLOOD.
  42(AR):SUMMER70-266
OATES, W.J. & L.F. A REVISED LINGUISTIC
  SURVEY OF AUSTRALIA.
  D.T. TRYON, 67:NOV72-263
OBERG, E. - SEE AMPHILOCHIUS
OBERHELMAN, H.D. ERNESTO SÁBATO.
  D.L. SHAW, 402(MLR):APR72-449
OBERTI, E. PER UNA FONDAZIONE FENOMENO-
  LOGICA DELLA CONOSCIVITÀ DELL'ARTE.
  E. NAMER, 542:APR-JUN70-253
OBICHERE, B.I. WEST AFRICAN STATES AND
  EUROPEAN EXPANSION.
  676(YR):SUMMER72-XV
OBOLENSKY, D. THE BYZANTINE COMMON-
  WEALTH.*
  D. ABRAHAMSE, 32:SEP72-657
O'BRIAN, P. H.M.S. SURPRISE.
  M. LEVIN, 441:9DEC73-48
O'BRIEN, B.T. SUMMER OF THE BLACK SUN.*
  J. MILLS, 648:JUN70-35
O'BRIEN, C.C. ALBERT CAMUS OF EUROPE
  AND AFRICA.*
  R. GAMBINO, 477:WINTER71-146
O'BRIEN, C.C. STATES OF IRELAND.*
  O.D. EDWARDS, 441:11FEB73-6
  J. HORGAN, 453:3MAY73-29
  T. LASK, 441:3FEB73-31
O'BRIEN, C.C. - SEE BURKE, E.
O'BRIEN, C.H. IDEAS OF RELIGIOUS TOLERA-
  TION AT THE TIME OF JOSEPH II.
  P.W. SCHROEDER, 32:JUN72-459
O'BRIEN, D. EMPEDOCLES' COSMIC CYCLE.*
  J.M. LEE, 63:DEC72-292
  B.S. LLAMZON, 613:SUMMER70-308
  E.L. MINAR, JR., 121(CJ):APR-MAY72-367
  H. WISMANN, 98:MAY70-462
O'BRIEN, E. NIGHT.*
  P. ADAMS, 61:FEB73-103
  S. BLACKBURN, 441:28JAN73-6
  442(NY):10FEB73-114
O'BRIEN, F. - SEE UNDER NA GOPALEEN, M.
O'BRIEN, M. & C.C. THE STORY OF IRELAND.
  O.D. EDWARDS, 441:11FEB73-6
  J. HORGAN, 453:3MAY73-29
O'BRIEN, M.J. THE SOCRATIC PARADOXES AND
  THE GREEK MIND.*
  A.W.H. ADKINS, 479(PHQ):JAN71-74
O'BRIEN, P. THE WOMAN ALONE.
  442(NY):10SEP73-135
O'BRIEN, R.C. A REPORT FROM GROUP 17.*
  617(TLS):2FEB73-129
O'BRIEN, T. IF I DIE IN A COMBAT ZONE,
  BOX ME UP AND SHIP ME HOME.
  P. ADAMS, 61:MAY73-122
  A. GOTTLIEB, 441:1JUL73-10
  442(NY):16JUL73-80
  617(TLS):19OCT73-1269
OCAMPO, V. DIÁLOGO CON BORGES.
  C.A.W. CAPSAS, 238:MAR71-202
OCHS, I. WOLFRAMS "WILLEHALM"-EINGANG IM
  LICHTE DER FRÜHMITTELHOCHDEUTSCHEN
  GEISTLICHEN DICHTUNG.*
  P. OCHSENBEIN, 657(WW):NOV/DEC70-430
OCKHAM, WILLIAM OF. SCRIPTUM IN LIBRUM
  PRIMUM SENTENTIARUM, ORDINATIO. (VOL
  2) (S. BROWN & G. GÁL, EDS)
  O. LANG, 182:VOL24#7/8-338
O'CONNELL, D. THE CORRESPONDENCE OF
  DANIEL O'CONNELL. (VOLS 1&2) (M.R.
  O'CONNELL, ED)
  617(TLS):8JUN73-637

O'CONNELL, D.P. RICHELIEU.
    J.R. VIGNERY, 50(ARQ):AUTUMN70-280
O'CONNELL, M.R. THE OXFORD CONSPIRATORS.*
    L.F. BARMANN, 377:NOV72-186
    E. KELLY, 613:WINTER70-634
O'CONNELL, R.J. ST. AUGUSTINE'S EARLY
    THEORY OF MAN, A.D. 386-391.* ST.
    AUGUSTINE'S "CONFESSIONS."*
    M.T. CLARK, 258:SEP71-427
O'CONNOR, D.J. AQUINAS AND NATURAL LAW.*
    J.B., 543:MAR71-546
O'CONNOR, F. MYSTERY AND MANNERS.*
    (S. & R. FITZGERALD, EDS)
    F.P.W. MC DOWELL, 598(SOR):AUTUMN73-
    998
    W.A. SESSIONS, 573(SSF):SUMMER71-491
O'CONNOR, F. FLANNERY O'CONNOR: THE
    COMPLETE STORIES.*
    R. DRAKE, 396(MODA):SUMMER72-322
    M.J. FRIEDMAN, 578:SPRING73-116
    F.P.W. MC DOWELL, 598(SOR):AUTUMN73-
    998
O'CONNOR, F. A SET OF VARIATIONS. (H.
    O'DONOVAN, ED)
    G. CORE, 219(GAR):SUMMER70-257
O'CONNOR, F.V., ED. THE NEW DEAL ART
    PROJECTS.
    D. AARON, 473(PR):FALL72-615
    H. KRAMER, 441:28JAN73-1
O'CONNOR, J., ED. MODERN MATERIALISM.
    D.M. JOHNSON, 154:MAR71-175
O'CONNOR, J.D. BETTER ENGLISH PRONUNCIA-
    TION.
    W. PRAEGER, 38:BAND88HEFT1-119
O'CONNOR, J.J. "AMADIS DE GAULE" AND ITS
    INFLUENCE ON ELIZABETHAN LITERATURE.*
    K. DUNCAN-JONES, 447(N&Q):JUN71-233
    T.P. HARRISON, 551(RENQ):SUMMER71-265
    J.R. ROTHSCHILD, 207(FR):MAR71-811
O'CONNOR, P.F. OLD MORALS, SMALL CONTI-
    NENTS, DARKER TIMES.*
    M. ANANIA, 473(PR):FALL72-630
O'CONNOR, R. PRINCIPLES OF FARM BUSI-
    NESS ANALYSIS AND MANAGEMENT.
    617(TLS):19OCT73-1289
O'CONNOR, U. BRENDAN.
    M. PAGE, 397(MD):FEB72-485
O'CONOR, J.F., ED & TRANS. THE SOKOLOV
    INVESTIGATION OF THE ALLEGED MURDER OF
    THE RUSSIAN IMPERIAL FAMILY.
    617(TLS):9FEB73-144
O'DANIEL, T.B., ED. LANGSTON HUGHES,
    BLACK GENIUS.
    P. BUTCHER, 27(AL):MAR72-168
ODDIE, W. DICKENS AND CARLYLE.
    617(TLS):2MAR73-235
ODLE, R. SALT OF OUR YOUTH.*
    N. LEWIS, 362:23AUG73-255
O'DOHERTY, B. AMERICAN MASTERS.
    L. NOCHLIN, 441:2DEC73-30
O'DONNELL, K.P. & D.F. POWERS, WITH J.
    MC CARTHY. "JOHNNY, WE HARDLY KNEW
    YE."
    P. ADAMS, 61:JAN73-100
    C. LEHMANN-HAUPT, 441:12JAN73-35
    C.L. MEE, JR., 441:21JAN73-6
O'DONNELL, L. DON'T WEAR YOUR WEDDING
    RING.
    N. CALLENDAR, 441:19AUG73-13
O'DONOVAN, H. - SEE O'CONNOR, F.
O'DRISCOLL, R., ED. THEATRE AND NATION-
    ALISM IN TWENTIETH-CENTURY IRELAND.*
    T.R. HENN, 402(MLR):OCT72-879
    N.H. MAC KENZIE, 150(DR):AUTUMN71-433
    B.F. TYSON, 397(MD):FEB72-480
    102(CANL):WINTER72-104

OELLERS, N. SCHILLER - ZEITGENOSSE ALLER
    EPOCHEN. (PT 1)
    O. FAMBACH, 680(ZDP):BAND90HEFT4-588
OELMÜLLER, W. DIE UNBEFRIEDIGTE AUFKLÄR-
    UNG.
    W. STEINBECK, 342:BAND61HEFT4-529
OERTEL, R. EARLY ITALIAN PAINTING TO
    1400.
    B. COLE, 56:AUTUMN70-306
    A. SMART, 39:FEB70-163
OESER, E. BEGRIFF UND SYSTEMATIK DER
    ABSTRAKTION.*
    H. HOLZ, 53(AGP):BAND53HEFT2-208
OESTERLEY, H., ED. SHAKESPEARE'S JEST
    BOOK.
    M.A. SHAABER, 551(RENQ):WINTER71-568
OESTREICH, G. GEIST UND GESTALT DES
    FRÜHMODERNEN STAATES.
    G. STRAUSS, 182:VOL24#13/14-561
O'FAOLAIN, J. GODDED AND CODDED.
    J.P., 376:APR71-129
O'FAOLAIN, J. THREE LOVERS.
    P.M. SPACKS, 249(HUDR):SPRING72-163
O'FAOLAIN, J. & L. MARTINES. NOT IN GOD'S
    IMAGE.
    M. ELLMANN, 453:1NOV73-18
O'FAOLAIN, S. THE TALKING TREES.
    E. GLOVER, 565:VOL12#3-58
OFER, G. THE SERVICE SECTOR IN SOVIET
    ECONOMIC GROWTH.
    617(TLS):16NOV73-1406
OFFNER, R. & K. STEINWEG. A CORPUS OF
    FLORENTINE PAINTING: GIOVANNI DEL
    BIONDO.* (PT 1)
    B. COLE, 54:JUN70-200
OFFORD, M.Y., ED. THE BOOK OF THE KNIGHT
    OF THE TOWER. (W. CAXTON, TRANS)
    J.M. FERRIER, 382(MAE):1972/3-278
OGBURN, C. WINESPRING MOUNTAIN.
    M. LEVIN, 441:9SEP73-42
OGDEN, C.K. BASIC ENGLISH.
    J. THIELEMANS, 556(RLV):1970/6-684
OGDEN, J. ISAAC D'ISRAELI.*
    R.W. KING, 541(RES):FEB71-111
OGDEN, M.S. - SEE DE CHAULIAC, G.
OGILBY, J. THE FABLES OF AESOP PARA-
    PHRAS'D IN VERSE (1668).
    R. ELLRODT, 189(EA):JUL-SEP70-338
OGILVIE, E. STRAWBERRIES IN THE SEA.
    M. LEVIN, 441:26AUG73-32
OGILVIE, R.M. THE ROMANS AND THEIR GODS
    IN THE AGE OF AUGUSTUS.*
    G. LUCK, 24:APR72-373
OGILVY, J.D.A. BOOKS KNOWN TO THE ENG-
    LISH, 597-1066.
    H. GNEUSS, 38:BAND89HEFT1-129
OGLEY, R. THE UNITED NATIONS AND EAST-
    WEST RELATIONS.
    617(TLS):20APR73-434
O'GORMAN, D. DIDEROT THE SATIRIST.
    (FRENCH TITLE: DIDEROT SATIRIQUE.)
    G.N. LAIDLAW, 401(MLQ):JUN72-198
    J. MAYER, 557(RSH):OCT-DEC71-668
    I.H. SMITH, 67:MAY72-96
O'GORMAN, F. EDMUND BURKE.
    617(TLS):12OCT73-1260
O'GORMAN, J.F. - SEE FRANKL, P.
O'GRADY, A. OPERATION MIDAS.
    M. LEVIN, 441:15JUL73-16
O'GRADY, D. THE DYING GAUL. OFF
    LICENCE.
    S. FAUCHEREAU, 98:MAY70-438
OGUNBOWALE, P.O. THE ESSENTIALS OF THE
    YORUBA LANGUAGE.
    E.C. ROWLANDS, 315(JAL):VOL10PT2-61
O'HAGAN, T. - SEE POULANTZAS, N.

O'HARA, F. THE COLLECTED POEMS OF FRANK
O'HARA. (D. ALLEN, ED)
    W. DICKEY, 249(HUDR):SUMMER72-308
    M.G. PERLOFF, 659:WINTER73-97
    T. SHAPCOTT, 491:APR73-40
O'HARA, J. THE TIME ELEMENT AND OTHER
STORIES.*
    617(TLS):21SEP73-1072
O HEHIR, B. EXPANS'D HIEROGLYPHICKS.*
    H. CASTROP, 541(RES):MAY71-210
    A. WILLIAMS, 405(MP):MAY71-384
O HEHIR, B. A GAELIC LEXICON FOR "FINNE-
GANS WAKE."
    A.M.L. KNUTH, 433:JAN70-92
O HEHIR, B. HARMONY FROM DISCORDS.*
    H. BERRY, 551(RENQ):AUTUMN71-414
    H. KELLIHER, 541(RES):FEB71-79
    P. LEGOUIS, 189(EA):JUL-SEP71-292
    A. WILLIAMS, 405(MP):MAY71-384
O'HIGGINS, P. CENSORSHIP IN BRITAIN.
    617(TLS):5JAN73-4
"OHIO STATE UNIVERSITY: THE FIRST HUNDRED
YEARS."
    B.C. HARDING, 14:JAN71-63
OHKAWA, K. & OTHERS, EDS. AGRICULTURE
AND ECONOMIC GROWTH.
    H.T. PATRICK, 293(JAST):FEB71-463
OHL, H. BILD UND WIRKLICHKEIT.
    K. RICHTER, 657(WW):SEP/OCT70-354
    V. SANDER, 222(GR):MAY71-229
    H.C. SASSE, 220(GL&L):JAN72-153
    H. SCHLAFFER, 680(ZDP):BAND89HEFT2-
    287
OHLIN, L.E., ED. PRISONERS IN AMERICA.
    D.J. ROTHMAN, 441:27MAY73-4
ØHRGAARD, P. C.F. MEYER.*
    G. RODGER, 220(GL&L):JUL72-401
OIJI, T., ED. THE VISION OF PIERS PLOW-
MAN.
    R.H. ROBBINS, 439(NM):1970/3-524
OINAS, F. BASIC COURSE IN ESTONIAN.
(REV)
    A. RAUN, 361:VOL26#1-110
OINAS, F.J. STUDIES IN FINNIC-SLAVIC
FOLKLORE RELATIONS.*
    A. KURLENTS, 292(JAF):JUL-SEP71-346
OKAMOTO, S. THE JAPANESE OLIGARCHY AND
THE RUSSO-JAPANESE WAR.*
    P. DUUS, 293(JAST):AUG71-897
    P. LOWE, 575(SEER):JAN72-132
O'KANE, E.S. - SEE DE ESPINOSA, F.
OKASHA, E. HAND-LIST OF ANGLO-SAXON NON-
RUNIC INSCRIPTIONS.
    E.G. STANLEY, 447(N&Q):AUG71-305
O'KEEFFE, T., ED. MYLES.
    617(TLS):13JUL73-798
OKIN, J.P-D. & C.J. SCHMIDT. LE FRANÇAIS:
COMMENÇONS.
    E. POPPER, 207(FR):MAY71-1135
OKKEN, L. EIN BEITRAG ZUR ENTWIRRUNG
EINER KONTAMINIERTEN MANUSKRIPTTRADI-
TION.
    G.T. GILLESPIE, 220(GL&L):JUL72-388
OKLADNIKOV, A.P. & OTHERS, EDS. ISTORIIA
SIBIRIA. (VOL 2, SECTION 1)
    A.S. DONNELLY, 104:WINTER72-639
OKPAKU, J., ED. NIGERIA.*
    H.R. LYNCH, 441:7JAN73-30
OKUDZHAVA, B. THE EXTRAORDINARY ADVEN-
TURES OF SECRET AGENT SHIPOV IN PURSUIT
OF COUNT LEO TOLSTOY IN THE YEAR 1862.
    617(TLS):29JUN73-737
OLAFSON, F.A. PRINCIPLES AND PERSONS.*
    R.J.B., 543:DEC70-343
Ó LAOGHAIRE, A.T-A.P. MY OWN STORY.
    617(TLS):25MAY73-597

"THE OLD AND THE NEW TESTAMENTS OF THE
HOLY BIBLE." (REVISED STANDARD VERSION)
    617(TLS):2MAR73-243
OLDENBOURG, Z. THE HEIRS OF THE KING-
DOM.*
    42(AR):SUMMER71-284
OLDENBURG, C. PROPOSALS FOR MONUMENTS
AND BUILDINGS, 1965-69.*
    D. IRWIN, 39:APR71-342
OLDENOW, K. THE SPREAD OF PRINTING:
GREENLAND.
    R. CAVE, 503:SUMMER70-99
    B. JUEL-JENSEN, 354:MAR71-72
OLDEROGGE, D. NEGRO ART.*
    E.L.R. MEYEROWITZ, 39:JUL70-80
OLDEROGGE, D.A., ED. KAMUS NA HAUSA-
RASHANCI.
    A.H.M. KIRK-GREENE, 69:OCT71-348
OLEARIUS, A. VERMEHRTE NEWE BESCHREIBUNG
DER MUSCOWITISCHEN VND PERSISCHEN
REYSE. (D. LOHMEIER, ED)
    E. KUNZE, 439(NM):1971/3-572
O'LEARY, D.F. BOLÍVAR AND THE WAR OF
INDEPENDENCE. (R.F. MC NERNEY, JR.,
ED & TRANS)
    A.C. AMBROSE, 37:MAR71-42
    D.A. DEL RÍO, 263:APR-JUN72-168
OLIPHANT, L. ELGIN'S MISSION TO CHINA
AND JAPAN.
    M.V. LAMBERTI, 318(JAOS):OCT-DEC71-526
OLIVA, L.J., ED. CATHERINE THE GREAT.
    D.M. GRIFFITHS, 32:DEC72-886
OLIVA, L.J., ED. PETER THE GREAT.*
    J. CRACRAFT, 550(RUSR):JUL71-314
DE OLIVEIRA MARQUES, A.H. HISTORY OF
PORTUGAL.
    617(TLS):27JUL73-867
OLIVER, A. BENJAMIN CONSTANT.
    A. FAIRLIE, 208(FS):JAN72-83
OLIVER, A. PORTRAITS OF JOHN QUINCY
ADAMS AND HIS WIFE.
    J.D. MACOLL, 14:APR71-193
    639(VQR):SPRING71-LXXXIII
OLIVER, A. - SEE CURWEN, S.
OLIVER, C.F. & S. SILLS, EDS. CONTEMPOR-
ARY BLACK DRAMA.
    M. COINER, 397(MD):DEC71-362
OLIVER, H.J. - SEE SHAKESPEARE, W.
OLIVER, M., ED. TRAVEL IN AQUATINT AND
LITHOGRAPHY, 1770-1860.
    617(TLS):5JAN73-20
OLIVER, P. SAVANNAH SYNCOPATORS.*
    R.D. ABRAHAMS, 650(WF):APR71-150
OLIVER, P., ED. SHELTER AND SOCIETY.*
    A.B., 45:SEP70-141
    T. CROSBY, 46:SEP70-200
OLIVER, R. POEMS WITHOUT NAMES.
    S. MANNING, 589:APR72-334
    E. REISS, 301(JEGP):JAN72-112
    R.D. STEVICK, 141:SUMMER71-324
OLIVER, R.T. COMMUNICATION AND CULTURE
IN ANCIENT INDIA AND CHINA.
    G. PHIFER, 583:SPRING72-329
OLIVIER DE SARDAN, J-P. SYSTÈME DES RE-
LATIONS ÉCONOMIQUES ET SOCIALES CHEZ
LES WOGO (NIGER).
    E. BERNUS, 69:JAN71-64
OLIVIER DE SARDAN, J-P. LES VOLEURS
D'HOMMES.
    E. BERNUS, 69:JAN71-73
OLLER, J.S. - SEE UNDER SANZ OLLER, J.
OLLIER, C. ENIGMA.
    617(TLS):10AUG73-921
OLLIGS, H., ED. GERMAN HISTORY OF WALL-
PAPER.
    E.A.E., 135:FEB71-138
OLMO, A. - SEE DI SANTA ROSA, S.

OLMSTED, F.L. CIVILIZING AMERICAN
CITIES. (S.B. SUTTON, ED)
    H.H. REED, 44:OCT71-8
    I.R. STEWART, 576:DEC71-331
OLMSTED, F.L. LANDSCAPE INTO CITYSCAPE.
(A. FEIN, ED) THE COTTON KINGDOM.
(A.M. SCHLESINGER, ED) WALKS AND TALKS
OF AN AMERICAN FARMER IN ENGLAND.
    I.R. STEWART, 576:DEC71-331
OLMSTED, F.L., JR. & T. KIMBALL, EDS.
FREDERICK LAW OLMSTED.
    I.R. STEWART, 576:DEC71-331
OLNEY, R.J. LINCOLNSHIRE POLITICS 1832-
1885.
    617(TLS):16NOV73-1388
OLSON, A.G. & R.M. BROWN, EDS. ANGLO-
AMERICAN POLITICAL RELATIONS, 1675-1775.
    J.A. SCHUTZ, 656(WMQ):APR71-312
OLSON, C. ARCHAEOLOGIST OF MORNING.*
    A. CLUYSENAAR, 565:VOL12#4-68
    42(AR):SUMMER71-284
OLSON, C. THE MAXIMUS POEMS.
    T. EAGLETON, 565:VOL12#1-77
OLSON, E. TRAGEDY AND THE THEORY OF
DRAMA.
    V. KLOTZ, 38:BAND88HEFT1-130
OLSON, L. JAPAN IN POSTWAR ASIA.
    E.C. HARRELL, 293(JAST):FEB71-471
OLTHUIS, J.H. FACTS, VALUES AND ETHICS.
    M.B.M., 543:JUN71-752
O LUING, S. I DIE IN A GOOD CAUSE.
    M. ASHE, 159(DM):SUMMER/AUTUMN70-124
OLYMPIODORUS. IN PLATONIS GORGIAM COM-
MENTARIA. (L.G. WESTERINK, ED)
    P. LOUIS, 555:VOL45FASC2-343
"OMAGGIO A VICO."
    R. PARENTI, 548(RCSF):APR-JUN70-203
O'MALLEY, J.W. GILES OF VITERBO ON CHURCH
AND REFORM.
    D.J. FITZ GERALD, 551(RENQ):SPRING71-
    83
O'MALLEY, T.P. TERTULLIAN AND THE BIBLE.
    P. PETITMENGIN, 555:VOL45FASC1-119
OMAN, C. CAROLINE SILVER 1625-1688.
    I. FINLAY, 39:SEP71-246
    J.F.H., 135:JUL71-226
OMAN, C. THE GOLDEN AGE OF HISPANIC
SILVER, 1400-1665.
    C.H., 135:MAR70-200
    J.H. HARVEY, 39:MAY70-401
    P.E. MULLER, 54:DEC70-446
OMAN, C. THE WIZARD OF THE NORTH.
    617(TLS):4MAY73-494
OMAR KHAYYÁM. RUBAIJAT VON OMAR CHAJJAM.
(E. FITZ GERALD, TRANS; TRANS INTO
GERMAN BY H.W. NORDMEYER)
    M. LOI, 549(RLC):JUL-SEP71-438
O'NAN, M. THE ROLE OF MIND IN HUGO,
FAULKNER, BECKETT, AND GRASS.
    R. HARRISON, 219(GAR):FALL70-380
ONDAATJE, M. THE COLLECTED WORKS OF
BILLY THE KID.*
    R.S., 376:APR71-127
    A. SCHROEDER, 102(CANL):WINTER72-80
    P. STEVENS, 529(QQ):SUMMER71-326
ONDAATJE, M. RAT JELLY.
    B.D. BARRIE, 198:SUMMER73-119
"ONE HUNDRED AND TWENTY TALES FROM IRAQ."
    E. SCHOENFELD, 196:BAND11HEFT1/2-183
O'NEIL, R. & M. DONOVAN. CHILDREN,
CHURCH AND GOD.
    B. COOKE, 628:FALL71-82
O'NEILL, J. - SEE HYPPOLITE, J.
O'NEILL, J. - SEE MERLEAU-PONTY, M.
O'NEILL, J.C. THE RECOVERY OF PAUL'S
LETTER TO THE GALATIANS.
    617(TLS):18MAY73-559

O'NEILL, J.P. WORKABLE DESIGN.
    617(TLS):30NOV73-1467
O'NEILL, K. ANDRÉ GIDE AND THE "ROMAN
D'AVENTURE."*
    D. MOUTOTE, 535(RHL):MAR-APR71-327
O'NEILL, P.G. JAPANESE NAMES.
    617(TLS):29JUN73-757
O'NEILL, R.J. GENERAL GIAP.
    M. OSBORNE, 293(JAST):NOV70-239
ONETTI, J.C. JUNTACADÁVERES. (3RD ED)
    D. CASTIEL, 238:MAR71-209
ONG, W.J. THE PRESENCE OF THE WORD.
    D. CRYSTAL, 47(ARL):[N.S.]VOL1-102
    M. OPPENHEIMER, JR., 186(ETC.):MAR70-
    118
    T.S. VERNON, 599:SPRING70-169
ONIONS, C.T. MODERN ENGLISH SYNTAX.
(NEW ED PREPARED BY B.D.H. MILLER)
    R.W.Z., 179(ES):DEC71-592
ONORATO, M.P., ED. PHILIPPINE BIBLIO-
GRAPHY (1899-1946).
    E. WICKBERG, 318(JAOS):OCT-DEC71-521
ONORATO, R.J. THE CHARACTER OF THE POET.*
    T. MC FARLAND, 676(YR):WINTER72-279
    J. WORDSWORTH, 401(MLQ):DEC72-460
OOMEN, U. AUTOMATISCHE SYNTAKTISCHE
ANALYSE.
    U. SCHWARTZ, 260(IF):BAND75-245
    W. TOSH, 361:VOL25#3-322
VAN OORSCHOT, T.G.M. - SEE SPEE, F.
OOSTERHUIS, H. PRAYERS, POEMS & SONGS.
    G.B. HARRISON, 363:FEB71-62
OOSTHUIZEN, G.C. POST-CHRISTIANITY IN
AFRICA.
    F.B. WELBOURN, 69:APR71-175
OPDAHL, K.M. THE NOVELS OF SAUL BELLOW.*
    R.H. FOSSUM, 594:SPRING70-99
OPIE, I. & P. CHILDREN'S GAMES IN STREET
AND PLAYGROUND.
    N. CROOK, 97(CQ):SPRING71-266
OPIE, I. & P., EDS. THE OXFORD BOOK OF
CHILDREN'S VERSE.
    R. BLYTHE, 362:7JUN73-763
    C. LEHMANN-HAUPT, 441:16MAY73-45
OPITZ, M. MARTIN OPITZ: GESAMMELTE
WERKE.* (VOL 1) (G. SCHULZ-BEHREND,
ED)
    J-U. FECHNER, 190:BAND64HEFT3/4-433
OPITZ, M. WELTLICHE POEMATA 1644. (PT
1) (E. TRUNZ, ED) BUCH VON DER DEUT-
SCHEN POETEREY (1624). (C. SOMMER, ED)
    H. RÜDIGER, 52:BAND6HEFT1-77
OPPÉ, A.P. RAPHAEL. (C. MITCHELL, ED)
    J.D., 135:MAR71-215
    C. GOULD, 39:APR71-344
    C. PEDRETTI, 275(IQ):SPRING-SUMMER72-
    103
OPPEL, H. ENGLISCH-DEUTSCHE LITERATUR-
BEZIEHUNGEN.
    W.F. SCHIRMER, 72:BAND209HEFT1/3-135
OPPEL, H. DIE GERICHTSSZENE IN "KING
LEAR."*
    E. EISENBACH, 430(NS):FEB70-103
OPPEL, H., ED. DIE MODERNE ENGLISCHE
LYRIK.*
    H. BONHEIM, 38:BAND89HEFT4-549
OPPEN, G. DISCRETE SERIES.
    M. HELLER, 600:WINTER71-156
OPPENHEIM, L. LA MÉSOPOTAMIE.
    D. REUILLARD, 98:OCT71-910
OPPENHEIMER, J. IN TIME.
    T. OLSON, 600:WINTER71-150
OPPENHEJM, R. IN ANDALUSIEN SIND DIE
ESEL BLAU.
    C. SÁNCHEZ, 430(NS):OCT70-536
OPPERMANN, H. WILHELM RAABE IN SELBST-
ZEUGNISSEN UND BILDDOKUMENTEN.
    V. SANDER, 222(GR):MAY71-230

ORAM, D. AN INDIVIDUAL NOTE.
  T. CARY, 415:JUN72-564
ORBÁN, Á.P. LES DÉNOMINATIONS DU MONDE
  CHEZ LES PREMIERS AUTEURS CHRÉTIENS.
  H. MUSURILLO, 124:SEP71-25
ORBELL, M., ED. CONTEMPORARY MAORI
  WRITING.
  B. PEARSON, 368:MAR71-89
ORCIBAL, J. LE PROCÈS DES "MAXIMES DES
  SAINTS" DEVANT LE SAINT-OFFICE AVEC
  LA RELATION DES CONGRÉGATIONS CARDI-
  NALICES ET LES "OBSERVATIONES" INÉDITES
  DE BOSSUET.
  J-L. GORÉ, 535(RHL):JAN-FEB71-84
ORD-HUME, A.W.J.G. CLOCKWORK MUSIC.
  617(TLS):14SEP73-1046
ORDERIC VITALIS. THE ECCLESIASTICAL
  HISTORY OF ORDERIC VITALIS. (VOL 4,
  BKS 7 & 8) (M. CHIBNALL, ED & TRANS)
  617(TLS):10AUG73-937
ORDIN-NASHCHOKIN, A.L. RANNIAIA PEREPISKA
  A.L. ORDINA-NASHCHOKINA (1642-1645 GG.)
  (I.V. GALAKTIONOV, ED)
  C.B. O'BRIEN, 104:WINTER72-606
OREL, H. THE DEVELOPMENT OF W.B. YEATS.
  E. ENGELBERG, 636(VP):WINTER70-354
  N.H. MAC KENZIE, 529(QQ):AUTUMN71-462
OREL, H. ENGLISH ROMANTIC POETS AND THE
  ENLIGHTENMENT.
  617(TLS):21SEP73-1090
ORESME, N. LE LIVRE DU CIEL ET DU MONDE.
  (A.D. MENUT & A.J. DENOMY, EDS)
  P.J. ARCHAMBAULT, 593:WINTER72-378
  P. SHARRATT, 478:JUL70-177
ORESME, N. NICOLE ORESME AND THE MEDI-
  EVAL GEOMETRY OF QUALITIES AND MO-
  TIONS.* (M. CLAGETT, ED)
  P. SHARRATT, 478:JUL70-177
ORGAN, T.W. THE HINDU QUEST FOR THE PER-
  FECTION OF MAN.
  L.G., 543:JUN71-753
  J.M. KOLLER, 485(PE&W):JUL71-340
  S.C. THAKUR, 479(PHQ):JUL71-284
ORGEL, S. - SEE JONSON, B.
ORGEL, S. - SEE MARLOWE, C.
ORGILL, D. THE "JASIUS" PURSUIT.
  N. CALLENDAR, 441:22JUL73-12
  617(TLS):18MAY73-562
ORGILL, D. T-34 RUSSIAN ARMOR.
  E. O'BALLANCE, 32:SEP72-680
"ORIENTAL MUSIC: A SELECTED DISCOGRAPHY."
  F.J. GILLIS, 187:JAN73-135
ORLEANS, L.A. EVERY FIFTH CHILD.
  617(TLS):12JAN73-27
ORLOW, D. THE HISTORY OF THE NAZI PARTY.
  E. ROTH, 619(TC):VOL179#1047-48
ORMOND, J. DEFINITION OF A WATERFALL.
  617(TLS):19OCT73-1276
ORMOND, R. JOHN SINGER SARGENT.
  M.E., 135:FEB71-138
  M. KINGSBURY, 56:AUTUMN71-363
  M. LEVEY, 90:OCT71-615
  S. SPECTOR, 58:NOV70-I5
  M.S. YOUNG, 39:APR71-340
ORNEA, Z. ŢĂRĂNISMUL.
  P. EIDELBERG, 32:SEP72-720
ORR, D. ITALIAN RENAISSANCE DRAMA IN
  ENGLAND BEFORE 1625.
  R.D.S. JACK, 402(MLR):APR72-398
ORR, G. BURNING THE EMPTY NESTS.
  H. LEIBOWITZ, 441:12AUG73-5
ORR, J. A PORTRAIT OF JULIE.
  617(TLS):18MAY73-565
ORREY, L. A CONCISE HISTORY OF OPERA.
  617(TLS):5JAN73-14
ORRICK, A.H., ED. NORDICA ET ANGLICA.
  H. BECK, 38:BAND89HEFT3-378
  A.H. CHAPPEL, 353:JUL71-103

ORTALI, R. UN POÈTE DE LA MORT: JEAN-
  BAPTISTE CHASSIGNET.*
  G. DOTTIN, 557(RSH):APR-JUN70-318
ORTEGA Y GASSET, J. AN INTERPRETATION OF
  UNIVERSAL HISTORY.
  P. ADAMS, 61:JUL73-103
ORTEGA Y GASSET, J. SOME LESSONS IN
  METAPHYSICS.
  A. DONOSO, 258:DEC71-599
ORTH, R.H. & A.R. FERGUSON - SEE EMERSON,
  R.W.
ORTH, W. DIE PROVINZIALPOLITIK DES
  TIBERIUS.
  E.W. GRAY, 123:DEC72-383
  S.I. OOST, 122:JUL72-225
ORTIZ, A. & E. ZIERER. SET THEORY AND
  LINGUISTICS.*
  R.C. SCHANK, 353:JUN71-119
  A.M. ZWICKY, 206:NOV70-584
ORWELL, G. THE COLLECTED ESSAYS, JOURNAL-
  ISM AND LETTERS OF GEORGE ORWELL. (S.
  ORWELL & I. ANGUS, EDS)
  R. MC CORMACK, 606(TAMR):#58-77
OSBORN, M. & J. RIGGS. "MR. MAC."
  R.P. KYKER, 583:WINTER71-216
OSBORNE, C. - SEE STOKER, A.
OSBORNE, C. - SEE VERDI, G.
OSBORNE, H. AESTHETICS AND ART THEORY.*
  N. CALAS, 58:APR71-19
  S.C. PEPPER, 290(JAAC):SUMMER71-542
  639(VQR):WINTER71-XLIII
OSBORNE, H., ED. AESTHETICS IN THE
  MODERN WORLD.
  A. SHIELDS, 290(JAAC):WINTER70-271
OSBORNE, H. THE ART OF APPRECIATION.*
  R.K. ELLIOTT, 89(BJA):WINTER72-79
  D. WALSH, 479(PHQ):JUL71-283
OSBORNE, H., ED. THE OXFORD COMPANION TO
  ART.*
  J. MASHECK, 592:NOV70-212
  639(VQR):WINTER71-XLIV
OSBORNE, J. THE NATURALIST DRAMA IN GER-
  MANY.*
  W.A. REICHART, 406:SPRING72-86
OSBORNE, J. TIME PRESENT (AND) THE HOTEL
  IN AMSTERDAM.
  J.C. FIELD, 556(RLV):1971/3-345
OSBORNE, J. VERY MUCH LIKE A WHALE.
  L. RUSSELL, 376:OCT71-133
OSBORNE, J.W. JOHN CARTWRIGHT.
  617(TLS):5JAN73-9
OSBORNE, R., S. TILLES & C. PÉREZ. VOCES
  Y VISTAS.
  C.F. WHITMER, 238:MAR71-218
OSERS, E. CHINESE FOLKTALES.
  J. SIMPSON, 203:SUMMER71-169
OSGOOD, C.E. & T.A. SEBEOK, EDS. PSYCHO-
  LINGUISTICS [BOUND TOGETHER WITH] DIE-
  BOLD, A.R. A SURVEY OF PSYCHOLINGUIS-
  TIC RESEARCH, 1954-1964. (2ND ED)
  B. MASPFUHL, 682(ZPSK):BAND24HEFT1/2-
  133
OSGOOD, R.E. THE WEARY AND THE WARY.
  G. BARRACLOUGH, 453:14JUN73-27
O'SHARKEY, E.M. - SEE BERNANOS, G.
OSIČKA, A. & I. POLDAUF. ANGLICKO-ČESKÝ
  SLOVNÍK S DODATKY.
  S.E. MANN, 575(SEER):APR72-288
OSLEY, A.S. LUMINARIO.
  617(TLS):6APR73-400
OSLEY, A.S. MERCATOR.*
  G.R. CRONE, 354:SEP70-258
  R. LISTER, 503:WINTER69-188
  R. MC LEAN, 135:NOV70-216
OSMAN, N. KLEINES LEXIKON UNTERGEGANGEN-
  ER WÖRTER.
  E. ÖHMANN, 182:VOL24#23/24-857

OSTER, D. ON NE SE REFAIT PAS.
   H. MICHOT-DIETRICH, 207(FR):OCT70-181
OSTER, H. LIVING COUNTRY BLUES.
   R.D. ABRAHAMS, 650(WF):APR71-150
   B. JACKSON, 292(JAF):APR-JUN71-253
OSTER, P. LES DIEUX.
   R.R. HUBERT, 207(FR):DEC70-420
OSTHOFF, W. THEATERGESANG UND DARSTEL-
LENDE MUSIK IN DER ITALIENISCHEN
RENAISSANCE (15. UND 16. JAHRHUNDERT).
   H.M. BROWN, 414(MQ):OCT71-671
OSTROVSKY, A.N. ARTISTES AND ADMIRERS.*
   A. RENDLE, 157:AUTUMN70-77
   205(FMLS):APR71-193
OSTROVSKY, E. VOYEUR VOYANT.*
   42(AR):WINTER71/72-592
OSTWALD, M. NOMOS AND THE BEGINNINGS OF
THE ATHENIAN DEMOCRACY.*
   M. CHAMBERS, 24:APR72-367
   E. WILL, 555:VOL45FASC1-102
O'SULLIVAN, V., ED. AN ANTHOLOGY OF
TWENTIETH CENTURY NEW ZEALAND POETRY.*
   L.W. MICHAELSON, 134(CP):SPRING71-54
   D.C. WALKER, 368:DEC70-356
OSWALD, J.G., COMP & TRANS. SOVIET
IMAGE OF CONTEMPORARY LATIN AMERICA.
   W.E. RATLIFF, 550(RUSR):OCT71-404
   L.S. THOMPSON, 263:OCT-DEC72-412
OTIS, B. OVID AS AN EPIC POET. (2ND ED)
   W.S. ANDERSON, 124:SEP71-27
OTKUPŠČIKOV, J.V. IZ ISTORII INDOEVROP-
EJSKOGO SLOVO-OBRAZOVANIJA.
   R. KATIČIĆ, 260(IF):BAND75-284
   S. LEVIN, 215(GL):VOL10#1-49
O'TOOLE, G. AN AGENT ON THE OTHER SIDE.
   N. CALLENDAR, 441:25NOV73-49
O'TOOLE, S. CONFESSIONS OF AN AMERICAN
SCHOLAR.
   639(VQR):WINTER71-XXXIII
OTT, P. ZUR SPRACHE DER JÄGER IN DER
DEUTSCHEN SCHWEIZ.
   B.J. KOEKKOEK, 301(JEGP):APR72-295
   E.H. YARRILL, 182:VOL24#4-154
OTT, W. METRISCHE ANALYSEN ZUR "ARS
POETICA" DES HORAZ.
   M.J. MC GANN, 123:JUN72-273
   J. SOUBIRAN, 555:VOL45FASC2-365
   S.V.F. WAITE, 487:WINTER71-406
OTTAVIANO, C. LA LEGGE DELLA BELLEZZA
COME LEGGE UNIVERSALE DELLA NATURA.
   H. BREDIN, 89(BJA):WINTER72-90
OTTAVIANO, C. METAFISICA DELL'ESSERE
PARZIALE.
   E. NAMER, 542:JAN-MAR70-102
OTTAWAY, H. WALTON.
   C. PALMER, 415:DEC72-1185
OTTEN, H. & V. SOUČEK. DAS GELÜBDE DER
KÖNIGIN PUDUHEPA AN DIE GÖTTIN LELWANI.
   G. NEUMANN, 260(IF):BAND75-292
OTTEN, K. DER ENGLISCHE ROMAN VOM 16.
ZUM 19. JAHRHUNDERT.
   K.T. VON ROSADOR, 72:BAND209HEFT4/6-
414
OTTER, H.S. A FUNCTIONAL LANGUAGE EXAM-
INATION.
   G. DE LANDSHEERE, 556(RLV):1970/6-685
OTTO, W.F. DIONYSUS, MYTH AND CULT.*
(FRENCH TITLE: DIONYSOS.)
   A. HURAUT, 98:FEB70-190
OTTONELLO, P.P. BIBLIOGRAFIA DI SAN JUAN
DE LA CRUZ.
   E. SARMIENTO, 86(BHS):JAN72-69
OTTOSEN, K., ED. THE MANUAL FROM NOTMARK.
   H. BEKKER-NIELSEN, 589:OCT72-787
OUDENDIJK, J.K. STATUS AND EXTENT OF
ADJACENT WATERS.
   G. KÖBLER, 182:VOL24#13/14-535

"OUR BODIES, OURSELVES."
   C. LEHMANN-HAUPT, 441:13MAR73-41
   E. LESTER, 441:20MAY73-12
OUTKA, G. AGAPE.
   617(TLS):26OCT73-1319
OVENDEN, G. & R. MELVILLE. VICTORIAN
CHILDREN.
   442(NY):31MAR73-119
OVER, A. - SEE WHITER, W.
OVERY, P. DE STIJL.*
   T.M. BROWN, 576:OCT71-259
   S.C., 46:JUN70-456
   M. WELISH, 58:DEC70/JAN71-12
OVERY, P. KANDINSKY.*
   J.P. HODIN, 290(JAAC):WINTER70-274
   R-C.W. LONG, 54:JUN71-273
   F. WHITFORD, 592:MAR70-138
OVID. METAMORPHOSES, BOOK VIII.* (A.S.
HOLLIS, ED)
   F.R.D. GOODYEAR, 313:VOL61-306
   E.J. KENNEY, 123:JUN72-214
OVID. OVIDE, "LES FASTES." (VOL 1) (H.
LE BONNIEC, ED & TRANS)
   A. ERNOUT, 555:VOL45FASC2-358
OVID. OVID'S "HEROIDES."* (H.C. CANNON,
TRANS)
   W.C. SCOTT, 124:FEB72-204
OVID. OVID'S "METAMORPHOSES:" SELEC-
TIONS.* (C.P. WATSON & A.C. REYNELL,
EDS)
   R. GLEN, 123:MAR72-98
"OVID'S 'METAMORPHOSES'." (BKS 6-10)
(W.S. ANDERSON, ED)
   617(TLS):2FEB73-133
OVIEDO, J.M. MARIO VARGAS LLOSA.*
   J. HIGGINS, 86(BHS):OCT72-417
ØVSTEDAL, B. NORWAY.
   617(TLS):13JUL73-817
OWEN, A.E.B. HANDLIST OF THE POLITICAL
PAPERS OF STANLEY BALDWIN, FIRST EARL
BALDWIN OF BEWDLEY.
   617(TLS):29JUN73-739
OWEN, C.R. HEINE IM SPANISCHEN SPRACHGE-
BIET.
   G. RIBBANS, 86(BHS):JAN72-88
OWEN, D.D.R., ED. ARTHURIAN ROMANCE.
   J.M. COWEN, 447(N&Q):JUL71-267
OWEN, D.D.R. THE VISION OF HELL.*
   M.D. LEGGE, 382(MAE):1972/3-266
OWEN, G. THE FLIM-FLAM MAN AND THE
APPRENTICE GRIFTER.
   M. LEVIN, 441:7JAN73-34
OWEN, G. JOURNEY FOR JOEDEL.*
   J.D. DURANT, 577(SHR):SUMMER71-301
OWEN, H. AFTERMATH.
   H.D. SPEAR, 177(ELT):VOL14#2-149
OWEN, H., ED. THE NEXT PHASE IN FOREIGN
POLICY.
   617(TLS):21SEP73-1091
OWEN, H.P. CONCEPTS OF DEITY.
   D. BASTOW, 518:JAN72-28
OWEN, P. THE APPRECIATION OF THE ARTS:
PAINTING.*
   P. QUINLAN, 290(JAAC):SUMMER71-565
   639(VQR):SUMMER71-CXXXIV
OWEN, W. WAR POEMS AND OTHERS. (D.
HIBBERD, ED)
   617(TLS):21DEC73-1562
OWEN, W.J.B. WORDSWORTH AS CRITIC.*
   J.R. MAC GILLIVRAY, 627(UTQ):FALL70-73
   H. PESCHMANN, 175:AUTUMN70-104
   J.R. WATSON, 541(RES):MAY71-219
OWENS, B. SUBURBIA.
   S. SCHWARTZ, 441:2DEC73-94
OWENS, G., ED. GEORGE MOORE'S MIND AND
ART.
   C. BURKHART, 445(NCF):MAR71-500
   C. MOORE, 131(CL):SPRING72-176

OWENS, I. AFTER CLAUDE.
    A. BROYARD, 441:31MAY73-45
    L. MICHAELS, 441:27MAY73-7
    442(NY):2JUL73-75
OWENS, J. AN INTERPRETATION OF EXIS-
    TENCE.
    D. BINNIE, 154:JUN70-120
OWENS, J.L. THE GRADUATE'S GUIDE TO THE
    BUSINESS WORLD.
    617(TLS):27JUL73-884
OWENS, W.A. A SEASON OF WEATHERING.
    D. RADER, 441:18MAR73-18
OWENS, W.A. THREE FRIENDS.
    G.D. HENDRICKS, 649(WAL):SPRING70-70
OWINGS, N.A. THE SPACES IN BETWEEN.
    R. JELLINEK, 441:26AUG73-4
OWSLEY, F.L., JR. - SEE TALBERT, H.S. &
    T.H. BALL
"OXFORD LATIN DICTIONARY." (FASC 1)
    A. ERNOUT, 555:VOL45FASC2-298
"OXFORD LATIN DICTIONARY."* (FASC 2)
    A. ERNOUT, 555:VOL45FASC1-192
    A. ERNOUT, 555:VOL45FASC2-298
OXLEY, A., A. PRAVDA & A. RITCHIE, EDS.
    CZECHOSLOVAKIA.
    617(TLS):16FEB73-177
OXLEY, B. 25 POEMS.
    T. EAGLETON, 565:VOL12#2-59
VAN OYEN, H. ETHIK DES ALTEN TESTAMENTS.
    S. KAPLAN, 328:SUMMER70-363
OZ, A. ELSEWHERE, PERHAPS.
    C. LEHMANN-HAUPT, 441:14NOV73-37
    P. ZWEIG, 441:18NOV73-4
OZICK, C. THE PAGAN RABBI.*
    R.J. FEIN, 328:FALL71-507
OZMENT, S.E. MYSTICISM AND DISSENT.
    617(TLS):1JUN73-619


PAARDEKOPER, P.C. BEKNOPTE ABN-SYNTAK-
    SIS.
    J-P. WILLEMS, 556(RLV):1971/4-507
PABST, W. LUIS DE GONGORA IM SPIEGEL DER
    DEUTSCHEN DICHTUNG UND KRITIK.*
    M. FRANZBACH, 52:BAND5HEFT1-99
PABST, W., ED. DAS MODERNE FRANZÖSISCHE
    DRAMA.
    Z. TAKACS, 182:VOL24#19/20-732
PABST, W., ED. DER MODERNE FRANZÖSISCHE
    ROMAN.
    K. BAHNERS, 430(NS):MAR71-162
PACAUT, M. FREDERICK BARBAROSSA.
    J.M. POWELL, 589:JAN72-136
    J.F. POWERS, 613:AUTUMN71-474
PACCAGNINI, G. PISANELLO.
    J. CANADAY, 441:2DEC73-89
    617(TLS):20JUL73-828
PACCAGNINI, G., E. MARANI & C. PERINA.
    MANTOVA, LE ARTI.
    F. HARTT, 54:SEP70-315
PACCHIANO, G. SERRA.
    A·M·M·, 228(GSLI):VOL148FASC461-158
PACE, E. ANY WAR WILL DO.
    N. CALLENDAR, 441:15APR73-35
PACELLA, G. & S. TIMPANARO - SEE LEOPARDI,
    G.
PACEY, D. - SEE GROVE, F.P.
PACHECO, A. - SEE FRANCESC DE LA VIA
PACHECO, J.E. EL PRINCIPIO DEL PLACER.
    617(TLS):12OCT73-1216
PACHMAN, L. ATTACK AND DEFENCE IN MODERN
    CHESS TACTICS.
    617(TLS):13APR73-429
PACHMUSS, T. ZINAIDA HIPPIUS.*
    I. KIRILLOVA, 575(SEER):JUL72-455
    O. MATICH, 32:MAR72-196
PACHMUSS, T. - SEE HIPPIUS, Z.

PÄCHT, O. & J.J.G. ALEXANDER. ILLUMI-
    NATED MANUSCRIPTS IN THE BODLEIAN LIB-
    RARY, OXFORD.* (VOL 2)
    P.M. GILES, 382(MAE):1972/1-84
PÄCHT, O. & J.J.G. ALEXANDER. ILLUMI-
    NATED MANUSCRIPTS IN THE BODLEIAN
    LIBRARY OXFORD. (VOL 3)
    617(TLS):15JUN73-699
PACIFICI, S., ED. FROM VERISMO TO EXPER-
    IMENTALISM.
    L. BALLERINI, 275(IQ):SPRING71-147
PACIFICI, S. ITALIA: VITA E CULTURA.
    M. SCHNEIDER, 276:SUMMER71-275
PACIFICI, S. THE MODERN ITALIAN NOVEL
    FROM MANZONI TO SVEVO.
    C. FANTAZZI, 593:SPRING72-90
PACK, R. HOME FROM THE CEMETERY.*
    J.T. IRWIN, 598(SOR):SUMMER73-720
PACKENHAM, R.A. LIBERAL AMERICA AND THE
    THIRD WORLD.
    J.K. GALBRAITH, 441:7OCT73-4
PACKER, H.L. THE LIMITS OF THE CRIMINAL
    SANCTION.
    M.P. GOLDING, 482(PHR):JAN71-117
PACKER, R. BEING OUT OF ORDER.
    S.E. LEE, 581:DEC72-302
PADBERG, J.W. COLLEGES IN CONTROVERSY.
    F. VIAL, 207(FR):OCT70-201
PADFIELD, P. THE BATTLESHIP ERA.
    617(TLS):15JUN73-659
PADGETT, R. & D. SHAPIRO, EDS. AN ANTHOL-
    OGY OF NEW YORK POETS.*
    M.G. PERLOFF, 659:WINTER73-97
PADHYE, P. & S. BHAKTAL, EDS. INDIAN
    WRITING TODAY.
    J.P. GEMMILL, 352(LE&W):VOL15#1-164
PADMORE, E. WAGNER.
    W. DEAN, 415:MAR72-269
PADOAN, G. - SEE POLENTON, S.
PAETZ, B. KIRKE UND ODYSSEUS.
    J.B. HAINSWORTH, 123:JUN72-269
PAGANI, W. REPERTORIO TEMATICO DELLA
    SCUOLA POETICA SICILIANA.
    A. FREEDMAN, 402(MLR):JUL72-665
PAGDEN, A.R. - SEE CORTÉS, H.
PAGE, A. PHOTOGRAPHIC INTERPRETATION.
    617(TLS):8JUN73-653
PAGE, B.B. THE CZECHOSLOVAK REFORM
    MOVEMENT 1963-1968.
    617(TLS):5OCT73-1153
PAGE, D. - SEE AESCHYLUS
PAGE, J.A. & M-W. O'BRIEN. BITTER WAGES.
    M. KEMPTON, 453:8FEB73-11
PAGE, M., ED. KISS ME GOODNIGHT, SER-
    GEANT-MAJOR.
    617(TLS):2NOV73-1338
PAGE, N. - SEE DICKENS, C.
PAGE, P.K. CRY ARARAT!
    617(TLS):26OCT73-1306
PAGE, R. THE DIOCESAN PASTORAL COUNCIL.
    J.M. GOWER, 363:MAY71-87
PAGE, R. DOWN AMONG THE DOSSERS.
    617(TLS):6APR73-372
PAGE, R.I. AN INTRODUCTION TO ENGLISH
    RUNES.
    617(TLS):14DEC73-1545
PAGE, R.I. LIFE IN ANGLO-SAXON ENGLAND.
    R.M. WILSON, 175:AUTUMN71-96
PAGE, T. THE HEPHAESTUS PLAGUE.
    M. LEVIN, 441:4NOV73-81
PAGET, R.F. CENTRAL ITALY.
    617(TLS):8JUN73-648
"PAGINI DE VECHE ARTĂ ROMÂNEASCĂ DE LA
    ORIGINI PÎNĂ LA SFÎRȘITUL SECOLULUI AL
    XVI-LEA."*
    E.M. WALLNER, 182:VOL24#9/10-428

PAGLIARESI, N. RIME SACRE DI CERTA O
PROBABILE ATTRIBUZIONE. (G. VARANINI,
ED)
F. FORTI, 228(GSLI):VOL148FASC461-104
PAGNOL, M. SOUVENIRS D'ENFANCE. (P.J.
CAPRETZ, ED)
A. HULL, 207(FR):OCT70-154
PAHEL, K. & M. SCHILLER, EDS. READINGS
IN CONTEMPORARY ETHICAL THEORY.*
M.B.M., 543:JUN71-765
PAIM, A. A FILOSOFIA DA ESCOLA DO
RECIFE.
J.C. TORCHIA-ESTRADA, 37:FEB70-41
PAINE, L. GENTLEMAN JOHNNY.
617(TLS):5OCT73-1195
PAINTER, G.D. & D.B. CHRÁSTEK. PRINTING
IN CZECHOSLOVAKIA IN THE FIFTEENTH CEN-
TURY.
J.S.G. SIMMONS, 354:MAR70-63
PAL, H.B. TEMPLES OF RAJASTHAN.
H. GOETZ, 318(JAOS):JAN-MAR71-155
PAL, P. THE ART OF TIBET.
M. LEESE, 293(JAST):MAY71-721
PALA, A. ISAAC NEWTON, SCIENZA E FILOSO-
FIA.*
617(TLS):1JUN73-615
DE PALACIO, J. MARY SHELLEY DANS SON
OEUVRE.*
J. VOISINE, 549(RLC):APR-JUN71-284
PALADINI, V. & E. CASTORINA. STORIA
DELLA LETTERATURA LATINA.
J-M. ANDRÉ, 555:VOL45FASC2-360
E.J. KENNEY, 123:MAR72-149
PALADINO, V. L'OPERA DI CORRADO ALVARO.
P.Z., 228(GSLI):VOL148FASC462/463-470
PALAZZESCHI, A. STEFANINO.
F.J. FATA, 275(IQ):WINTER71-127
PALEOLOGUE, M. AN AMBASSADOR'S MEMOIRS
1914-1917.
617(TLS):28SEP73-1138
PALEY, M.D. ENERGY AND THE IMAGINATION.
R.M. BAINE, 219(GAR):SUMMER71-238
I.H.C., 191(ELN):SEP71(SUPP)-31
R.F. GLECKNER, 401(MLQ):SEP71-326
J.E. GRANT, 191(ELN):MAR72-210
D. HUGHES, 418(MR):AUTUMN72-724
J.D. JUMP, 148:SPRING71-87
J.J. MC GANN, 405(MP):FEB72-261
P. MALEKIN, 541(RES):AUG71-352
R. MAYHEAD, 175:SUMMER71-59
481(PQ):JUL71-409
639(VQR):SUMMER71-CX
PALEY, M.D., ED. TWENTIETH-CENTURY IN-
TERPRETATIONS OF SONGS OF INNOCENCE AND
OF EXPERIENCE.
G.E. BENTLEY, JR., 627(UTQ):FALL70-86
PALIT, D.K., ED. HISTORY OF THE REGI-
MENT OF ARTILLERY, INDIAN ARMY.
617(TLS):23MAR73-333
"PALL MALL ENCYCLOPAEDIA OF ART."
D. HINTON, 135:DEC71-292
PALLARDÓ, F.G. - SEE UNDER GARRIDO PAL-
LARDÓ, F.
PALLISER, J. SOLITARY RAMBLES.
S. ATHERTON, 296:SUMMER73-110
PALLUCCHINI, R. TIZIANO.*
E. RUHMER, 683:BAND34HEFT2-147
PALMA, R. TRADICIONES PERUANAS.* (P.
FRANCIS, ED)
E.D. TERRY, 238:MAR71-232
PALMATIER, R.A. A DESCRIPTIVE SYNTAX OF
THE "ORMULUM."
U. OOMEN, 38:BAND89HEFT4-528
E.C. TRAUGOTT, 350:MAR72-182
PALMER, A. THE LANDS BETWEEN.
P.F. SUGAR, 32:MAR72-208
PALMER, A. RUSSIA IN WAR AND PEACE.
617(TLS):9FEB73-144

PALMER, C. IMPRESSIONISM IN MUSIC.
617(TLS):24AUG73-974
PALMER, D.J., ED. SHAKESPEARE: "TWELFTH
NIGHT."
617(TLS):13APR73-429
PALMER, D.J., ED. TENNYSON.
617(TLS):20JUL73-831
PALMER, F.L. - SEE FIRTH, J.R.
PALMER, H.E. & H.V. REDMAN. THE LANGUAGE-
LEARNING BUSINESS.
A. MOULIN, 556(RLV):1971/5-647
PALMER, J.A. JOSEPH CONRAD'S FICTION.*
E.K. HAY, 405(MP):NOV70-217
N. SHERRY, 402(MLR):OCT72-876
PALMER, R., ED. THE VALIANT SAILOR.
617(TLS):27JUL73-884
PALMER, R.E. HERMENEUTICS.*
A. CHILD, 223:MAR70-97
C.F. WALLRAFF, 50(ARQ):WINTER70-373
PALMIER, J.M. LES ECRITS POLITIQUES DE
HEIDEGGER.
J.D.C., 543:MAR71-547
PÁLSSON, H. - SEE "HRAFNKEL'S SAGA AND
OTHER ICELANDIC STORIES"
PÁLSSON, H. & P. EDWARDS - SEE "EYRBYGGJA
SAGA"
PALTER, R., ED. THE ANNUS MIRABILIS OF
SIR ISAAC NEWTON 1666-1966.*
617(TLS):1JUN73-615
PAMLÉNYI, E. - SEE TÖKEI, F.
"THE PAN AMERICAN HIGHWAY SYSTEM."
S.S. BENSON, 37:OCT71-41
PANCHANADIKAR, K.C. & J. DETERMINANTS OF
SOCIAL STRUCTURE AND SOCIAL CHANGE IN
INDIA AND OTHER PAPERS.
V. JESUDASON, 293(JAST):MAY71-697
PANCHENKO, A.M. RUSSKAYA STIKHOTVORNAYA
KULTURA XVII VEKA.
617(TLS):5OCT73-1177
PANDEY, B.N. THE BREAK-UP OF BRITISH
INDIA.
D.C. ELLINWOOD, JR., 637(VS):DEC70-224
PANET, L. PREMIÈRE EXPLORATION DU SAHARA
OCCIDENTAL.
H. DESCHAMPS, 69:JAN71-74
PANFILOV, V.Z. GRAMMAR AND LOGIC.*
J. ANDERSON, 297(JL):FEB70-144
F. JÜTTNER, 682(ZPSK):BAND23HEFT2/3-
295
PANGANIBAN, J.V. CONCISE ENGLISH-TAGALOG
DICTIONARY.*
H. MC KAUGHAN, 399(MLJ):JAN71-36
DE PANGE, J. JOURNAL (1934-1936).
F.B. CONEM, 557(RSH):OCT-DEC70-656
PANIGRAHI, L. BRITISH SOCIAL POLICY AND
FEMALE INFANTICIDE IN INDIA.
617(TLS):14SEP73-1065
PANNENBERG, W. THE APOSTLES' CREED.
617(TLS):18MAY73-559
PANNENBERG, W. BASIC QUESTIONS IN THE-
OLOGY. (VOL 3)
617(TLS):6JUL73-784
PANTER-BRICK, S.K., ED. NIGERIAN POLI-
TICS AND MILITARY RULE.
L. MAIR, 69:APR71-167
PANTER-DOWNES, M. AT "THE PINES."
F.A.C. WILSON, 648:APR72-13
PAPADOPOULOS, G.S. ENGLAND AND THE NEAR
EAST, 1896-98.
D. DAKIN, 303:VOL91-216
PAPALI, G.F. JACOB TONSON, PUBLISHER.*
T. BELANGER, 354:JUN70-166
PAPASTAMOS, D. MELISCHE AMPHOREN.
R.M. COOK, 123:JUN72-292
PAPE, H. KLOPSTOCKS AUTORENHONORARE UND
SELBSTVERLAGSGEWINNE.
T.E. CARTER, 220(GL&L):APR72-281
D. GUTZEN, 680(ZDP):BAND90HEFT4-586

273

PAPE, I. TRADITION UND TRANSFORMATION
DER MODALITÄT. (VOL 1)
R. BLANCHÉ, 542:OCT-DEC70-496
PAPE, W. INSTRUMENTENHANDBUCH.
J.A.W., 410(M&L):JUL72-333
"PAPERS OF THE BRITISH SCHOOL AT ROME."
(VOL 37)
R.M. OGILVIE, 123:MAR72-143
PAPMEHL, K.A. FREEDOM OF EXPRESSION IN
18TH CENTURY RUSSIA.
A. MC CONNELL, 32:DEC72-888
K. SANINE, 182:VOL24#23/24-885
PAPONE, A. ESISTENZA E CORPOREITÀ IN
SARTRE DALLE PRIME OPERE ALL'"ESSERE
E IL NULLA."*
E. NAMER, 542:OCT-DEC71-515
PAPP, F., COMP. REVERSE-ALPHEBETIZED
DICTIONARY OF THE HUNGARIAN LANGUAGE.
K. WODARZ-MAGDICS, 353:SEP70-119
PAPULI, G. GIROLAMO BALDUINO.
F. BOTTIN, 548(RCSF):JUL-SEP71-346
E. NAMER, 542:APR-JUN70-237
PAQUET, G., ED. THE MULTINATIONAL FIRM
AND THE NATION STATE.
M. BERNS, 99:MAR73-45
PAQUET, G. & J-P. WALLOT. PATRONAGE ET
POUVOIR DANS LE BAS-CANADA (1794-1812).
617(TLS):26OCT73-1321
PARANJPE, A.C. CASTE, PREJUDICE AND THE
INDIVIDUAL.
P. KOLENDA, 293(JAST):MAY71-696
DE' PARATESI, N.G. - SEE UNDER GALLI DE'
PARATESI, N.
PARATORE, E. TRADIZIONE E STRUTTURA IN
DANTE.
M. MARTI, 228(GSLI):VOL147FASC458/
459-437
PAREJA DIEZCANSECO, A. LAS PEQUEÑAS
ESTATURAS.
B. DULSEY, 238:DEC71-975
PARENT, M. CRÉATION THÉÂTRALE ET CRÉA-
TION ARCHITECTURALE.
D. KNOWLES, 208(FS):APR72-233
PARET, P., ED. FREDERICK THE GREAT.
617(TLS):2FEB73-133
PAREYSON, L. L'ESTETICA DI KANT.
M.E. BROWN, 290(JAAC):SPRING71-403
PAREYSON, L. VERITÀ E INTERPRETAZIONE.
M. RIESER, 319:JAN73-132
PARGETER, E. THE BLOODY FIELD.
P. ADAMS, 61:JUL73-104
PARINI, G. IL GIORNO. (VOLS 1&2) (D.
ISELLA, ED)
E. BONORA, 228(GSLI):VOL147FASC460-
603
PARIS, J. HAMLET ET PANURGE.
A.O.A., 149:DEC72-478
PARIS, J. RABELAIS AU FUTUR.
M. TETEL, 400(MLN):MAY71-573
PARISE, G. SILLABARIO N.1.
617(TLS):8JUN73-634
PARISIS, A. & J. PETIT. ORTHOGRAPHE
FRANÇAISE.
F. FLAGOTHIER, 556(RLV):1971/5-640
PARK, R. HAZLITT AND THE SPIRIT OF THE
AGE.
S. OLDFIELD, 89(BJA):SPRING72-207
PARKER, A.A. LITERATURE AND THE DELIN-
QUENT.*
G.S. ROUSSEAU, 173(ECS):SPRING71-336
PARKER, B. - SEE REANEY, J.
PARKER, C-A. MR. STUBBS THE HORSE PAINT-
ER.
R. EDWARDS, 39:DEC71-519
D. THOMAS, 135:DEC71-291
592:NOV71-218
PARKER, D. THE COLLECTED DOROTHY PARKER.
617(TLS):6APR73-395

PARKER, D. THE WEST COUNTRY.
617(TLS):4MAY73-509
PARKER, H. - SEE MELVILLE, G.
PARKER, M.E.E., ED. NORTH CAROLINA
HIGHER-COURT RECORDS, 1670-1696.*
H.A. JOHNSON, 656(WMQ):JAN71-157
PARKER, R.B. - SEE MIDDLETON, T.
PARKER, W.R. MILTON.*
B.K. LEWALSKI, 405(MP):AUG70-105
PARKES, C.M. BEREAVEMENT.
617(TLS):27JUL73-870
PARKES, M.B. ENGLISH CURSIVE BOOK HANDS,
1250-1500.*
J. BACKHOUSE, 354:MAR71-67
F.G. EMMISON, 551(RENQ):AUTUMN71-391
B. ROSS, 405(MP):FEB72-250
PARKES, R. THE GUARDIANS.
617(TLS):18MAY73-562
PARKIN, D. NEIGHBOURS AND NATIONALS IN
AN AFRICAN CITY WARD.
A. SOUTHALL, 69:OCT70-381
PARKIN, F. CLASS INEQUALITY AND POLITI-
CAL ORDER.
J.S. PRYBYLA, 32:SEP72-691
PARKIN, G., ED. THE EVOLUTION OF CANAD-
IAN LITERATURE IN ENGLISH. (VOL 3)
J.W. LENNOX, 296:FALL73-108
PARKINSON, C.N. DEVIL TO PAY.
M. LEVIN, 441:13MAY73-38
617(TLS):8JUN73-634
PARKINSON, C.N. LEFT LUGGAGE.
571:SPRING71-152
PARKINSON, G.H.R. LEIBNIZ ON HUMAN FREE-
DOM.
K.C. CLATTERBAUGH, 319:APR73-262
PARKINSON, G.H.R., ED. GEORG LUKÁCS.*
H.B., 543:DEC70-350
639(VQR):WINTER71-XXXIII
PARKINSON, G.H.R., ED. THE THEORY OF
MEANING.
R. BLANCHÉ, 542:OCT-DEC70-496
PARKINSON, R. BLOOD, TOIL, TEARS AND
SWEAT.
617(TLS):2MAR73-231
PARKINSON, R. THE PENINSULAR WAR.
617(TLS):17AUG73-957
PARKS, G. WHISPERS OF INTIMATE THINGS.
639(VQR):SUMMER71-CVIII
PARKS, G.B. - SEE MARTIN, G.
PARLASCA, K. REPERTORIO D'ARTE DELL'-
EGITTO GRECO-ROMANO. (SER B, VOL 1)
(A. ADRIANI, ED)
J. LECLANT, 182:VOL24#5-225
PARLAVANTZA-FRIEDRICH, U. TÄUSCHUNGS-
SZENEN IN DEN TRAGÖDIEN DES SOPHOKLES.*
P.E. EASTERLING, 123:MAR72-19
PARMELIN, H. LA MANIÈRE NOIRE.
B. KAY, 207(FR):APR71-965
PARMENTIER, A. LA PHILOSOPHIE DE WHITE-
HEAD ET LE PROBLÈME DE DIEU.
G. HÉLAL, 154:MAR71-194
PARMET, H.S. EISENHOWER AND THE AMERICAN
CRUSADES.
617(TLS):16FEB73-189
PAROISSIEN, D. - SEE DICKENS, C.
PARPOLA, A. THE ŚRAUTASŪTRAS OF LĀṬYĀ-
YANA AND DRĀHYĀYAṆA AND THEIR COMMEN-
TARIES. (VOL 1)
K. EUGSTER, 343:BAND13HEFT2-190
PARPOLA, A., ED & TRANS. THE ŚRAUTASŪTRAS
OF LĀṬYĀYANA AND DRĀHYĀYAṆA AND THEIR
COMMENTARIES. (VOL 1, PT 2)
L. STERNBACH, 318(JAOS):OCT-DEC71-543
PARPOLA, A. & OTHERS. DECIPHERMENT OF
THE PROTO-DRAVIDIAN INSCRIPTIONS OF
THE INDUS CIVILIZATION.*
M.B. EMENEAU, 318(JAOS):OCT-DEC71-541
W.P. SCHMID, 260(IF):BAND74-212

PARPOLA, A. & OTHERS. PROGRESS IN THE
DECIPHERMENT OF THE PROTO-DRAVIDIAN
INDUS SCRIPT. FURTHER PROGRESS IN THE
INDUS SCRIPT DECIPHERMENT.
M.B. EMENEAU, 318(JAOS):OCT-DEC71-541
PARR, R.P. GEOFFROY DE VINSAUF.
M. POLLET, 189(EA):OCT-DEC71-518
PARRA, N. EMERGENCY POEMS.*
V. YOUNG, 249(HUDR):WINTER72/73-666
PARRACK, J.D. THE NATURALIST IN MAJORCA.
617(TLS):10AUG73-936
PARREAUX, A. L'ARCHITECTURE EN GRANDE-
BRETAGNE.
N.P., 46:APR70-316
PARRINDER, G. THE INDESTRUCTIBLE SOUL.
617(TLS):19OCT73-1271
PARRIS, H. CONSTITUTIONAL BUREAUCRACY.
J.B. CHRISTOPH, 637(VS):DEC70-219
PARRIS, H. STAFF RELATIONS IN THE
CIVIL SERVICE.
617(TLS):23FEB73-221
PARRIS, L. LANDSCAPE IN BRITAIN C. 1750-
1850.
617(TLS):14DEC73-1528
PARRISH, J.A. JOURNAL OF A PLAGUE YEAR:
12, 20 & 5.*
617(TLS):22JUN73-717
PARRISH, M. THE SOVIET ARMED FORCES:
BOOKS IN ENGLISH, 1950-1967.*
R.G. WESSON, 550(RUSR):OCT71-414
PARRY, C. ENGLISH THROUGH DRAMA.
617(TLS):30MAR73-362
PARRY, G., ED. PARTICIPATION IN POLITICS.
617(TLS):13APR73-426
PARRY, M. THE MAKING OF HOMERIC VERSE.*
(A. PARRY, ED)
F.M. COMBELLACK, 122:JUL72-203
T.A. SHIPPEY, 402(MLR):JUL72-603
W. WHALLON, 131(CL):FALL72-359
M. WILLCOCK, 124:OCT71-60
PARSONS, J.B. THE PEASANT REBELLIONS OF
THE LATE MING DYNASTY.
R. HUANG, 293(JAST):NOV70-175
PARSONS, K.C. THE CORNELL CAMPUS.
R.P. DOBER, 505:FEB70-104
PARSONS, K.H. - SEE COMMONS, J.R.
PARSONS, T. & G.M. PLATT, WITH N.J. SMEL-
SER. THE AMERICAN UNIVERSITY.
P. BROOKS, 441:9DEC73-31
PARSONS, T.H. JOHN CROWE RANSOM.
R. BUFFINGTON, 219(GAR):FALL70-362
PARTLOW, R.B., JR., ED. DICKENS THE
CRAFTSMAN.
K.J. FIELDING, 541(RES):AUG71-364
R.D. MC MASTER, 445(NCF):SEP71-219
M.S., 155:MAY71-112
G. SMITH, 637(VS):JUN71-459
PARTLOW, R.B., JR. - SEE "DICKENS STUDIES
ANNUAL" (VOL 1)
PARTON, M. A JOURNEY THROUGH A LIGHTED
ROOM.
441:24JUN73-10
"'PARTONOPEU DE BLOIS,' A FRENCH ROMANCE
OF THE TWELFTH CENTURY." (VOL 2, PT 1)
(J. GILDEA, ED)
J. CANTERA, 202(FMOD):NOV71/FEB72-150
"'PARTONOPEU DE BLOIS,' A FRENCH ROMANCE
OF THE TWELFTH CENTURY." (VOL 2, PT 2)
(J. GILDEA, ED)
L. THORPE, 382(MAE):1972/3-263
F. WHITEHEAD, 208(FS):APR72-185
PARTRIDGE, A.C. ENGLISH BIBLICAL TRANS-
LATION.
617(TLS):2MAR73-243
PARTRIDGE, A.C. TUDOR TO AUGUSTAN ENG-
LISH.*
A.R. TELLIER, 189(EA):JUL-SEP71-320

PARTRIDGE, M. FARM TOOLS THROUGH THE
AGES.
617(TLS):11MAY73-533
PASCAL, P. LA RÉVOLTE DE POUGATCHÉV.
J.T. ALEXANDER, 32:DEC72-887
PASCAL, V. THE DISCIPLE AND HIS DEVIL.
W. HILLER, 572:JAN71-33
PASCASIUS RADBERTUS. DE CORPORE ET SAN-
GUINE DOMINI.* (B. PAULUS, ED)
M.L. COLKER, 589:JAN72-141
PASCHAL, A.G. - SEE DU BOIS, W.E.B.
PAS'CHIN, N. WÖRTERBUCH DER LANDWIRT-
SCHAFT.
M. ROUDNÝ, 75:1/1970-40
PASCHOUD, F. - SEE ZOSIMUS
PASHA, H.C.S. - SEE UNDER SINDERSON
PASHA, H.C.
PASINETTI, P.M. SUDDENLY TOMORROW.
A. BROYARD, 441:12FEB73-29
PASOLI, E., ED & TRANS. SCRIPTORES HIS-
TORIAE AUGUSTAE, IULIUS CAPITOLINUS:
"OPILIUS MACRINUS."*
A. CAMERON, 123:MAR72-115
PASOLINI, P.P. TRASUMANAR E ORGANIZZAR.
J-M. GARDAIR, 98:NOV71-1026
617(TLS):12OCT73-1253
PASQUALINI, J. - SEE UNDER BAO RUO-WANG
& R. CHELMINSKI
PASQUARIELLO, A.M. - SEE SASTRE, A.
PASQUINELLI, A. - SEE HEMPEL, C.
PASQUINI, E. INTORNO ALLA PRESUNTA "DIS-
PERSA" DEL PETRARCA "SOPRA LA RIVA OVE
'L SOL HA IN COSTUME."
M.M., 228(GSLI):VOL148FASC462/463-460
PASQUINI, E. - SEE SERDINI, S.
PASSAVANT, G. STUDIEN ÜBER DOMENICO EGI-
DIO ROSSI UND SEINE BAUKÜNSTLERISCHE
TÄTIGKEIT INNERHALB DER SÜDDEUTSCHEN
UND ÖSTERREICHISCHEN BAROCK.
S.L. FAISON, JR., 54:MAR70-108
PASSAVANT, G. VERROCCHIO.
C. GILBERT, 56:WINTER70-441
R.W. LIGHTBOWN, 39:FEB70-166
PASSELL, P. & L. ROSS. THE RETREAT FROM
RICHES.
J. EPSTEIN, 453:5APR73-13
R. SOLOW, 441:25FEB73-4
PASSERINI TOSI, C. DIZIONARIO DELLA
LINGUA ITALIANA.
R.C. MELZI, 276:SUMMER71-262
PASSERON, R. FRENCH PRINTS OF THE 20TH
CENTURY.
D.T., 135:DEC70-290
58:SEP/OCT70-16
PASSERON, R. L'OEUVRE PICTURALE ET LES
FONCTIONS DE L'APPARENCE.
P. DUFOUR, 98:AUG/SEP71-805
PASSLER, D.L. TIME, FORM, AND STYLE IN
BOSWELL'S "LIFE OF JOHNSON."
R.B. SCHWARTZ, 301(JEGP):JUL72-452
PASSMORE, J. THE PERFECTIBILITY OF MAN.*
D. EMMET, 479(PHQ):JUL71-280
617(TLS):12JAN73-29
PASTOR DÍAZ, N. OBRAS COMPLETAS DE DON
NICOMEDES-PASTOR DÍAZ. (J.M. CASTRO Y
CALVO, ED)
191(ELN):SEP71(SUPP)-179
PASTORELLI, P. - SEE SONNINO, S.
PASTOUREAU, H. - SEE UNDER JONES, H.
PATAI, R. THE ARAB MIND.
442(NY):10SEP73-133
"PATAÑJALI'S 'VYĀKARAŅA-MAHĀBHĀṢYA'."
(S.D. JOSHI, ED & TRANS)
R. ROCHER, 318(JAOS):APR-JUN71-315
PATCHEN, K. IN QUEST OF CANDLELIGHTERS.
M.G. PERLOFF, 659:WINTER73-97

PATEMAN, C. PARTICIPATION AND DEMOCRATIC
THEORY.
42(AR):SUMMER71-287
PATER, W. LETTERS OF WALTER PATER. (L.
EVANS, ED)
G. MONSMAN, 637(VS):JUN71-468
R.M. SCOTTO, 177(ELT):VOL14#2-150
PATERNOST, J. FROM ENGLISH TO SLOVEN-
IAN.*
E.A. NIDA, 215(GL):VOL11#2-131
PATERSON, A.K.G. - SEE TIRSO DE MOLINA
PATERSON, A.M. THE INFINITE WORLDS OF
GIORDANO BRUNO.
L.G., 543:DEC70-343
A.W. MUNK, 484(PPR):JUN71-610
PATRICK, J. A GLASGOW GANG OBSERVED.
S. CHAPLIN, 362:1MAR73-282
617(TLS):18MAY73-547
PATRIDES, C.A., ED. APPROACHES TO "PARA-
DISE LOST."*
G. BULLOUGH, 175:SPRING70-24
R.L. COLIE, 102(CANL):SPRING72-99
PATRIDES, C.A., ED. THE CAMBRIDGE PLAT-
ONISTS.*
639(VQR):WINTER71-XLIV
"DER PATRIOT."* (VOL 1) (W. MARTENS, ED)
[SHOWN IN PREV UNDER ED]
T.K. THAYER, 221(GQ):JAN71-86
PATRIZI, F. DELLA POETICA. (VOL 1)
(D.A. BARBAGLI, ED)
L. BOLZONI, 228(GSLI):VOL148FASC462/
463-427
A. STEGMANN, 549(RLC):JUL-SEP70-419
PATTEN, B. NOTES TO THE HURRYING MAN.
R. FULTON, 565:VOL11#1-68
PATTERSON, A.M. HERMOGENES AND THE
RENAISSANCE.*
J. GRUNDY, 402(MLR):OCT72-868
R.S. SYLVESTER, 401(MLQ):JUN72-188
PATTERSON, A.M. & F.D. GATTON, EDS.
NORTH CAROLINA; STATE DEPARTMENT OF
ARCHIVES AND HISTORY: THE MUNICIPAL
RECORDS MANUAL.
J. KATSAROS, 14:JUL71-324
PATTERSON, C.I., JR. THE DAEMONIC IN THE
POETRY OF JOHN KEATS.*
G.M. HARPER, 219(GAR):WINTER71-516
K. KROEBER, 405(MP):FEB72-267
R. MAYHEAD, 175:SUMMER71-59
A. RODWAY, 541(RES):AUG71-387
PATTERSON, G. T.S. ELIOT.
J. ESPEY, 27(AL):NOV72-507
D.E.S. MAXWELL, 402(MLR):JAN72-177
PATTERSON, W.C. NUCLEAR REACTORS.
617(TLS):7SEP73-1030
PATTI, E. GRAZIELLA.
B. MERRY, 270:VOL21#3-176
PATTISON, B. MUSIC AND POETRY OF THE
ENGLISH RENAISSANCE.* (2ND ED)
205(FMLS):JAN71-98
PATTISON, W.T. EL NATURALISMO ESPAÑOL.
R. PÉREZ DE LA DEHESA, 240(HR):JAN71-
49
PATTON, L. - SEE COLERIDGE, S.T.
PATTON, L. & P. MANN - SEE COLERIDGE, S.T.
PATURIER, M. - SEE MÉRIMÉE, P.
PATZE, H., ED. BIBLIOGRAPHIE ZUR THÜRING-
ISCHEN GESCHICHTE.
G.G. WINDELL, 182:VOL24#13/14-564
PATZE, H. & W. SCHLESINGER, EDS. GESCH-
ICHTE THÜRINGENS. (VOLS 1&3)
G.G. WINDELL, 182:VOL24#15/16-629
PATZIG, G. DIE ARISTOTELISCHE SYLLOGIS-
TIK. (3RD ED)
M-A. SINACEUR, 98:MAY71-446
PAUL, JON & CHARLOTTE. FIRE!
639(VQR):SPRING71-LXXVIII

PAUL, A. DIE BARMHERZIGKEIT DER GÖTTER
IM GRIECHISCHEN EPOS.
J.B. HAINSWORTH, 123:MAR72-117
PAUL, F. SYMBOL UND MYTHOS.*
A. AARSETH, 172(EDDA):1970/3-186
PAUL, H. DEUTSCHES WÖRTERBUCH. (5TH ED
REV BY W. BETZ)
W. BRAUN, 657(WW):MAY/JUN70-204
H. STOPP, 680(ZDP):BAND89HEFT3-466
PAUL, H. MITTELHOCHDEUTSCHE GRAMMATIK.
(20TH ED) (H. MOSER & I. SCHRÖBLER,
EDS)
W. BESCH, 680(ZDP):BAND90HEFT1-137
K. MATZEL, 224(GRM):BAND21HEFT4-463
R.K. SEYMOUR, 406:WINTER72-411
PAUL, J. DER PALAZZO VECCHIO IN FLORENZ,
URSPRUNG UND BEDEUTUNG SEINER FORM.
J.S. ACKERMAN, 576:MAR71-91
H. SAALMAN, 54:MAR71-115
PAUL, S. THE MUSIC OF SURVIVAL.*
M. MARCUS, 502(PRS):SUMMER70-179
J.N. RIDDEL, 405(MP):MAY71-402
PAUL, S., ED. SIX CLASSIC AMERICAN WRIT-
ERS.*
K. MC SWEENEY, 529(QQ):AUTUMN71-465
PAULOVÁ, M. TAJNÝ VÝBOR (MAFFIE) A
SPOLUPRÁCE S JIHOSLOVANY V LETECH
1916-1918.
J. KALVODA, 32:MAR72-219
PAULS-EISENBEISS, E. GERMAN PORCELAIN
OF THE 18TH CENTURY.
617(TLS):10AUG73-924
PAULSEN, W., ED. ASPEKTE DES EXPRESSION-
ISMUS.*
A. BEST, 220(GL&L):OCT71-31
K. KÄNDLER, 654(WB):10/1970-213
PAULSEN, W., ED. DER DICHTER UND SEINE
ZEIT.
M.B. BENN, 402(MLR):JAN72-231
PAULSEN, W., ED. DAS NACHLEBEN DER ROMAN-
TIK IN DER MODERNEN DEUTSCHEN LITERATUR.
J. TRAINER, 402(MLR):JUL72-707
PAULSON, I. THE OLD ESTONIAN FOLK RE-
LIGION.
F.J. OINAS, 32:SEP72-710
PAULSON, R. HOGARTH.* (VOL 1) [REVIEWS
SHOWN IN PREV ARE OF VOLS 1&2]
F.W. HILLES, 676(YR):SPRING72-428
R. LEIBOWITZ, 58:NOV71-14
566:SPRING72-92
PAULSON, R. HOGARTH.* (VOL 2)
F.W. HILLES, 676(YR):SPRING72-428
566:SPRING72-92
PAULSON, R., ED. SATIRE.
W. KINSLEY, 223:DEC71-348
566:AUTUMN71-28
PAULSON, R. SATIRE AND THE NOVEL IN
EIGHTEENTH-CENTURY ENGLAND.*
M. GOLDEN, 594:SUMMER70-222
P. ROGERS, 597(SN):VOL42#2-474
PAULSON, R. & T. LOCKWOOD, EDS. HENRY
FIELDING: THE CRITICAL HERITAGE.*
M. GEARIN-TOSH, 447(N&Q):SEP71-358
J. PRESTON, 184(EIC):JAN71-91
PAULUS, B. - SEE PASCASIUS RADBERTUS
PĂUNESCU, A. EVOLUŢIA UNELTELOR ŞI AR-
MELOR DE PIATRĂ CIOPLITĂ DESCOPERITE
PE TERITORIUL ROMÂNIEI.
R. PITTIONI, 182:VOL24#13/14-560
PAUSANIAS. GUIDE TO GREECE. (P. LEVI,
TRANS)
W.R. BIERS, 124:MAR72-241
DE PAUW-DE VEEN, L. DE BEGRIPPEN "SCHIL-
DER," "SCHILDEREY" EN "SCHILDEREN" IN
DE ZEVENTIENDE EEUW.
W. STECHOW, 54:JUN71-260
PAVESE, C. SAGGI LETTERARI.
M.A. DE KISCH, 189(EA):OCT-DEC71-544

PAVÓN, F.G. - SEE UNDER GARCÍA PAVÓN, F.
PAVONE, F. I CARMI LATINI DEL TASSO.
    A. DI BENEDETTO, 228(GSLI):VOL147FASC
    457-140
PAWLOWSKI, H-M. DAS STUDIUM DER RECHTS-
WISSENSCHAFT.
    F. GILLIARD, 182:VOL24#13/14-537
PAXTON, J., ED. THE STATESMAN'S YEAR-
BOOK 1973-1974.
    617(TLS):12OCT73-1235
PAXTON, R.O. VICHY FRANCE.
    S. HOFFMANN, 453:8FEB73-19
    N. WAHL, 441:28JAN73-5
PAXTON, T. RAMBLIN' BOY AND OTHER SONGS.
    J.O. WEST, 650(WF):JAN70-62
PAYEN, J-C. LE MOTIF DU REPENTIR DANS
    LA LITTÉRATURE FRANÇAISE MÉDIÉVALE
    (DES ORIGINES À 1230).*
    A. FOULET, 545(RPH):AUG71-137
PAYEN, J-C. & J-P. CHAUVEAU. LA POÉSIE
    DES ORIGINES À 1715.*
    N. CAZAURAN, 535(RHL):JAN-FEB70-125
PAYEN, J.C. LE MOYEN AGE I, DES ORIGINES
    À 1300.
    G.F. JONES, 207(FR):MAR71-815
PAYEN, J.C. - SEE ALARD DE CAMBRAI
PAYERLE, G. THE AFTERPEOPLE.
    H. ROSENGARTEN, 102(CANL):AUTUMN72-109
PAYNE, B. GETTING THERE WITHOUT DRUGS.
    A. BROYARD, 441:28FEB73-33
PAYNE, J.B. ERASMUS, HIS THEOLOGY OF THE
SACRAMENTS.
    A. HYMA, 551(RENQ):SUMMER71-242
PAYNE, L. THE BROTHERHOOD.
    617(TLS):18MAY73-547
PAYNE, R. THE LIFE AND DEATH OF ADOLF
HITLER.
    A. BULLOCK, 453:28JUN73-30
    J.K. GALBRAITH, 441:22APR73-4
    C. LEHMANN-HAUPT, 441:26APR73-47
    E. WEEKS, 61:MAY73-117
PAYNE, S.G. A HISTORY OF SPAIN AND
PORTUGAL.
    617(TLS):26OCT73-1304
PAYNTER, W. BRITISH TRADE UNIONS AND
THE PROBLEM OF CHANGE.
    E. HARRISON, 529(QQ):SPRING71-125
PAYTON, G. - SEE "WEBSTER'S DICTIONARY OF
PROPER NAMES"
PAZ, O. ALTERNATING CURRENT.
    P. ADAMS, 61:FEB73-103
    I. HOWE, 441:25MAR73-1
    442(NY):28APR73-147
PAZ, O. MARCEL DUCHAMP, OR THE CASTLE
OF PURITY.
    D. IRWIN, 39:JUN70-483
    42(AR):SPRING70-132
PAZ, O. THE OTHER MEXICO.
    C. FUENTES, 453:20SEP73-16
PAZ, O. POSDATA.
    Z.E. NELKEN, 238:SEP71-604
PAZ, O. VERSANT EST.
    P. CHAPPUIS, 98:JUL71-642
PEABODY, A.P. - SEE PLUMMER, W., JR.
PEABODY, J.B. - SEE "JOHN ADAMS"
PEACE, R. DOSTOYEVSKY.
    D. FANGER, 32:MAR72-191
    R. FREEBORN, 575(SEER):JAN72-120
    S.B. VLADIV, 67:NOV72-253
PEACOCK, C. SAMUEL PALMER: SHOREHAM AND
AFTER.*
    A.S. ROE, 54:SEP71-421
PEACOCK, K., ED. SONGS OF THE DOUKHOBORS.
    B. KRADER, 187:MAY73-339
    B. NETTL, 292(JAF):JUL-SEP71-348
PEACOCK, R. CRITICISM AND PERSONAL
TASTE.
    617(TLS):9FEB73-146

PEACOCK, T.L. MEMOIRS OF SHELLEY AND
    OTHER ESSAYS AND REVIEWS. (H. MILLS,
    ED)
    J. ESPEY, 445(NCF):JUN71-125
PEAKE, M. A BOOK OF NONSENSE.
    617(TLS):26JAN73-86
PEARCE, H.H. ON THE ORIGINS OF WALTZING
MATILDA.
    G.W. LEEPER, 381:DEC71-478
PEARCE, J.C. THE CRACK IN THE COSMIC
EGG.
    617(TLS):7SEP73-1034
PEARCE, R. STAGES OF THE CLOWN.
    B. GELFANT, 454:FALL71-94
PEARCE, R.H., ED. EXPERIENCE IN THE
NOVEL.*
    P. THOMSON, 597(SN):VOL42#1-247
PEARCE, R.H. HISTORICISM ONCE MORE.*
    J.K. ROBINSON, 598(SOR):SUMMER73-692
PEARCE, T.S. GEORGE ELIOT.
    617(TLS):17AUG73-950
PEARL, C. DUBLIN IN BLOOMTIME.*
    P. RECONDO, 202(FMOD):NOV70/FEB71-166
PEARL, J. VICTIMS.
    N. CALLENDAR, 441:28JAN73-20
PEARLMAN, D.D. THE BARB OF TIME.*
    L. CASPER, 613:WINTER70-614
    H. SERGEANT, 175:SUMMER71-63
    T.R. WHITAKER, 405(MP):AUG71-91
PEARS, D. WHAT IS KNOWLEDGE?*
    617(TLS):23FEB73-218
PEARSALL, D. JOHN LYDGATE.*
    D. FOX, 447(N&Q):AUG71-308
    R.M. WILSON, 402(MLR):JAN72-163
    639(VQR):SPRING71-LXVI
PEARSALL, D.A. & R.A. WALDRON, EDS. MED-
IEVAL LITERATURE AND CIVILIZATION.*
    M.W. BLOOMFIELD, 38:BAND89HEFT3-377
PEARSALL, R. VICTORIAN SHEET MUSIC
COVERS.
    A. LAMB, 415:DEC72-1188
PEARSALL, R. THE WORM IN THE BUD.*
    R. ACKERMAN, 637(VS):SEP70-107
PEARSON, A. 14 POEMS.*
    P. STEVENS, 628:SPRING72-103
PEARSON, J. JAMES BOND.
    E.S. TURNER, 362:25OCT73-563
PEARSON, J.D. & A. WALSH, COMPS. INDEX
    ISLAMICUS. (3RD SUPP 1966-1970)
    617(TLS):23FEB73-205
PEARSON, L.B. MIKE.* (VOL 1) (BRITISH
    TITLE: THROUGH DIPLOMACY TO POLITICS.)
    J.L. GRANATSTEIN, 99:FEB73-36
    617(TLS):24AUG73-967
PEARSON, R.J. ARCHAEOLOGY OF THE RYUKYU
ISLANDS.
    E. KANEKO, 293(JAST):FEB71-456
PECH, S.Z. THE CZECH REVOLUTION OF 1848.*
    R.J. RATH, 32:MAR72-218
    T.V. THOMAS, 575(SEER):APR72-305
PÉCHÈRE, F., ED & TRANS. TIERRA DE
ESPAÑA.
    J. VAN PRAAG-CHANTRAINE, 556(RLV):
    1970/5-554
PECK, E. THE BABY TRAP.
    P.M. SPACKS, 249(HUDR):SPRING72-160
PECK, J. SHAGBARK.
    V. YOUNG, 249(HUDR):WINTER72/73-670
PECK, R.A. - SEE GOWER, J.
PECK, R.N. A DAY NO PIGS WOULD DIE.
    V. CUNNINGHAM, 362:30AUG73-288
    C. LEHMANN-HAUPT, 441:4JAN73-39
    R. TODD, 61:APR73-114
    J. YARDLEY, 441:13MAY73-37
    442(NY):3FEB73-100
    617(TLS):17AUG73-945

PECKHAM, H. & C. GIBSON, EDS. ATTITUDES
OF COLONIAL POWERS TOWARD THE AMERICAN
INDIAN.
   A.T. VAUGHAN, 656(WMQ):APR71-331
PECKHAM, M. VICTORIAN REVOLUTIONARIES.*
   J.E. BAKER, 149:SEP72-344
   U.C. KNOEPFLMACHER, 191(ELN):MAR72-227
   R.A. LEVINE, 301(JEGP):APR72-267
   W.D. SHAW, 85:FALL70-35
   G.B. TENNYSON, 637(VS):JUN71-457
PECORARO, M. SAGGI VARI DA DANTE AL
TOMMASEO.
   A. BUCK, 72:BAND209HEFT1/3-202
PEDEN, M.S. - SEE CARBALLIDO, E.
PEDEN, W. TWILIGHT AT MONTICELLO.
   M. LEVIN, 441:3JUN73-33
PEDLEY, J.G. SARDIS IN THE AGE OF CROE-
SUS.*
   W.J. WILSON, 352(LE&W):VOL15#1-175
PEELE, G. THE DRAMATIC WORKS OF GEORGE
PEELE. (R.M. BENBOW, E. BLISTEIN &
F.S. HOOK, EDS)
   T.W. CRAIK, 447(N&Q):DEC71-468
   G.K. HUNTER, 551(RENQ):WINTER71-563
PEELE, G. THE LIFE AND WORKS OF GEORGE
PEELE. (VOL 3) (C.T. PROUTY, ED)
   E.A.J. HONIGMANN, 541(RES):NOV71-478
PEETERS, F. & M.A. VENTE, EDS. THE ORGAN
AND ITS MUSIC IN THE NETHERLANDS, 1500-
1800.
   W.L.S., 410(M&L):APR72-202
PEETERS, G.J. FRANS VERVOORT O.F.M. EN
ZIJN AFHANKELIJKHEID.
   F. VAN ELMBT, 556(RLV):1971/4-506
PEETERS, L. HISTORISCHE UND LITERARISCHE
STUDIEN ZUM DRITTEN TEIL DES KUDRUN-
EPOS.*
   K.C. KING, 220(GL&L):OCT71-26
PÉGUY, C. & ALAIN-FOURNIER. CORRESPON-
DANCE (1910-1914). (Y. REY-HERME, ED)
   617(TLS):14DEC73-1537
PEHNT, W. GERMAN ARCHITECTURE 1960-1970.
   S.C., 46:APR71-259
   W. LESNIKOWSKI, 45:OCT71-111
   L. SATKOWSKI, 576:MAY71-184
PEI, M. GLOSSARY OF LINGUISTIC TERMIN-
OLOGY.*
   G.F. MEIER & B. FLEGEL, 682(ZPSK):
   BAND23HEFT1-100
PEI, M. THE STORY OF THE ENGLISH LANGU-
AGE. (2ND ED)
   J.E. PIERCE, 353:DEC70-99
   A.R. TELLIER, 189(EA):APR-JUN70-224
PEI, M. WORDS IN SHEEP'S CLOTHING.
   R. LAWRENCE, 175:SPRING71-28
PEI, M.A. WHAT'S IN A WORD?
   P.V. CASSANO, 628:FALL71-80
PEIL, M. THE GHANAIAN FACTORY WORKER.
   617(TLS):23MAR73-333
PELIKÁN, J., ED. THE CZECHOSLOVAK POLITI-
CAL TRIALS, 1950-1954. DAS UNTERDRÜCKTE
DOSSIER. PANZER ÜBERROLLEN DEN PARTEI-
TAG.
   R.V. LUZA, 32:MAR72-221
PELIKAN, J., ED. ICI PRAGUE.
   617(TLS):3AUG73-892
PELIKÁN, J., ED. THE SECRET VYSOČANY
CONGRESS.
   F.L. CARSTEN, 575(SEER):APR72-321
PELLEGRINI, A. WIELAND E LA CLASSICITÀ
TEDESCA.
   C. SOMMER, 52:BAND5HEFT1-106
PELLEGRINI, G.B. & A.L. PROSDOCIMI. LA
LINGUA VENETICA.
   J. UNTERMANN, 343:BAND13HEFT2-137
PELLICER, C. ANTOLOGÍA.
   B. DULSEY, 238:MAR71-208

PELLICER, C. PRIMERA ANTOLOGÍA POÉTICA.
(G. FERNÁNDEZ, ED)
   E.J. MULLEN, 263:JUL-SEP72-268
PELLOW, J. WITH A LITTLE HELP FROM MY
FRIENDS.
   617(TLS):30NOV73-1485
PELTERS, W. LESSINGS STANDORT.
   617(TLS):6JUL73-777
PELTIER, L.C. GUIDEPOSTS TO THE STARS.
   617(TLS):6APR73-401
PENELHUM, T. SURVIVAL AND DISEMBODIED
EXISTENCE.*
   A. FLEW, 482(PHR):OCT71-528
   D. ODEGARD, 154:MAR71-203
   D. POLDEN, 483:APR71-176
   R. TRIGG, 393(MIND):OCT71-629
PENELHUM, T. & J.J. MAC INTOSH, EDS. THE
FIRST CRITIQUE.
   D. LEMON, 154:MAR71-167
   R. MALTER, 342:BAND62HEFT3-420
"PENGUIN MODERN STORIES 1-7."
   E. GLOVER, 565:VOL12#3-58
PENKERT, S. CARL EINSTEIN - BEITRÄGE ZU
EINER MONOGRAPHIE.
   H. GRABER, 657(WW):NOV/DEC71-431
   R.H. THOMAS, 402(MLR):JUL72-710
PENLINGTON, N., ED. ON CANADA.
   M. GILLETT, 651(WHR):WINTER72-80
   P.B. WAITE, 150(DR):SPRING71-113
PENNER, N., ED. WINNIPEG 1919.
   D. ORLIKOW, 99:NOV-DEC73-22
PENNY, R.J. EL HABLA PASIEGA.
   F. HODCROFT, 86(BHS):JUL72-290
   H. MEIER, 72:BAND209HEFT4/6-447
PENNYBACKER, J.H. & W.W. BRADEN, EDS.
BROADCASTING AND THE PUBLIC INTEREST.
   D.M. BERG, 583:SPRING71-296
PENROSE, H. BRITISH AVIATION.
   617(TLS):14DEC73-1545
PENROSE, R. MIRÓ.
   I. DUNLOP, 39:FEB71-150
PENROSE, R. & J. GOLDING, EDS. PICASSO
IN RETROSPECT.
   P. ADAMS, 61:DEC73-139
PENTECOST, H. THE BEAUTIFUL DEAD.
   N. CALLENDAR, 441:9DEC73-50
PENTECOST, H. WALKING DEAD MAN.
   N. CALLENDAR, 441:17JUN73-32
PENTIKÄINEN, J. THE NORDIC DEAD-CHILD
TRADITION.*
   B. ALVER, 196:BAND12HEFT1-100
PEÑUELAS, M.C. MR. CLARK NO TOMA POCA-
COLA.* (J.M. SHARP, ED)
   G.J. HASENAUER, 399(MLJ):JAN71-34
PEÑUELAS, M.C. CONVERSACIONES CON RAMÓN
J. SENDER.
   C.L. KING, 238:SEP71-601
PENZL, H. GESCHICHTLICHE DEUTSCHE LAUT-
LEHRE.*
   R.M.G. OSTER, 399(MLJ):MAY71-335
PENZL, H. LAUTSYSTEM UND LAUTWANDEL IN
DEN ALTHOCHDEUTSCHEN DIALEKTEN.
   M. CLYNE, 67:MAY72-104
   I. RAUCH, 301(JEGP):OCT72-561
"PEOPLE'S REPUBLIC OF CHINA: AN ECONOMIC
ASSESSMENT."
   617(TLS):12JAN73-27
PEPYS, S. THE DIARY OF SAMUEL PEPYS.*
(VOLS 1-3) (R. LATHAM & W. MATTHEWS,
EDS)
   D. UNDERDOWN, 639(VQR):SPRING71-310
PEPYS, S. THE DIARY OF SAMUEL PEPYS.*
(VOLS 4&5) (R. LATHAM & W. MATTHEWS,
EDS)
   568(SCN):SPRING72-6

PEPYS, S. THE DIARY OF SAMUEL PEPYS.*
(VOLS 6&7) (R. LATHAM & W. MATTHEWS,
EDS)
H. TREVOR-ROPER, 362:4JAN73-21
PERCHIK, S. WHICH HAND HOLDS THE BRO-
THER.*
M. CZARNECKI, 648:JUN70-37
PERCIVAL, A.C. VERY SUPERIOR MEN.
617(TLS):27APR73-469
PERCIVAL, J. EXPERIMENTAL DANCE.
N. GOODWIN, 415:JAN72-48
PERCY, W. LOVE IN THE RUINS.*
42(AR):SUMMER71-283
639(VQR):SUMMER71-XCVI
PERDIGÃO, J.D. - SEE UNDER DE AZEREDO
PERDIGÃO, J.
PEREC, G. LES CHOSES.* (J. LEBLON, ED)
J. DECOCK, 207(FR):APR71-1006
502(PRS):SPRING71-92
PERELLA, N.J. THE KISS SACRED AND PRO-
FANE.*
J.V. FLEMING, 276:WINTER71-497
L.J. FRIEDMAN, 401(MLQ):JUN72-181
PERELLA, N.J. NIGHT AND THE SUBLIME IN
GIACOMO LEOPARDI.
S. GAROFALO, 546(RR):OCT71-241
PERELLI, L., ED. ANTOLOGIA DELLA LETTERA-
TURA LATINA.
C.F. NATUNEWICZ, 124:DEC71-134
PERELLI, L. LUCREZIO, POETA DELL' ANGOS-
CIA.*
A. ERNOUT, 555:VOL45FASC1-165
PERELLI, L. STORIA DELLA LITTERATURA
LATINA AD USO DELLE SCUOLE MEDIE
SUPERIORI.
E.J. KENNEY, 123:MAR72-149
PERELMAN, C. JUSTICE.*
E.A.R., 543:DEC70-344
PERELMAN, C. & L. OLBRECHTS-TYTECA. THE
NEW RHETORIC.
E.J. AMENT, 290(JAAC):SUMMER71-569
M. GILBERT, 393(MIND):OCT71-626
J. KOZY, JR., 480(P&R):FALL70-249
PERELMAN, C. & L. OLBRECHTS-TYTECA.
TRAITÉ DE L'ARGUMENTATION. (2ND ED)
R. BLANCHÉ, 542:OCT-DEC70-497
F. LUSIGNAN, 154:SEP71-617
PERER, M.L.G. - SEE UNDER GATTI PERER,
M.L.
PERES, S. DAVID'S SLING.
S.L.A. MARSHALL, 390:APR71-63
PÉREZ ALFONZO, J.P. PETROLEO Y DEPEN-
DENCIA.
N. GALL, 453:15NOV73-29
PÉREZ DE AYALA, R. LA PATA DE LA RAPOSA.
(A. AMORÓS, ED)
N.J. LAMB, 86(BHS):APR72-194
PÉREZ GALDÓS, B. FORTUNATA AND JACINTA.
(L. CLARK, TRANS)
617(TLS):12OCT73-1227
PÉREZ GALDÓS, B. MIAU. (E.R. MULVIHILL
& R. SÁNCHEZ, EDS)
G. SMITH, 238:MAR71-226
PÉREZ GALLEGO, C. LITERATURA Y REBELDÍA
EN LA INGLATERRA ACTUAL.
F. TSCHUMI, 182:VOL24#17/18-679
"THE PERFORMING ARTS: PROBLEMS AND PROS-
PECTS."
M. PETERSON, 470:JAN66-43
PERICOT-GARCIA, L., J. GALLOWAY & A.
LOMMEL. PREHISTORIC AND PRIMITIVE ART.
H. AACH, 139:FEB71-8
PERIN, C. WITH MAN IN MIND.
S. KAPLAN, 44:DEC71-16
45:MAR71-45
PERITORE, G.A. NUOVA RACCOLTA DI STUDI.
P.A.T., 228(GSLI):VOL147FASC458/459-
478

PERKIN, H. THE ORIGINS OF MODERN ENGLISH
SOCIETY, 1780-1850.*
J. SAVILLE, 637(VS):MAR71-345
PERKINS, A. THE ART OF DURA-EUROPOS.
617(TLS):16NOV73-1394
PERKINS, J.A. THE CONCEPT OF THE SELF IN
THE FRENCH ENLIGHTENMENT.*
A.W. FAIRBAIRN, 402(MLR):APR72-415
PERKINS, J-G. SIMÉON LA ROQUE, POÈTE DE
L'ABSENCE (1550-1615).
H. LAFAY, 535(RHL):MAR-APR71-290
PERKINS, L.L. - SEE "JOHANNES LHÉRITIER:
OPERA OMNIA"
PERKINS, V.F. FILM AS FILM.
617(TLS):28SEP73-1109
PERLMAN, J. KACHINA.
W.H. PRITCHARD, 249(HUDR):SPRING72-121
PERLMANN, M. - SEE IBN KAMMŪNA, S.M.
PERLOFF, M. RHYME AND MEANING IN THE
POETRY OF YEATS.
G. GUNN, 405(MP):AUG71-87
M.F. SLATTERY, 290(JAAC):SUMMER71-567
PERMAN, D. CUBLINGTON.
617(TLS):27JUL73-849
PERNIOLA, M. L'ALIENAZIONE ARTISTICA.
H. BREDIN, 89(BJA):WINTER72-88
PERNOUD, R. HELOISE AND ABELARD.
617(TLS):18MAY73-546
PÉROL, J. MAINTENANT LES SOLEILS.
617(TLS):19JAN73-69
PÉROL, J. RUPTURES.
P. CHAPPUIS, 98:JAN71-91
PÉROUSE DE MONTCLOS, J-M. ETIENNE-LOUIS
BOULLÉE (1728-1799).*
J. GAUS, 683:BAND34HEFT2-158
D. WIEBENSON, 576:OCT71-250
PEROVIĆ, B. HRVATSKO DRUŠTVO U REVOLU-
CIONARNOM PROCESU.
M. MEŠTROVIĆ, 32:DEC72-930
PEROWNE, S. DEATH OF THE ROMAN REPUBLIC.*
M.R. GREEN, 123:MAR72-131
PERRAULT, C.B. & M.J. AFFRON - SEE SIL-
ONE, I.
PERRETT, G. DAYS OF SADNESS, YEARS OF
TRIUMPH.
A. CALDER, 441:9SEP73-36
453:5APR73-37
PERRIN, N. DR. BOWDLER'S LEGACY.
R. ACKERMAN, 637(VS):SEP70-107
PERROT, J. THE ORGAN FROM ITS INVENTION
IN THE HELLENISTIC PERIOD TO THE END OF
THE THIRTEENTH CENTURY.*
E.A. BOWLES, 317:SUMMER72-272
W.L.S., 410(M&L):APR72-201
PERROTTET, P. PRACTICAL STAGE MAKE-UP.
J.H. YOCUM, 570(SQ):WINTER70-93
"FRANÇOIS PERROUX INTERROGE HERBERT MAR-
CUSE...QUI RÉPOND."
J. WALCH, 542:OCT-DEC71-512
PERRY, D.L. THE CONCEPT OF PLEASURE.
A. PALMER, 393(MIND):APR71-308
PERRY, J.M. US AND THEM.
G. WILLS, 453:4OCT73-3
PERRY, K.L. THE RELIGIOUS SYMBOLISM OF
ANDRÉ GIDE.
J.C. MC LAREN, 207(FR):MAR71-797
PERRY, M.C. THE JAPAN EXPEDITION 1852-
1854. (R. PINEAU, ED)
B.B. SZCZESNIAK, 318(JAOS):JAN-MAR71-
147
PERRY, P.J., ED. BRITISH AGRICULTURE
1875-1914.
617(TLS):31AUG73-999
PERRY, R. A HARD MAN TO KILL.
N. CALLENDAR, 441:23SEP73-48
PERRY, R. NOWHERE MAN.
617(TLS):23FEB73-219

PERRY, R.  THE POLAR WORLDS.
   617(TLS):11MAY73-537
PERRY, R·L·  GALT U·S·A·
   G· LAX, 99:APR73-33
PERRY, T·A·  ART AND MEANING IN BERCEO'S
   "VIDA DE SANTA ORIA·"*
   B· DUTTON, 240(HR):JAN71-88
   H·T· OOSTENDORP, 433:JUL71-344
PERSE, S-J·  EXIL·  (R· LITTLE, ED)
   617(TLS):21DEC73-1562
PERSIUS·  A· PERSI FLACCI "SATURARUM LIB-
   ER·"*  (D· BO, ED)
   G· SCHMELING, 122:OCT72-303
PERSIUS - SEE UNDER HORACE AND PERSIUS
PERSONE, L·M·  PENSATORI LIBERI NELL'-
   ITALIA CONTEMPORANEA·
   F·J· JONES, 402(MLR):APR72-435
PERSONS, S·  THE DECLINE OF AMERICAN GEN-
   TILITY·
   I·R· DEE, 441:16DEC73-23
PERSSON, P·E·  SACRA DOCTRINA·
   J·B·, 543:DEC70-345
   J·F· WIPPEL, 589:OCT72-789
PERTUSI, A·, ED·  LA STORIOGRAFIA VENEZI-
   ANA FINO AL SECOLO XVI·
   F·C· LANE, 589:APR72-292
PESCE, D· - SEE LAMANNA, E·P·
PESCHKEN, B·  ENTSAGUNG IN WILHELM MEIS-
   TERS WANDERJAHREN·
   H· REISS, 220(GL&L):OCT71-39
PESCHMANN, H·, ED·  THE VOICE OF POETRY·
   (2ND ED)
   H· SERGEANT, 175:SPRING70-29
PESTALOZZI, K·  DIE ENTSTEHUNG DES LYR-
   ISCHEN ICH·
   R·D· SCHIER, 301(JEGP):JAN72-85
PETER THE VENERABLE·  PETRI VENERABILIS
   CONTRA PETROBRUSIANOS HERETICOS·  (J·
   FEARNS, ED)
   D· LUSCOMBE, 382(MAE):1972/2-141
PETER, H·  ENTSTEHUNG AUS AUSBILDUNG DER
   ITALIENISCHEN EISENBAHNTERMINOLOGIE·*
   W·T· ELWERT, 72:BAND209HEFT4/6-443
PETERFALVI, J-M·  INTRODUCTION À LA
   PSYCHOLINGUISTIQUE·
   E·P· HAMP, 269(IJAL):JUL71-211
PETERFALVI, J-M·  RECHERCHES EXPÉRIMEN-
   TALES SUR LE SYMBOLISME PHONÉTIQUE·
   M· CHASTAING, 182:VOL24#15/16-586
PETERKIEWICZ, J·  THE OTHER SIDE OF
   SILENCE·*
   D· DAVIE, 575(SEER):JUL72-456
   L·T·L·, 502(PRS):SUMMER70-184
   G·W· NITCHIE, 141:WINTER71-107
PETERKIN, J·  THE COLLECTED SHORT STORIES
   OF JULIA PETERKIN·  (F· DURHAM, ED)
   B· CHENEY, 569(SR):WINTER72-173
   L· HARTLEY, 577(SHR):SUMMER71-291
PETERMANN, K·  TANZBIBLIOGRAPHIE·  (VOLS
   1-6)
   J· DE LABAN, 650(WF):JAN70-64
   J· DE LABAN, 650(WF):APR71-154
PETERS, E·  CITY OF GOLD AND SHADOWS·
   617(TLS):16NOV73-1407
PETERS, E·  THE SHADOW KING·
   B· COTTLE, 301(JEGP):JAN72-111
   R·G· GIESEY, 589:OCT72-791
PETERS, F·E·  ARISTOTLE AND THE ARABS·*
   H· CATON, 480(P&R):SUMMER71-196
   L·E· GOODMAN, 485(PE&W):JAN70-92
   J·R·, 543:SEP70-141
PETERS, J·R·  ECONOMICS OF THE CANADIAN
   CORPORATE BOND MARKET·
   J·L· MC DOUGALL, 529(QQ):AUTUMN71-469
PETERS, M·  CHARLOTTE BRONTË·
   617(TLS):3AUG73-903

PETERS, R·A·  A LINGUISTIC HISTORY OF
   ENGLISH·
   T· GARDNER, 38:BAND89HEFT4-480
PETERS, R·S·, ED·  THE CONCEPT OF EDUCA-
   TION·
   R·J·B·, 543:SEP70-144
PETERS, R·S·  REASON AND COMPASSION·
   617(TLS):7DEC73-1498
PETERS, V·  NESTOR MAKHNO·*
   102(CANL):WINTER72-104
PETERSEN, A·  QUANTUM PHYSICS AND THE
   PHILOSOPHICAL TRADITION·
   J· BUB, 486:MAR70-156
PETERSEN, L·  PROSOPOGRAPHIA IMPERII
   ROMANI SAEC· I, II, III·  (REV) (PT 5,
   FASC 1)
   M·A·R· COLLEDGE, 123:JUN72-284
PETERSON, A·D·C·  THE FUTURE OF THE
   SIXTH FORM·
   617(TLS):18MAY73-552
PETERSON, H·  THE MAN WHO INVENTED BASE-
   BALL·
   R· SMITH, 441:20MAY73-42
PETERSON, K·D·  HOWLING WOLF·
   T·O· BALLINGER, 650(WF):JUL70-213
PETERSON, M·D·  THOMAS JEFFERSON AND THE
   NEW NATION·
   H· AMMON, 656(WMQ):JUL71-487
   A·C· LAND, 432(NEQ):MAR71-149
   V·P· LANNIE, 613:SUMMER71-309
   G·S· WOOD, 639(VQR):WINTER71-137
   185:OCT70-89
PETERSON, W·  INTERROGATING THE ORACLE·
   R·A· KING, JR·, 85:FALL71-56
PETERSSON, R·T·  THE ART OF ECSTASY·*
   M·R· BROWNELL, 290(JAAC):SUMMER71-567
   J·E· CHAMBERLIN, 249(HUDR):WINTER
   72/73-695
PETIT, H·, ED·  ALAIN ET ROMAIN ROLLAND·
   J· RELINGER, 535(RHL):MAR-APR70-344
PETIT, J· - SEE GREEN, J·
"LE PETIT PLET·"*  (B·S· MERRILEES, ED)
   M·D· LEGGE, 208(FS):JUL72-314
PETKOFF, T·  SOCIALISMO PARA VENEZUELA?
   N· GALL, 453:15NOV73-29
PETRAKIS, H·M·  IN THE LAND OF MORNING·
   R·P· BRICKNER, 441:11MAR73-47
   T· LASK, 441:10MAR73-35
PETRAN, T·  SYRIA·
   617(TLS):15JUN73-700
PETRARCA, F·  IL BUCOLICUM CARMEN E I
   SUOI COMMENTI INEDITI·  (A· AVENA, ED)
   L·T·, 275(IQ):SPRING-SUMMER72-114
PETRARCH·  LORD MORLEY'S "TRYUMPHES OF
   FRAUNCES PETRARCKE·"  (D·D· CARNI-
   CELLI, ED)
   G· WATSON, 382(MAE):1972/3-279
PETRIE, C·  THE GREAT TYRCONNEL·
   617(TLS):20APR73-454
PETRIE, G·  THE BRANCH-BEARERS·
   V· CUNNINGHAM, 362:26JUL73-125
   617(TLS):6JUL73-783
PETROCCHI, G· - SEE DANTE ALIGHIERI
PETRONIUS·  PETRONIO ARBITRO, "DAL SATYRI-
   CON: CENA TRIMALCHIONIS, TROIAE HALOSIS,
   BELLUM CIVILE·"  (E· CASTORINA, ED &
   TRANS)
   R· BROWNING, 123:JUN72-228
PETROV, V·P·  MONGOLIA·*
   P·S·H· TANG, 293(JAST):AUG71-904
PETROV, V·P·  SKIFY - MOVA I ETNOS·
   L·M·L· ONYSHKEVYCH, 424:MAR71-59
PETRUCCI, O·  OTTAVIANO PETRUCCI: CANTI B
   NUMERO CINQUANTA (VENICE, 1502)·*  (H·
   HEWITT, ED)
   N· BRIDGMAN, 551(RENQ):AUTUMN71-363
PETRUCCIANI, M· - SEE PRAGA, E·
PETRY, M·J· - SEE HEGEL, G·W·F·

PETTER, H. THE EARLY AMERICAN NOVEL.*
 T. MARTIN, 579(SAQ):SUMMER72-438
PETTIT, F.H. AMERICA'S PRINTED AND
 PAINTED FABRICS.
 M. LYON, 139:DEC70-9
PETTIT, H. - SEE YOUNG, E.
PETTIT, P. ON THE IDEA OF PHENOMENOLOGY.*
 L.G., 543:MAR71-547
PETZET, H.W. VON WORPSWEDE NACH MOSKAU:
 HEINRICH VOGELER.
 617(TLS):30MAR73-344
PETZOLD, K-E. STUDIEN ZUR METHODE DES
 POLYBIOS UND ZU IHRER HISTORISCHEN
 AUSWERTUNG.*
 J.J. FARBER, 24:OCT72-638
PETZOLDT, L., ED. DEUTSCHE VOLKSSAGEN.
 R. MICHAELIS-JENA, 203:WINTER71-336
PETZOLDT, L. DER TOTE ALS GAST.
 G. PETSCHEL, 680(ZDP):BAND90HEFT4-628
PETZOLDT, L., ED. VERGLEICHENDE SAGEN-
 FORSCHUNG.
 F. HARKORT, 196:BAND12HEFT1-102
PETZSCH, C. DAS LOCHAMER - LIEDERBUCH.
 P. OCHSENBEIN, 657(WW):MAY/JUN70-213
 N.T.J. VOORWINDEN, 433:OCT70-428
PEUCKERT, W-E. GABALIA.
 I. HAMPP, 680(ZDP):BAND89HEFT1-140
PEUCKERT, W-E. NIEDERSÄCHSISCHE SAGEN
 I-IV.
 H. LIXFELD, 196:BAND12HEFT1-103
PEUCKERT, W-E. SCHLESISCHE SAGEN. (2ND
 ED)
 F. HARKORT, 196:BAND12HEFT2/3-284
VAN PEURSEN, C.A. LEIBNIZ.*
 E.A.R., 543:DEC70-348
PEVSNER, N. THE BUILDINGS OF ENGLAND:
 LONDON. (VOL 1) (3RD ED REV BY B.
 CHERRY)
 617(TLS):15JUN73-700
PEVSNER, N. THE SOURCES OF MODERN ARCHI-
 TECTURE AND DESIGN.*
 S. ANDERSON, 54:JUN71-274
PEVSNER, N. STUDIES IN ART, ARCHITECTURE
 AND DESIGN.*
 J. WILTON-ELY, 39:JAN70-82
PEVSNER, N. & J.M. RICHARDS, EDS. THE
 ANTI-RATIONALISTS.
 G. WOODCOCK, 99:NOV-DEC73-41
PEYRE, H. HISTORICAL AND CRITICAL
 ESSAYS.*
 S. FRAISSE, 535(RHL):JAN-FEB70-165
 L.T. LEMON, 502(PRS):FALL70-263
PEYRE, H. LITERATURE AND SINCERITY.
 A.J. FRY, 433:JUL70-321
 H.T. MASON, 447(N&Q):SEP71-359
 R. THEIS, 52:BAND5HEFT2-200
PEYRE, H. RENAN.
 R. GALAND, 207(FR):MAY71-1131
 K. GORE, 208(FS):JAN72-89
PEYRE, H. JEAN-PAUL SARTRE.*
 R. GOLDTHORPE, 208(FS):JAN72-95
PEYRE, H. - SEE RENAN, J.E.
PEYROT, L. MA MORT EST TA VIE.
 F.F. BRUCE, 182:VOL24#5-200
PEYTARD, J. & E. GENOUVRIER. LINGUISTIQUE
 ET ENSEIGNEMENT DU FRANÇAIS.
 N. GUEUNIER, 209(FM):OCT71-353
 G. SCHWEIG, 430(NS):FEB71-101
PFÄNDER, A. PHENOMENOLOGY OF WILLING AND
 MOTIVATION.
 A.D.M., 543:DEC70-345
PFEFFER, J.A. GERMAN REVIEW GRAMMAR.
 (2ND ED)
 E.M. BISCHOFF, 221(GQ):NOV71-624
PFEFFER, J.A. GRUNDDEUTSCH.*
 K. BAHNICK, 221(GQ):MAY71-436
PFEFFER, K. NIETZSCHE.
 J. STAMBAUGH, 311(JP):24MAY73-302

PFEIFFER, E., ED. FRIEDRICH NIETZSCHE/
 PAUL RÉE/LOU VON SALOMÉ.
 J.A. KRUSE, 182:VOL24#9/10-423
PFEIFFER, E. - SEE FREUD, S. & L. ANDREAS-
 SALOMÉ
PFEIFFER, F. & K. BARTSCH. BRIEFWECHSEL.
 (H-J. KOPPITZ, ED)
 F.R. SCHRÖDER, 224(GRM):BAND21HEFT2-
 245
 F. WHITEHEAD, 208(FS):APR72-242
PFEIFFER, G. KUNST UND KOMMUNIKATION.
 617(TLS):12OCT73-1255
PFIFFIG, A.J. STUDIEN ZU DEN AGRAMER
 MUMIENBINDEN.
 A. HUS, 343:BAND13HEFT1-107
PFIFFIG, A.J. UNI-HERA-ASTARTE.
 A. HUS, 343:BAND13HEFT2-210
PFLUG, G. HENRI BERGSON, QUELLEN UND
 KONSEQUENZEN EINER INDUKTIVEN META-
 PHYSIK.
 R. VIOLETTE, 542:OCT-DEC71-443
PHAEDRUS. PHAEDRI AUGUSTI LIBERTI "LIBER
 FABULARUM."* (A. GUAGLIANONE, ED)
 F.R.D. GOODYEAR, 123:MAR72-50
 P.K. MARSHALL, 24:JUL72-506
PHAYRE, A.P. HISTORY OF BURMA INCLUDING
 BURMA PROPER, PEGU, TAUNGU, TENASSERIM,
 AND ARAKAN.
 D.K. WYATT, 293(JAST):NOV70-228
PHELAN, J. & R. POZEN. THE COMPANY
 STATE.
 R. SHERRILL, 441:4MAR73-3
PHELPS, G. THE OLD BELIEVER.
 V. CUNNINGHAM, 362:30AUG73-288
 617(TLS):31AUG73-993
PHELPS, R. - SEE COCTEAU, J.
PHELPS, R. & R. LIMMER - SEE BOGAN, L.
PHELPS, R. & J.M. STEIN. THE GERMAN
 HERITAGE. (3RD ED)
 G.W. DUNNINGHAM, 399(MLJ):OCT71-410
PHILIPP, M. PHONOLOGIE DES GRAPHIES ET
 DES RIMES.*
 I.T. PIIRAINEN, 182:VOL24#13/14-540
PHILIPP, M. LE SYSTÈME PHONOLOGIQUE DU
 PARLER DE BLAESHEIM.
 G. LERCHNER, 682(ZPSK):BAND23HEFT2/3-
 309
PHILIPPEN, J. DE OUDE VLAAMSE BEDEVAART-
 VAANTJES.*
 H. PAUL, 650(WF):APR71-152
PHILIPPI, D.L. - SEE "KOJIKI"
PHILIPS, J. THE LARKSPUR CONSPIRACY.
 N. CALLENDAR, 441:18NOV73-56
PHILIPS, J. THE VANISHING SENATOR.*
 617(TLS):17AUG73-959
PHILLIPS, A.A., ED. COAST TO COAST
 1967-8.
 M. WILDING, 381:JUN71-255
PHILLIPS, A.A. HENRY LAWSON.
 L. CANTRELL, 71(ALS):MAY73-99
PHILLIPS, C.E.L. - SEE UNDER LUCAS PHIL-
 LIPS, C.E.
PHILLIPS, D. NO POETS' CORNER IN THE
 ABBEY.
 R. MC KINNON, 619(TC):VOL179#1048-55
PHILLIPS, D. WAVE.* THE COHERENCE.
 D. BARBOUR, 102(CANL):SPRING72-77
PHILLIPS, D.Z. DEATH AND IMMORTALITY.*
 H. PAGE, 150(DR):WINTER71/72-598
PHILLIPS, D.Z. & H.O. MOUNCE. MORAL
 PRACTICES.*
 R.F. ATKINSON, 483:APR71-179
PHILLIPS, E.D. GREEK MEDICINE.
 617(TLS):4MAY73-506
PHILLIPS, E.D. THE MONGOLS.
 R. MC GUIRK, 244(HJAS):VOL30-281
PHILLIPS, E.D. LES NOMADES DE LA STEPPE.
 P. GUERRE, 98:DEC71-1093

PHILLIPS, G.A. & R.T. MADDOCK. THE
GROWTH OF THE BRITISH ECONOMY 1918-1968.
617(TLS):12OCT73-1224
PHILLIPS, G.R. JOHN ATKINSON GRIMSHAW
1836-1893.
617(TLS):2FEB73-121
PHILLIPS, J.R.S. AYMER DE VALENCE EARL
OF PEMBROKE 1307-1324.
617(TLS):30MAR73-355
PHILLIPS, R., ED. ASPECTS OF ALICE.*
G. SOULE, 109:FALL/WINTER72/73-102
PHILLIPS, R.A.J. CANADA'S NORTH.
D.W. SWAINSON, 529(QQ):SUMMER71-323
PHILLIPS, W. & R. KEATLEY. CHINA BEHIND
THE MASK.
J.K. FAIRBANK, 453:1NOV73-3
PHILLIPSON, D. SMUGGLING.
617(TLS):2NOV73-1352
PHILMUS, R.M. INTO THE UNKNOWN.
C.C. DOYLE, 173(ECS):SPRING71-352
J. RUSS, 128(CE):DEC71-368
W.D. SCHAEFER, 445(NCF):DEC70-381
"PHILOLOGIA FRISICA ANNO 1966."
B. SJÖLIN, 597(SN):VOL43#1-285
PHILONENKO, A. L'OEUVRE DE KANT. (VOL
1)
R. MALTER, 342:BAND62HEFT1-140
PHILONENKO, A. THÉORIE ET PRAXIS DANS LA
PENSÉE MORALE ET POLITIQUE DE KANT ET
DE FICHTE EN 1793.
K. OEDINGEN, 342:BAND61HEFT1-135
PHILONENKO, A. - SEE KANT, I.
"PHILOSOPHIA: YEARBOOK OF THE RESEARCH
CENTER FOR GREEK PHILOSOPHY OF THE
ACADEMY OF ATHENS." (1971)
G. ANAGNOSTOPOULOS, 319:APR73-252
"PHILOSOPHY AND THE ARTS."
617(TLS):29JUN73-753
"PHILOSOPHY AND THE FUTURE OF MAN."
P. DUBOIS, 542:JUL-SEP70-354
PHILOSTRATUS. LIFE OF APOLLONIUS. (C.P.
JONES, TRANS; ED & ABRIDGED BY G.W.
BOWERSOCK)
H.B. TIMOTHY, 124:NOV71-95
PHILOSTRATUS. PHILOSTRATOS, "DIE BILDER
(EIKONES)." (O. SCHÖNBERGER, ED &
TRANS)
J.M. COOK, 123:MAR72-105
PHILPOT, A.R. DICTIONARY OF PUPPETRY.
J.B. MYERS, 139:FEB71-10
PHORIS, B.D. ANTISTROPHOS PINAKAS TŌN
EPIRREMATŌN SE//ŌS TĒS ARCHAIAS HELLĒN-
IKĒS.
A.F. GARVIE, 123:JUN72-282
PHYSICK, J. DESIGNS FOR ENGLISH SCULP-
TURE 1680-1860.*
J.L-M., 135:AUG70-288
PHYSICK, J. THE WELLINGTON MONUMENT.
M. GIROUARD, 46:NOV71-324
P. SYNGE-HUTCHINSON, 135:NOV71-216
PHYSICK, J. & M. DARBY. MARBLE HALLS.
617(TLS):26OCT73-1298
PIA, P. - SEE LAFORGUE, J.
PIAGET, A. - SEE LE FRANC, M.
PIAGET, J., ED. LOGIQUE ET CONNAISSANCE
SCIENTIFIQUE.
R. BLANCHÉ, 542:OCT-DEC70-498
PIAGET, J. PSYCHOLOGY AND EPISTEMOLOGY.
617(TLS):29JUN73-753
PIAGET, J. SAGGEZZA E ILLUSIONI DELLA
FILOSOFIA.
M. ANTOMELLI, 548(RCSF):OCT-DEC71-469
PIAGET, J. LE STRUCTURALISME.
K. OHNESORG, 353:MAR71-94
PIAGET, J. & OTHERS. EPISTÉMOLOGIE ET
PSYCHOLOGIE DE LA FONCTION.
R. BLANCHÉ, 542:OCT-DEC70-500

PIAGET, J. & OTHERS. L'ÉPISTÉMOLOGIE DU
TEMPS.
R. BLANCHÉ, 542:OCT-DEC70-498
PIANEZZOLA, E. TRADUZIONE E IDEOLOGIA.*
J-C. DUMONT, 555:VOL45FASC1-172
PIAULT, M.H. HISTOIRE MAWRI.
I.A. DER MAUR, 182:VOL24#21/22-828
PIBLIS, S. PANATHENAEA, THE GREATEST
FESTIVAL OF ANCIENT ATHENS.
J.M. COOK, 123:DEC72-431
PICA, A. PIER LUIGI NERVI.
S. BUZAS, 46:MAR70-234
PICARD, G. ROMAN PAINTING.*
R. HIGGINS, 39:AUG71-162
D.E. STRONG, 123:JUN72-259
PICARD, R. GÉNIE DE LA LITTÉRATURE FRAN-
ÇAISE (1600-1800).
J. DUBU, 535(RHL):MAY-JUN71-501
PICARD, R. TWO CENTURIES OF FRENCH LIT-
ERATURE (1600-1800).
P.J. YARROW, 208(FS):JUL72-323
PICASSO, P. PICASSO ON ART.* (D. ASH-
TON, ED)
A. BLUNT, 453:14JUN73-31
617(TLS):17AUG73-944
"PICASSO'S PRIVATE DRAWINGS."
J.P., 376:JUL70-117
PICCARD, J. THE SUN BENEATH THE SEA.
617(TLS):13JUL73-815
PICCHIO, L.S. - SEE UNDER STEGAGNO PIC-
CHIO, L.
PICCIONI, L. VITA DI UN POETA.
M. PUCCINI, 275(IQ):SUMMER71-114
PICCOLOMINI, A. RAFFAELLA. (J. NEVIN-
SON, TRANS)
F. CERRETA, 276:AUTUMN71-391
PICCOLOMINI, A.S. SELECTED LETTERS OF
AENEAS SILVIUS PICCOLOMINI.* (A.R.
BACA, TRANS)
C.H. CLOUGH, 377:MAR72-53
PICHOIS, C. - SEE COLETTE
PICHOIS, C. & R. FORBIN - SEE COLETTE
PICHOIS, C. & A-M. ROUSSEAU. LA LITTÉRA-
TURE COMPARÉE.*
H.H.H. REMAK, 549(RLC):OCT-DEC70-547
PICHT, G. & H.E. TÖDT, EDS. STUDIEN ZUR
FRIEDENSFORSCHUNG. (VOL 1)
M. ROCK, 182:VOL24#6-265
PICKERING, F.P., ED. THE ANGLO-NORMAN
TEXT OF THE HOLKHAM BIBLE PICTURE BOOK.
W.O. HASSALL, 382(MAE):1972/2-149
PICKERING, F.P. AUGUSTINUS ODER
BOETHIUS?*
P.C. KERN, 657(WW):JAN/FEB71-66
J.G. KUNSTMANN, 221(GQ):MAR71-248
PICKERING, F.P. LITERATURE AND ART IN
THE MIDDLE AGES.
D.S. BREWER, 402(MLR):APR72-392
J.E. CHAMBERLIN, 249(HUDR):WINTER
72/73-696
A.C. SPEARING, 111:13NOV70-66
PICKERODT, G. HOFMANNSTHALS DRAMEN.
H.K. DOSWALD, 222(GR):MAY71-235
PICKERSGILL, J.W. & D.F. FORSTER - SEE
KING, W.L.M.
PICKLES, D. THE GOVERNMENT AND POLITICS
OF FRANCE.
617(TLS):21DEC73-1560
PICO DELLA MIRANDOLA, G. DE DIGNITATE
HOMINIS. (E. GARIN, ED)
F.G. SIEVEKE, 224(GRM):BAND21HEFT4-
472
J. THOMAS, 52:BAND5HEFT3-315
PICOCHE, J. UN VOCABULAIRE PICARD
D'AUTREFOIS.
R. ARVEILLER, 545(RPH):FEB72-340
F. CARTON, 209(FM):JUL71-264

PICÓN-SALAS, M. PEDRO CLAVER, EL SANTO
DE LOS ESCLAVOS.
  B. DULSEY, 238:SEP71-603
"A PICTORIAL ENCYCLOPEDIA OF THE ORIENTAL
ARTS."
  A. SOPER, 57:VOL32#1-94
PIEHLER, P. THE VISIONARY LANDSCAPE.
  K.A. BLEETH, 589:JAN72-138
  S. DELANY, 648:JAN72-79
  R.M. WILSON, 175:AUTUMN71-96
PIEPERS, N. LA "REVUE GÉNÉRALE" DE 1865
À 1940.
  A. ZUMKIR, 556(RLV):1971/4-511
PIERCE, F. - SEE DE CERVANTES SAAVEDRA, M.
PIERCE, J-R. SYMBOLES, SIGNAUX ET BRUIT.
LE CONCEPT D'INFORMATION DANS LA SCI-
ENCE CONTEMPORAINE.
  J.E. MORÈRE, 542:APR-JUN70-175
PIERCE, N. MESSENGER FROM MUNICH.
  N. CALLENDAR, 441:22JUL73-14
PIERCE, R.B. SHAKESPEARE'S HISTORY PLAYS.
  C.C. HUFFMAN, 301(JEGP):JUL72-441
PIERCY, M. BREAKING CAMP.*
  M. MARCUS, 502(PRS):FALL71-275
PIERCY, M. DANCE THE EAGLE TO SLEEP.*
  639(VQR):SUMMER71-XCVII
PIERCY, M. HARD LOVING.
  V. CONTOSKI, 600:FALL70-130
PIERCY, M. SMALL CHANGES.
  S. BLACKBURN, 441:12AUG73-2
  R. TODD, 61:SEP73-105
PIERI, S. TOPONOMASTICA DELLA TOSCANA
MERIDIONALE (VALLI DELLA FIORA, DELL'-
OMBRONE, DELLA CECINA E FIUMI MINORI)
E DELL'ARCIPELAGO TOSCANO.
  J.G. FUCILLA, 424:JUN70-125
PIERIUS, U. GESCHICHTE DER KURSÄCHSIS-
CHEN KIRCHEN- UND SCHULREFORMATION.
  E.G. SCHWIEBERT, 182:VOL24#9/10-439
PIERRET, M. RICHELIEU, OU LA DÉRAISON
D'ETAT.
  617(TLS):27JUL73-878
PIERRO, A. CURTELLE A LU SÓUE.
  617(TLS):5OCT73-1176
PIERROT, R. - SEE DE BALZAC, H.
PIERSON, S. MARXISM AND THE ORIGINS OF
BRITISH SOCIALISM.
  617(TLS):21SEP73-1079
PIERSON, W.H., JR. AMERICAN BUILDINGS
AND THEIR ARCHITECTS.
  L. WODEHOUSE, 576:DEC71-333
PIÉTRI, M. HISTOIRES DU RELIEF.
  R.B. JOHNSON, 207(FR):APR71-966
PIETROSI BARROW, L. DAL NEOREALISMO ALLO
SPERIMENTALISMO.
  R. KOFFLER, 276:SPRING71-104
PIGAFETTA, A., MAXIMILIAN OF TRANSYLVANIA
& G. CORRÊA. MAGELLAN'S VOYAGE AROUND
THE WORLD: THREE CONTEMPORARY ACCOUNTS.
(C.E. NOWELL, TRANS)
  W.G. BOLTZ, 545(RPH):MAY72-430
PIGEAUD, T.G.T. LITERATURE OF JAVA.
(VOLS 2&3)
  J.M. ECHOLS, 318(JAOS):OCT-DEC71-561
PIGNATTI, T., ED. CANALETTO: SELECTED
DRAWINGS.*
  F.J.B. WATSON, 39:SEP71-244
PIGNATTI, T. GIORGIONE.
  M.V. ALPER, 58:APR72-27
  G. ROBERTSON, 90:AUG71-475
PIGNATTI, T. PIETRO LONGHI.*
  M. LEVEY, 54:DEC70-463
  R. PAULSON, 173(ECS):SUMMER71-458
  D.T., 135:JAN71-55
PIIRAINEN, I.T. GRAPHEMATISCHE UNTER-
SUCHUNGEN ZUM FRÜHNEUHOCHDEUTSCHEN.*
  J. GOHEEN, 564:OCT70-241
                            [CONTINUED]

[CONTINUING]
  H. VAN DER KOLK, 433:OCT71-468
  H. SINGER, 657(WW):JUL/AUG70-272
PIKE, D. WAR, PEACE, AND THE VIET CONG.
  F.N. TRAGER, 293(JAST):AUG71-925
PIKE, E.R. THE STRANGE WAYS OF MAN.
  P.E. LEIS, 650(WF):APR70-141
PIKE, F.B. SPANISH AMERICA 1900-1970.
  617(TLS):14DEC73-1532
PIKE, N. GOD AND TIMELESSNESS.*
  M. KNEALE, 483:APR71-178
  W. NEWTON-SMITH, 154:MAR71-201
  S.R. SUTHERLAND, 479(PHQ):APR71-187
PILAT, O. DREW PEARSON.
  W.V. SHANNON, 441:29APR73-4
PILBROW, R. STAGE LIGHTING.
  J. WYCKHAM, 157:SUMMER71-81
PILCH, H. ALTENGLISCHE GRAMMATIK.* ALT-
ENGLISCHER LEHRGANG.*
  H. KOZIOL, 72:BAND209HEFT1/3-139
PILCH, H. & U. STEWART - SEE MOSSÉ, F.
PILKINGTON, J., JR. HENRY BLAKE FULLER.*
  J. SCHIFFMAN, 579(SAQ):WINTER72-133
PILL, D.H. THE ENGLISH REFORMATION.
  617(TLS):21SEP73-1093
PILLAI, P.M.J.S. - SEE UNDER SOMASUNDARAM
PILLAI, P.M.J.
PILLEMENT, G. UNKNOWN GREECE.
  617(TLS):9MAR73-277
PILLININI, G. IL SISTEMA DEGLI STATI
ITALIANI, 1454-1494.
  V. ILARDI, 589:OCT72-793
PILLSBURY, P.W. DESCRIPTIVE ANALYSIS OF
DISCOURSE IN LATE WEST SAXON TEXTS.
  B. CARSTENSEN, 38:BAND89HEFT2-246
  R.E. PALMER, JR., 361:VOL26#1-96
PIMSLEUR, P. C'EST LA VIE.
  J. CAROS, 399(MLJ):FEB71-119
  H. JAECKEL, 207:DEC70-430
PIÑAL, F.A. - SEE UNDER AGUILAR PIÑAL, F.
PINBORG, J. & H. ROOS, WITH S.S. JENSEN
- SEE "BOETHII DACI OPERA"
PINCHER, C. SEX IN OUR TIME.
  617(TLS):20JUL73-835
PINCUS, C. COME FROM THE FOUR WINDS.
  L. ELKIN, 287:MAY71-24
  A. HERTZBERG, 390:MAR71-78
PINDAR. DIE ISTHMISCHEN GEDICHTE.* (E.
THUMMER, ED & TRANS)
  D.E. GERBER, 487:SPRING71-74
PINE, L.G. THE NEW EXTINCT PEERAGE
1884-1971.
  617(TLS):3AUG73-906
PINEAS, R. THOMAS MORE AND TUDOR POLEM-
ICS.
  R. KOEHL, 480(P&R):SUMMER71-181
PINEAU, R. - SEE PERRY, M.C.
PING, C. & D. BLOODWORTH. HEIRS APPAR-
ENT.
  S. TOPPING, 441:11AUG73-17
  617(TLS):16MAR73-287
PING-TI, H. - SEE UNDER HO PING-TI
PINGAUD, B. LA VOIX DE SON MAÎTRE.
  617(TLS):17AUG73-945
PINGEL, V. DIE GLATTE DREHSCHEIBEN-
KERAMIK VON MANCHING.
  R. PITTIONI, 182:VOL24#21/22-801
PINGET, R. LE LIBERA.
  M.G. ROSE, 207(FR):OCT70-182
PINGET, R. PASSACAILLE.
  A. CISMARU, 207(FR):OCT70-183
  R. HENKELS, JR., 454:SPRING72-274
PINGREE, D. - SEE ABŪ MA'SHAR
PINGUENTINI, G. NUOVO DIZIONARIO DEL
DIALETTO TRIESTINO.
  R.O.J. VAN NUFFEL, 549(RLC):JUL-SEP
  70-415

PINI, I. BEITRÄGE ZUR MINOISCHEN GRÄBER-
KUNDE.*
J.E. COLEMAN, 54:SEP71-394
PINILLA, R. EN EL TIEMPO DE LOS TALLOS
VERDES.
J.W. DÍAZ, 238:MAY71-395
PINION, F.B. A JANE AUSTEN COMPANION.
617(TLS):26JAN73-99
PINKNEY, D.H. THE FRENCH REVOLUTION OF
1830.
617(TLS):27JUL73-878
PINKNEY, H.R. CHRISTOPHER GORE.
R.F. BANKS, 656(WMQ):OCT71-686
PINNA, G. THE DAWN OF LIFE.
617(TLS):16MAR73-305
DEL PINO, C.C. - SEE UNDER CASTILLA DEL
PINO, C.
PINSENT, J. GREEK MYTHOLOGY.*
R. HIGGINS, 39:AUG71-160
PINSKY, R. LANDOR'S POETRY.*
R. LAWRENCE, 175:SUMMER70-69
PINTER, H. FIVE SCREENPLAYS.
P. ROBERTS, 565:VOL12#4-60
PINTER, H. LANDSCAPE, SILENCE [AND]
NIGHT.
PINTER, H. MIXED DOUBLES.
P. ROBERTS, 565:VOL12#1-64
PINTER, H. TEA PARTY AND OTHER PLAYS
BY HAROLD PINTER.
S. DAY-LEWIS, 157:AUTUMN70-76
P. ROBERTS, 565:VOL12#1-64
PINTO, E.H. TREEN AND OTHER WOODEN BY-
GONES.
E.T.J., 135:AUG70-289
PINTO, V.D. - SEE UNDER DE SOLA PINTO, V.
PIPA, A. MONTALE AND DANTE.*
G. SINGH, 276:AUTUMN71-402
PIPA, F. ELEMENTARY ALBANIAN.
S.E. MANN, 575(SEER):JUL72-450
PIPER, D. THE DEVELOPMENT OF THE BRITISH
LITERARY PORTRAIT.
R. EDWARDS, 39:JAN71-69
K. GARLICK, 447(N&Q):AUG71-315
PIPER, D.G.B. V.A. KAVERIN.
E.J. BROWN, 32:MAR72-198
PIPER, D.W., ED. READINGS IN ART AND
DESIGN EDUCATION.
617(TLS):21SEP73-1078
PIPER, W.B. THE HEROIC COUPLET.*
W. BLISSETT, 627(UTQ):WINTER71-183
O.F. SIGWORTH, 50(ARQ):AUTUMN71-279
PIPES, R. STRUVE.*
W.E. MOSSE, 575(SEER):JAN72-126
L. SCHAPIRO, 550(RUSR):JUL71-294
PIPPIDI, D.M. CONTRIBUȚII LA ISTORIA
VECHE A ROMÂNIEI.
W.G. FORREST, 303:VOL91-198
"PIRACY AND PRIVATEERING."
617(TLS):1JUN73-625
PIRANDELLO, L. THREE PLAYS.* (F. FIRTH,
ED)
L. KLEM, 462(OL):VOL26#1-79
PIRANESI, G.B. THE POLEMICAL WORKS.
(J. WILTON-ELY, ED)
617(TLS):2MAR73-236
"GIOVANNI BATTISTA PIRANESI: DRAWINGS
AND ETCHINGS AT COLUMBIA UNIVERSITY."
617(TLS):2MAR73-236
PIRANI, E. GOTHIC ILLUMINATED MANU-
SCRIPTS.
J. BECKWITH, 39:OCT71-322
PIRIE, D. A HERITAGE OF HORROR.
617(TLS):23NOV73-1418
PIRON, M. LE PROBLÈME DES LITTÉRATURES
FRANÇAISES MARGINALES.
M.E. GILES, 545(RPH):AUG71-151
PIRROTTA, N. LI DUE ORFEI.
H.M. BROWN, 414(MQ):OCT71-671

DE PISAN, C. THE EPISTLE OF OTHEA. (S.
SCROPE, TRANS; C.F. BÜHLER, ED)
M.W. BLOOMFIELD, 589:OCT72-803
D. PEARSALL, 382(MAE):1972/3-274
PISANI, V. L'ETIMOLOGIA. (2ND ED)
R. KATIČIĆ, 260(IF):BAND75-280
PISANI, V. LE LINGUE DELL'ITALIA ANTICA
OLTRE IL LATINO. (2ND ED)
C. DE SIMONE, 260(IF):BAND74-246
PITCHER, G. A THEORY OF PERCEPTION.
J.W.R. COX, 518:MAY72-26
PITOU, S. THE TEXT AND SOURCES OF CHAT-
EAUBRUN'S LOST "AJAX."
J.H. DAVIS, JR., 546(RR):FEB71-59
"PITSEOLAK: PICTURES OUT OF MY LIFE."
(D.H. EBER, ED & TRANS)
H.P. GUNDY, 529(QQ):WINTER71-641
PITTOCK, J. THE ASCENDANCY OF TASTE.
617(TLS):5OCT73-1178
PITZ, E. ÜBERSICHT ÜBER DIE BESTÄNDE DES
NIEDERSÄCHSISCHEN STAATSARCHIVS IN
HANNOVER. (VOL 2)
C.A.F. MEEKINGS, 325:APR71-251
PIVIDAL, R. TENTATIVE DE VISITE À UNE
BASE ÉTRANGÈRE.
P.J. JOHNSON, 207(FR):MAY71-1125
PIZER, D. - SEE GARLAND, H.
PIZZORUSSO, A. TEORIE LETTERARIE IN
FRANCIA.
J. BRODY, 546(RR):OCT71-235
J-M. GARDAIR, 98:JAN70-25
S. MENANT, 535(RHL):MAY-JUN71-508
O. RAGUSA, 207(FR):DEC70-478
PLAATJE, S.T. THE BOER WAR DIARY OF SOL
T. PLAATJE. (J.L. COMAROFF, ED)
617(TLS):30NOV73-1472
PLACE, E.B., ED. AMADÍS DE GAULA.* (VOLS
1-4)
C.C. SMITH, 402(MLR):JAN72-192
DES PLACES, E. LA RELIGION GRECQUE.*
J. POLLARD, 303:VOL91-171
Z. STEWART, 241:APR72-361
F. VIAN, 555:VOL45FASC1-132
PLAMENATZ, J. DEMOCRACY AND ILLUSION.
J. DUNN, 362:23AUG73-252
617(TLS):11MAY73-520
PLANO, J.C. INTERNATIONAL APPROACHES TO
THE PROBLEMS OF MARINE POLLUTION.
617(TLS):20APR73-434
PLANT, H.R. SYNTAKTISCHE STUDIEN ZU DEN
MONSEER FRAGMENTEN.
B. MURDOCH, 220(GL&L):APR72-315
PLANT, R. HEGEL.
617(TLS):12OCT73-1237
PLANTINGA, A. GOD AND OTHER MINDS.*
G.I. MAVRODES, 543:SEP70-82
PLANTY-BONJOUR, G. - SEE HEGEL, G.W.F.
PLANYAVSKY, A. GESCHICHTE DES KONTRA-
BASSES.
R.S., 410(M&L):JUL72-324
PLATH, S. THE BELL JAR.*
P.M. SPACKS, 249(HUDR):SPRING72-163
639(VQR):SUMMER71-XCVI
PLATH, S. THE COLOSSUS AND OTHER POEMS.
C. STUBBLEFIELD, 502(PRS):SPRING71-83
PLATH, S. CROSSING THE WATER.*
E.M. AIRD, 148:AUTUMN71-286
M. PERLOFF, 295:NOV72-581
W.H. PRITCHARD, 249(HUDR):SPRING72-124
H. SERGEANT, 175:AUTUMN71-106
R. SKELTON, 376:OCT71-137
42(AR):WINTER71/72-587
PLATH, S. WINTER TREES.*
M. PERLOFF, 295:NOV72-581
PLATO. PHAEDRUS AND THE SEVENTH AND
EIGHTH LETTERS. (W. HAMILTON, TRANS)
617(TLS):30NOV73-1485

PLATO. PLATON. (P.J. ABOUT, ED)
P. SOMVILLE, 542:JUL-SEP71-388
PLATO. PLATON: "PHÉDON." (P. VICAIRE,
ED & TRANS)
N. GULLEY, 123:MAR72-103
PLATON, N. CORPUS DER MINOISCHEN UND
MYKENISCHEN SIEGEL. (VOL 2, PT 1)
J. BOARDMAN, 123:MAR72-139
PLATT, K. THE PRINCESS STAKES MURDER.
N. CALLENDAR, 441:11MAR73-50
PLATTS, B. A HISTORY OF GREENWICH.
617(TLS):16FEB73-189
PLAUTUS. AMPHITRUO.* (T. CUTT, ED) (REV)
W.S. THURMAN, 399(MLJ):DEC71-532
PLAUTUS. PLAUTE, "MOSTELLARIA" (LA FARCE
DU FANTÔME).* (J. COLLART, ED)
A. ERNOUT, 555:VOL45FASC2-357
PLAUTUS. PLAUTO, "CURCULIO." (G. MONACO,
ED)
A. ERNOUT, 555:VOL45FASC2-356
PLAUTUS. RUDENS. (H.C. FAY, ED)
R. GLEN, 123:MAR72-98
PLAYER, I. THE WHITE RHINO SAGA.
617(TLS):10AUG73-936
PLAYER, R. OH! WHERE ARE BLOODY MARY'S
EARRINGS?*
M. LEVIN, 441:1APR73-33
PLAZA, G. LATIN AMERICA TODAY AND TOMOR-
ROW.*
G.D., 37:JUN-JUL71-41
PLEKET, H.W. EPIGRAPHICA. (VOL 2)
D.M. LEWIS, 123:MAR72-130
PLEPELITS, K. DIE FRAGMENTE DER DEMEN
DES EUPOLIS.
N.G. WILSON, 123:DEC72-405
PLESCIA, J. THE OATH AND PERJURY IN
ANCIENT GREECE.*
D.M. MAC DOWELL, 123:JUN72-281
F.W. MITCHEL, 24:JUL72-489
C.B. PASCAL, 122:OCT72-310
PLESSEN, J. PROMENADE ET POÉSIE.
E.J. AHEARN, 188(ECR):WINTER70-343
PLEUSER, C. DIE BENENNUNGEN UND DER
BEGRIFF DES LEIDES BEI J. TAULER.*
J. MARGETTS, 220(GL&L):APR72-324
B. SOWINSKI, 657(WW):JAN/FEB70-67
PLIMPTON, G. MAD DUCKS AND BEARS.
C. LEHMANN-HAUPT, 441:12NOV73-37
442(NY):17DEC73-154
PLINY. PLINE L'ANCIEN, "HISTOIRE NATUR-
ELLE."* (BKS 21 & 22) (J. ANDRÉ, ED &
TRANS)
D.E. EICHHOLZ, 123:MAR72-113
PLOMMER, H. VITRUVIUS AND LATER ROMAN
BUILDING MANUALS.
617(TLS):7SEP73-1036
PLOTKIN, V.Y. DINAMIKA ANGLIJSKOJ FONO-
LOGIČESKOJ SISTEMY.
J. KRÁMSKÝ, 361:VOL25#2-178
PLOTT, J.C. & P.D. MAYS. SARVA-DARŚANA-
SANGRAHA: A BIBLIOGRAPHICAL GUIDE TO
THE GLOBAL HISTORY OF PHILOSOPHY.
J.B.L., 543:DEC70-346
PLOURDE, M. PAUL CLAUDEL - UNE MUSIQUE
DU SILENCE.
E. BEAUMONT, 208(FS):JUL72-350
M. LIOURE, 535(RHL):MAY-JUN71-530
H.A. WATERS, 207(FR):FEB71-609
PLOWDEN, D. LINCOLN AND HIS AMERICA,
1809-1865.
639(VQR):SUMMER71-CXXXIV
PLOWDEN, S. TOWNS AGAINST TRAFFIC.
617(TLS):23FEB73-204
PLUCKROSE, H. & F. PEACOCK - SEE DICKENS,
C.

PLUMB, J.H. IN THE LIGHT OF HISTORY.*
J.A. GARRATY, 441:18MAR73-14
W.L. GUNDERSHEIMER, 31(ASCH):SUMMER73-
529
PLUMB, J.H. & V.A. DEARING. SOME ASPECTS
OF EIGHTEENTH-CENTURY ENGLAND.
566:SPRING72-88
PLUMLY, S. IN THE OUTER DARK.
J.T. IRWIN, 598(SOR):SUMMER73-720
S.G. RADHUBER, 448:SPRING71-84
H. SUMMERS, 600:SPRING71-181
639(VQR):SPRING71-LXI
PLUMMER, A. THE LONDON WEAVERS' COMPANY
1600-1970.
617(TLS):23FEB73-207
PLUMMER, J. OLD TESTAMENT MINIATURES.*
J. BACKHOUSE, 90:MAY71-279
PLUMMER, W. WILLIAM PLUMMER'S MEMORANDUM
OF PROCEEDINGS IN THE UNITED STATES
SENATE 1803-1807. (E.S. BROWN, ED)
L.H. BUTTERFIELD, 432(NEQ):SEP71-525
PLUMMER, W., JR. LIFE OF WILLIAM PLUMER.
(A.P. PEABODY, ED)
L.H. BUTTERFIELD, 432(NEQ):SEP71-525
PLUTARCH. DE ISIDE ET OSIRIDE. (J.G.
GRIFFITHS, ED & TRANS)
R.E. WITT, 123:JUN72-207
R.E. WITT, 303:VOL91-155
PLUTARCH. PLUTARCHUS, "VITAE PARALLELAE."
(VOL 2, FASC 2) (2ND ED) (K. ZIEGLER,
ED)
A.J. GOSSAGE, 123:MAR72-24
PLUTARCH. PLUTARQUE, "DE LA VERTU ÉTH-
IQUE." (D. BABUT, ED & TRANS)
É. DES PLACES, 555:VOL45FASC2-353
PLUTARCH. PLUTARQUE, "LE DÉMON DE SOC-
RATE." (A. CORLU, ED & TRANS)
G.M. PEPE, 124:OCT71-62
É. DES PLACES, 555:VOL45FASC2-354
PLUTARCH. PLUTARQUE, "VIES."* (VOL 5)
(R. FLACELIÈRE & É. CHAMBRY, EDS &
TRANS)
R.M. ERRINGTON, 123:MAR72-105
PLUTARCH. PLUTARQUE, "VIES." (VOL 6)
(R. FLACELIÈRE & É. CHAMBRY, EDS &
TRANS)
P.A. STADTER, 124:MAR72-234
POCHODA, E.T. ARTHURIAN PROPAGANDA.
639(VQR):AUTUMN71-CLXXII
POCOCK, D.F. KANBI AND PATIDAR.
617(TLS):19JAN73-67
POCOCK, G. CORNEILLE AND RACINE.
617(TLS):7DEC73-1504
POCOCK, T. FIGHTING GENERAL.
617(TLS):17AUG73-947
PODLEWSKI, A.M. UN ESSAI D'OBSERVATION
PERMANENTE DES FAITS D'ÉTAT CIVIL DANS
L'ADAMAOUA.
A.H.M. KIRK-GREENE, 69:OCT71-343
PODRO, M. THE MANIFOLD IN PERCEPTION.
R. WOLLHEIM, 362:19APR73-519
617(TLS):26JAN73-96
POE, E.A. COLLECTED WORKS OF EDGAR ALLAN
POE.* (VOL 1: POEMS.) (T.O. MABBOTT,
ED)
R.S. MOORE, 219(GAR):WINTER71-481
POE, E.A. COMIC TALES OF EDGAR ALLAN
POE. (A.W. MURRAY, ED)
617(TLS):23NOV73-1416
VAN DER POEL, J. - SEE SMUTS, J.C.
"POEMS FROM THE SANSKRIT." (J. BROUGH,
TRANS)
C. COPPOLA, 352(LE&W):VOL15#1-170
POESSE, W., ED. HOMAGE TO JOHN M. HILL
IN MEMORIAM.
W.T. MC CREADY, 240(HR):APR71-214

POLONSKY, A. POLITICS IN INDEPENDENT
POLAND 1921-1939.
617(TLS):23FEB73-207
POLT, J.H.R. - SEE FORNER Y SEGARRA, J.P.
POLUNIN, O. & B.E. SMYTHIES. FLOWERS OF
SOUTH-WEST EUROPE.
617(TLS):3AUG73-908
POLVINEN, T. VENÄJÄN VALLANKUMOUS JA
SUOMI 1917-1920.
D. KIRBY, 575(SEER):OCT72-618
POLWARTH, G. & M., COMPS. NORTH COUNTRY
SONGS.
M. HUDLESTON, 203:SUMMER70-150
POLWARTH, G.M. COME YOU NOT FROM NEW-
CASTLE.
617(TLS):23FEB73-221
POMEAU, R. LA RELIGION DE VOLTAIRE.
(NEW ED)
F.J. CROWLEY, 207(FR):OCT70-243
R. MERCIER, 557(RSH):JAN-MAR70-159
POMERANCE, L. THE FINAL COLLAPSE OF
SANTORINI (THERA): 1400 B.C. OR 1200
B.C.?
W.R. BIERS, 124:SEP71-26
POMFRET, J.E., WITH F.M. SHUMWAY. FOUND-
ING THE AMERICAN COLONIES.
639(VQR):SPRING71-LXXIII
POMMIER, J. LE SPECTACLE INTÉRIEUR,
ESSAI.
R. LEBÈGUE, 535(RHL):JUL-AUG71-722
POMORSKA, K., ED. FIFTY YEARS OF RUSSIAN
PROSE.
V. YOUNG, 249(HUDR):AUTUMN72-513
POMORSKA, K. RUSSIAN FORMALIST THEORY
AND ITS POETIC AMBIANCE.*
J. HOLTHUSEN, 490:JUL/OCT70-646
POMPER, P. PETER LAVROV AND THE RUSSIAN
REVOLUTIONARY MOVEMENT.
617(TLS):18MAY73-560
PONASSE, D. LOGIQUE MATHÉMATIQUE.
A. BORGERS, 316:DEC70-579
PONCEAU, A. TIMOLÉON, RÉFLEXIONS SUR LA
TYRANNIE.
P-M.S., 542:OCT-DEC71-513
PONCELA, S.S. - SEE UNDER SERRANO PONCELA,
S.
POND, D. COUNSELLING IN RELIGION AND
PSYCHIATRY.
617(TLS):21SEP73-1080
PONGE, F. THINGS.* (C. CORMAN, ED &
TRANS)
K. HARRISON, 109:SPRING/SUMMER73-111
PONGS, H. DAS BILD IN DER DICHTUNG.*
(VOL 3)
K. VON WANGENHEIM, 430(NS):NOV71-613
PONICSAN, D. ANDOSHEN, PA.
M. LEVIN, 441:13MAY73-38
PONICSAN, D. CINDERELLA LIBERTY.
M. LEVIN, 441:27MAY73-19
PONNIAH, S.M. - SEE "SRI PADUKA"
PONS, C. & J. DULCK. S. RICHARDSON:
"PAMELA" - H. FIELDING: "JOSEPH AN-
DREWS."
J. GURY, 549(RLC):JAN-MAR71-116
PONS, J.R. - SEE UNDER ROCA PONS, J.
PONS, M. CHTO!
B. KAY, 207(FR):APR71-967
PONS, V. STANLEYVILLE.
P. MAYER, 69:OCT70-380
PONTIERO, G., ED. AN ANTHOLOGY OF BRAZ-
ILIAN MODERNIST POETRY.
W. MARTINS, 399(MLJ):MAR71-198
205(FMLS):APR70-203
PONTON, J. LA RELIGIEUSE DANS LA LITTÉRA-
TURE FRANÇAISE.
P. MOREAU, 535(RHL):JUL-AUG70-736

POOL, F. INTERPRETAZIONE DELL'ORLANDO
FURIOSO.
A. FRANCESCHETTI, 276:SPRING71-98
POOLE, C.H. THE CUSTOMS, SUPERSTITIONS
& LEGENDS OF THE COUNTY OF SOMERSET.
T. BROWN, 203:AUTUMN70-235
POOLE, L. & G. SCHLIEMANN À LA DÉCOUVERTE
DE TROIE.
P. CHANTRAINE, 555:VOL45FASC1-142
POOLE, P.A. THE VIETNAMESE IN THAILAND.
F.C. DARLING, 293(JAST):MAY71-725
"POOR LAW IN HAMPSHIRE THROUGH THE CEN-
TURIES."
B.R. MASTERS, 325:OCT71-344
POPA, V. EARTH ERECT.
617(TLS):23NOV73-1452
POPE, A. A CHOICE OF POPE'S VERSE. (P.
PORTER, ED)
566:AUTUMN71-10
POPE, A. ALEXANDER POPE: SELECTED POETRY
AND PROSE. (2ND ED) (W.K. WIMSATT, ED)
566:SPRING72-88
POPE, A. - SEE UNDER HOGGE, T.
POPE, D. GOVERNOR RAMAGE, R.N.
M. LEVIN, 441:18NOV73-54
POPE, J.A. & OTHERS. THE FREER CHINESE
BRONZES.* (VOL 1)
W. FAIRBANK, 244(HJAS):VOL30-240
V.C. KANE, 57:VOL33#1/2-152
A.C. SOPER, 54:MAR71-105
POPE, J.C. - SEE AELFRIC
POPE, R.G. THE HALF-WAY COVENANT.*
R.S. DUNN, 656(WMQ):JUL71-493
POPE, W.B. - SEE BARRETT, E.B. & B.R. HAY-
DON
POPE-HENNESSY, J. ESSAYS ON ITALIAN
SCULPTURE.*
D.A. COVI, 54:SEP70-316
POPE-HENNESSY, J. ITALIAN GOTHIC SCULP-
TURE.
617(TLS):24AUG73-980
POPE-HENNESSY, J. ITALIAN HIGH RENAIS-
SANCE AND BAROQUE SCULPTURE.
J. DANIELS, 135:DEC71-290
POPE-HENNESSY, J. RAPHAEL.
J.D., 135:MAR71-215
C. GOULD, 39:APR71-344
POPE-HENNESSY, J. PAOLO UCCELLO.
C. GILBERT, 56:WINTER70-441
POPE-HENNESSY, J. & A.J. RADCLIFFE. THE
FRICK COLLECTION.* (VOL 3)
A.C. RITCHIE, 54:JUN71-265
D.T., 135:JAN71-55
58:SEP/OCT70-16
POPE-HENNESSY, J., A.J. RADCLIFFE &
T.W.I. HODGKINSON. THE FRICK COLLEC-
TION. (VOLS 1&2)
A.C. RITCHIE, 54:JUN71-265
POPE-HENNESSY, J., A.J. RADCLIFFE &
T.W.I. HODGKINSON. THE FRICK COLLEC-
TION.* (VOL 4)
A.C. RITCHIE, 54:JUN71-265
D.T., 135:JAN71-55
58:SEP/OCT70-16
POPE HENNESSY, J. ANTHONY TROLLOPE.*
M. MUDRICK, 249(HUDR):AUTUMN72-487
POPHAM, M.R. THE DESTRUCTION OF THE
PALACE AT KNOSSOS.
R.J. BUCK, 487:WINTER71-404
POPITZ, H. DER ENTFREMDETE MENSCH.
W.G. BROCK, 182:VOL24#6-259
POPOV, K. JAPAN.
M.B. JANSEN, 293(JAST):FEB71-454
POPPE, N. MONGOLIAN LANGUAGE HANDBOOK.
J.C. STREET, 350:MAR72-212
POPPE, N., JR. STUDIES OF TURKIC LOAN
WORDS IN RUSSIAN.
Z. FOLEJEWSKI, 32:SEP72-740

POPPER, K.R. OBJECTIVE KNOWLEDGE.*
  617(TLS):16FEB73-171
POPPERWELL, R.G., ED. THE YEAR'S WORK IN
  MODERN LANGUAGE STUDIES. (VOL 32, 1970)
  S. ULLMANN, 208(FS):OCT72-490
POPS, M.L. THE MELVILLE ARCHETYPE.*
  L. BUELL, 432(NEQ):SEP71-517
  H. PARKER, 401(MLQ):MAR72-54
  M.R. STERN, 219(GAR):FALL71-369
PORCELLI, B. STUDI SULLA DIVINA COMMEDIA.
  D.H. HIGGINS, 402(MLR):OCT72-918
PÖRKSEN, U. DER ERZÄHLER IM MITTELHOCH-
  DEUTSCHEN EPOS.
  I.R. CAMPBELL, 67:NOV72-246
  C. GELLINEK, 301(JEGP):APR72-296
PÖRNBACHER, K. - SEE VON BIRKEN, S.
PÖRNBACHER, K. - SEE "FRANZ GRILLPARZER"
PORPHYRY. PORPHYRIS, "PROS MARKELLAN."
  (W. PÖTSCHER, ED & TRANS)
  R.T. WALLIS, 123:DEC72-344
"PORPHYRY: THE CAVE OF THE NYMPHS IN THE
  'ODYSSEY'."
  F.M. COMBELLACK, 122:APR72-146
PORSET, C., ED. VARIA LINGUISTICA.
  J-C. CHEVALIER, 535(RHL):JUL-AUG71-
  703
  L. WOLF, 72:BAND209HEFT4/6-393
PORSET, C. - SEE ROUSSEAU, J-J.
PORTAL, R. RUSSES ET UKRAINIENS.*
  J.S. RESHETAR, JR., 32:MAR72-172
PORTAL, R. THE SLAVS.* (FRENCH TITLE:
  LES SLAVES.)
  W.S. VUCINICH, 550(RUSR):JUL71-304
PORTE, J. THE ROMANCE IN AMERICA.*
  R.H. FOGLE, 445(NCF):JUN70-110
  E. STOCK, 454:FALL71-84
PORTER, D.B., COMP. THE NEGRO IN THE
  UNITED STATES.*
  M.L. FISHER, 432(NEQ):JUN71-322
PORTER, E. CAMBRIDGESHIRE CUSTOMS AND
  FOLKLORE.
  T. BROWN, 203:SPRING71-79
PORTER, E. - SEE RANDELL, A.
PORTER, H. MR. BUTTERFRY AND OTHER
  TALES OF NEW JAPAN.
  M. WILDING, 381:JUN71-265
PORTER, J. DOVER STRIKES AGAIN.
  N. CALLENDAR, 441:27MAY73-18
PORTER, J. IT'S MURDER WITH DOVER.
  N. CALLENDAR, 441:9DEC73-50
  617(TLS):31AUG73-1007
PORTER, K. MEDIEVAL ARCHITECTURE. LOM-
  BARD ARCHITECTURE. ROMANESQUE SCULP-
  TURE OF THE PILGRIM ROADS. SPANISH
  ROMANESQUE SCULPTURE.
  J. BECKWITH, 39:DEC70-494
PORTER, K.A. THE COLLECTED ESSAYS AND
  OCCASIONAL WRITINGS OF KATHERINE ANNE
  PORTER.
  E.C. BUFKIN, 219(GAR):SUMMER71-247
  J. PINKERTON, 418(MR):SUMMER72-511
PORTER, P. AFTER MARTIAL.* PREACHING TO
  THE CONVERTED.*
  A. MACLEAN, 362:22MAR73-389
PORTER, P. THE LAST OF ENGLAND.*
  A. CLUYSENAAR, 565:VOL12#1-72
  K.L. GOODWIN, 381:SEP71-369
PORTER, P. - SEE POPE, A.
PORTER, R.G. THE PREPARATION OF A COM-
  PUTERIZED INDEX TO THE NON-FICTION OF
  THOMAS MANN.
  K.W. JONAS, 400(MLN):OCT71-743
"PORTFOLIO FOR HEALTH."
  617(TLS):23NOV73-1456
PORTIS, C. TRUE GRIT.
  D.A. HOGLIN, 649(WAL):SUMMER70-158
PÖRTNER, P. - SEE VAN HODDIS, J.

PORTOGHESI, P. BORROMINI.
  A. BLUNT, 90:NOV71-670
PORTOGHESI, P. ROMA BAROCCA.*
  A. BLUNT, 46:OCT71-259
PORTOGHESI, P. BERNARDO VITTONE.*
  R. POMMER, 54:MAR71-124
PORZIO, D. - SEE BUZZATI, D.
POSCH, S. BEOBACHTUNGEN ZUR THEOKRITNACH-
  WIRKUNG BEI VERGIL.*
  M.L. CLARKE, 123:MAR72-61
PÖSCHL, V. HORAZISCHE LYRIK.
  G.W. WILLIAMS, 123:JUN72-272
VON POSER, M. DER ABSCHWEIFENDE ERZÄH-
  LER.
  G. HAAS, 52:BAND6HEFT2-213
POSNANSKY, M. - SEE FISHER, R.
POSNER, D. ANNIBALE CARRACCI.*
  J. CANADAY, 441:2DEC73-89
POSNER, D. WATTEAU: A LADY AT HER TOILET.
  R. DOWNES, 441:2DEC73-92
  617(TLS):6JUL73-766
POSNER, R. - SEE IORDAN, I. & J. ORR
POSPIELOVSKY, D. RUSSIAN POLICE TRADE
  UNIONISM.
  J. SCHNEIDERMAN, 32:SEP72-670
POSSONY, S.T. & J.E. POURNELLE. THE
  STRATEGY OF TECHNOLOGY.
  L.W. BEILENSON, 396(MODA):WINTER72-101
POST, K. & M. VICKERS. STRUCTURE AND
  CONFLICT IN NIGERIA 1960-1966.
  617(TLS):31AUG73-995
POST, K.W.J. & G.D. JENKINS. THE PRICE
  OF LIBERTY.
  617(TLS):27APR73-480
POST, M.D. THE STRANGE SCHEMES OF RAN-
  DOLPH MASON.
  N. CALLENDAR, 441:2SEP73-18
POSTAL, B. & H.W. LEVY. AND THE HILLS
  SHOUTED FOR JOY.
  R. ST. JOHN, 441:18MAR73-30
POSTAL, P.M. ASPECTS OF PHONOLOGICAL
  THEORY.
  E.V. PIKE, 361:VOL25#1-30
POSTAN, A. THE COMPLETE GRAPHIC WORK OF
  PAUL NASH.
  617(TLS):27JUL73-879
POSTAN, M.M. ESSAYS ON MEDIEVAL AGRICUL-
  TURE AND GENERAL PROBLEMS OF THE
  MEDIEVAL ECONOMY. MEDIEVAL TRADE AND
  FINANCE.
  617(TLS):17AUG73-941
POSTAN, M.M. THE MEDIEVAL ECONOMY AND
  SOCIETY.
  617(TLS):9FEB73-155
POSTER, M. THE UTOPIAN THOUGHT OF RESTIF
  DE LA BRETONNE.
  A. ROSENBERG, 173(ECS):SUMMER72-604
POSTIC, M. MAETERLINCK ET LE SYMBOLISME.
  K. CORNELL, 207(FR):MAR71-800
  M. SCHAETTEL, 557(RSH):OCT-DEC70-649
POSTMAN, N., C. WEINGARTNER & T.P. MORGAN,
  EDS. LANGUAGE IN AMERICA.
  R. OHMANN, 599:SPRING71-170
"THE POSTWAR DEVELOPMENT OF THE REPUBLIC
  OF VIETNAM."
  F.J. CORLEY, 613:SPRING71-156
"THE POTENTIAL FOR ENERGY CONSERVATION."
  E. ROTHSCHILD, 453:9AUG73-29
POTHOLM, C.P. FOUR AFRICAN POLITICAL
  SYSTEMS.
  L. MAIR, 69:OCT71-330
POTICHNYJ, P.J. SOVIET AGRICULTURAL
  TRADE UNIONS, 1917-70.
  617(TLS):9FEB73-148
POTICHNYJ, P.J. - SEE MAZLAKH, S. & V.
  SHAKHRAI

POTOK, C. THE PROMISE.
  L. ELKIN, 287:MAR70-25
  M.T. GILMORE, 390:JAN70-76
PÖTSCHER, W. - SEE PORPHYRY
POTTER, D. HIDE AND SEEK.
  R. GARFITT, 362:15NOV72-674
  617(TLS):9NOV73-1361
POTTER, D. & G.L. THOMAS, EDS. THE
  COLONIAL IDIOM.
  H. MIXON, 583:SUMMER71-401
POTTER, D.M. HISTORY AND AMERICAN SOCI-
  ETY. (D.E. FEHRENBACHER, ED)
  J.A. GARRATY, 441:1APR73-5
  K. JEFFREY, 109:SPRING/SUMMER73-156
POTTER, S. & L. SARGENT. PEDIGREE.
  617(TLS):14DEC73-1545
PÖTTERS, W. UNTERSCHIEDE IM WORTSCHATZ
  DER IBEROROMANISCHEN SPRACHEN.
  D. WOLL, 72:BAND209HEFT4/6-439
POTTIER, B. SYSTÉMATIQUE DES ÉLÉMENTS
  DE RELATION.
  R.S. MEYERSTEIN, 353:JUN70-103
POTTINGER, G. MUIRFIELD AND THE HONOUR-
  ABLE COMPANY.*
  K. MILLER, 362:15MAR73-346
POUGET, J. UN CERTAIN CAPITAINE DE
  GAULLE.
  617(TLS):5OCT73-1152
POULANTZAS, N. POLITICAL POWER AND
  SOCIAL CLASSES. (TRANS ED BY T. O'HAG-
  AN)
  617(TLS):30NOV73-1462
POULAT, E. INTÉGRISME ET CATHOLICISME
  INTÉGRAL.
  H. PEYRE, 207(FR):DEC70-401
POULET, G. TROIS ESSAIS DE MYTHOLOGIE
  ROMANTIQUE.
  J. BELLEMIN-NOËL, 535(RHL):MAY-JUN70-
  523
POULIN, A., JR., ED. CONTEMPORARY AMERI-
  CAN POETRY.
  H. ISBELL, 134(CP):SPRING71-52
POULIN, A., JR. IN ADVENT.
  M. WATERS, 398:VOL3#5-237
POULTON, D. JOHN DOWLAND.*
  J. NOBLE, 415:NOV72-1085
POUND, E. DRAFTS AND FRAGMENTS OF
  CANTOS CX-CXVII.*
  D. HOLBROOK, 619(TC):VOL178#1045-56
  H. SERGEANT, 175:SUMMER71-63
POUND, E. SELECTED PROSE 1909-1965. (W.
  COOKSON, ED)
  442(NY):27AUG73-91
  617(TLS):16MAR73-292
POUND, O.S., ED & TRANS. ARABIC AND
  PERSIAN POEMS.
  A. CLUYSENAAR, 565:VOL12#3-72
  J. KRITZECK, 318(JAOS):OCT-DEC71-540
POUNDS, N.J.G. AN HISTORICAL GEOGRAPHY
  OF EUROPE 450 B.C.-A.D. 1330.
  617(TLS):24AUG73-975
POUPON, M. APOLLINAIRE ET CENDRARS.
  C. TOURNADRE, 535(RHL):MAR-APR71-325
POURSIN, J-M. LA POPULATION MONDIALE.
  J. PIEL, 98:DEC71-1113
POUSSEUR, H. MUSIQUE, SÉMANTIQUE,
  SOCIÉTÉ.
  617(TLS):5OCT73-1167
POWELL, A. BOOKS DO FURNISH A ROOM.*
  M. MUDRICK, 249(HUDR):SPRING72-142
POWELL, A. THE MILITARY PHILOSOPHERS.
  J.C. FIELD, 556(RLV):1971/1-91
  M. MUDRICK, 249(HUDR):SPRING72-142
POWELL, A. TEMPORARY KINGS.
  A. BROYARD, 441:12OCT73-47
  L. CHAZEN, 441:14OCT73-46
  R. FULLER, 362:21JUN73-839
                              [CONTINUED]

[CONTINUING]
  M. WOOD, 453:1NOV73-20
  617(TLS):22JUN73-709
POWELL, A. THE VALLEY OF BONES. THE
  SOLDIER'S ART.
  M. MUDRICK, 249(HUDR):SPRING72-142
POWELL, D. THE VILLA ARIADNE.
  617(TLS):9NOV73-1368
POWELL, E. NO EASY ANSWERS.
  617(TLS):12OCT73-1254
POWELL, E.H. THE DESIGN OF DISCORD.
  639(VQR):SUMMER71-CXXX
POWELL, G. THE KANDYAN WARS.
  617(TLS):20APR73-454
POWELL, H. - SEE GRYPHIUS, A.
POWELL, J.D. POLITICAL MOBILIZATION OF
  THE VENEZUELAN PEASANT.
  N. GALL, 453:15NOV73-29
POWELL, J.M., ED & TRANS. THE LIBER
  AUGUSTALIS OR CONSTITUTIONS OF MELFI
  PROMULGATED BY THE EMPEROR FREDERICK II
  FOR THE KINGDOM OF SICILY IN 1231.
  J. RICHARD, 182:VOL24#15/16-632
POWELL, L.C. CALIFORNIA CLASSICS.
  F. GAIGE, 50(ARQ):WINTER71-369
POWELL, N. FUSELI: THE NIGHTMARE.
  R. DOWNES, 441:2DEC73-93
POWELL, T. - SEE CAMERON, J.M.
POWELL, V. A COMPTON-BURNETT COMPENDIUM.
  T. DRIBERG, 362:22MAR73-388
  617(TLS):6APR73-371
POWERS, J.R. THE LAST CATHOLIC IN
  AMERICA.
  E.B. FISKE, 441:31MAR73-33
  M. LEVIN, 441:22APR73-28
POWERS, L.H. HENRY JAMES.
  W. WALLIS, 502(PRS):SUMMER71-179
POWERS, L.H. HENRY JAMES AND THE NATURAL-
  IST MOVEMENT.
  M. BANTA, 432(NEQ):DEC71-681
  G. CORE, 385(MQR):WINTER73-82
  L. EDEL, 445(NCF):MAR72-498
  D.K. KIRBY, 579(SAQ):SPRING72-274
  D.A. LEEMING, 131(CL):FALL72-374
  G. MONTEIRO, 27(AL):NOV72-493
POWERS, T. THE WAR AT HOME.
  J. KIFNER, 441:14OCT73-32
POWLEDGE, F. MODEL CITY.
  V. SCULLY, 441:APR71-71
POWNALL, H. CHIEF OF STAFF. (VOL 1)
  (B. BOND, ED)
  617(TLS):11MAY73-534
POYATOS, F. ESPAÑA POR DENTRO.*
  P.W. O'CONNOR, 399(MLJ):OCT71-410
POYER, J. THE SHOOTING OF THE GREEN.
  N. CALLENDAR, 441:25NOV73-49
POYNTER, J.R. SOCIETY AND PAUPERISM.
  G. HIMMELFARB, 637(VS):DEC70-203
"PRAEGER ENCYCLOPEDIA OF ART."
  P. RUTA, 58:FEB72-20
PRAGA, E. POESIE. (M. PETTRUCCIANI, ED)
  M.P., 228(GSLI):VOL147FASC458/459-475
"PRAGUE STUDIES IN ENGLISH XIII."
  C.J.E. BALL, 447(N&Q):APR71-159
PRAK, N.L. THE LANGUAGE OF ARCHITECTURE.
  G. HILDEBRAND, 576:MAR70-74
PRAKASH, V. NEW TOWNS IN INDIA.
  E.J. VANDER VELDE, JR., 293(JAST):
  FEB71-488
PRANG, H. GESCHICHTE DES LUSTSPIELS.
  E. LEFÈVRE, 490:JAN/APR70-318
PRATT, C. THE SILENT ANCESTORS.
  C. THOMAS, 102(CANL):SPRING72-84
PRATT, G.C. SPELLBOUND IN DARKNESS.
  W. MARKFIELD, 441:2DEC73-96
PRAUSS, G. ERSCHEINUNG BEI KANT.
  J. SCHMUCKER, 342:BAND62HEFT4-511

PRAWER, S. HEINE'S SHAKESPEARE.
    J.L.S., 191(ELN):SEP71(SUPP)-136
PRAWER, S., ED. THE ROMANTIC PERIOD IN
    GERMANY.*
    W.J. LILLYMAN, 221(GQ):MAY71-397
    E. STOPP, 402(MLR):JUL72-693
PRAWER, S.S., R.H. THOMAS & L. FORSTER,
    EDS. ESSAYS IN GERMAN LANGUAGE, CUL-
    TURE, AND SOCIETY.
    M.B. BENN, 402(MLR):JAN72-214
PRAZ, M. MNEMOSYNE.*
    L. ALLOWAY, 58:SEP/OCT70-42
    J.E. CHAMBERLIN, 249(HUDR):WINTER
    72/73-693
    B. RICHARDS, 184(EIC):JUL71-318
    P. SLOANE, 127:FALL71-95
    D. SUTTON, 39:OCT70-246
    B. VANNIER, 400(MLN):MAY71-597
    639(VQR):SPRING71-LXXXII
PRAZ, M. ON NEO-CLASSICISM.*
    C.M., 135:JUL70-213
PREBBLE, J. SPANISH STIRRUP.
    M. LEVIN, 441:15JUL73-17
PRECLAIRE, M. UNE POETIQUE DE L'HOMME.
    V. THERRIEN, 154:DEC71-863
PREDMORE, R.L. CERVANTES.
    W. BEAUCHAMP, 441:23DEC73-10
    442(NY):15OCT73-188
    617(TLS):5OCT73-1164
PRELOT, M. & F. GALLOUÉDEC-GENUYS, EDS.
    LE LIBÉRALISME CATHOLIQUE.
    L. LE GUILLOU, 535(RHL):JAN-FEB71-109
    J.N. MOODY, 207(FR):FEB71-582
PREMCHAND. THE GIFT OF A COW.* (G.C.
    ROADARMEL, TRANS)
    R.O. SWAN, 293(JAST):NOV70-218
PREMCHAND. THE WORLD OF PREMCHAND. (D.
    RUBIN, TRANS)
    A. & S. CHANDOLA, 352(LE&W):VOL15#1-
    158
    G.C. ROADARMEL, 293(JAST):FEB71-497
PREMINGER, A., ED. ENCYCLOPEDIA OF
    POETRY AND POETICS.
    L.C. BONNEROT, 189(EA):JAN-MAR70-101
PRENTICE, T.M. WEEDS AND WILDFLOWERS OF
    EASTERN NORTH AMERICA. (TEXT BY E.O.
    SARGENT)
    442(NY):10DEC73-200
PRESCOTT, O. PRINCES OF THE RENAISSANCE.
    C.H. CLOUGH, 39:NOV70-398
PRESNIAKOV, A.E. THE FORMATION OF THE
    GREAT RUSSIAN STATE.
    C.B. O'BRIEN, 550(RUSR):JUL71-313
PRESS, J. THE LENGTHENING SHADOWS.
    H. SERGEANT, 175:AUTUMN71-106
PRESS, J. A MAP OF MODERN ENGLISH VERSE.
    H. SERGEANT, 175:SUMMER70-68
PRESSEAULT, J. L'ÊTRE-POUR-AUTRUI DANS
    LA PHILOSOPHIE DE JEAN-PAUL SARTRE.
    R. LAPOINTE, 154:SEP71-634
PRESSMAN, J.L. & A.B. WILDAVSKY. IMPLE-
    MENTATION.
    H. SCHWARTZ, 441:3SEP73-13
PRESTON, A. BATTLESHIPS OF WORLD WAR I.
    617(TLS):15JUN73-700
PRESTON, J. THE CREATED SELF.
    P-G. BOUCÉ, 189(EA):OCT-DEC71-535
    L. BRAUDY, 481(PQ):JUL71-394
    A.J. HASSALL, 67:NOV72-227
    J.J. RICHETTI, 141:FALL71-427
PRESTON-DUNLOP, V. PRACTICAL KINETOGRA-
    PHY LABAN.
    A. PAGE, 290(JAAC):SUMMER71-552
PRETO-RODAS, R.A. NEGRITUDE AS A THEME
    IN THE POETRY OF THE PORTUGUESE-SPEAK-
    ING WORLD.*
    J.C. VINCENT, 238:MAY71-399

PRÉVERT, J. CHOSES ET AUTRES.
    617(TLS):19JAN73-69
"PRÉVERT I." "PRÉVERT II." (T. SAVORY,
    TRANS)
    J. HART, 661:SUMMER70-113
PREVIN, A. & A. HOPKINS. MUSIC FACE TO
    FACE.*
    K. SPENCE, 415:JUL72-672
PRÉVOST, C.M. LA PSYCHO-PHILOSOPHIE DE
    PIERRE JANET.
    617(TLS):14DEC73-1535
PRICE, A. COLONEL BUTLER'S WOLF.*
    N. CALLENDAR, 441:17JUN73-32
PRICE, A.F. & WONG MOU-LAM - SEE "THE
    DIAMOND SUTRA AND THE SUTRA OF HUI
    NENG"
PRICE, C. THEATRE IN THE AGE OF GARRICK.
    617(TLS):19OCT73-1272
PRICE, E.C. THE STATE OF THE UNION.
    J. DITSKY, 628:SPRING72-108
PRICE, G. THE FRENCH LANGUAGE.
    B. FOSTER, 208(FS):OCT72-491
PRICE, H. STELLA C. (J. TURNER, ED)
    617(TLS):28SEP73-1137
PRICE, H.H. BELIEF.*
    R. BAMBROUGH, 479(PHQ):JAN71-78
    A.P. GRIFFITHS, 483:JAN71-63
PRICE, J.G. THE UNFORTUNATE COMEDY.*
    R.A. FOAKES, 175:SPRING70-22
PRICE, N. A NATURAL DEATH.
    J. YARDLEY, 441:23DEC73-11
PRICE, R. AN IMPERIAL WAR AND THE BRIT-
    ISH WORKING CLASS.
    617(TLS):9MAR73-259
PRICE, R. LOVE AND WORK.
    M. LA FRANCE, 573(SSF):SPRING71-345
PRICE, R. PERMANENT ERRORS.*
    J.H. WILDMAN, 598(SOR):WINTER73-233
PRICE, R.F. EDUCATION IN COMMUNIST
    CHINA.*
    W.H. LIU, 293(JAST):FEB71-446
PRICE, R.M. - SEE DE QUEVEDO Y VILLEGAS,
    F.G.
PRICE, V. - SEE BÜCHNER, G.
PRICHARD, C. FULL MOON.
    617(TLS):26JAN73-84
PRICKETT, S. COLERIDGE AND WORDSWORTH.*
    I.H.C., 191(ELN):SEP71(SUPP)-41
    D. EMMET, 541(RES):AUG71-358
    R.D. HUME, 290(JAAC):SPRING71-428
    J.R.D. JACKSON, 529(QQ):SPRING71-155
    H. PESCHMANN, 175:AUTUMN70-104
    C. WOODRING, 405(MP):MAY72-356
"PRIDE OF PLACE."
    617(TLS):6APR73-401
PRIDEAUX, T. THE WORLD OF WHISTLER
    (1834-1903).
    58:SEP/OCT70-18
DU PRIER, J. - SEE UNDER JEAN DU PRIER
PRIESTLEY, J.B. CHARLES DICKENS AND HIS
    WORLD.
    S. MONOD, 189(EA):APR-JUN70-223
PRIESTLEY, J.B. THE ENGLISH.
    E. TENNANT, 362:27SEP73-418
    617(TLS):14SEP73-1057
PRIESTLEY, J.B. LONDON END.
    J.C. FIELD, 556(RLV):1971/3-335
PRIESTLEY, J.B. THE PRINCE OF PLEASURE
    AND HIS REGENCY.
    C.M., 135:JUN70-133
PRIESTLEY, J.B. THEY CAME TO A CITY/SOU-
    DAIN...UNE VILLE. (L. CABOCHE, ED &
    TRANS)
    G. NIGOT, 189(EA):OCT-DEC71-541
PRIESTLEY, M. WEST AFRICAN TRADE AND
    COAST SOCIETY.
    J.A. LANGLEY, 69:OCT70-397

PRIETO, L.J. MESSAGES ET SIGNAUX.
G.F. MEIER, 682(ZPSK):BAND23HEFT2/3-
316
L. ZGUSTA, 353:JUN71-112
PRINCE, F.T. MEMOIRS OF OXFORD.*
A. CLUYSENAAR, 565:VOL12#1-72
PRINCE, G.J. MÉTAPHYSIQUE ET TECHNIQUE
DANS L'OEUVRE ROMANESQUE DE SARTRE.
R. GOLDTHORPE, 208(FS):JAN72-95
B. SUHL, 546(RR):APR71-157
PRINCIPE, W.H. THE THEOLOGY OF THE HYPO-
STATIC UNION IN THE EARLY THIRTEENTH
CENTURY.
A.S. MC GRADE, 589:APR72-335
PRINGLE, J.D. HAVE PEN: WILL TRAVEL.
617(TLS):16NOV73-1395
PRINGLE, R. THE LETTERBOOK OF ROBERT
PRINGLE. (W.B. EDGAR, ED)
617(TLS):19JAN73-70
PRINGLE, R. RAJAHS AND REBELS.
D. FREEMAN, 293(JAST):MAY71-734
PRINS, A.A. A HISTORY OF ENGLISH PHO-
NEMES.
E.H. FLINT, 67:NOV72-269
"PRINTING PATENTS, ABRIDGEMENTS OF PATENT
SPECIFICATIONS RELATING TO PRINTING
1617-1857."
R. STOKES, 354:JUN70-173
PRINTZ-PÅHLSON, G. ÅTTA DIKTER.
L. SJÖBERG, 563(SS):SPRING72-282
PRINZ, J. DIE SLAVISIERUNG BALTISCHER
UND DIE BALTISIERUNG SLAVISCHER ORTS-
NAMEN IM GEBIET DES EHEMALIGEN GOUVERNE-
MENTS SUWAŁKI.
E. DICKENMANN, 343:BAND13HEFT2-205
PRINZHORN, H. ARTISTRY OF THE MENTALLY
ILL.
C. ROBINS, 441:8APR73-7
PRIOR, A. PARADISO.
M. LEVIN, 441:24JUN73-12
PRIOR, A.N. PAPERS ON TIME AND TENSE.
R. BLANCHE, 542:OCT-DEC70-500
J.E. TOMBERLIN, 543:SEP70-57
PRIOR, M. THE LITERARY WORKS OF MATTHEW
PRIOR.* (2ND ED) (H.B. WRIGHT & M.K.
SPEARS, EDS)
M. BAUMANN, 72:BAND209HEFT4/6-412
D.L. PASSLER, 568(SCN):FALL-WINTER72-
58
566:SPRING72-94
PRISK, B. & J.A. BYERS. COSTUMING.
J. KESLER, 583:SUMMER72-448
PRITCHARD, J.B., ED. THE ANCIENT NEAR
EAST.*
R.A. FAZZINI, 57:VOL33#1/2-143
PRITCHARD, N.H. EECCHHOOEESS.
W.H. PRITCHARD, 249(HUDR):SPRING72-119
PRITCHARD, W.H. WYNDHAM LEWIS.*
J. FLETCHER, 184(EIC):APR71-204
PRITCHETT, V.S. BALZAC.
J. BAYLEY, 453:4OCT73-25
A. BROYARD, 441:18OCT73-51
M. DRABBLE, 362:6SEP73-318
R. LOCKE, 441:14OCT73-5
442(NY):29OCT73-182
617(TLS):14SEP73-1053
PRITCHETT, V.S. BLIND LOVE AND OTHER
STORIES.
J.M. FLORA, 573(SSF):SPRING71-348
PRITCHETT, V.S. GEORGE MEREDITH AND
ENGLISH COMEDY.
R.B. HENKLE, 454:SPRING72-269
F. LÉAUD, 189(EA):APR-JUN71-203
I. WILLIAMS, 541(RES):AUG71-389
PRITCHETT, W.K. THE CHOISEUL MARBLE.
D.M. LEWIS, 123:JUN72-256
P. ROESCH, 555:VOL45FASC1-130

PRITCHETT, W.K. STUDIES IN ANCIENT GREEK
TOPOGRAPHY.* (PT 2)
J.M. COOK, 123:MAR72-130
"PROBLEMAS Y PRINCIPIOS DEL ESTRUCURAL-
ISMO LINGÜÍSTICO."
K. TOGEBY, 545(RPH):AUG71-97
"PROBLEMI ATTUALI DELLA PIANIFICAZIONE
NELL'EST EUROPEO (SEMINARIO CESES DI
SORRENTO)."
E. CLAYTON, 32:DEC72-907
PROCACCI, G. HISTORY OF THE ITALIAN
PEOPLE.
D. VITTORINI, 275(IQ):SPRING71-153
676(YR):WINTER72-VI
"PROCEEDINGS OF THE BRITISH ACADEMY."
(VOL 57, 1971)
617(TLS):16MAR73-305
PROCLUS. COMMENTARY ON THE FIRST BOOK
OF EUCLID'S "ELEMENTS."* (G.R. MORROW,
TRANS)
I. BULMER-THOMAS, 123:DEC72-345
639(VQR):SUMMER71-CXXXVI
PROCOPIUS. PROKOP, WERKE. (VOLS 3&4)
(O. VEH, ED & TRANS)
W.G. SINNIGEN, 124:APR-MAY72-276
PROCTOR, D. - SEE DICKINSON, G.L.
PROFETI, M.G. - SEE UNDER GRAZIA PROFETI,
M.
PROFETI, M.G. - SEE VÉLEZ DE GUEVARA, L.
PROFFER, C.R., ED. FROM KARAMZIN TO
BUNIN.
T.L. AMAN, 550(RUSR):JAN71-95
PROFFER, C.R., ED & TRANS. SOVIET CRITI-
CISM OF AMERICAN LITERATURE IN THE
SIXTIES.
N. BALAKIAN, 441:14FEB73-43
PROFFER, C.R. - SEE DOSTOEVSKY, F.M.
PROFFER, C.R. - SEE PUSHKIN, A.S.
PROFFER, C.R. & E., EDS. CONTEMPORARY
RUSSIAN LITERATURE.
C. BROWN, 441:28OCT73-24
"PROFILE OF A CITY."
617(TLS):1JUN73-623
PROFITLICH, U. DER SEELIGE LESER.
H-J. MODLMAYR, 402(MLR):JAN72-216
J.W. SMEED, 220(GL&L):JAN72-145
PROHASKA, D. RAIMUND AND VIENNA.
J.D. BARLOW, 406:SUMMER72-180
205(FMLS):JUL71-298
617(TLS):27APR73-475
PROMIES, W. DIE BÜRGER UND DER NARR ODER
DAS RISIKO DER PHANTASIE.
J. FINCK, 556(RLV):1971/4-494
PROMIES, W. - SEE LICHTENBERG, G.C.
PRONZINI, B. UNDERCURRENT.
N. CALLENDAR, 441:12AUG73-10
442(NY):17SEP73-156
PRONZINI, B. THE VANISHED.
N. CALLENDAR, 441:25MAR73-49
PROPERTIUS. THE POEMS OF PROPERTIUS.
(J. WARDEN, TRANS)
R. LATTIMORE, 249(HUDR):AUTUMN72-482
E. SEGAL, 441:23DEC73-6
PROPERTIUS. THE POEMS OF SEXTUS PROPER-
TIUS. (J.P. MC CULLOCH, TRANS)
E. SEGAL, 441:23DEC73-6
PROSE, F. JUDAH THE PIOUS.
R. GARFITT, 362:13DEC73-828
T. LASK, 441:17FEB73-33
D.K. MANO, 441:25FEB73-2
PROSER, M.N. THE HEROIC IMAGE IN FIVE
SHAKESPEARE TRAGEDIES.
P. MORTENSON, 570(SQ):WINTER70-92
PROSPERI, M. ANGELO BEOLCO DETTO RUZAN-
TE.
L.T., 275(IQ):SPRING-SUMMER72-117
PROSSER, E. HAMLET AND REVENGE.*
R. BORGMEIER, 38:BAND88HEFT3-385

PROST, A. L'ENSEIGNEMENT EN FRANCE,
1800-1967.
   M. REBERIOUX, 557(RSH):JAN-MAR71-143
PROTASE, D. RITURILE FUNERARE LA DACI ŞI
DACO-ROMANI.
   J. NANDRIS, 575(SEER):JUL72-487
PROTAS'EVA, T.N. OPISANIYE RUKOPISEY
SINODAL'NOGO SOBRANIYA (NE VOSHEDSHIKH
V OPISANIYE A.V. GORSKOGO I K.I. NEVO-
STRUYEVA). (PT 1)
   W.F. RYAN & J.S.G. SIMMONS, 575(SEER):
   APR72-293
"PROTO-INDICA: 1968."
   M.B. EMENEAU, 318(JAOS):OCT-DEC71-541
PROUDFIT, C.L. - SEE LANDOR, W.S.
PROUST, M. LES PASTICHES DE PROUST. (J.
MILLY, ED)
   L.B. PRICE, 207(FR):MAR71-799
PROUST, M. MARCEL PROUST, CORRESPON-
DANCE. (VOL 1) (P. KOLB, ED)
   J.M. COCKING, 208(FS):OCT72-472
   Y. SANDRE, 535(RHL):SEP-DEC71-993
PROUST, M. TEXTES RETROUVÉS.* (P. KOLB
& L.B. PRICE, EDS)
   617(TLS):13APR73-423
PROUTY, C.T. - SEE PEELE, G.
PRØYSEN, A. DET VAR DA DET OG ITTE NÅ.
LØRDAGSKVELDSVISER.
   270:VOL22#4-86
PRÜCKNER, H. DIE LOKRISCHEN TONRELIEFS.*
   R. HIGGINS, 54:SEP71-396
   G.M.A. RICHTER, 303:VOL91-200
PRUDHOE, J. THE THEATRE OF GOETHE AND
SCHILLER.
   617(TLS):24AUG73-982
PRÜMM, K. GNOSIS AN DER WURZEL DES CHRIS-
TENTUMS?
   F.F. BRUCE, 182:VOL24#23/24-843
PRUNIÈRES, H. MONTEVERDI.
   D. ARNOLD, 415:DEC72-1185
PRŮŠEK, J. CHINESE HISTORY AND LITERA-
TURE.
   J.L.B., 244(HJAS):VOL31-351
PRŮŠEK, J. THREE SKETCHES OF CHINESE
LITERATURE.
   W.R. SCHULTZ, 352(LE&W):VOL15#1-151
PRUSSIN, L. ARCHITECTURE IN NORTHERN
GHANA.
   E. GOODY, 69:OCT71-345
PRUTZ, R. DAS ENGELCHEN. (E. EDLER, ED)
   J. HERMAND, 406:SUMMER72-163
VON PRYBRAM-GLADONA, C. UNBEKANNTE
ZEICHNUNGEN ALTER MEISTER AUS EUROPÄI-
SCHEM PRIVATBESITZ.
   G. BERGSTRÄSSER, 182:VOL24#21/22-799
PRYBYLA, J.S. THE POLITICAL ECONOMY OF
COMMUNIST CHINA.
   S-C. LENG, 293(JAST):MAY71-668
PRYCE-JONES, D. THE FACE OF DEFEAT.*
   A. ELON, 441:13MAY73-4
   T. MANGOLD, 362:8FEB73-189
   442(NY):12MAY73-146
   453:3MAY73-35
PRYCE-JONES, D., ED. EVELYN WAUGH AND
HIS WORLD.
   W. PRITCHARD, 362:1NOV73-603
   617(TLS):2NOV73-1338
PRYDE, D. NUNAGA.*
   G.W., 102(CANL):AUTUMN72-115
PRYKE, R. PUBLIC ENTERPRISE IN PRACTICE.*
   M. HOPPE, 619(TC):VOL179#1048-52
PRYNNE, J. BRASS.
   M. LONG, 111:19NOV71-62
PSEUDO-CALLISTHENES. THE ROMANCE OF ALEX-
ANDER THE GREAT BY PSEUDO-CALLISTHENES.
(A.M. WOLOHOJIAN, ED & TRANS)
   E.D. PHILLIPS, 123:MAR72-106

PUCCETTI, R. THE DEATH OF THE FUHRER.
   N. CALLENDAR, 441:22APR73-24
PUCCIANI, O.F. - SEE ROBBE-GRILLET, A.
PUDNEY, J. SELECTED POEMS 1967-1973.
   617(TLS):21DEC73-1562
PUGH, R.B., ED. COURT ROLLS OF THE WILT-
SHIRE MANORS OF ADAM DE STRATTON.
   A.J. DUGGAN, 447(N&Q):APR71-160
PUHLE, H-J. TRADITION UND REFORMPOLITIK
IN BOLIVIEN.
   C.W. ARNADE, 263:JAN-MAR72-46
PUHVEL, J., ED. SUBSTANCE AND STRUCTURE
OF LANGUAGE.
   B. MALMBERG, 596(SL):VOL25#1-52
PUIG, M. THE BUENOS AIRES AFFAIR.
   617(TLS):31AUG73-1007
PUIG, M. HEARTBREAK TANGO.
   D. GALLAGHER, 441:16DEC73-14
   C. LEHMANN-HAUPT, 441:28NOV73-49
   M. WOOD, 453:13DEC73-19
PUJOL, J. OBRA POÈTICA. (K-H. ANTON,
ED)
   A. PACHECO, 86(BHS):OCT72-412
PUKUI, M.K. & S.H. ELBERT. PLACE NAMES
OF HAWAII.*
   J.B. MC MILLAN, 650(WF):APR70-137
DEL PULGAR, F. FERNANDO DEL PULGAR:
CLAROS VARONES DE CASTILLA. (R.B.
TATE, ED)
   A. MACKAY, 402(MLR):JAN72-193
   E.M. WILSON, 382(MAE):1972/2-170
PULLAN, B. A HISTORY OF EARLY RENAIS-
SANCE ITALY.
   617(TLS):20APR73-436
PULLAN, B. RICH AND POOR IN RENAISSANCE
VENICE.*
   J.M. FLETCHER, 90:DEC71-747
PULLINI, G. LA NOVELA ITALIANA DE LA
POSTGUERRA.
   M. ARIZMENDI, 202(FMOD):JUN70-348
"THE PUPPET THEATRE OF THE MODERN WORLD."
   J.B. MYERS, 139:FEB71-10
PUPPI, L., COMP. THE COMPLETE PAINTINGS
OF CANALETTO.
   F.J.B. WATSON, 39:SEP71-244
PUPPI, L. - SEE FARINATI, P.
PUPPO, M. - SEE MACHIAVELLI, N.
PURDY, A., ED. STORM WARNING.*
   P. STEVENS, 628:SPRING72-103
PURDY, A.W. LOVE IN A BURNING BUILDING.*
   D. BARBOUR, 150(DR):SUMMER71-289
PURDY, J. I AM ELIJAH THRUSH.*
   T. TANNER, 473(PR):FALL72-609
PURDY, J. JEREMY'S VERSION.
   42(AR):FALL/WINTER70/71-458
   639(VQR):SPRING71-LVI
PUSHKIN, A.S. THE CRITICIAL PROSE OF ALEX-
ANDER PUSHKIN.* (C-R. PROFFER, ED &
TRANS)
   R.P. HUGHES, 550(RUSR):JAN71-96
   A.B. MC MILLIN, 575(SEER):JAN72-142
PUSHKIN, A.S. PUSHKIN ON LITERATURE.
(T. WOLFF, ED & TRANS)
   R.A. GREGG, 32:JUN72-507
PUSHKIN, A.S. PUSHKIN THREEFOLD. (W.
ARNDT, ED & TRANS)
   V. YOUNG, 249(HUDR):WINTER72/73-663
PUTNAM, H. PHILOSOPHY OF LOGIC.
   617(TLS):9FEB73-157
PUTNAM, H. THE COLLECTED POEMS OF H.
PHELPS PUTNAM. (C.R. WALKER, ED)
   J. ATLAS, 491:JAN73-229
   W.H. PRITCHARD, 249(HUDR):SPRING72-127
PUTNAM, M.C.J. VIRGIL'S PASTORAL ART.*
   E. JENKINSON, 313:VOL61-304
   P.L. SMITH, 487:AUTUMN71-288
   G.W. WILLIAMS, 123:JUN72-274

VAN DER PUTTEN, J.M.P.B. ARNOBII ADVERSUS
NATIONES 3, 1-19.
A. HUDSON-WILLIAMS, 123:DEC72-416
H. LE BONNIEC, 555:VOL45FASC2-369
PÜTZ, P. DIE ZEIT IM DRAMA/ZUR TECHNIK
DRAMATISCHER SPANNUNG.
D.G. DAVIAU, 406:WINTER72-413
PY, A. - SEE RIMBAUD, A.
PYBUS, R. IN MEMORIAM MILENA.
617(TLS):5OCT73-1154
PYE, J. PATRONAGE OF BRITISH ART.
R. EDWARDS, 39:APR71-341
PYE, M. COMPARATIVE RELIGION.
617(TLS):19JAN73-74
PYKE, E.J. A BIOGRAPHICAL DICTIONARY OF
WAX MODELLERS.
617(TLS):31AUG73-998
PYLE, F. "THE WINTER'S TALE."*
R.A. FOAKES, 175:SPRING70-22
PYLE, K.B. THE NEW GENERATION IN MEIJI
JAPAN.
G.B. BIKLE, JR., 318(JAOS):APR-JUN71-
352
PYNCHON, T. GRAVITY'S RAINBOW.
R. GARFITT, 362:15NOV72-674
C. LEHMANN-HAUPT, 441:9MAR73-31
R. LOCKE, 441:11MAR73-1
M. MADDOCKS, 61:MAR73-98
E. SHORRIS, 231:JUN73-78
L.E. SISSMAN, 442(NY):19MAY73-138
M. WOOD, 453:22MAR73-22
617(TLS):16NOV73-1389
PYNCHON, T. V. THE CRYING OF LOT 49.
E. SHORRIS, 231:JUN73-78


"QUADERNI URBINATI DI CULTURA CLASSICA,
8."
D.A. CAMPBELL, 123:MAR72-120
QUAINTON, M. - SEE DE BAÏF, J-A.
QUAM, A. - SEE "THE ZUÑIS"
QUATREPOINT, R. MORT D'UN GREC.
H. MICHOT-DIETRICH, 207(FR):APR71-968
QUAYLE, E. THE RUIN OF SIR WALTER SCOTT.*
J.R. MAC GILLIVRAY, 627(UTQ):FALL70-73
QUDDUSI, I.H. TADHKIRA-I-SHURAI SARHAD.
Q.K. HUSAINI, 273(IC):JUL70-191
QUELCH, E. PERFECT DARLING.*
617(TLS):5JAN73-9
QUELLET, H. LES DÉRIVÉS LATINS EN "-OR."*
A.C. MOORHOUSE, 123:MAR72-126
QUEMADA, B. LES DICTIONNAIRES DU FRAN-
ÇAIS MODERNES, 1539-1863.*
A. REY, 98:FEB70-163
QUENEAU, R. THE BARK TREE.
P. LENTZ, 385(MQR):WINTER73-93
QUENEAU, R. FENDRE LES FLOTS.
A. BERGENS, 207(FR):OCT70-184
QUENEAU, R. THE FLIGHT OF ICARUS.
R. BRYDEN, 362:5JUL73-25
617(TLS):3AUG73-893
QUENEAU, R. LE VOL D'ICARE.
L. JONES, 207(FR):OCT70-185
QUENEAU, R. LE VOYAGE EN GRÈCE.
617(TLS):8JUN73-638
QUENNELL, P. SAMUEL JOHNSON: HIS FRIENDS
AND ENEMIES.*
A. BROYARD, 441:8FEB73-45
F. STEEGMULLER, 441:15APR73-24
442(NY):28APR73-147
QUENNELL, P., ED. MARCEL PROUST.*
G. WERSON, 619(TC):VOL179#1048-53
QUENNELL, P. ROMANTIC ENGLAND.
D.T., 135:MAR71-215
639(VQR):SUMMER71-CXXXIV

QUESTED, R.K.I. THE EXPANSION OF RUSSIA
IN EAST ASIA, 1857-1860.*
J. FLETCHER, 244(HJAS):VOL31-303
A. LAMB, 302:JAN71-178
DE QUEVEDO Y VILLEGAS, F.G. AN ANTHOLOGY
OF QUEVEDO'S POETRY. (R.M. PRICE, ED)
D.L. BAUM, 238:MAY71-412
DE QUEVEDO Y VILLEGAS, F.G. OBRA POÉTICA.
(VOL 1) (J.M. BLECUA, ED)
A. REY, 238:MAR71-196
QUIGLEY, M., JR. & R. GERTNER. FILMS IN
AMERICA 1929-1969.
A.H. WHITHAM, 200:AUG-SEP71-434
QUILICI, V., ED. L'ARCHITETTURA DEL
COSTRUTTIVISMO.*
S.F. STARR, 576:MAY71-171
QUILLIOT, R. THE SEA AND PRISONS.*
(FRENCH TITLE: LA MER ET LES PRISONS.)
L.D. JOINER, 207(FR):APR71-978
QUINE, W.V. ELEMENTARY LOGIC. (REV)
R.L. STANLEY, 316:MAR70-166
QUINN, A. THE ORIGINAL SIN.*
617(TLS):18MAY73-563
QUINN, J. WORD OF MOUTH.
N. HAZELTON, 441:11MAR73-18
QUINN, K. CATULLUS: AN INTERPRETATION.
617(TLS):12JAN73-28
QUINN, K. - SEE CATULLUS
QUINONES, R.J. THE RENAISSANCE DISCOVERY
OF TIME.
617(TLS):31AUG73-1004
QUINTILIAN. QUINTILIANI INSTITUTIONIS
ORATORIAE LIBRI XII. (M. WINTERBOTTOM,
ED)
G. KENNEDY, 313:VOL61-308
H. NORTH, 124:SEP71-29
QUINTON, A. THE NATURE OF THINGS.
A. KENNY, 362:1FEB73-154
617(TLS):23MAR73-330
QUINTON, A. UTILITARIAN ETHICS.
617(TLS):19OCT73-1286
QUINTUS OF SMYRNA. THE WAR AT TROY.*
(F.M. COMBELLACK, ED & TRANS)
J. FONTENROSE, 131(CL):SUMMER72-275
"LES QUINZE JOYES DE MARIAGE." (J. CROW,
ED)
W.W. KIBLER, 207(FR):DEC70-465
J.C. LAIDLAW, 208(FS):JAN72-63
QUIRK, R. ESSAYS ON THE ENGLISH LAN-
GUAGE, MEDIEVAL AND MODERN.
N.E. ENKVIST, 597(SN):VOL42#1-249
QUIRK, R. & OTHERS. A GRAMMAR OF CON-
TEMPORARY ENGLISH.
617(TLS):2FEB73-123
QUIRK, R. & S. GREENBAUM. A UNIVERSITY
GRAMMAR OF ENGLISH.
617(TLS):12OCT73-1260
QUITSLUND, S.A. BEAUDUIN.
C.E. SIMCOX, 441:8JUL73-14
QUONDAM, A. CULTURA E IDEOLOGIA DI GIAN-
VINCENZO GRAVINA. FILOSOFIA DELLA LUCE
E LUMINOSI NELLE EGLOGHE DEL GRAVINA.
M. FUBINI, 228(GSLI):VOL148FASC462/
463-398
QURAISHI, Z.M. LIBERAL NATIONALISM IN
EGYPT.
S. AKHTAR, 468:VOL23#4-421
QVARNSTRÖM, G. THE ENCHANTED PALACE.*
E. MERTNER, 38:BAND88HEFT2-268
R.A. PECK, 179(ES):DEC71-550
QVARNSTRÖM, G. POETRY AND NUMBERS.
R.A. PECK, 179(ES):JUN71-269


RAAB, L. MYSTERIES OF THE HORIZON.
J. AARON, 398:WINTER73-334
D. KENWORTHY, 31(ASCH):SUMMER73-514
R.B. SHAW, 491:SEP73-344

RAABE, P., ED. INDEX EXPRESSIONISMUS.
617(TLS):23MAR73-332
RAABE, W. STOPFKUCHEN. (W.P. HANSON,
ED)
H.R. KLIENEBERGER, 402(MLR):OCT72-948
205(FMLS):JUL71-298
RAASCH, A. FRANZÖSISCHER MINDESTWORT-
SCHATZ.
G. VARGES, 430(NS):JUL71-395
RABA, J. ROBOTNICY ŚLĄSCY, 1850-1870,
PRACA I BYT.
J. KOLAJA, 497(POLR):AUTUMN70-117
RABELAIS, F. CONTES CHOISIS. (A.C. KEL-
LER, ED)
M-C. WRAGE, 399(MLJ):MAR71-193
RABELAIS, F. GARGANTUA AND PANTAGRUEL.
I. BAIN, 503:WINTER70-227
RABELAIS, F. PANTAGRUEL, ROY DES DIP-
SODES, RESTITUÉ A SON NATUREL, AVEC SES
FAICTZ ET PROUESSES ESPOVENTABLES.
(V-L. SAULNIER & J-Y. POUILLOUX, EDS)
D. COLEMAN, 208(FS):JAN72-71
RABI, I.I. SCIENCE.
A.B. WEAVER, 50(ARQ):SUMMER71-189
RABIBHADANA, M.R.A. - SEE UNDER AKIN
RABIBHADANA, M.R.
RABIL, A., JR. MERLEAU-PONTY.
P. DUBOIS, 542:OCT-DEC71-504
RABINOWITCH, A. PRELUDE TO REVOLUTION.*
G. KATKOV, 32:DEC72-896
RABINOWITCH, A. & J., WITH L.K.D. KRIS-
TOF, EDS. REVOLUTION AND POLITICS IN
RUSSIA.
617(TLS):24AUG73-983
RABINOWITSCH, W.Z. LITHUANIAN HASIDISM.
E. MENDELSOHN, 32:SEP72-712
RABKIN, N., ED. REINTERPRETATIONS OF
ELIZABETHAN DRAMA.*
R.A. FOAKES, 175:AUTUMN70-98
M. MINCOFF, 447(N&Q):DEC71-469
S. WELLS, 597(SN):VOL42#2-467
205(FMLS):OCT70-423
RABUSE-SCHÜTZNER-DENOUAL. FRANZÖSISCHE
GESCHÄFTSBRIEFE, RICHTIG SCHREIBEN.
K. LICHEM, 430(NS):JUL70-366
DE RACHEWILTZ, I. & MIYOKO NAKANO. INDEX
TO BIOGRAPHICAL MATERIAL IN CHIN AND
YÜAN LITERARY WORKS. (1ST SER)
T. CONNOR, 244(HJAS):VOL31-352
DE RACHEWILTZ, M. DISCRETIONS.*
G. DAVENPORT, 639(VQR):AUTUMN71-638
H. REGNERY, 396(MODA):FALL72-420
R.E. TEELE, 352(LE&W):VOL15#2-327
RACINE, J. PHAEDRA OF RACINE. (R.
LOWELL, TRANS)
A. RENDLE, 157:AUTUMN71-82
RACKHAM, B. MEDIEVAL ENGLISH POTTERY.
(NEW ED)
617(TLS):9MAR73-277
RACKMAN, E. ONE MAN'S JUDAISM.
P. BIRNBAUM, 287:MAR71-25
RÁCZ, I. THE UNKNOWN GOD.
W.S. KEENEY, 290(JAAC):SUMMER71-566
RADBERTUS, P. - SEE UNDER PASCASIUS RAD-
BERTUS
RADCLIFF-UMSTEAD, D. THE BIRTH OF MODERN
COMEDY IN RENAISSANCE ITALY.*
A.M. CRINÒ, 551(RENQ):WINTER71-528
RADER, D. BLOOD DUES.
G. BURNSIDE, 441:4NOV73-72
RADER, M. WORDSWORTH.*
W. FRANKE, 38:BAND88HEFT2-274
RADIG, W. DAS BAUERNHAUS IN BRANDENBURG
UND IM MITTELGEBIET.
R.L. WELSCH, 650(WF):APR70-131
RADL, S.L. MOTHER'S DAY IS OVER.
L.C. POGREBIN, 441:17JUN73-2

RÄDLE, H. UNTERSUCHUNGEN ZUM GRIECHIS-
CHEN FREILASSUNGSWESEN.
R. SEAGER, 123:MAR72-129
RADLEY, J. SCARRED TEMPLE.
617(TLS):31AUG73-996
RADNER, L. EICHENDORFF.
R. IMMERWAHR, 564:OCT71-244
W.J. LILLYMAN, 406:SUMMER72-170
K.T. LOCHER, 401(MLQ):SEP72-337
J. PURVER, 402(MLR):JAN72-220
E.M. SZAROTA, 301(JEGP):JAN72-74
RADNITZKY, G. ANGLO-SAXON SCHOOLS OF
METASCIENCE.
J.J.E., 543:MAR71-548
RADOEV, I. RED AND BROWN.
270:VOL22#2-35
RADVANY, E. METTERNICH'S PROJECTS FOR
REFORM IN AUSTRIA.
G.A. CRAIG, 32:DEC72-913
RADWAY, G.F. BRAHMINS & BULLYBOYS. (S.
& B. HALPERT, EDS)
S. SCHWARTZ, 441:2DEC73-95
RAEBURN, A. THE MILITANT SUFFRAGETTES.
617(TLS):11MAY73-515
RAEFF, M., ED. CATHERINE THE GREAT.
D-M. GRIFFITHS, 32:DEC72-886
617(TLS):2FEB73-133
RAEFF, M. IMPERIAL RUSSIA, 1682-1825.
J. CRACRAFT, 550(RUSR):OCT71-394
RAFAELLE, DUCHESS OF LEINSTER. SO BRIEF
A DREAM.
617(TLS):27JUL73-884
RAFFEL, B., ED & TRANS. RUSSIAN POETRY
UNDER THE TSARS.
D.H. STEWART, 651(WHR):WINTER72-83
RAFFEL, B. - SEE ANWAR, C.
RAGGHIANTI, C.L. - SEE FANELLI, G.
RAGGIUNTI, R. HUSSERL DALLA LOGICA ALLA
FENOMENOLOGIA.
E. NAMER, 542:APR-JUN70-254
RAGGIUNTI, R. LOGICA ELINGUISTICA NEL
PENSIERO DI GUIDO CALOGERO.
S. CECCATO, 206:AUG70-443
"RAGGUAGLI BORROMINIANI, MOSTRA DOCUMEN-
TARIA."
A. BLUNT, 90:NOV71-672
RAGNI, G. & J. RADO. HAIR.
M. PETERSON, 470:JAN71-45
RAGONESE, G. - SEE GUERRAZZI, F.D.
RAGUSA, O. LUIGI PIRANDELLO.
205(FMLS):JUL70-313
RAHNER, K. THE TRINITY.
M. HOLLERAN, 613:AUTUMN71-447
RAHTZ, P.A. EXCAVATIONS AT KING JOHN'S
HUNTING LODGE, WRITTLE, ESSEX, 1955-57.
U.T. HOLMES, 589:APR72-337
RAHUL, R. THE GOVERNMENT AND POLITICS OF
TIBET.
P. CARRASCO, 293(JAST):NOV70-245
RAHV, P. LITERATURE AND THE SIXTH
SENSE.
L.T. LEMON, 502(PRS):FALL70-263
P. PARRINDER, 111:7MAY71-163
RAIBLE, W. ARISTOTELES UND DER RAUM.*
P. LOUIS, 555:VOL45FASC1-154
RAILLARD, G. BUTOR.*
F. FLAGOTHIER, 556(RLV):1971/5-636
RAIM, W. - SEE "THE MITCHELL TRIO SONG
BOOK"
RAIMBAUD. REIMBALDI LEODIENSIS OPERA
OMNIA. (C. DE CLERCQ, ED)
D. LUSCOMBE, 382(MAE):1972/2-141
RAIMON DE MIRAVAL. LES POÉSIES DU TROU-
BADOUR RAIMON DE MIRAVAL. (L.T. TOPS-
FIELD, ED)
J.H. MARSHALL, 208(FS):APR72-186
T. NEWCOMBE, 382(MAE):1972/3-264

RAIMOND, J. ROBERT SOUTHEY.*
    G. CARNALL, 402(MLR):JAN72-174
RAINA, P.K. WŁADYSŁAW GOMUŁKA, ŻYCIORYS
  POLITYCZNY.
    A. BROMKE, 497(POLR):SPRING71-119
RAINBIRD, G. & R. SEARLE. THE SUBTLE AL-
  CHEMIST.
    617(TLS):15JUN73-700
RAINE, J.W. THE LAND OF SADDLE-BAGS.
    M.W. CLARKE, 292(JAF):JUL-SEP71-355
    L. MONTELL, 582(SFQ):DEC71-368
RAINE, K. WILLIAM BLAKE.
    J.E. GRANT, 481(PQ):JUL71-409
RAINE, K. BLAKE AND TRADITION.*
    G.E. BENTLEY, JR., 627(UTQ):FALL70-86
    J.H. HAGSTRUM, 405(MP):AUG70-76
    B. KENNELLY, 159(DM):SPRING70-104
    P. MALEKIN, 541(RES):FEB71-93
    A. ORAS, 569(SR):WINTER72-200
    D. WEEKS, 290(JAAC):SPRING71-424
RAINE, K. DEFENDING ANCIENT SPRINGS.
    K.P.S. JOCHUM, 38:BAND89HEFT1-143
    A. ORAS, 569(SR):WINTER72-200
RAINE, K. FAREWELL HAPPY FIELDS.
    617(TLS):14DEC73-1533
RAINE, K. THE LOST COUNTRY.*
    H. NEMEROV, 569(SR):SUMMER72-468
    J.C. OATES, 598(SOR):AUTUMN73-1014
RAINE, K. YEATS, THE TAROT AND THE
  GOLDEN DAWN.
    W. EMPSON, 453:13DEC73-43
    617(TLS):1JUN73-620
RAINE, K. & G.M. HARPER - SEE TAYLOR, T.
RAINES, J.C. & T. DEAN, EDS. MARXISM AND
  RADICAL RELIGION.
    H.L. PARSONS, 484(PPR):DEC71-286
RAINEY, A. MOSAICS IN ROMAN BRITAIN.
    617(TLS):8JUN73-653
RAISON, J. LE GRAND PALAIS DE KNOSSOS.
    J.T. HOOKER, 303:VOL91-200
RAISON, J. LES VASES À INSCRIPTIONS
  PEINTES DE L'ÂGE MYCÉNIEN ET LEUR CON-
  TEXTE ARCHÉOLOGIQUE.*
    R. SCHMITT, 343:BAND13HEFT2-190
RAISTRICK, A. INDUSTRIAL ARCHAEOLOGY.
    617(TLS):31AUG73-999
RAITIÈRE, A. L'ART DE L'ACTEUR SELON
  DORAT ET SAMSON.*
    J-M. PIEMME, 556(RLV):1971/3-365
RAJAN, B. THE LOFTY RHYME.*
    G. BULLOUGH, 175:AUTUMN70-101
    L.S. CHAMPION, 551(RENQ):WINTER71-585
RAJAN, B., ED. "PARADISE LOST:" A TER-
  CENTENARY TRIBUTE.*
    G. BULLOUGH, 175:AUTUMN70-101
    R.L. COLIE, 102(CANL):SPRING72-99
RAJAN, B., ED. THE PRISON AND THE PIN-
  NACLE.
    617(TLS):20JUL73-831
RAJASEKHARAIAH, T.R. THE ROOTS OF WHIT-
  MAN'S GRASS.*
    D.K. KIRBY, 646(WWR):JUN71-65
RAJU, P.T. INTRODUCTION TO COMPARATIVE
  PHILOSOPHY.
    N.L. CHOBOT, 485(PE&W):JAN71-95
    J.B.L., 543:MAR71-549
    A.W. MUNK, 484(PPR):JUN72-587
RAKOWSKA-HARMSTONE, T. RUSSIA AND NATION-
  ALISM IN CENTRAL ASIA.*
    F. KAZAMZADEH, 550(RUSR):APR71-186
RAM, M. INDIAN COMMUNISM.
    N.D. PALMER, 293(JAST):FEB71-492
RAM, M. POLITICS OF SINO-INDIAN CONFRON-
  TATION.
    617(TLS):30NOV73-1485
RAMACHANDRAN, T.P. THE CONCEPT OF THE
  VYĀVAHĀRIKA IN ĀDVAITA VEDĀNTA.
    J.B.L., 543:MAR71-549

RĀMĀNUJA. THE GITABHASHYA OF RAMANUJA.
    W.H. MAURER, 318(JAOS):OCT-DEC71-551
RAMAT, R. SAGGI SUL RINASCIMENTO. (W.
  BINNI, ED)
    M. PUCCINI, 275(IQ):FALL-WINTER71-101
RAMAZANI, R.K. THE PERSIAN GULF: IRAN'S
  ROLE.
    617(TLS):19JAN73-60
"JEAN-PHILIPPE RAMEAU: COMPLETE THEORETI-
  CAL WRITINGS." (VOL 1) (E.R. JACOBI,
  ED)
    P.H.L., 414(MQ):OCT71-677
"JEAN-PHILIPPE RAMEAU: COMPLETE THEORETI-
  CAL WRITINGS." (VOLS 2-5) (E.R. JACOBI,
  ED)
    P.H.L., 414(MQ):OCT71-677
    J.A.W., 410(M&L):JAN72-81
RAMM, A. SIR ROBERT MORIER.
    617(TLS):17AUG73-947
RAMNOUX, C. ÉTUDES PRÉSOCRATIQUES.
    Y. LAFRANCE, 154:SEP71-611
RAMPERSAD, A. MELVILLE'S "ISRAEL POT-
  TER."*
    C. NICHOLS, 454:WINTER72-181
    M.E. RUCKER, 50(ARQ):SUMMER70-182
RAMSAY, A. THE WORKS OF ALLAN RAMSAY.
  (VOL 4) (A.M. KINGHORN & A. LAW, EDS)
    M.P. MC DIARMID, 402(MLR):JUL72-620
RAMSAY, A. THE WORKS OF ALLAN RAMSAY.
  (VOL 5) (A.M. KINGHORN & A. LAW, EDS)
    617(TLS):3AUG73-911
RAMSAY, D. DEADLY DISCRETION.
    617(TLS):18MAY73-562
RAMSAY, W. & C. ANDERSON. MANAGING THE
  ENVIRONMENT.
    617(TLS):12OCT73-1246
RAMSDEN, H. ANGEL GANIVET'S "IDEARIUM
  ESPAÑOL."*
    205(FMLS):OCT70-422
RAMSEY, P. THE ART OF JOHN DRYDEN.*
    R. LAWRENCE, 175:AUTUMN70-107
RAMSEY, P. THE DOORS.
    J. TIPTON, 577(SHR):SPRING71-196
RAMSEY, W., ED. JULES LAFORGUE.*
    A. SONNENFELD, 188(ECR):WINTER71-68
RAMSEYER, U. SOZIALE BEZÜGE DES MUSIZ-
  IERENS IN NATURVOLKKULTUREN.
    K.P. ETZKORN, 187:JAN73-136
RAMTHUN, H., ED. BERTOLT-BRECHT-ARCHIV.
  (VOLS 1&2)
    J.A. KRUSE, 182:VOL24#11/12-484
RAMTHUN, H., ED. BERTOLT-BRECHT-ARCHIV.
  (VOL 3)
    617(TLS):23NOV73-1413
RAMTHUN, H., ED. BERTOLT-BRECHT-ARCHIV.
  (VOL 4)
    617(TLS):28DEC73-1591
RAMUS, P. THE LOGIKE OF THE MOST EXCEL-
  LENT PHILOSOPHER P. RAMUS MARTYR.* (R.
  MAC ILMAINE, TRANS; C.M. DUNN, ED)
    W.J. ONG, 551(RENQ):SPRING71-87
RANCOEUR, R. BIBLIOGRAPHIE DE LA LITTÉR-
  ATURE FRANÇAISE DU MOYEN AGE À NOS
  JOURS: 1968.
    A. CIORANESCU, 549(RLC):OCT-DEC71-615
    R. MERCIER, 557(RSH):JUL-SEP70-473
RANCOEUR, R. BIBLIOGRAPHIE DE LA LITTÉR-
  ATURE FRANÇAISE DU MOYEN AGE À NOS
  JOURS, 1969.
    R. MERCIER, 557(RSH):JUL-SEP71-467
RAND, E. CONSTRUCTING DIALOGS.
    J. ORNSTEIN, 215(GL):VOL10#1-56
    C. JAMES, 399(MLJ):FEB71-128
RAND, E. CONSTRUCTING SENTENCES.
    L. PAŽUSIS, 215(GL):VOL11#2-110
RANDALL, D., ED. THE BLACK POETS.
    W. DICKEY, 249(HUDR):SUMMER72-297

RANDALL, D.B.J. JOSEPH CONRAD AND WAR-
RINGTON DAWSON.*
A.T. SCHWAB, 405(MP):MAY71-364
RANDALL, F.E. HALDANE STATION.
M. LEVIN, 441:5AUG73-16
RANDALL, J.H. HELLENISTIC WAYS OF DELIV-
ERANCE AND THE MAKING OF THE CHRISTIAN
SYNTHESIS.*
H. CHADWICK, 123:DEC72-430
RANDALL, J.H., JR. PLATO.*
W. CHARLTON, 123:JUN72-270
L.G., 543:JUN71-753
J. MITTELSTRASS, 322(JHI):JUL-SEP71-
459
F.H. PAGE, 150(DR):SPRING71-121
R.A. SHINER, 154:SEP71-568
RANDALL, L.M.C. IMAGES IN THE MARGINS OF
GOTHIC MANUSCRIPTS.
L.F. SANDLER, 54:MAR70-95
RANDEL, M.G. THE HISTORICAL PROSE OF
FERNANDO DE HERRERA.*
A. MAC KAY, 402(MLR):APR72-440
RANDEL, W.P. THE AMERICAN REVOLUTION.
G.F. SCHEER, 441:25NOV73-22
RANDELL, A. FENLAND MEMORIES. (E. POR-
TER, ED)
T. BROWN, 203:SPRING70-78
RANDLE, R.F. GENEVA, 1954.*
A.E. GOODMAN, 293(JAST):FEB71-510
RANDOLPH, E. HISTORY OF VIRGINIA. (A.H.
SHAFFER, ED)
M.L. NICHOLLS, 656(WMQ):JAN71-146
RANGER, T.O. REVOLT IN SOUTHERN RHODESIA
1896-7.
R.P. WERBNER, 69:APR71-174
RANGER, T.O. & I.N. KIMAMBO, EDS. THE
HISTORICAL STUDY OF AFRICAN RELIGION.
617(TLS):23NOV73-1419
RANKE, F. ALTNORDISCHES ELEMENTARBUCH.
(3RD ED REV BY D. HOFMANN)
K. DÜWEL, 260(IF):BAND74-310
RANKE, F. KLEINERE SCHRIFTEN. (H. RUPP
& E. STUDER, EDS)
J.A. ASHER, 220(GL&L):APR72-303
E. ETTLINGER, 203:AUTUMN71-253
RANSOM, H.H. THE INTELLIGENCE ESTABLISH-
MENT.
639(VQR):WINTER71-XL
RANSOM, J.C. BEATING THE BUSHES.*
R. BUFFINGTON, 396(MODA):FALL72-440
RANSOM, J.C. SELECTED POEMS.
J. GLOVER, 565:VOL12#3-66
RANSOM, P.J.G. RAILWAYS REVIVED.
617(TLS):31AUG73-1009
RAO, K.R. GANDHI AND PRAGMATISM.
E.J. QUIGLEY, 485(PE&W):JUL70-330
RAO, K.V.N. THE EMERGENCE OF ANDHRA PRA-
DESH.
617(TLS):7SEP73-1037
RAO, K.V.N. TELANGANA.
617(TLS):20JUL73-842
RAO, P.R.R. CONTEMPORARY INDIAN ART.*
M.A., 135:FEB71-139
RAO, T.V.S. - SEE UNDER SUBBA RAO, T.V.
RAPER, J.R. WITHOUT SHELTER.
N. BAYM, 301(JEGP):APR72-291
F.P.W. MC DOWELL, 27(AL):MAR72-163
B. ROUSE, 579(SAQ):SPRING72-275
A.F. SCOTT, 639(VQR):AUTUMN71-634
RAPHAEL, F. RICHARD'S THINGS.
E. FEINSTEIN, 362:22NOV73-721
617(TLS):23NOV73-1455
RAPHAEL, M. THE DEMANDS OF ART.
D. SUTTON, 39:APR70-320
D.T. WIECK, 290(JAAC):WINTER70-273
"THE RAPHAEL CARTOONS."
617(TLS):16MAR73-284

RAPIN, R. LES RÉFLEXIONS SUR LA POÉTIQUE
DE CE TEMPS ET SUR LES OUVRAGES DES
POÈTES ANCIENS ET MODERNES. (E.T.
DUBOIS, ED)
P. FRANCE, 208(FS):JAN72-74
RAPOPORT, A. HOUSE FORM AND CULTURE.
W.P. THOMPSON, 45:JAN71-49
RAPP, H. DAS PARTEIENPRIVILEG DES GRUND-
GESETZES UND SEINE AUSWIRKUNGEN AUF DAS
STRAFRECHT.
G. STRICKRODT, 182:VOL24#23/24-846
RASCH, W., ED. DICHTERISCHE PROSA UM
1900.
T.A. SCHEUFELE, 400(MLN):OCT71-726
RASCOE, J. YOURS, AND MINE.
C. LEHMANN-HAUPT, 441:27JUL73-35
RASKIN, B. LOOSE ENDS.
M. LEVIN, 441:4NOV73-81
RASKIN, M. BEING AND DOING.
42(AR):SUMMER71-286
RASMUSSEN, D.M. MYTHIC-SYMBOLIC LAN-
GUAGE AND PHILOSOPHICAL ANTHROPOLOGY.
J. BRUN, 182:VOL24#23/24-838
RASMUSSEN, S.E. TOWNS AND BUILDINGS.
W. CREESE, 505:MAR70-138
RASS, H.H. GROSSBRITANNIEN: EINE POLI-
TISCHE LANDESKUNDE.
B. WÖLFL, 430(NS):DEC71-678
RASSAM, J. LA MÉTAPHYSIQUE DE SAINT
THOMAS.*
A. FOREST, 542:APR-JUN70-235
RATCLIFFE, M. THE NOVEL TODAY.
J.C. FIELD, 556(RLV):1971/2-233
RATIÈRE, A. L'ART DE L'ACTEUR SELON
DORAT ET SAMSON.
M. DESCOTES, 535(RHL):MAR-APR70-314
RATTENBURY, A. MAN THINKING.
617(TLS):20APR73-442
RATTRAY, R.S. HAUSA FOLKLORE, CUSTOMS,
PROVERBS.
A.H.M. KIRK-GREENE, 69:JAN71-80
RAU, W. - SEE KIELHORN, F.
RAUBITSCHEK, A.E. & OTHERS. L'ÉPIGRAMME
GRECQUE.* [SHOWN IN PREV UNDER TITLE]
D.A. CAMPBELL, 123:MAR72-59
RAUBITSCHEK, I.K. THE HEARST HILLSBOROUGH
VASES.
B.A. SPARKES, 303:VOL91-209
RAUCH, E.M. DIRTY PICTURES FROM THE PROM.
S.B., 502(PRS):SUMMER71-184
L.T. LEMON, 502(PRS):FALL71-270
RAUENHORST, D. ANNETTE KOLB, IHR LEBEN
UND IHR WERK.
J. BODY, 549(RLC):JUL-SEP71-432
RAUH, M. FÖDERALISMUS UND PARLAMENTAR-
ISMUS IM WILHELMINISCHEN REICH.
617(TLS):13JUL73-813
RAUHALA, L. INTENTIONALITY AND THE PROB-
LEM OF THE UNCONSCIOUS.
A. BORGMANN, 485(PE&W):OCT70-431
RAVÀ, A. SCRITTI MINORI DI FILOSOFIA
DEL DIRITTO.
E. NAMER, 542:JAN-MAR70-104
RAVEN, S. ROME IN AFRICA.
A.G. MC KAY, 487:SPRING71-88
RAVENSCROFT, A. CHINUA ACHEBE.
H. MAES-JELINEK, 179(ES):AUG71-399
RAWLINGS, J.D.R. PICTORIAL HISTORY OF
THE FLEET AIR ARM.
617(TLS):12OCT73-1260
RAWLINS, D. PEARY AT THE NORTH POLE -
FACT OR FICTION?
P. ADAMS, 61:AUG73-103
C. LEHMANN-HAUPT, 441:31JUL73-31
442(NY):30JUL73-72
RAWLINSON, D.H. THE PRACTICE OF CRITI-
CISM.*
A. RODWAY, 447(N&Q):JUL71-269

RAWLINSON, H. ENGLAND AND RUSSIA IN THE
EAST.
E. WIDMER, 293(JAST):MAY71-694
RAWLINSON, J.L. CHINA'S STRUGGLE FOR
NAVAL DEVELOPMENT, 1839-1895.
N.R. BENNETT, 302:JAN71-176
RAWLINSON, R. FOUR HUNDRED YEARS OF
BRITISH AUTOGRAPHS.
B. SAVAGE, 503:SUMMER71-95
RAWLS, J. A THEORY OF JUSTICE.*
K.J. ARROW, 311(JP):10MAY73-245
J. FEINBERG, 311(JP):10MAY73-263
S. GORDON, 311(JP):10MAY73-275
RAWORTH, T. ACT.
617(TLS):23NOV73-1452
RAWSON, C., ED. FOCUS: SWIFT.
C.T. PROBYN, 566:AUTUMN71-20
RAWSON, C.J. HENRY FIELDING AND THE
AUGUSTAN IDEAL UNDER STRESS.
617(TLS):11MAY73-525
RAWSON, C.J. GULLIVER AND THE GENTLE
READER.
617(TLS):5OCT73-1178
RAWSON, N. SHARDS.
617(TLS):1JUN73-610
RAWSON, P. THE APPRECIATION OF THE ARTS:
CERAMICS.*
M. EASTHAM, 89(BJA):AUTUMN72-407
RAWSON, P. THE APPRECIATION OF THE ARTS:
DRAWING.
S. ROSENTHAL, 58:MAR71-15
RAWSON, P. EROTIC ART OF THE EAST.*
J. UPDIKE, 441:28OCT73-4
RAWSON, P., ED. PRIMITIVE EROTIC ART.
J. UPDIKE, 441:28OCT73-4
RAY, C. COGNAC.
617(TLS):14DEC73-1548
RAY, G.E. WILY WOMEN OF THE WEST.
W. GARD, 584(SWR):SUMMER72-V
RAY, J.M., ED. THE PRESIDENT.
M.C. MC GEE, 583:SPRING71-292
RAY, L. L'INTERDIT EST MON OPÉRA.
617(TLS):1JUN73-610
RAY, N. NATIONALISM IN INDIA.
617(TLS):28DEC73-1595
RAY, P.S. LINGUISTIC MATRICES.*
E. ROULET, 343:BAND13HEFT2-177
RAY, T.F. THE POLITICS OF THE BARRIOS OF
VENEZUELA.
N. GALL, 453:15NOV73-29
RAYFIELD, J.R. THE LANGUAGES OF A BILIN-
GUAL COMMUNITY.
J.A. FISHMAN, 350:DEC72-969
RAYMOND, E. THE MOUNTAIN FARM.
M. LEVIN, 441:16DEC73-16
RAYMOND, M. ÉTUDES SUR JACQUES RIVIÈRE.
617(TLS):12OCT73-1257
RAYMOND, W.O. THE INFINITE MOMENT AND
OTHER ESSAYS IN ROBERT BROWNING.
L. BONNEROT, 189(EA):OCT-DEC70-448
RAYNOR, H. A SOCIAL HISTORY OF MUSIC
FROM THE MIDDLE AGES TO BEETHOVEN.
E.D. MACKERNESS, 415:AUG72-773
J.A.W., 410(M&L):OCT72-451
617(TLS):1JUN73-611
RAZ, J. THE CONCEPT OF A LEGAL SYSTEM.
D.N. MAC CORMICK, 479(PHQ):OCT71-380
"MISS READ" - SEE UNDER MISS
READ, D. EDWARDIAN ENGLAND 1901-15.
617(TLS):9MAR73-259
READ, H., J. CASSOU & J. SMITH. JAN LE
WITT.
R. LEBOWITZ, 58:DEC71/JAN72-24
READ, P.P. THE UPSTART.
R. BLYTHE, 362:6SEP73-320
C. LEHMANN-HAUPT, 441:22MAY73-45
D.K. MANO, 441:20MAY73-6
[CONTINUED]

[CONTINUING]
K. MILLER, 453:15NOV73-26
442(NY):13AUG73-87
617(TLS):7SEP73-1017
READE, B., ED. SEXUAL HERETICS.*
S. HEYWOOD, 111:29JAN71-108
REAL, H.J. UNTERSUCHUNGEN ZUR LUKREZ-
ÜBERSETZUNG VON THOMAS CREECH.
R. SELDEN, 173(ECS):WINTER71/72-335
"REAL ACADEMIA ESPAÑOLA, DICCIONARIO DE
LA LENGUA ESPAÑOLA."* (10TH ED)
F. GURRI, 263:JUL-SEP72-297
REALE, G. - SEE LEVI, A.
REANEY, G. GUILLAUME DE MACHAUT.*
M. BENT, 415:FEB72-155
REANEY, J. MASKS OF CHILDHOOD. (B. PAR-
KER, ED) LISTEN TO THE WIND.
G. WARKENTIN, 296:WINTER73-88
REANEY, J. POEMS.
D.W. DOERKSEN, 198:SUMMER73-120
F.W. WATT, 99:AUG73-32
REAVER, J.R., COMP. AN O'NEILL CONCOR-
DANCE.*
D. ALEXANDER, 397(MD):SEP70-226
R.S. WACHAL, 397(MD):SEP70-228
REB, P. CONFESSIONS OF A FUTURE SCOTSMAN.
P. THEROUX, 441:14OCT73-38
REBAY, L. ALBERTO MORAVIA.
D. HEINEY, 546(RR):OCT71-246
REBHOLZ, R.A. THE LIFE OF FULKE GREVILLE,
FIRST LORD BROOKE.*
N.K. FARMER, JR., 67:NOV72-220
F.J. LEVY, 401(MLQ):DEC72-433
REBSAMEN, F.R., ED & TRANS. BEOWULF IS
MY NAME.
A.M. KINLOCH, 255(HAB):FALL71-66
Y. MALKIEL, 545(RPH):FEB72-369
REBUFFAT, G. MEN AND THE MATTERHORN.
W.H. HONAN, 441:2DEC73-97
RECHENBACH, C.W. & OTHERS. SWAHILI-
ENGLISH DICTIONARY.*
M. VAN SPAANDONCK, 315(JAL):VOL10PT2-
64
"LA RECHERCHE EN PHILOSOPHIE ET EN THÉ-
OLOGIE."
C. PANACCIO, 154:DEC71-788
"RECHERCHE ET LITTÉRATURE CANADIENNE-
FRANÇAISE."
A. VIATTE, 549(RLC):JUL-SEP70-414
RECHY, J. THIS DAY'S DEATH.
L.T. LEMON, 502(PRS):FALL71-270
RECIO FLORES, S. DICCIONARIO COMPARADO
DE REFRANES Y MODISMOS: ESPAÑOL-ENGLISH.
E. O'KANE, 238:MAR71-223
RECK, A.J. THE NEW AMERICAN PHILOSO-
PHERS.*
R. SIMONDS, 321:WINTER70[VOL5#1]-64
185:OCT70-89
RECK, R.D. LITERATURE AND RESPONSIBIL-
ITY.*
R.M. ALBÉRÈS, 535(RHL):JAN-FEB71-144
J.V. ALTER, 405(MP):MAY72-371
V. CONLEY, 594:FALL71-348
P. FITTING, 188(ECR):FALL70-262
E. MOROT-SIR, 546(RR):FEB71-82
RECK-MALLECZEWEN, F.P. DIARY OF A MAN
IN DESPAIR.
M. SYRKIN, 390:DEC70-50
RECKFORD, K.J. HORACE.*
W.R. JOHNSON, 121(CJ):OCT-NOV71-83
"RECORDS OF AGRICULTURAL AGENCIES IN THE
OREGON STATE ARCHIVES." (RECORD GROUP
A-2)
L.C. WAFFEN, 14:APR71-197
"LE RECUEIL DU BRITISH MUSEUM."
R. LEBÈGUE, 535(RHL):MAY-JUN71-495
RED FOX. THE MEMOIRS OF CHIEF RED FOX.
639(VQR):SUMMER71-CXVII

297

REDDAWAY, W.B. & OTHERS. EFFECTS OF
SELECTIVE EMPLOYMENT TAX.
617(TLS):27APR73-466
REDEKOP, E. MARGARET AVISON.
W.H. NEW, 102(CANL):AUTUMN72-90
REDER, G. CLOCKWORK, STEAM AND ELECTRIC.
617(TLS):12JAN73-50
REDER, P. - SEE VON LENZ, W.
REDFERN, J. A GLOSSARY OF FRENCH LITER-
ARY EXPRESSION.
E.C. KNOX, 207(FR):DEC70-437
REDFERN, W.D. PAUL NIZAN.
617(TLS):1JUN73-622
REDGROVE, P. DR. FAUST'S SEA-SPIRAL
SPIRIT.*
A. MACLEAN, 362:22MAR73-389
REDGROVE, P. IN THE COUNTRY OF THE SKIN.
J. FULLER, 362:22MAR73-390
617(TLS):23MAR73-312
REDGROVE, P. LOVE'S JOURNEYS.
W.G. SHEPHERD, 493:SUMMER71-204
REDGROVE, P. & P. SHUTTLE. THE HERMA-
PHRODITE ALBUM.
A. MACLEAN, 362:25OCT73-565
617(TLS):20JUL73-826
REDIG DE CAMPOS, D. I PALAZZI VATICANI.
H.A. MILLON, 576:MAY70-194
RED'KO, J.K. DOVIDNYK UKRAJINS'KYX
PRIZVYŠČ.
L.M.L. ONYSHKEVYCH, 424:DEC70-321
REDMAN, E. THE DANCE OF LEGISLATION.
W.V. SHANNON, 441:16SEP73-3
442(NY):8OCT73-170
REDMOND, W.B. BIBLIOGRAPHY OF THE PHIL-
OSOPHY IN THE IBERIAN COLONIES OF
AMERICA.
A. DONOSO, 319:JUL73-413
REDPATH, T. - SEE DONNE, J.
REECE, R. ROMAN COINS.
R. HIGGINS, 39:AUG71-161
REED, A. BRITAIN'S AIRCRAFT INDUSTRY.
617(TLS):29JUN73-756
REED, B., ED. LOCOMOTIVES IN PROFILE.
(VOL 2)
617(TLS):19JAN73-74
REED, G. THE PSYCHOLOGY OF ANOMALOUS
EXPERIENCE.
617(TLS):2MAR73-247
REED, I. CONJURE.
W. HEYEN, 491:JUL73-237
G. LAMMING, 441:6MAY73-36
N. SCHMITZ, 398:AUTUMN73-218
REED, I., ED. 19 NECROMANCERS FROM NOW.
639(VQR):WINTER71-XV
REED, J. SCHUBERT: THE FINAL YEARS.*
M.J.E. BROWN, 415:DEC72-1184
REED, J.D. EXPRESSWAYS.
J. HARRISON, 600:FALL69-143
REED, J.W., JR. FAULKNER'S NARRATIVE.
617(TLS):31AUG73-1003
REED, J.W., JR. - SEE BODICHON, B.L.S.
REED, R.R., JR. THE OCCULT ON THE TUDOR
AND STUART STAGE.
R.H. WEST, 570(SQ):WINTER70-86
REEDY, D.R. & J.R. JONES, EDS. NARRA-
CIONES EJEMPLARES DE HISPANOAMÉRICA.
L.F. LYDAY, 238:DEC71-991
E.D. TERRY, 399(MLJ):FEB71-107
REEMAN, D. HIS MAJESTY'S U-BOAT.
M. LEVIN, 441:12AUG73-20
REEMAN, D. A PRAYER FOR THE SHIP.
M. LEVIN, 441:18MAR73-40
REES, B. PROPHET OF THE WIND.
M. LEVIN, 441:23SEP73-48
REES, B.R., ED. CLASSICS.
E.D. PHILLIPS, 123:JUN72-267

REES, J. FULKE GREVILLE, LORD BROOKE,
1554-1628.
F.J. LEVY, 401(MLQ):DEC72-433
B. SHERRY, 67:MAY72-75
568(SCN):SPRING72-15
REES, L. THE MAKING OF AUSTRALIAN DRAMA.
R. GOSTAND, 71(ALS):OCT73-214
REES, P.M. THE MIRACULOUS YEAR.
I. BROWN, 157:SUMMER71-85
REES, R. - SEE WEIL, S.
REESE, G. FOURSCORE CLASSICS OF MUSIC
LITERATURE.*
412:MAY72-148
REESE, G. & R.J. SNOW, EDS. ESSAYS IN
MUSICOLOGY IN HONOR OF DRAGAN PLAMENAC
ON HIS 70TH BIRTHDAY.
N.C. CARPENTER, 219(GAR):FALL70-380
REESE, G.H., COMP. THE CORNWALLIS PAPERS.
F.B. WICKWIRE, 656(WMQ):APR71-341
REESE, J.M. HELLENISTIC INFLUENCE ON THE
BOOK OF WISDOM AND ITS CONSEQUENCES.
É. DES PLACES, 555:VOL45FASC2-352
REEVE, F.D. THE BLUE CAT.
R.B. SHAW, 491:SEP73-344
REEVE, F.D. THE BROTHER.
639(VQR):SUMMER71-XCVII
REEVE, F.D. THE RUSSIAN NOVEL.
H. MC LEAN, 454:WINTER72-174
REEVE, F.D. WHITE COLORS.
J.D. O'HARA, 441:23DEC73-12
REEVES, D. GULLAH.
F.L. UTLEY, 582(SFQ):DEC70-365
REEVES, G.M. - SEE COINDREAU, M.E.
REEVES, J. COMMITMENT TO POETRY.
H. SERGEANT, 175:SUMMER70-68
REEVES, J.K. - SEE HOWELLS, W.D.
REEVES, M. & B. HIRSCH-REICH. THE "FIG-
URAE" OF JOACHIM OF FIORE.
617(TLS):16NOV73-1386
REEVES, P. THOMAS WOLFE'S ALBATROSS.*
R.S. KENNEDY, 219(GAR):FALL70-371
REGALADO, N.F. POETIC PATTERNS IN RUTE-
BEUF.
A. FOULET, 401(MLQ):MAR72-67
E.M. RUTSON, 382(MAE):1972/1-68
REGEHR, T.D. - SEE NORDEGG, M.
REGENSTEINER, E. THE ART OF WEAVING.
K. ROSSBACH, 139:DEC70-9
REGINA, U. HEIDEGGER, DAL NICHILISMO
ALLA DIGNITÀ DELL'UOMO.
E. NAMER, 542:OCT-DEC71-473
"LA RÉGIONALISATION DE L'ESPACE AU
BRÉSIL."
H. GUTERSOHN, 182:VOL24#23/24-890
REGUL, J. DIE ANTIMARCIONITISCHEN EVAN-
GELIENPROLOGE.
P. COURCELLE, 555:VOL45FASC2-376
REGULA, M. KURZGEFASSTE ERKLÄRENDE SATZ-
KUNDE DES NEUHOCHDEUTSCHEN.*
C.V.J. RUSS, 402(MLR):JUL72-681
REGULA, M. & J. JERNEJ. GRAMMATICA ITAL-
IANA DESCRITTIVA SU BASI STORICHE E
PSICOLOGICHE.
L. ROMEO, 353:JUN70-118
REHDER, H., U. THOMAS & F. TWADDELL.
ERSTE STUFE. ZWEITE STUFE.
R.A. AMAN, 221(GQ):NOV71-622
REHDER, H., U. THOMAS & F. TWADDELL.
VERSTEHEN UND SPRECHEN.* (REV)
R.A. AMAN, 221(GQ):NOV71-622
N.A. BUSCH, 399(MLJ):JAN71-45
B.J. KOEKKOEK, 399(MLJ):OCT71-409
REICH, C.A. THE GREENING OF AMERICA.*
L.J. CLANCY, 381:JUN71-246
REICH, P. A BOOK OF DREAMS.
P. ADAMS, 61:JUN73-123
R.P. BRICKNER, 441:29JUL73-5

REICH, S. JOHN MARIN.*
  T. BRUNIUS, 290(JAAC):SPRING71-428
  A.A. DAVIDSON, 127:SPRING72-358
REICH, W. SCHOENBERG.*
  M.C., 410(M&L):APR72-209
REICH-RANICKI, M., ED. ANBRUCH DER GEGEN-
WART.
  R. GRIMM, 406:SUMMER72-193
REICHARDT, J. THE COMPUTER IN ART.
  C. MOORCRAFT, 592:MAR71-134
  505:AUG71-85
REICHE, R. SEXUALITY AND CLASS STRUGGLE.
  J. CARROLL, 111:7MAY71-161
REICHEL-DOLMATOFF, G. SAN AGUSTÍN.
  617(TLS):12JAN73-42
REICHENBACH, H. AXIOMATIZATION OF THE
  THEORY OF RELATIVITY.* (M. REICHEN-
  BACH, ED & TRANS)
  G. WYLLIE, 478:JUL71-133
REICHENKRON, G. DAS DAKISCHE.
  W. ROTHE, 260(IF):BAND74-263
REICHLING, A.J.B.N., E.M. UHLENBECK &
  W.S. ALLEN, EDS. WORD CLASSES.
  D.T. LANGENDOEN, 206:FEB70-138
REICHMANN, E., ED. THE TEACHING OF GER-
MAN.
  W. LEPPMANN, 221(GQ):NOV71-611
REICHMANN, O. DEUTSCHE WORTFORSCHUNG.*
  J.L. FLOOD, 220(GL&L):APR72-319
  M. KAEMPFERT, 680(ZDP):BAND89HEFT3-
  465
REID, A. ALL I CAN MANAGE, MORE THAN
  I COULD.*
  R. MACLEAN, 157:SUMMER70-72
REID, A. A CHECK-LIST OF THE BOOK ILLUS-
  TRATIONS OF JOHN BUCKLAND WRIGHT, TO-
  GETHER WITH A PERSONAL MEMOIR.
  S. CARTER, 354:JUN70-175
REID, A. THE CONTEST FOR NORTH SUMATRA.
  R. VAN NIEL, 318(JAOS):OCT-DEC71-527
  P.W. VAN DER VEUR, 293(JAST):AUG71-918
REID, B.L. THE LONG BOY AND OTHERS.
  P-G. BOUCÉ, 189(EA):APR-JUN71-201
  H.K. RUSSELL, 219(GAR):SUMMER70-241
REID, C. DO YOU TAKE THIS WOMAN?
  617(TLS):1JUN73-625
REID, D. LE GROUPE DES SEPT/THE GROUP
  OF SEVEN.*
  W. TOWNSEND, 592:NOV70-210
REID, G. THE ELABORATE FUNERAL.
  617(TLS):5JAN73-18
REID, G.L., K. ALLEN & D.J. HARRIS. THE
  NATIONALIZED FUEL INDUSTRIES.
  617(TLS):16MAR73-300
REID, J. THE BEST LITTLE BOY IN THE
  WORLD.
  D. BRUDNOY, 441:7OCT73-18
REID, J.C. BUCKS AND BRUISERS.*
  H.G. IVENS, 619(TC):VOL179#1047-49
REID, L. CHARLES JAMES FOX.
  O. PETERSON, 583:FALL70-92
REID, L.A. MEANING IN THE ARTS.
  R. SAW, 483:OCT71-361
REID, P. HARRIS IN WONDERLAND.
  617(TLS):3AUG73-911
REID, T. ESSAYS ON THE ACTIVE POWERS OF
  THE HUMAN MIND.
  M.B.M., 543:SEP70-141
REID, T. AN INQUIRY INTO THE HUMAN MIND.
  (T. DUGGAN, ED)
  W.P.G., 543:JUN71-754
REIDELBACH, J.A., JR. MODULAR HOUSING
  IN THE REAL.
  C.P., 505:MAY71-144
REIGSTAD, P. RÖLVAAG, HIS LIFE AND ART.
  J.T. FLANAGAN, 27(AL):JAN73-692

REILLY, A.P. AMERICA IN CONTEMPORARY
  SOVIET LITERATURE.
  B. SCHERR, 32:MAR72-199
REILLY, E.R. QUANTZ AND HIS "VERSUCH."
  P. DRUMMOND, 415:JUN72-565
REILLY, F.E. CHARLES PEIRCE'S THEORY OF
  SCIENTIFIC METHOD.
  S.M. HARRISON, 613:AUTUMN71-464
REIMAN, D.H., ED. THE ROMANTICS REVIEWED.
  617(TLS):30MAR73-358
REIMAN, D.H. PERCY BYSSHE SHELLEY.*
  A. GROB, 301(JEGP):APR72-261
REIMANN, B.W. PSYCHOANALYSE UND GESELL-
  SCHAFTSTHEORIE.
  617(TLS):24AUG73-985
REIMER, E. SCHOOL IS DEAD.*
  R. FREEMAN, 111:19NOV71-47
REIMER, P. & H-M. SASS - SEE BARNIKOL, E.
REINECKE, H-P. CENTS FREQUENCY PERIOD.
  F. LIEBERMAN, 187:JAN73-137
REINER, E. LA PLACE DE L'ADJECTIF ÉPI-
  THÈTE EN FRANÇAIS.
  R. ARVEILLER, 209(FM):APR70-159
  H. GECKELER, 490:JUL/OCT70-606
  W. ZWANENBURG, 433:APR70-191
REINES, A.J. MAIMONIDES AND ABRABANEL
  ON PROPHECY.
  H. DAVIDSON, 589:OCT72-796
REINHARD, K. & U. LES TRADITIONS MUSI-
  CALES IV: TURQUIE.
  K. SIGNELL, 187:MAY73-340
REINHARDT, R., ED. WORKIN' ON THE RAIL-
  ROAD.
  G.F. ACKERMAN, 649(WAL):FALL70-238
REINHARDT, S., ED. LIEBESDICHTUNG DES
  DEUTSCHEN ROKOKO.
  A. ANGER, 406:FALL72-316
REINHOLD, H., ED. CHARLES DICKENS.
  F.L. BURWICK, 445(NCF):DEC71-358
  S. MONOD, 189(EA):APR-JUN70-216
  W.D. ROBSON-SCOTT, 155:JAN71-52
  J.M.S. TOMPKINS, 597(SN):VOL42#2-478
REINHOLD, J. POLEN/LITAUEN AUF DEN LEIP-
  ZIGER MESSEN DES 18. JAHRHUNDERTS.
  H.C. PEYER, 182:VOL24#13/14-565
REINHOLD, M. HISTORY OF PURPLE AS A
  STATUS SYMBOL IN ANTIQUITY.
  O. MURRAY, 123:JUN72-293
  S.I. OOST, 122:JAN72-75
REINHORN, M. DICTIONNAIRE LAOTIEN-FRAN-
  ÇAIS. (VOL 1)
  K. WENK, 182:VOL24#3-99
REISCHAUER, E.O. TOWARD THE 21ST CEN-
  TURY.
  E. WEEKS, 61:DEC73-135
  441:14OCT73-49
REISS, A.H. THE ARTS MANAGEMENT HAND-
  BOOK.
  D. HERING, 151:AUG71-98
REISS, B. & J. - SEE DICKEY, J.
REISS, G. "ALLEGORISIERUNG" UND MODERNE
  ERZÄHLKUNST.*
  T-J. REED, 402(MLR):OCT72-953
REISS, H. GOETHE'S NOVELS.*
  C.E. SCHWEITZER, 406:SUMMER72-177
REISS, H. - SEE KANT, I.
REISS, S. THE UNIVERSE OF MEANING.
  P. SMITH, 316:DEC71-672
REITER, U. JAKOB VAN HODDIS.*
  R. MAJUT, 220(GL&L):APR72-270
REITLINGER, G. THE ECONOMICS OF TASTE.
  (VOL 3)
  B. DENVIR, 592:MAR71-134
  K. ROBERTS, 90:SEP71-555
REITMEISTER, L.A. A PHILOSOPHY OF FREE-
  DOM.
  J.L. CARAFIDES, 484(PPR):JUN72-586

REITZENSTEIN, E. ÜBER DIE ELEGIE DES
PROPERTIUS AUF DEN TOD DER CORNELIA.
E.J. KENNEY, 123:DEC72-413
T.A. SUITS, 124:APR-MAY72-275
REMACLE, L. DOCUMENTS LEXICAUX EXTRAITS
DES ARCHIVES SCABINALES DE ROANNE (LA
GLEIZE) 1492-1794.
L. BONDY, 209(FM):APR71-172
VON REMESIANA, N. - SEE UNDER NICETA VON
REMESIANA
REMINGTON, R.A. THE WARSAW PACT.*
R.F. STAAR, 32:SEP72-703
REMNANT, G.L. A CATALOGUE OF MISERICORDS
IN GREAT BRITAIN.
J. BECKWITH, 39:JAN70-84
REMPEL, R.A. UNIONISTS DIVIDED.
617(TLS):9MAR73-259
RENAN, J.E. SAGESSE DE RENAN. (H. PEYRE,
ED)
R.M. CHADBOURNE, 207(FR):OCT70-196
RENARD, C. - SEE STENDHAL
RENARD, J-C. LA BRAISE ET LA RIVIÈRE.
G. BRÉE, 207(FR):DEC70-404
RENATO, C. OPERE, DOCUMENTI E TESTIMON-
IANZE. (A. ROTONDO, ED)
R.P. LIEBOWITZ, 551(RENQ):AUTUMN71-379
RENAUD, P. LECTURE D'APOLLINAIRE.*
S.I. LOCKERBIE, 208(FS):JAN72-91
C. TOURNADRE, 535(RHL):JAN-FEB71-129
RENAULT, M. THE PERSIAN BOY.*
M. LEVIN, 441:7JAN73-34
RENCHON, H. ÉTUDES DE SYNTAXE DESCRIP-
TIVE.
W. MAŃCZAK, 353:SEP70-114
RENDALL, F.G. THE CLARINET. (3RD ED,
REV BY P. BATE)
N. SHACKLETON, 415:APR72-365
RENDELL, R. SOME LIE AND SOME DIE.
N. CALLENDAR, 441:16DEC73-18
617(TLS):18MAY73-562
RENEHAN, R. GREEK TEXTUAL CRITICISM.*
N.G. WILSON, 123:MAR72-146
RENFREW, C. BEFORE CIVILIZATION.
G. BIBBY, 441:4NOV73-4
RENFREW, J.M. PALAEOETHNOBOTANY.
617(TLS):3AUG73-908
RENGSTORF, K.H. & S. VON KORTZFLEISCH,
EDS. KIRCHE UND SYNAGOGE.
G. MAY, 182:VOL24#9/10-401
RENGSTORFF, K.H., ED. DAS PAULUS-BILD IN
DER NEUEREN DEUTSCHEN FORSCHUNG.
M.J.V., 543:JUN71-764
RENNÉ, R. INHALTSANALYSE DER ENGLISCHEN
FUNKTOREN "MAY, CAN, MUST, WILL, SHALL,
WOULD, SHOULD."
G. STÖTZEL & B. HENN, 38:BAND88HEFT3-
349
RENOIR, A. THE POETRY OF JOHN LYDGATE.*
J. NORTON-SMITH, 179(ES):AUG71-361
RENSCH, B. HOMO SAPIENS.
617(TLS):12JAN73-34
RENTZEL, L. WHEN ALL THE LAUGHTER DIED
IN SORROW.*
P. AXTHELM, 441:7JAN73-28
REPLOGLE, J. AUDEN'S POETRY.*
J.K. ROBINSON, 598(SOR):SUMMER73-692
H. SERGEANT, 175:SUMMER70-68
"REPORT OF THE ROYAL COMMISSION ON THE
STATUS OF WOMEN IN CANADA."
E.H. MORTON, 529(QQ):SUMMER71-304
"REPORT ON THE CASE LOAD OF THE SUPREME
COURT."
P. WESTEN, 453:22FEB73-29
REPS, J.W. TOWN PLANNING IN FRONTIER
AMERICA.
H. PARKER, 173(ECS):FALL70-113

RESCHER, N. THE COHERENCE THEORY OF
TRUTH.
617(TLS):19OCT73-1286
RESCHER, N. ESSAYS IN PHILOSOPHICAL
ANALYSIS.*
L.J. COHEN, 536:JUN71-96
H.W. JOHNSTONE, JR., 484(PPR):DEC70-
308
RESCHER, N. GALEN AND THE SYLLOGISM.
M. JAGER, 206:FEB70-104
RESCHER, N. INTRODUCTION TO LOGIC.
W.E. GOULD, 316:DEC70-579
RESCHER, N. INTRODUCTION TO VALUE
THEORY.*
A. BERLEANT, 321:SUMMER71-235
L.A. ELIOSEFF, 290(JAAC):FALL70-133
185:OCT70-90
RESCHER, N. MANY-VALUED LOGIC.
G. PEARCE, 154:DEC71-810
RESCHER, N. SCIENTIFIC EXPLANATION.
R.H.K., 543:JUN71-754
RESCHER, N. STUDIES IN ARABIC PHILOSO-
PHY.*
R.T. BLACKWOOD, 485(PE&W):APR70-199
W.S., 543:JUN71-755
RESCHER, N., ED. STUDIES IN THE PHILOSO-
PHY OF SCIENCE.
R. BLANCHÉ, 542:OCT-DEC70-501
RESCHER, N., ED. STUDIES IN THE THEORY
OF KNOWLEDGE.
R. BLANCHÉ, 542:OCT-DEC70-501
L. TALLON, 154:JUN71-384
RESCHER, N. TOPICS IN PHILOSOPHICAL
LOGIC.*
J.E. TOMBERLIN, 484(PPR):SEP70-141
RESCHER, N. & M.E. MARMURA, EDS & TRANS.
THE REFUTATION BY ALEXANDER OF APHRO-
DISIAS OF GALEN'S TREATISE ON THE THEORY
OF MOTION.
J. VAN ESS, 182:VOL24#15/16-580
RESHETAR, J.S., JR. THE SOVIET POLITY.
E. MICKIEWICZ, 32:MAR72-180
RESHEVSKY, S. CHESS: THE FISCHER-SPASSKY
GAMES.
617(TLS):23MAR73-333
RESTAINO, F. J.S. MILL E LA CULTURA FIL-
OSOFICA BRITANNICA.
M.M.M., 543:JUN71-755
RESTIF DE LA BRETONNE. LA VIE DE MON
PÈRE. (G. ROUGER, ED)
J. MAYER, 557(RSH):JUL-SEP71-481
V. MYLNE, 208(FS):APR72-207
M.R. RUBIN, 207(FR):OCT70-233
RESTLE, M. BYZANTINE WALL PAINTING IN
ASIA MINOR.
J. BECKWITH, 39:JUL70-79
S.K. KOSTOF, 54:MAR70-88
RESTON, J., JR. THE AMNESTY OF JOHN
DAVID HERNDON.
P. ADAMS, 61:MAR73-107
T.P. ALDER, 441:18MAR73-5
E.Z. FRIEDENBERG, 453:20SEP73-40
RÉTAT, P. LE DICTIONNAIRE DE BAYLE ET LA
LUTTE PHILOSOPHIQUE AUX XVIIIE SIÈCLE.
J. ROGER, 319:OCT73-543
RETTIG, R.B. GUIDE TO CAMBRIDGE ARCHI-
TECTURE.
C. ROBINSON, 576:DEC70-357
REUCHLIN, J. DE ARTE CABALISTICA.
J. ROUDAUT, 98:JAN71-26
REUSS, R.A. A WOODY GUTHRIE BIBLIOGRAPHY
1912-1967.
R.S. DENISOFF, 650(WF):JAN71-67
REUTER, H-H. FONTANE.*
G. FRIEDRICH, 190:BAND64HEFT2-236
P.U. HOHENDAHL, 224(GRM):AUG70-361
B. VÖLKER-HEZEL, 556(RLV):1970/2-220

VAN HET REVE, G.K.  DE TAAL DER LIEFDE.
  A. DIXON, 270:VOL22#4-79
REVERDIN, O. - SEE "ENTRETIENS SUR L'AN-
  TIQUITÉ CLASSIQUE"  (VOL 15)
REVERDY, P.  SELECTED POEMS.
  617(TLS):2NOV73-1348
REVZIN, I.I.  MODELS OF LANGUAGE.
  H. SPITZBARDT, 682(ZPSK):BAND23HEFT6-
  639
REWALD, J.  THE HISTORY OF IMPRESSIONISM.
  (4TH ED)
  J.R. MELLOW, 441:2DEC73-6
REX, J.  DISCOVERING SOCIOLOGY.
  617(TLS):13JUL73-804
REX, J.  RACE, COLONIALISM AND THE CITY.
  617(TLS):10AUG73-926
REXROTH, K.  AMERICAN POETRY IN THE
  TWENTIETH CENTURY.
  L. GOLDMAN, 502(PRS):WINTER71/72-365
  B. WEBER, 27(AL):MAR72-173
REXROTH, K., ED & TRANS.  LOVE AND THE
  TURNING YEAR.*
  T-H. KUO, 352(LE&W):VOL15#1-153
  R.S., 376:APR71-128
REXROTH, T. - SEE BENJAMIN, W.
REY, A.  LA LEXICOLOGIE.
  J. NICHOLS, 545(RPH):NOV71-241
REY, J-M.  L'ENJEU DES SIGNES.
  P. TROTIGNON, 542:JUL-SEP71-377
DEL REY, L.  PSTALEMATE.*
  617(TLS):2FEB73-129
REY, W.H.  ARTHUR SCHNITZLER.*
  A.D. KLARMANN, 401(MLQ):SEP72-343
  R. PLANT, 222(GR):JAN71-81
  B. SUROWSKA, 654(WB):2/1971-220
REY-FLAUD, H.  LE CERCLE MAGIQUE.
  617(TLS):25MAY73-596
REY-HERME, Y. - SEE PÉGUY, C. & ALAIN-
  FOURNIER
REYCHMANA, J., ED.  SZKICE Z DZIEJÓW POL-
  SKIEJ ORIENTALISTYKI.
  L. STERNBACH, 318(JAOS):OCT-DEC71-544
REYNOLDS, B.J.  THE TRUTH ABOUT UNICORNS.
  M. LEVIN, 441:11FEB73-31
REYNOLDS, D.E.  EDITORS MAKE WAR.
  639(VQR):SPRING71-LXXVI
REYNOLDS, E.E.  THE ROMAN CATHOLIC
  CHURCH IN ENGLAND AND WALES.
  617(TLS):14SEP73-1065
REYNOLDS, G.  CATALOGUE OF THE CONSTABLE
  COLLECTION.  (2ND ED)
  617(TLS):31AUG73-1009
REYNOLDS, G.  FULL SWELL.
  A. BOND, 415:NOV72-1091
REYNOLDS, G.  TURNER.*
  R.E., 135:MAY70-48
REYNOLDS, G.F.  ON SHAKESPEARE'S STAGE.
  (R.K. KNAUB, ED)
  I. SMITH, 570(SQ):WINTER70-87
REYNOLDS, J.  SEVEN DISCOURSES DELIVERED
  IN THE ROYAL ACADEMY BY THE PRESIDENT.
  H. OSBORNE, 89(BJA):SPRING72-200
REYNOLDS, J.H.  THE LETTERS OF JOHN HAM-
  ILTON REYNOLDS.  (L.M. JONES, ED)
  617(TLS):19OCT73-1268
REYNOLDS, L.D. & N.G. WILSON.  SCRIBES
  AND SCHOLARS.*
  G. HERMANSEN, 487:SUMMER71-195
REZMERSKI, J.C.  HELD FOR QUESTIONING.
  V. CONTOSKI, 600:FALL70-129
RHEES, R.  DISCUSSIONS OF WITTGENSTEIN.*
  185:OCT70-90
RHEES, R. - SEE WITTGENSTEIN, L.
RHEIMS, M.  DICTIONNAIRE DES MOTS SAU-
  VAGES (ÉCRIVAINS DES XIXE ET XXE
  SIÈCLES).*
  F. KOENIG, 207(FR):OCT70-211

RHEIN, P.H.  ALBERT CAMUS.
  R.D. COTTRELL, 207(FR):MAR71-796
  J. CRUICKSHANK, 208(FS):APR72-227
RHEINFELDER, H.  PHILOLOGISCHE SCHATZ-
  GRÄBEREIEN.
  R. BAEHR, 430(NS):JUL71-394
"RHEINISCHE AUSGRABUNGEN, 1."
  E. KUHN-SCHNYDER, 182:VOL24#21/22-803
RHIND, N.  A SCOTTISH PAINTER AND HIS
  WORLD: GORDON GUNN.
  617(TLS):16MAR73-305
RHINE, J.B., ED.  PROGRESS IN PARAPSY-
  CHOLOGY.
  J.L. RANDALL, 619(TC):VOL179#1048-54
RHODES, A.  THE VATICAN IN THE AGE OF
  THE DICTATORS, 1922-1945.
  J. BOSSY, 362:26APR73-558
  617(TLS):15JUN73-693
RHODES, D.E., ED.  ESSAYS IN HONOUR OF
  VICTOR SCHOLDERER.
  N. BARKER, 78(BC):AUTUMN71-391
RHODES, D.E.  THE SPREAD OF PRINTING:
  INDIA, PAKISTAN, CEYLON, BURMA AND
  THAILAND.
  B.C. BLOOMFIELD, 354:MAR71-70
  R. CAVE, 503:SUMMER70-99
RHODES, I.S.  THE PAPERS OF JOHN MAR-
  SHALL: A DESCRIPTIVE CALENDAR.*
  R.K. FAULKNER, 656(WMQ):APR71-321
  K.J. PIKE, 14:OCT70-410
RHODES, P.J.  THE ATHENIAN BOULE.
  617(TLS):23FEB73-209
RHODES, R.  THE UNGODLY.
  P. ADAMS, 61:AUG73-103
  C. LEHMANN-HAUPT, 441:25JUN73-37
  M. MEWSHAW, 441:29JUL73-12
  617(TLS):5OCT73-1158
RHODES JAMES, R.  STAFFING OF THE UNITED
  NATIONS SECRETARIAT.
  617(TLS):20APR73-434
RHOODIE, N.J., ED.  SOUTH AFRICAN DIA-
  LOGUE.
  617(TLS):8JUN73-653
RHYS, J.  AFTER LEAVING MR. MACKENZIE.*
  M. COOKE, 676(YR):SUMMER72-599
RIABCHIKOV, E.  RUSSIANS IN SPACE.*
  (N.P. KAMANIN, ED)
  A. PARRY, 32:SEP72-696
RIASANOVSKY, N.V. & G. STRUVE, EDS.  CAL-
  IFORNIA SLAVIC STUDIES.*  (VOL 5)
  G. DONCHIN, 575(SEER):APR72-326
  R.L. STRONG, JR., 550(RUSR):APR71-198
RIBARD, J.  UN MÉNESTREL DU XIVE SIÈCLE:
  JEAN DE CONDÉ.*
  J.H. WATKINS, 208(FS):JAN72-62
RIBARD, J. - SEE DE CONDÉ, J.
RIBBANS, G.  NIEBLA Y SOLEDAD.
  617(TLS):23NOV73-1421
RIBBAT, E.  DIE WAHRHEIT DES LEBENS IM
  FRÜHEN WERK ALFRED DÖBLINS.
  H. GRABER, 401(MLQ):JUN71-233
  W. GROTHE, 597(SN):VOL43#2-563
  K. MÜLLER-SALGET, 680(ZDP):BAND90
  HEFT2-301
RICARDOU, J.  LA PRISE DE CONSTANTINOPLE.
  T.H. JONES, 659:SUMMER73-296
RICARDOU, J. & F. VAN ROSSUM-GUYON, EDS.
  NOUVEAU ROMAN: HIER, AUJOURD'HUI.
  617(TLS):12JAN73-33
RICAUT, P.  THE PRESENT STATE OF THE
  GREEK AND ARMENIAN CHURCHES, ANNO
  CHRISTI, 1678.
  C.S. CALIAN, 32:DEC72-936
RICCIOLI, G.  L'AMBIZIONE, LA MORTE NELL'
  "ADOLPHE" DI B. CONSTANT.
  P. DELBOUILLE, 535(RHL):MAR-APR70-317

RICE, D.T. THE APPRECIATION OF BYZANTINE
ART.
617(TLS):2FEB73-128
RICE, D.T. BYZANTINE ART AND ITS INFLU-
ENCES.
617(TLS):12OCT73-1245
RICE, D.T. BYZANTINE PAINTING: THE LAST
PHASE.*
J. BECKWITH, 39:JAN70-84
RICE, E. THE MAN IN THE SYCAMORE TREE.
A.W. GODFREY, 363:AUG71-113
R.W. THOM, 648:JAN72-77
RICE, E.E. MAO'S WAY.
R. TERRILL, 441:14JAN73-5
RICE, H.C., JR. & A.S.K. BROWN, EDS &
TRANS. THE AMERICAN CAMPAIGNS OF
ROCHAMBEAU'S ARMY 1780, 1781, 1782,
1783.*
617(TLS):21SEP73-1081
RICE, L.D. THE NEGRO IN TEXAS, 1874-
1900.
639(VQR):AUTUMN71-CLXXVII
RICE, O.K. THE ALLEGHENY FRONTIER.
P. WATLINGTON, 656(WMQ):JAN71-154
RICE, T.T. ELIZABETH, EMPRESS OF RUSSIA.
T.L. MANN, 173(ECS):FALL71-195
RICH, A. DIVING INTO THE WRECK.
M. ATWOOD, 441:30DEC73-1
R. HOWARD, 231:DEC73-120
H. SHAPIRO, 441:25AUG73-21
R. TONKS, 453:4OCT73-8
RICH, A. THE WILL TO CHANGE.*
617(TLS):20APR73-442
RICH, J.C. SCULPTURE IN WOOD.
M. EASTHAM, 89(BJA):WINTER72-109
RICH, V., ED & TRANS. LIKE WATER: LIKE
FIRE.
A.B. MC MILLIN, 575(SEER):JAN72-118
RICHARD, J-J. LOUIS RIEL EXOVIDE.
M. SILVERSIDES, 296:SPRING73-93
RICHARD, J-P. PAYSAGE DE CHATEAUBRIAND.
J. MOUROT, 535(RHL):SEP-DEC70-1079
RICHARDS, A. DAI COUNTRY.
617(TLS):16NOV73-1407
RICHARDS, A., E. LAMBERT & L. GEORGE.
GOD ALIVE!
617(TLS):17AUG73-961
RICHARDS, D.A.J. A THEORY OF REASONS FOR
ACTION.
B. MAYO, 518:MAY72-28
RICHARDS, D.H., ED. ISLAMIC CIVILISA-
TION 950-1150.
617(TLS):16NOV73-1404
RICHARDS, D.R. THE GERMAN BESTSELLER IN
THE 20TH CENTURY.*
M.S. OFFER, 220(GL&L):OCT71-51
RICHARDS, E. FEW COMFORTS OR SURPRISES.
S. SCHWARTZ, 441:2DEC73-94
RICHARDS, E. THE LEVIATHAN OF WEALTH.
617(TLS):4MAY73-490
RICHARDS, I. ABBEYS OF EUROPE.
J. WILSON-ELY, 39:APR70-318
RICHARDS, I.A. THE PHILOSOPHY OF RHET-
ORIC.
R.M. BABICH, 480(P&R):SPRING70-120
RICHARDS, J. AN AFFAIR WITH THE SEA.
617(TLS):24AUG73-986
RICHARDS, J. PRINCESS.
C. LEHMANN-HAUPT, 441:7JUN73-49
RICHARDS, J. VISIONS OF YESTERDAY.
617(TLS):14DEC73-1542
RICHARDS, J.M. & N. PEVSNER, EDS. THE
ANTI-RATIONALISTS.
617(TLS):23FEB73-202
RICHARDS, M., ED. AN ATLAS OF ANGLESEY.
I. FRASER, 595(SCS):VOL16PT2-191

RICHARDS, M.K. ELLEN GLASGOW'S DEVELOP-
MENT AS A NOVELIST.
W.W. KELLY, 27(AL):JAN73-690
RICHARDS, P.G. THE REFORMED LOCAL GOV-
ERNMENT SYSTEM.
617(TLS):14SEP73-1065
RICHARDS, S., ED. BEST SHORT PLAYS 1970.
J. SCHWARTZ, 160:WINTER70/71-133
RICHARDSON, A.W. & D.R. CUTLER, EDS.
TRANSCENDENCE.
J.B.L., 543:SEP70-147
RICHARDSON, B. THE FUTURE OF CANADIAN
CITIES.
R. SYKES, 99:FEB73-38
RICHARDSON, E. THE TEACHER, THE SCHOOL
AND THE TASK OF MANAGEMENT.
617(TLS):23NOV73-1450
RICHARDSON, F. NAPOLEON.
617(TLS):23MAR73-326
RICHARDSON, F.E. - SEE "SIR EGLAMOUR OF
ARTOIS"
RICHARDSON, G. THE NEW VIRTRUVIUS BRIT-
ANNICUS.
617(TLS):23FEB73-216
RICHARDSON, H.E. WILLIAM FAULKNER.
P. ROSENBLATT, 50(ARQ):WINTER70-377
RICHARDSON, J. BLAMETH NAT ME.
J.V. FLEMING, 589:OCT72-797
B. HILL, 382(MAE):1972/3-270
RICHARDSON, J. AN ESSAY ON THE THEORY OF
PAINTING. (2ND ED)
H. OSBORNE, 89(BJA):SPRING72-200
RICHARDSON, J. THE REGENCY.
617(TLS):5OCT73-1196
RICHARDSON, J. ENID STARKIE.
M-K. WILMERS, 362:11OCT73-491
617(TLS):31AUG73-992
RICHARDSON, J. WESTBROOK THE OUTLAW; OR,
THE AVENGING WOLF.
W.F.E. MORLEY, 296:SUMMER73-112
RICHARDSON, J.A. MODERN ART AND SCIEN-
TIFIC THOUGHT.*
R. WOODFIELD, 89(BJA):SUMMER72-303
RICHARDSON, K. & D. SPEARS. RACE CULTURE
AND INTELLIGENCE.
R. LYNN, 619(TC):VOL179#1049-53
RICHARDSON, K. & D. SPEARS, WITH M.
RICHARDS, EDS. RACE, CULTURE AND EDU-
CATION.
617(TLS):6APR73-372
RICHARDSON, M. FUNDAMENTALS OF MATHEMAT-
ICS. (3RD ED)
W.E. GOULD, 316:DEC71-678
RICHARDSON, S. THE HISTORY OF SIR
CHARLES GRANDISON. (J. HARRIS, ED)
617(TLS):26JAN73-98
RICHER, J. - SEE DE NERVAL, G.
RICHETTI, J.J. POPULAR FICTION BEFORE
RICHARDSON.*
P-G. BOUCÉ, 189(EA):JUL-SEP70-342
M. GEARIN-TOSH, 447(N&Q):SEP71-358
L-M. GUILHAMET, 173(ECS):FALL71-192
M.E. NOVAK, 405(MP):FEB71-312
J. PRESTON, 541(RES):FEB71-87
RICHEY, M.F. ESSAYS ON MEDIAEVAL GERMAN
POETRY.*
P. SALMON, 220(GL&L):OCT71-25
RICHIE, D. THE FILMS OF KUROSAWA.
H. LEE, 200:AUG-SEP71-436
RICHIE, D. JAPANESE CINEMA.
617(TLS):18MAY73-563
RICHLER, M. ST. URBAIN'S HORSEMAN.*
A. THOMAS, 102(CANL):WINTER72-83
G. WOODCOCK, 606(TAMR):#58-65
RICHLER, M. SHOVELLING TROUBLE.*
F. SUTHERLAND, 296:WINTER73-95
RICHMOND, A. A LONG VIEW FROM THE LEFT.
N. HENTOFF, 441:8JUL73-5

RICHMOND, A.H., WITH OTHERS. MIGRATION
AND RACE RELATIONS IN AN ENGLISH CITY.
617(TLS):22JUN73-707
RICHMOND, H.M. THE SCHOOL OF LOVE.
R. ELLRODT, 189(EA):OCT-DEC71-524
D. WEEKS, 290(JAAC):WINTER70-278
RICHMOND, H.M. SHAKESPEARE'S SEXUAL
COMEDY.
R.C. CLARK, 544:FALL72-187
RICHMOND, I. ROMAN ARCHAEOLOGY AND ART.*
(P. SALWAY, ED)
R. HIGGINS, 39:AUG71-162
RICHMOND, I. - SEE COLLINGWOOD, R.G.
RICHMOND, J. THEOLOGY AND METAPHYSICS.
I. TRETHOWAN, 479(PHQ):APR71-190
RICHOUX, P. THE STARDUST KID.
M. WATKINS, 441:28AUG73-39
RICHTER, A. - SEE VERGIL
RICHTER, D. DIE DEUTSCHE ÜBERLIEFERUNG
DER PREDIGTEN BERTHOLDS VON REGENSBURG.*
E. BAUER, 597(SN):VOL42#1-294
RICHTER, G.M.A. ENGRAVED GEMS OF THE
ROMANS.
H.L. BLACKMORE, 135:NOV71-215
R. HIGGINS, 39:AUG71-161
C.C. VERMEULE, 124:OCT71-64
RICHTER, G.M.A. A HANDBOOK OF GREEK
ART.* (6TH ED)
J.P. BARRON, 123:MAR72-140
R. HIGGINS, 39:JUL70-82
RICHTER, G.M.A. KORAI.*
B.S. RIDGWAY, 54:JUN70-195
RICHTER, G.M.A. KOUROI. (3RD ED)
J. BOARDMAN, 123:JUN72-291
R. HIGGINS, 39:AUG71-159
RICHTER, G.M.A. PERSPECTIVE IN GREEK AND
ROMAN ART.*
R. HIGGINS, 39:AUG71-159
D.E. STRONG, 123:DEC72-394
RICHTER, H. VIRGINIA WOOLF.*
C. OHMANN, 659:SPRING73-260
RICHTER, I. POLITICAL PURPOSE IN TRADE
UNIONS.
617(TLS):28SEP73-1108
RICHTER, J.P. - SEE LEONARDO DA VINCI
RICHTER, M. LA FORMAZIONE FRANCESE DI
ARDENGO SOFFICI.
P.Z., 228(GSLI):VOL148FASC462/463-469
RICHTER, M.N., JR. SCIENCE AS A CULTURAL
PROCESS.
617(TLS):12OCT73-1259
RICHTER, W. HISTORISCHE ENTWICKLUNG UND
JUNGER WANDEL DER AGRARLANDSCHAFT IS-
RAELS, DARGESTELLT INSBESONDERE AM
BEISPIEL NORDGALILÄAS.
P. VOSSELER, 182:VOL24#4-188
VON RICHTHOFEN, E. NUEVOS ESTUDIOS
ÉPICOS MEDIEVALES.
H.T. STURCKEN, 238:SEP71-596
RICKARD, P. LA LANGUE FRANÇAISE AU XVIE
SIÈCLE.
J. PICOCHE, 209(FM):JUL70-368
K. VARTY, 47(ARL):[N.S.]VOL1-97
RICKARDS, M., COMP. POSTERS OF PROTEST
AND REVOLUTION.
J. ELDERFIELD, 592:JUL-AUG70-49
RICKARDS, M. THE PUBLIC NOTICE.
617(TLS):7SEP73-1019
RICKLEFS, R.E. ECOLOGY.
617(TLS):12OCT73-1246
RICKMAN, G. ROMAN GRANARIES AND STORE
BUILDINGS.
H.C. BOREN, 124:NOV71-103
RICKS, C. TENNYSON.*
J.D. ROSENBERG, 441:18MAR73-7
RICKS, C. - SEE TENNYSON, A.
RICO, F. EL PEQUEÑO MUNDO DEL HOMBRE.
R.B. TATE, 402(MLR):APR72-436

RICO, F. - SEE LOPE DE VEGA
RICO, M. ENSAYO DE BIBLIOGRAFÍA PIN-
DÁRICA.*
M.M. WILLCOCK, 123:MAR72-101
RICOEUR, P. LE CONFLIT DES INTERPRÉ-
TATIONS.*
E. CLÉMENS, 98:JUN70-546
R. HÉBERT, 154:MAR71-179
RICOEUR, P. FREUD AND PHILOSOPHY.
J.M. HEMS, 484(PPR):SEP71-135
B.S. LLAMZON, 613:WINTER71-628
E. VIVAS, 321:WINTER71-310
RIDDLE, A. A SINGER AND HER SONGS.
(R.D. ABRAHAMS, ED)
R.D. BETHKE, 582(SFQ):DEC71-354
M. KARPELES, 203:AUTUMN71-249
RIDEOUT, R.W. TRADE UNIONS AND THE LAW.
617(TLS):17AUG73-958
RIDER, F. THE DIALECTIC OF SELFHOOD IN
MONTAIGNE.
617(TLS):5OCT73-1186
RIDGE, G.R. JORIS-KARL HUYSMANS.
A. ARTINIAN, 546(RR):FEB71-70
RIDGEWAY, J. THE LAST PLAY.
C. WELLES, 441:25FEB73-12
RIDGWAY, B.S. THE SEVERE STYLE IN GREEK
SCULPTURE.*
J. BOARDMAN, 90:OCT71-613
R. HIGGINS, 39:AUG71-160
RIDGWAY, M.H. THE CHESTER GOLDSMITHS
FROM EARLY TIMES TO 1726.*
R.C.B., 135:MAR70-201
RIDGWAY, R.S. VOLTAIRE AND SENSIBILITY.
617(TLS):17AUG73-961
RIDING, L. SELECTED POEMS.
M. KIRKHAM, 97(CQ):SPRING71-302
J. SAUNDERS, 565:VOL11#4-68
617(TLS):9FEB73-151
RIDLER, A. - SEE TRAHERNE, T.
RIDLER, W. BRITISH MODERN PRESS BOOKS.
D. CHAMBERS, 503:WINTER71-197
RIDOLFI, R. STUDI SULLE COMMEDIE DEL
MACHIAVELLI.
V.S., 275(IQ):SPRING-SUMMER72-118
RIEDEL, F.W. & H. UNVERRICHT, EDS. SYM-
BOLAE HISTORIAE MUSICAE (HELLMUT FEDER-
HOFER ZUM 60. GEBURTSTAG).
G. ABRAHAM, 415:JUN72-565
RIEDEL, W. DER NEUE MENSCH.
H.G. HERMANN, 406:SUMMER72-176
RIEFSTAHL, E. ANCIENT EGYPTIAN GLASS AND
GLAZES IN THE BROOKLYN MUSEUM.
T.G.H. JAMES, 39:FEB71-147
RIEGER, D. JACQUES CAZOTTE.
G. DÉCOTE, 535(RHL):MAR-APR71-305
C. THACKER, 208(FS):JAN72-81
RIEGER, L. ALGEBRAIC METHODS OF MATHE-
MATICAL LOGIC.
D. MONK, 316:SEP70-440
RIEGL, A. HISTORISCHE GRAMMATIK DER
BILDENDEN KÜNSTE.
J. GUTMANN, 290(JAAC):SUMMER71-565
VON RIEKHOFF, H. GERMAN-POLISH RELATIONS,
1918-1933.
E.D. WYNOT, JR., 32:DEC72-917
RIEMER, A.P. A READING OF SHAKESPEARE'S
"ANTONY AND CLEOPATRA."
R.A. FOAKES, 175:SPRING70-22
M. SPEVACK, 570(SQ):SPRING70-180
DE RIENZE, G. & G. MIRANDOLA. GIUSEPPE
GIACOSA ED ÉDOUARD ROD.
M.G. LERNER, £08(FS):OCT72-470
RIEPE, D. THE PHILOSOPHY OF INDIA AND
ITS IMPACT ON AMERICAN THOUGHT.* (M.
FARBER, ED)
K.K. INADA, 485(PE&W):APR71-219
D.C. MATHUR, 484(PPR):SEP71-113
[CONTINUED]

RIEPE, D. THE PHILOSOPHY OF INDIA AND
ITS IMPACT ON AMERICAN THOUGHT.* (M.
FARBER, ED) [CONTINUING]
  S. MAYEDA, 293(JAST):MAY71-711
  R. PAGEARD, 549(RLC):OCT-DEC71-617
RIES, W. GERÜCHT, GEREDE, ÖFFENTLICHE
MEINUNG.
  R.H. MARTIN, 123:MAR72-112
RIESE, T.A. & D. RIESNER, EDS. VERSDICH-
TUNG DER ENGLISCHEN ROMANTIK.*
  P. GOETSCH, 430(NS):NOV70-586
  P. MALEKIN, 597(SN):VOL42#1-236
RIESEL, E. DER STIL DER DEUTSCHEN
ALLTAGSREDE.
  G.L. TRACY, 564:MAR71-76
RIESER, M. AN ANALYSIS OF POETIC THINK-
ING.*
  M.F. SLATTERY, 290(JAAC):SUMMER71-554
RIEWALD, J.G. REYNIER JANSEN OF PHILA-
DELPHIA, EARLY AMERICAN PRINTER.
  H. EDELMAN, 517(PBSA):JUL-SEP72-335
RIEWALD, J.G. - SEE BEERBOHM, M.
RIEZLER, K. KURT RIEZLER: TAGEBÜCHER,
AUFSÄTZE, DOKUMENTE. (K.D. ERDMANN,
ED)
  617(TLS):31AUG73-1006
RIFFATERRE, H.B. L'ORPHISME DANS LA
POÉSIE ROMANTIQUE.
  R. CHAMBERS, 67:MAY72-98
  M. SCHAETTEL, 557(RSH):APR-JUN71-322
RIGAUT, J. ECRITS. (M. KAY, ED)
  H.S. GERSHMAN, 207(FR):DEC70-421
RIGBY, P. CATTLE AND KINSHIP AMONG THE
GOGO.
  R.G. WILLIS, 69:JAN71-64
RIGG, A.G. A GLASTONBURY MISCELLANY OF
THE FIFTEENTH CENTURY.*
  J.A.W. BENNETT, 354:MAR70-162
  R.H. ROBBINS, 38:BAND89HEFT1-140
RIGGS, D. SHAKESPEARE'S HEROICAL HIS-
TORIES.
  C.C. HUFFMAN, 301(JEGP):JUL72-441
  E.M. WAITH, 676(YR):SPRING72-441
RIGGS, J.B. A GUIDE TO THE MANUSCRIPTS
IN THE ELEUTHERIAN MILLS HISTORICAL
LIBRARY.
  R.W. LOVETT, 14:APR71-198
RIGGS, W.G. THE CHRISTIAN POET IN "PARA-
DISE LOST."
  617(TLS):15JUN73-697
RIGHINI, V. LINEAMENTI DI STORIA ECONO-
MICA DELLA GALLIA CISALPINA.
  J.P. WILD, 123:JUN72-283
RIGOBELLO, A. DIE GRENZEN DES TRANSZEN-
DENTALEN BEI KANT.
  W. STEINBECK, 342:BAND61HEFT2-274
RIHA, T. A RUSSIAN EUROPEAN.*
  N.D. ROODKOWSKY, 613:SUMMER70-319
RIKHOFF, J. BUTTES LANDING.
  M. LEVIN, 441:18MAR73-40
RILEY, A.W. ELISABETH LANGGÄSSER BIBLI-
OGRAPHIE MIT NACHLASSBERICHT.
  R.K. ANGRESS, 564:OCT71-245
  H.R. KLIENEBERGER, 402(MLR):JAN72-229
RILEY, P. - SEE LEIBNIZ, G.W.
RILKE, R.M. BRIEFE AN SIDONIE NÁDHERNÝ
VON BORUTIN. (B. BLUME, ED)
  617(TLS):28DEC73-1582
RIMBAUD, A. ILLUMINATIONS.* (A. PY, ED)
  J.U. HALPERIN, 402(MLR):JUL72-645
RINGBOM, H. STUDIES IN THE NARRATIVE
TECHNIQUE OF "BEOWULF" AND LAWMAN'S
"BRUT."*
  D.A.H. EVANS, 597(SN):VOL42#1-253
RINGE, D.A. THE PICTORIAL MODE.
  T. PHILBRICK, 27(AL):NOV72-484

RINGER, A.L., ED. YEARBOOK OF THE INTER-
NATIONAL FOLK MUSIC COUNCIL. (VOL 1)
  F. HOWES, 415:MAR72-271
RINGER, F.K. THE DECLINE OF THE GERMAN
MANDARINS.
  S.M. POPPEL, 390:JAN70-68
RINGGER, K. AMBIENTI ED INTRECCI NELLE
COMMEDIE DE CARLO GOLDONI.
  H. FELDMANN, 72:BAND209HEFT4/6-462
RINGGREN, H. RELIGIONS OF THE ANCIENT
NEAR EAST.
  617(TLS):6JUL73-784
RINSLER, N. GÉRARD DE NERVAL.
  617(TLS):21DEC73-1562
RINSLER, N. - SEE DE NERVAL, G.
VON RINTELEN, F-J. CONTEMPORARY GERMAN
PHILOSOPHY AND ITS BACKGROUND.
  W.V. DONIELA, 63:AUG72-200
  W. SCHWARZ, 484(PPR):JUN71-614
DE DEL RÍO, A.A. - SEE UNDER AGOSTINI DE
DEL RÍO, A.
DEL RÍO, D.A. SIMÓN BOLÍVAR.
  P.F. LAVÍN, 37:MAR71-43
RIOUX, M. QUEBEC IN QUESTION.
  D. DUFFY, 331:AUG71-60
  G. WOODCOCK, 102(CANL):WINTER72-73
RIOUX, M. LA QUESTION DU QUÉBEC.
  J. DAVID, 207(FR):OCT70-212
"CESARE RIPA: BAROQUE AND ROCOCO PICTOR-
IAL IMAGERY." (E.A. MASER, ED & TRANS)
  568(SCN):SPRING72-17
RIPIN, E.M., ED. KEYBOARD INSTRUMENTS.*
  H.M. BROWN, 415:NOV72-1089
RIPOLL, C. "LA CELESTINA" A TRAVÉS DEL
DECÁLOGO Y OTRAS NOTAS SOBRE LA LITERA-
TURA DE LA EDAD DE ORO.*
  D.S. SEVERIN, 545(RPH):MAY72-479
RIPOLL, C., ED. ESCRITOS DESCONOCIDOS DE
JOSÉ MARTÍ.*
  J.A. BALSEIRO, 238:DEC71-975
RIPPLEY, L. OF GERMAN WAYS.
  T. HUEBENER, 221(GQ):NOV71-608
DE RIQUER, M. - SEE MATORELL, J. & M.
JOAN DE GALBA
RIS, R. DAS ADJEKTIV "REICH" IM MITTEL-
ALTERLICHEN DEUTSCH.
  B.J. KOEKKOEK, 301(JEGP):OCT72-564
RISK, J.C. THE HISTORY OF THE ORDER OF
THE BATH AND ITS INSIGNIA.
  617(TLS):19JAN73-73
RISSANEN, M. THE USES OF "ONE" IN OLD
AND EARLY MIDDLE ENGLISH.
  G. BAUER, 179(ES):DEC71-543
  B. CARSTENSEN, 38:BAND89HEFT4-492
  T. KISBYE, 597(SN):VOL42#1-250
  H.H. MEIER, 72:BAND209HEFT1/3-147
RIST, J. SÄMTLICHE WERKE. (VOL 2) (E.
MANNACK, ED)
  S. ATKINS, 301(JEGP):OCT72-574
RIST, J.M. EPICURUS, AN INTRODUCTION.
  617(TLS):9FEB73-157
RIST, J.M. PLOTINUS.*
  L. TARÁN, 24:OCT72-637
RIST, J.M. STOIC PHILOSOPHY.*
  P.M. HUBY, 479(PHQ):JAN71-75
  P. LOUIS, 555:VOL45FASC2-350
  M.E. REESOR, 487:SPRING71-78
  J.B. SKEMP, 123:DEC72-366
  C. STOUGH, 482(PHR):JUL71-407
RISTAT, J. LE LIT DE NICOLAS BOILEAU ET
DE JULES VERNE. DE COUP D'ETAT EN LIT-
TÉRATURE.
  J-P. ATTAL, 98:JAN71-20
RITCHESON, C.R. AFTERMATH OF REVOLU-
TION.*
  D.G. BARNES, 173(ECS):WINTER71-218
RITCHIE, J.M. - SEE VON EICHENDORFF, J.
RITCHIE, J.M. - SEE STERNHEIM, C.

RITCHIE, J.M. - SEE STORM, T.
RITCHIE, J.M. & J.D. STOWELL - SEE
"VISION AND AFTERMATH"
RITTENHOUSE, J.D. MAVERICK TALES.
W. GARD, 584(SWR):WINTER72-76
RITTER, A. THE POLITICAL THOUGHT OF
PIERRE-JOSEPH PROUDHON.
D. JOHNSON, 208(FS):JUL72-343
RITTER, F. HUGO VON HOFFMANNSTHAL UND
ÖSTERREICH.
D.A. JOYCE, 564:JUN70-180
RITTER, J. HEGEL ET LA RÉVOLUTION FRAN-
ÇAISE.
Y. GAUTHIER, 154:MAR71-149
RITTER, J., ED. HISTORISCHES WÖRTERBUCH
DER PHILOSOPHIE. (VOL 1)
W.V. DONIELA, 63:MAY72-100
A. STERN, 182:VOL24#7/8-327
DE RIVAUDEAU, A. AMAN.* (K. CAMERON,
ED)
E. BALMAS, 535(RHL):JUL-AUG71-691
J. PINEAUX, 557(RSH):JAN-MAR70-155
RIVELAYGUE, J., ED. ROUSSEAU.
P. ROBINSON, 208(FS):APR72-205
RIVERO, E.S. EL GRAN AMOR DE PABLO
NERUDA.
D.L. SHAW, 402(MLR):OCT72-932
617(TLS):11MAY73-532
RIVERS, E.L. - SEE ALONSO, D.
RIVERS, I. THE POETRY OF CONSERVATISM,
1600-1745.
617(TLS):16FEB73-187
RIVERS, P. THE RESTLESS GENERATION.
617(TLS):2FEB73-131
RIVERSO, E. LA FILOSOFIA ANALITICA IN
INGHILTERRA.
L.M.P., 543:JUN71-756
L. THIRY, 154:SEP71-597
RIVOALLAN, A. LEXOBIE ET AUTRES LÉGENDES
DES CELTES.
R. FRÉCHET, 189(EA):APR-JUN71-213
RIX, H. DAS ETRUSKISCHE COGNOMEN.
C. DE SIMONE, 260(IF):BAND74-321
RIX, M.B. BOARS HILL, OXFORD.
T. BROWN, 203:SUMMER70-154
ROA BASTOS, A. HIJO DE HOMBRE.
T. HOLZAPFEL, 399(MLJ):NOV71-481
ROACHE, J. RICHARD EBERHART.
639(VQR):SUMMER71-CXX
ROAF, C. - SEE CAVALCANTI, B.
ROAZEN, P. BROTHER ANIMAL.*
Y. BRÈS, 542:APR-JUN71-189
ROBB, D.M. THE ART OF THE ILLUMINATED
MANUSCRIPT.
J. CANADAY, 441:2DEC73-90
ROBBE-GRILLET, A. PROJECT FOR A REVOLU-
TION IN NEW YORK.* (FRENCH TITLE: PRO-
JET POUR UNE RÉVOLUTION À NEW YORK.)
J. HUNTER, 362:1FEB73-156
J. RICARDOU, 98:MAR71-210
R. SALE, 249(HUDR):WINTER72/73-703
617(TLS):9MAR73-257
ROBBE-GRILLET, A. LE VOYEUR. (O.F.
PUCCIANI, ED)
A.M. BEICHMAN, 399(MLJ):MAY71-328
ROBBERECHTS, L. HUSSERL.
F. HEIDSIECK, 542:OCT-DEC71-478
LORD ROBBINS. AUTOBIOGRAPHY OF AN ECONO-
MIST.
P. JOHNSON, 441:7JAN73-6
ROBBINS, B.L. THE DEFINITE ARTICLE IN
ENGLISH TRANSFORMATIONS.
R.S. JACKENDOFF, 206:FEB71-138
ROBBINS, J.A., ED. AMERICAN LITERARY
SCHOLARSHIP, AN ANNUAL/1969.
A. BOND, 517(PBSA):JUL-SEP72-333
ROBBINS, M. A REPLY TO THE HEADLINES.
R.P. DICKEY, 649(WAL):SUMMER71-151

ROBBINS, R.H. & J.L. CUTLER. SUPPLEMENT
TO THE INDEX OF MIDDLE ENGLISH VERSE.
A.A. PRINS, 179(ES):FEB71-57
ROBE, S.L., ED. MEXICAN TALES AND LEG-
ENDS FROM LOS ALTOS.*
E. ETTLINGER, 203:AUTUMN71-258
ROBERSON, E. WHEN THY KING IS A BOY.*
L. HART, 661:SUMMER/FALL71-85
C. PEEK, 502(PRS):SPRING71-84
"ROBERT DE BLOIS'S 'FLORIS ET LYRIOPÉ'."*
(P. BARRETTE, ED)
F. KOENIG, 545(RPH):MAY72-457
ROBERT, P. AVENTURES ET MÉSAVENTURES
D'UN DICTIONNAIRE.
P.F. CINTAS, 207(FR):FEB71-583
N.C.W. SPENCE, 208(FS):APR72-241
ROBERT, W.C.H. THE EXPLORATIONS, 1696-
1697, OF AUSTRALIA BY WILLEM DE VLA-
MINGH.
617(TLS):2FEB73-133
ROBERT-BLUNN, J. NORTHERN ACCENT.
M. KENNEDY, 415:OCT72-977
ROBERTET, J. OEUVRES. (M. ZSUPPÁN, ED)
J-P. CHAUVEAU, 535(RHL):JUL-AUG71-689
K.M. HALL, 402(MLR):JAN72-184
F. SUARD, 557(RSH):JUL-SEP71-469
ROBERTO, E., ED. CAHIER CANADIEN CLAUDEL
6.
J. HOURIEZ, 557(RSH):JUL-SEP70-495
J. DE LABRIOLLE, 549(RLC):JAN-MAR70-
141
ROBERTO, E. - SEE CLAUDEL, P. & A. MEYER
ROBERTS, B. SPACEWALKS.
W.H. PRITCHARD, 249(HUDR):SPRING72-119
ROBERTS, B.C. & OTHERS. RELUCTANT
MILITANTS.
617(TLS):5JAN73-4
ROBERTS, C.G.D. THE LAST BARRIER AND
OTHER STORIES.
J. LENNOX, 296:SUMMER73-121
ROBERTS, C.M. FIRST ROUGH DRAFT.
E. WEEKS, 61:JUL73-102
441:210CT73-18
ROBERTS, D. ARTISTIC CONSCIOUSNESS AND
POLITICAL CONSCIENCE.
H.W. REICHERT, 406:FALL72-300
ROBERTS, D. DEBORAH.
J. BONI, 649(WAL):WINTER71-315
ROBERTS, E. WORKERS' CONTROL.
617(TLS):1JUN73-625
ROBERTS, E.V. - SEE FIELDING, H.
ROBERTS, E.V. - SEE GAY, J.
ROBERTS, G. - SEE JOSEPH OF EXETER
ROBERTS, J.S. BLACK MUSIC OF TWO WORLDS.
617(TLS):260CT73-1323
ROBERTS, K. MACHINES AND MEN.
617(TLS):18MAY73-562
ROBERTS, L. OLD GREASYBEARD.
H. GLASSIE, 292(JAF):APR-JUN71-263
B.A. ROSENBERG, 219(GAR):WINTER70-502
ROBERTS, M. GUSTAVUS ADOLPHUS AND THE
RISE OF SWEDEN.
617(TLS):30NOV73-1482
ROBERTS, P.C. ALIENATION AND THE SOVIET
ECONOMY.
E.G. DOLAN, 32:JUN72-444
ROBERTS, R.O., ED. FARMING IN CAERNAR-
VONSHIRE AROUND 1800.
617(TLS):22JUN73-728
ROBERTS, S.E. ALBERTA HOMESTEAD. (L.E.
ROBERTS, ED)
R. WIEBE, 649(WAL):WINTER72-262
ROBERTS, S.E. ED & TRANS. ESSAYS IN
RUSSIAN LITERATURE.*
R.D.B. THOMSON, 575(SEER):APR72-300
ROBERTS, T.A. THE CONCEPT OF BENEVOLENCE.
617(TLS):9NOV73-1379

ROBERTS, W.R.  TITO, MIHAILOVIC AND THE
ALLIES, 1941-1945.
    D. BINDER, 441:28OCT73-22
ROBERTSON, A.  THE CHURCH CANTATAS OF
J.S. BACH.
    S. DAW, 415:OCT72-975
ROBERTSON, A.S.  ROMAN IMPERIAL COINS IN
THE HUNTER COIN CABINET, UNIVERSITY OF
GLASGOW.  (VOL 2)
    C.C. VERMEULE, 124:FEB72-208
ROBERTSON, D.  SURVIVE THE SAVAGE SEA.
    R. BLYTHE, 362:19JUL73-92
    A. BROYARD, 441:27AUG73-27
    E. WEEKS, 61:SEP73-115
    A.B.C. WHIPPLE, 441:19AUG73-7
    617(TLS):3AUG73-901
ROBERTSON, D.S.  GREEK AND ROMAN ARCHI-
TECTURE.
    R. HIGGINS, 39:JAN70-88
ROBERTSON, E.G.  ORNAMENTAL CAST IRON IN
MELBOURNE.  EARLY BUILDING OF SOUTHERN
TASMANIA.
    617(TLS):31AUG73-998
ROBERTSON, G.  GIOVANNI BELLINI.*
    D. ROSAND, 56:SPRING70-72
ROBERTSON, J. - SEE SIDNEY, P.
ROBERTSON, J.G.  A HISTORY OF GERMAN LIT-
ERATURE.  (6TH ED)
    E. STOPP, 402(MLR):OCT72-934
ROBERTSON, J.G. & E. PURDIE.  GESCHICHTE
DER DEUTSCHEN LITERATUR.
    A.M. HAAS, 657(WW):NOV/DEC70-428
ROBEY, D., ED.  STRUCTURALISM.
    617(TLS):3AUG73-913
ROBICHEZ, J. - SEE VERLAINE, P.
ROBICSEK, F.  COPAN, HOME OF THE MAYAN
GODS.
    W.H. HONAN, 441:2DEC73-97
DE ROBIEN, L.  THE DIARY OF A DIPLOMAT IN
RUSSIA, 1917-1918.
    V.D. MEDLIN, 550(RUSR):APR71-209
    A. RABINOWITCH, 32:DEC72-898
ROBIN, M.  THE RUSH FOR SPOILS.  PILLARS
OF PROFIT.
    H.V. NELLES, 99:NOV-DEC73-20
ROBIN, R.  HISTOIRE ET LINGUISTIQUE.
    617(TLS):5OCT73-1171
ROBINET, A.  PÉGUY ENTRE JAURÈS, BERGSON
ET L'ÉGLISE, MÉTAPHYSIQUE ET POLITIQUE.
    S. FRAISSE, 535(RHL):JAN-FEB70-153
ROBINS, R.H.  GENERAL LINGUISTICS.*
    M. RENSKÝ, 206:AUG70-436
ROBINS, R.H.  A SHORT HISTORY OF LINGUIS-
TICS.
    M. LEROY, 297(JL):FEB70-148
ROBINSON, D.  BENEFICED CLERGY IN CLEVE-
LAND AND THE EAST RIDING 1306-1340.
    E. WELCH, 325:APR71-249
ROBINSON, D.  ROTTEN WITH HONOUR.
    N. CALLENDAR, 441:28OCT73-49
    617(TLS):3AUG73-911
ROBINSON, D.  WORLD CINEMA.
    617(TLS):14DEC73-1542
ROBINSON, D.L.  SLAVERY IN THE STRUCTURE
OF AMERICAN POLITICS, 1765-1820.
    D.B. DAVIS, 676(YR):AUTUMN71-117
ROBINSON, D.S.  ROYCE AND HOCKING.*
    J.H. COTTON, 321:SPRING70-76
    H.A. LARRABEE, 432(NEQ):JUN71-327
ROBINSON, E. & G. SUMMERFIELD - SEE CLARE,
J.
ROBINSON, E.A.  EDWIN ARLINGTON ROBIN-
SON'S LETTERS TO EDITH BROWER.  (R.
CARY, ED)
    J.E. FISHER, 502(PRS):WINTER70/71-365
    P. REEVES, 219(GAR):SUMMER70-238

ROBINSON, E.A.  SELECTED POEMS OF EDWIN
ARLINGTON ROBINSON.  (M.D. ZABEL, ED)
SELECTED EARLY POEMS AND LETTERS.
(C.T. DAVIS, ED)
    I.D. MAC KILLOP, 184(EIC):JUL71-297
ROBINSON, F.C.  OLD ENGLISH LITERATURE.
    R.D., 179(ES):APR71-192
    D.A.H. EVANS, 597(SN):VOL42#2-485
ROBINSON, F.G.  THE SHAPE OF THINGS
KNOWN.
    617(TLS):14SEP73-1063
ROBINSON, F.G. - SEE SIDNEY, P.
ROBINSON, I.  CHAUCER AND THE ENGLISH
TRADITION.
    D. BIGGINS, 67:NOV72-214
ROBINSON, I.  CHAUCER'S PROSODY.
    J.J. ANDERSON, 148:WINTER71-378
    J.A. BURROW, 97(CQ):SUMMER/AUTUMN71-
389
    J. DAALDER, 67:MAY72-73
    R.M. WILSON, 175:AUTUMN71-96
ROBINSON, I.  THE SURVIVAL OF ENGLISH.
    P.N. FURBANK, 362:16AUG73-220
    617(TLS):7SEP73-1027
ROBINSON, J., ED.  AFTER KEYNES.
    617(TLS):12OCT73-1224
ROBINSON, J., ED.  FAITH AND REFORM.
    R.W. ROUSSEAU, 613:SPRING71-140
ROBINSON, J.  HIGHWAYS AND OUR ENVIRON-
MENT.
    J. LOBELL, 505:SEP71-172
ROBINSON, J.A.T.  THE HUMAN FACE OF GOD.
    617(TLS):6APR73-397
ROBINSON, J.O.  AN ANNOTATED BIBLIOGRAPHY
OF MODERN LANGUAGE TEACHING.
    A. ERISAU, 556(RLV):1971/5-644
ROBINSON, K.F. & A.B. BECKER.  EFFECTIVE
SPEECH FOR THE TEACHER.
    R.G. REA, 583:FALL71-108
ROBINSON, M.  THE LONG SONATA OF THE
DEAD.*
    F.G. BLAHA, 502(PRS):SUMMER71-180
    J. FLETCHER, 188(ECR):FALL71-67
ROBINSON, M.F.  NAPLES AND NEAPOLITAN
OPERA.
    617(TLS):5JAN73-14
ROBINSON, R.  ALTJERINGA AND OTHER ABOR-
IGINAL POEMS.
    S.E. LEE, 581:1971/3-227
ROBINSON, R.  ESSAYS IN GREEK PHILOSOPHY.*
    H.J. EASTERLING, 123:MAR72-56
    J.J. MULHERN, 484(PPR):DEC70-315
ROBINSON, R. - SEE ARISTOTLE
ROBINSON, R.H.  THE BUDDHIST RELIGION.
    W.L. HIGHFILL, 293(JAST):NOV70-167
ROBINSON, T.M.  PLATO'S PSYCHOLOGY.*
    P. LOUIS, 555:VOL45FASC1-152
    J. PHILIP, 154:JUN71-347
    J.B. SKEMP, 123:DEC72-335
    R.K. SPRAGUE, 122:JAN72-63
    M.A. STEWART, 479(PHQ):APR71-172
ROBINSON, W.A.  RETURN TO THE SEA.
    617(TLS):17AUG73-956
ROBINSON, W.H.  INVENTIONS.
    D.A.N. JONES, 362:22NOV73-718
    617(TLS):23NOV73-1450
ROBINSON, W.P. & S.J. RACKSTRAW.  A QUES-
TION OF ANSWERS.
    617(TLS):29JUN73-745
ROBISON, G.B.  AN INTRODUCTION TO MATHE-
MATICAL LOGIC.
    W.E. GOULD, 316:DEC71-679
ROBSON, J., ED.  POETRY DIMENSION I.
    617(TLS):7DEC73-1513
ROBSON, J.M. - SEE MILL, J.S.
ROBSON, L.L.  THE FIRST A.I.F.
    J.M. MAIN, 381:DEC71-476

ROBSON, P. & D.A. LURY, EDS. THE ECONO-
MIES OF AFRICA.
T.D. WILLIAMS, 69:OCT70-399
ROBSON, W.A. & D.E. REGAN, EDS. GREAT
CITIES OF THE WORLD.
617(TLS):30MAR73-359
ROBSON, W.W., ED. ESSAYS AND POEMS PRE-
SENTED TO LORD DAVID CECIL.
G. THOMAS, 175:SUMMER71-62
ROBSON, W.W. MODERN ENGLISH LITERATURE.*
639(VQR):WINTER71-XXIV
ROCA, P.M. PATHS OF THE PADRES THROUGH
SONORA.
M. WHIFFEN, 576:MAY70-201
ROCA PONS, J. INTRODUCCIÓN A LA GRAMÁ-
TICA. (2ND ED)
R. SANTIAGO, 202(FMOD):NOV70/FEB71-
167
ROCHE, D. LE MÉCRIT. 3 POURRISSEMENTS
POÉTIQUES.
617(TLS):19JAN73-69
ROCHE, J. THE MADRIGAL.
617(TLS):9FEB73-156
ROCHE, J. PALESTRINA.*
L. LOCKWOOD, 415:APR72-364
ROCHER, R. LA THÉORIE DES VOIX DU VERBE
DANS L'ÉCOLE PĀṆINÉENNE (LE 14E ĀHN-
IKA).*
G. CARDONA, 361:VOL25#2-210
B.A. VAN NOOTEN, 206:NOV71-592
ROCHESTER, J. COMPLETE POEMS OF ROCHES-
TER. (D.M. VEITH, ED)
M. GEARIN-TOSH, 597(SN):VOL42#1-235
ROCHLIN, G. MAN'S AGGRESSION.
J. KOVEL, 441:18MAR73-34
ROCKHILL, W.W. CHINA'S INTERCOURSE WITH
KOREA FROM THE XVTH CENTURY TO 1895.
B.H. HAZARD, 318(JAOS):OCT-DEC71-523
ROCKS, L. & R.P. RUNYON. THE ENERGY
CRISIS.
P. ADAMS, 61:JAN73-100
C. WELLES, 441:25FEB73-12
ROCQ, M.M., ED. CALIFORNIA LOCAL HIS-
TORY.* (2ND ED)
P.A. BLEICH, 14:JAN71-65
RODAS, V. 1970: HABRÁ UN DÍA Y OTROS
POEMAS.
E.B. LABRADA, 37:OCT70-40
RODAX, Y. THE REAL AND THE IDEAL IN THE
NOVELLA OF ITALY, FRANCE AND ENGLAND.*
R.J. SCHOECK, 546(RR):FEB71-44
RODERICK, C., ED. HENRY LAWSON CRITI-
CISM 1894-1971.
L. CANTRELL, 71(ALS):MAY73-99
RODERICK, C. - SEE LAWSON, H.
RODEWALD, D. ROBERT WALSERS PROSA.
G.C. AVERY, 401(MLQ):JUN72-211
J.J. WHITE, 402(MLR):JUL72-708
RODGERS, G.B. DIDEROT AND THE EIGHT-
EENTH CENTURY FRENCH PRESS.
617(TLS):21SEP73-1090
RODGERS, W.R. COLLECTED POEMS.*
T. SHAPCOTT, 491:APR73-40
RODGERS, W.R., ED. IRISH LITERARY POR-
TRAITS.*
N. BALAKIAN, 441:28APR73-37
RODINI, R.J. ANTONFRANCESCO GRAZZINI.*
E.B., 228(GSLI):VOL148FASC462/463-462
E. GIANTURCO, 275(IQ):SUMMER71-102
B. MITCHELL, 546(RR):OCT71-233
A. PALERMO, 149:SEP72-336
RODINSON, M. MARXISME ET MONDE MUSULMAN.
617(TLS):23FEB73-205
RODITI, E. MAGELLAN OF THE PACIFIC.
617(TLS):12JAN73-32
RODNEY, W. A HISTORY OF THE UPPER
GUINEA COAST 1545-1800.
H. DESCHAMPS, 69:JAN71-73

RODNICK, D. THE STRANGLED DEMOCRACY.
A.H. BROWN, 575(SEER):JUL72-478
RODRIGUE, E. HEROÍNA.
G.R. MC MURRAY, 238:MAR71-205
RODRIGUEZ, A. A HISTORY OF MEXICAN MURAL
PAINTING.*
J. SPENCER, 363:FEB71-35
RODRÍGUEZ-MOÑINO, A. DICCIONARIO BIBLIO-
GRÁFICO DE PLIEGOS SUELTOS POÉTICOS
(SIGLO XVI).
E.M. WILSON, 545(RPH):FEB72-298
RODRÍGUEZ-MOÑINO, A. POESÍA Y CANCION-
EROS (SIGLO XVI).*
K. WHINNOM, 240(HR):JAN71-91
RODRÍGUEZ-PERALTA, P.W. JOSÉ SANTOS
CHOCANO.
H. CASTILLO, 238:SEP71-605
A.M.R. RAMBO, 399(MLJ):DEC71-542
RODWAY, A. THE TRUTHS OF FICTION.
J. KILLHAM, 89(BJA):SPRING72-209
ROEBUCK, C., ED. THE MUSES AT WORK.
P.P. BETANCOURT, 127:SPRING72-350
D.E. STRONG, 123:JUN72-261
ROECKER, W.A. WILLAMETTE.
R. SHELTON, 600:SPRING71-179
ROELS, J. LE CONCEPT DE REPRÉSENTATION
POLITIQUE AU XVIIIE SIÈCLE FRANÇAIS.
J. GODECHOT, 182:VOL24#6-317
ROEMING, R.F., ED. CAMUS: A BIBLIOGRA-
PHY.*
A. ANTONINI, 535(RHL):JAN-FEB71-142
J-M. KLINKENBERG, 556(RLV):1971/6-780
ROETHKE, T. SELECTED LETTERS OF THEODORE
ROETHKE.* (R.J. MILLS, JR., ED)
H. SERGEANT, 175:AUTUMN71-106
ROETHKE, T. STRAW FOR THE FIRE.* (D.
WAGONER, ED)
G. BURNS, 584(SWR):SUMMER72-255
K. MALKOFF, 598(SOR):SUMMER73-717
R.B. SHAW, 491:MAR73-341
ROETHLISBERGER, M. BARTHOLOMEUS BREEN-
BERGH, HANDZEICHNUNGEN.
J.Q.V. ALTENA, 54:DEC71-536
ROETHLISBERGER, M. CLAUDE LORRAIN: THE
DRAWINGS.*
M. CHIARINI, 54:JUN71-257
ROGER-MARX, C. & S. COTTE. DELACROIX.
R. LEBOWITZ, 58:MAY71-14
ROGERS, B.G. THE NOVELS AND STORIES OF
BARBEY D'AUREVILLY.
G. CORBIÈRE-GILLE, 546(RR):FEB71-67
ROGERS, C.R. BECOMING PARTNERS.
B. DE MOTT, 61:DEC73-122
J.S. GORDON, 441:28JAN73-2
ROGERS, C.R. & B. STEVENS. PERSON TO
PERSON.
617(TLS):24AUG73-985
ROGERS, E.S. NEW GUINEA.
J.A. WILLMOTT, 529(QQ):SUMMER71-339
ROGERS, F.R. - SEE TWAIN, M.
ROGERS, F.R. & P. BAENDER - SEE TWAIN, M.
ROGERS, H., JR. THEORY OF RECURSIVE
FUNCTIONS AND EFFECTIVE COMPUTABILITY.
C.E.M. YATES, 316:MAR71-141
ROGERS, H.C.B. THE CONFEDERATES AND
FEDERALS AT WAR.
617(TLS):14SEP73-1065
ROGERS, J.A. WORLD'S GREAT MEN OF COLOR.
(J.H. CLARKE, ED)
J.R. WILLIS, 441:4FEB73-21
ROGERS, L.R. THE APPRECIATION OF THE
ARTS: SCULPTURE.
S. ROSENTHAL, 58:MAR71-15
M. WELISH, 58:FEB71-14
ROGERS, M. MINDFOGGER.
M. LEVIN, 441:13MAY73-38
ROGERS, N. SHELLEY AT WORK.* (2ND ED)
F. WIESELHUBER, 38:BAND88HEFT3-404

ROGERS, N. - SEE SHELLEY, P.B.
ROGERS, P., ED. DEFOE: THE CRITICAL
HERITAGE.
617(TLS):5JAN73-6
ROGERS, P., ED. FLORILEGIO DE CUENTOS
HISPANOAMERICANOS.
G. SMITH, 399(MLJ):OCT71-411
ROGERS, S.T. & B.H. DAVEY. THE COMMON
AGRICULTURAL POLICY AND BRITAIN.
617(TLS):22JUN73-728
ROGERS, T.J. TECHNIQUES OF SOLIPSISM.*
205(FMLS):JAN71-99
ROGGERONE, G.A. BENEDETTO CROCE E LA
FONDAZIONE DEL CONCETTO DI LIBERTÀ.
E. NAMER, 542:APR-JUN70-252
ROGGERONE, G.A. DA KANT AD OGGI.
K. OEDINGEN, 342:BAND62HEFT3-410
ROGOW, A.A. THE PSYCHIATRISTS.
P.A. FRIEDMAN, 619(TC):VOL179#1048-53
ROH, F. GERMAN ART IN THE 20TH CENTURY.*
P. SELZ, 54:MAR70-109
"THE ROHAN MASTER."
J. POPE-HENNESSY, 441:2DEC73-99
ROHDE, E.S. THE OLD ENGLISH HERBALS.
THE OLD ENGLISH GARDENING BOOKS.
617(TLS):26JAN73-102
ROHDICH, H. DIE EURIPIDEISCHE TRAGÖDIE.*
E-R. SCHWINGE, 490:JUL/OCT70-620
ROHLFS, G. FROM VULGAR LATIN TO OLD
FRENCH.
J. KLAUSENBURGER, 399(MLJ):FEB71-109
ROHLFS, G. GRAMMATICA STORICA DELLA LIN-
GUA ITALIANA E DEI SUOI DIALETTI.
G. LEPSCHY, 402(MLR):JUL72-660
ROHLFS, G. VOCABOLARIO SUPPLEMENTARE DEI
DIALETTI DELLE TRE CALABRIE.
A. KAMBYLIS, 72:BAND209HEFT1/3-186
ROHOU, G. GRIS TOURTERELLE.
617(TLS):7DEC73-1512
ROHR, R. EINFÜHRUNG IN DAS STUDIUM DER
ROMANISTIK.
S. JAUERNICK, 224(GRM):AUG70-364
ROHRER, C. DIE WORTZUSAMMENSETZUNG IM
MODERNEN FRANZÖSISCH.
R.W. LANGACKER, 206:NOV70-569
W. ROTHE, 260(IF):BAND75-326
RÖHRICH, L. ADAM UND EVA.
F.R. SCHRÖDER, 224(GRM):JAN70-109
RÖHRICH, L. ERZÄHLUNGEN DES SPÄTEN MIT-
TELALTERS UND IHR WEITERLEBEN IN LIT-
ERATUR UND VOLKSDICHTUNG BIS ZUR
GEGENWART.
H. ZIMMERMANN, 657(WW):JAN/FEB71-65
RÖHRICH, L. GEBÄRDE, METAPHER, PARODIE.
R. SCHMIDT-WIEGAND, 680(ZDP):BAND89
HEFT3-474
RÖHRICH, L. MÄRCHEN UND WIRKLICHKEIT.
G. LUTZ, 196:BAND11HEFT1/2-193
ROIDER, K.A., JR. THE RELUCTANT ALLY.
617(TLS):14SEP73-1048
ROIG, A.A. LOS KRAUSISTAS ARGENTINOS.
J.C. TORCHIA-ESTRADA, 263:APR-JUN72-
181
DE ROJAS ZORRILLA, F. DEL REY ABAJO, NIN-
GUNO. (R.R. MAC CURDY, ED)
J.E. DIAL, 238:MAY71-414
ROLBANT, S. THE ISRAELI SOLDIER.
S.L.A. MARSHALL, 390:APR71-63
ROLI, R. I DESIGNI ITALIANI DEL SEI-
CENTO.
A.S. HARRIS, 54:SEP71-404
ROLLAND, R. ROMAIN ROLLAND ET LE MOUVE-
MENT FLORENTIN DE "LA VOCE." (H.
GIORDAN, ED)
P. RENARD, 535(RHL):MAY-JUN70-533
V. TASCA, 549(RLC):OCT-DEC70-579

ROLLAND, R. ROMAIN ROLLAND, UN BEAU
VISAGE À TOUS SENS. (M.R. ROLLAND, ED)
J. RELINGER, 535(RHL):MAR-APR70-343
ROLLAND, S.C. REFLECTIONS.
H.P. GUNDY, 529(QQ):SPRING71-163
RÖLLEKE, H. - SEE VON DROSTE-HÜLSHOFF, A.
ROLLESTON, J. RILKE IN TRANSITION.
H. ADOLF, 400(MLN):OCT71-742
B.L. BRADLEY, 222(GR):NOV71-315
S.B. PUKNAT, 406:SPRING72-59
J. RYAN, 401(MLQ):SEP71-330
ROLLET, P. - SEE MISTRAL, F.
ROLLIN, F. LA PHÉNOMÉNOLOGIE AU DÉPART.
M. DUFOUR, 154:SEP70-285
ROLLINS, E.W. & H. ZOHN - SEE BUBER, M. &
A. GOES
ROLO, J.P.V. ENTENTE CORDIALE.*
R.A. COSGROVE, 50(ARQ):WINTER70-369
ROLOFF, D. PLOTIN: DIE GROSS-SCHRIFT
III, 8; V, 8; V, 5; II, 9.
L.G. WESTERINK, 124:NOV71-95
ROLOFF, H-G. - SEE WICKRAM, G.
ROLPH, C.H. KINGSLEY.
R. CROSSMAN, 362:12APR73-485
617(TLS):13APR73-419
ROLT, L.T.C. FROM SEA TO SEA.
617(TLS):19OCT73-1287
"ROMAN ET LUMIÈRES AU XVIIIE SIÈCLE."
R. MERCIER, 557(RSH):OCT-DEC71-631
ROMANI, D., G. ALLSUP & R. HATTON. HOMBRE
HISPÁNICO.
R. MUNGUÍA, 238:SEP71-611
"ROMANIAN SHORT STORIES."
E-D. TAPPE, 575(SEER):OCT72-638
"ROMANISCHE FORSCHUNGEN: REGISTERBAND
1935-1965."
H. MEIER, 72:BAND209HEFT1/3-174
ROMANO, O.I., ED. EL ESPEJO - THE MIRROR.
C.M. TATUM, 399(MLJ):DEC71-540
"ROMANPROBLEMER."
I. HAVNEVIK, 172(EDDA):1971/2-126
"ROMANTISME ET POLITIQUE, 1815-1851."
O-A. HAAC, 207(FR):APR71-987
RÖMER, R. DIE SPRACHE DER ANZEIGENWER-
BUNG.
K. DANIELS, 657(WW):JUL/AUG70-275
ROMERALO, A.S. - SEE UNDER SÁNCHEZ ROMER-
ALO, A.
ROMEU FIGUERAS, J., ED. LA MÚSICA EN LA
CORTE DE LOS REYES CATÓLICOS, IV.
D. BECKER, 545(RPH):FEB72-357
RØMHILD, L.P. LAESERE.
J.L. SAMMONS, 563(SS):SPRING72-268
DE ROMILLY, J. LA TRAGÉDIE GRECQUE.
E.W. WHITTLE, 123:DEC72-419
RÓNAI, P. DER KAMPF GEGEN BABEL ODER DAS
ABENTEUER DER UNIVERSALSPRACHEN.
H-R., 430(NS):AUG70-420
RONAN, C.A. ASTRONOMY.
617(TLS):9MAR73-277
RONAY, G. THE TRUTH ABOUT DRACULA.
G. STADE, 441:14JAN73-2
RONFELDT, D. ATENCINGO.
617(TLS):20JUL73-839
RONGE, P. POLEMIK, PARODIE UND SATIRE
BEI IONESCO.
K. RINGGER, 224(GRM):JAN70-115
RONNET, G. SOPHOCLE, POÈTE TRAGIQUE.*
P.E. EASTERLING, 123:MAR72-17
DE RONSARD, P. LES OEUVRES DE PIERRE DE
RONSARD.* (VOLS 3&4) (I. SILVER, ED)
V.E. GRAHAM, 546(RR):APR71-139
DE RONSARD, P. LES OEUVRES DE PIERRE DE
RONSARD.* (VOLS 5&6) (I. SILVER, ED)
V.E. GRAHAM, 546(RR):APR71-139
B.L.O. RICHTER, 207(FR):OCT70-247

DE RONSARD, P. LES OEUVRES DE PIERRE DE
RONSARD. (VOLS 7&8) (I. SILVER, ED)
W.L. WILEY, 551(RENQ):WINTER71-546
DE RONSARD, P. SONNETS POUR HÉLÈNE.*
(M. SMITH, ED)
J. PINEAUX, 557(RSH):APR-JUN71-311
G.M. SUTHERLAND, 402(MLR):OCT72-884
RONSLEY, J. YEATS'S AUTOBIOGRAPHY.*
H. PESCHMANN, 175:SPRING70-28
RONY, J., ED. LE JEU DE LA FEUILLÉE.
205(FMLS):OCT70-421
ROOKE, B.E. - SEE COLERIDGE, S.T.
ROOSE-EVANS, J. EXPERIMENTAL THEATRE
FROM STANISLAVSKY TO TODAY.
B.L. KNAPP, 160:VOL8#2-149
H. MORRISON, 157:AUTUMN70-73
ROOSEVELT, E. & J. BROUGH. THE ROOSE-
VELTS OF HYDE PARK: AN UNTOLD STORY.
K.S. DAVIS, 441:20MAY73-4
442(NY):2JUN73-123
ROOSEVELT, F.D. & W.C. BULLITT. FOR THE
PRESIDENT, PERSONAL AND SECRET.* (O.H.
BULLITT, ED)
442(NY):6JAN73-75
ROOT, I., ED. CROMWELL.
B. WORDEN, 453:15NOV73-24
ROOT, W.P. THE STORM AND OTHER POEMS.*
D. LAWDER, 448:FALL70-118
ROOTH, E., ED. NIEDERDEUTSCHE BREVIER-
TEXTE DES 14. JAHRHUNDERTS AUS WEST-
FALEN.
J.E. HÄRD, 597(SN):VOL43#2-543
DE ROOVER, R. THE BRUGES MONEY MARKET
AROUND 1400.
J.F. BERGIER, 589:OCT72-756
ROPER, A. ARNOLD'S POETIC LANDSCAPES.*
G. JOSEPH, 405(MP):AUG71-82
J.D. JUMP, 541(RES):MAY71-234
R. KEEFE, 149:DEC72-476
P. MC CARTHY, 637(VS):SEP70-110
W.A. MADDEN, 636(VP):WINTER70-351
ROPER, R. ROYO COUNTY.
J.R. FRAKES, 441:16SEP73-4
C. LEHMANN-HAUPT, 441:13SEP73-51
DE ROPP, R.S. THE NEW PROMETHEANS.
617(TLS):9FEB73-158
ROREM, N. CRITICAL AFFAIRS.
639(VQR):SPRING71-LXX
RORTY, R., ED. THE LINGUISTIC TURN.*
R. BLANCHÉ, 542:OCT-DEC70-501
ROSCI, M. IL TRATTATO DI ARCHITETTURA DE
SEBASTIANO SERLIO. (VOL 1) SESTO
LIBRO DELLE HABITATIONI DI TUTTI LI
GRADI DEGLI HOMINI. (VOL 2)
M.N. ROSENFELD, 54:SEP70-319
ROSCIONI, G.C. LA DISARMONIA PRESTABIL-
ITA, STUDIO SU GADDA.
J. RISSET, 98:NOV70-944
ROSE, B. AMERICAN ART SINCE 1900.*
C.W. MILLARD, 56:SUMMER70-180
ROSE, B. JACKSON POLLOCK: WORKS ON
PAPER.
J.B. MYERS, 139:AUG70-7
ROSE, G. A CLEAR ROAD TO ARCHANGEL.
617(TLS):23FEB73-219
ROSE, G. A COUNTRYWOMAN'S YEAR.
617(TLS):23NOV73-1456
ROSE, L.E. ARISTOTLE'S SYLLOGISTIC.
I. BOH, 316:DEC71-670
ROSE, L.E. & M.W. FISHER. THE POLITICS
OF NEPAL.
F.H. GAIGE, 318(JAOS):OCT-DEC71-560
R.L. JONES, 293(JAST):AUG71-915
ROSE, M. ARTIST POTTERS IN ENGLAND.
M. ARCHER, 39:JUN71-528
ROSE, M. HEROIC LOVE.*
H. SMITH, 551(RENQ):WINTER71-556

ROSE, N.A. THE GENTILE ZIONISTS.
617(TLS):14SEP73-1050
ROSE, N.A. - SEE DUGDALE, B.
ROSE, P. WINDOW ON MOUNT ZION.
617(TLS):13JUL73-799
ROSEMONT, F. THE MORNING OF THE MACHINE
GUN.
N. WHITING, 600:SPRING71-178
ROSEN, B., ED. WITCHCRAFT.*
C.A. BURLAND, 203:AUTUMN70-231
ROSEN, C. THE CLASSICAL STYLE.*
R. SIMPSON, 97(CQ):SUMMER/AUTUMN71-
384
W.H. YOUNGREN, 249(HUDR):WINTER72/73-
633
ROSÉN, H.B. STRUKTURALGRAMMATISCHE
BEITRÄGE ZUM VERSTÄNDNIS HOMERS.
K. STRUNK, 260(IF):BAND75-315
ROSEN, M. POPCORN VENUS.
C. LEHMANN-HAUPT, 441:18DEC73-39
ROSEN, S. NIHILISM.
K. DORTER, 154:DEC71-797
B. MURCHLAND, 484(PPR):DEC71-277
ROSEN, S. PLATO'S "SYMPOSIUM."*
J.D. MOORE, 24:OCT72-612
L.E. ROSE, 484(PPR):DEC71-279
ROSEN, S.M. EDUCATION AND MODERNIZATION
IN THE USSR.
W.L. MATHES, 32:JUN72-449
ROSENBAUER, H. BRECHT UND DER BEHAVIOR-
ISMUS.
U. WEISSTEIN, 221(GQ):MAY71-400
ROSENBERG, B.A. THE ART OF THE AMERICAN
FOLK PREACHER.
G.B. GUNN, 405(MP):FEB72-281
A.W. WONDERLEY, 582(SFQ):JUN71-171
639(VQR):WINTER71-XLIII
ROSENBERG, H. ARTWORKS AND PACKAGES.*
D. ASHTON, 505:MAR70-114
R. HOWARD, 139:MAR-APR70-9
M. MUDRICK, 55:MAR70-47
ROSENBERG, J. DOROTHY RICHARDSON.
N. LEWIS, 362:23AUG73-255
617(TLS):15JUN73-660
ROSENBERG, M. THE MASKS OF KING LEAR.*
617(TLS):12JAN73-44
ROSENBLOOD, N., ED. SHAW: SEVEN CRITICAL
ESSAYS.*
J.P. SMITH, 150(DR):SPRING71-114
ROSENBLUETH, A. MIND AND BRAIN.
J. TROYER, 482(PHR):OCT71-522
ROSENBLUM, R. JEAN-AUGUSTE-DOMINIQUE
INGRES.*
N. SCHLENOFF, 54:JUN71-267
ROSENBLUM, R. THE MUSHROOM CAVE.
N. CALLENDAR, 441:15APR73-35
ROSENBLUM, R. FRANK STELLA.
T. HILTON, 592:MAR71-129
ROSENBLUM, R. TRANSFORMATIONS IN LATE
EIGHTEENTH CENTURY ART.*
G. LEVITINE, 54:DEC71-539
ROSENFELD, A.H., ED. WILLIAM BLAKE.*
G.E. BENTLEY, JR., 627(UTQ):FALL70-86
P. MALEKIN, 541(RES):FEB71-93
M.F. SCHULZ, 173(ECS):WINTER71-223
ROSENFELD, A.H. - SEE WHEELWRIGHT, J.
ROSENFIELD, J.M. & S. SHIMADA. TRADI-
TIONS OF JAPANESE ART.
T. BOWIE, 127:SUMMER72-472
M. SULLIVAN, 127:SUMMER72-476
ROSENGARTEN, F. THE ITALIAN ANTI-FASCIST
PRESS (1919-1945).
A.W. SALOMONE, 276:SUMMER71-253
ROSENGREN, I. INHALT UND STRUKTUR.*
H. GÖTZ, 680(ZDP):BAND90HEFT1-131
ROSENGREN, I. SEMANTISCHE STRUKTUREN.
H. SITTA, 556(RLV):1970/1-110

ROSENGREN, I. SPRACHE UND VERWANDTSCHAFT EINIGER ALTHOCHDEUTSCHEN UND ALTSÄCHSISCHEN EVANGELIENGLOSSEN.
   G. MÜLLER, 681(ZDS):BAND26HEFT1/2-121
ROSENKRANZ, R. ACROSS THE BARRICADES.
   C.P., 505:NOV71-130
ROSENMEYER, T.G. THE GREEN CABINET.*
   M.L. CLARKE, 123:MAR72-120
   P.V. MARINELLI, 487:AUTUMN71-292
   J.B. VAN SICKLE, 24:APR72-348
ROSENSTIEL, A. FRENCH OMNIBUS.
   R-M. DAELE-GUINAN, 207(FR):FEB71-592
ROSENTHAL, E. THE ILLUMINATIONS OF THE VERGILIUS ROMANUS.
   617(TLS):26JAN73-96
ROSENTHAL, E.T. DAS FRAGMENTARISCHE UNIVERSUM.
   M.E. COCK, 402(MLR):OCT72-955
   D. SEVIN, 406:SUMMER72-167
ROSENTHAL, M.L. THE VIEW FROM THE PEACOCK'S TAIL.
   R.B. SHAW, 491:SEP73-344
   P.D. ZIVKOVIC, 109:SPRING/SUMMER73-141
   617(TLS):31AUG73-996
ROSETTI, A. LINGUISTICA.*
   G.F. MEIER, 682(ZPSK):BAND23HEFT6-644
ROSEVEARE, H. THE TREASURY 1660-1870.
   617(TLS):16NOV73-1388
ROSITZKE, H. LEFT ON!
   M. LEVIN, 441:16DEC73-16
ROSITZKE, H. THE USSR TODAY.
   617(TLS):5OCT73-1153
ROSKILL, M. VAN GOGH, GAUGUIN AND THE IMPRESSIONIST CIRCLE.
   R. LEBOWITZ, 58:NOV70-I8
ROSKILL, M.W. DOLCE'S "ARETINO" AND VENETIAN ART THEORY OF THE CINQUECENTO.*
   D. ROSAND, 56:SUMMER71-240
ROSKILL, S. HANKEY. (VOL 1)
   P. JOHNSON, 441:7JAN73-7
ROSKOLENKO, H. THE TIME THAT WAS THEN.
   F. HIRSCH, 328:FALL71-500
RÖSLER, W. REFLEXE VORSOKRATISCHEN DENKENS BEI AISCHYLOS.
   A.F. GARVIE, 123:DEC72-404
ROSS, A. THE DUNFERMLINE AFFAIR.
   617(TLS):17AUG73-959
ROSS, A., ED. LONDON MAGAZINE STORIES 8.
   V. CUNNINGHAM, 362:8NOV73-638
   617(TLS):28SEP73-1100
ROSS, A., ED. POETRY OF THE AUGUSTAN AGE.
   566:AUTUMN71-29
ROSS, A.S.C. DON'T SAY IT.
   617(TLS):14DEC73-1541
ROSS, D.J.A. ALEXANDER AND THE FAITHLESS LADY.
   H.C.R. LAURIE, 402(MLR):JAN72-183
ROSS, D.O., JR. STYLE AND TRADITION IN CATULLUS.*
   R.A. HORNSBY, 599:FALL71-315
   R.O.A.M. LYNE, 123:MAR72-34
   K. QUINN, 487:SPRING71-82
ROSS, I.S. LORD KAMES AND THE SCOTLAND OF HIS DAY.
   R. MITCHISON, 362:25OCT73-568
   617(TLS):5JAN73-7
ROSS, J.D. THE HEART MACHINE.
   617(TLS):2MAR73-250
ROSS, J.F. INTRODUCTION TO THE PHILOSOPHY OF RELIGION.
   M.B.M., 543:MAR71-550
ROSS, J.F. PHILOSOPHICAL THEOLOGY.*
   A.F. HOLMES, 321:SPRING71-153
   G.I. MAVRODES, 543:SEP70-82
ROSS, M. TOTEM.
   617(TLS):10AUG73-921

ROSS, M.C. CATALOGUE OF THE BYZANTINE AND EARLY MEDIEVAL ANTIQUITIES IN THE DUMBARTON OAKS COLLECTION. (VOL 2)
   I.H. FORSYTH, 56:AUTUMN70-312
ROSS, T.W. - SEE KYD, T.
ROSS-CRAIG, S. DRAWINGS OF BRITISH PLANTS. (PT 30)
   617(TLS):9FEB73-161
ROSSELET, C. CATALOGUE DE LA CORRESPONDANCE DE J-J. ROUSSEAU. (PTS 1&2)
   E.R. BRIGGS, 402(MLR):JAN72-191
ROSSELLI, A. EPISODI DI GUERRIGLIA URBANA.
   617(TLS):25MAY73-575
ROSSETTI, D.G. LETTERS OF DANTE GABRIEL ROSSETTI.* (VOLS 1-4) (O. DOUGHTY & J.R. WAHL, EDS)
   M. PAGÈS, 189(EA):JUL-SEP70-311
ROSSETTI, G. SOCIETÀ E ISTITUZIONI NEL CONTADO LOMBARDO DURANTE IL MEDIOEVO.
   D. HERLIHY, 589:APR72-338
ROSSI, F. MOSAICS.
   J. BECKWITH, 39:OCT71-322
   B. BETTINSON, 363:NOV70-26
ROSSI, G.C. ESTUDIOS SOBRE LAS LETRAS EN EL SIGLO XVIII.* LA LETTERATURA ITALIANA E LE LETTERATURE DI LINGUA PORTOGHESE.
   M. FRANZBACH, 52:BAND5HEFT3-311
ROSSI, G.C. LETTERATURA BRASILIANA.
   E.M. REALI, 149:MAR72-106
ROSSI, M., ED. SEBASTIANO SERLIO.
   A. BLUNT, 90:JUL71-410
ROSSI, P. GIROLAMO CAMPAGNA.
   J. SCHULZ, 54:JUN71-250
ROSSI, P. LO STORICISMO TEDESCO CONTEMPORANEO. STORIA E STORICISMO DELLA FILOSOFIA CONTEMPORANEA.
   E. NAMER, 542:JAN-MAR70-104
ROSSI, P.A. & D.C. HUNT. THE ART OF THE OLD WEST.*
   617(TLS):5JAN73-21
ROSSI, V. ANDRÉ GIDE.*
   M. GIRARD, 546(RR):FEB71-71
   D. MOUTOTE, 535(RHL):MAR-APR70-337
ROSSI-LANDI, F. IL LINGUAGGIO COME LAVORO E COME MERCATO.
   G.C. LEPSCHY, 353:OCT70-105
RÜSSING-HAGER, M. WORTINDEX ZU GEORG BÜCHNER.
   M. GRÄFE, 680(ZDP):BAND90HEFT4-594
ROSSITER, A.P. ANGEL WITH HORNS. (G. STOREY, ED)
   J.B. FORT, 189(EA):APR-JUN71-195
ROSSIYANSKY, M. UTRO VNUTRI.
   R.D.B. THOMSON, 575(SEER):APR72-301
RÖSSLER, D. VOLUNTAD BEI CERVANTES.
   C. MORÓN ARROYO, 240(HR):JUL71-324
RÖSSLER, R. KIRCHE UND REVOLUTION IN RUSSLAND.
   B.R. BOCIURKIW, 32:JUN72-442
ROSSMAN, M. ON LEARNING AND SOCIAL CHANGE.*
   K.B. CLARK, 31(ASCH):WINTER72/73-156
ROSSO, C. ILLUMINISMO, FELICITÀ, DOLORE, MITI E IDEOLOGIE FRANCESI.
   A. MASSON, 98:NOV70-979
   A. SCAGLIONE, 131(CL):FALL72-362
ROSTAND, C. LISZT.
   H. SEARLE, 415:NOV72-1088
ROSTAND, J. HUMANLY POSSIBLE.
   T. DOBZHANSKY, 441:11MAR73-44
ROSTAND, R. THE KILLER ELITE.
   N. CALLENDAR, 441:11MAR73-50
ROSTEN, N. MARILYN.
   A. BROYARD, 441:14SEP73-43
ROSTON, M. BIBLICAL DRAMA IN ENGLAND.*
   J.H. SIMS, 577(SHR):WINTER71-87

ROSTOW, E.V. PEACE IN THE BALANCE.*
R. STEEL, 453:14JUN73-33
ROSTOW, W.W. THE DIFFUSION OF POWER.*
A. LEWIS, 453:8FEB73-23
ROSTOW, W.W. POLITICS AND THE STAGES OF
GROWTH.
K.E. BOULDING, 639(VQR):AUTUMN71-602
ROSZAK, T. THE MAKING OF A COUNTER CUL-
TURE.
J. ELDERFIELD, 592:JUL-AUG70-49
W.J. GAVIN, 258:JUN71-279
J. GRANGE, 613:SUMMER71-313
ROSZAK, T. WHERE THE WASTELAND ENDS.*
D. CAUTE, 362:19APR73-518
617(TLS):25MAY73-574
ROTBERG, R.I. JOSEPH THOMSON AND THE
EXPLORATION OF AFRICA.
676(YR):AUTUMN71-XXVIII
ROTERS, E. PAINTERS OF THE BAUHAUS.
I.L. FINKELSTEIN, 54:DEC70-469
ROTH, C. & G. WIGODER - SEE "ENCYCLOPAE-
DIA JUDAICA"
ROTH, P. THE BREAST.*
M. DRABBLE, 362:22MAR73-378
R. SALE, 249(HUDR):WINTER72/73-703
617(TLS):23MAR73-313
ROTH, P. THE GREAT AMERICAN NOVEL.
T.R. EDWARDS, 441:6MAY73-27
W.H. GASS, 453:31MAY73-7
F. KERMODE, 362:27SEP73-424
C. LEHMANN-HAUPT, 441:14MAY73-29
J. LEONARD, 61:JUN73-114
617(TLS):21SEP73-1073
ROTH, P. OUR GANG.*
A.B. KERNAN, 676(YR):SPRING72-407
M. MUDRICK, 249(HUDR):SPRING72-142
42(AR):FALL71-440
ROTH, P. PORTNOY'S COMPLAINT.*
J.C. FIELD, 556(RLV):1971/6-768
P-Y. PÉTILLON, 98:OCT70-820
ROTHBAUER, A.M. - SEE DE CERVANTES
SAAVEDRA, M.
ROTHE, A. DER DOPPELTITEL.
G. HAINSWORTH, 208(FS):JUL72-363
ROTHE, F. FRANK WEDEKINDS DRAMEN -
JUGENDSTIL UND LEBENSPHILOSOPHIE.
H.F. GARTEN, 220(GL&L):OCT71-64
ROTHE, H. N.M. KARAMZINS EUROPÄISCHE
REISE.
H. SCHROEDER, 52:BAND5HEFT2-212
G.S. SMITH, 402(MLR):APR72-479
ROTHE, H-J. & R. SZESKUS, EDS. FELIX
MENDELSSOHN BARTHOLDY.
E. SAMS, 415:DEC72-1184
ROTHE, J. JOHANNES ROTHES "RATSGEDICHTE."
(H. WOLF, ED)
I.R. CAMPBELL, 67:NOV72-248
J.S. GROSECLOSE, 406:WINTER72-398
ROTHE, W., ED. EXPRESSIONISMUS ALS LIT-
ERATUR.*
R. GRIMM, 406:SPRING72-61
D. KASANG, 597(SN):VOL43#1-295
J. OSBORNE, 220(GL&L):APR72-283
ROTHE, W. STRUKTUREN DES KONJUNKTIVS IM
FRANZÖSISCHEN.
J. THIEL, 430(NS):JUN71-335
ROTHENBERG, J. THE JEWISH RELIGION IN
THE SOVIET UNION.
W.C. FLETCHER, 32:SEP72-700
ROTHENBERG, J. & G. QUASHA, EDS. AMERICA
A PROPHECY.
H. VENDLER, 441:30DEC73-7
ROTHENBERG, K-J. DAS PROBLEM DES REAL-
ISMUS BEI THOMAS MANN.*
G. KLUGE, 680(ZDP):BAND89HEFT4-633
H-H. REUTER, 433:OCT71-461

ROTHENBERG, M. THE BREATH-STREAM DYNAM-
ICS OF SIMPLE-RELEASED-PLOSIVE PRODUC-
TION.
G. HEIKE, 260(IF):BAND75-364
A. MALÉCOT, 361:VOL27#4-390
ROTHENSTEIN, J. TIME'S THIEVISH PRO-
GRESS.
R.E., 135:NOV70-214
T. HILTON, 592:NOV70-214
ROTHKRUG, L. OPPOSITION TO LOUIS XIV.
J. LOUGH, 208(FS):JAN72-73
ROTHMAN, D. THE DISCOVERY OF THE ASYLUM.
42(AR):SUMMER71-286
ROTHMAN, H. MURDEROUS PROVIDENCE.
617(TLS):2FEB73-131
ROTHSCHILD, E. PARADISE LOST.
A. BROYARD, 441:13DEC73-51
R. SHERRILL, 441:28OCT73-1
442(NY):26NOV73-200
DE ROTHSCHILD, P., ED & TRANS. POÈMES
ÉLISABÉTHAINS (1525-1650).
J-M. BENOIST, 98:AUG/SEP71-730
ROTONDI, P. THE DUCAL PALACE OF URBINO.
H. SAALMAN, 90:JAN71-46
ROTONDO, A. - SEE RENATO, C.
ROTSTEIN, A., ED. POWER CORRUPTED.
D. DUFFY, 331:AUG71-59
ROTTENSTEINER, F., ED. VIEW FROM ANOTHER
SHORE.
T. STURGEON, 441:23SEP73-38
ROTTMANN, L., J. BARRY & B.T. PAQUET, EDS.
WINNING HEARTS AND MINDS.*
S. SPENDER, 453:8FEB73-3
ROUBARD, J. ∈.
J. GUERON, 98:AUG-SEP70-727
ROUBICZEK, P. ETHICAL VALUES IN THE AGE
OF SCIENCE.*
D.A.L. THOMAS, 393(MIND):JAN71-152
ROUDIEZ, L.S. FRENCH FICTION TODAY.
617(TLS):12JAN73-33
ROUDIL, J., ED. LES FUEROS D'ALCARAZ ET
D'ALARCÓN.*
E. SLAGER, 433:APR70-194
ROUGER, G. - SEE RESTIF DE LA BRETONNE
ROUGERIE, J. PARIS LIBRE, 1871.
M. REBÉRIOUX, 98:NOV71-979
ROUGIER, L. LE GÉNIE DE L'OCCIDENT.
J. KOLBERT, 207(FR):FEB71-580
ROULET, E. SYNTAXE DE LA PROPOSITION
NUCLÉAIRE EN FRANÇAIS PARLÉ.
J. CASAGRANDE, 207(FR):MAR71-788
J. DARBELNET, 207(FR):DEC70-438
J. DUBOIS, 209(FM):JUL70-359
R. HUDDLESTON, 297(JL):SEP70-277
R.W. LANGACKER, 399(MLJ):JAN71-37
M. WANDRUSZKA, 430(NS):FEB71-106
W. ZWANENBURG, 353:AUG71-121
ROUNER, L.S. WITHIN HUMAN EXPERIENCE.
N. CHOBOT, 485(PE&W):OCT70-435
J. HOWIE, 154:JUN71-373
ROUQUET, A. PRESENT STATE OF THE ARTS IN
ENGLAND.
R. EDWARDS, 39:APR71-341
ROUSE, P., JR. JAMES BLAIR OF VIRGINIA.*
617(TLS):9FEB73-159
ROUSSEAU, G.S. & P-G. BOUCÉ, EDS. TOBIAS
SMOLLETT.
L. HARTLEY, 579(SAQ):SUMMER72-455
617(TLS):26JAN73-98
ROUSSEAU, J-J. CORRESPONDANCE COMPLÈTE
DE JEAN-JACQUES ROUSSEAU.* (VOL 5)
(R.A. LEIGH, ED)
R. MERCIER, 557(RSH):JAN-MAR70-160
ROUSSEAU, J-J. CORRESPONDANCE COMPLÈTE
DE JEAN-JACQUES ROUSSEAU.* (VOLS 6-8)
(R.A. LEIGH, ED)
R. MERCIER, 557(RSH):JAN-MAR70-160
M.L. PERKINS, 399(MLJ):JAN71-32

ROUSSEAU, J-J. CORRESPONDANCE COMPLÈTE
DE JEAN-JACQUES ROUSSEAU. (VOLS 9&10)
(R.A. LEIGH, ED)
    E.R. BRIGGS, 402(MLR):JAN72-189
    H. BROWN, 207(FR):DEC70-459
    R. MERCIER, 557(RSH):OCT-DEC71-665
    J.S. SPINK, 208(FS):APR72-203
ROUSSEAU, J-J. CORRESPONDANCE COMPLÈTE
DE JEAN-JACQUES ROUSSEAU. (VOLS 11&12)
(R.A. LEIGH, ED)
    E.R. BRIGGS, 402(MLR):JAN72-189
    R. MERCIER, 557(RSH):OCT-DEC71-665
    J.S. SPINK, 208(FS):APR72-203
ROUSSEAU, J-J. CORRESPONDANCE COMPLÈTE
DE JEAN-JACQUES ROUSSEAU. (VOLS 13&14)
(R.A. LEIGH, ED)
    R. MERCIER, 557(RSH):OCT-DEC71-665
    J.S. SPINK, 208(FS):APR72-203
ROUSSEAU, J-J. ESSAI SUR L'ORIGINE DES
LANGUES.* (C. PORSET, ED)
    M. DUCHET, 535(RHL):JUL-AUG70-718
ROUSSEAU, J-J. OEUVRES COMPLÈTES. (VOL
15) (B. GAGNEBIN & M. RAYMOND, EDS)
    J-L. LECERCLE, 535(RHL):JAN-FEB71-104
ROUSSEAU, J-J. LES RÊVERIES DU PROMENEUR
SOLITAIRE. (R. GEEN, ED)
    A.S. DE FABRY, 399(MLJ):FEB71-125
ROUSSEAU, J-J. ROUSSEAU RELIGIOUS WRIT-
INGS. (R. GRIMSLEY, ED)
    J.H. BROOME, 208(FS):JUL72-336
    D. CAMERON, 154:SEP71-598
    P. FRANCE, 402(MLR):JAN72-188
    A.C. KEYS, 67:MAY72-99
ROUSSEAU, J-J. THE SOCIAL CONTRACT AND
DISCOURSES. (G.D.H. COLE, TRANS; REV
& AUGMENTED BY J.H. BRUMFITT & J.C.
HALL)
    617(TLS):22JUN73-724
ROUSSEAU, M.F. - SEE "THE APPLE OR ARIS-
TOTLE'S DEATH"
ROUSSEL, D. LES SICILIENS ENTRE LES
ROMAINS ET LES CARTHAGINOIS À L'ÉPOQUE
DE LA PREMIÈRE GUERRE PUNIQUE.
    J-C. DUMONT, 555:VOL45FASC2-380
ROUSSEL, R. THE METAPHYSICS OF DARKNESS.
    617(TLS):15JUN73-664
ROUSSET, J. L'INTÉRIEUR ET L'EXTÉRIEUR.*
    J-L. BACKÈS, 98:JAN70-32
    M. FUMAROLI, 535(RHL):JAN-FEB71-87
ROUSSET, J. LA LITTÉRATURE DE L'ÂGE
BAROQUE EN FRANCE. FORME ET SIGNIFI-
CATION. LES CHEMINS ACTUELS DE LA
CRITIQUE.
    J-L. BACKÈS, 98:JAN70-32
ROUSSET, J. NARCISSE ROMANCIER.
    617(TLS):12OCT73-1243
ROUSSOS, E.N. HERAKLIT-BIBLIOGRAPHIE.
    F. LASSERRE, 182:VOL24#23/24-880
ROUT, L.B., JR. POLITICS OF THE CHACO
PEACE CONFERENCE, 1935-1939.
    P.H. KELSO, 50(ARQ):WINTER71-371
ROUTH, F. CONTEMPORARY BRITISH MUSIC.
    A.W., 410(M&L):OCT72-449
ROUTH, F. EARLY ENGLISH ORGAN MUSIC
FROM THE MIDDLE AGES TO 1837.
    617(TLS):30MAR73-345
ROUTILA, L. DIE ARISTOTELISCHE IDEE DER
ERSTEN PHILOSOPHIE.
    E. KÖNIG, 53(AGP):BAND53HEFT3-300
DE ROUX, D. MAISON JAUNE.
    B.L. KNAPP, 207(FR):DEC70-422
ROVIGHI, S.V. INTRODUZIONE ALLO STUDIO
DI KANT.
    K. OEDINGEN, 342:BAND61HEFT3-420
ROVIGHI, S.V. - SEE D'AOSTA, A.
ROWBOTHAM, D. THE MAKERS OF THE ARK.
    K.L. GOODWIN, 381:SEP71-373

ROWBOTHAM, S. HIDDEN FROM HISTORY.
    617(TLS):30NOV73-1473
ROWBOTHAM, S. WOMEN, RESISTANCE AND
REVOLUTION.
    F. HOWE, 31(ASCH):AUTUMN73-676
    617(TLS):23MAR73-321
ROWE, W.L. RELIGIOUS SYMBOLS AND GOD.*
    I. RAMSEY, 479(PHQ):APR71-188
    T. REGAN, 321:WINTER71-318
ROWE, W.W. NABOKOV'S DECEPTIVE WORLD.*
    A. FIELD, 659:WINTER73-132
    J.D. O'HARA, 651(WHR):SPRING72-171
    D. STUART, 401(MLQ):SEP72-347
ROWELL, G., ED. LATE VICTORIAN PLAYS,
1890-1914.*
    P.D. HERRING, 405(MP):AUG70-83
ROWELL, G., ED. THE LYONS MAIL.
    A. RENDLE, 157:SUMMER70-75
ROWEN, H.H., ED. THE LOW COUNTRIES IN
EARLY MODERN TIMES.
    617(TLS):27JUL73-884
ROWLAND, B., ED. COMPANION TO CHAUCER
STUDIES.*
    D. MEHL, 38:BAND88HEFT4-535
ROWLAND, J. COMMUNITY DECAY.
    617(TLS):29JUN73-757
ROWLAND, J.R. SNOW AND OTHER POEMS.
    S.E. LEE, 581:DEC72-302
ROWLANDS, P. CHILDREN APART.
    617(TLS):9NOV73-1381
ROWLANDSON, T. LOYAL VOLUNTEERS OF LON-
DON AND ENVIRONS.
    617(TLS):20APR73-453
ROWLEY, D.E. IN NEED OF CARE.
    A. RENDLE, 157:SPRING70-71
ROWLEY, N., ED. ESSEX TOWNS 1540-1640.
    S. BOND, 325:OCT71-343
ROWSE, A.L. SHAKESPEARE THE MAN.
    P. ADAMS, 61:AUG73-103
    A. BROYARD, 441:3AUG73-29
    J. CAREY, 362:   Y73-589
    D.L. STEVENSON, 441:23SEP73-46
    617(TLS):27APR73-457
ROWSE, A.L. - SEE FROUDE, J.A.
ROWSE, A.L. - SEE SHAKESPEARE, W.
ROY, E.E. LES CAUSES DU DÉCLIN DE LA
PRESSE FRANCO-AMÉRICAINE.
    G.J. BRAULT, 207(FR):FEB71-632
ROY, G. CET ÉTÉ QUI CHANTAIT.
    L. SHOHET, 296:SPRING73-84
ROY, R. LE CHANT DE L'ALOUETTE.
    M. KARPELES, 203:SUMMER70-154
ROYCE, J. THE BASIC WRITINGS OF JOSIAH
ROYCE.* (J.J. MC DERMOTT, ED)
    P. FUSS, 319:APR73-283
    R. IMBELLI, 258:JUN70-326
ROYCE, J. THE LETTERS OF JOSIAH ROYCE.*
(J. CLENDENNING, ED)
    H.M. KALLEN, 484(PPR):MAR71-454
    B. KUKLICK, 321:SUMMER71-229
    185:JAN72-179
ROYCE, K. THE MASTERPIECE AFFAIR.
    N. CALLENDAR, 441:16SEP73-31
ROYCE, K. SPIDER UNDERGROUND.
    617(TLS):26OCT73-1324
ROYKO, M. BOSS.
    639(VQR):SUMMER71-CXXXI
ROZANOV, V.V. IZBRANNOE.
    L.J. SHEIN, 550(RUSR):OCT71-415
ROZENTAL, A.A. FINANCE AND DEVELOPMENT
IN THAILAND.
    E.B. AYAL, 293(JAST):FEB71-504
RÓŻEWICZ, T. FACES OF ANXIETY.*
    M. CZAJKOWSKA, 497(POLR):SUMMER70-78
    L. SHAYKIN, 114(CHIR):WINTER72-114
RUANO, A. LÓGICA Y MÍSTICA.
    H. HATZFELD, 551(RENQ):AUTUMN71-406
    E. SARMIENTO, 86(BHS):JAN72-69

RUARK, G. A PROGRAM FOR SURVIVAL.
   A. BARSON, 398:VOL3#6-280
   F.D. REEVE, 491:MAR73-348
   639(VQR):AUTUMN71-CLXIV
RUBENS, B. GO TELL THE LEMMING.
   R. GARFITT, 362:15NOV72-674
   617(TLS):9NOV73-1361
RUBIA BARCIA, J. & M.A. ZEITLIN, EDS.
UNAMUNO.*
   J. MARTIN, 131(CL):WINTER72-77
RUBIN, J. NATIONAL BILINGUALISM IN PARA-
GUAY.
   D.L. OLMSTED, 353:NOV71-127
RUBIN, L.D., JR., ED. A BIBLIOGRAPHICAL
GUIDE TO THE STUDY OF SOUTHERN LITERA-
TURE.*
   J.W. LEE, 577(SHR):SUMMER71-288
RUBIN, L.D., JR. GEORGE W. CABLE.*
   R.L. HOUGH, 502(PRS):SPRING70-77
   R.M. WILLINGHAM, JR., 219(GAR):SUM-
MER71-254
RUBIN, W.S. DADA AND SURREALIST ART.*
   D. IRWIN, 39:FEB71-149
   B. REISE, 592:NOV70-214
RUBIN, W.S. MIRO IN THE COLLECTION OF
THE MUSEUM OF MODERN ART.
   J.R. MELLOW, 441:2DEC73-16
RUBINOFF, L. COLLINGWOOD AND THE REFORM
OF METAPHYSICS.
   R.E. ROBLIN, 484(PPR):JUN72-588
RUBINOFF, L. THE PORNOGRAPHY OF POWER.*
   A. VACHET, 154:DEC70-451
RUBINOFF, L. - SEE BRADLEY, F.H.
RUBINSTEIN, A. MY YOUNG YEARS.
   P. ADAMS, 61:JUL73-104
   D. HENAHAN, 441:19MAY73-41
   H. KELLER, 362:6DEC73-790
   H.C. SCHONBERG, 441:3JUN73-28
   442(NY):9JUN73-115
   617(TLS):2NOV73-1339
RUBINSTEIN, D. SCHOOL ATTENDANCE IN LON-
DON 1870-1904.
   M.B. KATZ, 637(VS):SEP70-100
RUBINSTEIN, E., ED. "PRIDE AND PREJU-
DICE."
   502(PRS):SPRING70-89
RUBINSTEIN, H. SHYLOCK'S END AND OTHER
PLAYS.
   I. BROWN, 157:AUTUMN71-85
RUBINSTEIN, H. & S. BUSH. THE PENGUIN
FREEZER COOKBOOK.
   617(TLS):19OCT73-1289
RUBINSTEIN, J. CITY POLICE.
   C. LEHMANN-HAUPT, 441:19JUN73-43
   441:26AUG73-14
RUCHAMES, L. - SEE GARRISON, W.L.
RUCK, C.A.P. ANCIENT GREEK.
   R. GLEN, 123:MAR72-97
RÜCKERT, J. BEMERKUNGEN ÜBER WEIMAR
1799. (E. HAUFE, ED)
   G. HARTUNG, 654(WB):9/1970-217
RUDD, N. - SEE HORACE AND PERSIUS
RUDÉ, G. THE HISTORY OF LONDON: HANOVER-
IAN LONDON 1714-1808.
   566:AUTUMN71-26
RUDENKO, S.I. FROZEN TOMBS OF SIBERIA.*
   E. DUNN, 550(RUSR):OCT71-407
   293(JAST):NOV70-246
RUDENSTINE, N.L. SIDNEY'S POETIC DEVEL-
OPMENT.*
   R.G. TWOMBLY, 599:SPRING71-196
RÜDIGER, H. & E. KOPPEN - SEE "KLEINES
LITERARISCHES LEXIKON"
RUDISILL, R. MIRROR IMAGE.
   C. CHIARENZA, 127:SPRING72-338
RUDNER, R. & I. SCHEFFLER, EDS. LOGIC AND
ART.
   P. JONES, 89(BJA):AUTUMN72-403

RUDNYCKYJ, J.B. MANITOBA MOSAIC OF PLACE
NAMES.
   E.C. SMITH, 424:MAR71-58
RUDOLF, J. HÄNDELRENAISSANCE. (VOL 2)
   C. TRÄGER, 654(WB):6/1971-168
RUDOLF, P.R. - SEE VON LANGENSTEIN, H.
RUDOLPH, A. - SEE "MODERN POETRY IN TRANS-
LATION" (NO. 16)
RUDOLPH, D.K. & G.A. HISTORICAL DICTION-
ARY OF VENEZUELA.
   V. DE ROZENTAL, 37:NOV-DEC71-37
RUDOLPH, H. KULTURKRITIK UND KONSERVATIVE
REVOLUTION.
   K. MENGES, 406:WINTER72-396
RUDOLPH, K., R. HELLER & E. WALTER, EDS.
FESTSCHRIFT WALTER BAETKE.
   H. UECKER, 680(ZDP):BAND89HEFT1-143
RUEFF, J. THE MONETARY SIN OF THE WEST.*
(FRENCH TITLE: LE PÉCHÉ MONÉTAIRE DE
L'OCCIDENT.)
   M. BELGION, 619(TC):VOL179#1049-51
RUEFF, J. DES SCIENCES PHYSIQUES AUX
SCIENCES MORALES, UN ESSAI DE 1922
RECONSIDÉRÉ EN 1969.
   R. BLANCHÉ, 542:JAN-MAR71-123
RUEL, M. LEOPARDS AND LEADERS.
   R. BRAIN, 69:OCT70-389
RUELLE, P. LES DITS DU CLERC DE VAUDOY.*
   M. THIRY-STASSIN, 556(RLV):1971/4-482
RUESCH, H. BACK TO THE TOP OF THE WORLD.
   P. ADAMS, 61:JUL73-103
   M. LEVIN, 441:17JUN73-28
   442(NY):10SEP73-133
RUETHER, R.R. GREGORY OF NAZIANZUS.
   R.J. MURRAY, 121(CJ):DEC71/JAN72-188
RUETHER, R.R. LIBERATION THEOLOGY.
   J.M. CAMERON, 453:31MAY73-19
RUF, G. WEGE DER SPÄTROMANTIK.
   J.L.S., 191(ELN):SEP71(SUPP)-136
RÜFNER, V. PSYCHOLOGIE.
   F.J.J. BUYTENDIJK, 182:VOL24#3-79
RUGE, F. SCAPA FLOW 1919. (A.J. WATTS,
ED)
   617(TLS):5OCT73-1195
RUGE, H. ZUR ENTSTEHUNG DER NEUGRIECH-
ISCHEN SUBSTANTIVDEKLINATION.*
   R. BROWNING, 123:MAR72-125
RUGGERI, U. FRANCESCO MONTI, BOLOGNESE
(1685-1768).
   D.C. MILLER, 56:SPRING70-74
RUGGIU, L. TEMPO, COSCIENZA E ESSERE
NELLA FILOSOFIA DI ARISTOTELE.
   V. TEJERA, 319:JAN73-111
RUHEMANN, H. THE CLEANING OF PAINTINGS.*
   T. CROMBIE, 39:JAN70-85
RÜHLE, G. - SEE FLEISSER, M.
RÜHLE, J. LITERATURE AND REVOLUTION.*
(REV)
   M. SLONIM, 550(RUSR):JAN71-71
RUIGH, R.E. THE PARLIAMENT OF 1624.*
   568(SCN):SPRING72-13
   639(VQR):AUTUMN71-CLXXVII
RUIJGH, C.J. ÉTUDES SUR LA GRAMMAIRE ET
LE VOCABULAIRE DU GREC MYCÉNIEN.*
   A. HEUBECK, 260(IF):BAND75-312
   M. LEJEUNE, 361:VOL25#1-78
RUIN, H. HÖJDER OCH STUP HOS IBSEN OCH
NÅGRA ANDRA.
   W.A. BERENDSOHN, 182:VOL24#19/20-737
RUITENBEEK, H.M., ED. FREUD AS WE KNEW
HIM.
   617(TLS):2NOV73-1352
RUIZ, J. LIBRO DE BUEN AMOR. (R.S.
WILLIS, ED & TRANS)
   617(TLS):2FEB73-128
RUIZ, J.M. - SEE UNDER MARTÍNEZ RUIZ, J.

RUIZ IRIARTE, V. EL CARRUSELL. (M.P.
HOLT, ED)
    J.E. DIAL, 238:SEP71-614
    M. MONTES HUIDOBRO, 399(MLJ):OCT71-412
RUIZ IRIARTE, V. TRES TELECOMEDIAS DE
ESPAÑA. (M.P. HOLT & G.W. WOODYARD,
EDS)
    D.R. MC KAY, 399(MLJ):DEC71-525
RŪĶE-DRAVIŅA, V., ED. DONUM BALTICUM.
    E.P. HAMP, 424:DEC71-284
RŪĶE-DRAVIŅA, V. MEHRSPRACHIGKEIT IM
VORSCHULALTER.*
    G.F. MEIER, 682(ZPSK):BAND24HEFT5-446
RUKEYSER, M. THE TRACES OF THOMAS HAR-
IOT.*
    R.W. FRENCH, 568(SCN):SPRING72-16
RUKSER, U. BIBLIOGRAFÍA DE ORTEGA.
    H.C. WOODBRIDGE, 517(PBSA):OCT-DEC72-
    447
RULAND, R., ED. TWENTIETH CENTURY INTER-
PRETATIONS OF "WALDEN."
    M. POLI, 189(EA):APR-JUN70-232
RULE, J. AGAINST THE SEASON.*
    J. MILLS, 648:OCT71-55
RULE, J.B. PRIVATE LIVES AND PUBLIC SUR-
VEILLANCE.
    617(TLS):25MAY73-574
"THE RULE OF ST. BENEDICT." (D.H. FAR-
MER, ED)
    H. GNEUSS, 38:BAND88HEFT3-368
    C.E. WRIGHT, 382(MAE):1972/2-132
RULFO, J. PEDRO PÁRAMO. (L. LEAL, ED)
    M.R. ASSARDO, 238:DEC71-986
RUMANES, G.N. THE MAN WITH THE BLACK
WORRYBEADS.
    N. CALLENDAR, 441:19AUG73-13
RUMBELOW, D. THE HOUNDSDITCH MURDERS
AND THE SIEGE OF SIDNEY STREET.
    617(TLS):5OCT73-1182
RUMBLE, T.C., ED. THE BRETON LAYS IN
MIDDLE ENGLISH.
    D. MEHL, 38:BAND88HEFT2-253
COUNT RUMFORD - SEE UNDER THOMPSON, B.
RUMPLER, H. DIE PROTOKOLLE DES ÖSTER-
REICHISCHEN MINISTERRATES, 1848-1867.
    W.A. JENKS, 32:MAR72-207
RUNCIMAN, S. THE GREAT CHURCH IN CAP-
TIVITY.*
    T.G. STAVROU, 32:JUN72-413
RUNCIMAN, S. THE LAST BYZANTINE RENAIS-
SANCE.*
    R. BROWNING, 303:VOL91-214
RUNCIMAN, W.G. A CRITIQUE OF MAX WEBER'S
PHILOSOPHY OF SOCIAL SCIENCE.*
    D.E. MILLIGAN, 518:OCT72-29
RUNCIMAN, W.G. SOCIOLOGY IN ITS PLACE.*
    J.G. MORGAN, 150(DR):SPRING71-128
RUNDELL, W., JR. IN PURSUIT OF AMERICAN
HISTORY.
    D.H. WINFREY, 14:JAN71-57
RUNEBERG, J.L. SAMLADE SKRIFTER IX.
    G.C. SCHOOLFIELD, 563(SS):SPRING72-290
RUNES, D.D. PHILOSOPHY FOR EVERYMAN.
    J.F. HARRIS, 219(GAR):SPRING70-83
RUNGE, E. REISE NACH ROSTOCK, DDR.
    617(TLS):20JUL73-836
RUNGTA, R.S. THE RISE OF BUSINESS COR-
PORATIONS IN INDIA: 1851-1900.
    I. SINGH, 293(JAST):FEB71-483
RUO-WANG, B. & R. CHELMINSKI - SEE UNDER
BAO RUO-WANG & R. CHELMINSKI
RUPP, H., ED. WOLFRAM VON ESCHENBACH.
    G. MEISSBURGER, 657(WW):MAY/JUN70-206
RUPP, H. - SEE KOSCH, W.
RUPP, H. & E. STUDER - SEE RANKE, F.
RUSH, J. THE INGENIOUS BEILBYS.
    617(TLS):31AUG73-998

RUSKIN, J. THE BRANTWOOD DIARY OF JOHN
RUSKIN.* (H.G. VILJOEN, ED)
    J.S.D., 135:JUL71-226
    P. FONTANEY, 189(EA):JUL-SEP71-343
    G.P. LANDOW, 301(JEGP):APR72-277
RUSKIN, J. THE WINNINGTON LETTERS.*
(V.A. BURD, ED)
    J.S.D., 135:APR70-276
    P. FONTANEY, 189(EA):JUL-SEP71-342
    R. LAWRENCE, 175:SPRING71-28
    M. LUTYENS, 39:MAR70-249
    R. TRICKETT, 637(VS):DEC70-201
RUSS, C., ED. DER SCHRIFTSTELLER SIEG-
FRIED LENZ.
    617(TLS):14DEC73-1547
RUSS, C.A.H. - SEE LENZ, S.
RUSSELL, B. THE AUTOBIOGRAPHY OF BER-
TRAND RUSSELL, 1872-1914.* THE AUTOBI-
OGRAPHY OF BERTRAND RUSSELL, 1914-1944.*
(FRENCH TITLE: AUTOBIOGRAPHIE. [VOLS
1&2])
    E. DELAVENAY, 189(EA):JAN-MAR70-98
    Y. LAMONDE, 154:JUN70-101
RUSSELL, B. CALKED BOOTS AND OTHER
NORTHWEST WRITINGS.
    B. MELDRUM, 649(WAL):WINTER71-317
RUSSELL, B. ESSAYS IN ANALYSIS. (D.
LACKEY, ED)
    617(TLS):7DEC73-1498
RUSSELL, C., ED. THE ORIGINS OF THE
ENGLISH CIVIL WAR.
    617(TLS):10AUG73-927
"CARL PARCHER RUSSELL: AN INDEXED REGIS-
TER OF HIS SCHOLARLY AND PROFESSIONAL
PAPERS, 1920-1967."
    J.P. BUTLER, 14:APR71-200
RUSSELL, D.A. PLUTARCH.
    617(TLS):30MAR73-356
RUSSELL, J. ANTHONY POWELL.
    A. MIZENER, 454:FALL71-79
    R.K. MORRIS, 141:FALL71-415
    P. WOLFE, 594:SPRING71-126
RUSSELL, J. THE GOLDEN CHAIN.
    A. OBERG, 598(SOR):WINTER73-243
RUSSELL, R. BIRD LIVES!
    S. BROWN, 362:16AUG73-222
    R. LOCKE, 441:1MAY73-37
    I. REED, 441:25MAR73-4
    617(TLS):28DEC73-1593
RUSSELL, R. THE ISLAND.
    P. THEROUX, 441:14OCT73-38
RUSSELL, R. & K. ISLAM, EDS & TRANS.
GHALIB: 1797-1869. (VOL 1)
    Z. GHOSE, 249(HUDR):SUMMER72-309
    G.C. NARANG, 293(JAST):MAY71-714
RUSSELL, T. BLACKS, WHITES AND BLUES.*
    R.D. ABRAHAMS, 650(WF):APR71-150
    N.V. ROSENBERG, 650(WF):APR71-147
RUSSELL-COBB, T. PAYING THE PIPER.
    412:FEB72-67
RUSSETT, B.M. NO CLEAR AND PRESENT DAN-
GER.
    P.F. BOLLER, JR., 584(SWR):AUTUMN72-V
"A RUSSIAN-CHINESE-ENGLISH GLOSSARY OF
EDUCATION." (C.T. HU & B. BEACH, TRANS)
    A. LEONG, 32:JUN72-450
RUSSIER, G. THE AFFAIR OF GABRIELLE
RUSSIER.
    M. MEWSHAW, 362:4JAN73-24
    617(TLS):19JAN73-58
"RUSSKAJA LITERATURA NA RUBEŽE DVUCH
EPOCH, XVII - NAČALO XVIII VEKA."
    D. TSCHIŽEWSKIJ, 72:BAND209HEFT1/3-
    228
RUSSO, V. ESPERIENZE E/DI LETTURE DAN-
TESCHE (TRA IL 1966 E IL 1970).
    M.M., 228(GSLI):VOL148FASC464-625

RUSSU, I.I. ELEMENTE AUTOHTONE ÎN LIMBA
ROMÂNA.
  E.M. WALLNER, 182:VOL24#1/2-16
RUSTERHOLZ, P. THEATRUM VITAE HUMANAE.*
  F.L. BORCHARDT, 221(GQ):MAY71-415
  P. SKRINE, 402(MLR):JAN72-210
RUTBERG, S. TEN CENTS ON THE DOLLAR.
  L. WILLIAMS, 441:1JUL73-17
RUTENBERG, M.E. EDWARD ALBEE.
  W. WILLEFORD, 397(MD):FEB71-450
RUTGERS, A. & K.A. NORRIS, EDS. ENCYCLO-
PAEDIA OF AVICULTURE. (VOL 2)
  617(TLS):8JUN73-653
RUTHERFORD, A., ED. TWENTIETH CENTURY
INTERPRETATIONS OF "A PASSAGE TO INDIA."
  K. MC SWEENEY, 529(QQ):SUMMER71-337
RUTHERFORD, A. & D. HANNAH, EDS. COMMON-
WEALTH SHORT STORIES.
  H.W. RHODES, 368:SEP71-307
RUTHERFORD, J. MEXICAN SOCIETY DURING
THE REVOLUTION.*
  M. GONZALEZ, 111:5MAY72-128
RUTHERFORD, W. THE UNTIMELY SILENCE.
  617(TLS):18MAY73-547
RUTHVEN, K.K. THE CONCEIT.
  205(FMLS):OCT70-420
RUTHVEN, K.K. A GUIDE TO EZRA POUND'S
"PERSONAE" (1926).*
  M.E. BROWN, 290(JAAC):SPRING71-412
  T.R. WHITAKER, 405(MP):AUG71-91
RUTISHAUSER, B. MAX SCHELERS PHÄNOMENO-
LOGIE DES FÜHLENS.
  F. KERSTEN, 484(PPR):MAR71-456
RUTLAND, H. TRINITY COLLEGE OF MUSIC.
  K. SPENCE, 415:AUG72-777
RUTLAND, R.A. THE NEWSMONGERS.
  441:2SEP73-8
RUTLAND, R.A. - SEE MASON, G.
RUTMAN, D.B. AMERICAN PURITANISM.*
  M. MC GIFFERT, 656(WMQ):APR71-327
RUTMAN, D.B., ED. THE GREAT AWAKENING:
EVENT AND EXEGISIS.
  E.S. GAUSTAD, 656(WMQ):APR71-315
RUTT, R., ED & TRANS. THE BAMBOO GROVE.
  G. LEDYARD, 352(LE&W):VOL15#2-319
RÜTTEN, R. SYMBOL UND MYTHUS IM ALT-
FRANZÖSISCHEN ROLANDSLIED.
  D. KELLY, 589:JAN72-142
  F. WHITEHEAD, 208(FS):APR72-182
RUTTKOWSKI, W.V. & R.E. BLAKE. LITERA-
TURWÖRTERBUCH/GLOSSARY OF LITERARY
TERMS/GLOSSAIRE DE TERMES LITTÉRAIRES.
  H.O. THIEME, 430(NS):JUN70-309
DE RUVO, V. IL PENSIERO FILOSOFICO DI E.
KANT, OVVERO PROBLEMI DI CRITICA KAN-
TIANA.
  E. NAMER, 542:APR-JUN70-247
RUWET, N. INTRODUCTION À LA GRAMMAIRE
GÉNÉRATIVE.*
  C. ASSELIN, 269(IJAL):JAN71-52
  W.G. KLOOSTER, 206:FEB70-148
  C. ROHRER, 490:JUL/OCT70-601
  E. ROULET, 343:BAND13HEFT1-27
RUWET, N. LANGAGE, MUSIQUE, POÉSIE.
  617(TLS):16FEB73-175
RYAN, A. THE PHILOSOPHY OF JOHN STUART
MILL.*
  J.O. URMSON, 479(PHQ):OCT71-373
RYAN, J., ED. A BASH IN THE TUNNEL.
  K. SULLIVAN, 159(DM):SPRING71-118
RYAN, M.G. - SEE FUTABATEI SHIMEI
RYAN, R. LEDGES.
  R.S., 376:OCT70-91
RYBALKA, M. BORIS VIAN.
  S.M. BELL, 208(FS):JUL72-361
  B.A. LENSKI, 207(FR):DEC70-442
  M. PICARD, 535(RHL):JAN-FEB71-138

RYBOT, D. IT BEGAN BEFORE NOAH.
  617(TLS):20APR73-453
RYCHLAK, J.F. A PHILOSOPHY OF SCIENCE
FOR PERSONALITY THEORY.
  R. ARDILA, 486:JUN70-315
RYCHNER, J. FORMES ET STRUCTURES DE LA
PROSE FRANÇAISE MÉDIÉVALE: L'ARTICULA-
TION DES PHRASES NARRATIVES DANS LA
"MORT ARTU."* [SHOWN IN PREV UNDER
SUB-TITLE]
  B. FOSTER, 208(FS):OCT72-493
RYCK, F. GREEN LIGHT, RED CATCH.
  N. CALLENDAR, 441:25FEB73-50
RYDBECK, L. FACHPROSA, VERMEINTLICHE
VOLKSSPRACHE UND NEUES TESTAMENT.*
  H. CHADWICK, 123:MAR72-125
RYDÉN, L. BEMERKUNGEN ZUM LEBEN DES
HEILIGEN NARREN SYMEON VON LEONTIOS
VON NEAPOLIS.
  R. BROWNING, 123:DEC72-416
RYDER, A.F.C. BENIN AND THE EUROPEANS,
1485-1897.
  J. VANSINA, 69:OCT70-384
RYDER, A.J. TWENTIETH-CENTURY GERMANY.
  442(NY):17SEP73-154
  617(TLS):22JUN73-714
RYDER, F.G., ED. DIE NOVELLE.
  L.E. BRISTER, 406:FALL72-294
RYDER, J. TREVAYNE.
  N. CALLENDAR, 441:28JAN73-20
RYDJORD, J. INDIAN PLACE NAMES.*
  J.B. MC MILLAN, 650(WF):APR70-137
RYGA, G. CAPTIVES OF THE FACELESS DRUM-
MER.
  N. CARSON, 102(CANL):SPRING72-92
RYKEN, L. THE APOCALYPTIC VISION IN
"PARADISE LOST."*
  A.W. FIELDS, 577(SHR):SPRING71-202
  M. FIXLER, 405(MP):NOV71-163
  C. HUCKABAY, 219(GAR):FALL71-378
  M. HUGHES, 549(RLC):APR-JUN71-270
RYKWERT, J. ON ADAM'S DREAM HOUSE IN
PARADISE.
  E.H. GOMBRICH, 453:29NOV73-35
RYLE, G. COLLECTED PAPERS BY GILBERT
RYLE.
  A.R. WHITE, 518:JAN72-29
RYPKA, J. & OTHERS. HISTORY OF IRANIAN
LITERATURE.* (REV)
  R.C. CLARK, 544:SPRING71-182
RYSKAMP, C. WILLIAM BLAKE ENGRAVER.
  G.E. BENTLEY, JR., 627(UTQ):FALL70-86
RYTKÖNEN, S. BARTHOLD GEORG NIEBUHR ALS
POLITIKER UND HISTORIKER.
  H.F. YOUNG, 182:VOL24#11/12-506

SAAKE, H. ZUR KUNST SAPPHOS.
  F. LASSERRE, 182:VOL24#21/22-811
SAALMAN, H. THE BIGALLO.
  A. BLUNT, 90:JUL71-410
  M. TRACHTENBERG, 54:DEC71-521
SAAM, J. DAS BASSETTHORN, SEINE ERFIN-
DUNG UND WEITERBILDUNG.
  N. SHACKLETON, 415:APR72-365
SAAME, O. - SEE LEIBNIZ, G.W.
"EERO SAARINEN ON HIS WORK." (REV) (A.
SAARINEN, ED)
  G. HILDEBRAND, 576:MAY70-206
SAAVEDRA, M.D. - SEE UNDER DE CERVANTES
SAAVEDRA, M.
VON SAAZ, J. DER ACKERMANN AUS BÖHMEN.
(VOL 1) (G. JUNGBLUTH, ED)
  J.L. FLOOD, 220(GL&L):APR72-305
  A. HRUBÝ, 301(JEGP):JAN72-59
SABAIS, H.W. GENERATION.
  J. TIPTON, 661:SPRING71-64

315

SABALIŪNAS, L. LITHUANIA IN CRISIS.
   A. EZERGAILIS, 32:SEP72-711
SABATIER, R. LES CHÂTEAUX DES MILLIONS
  D'ANNÉES.
   G. BRÉE, 207(FR):DEC70-404
SABATINI, R. CAPTAIN BLOOD. SCARAMOUCHE.
   617(TLS):22JUN73-725
SÁBATO, E. ITINERARIO.
   C. GIACONI, 37:SEP71-40
SABBEN-CLARE, J. CAESAR AND ROMAN POLI-
  TICS 60-50 B.C.
   E.G. HUZAR, 124:MAR72-239
SABINES, J. MALTIEMPO.
   617(TLS):18MAY73-548
SABIR, M. TÜRKCE-URDUCA LUGAT.
   468:VOL22#2-163
SACCHETTI, R. ENTUSIASMI. (C. COLICCHI,
  ED)
   M.P., 228(GSLI):VOL147FASC460-635
SACCIO, P. THE COURT COMEDIES OF JOHN
  LYLY.*
   I. BROWN, 157:SUMMER70-70
   G.K. HUNTER, 141:WINTER71-110
   M. MINCOFF, 447(N&Q):DEC71-469
SACHAR, H.M. EUROPE LEAVES THE MIDDLE
  EAST, 1936-1954.
   P. GROSE, 441:21JAN73-4
VON SACHER-MASOCH, L. CONTES ET ROMANS.
  (G-P. VILLA, ED)
   C. RABANT, 98:FEB70-142
DE SACHER-MASOCH, W. CONFESSION DE MA
  VIE.
   C. RABANT, 98:FEB70-142
SACHS, A. JUSTICE IN SOUTH AFRICA.
   J. BIDDULPH, 362:23AUG73-254
   617(TLS):7SEP73-1015
SACHS, A. PASSIONATE INTELLIGENCE.
   J.T. BOULTON, 179(ES):JUN71-274
SACHS, B. MIST OF MEMORY.
   617(TLS):16MAR73-286
SACHS, M. THE SEARCH FOR A THEORY OF
  MATTER.
   M. MC VAUGH, 385(MQR):SUMMER73-294
SACHSE, W.L., COMP. RESTORATION ENGLAND
  1660-1689.
   568(SCN):SPRING72-19
SACKS, O. AWAKENINGS.
   R. GREGORY, 362:28JUN73-869
   617(TLS):14DEC73-1535
SACKTON, A.H. RHETORIC AS A DRAMATIC
  LANGUAGE IN BEN JONSON.
   E. LEHMANN, 38:BAND89HEFT3-391
SADA, L., C. SCORCIA & V. VALENTE. BARI
  MITO.
   S.F. SANDERSON, 203:SUMMER71-167
   R. WIS, 439(NM):1970/4-718
SADDHĀTISSA, H. BUDDHIST ETHICS.
   639(VQR):SUMMER71-CXXXVI
SADDLEMYER, A. - SEE SYNGE, J.M.
MARQUIS DE SADE. LES INFORTUNES DE LA
  VERTU.* (J-M. GOULEMOT, ED)
   205(FMLS):OCT70-423
"LE MARQUIS DE SADE; ACTES DU COLLOQUE
  D'AIX-EN-PROVENCE DES 19 ET 20 FÉVRIER
  1966."
   M. TOURNÉ, 535(RHL):SEP-DEC70-1074
SADIE, S. MOZART.
   M. PETERSON, 470:MAY71-35
SADKA, E. THE PROTECTED MALAY STATES:
  1874-1895.
   W.R. ROFF, 293(JAST):NOV70-237
SADLER, M. CIRCLE OF FIRE.
   N. CALLENDAR, 441:27MAY73-19
SADLER, W.A., JR. EXISTENCE AND LOVE.
   B.S. LLAMZON, 613:AUTUMN70-463
DE SÁENZ, P.G.S. - SEE UNDER SUELTO DE
  SÁENZ, P.G.

SAFDIE, M. BEYOND HABITAT. (J. KETTLE,
  ED)
   R. BANHAM, 44:JUL/AUG71-10
   L. LERNER, 505:MAR71-120
   R.E. WHEELER, 58:APR71-16
   F. WILSON, 505:MAR71-120
SAFIRE, W. THE NEW LANGUAGE OF POLITICS.
  (REV)
   M. PEI, 396(MODA):SUMMER72-334
SAGAN, C. & T. PAGE, EDS. UFO'S - A
  SCIENTIFIC DEBATE.
   617(TLS):15JUN73-658
SAGARRA, E. TRADITION AND REVOLUTION.
   676(YR):SUMMER72-X
SAGE, B.L. ALASKA AND ITS WILDLIFE.
   617(TLS):20JUL73-837
SAGNES, G. L'ENNUI DANS LA LITTÉRATURE
  FRANÇAISE DE FLAUBERT À LAFORGUE (1848-
  1884).
   E. CARASSUS, 535(RHL):JUL-AUG70-731
   P. MOREAU, 557(RSH):JUL-SEP70-491
SAHER, P.J. HAPPINESS AND IMMORTALITY.
   A. BLOOM, 485(PE&W):JUL71-346
SAHLINS, M. STONE AGE ECONOMICS.
   617(TLS):19JAN73-67
SA'ID, M.F. LEXICAL INNOVATION THROUGH
  BORROWING IN MODERN STANDARD ARABIC.*
   F.J. CADORA, 318(JAOS):APR-JUN71-343
SAINE, T.P. DIE ÄSTHETISCHE THEODIZEE.
   M.K. TORBRUEGGE, 406:WINTER72-407
ST. JOHN, D. THE COVEN.*
   G. VIDAL, 453:13DEC73-6
ST. JOHN, J. TO THE WAR WITH WAUGH.
   C. SYKES, 362:21JUN73-839
   617(TLS):1JUN73-625
ST. JOHN, R. EBAN.
   617(TLS):13JUL73-799
DE ST. JORRE, J. THE BROTHERS' WAR.*
  (BRITISH TITLE: THE NIGERIAN CIVIL WAR.)
   H.R. LYNCH, 441:7JAN73-30
DE ST. JORRE, J. & B. SHAKESPEARE. THE
  PATRIOT GAME.
   N. CALLENDAR, 441:11NOV73-50
DE STE. CROIX, G.E.M. THE ORIGINS OF THE
  PELOPONNESIAN WAR.*
   617(TLS):18MAY73-541
SAINTE-BEUVE, C-A. LITERARY CRITICISM
  OF SAINTE-BEUVE. (E.R. MARKS, ED &
  TRANS)
   502(PRS):FALL71-281
SAINTE-BEUVE, C-A. VOLUPTÉ. (R. MOLHO,
  ED)
   T.G.S. COMBE, 208(FS):JAN72-87
   F-B. CONEM, 557(RSH):JAN-MAR70-164
SAITTA, A. SINISTRA HEGELIANA E PROBLEMA
  ITALIANO NEGLI SCRITTI DI A.L. MAZZINI.
   G.M. BRAVO, 548(RCSF):JUL-SEP70-346
SAJAVAARA, K. - SEE GROSSETESTE, R.
SAJNOVICS, J. DEMONSTRATIO.
   H.M. HOENIGSWALD, 318(JAOS):OCT-DEC71-
   564
SAJÓ, G. & E. SOLTÉSZ. CATALOGUS INCUN-
  ABULORUM QUAE IN BIBLIOTHECIS PUBLICIS
  HUNGARIAE ASSERVANTUR.*
   D.E. RHODES, 354:DEC70-357
SAKAMOTO, M. & S. UEHARA. KOKUHŌ CHŌZŌ.
   A. SOPER, 57:VOL32#1-89

SAKHAROV, A.M. OBRAZOVANIE I RAZVITIE
ROSSIISKOGO GOSUDARSTVA V XIV-XVII VV.
J. RABA, 104:WINTER72-649
SAKSENA, S.K. ESSAYS ON INDIAN PHILOSO-
PHY.
J.B.L., 543:JUN71-756
SALAMAN, E. THE GREAT CONFESSION.
P. BEER, 362:22MAR73-387
617(TLS):16MAR73-289
SALAMANCA, J.R. EMBARKATION.
M. LEVIN, 441:25NOV73-48
SALARRUÉ. O-YARKANDAL. (2ND ED)
H. LINDO, 263:JUL-SEP72-294
SALAS, F. WHAT NOW MY LOVE.
L.T. LEMON, 502(PRS):FALL71-268
SALE, K. SDS.
W.C. MC WILLIAMS, 441:6MAY73-3
H. MITGANG, 441:2JUN73-29
R. TODD, 61:JUL73-98
SALE, R. MODERN HEROISM.
F. KERMODE, 362:20SEP73-382
H. LEIBOWITZ, 441:29JUL73-6
D. WILLARD, 31(ASCH):AUTUMN73-684
617(TLS):27JUL73-848
SALGADO, M.A. EL ARTE POLIFACETICO DE
LAS "CARICATURAS LIRICAS" JUANRAMONI-
ANAS.*
A.P. DEBICKI, 238:SEP71-598
SALGARI, E. IL PRIMO CICLO DELLA JUNGLA.
(M. SPAGNOL, ED) I PIRATI DELLA MAL-
ESIA. I MISTERI DELLA JUNGLA NERA. LE
TIGRI DI MOMPRACEM. LE DUE TIGRI. IL
RE DEL MARE.
G. GENOT, 98:JUL71-635
SALINAS, J.S. - SEE UNDER SILES SALINAS,
J.
SALINAS DE MARICHAL, S. EL MUNDO POÉTICO
DE RAFAEL ALBERTI.*
L. MONGUIÓ, 405(MP):AUG71-94
SALISBURY, C.Y. CHINA DIARY.
H.L. BOORMAN, 441:22APR73-5
SALISBURY, H.E. TO PEKING - AND BEYOND.
M. BERNAL, 453:9AUG73-21
H.L. BOORMAN, 441:22APR73-5
C. LEHMANN-HAUPT, 441:15MAR73-47
617(TLS):16NOV73-1397
SALISBURY, H.E. WAR BETWEEN RUSSIA AND
CHINA.*
S-Y. DAI, 550(RUSR):JAN71-91
SALIVAROVA, Z. SUMMER IN PRAGUE.
J. HUNTER, 362:29MAR73-423
M. LEVIN, 441:4MAR73-39
G. STEINER, 442(NY):12MAY73-142
617(TLS):2FEB73-113
SALKEY, A. ANANCY'S SCORE.
617(TLS):20JUL73-825
SALKEY, A. GEORGETOWN JOURNAL.
617(TLS):16MAR73-283
SALLES, I.B.A. - SEE UNDER ALBIA SALLES,
I.B.
SALLESE, N.F. & O. FERNÁNDEZ DE LA VEGA.
AUDIO-LINGUAL SPANISH.
F.J. SHAMBERG, 399(MLJ):OCT71-413
SALLIS, J., ED. HEIDEGGER AND THE PATH
OF THINKING.
J.D.C., 543:DEC70-350
SALLUST. ROME AND JUGURTHA.* (J.R.
HAWTHORN, ED)
R. GLEN, 123:MAR72-98
SALMEN, J. IMMANUEL KANTS LEHRE UND IHRE
AUSWIRKUNGEN.
W. STEINBECK, 342:BAND62HEFT4-515
SALMEN, W. & H.E. SCHWAB, EDS. MUSIK-
GESCHICHTE SCHLESWIG-HOLSTEINS IN BIL-
DERN.
J.A.W., 410(M&L):OCT72-460
SALMON, E.T. SAMNIUM AND THE SAMNITES.*
T.R.S. BROUGHTON, 627(UTQ):FALL70-105

SALMON, J.H.M. CARDINAL DE RETZ.
D.A. WATTS, 208(FS):OCT72-453
SALMON, P.B. INTRODUCTIONS TO GERMAN
LITERATURE.* (VOL 1: LITERATURE IN
MEDIEVAL GERMANY.)
L.P. JOHNSON, 382(MAE):1972/3-253
K.J. NORTHCOTT, 402(MLR):APR72-460
SALMON, W.C., WITH R.C. JEFFREY & J.G.
GREENO. STATISTICAL EXPLANATION AND
STATISTICAL RELEVANCE.
L.J. COHEN, 518:OCT72-30
SALOVAARA, S. ON SET THEORETICAL FOUNDA-
TIONS OF SYSTEM THEORY.
L.A. ZADEH, 316:DEC70-597
SALTER, C.L. - SEE HSIEH, C-M.
SALTER, E. MEDIEVAL POETRY AND THE
FIGURAL VIEW OF REALITY.*
D. FOX, 447(N&Q):SEP71-349
SALUS, P.H., ED. ON LANGUAGE.
E.F.K. KOERNER, 361:VOL25#4-419
W.K. PERCIVAL, 215(GL):VOL10#1-51
SALUSBURY, T. MATHEMATICAL COLLECTIONS
AND TRANSLATIONS.
A.R. HALL, 78(BC):AUTUMN71-395
SALWAY, P. - SEE RICHMOND, I.
SALZINGER, H. SWINGING BENJAMIN.
617(TLS):14DEC73-1539
SALZMANN, W. MOLIÈRE UND DIE LATEINISCHE
KOMÖDIE.*
H. KÖHLER, 535(RHL):JUL-AUG70-702
SAMACHSON, D. & J. THE FIRST ARTISTS.
M. LAVANOUX, 363:FEB71-60
SAMARIN, W.J. THE GBEYA LANGUAGE.
H. JUNGRAITHMAYR, 361:VOL27#2/3-297
SAMMONS, J.L. HEINRICH HEINE.*
G.W. FIELD, 564:JUN71-156
S-S. PRAWER, 405(MP):FEB71-307
H. REISS, 220(GL&L):JAN72-178
SAMPSON, A. THE SOVEREIGN STATE OF I.T.T.
(BRITISH TITLE: SOVEREIGN STATE.)
M.J. GREEN, 441:8JUL73-1
M.C. JENSEN, 441:9JUL73-31
J. VAIZEY, 362:26JUL73-124
617(TLS):3AUG73-892
SAMPSON, G. THE CONCISE CAMBRIDGE HIS-
TORY OF ENGLISH LITERATURE. (3RD ED
REV BY R.C. CHURCHILL)
B. COTTLE, 541(RES):MAY71-174
R.D., 179(ES):FEB71-95
SAMPSON, R.V. TOLSTOY.
617(TLS):7DEC73-1503
SAMUEL, C. PROKOFIEV.*
R.M., 410(M&L):APR72-206
R. MC ALLISTER, 415:FEB72-153
SAMUEL, E. - SEE VAN DOREN, M. & M.
SAMUEL
SAMUEL, M. IN PRAISE OF YIDDISH.
M.S. CHERTOFF, 287:SEP71-31
M. HINDUS, 390:DEC71-63
SAMUEL, R., WITH H-J. MÄHL & G. SCHULZ -
SEE NOVALIS
SAMUEL, R. & R.H. THOMAS. EXPRESSIONISM
IN GERMAN LIFE, LITERATURE AND THE THE-
ATRE (1910-1924).
L. MARTIN, 406:SUMMER72-195
SAMUELS, C.T. THE AMBIGUITY OF HENRY
JAMES.*
M. BEEBE, 579(SAQ):SUMMER72-447
G. CORE, 385(MQR):WINTER73-82
L.B. LEVY, 27(AL):MAY72-328
SAMUELS, C.T. ENCOUNTERING DIRECTORS.
D. BROMWICH, 441:14JAN73-7
M. WOOD, 453:8MAR73-3
SAMUELS, C.T. JOHN UPDIKE.
R. ASSELINEAU, 189(EA):APR-JUN70-233
SANBORN, F.B. THE LIFE OF HENRY DAVID
THOREAU.
L. LANE, JR., 255(HAB):SPRING70-60

SANCHEZ, J. - SEE CORNEILLE, P.
SÁNCHEZ, L.A. VALDELOMAR O LA BELLE
ÉPOQUE.
B. DULSEY, 238:SEP71-605
SÁNCHEZ, N. 20 NUEVOS NARRADORES ARGEN-
TINOS.
J.A. HERNÁNDEZ, 263:JUL-SEP72-296
SÁNCHEZ, R.D. - SEE UNDER DÍAZ SÁNCHEZ,
R.
SANCHEZ, T. RABBIT BOSS.
P. ADAMS, 61:JUN73-123
SÁNCHEZ-CUTILLAS, C. UN MON REBEL. (C.
KEUL & I.M. MUÑOZ, TRANS)
J. GULSOY, 545(RPH):AUG71-151
SÁNCHEZ-REULET, A., ED. HOMENAJE A RUBÉN
DARÍO (1867-1967).
E.U. IRVING, 238:DEC71-973
SÁNCHEZ BARBUDO, A. ESTUDIOS SOBRE GAL-
DÓS.
M. DURÁN, 240(HR):JUL71-337
SÁNCHEZ DE BADAJOZ, D. RECOPILACIÓN EN
METRO (SEVILLA, 1554).* (F.W. DE KUR-
LAT, ED)
P. GALLAGHER, 86(BHS):APR72-183
SÁNCHEZ ESPESO, G. SÍNTOMAS DE ÉXODO.
J.W. KRONIK, 238:MAY71-397
SÁNCHEZ FERLOSIO, R. INDUSTRIAS Y AN-
DANZAS DE ALFANHUÍ.* (S. & A.H.
CLARKE, EDS)
S. BACARISSE, 205(FMLS):JAN71-52
SÁNCHEZ ROMERALO, A. EL VILLANCICO (ES-
TUDIOS SOBRE LA LÍRICA POPULAR EN LOS
SIGLOS XV Y XVI).*
E.L. RIVERS, 400(MLN):MAR71-302
SAND, G. CORRESPONDANCE. (VOL 3) (G.
LUBIN, ED)
R. MERKER, 207(FR):DEC70-451
SAND, G. CORRESPONDANCE. (VOLS 4&5)
(G. LUBIN, ED)
J. GAULMIER, 535(RHL):MAR-APR70-322
R. MERKER, 207(FR):DEC70-451
SAND, G. CORRESPONDANCE. (VOL 6) (G.
LUBIN, ED)
T.G.S. COMBE, 208(FS):JUL72-341
617(TLS):30NOV73-1478
SAND, G. CORRESPONDANCE. (VOLS 7-9)
(G. LUBIN, ED)
617(TLS):30NOV73-1478
SAND, G. MAUPRAT. (C. SICARD, ED)
T.G.S. COMBE, 208(FS):JAN72-88
SANDARS, N.K. PREHISTORIC ART IN EUROPE.
F.O. WAAGE, 54:DEC70-423
SANDBACH, F.H. - SEE MENANDER
SANDBERG, K.C. AT THE CROSSROADS OF
FAITH AND REASON.
J.M.S., 543:JUN71-757
SANDBERG-BRAUN, B. WEGE ZUM SYMBOLISMUS.*
A. BURKHARD, 400(MLN):OCT71-739
P.K. JANSEN, 405(MP):FEB72-269
SANDBY, W. THE HISTORY OF THE ROYAL
ACADEMY OF ARTS.
R. EDWARDS, 39:APR71-341
SANDER, G. AUGUST SANDER: PHOTOGRAPHER
EXTRAORDINARY.
617(TLS):31AUG73-1009
SANDER, H-D. MARXISTISCHE IDEOLOGIE UND
ALLGEMEINE KUNSTTHEORIE.
Z. TAKACS, 182:VOL24#4-132
SANDERBERG-BRAUN, B. WEGE ZUM SYMBOLIS-
MUS.
W.D. WILLIAMS, 220(GL&L):OCT71-36
SANDERLIN, D. THE MEDIAEVAL STATUTES OF
THE COLLEGE OF AUTUN AT THE UNIVERSITY
OF PARIS.
J.M. FLETCHER, 382(MAE):1972/3-288
SANDERS, C.R. - SEE CARLYLE, T. & J.W.
SANDERS, D.A. AURAL REHABILITATION.
L.L. KOPRA, 583:SUMMER72-450

SANDERS, E. THE SHARDS OF GOD.
42(AR):FALL/WINTER70/71-459
SANDERS, L. THE FIRST DEADLY SIN.
M. LEVIN, 441:14OCT73-48
H. MITGANG, 441:20OCT73-29
442(NY):22OCT73-174
SANDERS, M.K. DOROTHY THOMPSON.
M. BENDER, 441:25MAY73-39
D. TRILLING, 441:22APR73-1
SANDERS, S. D.H. LAWRENCE.
617(TLS):28DEC73-1595
SANDERS, W. JOHN DONNE'S POETRY.
P. DANE, 67:MAY72-83
W.R. DAVIS, 568(SCN):SUMMER72-33
D.L. GUSS, 551(RENQ):WINTER71-566
SANDERSON, M. THE UNIVERSITIES AND BRIT-
ISH INDUSTRY, 1850-1970.
617(TLS):13APR73-412
SANDERSON, P. ENGLISH CONSONANT CLUSTERS.
K. FAISS, 353:DEC70-96
SANDESARA, B.J. & J.P. THAKER. LEXICO-
GRAPHICAL STUDIES IN "JAINA SANSKRIT."
C. MALAMOUD, 343:BAND13HEFT1-99
SANDFORD, J. GYPSIES.
617(TLS):3AUG73-892
SANDHU, K.S. INDIANS IN MALAYA.
M. RUDNER, 318(JAOS):APR-JUN71-325
R.W. TELLANDER, 293(JAST):NOV70-232
K.N. VAID, 302:JUL71-381
SANDIROCCO, M. - SEE GENTILE, G. & D.
JAJA
SANDKÜHLER, H.J. FRIEDRICH WILHELM
JOSEPH SCHELLING.
C. CESA, 548(RCSF):OCT-DEC71-463
SANDLER, I. ABSTRACT EXPRESSIONISM.
B. REISE, 592:MAR71-137
SANDLER, I. & B. BERKSON, EDS. ALEX
KATZ.
S.L. SCHWARTZ, 58:SEP/OCT71-16
SANDON, H. ROYAL WORCESTER PORCELAIN
FROM 1862 TO THE PRESENT DAY.
617(TLS):20JUL73-828
SANDOZ, E. POLITICAL APOCALYPSE.
G.A. PANICHAS, 396(MODA):FALL72-416
V. TERRAS, 32:JUN72-507
617(TLS):2MAR73-235
SANDROW, N. SURREALISM.
617(TLS):27JUL73-884
SANDVED, A.O. STUDIES IN THE LANGUAGE
OF CAXTON'S MALORY AND THAT OF THE WIN-
CHESTER MANUSCRIPT.*
K. FAISS, 353:DEC70-103
P.H. SALUS, 179(ES):JUN71-264
E.G. WILLIAMS, 47(ARL):[N.S.]VOL1-104
SANDY, S. ROOFS.*
42(AR):FALL71-440
SANFAÇON, R. L'ARCHITECTURE FLAMBOYANTE
EN FRANCE.
H. ROSENAU, 89(BJA):SUMMER72-311
SANFORD, D. WHO PUT THE CON IN CONSUMER?
S.E. COHEN, 441:25FEB73-20
SANGERMANO, V. A DESCRIPTION OF THE BUR-
MESE EMPIRE.
D.K. WYATT, 293(JAST):NOV70-228
SANGHASENA, ED. SPHUTĀRTHĀ ŚRĪGHANĀCĀR-
ASAŊGRAHAṬĪKĀ.
C.S. GEORGE, 318(JAOS):OCT-DEC71-555
SANGUINETTI, E. MC BEE'S STATION.
639(VQR):AUTUMN71-CLXI
SAN JUAN, E., JR. JAMES JOYCE AND THE
CRAFT OF FICTION.
J.R. BAKER, 329(JJQ):SPRING73-364
SANKEY, B. A COMPANION TO WILLIAM CARLOS
WILLIAMS' "PATERSON."
B. DUFFEY, 659:SUMMER73-406
P. MARIANI, 418(MR):AUTUMN72-667
R.H. PEARCE, 27(AL):JAN73-695

SANMINIATELLI, D. DOMENICO BECCAFUMI.
K.W. FORSTER, 54:SEP71-402
SANNES, G.W. AFRICAN PRIMITIVES.
D. DUERDEN, 111:23OCT70-30
SANS, E. RICHARD WAGNER ET LA PENSÉE
SCHOPENHAUERIENNE.
L. BOUGIE, 154:DEC71-864
SANSOM, C. THE WITNESSES.
T. EAGLETON, 565:VOL12#3-68
SANSOM, K. SIR GEORGE SANSOM AND JAPAN.
617(TLS):5JAN73-16
SANSOM, R.L. THE ECONOMICS OF INSURGENCY
IN THE MEKONG DELTA OF VIETNAM.
C. WOLF, JR., 293(JAST):FEB71-508
SANSOM, W. THE MARMALADE BIRD.
V. CUNNINGHAM, 362:8NOV73-638
617(TLS):14SEP73-1045
SANSOM, W. PROUST AND HIS WORLD.
617(TLS):14SEP73-1053
SANSONE, G.E., ED. IL CARRIAGGIO DI
NÎMES.*
F. KOENIG, 545(RPH):AUG71-135
SANTANDREA, S. BRIEF GRAMMAR OUTLINES
OF THE YULU AND KARA LANGUAGES. LAN-
GUAGES OF THE BANDA AND ZANDE GROUPS.
NOTE GRAMMATICALI E LESSICALI SUL
GRUPPO FEROGE E SUL MUNDU (SUDAN).
A.N. TUCKER, 69:OCT71-350
SANTANDREA, S. LUCI E OMBRE DELL'AMMIN-
ISTRAZIONE BRITANNICA NEL BAHR EL
GHAZAL (1898-1955).
G.N. SANDERSON, 69:OCT71-341
SANTARELLI, G. I CAPPUCCINI NEL ROMANZO
MANZONIANO.
E.B., 228(GSLI):VOL148FASC462/463-466
DI SANTA ROSA, S. LETTERE DALL'ESILIO
(1821-1825). (A. OLMO, ED)
M. FUBINI, 228(GSLI):VOL147FASC458/
459-461
SANTAYANA, G. LOTZE'S SYSTEM OF PHILOSO-
PHY. (P.G. KUNTZ, ED)
H.W. SCHNEIDER, 319:JUL73-424
SANTAYANA, G. PHYSICAL ORDER AND MORAL
LIBERTY. (J. & S. LACHS, EDS)
V.M. AMES, 290(JAAC):FALL70-145
A.R. PERREIAH, 154:JUN70-113
A.J. RECK, 577(SHR):FALL71-415
DE SANTILLANA, G. & H. VON DECHEND. HAM-
LET'S MILL.*
G.K. GRESSETH, 292(JAF):APR-JUN71-246
SANTINELLO, G. STUDI SULL'UMANESIMO
EUROPEO.
T.G. BERGIN, 551(RENQ):SUMMER71-232
SANTINI, P. TERMINOLOGIA RETORICA E
CRITICA DEL "DIALOGUS DE ORATORIBUS."
J-M. ANDRÉ, 555:VOL45FASC1-176
SANTINI, P.C. MODERN LANDSCAPE PAINTING.
617(TLS):20APR73-438
SANTONI, R.E., ED. RELIGIOUS LANGUAGE
AND THE PROBLEM OF RELIGIOUS KNOWLEDGE.
W. HOROSZ, 484(PPR):DEC71-275
SANTOS, L.M. - SEE UNDER MARTÍN SANTOS, L.
DOS SANTOS SIMÕES, J.M. AZULEJARIA EM
PORTUGAL NOS SÉCULOS XV E XVI.
T. CROMBIE, 39:MAR71-230
R.C. SMITH, 90:JUL71-415
SANTUCCI, L. DAS KIND, SEIN MYTHOS UND
SEIN MÄRCHEN.
H. LIXFELD, 196:BAND11HEFT1/2-193
SANTUCCI, L. WRESTLING WITH CHRIST.
617(TLS):16MAR73-299
SANZ OLLER, J. ENTRE EL FRAUDE Y LA
ESPERANZA.
617(TLS):15JUN73-696
SAPIO, V.A. PENNSYLVANIA & THE WAR OF
1812.
H.M. TINKCOM, 656(WMQ):JAN71-143

SAPIR, B., ED. "VPERED!" 1873-1877.
P. POMPER, 32:MAR72-157
SAPIR, E. & H. HOIJER. THE PHONOLOGY
AND MORPHOLOGY OF THE NAVAHO LANGUAGE.
M.E. KRAUSS, 269(IJAL):JUL70-220
SAPORTA, S. & H. CONTRERAS. A PHONOLOGI-
CAL GRAMMAR OF SPANISH.
O.T. MYERS, 545(RPH):MAY72-412
SAPPLER, P., ED. DAS KÖNIGSTEINER LIEDER-
BUCH: MS. GERM. QU. 719 BERLIN.
R. HARVEY, 382(MAE):1972/3-261
E. SIMON, 589:APR72-340
SARAN, R. POLICY-MAKING IN SECONDARY
EDUCATION.
617(TLS):14DEC73-1549
DE SARDAN, J-P.O. - SEE UNDER OLIVIER DE
SARDAN, J-P.
SAREIL, J., ED. EXPLICATION DE TEXTE.
(2ND ED)
M-C. WRAGE, 207(FR):MAY71-1140
SAREIL, J. LES TENCIN.*
J. LOUGH, 208(FS):APR72-199
SAREIL, J. & J. ROMANCIERS DU VINGTIÈME
SIÈCLE.
R.L. ADMUSSEN, 207(FR):MAY71-1136
R. ROZA, 399(MLJ):FEB71-111
SARGANT, W. THE MIND POSSESSED.
617(TLS):23NOV73-1419
SARGEANT, W. DIVAS.
D. HENAHAN, 441:18MAR73-6
SARGENT, A.W. VOICES, PIPES AND PEDALS.
A. BOND, 415:APR72-367
SARGENT, E.O. - SEE PRENTICE, T.M.
SARIOLA, M. THE TORVICK AFFAIR.
N. CALLENDAR, 441:18MAR73-41
SARKANY, S. PAUL MORAND ET LE COSMOPO-
LITISME LITTÉRAIRE, SUIVI DE TROIS
ENTRETIENS INÉDITS AVEC L'ECRIVAIN.
M. PICARD, 535(RHL):JAN-FEB71-133
SARMA, E.R.S. - SEE UNDER SREEKRISHNA
SARMA, E.R.S.
SARMA, M.V.R. THE HEROIC ARGUMENT.
W.B. HUNTER, 568(SCN):SPRING72-7
SARMIENTO, D.F. - SEE UNDER FAUSTINO
SARMIENTO, D.
SARMIENTO, E. CONCORDANCIAS DE LA OBRAS
POÉTICAS EN CASTELLANO DE GARCILASO DE
LA VEGA.*
J.G. FUCILLA, 551(RENQ):SUMMER71-260
R.O. JONES, 86(BHS):APR72-185
H. SIEBER, 400(MLN):MAR71-297
SAROCCHI, J. JULIEN BENDA, PORTRAIT D'UN
INTELLECTUEL.*
R.J. NIESS, 207(FR):OCT70-225
SÁROSI, B. CIGÁNYZENE.
L. VINCZE, 187:JAN73-138
SAROYAN, W. I USED TO BELIEVE I HAD FOR-
EVER, NOW I'M NOT SO SURE. DAYS OF
LIFE AND DEATH AND ESCAPE TO THE MOON.
K.P. SHOREY, 396(MODA):SPRING72-218
SAROYAN, W. PLACES WHERE I'VE DONE TIME.*
617(TLS):22JUN73-717
SARPI, P. SCRITTI SCELTI. (G. DA POZZO,
ED) OPERE. (G. & L. COZZI, EDS)
M. POZZI, 228(GSLI):VOL148FASC462/
463-384
SARRAUTE, N. DO YOU HEAR THEM?
P. ADAMS, 61:MAR73-107
N. BLIVEN, 442(NY):17MAR73-128
R.Z. TEMPLE, 441:4FEB73-5
J. WEIGHTMAN, 453:19APR73-30
SARRAUTE, N. "ISMA" SUIVI DE "LE SILENCE"
ET "LE MENSONGE."
C. LAUCKNER, 207(FR):MAR71-785
SARRIS, A. THE PRIMAL SCREEN.
D. BROMWICH, 441:20MAY73-5
SARTON, M. AS WE ARE NOW.
E. DOUGLAS, 441:4NOV73-77

SARTON, M.  A GRAIN OF MUSTARD SEED.*
    F.D. REEVE, 491:MAR73-348
SARTON, M.  JOURNAL OF A SOLITUDE.
    P. MERAS, 441:13MAY73-14
SARTON, M.  KINDS OF LOVE.
    J.L. HALIO, 598(SOR):SPRING73-455
SARTRE, J-P.  L'IDIOT DE LA FAMILLE.*
    (VOLS 1&2)
    C. MOUCHARD, 98:DEC71-1029
    J. WEIGHTMAN, 111:19NOV71-49
SARTRE, J-P.  POLITICS AND LITERATURE.
    617(TLS):4MAY73-502
SASS, E.K.  THORVALDSENS PORTRAETBUSTER.
    F. LIGHT, 54:SEP70-334
SASSE, K.  LA DÉCOUVERTE DE LA "COURTI-
    SANE VERTUEUSE" DANS LA LITTÉRATURE
    FRANÇAISE DU DIX-HUITIÈME SIÈCLE.
    J. MAYER, 557(RSH):APR-JUN70-323
SASSEN, A.  ZEVENTIENDE-EEUWSE TEKSTEN.
    J. BARTHELS, 556(RLV):1970/6-676
SASTRE, A.  ESCUADRA HACIA LA MUERTE.*
    (A.M. PASQUARIELLO, ED)
    S.M. CYPESS, 238:SEP71-620
    R. LIMA, 238:DEC71-992
SATO, K.  THE ZEN LIFE.
    617(TLS):18MAY73-559
SATOW, E.  A DIPLOMAT IN JAPAN.
    A. CRAIG, 244(HJAS):VOL31-353
SAUERBECK, K.O.  GRAMMATIK DES FRÜHNEU-
    HOCHDEUTSCHEN: VOKALISMUS DER NEBEN-
    SILBEN.  (VOL 1)
    J.R. ASHCROFT, 402(MLR):OCT72-934
SAUERLÄNDER, W.  GOTHIC SCULPTURE IN
    FRANCE 1140-1270.
    J. CANADAY, 441:2DEC73-90
    617(TLS):13APR73-410
SAUERMANN, H., ED.  BEITRÄGE ZUR EXPERI-
    MENTELLEN WIRTSCHAFTSFORSCHUNG.  (VOL 2)
    A. HÜFNER, 182:VOL24#6-284
SAUGNIEUX, J.  UN PRÉLAT ECLAIRÉ.
    J. NADAL, 86(BHS):JAN72-83
SAUL, G.B.  QUINTET.
    J.G. RIEWALD, 179(ES):JUN71-286
SAUL, G.B.  THE WILD QUEEN.
    S. EISNER, 50(ARQ):SUMMER70-185
SAULNIER, V-L. & J-Y. POUILLOUX - SEE
    RABELAIS, F.
ŠAUMJAN, S.K.  PROBLEMS OF THEORETICAL
    PHONOLOGY.
    K. KOHLER, 297(JL):SEP70-285
SAUNDERS, A.  REGENT'S PARK.
    B. WHITAKER, 46:APR70-316
SAUNERON, S.  LE PAPYRUS MAGIQUE ILLUSTRÉ
    DE BROOKLYN.
    M. SCHATKIN, 124:NOV71-99
SAUR, K-O. & G. GRINGMUTH, EDS.  TECHNIK
    UND WIRTSCHAFT IN FREMDEN SPRACHEN.
    G.F. MEIER, 682(ZPSK):BAND24HEFT1/2-
    149
DE SAUSMAREZ, M., ED.  BEN NICHOLSON.
    R.S., 376:JUL70-119
DE SAUSSURE, F.  COURS DE LINGUISTIQUE
    GÉNÉRALE.*  (FASC 1-3)  (R. ENGLER, ED)
    R.H. ROBINS, 297(JL):SEP70-302
DE SAUSSURE, F.  COURS DE LINGUISTIQUE
    GÉNÉRALE.*  (VOL 1)  (R. ENGLER, ED)
    E.F.K. KOERNER, 350:SEP72-682
DE SAUSSURE, F.  GRUNDFRAGEN DER ALLGE-
    MEINEN SPRACHWISSENSCHAFT.  (2ND ED)
    (C. BALLY & A. SECHEHAYE, EDS)
    H. GELHAUS, 657(WW):JAN/FEB70-65
    L. SÖLL, 260(IF):BAND74-180
SAUVAGE, O. - SEE SIGÉE, L.
DE SAUZÉ, E.B., E.K. DAWSON & B.J. GIL-
    LIAM.  UN PEU DE TOUT.  (3RD ED)
    W.W. THOMAS, 399(MLJ):OCT71-417
SAVAGE, C.  ROGER MARTIN DU GARD.*
    C. SICARD, 535(RHL):JAN-FEB71-135

SAVAGE, E.  THE LAST NIGHT AT THE RITZ.
    M. LEVIN, 441:19AUG73-10
SAVAGE, G.  FRENCH DECORATIVE ART 1638-
    1793.
    G. DE BELLAIGUE, 39:MAY71-435
SAVAGE, N.D., ED.  LE FRANÇAIS ÉLÉMEN-
    TAIRE PAR LA LITTÉRATURE (CLASSIQUES
    D'AUJOURD'HUI ET D'HIER).
    D. NOAKES, 207(FR):DEC70-427
SAVAGE, T.  DADDY'S GIRL.
    639(VQR):WINTER71-IX
SAVARESE, G.  SAGGIO SUI "PARALIPOMENI"
    DI GIACOMO LEOPARDI.
    E.G. CASERTA, 275(IQ):WINTER71-130
    O. FOSSATI, 228(GSLI):VOL147FASC457-
    143
    V.S., 275(IQ):SPRING-SUMMER72-120
SAVESON, J.E.  JOSEPH CONRAD: THE MAKING
    OF A MORALIST.
    617(TLS):15JUN73-664
VON SAVIGNY, E.  DIE PHILOSOPHIE DER NOR-
    MALEN SPRACHE.
    J.E. LLEWELYN, 479(PHQ):APR71-176
SAVIGNY, W.B.  HEITERES ZUM LESEN.
    G.F. MEIER, 682(ZPSK):BAND24HEFT1/2-
    149
SAVIOZZO - SEE UNDER SERDINI, S.
SAVORY, T. - SEE UNDER "CORBIÈRE;"
    "JAMMES;" "SUPERVIELLE;" "PRÉVERT I;"
    "PRÉVERT II;" "GUILLEVIC"
SAVORY, T.H.  THE LANGUAGE OF SCIENCE.
    (REV)
    K.J. FRANKLIN, 353:MAY70-105
SAXL, F.  A HERITAGE OF IMAGES.  (H.
    HONOUR & J. FLEMING, EDS)
    J. MASHECK, 592:NOV70-219
    D. SUTTON, 39:OCT70-246
SAXL, F. & R. WITTKOWER.  BRITISH ART AND
    THE MEDITERRANEAN.*  (NEW ED)
    S.J.F., 135:JUN71-151
SAYCE, O., ED.  POETS OF THE MINNESANG.
    H. TERVOOREN, 657(WW):JAN/FEB70-68
SAYDAH, J.R.  THE ETHICAL THEORY OF CLAR-
    ENCE IRVING LEWIS.
    J.T. STEVENSON, 154:DEC70-462
SAYERS, J.E.  PAPAL JUDGES DELEGATE IN
    THE PROVINCE OF CANTERBURY 1198-1254.*
    R. HILL, 382(MAE):1972/3-283
SAYLOR, D.J.  JACKSON HOLE, WYOMING.
    T.J. LYON, 649(WAL):WINTER72-264
SAYRE, K.M.  CONSCIOUSNESS.
    W. EASTMAN, 154:DEC71-836
SAYRE, K.M.  PLATO'S ANALYTIC METHOD.*
    R.C. CROSS, 479(PHQ):JUL71-261
    L.E. ROSE, 484(PPR):DEC71-280
SAYRE, N.  SIXTIES GOING ON SEVENTIES.
    R.R. LINGEMAN, 441:21APR73-25
    R. SHERRILL, 441:4FEB73-3
    442(NY):27JAN73-95
SBORDONE, F., ED.  RICERCHE SUI PAPIRI
    ERCOLANESI.  (VOL 1)
    E.K. BORTHWICK, 123:DEC72-396
    G.M. BROWNE, 24:OCT72-635
SCALAPINO, R.A. & C-S. LEE.  COMMUNISM
    IN KOREA.
    617(TLS):13JUL73-810
SCAMOZZI, O.B. - SEE UNDER BERTOTTI SCA-
    MOZZI, O.
SCANFERLATO, A.  LEZIONI D'ITALIANO.
    (2ND ED)  (H. HINTERHÄUSER, ED)
    G. ERNST, 430(NS):SEP70-475
SCARPAT, G.  LA LETTERA 65 DI SENECA.
    (2ND ED)
    M. WINTERBOTTOM, 123:JUN72-224
DE SCAZZOCCHIO, L.S.  LENGUA Y CIVILIZA-
    CIÓN MICÉNICAS, Y EL MUNDO DE HOMERO.
    J-P. KENT, 343:BAND13HEFT1-10!
SCELLES-MILLIE, J. - SEE MEDJDOUB

"SCENERY OF GREAT BRITAIN IN AQUATINT
AND LITHOGRAPHY, 1770-1860."
617(TLS):5JAN73-20
SCHAAD, H. LE THÈME DE L'ÊTRE ET DU
PARAÎTRE DANS L'OEUVRE DE MARIVAUX.
O.A. HAAC, 207(FR):FEB71-622
SCHABRAM, H. SUPERBIA I.
C.A. LADD, 447(N&Q):MAY71-186
SCHACH, P. - SEE SVEINSSON, E.Ó.
SCHACHT, R. ALIENATION.
J. GRANGE, 484(PPR):MAR72-430
SCHADE, G. EINFÜHRUNG IN DIE SPRACHE DER
WISSENSCHAFTEN.
H. ERK, 657(WW):NOV/DEC70-425
SCHAEDER, G. - SEE BUBER, M.
SCHAEFER, H. NINETEENTH CENTURY MODERN.
E. KAUFMANN, JR., 576:MAY71-183
SCHAEFER, L.C. WOMEN AND SEX.
L. DICKSTEIN, 441:70CT73-19
F. HOWE, 31(ASCH):AUTUMN73-676
SCHAEFFER, G. LE VOYAGE EN ORIENT DE
NERVAL.
A. VIATTE, 549(RLC):JAN-MAR70-137
SCHAEFFER, S.F. FALLING.
W.C. BOOTH, 441:20MAY73-56
SCHÄFER, E. LAUDATIO ORGANI.
P. WILLIAMS, 415:NOV72-1091
SCHAFER, E.H. SHORE OF PEARLS.*
R.C. MIAO, 293(JAST):FEB71-433
W. SCHULTZ, 352(LE&W):VOL15#2-331
R.A. STEIN, 318(JAOS):OCT-DEC71-519
SCHÄFER, H.D. WILHELM LEHMANN.
U. PÖRKSEN, 680(ZDP):BAND89HEFT2-312
SCHÄFER, J. WORT UND BEGRIFF "HUMOUR"
IN DER ELISABETHANISCHEN KOMÖDIE.
E. PLATZ-WAURY, 38:BAND88HEFT2-261
SCHAFER, W.J. & J. RIEDEL. THE ART OF
RAGTIME.
617(TLS):260CT73-1323
SCHALK, D.L. ROGER MARTIN DU GARD.
A. DASPRE, 535(RHL):MAY-JUN70-535
SCHALLER, G.B. GOLDEN SHADOWS, FLYING
HOOVES.
C.P. HASKINS, 441:11NOV73-10
SCHALLER, G.B. SERENGETI.*
617(TLS):25MAY73-597
SCHALLER, G.B. THE SERENGETI LION.*
C. CONNOLLY, 453:25JAN73-19
SCHANG, F.C. VISITING CARDS OF CELEBRI-
TIES.
A. LAMB, 415:DEC72-1189
SCHANZE, H. DIE ÜBERLIEFERUNG VON WOL-
FRAMS WILLEHALM.
G. MEISSBURGER, 657(WW):MAY/JUN70-210
SCHAPERA, I. TRIBAL INNOVATORS.
A. KUPER, 69:OCT71-333
SCHÄRER, K. THÉMATIQUE DE NERVAL.
J. BELLEMIN-NOËL, 535(RHL):MAY-JUN70-
523
SCHARF, A. ART AND PHOTOGRAPHY.
C. CHIARENZA, 127:SPRING72-338
SCHARF, B. ENGINEERING AND ITS LANGUAGE.
X., 75:4/1971-49
SCHARFSCHWERDT, J. THOMAS MANN UND DER
DEUTSCHE BILDUNGSROMAN.
M. DUNSBY, 220(GL&L):OCT71-33
SCHARFSTEIN, B-A. MYSTICAL EXPERIENCE.
617(TLS):2NOV73-1349
SCHATOFF, M., COMP. HALF A CENTURY OF
RUSSIAN SERIALS: CUMULATIVE INDEX OF
SERIALS PUBLISHED OUTSIDE THE USSR.
(N.A. HALE, ED)
P. VALOIS, 575(SEER):OCT72-640
SCHATZ, W., ED. DIRECTORY OF AFRO-
AMERICAN RESOURCES.
R.L. CLARKE, 14:OCT71-385

SCHATZMAN, M. SOUL MURDER.
J.S. GORDON, 441:28JAN73-2
D.W. HARDING, 453:14JUN73-24
G. NEUBECK, 109:SPRING/SUMMER73-150
R. WOLLHEIM, 362:17MAY73-656
617(TLS):13JUL73-803
SCHAU, A. MÄRCHENFORMEN BEI EICHENDORFF.
L. RADNER, 406:FALL72-315
O. SEIDLIN, 301(JEGP):OCT72-578
SCHAUB, F. OTTO WIRZ.
P. SPYCHER, 301(JEGP):APR72-308
VON SCHAUBERT, E. SHELLEYS TRAGÖDIE THE
CENCI UND MARLOWES DOPPELDRAMA TAMBUR-
LAINE.
R. FRICKER, 38:BAND88HEFT1-148
DE SCHAUENSEE, R.M. A GUIDE TO THE BIRDS
OF SOUTH AMERICA. THE SPECIES OF BIRDS
OF SOUTH AMERICA WITH THEIR DISTRIBU-
TION. THE BIRDS OF COLOMBIA AND ADJA-
CENT AREAS OF SOUTH AND CENTRAL AMER-
ICA.
S.S. BENSON, 37:OCT71-38
SCHECHNER, R. DIONYSUS IN 69.
R.C. LAMONT, 418(MR):SUMMER72-515
SCHEDLER, K. NATUR UND GNADE.
G. PHILIPS, 182:VOL24#4-140
SCHEEL, K. KRIEG ÜBER ÄTHERWELLEN.
E. RICHTER, 654(WB):7/1971-181
SCHEFFLER, I. REASON AND TEACHING.
617(TLS):29JUN73-753
SCHEFFLER, W. THE GOLDSMITHS OF BERLIN.
G.S., 135:SEP70-62
SCHEIBE, F.K. WALTHER VON DER VOGELWEIDE,
TROUBADOUR OF THE AGES.
H.W. BRANN, 221(GQ):NOV71-595
SCHEIBE, S. - SEE VON GOETHE, J.W.
SCHEIBLER, R. THE LATE PLAYS OF EUGENE
O'NEILL.
G. KNOX, 182:VOL24#13/14-547
M. MATLAW, 397(MD):DEC71-358
SCHEINER, I. CHRISTIAN CONVERTS AND
SOCIAL PROTEST IN MEIJI JAPAN.
J.W. BENNETT, 293(JAST):NOV70-192
F.G. NOTEHELFER, 244(HJAS):VOL31-339
SCHELLING, F.W.J. BRIEFE UND DOKUMENTE.
(VOL 2) (H. FUHRMANS, ED)
617(TLS):28DEC73-1582
SCHELLING, F.W.J. INITIA PHILOSOPHIAE
UNIVERSAE. (H. FUHRMANS, ED)
C. CESA, 548(RCSF):JUL-SEP70-340
SCHELLING, U. IDENTITÄT UND WIRKLICHKEIT
BEI ROBERT MUSIL.
M. DURZAK, 190:BAND65HEFT2-211
SCHELLING-SCHÄR, E. DIE GESTALT DER
OTTILIE.*
H. REISS, 220(GL&L):JAN72-176
SCHENDEL, E. HERRSCHAFT UND UNTERWER-
FUNG CHRISTI.
F.F. BRUCE, 182:VOL24#11/12-465
SCHENKER, A.M. BEGINNING POLISH.
J.J. BRENCKLE, JR., 497(POLR):SUMMER
70-72
SCHENKER, A.M., ED. FIFTEEN MODERN POL-
ISH SHORT STORIES.*
B.W. MAZUR, 575(SEER):APR72-326
SCHENKER, W. DIE SPRACHE MAX FRISCHS IN
DER SPANNUNG ZWISCHEN MUNDART UND
SCHRIFTSPRACHE.
R.E. KELLER, 220(GL&L):APR72-294
SCHER, S.P. VERBAL MUSIC IN GERMAN
LITERATURE.*
J. FETZER, 222(GR):MAR71-129
T-M. MARSHALL, 405(MP):MAY71-408
R.P. NEWTON, 400(MLN):OCT71-723
SCHERER, A. - SEE HOFFMANN, O.
SCHÉRER, R. STRUCTURE ET FONDEMENT DE
LA COMMUNICATION HUMAINE.
R. BLANCHÉ, 542:JUL-SEP70-360

SCHERMAN, D.E., ED. THE BEST OF LIFE.
C. LEHMANN-HAUPT, 441:6DEC73-51
H. KRAMER, 441:16SEP73-23
SCHERMAN, K. TWO ISLANDS.
639(VQR):AUTUMN71-CLXXXVIII
SCHERNBERG, D. DIETRICH SCHERNBERG: EIN
SCHÖN SPIEL VON FRAU JUTTEN. (M. LEM-
MER, ED)
P.F. GANZ, 382(MAE):1972/1-81
J.S. GROSECLOSE, 406:WINTER72-379
W.F. MICHAEL, 301(JEGP):JAN72-65
SCHERPE, K.R. GATTUNGSPOETIK IM 18.
JAHRHUNDERT.*
G. OESTERLE, 490:JAN/APR70-323
SCHERPE, K.R. WERTHER UND WERTHERWIRKUNG.
L.E. KURTH, 301(JEGP):JAN72-72
M.K. TORBRUEGGE, 406:FALL72-311
SCHERRER, P. & H. WYSLING. QUELLENKRIT-
ISCHE STUDIEN ZUM WERK THOMAS MANNS.*
E.A. WIRTZ, 220(GL&L):OCT71-34
SCHEURWEGHS, G., ED. ANALYTICAL BIBLI-
OGRAPHY OF WRITINGS ON MODERN ENGLISH
MORPHOLOGY AND SYNTAX 1877-1960.*
(VOL 3)
G. GRABAND, 38:BAND89HEFT2-240
SCHEVILL, J. VIOLENCE AND GLORY.
J.H. JUSTUS, 598(SOR):WINTER73-261
SCHEYER, E. THE CIRCLE OF HENRY ADAMS.*
R. LEHAN, 445(NCF):SEP71-245
639(VQR):AUTUMN71-CLXXIII
SCHIAFFINI, A. MERCANTI, POETI, UN
MAESTRO.
D.D., 275(IQ):SPRING-SUMMER72-123
SCHIAFFINI, A. - SEE ALINEI, M.L.
SCHIAVONE, M. PROBLEMI ED ASPETTI
DELL'UMANESIMO.
E. NAMER, 542:JUL-SEP70-361
SCHIBSBYE, K. A MODERN ENGLISH GRAMMAR.
A.R. TELLIER, 189(EA):JUL-SEP71-320
SCHICK, J.M. THE BERLIN CRISIS, 1958-
1962.*
H.S. DINERSTEIN, 32:SEP72-682
SCHICK, U. ZUR ERZÄHLTECHNIK IN VOL-
TAIRES "CONTES."
J. VERCRUYSSE, 535(RHL):JUL-AUG70-717
SCHIER, R.D. DIE SPRACHE GEORG TRAKLS.*
R. FURNESS, 402(MLR):OCT72-951
SCHIFF, Z. & R. ROTHSTEIN. FEDAYEEN.*
617(TLS):23FEB73-205
SCHIFFER, R. & H.J. WEIAND, EDS. INSIGHT
III.
H. OPPEL, 430(NS):FEB71-105
SCHIFFER, S.R. MEANING.
617(TLS):31AUG73-1004
SCHILBACH, E. BYZANTINISCHE METROLOGIE.
D.M. NICOL, 123:JUN72-264
D. PINGREE, 589:APR72-344
SCHILBACH, E. BYZANTINISCHE METROLOGISCHE
QUELLEN.
D.M. NICOL, 123:JUN72-264
SCHILLEBEECKX, E., ED. DOGMA AND PLURAL-
ISM.
R. SKALITZKY, 613:WINTER70-626
SCHILLER, F. KABALE UND LIEBE.* (H.
KRAFT, ED)
H.C. SEEBA, 221(GQ):JAN71-112
SCHILLER, F. KALLIAS ODER ÜBER DIE
SCHÖNHEIT. (K.L. BERGHAHN, ED)
C.E. SCHWEITZER, 406:FALL72-312
SCHILLER, F. ON THE AESTHETIC EDUCATION
OF MAN IN A SERIES OF LETTERS. (E.
WILKINSON & L.A. WILLOUGHBY, EDS &
TRANS)
F. WIEDEN, 564:MAR70-85
SCHILLER, F. SCHILLERS WERKE. [VOLS UN-
KNOWN] (D. GERMANN & E. HAUFE, EDS)
F.W. WENTZLAFF-EGGEBERT, 680(ZDP):
BAND89HEFT2-279

SCHILLER, F. SELECTED POEMS. (F.M.
FOWLER, ED)
J. ANNABLE, 402(MLR):APR72-468
H.B. GARLAND, 220(GL&L):JAN72-182
205(FMLS):JUL70-313
SCHILLER, F. WALLENSTEIN. (S. KIRSHNER,
ED)
B. DUNCAN, 221(GQ):MAY71-430
SCHILLER, F. WILHELM TELL. (J. PRUDHOE,
TRANS)
A. RENDLE, 157:SPRING71-77
205(FMLS):JAN71-100
"FRIEDRICH SCHILLER."* (B. LECKE, ED)
F. STOCK, 52:BAND6HEFT1-106
SCHILLER, G. ICONOGRAPHY OF CHRISTIAN
ART. (VOL 2)
617(TLS):12JAN73-47
VON SCHILLER, J.C.F. WILHELM TELL.
(W.F. MAINLAND, ED & TRANS)
617(TLS):5OCT73-1185
SCHILLER, J.P. I.A. RICHARDS'S THEORY OF
LITERATURE.*
W.H. CLARK, JR., 290(JAAC):FALL70-137
G.D. KLINGOPULOS, 402(MLR):JAN72-152
SCHILPP, P.A., ED. ERNST CASSIRER.
J.F.S., 206:NOV70-598
SCHILPP, P.A., ED. THE PHILOSOPHY OF
C.I. LEWIS.
J. HULLETT, 484(PPR):SEP70-137
SCHINDLER, M.S. THE SONNETS OF ANDREAS
GRYPHIUS.
B.L. SPAHR, 401(MLQ):DEC72-453
SCHIØRRING, N., ED. FESTSKRIFT JENS
PETER LARSEN.
S. SADIE, 415:NOV72-1089
SCHIOTZ, A. & P. DAHLSTROM. COLLINS
GUIDE TO AQUARIUM FISHES AND PLANTS.
617(TLS):9FEB73-158
SCHIRMER, K-H. STIL- UND MOTIVUNTERSUCH-
UNGEN ZUR MITTELHOCHDEUTSCHEN VERS-
NOVELLE.
B. SOWINSKI, 657(WW):SEP/OCT70-353
SCHISCHKOFF, G. PETER BERON (1798-1871),
FORSCHERDRANG AUS DEM GLAUBEN AN DIE
GESCHICHTLICHE SENDUNG DER SLAWEN.
A. MERCIER, 182:VOL24#17/18-647
SCHITTER, H.G. DIE DREI LETZTEN ROMANE
F. SCOTT FITZGERALDS.*
A. HELLER, 430(NS):APR71-221
SCHLAFFER, H. MUSA IOCOSA.
N.H. SMITH, 182:VOL24#17/18-680
SCHLAFFKE, W. HEINRICH WITTENWEILERS
RING.*
G.F. JONES, 400(MLN):OCT71-731
E. MITTLER, 182:VOL24#13/14-551
SCHLANT, E. DIE PHILOSOPHIE HERMANN
BROCHS.*
J.N. HARDIN, 301(JEGP):APR72-304
SCHLAUCH, M. ENGLISH MEDIEVAL LITERATURE
AND ITS SOCIAL FOUNDATIONS.*
D. GRAY, 447(N&Q):JAN71-40
SCHLAUCH, M. LANGUAGE AND THE STUDY OF
LANGUAGES TODAY.
J. FOX, 399(MLJ):APR71-264
SCHLAWE, F. DIE BRIEFSAMMLUNGEN DES 19.
JAHRHUNDERTS.
J-U. FECHNER, 220(GL&L):OCT71-87
J.R. FREY, 149:JUN72-239
SCHLEGEL, A.W. VORLESUNGEN ÜBER DAS
AKADEMISCHE STUDIUM. (F. JOLLES, ED)
W.J. LILLYMAN, 406:SUMMER72-169
SCHLEGEL, F. DIALOGUE ON POETRY AND LIT-
ERARY APHORISMS.* (E. BEHLER & R.
STRUC, EDS & TRANS)
E. STOPP, 220(GL&L):OCT71-64

SCHLEGEL, F. KRITISCHE AUSGABE SEINER
WERKE. (VOL 2: CHARAKTERISTIKEN UND
KRITIKEN.) (H. EICHNER, ED)
J.W. DYCK, 564:MAR70-86
SCHLEGEL, F. KRITISCHE AUSGABE SEINER
WERKE. (VOL 19: PHILOSOPHISCHE LEHR-
JAHRE, 1796-1806.) (E. BEHLER, ED)
W.H.W., 319:JUL73-434
SCHLEGEL, F. FRIEDRICH SCHLEGEL'S "LUCIN-
DE" AND THE FRAGMENTS. (P. FIRCHOW,
TRANS)
J.L. GREENWAY, 406:WINTER72-382
SCHLEGEL, R. COMPLETENESS IN SCIENCE.
R.L. CAUSEY, 316:DEC70-576
SCHLEIFENBAUM, R. MEHRHEITSMACHT UND
SCHUTZ DER BETEILIGUNG IN DEN AKTIEN-
RECHTEN DER USA, INSBESONDERE BEIM
MERGERVERFAHREN.
E. STASSYNS, 182:VOL24#6-280
SCHLEINER, W. THE IMAGERY OF JOHN
DONNE'S SERMONS.*
R. BOSTON, 401(MLQ):DEC71-431
P. LEGOUIS, 189(EA):OCT-DEC71-529
P.S. MACAULAY, 179(ES):JUN71-266
W.R. MUELLER, 191(ELN):SEP71-64
S.G. PUTT, 175:AUTUMN70-102
B. VICKERS, 541(RES):AUG71-342
SCHLEPP, W. SAN-CH'Ü.
M. LOI, 549(RLC):JUL-SEP71-406
P.F-M. YANG, 293(JAST):AUG71-886
SCHLESINGER, A.M. - SEE OLMSTED, F.L.
SCHLESINGER, A.M., JR., ED. HISTORY OF
US POLITICAL PARTIES.
617(TLS):2NOV73-1332
SCHLESINGER, A.M., JR. THE IMPERIAL
PRESIDENCY.
A. KAZIN, 453:13DEC73-23
C. LEHMANN-HAUPT, 441:16NOV73-39
R.H. ROVERE, 442(NY):10DEC73-190
G. WILLS, 441:18NOV73-1
SCHLESINGER, A.M., JR. & F.L. ISRAEL,
EDS. HISTORY OF AMERICAN PRESIDENTIAL
ELECTIONS.
W.E. LAMPTON, 583:SUMMER72-444
SCHLESINGER, I.M. SENTENCE STRUCTURE AND
THE READING PROCESS.
R. WARDHAUGH, 206:AUG71-446
SCHLEUSSNER, B. DER NEOPIKARESKE ROMAN.*
H.O., 430(NS):APR70-208
U. WICKS, 454:FALL71-71
SCHLIER, H.C., ED. EASTERN EUROPE.
B. DMYTRYSHYN, 550(RUSR):JAN71-98
SCHLÖSSER, A. & A-G. KUCKHOFF, EDS.
SHAKESPEARE JAHRBUCH. (VOL 102)
V.B. HELTZEL, 570(SQ):AUTUMN70-505
SCHLUETER, P. THE NOVELS OF DORIS LES-
SING.
J. GINDIN, 659:AUTUMN73-586
SCHLÜTER, K. KURIOSE WELT IM MODERNEN
ENGLISCHEN ROMAN.*
J.M.S. TOMPKINS, 597(SN):VOL42#2-480
SCHLÜTER, K. DER MENSCH ALS SCHAUSPIELER.
(2ND ED)
K. SMIDT, 179(ES):APR71-183
SCHLÜTTER, H-J. GOETHES SONETTE.
H.R. VAGET, 222(GR):MAR71-155
SCHMALENBACH, W. KURT SCHWITTERS.*
M. HERBAN 3D, 127:WINTER71/72-228
F. WHITFORD, 592:NOV71-216
SCHMEJA, H. DER MYTHOS VON DEN ALPEN-
GERMANEN.*
H. BECK, 260(IF):BAND75-359
R. RIS, 343:BAND13HEFT2-151
SCHMIDT, A. ZETTEL'S TRAUM.
617(TLS):7DEC73-1512

SCHMIDT, A., K. SCHÜTTE & E.J. THIELE,
EDS. CONTRIBUTIONS TO MATHEMATICAL
LOGIC.
A. SKIDMORE, 486:DEC70-623
SCHMIDT, A-M. LA POÉSIE SCIENTIFIQUE EN
FRANCE AU XVIE SIÈCLE.
R. MERCIER, 557(RSH):APR-JUN70-319
SCHMIDT, D. DIE RECHTEN NEBENFLÜSSE DES
RHEINS VON DER WUPPER BIS ZUR LIPPE.
E. DICKENMANN, 260(IF):BAND74-204
SCHMIDT, F.W. "VERTELL."
A. CAMMANN, 196:BAND11HEFT1/2-194
SCHMIDT, G. KYPRISCHE BILDWERKE AUS DEM
HERAION VON SAMOS.*
K. NICOLAOU, 303:VOL91-201
SCHMIDT, H. NIKOLAUS LENAU.
H. SLESSAREV, 406:SPRING72-87
SCHMIDT, H.J. SATIRE, CARICATURE, AND
PERSPECTIVISM IN THE WORKS OF GEORG
BÜCHNER.
M.B. BENN, 402(MLR):JAN72-221
P.F. VEIT, 406:SPRING72-96
SCHMIDT, J. HÖLDERLINS ELEGIE "BROT UND
WEIN."
G.L. JONES, 220(GL&L):OCT71-86
SCHMIDT, J. HÖLDERLINS LETZTE HYMNEN.
M.B. BENN, 402(MLR):JAN72-219
F.M. WASSERMANN, 406:SUMMER72-169
SCHMIDT, J. VIE ET MORT DES ESCLAVES
DANS LA ROME ANTIQUE.
617(TLS):13JUL73-812
SCHMIDT, J.D. RAMESSES II.
617(TLS):21DEC73-1561
SCHMIDT, L. VOLKSGESANG UND VOLKSLIED.
G. RODGER, 402(MLR):OCT72-939
SCHMIDT, M. RUDOLF VON BIBERACH DIE
SIEBEN STRASSEN ZU GOT DIE HOCHALEMANN-
ISCHE ÜBERTRAGUNG NACH DER HANDSCHRIFT
EINSIEDELN 278.
A-M. SCHURR-LORUSSO, 133:1970/2&3-292
SCHMIDT, M. IT WAS MY TREE.
617(TLS):12JAN73-36
SCHMIDT, M. - SEE VON BIBERACH, R.
SCHMIDT, P. DIE WORTSCHATZ VON GOETHES
"IPHIEGENIE."
M. GRÄFE, 680(ZDP):BAND90HEFT4-594
SCHMIDT, P.L. IULIUS OBSEQUENS UND DAS
PROBLEM DER LIVIUS-EPITOME.*
A. HUS, 555:VOL45FASC1-173
SCHMIDT, R. - SEE KANT, I.
SCHMIDT, S.J. ÄSTHETIZITÄT.
H.U. GUMBRECHT, 490:OCT71-554
SCHMIDT, V. SPRACHLICHE UNTERSUCHUNGEN
ZU HERONDAS.*
B. FORSSMAN, 260(IF):BAND75-322
SCHMIDT, W., ED. GESCHICHTE DER DEUTSCHEN
SPRACHE.
R.L. KYES, 399(MLJ):OCT71-404
SCHMIDT-HENKEL, G. MYTHOS UND DICHTUNG.
G.P. KNAPP, 657(WW):JUL/AUG70-288
SCHMIDT-RADEFELT, J. PAUL VALÉRY LIN-
GUISTE DANS LES CAHIERS.
A. NICOLAS, 557(RSH):OCT-DEC71-675
SCHMIT, M. BEDLAM AND THE OAK-WOOD.
A. CLUYSENAAR, 565:VOL12#2-63
SCHMITT, A.R., ED. FESTSCHRIFT FÜR DET-
LEV W. SCHUMANN ZUM 70. GEBURTSTAG.
K. HARRIS, 400(MLN):OCT71-715
W. WITTKOWSKI, 221(GQ):NOV71-559
SCHMITT, A.R., ED. DES MELCHIOR ADAM
PASTORIUS VON 1670 BIS 1696 BÜRGERMEIS-
TERS DER REICHSSTADT WINDSHEIM LEBEN
UND REISEBESCHREIBUNGEN VON IHM SELBST
ERZÄHLT UND NEBST DESSEN LYRISCHEN GE-
DICHTEN ALS BEITRAG ZUM DEUTSCHEN
BAROCK.
H.E. HUELSBERGEN, 221(GQ):MAY71-395

SCHMITT, C.B. A CRITICAL SURVEY AND BIB-
LIOGRAPHY OF STUDIES ON RENAISSANCE
ARISTOTELIANISM 1958-69.
W. HALBFASS, 182:VOL24#21/22-769
SCHMITT, C.B. GIANFRANCESCO PICO DELLA
MIRANDOLA (1469-1533) AND HIS CRITIQUE
OF ARISTOTLE.*
G. GAWLICK, 53(AGP):BAND53HEFT3-306
E. NAMER, 542:JUL-SEP70-361
SCHMITT, G. THE GODFORGOTTEN.*
617(TLS):20APR73-451
SCHMITT, H.H. DIE STAATSVERTRÄGE DES
ALTERTUMS.* (VOL 3)
F.W. WALBANK, 303:VOL91-195
SCHMITT, L.E., ED. KURZER GRUNDRISS DER
GERMANISCHEN PHILOLOGIE BIS 1500.*
(VOLS 1&2)
T.L. MARKEY, 589:OCT72-799
W.W. SEEGER, 406:SUMMER72-187
SCHMITT, L.E., ED. SCHLESISCHER SPRACH-
ATLAS.
P. WIESINGER, 680(ZDP):BAND89HEFT3-
469
SCHMITT, L.E. UNTERSUCHUNGEN ZU ENTSTE-
HUNG UND STRUKTUR DER "NEUHOCHDEUTSCHEN
SCHRIFTSPRACHE." (VOL 1)
R. BERGMANN, 260(IF):BAND74-314
SCHMITT, L.E., ED. VERHANDLUNGEN DES
ZWEITEN INTERNATIONALEN DIALEKTOLOGEN-
KONGRESS.
J. GÖSCHEL, 260(IF):BAND74-177
SCHMITT, L.E. - SEE MITZKA, W.
SCHMITT, R. DICHTUNG UND DICHTERSPRACHE
IN INDOGERMANISCHER ZEIT.*
F. LOCHNER-HUTTENBACH, 260(IF):BAND
74-199
A. SCHERER, 343:BAND13HEFT1-41
SCHMITT, R. DIE NOMINALBILDUNG IN DEN
DICHTUNGEN DES KALLIMACHOS VON KYRENE.
D.A. CAMPBELL, 123:DEC72-407
SCHMITT-BRANDT, R. DIE ENTWICKLUNG DES
INDOGERMANISCHEN VOKALSYSTEMS.
J. SAFAREWICZ, 343:BAND13HEFT1-44
SCHMITTER, P.C. INTEREST CONFLICT AND
POLITICAL CHANGE IN BRAZIL.
T.E. SKIDMORE, 263:JUL-SEP72-302
SCHMITZ, D. WE WEEP FOR OUR STRANGENESS.
R. BROTHERSON, 661:SPRING71-69
SCHMITZ-MAYR-HARTING, E., ED. GRILLPAR-
ZER-FORUM-FORCHTENSTEIN.
P.K. WHITAKER, 133:1970/2&3-333
SCHNABEL, J.G. INSEL FELSENBURG. (W.
VOSSKAMP, ED)
J-U. FECHNER, 220(GL&L):OCT71-89
SCHNAPP, F. - SEE HOFFMANN, E.T.A.
SCHNAPPER, A. TABLEAUX POUR LE TRIANON
DE MARBRE, 1688-1714.*
C. GOLDSTEIN, 54:DEC70-453
SCHNAPPER, B. LE REMPLACEMENT MILITAIRE
EN FRANCE.
W. ARZÜ, 207(FR):MAR71-776
SCHNEEDE, U.M. MAX ERNST.
J-R. MELLOW, 441:2DEC73-16
SCHNEIDAU, H.N. EZRA POUND.*
M.E. BROWN, 290(JAAC):SPRING71-412
L. CASPER, 613:SUMMER70-301
D.V. FULLER, 50(ARQ):SPRING70-92
T.R. WHITAKER, 405(MP):AUG71-91
SCHNEIDER, B.R., JR. THE ETHOS OF RES-
TORATION COMEDY.
G. MARSHALL, 568(SCN):FALL-WINTER72-
68
566:SPRING72-95
SCHNEIDER, C. KULTURGESCHICHTE DES HEL-
LENISMUS. (VOL 2)
F.M. WASSERMANN, 121(CJ):OCT-NOV71-80

SCHNEIDER, E.W. THE DRAGON IN THE GATE.*
M. BOWEN, 405(MP):AUG71-85
W.R. MUNDT, 598(SOR):AUTUMN73-1029
SCHNEIDER, G. DER LIBERTIN.
W. KRAUSS, 72:BAND209HEFT1/3-213
SCHNEIDER, H. JAKOB VAN HODDIS.
R. MAJUT, 220(GL&L):APR72-270
SCHNEIDER, H.K. THE WAHI WANYATURU.
A. SOUTHALL, 69:OCT71-334
SCHNEIDER, K. DER "TROJANISCHE KRIEG"
IM SPÄTEN MITTELALTER.*
H. FISCHER, 680(ZDP):BAND90HEFT1-123
G.F. JONES, 133:1970/2&3-290
P.C. KERN, 657(WW):JAN/FEB71-71
SCHNEIDER, K.L. & G. BURCKHARDT - SEE
HEYM, G.
SCHNEIDER, K.R. AUTOKIND VS. MANKIND.
J. LOBELL, 505:SEP71-172
SCHNEIDER, L. & C.M. BONJEAN, EDS. THE
IDEA OF CULTURE IN THE SOCIAL SCIENCES.
617(TLS):14DEC73-1534
SCHNEIDER, M. ETÜDEN ZUM LESEN SPRACH-
LICHER FORMEN IN GOETHES WILHELM
MEISTER.
N.H. SMITH, 182:VOL24#23/24-871
SCHNEIDER, M. NEUROSE UND KLASSENKAMPF.
617(TLS):24AUG73-985
SCHNELLE, H. & OTHERS. METHODEN DER
SPRACHWISSENSCHAFT.
I. REVZIN, 353:JUN71-107
SCHNITZLER, A. FRÜHE GEDICHTE.* (H.
LEDERER, ED)
W. NEHRING, 221(GQ):NOV71-607
SCHNITZLER, A. MY YOUTH IN VIENNA.*
(GERMAN TITLE: JUGEND IN WIEN.) (T.
NICKL & H. SCHNITZLER, EDS)
F.H. HELLER, 397(MD):MAY70-101
E. PAWEL, 390:MAR71-71
SCHNITZLER, O. - SEE NEHMAD, M.
VON SCHNÜFFIS, L. MIRANTISCHES FLÖTLEIN.
A. MENHENNET, 220(GL&L):JAN72-150
SCHOELLER, B. GELÄCHTER UND SPANNUNG.
N.H. SMITH, 182:VOL24#21/22-797
SCHOEN, S., ED. SING SING.
441:27MAY73-5
SCHOENBAUM, S. SHAKESPEARE'S LIVES.*
R.A. FOAKES, 175:AUTUMN71-98
J-B. FORT, 189(EA):OCT-DEC71-521
D. HAMER, 541(RES):NOV71-482
P.A. JORGENSEN, 401(MLQ):DEC71-429
D. MEHL, 72:BAND209HEFT1/3-157
J.M. OSBORN, 481(PQ):JUL71-396
B. VICKERS, 111:220CT71-24
L.B. WRIGHT, 639(VQR):SPRING71-305
SCHOENBRUN, D., WITH R. & L. SZEKELY.
THE NEW ISRAELIS.
T. PRITTIE, 441:18MAR73-4
SCHOENER, A., ED. PORTAL TO AMERICA.
M. MUDRICK, 249(HUDR):SUMMER72-338
SCHOFIELD, M. THE SEXUAL BEHAVIOUR OF
YOUNG ADULTS.
617(TLS):21DEC73-1563
SCHOGT, H.G. LE SYSTÈME VERBAL DU FRAN-
ÇAIS CONTEMPORAIN.*
D. BOUVEROT, 209(FM):APR70-170
SCHOLBERG, H. THE DISTRICT GAZETTEERS OF
BRITISH INDIA.
N.G. BARRIER, 293(JAST):MAY71-713
SCHOLEFIELD, A. THE HAMMER OF GOD.
M. LEVIN, 441:27MAY73-18
617(TLS):30MAR73-340
SCHOLEM, G. THE MESSIANIC IDEA IN JUDA-
ISM AND OTHER ESSAYS ON JEWISH SPIRIT-
UALITY.
617(TLS):15JUN73-695

SCHOLEM, G. SABBATAI SEVI: THE MYSTICAL
MESSIAH.
G. STEINER, 442(NY):22OCT73-152
D.P. WALKER, 453:4OCT73-17
SCHOLES, P.A. THE CONCISE OXFORD DIC-
TIONARY OF MUSIC. (2ND ED)
M. PETERSON, 470:MAY71-35
SCHOLES, P.A. THE OXFORD COMPANION TO
MUSIC.* (10TH ED) (J.O. WARD, ED)
J.P., 376:JAN71-134
SCHOLES, R. THE FABULATORS.*
U. BROICH, 38:BAND88HEFT2-275
SCHOLES, R. & R. KELLOGG. THE NATURE OF
NARRATIVE.
A. RODWAY, 447(N&Q):JUL71-269
SCHOLES, R.J. PHONOTACTIC GRAMMATICAL-
ITY.*
M. LEHTINEN, 215(GL):VOL10#1-41
SCHOLZ, H. CONCISE HISTORY OF LOGIC.
G.T. KNEEBONE, 316:DEC71-676
SCHOLZ, M.G., ED. BIBLIOGRAPHIE ZU WAL-
THER VON DER VOGELWEIDE.*
O. SAYCE, 402(MLR):JAN72-205
K. SMITS, 67:MAY72-105
H.B. WILLSON, 220(GL&L):APR72-312
SCHOLZ, R. DIE ORGELWERKE VON FRANZ
SCHMIDT.
S.J., 410(M&L):APR72-200
SCHÖNAU, W. SIGMUND FREUDS PROSA.*
A. GLÜCK, 657(WW):JUL/AUG70-285
SCHONBERG, H.C. GRANDMASTERS OF CHESS.
C. LEHMANN-HAUPT, 441:24DEC73-11
SCHÖNBERGER, O. UNTERSUCHUNGEN ZUR WIE-
DERHOLUNGSTECHNIK LUCANS. (2ND ED)
O.C. PHILLIPS, JR., 122:OCT72-314
SCHÖNBERGER, O. - SEE PHILOSTRATUS
SCHÖNDORF, K.E. DIE TRADITION DER DEUT-
SCHEN PSALMENÜBERSETZUNG.
P. ASSION, 224(GRM):BAND21HEFT4-465
A. MASSER, 680(ZDP):BAND89HEFT3-458
SCHÖNERT, J. ROMAN UND SATIRE IM 18.
JAHRHUNDERT.
D. VAN ABBE, 220(GL&L):OCT71-79
SCHÖNFELDER, K-H. & K-H. WIRZBERGER.
AMERIKANISCHE LITERATUR IM ÜBERBLICK -
VOM BÜRGERKRIEG BUS ZUR GEGENWART.
M. SCHULZE, 72:BAND209HEFT4/6-431
SCHÖNHAAR, R.F. NOVELLE UND KRIMINAL-
SCHEMA.*
V. NEUHAUS, 52:BAND6HEFT3-321
SCHONHORN, M. - SEE DEFOE, D.
SCHÖNLE, G. DEUTSCH-NIEDERLÄNDISCHE BE-
ZIEHUNGEN IN DER LITERATUR DES 17.
JAHRHUNDERTS.
J. MENDELS, 400(MLN):OCT71-748
SCHOOP, H. ENTSTEHUNG UND VERWENDUNG DER
HANDSCHRIFT OXFORD, BODLEIAN LIBRARY,
CANONICI MISC. 213.
P.M.D., 410(M&L):JUL72-332
SCHOOP, W. VERGLEICHENDE UNTERSUCHUNGEN
ZUR AGRARKOLONISATION DER HOCHLANDIN-
DIANER AM ANDENABFALL UND IM TIEFLAND
OSTBOLIVIENS.
P. VOSSELER, 182:VOL24#23/24-893
SCHOPENHAUER, A. DER HANDSCHRIFTLICHE
NACHLASS. (VOL 5) (A. HÜBSCHER, ED)
H.W. BRANN, 258:DEC70-664
SCHOPF, A. UNTERSUCHUNGEN ZUR WECHSELBE-
ZIEHUNG ZWISCHEN GRAMMATIK UND LEXIK
IM ENGLISCHEN.
A.R. TELLIER, 189(EA):JUL-SEP71-318
SCHÖPFLIN, G., ED. THE SOVIET UNION AND
EASTERN EUROPE.*
H. HANAK, 575(SEER):APR72-329
SCHOPLICK, V. DER PLATONISCHE DIALOG
LYSIS.
P.M. HUBY, 123:MAR72-103

SCHOTT, H. PLAYING THE HARSICHORD.*
H.F., 410(M&L):APR72-210
P. WILLIAMS, 415:JAN72-48
SCHOTT, W. - SEE WILLIAMS, W.C.
SCHOTTEL, J.G. FRUCHTBRINGENDER LUST-
GARTE. (M. BURKHARD, ED)
B.L. SPAHR, 133:1971/1&2-197
SCHOTTELIUS, J.G. AUSFÜHRLICHE ARBEIT
VON DER TEUTSCHEN HAUBTSPRACHE 1663
I-II.* (W. HECHT, ED)
H. RÜDIGER, 52:BAND6HEFT1-77
SCHOU, S., ED. 60'ERNES DANSKE KRITIK.
H.J. CHRISTENSEN, 172(EDDA):1971/5-
316
SCHRADER, L. SINNE UND SINNESVERKNÜPFUN-
GEN.
S. ULLMANN, 208(FS):OCT72-502
L. WELCH, 290(JAAC):SUMMER71-545
SCHRAG, C.O. EXPERIENCE AND BEING.
D.H. DEGROOD, 484(PPR):JUN71-613
J.N. MOHANTY, 311(JP):8MAR73-134
SCHRAG, P. OUT OF PLACE IN AMERICA.
639(VQR):SUMMER71-CXXX
SCHRAM, R. A HISTORY OF THE NIGERIAN
HEALTH SERVICES.
617(TLS):16MAR73-305
SCHRAM, S.R., ED. AUTHORITY, PARTICIPA-
TION AND CULTURAL CHANGE IN CHINA.
617(TLS):14DEC73-1527
SCHRAMM, R. ROOTED IN SILENCE.
E. LUEDERS, 651(WHR):SUMMER72-295
R. PINSKY, 491:JUN73-168
SCHRAN, P. THE DEVELOPMENT OF CHINESE
AGRICULTURE 1950-1959.
W. KLATT, 293(JAST):FEB71-451
SCHRAPEL, D. DIE ENTZIFFERUNG DES YAT-
ISCHEN.
M.B. EMENEAU, 318(JAOS):OCT-DEC71-541
SCHRECKENBACH, H-J., ED. BIBLIOGRAPHIE
ZUR GESCHICHTE DER MARK BRANDENBURG.
(PT 2)
T. KLEIN, 182:VOL24#13/14-567
SCHREIBER, F.R. SYBIL.
P. ADAMS, 61:JUN73-123
J.S. GORDON, 441:17JUN73-30
D.W. HARDING, 453:14JUN73-24
SCHREIBER, K. BIBLIOGRAPHIE LAUFENDER
BIBLIOGRAPHIEN ZUR ROMANISCHEN LITERA-
TURWISSENSCHAFT.
H. MEIER, 72:BAND209HEFT1/3-174
SCHREUDER, D. GLADSTONE AND KRUGER.
J. BUTLER, 637(VS):DEC70-216
"SCHRIFTEN DER THEODOR-STORM-GESELL-
SCHAFT." (SCHRIFT 18)
F.R. SAMMERN-FRANKENEGG, 597(SN):
VOL42#2-535
SCHRIJVERS, P.H. HORROR AC DIVINA VOLUP-
TAS.
P. BOYANCÉ, 487:AUTUMN71-285
E.J. KENNEY, 123:DEC72-348
SCHRIMPF, H.J. - SEE MORITZ, K.P.
SCHRIVER, E.O. GO FREE.
W.S. MC FEELY, 432(NEQ):JUN71-325
SCHROCK, G. LETTERS FROM ALF.
M. LEVIN, 441:7OCT73-47
SCHRÖDER, H-J. DEUTSCHLAND UND DIE VER-
EINIGTEN STAATEN 1933-39.
H.F. YOUNG, 182:VOL24#11/12-509
SCHRÖDER, R. NOVELLE UND NOVELLENTHEORIE
IN DER FRÜHEN BIEDERMEIERZEIT.
J. HERMAND, 406:FALL72-296
B. VON WIESE, 680(ZDP):BAND90HEFT4-
603
SCHRÖDER, W. VELDEKE-STUDIEN.
C. MINIS, 182:VOL24#9/10-417

SCHRÖDER, W., ED. WOLFRAM-STUDIEN.
V. GÜNTHER, 182(GQ):VOL24#21/22-781
H. KRATZ, 221(GQ):MAY71-390
J.F. POAG, 406:SUMMER72-195
SCHRÖDER, W. - SEE WOLFF, L.
SCHRÖDER, W.J. & G. HOLLANDT - SEE
WOLFRAM VON ESCHENBACH, W.
SCHROEDER, A. FILE OF UNCERTAINTIES.
J. DITSKY, 628:SPRING72-108
VON SCHROEDER, L., ED. KĀṬHAKA.
H-P. SCHMIDT, 318(JAOS):OCT-DEC71-552
SCHRÖER, F. DAS HAVELLAND IM DREISSIG-
JÄHRIGEN KRIEG.
W.A. BOELCKE, 182:VOL24#21/22-819
SCHRÖER, M.M.A. ENGLISCHES HANDWÖRTER-
BUCH. (PTS 10-24) (P.L. JAEGER, ED)
M. LEHNERT, 682(ZPSK):BAND23HEFT2/3-
308
SCHRÖER, M.M.A. ENGLISCHES HANDWÖRTER-
BUCH. (PT 26) (P.L. JAEGER, ED)
M. LEHNERT, 682(ZPSK):BAND24HEFT1/2-
131
SCHRÖTER, K. LITERATUR UND ZEITGESCHICH-
TE.
R. GRIMM, 222(GR):MAY71-228
SCHRÖTER, K., ED. THOMAS MANN IM URTEIL
SEINER ZEIT.*
D. ASSMANN, 439(NM):1971/4-764
B. VÖLKER-HEZEL, 556(RLV):1971/6-776
SCHUBEL, F. ENGLISCHE LITERATURGE-
SCHICHTE. (VOL 1)
E.G. STANLEY, 38:BAND88HEFT3-356
F.C. DE VRIES, 433:APR70-212
SCHUBIGER, J. FRANZ KAFKA.
E. BOA, 402(MLR):JAN72-226
SCHUBIGER, M. EINFÜHRUNG IN DIE PHON-
ETIK.
F.W. GESTER, 38:BAND89HEFT4-502
SCHUCHARD, B. "VALOR."
B. FOSTER, 208(FS):JUL72-368
SCHUCHARDT, H. PRIMITIAE LINGUAE VAS-
CONUM.
H. BERGER, 260(IF):BAND75-372
SCHUCHHARDT, W-H. GREEK ART.* (GERMAN
TITLE: GRIECHISCHE KUNST.)
617(TLS):16FEB73-184
SCHUELER, H.J. HANS FALLADA.
E.M. CHICK, 221(GQ):MAR71-247
SCHUELLER, H.M. & R.L. PETERS - SEE
SYMONDS, J.A.
SCHUH, W. UMGANG MIT MUSIK.
P.J.B., 410(M&L):JAN72-82
SCHUHL, P-M. L'IMAGINATION ET LE MER-
VEILLEUX (LA PENSÉE ET L'ACTION).
P. SOMVILLE, 556(RLV):1971/5-634
SCHUHMANN, K. UNTERSUCHUNGEN ZUR LYRIK
BRECHTS THEMEN, FORMEN, WEITERUNGEN.
617(TLS):28DEC73-1591
SCHULIN, E. HANDELSSTAAT ENGLAND.
R. HOWELL, JR., 182:VOL24#4-183
SCHULMAN, E. A HISTORY OF JEWISH EDUCA-
TION IN THE SOVIET UNION.
L. KOCHAN, 32:JUN72-447
SCHULMAN, I.A. - SEE MARTÍ, J.
SCHULMAN, I.A. & M.P. GONZÁLEZ. MARTÍ,
DARÍO Y EL MODERNISMO.*
J. GONZÁLEZ MUELA, 202(FMOD):NOV70/
FEB71-163
SCHULTE, H.F. THE SPANISH PRESS, 1470-
1966.
P-L. ULLMAN, 238:MAR71-213
SCHULTE-SASSE, J. LITERARISCHE WERTUNG.
L. BORNSCHEUER, 406:FALL72-291
SCHULTE-SASSE, J. - SEE LESSING, G.E.,
M. MENDELSSOHN & F. NICOLAI
SCHULTHEIS, W. DRAMATISIERUNG VON VOR-
GESCHICHTE.
G. BENDA, 406:FALL72-292

SCHULTZE, C.L. & OTHERS. SETTING NATIONAL
PRIORITIES.*
P. PASSELL & L. ROSS, 453:22MAR73-26
SCHULZ, G. - SEE NOVALIS
SCHULZ, J. VENETIAN PAINTED CEILINGS OF
THE RENAISSANCE.*
C. GOULD, 54:MAR71-121
G. ROBERTSON, 90:JUN71-337
SCHULZ, K. ART UND HERKUNFT DES VARIIER-
ENDEN STILS IN OTFRIDS EVANGELIENDICH-
TUNG.
V. GÜNTHER, 182:VOL24#6-290
SCHULZ, M.F. RADICAL SOPHISTICATION.
C.E. LLOYD, 573(SSF):FALL71-648
M.G. PORTER, 594:FALL71-332
SCHULZ-BEHREND, G. - SEE OPITZ, M.
SCHULZ-BUSCHHAUS, U. DAS MADRIGAL.*
J. RIESZ, 52:BAND6HEFT2-203
SCHULZ-VANHEYDEN, E. PROPERZ UND DAS
GRIECHISCHE EPIGRAMM.
E.J. KENNEY, 123:MAR72-111
SCHUMACHER, E.F. SMALL IS BEAUTIFUL.
617(TLS):28SEP73-1108
SCHUPPENHAUER, C. DER KAMPF UM DEN REIM
IN DER DEUTSCHEN LITERATUR DES 18.
JAHRHUNDERTS.
F. NEUMANN, 224(GRM):BAND21HEFT4-477
SCHUR, M. FREUD: LIVING AND DYING.*
617(TLS):23MAR73-317
SCHÜRER, E. GEORG KAISER UND BERTOLT
BRECHT.
E. KRISPYN, 406:SUMMER72-204
SCHÜRMANN, U. CENTRAL ASIAN RUGS.
M.H.B., 135:OCT70-138
SCHÜRR, F. ERLEBNIS, SINNBILD, MYTHOS.
H.R., 430(NS):AUG71-451
SCHUSTER, P. HENRY WICKHAM STEED UND DIE
HABSBURGERMONARCHIE.
H. HANAK, 575(SEER):OCT72-615
SCHÜTRUMPF, E. DIE BEDEUTUNG DES WORTES
ÉTHOS IN DER "POETIK" DES ARISTOTELES.*
P. LOUIS, 555:VOL45FASC2-349
SCHÜTTE, K. VOLLSTANDIGE SYSTEME MODALER
UND INTUITIONISTISCHER LOGIK.
R.E. VESLEY, 316:SEP71-522
SCHUTZ, A. THE PHENOMENOLOGY OF THE
SOCIAL WORLD.*
K. HARRIES, 321:SPRING70-65
SCHUTZ, A. REFLECTIONS ON THE PROBLEM OF
RELEVANCE.* (R.M. ZANER, ED)
V.J. MC GILL, 484(PPR):SEP71-112
SCHÜTZ, A.J. NGUNA GRAMMAR.
D.S. WALSH, 350:SEP72-730
SCHÜTZ, A.J. NGUNA TEXTS.
A. CAPELL, 215(GL):VOL10#1-59
D.S. WALSH, 350:SEP72-730
SCHÜTZEICHEL, R. ALTHOCHDEUTSCHES WÖR-
TERBUCH.*
H. GNEUSS, 38:BAND88HEFT3-354
SCHUYLER, J. THE CRYSTAL LITHIUM.*
D. SHAPIRO, 491:JUL73-235
S. SPENDER, 453:20SEP73-8
SCHWAB, F.M. DAVID OF AUGSBURG'S "PATER-
NOSTER" AND THE AUTHENTICITY OF HIS
GERMAN WORKS.
J.S. GROSECLOSE, 406:WINTER72-409
SCHWAB, R.N. & W.E. REX. INVENTORY OF
DIDEROT'S ENCYCLOPÉDIE. (VOLS 4-6)
617(TLS):19JAN73-59
SCHWAMBORN, F. DAS SPANIENBILD DOMINGO
FAUSTINO SARMIENTOS.*
F. NIEDERMAYER, 430(NS):AUG71-448
SCHWARTZ, A., COMP. A TWISTER OF TWISTS,
A TANGLER OF TONGUES.
A. TAYLOR, 70(ANQ):MAR73-110
SCHWARTZ, B., ED. THE BILL OF RIGHTS.
I. DILLIARD, 31(ASCH):SPRING73-347

SCHWARTZ, C. GERSHWIN.
    W. CLEMONS, 441:23SEP73-3
SCHWARTZ, E. ELECTRONIC MUSIC.
    617(TLS):7SEP73-1024
SCHWARTZ, H. EASTERN EUROPE IN THE
    SOVIET SHADOW.
    617(TLS):5OCT73-1153
SCHWARTZ, K. VICENTE ALEIXANDRE.
    C.W. COBB, 238:MAR71-211
SCHWARTZ, K. THE MEANING OF EXISTENCE
    IN CONTEMPORARY HISPANIC LITERATURE.
    J.W. DÍAZ, 238:MAR71-201
SCHWARTZ, L.M. KEATS REVIEWED BY HIS
    CONTEMPORARIES.
    617(TLS):7SEP73-1025
SCHWARTZ, M-A. L'AUTOMNE.
    C-L. FOULT, 98:DEC70-1068
SCHWARTZ, P. THE NEW POLITICAL ECONOMY
    OF J.S. MILL.
    617(TLS):9MAR73-263
SCHWARTZ, R.B. SAMUEL JOHNSON AND THE
    NEW SCIENCE.
    D. GREENE, 579(SAQ):SPRING72-269
SCHWARTZ, W.J. DER ERZÄHLER GÜNTER GRASS.
    M. FÜRSTENWALD, 564:MAR71-71
SCHWARZ, A. THE COMPLETE WORKS OF MARCEL
    DUCHAMP.*
    D. IRWIN, 39:JUN70-483
    R. REES, 592:JUL-AUG70-62
SCHWARZ, A. MARCEL DUCHAMP: NOTES AND
    PROJECTS FOR THE LARGE GLASS.
    D. IRWIN, 39:JUN70-483
SCHWARZ, B. MUSIC AND MUSICAL LIFE IN
    SOVIET RUSSIA 1917-1970.*
    R. MC ALLISTER, 415:AUG72-770
SCHWARZ, D. DIE KONZENTRATION DES BE-
    TRIEBSVERMÖGENS IN DER GEWERBLICHEN
    WIRTSCHAFT DER BUNDESREPUBLIK DEUTSCH-
    LAND 1953, 1957 UND 1960.
    K. MELLEROWICZ, 182:VOL24#11/12-472
SCHWARZ, D.W.H. SACHGÜTER UND LEBENSFOR-
    MEN.
    D. BLAMIRES, 402(MLR):JUL72-689
    U. DIRLMEIER, 182:VOL24#17/18-693
    E. ETTLINGER, 203:SPRING71-83
    H. MARTIN, 406:SPRING72-67
SCHWARZ, F. LITERARISCHES ZEITGESPRÄCH
    IM DRITTEN REICH, DARGESTELLT AN DER
    ZEITSCHRIFT "NEUE RUNDSCHAU."
    617(TLS):11MAY73-532
SCHWARZ, J. STUDENTEN IN DER WEIMARER
    REPUBLIK.
    E.J. COHN, 182:VOL24#7/8-373
SCHWARZ, R., ED. MENSCHLICHE EXISTENZ
    UND MODERNE WELT.
    C.O. SCHRAG, 485(PE&W):JAN70-83
SCHWARZ, W.J. DER ERZÄHLER UWE JOHNSON.*
    M.E. COCK, 402(MLR):OCT72-954
    H.H. JACKSON, 564:JUN71-160
SCHWARZ, W.J. DER ERZÄHLER MARTIN WALSER.
    D.F. NELSON, 301(JEGP):APR72-306
    G.B. PICKAR, 406:SUMMER72-202
SCHWARZ-BART, A. A WOMAN NAMED SOLITUDE.*
    (FRENCH TITLE: LA MULÂTRESSE SOLITUDE.)
    T.R. EDWARDS, 453:22MAR73-29
    A. FRIEDMAN, 441:11FEB73-1
    S. HILL, 362:17MAY73-658
    C. LEHMANN-HAUPT, 441:9FEB73-37
    E. WEEKS, 61:MAR73-105
    442(NY):10FEB73-114
    617(TLS):11MAY73-517
SCHWARZE, J. DIE BEURTEILUNG DES PERIKLES
    DURCH DIE ATTISCHE KOMÖDIE UND IHRE HIS-
    TORISCHE UND HISTORIOGRAPHISCHE BEDEU-
    TUNG.
    F. LASSERRE, 182:VOL24#9/10-433

SCHWARZENBACH, R. DIE STELLUNG DER MUN-
    DART IN DER DEUTSCHSPRACHIGEN SCHWEIZ.*
    L. SPULER, 400(MLN):OCT71-716
SCHWEICKERT, A. HEINRICH HEINES EIN-
    FLÜSSE AUF DIE DEUTSCHE LYRIK 1830-
    1900.*
    M.J. GONZÁLEZ, 202(FMOD):JUN70-358
SCHWEIKERT, U. - SEE "LUDWIG TIECK"
SCHWEIKLE, G., ED. DICHTER ÜBER DICHTER
    IN MITTELHOCHDEUTSCHER LITERATUR.
    D.H. GREEN, 402(MLR):JAN72-207
SCHWEINFURTH, U., WITH M. DOMRÖS, EDS.
    PROBLEMS OF LAND USE IN SOUTH ASIA.
    J.E. SCHWARTZBERG, 293(JAST):FEB71-476
SCHWEITZER, B. GREEK GEOMETRIC ART.*
    (GERMAN TITLE: DIE GEOMETRISCHE KUNST
    GRIECHENLANDS.)
    J. BOARDMAN, 90:DEC71-748
    R.V. SCHODER, 124:MAR72-236
SCHWEITZER, C. - SEE LESSING, G.E.
SCHWEIZER, W.R. MÜNCHHAUSEN UND MÜNCH-
    HAUSIADEN.*
    T. HALL, 402(MLR):JUL72-609
SCHWENCKE, O. DIE GLOSSIERUNG ALTTESTA-
    MENTLICHER BÜCHER IN DER LÜBECKER BIBEL
    VON 1494.
    G. STEER, 657(WW):MAR/APR70-141
SCHWITTERS, K. DAS LITERARISCHE WERK.
    (VOL 1) (F. LACH, ED)
    617(TLS):5OCT73-1186
SCHWOB, A. WEGE UND FORMEN DES SPRACH-
    AUSGLEICHS IN NEUZEITLICHEN OST- UND
    SÜDOSTDEUTSCHEN SPRACHINSELN.
    E. SKÁLA, 220(GL&L):JUL72-391
    E.H. YARRILL, 182:VOL24#19/20-724
SCIACCA, M.F. PLATONE.
    P. SOMVILLE, 542:APR-JUN70-227
SCIASCIA, L. IL CONTESTO.*
    270:VOL22#3-67
SCIASCIA, L. EQUAL DANGER.
    P. ADAMS, 61:AUG73-103
SCIASCIA, L. IL MARE COLORE DEL VINO.
    617(TLS):5OCT73-1155
SCOBBIE, I. SWEDEN.
    617(TLS):9FEB73-154
SCOBIE, A. ASPECTS OF THE ANCIENT
    ROMANCE AND ITS HERITAGE.*
    B.P. REARDON, 24:JUL72-503
    P.G. WALSH, 487:SPRING71-89
SCOBIE, S. IN THE SILENCE OF THE YEAR.
    J. PIVATO, 102(CANL):SPRING72-106
    P. STEVENS, 628:SPRING72-103
SCOLARI, A. PAGINE VERONESI.
    M.F., 228(GSLI):VOL148FASC461-151
SCORER, R.S. POLLUTION IN THE AIR.
    617(TLS):7DEC73-1521
SCOT, J. HOMÉLIE SUR LE PROLOGUE DE
    JEAN. (E. JEAUNEAU, ED)
    P. MICHAUD-QUANTIN, 542:JUL-SEP70-362
SCOTLAND, J. THE HISTORY OF SCOTTISH
    EDUCATION.
    J.A. RUSSELL, 478:JAN71-75
SCOTT, A.B. - SEE HILDEBERT OF LAVARDIN
SCOTT, A.C. - SEE "TRADITIONAL CHINESE
    PLAYS"
SCOTT, A.L. ON THE POETRY OF MARK TWAIN.
    L.T. DICKINSON, 179(ES):FEB71-82
SCOTT, A.L. MARK TWAIN AT LARGE.*
    R. LEHAN, 445(NCF):SEP71-245
SCOTT, C. BARTLEBY.*
    W.H. NEW, 102(CANL):SUMMER72-88
SCOTT, D.C. IN THE VILLAGE OF VIGER AND
    OTHER STORIES.
    G. STOW, 296:SUMMER73-123
SCOTT, F.R. THE DANCE IS ONE.
    D. PACEY, 198:FALL73-94
SCOTT, J. MANY HAPPY RETURNS.
    N. CALLENDAR, 441:6MAY73-41

SCOTT, J.M. DONS AND STUDENTS.
617(TLS):9NOV73-1364
SCOTT, J.M. A WALK ALONG THE APENNINES.
617(TLS):25MAY73-597
SCOTT, N.A., JR. THE BROKEN CENTER.
U. BRUMM, 38:BAND89HEFT1-148
SCOTT, N.A. JR. NEGATIVE CAPABILITY.*
A.J. FRY, 433:APR71-221
R. MACKSEY, 400(MLN):MAY71-608
S.J. SPÅNBERG, 597(SN):VOL43#1-327
SCOTT, N.A., JR. THE WILD PRAYER OF
LONGING.*
639(VQR):AUTUMN71-CLXXXVIII
SCOTT, R. GOODBYE DAUGHTER; DADDY'S
GOING ON THE BOARD.
617(TLS):13JUL73-817
SCOTT, R.H.F. JEAN-BAPTISTE LULLY.
617(TLS):28SEP73-1139
SCOTT, R.L. THE SPEAKER'S READER.
J.W. PATTERSON, 583:WINTER70-187
SCOTT, T. DUNBAR.
G.S. FRASER, 179(ES):APR71-165
SCOTT, W. THE JOURNAL OF SIR WALTER
SCOTT. (W.E.K. ANDERSON, ED)
K. MILLER, 362:15MAR73-346
617(TLS):5JAN73-17
SCOTT, W. TERROR AND REPRESSION IN
REVOLUTIONARY MARSEILLES.
617(TLS):17AUG73-957
SCOTT, W.N. BROTHER AND BROTHER.
S.E. LEE, 581:DEC72-302
SCOTT-SUTHERLAND, C. ARNOLD BAX.
617(TLS):7SEP73-1024
"SCOTTISH SHORT STORIES."
617(TLS):6JUL73-769
SCOUTEN, A.H. THE LONDON STAGE, 1729-
1747.
C. PRICE, 570(SQ):WINTER71-67
SCOWCROFT, R. BACK TO FIRE MOUNTAIN.
M. LEVIN, 441:11MAR73-49
SCRIMIERI, G. LA FORMAZIONE DELLA FENOM-
ENOLOGIA DI E. HUSSERL.
E. NAMER, 542:APR-JUN70-255
"SCRITTI IN ONORE DI LUIGI STEFANINI."
E. NAMER, 542:OCT-DEC71-516
SCRIVANO, R. BENEDETTO CROCE CRITICO
LETTERARIO E I FONDAMENTI DELLA CULTURA
LETTERARIA DEL NOVECENTO.
E.G. CASERTA, 275(IQ):SPRING71-155
SCRIVNER, F.C. MOHAVE PEOPLE.
B. TOELKEN, 650(WF):OCT70-268
SCROPE, S. THE EPISTLE OF OTHEA. (C.F.
BÜHLER, ED)
R.W. HANNING, 551(RENQ):AUTUMN71-355
SCUDDER, G. BIBLIOGRAFIA DEGLI SCRITTI
DI EMILIO CECCHI.
S. GAMBERINI, 402(MLR):OCT72-923
SCUDERI, E. FEDERICO DE ROBERTO E LA
LETTERATURA D'OGGI.
J-P. DE NOLA, 549(RLC):JAN-MAR71-125
SCULLARD, H.H. SCIPIO AFRICANUS.*
A.E. ASTIN, 313:VOL61-272
E.S. GRUEN, 24:APR72-377
SCULLY, C., WITH A. TUPPER & P. MAC CAR-
THY, EDS. UNIVERSITY OF LEEDS, PHONET-
ICS DEPARTMENT, REPORT NO. 1.
G.F. MEIER, 682(ZPSK):BAND23HEFT4-427
SCULLY, J. AVENUE OF THE AMERICAS.*
M.G. PERLOFF, 659:WINTER73-97
SCULLY, V. AMERICAN ARCHITECTURE AND
URBANISM.
C.W. CONDIT, 56:SUMMER70-179
W.S. RUSK, 127:FALL71-106
SCUPHAM, P. THE GIFT.
617(TLS):2NOV73-1348
SCUPHAM, P. THE SNOWING GLOBE.
617(TLS):17AUG73-946

SEABORNE, M. THE ENGLISH SCHOOL - ITS
ARCHITECTURE AND ORGANISATION: 1370-
1870.
O. VAN OSS, 135:SEP71-62
SEABORNE, M., ED. HISTORY OF EDUCATION.
(VOL 1)
617(TLS):2FEB73-115
SEAGER, A. THE GLASS HOUSE.*
D. SHEEHAN, 405(MP):AUG70-123
SEALE, M.S. MUSLIM THEOLOGY.
S. VAHIDUDDIN, 273(IC):APR71-137
SEALE, P. & M. MC CONVILLE. THE HILTON
ASSIGNMENT.
617(TLS):27JUL73-850
SEALE, P. & M. MC CONVILLE. PHILBY.
R. CROSSMAN, 362:19JUL73-91
D. RABINOWITZ, 441:18NOV73-38
617(TLS):27JUL73-855
SEAMAN, B. FREE AND FEMALE.*
F. HOWE, 31(ASCH):AUTUMN73-676
SEAMAN, L.C.B. LIFE IN VICTORIAN LONDON.
617(TLS):23NOV73-1424
SEAMAN, W.A.L. & J.R. SEWELL - SEE LADY
LONDONDERRY
SEARLE, J.R. SPEECH ACTS.*
N. BROWN, 154:DEC70-431
L.W. COLTER, 477:WINTER71-114
J.R. STEWART, 480(P&R):WINTER71-59
SEARLE, S.A. ENVIRONMENT AND PLANT LIFE.
617(TLS):12OCT73-1246
SEARS, S. THE NEGATIVE IMAGINATION.*
M. ALLOTT, 541(RES):FEB71-104
L. EDEL, 445(NCF):JUN70-116
M.J. LYDE, 577(SHR):SPRING71-204
SEARY, E.R. PLACE NAMES OF THE AVALON
PENINSULA OF THE ISLAND OF NEWFOUND-
LAND.
L.A. DUCHEMIN, 150(DR):AUTUMN71-428
A.R. DUCKERT, 320(CJL):FALL71-63
SEATON, A. THE RUSSO-GERMAN WAR, 1941-45.
A. DALLIN, 32:JUN72-431
SEAVER, P.S. THE PURITAN LECTURESHIPS.
C. HILL, 551(RENQ):AUTUMN71-410
SEAY, J. LET NOT YOUR HART.*
B. GUNTER, 219(GAR):WINTER70-517
J.T. IRWIN, 598(SOR):SUMMER73-720
SEBALD, W.G. CARL STERNHEIM.
J. OSBORNE, 402(MLR):APR72-471
SEBEOK, T.A., ED. PORTRAITS OF LINGUISTS.
G.C. LEPSCHY, 353:MAY70-100
SEBEOK, T.A. - SEE LEHTINEN, M.
SEBOLD, R.P. EL RAPTO DE LA MENTE.
J. DOWLING, 238:DEC71-970
SECCHI, S. ANTONIO FOSCARINI.
R.A., 228(GSLI):VOL147FASC458/459-473
SECCI, L. IL MITO GRECO NEL TEATRO
TEDESCA ESPRESSIONISTICA.
A. ARNOLD, 222(GR):MAR71-137
SECO, M. ARNICHES Y EL HABLA DE MADRID.
L. MARISTANY, 86(BHS):APR72-190
SECRET, F. BIBLIOGRAPHIE DES MANUSCRITS
DE GUILLAUME POSTEL.*
E. ARMSTRONG, 208(FS):JUL72-320
C-G. DUBOIS, 535(RHL):JUL-AUG71-689
J. PINEAUX, 557(RSH):JUL-SEP71-470
SECRET, F. L'ÉSOTÉRISME DE GUY LE
FÈVRE DE LA BODERIE.*
J. MC CLELLAND, 405(MP):MAY71-380
D. MASKELL, 182:VOL24#1/2-26
A. SPINA, 535(RHL):JAN-FEB71-69
SEDWICK, F. CONVERSATION IN SPANISH.
R. MUNGUÍA, 238:MAY71-411
VON SEE, K. DEUTSCHE GERMANEN-IDEOLOGIE.
E.A. PHILIPPSON, 301(JEGP):JUL72-407
VON SEE, K. GERMANISCHE VERSKUNST.
P. OCHSENBEIN, 657(WW):JAN/FEB71-63
SEEBERG-ELVERFELDT, R. REVALER REGESTEN.
C.A.F. MEEKINGS, 325:APR71-251

SEEBOLD, E. - SEE KRAHE, H.
SEEGER, L.G. DIE DEMASKIERUNG DER
LEBENSLÜGE.*
E. BOA, 402(MLR):JAN72-226
J.H. REID, 182:VOL24#13/14-553
U. SCHELLING, 657(WW):JUL/AUG70-284
D.J. WILSON, 301(JEGP):JAN72-89
SEEL, A., ED. "LAUS PISONIS."
E.J. KENNEY, 123:JUN72-279
SEELEY, C. TO A YOUNG MUSIC LOVER.
P. STANDFORD, 415:FEB72-158
SEELHAMMER, R. HOPKINS COLLECTED AT
GONZAGA.
W.F. GLEESON, 613:SUMMER71-304
W.R. MUNDT, 598(SOR):AUTUMN73-1029
J. PICK, 636(VP):SUMMER70-176
SEELIG, H., ED. NEUE WEGE.
R.C. ANDREWS, 220(GL&L):APR72-301
SEELYE, J. THE KID.*
M. ANANIA, 473(PR):FALL72-630
SEELYE, J. MELVILLE.*
C. FEIDELSON, 445(NCF):SEP71-228
L. LANE, JR., 594:SPRING71-128
H. PARKER, 401(MLQ):MAR72-54
SEEMANN, E., D. STRÖMBÄCK & B.R. JONSSON,
EDS. EUROPEAN FOLK BALLADS.
A. JABBOUR, 650(WF):JUL70-207
SEGAL, C.P. LANDSCAPE IN OVID'S "META-
MORPHOSES."*
G. LUCK, 52:BAND6HEFT1-96
SEGAL, E. FAIRY TALE.
P. ADAMS, 61:APR73-128
S.P. LEE & L. ROSS, 441:25MAR73-46
442(NY):7APR73-151
SEGAL, E. ROMAN LAUGHTER.*
J-C. DUMONT, 555:VOL45FASC1-162
SEGAL, L. & M. SENDAK - SEE GRIMM, J. &
W.
SEGAL, O. THE LUCID REFLECTOR.*
J. BRYSON, 597(SN):VOL43#1-322
J. DELBAERE-GARANT, 556(RLV):1971/4-
490
D. HEWITT, 541(RES):AUG71-371
R. LAWRENCE, 175:SPRING71-28
J.P. LOVERING, 613:SPRING71-129
W.T. STAFFORD, 445(NCF):SEP70-237
J.A. WARD, 141:WINTER71-104
639(VQR):WINTER71-XXVI
SEGAL, R. WHOSE JERUSALEM?
617(TLS):18MAY73-544
SEGALEN, V. CHINE: LA GRANDE STATUAIRE.
617(TLS):22JUN73-722
SEGARRA, J.P.F. - SEE UNDER FORNER Y SEG-
ARRA, J.P.
SEGEBRECHT, W. - SEE HOFFMANN, E.T.A.
SEGER, I. INTRODUCTION TO SOCIOLOGY.
617(TLS):16FEB73-190
SEGERBÄCK, B. LA RÉALISATION D'UNE
OPPOSITION DE TONÈMES DANS DES DIS-
SYLLABES CHUCHOTÉS.
H.G. SCHOGT, 353:JAN71-119
SEGERBERG, O., JR. WHERE HAVE ALL THE
FLOWERS, FISHES, BIRDS, TREES, WATER
AND AIR GONE?
42(AR):WINTER71/72-598
SEGESSER, E. AM GOLDENEN TOR.
G. RODGER, 220(GL&L):OCT71-47
SEGHERS, A. DIE HOCHZEIT VON HAITI.
(W.F. TULASIEWICZ & K. SCHEIBLE, EDS)
R.C. ANDREWS, 220(GL&L):APR72-301
SEGHERS, P. LE LIVRE D'OR DE LA POÉSIE
FRANÇAISE. (PT 2)
G. BRÉE, 207(FR):DEC70-404
P.F. CINTAS, 207(FR):DEC70-423
SEGHERS, P. LES MOTS COUVERTS.
G. BRÉE, 207(FR):DEC70-404
SEGOVIA, T. TERCETO.
617(TLS):12OCT73-1216

SEGRE, C. CRÍTICA BAJO CONTROL.
R.G. KEIGHTLEY, 402(MLR):OCT72-863
SÉGUIER, M. LA HALTE.
M. SAKHAROFF, 207(FR):FEB71-645
SEGY, L. AFRICAN SCULPTURE SPEAKS. (3RD
ED)
G.I. JONES, 69:APR71-178
SEIBERT, J. UNTERSUCHUNGEN ZUR GESCHICHTE
PTOLEMAIOS' I.*
J. BRISCOE, 123:MAR72-84
SEIBICKE, W. TECHNIK.
R. RÖMER, 680(ZDP):BAND90HEFT1-133
SEIBT, F. BOHEMICA.
O. ODLOŽILÍK, 32:SEP72-708
SEIDLER, G.L. THE EMERGENCE OF THE EAST-
ERN WORLD.
P. BURKE, 483:JAN71-78
SEIDMAN, H. POLITICS, POSITION AND
POWER.
639(VQR):WINTER71-XL
SEIGEL, J.E. RHETORIC AND PHILOSOPHY IN
RENAISSANCE HUMANISM.*
D. HAY, 447(N&Q):AUG71-317
E.J. KENNEY, 123:MAR72-124
SEILER, F. DEUTSCHE SPRICHWÖRTERKUNDE.
M. HAIN, 680(ZDP):BAND89HEFT1-139
SEILERN, A., COMP. CATALOGUE OF PAINT-
INGS AND DRAWINGS AT 56 PRINCES GATE,
LONDON SW7. (VOLS 6&7)
617(TLS):5JAN73-2
SEIRRA, P-O. GABRIEL CELAYA.
P. REDONDO, 202(FMOD):JUN70-352
SÉJOURNÉ, P. ASPECTS GÉNÉRAUX DU ROMAN
FÉMININ EN ANGLETERRE DE 1740 À 1800.
J. DELBAERE-GARANT, 179(ES):JUN71-276
SELA, O. THE BEARER PLOT.*
N. CALLENDAR, 441:25MAR73-49
SELA, O. THE PORTUGUESE FRAGMENT.
N. CALLENDAR, 441:4NOV73-79
EMPEROR HAILE SELASSIE I. HEYWATENNA
YA-ITYOPYA ERMEJA. (PT 1)
617(TLS):1JUN73-609
SELBOURNE, D. DORABELLA.
A. RENDLE, 157:AUTUMN70-77
SELBOURNE, D. THE TWO BACKED BEAST.
A. RENDLE, 157:SPRING70-71
SELBY, J. OVER THE SEA TO SKYE.
617(TLS):18MAY73-561
SELDEN, S. THEATRE DOUBLE GAME.
A. MATHIESON, 157:SPRING70-64
SELGE, G. ANTON ČECHOVS MENSCHENBILD.
H.J. PITCHER, 575(SEER):APR72-298
SELIGSON, M. THE ETERNAL BLISS MACHINE.
R. LASSON, 441:6MAY73-5
DE SELINCOURT, E. - SEE WORDSWORTH, W. &
D.
SELLARS, R.W. LENDING A HAND TO HYLAS.*
J. COLLINS, 486:MAR70-158
SELLARS, R.W. THE PRINCIPLES, PERSPEC-
TIVES, AND PROBLEMS OF PHILOSOPHY.
PRINCIPLES OF EMERGENT REALISM. (W.P.
WARREN, ED OF 2ND TITLE ONLY)
A.H. JOHNSON, 154:DEC71-779
N. MELCHERT, 484(PPR):MAR72-414
SELLARS, R.W. REFLECTIONS ON AMERICAN
PHILOSOPHY FROM WITHIN.
M. FARBER, 484(PPR):DEC70-299
A.W.M., 477:AUTUMN70-548
SELLARS, R.W. SOCIAL PROBLEMS AND POLITI-
CAL HORIZONS.
A.H. JOHNSON, 154:DEC71-779
SELLARS, W. SCIENCE AND METAPHYSICS.*
J.A. BAILEY, 154:DEC71-793
B. GENDRON, 258:MAR70-129
D.H. MELLOR, 536:JUN71-93
J.C. NYÍRI, 262:AUTUMN70-321

SELLIN, P.R. DANIEL HEINSIUS AND STUART
ENGLAND.*
G.C. SCHOOLFIELD, 568(SCN):SPRING72-
14
SELTÉN, B. EARLY EAST-ANGLIAN NICKNAMES,
"SHAKESPEARE NAMES."
E.C. SMITH, 424:DEC71-286
SELTZER, L.F. THE VISION OF MELVILLE AND
CONRAD.
W.E. MESSENGER, 136:VOL3#1-111
SELZNICK, D.O. MEMO FROM DAVID O. SELZ-
NICK.* (R. BEHLMER, ED)
J. DIDION, 453:22MAR73-15
617(TLS):18MAY73-563
SEMBACH, K-J. INTO THE THIRTIES.*
P. OWEN, 89(BJA):SUMMER72-307
SEMBDNER, H. - SEE "HEINRICH VON KLEIST"
"SÉMEIŌTIKÉ (WORKS ON SEMIOTICS)." (VOL
3)
D. TSCHIŽEWSKIJ, 72:BAND209HEFT1/3-
233
SEMENZATO, C. CORPUS PALLADIANUM.*
(VOL 1: THE ROTUNDA OF ANDREA PAL-
LADIO.)
S. MILLIKIN, 90:SEP71-554
J. NEWMAN, 90:NOV71-675
F.J.B. WATSON, 39:NOV70-396
SEMERARI, G. DIALOGO STORIA VALORI.
E. NAMER, 542:JAN-MAR70-105
SEMMLER, C. THE ART OF BRIAN JAMES AND
OTHER ESSAYS ON AUSTRALIAN LITERATURE.
S. MURRAY-SMITH, 71(ALS):MAY73-104
SEMPRUN, J. THE SECOND DEATH OF RAMÓN
MERCADER.* (FRENCH TITLE: LA DEUXIÈME
MORT DE RAMÓN MERCADER.)
J. HUNTER, 362:1MAR73-284
617(TLS):13APR73-408
SEN, E. INDIRA GANDHI.
617(TLS):16NOV73-1400
SEN, L.K. OPINION LEADERSHIP IN INDIA.
A.R. BEALS, 293(JAST):FEB71-513
SEN, T., ED. SHAKESPEARE COMMEMORATION
VOLUME.
A.C. KIRSCH, 570(SQ):SPRING70-187
SENA, J.F. A BIBLIOGRAPHY OF MELANCHOLY:
1660-1800.*
N. DEWEY, 481(PQ):JUL71-329
SENCOURT, R. T.S. ELIOT: A MEMOIR.*
(D. ADAMSON, ED)
J. ESPEY, 27(AL):NOV72-507
R. KIRK, 569(SR):SUMMER72-470
J.D. MARGOLIS, 651(WHR):SUMMER72-279
W.H. PRITCHARD, 249(HUDR):SPRING72-132
G. WERSON, 619(TC):VOL179#1049-53
42(AR):WINTER71/72-594
SENECA. MEDEA. (C.D.N. COSTA, ED)
617(TLS):21DEC73-1574
SENECA. SÄMTLICHE TRAGÖDIEN. (VOL 2)
(T. THOMANN, ED & TRANS)
H. RÜDIGER, 52:BAND6HEFT3-313
SENECA. SÉNÈQUE: "DE VITA BEATA." (P.
GRIMAL, ED)
A. ERNOUT, 555:VOL45FASC1-175
J.R.G. WRIGHT, 123:DEC72-414
SENELIER, J. - SEE DE NERVAL, G.
VON SENGER, H. KAUFVERTRÄGE IM TRADITION-
ELLEN CHINA.
W. EBERHARD, 293(JAST):AUG71-875
SENGHAAS-KNOBLOCH, E. FRIEDEN DURCH
INTEGRATION AND ASSOZIATION.
M. ROCK, 182:VOL24#6-265
SENGLE, F. BIEDERMEIERZEIT. (VOL 2)
617(TLS):19JAN73-73
SENGLE, F. DAS HISTORISCHE DRAMA IN
DEUTSCHLAND. (2ND ED)
G. RODGER, 220(GL&L):APR72-282
SEN GUPTA, B. THE FULCRUM OF ASIA.
C.V. CRABB, JR., 293(JAST):FEB71-473

SENN, A.E. THE RUSSIAN REVOLUTION IN
SWITZERLAND, 1914-1917.*
H. SHUKMAN, 575(SEER):JUL72-476
C.J. SMITH, 32:MAR72-164
SENNETT, R. & J. COBB. THE HIDDEN INJUR-
IES OF CLASS.*
M. KEMPTON, 453:8FEB73-11
SENUNGETUK, J. GIVE OR TAKE A CENTURY.
W.C. STURTEVANT, 441:18MAR73-38
ŠEPIĆ, D. ITALIJA, SAVEZNICI I JUGO-
SLAVENSKO PITANJE, 1914-1918.
B. RADITSA, 32:DEC72-929
ŠEPIĆ, D., ED. FRANO SUPILO.
B. RADITSA, 32:DEC72-929
SEPPÄNEN, L. ZUR LIEBESTERMINOLOGIE IN
MITTELHOCHDEUTSCHEN GEISTLICHEN TEXTEN.
R.M. KULLY, 657(WW):MAY/JUN70-211
D.A. WELLS, 433:APR70-200
"VIIe CONGRÈS INTERAMÉRICAIN DE PHILOSO-
PHIE, 1967." (VOL 1)
P. DUBOIS, 542:JUL-SEP70-357
SERAO, M. IL VENTRE DI NAPOLI. (NEW ED)
617(TLS):21DEC73-1558
SERDINI, S. SIMONE SERDINI DA SIENA
DETTO IL SAVIOZZO, "RIME." (E. PAS-
QUINI, ED)
C. DELCORNO, 545(RPH):FEB72-310
SEREJSKI, M.H. EUROPA A ROZBIORY POLSKI.
D. STONE, 32:JUN72-467
SERENI, V. & F. FRANCESE. SEI POESIE E
SEI DISEGNI.
617(TLS):5OCT73-1176
SERENY, G. THE CASE OF MARY BELL.*
P. ADAMS, 61:NOV73-130
SERLE, G. THE RUSH TO BE RICH.*
W. BATE, 381:DEC71-474
SERMONETA, G. UN GLOSSARIO FILOSOFICO
EBRAICO-ITALIANO DEL XIII SECOLO.
J. MAIER, 182:VOL24#4-135
DE LA SERNA, R.G. - SEE UNDER GÓMEZ DE LA
SERNA, R.
SEROFF, V. THE REAL ISADORA.*
M. MARKS, 151:NOV71-110
SERPER, A. RUTEBEUF POÈTE SATIRIQUE.
J. FOX, 208(FS):JAN72-61
F. SUARD, 557(RSH):JUL-SEP71-468
SERRALTA, F. LA RENEGADA DE VALLADOLID.
M. MC KENDRICK, 86(BHS):JUL72-303
SERRANO-PLAJA, A. "MAGIC" REALISM IN
CERVANTES.*
J.B. AVALLE-ARCE, 402(MLR):APR72-441
SERRANO PONCELA, S. LA METÁFORA.
R.S. MEYERSTEIN, 545(RPH):FEB72-328
SERRAU, G. CHER POINT DU MONDE.
M.G. ROSE, 207(FR):FEB71-647
SERRES, M. LE SYSTÈME DE LEIBNIZ ET SES
MODÈLES MATHÉMATIQUES.*
M-A. SINACEUR, 98:JUL70-626
SERRIN, W. THE COMPANY AND THE UNION.
N. BLIVEN, 442(NY):9JUL73-69
T.J. JACOBS, 441:18MAR73-27
M. KEMPTON, 453:8FEB73-11
SESSIONS, R. QUESTIONS ABOUT MUSIC.*
H.M. SCHUELLER, 290(JAAC):SUMMER71-551
SESSIONS, W.A., ED. THE LEGACY OF FRAN-
CIS BACON.
M. KIERNAN, 568(SCN):SPRING72-1
DE' SETA, C. CARTOGRAFIA DELLA CITTA DI
NAPOLI.
A. BLUNT, 46:APR71-259
SETH, R. ENCYCLOPEDIA OF ESPIONAGE.
617(TLS):8JUN73-648
SETH, R. JACKALS OF THE REICH.
617(TLS):19JAN73-71
SETHI, J.D. INDIA'S STATIC POWER STRUC-
TURE.
T.A. RUSCH, 293(JAST):NOV70-204

SETON, A.  GREEN DARKNESS.
    M. LEVIN, 441:21JAN73-22
SETON, C.P.  THE SEA CHANGE OF ANGELA
  LEWES.
    P.M. SPACKS, 249(HUDR):SPRING72-166
SEUREN, P.A.M.  OPERATORS AND NUCLEUS.
    B. CARSTENSEN, 430(NS):SEP71-505
    R.A. HUDSON, 297(JL):OCT71-277
    205(FMLS):OCT70-423
SÈVE, L.  LA PHILOSOPHIE FRANÇAISE CON-
  TEMPORAINE.
    M. BARTHÉLEMY-MADAULE, 542:JUL-SEP70-
    363
"THE SEVENTH DAY."
    S.L·A. MARSHALL, 390:APR71-63
SEVERIN, D.S.  MEMORY IN "LA CELESTINA."
    L.P. HARVEY, 382(MAE):1972/1-76
    J.H. MARTIN, 131(CL):FALL72-357
    G. MARTÍNEZ LACALLE, 402(MLR):JUL72-
    672
    K. WHINNOM, 86(BHS):JUL72-297
SEVERIN, T.  THE AFRICAN ADVENTURE.
    617(TLS):28DEC73-1580
SEVERINO, R.  EQUIPOTENTIAL SPACE.
    M. BRILL, 44:JUN71-8
SEWALL, B.  FOOTNOTE TO THE NINETIES.
    E. ENGELBERG, 637(VS):DEC70-205
    R.K.R. THORNTON, 447(N&Q):MAR71-118
SEWARD, D.  PRINCE OF THE RENAISSANCE.
    W. BEAUCHAMP, 441:23DEC73-10
    617(TLS):14DEC73-1546
SEWELL, J.  UP AGAINST CITY HALL.
    E. FRERICHS, 99:APR73-34
SEXTON, A.  TRANSFORMATIONS.*
    L.L. MARTZ, 676(YR):SPRING72-410
    R. PHILLIPS, 398:VOL3#4-185
SEYERSTED, P.  KATE CHOPIN.
    J. ESPEY, 445(NCF):SEP70-242
SEYERSTED, P. - SEE CHOPIN, K.
SEYMOUR, A.  A SQUARE MILE OF OLD ENG-
  LAND.  (M. BAKER, ED)
    617(TLS):4MAY73-509
SEYMOUR, C., JR.  EARLY ITALIAN PAINTINGS
  IN THE YALE UNIVERSITY ART GALLERY.
    B.B. FREDERICKSEN, 56:SUMMER71-245
SEYMOUR, C., JR.  JACOPO DELLA QUERCIA,
  SCULPTOR.
    617(TLS):30NOV73-1475
SEYMOUR, J. & S.  SELF-SUFFICIENCY.
    617(TLS):13JUL73-817
SEYMOUR, R.K.  A BIBLIOGRAPHY OF WORD
  FORMATION IN THE GERMANIC LANGUAGES.*
    K.R. GRINDA, 38:BAND89HEFT2-241
    P. SCHACH, 221(GQ):MAY71-425
SEYMOUR, W.  ORDEAL BY AMBITION.
    617(TLS):9FEB73-155
SEYMOUR, W.N., JR.  WHY JUSTICE FAILS.
    J.C. GOULDEN, 441:28OCT73-37
    442(NY):17DEC73-154
SEYMOUR-SMITH, M.  REMINISCENCES OF
  NORMA.*
    A. CLUYSENAAR, 565:VOL12#4-68
SEZNEC, J. - SEE DIDEROT, D.
SGARD, J.  PRÉVOST ROMANCIER.*
    H. COULET, 535(RHL):JUL-AUG70-704
SHABAN, M.A.  THE 'ABBĀSID REVOLUTION.
    D.M. DUNLOP, 589:OCT72-804
SHABAN, M.A.  ISLAMIC HISTORY, A.D. 600-
  750 (A.H. 132).*
    A. AHMAD, 589:OCT72-806
SHACKLE, G.L.S.  AN ECONOMIC QUERIST.
    617(TLS):12OCT73-1224
SHACKLETON BAILEY, D.R.  CICERO.*
    S.J. SIMON, 651(WHR):AUTUMN72-378
SHADBOLT, M.  AN EAR OF THE DRAGON.
    K.O. ARVIDSON, 368:DEC71-469
SHADBOLT, M.  STRANGERS AND JOURNEYS.*
    M. LEVIN, 441:5AUG73-12

SHAFFER, A.H. - SEE RANDOLPH, E.
SHAFFER, J·A.  PHILOSOPHY OF MIND.
    J.A. FODOR, 482(PHR):JAN71-104
SHAFFER, J.A., ED.  VIOLENCE.*
    W. WICK, 185:JAN72-177
SHAH, C.G.  ENDS AND MEANS.
    617(TLS):1JUN73-606
SHAH, W.  THE ADVENTURES OF HIR AND RAN-
  JHA.
    R. BRYDEN, 362:15FEB73-219
SHAHN, B.B.  BEN SHAHN.
    E. WEEKS, 61:FEB73-101
SHAKESPEARE, W.  ANTHONY AND CLEOPATRA.
  (G. SKILLON, ED)
    A. RENDLE, 157:SPRING71-77
SHAKESPEARE, W.  THE COMPLETE WORKS.  (A.
  HARBAGE, GENERAL ED)
    R.A. FOAKES, 175:AUTUMN70-98
SHAKESPEARE, W.  FIRST FOLIO OF SHAKE-
  SPEARE.  (C. HINMAN, ED)
    D. BEVINGTON, 405(MP):AUG70-98
SHAKESPEARE, W.  HAMLET.  OTHELLO.  EIN
  SOMMERNACHTSTRAUM.  ZWÖLFTE NACHT ODER
  WAS IHR WOLLT.  ANTONIUS UND KLEOPATRA.
  PERIKLES.  VIEL GETU UM NICHTS.  DIE
  LUSTIGEN WEIBER VON WINDSOR.  KÖNIG
  CYMBELIN.  ZWEI HERREN AUS VERONA.
  RICHARD II.  HEINRICH V.  (ALL TRANS BY
  E. FRIED)
    617(TLS):2FEB73-126
SHAKESPEARE, W.  KING LEAR.  (3 EDITIONS:
  1.  K. MUIR, ED; 2.  G.I. DUTHIE & J.D.
  WILSON, EDS; 3.  O.J. CAMPBELL, A.
  ROTHSCHILD & S. VAUGHAN, EDS)
    A. GREEN, 98:JAN71-3
SHAKESPEARE, W.  MEASURE FOR MEASURE.
  (R.E.C. HOUGHTON, ED)
    M. ECCLES, 570(SQ):AUTUMN71-408
SHAKESPEARE, W.  THE MERRY WIVES OF WIND-
  SOR.  (H.J. OLIVER, ED)
    G.R. HIBBARD, 402(MLR):OCT72-870
SHAKESPEARE, W.  PEINES D'AMOUR PERDUES.
  (A. BERTHET, TRANS)
    M. GRIVELET, 189(EA):OCT-DEC71-523
SHAKESPEARE, W.  RICHARD THE SECOND
  (1597); [AND] HENRY THE FOURTH, PART
  1 (1598).  (BOTH ED BY W.W. GREG &
  C. HINMAN)
    K. SMIDT, 179(ES):FEB71-67
    W. WEISS, 38:BAND88HEFT1-138
SHAKESPEARE, W.  THE SECOND PART OF KING
  HENRY IV.  (A.R. HUMPHREYS, ED)
    W. WEISS, 38:BAND88HEFT1-139
SHAKESPEARE, W.  SHAKESPEARE'S SONNETS.
  (2ND ED) (A.L. ROWSE, ED)
    D.L. STEVENSON, 441:23SEP73-46
    617(TLS):10AUG73-919
SHAKESPEARE, W.  LA TRAGÉDIE DU ROI
  RICHARD II.  (M. GRIVELET, ED & TRANS)
    M.W. BLACK, 570(SQ):WINTER70-86
SHAKESPEARE, W.  LA TRAGÉDIE DU ROI
  RICHARD II.  (G. LAMBIN, TRANS) PÉRI-
  CLÈS, PRINCE DE TYR.  (G. LAMBIN,
  TRANS)
    M. GRIVELET, 189(EA):JAN-MAR70-89
SHAKESPEARE, W.  THE TRAGEDY OF JULIUS
  CAESAR.*  (M. CHARNEY, ED)
    J.W. VELZ, 570(SQ):WINTER71-73
"SHAKESPEARE: AN EXCERPT FROM THE GENERAL
  CATALOGUE OF PRINTED BOOKS IN THE BRIT-
  ISH MUSEUM."
    G.E. DAWSON, 570(SQ):WINTER71-73
"A SHAKESPEARE BIBLIOGRAPHY: THE CATA-
  LOGUE OF THE BIRMINGHAM SHAKESPEARE
  LIBRARY."  (PTS 1&2)
    617(TLS):14DEC73-1525
"SHAKESPEARE JAHRBUCH."  (VOL 102) - SEE
  UNDER SCHLÖSSER, A. & A-G. KUCKHOFF

SHALOM, A.  R.G. COLLINGWOOD, PHILOSOPHE
   ET HISTORIEN.
   C. LOCAS, 154:SEP71-628
SHANKAR, R.  MY MUSIC, MY LIFE.
   N. KAY, 607:SPRING71-25
SHANLEY, J.L. - SEE THOREAU, H.D.
SHANNON, D.  SPRING OF VIOLENCE.
   N. CALLENDAR, 441:30DEC73-19
SHANNON, D.  WITH INTENT TO KILL.*
   617(TLS):18MAY73-562
SHANNON, J.J.  THE ORPHAN.
   R.P. BRICKNER, 441:11FEB73-28
SHAPCOTT, T.W.  BEGIN WITH WALKING.
   617(TLS):120CT73-1216
SHAPIRA, A., ED.  THE SEVENTH DAY.
   D. KAUFMAN, 287:APR71-37
SHAPIRO, B.J.  JOHN WILKINS, 1614-1672.*
   M. NORMAN, 405(MP):MAY72-344
   R.B. SCHWARTZ, 173(ECS):FALL71-187
SHAPIRO, D.  A MAN HOLDING AN ACOUSTIC
   PANEL.
   J. ATLAS, 491:JAN73-229
SHAPIRO, K.  EDSEL.
   42(AR):FALL71-439
SHAPIRO, K.  SELECTED POEMS.
   E.L. MAYO, 448:FALL70-114
SHAPIRO, K.  WHITE-HAIRED LOVER.
   J.H. JUSTUS, 598(SOR):WINTER73-261
SHAPIRO, M.  ASPECTS OF RUSSIAN MORPHOL-
   OGY.*
   D. WARD, 402(MLR):JAN72-236
SHAPLEY, F.R.  PAINTINGS FROM THE SAMUEL
   H. KRESS COLLECTION: ITALIAN SCHOOLS
   XVI-XVIII CENTURY.
   617(TLS):17AUG73-944
SHARELL, R.  NEW ZEALAND INSECTS AND
   THEIR STORY.
   617(TLS):9FEB73-161
SHARMA, J.P.  REPUBLICS IN ANCIENT INDIA.
   J.W. SPELLMAN, 293(JAST):MAY71-712
SHARMA, R.S.  ASPECTS OF POLITICAL IDEAS
   AND INSTITUTIONS IN ANCIENT INDIA.*
   J.W. SPELLMAN, 318(JAOS):JAN-MAR71-157
SHARMAN, G.  FILIGREE IN SOUND.*
   N. KAY, 607:SPRING71-25
SHARON, A.  PLANNING JERUSALEM.
   617(TLS):2NOV73-1344
SHARP, D., ED.  MANCHESTER.
   T. WRIGHT, 46:FEB70-166
SHARP, D., ED.  PLANNING AND ARCHITEC-
   TURE.
   R.P. DOBER, 505:JAN70-190
SHARP, D.  A VISUAL HISTORY OF TWENTIETH-
   CENTURY ARCHITECTURE.
   617(TLS):9MAR73-264
SHARP, J.  OPEN SCHOOL.
   617(TLS):29JUN73-738
SHARP, J.M.  CREDIT REPORTING AND PRIVACY.
   D.H. BONHAM, 529(QQ):SPRING71-146
SHARP, J.M. - SEE PEÑUELAS, M.C.
SHARP, J.R.  THE JACKSONIANS VERSUS THE
   BANKS.
   639(VQR):SPRING71-LXXIV
SHARP, T.  TOWN AND TOWNSCAPE.
   J. WILTON-ELY, 39:APR70-319
SHARP, W.L.  LANGUAGE IN DRAMA.
   J.R. BROWN, 157:SPRING71-67
SHARPE, C.  THE BISHOPRICK GARLAND.
   T. BROWN, 203:SUMMER70-154
SHARPE, M.E.  JOHN KENNETH GALBRAITH AND
   THE LOWER ECONOMICS.
   617(TLS):2NOV73-1350
SHARPE, T.  INDECENT EXPOSURE.
   J. HUNTER, 362:29MAR73-423
   617(TLS):30MAR73-340
SHARPE, T.  RIOTOUS ASSEMBLY.
   M. WHITEHOUSE, 111:28MAY71-226

SHARPLESS, F.P.  THE LITERARY CRITICISM
   OF JOHN STUART MILL.
   M. ADAMS, 637(VS):MAR71-355
SHARROCK, R., ED.  THE PELICAN BOOK OF
   ENGLISH PROSE.
   J. GURY, 549(RLC):JAN-MAR71-102
SHAVER, C.L. - SEE WORDSWORTH, W. & D.
SHAW, A.  THE WORLD OF SOUL.
   M. PETERSON, 470:JAN71-44
SHAW, B.  TOMORROW LIES IN AMBUSH.
   617(TLS):20APR73-451
SHAW, D.L.  THE NINETEENTH CENTURY.
   617(TLS):23MAR73-331
SHAW, D.L. - SEE BAROJA, P.
SHAW, G.  DAS PROBLEM DES DINGES AND SICH
   IN DER ENGLISCHEN KANTINTERPRETATION.
   R. MALTER, 342:BAND61HEFT2-279
SHAW, G.B.  THE BODLEY HEAD BERNARD SHAW.*
   (VOL 1) (D.H. LAURENCE, ED)
   T.F. EVANS, 571:SPRING71-140
   F.P.W. MC DOWELL, 295:FEB73-120
   R. MACLEAN, 157:AUTUMN70-68
   S. WEINTRAUB, 572:SEP71-138
SHAW, G.B.  THE BODLEY HEAD BERNARD SHAW.
   (VOL 2) (D.H. LAURENCE, ED)
   F.P.W. MC DOWELL, 295:FEB73-120
   S. WEINTRAUB, 572:SEP71-138
SHAW, G.B.  THE BODLEY HEAD BERNARD SHAW.*
   (VOLS 3 & 4) (D.H. LAURENCE, ED)
   F.P.W. MC DOWELL, 295:FEB73-120
SHAW, G.B.  THE BODLEY HEAD BERNARD SHAW.
   (VOL 6)
   617(TLS):27APR73-481
SHAW, G.B.  COLLECTED LETTERS, 1898-1910.*
   (D.H. LAURENCE, ED)
   G. GERSH, 109:SPRING/SUMMER73-122
SHAW, G.B.  THE ROAD TO EQUALITY.  (L.
   CROMPTON, WITH H. CAVANAUGH, EDS)
   F.P.W. MC DOWELL, 295:FEB73-120
SHAW, G.B.  SAINT JOAN, A SCREENPLAY.*
   (B.F. DUKORE, ED)
   C. SLATER, 571:SUMMER70-102
SHAW, G.B.  SHAW: AN AUTOBIOGRAPHY 1856-
   1898.  (S. WEINTRAUB, ED)
   A.S. DOWNER, 572:JAN70-35
   J. GRIGG, 571:SPRING71-136
   F.P.W. MC DOWELL, 295:FEB73-120
   R. MACLEAN, 157:AUTUMN70-68
SHAW, G.B.  SHAW: AN AUTOBIOGRAPHY, 1898-
   1950.  (S. WEINTRAUB, ED)
   C.A. BERST, 572:JAN71-36
   F.P.W. MC DOWELL, 295:FEB73-120
   R.J. SMITH, 157:AUTUMN71-78
SHAW, G.F. - SEE UNDER FERNÁNDEZ SHAW, G.
SHAW, H.  OUT OF DARK.
   B. MANHIRE, 368:MAR70-88
SHAW, I.  EVENING IN BYZANTIUM.
   P. ADAMS, 61:MAY73-122
   A. BROYARD, 441:28MAR73-49
   J.R. FRAKES, 441:1APR73-6
   442(NY):23JUN73-90
SHAW, I.  GOD WAS HERE BUT HE LEFT EARLY.
   A. BROYARD, 441:15JAN73-27
   M. LEVIN, 441:4FEB73-27
   E. WEEKS, 61:FEB73-102
SHAW, I.  RICH MAN, POOR MAN.
   639(VQR):SPRING71-LVI
SHAW, L.R.  THE PLAYWRIGHT AND HISTORICAL
   CHANGE.*
   B.K. BENNETT, 221(GQ):JAN71-75
   N.J. CALARCO, 397(MD):MAY71-122
   S. GITTLEMAN, 222(GR):MAY71-232
   C.P. MAGILL, 220(GL&L):JAN72-190
   U. WEISSTEIN, 400(MLN):OCT71-727
SHAW, R.  CAUSES.
   617(TLS):20APR73-442
SHAW, R.  RUNNING.
   N. CALLENDAR, 441:4FEB73-16

SHAW, R.B. IN WITNESS.
617(TLS):12JAN73-36
SHAW, W.D. THE DIALECTICAL TEMPER.*
F.E.L. PRIESTLEY, 85:FALL71-53
T. SLOAN, 480(P&R):SUMMER70-189
SHAWCROSS, J.T., ED. MILTON 1732-1801:
THE CRITICAL HERITAGE.
617(TLS):15JUN73-697
SHAWCROSS, W. DUBCEK.
S. BORSODY, 32:MAR72-222
SHAY, D. CONVERSATIONS.
A.E. WITHAM, 200:MAY70-291
SHE, L. - SEE UNDER LAO SHE
SHEA, W.R. GALILEO'S INTELLECTUAL REVO-
LUTION.
617(TLS):24AUG73-979
SHEAFFER, L. O'NEILL: SON AND ARTIST.
D. TRILLING, 441:25NOV73-1
SHEARMAN, J. RAPHAEL'S CARTOONS IN THE
COLLECTION OF HER MAJESTY THE QUEEN
AND THE TAPESTRIES FOR THE SISTINE
CHAPEL.
617(TLS):16MAR73-284
SHEARMAN, J. ANDREA DEL SARTO.
I.H. CHENEY, 54:DEC71-532
SHECKLEY, R. THE ROBERT SHECKLEY OMNI-
BUS. (R. CONQUEST, ED)
617(TLS):9NOV73-1376
SHEED, W. THE MORNING AFTER.
42(AR):FALL71-442
SHEED, W. PEOPLE WILL ALWAYS BE KIND.
A. BROYARD, 441:11APR73-39
T.R. EDWARDS, 453:17MAY73-35
G. STADE, 441:8APR73-1
E. WEEKS, 61:MAY73-119
442(NY):21APR73-133
SHEEHAN, N. THE ARNHEITER AFFAIR.*
C. QUIMBY, 109:FALL/WINTER72/73-117
SHEEHY, G. HUSTLING.
C. LEHMANN-HAUPT, 441:10AUG73-29
SHEEHY, M., ED. MICHAEL/FRANK.
W.L. BEASLEY, 573(SSF):FALL71-661
SHELBY, L.R. JOHN ROGERS.*
H. DE LA CROIX, 54:DEC70-445
SHELDRICK, D. THE TSAVO STORY.
617(TLS):5OCT73-1189
SHELL, A.G. SUPERMARKET COUNTER POWER.
J.L. HESS, 441:23DEC73-9
SHELLEY, H. - SEE COLETTE
SHELLEY, P.B. THE COMPLETE POETICAL
WORKS OF PERCY BYSSHE SHELLEY. (VOL 1)
(N. ROGERS, ED)
617(TLS):2MAR73-246
SHELLEY, P.B. POSTHUMOUS POEMS OF SHEL-
LEY.* (I. MASSEY, ED)
J.R. MAC GILLIVRAY, 627(UTQ):FALL70-73
SHELLEY, P.B. SHELLEY'S "PROMETHEUS
UNBOUND."* (L.J. ZILLMAN, ED)
J.R. MAC GILLIVRAY, 627(UTQ):FALL70-73
G. O'MALLEY, 405(MP):FEB71-308
SHELTON, R. OF ALL THE DIRTY WORDS.
W. HEYEN, 491:JUL73-237
SHELTON, R. THE TATTOOED DESERT.*
D. ROSOCHACKI, 600:FALL71-138
SHELTON, W.J. ENGLISH HUNGER AND INDUS-
TRIAL DISORDERS.
617(TLS):19OCT73-1275
SHEN, T.H. THE SINO-AMERICAN JOINT COM-
MISSION ON RURAL RECONSTRUCTION.
R. MYERS, 293(JAST):MAY71-665
SHENKEL, J.D. CHRONOLOGY AND RECENSIONAL
DEVELOPMENT IN THE GREEK TEXT OF KINGS.
S.D. WALTERS, 318(JAOS):APR-JUN71-304
SHEPARD, L. THE HISTORY OF STREET LITER-
ATURE.
617(TLS):20JUL73-836

SHEPARD, L. JOHN PITTS.
N. BARKER, 78(BC):SPRING71-121
F.A. DE CARO, 292(JAF):JUL-SEP71-349
SHEPARD, O. THE LORE OF THE UNICORN.
R. SCHENDA, 196:BAND11HEFT1/2-195
SHEPARDSON, M. & B. HAMMOND. THE NAVAJO
MOUNTAIN COMMUNITY.
B. TOELKEN, 650(WF):OCT70-268
SHEPHERD, W., COMP. SHEPHERD'S GLOSSARY
OF GRAPHIC SIGNS AND SYMBOLS.*
V. FILBY, 70(ANQ):NOV72-45
SHEPPARD, F.H.W., ED. SURVEY OF LONDON.*
(VOL 35)
J. HAYES, 90:NOV71-679
J. HESTER, 157:SPRING70-68
P. METCALF, 46:DEC70-396
SHEPPARD, F.H.W., ED. SURVEY OF LONDON.
(VOL 36)
J.D., 135:JUL71-227
J. HAYES, 90:NOV71-679
J. HESTER, 157:SPRING71-75
SHEPPARD, F.H.W., GENERAL ED. SURVEY OF
LONDON. (VOL 37)
617(TLS):1JUN73-623
SHEPPARD, H.L. & N.Q. HERRICK. WHERE
HAVE ALL THE ROBOTS GONE?*
M. KEMPTON, 453:8FEB73-11
SHEPPARD, M. TAMAN INDERA.
617(TLS):27APR73-481
SHERATON, T. THE CABINET MAKERS AND UP-
HOLSTERERS DRAWING BOOK. THE CABINET
DICTIONARY.
R. EDWARDS, 39:JUL71-75
SHERBO, A. STUDIES IN THE EIGHTEENTH
CENTURY NOVEL.*
J. TRAUGOTT, 481(PQ):JUL71-398
SHERBO, A. - SEE JOHNSON, S.
SHERBURNE, J. STAND LIKE MEN.
M. LEVIN, 441:29JUL73-13
SHERBURNE, J.C. JOHN RUSKIN OR THE AM-
BIGUITIES OF ABUNDANCE.
617(TLS):26OCT73-1296
SHERFEY, M.J. THE NATURE AND EVOLUTION
OF FEMALE SEXUALITY.*
F. HOWE, 31(ASCH):AUTUMN73-676
SHERIDAN, W. THE FALL AND RISE OF JIMMY
HOFFA.
T. BETHELL, 441:4FEB73-10
M. KEMPTON, 231:MAY73-96
A.H. RASKIN, 441:19JAN73-35
SHERK, R.K. ROMAN DOCUMENTS FROM THE
GREEK EAST.
A. CHASTAGNOL, 555:VOL45FASC2-381
E.W. GRAY, 123:MAR72-87
J. REYNOLDS, 313:VOL61-284
SHERMAN, C.R. THE PORTRAITS OF CHARLES V
OF FRANCE (1338-1380).
G. SCHMIDT, 683:BAND34HEFT1-72
S. WHITTINGHAM, 90:SEP71-552
SHERRILL, R. THE SATURDAY NIGHT SPECIAL.
C. LEHMANN-HAUPT, 441:4DEC73-49
E. REDMAN, 441:9DEC73-1
SHERRINGTON, R.J. THREE NOVELS BY FLAU-
BERT.*
F. BASSAN, 141:FALL71-425
A.S.G. BUTLER, 67:MAY72-97
SHERRY, N. CHARLOTTE AND EMILY BRONTË.
D. HEWITT, 447(N&Q):NOV71-429
SHERRY, N. CONRAD AND HIS WORLD.
617(TLS):15JUN73-664
SHERRY, N., ED. CONRAD - THE CRITICAL
HERITAGE.
617(TLS):15JUN73-664
SHERRY, N. CONRAD'S WESTERN WORLD.*
J.K. BOSWELL, 136:VOL3#1-126
R. LEHAN, 445(NCF):DEC71-367
J.E. SAVESON, 454:SPRING72-266
[CONTINUED]

SHERRY, N. CONRAD'S WESTERN WORLD.*
[CONTINUING]
 A. SHELSTON, 148:AUTUMN71-285
 I. VIDAN, 163:VOL3#2-105
SHERWANI, H.K. THE ALIGARH MOVEMENT.
 B. TYABJI, 273(IC):APR71-139
SHERWIN, J.J. IMPOSSIBLE BUILDINGS.
 H. VENDLER, 441:12AUG73-6
SHERWIN-WHITE, A.N. RACIAL PREJUDICE IN
IMPERIAL ROME.
 J.A. CROOK, 313:VOL61-276
SHERWOOD, J. NO GOLDEN JOURNEY.
 617(TLS):23NOV73-1451
SHERWOOD, W.R. CIRCUMFERENCE AND CIR-
CUMSTANCE.*
 W. BINDER, 38:BAND88HEFT4-552
 D. DUNCAN, 179(ES):DEC71-562
SHESTOV, L. DOSTOEVSKY, TOLSTOY, AND
NIETZSCHE.*
 R.L. STRONG, JR., 550(RUSR):JUL71-314
SHESTOV, L. KIERKEGAARD AND THE EXISTEN-
TIAL PHILOSOPHY.
 W.A.J., 543:JUN71-757
SHEWELL-COOPER, W.E. THE BASIC BOOK OF
VEGETABLE GROWING.
 617(TLS):5JAN73-21
SHEWMAKER, K.E. AMERICANS AND CHINESE
COMMUNISTS 1927-1945.
 42(AR):FALL71-444
SHIBLES, W. PHILOSOPHICAL PICTURES.
 G.E. MYERS, 480(P&R):WINTER70-67
SHIEH, M.J.T., ED. THE KUOMINTANG.*
 G.T. YU, 293(JAST):NOV70-181
SHIH-HONG, L. - SEE UNDER LIU SHIH-HONG
"THE IZUMI SHIKIBU DIARY" - SEE UNDER
IZUMI
SHILS, E. THE INTELLECTUALS AND THE
POWERS AND OTHER ESSAYS.
 A. RYAN, 362:4JAN73-23
 S.S. WOLIN, 441:30SEP73-31
 617(TLS):26JAN73-93
SHIMADA, S., ED. ZAIGAI HIHŌ.
 A. SOPER, 57:VOL32#1-93
SHIMEI, F. - SEE UNDER FUTABATEI SHIMEI
SHIMOSE, P. QUIERO ESCRIBIR, PERO ME
SALE SPUMA.
 617(TLS):12OCT73-1216
SHIN, L.B. - SEE UNDER BA SHIN, L.
SHINAGEL, M. DANIEL DEFOE AND MIDDLE-
CLASS GENTILITY.*
 I. RIVERS, 148:AUTUMN71-282
 F. WÖLCKEN, 38:BAND89HEFT3-400
SHINE, F.L. JOHNNY NOON.
 M. LEVIN, 441:14OCT73-48
SHINE, M.G. THE FICTIONAL CHILDREN OF
HENRY JAMES.*
 R. LAWRENCE, 175:AUTUMN70-107
 W.T. STAFFORD, 445(NCF):SEP70-237
SHINKICHI, T. - SEE UNDER ETŌ SHINKICHI
SHINWELL, E. I'VE LIVED THROUGH IT ALL.
 617(TLS):30NOV73-1463
SHIPTON, C.K. BIOGRAPHICAL SKETCHES OF
THOSE WHO ATTENDED HARVARD COLLEGE IN
THE CLASSES 1761-1763, WITH BIBLIO-
GRAPHICAL AND OTHER NOTES.*
 J.A. SCHUTZ, 656(WMQ):JAN71-148
SHIPTON, C.K. & J.E. MOONEY. NATIONAL
INDEX OF AMERICAN IMPRINTS THROUGH
1800: THE SHORT TITLE EVANS.*
 J.A.L. LEMAY, 165:SPRING73-66
SHIRAKAWA, Y. THE HIMALAYAS.
 A. BROYARD, 441:15NOV73-49
 E. HOAGLAND, 441:2DEC73-3
SHIRE, H.M. SONG, DANCE AND POETRY OF
THE COURT OF SCOTLAND UNDER KING JAMES
VI.*
 M. DEAN-SMITH, 203:SPRING70-74
[CONTINUED]

[CONTINUING]
 R.D.S. JACK, 541(RES):FEB71-77
 W. TORTOLANO, 363:FEB71-54
 205(FMLS):JUL70-314
SHIRER, W.L. THE COLLAPSE OF THE THIRD
REPUBLIC.*
 N. HAMPSON, 208(FS):JAN72-113
SHIRŌ HATTORI, ED. AN AINU DIALECT DIC-
TIONARY.
 G. SIMEON, 353:APR71-105
SHIROKOGOROFF, S.M. ETHNOLOGICAL AND
LINGUISTICAL ASPECTS OF THE URAL-ALTAIC
HYPOTHESIS.
 C.F. CARLSON, 293(JAST):NOV70-166
SHKLAR, J.N. MEN AND CITIZENS.*
 D. CAMERON, 154:SEP71-598
 B.C. FINK, 207(FR):OCT70-234
 J. SAREIL, 188(ECR):WINTER70-329
SHMEAD, L.P.A. - SEE ASIMOV, I.
SHNEIDMAN, J.L. THE RISE OF THE ARAGON-
ESE-CATALAN EMPIRE, 1200-1350.
 J.N. HILLGARTH, 589:APR72-345
SHOGAN, R. A QUESTION OF JUDGMENT.*
 I. DILLIARD, 31(ASCH):SPRING73-347
SHOLEM, G. THE MESSIANIC IDEA IN JUDAISM
AND OTHER ESSAYS ON JEWISH SPIRITUALITY.
 S. CAIN, 390:DEC71-35
SHOMON, J. OPEN LAND FOR URBAN AMERICA.
 42(AR):FALL71-445
SHŌNAGON, S. THE PILLOW BOOK OF SEI
SHŌNAGON.* (I. MORRIS, ED & TRANS)
 L. ALLEN, 447(N&Q):MAY71-192
 A.H. MARKS, 352(LE&W):VOL15#1-148
SHONFIELD, A. EUROPE.
 R. PRYCE, 362:9AUG73-189
"SHŌRAI BIJUTSU, 'THE BUDDHIST ART FROM
CHINA FROM THE 6TH CENTURY TO 10TH
CENTURY'."
 A. SOPER, 57:VOL32#1-89
SHORES, C.F. PICTORIAL HISTORY OF THE
MEDITERRANEAN AIR WAR. (VOL 2)
 617(TLS):12OCT73-1260
"A SHORT-TITLE CATALOGUE OF FOREIGN BOOKS
PRINTED UP TO 1600; BOOKS PRINTED OR
PUBLISHED OUTSIDE THE BRITISH ISLES NOW
IN THE NATIONAL LIBRARY OF SCOTLAND AND
THE LIBRARY OF THE FACULTY OF ADVOCATES,
EDINBURGH."
 J. BENZING, 182:VOL24#17/18-643
 C.F. BÜHLER, 551(RENQ):WINTER71-548
SHOWALTER, E., JR. THE EVOLUTION OF THE
FRENCH NOVEL 1641-1782.
 617(TLS):29JUN73-740
SHUB, J. MOSCOW BY NIGHTMARE.
 N. CALLENDAR, 441:17JUN73-32
 617(TLS):18MAY73-562
SHUKMAN, H. LENIN AND THE RUSSIAN REVO-
LUTION.*
 H.J. ELLISON, 32:JUN72-426
SHULMAN, A.K. MEMOIRS OF AN EX-PROM
QUEEN.*
 D. MAHON, 362:26APR73-560
 P.M. SPACKS, 249(HUDR):AUTUMN72-497
 617(TLS):11MAY73-535
SHULMAN, F.J., COMP. JAPAN AND KOREA.
 293(JAST):FEB71-512
SHULMAN, M. THE LEAST WORST TELEVISION
IN THE WORLD.
 D.A.N. JONES, 362:22MAR73-396
 617(TLS):13APR73-411
SHULMAN, M. POTATOES ARE CHEAPER.
 617(TLS):9MAR73-257
SHULMAN, M. THE RAVENOUS EYE.
 D.A.N. JONES, 362:29NOV73-759
SHULVASS, M.A. FROM EAST TO WEST.
 E. MENDELSOHN, 32:SEP72-712

SHUMAKER, W. THE OCCULT SCIENCES IN THE
RENAISSANCE.
F. YATES, 453:25JAN73-39
617(TLS):12JAN73-34
SHUTE, N. THE ESCAPIST GENERATIONS.
617(TLS):13JUL73-817
SHVIDKOVSKY, O.A. BUILDINGS IN THE
U.S.S.R., 1917-1932.
45:OCT71-218
SICA, P. L'IMMAGINE DELLA CITTÀ DA
SPARTA A LAS VEGAS.
G. FANELLI, 576:DEC71-338
SICARD, C. - SEE SAND, G.
SICES, D. MUSIC AND THE MUSICIAN IN
"JEAN-CHRISTOPHE."*
W.S. WILLIS, 207(FR):FEB71-610
SICILIANO, E. DIETRO DI ME.
270:VOL22#2-40
SICILIANO, I. LES CHANSONS DE GESTE ET
L'ÉPOPÉE.*
W. CALIN, 546(RR):APR71-133
D. MC MILLAN, 208(FS):APR72-179
SIDDĪQĪ, M. CONCEPT OF MUSLIM CULTURE IN
IQBĀL.
R. WIELANDT, 182:VOL24#11/12-466
SIDDIQI, N.A. LAND REVENUE ADMINISTRA-
TION UNDER THE MUGHALS (1700-1750).
M.N. PEARSON, 318(JAOS):OCT-DEC71-560
SIDERAS, A. AESCHYLUS HOMERICUS.
W.C. SCOTT, 124:APR-MAY72-277
SIDNELL, M.J., G.P. MAYHEW & D.R. CLARK,
EDS. DRUID CRAFT.
R.J. FINNERAN, 295:FEB73-129
SIDNEY, P. AN APOLOGY FOR POETRY. (F.G.
ROBINSON, ED)
J. RACIN, 399(MLJ):NOV71-486
SIDNEY, P. THE COUNTESS OF PEMBROKE'S
"ARCADIA." (J. ROBERTSON, ED)
617(TLS):14SEP73-1063
THE DUCHESS OF MEDINA SIDONIA - SEE UNDER
MEDINA
SIDONIUS. SIDOINE APOLLINAIRE, "LETTRES."
(VOLS 2&3) (A. LOYEN, ED & TRANS)
R. BROWNING, 123:DEC72-357
A. ERNOUT, 555:VOL45FASC2-374
SIEBENMANN, G. - SEE CALDERÓN DE LA BARCA,
P.
SIEBERER, A. LAUTWANDEL UND SEINE TRIEB-
KRÄFTE.
R. SCHMITT, 343:BAND13HEFT2-178
SIEBRASSE, G. MAN: UNMAN.
L. THOMPSON, 628:FALL70-86
SIEBS, B.E. DIE PERSONENNAMEN DER GER-
MANEN.
G.B. DROEGE, 424:MAR71-57
SIEFKES, F. ZUR FORM DER ŽITIE FEODOSÝA.
B. CONRAD, 72:BAND209HEFT1/3-223
SIEGEL, B. ISAAC BASHEVIS SINGER.
R. ASSELINEAU, 189(EA):JUL-SEP71-349
SIEGEL, P.N. SHAKESPEARE IN HIS TIME AND
OURS.*
R. WARREN, 447(N&Q):OCT71-390
SIEMENS, R. THE WORDSWORTH COLLECTION.
A.J. HARTLEY, 150(DR):AUTUMN71-441
SIERS, J. HAWAII.
W.H. HONAN, 441:2DEC73-97
SIERTSEMA, B. A STUDY OF GLOSSEMATICS.
(2ND ED)
L. ZGUSTA, 353:JUN71-113
SIEVEKE, F.G. - SEE VON GRIMMELSHAUSEN,
H.J.C.
SIEVERS, H. JOHANN GEORG HAMANNS BEKEH-
RUNG.
W. SCHMIDT, 182:VOL24#19/20-710

SIGÉE, L. DIALOGUE DE DEUX JEUNES FILLES
SUR LA VIE DE COUR ET LA VIE DE RE-
TRAITE (1552).* (O. SAUVAGE, ED &
TRANS)
H. HATZFELD, 551(RENQ):AUTUMN71-406
SIGEL, E. THE KERMANSHAH TRANSFER.
N. CALLENDAR, 441:3JUN73-34
SIGELSCHIFFER, S. THE AMERICAN CON-
SCIENCE.
S.P. LEE, 441:23DEC73-10
SIGMANN, J. EIGHTEEN-FORTYEIGHT.
617(TLS):21SEP73-1081
SIGURD, B. PHONOTACTIC STRUCTURES IN
SWEDISH.
W. THÜMMEL, 206:NOV70-572
SIGWORTH, O.F., ED. CRITICISM AND
AESTHETICS 1660-1800.
G. MC FADDEN, 566:AUTUMN71-29
SIH, P.K.T., ED. THE STRENUOUS DECADE.*
J.E. SHERIDAN, 293(JAST):AUG71-879
SIHANOUK, N., WITH W. BURCHETT. MY WAR
WITH THE CIA.
J.C. THOMSON, JR., 441:26AUG73-3
617(TLS):23FEB73-198
ŠIK, O. DER DRITTE WEG.
617(TLS):2FEB73-116
ŠILBAJORIS, R. PERFECTION OF EXILE.
B. CIPLIJAUSKAITÉ, 32:MAR72-217
SILBER, M. - SEE TILTON, G.W. & F.W.
RECORD
SILBERMAN, C. CRISIS IN THE CLASSROOM.
639(VQR):SPRING71-LXXIX
SILBERSCHMIDT, M. THE UNITED STATES AND
EUROPE.
G. BARRACLOUGH, 453:31MAY73-9
SILCOCK, T.H. THE ECONOMIC DEVELOPMENT OF
THAI AGRICULTURE.
J.A. HAFNER, 293(JAST):AUG71-920
SILES SALINAS, J. LA LITERATURA DE LA
GUERRA DEL CHACO.
E. ECHEVARRÍA, 400(MLN):MAR71-317
SILKE, J.J. KINSALE.
A.J. LOOMIE, 613:SUMMER71-312
SILKIN, J. AMANA GRASS.*
L.L. MARTZ, 676(YR):SPRING72-410
M.G. PERLOFF, 659:WINTER73-97
R. SCHRAMM, 651(WHR):AUTUMN72-389
SILKIN, J., ED. POETRY OF THE COMMITTED
INDIVIDUAL.
A. MACLEAN, 362:16AUG73-223
617(TLS):20APR73-442
SILLER, V. THE OLD FRIEND.
N. CALLENDAR, 441:21OCT73-49
SILLITOE, A. GUZMAN, GO HOME AND OTHER
STORIES.
J.L. HALIO, 598(SOR):SPRING73-455
SILLITOE, A. LOVE IN THE ENVIRONS OF
VORONEZH.
P. CALLAHAN, 502(PRS):SUMMER71-178
SILLITOE, A. MEN WOMEN AND CHILDREN.
V. CUNNINGHAM, 362:8NOV73-638
617(TLS):19OCT73-1269
SILLITOE, A. RAW MATERIAL.*
442(NY):31DEC73-59
SILMAN, T.I. STILANALYSEN.
G.L. TRACY, 564:MAR71-76
SILONE, I. FONTAMARA. (C.B. PERRAULT &
M.J. AFFRON, EDS)
A. TRALDI, 276:SUMMER71-277
SILONE, I. THE STORY OF A HUMBLE CHRIS-
TIAN.
R. MAZZOCCO, 453:31MAY73-26
SILVAIN, P. LE GRAND THÉÂTRE.
617(TLS):14DEC73-1547
SILVAIN, P. LA PROMENADE EN BARQUE.
M.G. ROSE, 207(FR):OCT70-185
SILVER, C. CLASSIC LIVES.
617(TLS):6JUL73-789

SIMÓN DÍAZ, J. BIBLIOGRAFÍA DE LA LIT-
ERATURA HISPÁNICA. (VOL 7)
A.L. MACKENZIE, 86(BHS):JUL72-299
SIMÓN DÍAZ, J. BIBLIOGRAFÍA DE LA LITERA-
TURA HISPÁNICA. (VOL 8)
G. STAGG, 86(BHS):OCT72-401
H.C. WOODBRIDGE, 517(PBSA):APR-JUN72-
215
SIMONCINI, G. ARCHITETTI E ARCHITETTURA
NELLA CULTURA DEL RINASCIMENTO.
S. LANG, 46:MAR70-234
DE SIMONE, C. DIE GRIECHISCHEN ENTLEH-
NUNGEN IM ETRUSKISCHEN. (VOL 1)
K. OLZSCHA, 260(IF):BAND74-332
H. RIX, 343:BAND13HEFT2-166
DE SIMONE, C. DIE GRIECHISCHEN ENTLEH-
NUNGEN IM ETRUSKISCHEN. (VOL 2)
A.M. DEVINE, 303:VOL91-166
SIMONE, F., ED. DIZIONARIO CRITICO
DELLA LETTERATURA FRANCESE.
617(TLS):12JAN73-33
SIMONE, F. THE FRENCH RENAISSANCE.*
W.H. BOWEN, 551(RENQ):SUMMER71-253
F. SIMONE, 205(FMLS):OCT70-342
SIMONE, F., ED. MISCELLANEA DI STUDI E
RICERCHE SUL QUATTROCENTO FRANCESE.*
R. TROUSSON, 549(RLC):JAN-MAR70-128
SIMONE, F. UMANESIMO, RINASCIMENTO,
BAROCCO IN FRANCIA.*
J. BAILBÉ, 535(RHL):JAN-FEB70-121
G. MOMBELLO, 549(RLC):APR-JUN71-262
SIMONELLI, M. MATERIALI PER UN'EDIZIONE
CRITICA DEL "CONVIVO" DI DANTE.
L.W., 275(IQ):SPRING-SUMMER72-112
SIMONETT, C. DIE BAUERNHÄUSER DES KAN-
TONS GRAUBÜNDEN. (VOL 2)
R.L. WELSCH, 650(WF):APR70-131
SIMONS, J. - SEE CAMPION, E.
SIMONSON, H.P. THE CLOSED FRONTIER.
M. LEWIS, 649(WAL):WINTER72-259
SIMPLE, P. THE WORLD OF PETER SIMPLE.
617(TLS):28DEC73-1595
SIMPSON, C. A COMPENDIUM OF PRACTICAL
MUSIC, IN FIVE PARTS.
412:MAY72-148
SIMPSON, C. THE LUSITANIA.*
R.D. POLLACK, 441:6MAY73-6
E. WEEKS, 61:AUG73-101
SIMPSON, J. THE FOLKLORE OF SUSSEX.
617(TLS):22JUN73-728
SIMPSON, L. ADVENTURES OF THE LETTER I.*
W.V. DAVIS, 398:WINTER73-339
R. LATTIMORE, 249(HUDR):AUTUMN72-477
SIMPSON, L. ARKWRIGHT.*
R.M. BROWN, 102(CANL):AUTUMN72-93
SIMPSON, L. NORTH OF JAMAICA.
H. BEVINGTON, 441:8APR73-3
SIMPSON, L.P. THE MAN OF LETTERS IN NEW
ENGLAND AND THE SOUTH.
A. TURNER, 578:FALL73-111
SIMPSON, M. SORRY WRONG NUMBER.
617(TLS):26OCT73-1324
SIMPSON, R. APRIL'S THERE.
M. LEVIN, 441:14OCT73-48
SIMPSON, R.A. DIVER.
S.E. LEE, 581:DEC72-302
617(TLS):12OCT73-1216
SIMPSON, R.C. & J. WOOD. INDUSTRIAL
RELATIONS AND THE 1971 ACT.
617(TLS):30NOV73-1469
SIMPSON, R.H. & J.F. LAZENBY. THE CATA-
LOGUE OF THE SHIPS IN HOMER'S "ILIAD."*
F.M. COMBELLACK, 122:JAN72-72
M.L. LANG, 24:OCT72-602
SIMS, G.O., ED. THE BOOK OF KELLS.
R. HYDE, 325:APR71-242

SIMS, J.H. DRAMATIC USES OF BIBLICAL
ALLUSIONS IN MARLOWE AND SHAKESPEARE.
W. RIEHLE, 38:BAND88HEFT1-137
SIMS, J.M. LONDON AND MIDDLESEX PUB-
LISHED RECORDS.
I.F. MAXTED, 325:APR71-245
SIMS, J.M. THE STORY OF MY LIFE.
J.H. BURN, 447(N&Q):MAR71-119
SINARI, R.A. THE STRUCTURE OF INDIAN
THOUGHT.
D.C. MATHUR, 484(PPR):JUN72-576
M. SPRUNG, 154:JUN71-375
SINCLAIR, A. MAGOG.*
P.M. SPACKS, 249(HUDR):AUTUMN72-502
SINCLAIR, C. BIBLIOSEXUALITY.
617(TLS):27JUL73-851
SINCLAIR, K.V. DESCRIPTIVE CATALOGUE OF
MEDIEVAL AND RENAISSANCE WESTERN MANU-
SCRIPTS IN AUSTRALIA.*
J. BACKHOUSE, 354:DEC70-355
SINCLAIR, M. THE DOLLAR COVENANT.
N. CALLENDAR, 441:30SEP73-18
SINCLAIR-DE ZWART, H. ACQUISITION DU
LANGAGE ET DÉVELOPPEMENT DE LA PENSÉE.
B.T. TERVOORT, 206:FEB70-110
SINDERSON PASHA, H.C. TEN THOUSAND AND
ONE NIGHTS.
617(TLS):21DEC73-1556
SINELNIKOFF, C. L'OEUVRE DE WILHELM
REICH.
J. BERNHARDT, 542:OCT-DEC71-514
SINGER, A. & B.V. STREET, EDS. ZANDE
THEMES.
617(TLS):19JAN73-67
SINGER, B. THE COLLECTED POEMS.
A. CLUYSENAAR, 565:VOL12#1-72
SINGER, B.J. THE RATIONAL SOCIETY.
A.T., 543:MAR71-551
SINGER, I.B. A CROWN OF FEATHERS.
A. BROYARD, 441:17DEC73-41
A. KAZIN, 441:4NOV73-1
SINGER, I.B. ENEMIES, A LOVE STORY.*
R. SALE, 249(HUDR):WINTER72/73-703
SINGER, I.B. A FRIEND OF KAFKA AND
OTHER STORIES.*
J.L. HALIO, 598(SOR):SPRING73-455
R. MC KEAN, 114(CHIR):JAN-FEB71-167
S. PINSKER, 573(SSF):SPRING71-339
W.W., 502(PRS):SUMMER71-184
639(VQR):WINTER71-XIV
SINGER, I.J. OF A WORLD THAT IS NO MORE.
C. LEVIANT, 390:AUG/SEP71-76
SINGER, J.K. THE UNHOLY BIBLE.
D.V.E., 191(ELN):SEP71(SUPP)-33
SINGER, K. MIRROR, SWORD AND JEWEL.
617(TLS):2MAR73-237
SINGER, L. THAT'S THE HOUSE, THERE.
N. CALLENDAR, 441:11NOV73-50
SINGER, M. WHEN A GREAT TRADITION MOD-
ERNIZES.
617(TLS):6JUL73-774
SINGER, P. DEMOCRACY AND DISOBEDIENCE.
J. DUNN, 362:23AUG73-252
617(TLS):20JUL73-838
SINGH, A. TIGER HAVEN.
617(TLS):24AUG73-986
SINGH, G. LEOPARDI E L'INGHILTERRA.*
B. CORRIGAN, 546(RR):OCT71-239
A.G. HILL, 205(FMLS):APR70-192
SINGH, G. - SEE "CONTEMPORARY ITALIAN
VERSE"
SINGH, H. GURU NANAK AND ORIGINS OF THE
SIKH FAITH.
S.C. CRAWFORD, 485(PE&W):JUL71-348
SINGH, R.J., ED. WORLD PERSPECTIVES IN
PHILOSOPHY, RELIGION AND CULTURE.*
J.S. WU, 485(PE&W):APR70-197

SINGH, T. TOWARDS AN INTEGRATED SOCIETY.
M.R. GOODALL, 293(JAST):MAY71-707
SINGHAL, D.P. INDIA AND WORLD CIVILIZA-
TION.
617(TLS):8JUN73-641
SINGLETON, C.S., ED. ART, SCIENCE, AND
HISTORY IN THE RENAISSANCE.
L.W. SPITZ, 613:SUMMER70-317
SINGLETON, C.S., ED. INTERPRETATION.
M.C. BEARDSLEY, 322(JHI):JAN-MAR71-
143
SINGLETON, C.S. VIAGGIO A BEATRICE.
M. MARTI, 228(GSLI):VOL148FASC464-589
SINGLETON, C.S. - SEE DANTE ALIGHIERI
SINOR, D. INNER ASIA, HISTORY - CIVILI-
ZATION - LANGUAGES.
F. HUDDLE, JR., 244(HJAS):VOL30-279
SIPE, D.L. SHAKESPEARE'S METRICS.*
W. WEISS, 72:BAND209HEFT1/3-163
"SIR GAWAIN AND THE GREEN KNIGHT."*
(J.R.R. TOLKIEN & E.V. GORDON, EDS;
2ND ED REV BY N. DAVIS)
K.H. GÖLLER, 38:BAND88HEFT2-256
SIRCAR, D.C. STUDIES IN INDIAN COINS.*
L. ROCHER, 318(JAOS):OCT-DEC71-549
SIREN, O. CHINESE SCULPTURE FROM THE
FIFTH TO THE FOURTEENTH CENTURY. A
HISTORY OF EARLY CHINESE ART.
A. SOPER, 57:VOL32#4-336
SIROIS, A. MONTRÉAL DANS LE ROMAN CANA-
DIEN.*
J. WARWICK, 399(MLJ):MAY71-325
SIRSIKAR, V.M. SOVEREIGNS WITHOUT
CROWNS.
617(TLS):7SEP73-1037
SISAM, C. & K., EDS. THE OXFORD BOOK OF
MEDIEVAL ENGLISH VERSE.*
S.I. TUCKER, 382(MAE):1972/1-72
G.A.W., 581:MAR72-78
R.M. WILSON, 402(MLR):JAN72-163
SISSMAN, L.E. SCATTERED RETURNS.*
J. ATLAS, 114(CHIR):AUTUMN70-131
SITHOLE, N. THE POLYGAMIST.*
617(TLS):31AUG73-993
SITNEY, P.A., ED. FILM CULTURE.
P. GIDAL, 592:NOV71-214
SITTER, J.E. THE POETRY OF POPE'S "DUN-
CIAD."
617(TLS):5JAN73-6
SITWELL, S. CONVERSATION PIECES. NAR-
RATIVE PICTURES.
R. EDWARDS, 39:JUN70-488
SITWELL, S. FOR WANT OF THE GOLDEN CITY.
J. CAREY, 362:2AUG73-154
P. WEST, 441:7OCT73-6
617(TLS):10AUG73-920
SITWELL, S. GOTHIC EUROPE.*
W. KIDNEY, 505:MAR70-128
SIUTS, H. DIE ANSINGELIEDER ZU DEN
KALENDERFESTEN.
D-R. MOSER, 196:BAND12HEFT2/3-285
SIVERTSEN, E. FONOLOGI.*
J. VACHEK, 353:JAN71-117
SIXSMITH, E.K.G. EISENHOWER AS MILITARY
COMMANDER.
441:25MAR73-26
617(TLS):23FEB73-212
SIXTL, F. MESSMETHODEN DER PSYCHOLOGIE.
H. PETZOLD, 682(ZPSK):BAND24HEFT5-448
SJÖGREN, G. SHAKESPEARES SAMTIDA OCH
DERAS DRAMATIK.
A. MIDGAARD, 172(EDDA):1970/2-120
SJÖLIN, B. EINFÜHRUNG IN DAS FRIESISCHE.*
O. ROGBY, 597(SN):VOL43#1-289
M.O. WALSHE, 220(GL&L):OCT71-18
SJÖWALL, M. & P. WAHLÖÖ. THE ABOMINABLE
MAN.*
617(TLS):31AUG73-1007

SJÖWALL, M. & P. WAHLÖÖ. THE LOCKED ROOM.
N. CALLENDAR, 441:4NOV73-78
SKAPSKI, M.J. FROM THE MESHES.
J. DITSKY, 628:SPRING72-108
SKARD, S., ED. AMERICANA NORVEGICA.
(VOL 1)
R. ASSELINEAU, 189(EA):APR-JUN71-221
SKARD, S., ED. AMERICANA NORVEGICA.
(VOL 2)
R. ASSELINEAU, 189(EA):APR-JUN71-221
H.O., 430(NS):SEP70-478
SKELTON, J. POEMS.* (R.S. KINSMAN, ED)
J. CHALKER, 597(SN):VOL43#2-581
P. INGHAM, 541(RES):MAY71-185
P. THOMSON, 447(N&Q):JUN71-231
SKELTON, R., ED. THE CAVALIER POETS.*
P.G. STANWOOD, 102(CANL):SPRING72-98
SKELTON, R. THE HUNTING DARK.*
A. HUTCHINSON, 102(CANL):WINTER72-78
J. SAUNDERS, 565:VOL12#4-63
SKELTON, R. THE PRACTICE OF POETRY.
H. SERGEANT, 175:AUTUMN71-106
SKELTON, R. PRIVATE SPEECH.*
J. DITSKY, 628:SPRING72-108
A. HUTCHINSON, 102(CANL):WINTER72-78
SKELTON, R., ED. HERBERT READ.
M.E., 135:JUN70-135
T. HILTON, 592:JUL-AUG70-52
SKELTON, R. SELECTED POEMS, 1947-1967.*
H. SERGEANT, 175:SPRING70-29
SKELTON, R. J.M. SYNGE AND HIS WORLD.
R. HOGAN, 397(MD):FEB72-487
639(VQR):AUTUMN71-CLXXIV
SKELTON, R. THE WRITINGS OF J.M. SYNGE.
R. HOGAN, 397(MD):FEB72-487
102(CANL):WINTER72-103
639(VQR):AUTUMN71-CLXIX
SKELTON, R. - SEE SYNGE, J.M.
SKELTON, R.A. EXPLORER'S MAPS.
G. WILLS, 39:JUL71-79
SKIDMORE, I. ESCAPE FROM THE RISING SUN.
617(TLS):30NOV73-1485
SKILLING, H.G. & F. GRIFFITHS, EDS. IN-
TEREST GROUPS IN SOVIET POLITICS.
M. GARRISON, 550(RUSR):OCT71-406
M. MC CAULEY, 575(SEER):APR72-316
D.E. POWELL, 32:MAR72-181
639(VQR):SUMMER71-CXXXIV
SKILLON, G. - SEE SHAKESPEARE, W.
SKINNER, B.F. BEYOND FREEDOM AND DIG-
NITY.*
P.F. BOLLER, JR., 584(SWR):WINTER72-
80
S.J. HARTENBERG, 185:JUL72-353
A. MC LAUGHLIN, 473(PR):SPRING72-282
M. MORGAN, 111:19NOV71-58
SKINNER, M.L. THE FIFTH SPARROW.
617(TLS):1JUN73-625
SKINNER, N. - SEE EDGAR, F.
ŠKLOVSKIJ, V. LETTURA DEL DECAMERON.
A.D.B., 228(GSLI):VOL147FASC460-632
SKOLEM, T.A. ABSTRACT SET THEORY.
P. SMITH, 316:DEC71-680
SKOLIMOWSKI, H. POLISH ANALYTICAL PHIL-
OSOPHY.
A. ORENSTEIN, 497(POLR):AUTUMN71-82
SKOUMAL, A. - SEE SWIFT, J.
SKRINE, C.P. & P. NIGHTINGALE. MACARTNEY
AT KASHGAR.
617(TLS):8JUN73-641
SKRIPNIK, M. VLES-KNYHA.
M. SAMILOV, 575(SEER):OCT72-640
SKRJABINA, E. SIEGE AND SURVIVAL. (N.
LUXENBURG, ED & TRANS)
L. GOURE, 32:JUN72-432
SKRZYNECKI, P. THERE, BEHIND THE LIDS.*
K.L. GOODWIN, 381:SEP71-375

SKUTCH, M. & W.G. HAMLIN. CHILDREN AT
  WORK.
  617(TLS):7DEC73-1521
SKVORECKY, J. ALL THE BRIGHT YOUNG MEN
  AND WOMEN.
  N. ASCHERSON, 453:5APR73-34
ŠKVORECKÝ, J. MIRAKL.
  617(TLS):13APR73-408
SLADE, H. & OTHERS. REPUBLIC OF KENYA:
  REPORT OF THE COMMISSION ON THE LAW OF
  SUCCESSION.
  C.M. MC DOWELL, 69:OCT71-337
SLADE, L. SLADE'S ANATOMY OF THE HORSE.
  617(TLS):12OCT73-1216
SLADE, M. LANGUAGE OF CHANGE.
  T. RYAN, 96:AUG/SEP71-53
SLADER, J.M. THE CHURCHES OF DEVON.
  617(TLS):6JUL73-789
SLATER, G., ED. MY WARRIOR SONS.
  617(TLS):18MAY73-549
SLATER, J. INTERVENTION AND NEGOTIATION.
  J.F. THORNING, 613:AUTUMN71-477
SLATER, L. THE PLEDGE.
  M.L. ABRAMS, 287:JAN71-28
SLATER, M., ED. DICKENS 1970.*
  K.J. FIELDING, 541(RES):AUG71-364
  R.D. MC MASTER, 445(NCF):SEP71-219
  J.C. MAXWELL, 447(N&Q):NOV71-427
  S. MONOD, 189(EA):JAN-MAR71-98
  G. SMITH, 637(VS):JUN71-459
  G. THOMAS, 175:SPRING71-25
  S. WALL, 184(EIC):JUL71-261
SLATER, W.J. LEXICON TO PINDAR.*
  M.M. WILLCOCK, 123:MAR72-14
SLATOFF, W.J. WITH RESPECT TO READERS.*
  K.J. ATCHITY, 529(QQ):AUTUMN71-475
  J. MC CONKEY, 181:WINTER71-203
SLATTERY, W.C., ED. THE RICHARDSON-
  STINSTRA CORRESPONDENCE AND STINSTRA'S
  PREFACES TO "CLARISSA."*
  J. CARROLL, 541(RES):MAY71-218
  R.A. DAY, 454:WINTER72-189
  M. GEARIN-TOSH, 447(N&Q):SEP71-358
SLAVITT, D.R. ABCD.
  M. LEVIN, 441:14JAN73-25
SLAVITT, D.R. CHILD'S PLAY.
  J.C. OATES, 598(SOR):AUTUMN73-1014
SLAVITT, D.R. THE ECLOGUES OF VIRGIL.
  L.L. MARTZ, 676(YR):SPRING72-410
SLAVITT, D.R. THE OUTER MONGOLIAN.
  M. LEVIN, 441:8JUL73-22
SLAWIK, A. DIE ORTSNAMEN DER AINU.
  G.B. DROEGE, 424:MAR70-51
  G.B. DROEGE, 424:JUN70-127
SLEEMAN, W.H. RAMBLES AND RECOLLECTIONS
  OF AN INDIAN OFFICIAL. (V. SMITH, ED)
  617(TLS):28SEP73-1138
SLEEPER, J.A. & A.L. MINTZ, EDS. THE
  NEW JEWS.
  A.A. COHEN, 390:JUN/JUL71-71
SLESINGER, W. FIELD WITH FIGURATIONS.
  L.L. MARTZ, 676(YR):SPRING72-410
SLETTENGREN/WIDÉN. MODERNE ENGLISCHE
  KURZGRAMMATIK.
  R. AHRENS, 430(NS):SEP71-500
SLIM, H.C. A GIFT OF MADRIGALS AND
  MOTETS.
  617(TLS):29JUN73-751
SLIVE, S. FRANS HALS.
  G. MARTIN, 39:SEP71-242
SLIVKA, R., A.O. WEBB & M.M. PATCH. THE
  CRAFTS OF THE MODERN WORLD.
  L. LASTRA, 37:MAR70-43
ŚLIWOWSKI, R. OD TURGIENIEWA DO CZECH-
  OWA.*
  G. DONCHIN, 575(SEER):APR72-328
SLOAN, J.P. WAR GAMES.
  R. TRICKETT, 676(YR):AUTUMN71-121

SLOBIN, D.I. PSYCHOLINGUISTICS.
  H.D. BROWN, 351(LL):DEC71-249
SLOCHOWER, H. MYTHOPOESIS.
  502(PRS):FALL70-277
SLOMAN, A. & A. KING. WESTMINSTER AND
  BEYOND.
  617(TLS):3AUG73-906
SLONIMSKY, N. MUSIC SINCE 1900. (4TH ED)
  J.A.W., 410(M&L):OCT72-447
SLOTE, M.A. REASON AND SCEPTICISM.*
  B. FREED, 154:DEC71-799
  T. GREENWOOD, 483:OCT71-363
  D. MOSS, 479(PHQ):OCT71-377
SLOTKIN, R. REGENERATION THROUGH VIO-
  LENCE.
  J. DITSKY, 31(ASCH):SUMMER73-526
SLOYAN, V. & G. HUCK, EDS. CHILDREN'S
  LITURGIES.
  C.J. MC NASPY, 363:MAY71-84
SLUSSER, R.M. THE BERLIN CRISIS OF 1961.
  617(TLS):31AUG73-1006
SMALL, C.S. RAILS TO THE SETTING SUN.
  617(TLS):16MAR73-305
SMALL, W. TO KILL A MESSENGER.
  J.M. RIPLEY, 583:FALL71-110
"SMALL - ON SAFETY."
  R. SHERRILL, 441:4MAR73-3
SMALLEY, B. THE BECKET CONFLICT AND THE
  SCHOOLS.
  617(TLS):7SEP73-1035
SMALLEY, W.A. & OTHERS. ORTHOGRAPHY
  STUDIES.
  D. ABERCROMBIE, 47(ARL):VOL17FASC1-50
SMALLWOOD, J.R. I CHOSE CANADA.
  P. NEARY, 99:NOV-DEC73-14
SMART, A. THE ASSISI PROBLEM AND THE ART
  OF GIOTTO.
  F.A. AMES-LEWIS, 89(BJA):WINTER72-108
SMART, A. THE RENAISSANCE AND MANNERISM
  IN ITALY. THE RENAISSANCE AND MANNER-
  ISM OUTSIDE ITALY.
  G.T. NOSZLOPY, 89(BJA):AUTUMN72-404
SMART, G.K. RELIGIOUS ELEMENTS IN FAULK-
  NER'S EARLY NOVELS.
  F. GADO, 597(SN):VOL42#1-240
SMART, J.J.C. & B. WILLIAMS. UTILITAR-
  IANISM FOR AND AGAINST.
  617(TLS):9NOV73-1379
SMART, N. THE PHENOMENON OF RELIGION.
  617(TLS):1JUN73-619
SMETANA, J. & M-R. MYRON. MÉLANGE LITTÉR-
  AIRE.
  G.J. HASENAUER, 207(FR):MAY71-1138
  M. OPPENHEIMER, JR., 399(MLJ):FEB71-
  125
SMETS, A. & M. VAN ESBROECK - SEE BASIL
  THE GREAT
SMIBERT, J. THE NOTEBOOK OF JOHN SMI-
  BERT.* (D. EVANS, J. KERSLAKE & A.
  OLIVER, EDS)
  M. ALLENTUCK, 14:JUL70-339
  J.D. PROWN, 54:SEP70-330
SMIDT, K. MEMORIAL TRANSMISSION AND
  QUARTO COPY IN "RICHARD III."
  A. SMITH, 354:DEC71-352
SMILEY, D.V. CANADA IN QUESTION.
  P. CLARKE, 99:JAN73-25
SMIRNOV, A. IZ ISTORII ZAPADNO-EVROPJSKOJ
  LITERATURY.
  P.F. DEMBOWSKI, 545(RPH):MAY72-442
SMIT, J.W. STUDIES ON THE LANGUAGE AND
  STYLE OF COLUMBA THE YOUNGER (COLUM-
  BANUS)
  M. WINTERBOTTOM, 382(MAE):1972/3-243
SMITH, A. DICTIONARY OF CITY OF LONDON
  STREET NAMES.
  E.B. VEST, 424:JUN71-149

SMITH, A. DISCOVERING FOLKLORE IN INDUS-
TRY.
  H.R.E. DAVIDSON, 203:WINTER70-321
SMITH, A. THE ILLUSTRATED GUIDE TO
LIVERPOOL HERCULANEUM POTTERY.
  P.S.H., 135:MAR71-214
SMITH, A. LECTURES ON RHETORIC AND
BELLES LETTRES. (J.M. LOTHIAN, ED)
  A. PARREAUX, 189(EA):OCT-DEC71-537
SMITH, A. LA NUIT DE LOUIS-FERDINAND
CÉLINE.
  617(TLS):13JUL73-816
SMITH, A. SALFORD AS IT WAS.
  617(TLS):21DEC73-1573
SMITH, A. THE SHADOW IN THE CAVE.
  D.A.N. JONES, 362:29NOV73-759
  617(TLS):16NOV73-1395
SMITH, A. & J. SOUTHAM. GOOD BEACH
GUIDE.
  617(TLS):8JUN73-653
SMITH, A.B. IDEAL AND REALITY IN THE
FICTIONAL NARRATIVES OF THÉOPHILE
GAUTIER.*
  J. DECOTTIGNIES, 535(RHL):JUL-AUG71-
  713
  J.G. LOWIN, 188(ECR):SPRING70-88
SMITH, A.G.R. SCIENCE AND SOCIETY IN
THE SIXTEENTH AND SEVENTEENTH CENTUR-
IES.
  617(TLS):13APR73-425
SMITH, A.H. THE PLACE-NAMES OF WESTMOR-
LAND. (PTS 1 & 2)
  G. KRISTENSSON, 179(ES):OCT71-466
SMITH, A.J.M., ED. THE BOOK OF CANADIAN
POETRY.
  W. STUCK, 430(NS):JAN70-48
SMITH, A.J.M., ED. THE BOOK OF CANADIAN
PROSE. (VOL 1)
  W. STUCK, 430(NS):JAN70-50
"ADAM SMITH." $UPERMONEY.*
  617(TLS):3AUG73-898
SMITH, B. & W-G. WENG. CHINA.
  617(TLS):21DEC73-1568
SMITH, B.H. POETIC CLOSURE.
  J.B. BENDER, 290(JAAC):WINTER70-270
SMITH, B.S. BUT ALWAYS AS FRIENDS.
  A.H.M. KIRK-GREENE, 69:OCT70-396
SMITH, C., WITH M. BERMEJO MARCOS & E.
CHANG-RODRÍGUEZ, COMPS. COLLINS
SPANISH-ENGLISH ENGLISH-SPANISH DIC-
TIONARY.
  R.J. PENNY, 402(MLR):JUL72-668
SMITH, C.B. - SEE BABINGTON SMITH, C.
SMITH, C.M. THE WORKING MAN'S WAY IN THE
WORLD. (E. HOWE, ED)
  S. NOWELL-SMITH, 354:MAR70-75
SMITH, D. BLEEDING HEARTS...BLEEDING
COUNTRY.
  D. DUFFY, 331:AUG71-51
  A.N. RASPA, 150(DR):WINTER71/72-584
  G. WOODCOCK, 102(CANL):WINTER72-73
SMITH, D.H. CONFUCIUS.
  617(TLS):4MAY73-508
SMITH, D.I.B., ED. EDITING EIGHTEENTH-
CENTURY TEXTS.*
  R.R. ALLEN, 173(ECS):SPRING71-345
  G.D. STOUT, JR., 405(MP):AUG70-111
SMITH, D.I.B. - SEE MARVELL, A.
SMITH, D.M. - SEE UNDER MACK SMITH, D.
SMITH, E. GETTING OUT.
  441:25FEB73-22
SMITH, E.C. AMERICAN SURNAMES.
  K.B. HARDER, 424:MAR70-57
SMITH, E.C. NAMING YOUR BABY. (2ND ED)
  K.B. HARDER, 424:DEC70-320

SMITH, F. & G.A. MILLER, EDS. THE GENE-
SIS OF LANGUAGE.
  H.C.J. DUIJKER, 206:NOV70-580
  V. RŪĶE-DRAVIŅA, 353:OCT71-96
SMITH, F.B. RADICAL ARTISAN.
  617(TLS):23NOV73-1420
SMITH, G. CANADA AND THE CANADIAN QUES-
TION.
  W.F.E. MORLEY, 296:WINTER73-85
  G.W., 102(CANL):AUTUMN72-113
SMITH, G. A COLLECTION OF DESIGNS FOR
HOUSEHOLD FURNITURE.
  R. EDWARDS, 39:JUL71-75
SMITH, G. DICKENS, MONEY, AND SOCIETY.*
  L. LANE, JR., 594:FALL70-377
SMITH, G. - SEE HUXLEY, A.
SMITH, G.A. & C.D., EDS. THE ARMCHAIR
MOUNTAINEER.
  J. BONI, 649(WAL):SUMMER70-162
SMITH, G.E. & M.P. LEAMON, EDS. EFFEC-
TIVE FOREIGN LANGUAGE INSTRUCTION IN
THE SECONDARY SCHOOL.
  E.C. CONDON, 207(FR):FEB71-601
SMITH, H. SHAKESPEARE'S ROMANCES.
  617(TLS):29JUN73-752
SMITH, H.H. ETHNOBOTANY OF THE MENOMINI
INDIANS.
  E.P. HAMP, 269(IJAL):APR71-136
SMITH, I. THE DEATH OF A WOMBAT.
  617(TLS):20JUL73-842
SMITH, I.C. - SEE UNDER CRICHTON SMITH,
I.
SMITH, J. COLONIAL CADET IN NIGERIA.
  A.H.M. KIRK-GREENE, 69:OCT70-396
  P. SALMON, 182:VOL24#9/10-445
SMITH, J. ENTERING ROOMS.
  617(TLS):11MAY73-516
SMITH, J.E. THEMES IN AMERICAN PHILOSO-
PHY.
  J. GRANGE, 613:SUMMER71-313
SMITH, J.H. CONSTANTINE THE GREAT.
  J.W. BARKER, 651(WHR):WINTER72-77
  J. DAHMUS, 124:DEC71-136
SMITH, J.H. FRANCIS OF ASSISI.
  617(TLS):27APR73-479
SMITH, J.M. & T. CAWKWELL, EDS. THE
WORLD ENCYCLOPEDIA OF FILM.
  617(TLS):2MAR73-228
SMITH, J.R. FOCKE-WULF.
  617(TLS):14SEP73-1065
SMITH, K. WORK, DISTANCES/POEMS.
  617(TLS):11MAY73-516
SMITH, K.J. THE PITY.
  C. LEVENSON, 529(QQ):SUMMER71-309
SMITH, L. FANCY STRUT.
  M. LEVIN, 441:7OCT73-47
SMITH, L. THE ORIGINAL.
  E.S. RABKIN, 385(MQR):SUMMER73-291
SMITH, L. SOMETHING IN THE WIND.
  639(VQR):SUMMER71-XCVI
SMITH, M. CANTO FOR A GYPSY.
  N. CALLENDAR, 441:21JAN73-26
SMITH, M. FINE ENGLISH COOKERY.
  617(TLS):30NOV73-1485
SMITH, M. THE SECRET GOSPEL. CLEMENT OF
ALEXANDRIA AND A SECRET GOSPEL OF MARK.
  W.H.C. FREND, 453:9AUG73-24
  P. PARKER, 441:22JUL73-5
SMITH, M. - SEE BRONTË, C.
SMITH, M. - SEE DE RONSARD, P.
SMITH, M.A. FRANÇOIS MAURIAC.*
  C.S. BROSMAN, 207(FR):MAR71-795
SMITH, M.A., S. PARKER & C.S. SMITH, EDS.
LEISURE AND SOCIETY IN BRITAIN.
  617(TLS):14DEC73-1534

SMITH, M.J., COMP. JOHN E. FOGARTY, AN
INVENTORY OF HIS PAPERS IN THE ARCHIVES
AND MANUSCRIPT COLLECTIONS OF THE LIB-
RARY OF PROVIDENCE COLLEGE.
   P. MC CARTHY, 14:JUL71-315
SMITH, P.D. FOREVER ISLAND.
   M. LEVIN, 441:25MAR73-48
SMITH, P.D., JR. A COMPARISON OF THE
COGNITIVE AND AUDIOLINGUAL APPROACHES
TO FOREIGN LANGUAGE INSTRUCTION.
   T. ANDERSSON, 238:MAR71-216
   R.C. CONRAD, 221(GQ):MAR71-259
   R. STEELE, 67:NOV72-274
SMITH, P.M. LAST RITES.
   R. TRICKETT, 676(YR):AUTUMN71-121
SMITH, P.M. CLÉMENT MAROT, POET OF THE
FRENCH RENAISSANCE.
   F. GRAY, 401(MLQ):JUN72-186
   F. JOUKOVSKY, 545(RPH):MAY72-478
SMITH, R., COMP. THE ARCHIVES OF THE
FRENCH PROTESTANT CHURCH OF LONDON.
(QUARTO SER, VOL 50)
   617(TLS):16MAR73-305
SMITH, R. KINGDOMS OF THE YORUBA.
   J.D.Y. PEEL, 69:JAN70-84
SMITH, R. LYRIC AND POLEMIC.
   617(TLS):8JUN73-646
SMITH, R.A., ED. AESTHETIC CONCEPTS AND
EDUCATION.
   S. ROUVE, 89(BJA):SPRING72-195
SMITH, R.C. THE ART OF PORTUGAL.
   T. CROMBIE, 39:MAR71-230
   E.T.J., 135:APR70-277
SMITH, R.K. SADIE SHAPIRO'S KNITTING
BOOK.
   M. LEVIN, 441:13MAY73-39
   617(TLS):16NOV73-1407
SMITH, R.P. CAIUS MARIUS. (N.M. WEST-
LAKE, ED)
   V.J. CLEARY, 124:DEC71-132
SMITH, S. ESP AND HYPNOSIS.
   M. GARDNER, 453:3MAY73-16
SMITH, S. A GRAVE AFFAIR.
   N. CALLENDAR, 441:17JUN73-32
   442(NY):9JUL73-72
SMITH, T.C. THE AGRARIAN ORIGINS OF
MODERN JAPAN.
   M.V. LAMBERTI, 318(JAOS):OCT-DEC71-526
SMITH, T.D - SEE UNDER D'ARCH SMITH, T.
SMITH, V. - SEE SLEEMAN, W.H.
SMITH, V.L. ANTON CHEKHOV AND THE LADY
WITH THE DOG.
   617(TLS):21SEP73-1086
SMITH, W. THE SUNBIRD.
   M. LEVIN, 441:29JUL73-13
SMITH, W., JR. THE HISTORY OF THE PRO-
VINCE OF NEW YORK. (M. KAMMEN, ED)
   617(TLS):26JAN73-103
SMITH, W.E. NYERERE OF TANZANIA.
   617(TLS):2MAR73-244
SMITH, W.J. NEW AND SELECTED POEMS.*
   J.T. IRWIN, 598(SOR):SUMMER73-720
SMITHSON, A. & P. THE EUSTON ARCH AND
THE GROWTH OF THE LONDON, MIDLAND AND
SCOTTISH RAILWAY.
   J.R.F.T., 135:MAR70-201
SMITHSON, A. & P. ORDINARINESS AND
LIGHT.
   P.D. EISENMAN, 44:MAY71-76
SMITHSON, A. & P. WITHOUT RHETORIC.
   617(TLS):21DEC73-1558
SMITHYMAN, K. EARTHQUAKE WEATHER.
   617(TLS):27APR73-474
SMITS, R., COMP. HALF A CENTURY OF
SOVIET SERIALS, 1917-1968.*
   P. VALOIS, 575(SEER):JAN72-149

SMOCK, D.R. CONFLICT AND CONTROL IN AN
AFRICAN TRADE UNION.
   R.D. GRILLO, 69:JAN71-75
SMOLLETT, T. THE ADVENTURES OF FERDI-
NAND COUNT FATHOM. (D. GRANT, ED)
   P-G. BOUCÉ, 189(EA):OCT-DEC71-536
SMOLLETT, T. THE LETTERS OF TOBIAS SMOL-
LETT, M.D.* (L.M. KNAPP, ED)
   P-G. BOUCÉ, 189(EA):JAN-MAR71-95
   J.D. FLEEMAN, 447(N&Q):SEP71-357
   G.S. ROUSSEAU, 173(ECS):SPRING71-336
   481(PQ):JUL71-482
SMOLLETT, T. TRAVELS THROUGH FRANCE AND
ITALY.
   P-G. BOUCÉ, 189(EA):JAN-MAR70-93
SMUTS, J.C. SELECTIONS FROM THE SMUTS
PAPERS. (VOLS 5-7) (J. VAN DER POEL,
ED)
   617(TLS):9NOV73-1359
SMUTS, J.C. WALT WHITMAN. (A.L. MC LEOD,
ED)
   617(TLS):21SEP73-1086
SMYTH, P. NATIVE GRASS.
   R. HOWARD, 491:SEP73-351
SMYTH, W.R. THESAURUS CRITICUS AD SEXTI
PROPERTII TEXTUM.
   G.P. GOOLD, 487:AUTUMN71-294
SNAITH, W. ON THE WIND'S WAY.
   W.F. BUCKLEY, JR., 441:18NOV73-7
SNELGROVE, D., WITH J. MAYNE & B. TAYLOR
- SEE HARDIE, M.
SNELL, B. SZENEN AUS GRIECHISCHEN DRAMEN.
   L. GOLDEN, 124:JAN72-171
SNELL, B. TYRTAIOS UND DIE SPRACHE DES
EPOS.*
   C. DOBIAS-LALOU, 555:VOL45FASC1-148
SNELL, B., H. ERBSE & E-M. VOIGT. LEXICON
DES FRÜHGRIECHISCHEN EPOS. (PT 6)
   P. CHANTRAINE, 555:VOL45FASC2-330
   M.M. WILLCOCK, 123:MAR72-99
SNELLGROVE, D.L. FOUR LAMAS OF DOLPO.
(VOL 2)
   P.J.H., 543:DEC70-346
SNELLING, L. THE HERESY.
   N. CALLENDAR, 441:7OCT73-44
SNETHLAGE, J.L. HEINRICH HEINE 1797-1856.
   J.L.S., 191(ELN):SEP71(SUPP)-137
SNIDER, L. - SEE COWARD, N.
SNOW, C.P. LAST THINGS.*
   J.L. HALIO, 598(SOR):SPRING73-455
   C. SHAPIRO, 454:FALL71-87
SNOW, C.P. THE MALCONTENTS.*
   P.M. SPACKS, 249(HUDR):AUTUMN72-505
SNOW, C.P. THE SLEEP OF REASON.
   J.C. FIELD, 556(RLV):1971/1-93
   S. MONOD, 189(EA):JUL-SEP70-350
SNOW, E. THE LONG REVOLUTION.*
   H.E. SALISBURY, 441:14JAN73-4
   617(TLS):16MAR73-287
SNOW, L.W. CHINA ON STAGE.
   J. SPENCE, 441:14JAN73-4
SNOW, V.F. ESSEX THE REBEL.
   E. LE COMTE, 551(RENQ):WINTER71-577
SNOWDEN, F.M., JR. BLACKS IN ANTIQUITY.*
   J.M. COOK, 123:JUN72-253
   H. DESCHAMPS, 69:JAN71-68
   C.R. WHITTAKER, 487:SUMMER71-186
SNUKAL, R. HIGH TALK.
   617(TLS):31AUG73-996
SNYDER, G. EARTH HOUSE HOLD.* THE BACK
COUNTRY.
   D. GERBER, 600:FALL69-147
SNYDER, G. REGARDING WAVE.*
   M.G. PERLOFF, 659:WINTER73-97
   R.I. SCOTT, 648:APR71-6
   639(VQR):SPRING71-LX

SNYDER, H.H. THE HALL OF THE MOUNTAIN
KING.
P. ADAMS, 61:SEP73-118
SNYDER, W.A. SOUTHERN PUGET SOUND SAL-
ISH.
P. AMOSS, 269(IJAL):APR71-134
SOBEL, I.P. THE HOSPITAL MAKERS.
M. LEVIN, 441:18MAR73-40
SODANO, A.R. PORPHYRII QUAESTIONUM HOM-
ERICARUM LIBER I.
N.G. WILSON, 123:DEC72-412
SÖDERGÅRD, Ö. - SEE BENOÎT
SOHL, J. THE RESURRECTION OF FRANK BOR-
CHARD.
M. LEVIN, 441:15APR73-35
SOKOLOFF, A.H. HADLEY.
442(NY):16JUN73-111
DE SOLA PINTO, V. THE CITY THAT SHONE.
R. LAWRENCE, 175:SPRING70-33
P. LEGOUIS, 189(EA):JAN-MAR71-104
T.F. STALEY, 295:NOV72-576
SOLBERG, C. IMMIGRATION AND NATIONALISM.
A.F. CORWIN, 263:JAN-MAR72-54
SOLDATI, M. THE MALACCA CANE.
617(TLS):15JUN73-661
SOLDATOV, G.M. ARSENII MATSEEVICH MIT-
ROPOLIT ROSTOVSKII, 1696-1772.
E. BENOWITZ, 32:JUN72-416
"SOLDIER AND BRAVE."
W. GARD, 584(SWR):SUMMER72-V
SOLER, F. ELS HEROIS I LES GRANDESES.
(X. FÀBREGAS, ED)
J-L. MARFANY, 86(BHS):JUL72-323
SOLERI, P. ARCOLOGY.
J.H., 45:APR70-129
M. MILLS, 363:FEB71-56
SOLIN, H. BEITRÄGE ZUR KENNTNIS DER
GRIECHISCHEN PERSONENNAMEN IN ROM.
C. DOBIAS-LALOU, 182:VOL24#21/22-813
SOLIN, H. EINE NEUE FLUCHTAFEL AUS
OSTIA.*
J.M. REYNOLDS, 123:MAR72-143
SOLL, I. AN INTRODUCTION TO HEGEL'S "MET-
APHYSICS."
R.J.B., 543:DEC70-346
SÖLL, L. DIE BEZIECHNUNGEN FÜR DEN WALD
IN DEN ROMANISCHEN SPRACHEN.
M. BAMBECK, 260(IF):BAND74-284
H. KAHANE, 545(RPH):MAY72-427
SOLLERS, P. H.
617(TLS):2NOV73-1333
SOLLERS, P. LOGIQUES.
L. FINAS, 98:JUL70-600
R. LAPORTE, 98:OCT70-813
SOLMI, S. SCRITTI LEOPARDIANI.*
M. FUBINI, 228(GSLI):VOL147FASC460-
617
SOLMSEN, F. - SEE HESIOD
SOLOMON, A., WITH S. PERRY & R. DEVINE.
INTERPERSONAL COMMUNICATION.
W.C. REDDING, 583:WINTER70-184
SOLOMON, M. MAGADAN.
J. WALKIN, 32:DEC72-902
SOLOMON, M.C. ETERNAL GEOMATER.*
J.C. SHERWOOD, 648:OCT70-84
SOLOTAROFF, T. THE RED HOT VACUUM.
42(AR):FALL/WINTER70/71-460
SOLOTAROFF, T. - SEE "AMERICAN REVIEW 16"
SOLOVEY, M.M. THE BYZANTINE DIVINE LIT-
URGY.
J. MEYENDORFF, 32:MAR72-149
SOLOVIEFF, G. - SEE MADAME DE STAËL &
OTHERS
SOLOWAY, R. PRELATES AND PEOPLE.
D. ROBERTS, 637(VS):SEP70-95
SOLSTAD, D. IRR! GRÖNT!
I.T. SVENNING, 270:VOL21#2-151

SOLZHENITSYN, A. AUGUST 1914.* (RUSSIAN
TITLE: AVGUST CHETYRNADTSATOGO.)
N. CHRISTESEN, 381:DEC71-402
J. KORG, 31(ASCH):WINTER72/73-164
E. PAWEL, 390:DEC71-68
SOLZHENITSYN, A. CANCER WARD.*
J.L. HALIO, 598(SOR):SPRING73-455
SOLZHENITSYN, A. CANDLE IN THE WIND.
H.E. SALISBURY, 441:9SEP73-43
R. WILLIAMS, 362:29NOV73-750
SOLZHENITSYN, A. NOBEL LECTURE.
E. WEEKS, 61:APR73-124
SOLZHENITSYN, A. "ONE WORD OF TRUTH..."*
D. CAUTE, 362:8FEB73-188
SOMASUNDARAM PILLAI, P.M.J. A HISTORY OF
TAMIL LITERATURE.
S. VAIDYANATHAN, 318(JAOS):APR-JUN71-
322
SOMERVILLE, E. & M. ROSS. THE REAL CHAR-
LOTTE. (NEW ED)
J. BAYLEY, 362:11JAN73-57
SOMFAI, L., COMP. JOSEPH HAYDN: HIS LIFE
IN CONTEMPORARY PICTURES.*
P.H.L., 414(MQ):APR70-295
SOMJEE, A.H. DEMOCRACY AND POLITICAL
CHANGE IN VILLAGE INDIA.
617(TLS):7SEP73-1037
SOMMER, C. - SEE OPITZ, M.
SOMMERSTEIN, A.H. THE SOUND PATTERN OF
ANCIENT GREEK.
617(TLS):30MAR73-361
DE' SOMMI, L. QUATTRO DIALOGHI IN MA-
TERIA DI RAPPRESENTAZIONI SCENICHE.
(F. MAROTTI, ED)
R.C., 228(GSLI):VOL147FASC458/459-471
SONDEREGGER, S. ALTHOCHDEUTSCH IN ST.
GALLEN.
R.H. LAWSON, 301(JEGP):JAN72-56
H. TIEFENBACH, 182:VOL24#3-100
SONDEREGGER, S. ANDREAS HEUSLER UND DIE
SPRACHE.
K. MATZEL, 343:BAND13HEFT1-104
SONDEREGGER, S., A.M. HAAS & H. BURGER,
EDS. TYPOLOGIA LITTERARUM.
P.F. GANZ, 220(GL&L):APR72-302
SONE, R., ED. LES FANTAISIES AMOUR-
EUSES.
R. ZUBER, 535(RHL):JAN-FEB71-70
SONKES, M. DESSINS DU XVE SIÈCLE,
GROUPE VAN DER WEYDEN.
K.G. BOON, 90:MAY71-277
SÖNMEZ, E. THE NOVELIST GEORGE MEREDITH.
617(TLS):16MAR73-305
SONNICHSEN, C.L. PASS OF THE NORTH.
(2ND ED) (S.D. MYRES, ED)
J.D. MC KEE, 649(WAL):FALL70-239
SONNINO, L.A. A HANDBOOK TO SIXTEENTH-
CENTURY RHETORIC.*
D. NEWTON-DE MOLINA, 148:SUMMER71-189
SONNINO, P. - SEE LOUIS XIV
SONNINO, S. DIARIO. (VOL 1 ED BY B.F.
BROWN, VOLS 2&3 ED BY P. PASTORELLI)
SCRITTI E DISCORSI EXTRAPARLAMENTARI.
(B.F. BROWN, ED)
617(TLS):21DEC73-1569
SONSTROEM, D. ROSSETTI AND THE LADY
FAIR.
P.M. PITTMAN, 637(VS):MAR71-352
SONTAG, F. THE EXISTENTIALIST PROLEGOM-
ENA TO A FUTURE METAPHYSICS.*
J. HOWIE, 154:JUN71-380
SONTAG, F. & J.K. ROTH. THE AMERICAN
RELIGIOUS EXPERIENCE.
V.M. AMES, 319:JAN73-125
SONTAG, S. STYLES OF RADICAL WILL.
C. FOX, 592:MAR70-135

SOOM, A. DIE ZUNFTHANDWERKER IN REVAL
IM SIEBZEHNTEN JAHRHUNDERT.
W. KIRCHNER, 32:DEC72-912
SOPHOCLES. ELECTRA. (J.H. KELLS, ED)
617(TLS):23MAR73-333
SOPHOCLES. OEDIPUS THE KING BY SOPHOCLES.
(T. GOULD, TRANS)
S.G. DAITZ, 124:OCT71-60
SOPHOCLES. PHILOCTETES.* (T.B.L. WEB-
STER, ED)
H. LLOYD-JONES, 123:MAR72-102
SOPHOCLES. SOPHOKLES, "KÖNIG ÖDIPUS."
(K.A. PFEIFF, TRANS)
H. LLOYD-JONES, 123:JUN72-235
SOR, F. METHOD FOR THE SPANISH GUITAR.
L. SALTER, 415:JAN72-49
SORAI, O. DISTINGUISHING THE WAY.
T. KUWAHARA, 293(JAST):NOV70-190
R.K. SAKAI, 485(PE&W):JAN71-92
SÖRBOM, G. MIMESIS AND ART.
A. BERLEANT, 186(ETC.):DEC70-467
SORDI, M. ROMA E I SANNITI NEL IV SECOLO
A.C.*
J. PINSENT, 313:VOL61-271
SOREIL, A. LANCES ROMPUES - PROPOS
CRITIQUES.
J. DE CALUWÉ, 556(RLV):1970/1-111
SORELL, W. THE DUALITY OF VISION.
C. HEIMSATH, 363:FEB71-62
SORELL, W. THE SWISS.*
617(TLS):22JUN73-721
SORIANO, M. LES CONTES DE PERRAULT,
CULTURE SAVANTE ET TRADITIONS POPU-
LAIRES.*
M. DE MEYER, 196:BAND12HEFT1-106
SORIANO, M. LE DOSSIER PERRAULT.
617(TLS):4MAY73-507
SORRENTINO, G. IMAGINATIVE QUALITIES OF
ACTUAL THINGS.*
42(AR):FALL71-440
SORRENTINO, G. STEELWORK.
42(AR):SPRING71-132
SŌSEKI, N. BOTCHAN.
S. HILL, 362:22FEB73-251
617(TLS):30MAR73-340
SŌSEKI, N. GRASS ON THE WAYSIDE (MICHI-
KUSA).*
R.H.B., 648:OCT70-81
YOSHIO IWAMOTO, 244(HJAS):VOL30-258
SŌTER, I. ASPECTS ET PARALLÉLISMES DE LA
LITTÉRATURE HONGROISE.
R.C. BALL, 131(CL):WINTER72-79
SOUBIRAN, J. - SEE VITRUVIUS
SOUDEK, L. STRUCTURE OF SUBSTANDARD
WORDS IN BRITISH AND AMERICAN ENGLISH.
J.E. PIERCE, 353:DEC70-108
SOULE, L. THE EYE OF THE CEDAR.
M. FIAMENGO, 102(CANL):SUMMER72-104
SOUPAULT, P. POÈMES ET POÉSIES (1917-
1973).
617(TLS):1JUN73-610
SOUTER, G. THE IDLE HILL OF SUMMER.
617(TLS):6JUL73-789
"SOUTH AMERICAN TRAVEL GUIDE."
S.S. BENSON, 37:OCT71-43
SOUTHAM, B.C., ED. CRITICAL ESSAYS ON
JANE AUSTEN.*
I. RIVERS, 148:AUTUMN71-282
SOUTHERN, R. THE STAGING OF PLAYS BEFORE
SHAKESPEARE.
617(TLS):24AUG73-982
SOUTHERN, R. THE VICTORIAN THEATRE.
J.C. TREWIN, 157:SPRING71-69
SOUTHERN, R.W. MEDIEVAL HUMANISM AND
OTHER STUDIES.
J.D. ADAMS, 589:APR72-353

SOUTHERN, T. BLUE MOVIE.
V. CUNNINGHAM, 362:31MAY73-728
617(TLS):1JUN73-604
LORD SOUTHESK. SASKATCHEWAN AND THE
ROCKY MOUNTAINS.
L.R. RICOU, 296:SUMMER73-116
SOUTHEY, R. & S.T. COLERIDGE. OMNIANA
OR HORAE OTIOSIORES. (R. GITTINGS, ED)
J. RAIMOND, 189(EA):APR-JUN70-227
SOVIJÄRVI, A. DER LAUTÜBERGANG IM LICHTE
VON RÖNTGENFILMEN UND SPECTROGRAMMEN.
I.H. SLIS, 361:VOL26#2-209
SOW, A.I., ED & TRANS. CHRONIQUES ET
RÉCITS DU FOÛTA DJALON.
M. DUPIRE, 69:APR70-185
L.H. STENNES, 315(JAL):VOL10PT2-63
SOWDEN, H. TOWARDS AN AUSTRALIAN ARCHI-
TECTURE.
J.M.R., 46:APR70-316
SOWELL, T. SAY'S LAW.
617(TLS):27JUL73-880
SOWERBY, B. THE DISINHERITED.
617(TLS):30NOV73-1478
SOWINSKI, A. LES MUSICIENS POLONAIS ET
SLAVES.
J. TYRRELL, 415:JUN72-567
SOYINKA, W. THE MAN DIED.*
G. WEALES, 441:29JUL73-10
617(TLS):2MAR73-244
SOYINKA, W. SEASON OF ANOMY.
617(TLS):14DEC73-1529
SOZZI, G.P. GERMAIN NOUVEAU.
M. SCHAETTEL, 557(RSH):APR-JUN71-328
SPACKS, B. THE COMPANY OF CHILDREN.
G. KUZMA, 502(PRS):WINTER70/71-358
SPACKS, B. SOMETHING HUMAN.
J. KESSLER, 491:FEB73-292
SPACKS, P.M. AN ARGUMENT OF IMAGES.
T.R. EDWARDS, 301(JEGP):OCT72-546
SPACKS, P.M., ED. LATE AUGUSTAN PROSE.
566:AUTUMN71-29
SPADARO, M.D. SULLE EGLOGHE POLITICHE DI
TITO CALPURNIO SICULO.
S. VIARRE, 555:VOL45FASC2-363
SPADOLINI, G. IL MONDO DI GIOLITTI.
B. MERRY, 270:VOL21#4-195
SPAGNOL, M. - SEE SALGARI, E.
SPAHR, B.L. ANTON ULRICH AND ARAMENA.
G. SCHULZ-BEHREND, 400(MLN):APR71-425
E-P. WIECKENBERG, 680(ZDP):BAND89
HEFT2-274
SPALEK, J.M. ERNST TOLLER AND HIS CRIT-
ICS.*
A.J. DICKSON, 354:MAR70-80
M. RESO, 654(WB):7/1970-207
SPARK, M. THE DRIVER'S SEAT.*
42(AR):FALL/WINTER70/71-458
SPARK, M. THE HOTHOUSE BY THE EAST
RIVER.
P. ADAMS, 61:MAY73-122
R.P. BRICKNER, 441:29APR73-24
D. MAY, 362:1MAR73-283
617(TLS):2MAR73-229
SPARK, M. NOT TO DISTURB.*
P.M. SPACKS, 249(HUDR):AUTUMN72-502
SPARKES, B.A. & L. TALCOTT. THE ATHENIAN
AGORA. (VOL 12, PTS 1 & 2)
J. FREL, 124:SEP71-25
SPARKS, B.W. & R.G. WEST. THE ICE AGE
IN BRITAIN.
617(TLS):30MAR73-359
SPARROW, J. VISIBLE WORDS.*
F.M. COMBELLACK, 122:JUL72-208
D.A. COVI, 90:MAR71-158
N. GRAY, 354:SEP70-269
A.R. TURNER, 551(RENQ):WINTER71-539
SPARSHOTT, F.E. LOOKING FOR PHILOSOPHY.
617(TLS):16FEB73-190

SPATT, B.M. A PROPOSAL TO CHANGE THE
STRUCTURE OF CITY PLANNING.
505:AUG71-85
SPEAIGHT, R. GEORGES BERNANOS.
617(TLS):27JUL73-872
SPEAIGHT, R. THE PROPERTY BASKET.
J.C. TREWIN, 157:SUMMER71-78
SPEAR, A.T. BRANCUSI'S BIRDS.
A. BOWNESS, 592:NOV70-221
SPEARING, A.C. THE GAWAIN-POET.
J.J. ANDERSON, 148:SUMMER71-191
L.D. BENSON, 401(MLQ):JUN72-183
D.R. HOWARD, 589:JUL72-548
R.M. WILSON, 175:AUTUMN71-96
SPEARMAN, D. THE NOVEL AND SOCIETY.
N. WÜRZBACH, 430(NS):OCT70-532
SPEARS, M.K. DIONYSUS AND THE CITY.*
C. BROOKS, 569(SR):SPRING72-361
G. CAMBON, 141:FALL71-417
L. CASPER, 613:WINTER71-617
S.C. MOORE, 219(GAR):WINTER71-507
SPEARS, R.A. BASIC COURSE IN MENDE.
G. INNES, 69:JAN70-97
SPECHT, E.K. THE FOUNDATIONS OF WITTGEN-
STEIN'S LATE PHILOSOPHY.*
J. HARTNACK, 482(PHR):JUL71-391
L. POMPA, 478:JUL70-181
SPECK, R.V. & C.L. ATTNEAVE. FAMILY
NETWORKS.
E. FIRST, 441:23SEP73-20
"THE SPECTATOR." (D.F. BOND, ED)
A. MAUROCORDATO, 189(EA):JUL-SEP70-
282
SPECTOR, J.J. THE AESTHETICS OF FREUD.
J. HOFFELD, 441:11MAR73-38
617(TLS):4MAY73-495
SPECTOR, J.J. THE MURALS OF EUGÈNE DELA-
CROIX AT SAINT-SULPICE.
B. FARWELL, 54:MAR71-127
SPECTOR, R.D. ENGLISH LITERARY PERIODI-
CALS AND THE CLIMATE OF OPINION DURING
THE SEVEN YEARS' WAR.
P-G. BOUCÉ, 189(EA):APR-JUN71-199
SPECTOR, R.D. TOBIAS GEORGE SMOLLETT.
P-G. BOUCÉ, 189(EA):JAN-MAR70-91
G.S. ROUSSEAU, 173(ECS):SPRING71-336
SPEE, F. GÜLDENES TUGEND-BUCH. (T.G.M.
VAN OORSCHOT, ED)
B.L. SPAHR, 133:1971/1&2-198
SPEER, A. ERINNERUNGEN.
R. GILL, 220(GL&L):OCT71-58
SPEER, A. INSIDE THE THIRD REICH.
M. SYRKIN, 390:DEC70-50
K.P. TAUBER, 639(VQR):WINTER71-145
SPEIGHT, J. ALF GARNETT.
F. DILLON, 362:6DEC73-788
SPEIGHT, J. IT STANDS TO REASON.
F. DILLON, 362:6DEC73-788
617(TLS):19OCT73-1273
SPEIRS, J. POETRY TOWARDS NOVEL.
J.D. JUMP, 148:SUMMER71-187
SPEIRS, L. TOLSTOY AND CHEKHOV.
J.M. CURTIS, 550(RUSR):OCT71-415
R. FREEBORN, 575(SEER):JAN72-120
K.D. KRAMER, 32:MAR72-190
K. SANINE, 182:VOL24#9/10-426
SPELLERBERG, G. VERHÄNGNIS UND GESCHICH-
TE.
G. GILLESPIE, 301(JEGP):JUL72-413
SPENCE, C.H. CLARA MORISON. (S. EADE,
ED)
B.H. BENNETT, 71(ALS):OCT73-220
SPENCE, K. THE COMPANION GUIDE TO KENT
AND SUSSEX.
617(TLS):27JUL73-884
SPENCER, H., ED. THE PENROSE ANNUAL 1970.
(VOL 63)
A. FROSHAUG, 592:JUL-AUG70-60

SPENCER, H., ED. THE PENROSE GRAPHIC
ARTS INTERNATIONAL ANNUAL 66, 1973.
617(TLS):10AUG73-936
SPENCER, H. PIONEERS OF MODERN TYPOGRA-
PHY.
A. FROSHAUG, 592:JUL-AUG70-60
SPENCER, H., ED. READINGS IN ART HIS-
TORY.
R.M. CAPERS, 54:DEC71-550
SPENCER, M.C. THE ART CRITICISM OF THÉO-
PHILE GAUTIER.*
R. DEMORIS, 557(RSH):JUL-SEP71-484
205(FMLS):JUL70-314
SPENCER, S. LAST NIGHT AT THE BRAIN
THIEVES BALL.
M. LEVIN, 441:16SEP73-32
SPENCER, S. THE SPACE BETWEEN.
M. LEVIN, 441:8JUL73-24
442(NY):17SEP73-154
SPENCER, S. SPACE, TIME AND STRUCTURE IN
THE MODERN NOVEL.
D.D. GALLOWAY, 659:SUMMER73-398
SPENCER, S. WAYS OF FISHING.
617(TLS):12JAN73-49
SPENCER, T.J.B. & R.L. SMALLWOOD - SEE
"THE YEARBOOK OF ENGLISH STUDIES"
SPENCER, T.J.B. & S.M. WELLS - SEE "A
BOOK OF MASQUES"
SPENDER, S. THE GENEROUS DAYS.*
P.J. CALLAHAN, 569(SR):AUTUMN72-639
W.H. PRITCHARD, 249(HUDR):SPRING72-127
SPENDER, S., ED. D.H. LAWRENCE.
A. BROYARD, 441:9NOV73-45
W. PRITCHARD, 362:1NOV73-603
442(NY):24DEC73-80
617(TLS):9NOV73-1369
SPENDER, S. & D. HALL, EDS. THE CONCISE
ENCYCLOPEDIA OF ENGLISH AND AMERICAN
POETS AND POETRY.
L.C. BONNEROT, 189(EA):JAN-MAR70-100
SPERATI-PIÑERO, E.S. DE "SONATA DE OTOÑO"
AL ESPERPENTO (ASPECTOS DEL ARTE DE
VALLE-INCLÁN).*
A. ADELL, 270:VOL21#1-108
SPERBER, H. EINFÜHRUNG IN DIE BEDEUTUNGS-
LEHRE. (3RD ED)
R. RIS, 343:BAND13HEFT2-202
SPERK, K., ED. MEDIEVAL ENGLISH SAINTS'
LEGENDS.
R.M. WILSON, 402(MLR):JAN72-163
SPERONI, C. THE APHORISMS OF ORAZIO RIN-
ALDI, ROBERT GREENE, AND LUCAS GRACIÁN
DANTISCO.*
M.E. BARRICK, 292(JAF):APR-JUN71-258
SPETTIGUE, D.O. FREDERICK PHILIP GROVE.*
B. NESBITT, 648:OCT70-72
SPEVACK, M. A COMPLETE AND SYSTEMATIC
CONCORDANCE TO THE WORKS OF SHAKE-
SPEARE.* (VOLS 1&2)
E. LEISI, 38:BAND89HEFT3-387
SPEVACK, M. A COMPLETE AND SYSTEMATIC
CONCORDANCE TO THE WORKS OF SHAKE-
SPEARE. (VOL 3)
E. LEISI, 38:BAND89HEFT3-387
M. ROSENBERG, 290(JAAC):WINTER70-279
SPEYER, W. BÜCHERFUNDE IN DER GLAUBENS-
WERBUNG DER ANTIKE.
C.B. PASCAL, 122:JUL72-214
N.G. WILSON, 354:DEC70-355
SPICER, E.H. & R.H. THOMPSON, EDS. PLURAL
SOCIETY IN THE SOUTHWEST.
W. GARD, 584(SWR):AUTUMN72-330
SPIEGELBERG, R. THE CITY.
617(TLS):3AUG73-898
SPIKE, P. PHOTOGRAPHS OF MY FATHER.
R.P. BRICKNER, 441:29JUL73-5
E.Z. FRIEDENBERG, 453:20SEP73-40
C. LEHMANN-HAUPT, 441:21JUN73-45

SPILLANE, M.  THE ERECTION SET.*
  R. BRYDEN, 362:10MAY73-623
SPILLANE, M.  THE LAST COP OUT.
  N. CALLENDAR, 441:20MAY73-22
SPILLER, B.  VICTORIAN PUBLIC HOUSES.
  617(TLS):5JAN73-22
SPINNER, T.J., JR.  GEORGE JOACHIM GOS-
  CHEN.
  617(TLS):28DEC73-1580
SPINNEY, D.  RODNEY.
  T.W. PERRY, 656(WMQ):JAN71-139
SPIRITO, U.  SIGNIFICATO DEL NOSTRO
  TEMPO.
  E. NAMER, 542:JAN-MAR70-105
SPIRITO, U.  STORIA ANTOLOGICA DEI PROB-
  LEMI FILOSOFICI.  (TEORETICA, 2)
  MACHIAVELLI E GUICCIARDINI.
  E. NAMER, 542:JUL-SEP70-367
SPIRITO, U.  STORIA DELLA MIA RICERCA.
  P. PICCONE, 484(PPR):MAR72-435
SPIRITO, U.  TRASCENDENZA E METAFISICA.
  E. NAMER, 542:JAN-MAR70-106
SPITERIS, T.  THE ART OF CYPRUS.
  R. HIGGINS, 39:AUG71-161
SPITZER, A.B.  OLD HATREDS AND YOUNG
  HOPES.
  617(TLS):16MAR73-304
SPITZER, L.  ETUDES DE STYLE.
  J. BOREL, 98:DEC71-1060
  R. CHAMPIGNY, 207(FR):APR71-995
SPIVAK, T.  THE BRIDE WORE THE TRADITION-
  AL GOLD.*
  P.M. SPACKS, 249(HUDR):AUTUMN72-497
SPLETT, J.  RÜDIGER VON BECHELAREN.
  B. NAGEL, 680(ZDP):BAND90HEFT3-456
  B. SOWINSKI, 657(WW):SEP/OCT70-347
SPONGANO, R., ED.  LA RIME DEI DUE BUON-
  ACCORSO DA MONTEMAGNO.
  C. MAZZOTTA, 228(GSLI):VOL148FASC
  462/463-422
SPONGANO, R., ED.  RISPETTI E STRAMBOTTI
  DEL QUATTROCENTO.
  L.T., 275(IQ):SPRING-SUMMER72-116
SPRAGENS, T.A., JR.  THE POLITICS OF
  MOTION.
  617(TLS):28DEC73-1594
SPRAGGETT, A., WITH W.V. RAUSCHER.  ARTHUR
  FORD.
  M. GARDNER, 453:3MAY73-16
SPRAGUE, A.C. & J.C. TREWIN.  SHAKE-
  SPEARE'S PLAYS TO-DAY.
  R.H. BALL, 570(SQ):AUTUMN71-405
  I. BROWN, 157:SPRING71-65
SPRAGUE, C., ED.  VIRGINIA WOOLF.
  C. OHMANN, 659:SPRING73-260
SPRANGER, E.  KULTURPHILOSOPHIE UND KUL-
  TURKRITIK.  (H. WENKE, ED)
  M. ROCK, 182:VOL24#21/22-771
SPRIET, P.  SAMUEL DANIEL.
  J. REES, 189(EA):OCT-DEC70-399
SPRIGGE, E.  THE LIFE OF IVY COMPTON-
  BURNETT.
  T. DRIBERG, 362:22MAR73-388
  C-G. HEILBRUN, 441:1JUL73-20
  J. UPDIKE, 442(NY):2JUN73-119
  617(TLS):6APR73-371
SPRIGGE, T.L.S.  FACTS, WORDS AND BELIEFS.
  A. COLLINS, 311(JP):26APR73-236
  A.R. WHITE, 479(PHQ):JUL71-277
SPRING, G.M.  MAN'S INVINCIBLE SURMISE.*
  F.C. COPLESTON, 546(RR):DEC71-308
SPRING, J.H.  EDUCATION AND THE RISE OF
  THE CORPORATE STATE.*
  C. LASCH, 453:17MAY73-19
SPRINGER, J.  THE FONDAS.
  200:AUG-SEP71-433
SPRINGER, J.L.  THE MUTUAL FUND TRAP.
  S.H. BROWN, 441:18FEB73-22

SPRY, J.F. & OTHERS.  REPUBLIC OF KENYA:
  REPORT OF THE COMMISSION ON THE LAW OF
  MARRIAGE AND DIVORCE.
  C.M. MC DOWELL, 69:OCT71-337
SPUFFORD, P.  MONETARY PROBLEMS AND POLI-
  CIES IN THE BURGUNDIAN NETHERLANDS,
  1433-1496.
  H.A. MISKIMIN, 589:OCT72-807
SPULBER, N.  SOCIALIST MANAGEMENT AND
  PLANNING.
  J. THORNTON, 32:JUN72-465
SPURLIN, P.M.  ROUSSEAU IN AMERICA.*
  M. KIMBROUGH, 207(FR):OCT70-235
  J. SAREIL, 188(ECR):WINTER70-329
SPYRIDAKIS, S.  PTOLEMAIC ITANOS AND
  HELLENISTIC CRETE.
  R.S. BAGNALL, 487:WINTER71-405
SQUIBB, G.D.  FOUNDERS' KIN.
  617(TLS):30MAR73-360
SQUIRES, R.  ALLEN TATE.*
  R. BUFFINGTON, 578:SPRING73-102
  L. COWAN, 569(SR):SPRING72-377
  J.L. DAVIS, 385(MQR):FALL73-375
  H. SMITH, 376:OCT71-135
  H. TAYLOR, 651(WHR):SPRING72-179
  A. WARREN, 598(SOR):AUTUMN73-753
SQUIRES, R., ED.  ALLEN TATE AND HIS
  WORK.
  R. BUFFINGTON, 578:SPRING73-102
  J.L. DAVIS, 385(MQR):FALL73-375
  A. WARREN, 598(SOR):AUTUMN73-753
SQUIRRU, R.  CREDO PARA EL HOMBRE NUEVO.
  A. PLANNELS, 37:MAY70-40
SREEKRISHNA SARMA, E.R., ED.  KAUṢĪTAKI-
  BRĀHMAṆA.  (VOL 1)
  L. ROCHER, 318(JAOS):JAN-MAR71-153
"SRI PADUKA: THE EXILE OF THE PRINCE OF
  AYODHYA."*  (S.M. PONNIAH, TRANS)
  C. COPPOLA, 352(LE&W):VOL15#1-163
ŚRĪJĪVA, G.  TATTVASANDARBHA.  (S. GOS-
  WAMI, ED)
  J.B.L., 543:SEP70-142
STAAL, J.F.  WORD ORDER IN SANSKRIT AND
  UNIVERSAL GRAMMAR.*
  W. THOMAS, 260(IF):BAND74-220
STAATS, A.  EDGAR ALLAN POES SYMBOLIS-
  TISCHE ERZÄHLKUNST.
  K. LUBBERS, 38:BAND88HEFT2-277
STACK, P.  MOVEMENT IN LIFE.
  617(TLS):15JUN73-660
VON STACKELBERG, J., ED.  DAS FRANZÖ-
  SISCHE THEATER.
  F. WOLFZETTEL, 224(GRM):BAND21HEFT3-
  358
VON STACKELBERG, J.  VON RABELAIS BIS
  VOLTAIRE.
  A.C. KELLER, 131(CL):SPRING72-180
  F. WOLFZETTEL, 224(GRM):BAND21HEFT4-
  474
STACPOOLE, A. & OTHERS, EDS.  THE NOBLE
  CITY OF YORK.
  617(TLS):13APR73-429
STADELMANN, R.  SYRISCH-PALÄSTINENSISCHE
  GOTTHEITEN IN ÄGYPTEN.
  M.C. ASTOUR, 318(JAOS):OCT-DEC71-530
STÄDTLER, I. & W.  ENGLISCH: SYMBOLIK UND
  FACHAUSDRÜCKE - MATHEMATIK, PHYSIK,
  CHEMIE.
  J. CAIRNS, 75:4/1970-218
STAEHELIN, B. & S. JENNY, EDS.  DAS BILD
  VOM MENSCHEN.
  S. DECLOUX, 182:VOL24#11/12-451
MADAME DE STAËL.  TEN YEARS OF EXILE.
  (D. BEIK, TRANS)
  441:11MAR73-46
  442(NY):17FEB73-111

STARK, R. PLUNDER SQUAD.*
N. CALLENDAR, 441:7JAN73-35
STARKE, C.J. BLACK PORTRAITURE IN AMERI-
CAN FICTION.
N.M. TISCHLER, 27(AL):MAR72-172
STARKIE, E. FLAUBERT: THE MAKING OF THE
MASTER.
J. BRUNEAU, 535(RHL):JAN-FEB70-146
STAROBIN, J.R. AMERICAN COMMUNISM IN
CRISIS 1943-1957.*
S.B. RYERSON, 99:FEB73-40
STAROBINSKI, J. HAMLET ET FREUD.
J-F. LYOTARD, 98:JUN70-530
STAROBINSKI, J. L'OEIL VIVANT.
J. BOREL, 98:JUL70-604
STARR, C.G. THE ANCIENT GREEKS.
639(VQR):SUMMER71-CXXVII
STARR, C.G. ATHENIAN COINAGE 480-449
B.C.
J.J. FARBER, 124:NOV71-97
STARR, G.A. DEFOE AND CASUISTRY.
M.C. BATTESTIN, 301(JEGP):JAN72-140
M.E. NOVAK, 401(MLQ):DEC72-456
K. STEWART, 191(ELN):JUN72-306
639(VQR):AUTUMN71-CLXIX
STARR, H.W. & J.R. HENDRICKSON - SEE
GRAY, T.
STARR, K. AMERICANS AND THE CALIFORNIA
DREAM: 1850-1915.
R. COLES, 442(NY):6AUG73-82
J. SEELYE, 441:5AUG73-4
STARR, S.F. DECENTRALIZATION AND SELF-
GOVERNMENT IN RUSSIA, 1830-1870.
617(TLS):18MAY73-560
STARR, S.F. - SEE VON HAXTHAUSEN, A.
STASOV, V.V. SELECTED ESSAYS ON MUSIC.*
R.S. BECKWITH, 317:SPRING72-115
STASSINOPOULOS, A. THE FEMALE WOMAN.
G. GREER, 362:15NOV73-671
617(TLS):14DEC73-1534
STATES, B.O. IRONY AND DRAMA.
R.T. ALLEN, 89(BJA):SPRING72-210
W. SMART, 651(WHR):WINTER72-75
STATHIS, J.J., ED. A BIBLIOGRAPHY OF
SWIFT STUDIES 1945-1965.
P. DANCHIN, 179(ES):AUG71-369
"STATISTIQUE ET ANALYSE LINGUISTIQUE."
W. ZWANENBURG, 353:MAY70-107
STATIUS. STACE, "ACHILLÉIDE." (J. MÉ-
HEUST, ED & TRANS)
R.D. SWEENEY, 124:MAR72-237
STATLER, O. SHIMODA STORY.
293(JAST):NOV70-245
STÄUBLE, A. LA COMMEDIA UMANISTICA DEL
QUATTROCENTO.*
I.A. PORTNER, 405(MP):AUG70-93
STAVAN, H.A. GABRIEL SÉNAC DE MEILHAN
(1736-1803).*
L. VERSINI, 535(RHL):JUL-AUG70-724
STAVE, B.M. THE NEW DEAL AND THE LAST
HURRAH.
639(VQR):SPRING71-LXXVIII
STEAD, C. THE PUZZLEHEADED GIRL.
M. WILDING, 381:JUN71-263
STEAD, C.K. CROSSING THE BAR.
617(TLS):27APR73-474
STEADMAN, J.M. MILTON AND THE RENAIS-
SANCE HERO.*
E. MERTNER, 38:BAND88HEFT2-267
STEADMAN, J.M. MILTON'S EPIC CHARAC-
TERS.*
G. BULLOUGH, 175:SPRING70-24
A. HIMY, 98:AUG-SEP70-705
R.B. WADDINGTON, 405(MP):NOV70-201
STECHOW, W. DUTCH LANDSCAPE PAINTING OF
THE SEVENTEENTH CENTURY.
S. SLIVE, 54:JUN71-261

STECHOW, W. RUBENS AND THE CLASSICAL
TRADITION.*
G. MARTIN, 39:FEB70-168
J.R. MARTIN, 54:MAR71-122
STEDINGH, W. FROM A BELL TOWER.
J. DITSKY, 628:SPRING72-108
STEDJE, A. DIE NÜRNBERGER HISTORIENBIBEL.
B. STOLT, 597(SN):VOL42#2-523
STEEGMAN, J. VICTORIAN TASTE.
R.E., 135:JUN71-150
STEEGMULLER, F. COCTEAU.
639(VQR):WINTER71-XXXVI
STEEGMULLER, F. - SEE FLAUBERT, G.
STEELE, F. WALKING TO THE WATERFALL.
J. TIPTON, 577(SHR):SPRING71-196
STEELE, R. THE PLAYS OF RICHARD STEELE.
(S.S. KENNY, ED)
566:SPRING72-88
STEER, G. - SEE WENCK VON HERRENBERG, J.
STEER, J. A CONCISE HISTORY OF VENETIAN
PAINTING.
J.D. GRIFFIN, 58:NOV70-17
STEERE, D.V. GOD'S IRREGULAR.
617(TLS):15JUN73-695
STÉFAN, J. IDYLLES SUIVI DE CIPPES.
617(TLS):1JUN73-610
STÉFAN, J. LIBÈRES.
R.R. HUBERT, 207(FR):APR71-971
STEFANINI, J. UN PROVENÇALISTE MARSEIL-
LAIS L'ABBÉ FÉRAUD.
P. LARTHOMAS, 209(FM):APR71-173
DI STEFANO, G. - SEE COURTECUISSE, J.
STEFENELLI, A. DER SYNONYMENREICHTUM DER
ALTFRANZÖSISCHEN DICHTERSPRACHE.
W. SAYERS, 545(RPH):AUG71-112
STEFFAN, T.G. LORD BYRON'S "CAIN."*
J.D. BONE, 447(N&Q):MAY71-195
K.A. BRUFFEE, 405(MP):AUG70-115
STEFFAN, T.G., E. STEFFAN & W.W. PRATT -
SEE LORD BYRON
STEFFEN, H., ED. DAS DEUTSCHE LUST-
SPIEL. (PT 2)
C.P. MAGILL, 220(GL&L):JAN72-194
STEGAGNO PICCHIO, L. RICERCHE SUL TEATRO
PORTOGHESE.
T.R. HART, 400(MLN):MAR71-289
STEGAGNO PICCHIO, L. - SEE MOYA, M.
STEGER, H. SPRACHRAUMBILDUNG UND LANDES-
GESCHICHTE IM ÖSTLICHEN FRANKEN.
E. STRASSNER, 657(WW):JUL/AUG70-273
STEGMANN, A. L'HÉROÏSME CORNÉLIEN.*
(VOL 1)
M. FUMAROLI, 535(RHL):JAN-FEB71-71
D.A. WATTS, 402(MLR):OCT72-886
STEGMANN, A. L'HÉROÏSME CORNÉLIEN.*
(VOL 2)
M. FUMAROLI, 535(RHL):JAN-FEB71-76
D.A. WATTS, 402(MLR):OCT72-886
STEGMÜLLER, W. MAIN CURRENTS IN CONTEM-
PORARY GERMAN, BRITISH, AND AMERICAN
PHILOSOPHY.
185:JAN72-180
STEGMÜLLER, W. PROBLEME UND RESULTATE
DER WISSENSCHAFTSTHEORIE UND ANALYT-
ISCHE PHILOSOPHIE. (VOL 1)
J.J. KOCKELMANS, 486:MAR71-126
STEGMÜLLER, W. DAS WAHRHEITSPROBLEM UND
IDEE DER SEMANTIK. (2ND ED)
R.F.M., 543:JUN71-759
STEGMÜLLER, W. WISSENSCHAFTLICHE ERKLÄR-
UNG UND BEGRÜNDUNG.
R.F.M., 543:MAR71-551
STEGNER, W. ANGLE OF REPOSE.
J.S. BULLEN, 649(WAL):SPRING71-60
STEIN, A. ANSWERABLE STYLE.
F.R. BARUCH, 599:WINTER70-77
STEIN, A. GEORGE HERBERT'S LYRICS.*
G. THOMAS, 175:SPRING70-26

STEIN, A., ED.  ON MILTON'S POETRY.
  M.A. DI CESARE, 551(RENQ):WINTER71-587
STEIN, A.  PESTALOZZI UND DIE KANTISCHE
  PHILOSOPHIE.  (2ND ED)
  W. RITZEL, 342:BAND62HEFT4-507
STEIN, A.M.  THE FINGER.
  N. CALLENDAR, 441:18FEB73-29
  442(NY):10MAR73-136
STEIN, A.M.  LOCK AND KEY.
  N. CALLENDAR, 441:16SEP73-31
STEIN, G., WITH E.K. BERNDT & E. ZICKEL,
  EDS.  DIE SILBERFRACHT.  (8TH ED)
  K.F. OTTO, JR., 221(GQ):JAN71-116
STEIN, W.  CRITICISM AS DIALOGUE.
  J. FRANK, 149:SEP72-335
  R. LAWRENCE, 175:SPRING71-28
STEIN, W.B.  THE POETRY OF MELVILLE'S
  LATE YEARS.*
  L. BUELL, 432(NEQ):SEP71-517
  H. PARKER, 401(MLQ):MAR72-54
  H.P. VINCENT, 27(AL):MAY72-325
STEINBERG, A.  THE BOSSES.
  617(TLS):2MAR73-230
STEINBERG, L.  OTHER CRITERIA.
  H. KRAMER, 441:8APR73-6
STEINBERG, S.  THE INSPECTOR.
  J. CANADAY, 441:1APR73-3
STEINBERG, S.H., ED.  CASSELL'S ENCYCLO-
  PAEDIA OF WORLD LITERATURE.  (REV BY
  J. BUCHANAN-BROWN)
  617(TLS):28SEP73-1136
STEINBUCH, K.  FALSCH PROGRAMMIERT.
  K. FUCHS, 430(NS):MAY70-253
STEINBUCH, K. & S.W. WAGNER, EDS.  NEUE
  ERGEBNISSE DER KYBERNETIK.
  G.F. MEIER, 682(ZPSK):BAND24HEFT1/2-
  142
STEINECKE, H.  HERMANN BROCH UND DER
  POLYHISTORISCHE ROMAN.
  G. WIENOLD, 680(ZDP):BAND90HEFT2-311
STEINECKE, H., ED.  THEORIE UND TECHNIK
  DES ROMANS IM 19. JAHRHUNDERT.
  L.E. KURTH, 221(GQ):MAR71-236
STEINECKE, H. - SEE LENAU, N.
STEINER, E.  THE SLOVAK DILEMMA.
  617(TLS):27JUL73-860
STEINER, G.  IN BLUEBEARD'S CASTLE.*
  B. KINGSTONE, 628:SPRING72-112
  42(AR):FALL71-442
STEINER, G., ED.  POEM INTO POEM.
  R.S., 376:JUL71-122
  R.K.G. TEMPLE, 493:SUMMER71-188
STEINER, G.  THE SPORTING SCENE.
  D. CAUTE, 362:7JUN73-771
  617(TLS):18MAY73-550
STEINER, N.H.  A CLOSER LOOK AT ARIEL.
  P. ADAMS, 61:MAR73-107
STEINER, Z.S.  THE FOREIGN OFFICE AND FOR-
  EIGN POLICY 1898-1914.*
  M. ROPER, 325:APR71-239
STEINGASS, D.  BODY COMPASS.*
  G. KUZMA, 502(PRS):FALL70-271
STEINGRUBER, J.D.  ARCHITECTURAL ALPHABET
  1773.
  617(TLS):23FEB73-216
STEINHAGEN, H.  DIE STATISCHEN GEDICHTE
  VON GOTTFRIED BENN.*
  R. FURNESS, 220(GL&L):JUL72-398
STEINHAUER, H. & R. KONRAD.  STILVOLLES
  DEUTSCH.
  G. HÜNERT, 221(GQ):JAN71-123
  H.C. KAYSER, 399(MLJ):FEB71-115
STEINITZ, R., WITH E. LANG.  ADVERBIAL-
  SYNTAX.*
  W. ABRAHAM, 343:BAND13HEFT2-213

STEINMETZ, H., ED.  LESSING - EIN UNPOET-
  ISCHER DICHTER.
  H. FRIEDERICI, 654(WB):1/1971-219
  617(TLS):6JUL73-777
STEINMETZ, H.  EDUARD MÖRIKES ERZÄHLUN-
  GEN.
  L. THOMAS, 220(GL&L):JUL72-399
STEINWEG, R.  DAS LEHRSTÜCK.
  617(TLS):28DEC73-1591
STEINWEG, R. - SEE BRECHT, B.
STELAND, D.  DIALEKTISCHE GEDANKEN IN
  STÉPHANE MALLARMÉS DIVAGATIONS.
  W. ENGLER, 430(NS):SEP70-474
STEMMLER, T.  LITURGISCHE FEIERN UND
  GEISTLICHE SPIELE.
  E. SIMON, 589:APR72-356
STENBORG, E.  PIERROT OCH PILGRIM.
  Y.L. SANDSTROEM, 563(SS):SPRING72-281
STENDHAL.  LIVES OF HAYDN, MOZART AND
  METASTASIO BY STENDHAL (1814).*  (R.N.
  COE, ED & TRANS)
  J.W.K., 410(M&L):OCT72-444
STENDHAL.  LE ROUGE ET LE NOIR.  (C.
  RENARD, ED)
  B.R. WOSHINSKY, 399(MLJ):MAR71-197
STENERSON, D.C.  H.L. MENCKEN.*
  T.A. KRUEGER, 149:SEP72-348
STENSON, S.H.  SENSE AND NONSENSE IN
  RELIGION.
  A.W.M., 477:AUTUMN70-549
  G.M. PATERSON, 154:JUN71-377
  R.E. SANTONI, 258:MAR70-155
STENZEL, J.  PHILOSOPHIE DER SPRACHE.
  L. ZGUSTA, 353:JUN71-115
STENZEL, J.  ZEICHENSETZUNG.
  H. ZIMMERMANN, 657(WW):MAR/APR71-143
STENZL, J.  DIE VIERZIG CLAUSULAE DER
  HANDSCHRIFT PARIS BIBLIOTHÈQUE NATION-
  ALE LATIN 15139 (SAINT VICTOR-CLAUSU-
  LAE).
  H. TISCHLER, 317:SPRING72-107
STEPANCHEV, S.  THE MAD BOMBER.
  R.E. LONG, 398:AUTUMN73-237
STEPHAN, J.J.  SAKHALIN.*
  P.F. LANGER, 32:JUN72-433
STEPHAN, R., ED.  ÜBER MUSIK UND KRITIK.
  E. SAMS, 415:OCT72-979
STEPHANIDES, T.  ISLAND TRAILS.
  617(TLS):19OCT73-1287
STEPHANY, U.  ADJEKTIVISCHE ATTRIBUTKON-
  STRUKTIONEN DES FRANZÖSISCHEN, UNTER-
  SUCHT NACH DEM MODELL DER GENERATIVEN
  GRAMMATIK.
  N.C.W. SPENCE, 208(FS):OCT72-498
STEPHENS, A.  RAINER MARIA RILKE'S "GE-
  DICHTE AN DIE NACHT."
  617(TLS):9NOV73-1369
STEPHENS, A.  TREE MEDITATION AND OTHERS.*
  R.P. DICKEY, 649(WAL):SUMMER71-151
STEPHENS, E.  THE SUBMARINER.
  M. LEVIN, 441:16SEP73-32
STEPHENS, J.E. - SEE AUBREY, J.
STEPHENS, W.B.  SOURCES FOR ENGLISH LOCAL
  HISTORY.
  617(TLS):27APR73-481
STEPHENSON, C.  MERRILY ON HIGH.
  617(TLS):16FEB73-176
STEPHENSON, G.  RUSSIA FROM 1812 TO 1945.*
  E.W. BROOKS, 550(RUSR):JAN71-90
STERMER, D.  THE ART OF REVOLUTION.
  592:NOV70-222
STERN, F.  THE POLITICS OF CULTURAL DES-
  PAIR.
  S.M. POPPEL, 390:JAN70-67
STERN, G., ED.  LESSING YEARBOOK III.
  617(TLS):6JUL73-777
STERN, G.  WAR, WEIMAR, AND LITERATURE.
  J. HERMAND, 406:WINTER72-390

STERN, H.H. PERSPECTIVES ON SECOND
LANGUAGE TEACHING.
J.C. DAVIS, 238:MAY71-410
STERN, J.P. IDYLLS AND REALITIES.
R.K. ANGRESS, 406:WINTER72-403
STERN, J.P. ON REALISM.
617(TLS):9FEB73-146
STERN, M.B. HEADS & HEADLINES.
H. ASPIZ, 646(WWR):DEC71-139
STERN, M.R. THE GOLDEN MOMENT.*
H.T. MOORE, 594:FALL71-350
W. RUECKERT, 141:SUMMER71-326
STERN, P.M. THE RAPE OF THE TAXPAYER.
M. BENDER, 441:20APR73-31
P. PASSELL & L. ROSS, 453:19APR73-39
S.S. SURREY, 441:8APR73-10
STERN, R. THE BOOKS IN FRED HAMPTON'S
APARTMENT.
H. KENNER, 441:25MAR73-6
C. NEWMAN, 231:NOV73-116
STERN, R. OTHER MEN'S DAUGHTERS.
A. BROYARD, 441:16OCT73-47
B. DE MOTT, 61:DEC73-126
J.R. FRAKES, 441:18NOV73-4
M. WOOD, 453:13DEC73-19
442(NY):19NOV73-246
STERN, R.A.M. NEW DIRECTIONS IN AMERICAN
ARCHITECTURE.
R.J., 45:APR70-130
T. SCHUMACHER, 44:MAR70-58
STERN, R.M. DEATH IN THE SNOW.
N. CALLENDAR, 441:22APR73-24
STERN, R.M. THE TOWER.
C. LEHMANN-HAUPT, 441:19OCT73-47
M. LEVIN, 441:30SEP73-20
STERN, S.M. ARISTOTLE ON THE WORLD-STATE.
D.M. LEWIS, 123:JUN72-271
STERN, S.M. - SEE GOLDZIHER, I.
STERNBACH, L. THE SPREADING OF CĀNAKYA'S
APHORISM OVER "GREATER INDIA."
H. BECHERT, 318(JAOS):APR-JUN71-313
STERNBACH, L., ED. VYĀSASUBHĀṢITASAṂ-
GRAHAḤ (THE VYĀSA-SUBHĀṢITASAṂGRAHA).
H. BECHERT, 318(JAOS):APR-JUN71-312
STERNBERG, E.D. & B.E. COMMUNITY CENTERS
AND STUDENT UNIONS.
505:DEC71-100
STERNBERG, S. - SEE GANDZ, S.
STERNBERGER/STORZ/SÜSKIND. AUS DEM
WÖRTERBUCH DES UNMENSCHEN. (3RD ED)
M. KAEMPFERT, 680(ZDP):BAND90HEFT1-
144
STERNFELD, F.W., ED. A HISTORY OF WESTERN
MUSIC. (VOL 5)
617(TLS):14SEP73-1046
STERNFELD, F.W. & D. GREER - SEE FELLOWES,
E.H.
STERNHEIM, C. BÜRGER SCHIPPEL. (D. BAR-
LOW, ED)
J.M. RITCHIE, 220(GL&L):JAN72-163
205(FMLS):JUL70-314
STERNHEIM, C. SCENES FROM THE HEROIC
LIFE OF THE MIDDLE CLASSES. (J.M.
RITCHIE, ED)
D. BARLOW, 220(GL&L):OCT71-43
J. OSBORNE, 402(MLR):APR72-471
STÉTIÉ, S. L'EAU FROIDE GARDÉE.
617(TLS):12OCT73-1244
STETLER, R., ED. PALESTINE.*
P. GROSE, 441:21JAN73-4
STEUERWALD, U. DER AMERIKANISCHE WELT-
KRIEGSROMAN 1919-1939.
R. ASSELINEAU, 189(EA):OCT-DEC71-546
STEVENS, D., ED. A HISTORY OF SONG.
M. PETERSON, 470:MAY71-35
STEVENS, G. STANFIELD.
J.M. BECK, 99:NOV-DEC73-19

STEVENS, H. THE LIFE AND MUSIC OF BÉLA
BARTÓK. (REV)
M. PETERSON, 470:MAY71-35
STEVENS, J. MEDIEVAL ROMANCE.
617(TLS):31AUG73-1008
STEVENS, J. - SEE TAYLOR, M.
STEVENS, M. V. SACKVILLE-WEST.
617(TLS):9MAR73-261
STEVENS, P.T. - SEE EURIPIDES
STEVENS, S. DEAD CITY.
F. BUSCH, 441:9DEC73-24
STEVENS, W. THE PALM AT THE END OF THE
MIND.* (H. STEVENS, ED)
B. HERINGMAN, 398:VOL3#6-282
STEVENS, W.B. THE JOURNAL OF THE REV.
WILLIAM BAGSHAW STEVENS. (G. GALBRAITH,
ED)
A. PARREAUX, 189(EA):OCT-DEC71-538
STEVENSON, A.E. THE PAPERS OF ADLAI E.
STEVENSON. (VOL 2) (W. JOHNSON, WITH
C. EVANS, EDS)
R.J. WALTON, 441:18FEB73-7
STEVENSON, C.H. THE SPANISH LANGUAGE
TODAY.
K. ADAMS, 402(MLR):APR72-435
D.N. CÁRDENAS, 238:DEC71-982
C. PRATT, 86(BHS):JAN72-66
N.P. SACKS, 350:DEC72-954
STEVENSON, D.E. MRS. TIM CARRIES ON.
M. LEVIN, 441:9DEC73-49
STEVENSON, L. THE PRE-RAPHAELITE POETS.
617(TLS):22JUN73-712
STEVENSON, O. CLAIMANT OR CLIENT?
617(TLS):4MAY73-487
STEVENSON, R. MUSIC IN AZTEC & INCA
TERRITORY.*
M. PETERSON, 470:NOV70-44
STEVENSON, W. THE BORMANN BROTHERHOOD.
441:13MAY73-40
STEVENSON, W. ZANEK!
S.L.A. MARSHALL, 390:APR71-63
STEVENSON, W.H. EMILY AND ANNE BRONTË.
S.C. GILL, 447(N&Q):FEB71-80
STEVENSON, W.T. HISTORY AS MYTH.
J.Y. FENTON, 480(P&R):WINTER71-65
STEVICK, P., ED. ANTI-STORY.
42(AR):SPRING71-132
STEVICK, P. THE CHAPTER IN FICTION.*
K. KROEBER, 454:FALL71-77
P.W. ROGERS, 529(QQ):AUTUMN71-477
STEVICK, R.D. SUPRASEGMENTALS, METER,
AND THE MANUSCRIPT OF "BEOWULF."*
J.M. LUECKE, 353:OCT70-110
G. STORMS, 179(ES):APR71-157
STEWARD, D. THE ACUPUNCTURE MURDERS.
N. CALLENDAR, 441:29JUL73-13
STEWART, E. THEY'VE SHOT THE PRESIDENT'S
DAUGHTER!
N. CALLENDAR, 441:22JUL73-12
C. LEHMANN-HAUPT, 441:23JUL73-29
STEWART, F.M. THE MANNINGS.
M. LEVIN, 441:28OCT73-48
G. WALKER, 441:1DEC73-37
STEWART, G.R. AMERICAN PLACE-NAMES.
E.P. HAMP, 269(IJAL):APR71-135
STEWART, H. - SEE "A CHIME OF WINDBELLS"
STEWART, J. - SEE DELACROIX, E.
STEWART, J.I.M. THOMAS HARDY.
A. WELSH, 676(YR):SPRING72-459
STEWART, J.I.M. MUNGO'S DREAM.
V. CUNNINGHAM, 362:8FEB73-189
M. LEVIN, 441:24JUN73-12
617(TLS):2FEB73-113
STEWART, M. THE HOLLOW HILLS.
R. BRYDEN, 362:7JUN73-772
M. LEVIN, 441:29JUL73-13
STEWART, N. EVIL EYE.
D. MAHON, 362:21JUN73-840

STEWART, P.D. INNOCENT GENTILLET E LA
SUA POLEMICA ANTIMACHIAVELLICA.
A. CIORANESCU, 549(RLC):JUL-SEP70-417
C. CORDIÉ, 228(GSLI):VOL147FASC458/
459-452
STEWART, P.R. IMITATION AND ILLUSION IN
THE FRENCH MEMOIR-NOVEL, 1700-1750.*
P. BROOKS, 149:MAR72-119
R.L. FRAUTSCHI, 401(MLQ):JUN71-223
V. MYLNE, 208(FS):JAN72-77
R.F. O'REILLY, 207(FR):OCT70-258
R.G. SAISSELIN, 290(JAAC):WINTER70-284
E. SHOWALTER, JR., 173(ECS):SPRING72-
467
205(FMLS):OCT70-423
STEWART, R. THE APPARITION.
N. CALLENDAR, 441:24JUN73-34
STEWART, S. THE EXPANDED VOICE.*
G.R. GUFFEY, 141:SPRING71-213
M.W. MARSHALL, 551(RENQ):SUMMER71-287
A. RIDLER, 541(RES):NOV71-498
B. WOODWARD, 290(JAAC):SPRING71-429
STEWART, W. DIVIDE AND CON.
P. STEVENS, 99:NOV-DEC73-22
STIEBER, Z. THE PHONOLOGICAL DEVELOPMENT
OF POLISH.*
F.Y. GLADNEY, 215(GL):VOL10#1-22
STIEGLITZ, A., ED. CAMERA WORK.
R.P. HULL, 127:FALL71-104
STIEHM, L., ED. ADALBERT STIFTER.*
L.W. KAHN, 222(GR):MAR71-143
STIELER, K. DER TEUTSCHEN SPRACHE STAMM-
BAUM UND FORTWACHS/ODER TEUTSCHER
SPRACHSCHATZ.
B.L. SPAHR, 133:1971/1&2-197
STIERLE, K. DUNKELHEIT UND FORM IN NER-
VALS "CHIMÈRES."
A. DUBRUCK, 535(RHL):MAY-JUN70-526
STIFTER, A. DER BESCHRIEBENE TÄNNLING.
(C. HAYES, ED)
L.L. TITCHE, JR., 399(MLJ):OCT71-417
STILL, J. EARLY RECOLLECTIONS AND LIFE
OF DR. JAMES STILL.
M. PHILLIPS, 441:28DEC73-27
STILL, W.N., JR. IRON AFLOAT.
639(VQR):SUMMER71-CXXII
STILLER, J. SCHRIFTTUM ÜBER POLEN (OHNE
POSENER LAND) 1961-1962 UND NACHTRÄGE
(AUSWAHL).
P. VALOIS, 575(SEER):JUL72-485
STILLWELL, M.B. THE AWAKENING INTEREST
IN SCIENCE DURING THE FIRST CENTURY OF
PRINTING 1450-1550.*
A.R. HALL, 78(BC):SPRING71-113
STILZ, G. DIE DARSTELLUNG UND FUNKTION
DES TIERES IN DER ENGLISCHEN LYRIK DES
20. JAHRHUNDERTS.
W. ZACHARASIEWICZ, 224(GRM):BAND21
HEFT1-118
STIMPSON, C. J.R.R. TOLKIEN.
502(PRS):SPRING70-88
STIMSON, G.V. HEROIN AND BEHAVIOUR.
617(TLS):7SEP73-1023
STIVENS, D. SELECTED STORIES 1936-68.
M. WILDING, 381:JUN71-261
STOCK, B. MYTH AND SCIENCE IN THE
TWELFTH CENTURY.
617(TLS):15JUN73-658
STOCK, B. - SEE "MEDIEVAL LATIN LYRICS"
STOCK, N. THE LIFE OF EZRA POUND.*
D. BARBOUR, 529(QQ):SPRING71-138
L. CASPER, 613:AUTUMN71-466
U. SCHNEIDER, 72:BAND209HEFT1/3-168
H. SERGEANT, 175:SUMMER71-63
639(VQR):SPRING71-LXVI

VON STOCKERT, F.K.R. ZUR ANATOMIE DES
REALISMUS.
J.L. HODGE, 221(GQ):MAY71-403
L.H.C. THOMAS, 402(MLR):OCT72-947
STOCKERT, W. KLANGFIGUREN UND WORTRES-
PONSIONEN BEI PINDAR.
D.C. INNES, 123:DEC72-323
STOCKHAUSEN, K. TEXTE 1952-1970.
617(TLS):2MAR73-239
STOCKING, M.K. & D.M. - SEE CLAIRMONT, C.
STOCKMANN, E., ED. STUDIA INSTRUMENTORUM
MUSICAE POPULARIS. I.
J.P.S. MONTAGU, 187:MAY73-346
STOCKS, M. STILL MORE COMMONPLACE.
617(TLS):21DEC73-1574
STOCKTON, D. CICERO.
R. SEAGER, 313:VOL61-273
STOCKWELL, R.P., P. SCHACHTER & B.H. PAR-
TEE. INTEGRATION OF TRANSFORMATIONAL
THEORIES ON ENGLISH SYNTAX.
P.G. CHAPIN, 350:SEP72-645
STODDARD, R.E. A CATALOGUE OF BOOKS AND
PAMPHLETS UNRECORDED IN OSCAR WEGELIN'S
"EARLY AMERICAN POETRY, 1650-1820."
S.M. COCKCROFT, 354:MAR71-78
J.A.L. LEMAY, 165:SPRING73-66
STOEBKE, R. DIE VERHÄLTNISWÖRTER IN DEN
OSTSEEFINNISCHEN SPRACHEN.
K. MAITINSKAJA, 353:SEP71-114
F.J. OINAS, 215(GL):VOL10#1-70
STOEKL, G. TESTAMENT UND SIEGEL IVANS IV.
P. SCHEIBERT, 104:FALL72-498
STOKER, A. THE BRAM STOKER BEDSIDE COM-
PANION. (C. OSBORNE, ED)
617(TLS):11MAY73-517
STOKES, J. RESISTIBLE THEATRES.
617(TLS):11MAY73-521
STOKES, M.C. ONE AND MANY IN PRESOCRATIC
PHILOSOPHY.
A.R. LACEY, 518:OCT72-34
N.P. WHITE, 124:APR-MAY72-278
STOKES, T. CRIMES OF PASSION.
A. BARSON, 398:AUTUMN73-239
H. LEIBOWITZ, 441:12AUG73-5
STOKES, T. NATURAL DISASTERS.
W.H. PRITCHARD, 249(HUDR):SPRING72-120
STOLBERG-WERNIGERODE, O. DIE UNENTSCHIE-
DENE GENERATION.
M. STERNE, 182:VOL24#5-252
STOLL, C.T. DIE RECHTSSTELLUNG DER DEUT-
SCHEN STAATSANGEHÖRIGEN IN DEN POL-
NISCH VERWALTETEN GEBIETEN.
M. MANELI, 32:JUN72-472
STOLL, J.E. THE GREAT DELUGE.
R.J. FINNERAN, 295:FEB73-129
STOLOFF, C. STEPPING OUT.
42(AR):WINTER71/72-587
STONE, A. THE BANISHMENT.
M. LEVIN, 441:18NOV73-54
STONE, G. THE SMALLEST SLAVONIC NATION.*
P. BROCK, 32:DEC72-922
STONE, G.W., JR. THE LONDON STAGE, 1747-
1776.
C. PRICE, 570(SQ):WINTER71-67
STONE, H. - SEE DICKENS, C.
STONE, I.F. THE BEST OF I.F. STONE'S
WEEKLY. (N. MIDDLETON, ED)
B. DE MOTT, 61:OCT73-118
617(TLS):9FEB73-139
STONE, J. COLONIST OR UITLANDER?
617(TLS):22JUN73-707
STONE, J. LEGAL SYSTEM AND LAWYERS'
REASONINGS.
D.P. CUSHMAN, 480(P&R):SUMMER71-185
K. SEGERBERG, 316:DEC70-578
STONE, L. FAMILY AND FORTUNE.
K. THOMAS, 362:16AUG73-222
617(TLS):13JUL73-805

STONE, T.R. BEYOND THE AUTOMOBILE.
J. LOBELL, 505:SEP71-172
STONE, W. THE CAVE AND THE MOUNTAIN.
H-J. MÜLLENBROCK, 38:BAND88HEFT3-419
STONEHOUSE, B. ANIMALS OF THE ANTARCTIC.
617(TLS):8JUN73-649
STOOKINS, J.S. LECTURES POUR LE COURS
AVANCE 1970-1972.
N. KOVACS, 207(FR):MAR71-823
STORER, N.W. - SEE MERTON, R.K.
STOREY, A. THE CENTRE HOLDS.
617(TLS):12OCT73-1210
STOREY, D. A TEMPORARY LIFE.
E. FEINSTEIN, 362:27SEP73-426
617(TLS):21SEP73-1073
STOREY, G. - SEE ROSSITER, A.P.
STOREY, M., ED. CLARE: THE CRITICAL
HERITAGE.
617(TLS):27JUL73-856
STOREY, R.L. CHRONOLOGY OF THE MEDIEVAL
WORLD 800 TO 1491.
617(TLS):16FEB73-189
STORK, T. NIL IGITUR MORS EST AD NOS.
E.J. KENNEY, 123:DEC72-413
STORM, C., COMP. A CATALOG OF THE
EVERETT D. GRAFF COLLECTION OF WESTERN
AMERICANA.
C.E. DEWING, 14:APR70-214
STORM, H. SEVEN ARROWS.*
W.C. STURTEVANT, 441:18MAR73-37
STORM, T. DREI NOVELLEN. (D. BRETT-
EVANS, ED)
J.W. SMEED, 220(GL&L):JAN72-143
STORM, T. IMMENSEE. (J.M. RITCHIE, ED)
205(FMLS):OCT70-424
STORM, T. & P. HEYSE. BRIEFWECHSEL.*
(VOL 1) (C.A. BERND, ED)
P. PROCHNIK, 182:VOL24#13/14-546
W. SCHUMANN, 221(GQ):JAN71-80
M. SCHUNICHT, 52:BAND5HEFT3-330
J.W. SMEED, 220(GL&L):JAN72-142
STORM, T. & P. HEYSE. BRIEFWECHSEL.*
(VOL 2) (C.A. BERND, ED)
P. PROCHNIK, 182:VOL24#13/14-546
STORR, A. THE DYNAMICS OF CREATION.*
R. COLES, 453:22FEB73-15
R. SENNETT, 441:25FEB73-32
STORR, A. HUMAN DESTRUCTIVENESS.
617(TLS):14SEP73-1057
STORR, A. - C.G. JUNG.
R. DAVIES, 441:25FEB73-31
STORY, J.T. LETTERS TO AN INTIMATE
STRANGER.
617(TLS):19JAN73-73
STORY, N. THE OXFORD COMPANION TO CANAD-
IAN HISTORY AND LITERATURE.*
P. GOETSCH, 38:BAND89HEFT3-413
STORZ, G. HEINRICH HEINES LYRISCHE
DICHTUNG.
S. ATKINS, 401(MLQ):SEP72-341
G. BENDA, 406:SPRING72-98
H. HULTBERG, 301(JEGP):JAN72-78
STORZ, G. EDUARD MÖRIKE.*
G. NEUMANN, 657(WW):JAN/FEB70-63
R. POHL, 680(ZDP):BAND89HEFT2-282
STORZ, G. DER VERS IN DER NEUEREN DEUT-
SCHEN DICHTUNG.
L.W. KAHN, 406:SUMMER72-192
H-J. SCHLÜTTER, 301(JEGP):JUL72-424
STOTT, R.T. A BIBLIOGRAPHY OF THE WORKS
OF SOMERSET MAUGHAM.
617(TLS):17AUG73-960
STOUGH, C.L. GREEK SKEPTICISM.*
D.Z. ANDRIOPOULOS, 484(PPR):MAR72-417
M. FREDE, 311(JP):6DEC73-805
A.A. LONG, 483:JAN71-77
C.G. PRADO, 154:JUN70-118

STOURZH, G. ALEXANDER HAMILTON AND THE
IDEA OF REPUBLICAN GOVERNMENT.
A. KOCH, 656(WMQ):OCT71-661
J. SHY, 432(NEQ):MAR71-141
STOUT, R. PLEASE PASS THE GUILT.
F. JELLINEK, 441:11NOV73-7
H. MITGANG, 441:20OCT73-29
STOUT, R. & OTHERS. THE NERO WOLFE COOK
BOOK.
N-W. POLSBY, 231:AUG73-93
STOVALL, F. EDGAR POE THE POET.*
R.S. MOORE, 219(GAR):WINTER71-481
STOVE, D.C. PROBABILITY AND HUME'S
INDUCTIVE SCEPTICISM.
617(TLS):10AUG73-935
STOVÍČKOVÁ, D. & M. CHINESE FAIRY TALES.
N-T. TING, 292(JAF):APR-JUN71-251
STOWELL, R.F. A THOREAU GAZETTEER.*
(W.L. HOWARTH, ED)
M.I. LOWANCE, JR., 432(NEQ):JUN71-316
STRABO. STRABON, "GÉOGRAPHIE."* (VOL 1
ED & TRANS BY G. AUJAC, VOL 3 ED & TRANS
BY F. LASSERRE)
E.H. WARMINGTON, 303:VOL91-150
STRACHAN, W.J. THE ARTIST AND THE BOOK
IN FRANCE: THE 20TH CENTURY LIVRE
D'ARTISTE.*
J. TEPLIN, 503:SPRING70-45
STRACHEY, J. & OTHERS - SEE FREUD, S.
STRACHEY, J. & A. RICHARDS - SEE FREUD,
S.
STRACHEY, L. THE REALLY INTERESTING
QUESTION AND OTHER PAPERS.* (P. LEVY,
ED)
E. HARDWICK, 453:8FEB73-15
STRADA, V. TRADIZIONE E RIVOLUZIONE NELLA
LETTERATURA RUSSA.
R.L. COX, 550(RUSR):APR71-209
STRAHS, J. SEED JOURNAL.
A. GOTTLIEB, 441:1JUL73-10
STRAND, M. DARKER.*
M. BOWERS, 398:VOL3#6-275
A. HELMS, 473(PR):FALL72-621
42(AR):FALL/WINTER70/71-464
639(VQR):WINTER71-XX
STRAND, M. THE STORY OF OUR LIVES.
H. SHAPIRO, 441:22SEP73-29
STRANG, B.M.H. A HISTORY OF ENGLISH.
R.E. PALMER, JR., 350:DEC72-941
R.M. WILSON, 175:SPRING71-22
STRANG, B.M.H. MODERN ENGLISH STRUC-
TURE.* (2ND ED)
W. KUHLWEIN, 38:BAND88HEFT1-114
A.R. TELLIER, 189(EA):APR-JUN70-223
STRANGE, M. CAPE TO CAIRO.
617(TLS):7DEC73-1521
STRANKS, C.J. THIS SUMPTUOUS CHURCH.
617(TLS):10AUG73-937
STRATENWERTH, H. DIE REFORMATION IN DER
STADT OSNABRÜCK.
T.A. BRADY, JR., 182:VOL24#23/24-887
STRATFORD, A.H. AIR TRANSPORT ECONOMICS
IN THE SUPERSONIC ERA.
617(TLS):29JUN73-756
STRATHERN, P. ONE MAN'S WAR.
V. CUNNINGHAM, 362:31MAY73-728
617(TLS):6JUL73-783
STRATMAN, C.J. BRITAIN'S THEATRICAL
PERIODICALS, 1720-1967. (2ND ED)
617(TLS):9FEB73-161
STRATMANN, G., ED. AUGUSTAN POETRY.
B.F., 566:AUTUMN71-5
STRATMANN, G. ENGLISCHE ARISTOKRATIE UND
KLASSIZISTISCHE DICHTUNG.
B. FABIAN, 38:BAND88HEFT1-143

STRAUB, P. MARRIAGES.
  R. BRYDEN, 362:15MAR73-348
  M. LEVIN, 441:18MAR73-40
  617(TLS):23MAR73-313
STRAUB, P. OPEN AIR.
  617(TLS):16FEB73-183
STRAUMANN, H. WILLIAM FAULKNER.
  A. BLEIKASTEN, 189(EA):APR-JUN70-229
  A. HELLER, 430(NS):JUN71-330
STRAUS, E.W., M. NATHANSON & H. EY.
  PSYCHIATRY AND PHILOSOPHY.* (M. NATH-
  ANSON, ED)
  J.J. KOCKELMANS, 480(P&R):WINTER71-62
STRAUSS, D.F. THE LIFE OF JESUS CRITI-
  CALLY EXAMINED. (P.C. HODGSON, ED)
  617(TLS):20JUL73-821
STRAUSS, G., ED. MANIFESTATIONS OF DIS-
  CONTENT IN GERMANY ON THE EVE OF THE
  REFORMATION. PRE-REFORMATION GERMANY.
  617(TLS):14DEC73-1546
STRAUSS, K. CERAMICS IN OLD LIVONIA
  (ESTHONIA AND LITHUANIA).
  F.A.D., 135:MAR71-215
STRAUSS, L. LIBERALISM.
  W.J. STANKIEWICZ, 154:JUN71-365
STRAUSS, L. XENOPHON'S SOCRATIC DIS-
  COURSE.
  J.K. ANDERSON, 124:MAR72-240
  J.A. SCHWANDT, 613:SUMMER71-315
STRAUSS, W.A. DESCENT AND RETURN.
  K. MC SWEENEY, 529(QQ):AUTUMN71-478
STRAUSS, W.L. CHIAROSCURO.
  617(TLS):21DEC73-1568
STRAVINSKY, I. POETICS OF MUSIC IN THE
  FORM OF SIX LESSIONS.*
  H.M. SCHUELLER, 290(JAAC):SUMMER71-551
STRAVINSKY, T. CATHERINE & IGOR STRAVIN-
  SKY.
  617(TLS):26OCT73-1323
STRAWSON, J. THE BATTLE FOR THE ARDENNES.
  617(TLS):19JAN73-71
STRAWSON, P.F. THE BOUNDS OF SENSE.
  L. GUILLERMIT, 53(AGP):BAND53HEFT2-
  198
STRAWSON, P.F. LOGICO-LINGUISTIC PAPERS.
  M. DURRANT, 518:JAN72-32
STRAWSON, P.F., ED. PHILOSOPHIC LOGIC.
  R. BLANCHÉ, 542:OCT-DEC70-502
STRAYER, J.R. LES GENS DE JUSTICE DU
  LANGUEDOC SOUS PHILIPPE LE BEL.
  T.N. BISSON, 589:JAN72-144
STRAYER, J.R. MEDIEVAL STATECRAFT AND
  THE PERSPECTIVES OF HISTORY.*
  J. RICHARD, 182:VOL24#15/16-633
STRAYER, J.R. ON THE MEDIEVAL ORIGINS
  OF THE MODERN STATE.
  W. ULLMANN, 382(MAE):1972/1-79
STRECH, H. THEODOR FONTANE; DIE SYNTHESE
  VON ALT UND NEU.*
  T. ALT, 406:FALL72-307
  E.F. GEORGE, 182:VOL24#3-106
STREKALOVA, Z.N. IZ ISTORII POL'SKOGO
  GLAGOL'NOGO VIDA.*
  H.D. POHL, 353:AUG71-124
STRELKA, J. VERGLEICHENDE LITERATURKRIT-
  IK.*
  L.L. DUROCHE, 301(JEGP):JAN72-96
  H.H. RUDNICK, 399(MLJ):DEC71-530
STRIBLING, M.L. ART FROM FOUND MATERIALS
  DISCARDED AND NATURAL.
  M. EASTHAM, 89(BJA):WINTER72-110
STRICKLAND, W.G. A DICTIONARY OF IRISH
  ARTISTS.
  M. WYNNE, 39:APR70-323
STRIKER, G. PERAS UND APEIRON.
  P.M. HUBY, 123:DEC72-332
  J.D. MOORE, 124:DEC71-132

STRINDBERG, A. GETTING MARRIED.* (M.
  SANDBACH, TRANS)
  R. COLES, 442(NY):10SEP73-126
  V.S. PRITCHETT, 453:22MAR73-13
STRINDBERG, A. WORLD HISTORICAL PLAYS.
  (A. PAULSON, TRANS)
  Y.L. SANDSTROEM, 563(SS):WINTER72-146
STRODACH, G.K. - SEE LUCRETIUS
STRÖMBÄCK, D. THE EPIPHANY IN RUNIC ART.
  C.W. THOMPSON, 563(SS):WINTER72-130
STRÖMBACK, D. & OTHERS, EDS. BIOGRAPH-
  ICA.
  R. GRAMBO, 196:BAND12HEFT2/3-260
STRONG, J. SEARCH THE SOLAR SYSTEM.
  617(TLS):17AUG73-961
STRONG, R. THE ELIZABETHAN IMAGE.
  C. WHITFIELD, 592:MAR70-130
STRONG, R. THE ENGLISH ICON.*
  M.V. ALPER, 58:APR71-19
  J.K., 135:APR70-276
  C. WHITFIELD, 592:MAR70-130
STRONG, R. TUDOR AND JACOBEAN PORTRAITS:
  NATIONAL PORTRAIT GALLERY.*
  R.E., 135:JUN70-134
STRONG, R. VAN DYCK: CHARLES I ON HORSE-
  BACK.*
  R. DOWNES, 441:2DEC73-92
STROUD, D. GEORGE DANCE.*
  J. DANIELS, 135:NOV71-214
  J. LEES-MILNE, 39:DEC71-522
STROUD, R.S. DRAKON'S LAW ON HOMICIDE.*
  B.M. CAVEN, 303:VOL91-193
  F.W. MITCHEL, 24:JUL72-489
STROUP, T.B. RELIGIOUS RITE AND CEREMONY
  IN MILTON'S POETRY.*
  E. MERTNER, 38:BAND88HEFT2-265
  J.M. STEADMAN, 72:BAND209HEFT4/6-407
STRUEVER, N.S. THE LANGUAGE OF HISTORY IN
  THE RENAISSANCE.*
  D. HAY, 402(MLR):OCT72-922
  639(VQR):SUMMER71-CIX
STRUGATSKI, B. & A. HARD TO BE A GOD.
  T. STURGEON, 441:23SEP73-39
STRUTTON, B. THE CARPACCIO CAPER.
  N. CALLENDAR, 441:28OCT73-49
"STRUTTURALISMO FILOSOFICO."
  E. NAMER, 542:JUL-SEP70-368
STRUVE, G. RUSSIAN LITERATURE UNDER
  LENIN AND STALIN, 1917-1953.
  V.S. DUNHAM, 32:MAR72-197
  L.A. FOSTER, 579(SAQ):WINTER72-134
STRYK, L. & T. IKEMOTO - SEE TAKAHASHI, S.
STUART, J. THE LAND BEYOND THE RIVER.
  M. LEVIN, 441:15APR73-34
STUART, J. MEMORIAL.
  V. CUNNINGHAM, 362:6DEC73-793
STUART, J. YELLOWHAWK.
  M. LEVIN, 441:6MAY73-40
STUBBINGS, H.U. RENAISSANCE SPAIN IN ITS
  LITERARY RELATIONS WITH ENGLAND AND
  FRANCE.*
  D.B. DRAKE, 399(MLJ):FEB71-127
  G. UNGERER, 402(MLR):APR72-399
STUBBLEBINE, J.H., ED. GIOTTO: THE
  ARENA CHAPEL FRESCOES.
  A. SMART, 39:FEB70-163
  D. WILKINS, 56:SPRING71-113
STUBBS, J. DEAR LAURA.
  617(TLS):18MAY73-562
STUBBS, J.C. THE PURSUIT OF FORM.
  J.D. CROWLEY, 445(NCF):JUN71-121
STUBELIUS, S. ENGELSK FONETIK.
  A. WIJK, 597(SN):VOL42#2-504
STUCKENSCHMIDT, H.H. MAURICE RAVEL.*
  A.F.L.T., 412:FEB72-68

STUCKENSCHMIDT, H.H. TWENTIETH CENTURY
COMPOSERS.* (VOL 2: GERMANY AND CENTRAL
EUROPE.)
A.W., 410(M&L):APR72-203
STUCKERT, K. UNTERSUCHUNGEN ÜBER DAS
VERHÄLTNIS VON PRÄFIX UND POSTVERBALER
PARTIKEL BEI LATEINISCHEN LEHNVERBEN IM
ENGLISCHEN, DARGESTELLT AN DEN GRUPPEN
DER AD- UND DIS-KOMPOSITA.
A. BRISAU, 556(RLV):1970/6-680
L. LIPKA, 38:BAND88HEFT3-352
STUCKEY, S. THE IDEOLOGICAL ORIGINS OF
BLACK NATIONALISM.
441:25MAR73-24
STUDENCKI, W. O WACŁAWIE BERENCIE.
J. BAER, 497(POLR):AUTUMN70-112
"STUDI AMERICANI." (NO. 13)
R. ASSELINEAU, 189(EA):APR-JUN71-221
"STUDI DE LITERATURĂ COMPARATĂ."
B. KÖPECZI, 549(RLC):JUL-SEP70-410
"STUDI DI FILOLOGIA E LETTERATURA." (VOL
1)
P.Z., 228(GSLI):VOL148FASC464-624
"STUDI IN ONORE DI ANTONIO CORSANO."
E. NAMER, 542:OCT-DEC71-463
"STUDI IN ONORE DI ARTURO MASSOLO."
E. NAMER, 542:OCT-DEC71-496
"STUDI SUL BORROMINI."
A. BLUNT, 90:NOV71-672
"STUDIEN ZU KANTS PHILOSOPHISCHER ENTWICK-
LUNG."
J. KOPPER, 342:BAND61HEFT2-255
"STUDIEN ZUR GRIECHISCHEN VASENMALEREI."
R.M. COOK, 123:JUN72-291
STUEWER, R.H., ED. HISTORICAL AND PHIL-
OSOPHICAL PERSPECTIVES OF SCIENCE.
M. RUSE, 154:DEC71-832
STURGEON, T. TO HERE AND THE EASEL.
617(TLS):9NOV73-1378
STURM, E. CONSCIENCE ET IMPUISSANCE CHEZ
DOSTOÏEVSKI ET CAMUS.
A.R. BETTLER, 207(FR):OCT70-221
STURM, S. THE LAY OF GUINGAMOR.
N.H.J. VAN DEN BOOGAARD, 433:OCT71-
454
M.D. LEGGE, 208(FS):JAN72-60
H. NIEDZIELSKI, 188(ECR):FALL70-257
W.S. WOODS, 546(RR):DEC71-290
STURROCK, J. THE FRENCH NEW NOVEL.*
J.V. ALTER, 207(FR):DEC70-470
B. MORRISSETTE, 149:SEP72-345
W.A. STRAUSS, 141:WINTER71-103
STURROCK, J. A WICKED WAY TO DIE.
617(TLS):26OCT73-1324
STURT-PENROSE, B. THE ART SCENE.
T. CROMBIE, 39:JUL70-82
STUTCHBURY, O. THE USE OF PRINCIPLE.
617(TLS):2NOV73-1340
STUVERAS, R. LE "PUTTO" DANS L'ART
ROMAIN.*
A. ERNOUT, 555:VOL45FASC2-387
STYAN, J.L. CHEKHOV IN PERFORMANCE.*
K.D. KRAMER, 32:JUN72-511
STYAN, J.L. THE DARK COMEDY.* (2ND ED)
K.P. STEIGER, 402(MLR):JUL72-611
STYAN, J.L. SHAKESPEARE'S STAGECRAFT.*
W.A. BACON, 570(SQ):SPRING70-187
SUBBA RAO, T.V. STUDIES IN INDIAN MUSIC.
N.A. JAIRAZBHOY, 187:MAY73-348
SUBHAN, A. "THE TARIKH-I-BANGALA-I-MAHA-
BATJANGI" OF YUSUF ALI KHAN.
K.S. LAL, 273(IC):OCT71-301
SUBRAHMANIAN, N. HISTORY OF TAMILNAD TO
A.D. 1336.
617(TLS):23FEB73-221
SUCH, P. SOUNDPRINTS.
L.C. MARSH, 99:NOV-DEC73-43
SUCHOFF, B. - SEE BARTÓK, B.

SUCIU, C. DICŢIONAR ISTORIC AL LOCALI-
TĂŢILOR DIN TRANSILVANIA.* (VOL 1)
E.P. HAMP, 215(GL):VOL11#2-138
SUCKLING, J. THE WORKS OF SIR JOHN SUCK-
LING: THE PLAYS.* (L.A. BEAURLINE, ED)
G.B. EVANS, 301(JEGP):OCT72-543
D.C. GUNBY, 67:NOV72-223
SUCKSMITH, H.P. THE NARRATIVE ART OF
CHARLES DICKENS.*
D. DE VRIES, 301(JEGP):JAN72-152
K.J. FIELDING, 637(VS):DEC70-211
S. GILL, 447(N&Q):NOV71-425
S. MONOD, 189(EA):JAN-MAR71-102
R.B. PARTLOW, JR., 445(NCF):MAR72-494
G. SMITH, 155:JAN71-49
M. STEIG, 141:SUMMER71-319
G. THOMAS, 175:SPRING71-25
P. THOMSON, 541(RES):NOV71-509
S. WALL, 184(EIC):JUL71-261
"SÜDHESSISCHES WÖRTERBUCH." (VOL 1)
H. STOPP, 680(ZDP):BAND89HEFT1-131
SUDHOF, S. - SEE BRENTANO, C.
SUELTO DE SÁENZ, P.G. EUGENIO D'ORS.
A. YATES, 86(BHS):APR72-200
"EL SUEÑO Y SU REPRESENTACIÓN EN EL BAR-
ROCO ESPAÑOL."
A. CIORANESCU, 549(RLC):APR-JUN70-270
SUGANA, G.M. THE COMPLETE PAINTINGS OF
TOULOUSE-LAUTREC.
617(TLS):16NOV73-1409
SUGAR, P.F., ED. NATIVE FASCISM IN THE
SUCCESSOR STATES, 1918-1945.
F.L. CARSTEN, 575(SEER):APR72-310
N.M. NAGY-TALAVERA, 32:SEP72-709
SUH, D-S., ED. DOCUMENTS OF KOREAN COM-
MUNISM 1918-1948.
H.C. KIM, 293(JAST):MAY71-692
SUHL, B. JEAN-PAUL SARTRE.*
E.T. DUBOIS, 182:VOL24#19/20-738
A.J. MC KENNA, 400(MLN):MAY71-604
SUKENICK, R. OUT.
L.J. DAVIS, 441:21OCT73-48
SUKIJASOVIĆ, M. YUGOSLAV FOREIGN IN-
VESTMENT LEGISLATION AT WORK.
D.D. MILENKOVITCH, 32:SEP72-726
SULIMIRSKI, T. THE SARMATIANS.
K.F. SMIRNOV, 32:DEC72-876
SULLIVAN, A. THE RAPIDS.
G.W., 102(CANL):AUTUMN72-113
SULLIVAN, D.M. - SEE BENEDETTI, A.
SULLIVAN, J.P., ED. EZRA POUND.
H. WITEMEYER, 659:SPRING73-240
SULLIVAN, M. THE ARTS OF CHINA. CHINESE
ART: RECENT DISCOVERIES.
617(TLS):21DEC73-1568
SULLIVAN, M.R. BROWNING'S VOICES IN "THE
RING AND THE BOOK."*
I. ARMSTRONG, 637(VS):DEC70-207
R. LAWRENCE, 175:SPRING70-33
J.F. LOUCKS 2D, 405(MP):MAY71-392
D.A. LOW, 205(FMLS):APR70-195
SULLIVAN, S., ED. CRITICS ON CHAUCER.
S.S. HUSSEY, 447(N&Q):FEB71-72
SULLIVAN, W. DEATH BY MELANCHOLY.
L.P. SIMPSON, 578:SPRING73-88
SULLOWAY, A.G. GERARD MANLEY HOPKINS AND
THE VICTORIAN TEMPER.
W.R. MUNDT, 598(SOR):AUTUMN73-1029
617(TLS):9FEB73-143
SULTANA, D. SAMUEL TAYLOR COLERIDGE IN
MALTA AND ITALY.*
J.B. BEER, 541(RES):FEB71-98
J. DUFFY, 399(MLJ):FEB71-108
J.R. MAC GILLIVRAY, 627(UTQ):FALL70-73
G. WHALLEY, 401(MLQ):MAR71-115
R.S. WOOF, 447(N&Q):MAY71-196
SULZBACH, H. WITH THE GERMAN GUNS.
617(TLS):26OCT73-1309

SULZBERGER, C.L. AN AGE OF MEDIOCRITY.
W. LAQUEUR, 441:25NOV73-44
442(NY):10DEC73-199
SULZBERGER, C.L. THE TOOTH MERCHANT.
N. CALLENDAR, 441:18FEB73-29
C. LEHMANN-HAUPT, 441:15FEB73-45
442(NY):3MAR73-114
617(TLS):17AUG73-959
SUMMERS, J.H. THE HEIRS OF DONNE AND
JONSON.*
R.L. COLIE, 401(MLQ):MAR72-75
D.L. GUSS, 551(RENQ):WINTER71-566
SUMMERSON, J., ED. CONCERNING ARCHITEC-
TURE.*
W. CREESE, 576:OCT70-275
J. WILTON-ELY, 39:JAN70-82
SUMMERSON, J. VICTORIAN ARCHITECTURE.
R.F. JORDAN, 637(VS):DEC70-225
N. PEVSNER, 46:APR71-259
SUMNER, L.W. & J. WOODS, EDS. NECESSARY
TRUTH.*
E.A.R., 543:DEC70-352
SUMOWSKI, W. CASPAR DAVID FRIEDRICH-
STUDIEN.*
K. ANDREWS, 39:DEC70-498
H. BÖRSCH-SUPAN, 683:BAND34HEFT4-314
SUNDARAM, K. THE SIMHACHALAM TEMPLE.
G.L. HART 3D, 293(JAST):FEB71-499
SÜNGER, M.T. STUDIEN ZUR STRUKTUR DER
WIENER UND MILLSTÄTTER GENESIS (MSS.
WIEN 2721 UND KLAGENFURT 6/19).
H. KUHN, 182:VOL24#1/2-18
SUNY, R.G. THE BAKU COMMUNE, 1917-1918.
R.G. HOVANNISIAN, 32:SEP72-673
SUPER, R.H. THE TIME-SPIRIT OF MATTHEW
ARNOLD.*
W.V. HARRIS, 191(ELN):SEP71-69
SUPER, R.H. - SEE ARNOLD, M.
"SUPERVIELLE." (T. SAVORY, TRANS)
J. HART, 661:SUMMER70-113
SUPERVIELLE-ÉTIEMBLE, J. CORRESPONDANCE
1936-1959. (J. ÉTIEMBLE, ED)
C-R. GIRARD, 535(RHL):JAN-FEB71-140
SUPIČIĆ, I. MUSIQUE ET SOCIÉTÉ.
J.A.W., 410(M&L):OCT72-451
SUPPES, P. & OTHERS. COMPUTER-ASSISTED
INSTRUCTION.
L.E. ALLEN, 316:JUN71-326
"A SUPPLEMENT TO THE OXFORD ENGLISH DIC-
TIONARY."* (VOL 1) (R.W. BURCHFIELD,
ED)
617(TLS):26JAN73-90
SURER, P. CINQUANTE ANS DE THÉÂTRE.
D. KNOWLES, 208(FS):APR72-231
J-J. ROUBINE, 535(RHL):MAR-APR71-330
SURTEES, V. THE PAINTINGS AND DRAWINGS
OF DANTE GABRIEL ROSSETTI (1828-1882).
P. FULLER, 135:SEP71-63
S.M. SMITH, 89(BJA):WINTER72-104
"SURVIVAL PRINTOUT."
T. STURGEON, 441:22APR73-16
SUSANN, J. ONCE IS NOT ENOUGH.
J. O'REILLY, 441:1APR73-6
"'SUSANNAH:' AN ALLITERATIVE POEM OF THE
FOURTEENTH CENTURY."* (A. MISKIMIN,
ED)
E.J. DOBSON, 447(N&Q):MAR71-110
A.M. KINLOCH, 255(HAB):WINTER70-54
T. TURVILLE-PETRE, 597(SN):VOL42#1-
262
SUTER, J.F. PHILOSOPHIE ET HISTOIRE CHEZ
WILHELM DILTHEY.
J. GRANIER, 542:OCT-DEC71-466
SUTHER, M. VISIONS OF XANADU.
J.R. BENNETT, 179(ES):FEB71-80
SUTHERLAND, E. LENT TERM.
617(TLS):17AUG73-945

SUTHERLAND, F. THE STYLE OF INNOCENCE.
J. ORANGE, 296:FALL73-95
SUTHERLAND, J. DANIEL DEFOE.*
A. SHERBO, 301(JEGP):APR72-251
K. STEWART, 191(ELN):JUN72-306
SUTHERLAND, J. OXFORD HISTORY OF ENGLISH
LITERATURE.* (VOL 6: ENGLISH LITERA-
TURE OF THE LATE SEVENTEENTH CENTURY.)
P. LEGOUIS, 189(EA):OCT-DEC70-402
I. SIMON, 556(RLV):1971/2-228
P. THORPE, 648:JUN70-41
G.A.W., 581:MAR72-78
SUTHERLAND, J. - SEE TROLLOPE, A.
SUTHERLAND, J.R., ED. EARLY EIGHTEENTH-
CENTURY POETRY.
566:SPRING72-90
SUTHERLAND, L. THE UNIVERSITY OF OXFORD
IN THE EIGHTEENTH CENTURY.
617(TLS):29JUN73-738
SUTHERLAND, N.M. THE MASSACRE OF ST.
BARTHOLOMEW AND THE EUROPEAN CONFLICT,
1559-1572.
C.V. WEDGWOOD, 362:6SEP73-306
617(TLS):7DEC73-1501
SUTHERLAND, R. FREDERICK PHILIP GROVE.
B. NESBITT, 648:OCT70-72
SUTHERLAND, R., ED. THE "ROMAUNT OF THE
ROSE" AND "LE ROMAN DE LA ROSE."
A.C. BAUGH, 179(ES):OCT71-450
L.J. FRIEDMAN, 545(RPH):AUG71-148
I. GLIER, 38:BAND89HEFT2-257
SUTHERLAND, R. SECOND IMAGE.
D. CAMERON, 102(CANL):SUMMER72-94
A. MITCHAM, 255(HAB):FALL71-65
SUTKOWSKI, A. & A. OSOSTOWICZ-SUTKOWSKA,
EDS. ANTIQUITATES MUSICAE IN POLONIA.
(VOLS 2-7)
G.S. GOLOS, 414(MQ):APR70-294
SUTTER, J., ED. THE NEO-IMPRESSIONISTS.
M.V. ALPER, 58:MAR71-12
SUTTON, A. & M. THE WILD PLACES.
W.H. HONAN, 441:2DEC73-97
SUTTON, A. & M. THE WILDERNESS WORLD OF
THE GRAND CANYON.
42(AR):SPRING71-136
SUTTON, A.C. WESTERN TECHNOLOGY AND
SOVIET ECONOMIC DEVELOPMENT, 1930-
1945.*
M.R. DOHAN, 32:DEC72-904
SUTTON, D. - SEE FRY, R.
SUTTON, D. - SEE WILSON, R.
SUTTON, S.B. CHARLES SPRAGUE SARGENT AND
THE ARNOLD ARBORETUM.
G.H. PRIDE, 432(NEQ):JUN71-314
SUTTON, S.B. - SEE OLMSTED, F.L.
SUYIN, H. - SEE UNDER HAN SUYIN
SUZUKI, D.T. SHIN BUDDHISM.
P.J.H., 543:DEC70-347
YOSHIFUMI UEDA & B.T. YAMASAKI, 485
(PE&W):JUL71-335
SVARTVIK, J. THE EVANS STATEMENTS.
J.A. VAN EK, 597(SN):VOL42#2-503
N.E. OSSELTON, 179(ES):JUN71-288
SVARTVIK, J. ON VOICE IN THE ENGLISH
VERB.*
J.E. PIERCE, 353:MAY70-125
J.M. SINCLAIR, 297(JL):FEB70-158
SVEINSSON, E.Ó. NJÁLS SAGA. (P. SCHACH,
ED & TRANS)
T-M. ANDERSSON, 301(JEGP):JAN72-100
SVENDSEN, C. THE LIFE AND DESTINY OF
ISAK DINESEN.
639(VQR):SUMMER71-CXX
SVEVO, I. FURTHER CONFESSIONS OF ZENO.
A.N. MANCINI, 573(SSF):SUMMER71-483
SVITÁK, I. THE CZECHOSLOVAK EXPERIMENT
1968-1969.
V.V. KUSIN, 575(SEER):OCT72-626

SWADOS, H.   STANDING FAST.*
  C. SHAPIRO, 454:FALL71-87
SWAHN, S.   SVENSK ANTOLOGI 1910-1970.
  Y.L. SANDSTROEM, 563(SS):SPRING72-286
SWAIN, J.O.   JUAN MARÍN-CHILEAN.
  G. CABRERA LEIVA, 263:APR-JUN72-173
SWAIN, M., ED.   INDUCTION, ACCEPTANCE AND
  RATIONAL BELIEF.
  R.H.K., 543:JUN71-763
SWAINSON, D., ED.   HISTORICAL ESSAYS ON
  THE PRAIRIE PROVINCES.
  N. WARD, 529(QQ):WINTER71-624
SWAINSON, D., ED.   OLIVER MOWATT'S
  ONTARIO.
  P. OLIVER, 99:SEP73-39
SWALES, M.   ARTHUR SCHNITZLER.
  W. SCHMIDT, 406:FALL72-317
  617(TLS):120CT73-1231
SWAN, A.J.   RUSSIAN MUSIC AND ITS SOURCES
  IN CHANT AND FOLK-SONG.
  617(TLS):120CT73-1247
SWAN, A.J.   SCRIABIN.
  F.W. STERNFELD, 447(N&Q):FEB71-80
SWAN, R.O.   MUNSHI PREMCHAND OF LAMHI
  VILLAGE.
  C. COPPOLA, 352(LE&W):VOL15#1-161
  L. ROCHER, 293(JAST):NOV70-225
SWANN, D., ED.   THE ROPE OF LOVE.
  617(TLS):50CT73-1167
SWANSON, D.C.   THE NAMES IN ROMAN VERSE.*
  E. MENSCHING, 260(IF):BAND74-278
  J. SAFAREWICZ, 353:OCT70-117
SWANSON, D.R.   THREE CONQUERORS.
  M. WILDING, 402(MLR):OCT72-875
SWANTON, M., ED.   THE DREAM OF THE ROOD.
  G. CLARK, 589:JUL72-551
  B.C. RAW, 382(MAE):1972/2-135
SWARTHOUT, G.   LUCK AND PLUCK.
  M. LEVIN, 441:11MAR73-49
SWEARINGEN, R., ED.   LEADERS OF THE
  COMMUNIST WORLD.
  B.S. MORRIS, 32:SEP72-686
SWEDENBERG, H.T., JR. - SEE DRYDEN, J.
SWEET, J.   THE LEGAL ASPECTS OF ARCHITEC-
  TURE, ENGINEERING AND THE CONSTRUCTION
  PROCESS.
  G.P. SIMONDS, 45:OCT71-112
SWENSON, M. - SEE TRANSTRÖMER, T.
SWETTENHAM, J., ED.   VALIANT MEN.
  J.L. GRANATSTEIN, 99:NOV-DEC73-26
SWEVEN, B.R., ED.   MODERN CALLIGRAPHY,
  AMERICAN AND BRITISH.
  617(TLS):15JUN73-698
SWIDLER, L. & A., EDS.   BISHOPS AND
  PEOPLE.
  R.E. BROWN, 363:AUG71-123
SWIFT, J.   AGRARIAN REFORM IN CHILE.
  N. GALL, 441:1JUL73-6
SWIFT, J.   A DISCOURSE OF THE CONTESTS
  AND DISSENTIONS BETWEEN THE NOBLES AND
  THE COMMONS IN ATHENS AND ROME...
  (F.H. ELLIS, ED)
  P. DANCHIN, 179(ES):FEB71-74
SWIFT, J.   POETICAL WORKS.   (H. DAVIS,
  ED)
  P. DANCHIN, 179(ES):APR71-178
  I. SIMON, 556(RLV):1971/6-774
SWIFT, J.   ZAKLETÝ DUCH.   (A. SKOUMAL,
  ED)
  566:AUTUMN71-6
SWINBURNE, A.C.   A CHOICE OF SWINBURNE'S
  VERSE.   (R. NYE, ED)
  617(TLS):25MAY73-597
SWINBURNE, R.   THE CONCEPT OF MIRACLE.*
  H. PAGE, 150(DR):WINTER71/72-598
  A.W. SPARKES, 63:DEC72-291
  R.C. WALLACE, 483:OCT71-366

SWINBURNE, R.   AN INTRODUCTION TO CON-
  FIRMATION THEORY.
  617(TLS):190CT73-1286
SWINDEN, P., ED.   GEORGE ELIOT: "MIDDLE-
  MARCH."
  617(TLS):17AUG73-950
SWINDEN, P.   UNOFFICIAL SELVES.
  617(TLS):27JUL73-862
SWINDLER, W.F.   COURT AND CONSTITUTION IN
  THE TWENTIETH CENTURY.
  I. DILLIARD, 31(ASCH):SPRING73-347
SWING, T.K.   KANT'S TRANSCENDENTAL LOGIC.*
  K. MARC-WOGAU, 482(PHR):JUL71-403
  J.A. REUSCHER, 258:DEC70-661
  E. SCHAPER, 483:JAN71-75
SWINSON, A., ED.   A REGISTER OF THE
  REGIMENTS AND CORPS OF THE BRITISH ARMY.
  617(TLS):23MAR73-329
SWISHER, C.B.   STEPHEN J. FIELD.
  R. GOEDECKE, 185:OCT70-77
SWITZER, R., ED.   CHATEAUBRIAND.
  F. LETESSIER, 535(RHL):MAY-JUN71-515
  J.B. SANDERS, 207(FR):DEC70-457
SYKES, A.   HAROLD PINTER.
  A.P. HINCHLIFFE, 397(MD):FEB72-486
SYKES, C.   NANCY.*
  N. ANNAN, 453:8FEB73-25
SYKES, P.   THE ELIZABETHAN GARDEN.
  M. LEVIN, 441:13MAY73-39
"SYLLOGE NUMMORUM GRAECORUM: THE COLLEC-
  TION OF THE AMERICAN NUMISMATIC SOCI-
  ETY." (PT 1: ETRURIA - CALABRIA.)
  D. KIANG, 124:OCT71-66
"SYLLOGE NUMMORUM GRAECORUM: THE COLLEC-
  TION OF THE AMERICAN NUMISMATIC SOCI-
  ETY." (PT 2: LUCANIA.)
  M.J. PRICE, 453:19JUL73-15
SYLVESTER, D.   HENRY MOORE.*
  R.E. KRAUSS, 54:SEP70-337
SYME, R.   AMMIANUS AND THE "HISTORIA
  AUGUSTA."*
  A. CAMERON, 313:VOL61-255
SYME, R.   EMPERORS AND BIOGRAPHY.
  S.I. OOST, 122:JAN72-75
  A.M. WARD, 124:NOV71-100
SYME, R.   TEN STUDIES IN TACITUS.
  J. CROOK, 123:JUN72-221
"LA SYMÉTRIE COMME PRINCIPE HEURISTIQUE
  DANS LES DIFFÉRENTES SCIENCES."
  Y. GAUTHIER, 154:SEP71-622
SYMMACHUS: PREFECT AND EMPEROR.   (R.H.
  BARROW, ED & TRANS)
  617(TLS):28DEC73-1584
SYMONDS, J.   PROPHECY AND THE PARASITES.
  J. HUNTER, 362:1FEB73-156
SYMONDS, J. - SEE CROWLEY, A.
SYMONDS, J. & K. GRANT - SEE CROWLEY, A.
SYMONDS, J.A.   THE LETTERS OF JOHN ADD-
  INGTON SYMONDS.*   (VOL 2) (H.M. SCHUEL-
  LER & R.L. PETERS, EDS)
  L. POSTON 3D, 502(PRS):FALL70-268
SYMONDS, J.A.   THE LETTERS OF JOHN ADD-
  INGTON SYMONDS.*   (VOL 3) (H.M. SCHUEL-
  LER & R.L. PETERS, EDS)
  S. DICK, 529(QQ):AUTUMN71-473
  E. ENGELBERG, 637(VS):DEC70-205
  L. POSTON 3D, 502(PRS):FALL70-268
SYMONDS, R.   INTERNATIONAL TARGETS FOR
  DEVELOPMENT.
  468:VOL23#4-429
SYMONDS, R. & M. CARDER.   THE UNITED
  NATIONS AND THE POPULATION QUESTION,
  1945-1970.
  617(TLS):4MAY73-496
SYMONDSON, A., ED.   THE VICTORIAN CRISIS
  OF FAITH.
  L.F. BARMANN, 613:AUTUMN71-451
  N.N. FELTES, 637(VS):MAR71-354

SYMONS, J. THE PLOT AGAINST ROGER RIDER.
N. CALLENDAR, 441:9DEC73-50
442(NY):10DEC73-200
617(TLS):17AUG73-959
SYMONS, L. RUSSIAN AGRICULTURE.
617(TLS):18MAY73-560
SYMONS, R.D. NORTH BY WEST.
R.M. BROWN, 296:FALL73-92
SYNGE, J.M. COLLECTED WORKS.* (VOLS
3&4) (A. SADDLEMYER, ED)
I. DONALDSON, 447(N&Q):JUL71-276
SYNGE, J.M. LETTERS TO MOLLY.* (A.
SADDLEMYER, ED)
102(CANL):WINTER72-103
SYNGE, J.M. RIDERS TO THE SEA. (R.
SKELTON, ED)
J.C. MAXWELL, 447(N&Q):JUL71-277
SYNGE, J.M. SOME SONNETS FROM "LAURA IN
DEATH," AFTER THE ITALIAN OF FRANCESCO
PETRARCH. (R. SKELTON, ED)
G. WATSON, 402(MLR):APR72-408
SYRETT, D. SHIPPING AND THE AMERICAN
WAR, 1775-83.
I.D. GRUBER, 656(WMQ):JUL71-500
SYRETT, H.C. - SEE HAMILTON, A.
SYRETT, I. THE NEW IRIS SYRETT COOKERY
BOOK. (H. LEES & M. LOVELL, EDS)
617(TLS):16NOV73-1409
SZABÓ, E. A MÜFORDÍTÁS.
T. ZSILKA, 75:3/1970-164
SZABÓ, L. SELKUP TEXTS.
E.K. RISTINEN, 350:MAR72-206
SZABOLCSI, M. JEL ÉS KIÁLTÁS.
G.F. CUSHING, 575(SEER):OCT72-608
SZARKOWSKI, J. LOOKING AT PHOTOGRAPHS.
E. HOAGLAND, 441:7OCT73-5
H. KRAMER, 441:4AUG73-21
442(NY):5NOV73-187
SZARKOWSKI, J. - SEE "E.J. BELLOCQ:
STORYVILLE PORTRAITS"
SZAROTA, E.M. KÜNSTLER, GRÜBLER UND
REBELLEN.
M. LEHTONEN, 439(NM):1970/2-328
M. ZUROWSKI, 654(WB):6/1970-219
SZAROTA, E.M. LOHENSTEINS ARMINIUS ALS
ZEITROMAN.*
G. HOFFMEISTER, 221(GQ):MAY71-379
E. SAGARRA & P. SKRINE, 402(MLR):
JUL72-689
J. SCHMIDT, 182:VOL24#19/20-741
P. SKRINE, 220(GL&L):JAN72-140
SZASZ, T.S. IDEOLOGY AND INSANITY.
617(TLS):15JUN73-662
SZCZEPANSKI, J. POLISH SOCIETY.
K. SYMMONS-SYMONOLEWICZ, 497(POLR):
SUMMER71-95
SZCZEPAŃSKI, J., ED. PRZEMYSŁ I SPOŁE-
CZEŃSTWO W POLSCE LUDOWEJ.
J.C. FISHER, 32:MAR72-214
VON SZELISKI, J. TRAGEDY AND FEAR.
S. WEINSTEIN, 651(WHR):AUTUMN72-386
SZEMKUS, K. GESELLSCHAFTLICHER WANDEL
UND SPRACHLICHE FORM.*
J. FUEGI, 149:SEP72-352
C. STEINER, 221(GQ):JAN71-106
SZÉNÁSSY, I.L. ARCHITECTUUR IN NEDER-
LAND: 1960-1967.
T.M. BROWN, 576:OCT71-259
SZIDAT, J. CAESARS DIPLOMATISCHE TÄTIG-
KEIT IM GALLISCHEN KRIEG.*
J.P.V.D. BALSDON, 123:DEC72-429
SZKLARSKA-LOHMANNOWA, A. POLSKO-CZECHO-
SŁOWACKIE STOSUNKI DYPLOMATYCZNE W
LATACH 1918-1925.
R.A. WOYTAK, 32:MAR72-212
R.A. WOYTAK, 497(POLR):AUTUMN71-89
SZONDI, P. HÖLDERLIN - STUDIEN.
E. RADCZUN, 654(WB):7/1970-210

SZONDI, P. LEKTÜREN UND LEKTIONEN.
CELAN-STUDIEN.
617(TLS):15JUN73-669
SZÖVÉRFFY, J. WELTLICHE DICHTUNGEN DES
LATEINISCHEN MITTELALTERS. (VOL 1)
M. WINTERBOTTOM, 382(MAE):1972/1-52
SZPORLUK, R. - SEE POKROVSKY, M.N.
SZULC, T. COMPULSIVE SPY.
G. VIDAL, 453:13DEC73-6
SZWED, J.F., ED. BLACK AMERICA.
R. GREEN, 292(JAF):OCT-DEC71-455
SZYROCKI, M. - SEE BUCHNER, A.

TAAFFE, J.G. - SEE COWLEY, A.
TABORI, P. & P. UNDERWOOD. THE GHOSTS
OF BORLEY.
617(TLS):28DEC73-1595
TACCOLA - SEE UNDER DI JACOPO, M.
TACEY, W.S. BUSINESS AND PROFESSIONAL
SPEAKING.
S.L. COLE, 583:SUMMER71-403
TADDESSE TAMRAT. CHURCH AND STATE IN
ETHIOPIA, 1270-1527.
617(TLS):19JAN73-72
TADIÉ, J-Y. PROUST ET LE ROMAN.* LEC-
TURES DE PROUST.*
J. BOREL, 98:DEC71-1060
TAEGER, B. ZAHLENSYMBOLIK BEI HRABAN, BEI
HINCMAR - UND IM "HEILAND?"
G. CORDES, 182:VOL24#19/20-727
D.H. GREEN, 402(MLR):JUL72-681
TAËNI, R. DRAMA NACH BRECHT.
J.C. HAMMER, 397(MD):MAY70-105
TAFAWA BALEWA, A. SHAIHU UMAR.
H. MAES-JELINEK, 556(RLV):1971/4-492
TAFURI, M. JACOPO SANSOVINO E L'ARCHI-
TETTURA DEL '500 A VENEZIA.
A.A. TAIT, 90:DEC71-748
TAFURI, M. TEORIE E STORIA DELL'ARCHI-
TETTURA.
M. RIESER, 290(JAAC):WINTER70-281
E. TEDESCHI, 46:MAR70-236
TAGLIACOZZO, G., WITH H.V. WHITE, EDS.
GIAMBATTISTA VICO.*
H.B., 543:JUN71-762
A.R. CAPONIGRI, 480(P&R):SPRING71-135
E. GIANTURCO, 275(IQ):FALL70-108
E. GIANTURCO, 551(RENQ):AUTUMN71-419
M. GORETTI, 276:WINTER71-463
F. GRANDE, 544:FALL70-293
H.S. HARRIS, 154:DEC70-410
D.S. ROBINSON, 484(PPR):SEP70-133
N.S. STRUEVER, 311(JP):6DEC73-801
D.P. VERENE, 258:JUN71-260
TAIMNI, I.K. THE SCIENCE OF YOGA.
K. WERNER, 485(PE&W):JAN71-96
"THE TAIN." (T. KINSELLA, TRANS)
S. FAUCHEREAU, 98:MAY70-438
D.F. MELIA, 589:JAN72-130
TAIRA, K. ECONOMIC DEVELOPMENT AND THE
LABOR MARKET IN JAPAN.
T. BLUMENTHAL, 293(JAST):AUG71-900
"THE TAIZÉ PICTURE BIBLE."
M. LAVANOUX, 363:AUG71-121
TAKAHASHI, A. LAND AND PEASANTS IN CEN-
TRAL LUZON.
B. FEGAN, 293(JAST):AUG71-927
TAKAHASHI, K. THE RISE AND DEVELOPMENT
OF JAPAN'S MODERN ECONOMY.
A.H. GLEASON, 293(JAST):MAY71-686
TAKAHASHI, S. AFTERIMAGES.* (L. STRYK &
T. IKEMOTO, EDS & TRANS)
W. DICKEY, 249(HUDR):SUMMER72-301
TAKASHI HATADA. A HISTORY OF KOREA.
W.E. HENTHORN, 293(JAST):NOV70-150

TAKATA, O., T. AKIYAMA & T. YANAGISAWA. TAKAO MANDARA.
    A. SOPER, 57:VOL32#1-90
TAKEDA AKIRA, ED. SŌRAE BAKU-BAKU.
    F.H. MAYER, 244(HJAS):VOL30-263
TAKEDA, S. KANT UND DAS PROBLEM DER ANALOGIE.
    M. KLEINSCHNIEDER, 342:BAND62HEFT2-253
TAKEUCHI, H., S. UYEDA & H. KANAMORI. DEBATE ABOUT THE EARTH.
    42(AR):WINTER71/72-596
TAKTSIS, C. THE THIRD WEDDING.*
    42(AR):WINTER71/72-588
TAL, U. CHRISTIANS AND JEWS IN THE "SECOND REICH" (1870-1914).
    I. SCHORSCH, 328:SUMMER70-373
TALBERT, H.S. & T.H. BALL. THE CREEK WAR OF 1813 AND 1814. (F.L. OWSLEY, JR., ED)
    J.F. DOSTER, 9(ALAR):JUL71-216
TALBOT, T. SOLDIER IN THE WEST. (P.V. HINE & S. LOTTINVILLE, EDS)
    W. GARD, 584(SWR):AUTUMN72-329
TALBOTT, S. - SEE KHRUSHCHEV, N.S.
"THE TALES OF HOFFMAN."
    F.D. MC CONNELL, 181:SPRING71-315
TALLIS, J. LONDON STREET VIEWS 1838-1840.*
    P. METCALF, 46:AUG70-130
    G. WILLS, 39:MAY70-405
TALMON, J.L. ISRAEL AMONG THE NATIONS.
    A. ELON, 390:MAR71-67
TAMÁS, A. AZ ÉLETKÉPEK (1846-1848).
    G. BARANY, 32:JUN72-480
TAMBIAH, S.J. BUDDHISM AND THE SPIRIT CULTS IN NORTH-EAST THAILAND.
    M. TOPLEY, 302:JUL71-373
TAMBIMUTTU, ED. FESTSCHRIFT FOR K.F.B.
    G. BARKER, 362:8MAR73-315
TAMBORNINO, A. & F.J. ZAPP. PERSPECTIVES.
    G. SCHWEIG, 430(NS):AUG71-444
TAMBURINI, L. LE CHIESE DI TORINO DAL RINASCIMENTO AL BAROCCO.
    R. POMMER, 576:MAY71-183
TAMINIAUX, J. LA NOSTALGIE DE LA GRÈCE À L'AUBE DE L'IDÉALISME ALLEMAND.
    K. OEDINGEN, 342:BAND61HEFT1-133
TAMMUZ, B. & L. YUDKIN, EDS. MEETINGS WITH THE ANGEL.
    R. BLYTHE, 362:29NOV73-752
TAMRAT, T. - SEE UNDER TADDESSE TAMRAT
TAMURA JITSUZŌ, IMANISHI SHUNJŪ & SATŌ HISASHI, EDS. GOTAI SHIMBUNKAN YAKKAI.
    D.M. FARQUHAR, 244(HJAS):VOL30-243
TANAKA, I., T. DOI & YAMANE YŪZŌ, EDS. SHŌHEKI-GA ZENSHŪ.
    A. SOPER, 57:VOL33#1/2-157
TANAVEC, P.V., ED. PROBLEMS OF THE LOGIC OF SCIENTIFIC KNOWLEDGE.
    F. WILSON, 154:SEP71-590
TANGE, K. KATSURA.
    617(TLS):13APR73-410
"TANGLED HAIR." (S. GOLDSTEIN & S. SHINODA, TRANS)
    639(VQR):AUTUMN71-CLXIV
TANIZAKI, J. IN-EI RAISAN.
    J. PIGEOT, 98:FEB71-132
TANN, J. GLOUCESTERSHIRE WOOLLEN MILLS.
    617(TLS):4MAY73-509
TANNAHILL, R. FOOD IN HISTORY.
    M.F.K. FISHER, 442(NY):12NOV73-213
    J.L. HESS, 441:4NOV73-5
    617(TLS):28DEC73-1583
TANNER, R.E.S. TRANSITION IN AFRICAN BELIEFS.
    R.G. ABRAHAMS, 69:APR71-173

TANNER, T. SAUL BELLOW.
    R.H. FOSSUM, 594:SPRING70-99
TANNER, T. CITY OF WORDS.*
    S. DICK, 529(QQ):WINTER71-631
    A. GUTTMANN, 27(AL):MAY72-342
    A.J. HANSEN, 454:SPRING72-263
    I. MALIN, 651(WHR):SPRING72-174
    S. SANDERS, 111:28MAY71-223
TANSELLE, G.T. GUIDE TO THE STUDY OF UNITED STATES IMPRINTS.*
    J.A.L. LEMAY, 165:SPRING73-66
T'AO CH'IEN. THE POETRY OF T'AO CH'IEN. (J.R. HIGHTOWER, ED & TRANS)
    H.H. FRANKEL, 244(HJAS):VOL31-313
    R.C. MIAO, 293(JAST):MAY71-627
    639(VQR):SUMMER71-CVIII
TAPIÉ, V-L. L'EUROPE DE MARIE-THÉRÈSE.
    617(TLS):14SEP73-1048
TAPIÉ, V-L. MONARCHIE ET PEUPLES DU DANUBE.
    M. MOLNÁR, 98:JAN70-72
TAPIÉ, V-L. THE RISE AND FALL OF THE HABSBURG MONARCHY.
    F.L. CARSTEN, 575(SEER):JUL72-463
    R.A. KANN, 32:SEP72-706
TARAFDAR, M.R. HUSAIN SHAHI BENGAL.
    K.S. LAL, 273(IC):JAN71-70
TARANOW, G. SARAH BERNHARDT.*
    D.R. FAULKNER, 676(YR):SUMMER72-615
TARATUTA, Y. S.M. STEPNIAK-KRAVCHINSKII.
    617(TLS):12OCT73-1238
TARBUCK, K.J. - SEE LUXEMBURG, R. & N. BUKHARIN
TARDIEU, J. LES PORTES DE TOILE.
    R.R. HUBERT, 207(FR):DEC70-424
TARDIEU, J. THE UNDERGROUND LOVERS AND OTHER EXPERIMENTAL PLAYS.
    D. KNOWLES, 208(FS):APR72-230
TARLING, N. BRITAIN, THE BROOKES AND BRUNEI.
    617(TLS):27APR73-481
TARLTON, C.D. FORTUNE'S CIRCLE.
    639(VQR):WINTER71-XXXVI
TARN, N. - SEE NERUDA, P.
TAROT, R. HUGO VON HOFMANNSTHAL.*
    P. GOFF, 133:1971/3-334
TAROT, R. - SEE VON GRIMMELSHAUSEN, H.J.C.
TARPLEY, F. PLACE NAMES OF NORTHEAST TEXAS.
    L.P. BOONE, 424:DEC70-318
TARR, H. A TIME FOR LOVING.
    M. LEVIN, 441:21JAN73-24
TARRANT, D. JAMES BRANCH CABELL.
    P.L. ARONS, 223:MAR70-64
TARSAÏDZÉ, A. CHETYRE MIFA.
    S. PUSHKAREV, 550(RUSR):JUL71-307
TARSAÏDZÉ, A. KATIA.
    W.E. MOSSE, 32:MAR72-156
    G. TOKMAKOFF, 550(RUSR):APR71-210
"TARTESSOS Y SUS PROBLEMAS."
    P. MAC KENDRICK, 124:DEC71-133
TARVAINEN, K. ZUR WORTGESTALT IN BAIRISCHEN CHRONIKEN DES 15. JAHRHUNDERTS.
    H.L. KUFNER, 405(MP):AUG70-96
TASALOV, V.I. PROMETEI ILI ORPHEI.
    S.F. STARR, 576:MAY71-174
TASSO, T. JERUSALEM DELIVERED. (J. TUSIANI, TRANS)
    W.J. KENNEDY, 275(IQ):FALL-WINTER71-99
TATARKIEWICZ, W. HISTORY OF AESTHETICS. (VOLS 1&2) (J. HARRELL & C. BARRETT, EDS)
    H. OSBORNE, 89(BJA):WINTER72-85
    A. SHIELDS, 319:JAN73-110
TATE, A. ESSAYS OF FOUR DECADES.*
    K. FIELDS, 569(SR):WINTER72-180

TATE, A., ED. SIX AMERICAN POETS.
H. MORRIS, 569(SR):AUTUMN72-627
TATE, A. THE SWIMMERS AND OTHER SELECTED
POEMS.*
J.L. DAVIS, 385(MQR):FALL73-375
TATE, J. ABSENCES.*
V. YOUNG, 249(HUDR):WINTER72/73-666
TATE, J. HINTS TO PILGRIMS.
W.H. PRITCHARD, 249(HUDR):SPRING72-123
D. ROSOCHACKI, 600:FALL71-138
42(AR):FALL71-441
TATE, J. THE OBLIVION HA-HA.*
M. HALPERIN, 134(CP):FALL70-75
F. MORAMARCO, 651(WHR):SPRING72-192
J.D. REED, 600:WINTER71-155
42(AR):SPRING70-135
TATE, J. ROW WITH YOUR HAIR.*
E. FEINSOD, 114(CHIR):JAN-FEB71-156
TATE, P. COUNTRY LOVE AND POISON RAIN.
N. CALLENDAR, 441:11MAR73-50
TATE, R.B. ENSAYOS SOBRE LA HISTORIO-
GRAFÍA PENINSULAR DEL SIGLO XV.
D.W. LOMAX, 86(BHS):APR72-181
TATE, R.B - SEE DEL PULGAR, F.
TATE, R.S., JR. PETIT DE BACHAUMONT.*
B. GUY, 207(FR):DEC70-460
L.A. OLIVIER, 400(MLN):MAY71-587
TATLOW, A. BRECHTS CHINESISCHE GEDICHTE.
617(TLS):28DEC73-1591
TATSEY, J. THE BLACK MOCCASIN. (P.T.
DE VORE, ED)
W.C. STURTEVANT, 441:18MAR73-38
TATSUO, A. - SEE UNDER ARIMA TATSUO
TAUBES, J.S. EINE BOTSCHAFT VOM GEISTE
HEINRICH HEINES.
J.L.S., 191(ELN):SEP71(SUPP)-138
TAULI, V. INTRODUCTION TO A THEORY OF
LANGUAGE PLANNING.*
O. BACK, 75:4/1970-233
B. JEGERS, 215(GL):VOL10#3-212
G. UNGEHEUER, 657(WW):NOV/DEC70-426
F-E. VINJE, 260(IF):BAND75-248
TAURO, A. ELEMENTOS DE LITERATURA PERU-
ANA. (2ND ED)
L. FOX, 263:APR-JUN72-175
TAVANI, G. POESIA DEL DUECENTO NELLA
PENISOLA IBERICA.*
T.R. HART, 400(MLN):MAR71-289
TAVANI, G. PREISTORIA E PROTOSTORIA
DELLE LINGUE ISPANICHE.
J. HORRENT, 556(RLV):1971/4-501
TAVERNIER-VEREECKEN, C. GENTSE NAAMKUNDE
VAN CA. 1000 TOT 1253.
G.B. DROEGE, 424:MAR70-50
TAYLER, I. BLAKE'S ILLUSTRATIONS TO THE
POEMS OF GRAY.
A. BLUNT, 676(YR):WINTER72-301
H. HONOUR, 453:25JAN73-34
D. HUGHES, 418(MR):AUTUMN72-722
W. JACKSON, 579(SAQ):WINTER72-131
B. WILKIE, 301(JEGP):JAN72-142
639(VQR):AUTUMN71-CLXVIII
TAYLEUR, W.H.T. THE PENGUIN BOOK OF
HOME BREWING AND WINE-MAKING.
617(TLS):19OCT73-1289
LORD TAYLOR OF MANSFIELD. UPHILL ALL THE
WAY.
617(TLS):12JAN73-49
TAYLOR, A.C., COMP. CURRENT RESEARCH IN
FRENCH STUDIES AT UNIVERSITIES AND
UNIVERSITY COLLEGES IN THE UNITED KING-
DOM 1970-1971.
D.M. SUTHERLAND, 208(FS):OCT72-487
TAYLOR, A.J. LAISSEZ-FAIRE AND STATE
INTERVENTION IN NINETEENTH-CENTURY
BRITAIN.
617(TLS):12JAN73-45

TAYLOR, A.J.P. BEAVERBROOK.*
R. BLYTHE, 453:8MAR73-29
TAYLOR, A.J.P. - SEE CROZIER, W.P.
TAYLOR, B. STUBBS.*
R. EDWARDS, 39:DEC71-519
D. THOMAS, 135:DEC71-291
592:NOV71-218
TAYLOR, C. THE PATTERN OF POLITICS.
G.A. RAWLYK, 529(QQ):SPRING71-142
TAYLOR, C.L., ED. AGGREGATE DATA ANALY-
SIS.
J.P. BELSHAW, 182:VOL24#3-97
TAYLOR, D. AFTER THE FIRST DEATH.
M. LEVIN, 441:22APR73-28
TAYLOR, D.S., WITH B.B. HOOVER - SEE
CHATTERTON, T.
TAYLOR, E. MRS. PALFREY AT THE CLARE-
MONT.*
P.M. SPACKS, 249(HUDR):SPRING72-166
TAYLOR, E. THE SERPENT UNDER IT.
N. CALLENDAR, 441:4FEB73-16
TAYLOR, E.R. WELCOME EUMENIDES.*
V. YOUNG, 249(HUDR):WINTER72/73-667
TAYLOR, G.O. THE PASSAGES OF THOUGHT.*
G. CORE, 219(GAR):SUMMER70-255
TAYLOR, H., ED. THE HUMANITIES AND THE
SCHOOLS.
C.W. STANSFIELD, 399(MLJ):APR71-257
TAYLOR, I. BLAKE'S ILLUSTRATIONS TO THE
POEMS OF GRAY.
W. VAUGHAN, 592:NOV71-210
TAYLOR, I. NAMES AND THEIR HISTORIES.
(2ND ED)
K.B. HARDER, 424:JUN71-144
TAYLOR, I. & L., EDS. POLITICS AND
DEVIANCE.
617(TLS):31AUG73-997
TAYLOR, I., P. WALTON & J. YOUNG. THE
NEW CRIMINOLOGY.
617(TLS):24AUG73-970
TAYLOR, J. PLANTING FOR PLEASURE.
617(TLS):9NOV73-1381
TAYLOR, J.G., ED. THE LITERATURE OF THE
AMERICAN WEST.
G. HASLAM, 649(WAL):WINTER71-313
TAYLOR, J.L., WITH P.C. MARTIN. A PORTU-
GUESE-ENGLISH DICTIONARY. (REV)
M.G. MACNICOLL, 238:MAR71-223
E.W. THOMAS, 399(MLJ):FEB71-113
TAYLOR, J.R. HAROLD PINTER.
S.H. GALE, 397(MD):FEB72-478
TAYLOR, J.R. - SEE GREENE, G.
TAYLOR, J.R. & B. BROOKE. THE ART
DEALERS.
T. CROMBIE, 39:JUL70-82
TAYLOR, J.W.R. AIRCRAFT 1974.
617(TLS):21SEP73-1093
TAYLOR, J.W.R. & D. MONDEY. SPIES IN
THE SKY.
617(TLS):19JAN73-73
TAYLOR, J.W.R. & G. SWANBROUGH. MILITARY
AIRCRAFT OF THE WORLD.
617(TLS):21SEP73-1093
TAYLOR, L.E. PASTORAL AND ANTI-PASTORAL
IN JOHN UPDIKE'S FICTION.*
W.T. STAFFORD, 295:NOV72-569
TAYLOR, M. MARY TAYLOR, FRIEND OF CHAR-
LOTTE BRONTË. (J. STEVENS, ED)
617(TLS):3AUG73-903
TAYLOR, M.A. A NEW LOOK AT THE OLD
SOURCES OF "HAMLET."
T.P. HARRISON, 570(SQ):AUTUMN70-504
TAYLOR, M.C. GABRIELA MISTRAL'S RELIG-
IOUS SENSIBILITY.
J. GIORDANO, 240(HR):APR71-229
TAYLOR, N. THE VILLAGE IN THE CITY.
G. ANNAN, 362:12JUL73-59
617(TLS):23NOV73-1424

TAYLOR, O.R. - SEE DE VOLTAIRE, F.M.A.
TAYLOR, P. THE COLLECTED STORIES OF
   PETER TAYLOR.
   J.P., 376:JUL70-115
   R. PHILLIPS, 573(SSF):SUMMER71-487
   639(VQR):WINTER71-XII
TAYLOR, P. - SEE GREENE, G.
TAYLOR, R. FLORIDA EAST COAST CHAMPION.
   T. GUNN, 491:JAN73-239
TAYLOR, R. NOISE.
   A.W. BAINS, 46:OCT71-259
TAYLOR, R., ED. THE ROMANTIC TRADITION
   IN GERMANY.
   P.H. ZOLDESTER, 221(GQ):NOV71-579
TAYLOR, R.J., ED. THE SUSQUEHANNAH COM-
   PANY PAPERS. (VOLS 7-9)
   W.S. HANNA, 656(WMQ):APR71-340
TAYLOR, S.W. & E. LUCIE-SMITH, EDS.
   FRENCH POETRY TODAY.*
   H. CIXOUS, 441:11FEB73-22
   V. YOUNG, 249(HUDR):WINTER72/73-659
TAYLOR, T. THOMAS TAYLOR THE PLATONIST.*
   (K. RAINE & G.M. HARPER, EDS)
   R.M. BAINE, 219(GAR):FALL71-380
   R. VOITLE, 173(ECS):SPRING72-496
TAYLOR, W. GREEK ARCHITECTURE.
   R. HIGGINS, 39:AUG71-160
   D.W. ROLLER, 124:NOV71-101
TEDESCHINI-LALLI, B., ED. REPERTORIO
   BIBLIOGRAFICO DELLA LETTERATURA AMERI-
   CANA IN ITALIA. (VOLS 1-3)
   R. ASSELINEAU, 189(EA):APR-JUN71-220
TEER, F. & J.D. SPENCE. POLITICAL OPIN-
   ION POLLS.
   617(TLS):31AUG73-997
TEETS, B.E. & H.E. GERBER, COMPS. JOSEPH
   CONRAD.
   617(TLS):15JUN73-664
TEGNER, H. NATURAL HISTORY IN NORTHUM-
   BERLAND AND DURHAM.
   617(TLS):9FEB73-161
TEH-CHANG, C. - SEE UNDER CHANG TEH-CHANG
TEILHARD DE CHARDIN, P. LETTERS TO TWO
   FRIENDS.* (R.N. ANSHEN, ED)
   617(TLS):20JUL73-841
TEILHARD DE CHARDIN, P. SCIENCE AND
   CHRIST.
   W.A.J., 543:JUN71-759
TEKEYAN, C. THE REVELATIONS OF A DISAP-
   PEARING MAN.
   M. COOKE, 676(YR):SUMMER72-599
TEKIN, S., ED. SOURCES OF ORIENTAL LAN-
   GUAGES AND LITERATURES.
   K.H. MENGES, 318(JAOS):OCT-DEC71-555
TELES, G.M. - SEE UNDER MENDONÇA TELES,
   G.
TELLER, W., ED. TWELVE WORKS OF NAIVE
   GENIUS.
   J. SEELYE, 441:4MAR73-14
TEMIANKA, H. FACING THE MUSIC.
   441:15APR73-32
TEMKIN, S.D. - SEE LEVY, F.A.
TEMKINE, R. L'ENTREPRISE THÉÂTRE.
   H.A. WATERS, 188(ECR):SUMMER70-160
TEMPEL, E. NEW JAPANESE ARCHITECTURE.
   L. SATKOWSKI, 576:MAY71-184
TEMPERLEY, H. BRITISH ANTI-SLAVERY
   1833-1870.
   617(TLS):19OCT73-1275
TEMPLE, R.Z. NATHALIE SARRAUTE.*
   R.R. HUBERT, 207(FR):DEC70-440
TEMPLIER, P-D. ERIK SATIE.*
   R. HAGGH, 502(PRS):SUMMER70-181
"LE TEMPS ET LA MORT DANS LA PHILOSOPHIE
   ESPAGNOLE CONTEMPORAINE."
   E. NAMER, 542:APR-JUN70-261

TENCA, C. SAGGI CRITICI. (G. BERARDI,
   ED)
   M. FUBINI, 228(GSLI):VOL147FASC458/
   459-415
TENDRYAKOV, V. THREE, SEVEN, ACE AND
   OTHER STORIES.
   S. HILL, 362:19APR73-520
   617(TLS):27APR73-461
TENISON, M.H. FOR BETTER, FOR WORSE.
   617(TLS):9FEB73-147
TENNANT, E. THE TIME OF THE CRACK.
   S. HILL, 362:14JUN73-808
   617(TLS):15JUN73-661
TENNANT, K. EVATT.
   D. AITKIN, 381:MAR71-118
TENNYSON, A. THE POEMS OF TENNYSON.*
   (C. RICKS, ED)
   J.C. MAXWELL, 447(N&Q):JUL71-274
   J. PETTIGREW, 636(VP):SUMMER70-161
TEODOR, P. EVOLUŢIA GÎNDIRII ISTORICE
   ROMÂNEŞTI.
   K. HITCHINS, 32:JUN72-486
TEPPE, J. LES CAPRICES DU LANGAGE.
   F. HELGORSKY, 209(FM):JUL71-267
TERESA, V., WITH T.C. RENNER. MY LIFE IN
   THE MAFIA.
   F. FERRETTI, 441:8APR73-5
"TERMINOLOGIE DE L'HYGIÈNE DU MILIEU."
   R. HAESERYN, 75:4/1971-49
TERRACE, E.L.B. EGYPTIAN PAINTINGS OF
   THE MIDDLE KINGDOM.
   J.D., 135:MAR70-201
   T.G.H. JAMES, 39:FEB71-147
   W. NEEDLER, 54:JUN71-240
TERRACE, E.L.B. & H.G. FISCHER. TREAS-
   URES OF EGYPTIAN ART FROM THE CAIRO
   MUSEUM.*
   S. ROSENTHAL, 58:APR71-18
TERRAY, E. L'ORGANISATION SOCIALE DES
   DIDA DE CÔTE D'IVOIRE.
   R. BRAIN, 69:APR71-165
TERREAUX, L. RONSARD CORRECTEUR DE SES
   OEUVRES.
   H. NAÏS, 209(FM):APR70-167
   I. SILVER, 546(RR):FEB71-36
   H. WEBER, 535(RHL):JUL-AUG70-693
TERRILL, R. R.H. TAWNEY AND HIS TIMES.
   P. JOHNSON, 441:30DEC73-4
TERRY, A., ED. AN ANTHOLOGY OF SPANISH
   POETRY, 1500-1700.* (PT 2)
   J. LOWE, 402(MLR):JAN72-195
TERRY, A. CATALAN LITERATURE.
   617(TLS):23MAR73-331
TERRY, A. ANTONIO MACHADO: CAMPOS DE
   CASTILLA.
   617(TLS):5OCT73-1191
TERRY, E.D., ED. ARTISTS AND WRITERS IN
   THE EVOLUTION OF LATIN AMERICA.
   S. KARSEN, 238:MAR71-213
   J. RUTHERFORD, 447(N&Q):NOV71-428
TERRY, M. COUPLINGS AND GROUPINGS.
   442(NY):10FEB73-116
TERSON, R. ZIGGER ZAGGER [AND] MOONEY
   AND HIS CARAVANS.
   A. RENDLE, 157:SUMMER70-75
TERSON, P. & P. CHEESEMAN. THE KNOTTY.
   A. RENDLE, 157:WINTER70-70
TERVOOREN, H. BIBLIOGRAPHIE ZUM MINNE-
   SANG UND ZU DEN DICHTERN AUS "DES
   MINNESANGS FRÜHLING."*
   M.E. GIBBS, 220(GL&L):APR72-313
   C. PETZSCH, 657(WW):JUL/AUG70-278
TERVOOREN, H. EINZELSTROPHE ODER STRO-
   PHENBINDUNG?
   M. KAEMPFERT, 680(ZDP):BAND89HEFT3-
   450
TE SELLE, E. AUGUSTINE THE THEOLOGIAN.
   R.J. O'CONNELL, 613:WINTER70-628

359

TESSARI, R. LA COMMEDIA DELL'ARTE NEL
  SEICENTO.
    R. ALONGE, 288(GSLI):VOL148FASC461-
    134
TESTA, A. DISCORSO DI FISICA.
    E. NAMER, 542:JUL-SEP70-369
TESTARD, M. SAINT JÉRÔME.*
    W.H.C. FREND, 123:MAR72-115
    P. LANGLOIS, 555:VOL45FASC1-181
    R.A. MARKUS, 313:VOL61-312
TETEL, M. MARGUERITE DE NAVARRE'S "HEP-
  TAMERON."
    617(TLS):20APR73-440
TEVETH, S. THE CURSED BLESSING.
    J. RIEMER, 287:JUN71-29
TEVETH, S. MOSHE DAYAN.
    617(TLS):23FEB73-212
TEZLA, A. HUNGARIAN AUTHORS.*
    G.F. CUSHING, 575(SEER):APR72-297
    T.R. MARK, 32:MAR72-236
THACKER, C. - SEE DE VOLTAIRE, F.M.A.
THACKERAY, W.M. THE LUCK OF BARRY LYNDON.
  (M.J. ANISMAN, ED)
    P.L. SHILLINGSBURG, 517(PBSA):APR-JUN
    72-219
THACKRAY, A. JOHN DALTON.
    617(TLS):14SEP73-1065
THADEN, E.C. RUSSIA SINCE 1801.
    B. DMYTRYSHYN, 32:MAR72-154
    W.E. MOSSE, 575(SEER):JUL72-466
VAN THAL, H., ED. LANDOR.
    617(TLS):21DEC73-1559
VAN THAL, H. - SEE KELLY, M.
VAN THAL, H. & J.S. NICKERSON - SEE
  BELLOC, H.
THALBERG, I. ENIGMAS OF AGENCY.
    617(TLS):1JUN73-612
THALMANN, M. DIE ROMANTIK DES TRIVIALEN.
    W.J. LILLYMAN, 301(JEGP):JUL72-432
    A. WARD, 402(MLR):OCT72-945
THALMANN, M. ROMANTIKER ALS POETOLOGEN.*
    L.R. FURST, 220(GL&L):JUL72-403
THALMANN, M. ZEICHENSPRACHE DER ROMANTIK.
    R. HABEL, 657(WW):JAN/FEB70-66
    P. KÜPPER, 433:JUL70-315
THATCHER, D.S. NIETZSCHE IN ENGLAND,
  1890-1914.*
    L. TUMMON, 150(DR):SPRING71-122
THAYER, H.S. MEANING AND ACTION.*
    H.W.S., 319:JUL73-435
THAYER, H.S. PRAGMATISM.
    W.J.L., 543:MAR71-552
THEALL, D.F. THE MEDIUM IS THE REAR VIEW
  MIRROR.
    D. DUFFY, 150(DR):SPRING71-119
    D.W. SMYTHE, 529(QQ):SUMMER71-321
"LE THÉÂTRE MODERNE DEPUIS LA DEUXIÈME
  GUERRE MONDIALE."* (VOL 2)
    R. PIGNARRE, 535(RHL):JAN-FEB70-159
THEIS, N. JOHN HENRY NEWMAN IN UNSERER
  ZEIT.
    617(TLS):27APR73-479
THEISS, W. EXEMPLARISCHE ALLEGORIK.*
    W. BLANK, 680(ZDP):BAND90HEFT3-472
    G.J. MARTIN-TEN WOLTHUIS, 433:APR71-
    214
THELEN, H. ZUR ENTSTEHUNGSGESCHICHTE DER
  HOCHALTAR-ARCHITEKTUR VON ST. PETER IN
  ROM.
    J. MONTAGU, 56:WINTER71-490
THELWELL, N. THREE SHEETS IN THE WIND.
    617(TLS):17AUG73-961
VAN THEMAAT, W.A.V. RÄUMLICHE VORSTEL-
  LUNG UND MATHEMATISCHES ERKENNTNISVER-
  MÖGEN. (VOLS 1&2)
    H. FREUDENTHAL, 316:MAR70-131

THEOCRITUS. THEOKRIT: DIE ECHTEN GEDICH-
  TE. (E. STAIGER, TRANS)
    D.N. LEVIN, 124:OCT71-63
    H. RÜDIGER, 52:BAND6HEFT3-313
THEOCRITUS. THEOKRIT: GEDICHTE." (F.P.
  FRITZ, ED)
    H. RÜDIGER, 52:BAND6HEFT3-313
THEODORAKIS, M. JOURNALS OF RESISTANCE.
    A. RYAN, 362:15FEB73-217
    617(TLS):30MAR73-342
THÉODORIDÈS, J. STENDHAL DU CÔTÉ DE LA
  SCIENCE.
    617(TLS):20APR73-450
THEODOULOU, C. GREECE AND THE ENTENTE,
  AUGUST 1, 1914 - SEPTEMBER 25, 1916.
    617(TLS):2MAR73-227
THEOGNIS - SEE UNDER HESIOD
THEOHARIS, A.G. THE YALTA MYTHS.
    E.B. TOMPKINS, 550(RUSR):OCT71-416
THEOPHILUS. THEOPHILUS OF ANTIOCH: "AD
  AUTOLYCUM." (R.M. GRANT, ED & TRANS)
    C.B. PASCAL, 124:NOV71-94
THERNSTROM, S. THE OTHER BOSTONIANS.
    I.R. DEE, 441:16DEC73-5
THEROUX, A. THREE WOGS.*
    V. CUNNINGHAM, 362:28JUN73-873
    617(TLS):6JUL73-783
THEROUX, P. GIRLS AT PLAY.*
    J.P., 376:JAN70-109
THEROUX, P. JUNGLE LOVERS.*
    639(VQR):AUTUMN71-CLXI
THEROUX, P. SAINT JACK.
    A. BROYARD, 441:10SEP73-33
    R.V. CASSILL, 441:9SEP73-5
    S. HILL, 362:19APR73-520
    E. WEEKS, 61:OCT73-128
    442(NY):10SEP73-132
    617(TLS):27APR73-460
THERRIEN, V. LA RÉVOLUTION DE GASTON
  BACHELARD EN CRITIQUE LITTÉRAIRE.
    E.K. KAPLAN, 207(FR):APR71-993
"THESAURUS LINGUAE LATINAE."
    A. ERNOUT, 555:VOL45FASC2-298
THIBAULT, C. BIBLIOGRAPHIA CANADIANA.
    J.L. GRANATSTEIN, 99:NOV-DEC73-27
THIEL, C. SENSE AND REFERENCE IN FREGE'S
  LOGIC.
    L. LINSKY, 482(PHR):APR71-263
VAN THIEL, H. DER ESELSROMAN. (VOL 1)
    F. LASSERRE, 182:VOL24#19/20-758
    C. SCHLAM, 124:JAN72-170
VAN THIEL, H. DER ESELSROMAN. (VOL 2)
    F. LASSERRE, 182:VOL24#19/20-758
THIELEMANS, M-R. BOURGOGNE ET ANGLE-
  TERRE.
    J.J.N. PALMER, 182:VOL24#1/2-53
THIELICKE, H. HOW TO BELIEVE AGAIN.
    617(TLS):29JUN73-755
THIEME, P. KLEINE SCHRIFTEN. (G. BUDD-
  RUSS, ED)
    H. HUMBACH, 182:VOL24#21/22-784
THIESS, W. EXEMPLARISCHE ALLEGORIK.
    P. SALMON, 220(GL&L):JAN72-151
THIHER, A. CÉLINE.
    617(TLS):13JUL73-816
THINÈS, G. LA PROBLÉMATIQUE DE LA PSY-
  CHOLOGIE.
    H. DECLÈVE, 154:DEC70-492
THION, S. - SEE MUS, P. & J. MC ALISTER,
  JR.
THIRION, A. RÉVOLUTIONNAIRES SANS RÉVO-
  LUTION.
    617(TLS):18MAY73-546
"THIRTY-THIRD BIENNIAL REPORT OF THE
  NORTH CAROLINA DEPARTMENT OF ARCHIVES
  AND HISTORY, JULY 1, 1968 THROUGH JUNE
  30, 1970."
    W.L. JORDAN, 14:OCT71-383

THISTLE, M. TIME TOUCH ME GENTLY.
F. COGSWELL, 529(QQ):SUMMER71-325
THODY, P. ALDOUS HUXLEY.
617(TLS):6APR73-371
THODY, P.M.W. LACLOS: "LES LIAISONS
DANGEREUSES."
P-E. LEVAYER, 535(RHL):MAY-JUN71-512
V. MYLNE, 208(FS):APR72-208
THOMANN, T. - SEE SENECA
THOMAS, A. HOPKINS THE JESUIT.
R. BOYLE, 636(VP):WINTER71-455
R. BRINLEE, 577(SHR):SUMMER71-297
W-F. GLEESON, 613:SPRING70-136
W.R. MUNDT, 598(SOR):AUTUMN73-1029
THOMAS, A. SONGS MY MOTHER TAUGHT ME.
J-D. O'HARA, 441:23DEC73-12
THOMAS, A.R.B. CHESS FOR THE LOVE OF IT.
617(TLS):21SEP73-1093
THOMAS, B. GEOMETRY IN PICTORIAL COM-
POSITION.
A.G., 135:JUN71-152
THOMAS, B. SELZNICK.
200:JAN71-31
THOMAS, D. COLLECTED POEMS 1934-1952.
J-J. MAYOUX, 98:AUG/SEP71-675
THOMAS, D. A LONG TIME BURNING.
D-F. FOXON, 354:JUN70-174
THOMAS, D., COMP. THE MIND OF ECONOMIC
MAN.
G. HUTTON, 619(TC):VOL179#1046-49
THOMAS, D. THE NOTEBOOKS OF DYLAN
THOMAS. (BRITISH TITLE: POET IN THE
MAKING.) (R. MAUD, ED)
A.R. TELLIER, 189(EA):JAN-MAR70-96
THOMAS, D. OEUVRES. (M. NATHAN & D.
ROCHE, EDS)
J-J. MAYOUX, 98:AUG/SEP71-675
THOMAS, D. THE POEMS OF DYLAN THOMAS.
(D. JONES, ED)
W.H. PRITCHARD, 249(HUDR):SPRING72-127
THOMAS, D.A. CRETE 1941.
617(TLS):23FEB73-222
THOMAS, D.S. & S.R. SMITH. SUMMER SAT-
URDAYS IN THE WEST.
617(TLS):25MAY73-597
THOMAS, E. LETTERS FROM EDWARD THOMAS TO
GORDON BOTTOMLEY. (R.G. THOMAS, ED)
R. LAWRENCE, 175:SUMMER70-69
THOMAS, E.W. THE SYNTAX OF SPOKEN BRA-
ZILIAN PORTUGUESE.*
F.P. HEBBLETHWAITE, 37:MAR70-42
205(FMLS):APR70-211
THOMAS, G. & M. MORGAN-WITTS. THE STRANGE
FATE OF THE MORRO CASTLE.
617(TLS):12JAN73-49
THOMAS, G.F. PHILOSOPHY AND RELIGIOUS
BELIEF.
T-S-P., 543:DEC70-347
M-K-S., 154:SEP71-643
THOMAS, H. CUBA.*
42(AR):FALL71-443
THOMAS, H. EUROPE.
R. MAYNE, 362:15FEB73-219
617(TLS):23FEB73-196
THOMAS, H. GOYA: THE THIRD OF MAY 1808.
R. DOWNES, 441:2DEC73-93
617(TLS):7SEP73-1021
THOMAS, H. SAINTE JEUNESSE.
617(TLS):6JUL73-783
THOMAS, H. JOHN STRACHEY.
R. CROSSMAN, 362:3MAY73-588
P. STANSKY, 441:30SEP73-2
442(NY):220CT73-175
617(TLS):11MAY73-515
THOMAS, J. & D.J. NORDLOH - SEE HOWELLS,
W.D.

THOMAS, J.J. THE THEORY AND PRACTICE OF
CREOLE GRAMMAR.*
A. VALDMAN, 207(FR):MAR71-791
J. VOORHOEVE, 361:VOL27#1-104
THOMAS, J.W. MEDIEVAL GERMAN LYRIC
VERSE.*
H. HOMANN, 400(MLN):APR71-423
THOMAS, K. ANALYSE DER ARBEIT.
K. MELLEROWICZ, 182:VOL24#7/8-344
THOMAS, K. RELIGION AND THE DECLINE OF
MAGIC.
K.M. BRIGGS, 203:SUMMER71-168
THOMAS, L. THE MAN WITH THE POWER.
J. CAREY, 362:22NOV73-719
THOMAS, L. WHEN EVEN ANGELS WEPT.
T. LASK, 441:10FEB73-33
442(NY):17FEB73-112
THOMAS, L.L. - SEE VINOGRADOV, V.V.
THOMAS, M. - SEE "THE GRANDES HEURES OF
JEAN, DUKE OF BERRY"
THOMAS, N.L. MODERN LOGIC.
W.E. GOULD, 316:SEP71-544
THOMAS, O. METAPHOR AND RELATED SUB-
JECTS.*
P. SWIGGART, 128(CE):DEC71-372
THOMAS, O. TRANSFORMATIONAL GRAMMAR AND
THE TEACHER OF ENGLISH.* (GERMAN
TITLE: TRANSFORMATIONELLE GRAMMATIK UND
ENGLISCHUNTERRICHT.)
H-O. THIEME, 430(NS):JUN71-333
THOMAS, P. THE TRAILING CORD.
M.T. LANE, 198:FALL73-105
THOMAS, P.W. SIR JOHN BERKENHEAD, 1617-
1679.*
G.E. AYLMER, 354:SEP70-263
M. CRUM, 541(RES):FEB71-81
THOMAS, R. IF YOU CAN'T BE GOOD.
N. CALLENDAR, 441:22JUL73-12
THOMAS, R.H. & W. VAN DER WILL. THE GER-
MAN NOVEL AND THE AFFLUENT SOCIETY.*
H. LEHNERT, 149:SEP72-361
THOMAS AQUINAS - SEE UNDER AQUINAS, T.
"SAINT THOMAS AUJOURD'HUI."
A. FOREST, 542:APR-JUN70-236
THOMASON, R.H. SYMBOLIC LOGIC.
H. HERMES, 316:DEC71-678
THOMES, F.C. LA RIVOLTA DI ARISTONICO E
LE ORIGINI DELLA PROVINCIA ROMANA
D'ASIA.
J. BRISCOE, 123:MAR72-132
THOMPSEN, M. LIVING POOR.
V-L-E., 37:MAY71-41
THOMPSON, A. THE DYNAMICS OF THE INDUS-
TRIAL REVOLUTION.
617(TLS):31AUG73-999
THOMPSON, A.W. & R.A. HART. THE UNCERTAIN
CRUSADE.*
J. WALKIN, 550(RUSR):JAN71-85
THOMPSON, A.W.J. & L.C. HUNTER. THE
NATIONALIZED TRANSPORT INDUSTRIES.
617(TLS):16MAR73-300
THOMPSON, B. [COUNT RUMFORD] THE COLLEC-
TED WORKS OF COUNT RUMFORD. (VOLS 3-5)
(S.C. BROWN, ED)
639(VQR):WINTER71-XLIV
THOMPSON, C.W. VICTOR HUGO AND THE GRA-
PHIC ARTS.
D. ADAMSON, 402(MLR):APR72-421
205(FMLS):OCT71-414
THOMPSON, D. ROBYN DENNY.
T. HILTON, 592:MAR71-129
THOMPSON, D. TOYS OF DEATH.
J. DITSKY, 628:SPRING72-108
THOMPSON, D.F. THE DEMOCRATIC CITIZEN.
W.R. MATHIE, 150(DR):AUTUMN71-443
THOMPSON, D.M., ED. NONCONFORMITY IN
THE NINETEENTH CENTURY.
617(TLS):16FEB73-190

THOMPSON, E.P. & E. YEO - SEE MAYHEW, H.
THOMPSON, G. PLANNING AND DESIGN OF
LIBRARY BUILDINGS.
　617(TLS):7DEC73-1519
THOMPSON, G.R. POE'S FICTION.
　P.F. QUINN, 578:FALL73-81
　617(TLS):13JUL73-800
THOMPSON, H.A. & R.E. WYCHERLEY. THE
ATHENIAN AGORA. (VOL 14)
　617(TLS):11MAY73-522
THOMPSON, H.S. FEAR AND LOATHING.
　C. LEHMANN-HAUPT, 441:18MAY73-27
　T. SELIGSON, 441:15JUL73-7
　R. TODD, 61:JUL73-99
　K. VONNEGUT, JR., 231:JUL73-92
　G. WILLS, 453:4OCT73-3
　442(NY):13AUG73-88
THOMPSON, J. DEATH CAP.
　617(TLS):3AUG73-911
THOMPSON, J. KIERKEGAARD.
　J.M. CAMERON, 453:20SEP73-14
THOMPSON, J.E.S., ED. THE DRESDEN CODEX.
　617(TLS):5OCT73-1194
THOMPSON, K. THE TENANTS WERE CORRIE AND
TENNIE.
　N. BAILEY, 296:FALL73-110
　R.F. HASSAN, 198:FALL73-108
THOMPSON, K.F. MODESTY AND CUNNING.
　I. RIBNER, 301(JEGP):APR72-246
　W.G. RICE, 385(MQR):SPRING73-202
THOMPSON, L. ROBERT FROST: THE YEARS OF
TRIUMPH, 1915-1938.*
　E. BARNARD, 418(MR):SUMMER72-506
　J.M. COX, 639(VQR):WINTER71-126
　J.J. MC ALEER, 613:AUTUMN71-469
　42(AR):SUMMER70-265
THOMPSON, L.S. A BIBLIOGRAPHY OF SPANISH
PLAYS ON MICROCARDS.
　N.D. SHERGOLD, 354:MAR70-84
THOMPSON, R.W. GENERALISSIMO CHURCHILL.
　M. HOWARD, 231:DEC73-116
　617(TLS):26OCT73-1309
THOMPSON, R.W. INTERNATIONAL TRADE AND
DOMESTIC PROSPERITY: CANADA 1926-38.
　P.B. HUBER, 150(DR):SPRING71-118
THOMPSON, S., ED. ONE HUNDRED FAVORITE
FOLKTALES.*
　F. HARKORT, 196:BAND12HEFT1-108
THOMPSON, T. RICHIE.
　D. RADER, 441:15JUL73-4
THOMPSON, T.W. WORDSWORTH'S HAWKSHEAD.
(R. WOOF, ED)
　N. NICHOLSON, 565:VOL12#3-45
THOMPSON, W.B. & J.D. RIDGE. CATALOGUE OF
THE NATIONAL COLLECTION OF GREEK AND
LATIN SCHOOL TEXTBOOKS (1800 ONWARDS).*
(PT 1)
　M.L. CLARKE, 303:VOL91-217
　R. MASCIANTONIO, 124:SEP71-32
THOMPSON, W.I. AT THE EDGE OF HISTORY.
　W.C. HAVARD, 639(VQR):SUMMER71-452
THOMPSON, W.S. "THE FREE STATE OF WIN-
STON."
　H.C. BAILEY, 9(ALAR):JAN70-79
THOMSEN, J.S., ED. VIRKELIGHEDEN DER
VOKSEDE.
　H.J. CHRISTENSEN, 172(EDDA):1971/5-
　316
THOMSON, D. WILD EXCURSIONS.*
　L. BRAUDY, 441:1APR73-30
　C. LEHMANN-HAUPT, 441:10JAN73-39
　442(NY):24FEB73-132
THOMSON, D.C., ED. QUEBEC SOCIETY AND
POLITICS.
　R. COOK, 99:OCT73-33
THOMSON, F.M. NEWCASTLE CHAPBOOKS IN THE
NEWCASTLE UPON TYNE UNIVERSITY LIBRARY.
　P.C.G. ISAAC, 354:MAR70-83

THOMSON, G.M. LORD CASTLEROSSE.
　E.S. TURNER, 362:6SEP73-319
　617(TLS):7SEP73-1019
THOMSON, R.W., ED & TRANS. THE TEACHING
OF SAINT GREGORY.
　N.G. GARSOÏAN, 589:JUL72-555
THOMSON, S.H. LATIN BOOKHANDS OF THE
LATER MIDDLE AGES 1100-1500.*
　L. BIELER, 382(MAE):1972/1-82
　B.B. BOYER, 551(RENQ):SPRING71-55
　J.A. BRUNDAGE, 121(CJ):OCT-NOV71-78
THONNESSEN, W. THE EMANCIPATION OF
WOMEN.
　617(TLS):30NOV73-1473
THONSSEN, L., A.C. BAIRD & W.W. BRADEN.
SPEECH CRITICISM. (2ND ED)
　C.C. ARNOLD, 583:FALL71-104
THOREAU, H.D. LA DÉSOBÉISSANCE CIVILE
(AND) PLAIDOYER POUR JOHN BROWN. (M.
FLAK, C. DEMOREL & L. VERNET, TRANS)
　M. POLI, 189(EA):JAN-MAR70-105
THOREAU, H.D. THE MAINE WOODS. (J.J.
MOLDENHAUER, ED)
　N. BAYM, 27(AL):JAN73-683
THOREAU, H.D. WALDEN. (J.L. SHANLEY,
ED)
　S. PAUL, 27(AL):MAR72-155
THORLBY, A. THE ROMANTIC MOVEMENT.
　F. GARBER, 131(CL):SPRING72-186
THORNBURG, N. TO DIE IN CALIFORNIA.
　M. MEWSHAW, 441:16SEP73-31
THORNDIKE, S. FAVOURITES.
　617(TLS):28DEC73-1593
THORNE, C. THE LIMITS OF FOREIGN POLICY.
　J. GITTINGS, 453:17MAY73-10
　617(TLS):2FEB73-111
THORNE, T. TENSE MOOD AND VOICE.
　K.L. GOODWIN, 381:SEP71-375
THORNLEY, G.C. AN OUTLINE OF ENGLISH
LITERATURE.
　J.C. FIELD, 556(RLV):1971/2-232
THORNS, D.C. SUBURBIA.
　617(TLS):5JAN73-4
THORNTON, A. PEOPLE AND THEMES IN
HOMER'S "ODYSSEY."
　F.M. COMBELLACK, 122:APR72-144
　J.B. HAINSWORTH, 123:DEC72-320
THORNTON, G. - SEE ANDERSEN, H.C.
THORNTON, R.C. THE COMINTERN AND THE
CHINESE COMMUNISTS, 1928-1931.*
　Y.J. CHIH, 318(JAOS):JAN-MAR71-150
　W.W. WHITSON, 293(JAST):NOV70-179
THORPE, J. PRINCIPLES OF TEXTUAL CRITI-
CISM.
　W.M. GIBSON, 27(AL):JAN73-704
THORPE, M. MATTHEW ARNOLD.*
　J.C. MAXWELL, 447(N&Q):NOV71-433
THORPE, M. BY THE NIGER.
　H. SERGEANT, 175:SUMMER71-65
THORPE, M., ED. CLOUGH: THE CRITICAL
HERITAGE.
　617(TLS):12JAN73-43
THORPE, M. SIEGFRIED SASSOON.*
　J.K. ROBINSON, 598(SOR):SUMMER73-692
THORSON, T.L., ED. PLATO.
　D. MEIKLEJOHN, 185:JAN71-181
THRAEDE, K. GRUNDZÜGE GRIECHISCH-RÖM-
ISCHER BRIEFTOPIK.*
　C.D.N. COSTA, 313:VOL61-302
THRALL, W.F. & A. HIBBARD. A HANDBOOK TO
LITERATURE. (3RD ED REV BY C.H. HOLMAN)
　J. SEELYE, 441:14JAN73-6
"THREE CZECH POETS."
　A. CLUYSENAAR, 565:VOL12#3-72
"THREE FILIPINO PLAYWRIGHTS: FLORENTINO,
NOLLEDO, PERALTA."
　L. CASPER, 352(LE&W):VOL15#1-176

THRING, M.W. & A. BLAKE. MAN, MACHINES
AND TOMORROW.
617(TLS):7SEP73-1030
THUCYDIDES. HISTORY OF THE PELOPONNESIAN
WAR. (R. WARNER, TRANS; M.I. FINLEY,
ED)
617(TLS):12JAN73-49
THUILLIER, J. & J. FOUCART. RUBENS'
LIFE OF MARIE DE' MEDICI.
J.S. HELD, 56:AUTUMN70-304
W. STECHOW, 127:WINTER71/72-212
THUILLIER, P. SOCRATE FONCTIONNAIRE.
A. GIGUERE, 154:SEP71-616
THUMMER, E. - SEE PINDAR
THUN, N. REDUPLICATIVE WORDS IN ENGLISH.
G. BOURCIER, 189(EA):JAN-MAR71-88
THUNIG-NITTNER, G. DIE TSCHECHOSLOWAK-
ISCHE LEGION IN RUSSLAND.
J.F.N. BRADLEY, 575(SEER):JUL72-477
"THÜRINGISCHES WÖRTERBUCH." (VOL 4, PTS
1-5)
J.P. PONTEN, 680(ZDP):BAND90HEFT4-625
THURLEY, K. & H. WIRDENIUS. SUPERVISION.
617(TLS):27APR73-466
THUROT, F. TABLEAU DES PROGRÈS DE LA
SCIENCE GRAMMATICALE. (A. JOLY, ED)
J-C. CHEVALIER, 535(RHL):JUL-AUG71-
703
THWAITE, A. INSCRIPTIONS.
A. MACLEAN, 362:25OCT73-565
617(TLS):18MAY73-548
THWAITES, B. THE FIRST TEN YEARS.
617(TLS):6APR73-401
THYNNE, A. THE CARRY-COT.
617(TLS):23FEB73-219
"DIE FRITZ THYSSEN STIFTUNG 1960-1970."
G. STRICKRODT, 182:VOL24#19/20-712
THYSSEN, K-W., ED. BEGEGNUNG UND VERANT-
WORTUNG.
F.F. BRUCE, 182:VOL24#6-275
TIBBETTS, P.R., ED. PERCEPTION.
M.B.M., 543:SEP70-147
TIBBLE, A. GREENHORN.
617(TLS):22JUN73-717
TIBBLE, A. LABYRINTH.
617(TLS):5JAN73-10
TIBBLE, A. THE STORY OF ENGLISH LITERA-
TURE.
R. LAWRENCE, 175:AUTUMN71-110
TIBERIUS. TIBERII "DE FIGURIS DEMOS-
THENICIS LIBELLUS CUM DEPERDITORUM
OPERUM FRAGMENTA."* (G. BALLAIRA, ED)
S. USHER, 303:VOL91-157
TICE, T.N. SCHLEIERMACHER-BIBLIOGRAPHIE.
C. CESA, 548(RCSF):APR-JUN70-214
TICHER, K. IRISH SILVER IN THE ROCOCO
PERIOD.
617(TLS):9MAR73-265
"LUDWIG TIECK."* (U. SCHWEIKERT, ED)
R. GRIMM, 406:SUMMER72-172
TIEDEMANN, R. - SEE ADORNO, T.W.
TIEDEMANN-BARTELS, H. - SEE BENJAMIN, W.
TIEFENTHALER, E. DIE RÄTOROMANISCHEN
FLURNAMEN DER GEMEINDEN FRASTANZ UND
NENZING.
G. FRANCESCATO, 433:JAN70-87
TIETZE, A. THE KOMAN RIDDLES AND TURKIC
FOLKLORE.
G. DOERFER, 196:BAND11HEFT1/2-196
TIFFANY, K. - SEE VON DROSTE-HÜLSHOFF, A.
TIGERSTEDT, E.N. PLATO'S IDEA OF POETI-
CAL INSPIRATION.
F.M. COMBELLACK, 122:APR72-145
TILANDER, G. LITTRÉ ET REMIGEREAU COMME
LEXICOGRAPHES [ET] MISCELLANEA CYNE-
GETICA.*
R. LEPELLEY, 209(FM):OCT70-456
TILLETT, J. - SEE DICKENS, C.

TILLETT, M. STENDHAL.
L. LUSIS, 67:NOV72-242
TILLEY, B. - SEE VERGIL
TILLICH, H. FROM TIME TO TIME.
H. COX, 441:14OCT73-31
E.B. FISKE, 441:27OCT73-35
TILLIER, L. ARNOLD BENNETT ET SES ROMANS
RÉALISTES.
J. DELBAERE-GARANT, 556(RLV):1970/6-
674
TILLIETTE, X. JULES LEQUIER OU LE TOUR-
MENT DE LA LIBERTÉ.
J. GRENIER, 542:JUL-SEP70-349
TILLINGHAST, R. SLEEP WATCH.*
J. ATLAS, 114(CHIR):AUTUMN70-131
W. CORBETT, 600:WINTER/SPRING70-233
TILLOTSON, G. - SEE LEISHMAN, J.B.
TILTON, G.W. & F.W. RECORD. THE FAMILY
ALBUM. (M. SILBER, COMP)
S. SCHWARTZ, 441:2DEC73-94
617(TLS):21DEC73-1573
"THE 'TIMES' OF LONDON ANTHOLOGY OF
DETECTIVE STORIES."*
442(NY):13NOV73-220
TIMM, W. THE GRAPHIC ART OF EDVARD
MUNCH.*
J.B. SMITH, 39:AUG70-159
TIMMERS, J.J.M. A HANDBOOK OF ROMANESQUE
ART.
J. BECKWITH, 39:OCT70-314
M. STOKSTAD, 290(JAAC):FALL70-145
TIMMS, N., ED. THE RECEIVING END.
617(TLS):6JUL73-789
TIMOFIEWITSCH, W. CORPUS PALLADIANUM.*
(VOL 3: THE CHIESA DEL REDENTORE.)
[SHOWN IN PREV UNDER SUBTITLE]
J. NEWMAN, 90:NOV71-675
TINBERGEN, E.A. & N. EARLY CHILDHOOD
AUTISM.
P.B. MEDAWAR, 453:8MAR73-21
TINBERGEN, N. THE ANIMAL IN ITS WORLD.
(VOL 1)
P.B. MEDAWAR, 453:8MAR73-21
617(TLS):20JUL73-837
TINDALL, G. DANCES OF DEATH.
R. BRYDEN, 362:5JUL73-25
J.C. OATES, 441:25NOV73-7
617(TLS):20JUL73-825
TINDALL, G.B. THE DISRUPTION OF THE
SOLID SOUTH.
L.C. MILAZZO, 584(SWR):AUTUMN72-346
TINDALL, W.Y. A READER'S GUIDE TO "FIN-
NEGANS WAKE."*
A. GOLDMAN, 541(RES):FEB71-105
TINNIN, D.B. JUST ABOUT EVERYBODY VERSUS
HOWARD HUGHES.
J. BROOKS, 441:23DEC73-3
TINNISWOOD, P. I DIDN'T KNOW YOU CARED.
V. CUNNINGHAM, 362:3MAY73-591
617(TLS):18MAY73-545
TINT, H. FRENCH FOREIGN POLICY SINCE THE
SECOND WORLD WAR.
617(TLS):12JAN73-37
TINTO, A. GLI ANNALI TIPOGRAFICI DI
EUCARIO E MARCELLO SILBER (1501-1527).
D.E. RHODES, 354:JUN70-163
TINTORI, G. GLI STRUMENTI MUSICALI.
H.M. BROWN, 415:AUG72-776
J.A.W., 410(M&L):JUL72-333
TIPPING, R. SOFT RIOTS.
617(TLS):12OCT73-1216
TIPPLE, J. CRISIS OF THE AMERICAN DREAM.
H.C. DAVIS, 9(ALAR):JAN70-75
TIRSO DE MOLINA. LA VENGANZA DE TAMAR.*
(A.K.G. PATERSON, ED)
J. JOSET, 556(RLV):1971/5-657
D. ROGERS, 402(MLR):JAN72-197

TISCHLER, N.M.  BLACK MASKS.
   M. FABRE, 189(EA):APR-JUN71-222
TITUS, H.H.  LIVING ISSUES IN PHILOSOPHY.
   (5TH ED)
   A.W. MUNK, 484(PPR):SEP71-130
TIVY, L. - SEE LEVERIDGE, A.
"TO HONOR ROMAN JAKOBSON."*
   E.M. UHLENBECK, 204(FDL):1970/1-71
TOBIAS, J.J.  NINETEENTH CENTURY CRIME.
   617(TLS):5JAN73-22
TODD, A.C. & P. LAWS.  INDUSTRIAL ARCHAE-
   OLOGY OF CORNWALL.
   617(TLS):31AUG73-999
TODD, C. - SEE DE LA HARPE, J.F.
TODD, C.L. & R.T. BLACKWOOD, EDS.  LAN-
   GUAGE AND VALUE.
   W.F. BOLTON, 297(JL):SEP70-305
TODD, M.  THE CORITANI.
   617(TLS):10AUG73-932
TODD, M.  EVERYDAY LIFE OF THE BARBAR-
   IANS.
   617(TLS):4MAY73-506
TODD, R.  WILLIAM BLAKE: THE ARTIST.
   R. LEBOWITZ, 58:MAR72-18
   W. VAUGHAN, 592:NOV71-212
TODD, W.  ANALYTICAL SOLIPSISM.
   T.L.S. SPRIGGE, 262:WINTER70-462
TODOROV, T.  GRAMMAIRE DU DÉCAMÉRON.
   W.A. KOCH, 490:OCT71-565
TODOROV, T.  INTRODUCTION À LA LITTÉRA-
   TURE FANTASTIQUE.
   S. LOTRINGER, 98:MAR71-195
   J-M. PIEMME, 556(RLV):1971/6-782
TODOROV, T.  LITTÉRATURE ET SIGNIFICA-
   TION.*
   S. LOTRINGER, 98:MAR71-195
   B. MALMBERG, 596(SL):VOL25#1-59
TODOROV, T. - SEE JAKOBSON, R.
TOELLNER, R.  ALBRECHT VON HALLER.
   K.S. GUTHKE, 406:WINTER72-386
TOENNIES, F.  ON SOCIOLOGY.  (W.J. CAHN-
   MAN & R. HEBERLE, EDS)
   639(VQR):SUMMER71-CXXXVII
TOFFLER, A.  FUTURE SHOCK.
   639(VQR):WINTER71-XLII
TOGEBY, K., ED.  OGIER LE DANNOYS.*
   L. LÖFSTEDT, 597(SN):VOL43#2-602
TOGEBY, K.  OGIER LE DANOIS DANS LES
   LITTÉRATURES EUROPÉENNES.*
   L. LÖFSTEDT, 597(SN):VOL43#2-602
TOITA YASUJI.  KABUKI, THE POPULAR THEA-
   TER.
   M. PRESS, 285(JAPQ):APR-JUN71-236
TŌKEI, F.  GENRE THEORY IN CHINA IN THE
   3RD-6TH CENTURIES (LIU HSIEH'S THEORY
   ON POETIC GENRES).
   R. WOODFIELD, 89(BJA):SUMMER72-305
TŌKEI, F.  SUR LE MODE DE PRODUCTION ASI-
   ATIQUE.  (E. PAMLÉNYI, ED)  ZUR FRAGE
   DER ASIATISCHEN PRODUKTIONSWEISE.  (J.
   HARTMANN, ED)
   G.L. ULMEN, 32:JUN72-438
TOKER, F.  THE CHURCH OF NOTRE DAME IN
   MONTREAL.
   A. GOWANS, 96:AUG/SEP71-44
   H. KALMAN, 576:OCT71-249
   J.D. STEWART, 529(QQ):SPRING71-137
TOKUTOMI, K.  FOOTPRINTS IN THE SNOW.
   B. ROBSON, 285(JAPQ):JAN-MAR71-109
DE TOLEDANO, R.  J. EDGAR HOOVER.
   C. LEHMANN-HAUPT, 441:10APR73-37
   M. ROGIN, 441:17JUN73-24
DE TOLEDO, A.M. - SEE UNDER MARTÍNEZ DE
   TOLEDO, A.
TOLIVER, H.E.  PASTORAL FORMS AND ATTI-
   TUDES.
   R.L. COLIE, 301(JEGP):JUL72-447
                              [CONTINUED]

[CONTINUING]
   G.D. LORD, 401(MLQ):DEC72-449
   P.E. MC LANE, 568(SCN):FALL-WINTER72-
   63
TOLKIEN, J.R.R. & E.V. GORDON - SEE "SIR
   GAWAIN AND THE GREEN KNIGHT"
DE TOLNAY, C.  MICHELANGELO: THE MEDICI
   CHAPEL.
   R.W. LIGHTBOWN, 39:JUN71-529
TOMASZEWSKI, W., ED.  THE UNIVERSITY OF
   EDINBURGH AND POLAND.*
   H.G. WEISSER, 497(POLR):WINTER71-128
TOMISON, M.  THE ENGLISH SICKNESS.
   617(TLS):30MAR73-342
TOMLIN, E.W.F., ED.  CHARLES DICKENS
   1812-1870.
   R.F. FLEISSNER, 594:FALL70-384
   R.D. MC MASTER, 445(NCF):SEP71-219
   S. MONOD, 189(EA):APR-JUN70-214
   G. SMITH, 637(VS):JUN71-459
TOMLIN, M.  ENGLISH FURNITURE.  CATA-
   LOGUE OF ADAM PERIOD FURNITURE.
   617(TLS):22JUN72-708
TOMLINSON, C.  WRITTEN ON WATER.*
   C. BEDIENT, 441:29APR73-7
TOMLINSON, J.W.C.  THE JOINT VENTURE PRO-
   CESS IN INTERNATIONAL BUSINESS.
   W. MALENBAUM, 293(JAST):MAY71-709
TOMLINSON, R.  DOWN UNDER IT ALL.
   J. DITSKY, 628:SPRING72-108
TOMMASEO, N.  RACCONTI BIBLICI E MEDITA-
   ZIONI SUI VANGELI.  (G. GAMBARIN, ED)
   B. BIRAL, 228(GSLI):VOL148FASC461-143
TOMORY, P.  THE LIFE AND ART OF HENRY
   FUSELI.*
   H. HONOUR, 453:25JAN73-34
   617(TLS):4MAY73-499
TOMPA, J.  UNGARISCHE GRAMMATIK.
   G.F. MEIER, 682(ZPSK):BAND24HEFT1/2-
   151
   K. WODARZ-MAGDICS, 353:AUG71-125
TOMPKINS, E.B.  ANTI-IMPERIALISM IN THE
   UNITED STATES.
   C.D. DAVIS, 579(SAQ):WINTER72-132
TOMPKINS, P. & C. BIRD.  THE SECRET LIFE
   OF PLANTS.
   E. FIRST, 441:30DEC73-15
   C. LEHMANN-HAUPT, 441:12DEC73-51
TOMSICH, J.  A GENTEEL ENDEAVOR.
   E.H. CADY, 27(AL):JAN73-698
   A.S. GORDENSTEIN, 191(ELN):JUN72-317
   639(VQR):AUTUMN71-CLXXIII
TONELLI, G.  A SHORT-TITLE LIST OF SUB-
   JECT DICTIONARIES OF THE SIXTEENTH,
   SEVENTEENTH AND EIGHTEENTH CENTURIES
   AS AIDS TO THE HISTORY OF IDEAS.
   M. JASENAS, 517(PBSA):OCT-DEC72-444
   L.C. ROSENFIELD, 319:JUL73-411
TÖNNIES, F. - SEE HOBBES, T.
"TÖNNIES FENNE'S LOW GERMAN MANUAL OF
   SPOKEN RUSSIAN, PSKOV, 1607" - SEE
   UNDER FENNE
TOOLEY, R.V.  MAPS AND MAPMAKERS.
   G. WILLS, 39:JUL71-79
TOPHAM, E.  LETTERS FROM EDINBURGH, 1774-
   1775.
   K. MILLER, 362:15MAR73-346
TOPOLSKI, F.  PARIS LOST.
   617(TLS):21DEC73-1558
TOPPEN, W.H.  CONSCIENCE IN SHAKESPEARE'S
   "MACBETH."
   C. UHLIG, 38:BAND88HEFT1-142
TOPSFIELD, L.T. - SEE RAIMON DE MIRAVAL
TOPUSOVA, V. - SEE KANT, I.
TORBOV, Z. - SEE KANT, I.
TORCELLAN, G.  SETTECENTO VENETO E ALTRI
   SCRITTI STORICI.
   M.F., 228(GSLI):VOL147FASC458/459-474

TORCHIO, M. THE WORLD BENEATH THE SEA.
617(TLS):16MAR73-305
TORMEY, A. THE CONCEPT OF EXPRESSION.*
H. OSBORNE, 89(BJA):SPRING72-186
TORNER, E.M. - SEE UNDER MARTÍNEZ TORNER,
E.
TÖRNQVIST, E. A DRAMA OF SOULS.
A.P. HINCHLIFFE, 148:AUTUMN71-283
L. SHEAFFER, 397(MD):MAY71-117
TORRANCE, D.W. & T.F. - SEE CALVIN, J.
TORRANCE, T.F. SPACE, TIME AND INCARNA-
TION.
P. MAIRET, 478:JAN71-76
TORRES, L. THE BLACK POETRY OF LUIS
PALÉS MATOS AND ITS SOURCES.
M.R. HOFF, 37:JAN71-40
TORRES, T. THE CONVERTS.
J. GREENFIELD, 287:SEP70-24
TORRES BODET, J. AÑOS CONTRA EL TIEMPO.
S. KARSEN, 238:MAR71-207
TORRES BODET, J. MEMORIAS. (VOL 2)
S. KARSEN, 263:APR-JUN72-176
DE TORRES VILLARROEL, D. LA BARCA DE
AQUERONTE (1731).* (G. MERCADIER, ED)
DIEGO DE TORRES Y VILLARROEL, SAINETES.
(J. HESSE, ED)
R.P. SEBOLD, 240(HR):APR71-219
TORTEL, J. INSTANTS QUALIFIÉS.
617(TLS):1JUN73-610
TŌRU MATSUI & TOSHIO YAMAZAKI, EDS. INDO-
SHI NI OKERU TOCHISEIDO TO KENRYOKU-
KŌZŌ.
T. MATSUI, 293(JAST):FEB71-474
"LA TOSCANA NEL REGIME FASCISTA (1922-
1939)."
617(TLS):2MAR73-225
TOSCO, U. THE FLOWERING WILDERNESS.
617(TLS):16MAR73-305
TOSI, C.P. - SEE UNDER PASSERINI TOSI, C.
TOSI, M. & A. ROCCATI. STELE E ALTRE
EPIGRAFI DI DEIR EL MEDINA.
617(TLS):6APR73-370
TOTTON, R.K. - SEE GIRAUDOUX, J.
TOUCHARD, H. LE COMMERCE MARITIME BRE-
TON À LA FIN DU MOYEN AGE.
G.T. BEECH, 589:JAN72-145
TOULEMONT, R. L'ESSENCE DE LA SOCIÉTÉ
SELON HUSSERL.
C. PRÉVOST, 542:OCT-DEC71-478
DE TOULOUSE-LAUTREC, H. UNPUBLISHED COR-
RESPONDENCE OF HENRI DE TOULOUSE-LAU-
TREC.* (L. GOLDSCHMIDT & H. SCHIMMEL,
EDS)
D.T., 135:JUN70-134
TOURNIER, M. THE OGRE.*
R. SALE, 249(HUDR):WINTER72/73-703
TOURNOUX, J-R. LA TRAGÉDIE DU GÉNÉRAL.
Y. COURTEVILLE, 207(FR):DEC70-400
TOUSSAINT, A. PORT LOUIS.
617(TLS):19OCT73-1289
TOUSSAINT, A. THE SPREAD OF PRINTING:
MAURITIUS, RÉUNION, MADAGASCAR AND THE
SEYCHELLES.
B.C. BLOOMFIELD, 354:MAR71-70
R. CAVE, 503:SUMMER70-99
TOWERS, B., T.G. WHITTINGHAM & A.W.
GOTTSCHALK, EDS. BARGAINING FOR CHANGE.
617(TLS):9FEB73-148
TOWLE, T. NORTH.*
J. SAUNDERS, 565:VOL12#4-63
TOWNSEND, W., ED. CANADIAN ART TODAY.*
R.S., 376:JUL70-118
TOYÉ, K. REGIONAL FRENCH COOKERY.
617(TLS):30NOV73-1485
TOYNBEE, A. CITIES ON THE MOVE.
639(VQR):WINTER71-XLIV

TOYNBEE, A. CONSTANTINE PORPHYROGENITUS
AND HIS WORLD.
M.I. FINLEY, 362:26APR73-555
617(TLS):11MAY73-523
TOYNBEE, A. EXPERIENCES.
J.F. POWERS, 613:SPRING70-158
TOYNBEE, A., ED. HALF THE WORLD.
617(TLS):28DEC73-1579
TOYNBEE, A. SOME PROBLEMS OF GREEK
HISTORY.*
J.K. ANDERSON, 121(CJ):DEC71/JAN72-184
L. RICHARD, 182:VOL24#5-235
TOYNBEE, A. A STUDY OF HISTORY.* (NEW
ED, REV & ABRIDGED BY A. TOYNBEE & J.
CAPLAN)
G. WOODCOCK, 99:JAN73-29
TOYNBEE, A. SURVIVING THE FUTURE.*
A.R. CHISHOLM, 67:NOV72-280
TOYNBEE, A. & OTHERS. MAN'S CONCERN WITH
DEATH.
J. VAN EVRA, 154:MAR71-206
TOYNBEE, A.J. LE CHANGEMENT ET LA TRA-
DITION.
J. NANTET, 98:FEB70-187
TOYNBEE, J.M.C. ANIMALS IN ROMAN LIFE
AND ART.
617(TLS):28DEC73-1584
TOYNBEE, J.M.C. DEATH AND BURIAL IN THE
ROMAN WORLD.
R.P.H. GREEN, 313:VOL61-283
W.S. THURMAN, 399(MLJ):NOV71-483
L.B. WARREN, 124:FEB72-210
TRABANT, J. ZUR SEMIOLOGIE DES LITERAR-
ISCHEN KUNSTWERKS.
G. WIENOLD, 490:OCT71-559
TRACEY, H. CHOPI MUSICIANS.
A.M. JONES, 69:OCT71-347
TRACHTENBERG, A. - SEE FRANK, W.
TRACHTENBERG, I. SO SLOW THE DAWNING.
M. LEVIN, 441:4FEB73-27
TRACY, B. & J.K. HOWAT. 19TH CENTURY
AMERICA.
58:SEP/OCT70-16
TRACY, C., ED. BROWNING'S MIND AND ART.*
I. ARMSTRONG, 637(VS):DEC70-208
TRACY, C. - SEE JOHNSON, S.
TRACY, D. THE ACHIEVEMENT OF BERNARD
LONERGAN.
C.M. GOING, 613:AUTUMN71-445
TRACY, H. WINTER IN CASTILLE.
A. BROYARD, 441:11DEC73-49
W.H. HONAN, 441:2DEC73-97
TRACY, T.J. PHYSIOLOGICAL THEORY AND THE
DOCTRINE OF THE MEAN IN PLATO AND ARIS-
TOTLE.*
R.G. HOERBER, 124:JAN72-171
E.D. PHILLIPS, 123:DEC72-419
F.E. SPARSHOTT, 487:SUMMER71-171
"TRADITIONAL CHINESE PLAYS." (VOL 2)
(A.C. SCOTT, TRANS)
A. RENDLE, 157:AUTUMN70-77
TRAGER, F.N. & W. HENDERSON, EDS. COM-
MUNIST CHINA, 1949-1969.
J. DREYER, 293(JAST):AUG71-882
639(VQR):AUTUMN71-CLXXXI
TRAGER, J. AMBER WAVES OF GRAIN.
J.L. HESS, 441:9SEP73-2
TRAHARD, P. LE MYSTÈRE POÉTIQUE.
W. ALBERT, 207(FR):MAR71-792
TRAHARD, P. "LA PORTE ÉTROITE" D'ANDRÉ
GIDE.
R. TARICA, 207(FR):FEB71-606
TRAHERNE, T. POEMS, CENTURIES AND THREE
THANKSGIVINGS. (A. RIDLER, ED)
S. SANDBANK, 179(ES):JUN71-270
TRAINA, A. VORTIT BARBARE.
E.J. KENNEY, 123:JUN72-231

TRAINER, J. LUDWIG TIECK.
  W.J. LILLYMAN, 220(GL&L):OCT71-60
TRAKL, G. DICHTUNGEN UND BRIEFE.* (W.
  KILLY & H. SZKLENAR, EDS)
  K.L. BERGHAHN, 221(GQ):MAR71-254
TRAMMELL, R. FAMOUS MEN.
  G. BURNS, 584(SWR):SPRING72-162
TRANH-NHA, N. TABLEAU ECONOMIQUE DU
  VIETNAM AUX XVIIE ET XVIIIE SIÈCLES.
  A. WOODSIDE, 293(JAST):AUG71-922
TRANSTRÖMER, T. WINDOWS AND STONES. (M.
  SWENSON, ED & TRANS)
  K. HARRISON, 109:SPRING/SUMMER73-111
TRANTER, J.E. PARALLAX.*
  K.L. GOODWIN, 381:SEP71-365
TRANTER, N.L., ED. POPULATION AND INDUS-
  TRIALIZATION.
  617(TLS):8JUN73-651
TRAPP, F.A. THE ATTAINMENT OF DELA-
  CROIX.*
  J.D. WELDON, 58:DEC70/JAN71-10
TRASK, D.F. CAPTAINS AND CABINETS.
  617(TLS):26OCT73-1325
TRASK, W., ED. CLASSIC BLACK AFRICAN
  POEMS.
  W. DICKEY, 249(HUDR):SUMMER72-297
TRAUTMANN, R. BALTISCH-SLAVISCHES WÖR-
  TERBUCH.
  R.J., 279:VOL14-210
"TRAVAUX LINGUISTIQUES DE PRAGUE." (VOL
  3)
  B. LOMMATZSCH, 682(ZPSK):BAND23HEFT1-
  90
TRAVEN, B. GENERAL FROM THE JUNGLE.
  A. CHEUSE, 441:26AUG73-24
TRAVIS, G. THE COTTAGE.
  M. LEVIN, 441:6MAY73-40
TREACY, S. A SMELL OF BROKEN GLASS.
  617(TLS):27JUL73-884
TREADGOLD, D.W. THE WEST IN RUSSIA AND
  CHINA.
  H. SCHWARTZ, 441:5MAY73-43
TREASURE, G.R.R. CARDINAL RICHELIEU AND
  THE DEVELOPMENT OF ABSOLUTISM.
  617(TLS):27JUL73-878
TREBELS, A.H. EINBILDUNGSKRAFT UND
  SPIEL.
  K-H. DICKOPP, 342:BAND61HEFT2-263
TREDGOLD, R. XHOSA.
  617(TLS):3AUG73-913
TREDINNICK, F. CARLOS.
  617(TLS):12OCT73-1209
TREGEAR, T.R. AN ECONOMIC GEOGRAPHY OF
  CHINA.
  L. VEILLEUX, 302:JUL71-377
TREGENZA, J. AUSTRALIAN LITTLE MAGAZINES
  1923-1954.
  P.H., 503:SUMMER68-82
TREGGIARI, S. ROMAN FREEDMEN DURING THE
  LATE REPUBLIC.*
  B. BALDWIN, 121(CJ):FEB-MAR72-289
TREHARNE, R.E. & I.J. SANDERS, EDS. DOC-
  UMENTS OF THE BARONIAL MOVEMENT OF RE-
  FORM AND REBELLION 1258-1267.
  617(TLS):7SEP73-1037
TREIP, M. MILTON'S PUNCTUATION AND CHANG-
  ING ENGLISH USAGE, 1582-1676.*
  A.C. PARTRIDGE, 180(ESA):MAR72-64
TREMAYNE, S. SELECTED AND NEW POEMS.
  617(TLS):20APR73-442
TREMBLAY, B. CRYING IN THE CHEAP SEATS.
  M.G. PERLOFF, 659:WINTER73-97
  W.H. PRITCHARD, 249(HUDR):SPRING72-122
TREMBLAY, J-P. A LA RECHERCHE DE
  NAPOLÉON AUBIN.
  R. MERCIER, 557(RSH):OCT-DEC70-663
  A. VIATTE, 207(FR):DEC70-450
  A. VIATTE, 549(RLC):OCT-DEC70-571

TREMBLEY, G. MARCEL SCHWOB.
  J.A. GREEN, 207(FR):FEB71-613
TREMEARNE, A.J.N. HAUSA SUPERSTITIONS
  AND CUSTOMS.
  A.H.M. KIRK-GREENE, 69:JAN71-80
TRÉNARD, L. SALVANDY EN SON TEMPS, 1795-
  1856.
  J. VOISINE, 535(RHL):JAN-FEB70-141
TRENCH, C.C. A HISTORY OF MARKSMANSHIP.
  617(TLS):23FEB73-212
TRENCKNER, V. A CRITICAL PĀLI DICTION-
  ARY. (VOL 2, FASC 4) (D. ANDERSEN &
  H. SMITH, EDS)
  C. CAILLAT, 260(IF):BAND74-223
TRENDALL, A.D. GREEK VASES IN THE FELTON
  COLLECTION. THE RED-FIGURED VASES OF
  LUCANIA, CAMPANIA AND SICILY.
  R. HIGGINS, 39:AUG71-161
"THE TRES RICHES HEURES OF JEAN, DUKE OF
  BERRY."* (BRITISH TITLE: LES TRÈS
  RICHES HEURES DU DUC DE BERRY.)
  J. BACKHOUSE, 90:MAY71-279
"TRÉSOR DE LA LANGUE FRANÇAISE." (VOL 2)
  (P. IMBS, GENERAL ED)
  617(TLS):3AUG73-909
TRETHOWAN, I. ABSOLUTE VALUE.*
  T. MAUTNER, 63:AUG72-196
TREVANIAN. THE LOO SANCTION.
  P. ADAMS, 61:DEC73-138
  A. BROYARD, 441:5NOV73-43
  N. CALLENDAR, 441:9DEC73-50
TREVELYAN, H. DIPLOMATIC CHANNELS.
  617(TLS):12OCT73-1205
TREVELYAN, J. WHAT THE CENSOR SAW.
  G. MILLAR, 362:18OCT73-527
TREVELYAN, R. PRINCES UNDER THE VOLCANO.*
  J. MANGIONE, 441:8APR73-14
TREVES, P. - SEE CARDUCCI, G.
TREVICK, H. THE CRAFT AND DESIGN OF
  MONUMENTAL BRASSES.
  C.B., 135:SEP70-63
TREVISAN, D. THE VAMPIRE OF CURITIBA AND
  OTHER STORIES.*
  M. WOOD, 453:19APR73-35
TREVOR, M. THE ARNOLDS.
  617(TLS):27APR73-469
TREVOR, W. ELIZABETH ALONE.
  E. FEINSTEIN, 362:25OCT73-572
  617(TLS):26OCT73-1299
TREVOR, W. THE LAST LUNCH OF THE SEASON.
  617(TLS):10AUG73-921
TREWIN, J.C. PORTRAIT OF PLYMOUTH.
  617(TLS):19OCT73-1289
"THE TRIBUNAL."
  S.P. ROSENBAUM, 99:JAN73-31
TRIEM, E. E.E. CUMMINGS.
  R. ASSELINEAU, 189(EA):APR-JUN71-223
TRIESCH, G. DIE MOTIVE IN "THIRST AND
  OTHER ONE-ACT PLAYS" UND IHRE VERAR-
  BEITUNG IN DEN SPÄTEREN WERKEN
  O'NEILLS.
  J. SCHLUNK, 430(NS):JUN71-337
TRIESCH, M., ED. PROBLEME DES DEUTSCHEN
  ALS FREMDSPRACHE.
  J. LEJEUNE, 556(RLV):1970/3-331
TRIGG, R. PAIN AND EMOTION.*
  O. HANFLING, 483:APR71-173
  L. HOLBOROW, 479(PHQ):APR71-182
  C.H. WHITELEY, 482(PHR):JUL71-388
TRIGG, R. REASON AND COMMITMENT.
  617(TLS):12OCT73-1254
DE TRILIA, B. - SEE UNDER BERNARDUS DE
  TRILIA
TRILLIN, C. U.S. JOURNAL.
  F.G. PATTON, 579(SAQ):WINTER72-130
TRILLING, L. MIND IN THE MODERN WORLD.*
  G.H. HARTMAN, 441:4FEB73-1

TRILLING, L.  SINCERITY AND AUTHENTICITY.*
P. FOOT, 453:8MAR73-23
G.H. HARTMAN, 441:4FEB73-1
TRINDER, B.  THE INDUSTRIAL REVOLUTION IN
SHROPSHIRE.
617(TLS):20JUL73-839
TRINKAUS, C.  IN OUR IMAGE AND LIKENESS.
H.A. OBERMAN, 589:OCT72-808
TRIPATHI, G.C.  DER URSPRUNG UND DIE ENT-
WICKLUNG DER VĀMANA-LEGENDE IN DER
INDISCHEN LITERATURE.
L. ROCHER, 318(JAOS):OCT-DEC71-546
TRIPP, R.T., ED.  THE INTERNATIONAL
THESAURUS OF QUOTATIONS.
617(TLS):2NOV73-1352
TRISELIOTIS, J.  IN SEARCH OF ORIGINS.
617(TLS):10AUG73-934
"TRISTRANT UND ISALDE." (A. BRANDSTETTER,
ED)
H. STOPP, 680(ZDP):BAND89HEFT1-121
TRIVICK, H.H.  THE CRAFT AND DESIGN OF
MONUMENTAL BRASSES.*
N. DOWNS, 589:JAN72-147
TROGU, G.  VARIANTI-INVARIABILI.
R. BLANCHÉ, 542:JAN-MAR71-124
TROLLOPE, A.  CAN YOU FORGIVE HER? (S.
WALL, ED) PHINEAS FINN, THE IRISH
MEMBER. (J. SUTHERLAND, ED)
617(TLS):20APR73-443
TROLLOPE, A.  SOUTH AFRICA.
617(TLS):28SEP73-1138
TROTIGNON, Y.  LA FRANCE AU XXE SIÈCLE.
M. ANDERSON, 208(FS):JUL72-364
TROTSKY, L.  1905.* (A. BOSTOCK, TRANS)
M. RAEFF, 676(YR):SUMMER72-625
TROTSKY, L.  RAPPORT DE LA DÉLÉGATION
SIBÉRIENNE. (D. AUTHIER, ED & TRANS)
NOS TÂCHES POLITIQUES. (B. FRAENKEL,
ED & TRANS)
F. GUATTARI, 98:JUN71-563
TROTSKY, L.  LEON TROTSKY SPEAKS. THE
SPANISH REVOLUTION. WRITINGS OF LEON
TROTSKY 1932-33.
617(TLS):18MAY73-560
TROTSKY, L.  THE YOUNG LENIN.* (GERMAN
TITLE: DER JUNGE LENIN.) (M. FRIEDBERG,
ED)
617(TLS):9FEB73-144
TROTTER, G.D. & K. WHINNOM - SEE "LA
COMEDIA THEBAIDA"
TROUSSON, R. - SEE FOUGERET DE MONBRON
TROWELL, M.  CLASSICAL AFRICAN SCULPTURE.
E.L.R. MEYEROWITZ, 39:DEC71-526
TROYAT, H.  DIVIDED SOUL.
H. MUCHNIC, 441:23DEC73-7
V.S. PRITCHETT, 442(NY):5NOV73-176
A. WHITMAN, 441:3NOV73-27
TROYAT, H.  PUSHKIN.
L.T. LEMON, 502(PRS):FALL71-277
B. ROBERTS, 50(ARQ):SUMMER71-182
TRUBETZKOY, N.S.  PRINCIPLES OF PHONOL-
OGY.*
W.K. PERCIVAL, 215(GL):VOL11#1-54
TRUDEAU, P.E.  APPROACHES TO POLITICS.
H.P. GUNDY, 529(QQ):SPRING71-163
TRUDEL, M.  THE BEGINNINGS OF NEW FRANCE
1524-1663.
617(TLS):26OCT73-1321
TRUEBLOOD, E.  ABRAHAM LINCOLN.
W. DAVISON, 441:29JUL73-14
TRUFFAUT, F. - SEE BAZIN, A.
TRUFFAUT, L.  GRUNDPROBLEME DER DEUTSCH-
FRANZÖSISCHEN ÜBERSETZUNG.
P. KUENTZ, 209(FM):JAN70-74
TRUMAN, D.  HARRY S. TRUMAN.*
K. KYLE, 362:13SEP73-351
617(TLS):7SEP73-1013

TRUMBO, D.  ADDITIONAL DIALOGUE.
200:AUG-SEP71-432
TRUNK, I.  JUDENRAT.*
N. ASCHERSON, 453:14JUN73-3
TRUNZ, E. - SEE OPITZ, M.
TRUSSLER, S., ED.  BURLESQUE PLAYS OF THE
EIGHTEENTH CENTURY.*
173(ECS):SUMMER71-499
TRUSSLER, S.  THE PLAYS OF JOHN OSBORNE.*
J.M. WARE, 397(MD):MAY71-118
TRUSSLER, S.  THE PLAYS OF HAROLD PINTER.
617(TLS):6JUL73-775
TRYON, D.T.  CONVERSATIONAL TAHITIAN.
A.S.C. ROSS, 447(N&Q):JUL71-268
TRYON, T.  HARVEST HOME.
P. ADAMS, 61:JUL73-103
G. WALKER, 441:6OCT73-21
J. YARDLEY, 441:1JUL73-22
442(NY):23JUL73-77
TRYPANIS, C.A.  THE GLASS ADONIS.
617(TLS):20APR73-442
TRYPANIS, C.A., ED & TRANS.  THE PENGUIN
BOOK OF GREEK VERSE.
G. DAVENPORT, 124:APR-MAY72-273
P. MACKRIDGE, 402(MLR):JUL72-718
TSANGAS, N.M.  CHARLES BAUDELAIRE.  [IN
GREEK]
R. BOSER & C. PICHOIS, 535(RHL):
MAR-APR71-314
TSAO, P.  CHIANG-HSI SSU-WEI-AI CHIH
CHIEN-LI CHI CH'I PENG-HUI (1931-1934).
H. PAK, 293(JAST):MAY71-669
TSATSOS, J.  THE SWORD'S FIERCE EDGE.
E. CURRENT-GARCIA, 577(SHR):WINTER71-
89
TSCHAKERT, I.  WANDLUNGEN PERSISCHER TANZ-
MUSIKGATTUNGEN UNTER WESTLICHEM EIN-
FLUSS.
J. KUCKERTZ, 187:MAY73-349
TSCHELIESNIG, K., ED.  LEHRLINGSPROTO-
KOLLE.
617(TLS):20JUL73-836
TSCHENKÉLI, K.  EINFÜHRUNG IN DIE GEORG-
ISCHE SPRACHE.
G.F. MEIER, 682(ZPSK):BAND24HEFT1/2-
153
TSCHENKÉLI, K.  GEORGISCH-DEUTSCHES WÖR-
TERBUCH. (COMPLETED BY Y. MARCHEV)
D.M. LANG, 402(MLR):OCT72-959
TSCHICHOLD, J.  CHINESE COLOUR PRINTS
FROM THE TEN BAMBOO STUDIO.
617(TLS):21SEP73-1077
TSCHIEDEL, H.J.  PHAEDRA UND HIPPOLYTUS.
S.A. BARLOW, 123:MAR72-123
R. SCHMIEL, 124:NOV71-96
TSCHIRCH, F.  GESCHICHTE DER DEUTSCHEN
SPRACHE. (VOL 1)
W.F. LEOPOLD, 221(GQ):JAN71-98
TSCHIRCH, F.  GESCHICHTE DER DEUTSCHEN
SPRACHE. (VOL 2)
E. ERÄMETSÄ, 439(NM):1970/3-515
W.F. LEOPOLD, 221(GQ):JAN71-98
TSCHIRKY, R.  HEIMITO VON DODERERS "POS-
AUNEN VON JERICHO."
E. KRISPYN, 301(JEGP):JUL72-434
W. SCHMIDT-DENGLER, 680(ZDP):BAND90
HEFT4-634
TSCHIŽEWSKIJ, D., ED.  DIE NESTOR-CHRONIK.
M. SZEFTEL, 32:JUN72-415
TSE-TUNG, M. - SEE UNDER MAO TSE-TUNG
TSUNG-MAO, F. - SEE UNDER FU TSUNG-MAO
TSUNG-SAN, M. - SEE UNDER MOU TSUNG-SAN
TSURUMI, K.  SOCIAL CHANGE AND THE INDI-
VIDUAL.*
J.V. KOSCHMANN, 285(JAPQ):APR-JUN71-
233
P.G. STEINHOFF, 293(JAST):FEB71-468

TSVETKOVA, B. PAMETNA BITKA NA NARODITE.
  W.S. VUCINICH, 32:MAR72-232
TUAN, Y-F. CHINA.
  C.L. SALTER, 293(JAST):MAY71-653
TUBACH, F.C. INDEX EXEMPLORUM.
  M. DE MEYER, 196:BAND12HEFT2/3-289
  F.L. UTLEY, 589:JUL72-557
  R. VIRTANEN, 582(SFQ):DEC71-361
TUCCI, G. DICETTE PULICENELLA...
  S. NEUMANN, 196:BAND11HEFT1/2-202
TUCHMAN, B.W. NOTES FROM CHINA.
  M. BERNAL, 453:9AUG73-21
  H.L. BOORMAN, 441:22APR73-6
TUCHMAN, M. ART AND TECHNOLOGY.
  S.L. SCHWARTZ, 58:SEP/OCT71-16
TUCHMAN, M., ED. THE NEW YORK SCHOOL.
  R. LEBOWITZ, 58:MAY71-12
  B. REISE, 592:MAR71-137
TUCKER, A. READING GAMES.
  617(TLS):10AUG73-934
TUCKER, A. THE WOMAN'S EYE.
  S. SCHWARTZ, 441:DEC73-94
TUCKER, J. & L.S. WINSTOCK, EDS. THE
  ENGLISH CIVIL WAR.
  617(TLS):23FEB73-212
TUCKER, R.C. STALIN AS REVOLUTIONARY
  1879-1929.
  H.E. SALISBURY, 441:23SEP73-4
TUCKER, R.W. A NEW ISOLATIONISM.
  R. STEEL, 453:31MAY73-29
TUCKER, S.I. PROTEAN SHAPE.*
  F.G.A.M. AARTS, 179(ES):OCT71-459
  J. DULCK, 189(EA):APR-JUN71-199
TUCKER, W. THE TIME MASTERS.
  617(TLS):18MAY73-562
TUCKEY, J.S. MARK TWAIN'S "THE MYSTERI-
  OUS STRANGER" AND THE CRITICS.
  R. LEHAN, 445(NCF):MAR71-502
TUCKEY, J.S. - SEE TWAIN, M.
TUDOR, D. CORPUS MONUMENTORUM RELIGIONIS
  EQUITUM DANUVINORUM. (VOL 1)
  R.E. WITT, 123:DEC72-388
TUDOR, D. PODURILE ROMANE DE LA DUNĂREA
  DE JOS.
  J. NANDRIS, 575(SEER):JUL72-486
TUDOR, H. POLITICAL MYTH.
  617(TLS):16MAR73-288
IBN TUFAYL AL QAYSI. IBN TUFAYL'S "HAYY
  IBN YAQZĀN." (L.E. GOODMAN, ED & TRANS)
  617(TLS):9NOV73-1358
TUFTE, V. THE POETRY OF MARRIAGE.
  T.M. GREENE, 551(RENQ):SUMMER71-267
TUGAN-BARANOVSKY, M.I. THE RUSSIAN FAC-
  TORY IN THE 19TH CENTURY.
  W.L. BLACKWELL, 32:SEP72-665
TUGWELL, R.G. IN SEARCH OF ROOSEVELT.*
  617(TLS):27JUL73-863
TUGWELL, R.G. OFF COURSE.*
  L.W. KOENIG, 639(VQR):SUMMER71-456
TUILIER, A. RECHERCHES CRITIQUES SUR LA
  TRADITION DU TEXTE D'EURIPIDE.*
  S. FOLLET, 555:VOL45FASC2-318
TULASIEWICZ, W.F. & K. SCHEIBLE - SEE
  SEGHERS, A.
TUÑÓN DE LARA, M. MEDIO SIGLO DE CULTURA
  ESPAÑOLA, 1885-1936.
  F. CAUDET, 86(BHS):APR72-192
TUOHY, F. FINGERS IN THE DOOR AND OTHER
  STORIES.
  K. CUSHMAN, 573(SSF):SUMMER71-485
TURBAYNE, C.M. - SEE BERKELEY, G.
TURBULL, P. & G. CELAYA, EDS. CASTILLA.
  V. BURBRIDGE, 238:MAR71-224
TURCHI, M. FRANCESCO FRANCHINI.
  E.B., 228(GSLI):VOL148FASC461-153
TÜRCK, D.G. KLAVIERSCHULE. (E.R. JACOBI,
  ED)
  H.R., 412:MAY72-152

TURCO, L. THE INHABITANT.
  J. GALASSI, 491:MAR73-344
TURGENEV, I.S. DVORYANSKOYE GNEZDO.*
  (P. WADDINGTON, ED)
  205(FMLS):APR70-211
TURGOT, A.R.J. TURGOT ON PROGRESS,
  SOCIOLOGY AND ECONOMICS. (R.L. MEEK,
  ED & TRANS)
  617(TLS):9MAR73-263
TURK, L.H. & A.M. ESPINOSA, JR. FOUNDA-
  TION COURSE IN SPANISH. (2ND ED)
  F.M. BRADFORD, 238:MAR71-219
TURK, L.H. & A.M. ESPINOSA, JR. MASTER-
  ING SPANISH.
  J.L. MARTIN, 238:SEP71-609
TURKHAN, K.H. ISLAMIC RUGS.
  D.N. WILBER, 318(JAOS):APR-JUN71-345
TURNER, B. HOT-FOOT.
  617(TLS):16MAR73-303
TURNER, B. A PLACE IN THE COUNTRY.
  617(TLS):5JAN73-22
TURNER, F. SHAKESPEARE AND THE NATURE OF
  TIME.
  R.A. FOAKES, 175:AUTUMN71-98
  E.M. WAITH, 676(YR):SPRING72-441
TURNER, F.J. & A.F.P. HOOPER. "DEAR
  LADY." (R.A. BILLINGTON, WITH W.M.
  WHITEHILL, EDS)
  S.E. MORISON, 432(NEQ):DEC71-676
TURNER, G.W. THE ENGLISH LANGUAGE IN
  AUSTRALIA AND NEW ZEALAND.
  H.E. KIJLSTRA, 353:JUN70-124
TURNER, H.L. TOWN DEFENCES IN ENGLAND
  AND WALES.
  J. BEELER, 589:OCT72-814
TURNER, J. GHOSTS IN THE SOUTH WEST.
  617(TLS):23NOV73-1456
TURNER, J. - SEE PRICE, H.
TURNER, J. & R. FICHTER, EDS. FREEDOM TO
  BUILD.
  N. SILVER, 362:23AUG73-239
TURNER, J.K. BARBAROUS MEXICO.
  R.C. EWING, 263:APR-JUN72-170
  50(ARQ):SPRING71-96
TURNER, M.A. THE YELLOW ROSE OF TEXAS.
  W. GARD, 584(SWR):SPRING72-V
TURNER, M.J. NEW DANCE.
  B. KING, 151:JUL71-90
TURNER, M.R., ED. THE PARLOUR SONG BOOK.
  (MUSIC ED BY A. MIALL)
  617(TLS):11MAY73-530
TURNER, V. THE FOREST OF SYMBOLS.
  D. BEN-AMOS, 650(WF):APR70-134
TURNER, V.W. THE RITUAL PROCESS.
  P.M. GARDNER, 292(JAF):OCT-DEC71-450
  R.G. WILLIS, 69:JAN71-70
TURNEY, C. BYRON'S DAUGHTER.
  F.W. BATESON, 453:22FEB73-32
TURSI, J., ED. FOREIGN LANGUAGE AND THE
  "NEW" STUDENT.
  S. LEVENSON, 238:MAR71-217
TURSMAN, R., ED. STUDIES IN PHILOSOPHY
  AND IN THE HISTORY OF SCIENCE.
  H.B., 543:JUN71-765
  P.H. HARE, 484(PPR):DEC71-284
  W.R. SHEA, 154:MAR71-182
TUSCANO, P. POETICA E POESIA DI TOMMASO
  CAMPANELLA.
  L. BOLZONI, 228(GSLI):VOL147FASC458/
  459-457
TUTE, W. THE DEADLY STROKE.
  617(TLS):3AUG73-913
TUTTLE, A. SONGS FROM THE NIGHT BEFORE.*
  R. BRYDEN, 362:15MAR73-348
  617(TLS):2FEB73-129
TUTTLE, A. - SEE BIHALY, A.

TUTTLE, E.X., JR. WITH BENEFIT OF ARCHI-
TECT.
505:OCT71-160
TUTTLE, H.N. WILHELM DILTHEY'S PHILOSO-
PHY OF HISTORICAL UNDERSTANDING.*
H.B., 543:DEC70-347
TUTTLE, I. CONCORDANCE TO VAUGHAN'S
"SILEX SCINTILLANS."
A. RUDRUM, 184(EIC):JAN71-86
K. WILLIAMSON, 597(SN):VOL43#2-587
TUTTLETON, J.W. THE NOVEL OF MANNERS IN
AMERICA.
F.B. FREEMAN, JR., 70(ANQ):OCT72-30
B. NEVIUS, 27(AL):JAN73-701
TUWHARE, H. COME RAIN HAIL.
G. COLLIER, 368:DEC70-418
TUYNMAN, P. & F.L. ZWAAN. PROEVEN VAN
TEKST EN COMMENTAAR VOOR DE UITGAVE VAN
HOOFTS LYRIEK. (VOL 2)
W. GOBBERS, 556(RLV):1970/6-678
TVINNEREIM, U. & A. VURDERINGER AV
SYNNØVE SOLBAKKEN.
A.H. LERVIK, 172(EDDA):1970/6-367
TWAIN, M. CLEMENS OF THE "CALL."* (E.M.
BRANCH, ED)
P. MORROW, 649(WAL):SUMMER70-155
B. POLI, 189(EA):APR-JUN71-222
TWAIN, M. MARK TWAIN'S FABLES OF MAN.
(J.S. TUCKEY, ED)
J.C. BARNES, 31(ASCH):SPRING73-343
TWAIN, M. MARK TWAIN'S HANNIBAL, HUCK &
TOM.* (W. BLAIR, ED)
E. WAGENKNECHT, 594:SPRING70-88
TWAIN, M. MARK TWAIN'S LETTERS TO HIS
PUBLISHERS, 1867-1894.* (H. HILL, ED)
H-J. LANG, 38:BAND88HEFT4-554
TWAIN, M. MARK TWAIN'S MYSTERIOUS
STRANGER MANUSCRIPTS.* (W.M. GIBSON,
ED)
R. LEHAN, 445(NCF):MAR71-502
E. WAGENKNECHT, 594:SPRING70-88
TWAIN, M. MARK TWAIN'S SATIRES & BUR-
LESQUES.* (F.R. ROGERS, ED)
H. KRUSE, 38:BAND88HEFT3-409
TWAIN, M. THE WORKS OF MARK TWAIN. (VOL
2: ROUGHING IT.) (F.R. ROGERS & P.
BAENDER, EDS)
H.A. POCHMANN, 27(AL):JAN73-687
TWAIN, M. & H.H. ROGERS. MARK TWAIN'S
CORRESPONDENCE WITH HENRY HUTTLESTON
ROGERS, 1893-1909.* (L. LEARY, ED)
E. WAGENKNECHT, 594:SPRING70-88
TWIGG, E., WITH R.H. BROD. ENA TWIGG:
MEDIUM.
G. ANNAN, 362:1FEB73-156
617(TLS):23FEB73-221
TWOMBLY, R.C. FRANK LLOYD WRIGHT.
R. JELLINEK, 441:26AUG73-5
442(NY):2JUN73-124
TWYMAN, M. LITHOGRAPHY 1800-1850.
R. MC LEAN, 135:NOV70-216
G. WAKEMAN, 354:JUN71-178
J. WALTON, 503:SPRING71-48
TWYMAN, M. PRINTING 1770-1970.
D. CHAMBERS, 503:SUMMER71-93
R. MC LEAN, 135:MAY71-63
TYLER, A. - THE CLOCK-WINDER.*
J. HUNTER, 362:1FEB73-156
TYLER, A. A SLIPPING-DOWN LIFE.
A. EDELSTEIN, 598(SOR):SUMMER73-736
TYLER, P. UNDERGROUND FILM.
P. GIDAL, 592:JUL/AUG71-42
TYLER, S.A. KOYA: AN OUTLINE GRAMMAR,
GOMMU DIALECT.*
G.F. MEIER, 682(ZPSK):BAND23HEFT4-426
TYNE, J. MISTER DR. BLO.
L.E. SISSMAN, 442(NY):7APR73-147
M. LEVIN, 441:11FEB73-31

TYNIANOV, I. LE DISGRACIÉ. LE LIEUTEN-
ANT KIJÉ. LA MORT DU VAZIR-MOUKHTAR.
R. MICHA, 98:JUL70-581
"TYPOLOGIA LITTERARUM."
V. GÜNTHER, 182:VOL24#6-299
TYRWHITT, J. - SEE BARTLETT, W.H.
TYSDAHL, B.J. JOYCE AND IBSEN.*
H. BONHEIM, 38:BAND89HEFT4-551
J. DELBAERE-GARANT, 556(RLV):1970/1-
104
K. RICHARDS, 597(SN):VOL42#1-239
TYSSENS, M. LA GESTE DE GUILLAUME
D'ORANGE DANS LES MANUSCRITS CYCLIQUES.
P.F. DEMBOWSKI, 405(MP):AUG70-71
TZERMIAS, P. NEUGRIECHISCHE GRAMMATIK.
B.E. NEWTON, 361:VOL26#2-214


"US ENERGY OUTLOOK."
E. ROTHSCHILD, 453:9AUG73-29
UBALDINI, F. VITA DI MONS. ANGELO COL-
OCCI. (V. FANELLI, ED)
M.P., 228(GSLI):VOL148FASC462/463-463
"ÜBER DIE SPRACHE."
P.W., 206:NOV70-599
UDOVITCH, A.L. PARTNERSHIP AND PROFIT IN
MEDIEVAL ISLAM.
A.S. EHRENKREUTZ, 589:JAN72-147
UEDA, M. LITERARY AND ART THEORIES IN
JAPAN.
V.H. VIGLIELMO, 485(PE&W):JAN70-91
UHLIG, C. TRADITIONELLE DENKFORMEN IN
SHAKESPEARES TRAGISCHER KUNST.
E. FAAS, 38:BAND88HEFT4-543
G. LAMBRECHTS, 189(EA):OCT-DEC70-440
UHNAK, D. LAW AND ORDER.
C. LEHMANN-HAUPT, 441:4MAY73-41
W. SCHOTT, 441:27MAY73-6
442(NY):28APR73-145
UIJTERWAAL, J. JULIEN GREEN.
R. BROUN, 556(RLV):1970/6-675
UITTI, K.D. LINGUISTICS AND LITERARY
THEORY.*
S. CHATMAN, 269(IJAL):OCT70-302
J. ONIMUS, 557(RSH):APR-JUN71-303
S. ULLMANN, 208(FS):APR72-244
G. WIENOLD, 490:JUL71-411
J.M. WILLIAMS, 405(MP):FEB71-316
UJFALUSSY, J. BÉLA BARTÓK.
A. CROSS, 415:APR72-365
A.W., 410(M&L):JUL72-322
"UKRAINS'KYI VISNYK: VYPUSK I-II, SICHEN'
1970-TRAVEN' 1970."
J.S. RESHETAR, JR., 32:DEC72-910
ULAM, A. THE FALL OF THE AMERICAN UNI-
VERSITY.
617(TLS):2FEB73-115
ULAM, A.B. THE RIVALS.
A. DALLIN, 32:JUN72-434
617(TLS):30NOV73-1481
ULBRICHT, H. WAYANG PURWA.
A.C. SCOTT, 293(JAST):AUG71-919
ULLAND, W. "JOUER D'UN INSTRUMENT" UND
DIE ALTFRANZÖSISCHEN BEZEICHNUNGEN DES
INSTRUMENTENSPIELS.
M. SANDMANN, 545(RPH):FEB72-364
ULLMAN, P.L. MARIANO DE LARRA AND SPANISH
POLITICAL RHETORIC.
J. BUTT, 402(MLR):JAN72-200
A. NOUGUÉ, 182:VOL24#17/18-682
ULLMANN, S. MEANING AND STYLE.
617(TLS):12OCT73-1242
ULLMANN, S. THE PRINCIPLES OF SEMANTICS.
(GERMAN TITLE: GRUNDZÜGE DER SEMANTIK.)
L.J. COHEN, 316:JUN70-310
M. FAUST, 260(IF):BAND74-183

ULLOM, J.C., COMP.  FOLKLORE OF THE NORTH
AMERICAN INDIANS.
  J.W. KEALIINOHOMOKU, 292(JAF):APR-JUN
  71-261
ULLRICH, F.M.C. - SEE UNDER CRUCITTI
ULLRICH, F.M.
ULLRICH, H.  DIE BLINDE GLASHARMONIKA-
VIRTUOSIN MARIANNE KIRCHGESSNER UND
WIEN.
  A.H.K., 410(M&L):JUL72-335
ULMANN, D.  THE APPALACHIAN PHOTOGRAPHS
OF DORIS ULMANN.
  J.C. SLOANE, 127:SPRING72-352
ULRICH, W.D.  THE TREE IN THE ROOM.
  J. DITSKY, 628:SPRING72-108
DE UNAMUNO, M.  DESDE EL MIRADOR DE LA
GUERRA (COLABORACIÓN AL PERIÓDICO "LA
NACIÓN" DE BUENOS AIRES). (L. URRUTIA,
ED)
  V. OUIMETTE, 86(BHS):JAN72-90
DE UNAMUNO, M.  OUR LORD DON QUIXOTE.*
THE AGONY OF CHRISTIANITY. (A. KERRI-
GAN, TRANS OF BOTH)
  A.A. COHEN, 441:16DEC73-19
DE UNAMUNO, M.  THE TRAGIC SENSE OF LIFE.
(A. KERRIGAN, TRANS)
  A.A. COHEN, 441:16DEC73-19
  617(TLS):1JUN73-612
DE UNAMUNO, M.  TRES NIVOLAS DE UNAMUNO.
(D. BASDEKIS, ED)
  J.W. SCHWEITZER, 238:DEC71-983
UNDERDOWN, D.  PRIDE'S PURGE.
  639(VQR):AUTUMN71-CLXXVII
UNDERDOWN, D.  SOMERSET IN THE CIVIL WAR
AND INTERREGNUM.
  617(TLS):25MAY73-597
UNDERHILL, R.M.  SINGING FOR POWER.*
  B. TOELKEN, 650(WF):OCT70-268
"UNDERSEA FEATURES." (UNITED STATES
BOARD ON GEOGRAPHIC NAMES)
  K.B. HARDER, 424:MAR71-55
UNDERWOOD, M.  REWARD FOR A DEFECTOR.
  617(TLS):16MAR73-303
UNDERWOOD, P.  A GAZETTEER OF BRITISH
GHOSTS.
  K.M. BRIGGS, 203:AUTUMN71-255
UNGER, H-J.  DIE LITERATUR DER CAMARGUE.
  C. ROSTAING, 535(RHL):MAR-APR71-315
UNGERER, M.  GOOD CHEAP FOOD.
  N. HAZELTON, 441:29APR73-30
"UNITED STATES MINERAL RESOURCES."
  E. ROTHSCHILD, 453:9AUG73-29
UNNITHAN, T.K.N. & OTHERS, EDS.  SOCIOLOGY
FOR INDIA.
  L. HOWARD, 293(JAST):NOV70-247
UNRAU, W.E.  THE KANSA INDIANS.
  W. GARD, 584(SWR):WINTER72-76
UNSELD, S., ED.  ZUR AKTUALITÄT WALTER
BENJAMIN.
  617(TLS):14DEC73-1539
UNSWORTH, B.  MOONCRANKER'S GIFT.
  R. BLYTHE, 362:1NOV73-605
  617(TLS):16NOV73-1389
UNTERECKER, J.  VOYAGER.*
  L. CASPER, 613:SUMMER70-299
UNTERKIRCHER, F. & A. DE SCHRIJVER, EDS.
FACSIMILE GEBETBUCH KARL DES KÜHNEN
VEL POTIUS STUNDENBUCH DER MARIA VON
BURGUND.
  K.G. BOON, 90:DEC71-749
UNTERSTEINER, M.  POSIDONIO NEI PLACITA
DI PLATONE SECONDO DIOGENE LAERZIO III.*
  A.A. LONG, 123:DEC72-408
UNTRACHT, O.  METAL TECHNIQUES FOR
CRAFTSMEN.
  F. PETTIT, 139:JAN-FEB70-11
UPADHYAYA, S.A. - SEE YAŚASVATSĀGARA, Ś.

UPADHYE, A.N., ED.  KUVALAYAMĀLĀ (PT 2)
AND KUVALAYAMĀLĀ KATHĀ.
  E. BENDER, 318(JAOS):OCT-DEC71-567
UPDIKE, J.  BECH: A BOOK.*
  D.L. KAUFMANN, 390:OCT70-67
  R. TOWNLEY, 573(SSF):SPRING71-343
  42(AR):SUMMER70-262
UPDIKE, J.  COUPLES.*
  J.C. FIELD, 556(RLV):1971/3-338
UPDIKE, J.  MUSEUMS AND WOMEN.*
  D. MAHON, 362:26APR73-560
  E.F. SUDERMAN, 109:SPRING/SUMMER73-153
  617(TLS):4MAY73-488
UPDIKE, J.  RABBIT REDUX.*
  M. COOKE, 676(YR):SUMMER72-599
  M. MUDRICK, 249(HUDR):SPRING72-142
  W.T. STAFFORD, 295:NOV72-569
UPHAM, W.  MINNESOTA GEOGRAPHIC NAMES.
  E.C. EHRENSPERGER, 424:JUN70-121
URANG, G.  SHADOWS OF HEAVEN.
  R.M. KAWANO, 651(WHR):SUMMER72-286
URBAN, M.  EMIL NOLDE - LANDSCAPES,
WATERCOLOURS AND DRAWINGS.*
  D. IRWIN, 39:JUN71-532
  D.T., 135:AUG70-288
  F. WHITFORD, 592:JUL-AUG70-59
URE, J.  CUCUMBER SANDWICHES IN THE
ANDES.
  617(TLS):2NOV73-1347
URE, P.  W.B. YEATS AND THE SHAKESPEAREAN
MOMENT.
  R. FRÉCHET, 189(EA):JAN-MAR71-91
URIBE ECHEVERRÍA, J.  PÍO BAROJA.
  M.A. SALGADO, 238:MAR71-198
URMSON, J.O.  PHILOSOPHICAL ANALYSIS.
(2ND ED)
  R. BLANCHÉ, 542:OCT-DEC70-502
  E. NAMER, 542:OCT-DEC71-435
URQUHART, B.  HAMMARSKJÖLD.
  W.H. AUDEN, 442(NY):26MAY73-130
  D.P. CALLEO, 441:25FEB73-44
  617(TLS):20APR73-433
URRUTIA, L. - SEE DE UNAMUNO, M.
URWIN, G.S.  THE NEGLECTED SHAKESPEARE.
  I. BROWN, 157:AUTUMN70-67
URWIN, K. - SEE "LANGENSCHEIDT STANDARD
DICTIONARY OF THE FRENCH AND ENGLISH
LANGUAGES"
USHER, S.  THE HISTORIANS OF GREECE AND
ROME.*
  R.M. OGILVIE, 313:VOL61-298
  É. WILL, 555:VOL45FASC2-328
USINGER, F.  DICHTUNG ALS INFORMATION.
  O.W. TETZLAFF, 221(GQ):JAN71-111
USPENSKIJ, B.A.  POÈTIKA KOMPOZICII.
  W. SCHMID, 490:JAN71-124
USPENSKY, B.A.  POETIKA KOMPOZITSII.
  A. SHUKMAN, 402(MLR):JUL72-713
USSHER, A.  THE TWENTY-TWO KEYS OF THE
TAROT.
  J.P. COPE, 159(DM):SUMMER/AUTUMN70-
  120
USSHER, R.G. - SEE ARISTOPHANES
USTINOV, N.B.  KLOP AND THE USTINOV
FAMILY.
  D.J. ENRIGHT, 362:7JUN73-770
  617(TLS):1JUN73-608
UYA, O.E.  FROM SLAVERY TO PUBLIC SERVICE.
  639(VQR):SPRING71-LXXII


VAAL, J.  TECHNISCHER FORTSCHRITT UND
FAKTORSUBSTITUTION IN DER WESTDEUTSCHEN
TEXTILINDUSTRIE (1950-65).
  K. MELLEROWICZ, 182:VOL24#5-204
VÄÄNÄNEN, V.  INTRODUZIONE AL LATINO
VOLGARE. (A. LIMENTANI, ED)
  R. HARRIS, 382(MAE):1972/1-81

VÄÄNÄNEN, V. - SEE CASTREN, P. & H. LILIUS
VACALOPOULOS, A.E. ORIGINS OF THE GREEK
  NATION.* (VOL 1)
    J.M. HUSSEY, 575(SEER):OCT72-611
VACCARO, A.J. LA NUMERACIÓN LATINA.
    D.A. MALCOLM, 123:MAR72-127
VACHEK, J. DYNAMIKA FONOLOGICKÉHO SYS-
  TÉMU SOUČASNÉ SPISOVNÉ ČEŠTINY.
    J. KRÁMSKÝ, 361:VOL25#2-178
    H.D. POHL, 353:DEC70-123
VACHEY, M. LA SNOW.
    S. MAX, 207(FR):APR71-973
VACHTOVÁ, L. FRANK KUPKA.
    J. MC ANDREW, 54:MAR71-132
VACULÍK, L. THE AXE.* (GERMAN TITLE:
  DAS BEIL.)
    R. BLYTHE, 362:6SEP73-320
    617(TLS):12OCT73-1209
VACULÍK, L. THE GUINEA PIGS.* (GERMAN
  TITLE: DIE MEERSCHWEINCHEN.)
    617(TLS):12OCT73-1209
VĀDIN DEVASŪRI. PRAMĀṆA-NAYA-TATTVĀLO-
  KĀLAṂKĀRA OF VĀDI DEVASŪRI. (H.S.
  BHATTACHARYA, ED & TRANS)
    W.H. MAURER, 485(PE&W):JAN71-98
VAILLAND, R. ECRITS INTIMES.
    Y. PIHAN, 98:APR70-383
VAILLANT, A. GRAMMAIRE COMPARÉE DES
  LANGUES SLAVES. (VOL 3)
    M. SAMILOV, 575(SEER):OCT72-636
VAILLANT, M. ESQUISSE GRAMMATICALE DU
  LOBIRI.
    W.A.A. WILSON, 69:JAN70-96
VAIZEY, J. THE ECONOMICS OF EDUCATION.
    617(TLS):10AUG73-934
VAJDA, A. VAKULÁSTÓL LÁTÁSIG.
    617(TLS):9FEB73-147
VALDASTRI, I. PREISSCHRIFT ÜBER DAS BÜR-
  GERLICHE TRAUERSPIEL. (A. WIERLACHER,
  ED)
    R.K. ANGRESS, 221(GQ):NOV71-579
VALDESPINO, A. JORGE MAÑACH Y SU GENERA-
  CIÓN EN LAS LETRAS CUBANAS.
    A. ARROYO, 263:OCT-DEC72-434
VALDEZ, L. & S. STEINER, EDS. AZTLÁN.*
    W. GARD, 584(SWR):AUTUMN72-330
VALENCY, M. THE CART AND THE TRUMPET.
    617(TLS):26OCT73-1316
VALENTINE, J. PILGRIMS.*
    A. RICH, 114(CHIR):AUTUMN70-128
VALENTINE, L.N. ORNAMENT IN MEDIEVAL
  MANUSCRIPTS.
    L.M.C. RANDALL, 39:JAN70-87
VALENTINER, T. KANT UND SEINE LEHRE.
    R. MALTER, 342:BAND62HEFT4-517
VALENTINER, T. - SEE KANT, I.
VALENTINI, F. STORIA ANTOLOGICA DEI
  PROBLEMI FILOSOFICI. (POLITICA, 1)
    E. NAMER, 542:JUL-SEP70-366
VALERIUS, M. M. VALERIO: BUCOLICHE.
  (2ND ED) (F. MUNARI, ED)
    H. COOPER, 382(MAE):1972/2-153
    P.G. WALSH, 123:DEC72-417
VALÉRY, P. ALIQUOT CARMINA (SERPENS -
  CANTICUM - SEPULCRA IUXTA MARE). (A.R.
  CHISHOLM, ED)
    I.D. MC FARLANE, 208(FS):OCT72-478
VALÉRY, P. CHARMES OU POÈMES. (C.G.
  WHITING, ED)
    617(TLS):21DEC73-1562
VALÉRY, P. THE COLLECTED WORKS OF PAUL
  VALÉRY.* (VOL 1) (J. MATHEWS, ED; D.
  PAUL & J.R. LAWLER, TRANS)
    R. LATTIMORE, 249(HUDR):SPRING72-135
VALÉRY, P. THE COLLECTED WORKS OF PAUL
  VALÉRY. (VOL 2) (H. CORKE, TRANS)
    R. GEEN, 399(MLJ):FEB71-112
    205(FMLS):JAN71-100

VALÉRY, P. THE COLLECTED WORKS OF PAUL
  VALÉRY. (VOL 6) (J. MATHEWS, ED &
  TRANS)
    617(TLS):23MAR73-333
VALESIO, P. STRUTTURE DELL'ALLITTERA-
  ZIONE.*
    G. FRANCESCATO, 361:VOL25#4-435
    R. STEFANINI, 276:AUTUMN71-367
    S. STURM, 599:WINTER71-95
VALETTE, R.M. ARTHUR DE GOBINEAU AND THE
  SHORT STORY.
    J. GAULMIER, 535(RHL):JUL-AUG70-730
VALGEMAE, M. ACCELERATED GRIMACE.
    S.S. STANTON, 385(MQR):FALL73-384
VÁLI, F.A. BRIDGE ACROSS THE BOSPORUS.*
    N. ITZKOWITZ, 32:SEP72-732
VALIANI, L. THE END OF AUSTRIA-HUNGARY.
    441:26AUG73-16
VALIANI, L. LA DISSOLUZIONE DELL'AUSTRIA-
  UNGHERIA.
    M. MOLNÁR, 98:JAN70-72
VALIENTE, D. AN ABC OF WITCHCRAFT PAST
  AND PRESENT.
    617(TLS):27APR73-482
VALIN, R. LA MÉTHODE COMPARATIVE EN LIN-
  GUISTIQUE HISTORIQUE ET EN PSYCHOMÉC-
  ANIQUE DU LANGAGE.
    L. ZGUSTA, 353:OCT71-103
VALLA, L. DE VERO FALSOQUE BONO.
    F. LASSERRE, 182:VOL24#7/8-367
DEL VALLE-INCLÁN, R. PÁGINAS SELECTA.
  (J. MICHEL, ED)
    S.M. GREENFIELD, 238:MAR71-227
VALLEJO, A.B. - SEE UNDER BUERO VALLEJO,
  A.
VALLEJO, C. POEMAS HUMANOS/HUMAN POEMS.
    G. BROTHERSTON, 565:VOL11#1-59
VALLEJO, C. CÉSAR VALLEJO, AN ANTHOLOGY
  OF HIS POETRY. (J. HIGGINS, ED)
    K.A. MC DUFFIE, 263:JAN-MAR72-55
    M.E. RUIZ, 238:SEP71-615
    D.L. SHAW, 86(BHS):JAN72-104
VALLIÈRES, P. CHOOSE.
    C. MILLER, 99:FEB73-37
VALLIÈRES, P. WHITE NIGGERS OF AMERICA.*
  (FRENCH TITLE: NÈGRES BLANCS D'AMÉR-
  IQUE.)
    P. AUBERY, 207(FR):OCT70-213
    M. MORF, 628:FALL71-83
    A.N. RASPA, 150(DR):SUMMER71-292
    G. WOODCOCK, 102(CANL):WINTER72-73
VALLONE, A. L'INTERPRETAZIONE DI DANTE
  NEL CINQUECENTO.
    M.P., 228(GSLI):VOL147FASC460-631
    R. WIS, 439(NM):1970/4-717
VALLONE, A. LA PROSA DEL "CONVIVIO."
    A. SCAGLIONE, 545(RPH):AUG71-150
VALLVERDÚ, F. DUES LLENGÜES, DUES FUN-
  CIONS?
    191(ELN):SEP71(SUPP)-175
VALSAN, E.H. COMMUNITY DEVELOPMENT PRO-
  GRAMS AND RURAL LOCAL GOVERNMENT.
    J.D. MONTGOMERY, 293(JAST):NOV70-207
VALSECCHIO, M. LANDSCAPE PAINTING OF THE
  19TH CENTURY.
    R. LEBOWITZ, 58:MAR72-18
VAMBERY, A. TRAVELS IN CENTRAL ASIA.
    E. WIDMER, 293(JAST):MAY71-694
VAN ALSTYNE, R.W. THE UNITED STATES AND
  EAST ASIA.
    G. BARRACLOUGH, 453:31MAY73-9
VAN BEEK, G.W. HAJAR BIN ḤUMEID.
    R.L. CLEVELAND, 318(JAOS):APR-JUN71-
    309
VAN BRUNT, H. ARCHITECTURE AND SOCIETY.*
  (W.A. COLES, ED)
    W.H. JORDY, 576:DEC71-330

VAN BRUNT, H.L. UNCERTAINTIES.
G. KUZMA, 502(PRS):FALL70-271
VAN BUREN, P.M. THE EDGES OF LANGUAGE.
617(TLS):10AUG73-933
VANCE, C.M. THE EXTRAVAGANT SHEPHERD.
617(TLS):13JUL73-816
VANCE, E. READING THE "SONG OF ROLAND."
G.J. BRAULT, 207(FR):FEB71-628
S.G. NICHOLS, JR., 589:JUL72-561
VAN CLEVE, T.C. THE EMPEROR FREDERICK II
OF HOHENSTAUFEN.
K. LEYSER, 362:16AUG73-208
VANDERBILT, K. THE ACHIEVEMENT OF WIL-
LIAM DEAN HOWELLS.*
M. BUCCO, 594:FALL70-379
W.M. GIBSON, 27(AL):MAY72-327
VAN DER EYKEN, W. & B. TURNER. ADVEN-
TURES IN EDUCATION.
N. CROOK, 97(CQ):SPRING71-266
VAN DER STARRE, E. RACINE ET LE THÉÂTRE
DE L'AMBIGUÏTÉ.*
P. DELBOUILLE, 556(RLV):1970/4-442
W.G. MOORE, 402(MLR):OCT72-891
VANDER VEER, G.L. BRADLEY'S METAPHYSICS
AND THE SELF.
G.R.G. MURE, 483:OCT71-357
W.H. WALSH, 479(PHQ):OCT71-374
VAN DE WAAL, H. DRIE EEUWEN VADERLAND-
SCHE GESCHIED-UITBEELDING, 1500-1800.
J. BIALSTOCKI, 54:JUN71-262
VAN DOREN, M. & M. SAMUEL. IN THE BEGIN-
NING, LOVE. (E. SAMUEL, ED)
W. DAVISON, 441:16SEP73-6
VAN DUYN, M. MERCIFUL DISGUISES.
H. LEIBOWITZ, 441:9DEC73-4
H. SHAPIRO, 441:22SEP73-29
VAN DUYN, M. TO SEE, TO TAKE.
A. OBERG, 598(SOR):WINTER73-243
42(AR):SPRING70-134
VANĚČEK, V. DĚJINY STÁTU A PRÁVA V
ČESKOSLOVENSKU DO ROKU 1945. (2ND ED)
R.F. WIERER, 32:JUN72-475
VAN EERDE, K.S. WENCESLAUS HOLLAR.*
O. ODLOZILIK, 551(RENQ):WINTER71-534
568(SCN):SPRING72-17
VAN FOSSEN, R.W. - SEE HEYWOOD, T.
VANGGAARD, T. PHALLÓS.
617(TLS):12JAN73-50
VAN HOECK, J. VOORLOPIG VONNIS.
J. GOFFART, 556(RLV):1971/6-786
VAN LAAN, T.F. THE IDIOM OF DRAMA.
S.G. PUTT, 175:AUTUMN71-101
O. REINERT, 401(MLQ):DEC71-425
VAN LIERDE, J. - SEE LUMUMBA, P.
VANN, J.D., ED. CRITICS ON HENRY JAMES.
G. CORE, 385(MQR):WINTER73-82
VANN, R.T. THE SOCIAL DEVELOPMENT OF
ENGLISH QUAKERISM, 1655-1755.
R. SCHLATTER, 656(WMQ):APR71-323
VAN NESS, P. REVOLUTION AND CHINESE
FOREIGN POLICY.
H.C. HINTON, 293(JAST):FEB71-444
VAN NIEL, R., ED. ECONOMIC FACTORS IN
SOUTHEAST ASIAN SOCIAL CHANGE.
C.O. HOUSTON, 293(JAST):FEB71-515
VANNUCCI, P. SAGGI VARI TRA CARDUCCIANI
E PASCOLIANI.
P.A.T., 228(GSLI):VOL148FASC461-157
VAN OS, H.W. MARIAS DEMUT UND VERHERR-
LICHUNG IN DER SIENESISCHEN MALEREI
1300-1450.
I. HUECK, 54:MAR71-116
VAN ROOTSELAAR, B. & J.F. STAAL, EDS.
LOGIC, METHODOLOGY AND PHILOSOPHY OF
SCIENCE III.
R.H. STOOTHOFF, 478:JUL70-179

VAN RYSSELBERGHE, T. LES CAHIERS DE LA
PETITE DAME.
617(TLS):22JUN73-717
VAN SONSBEECK, D. HET ZIJN ALS MYSTERIE.
P. SOMVILLE, 542:OCT-DEC71-495
VAN TIEGHEM, P. DICTIONNAIRE DE VICTOR
HUGO.
J. SEEBACHER, 535(RHL):MAR-APR71-311
VAN TOORN, P. LEEWAY GRASS.
D. BARBOUR, 150(DR):SPRING71-133
P. STEVENS, 628:SPRING72-103
VAN TRUMP, J.D. AN AMERICAN PALACE OF
CULTURE.
N. PEVSNER, 46:AUG71-128
VANTUCH, A., ED. DER ÖSTERREICHISCH-
UNGARISCHE AUSGLEICH 1867.
W.A. JENKS, 32:JUN72-460
VAN VOGT, A.E. THE THREE EYES OF EVIL
AND EARTH'S LAST FORTRESS.
617(TLS):9NOV73-1378
VAN VORIS, W.H. THE CULTIVATED STANCE.
D.R-M. WILKINSON, 179(ES):FEB71-73
VARANINI, G., ED. LAMENTI STORICI
PISANI.
L. BANFI, 228(GSLI):VOL148FASC462/
463-417
VARANINI, G. - SEE PAGLIARESI, N.
VARDAR, B. ETUDE LEXICOLOGIQUE D'UN
CHAMP NOTIONNEL.
G. MATORÉ, 209(FM):APR71-168
VARÈSE, L. VARÈSE.* (VOL 1: 1883-1928.)
617(TLS):2FEB73-118
VAREY, J.E., ED. GALDÓS STUDIES.*
R.M. FEDORCHEK, 238:SEP71-597
VAREY, J.E., N.D. SHERGOLD & J. SAGE -
SEE VÉLEZ DE GUEVERA, J.
VARGAS LLOSA, M. PANTALEÓN Y LAS VISITA-
DORAS.
617(TLS):12OCT73-1208
VARGISH, T. NEWMAN.
T. GIBERT, 189(EA):OCT-DEC71-539
G.L. LEVINE, 191(ELN):MAR72-223
VARGYAS, L. - SEE KODÁLY, Z.
"VARIATIONS ON A THEME: FOURTH ANNUAL
REVIEW, 1969-70."
R.C. ELLSWORTH, 529(QQ):SUMMER71-340
VARLEY, H.P. IMPERIAL RESTORATION IN
MEDIEVAL JAPAN.*
639(VQR):AUTUMN71-CLXXXIV
VARLEY, H.P. JAPANESE CULTURE.
M.B. JANSEN, 441:1APR73-29
617(TLS):29JUN73-757
VARMA, D.P., ED. GOTHIC NOVELS.
L. WOLF, 441:14JAN73-2
VARNHAGEN VON ENSE, R. RAHEL VARNHAGEN
UND IHRE ZEIT. (F. KEMP, ED)
D.L., 191(ELN):SEP71(SUPP)-163
VARTIKAR, V.S. COMMERCIAL POLICY AND
ECONOMIC DEVELOPMENT IN INDIA.
G.P. PAPANEK, 293(JAST):NOV70-205
VARTY, K. REYNARD THE FOX.
P.M. VERMEER, 179(ES):DEC71-545
VAS, I. CET HOMME SEUL, QUE VEUT-IL?
I. FENYÖ, 270:VOL22#1-17
VASARELY, V. & M. JORAY. VASARELY II.
M. BRUMER, 58:DEC70/JAN71-12
VASÍLIEVA-SHVEDE, O.K. & G.V. STEPÁNOV.
GRAMMÁTIKA ISPÁNSKOGO YAZYKÁ.
M. SÁNCHEZ PUIG, 202(FMOD):JUN70-352
VASSALLI, D.C. - SEE UNDER CHIOMENTI VAS-
SALLI, D.
VASSILIKOS, V. THE HARPOON GUN.
P. ADAMS, 61:MAY73-122
P. SOURIAN, 441:6MAY73-39
VASSILIKOS, V. OUTSIDE THE WALLS.
P. ADAMS, 61:MAY73-122
A. BAILEY, 441:6MAY73-38

VASTHOFF, J. SMALL FARM CREDIT AND DE-
VELOPMENT.
W. ALLAN, 69:JAN71-79
VATER, H. DAS SYSTEM DER ARTIKELFORMEN
IM GEGENWÄRTIGEN DEUTSCH.
K. SPALDING, 47(ARL):VOL17FASC1-48
VATUK, S. KINSHIP AND URBANISATION.
617(TLS):6JUL73-774
VATUK, V.P. THIEVES IN MY HOUSE.*
M. PANDIT, 650(WF):OCT70-287
VAUGHAN, G.L. THE COTTON RENTER'S SON.
E.M. THOMAS, 219(GAR):SPRING70-74
VAUGHAN, H.H. WELSH PROVERBS WITH ENG-
LISH TRANSLATIONS.
J.L. CUTLER, 582(SFQ):DEC70-375
VAUGHAN, P. THE PILL ON TRIAL.
617(TLS):9MAR73-277
VAUGHAN, W., H. BÖRSCH-SUPAN & H.J. NEID-
HARDT. CASPAR DAVID FRIEDRICH, 1774-
1840: ROMANTIC LANDSCAPE PAINTING IN
DRESDEN.*
C. ROSEN, 453:1NOV73-12
VAUGHAN WILLIAMS, R. NATIONAL MUSIC AND
OTHER ESSAYS.
H. OTTAWAY, 415:OCT72-974
VAUTHIER, J. CAPITAINE BADA. LES PRO-
DIGES.
J-N. VUARNET, 98:APR70-352
VAUTHIER, J. LE SANG.
B.L. KNAPP, 207(FR):DEC70-425
J-N. VUARNET, 98:APR70-352
DE VAUX, R. PALESTINE DURING THE NEO-
LITHIC AND CHALCOLITHIC PERIODS. (REV)
PALESTINE IN THE EARLY BRONZE AGE.
(REV)
G.E. WRIGHT, 318(JAOS):APR-JUN71-276
DEL VAYO, J.A. GIVE ME COMBAT.
442(NY):3SEP73-67
VÁZQUEZ MONTALBÁN, M. RECORDANDO A
DARDÉ.
C.W. BUTLER, 238:MAR71-199
VEATCH, H. FOR AN ONTOLOGY OF MORALS.
K. PAHEL, 185:JUL72-349
VEATCH, H.B. TWO LOGICS.*
R.G. MEYERS, 484(PPR):SEP70-136
C. WELCH, 154:SEP70-255
42(AR):SPRING70-133
VEBLEN, T. THE THEORY OF THE LEISURE
CLASS. [INTRODUCTION BY J.K. GALBRAITH]
A. BROYARD, 441:23APR73-31
DEL VECCHIO, G. NUOVA SILLOGE DI TEMI
GIURIDICI E FILOSOFICI.
E. NAMER, 542:APR-JUN70-260
VÉDRINE, H. LA CONCEPTION DE LA NATURE
CHEZ GIORDANO BRUNO.
E. NAMER, 542:JUL-SEP70-369
VAN DER VEEN, J. ORFEUS ONDER DE STERVE-
LINGEN.
C.F.P. STUTTERHEIM, 204(FDL):1970/1-
67
VAN'T VEER, P. DE ATJEH-OORLOG.
P-W. VAN DER VEUR, 293(JAST):AUG71-918
DE VEGA, L. - SEE UNDER LOPE DE VEGA
VEH, O. - SEE PROCOPIUS
VEIDLE, V. BEZYMIANNAIA STRANA.
R. HAGGLUND, 32:DEC72-941
VEILLON, E. & A. NOBEL. MEDICAL DIC-
TIONARY. (5TH ED)
H. FISCHBACH, 75:4/1970-216
VEIRAS, H.F. HEUTELIA. (W. WEIGUM, ED)
B.L. SPAHR, 133:1971/1&2-199
VEITH, D.M. - SEE ROCHESTER, J.
VAN DE VELDE, R.G. DE STUDIE VAN HET
GOTISCH IN DE NEDERLANDEN.
F. VAN DER RHEE, 433:JAN71-97
E. STUTZ, 260(IF):BAND74-300

VÉLEZ DE GUEVERA, J. LOS CELOS HACEN
ESTRELLAS.* (J.E. VAREY, N.D. SHERGOLD
& J. SAGE, EDS)
E.M. WILSON, 402(MLR):JAN72-198
VÉLEZ DE GUEVARA, L. LOS HIJOS DE LA
BARBUDA. (M.G. PROFETI, ED)
A.L. MACKENZIE, 86(BHS):OCT72-405
VELLACOTT, P. SOPHOCLES AND OEDIPUS.
C. MOULTON, 676(YR):SPRING72-455
VELZ, J.W. SHAKESPEARE AND THE CLASSICAL
TRADITION.*
R.A. FOAKES, 175:SPRING70-22
VENDITTI, A. CORPUS PALLADIANUM. (VOL 4)
J. NEWMAN, 90:NOV71-675
VENDLER, H.H. ON EXTENDED WINGS.*
L. CASPER, 613:AUTUMN70-452
I.G. MAC CAFFREY, 401(MLQ):JUN71-234
M. MUELLER, 72:BAND209HEFT1/3-170
C. TOMLINSON, 184(EIC):OCT71-404
VENDLER, Z. ADJECTIVES AND NOMINALIZA-
TIONS.*
C. GOOD, 353:DEC70-94
VENDLER, Z. LINGUISTICS IN PHILOSOPHY.*
L.J. COHEN, 206:FEB71-125
VENDLER, Z. RES COGITANS.
617(TLS):23MAR73-330
VENEZKY, R.L. THE STRUCTURE OF ENGLISH
ORTHOGRAPHY.*
A.R. TELLIER, 189(EA):JUL-SEP71-320
VENTERS, P. & B.C. KING. RÉPÉTITIONS.
W.N. FELT, 399(MLJ):DEC71-537
VENTURI, F. IL SETTECENTO RIFORMATORE.
J.T.S. WHEELOCK, 276:AUTUMN71-395
VENTURI, F. UTOPIA AND REFORM IN THE
ENLIGHTENMENT.
A. ROSENBERG, 173(ECS):SUMMER72-604
S. SCHAMA, 111:7MAY71-171
VENTURI, R., D.S. BROWN & S. IZENOUR.
LEARNING FROM LAS VEGAS.*
A.L. HUXTABLE, 453:18OCT73-45
N. SILVER, 441:29APR73-5
617(TLS):6APR73-366
VERBEECK, L. KONRAD WEISS.
H-R. KLIENEBERGER, 402(MLR):JAN72-229
VERCORS. THE BATTLE OF SILENCE. (FRENCH
TITLE: LA BATAILLE DU SILENCE.)
K. BIEBER, 207(FR):OCT70-186
VERCORS. LE RADEAU DE LA MÉDUSE.
K. BIEBER, 207(FR):OCT70-187
VERCRUYSSE, J. - SEE HÉLISENNE DE CRENNE
VERCRUYSSE, J. - SEE DE VOLTAIRE, F-M.A.
VERDI, G. LETTERS OF GIUSEPPE VERDI.*
(C. OSBORNE, ED & TRANS)
J.W.K., 410(M&L):APR72-191
M.J.P. MATZ, 415:FEB72-151
VERDIER, J-M. & OTHERS. STRUCTURES FON-
CIÈRES ET DÉVELOPPEMENT RURAL AU
MAGHREB.
E. GELLNER, 69:OCT70-395
VERDIER, P. THE WALTERS ART GALLERY:
CATALOGUE OF THE PAINTED ENAMELS OF
THE RENAISSANCE.*
R-W. LIGHTBOWN, 39:JUN70-487
VERDÍN DÍAZ, G. INTRODUCCIÓN AL ESTILO
INDIRECTO LIBRE EN ESPAÑOL.
P. RUSSELL-GEBBETT, 86(BHS):OCT72-400
VERDY, V. - SEE GAUTIER, T.
VEREMANS, J. ÉLÉMENTS SYMBOLIQUES DANS
LA IIIE BUCOLIQUE DE VERGILE.
A. ERNOUT, 555:VOL45FASC1-167
G.W. WILLIAMS, 123:MAR72-109
VEREY, D. THE BUILDINGS OF ENGLAND:
GLOUCESTERSHIRE: THE COTSWOLDS. THE
BUILDINGS OF ENGLAND: GLOUCESTERSHIRE:
THE VALE AND THE FOREST OF DEAN.
A.C-T., 135:DEC70-291
P. METCALF, 46:JAN71-66

VERGIL. THE AENEID: A RETELLING FOR
YOUNG PEOPLE. (F.M. GERDES, TRANS)
W.S. THURMAN, 399(MLJ):MAY71-330
VERGIL. THE "AENEID" OF VIRGIL.* (A.
MANDELBAUM, TRANS)
R. LATTIMORE, 249(HUDR):AUTUMN72-482
VERGIL. AENEIDOS XII. (B. TILLEY, ED)
R. GLEN, 123:MAR72-98
VERGIL. VIRGILE, "LA HUITIÈME BUCOLIQUE."
(A. RICHTER, ED & TRANS)
M.L. CLARKE, 123:JUN72-275
VERGIL. VIRGILIO: "LE GEORGICHE." (L.
FIRPO, ED)
H.H. DAVIS, 122:OCT72-304
VERGIL. PUBLIUS VERGILIUS MARO, "THE
GEORGICS." (K.R. MAC KENZIE, TRANS)
D. CHAMBERS, 503:WINTER69-190
L.P. WILKINSON, 123:MAR72-107
"VERGLEICHEN UND VERÄNDERN."
H. HATFIELD, 221(GQ):MAR71-246
VERHOFSTADT, E. DANIEL CASPER VON LOHEN-
STEIN.
G. LUTHER, 224(GRM):NOV70-470
VERLAINE, P. OEUVRES POÉTIQUES.* (J.
ROBICHEZ, ED)
G. ZAYED, 535(RHL):JUL-AUG70-728
VERLAINE, P. SAGESSE. (C. CHADWICK, ED)
617(TLS):21DEC73-1562
VERLÉE, L. L'ENSEIGNEMENT DES LANGUES
ET INFORMATION CULTURELLE.*
E.C. CONDON, 207(FR):FEB71-597
VERLÉE, L., I. LEFEBVRE & L. HEBBELINCK.
VOIES NOUVELLES 1, MÉTHODE DE FRAN-
ÇAIS. (10TH ED)
M-L. MOREAU, 556(RLV):1971/2-236
VERMES, G. JESUS THE JEW.
617(TLS):7DEC73-1516
VERMEULE, C.C. ROMAN IMPERIAL ART IN
GREECE AND ASIA MINOR.*
E. ALFÖLDI-ROSENBAUM, 487:SUMMER71-
179
D. BRINKERHOFF, 54:JUN71-244
VERNADSKY, G. THE TSARDOM OF MOSCOW 1547-
1682.*
H.W. DEWEY, 104:WINTER72-631
VERNADSKY, G. & OTHERS, EDS. A SOURCE
BOOK FOR RUSSIAN HISTORY FROM EARLY
TIMES TO 1917.
617(TLS):9MAR73-260
VERNANT, J-P., ED. PROBLÈMES DE LA
GUERRE EN GRÈCE ANCIENNE.*
P. GAUTHIER, 555:VOL45FASC1-134
S.C. HUMPHREYS, 303:VOL91-191
VERNE, J. HIER ET DEMAIN.
J. BELLEMIN-NOËL, 98:AUG-SEP70-692
VERNE, J. MICHEL STROGOFF.
M. SERRES, 98:JAN70-3
VERNEAUX, R. LE VOCABULAIRE DE KANT.
R. MALTER, 342:BAND61HEFT1-140
VERNEAUX, R. - SEE KANT, I.
VERNEY, J. SAMSON'S HOARD.
R. BLYTHE, 362:4OCT73-459
VERNIÈRE, P. & R. DESNE, EDS. DIX-
HUITIÈME SIÈCLE. (VOL 1: 1969)
D-A. BONNEVILLE, 207(FR):APR71-987
A.D. HYTIER, 173(ECS):WINTER71-216
VERNILLAT, F. & J. CARPENTREAU. DICTION-
NAIRE DE LA CHANSON FRANÇAISE.
D.R. BRODIN, 207(FR):OCT70-163
VERONESI, G. STYLE AND DESIGN, 1909-
1929. STILE 1925 ASCESA E CADUTA DELLE
"ARTS DÉCO."
E. KAUFMANN, JR., 54:SEP70-340
VERPEAUX, J., ED. PSEUDO-KODINOS, TRAITÉ
DES OFFICES.
P.J. ALEXANDER, 589:JUL72-569

VERSINI, L. LACLOS ET LA TRADITION.*
H. COULET, 535(RHL):JUL-AUG70-719
S. LOTRINGER, 98:MAR71-195
VERSINI, L. - SEE DUCLOS, C.
"VERSLAG VAN HET DERDE COLLOQUIUM VAN
HOOGLERAREN EN LECTOREN IN DE NEDER-
LANDISTIEK AAN BUITENLANDSE UNIVERSI-
TEITEN."
J.P. WILLEMS, 556(RLV):1971/4-511
VERSNEL, H.S. TRIUMPHUS.
A. MARSHALL, 487:WINTER71-391
VERSTEGEN, J. EEN ZON BIJ NACHT.
270:VOL21#1-122
VERZÁR, C. DIE ROMANISCHEN SKULPTUREN
DER ABTEI SAGRA DI SAN MICHELE, STUD-
IEN ZU MEISTER NICOLAUS UND ZUR
"SCUOLA DI PIACENZA."
C-D. SHEPPARD, 54:MAR71-113
"VERZEICHNISS DER BÜCHER DES VERSTORBENEN
PROFESSOR JOHANN FRIEDRICH GENSICHEN."
R. MALTER, 342:BAND61HEFT2-253
VERZERA, A. LA POESIA DI TOMMASO CAMPA-
NELLA.
L. BOLZONI, 228(GSLI):VOL147FASC458/
459-457
VERZONE, P. FROM THEODRIC TO CHARLE-
MAGNE.
J. BECKWITH, 39:JAN70-84
VESAAS, T. LIV VED STRAUMEN.
E. HASLUND, 270:VOL21#1-128
"THE VESPASIAN PSALTER."* (D.H. WRIGHT,
ED)
H. GNEUSS, 38:BAND88HEFT3-368
VESSEY, D. STATIUS AND THE THEBAID.
617(TLS):22JUN73-710
VETTER, T. DHARMAKĪRTI'S PRAMĀṆAVINIŚ-
CAYAḤ. (VOL 1)
A. WAYMAN, 318(JAOS):OCT-DEC71-550
VEYNE, P. COMMENT ON ÉCRIT L'HISTOIRE.
G. LEBRUN, 98:JUL71-648
DE LA VIA, F. - SEE UNDER FRANCESC DE LA
VIA
VIALATOUX, J. LA MORALE DE KANT. (5TH
ED)
R. MALTER, 342:BAND62HEFT1-147
VIALLANEIX, P. LE PREMIER CAMUS SUIVI
DE ECRITS DE JEUNESSE D'ALBERT CAMUS.
617(TLS):12OCT73-1252
VIALLANEIX, P. VIGNY PAR LUI-MÊME.
J-P. RICHARD, 98:FEB70-99
VIAN, R. & M. VOCABULAIRE ET PHRASÉOLO-
GIE MODERNES.
G. SCHWEIG, 430(NS):FEB71-104
VIANSINO, G. INTRODUZIONE ALLO STUDIO
CRITICO DELLA LETTERATURA LATINA.
E-J. KENNEY, 123:DEC72-420
F-A. SULLIVAN, 122:OCT72-315
VIANU, A. NASTEREA S-U-A.
G-E. TORREY & L.E. PENNINGTON,
656(WMQ):APR71-343
VIARD, J., ED. L'ESPRIT RÉPUBLICAIN.
617(TLS):12OCT73-1229
VIARD, J. LES OEUVRES POSTHUMES DE
CHARLES PÉGUY.
S. FRAISSE, 535(RHL):JAN-FEB71-128
B. GUYON, 557(RSH):APR-JUN70-333
"VIATOR." (VOL 1)
B. ROWLAND, 70(ANQ):SEP72-14
"VIATOR." (VOL 2)
R.J.P. KUIN, 70(ANQ):APR73-125
VIATTE, A. LA FRANCOPHONIE.
H. GODIN, 208(FS):APR72-242
G.J. JOYAUX, 399(MLJ):FEB71-114
L. TERREAUX, 209(FM):OCT71-359
VICAIRE, P. - SEE PLATO
VICINUS, M., ED. SUFFER AND BE STILL.
617(TLS):6APR73-372

VICKERS, B. THE ARTISTRY OF SHAKE-
SPEARE'S PROSE.
J. ALTIERI, 599:SPRING70-159
M. GRIVELET, 189(EA):OCT-DEC70-440
VICKERS, B. CLASSICAL RHETORIC IN ENG-
LISH POETRY.*
K. COCHRANE, 541(RES):MAY71-241
D. NEWTON-DE MOLINA, 184(EIC):JUL71-
288
C.N. SMITH, 111:13NOV70-67
R.A. SWANSON, 149:MAR72-107
H. WEINBROT, 173(ECS):WINTER71/72-340
VICKERS, B., ED. THE WORLD OF JONATHAN
SWIFT.*
I. SIMON, 556(RLV):1971/6-774
W.B. WARDE, JR., 577(SHR):SUMMER71-
298
VICKERY, W.N. ALEXANDER PUSHKIN.*
C. BRYNER, 550(RUSR):JAN71-80
"GIAMBATTISTA VICO NEL TERZO CENTENARIO
DELLA NASCITA."
F.S., 275(IQ):SPRING-SUMMER72-119
"VICTORIAN SHOPPING."
617(TLS):26JAN73-102
VIDAL, G. BURR.
G. DANGERFIELD, 441:28OCT73-2
M. KEMPTON, 453:15NOV73-6
C. LEHMANN-HAUPT, 441:25OCT73-51
E. WEEKS, 61:DEC73-134
442(NY):26NOV73-198
VIDAL, G. HOMAGE TO DANIEL SHAYS.*
S. SPENDER, 453:22MAR73-6
VIDAL JOVÉ, J.F. - SEE MATORELL, J. & M.
JOAN DE GALBA
VIDERMAN, S. LA CONSTRUCTION DE L'ESPACE
ANALYTIQUE.
F. DE GRUSON, 98:DEC71-1085
VIDMAN, L. SYLLOGE INSCRIPTIONUM RELIG-
IONIS ISIACAE ET SARAPIACAE.*
T.T. TINH, 487:SPRING71-80
VIDOR, K. ON FILM MAKING.
617(TLS):7SEP73-1020
VIDOS, B.E. HANDBUCH DER ROMANISCHEN
SPRACHWISSENSCHAFT.
H. BERSCHIN, 430(NS):AUG71-447
A. LOMBARD, 597(SN):VOL42#1-269
VIDYARTHI, L.P., ED. LEADERSHIP IN INDIA.
L. HOWARD, 293(JAST):NOV70-248
VIEBROCK, H., ED. DISRAELIS REDE IM
KRISTALLPALAST AM 24. JUNI 1872.
W. FRANKE, 38:BAND89HEFT3-403
VIEILLEFOND, J-R. - SEE JULIUS AFRICANUS
VIER, J. GIDE.
P. MOREAU, 557(RSH):JUL-SEP71-490
VIERL, P. DER STUCK.
H. HUTH, 54:MAR71-123
VIETH, D.M. - SEE WILMOT, J.
VIGÉE, C. LA LUNE D'HIVER.
F. GALAND, 207(FR):APR71-973
VIGNAU-SCHUURMAN, T.A.G.W. - SEE UNDER
WILBERG VIGNAU-SCHUURMAN, T.A.G.
VIGNE, R. A DWELLING PLACE OF OUR OWN.
617(TLS):30NOV73-1485
VIGOR, P.H. BOOKS ON COMMUNISM AND THE
COMMUNIST COUNTRIES.
M. WALLER, 575(SEER):OCT72-632
VIK, B. GRÅT ELSKEDE MANN.
S. LANGE-NIELSON, 270:VOL21#2-150
VILAR, E. THE MANIPULATED MAN.*
P. ADAMS, 61:FEB73-103
M. ELLMANN, 453:1NOV73-18
442(NY):20JAN73-103
VILJAMAA, T. NOUNS MEANING "RIVER" IN
CURTIUS RUFUS.
A. ERNOUT, 555:VOL45FASC1-178
VILJOEN, H.G. - SEE RUSKIN, J.

VILKUNA, K. FINNISCHES BRAUCHTUM IM
JAHRESLAUF.
R. VIRTANEN, 582(SFQ):DEC71-361
VILLA, G-P. - SEE VON SACHER-MASOCH, L.
VILLAIN-GANDOSSI, C. COMPTES DU SEL
(LIBRO DI RAGIONE E CONTO DI SALLE) DE
FRANCESCO DI MARCO DATINI POUR SA COM-
PAGNIE D'AVIGNON, 1376-1379.
R. DE ROOVER, 589:JAN72-149
VILLANUEVA, B.M. EL CONCEPTO DE "MIME-
SIS" EN PLATON.
P. LOUIS, 555:VOL45FASC1-152
VILLARROEL, D.D. - SEE UNDER DE TORRES
VILLARROEL, D.
VILLAS, J. GÉRARD DE NERVAL.*
W.T. BANDY, 535(RHL):MAY-JUN70-528
A. DU BRUCK, 546(RR):FEB71-66
VILLEGAS, F.G.D. - SEE UNDER DE QUEVEDO Y
VILLEGAS, F.G.
DE VILLEHARDOUIN, G. LE CONQUÊTE DE CON-
STANTINOPLE. (J. DUFOURNET, ED)
M.R. MORGAN, 208(FS):JAN72-60
VILLIERS, C. L'UNIVERS MÉTAPHYSIQUE DE
VICTOR HUGO.
J.C. MC LAREN, 188(ECR):SPRING71-95
DE VILLIERS, M. DIE GRAMMATIKA VAN TYD
EN MODALITEIT.
W.G. MOULTON, 350:DEC72-952
DE VILLIERS DE L'ISLE-ADAM, P.A.M. CON-
TES CRUELS, NOUVEAUX CONTES CRUELS.
(P-G. CASTEX, ED)
J-M. BELLEFROID, 535(RHL):MAY-JUN71-
524
VILLON, F. THE LEGACY, THE TESTAMENT,
AND OTHER POEMS. (P. DALE, TRANS)
617(TLS):5OCT73-1154
VILLON, F. OEUVRES. (A. LANLY, ED &
TRANS)
J. DUFOURNET, 535(RHL):MAR-APR71-293
VINAVER, E. MALORY.
J.M. COWEN, 447(N&Q):AUG71-310
VINAVER, E. A LA RECHERCHE D'UNE POÉT-
IQUE MÉDIÉVALE.
F. WHITEHEAD, 208(FS):JAN72-54
VINAVER, E. THE RISE OF ROMANCE.
D. MEHL, 72:BAND209HEFT1/3-136
C.E. PICKFORD, 208(FS):OCT72-439
VINAVER, E. - SEE MALORY, T.
VINCENT, H.P. THE TAILORING OF MELVILLE'S
"WHITE-JACKET."*
H. PARKER, 401(MLQ):MAR72-54
VINCENT, J.C. THE EXTRATERRITORIAL SYS-
TEM IN CHINA.
F.R. GLADECK, 293(JAST):NOV70-182
VINCENT, S. WHITE LIGHTS & WHALE HEARTS.
F.D. REEVE, 491:MAR73-348
DE VINCENZ, A. TRAITÉ D'ANTHROPONYMIE
HOUTZOULE.*
V.O. BUYNIAK, 32:MAR72-237
J.B. RUDNYĆKYJ, 424:DEC71-285
DA VINCI, L. - SEE UNDER LEONARDO DA
VINCI
VINCITORIO, G.L., ED. CRISIS IN THE
"GREAT REPUBLIC."
A.J. LOOMIE, 613:SUMMER71-308
VINCKE, J., WITH E. SCHRAMM & J. VIVES,
EDS. GESAMMELTE AUFSÄTZE ZUR KULTUR-
GESCHICHTE SPANIENS. (VOL 25)
A.L. MACKENZIE, 86(BHS):APR72-175
VINGE, L. THE NARCISSUS THEME IN WESTERN
EUROPEAN LITERATURE UP TO THE EARLY
19TH CENTURY.*
J. BARTHELS, 556(RLV):1970/5-553
LE VINIER, G. - SEE UNDER GUILLAUME LE
VINIER
VINNAI, G. FOOTBALL MANIA.
617(TLS):11MAY73-529

VINOGRADOV, V.V. THE HISTORY OF THE RUS-
SIAN LITERARY LANGUAGE FROM THE SEVEN-
TEENTH CENTURY TO THE NINETEENTH.*
(L.L. THOMAS, ED & TRANS)
    O. FRINK, 215(GL):VOL11#2-130
VINOKUR, G.O. THE RUSSIAN LANGUAGE.
(J. FORSYTH, ED)
    R. AUTY, 575(SEER):OCT72-606
    R. SUSSEX, 67:MAY72-118
"LA VIOLENCE DANS LE MONDE ACTUEL."
    A. VACHET, 154:DEC70-458
VIPPER, G. LA FORMATION DU CLASSICISME
DANS LA POÉSIE FRANÇAISE DU DÉBUT DU
XVIIe SIÈCLE.
    FR. DE LABRIOLLE, 535(RHL):MAR-APR70-
308
VIRGIL - SEE UNDER VERGIL
"THE VISCONTI HOURS."* (M. MEISS & E.W.
KIRSCH, EDS)
    617(TLS):2FEB73-128
VISCOTT, D.S. DORCHESTER BOY.
    G. BURNSIDE, 441:18NOV73-46
VISCOTT, D.S. THE MAKING OF A PSYCHIA-
TRIST.*
    J.S. GORDON, 441:28JAN73-2
VISHNEWSKI, S. - SEE DAY, D.
VISHNIAK, M. GODY EMIGRATSII, 1919-1969.*
    N.P. POLTORATZKY, 550(RUSR):APR71-200
"VISION AND AFTERMATH." (J.M. RITCHIE &
J.D. STOWELL, TRANS)
    G.P. BUTLER, 220(GL&L):OCT71-44
VISSCHER, C.J. LONDON BEFORE THE FIRE.
    617(TLS):7SEP73-1016
VISSER, F.T. AN HISTORICAL SYNTAX OF THE
ENGLISH LANGUAGE. (PT 2)
    E. STANDOP, 38:BAND88HEFT1-104
VISSER, F.T. AN HISTORICAL SYNTAX OF THE
ENGLISH LANGUAGE.* (PT 3, FIRST HALF)
    N. DAVIS, 541(RES):FEB71-64
    T. KISBYE, 597(SN):VOL43#1-329
VITA-FINZI, C. THE MEDITERRANEAN VAL-
LEYS.
    W.G. EAST, 303:VOL91-188
VITALE, P. LA RIFORMA DEGLI ISTITUTI DI
EMISSIONE E GLI "SCANDALI BANCARI" IN
ITALIA, 1892-1896.
    617(TLS):21DEC73-1569
VITALIS, O. - SEE UNDER ORDERIC VITALIS
VITIELLO, V. STORIOGRAFIA E STORIA NEL
PENSIERO DI BENEDETTO CROCE.
    G. OLDRINI, 548(RCSF):APR-JUN70-215
VITIER, C., ED. LA CRÍTICA LITERARIA Y
ESTÉTICA EN EL SIGLO XIX CUBANO.
    J. JOSET, 556(RLV):1971/5-658
VITOUX, F. LOUIS-FERDINAND CÉLINE.
    617(TLS):13JUL73-816
VITRUVIUS. VITRUVE: DE L'ARCHITECTURE.*
(BK 9) (J. SOUBIRAN, ED & TRANS)
    J. RUSSELL, 487:AUTUMN71-295
VIVANTE, P. THE HOMERIC IMAGINATION.
    A. AMORY, 122:APR72-136
    J.B. HAINSWORTH, 123:DEC72-318
VIVAS, E. CONTRA MARCUSE.*
    42(AR):SUMMER71-288
VIVIAN, F. THINKING PHILOSOPHICALLY.
    R.E.C., 154:JUN70-131
VIZZARD, J. SEE NO EVIL.
    C. NORTH, 200:JAN71-29
VLACHOS, T.N. DIE GESCHICHTE DER BYZAN-
TINISCHEN STADT MELENIKON.
    G. CANKOVA-PETKOVA, 303:VOL91-212
VLAD BORRELLI, L. - SEE UNDER "CORPUS
VASORUM ANTIQUORUM" (ITALIA, FASC 41)
VLADIMIROV, S.V., D.I. ZOLOTNITSKY & G.A.
LAPKINA, EDS. OCHERKI ISTORII RUSSKOI
SOVETSKOI DRAMATURGII. (VOLS 1-3)
    E.H. LEHRMAN, 32:MAR72-200

VLASTO, A.P. THE ENTRY OF THE SLAVS INTO
CHRISTENDOM.*
    O. ODLOZILIK, 589:OCT72-816
VLASTOS, G., ED. THE PHILOSOPHY OF
SOCRATES.
    D.Z. ANDRIOPOULOS, 484(PPR):JUN72-582
VLIEGHE, H. SAINTS. (VOL 1)
    617(TLS):19JAN73-68
VO DUC HANH, E. LA PLACE DU CATHOLICISME
DANS LES RELATIONS ENTRE LA FRANCE ET
LE VIET-NAM, 1851-1870.
    A. WOODSIDE, 293(JAST):FEB71-505
VODANOVIC, S. DEJA QUE LOS PERROS LAD-
REN - NOS TOMAMOS LA UNIVERSIDAD.
    H. CASTILLO, 238:MAY71-401
VOEGT, H. - SEE KNIGGE, A.F.
DE VOGEL, C.J. PHILOSOPHIA. (PT 1:
STUDIES IN GREEK PHILOSOPHY.)
    R. HATHAWAY, 124:OCT71-65
    R.K. SPRAGUE, 122:OCT72-298
VOGEL, L. THE COLUMN OF ANTONINUS PIUS.
    617(TLS):5OCT73-1561
VOGEL, M. APOLLINISCH UND DIONYSISCH.
    M. KAEMPFERT, 680(ZDP):BAND90HEFT4-
629
VOGEL, V.J. AMERICAN INDIAN MEDICINE.
    B. TOELKEN, 650(WF):OCT70-268
VOGLER, T.A. PRELUDES TO VISION.
    P. GRANT, 376:OCT71-128
    T. MC FARLAND, 676(YR):WINTER72-279
    B. WILKIE, 301(JEGP):APR72-255
VOGLER, T.A., ED. TWENTIETH-CENTURY
INTERPRETATIONS OF "TO THE LIGHTHOUSE."
    C. OHMANN, 659:SPRING73-260
VOGT, A.M. ART OF THE NINETEENTH CEN-
TURY.
    617(TLS):5OCT73-1195
VOGT, A.M. BOULLÉE'S NEWTON DENKMAL.*
    J. GAUS, 683:BAND34HEFT2-158
    H. ROSENAU, 46:MAY70-388
VOGT, J. KULTURWELT UND BARBAREN ZUM
MENSCHHEITSBILD DER SPÄTANTIKEN GESELL-
SCHAFT.
    W. LIEBESCHUETZ, 313:VOL61-281
VOGT, J. STRUKTUR UND KONTINUUM.
    H.A. SMITH, 221(GQ):NOV71-560
VOGT, M., ED. DIE ENTSTEHUNG DES YOUNG-
PLANS.*
    A. WAHL, 182:VOL24#7/8-375
VOJVODIC, M. & D. ŽIVOJINOVIĆ, EDS. VEL-
IKI RAT SRBIJE, 1914-1918.
    J.C. ADAMS, 32:JUN72-492
VÖLGYES, I., ED. HUNGARY IN REVOLUTION,
1918-19.
    F.L. CARSTEN, 575(SEER):APR72-308
VOLIN, L. A CENTURY OF RUSSIAN AGRICUL-
TURE.*
    R.D. LAIRD, 550(RUSR):JUL71-297
    R.F. MILLER, 32:MAR72-184
VOLINE. LA RÉVOLUTION INCONNUE, 1917-
1921.
    J.M. THOMPSON, 32:MAR72-165
VÖLKEL, P. HORNJOSERBSKO-NĚMSKI SŁOWNIK.
    G. STONE, 575(SEER):OCT72-603
VÖLKER, K., ED. BRECHT-CHRONIK.
    617(TLS):23NOV73-1413
VOLKMANN, H. GIOVANNI BAPTISTA PIRANESI.
    P. MOISY, 182:VOL24#21/22-800
VOLKMANN, H-E. DIE DEUTSCHE BALTIKUM-
POLITIK ZWISCHEN BREST-LITOVSK UND
COMPIEGNE.
    J.W. HIDEN, 575(SEER):JAN72-134
VOLLRATH, E. DIE THESE DER METAPHYSIK.
    T. BODAMMER, 53(AGP):BAND53HEFT2-187
DE VOLTAIRE, F.M.A. CANDIDE, OU L'OPTIM-
ISME.* (C. THACKER, ED)
    J. SAREIL, 546(RR):APR71-146

DE VOLTAIRE, F.M.A. THE COMPLETE WORKS
OF VOLTAIRE. (VOL 2) (O.R. TAYLOR, ED)
C. TODD, 402(MLR):OCT72-896
DE VOLTAIRE, F.M.A. THE COMPLETE WORKS
OF VOLTAIRE. (VOL 7) (J. VERCRUYSSE,
ED)
C. TODD, 402(MLR):OCT72-897
DE VOLTAIRE, F.M.A. THE COMPLETE WORKS
OF VOLTAIRE.* (VOL 59) (J.H. BRUMFITT,
ED)
H. BROWN, 207(FR):OCT70-240
C. TODD, 402(MLR):OCT72-899
DE VOLTAIRE, F.M.A. THE COMPLETE WORKS
OF VOLTAIRE.* (VOLS 81 & 82) (T. BES-
TERMAN, ED)
C. TODD, 402(MLR):OCT72-900
DE VOLTAIRE, F.M.A. THE COMPLETE WORKS
OF VOLTAIRE.* (VOLS 85-87) (T. BESTER-
MAN, ED)
G. MAILHOS, 535(RHL):MAY-JUN70-515
C. TODD, 402(MLR):OCT72-901
DE VOLTAIRE, F.M.A. THE COMPLETE WORKS
OF VOLTAIRE.* (VOLS 88-98) (T. BESTER-
MAN, ED)
C. TODD, 402(MLR):OCT72-901
DE VOLTAIRE, F.M.A. HISTOIRE DE CHARLES
XII. (G. MAILHOS, ED)
W.H. BARBER, 208(FS):OCT72-456
DE VOLTAIRE, F.M.A. VOLTAIRE ON SHAKE-
SPEARE. (T. BESTERMAN, ED)
G. MAILHOS, 535(RHL):MAY-JUN70-514
DE VOLTAIRE, F.M.A. VOLTAIRE'S HOUSEHOLD
ACCOUNTS 1760-1778. (T. BESTERMAN, ED)
W.H. BARBER, 208(FS):OCT72-457
O.R. TAYLOR, 402(MLR):JAN72-186
VON HEHN, J., H. VON RIMSCHA & H. WEISS,
EDS. VON DEN BALTISCHEN PROVINZEN ZU
DEN BALTISCHEN STAATEN.
J.W. HIDEN, 575(SEER):OCT72-617
VONNEGUT, K., JR. BETWEEN TIME AND
TIMBUKTU.
M. WOOD, 453:31MAY73-23
VONNEGUT, K., JR. BREAKFAST OF CHAMPIONS.
V. CUNNINGHAM, 362:26JUL73-125
C. LEHMANN-HAUPT, 441:2MAY73-47
N. SAYRE, 441:13MAY73-3
G. STADE, 231:MAY73-86
R. TODD, 61:MAY73-105
M. WOOD, 453:31MAY73-23
442(NY):12MAY73-146
617(TLS):20JUL73-825
VONNEGUT, K., JR. HAPPY BIRTHDAY, WANDA
JUNE.
617(TLS):20JUL73-825
VAN DER VOORT, P.J. THE PEN AND THE
QUARTER-DECK.
617(TLS):20JUL73-841
VORDTRIEDE, W., WITH G. BARTENSCHLAGER -
SEE "CLEMENS BRENTANO"
VORTRIEDE, W. & U. SCHWEIKERT. HEINE-
KOMMENTAR.*
J.L.S., 191(ELN):SEP71(SUPP)-138
H.S. SCHULTZ, 221(GQ):NOV71-586
DE VOS, H. KANT ALS THEOLOOG.
K. OEDINGEN, 342:BAND62HEFT3-404
VOSS, E. STUDIEN ZUR INSTRUMENTATION
RICHARD WAGNERS.
G.A., 410(M&L):JAN72-77
VOSS, J. & P.L. WARD, EDS. CONFRONTATION
AND LEARNED SOCIETIES.
A.H. MARCKWARDT, 350:MAR72-243
VOSSKAMP, W. UNTERSUCHUNGEN ZUR ZEIT-
UND GESCHICHTSAUFFASSUNG IM 17. JAHR-
HUNDERT BEI GRYPHIUS UND LOHENSTEIN.
V. MEID, 224(GRM):BAND21HEFT1-108
E.A. PHILIPPSON, 222(GR):MAR71-146
VOSSKAMP, W. - SEE SCHNABEL, J.G.

VOSTELL, W. & D. HIGGINS. FANTASTIC
ARCHITECTURE.
505:OCT71-166
VOVELLE, G. & M. VISION DE LA MORT ET DE
L'AU-DELÀ EN PROVENCE D'APRÈS LES AUTELS
DES ÂMES DU PURGATOIRE, XVE-XXE SIÈCLES.
R. DARNTON, 453:5APR73-25
VRABIE, G. FOLCLORUL.
B. GUNDA, 203:AUTUMN71-250
VRANICH, S.B. - SEE DE ARGUIJO, J.
VREEDE-DE STUERS, C. PARDA.
D. JACOBSON, 293(JAST):NOV70-213
DE VRIES, F.C. - SEE "FLORIS AND BLAUNCHE-
FLUR"
DE VRIES, J. KLEINE SCHRIFTEN. (K.
HEEROMA & A. KYLSTRA, EDS)
O. BANDLE, 680(ZDP):BAND89HEFT1-149
DE VRIES, L., WITH I. VAN AMSTEL, COMPS.
HISTORY AS HOT NEWS 1865-1897.
617(TLS):7SEP73-1019
VROMAN, A.C. DWELLERS AT THE SOURCE.
S. SCHWARTZ, 441:2DEC73-94
VUCINICH, A. SCIENCE IN RUSSIAN CULTURE,
1861-1917.*
N.V. RIASANOVSKY, 32:MAR72-159
W.B. WALSH, 550(RUSR):JUL71-296
VUILLEMIN, J. LEÇONS SUR LA PREMIÈRE
PHILOSOPHIE DE RUSSELL.
Y. GAUTHIER, 154:JUN71-391
VUILLEMIN, J. LA LOGIQUE ET LE MONDE
SENSIBLE.
Y. GAUTHIER, 154:DEC71-821
VŮLCHEV, V. IVAN VAZOV.
C.A. MOSER, 32:SEP72-729
VYGOTSKIJ, L.S. PSICHOLOGIJA ISKUSSTVA.
H. SCHMID, 490:JUL/OCT70-611


DE WAARD, C. - SEE MERSENNE, M.
WACHSMANN, K., ED. ESSAYS ON MUSIC AND
HISTORY IN AFRICA.
D.W. AMES, 187:MAY73-351
WÄCHTLER, K. DAS STUDIUM DER ENGLISCHEN
SPRACHE.
D. GÖTZ, 38:BAND88HEFT4-519
WÄCHTLER, K. - SEE GLEASON, H.A., JR.
WACKENHEIM, G. COMMUNICATION ET DEVENIR
PERSONNEL.
Y. BRÈS, 542:JAN-MAR71-122
WADDINGTON, C.H. BEHIND APPEARANCE.*
J. BENTHALL, 592:MAR70-133
D. IRWIN, 39:NOV70-396
WADDINGTON, C.H., ED. TOWARDS A THEOR-
ETICAL BIOLOGY. (VOL 4)
617(TLS):18MAY73-551
WADDINGTON, M. DRIVING HOME.
K. MULHALLEN, 99:MAR73-48
WADDINGTON, M. A.M. KLEIN.*
D.G. SPETTIGUE, 102(CANL):SUMMER72-
107
WADDINGTON, P. - SEE TURGENEV, I.S.
WADE, I.O. THE INTELLECTUAL DEVELOPMENT
OF VOLTAIRE.*
A.D. HYTIER, 399(MLJ):OCT71-416
A.J. KNODEL, 173(ECS):SUMMER71-471
J.S. SPINK, 546(RR):DEC71-297
R.S. TATE, JR., 207(FR):OCT70-242
WADE, I.O. THE INTELLECTUAL ORIGINS OF
THE FRENCH ENLIGHTENMENT.*
C.B. BRUSH, 319:JUL73-407
WADE, M. PETER ABRAHAMS.
617(TLS):27JUL73-876
WADEKAR, A. MY CRICKETING YEARS.
617(TLS):9FEB73-161
WÄDEKIN, K-E. FÜHRUNGSKRÄFTE IM SOWJET-
ISCHEN DORF.
S.P. DUNN, 32:MAR72-177

WÄDEKIN, K-E. THE PRIVATE SECTOR IN
SOVIET AGRICULTURE.
617(TLS):16NOV73-1406
WAGENER, H. DIE KOMPOSITION DER ROMANE
CHRISTIAN FRIEDRICH HUNOLDS.
J.K. SOWDEN, 220(GL&L):JAN72-148
WAGENHEIM, K., WITH O. JIMÉNEZ DE WAGEN-
HEIM, EDS. THE PUERTO RICANS.
J.M. GARCIA-PASSALACQUA, 441:7OCT73-
24
WAGENKNECHT, C.J. - SEE JOCHMANN, C.G.
WAGENKNECHT, E. AMBASSADORS FOR CHRIST.
617(TLS):16MAR73-299
WAGENKNECHT, E. WILLIAM DEAN HOWELLS.*
S.J. HASELTON, 613:AUTUMN70-448
R. LEHAN, 445(NCF):SEP70-248
WAGENKNECHT, E. JAMES RUSSELL LOWELL.*
P. CARTER, 579(SAQ):SUMMER72-441
A. TURNER, 191(ELN):JUN72-314
D. YANNELLA, 432(NEQ):SEP71-512
WAGENLEHNER, G. STAAT ODER KOMMUNISMUS.
(2ND ED)
A.G. MEYER, 32:JUN72-437
WAGNER, G. ON THE WISDOM OF WORDS.
A. RODWAY, 447(N&Q):JUL71-269
WAGNER, H. STUDIES IN THE ORIGINS OF THE
CELTS AND OF EARLY CELTIC CIVILISATION.
B.K. MARTIN, 67:NOV72-217
WAGNER, J. BLACK POETS OF THE UNITED
STATES.
B. BECKHAM, 441:1APR73-32
WAGNER, J. - SEE LÖWENSTEIN, K.
WAGNER, K.H. GENERATIVE GRAMMATICAL
STUDIES IN THE OLD ENGLISH LANGUAGE.
D. KASTOVSKY, 38:BAND89HEFT4-482
WAGNER, L.W. THE PROSE OF WILLIAM CARLOS
WILLIAMS.*
B. DUFFEY, 659:SUMMER73-406
P. MARIANI, 418(MR):AUTUMN72-670
WAGNER, M. MOLIÈRE AND THE AGE OF EN-
LIGHTENMENT.
617(TLS):21SEP73-1090
WAGNER, R.L. LA GRAMMAIRE FRANÇAISE.
M. ARRIVÉ, 209(FM):JAN70-69
WAGNER, R.L. LES VOCABULAIRES FRANÇAIS.
A. REY, 98:FEB70-163
WAGNER, W.J., ED. POLISH LAW THROUGHOUT
THE AGES.*
K. GRZYBOWSKI, 497(POLR):SUMMER71-104
WAGNER-RIEGER, R. DIE WIENER RINGSTRASSE
- DAS KUNSTWERKE IM BILD.
J. MAASS, 576:OCT70-281
WAGONER, D. RIVERBED.*
B. HERINGMAN, 398:WINTER73-331
J.R. REED, 491:SEP73-47
WAGONER, D. WHERE IS MY WANDERING BOY
TONIGHT?
639(VQR):WINTER71-IX
WAGONER, D. - SEE ROETHKE, T.
WAHRIG, G. NEUE WEGE IN DER WÖRTERBUCH-
ARBEIT.
F. DE TOLLENAERE, 433:APR70-195
WAIN, J. A HOUSE FOR THE TRUTH.
J. CAREY, 362:15FEB73-218
H. LEIBOWITZ, 441:29JUL73-6
WAIN, J. HURRY ON DOWN. (ABRIDGED & ED
BY R. MARTIN)
J.C. FIELD, 556(RLV):1971/3-361
WAIN, J. A WINTER IN THE HILLS.*
S. MONOD, 189(EA):OCT-DEC70-454
WAINGROW, M. - SEE BOSWELL, J.
WAINWRIGHT, A. MOVING OUTWARD.*
P. STEVENS, 529(QQ):SUMMER71-326
WAINWRIGHT, J. HIGH-CLASS KILL.
617(TLS):17AUG73-959
WAINWRIGHT, J. THE IMPORTANT MAN.
A. CLUYSENAAR, 565:VOL12#2-63

WAINWRIGHT, J. A PRIDE OF PIGS.
617(TLS):23FEB73-219
WAISMANN, F. HOW I SEE PHILOSOPHY. (R.
HARRÉ, ED)
G.J. WARNOCK, 482(PHR):APR71-274
WAIT, R.J.C. THE BACKGROUND TO SHAKE-
SPEARE'S SONNETS.
617(TLS):30MAR73-346
WAITE, P.B. CANADA 1874-1896.
G.W., 102(CANL):AUTUMN72-116
WAKEFIELD, D. STARTING OVER.
C. LEHMANN-HAUPT, 441:5JUL73-33
M. MEWSHAW, 441:29JUL73-12
WAKEFIELD, W.L. & A.P. EVANS, EDS &
TRANS. HERESIES OF THE HIGH MIDDLE
AGES.*
A.W. GODFREY, 363:MAY71-78
R.L. JONES, 325:APR71-254
WAKELIN, M.F. ENGLISH DIALECTS.
617(TLS):19JAN73-73
WAKEMAN, G. VICTORIAN BOOK ILLUSTRATION.
617(TLS):24AUG73-986
WAKOSKI, D. INSIDE THE BLOOD FACTORY.*
GREED. (PTS 1&2) THE DIAMOND MER-
CHANT.
P. HANNIGAN, 600:FALL69-141
WAKOSKI, D. THE MOTORCYCLE BETRAYAL
POEMS.*
W.H. PRITCHARD, 249(HUDR):SPRING72-124
WAKOSKI, D. ON BARBARA'S SHORE.
639(VQR):SUMMER71-CVIII
WAKOSKI, D. SMUDGING.*
V. YOUNG, 249(HUDR):WINTER72/73-667
WALBANK, F.W. THE AWFUL REVOLUTION.*
A. CHASTAGNOL, 555:VOL45FASC1-186
WALBANK, F.W. POLYBIUS.
617(TLS):13JUL73-812
WALCKER-MAYER, W. DIE RÖMISCHE ORGEL VON
AQUINCUM.*
E.K. BORTHWICK, 123:DEC72-364
WALCOTT, D. ANOTHER LIFE.
G. LAMMING, 441:6MAY73-36
617(TLS):3AUG73-894
WALDECK, P.B. DIE KINDHEITSPROBLEMATIK
BEI HERMANN BROCH.*
J.J. WHITE, 220(GL&L):OCT71-84
WALDHEIM, K. THE AUSTRIAN EXAMPLE.
617(TLS):24AUG73-981
WALDMAN, D. ROY LICHTENSTEIN.
C. NEMSER, 58:FEB72-20
"MYRA WALDO'S TRAVEL GUIDE TO SOUTH
AMERICA."
S.S. BENSON, 37:OCT71-43
WALDRIP, L. & S.A. BAUER. A BIBLIOGRAPHY
OF THE WORKS OF KATHERINE ANNE PORTER
AND A BIBLIOGRAPHY OF THE CRITICISM OF
THE WORKS OF KATHERINE ANNE PORTER.
C. ALLEN, 50(ARQ):SPRING70-95
WALDSCHMIDT, E. & R.L. NEPAL.
M. LEESE, 293(JAST):MAY71-721
WALICKI, A. FILOZOFIA A MESJANIZM.
W. WEINTRAUB, 32:JUN72-468
WALKER, A. LISZT.*
412:FEB72-69
WALKER, A., ED. FRANZ LISZT: THE MAN AND
HIS MUSIC.*
412:FEB72-69
WALKER, A. REVOLUTIONARY PETUNIAS AND
OTHER POEMS.
D. KENWORTHY, 31(ASCH):SUMMER73-514
WALKER, A., ED. ROBERT SCHUMANN.
C. ROSEN, 453:1NOV73-12
617(TLS):27APR73-476
WALKER, A. THE THIRD LIFE OF GRANGE
COPELAND.*
J.L. HALIO, 598(SOR):SPRING73-455

WALKER, B. SECOND TREASURY OF KNITTING
PATTERNS.
M.W. PHILLIPS, 139:APR71-8
WALKER, C. THOMAS BRASSEY, RAILWAY
BUILDER.
E.A. BATTISON, 637(VS):SEP70-112
WALKER, C.R. - SEE PUTNAM, H.P.
WALKER, D. - SEE LINDSAY, I.G.
WALKER, D.P. THE ANCIENT THEOLOGY.
F. YATES, 453:40CT73-19
617(TLS):2MAR73-243
WALKER, E.C. WILLIAM DELL: MASTER PURI-
TAN.
568(SCN):FALL-WINTER72-69
WALKER, H. - SEE MOLIÈRE, J.B.P.
WALKER, J. DISASTERS.
617(TLS):8JUN73-653
WALKER, K. MY PEOPLE.
S.E. LEE, 581:1971/3-227
WALKER, N. & S. MC CABE. CRIME AND
INSANITY IN ENGLAND. (VOL 2)
617(TLS):14DEC73-1535
WALKER, P.D. ÉMILE ZOLA.*
A. BOURGEOIS, 207(FR):DEC70-448
WALKER, T. GLOVES TO THE HANGMAN.
A. MACLEAN, 362:250CT73-565
617(TLS):8JUN73-646
WALKER, T. THE NIGHT BATHERS.
A. CLUYSENAAR, 565:VOL11#4-74
WALKER MORRIS, J. PRINCIPLES AND PRAC-
TICE OF JOB EVALUATION.
617(TLS):8JUN73-653
WALL, A., ED. MINDSCAPES.
D.G. JONES, 102(CANL):SUMMER72-81
WALL, J.F. ANDREW CARNEGIE.
H.J. SIEVERS, 613:WINTER71-632
639(VQR):WINTER71-XXX
WALL, S., ED. CHARLES DICKENS.
I. RANTAVAARA, 155:MAY71-109
WALL, S. - SEE TROLLOPE, A.
WALLA, M. DER VOGEL PHOENIX IN DER AN-
TIKEN LITERATUR UND DER DICHTUNG DES
LAKTANZ.
A. HUDSON-WILLIAMS, 123:MAR72-122
WALLACE, A.F.C., WITH S.C. STEEN. THE
DEATH AND REBIRTH OF THE SENECA.
W.R. JACOBS, 656(WMQ):JAN71-161
WALLACE, E.M. A BIBLIOGRAPHY OF WILLIAM
CARLOS WILLIAMS.
B.C. BLOOMFIELD, 354:MAR70-79
WALLACE, G.F. THE GUNS OF THE ROYAL AIR
FORCE, 1939-1945.
617(TLS):9FEB73-161
WALLACE, H.A. THE PRICE OF VISION. (J.M.
BLUM, ED)
C. PHILLIPS, 441:140CT73-40
WALLACE, I. DEATHSTAR VOYAGE.
617(TLS):2FEB73-129
WALLACE, K.R. FRANCIS BACON ON THE
NATURE OF MAN.
P. CRISTOFOLINI, 548(RCSF):JAN-MAR71-
97
WALLER, M. THE LANGUAGE OF COMMUNISM.
617(TLS):19JAN73-63
WALLERSTEIN, I. & P. STARR, EDS. THE
UNIVERSITY CRISIS READER.
D.J. LEAB, 432(NEQ):SEP71-489
WALLIA, C.S., ED. TOWARD CENTURY 21.
L. REYNOLDS, 321:SPRING71-151
WALLIS, J.H. PERSONAL COUNSELLING.
617(TLS):22JUN73-728
WALLMAN, S. TAKE OUT HUNGER.
A. KUPER, 69:JUL71-261
WALLNER, B., ED. A MIDDLE ENGLISH VERSION
OF THE INTRODUCTION TO GUY DE CHAULIAC'S
"CHIRURGIA MAGNA."
S.M. KUHN, 589:JUL72-544
WALLNER, B. - SEE DE CHAULIAC, G.

WALLOP, D. HOWARD'S BAG.
M. LEVIN, 441:25MAR73-48
WALLRAFF, G. NEUE REPORTAGEN, UNTER-
SUCHUNGEN UND LEHRBEISPIELE.
617(TLS):20JUL73-836
WALLRAFF, G. & J. HAGEN. WAS WOLLT IHR
DENN, IHR LEBT JA NOCH.
617(TLS):20JUL73-836
WALLWORK, E. DURKHEIM.
P. ROSENBERG, 441:15JUL73-21
617(TLS):6JUL73-770
WALLWORK, J.F. LANGUAGE AND LINGUISTICS.*
D. CRYSTAL, 297(JL):SEP70-307
WALNE, P. A CATALOGUE OF MANUSCRIPT
MAPS IN THE HERTFORDSHIRE RECORD OFFICE.
R.A. SKELTON, 325:APR71-247
WALPOLE, H. SELECTED LETTERS OF HORACE
WALPOLE. (W.S. LEWIS, ED)
617(TLS):14DEC73-1537
WALPOLE, H., J. CAZOTTE & W. BECKFORD.
FANTASTIČESKIE POVESTI. (V. ŽIRMUNSKIJ
& N. SIGAL, EDS)
J-L. BACKÈS, 549(RLC):APR-JUN71-273
WALSER, M. DER STURZ.
617(TLS):50CT73-1156
WALSER, R. BASTA. (H.G. HELMS, ED)
H.L. KAUFMAN, 221(GQ):MAR71-256
WALSER, R. JAKOB VON GUNTEN.*
H.M. WAIDSON, 220(GL&L):OCT71-42
J.J. WHITE, 402(MLR):JUL72-708
WALSH, C. GOD AT LARGE.
639(VQR):SPRING71-LXXXI
WALSH, D. LITERATURE AND KNOWLEDGE.*
V.C. ALDRICH, 482(PHR):APR71-265
WALSH, D. & OTHERS. VOICES UNDERGROUND.
P. O'FLAHERTY, 99:SEP73-42
WALSH, J. STRANGE HARP, STRANGE SYM-
PHONY.*
P. DANCHIN, 189(EA):JAN-MAR70-93
WALSH, P.G. THE ROMAN NOVEL.*
P.A. GEORGE, 313:VOL61-300
A. HEISERMAN, 122:OCT72-312
J.P. SULLIVAN, 487:SUMMER71-191
WALSH, S. THE LIEDER OF SCHUMANN.
E. SAMS, 415:JAN72-44
WALSH, T.J. OPERA IN DUBLIN 1705-1797.
617(TLS):28SEP73-1139
WALSH, W. COLERIDGE.
W. ARENS, 38:BAND89HEFT2-268
WALSH, W. COMMONWEALTH LITERATURE.
617(TLS):27JUL73-876
WALSH, W. A MANIFOLD VOICE.*
K.L. GOODWIN, 71(ALS):OCT73-218
R. LAWRENCE, 175:SPRING71-28
581:MAR72-77
WALSH, W.H. HEGELIAN ETHICS.
D.R. BELL, 479(PHQ):JAN71-88
WALSH, W.S. A HANDY BOOK OF CURIOUS
INFORMATION.
R. BURNS, 582(SFQ):DEC70-368
WALTER, H. FRÜHE SAMISCHE GEFÄSSE.
J.N. COLDSTREAM, 303:VOL91-202
WALTER, J-C. LE SISMOGRAPHE APPLIQUÉ.
R. VERNIER, 207(FR):OCT70-188
WALTERS, R.S. AMERICAN AND SOVIET AID.
J. HORVATH, 321:SEP72-695
WALTHER, E. & L. HARIG, EDS. MUSTER
MÖGLICHER WELTEN. EINE ANTHOLOGIE FÜR
MAX BENSE.
617(TLS):120CT73-1255
WALTMAN, F.M. CONCORDANCE TO "POEMA DE
MIO CID."
617(TLS):17AUG73-960
WALTON, P. & A. GAMBLE. FROM ALIENATION
TO SURPLUS VALUE.
617(TLS):9FEB73-142

WALTON, P. & S. HALL, EDS. SITUATING
  MARX.
  617(TLS):9FEB73-142
WALVIN, J. BLACK AND WHITE.
  617(TLS):11MAY73-524
WALZER, M. POLITICAL ACTION.
  639(VQR):SUMMER71-CXXXI
WALZER, P-O. - SEE COMTE DE LAUTRÉAMONT
WAMBAUGH, J. THE BLUE KNIGHT.*
  617(TLS):16MAR73-303
WAMBAUGH, J. THE ONION FIELD.
  J. CONAWAY, 441:2SEP73-5
  C. LEHMANN-HAUPT, 441:7SEP73-39
  E. WEEKS, 61:OCT73-129
"THE WANDERER." (R.F. LESLIE, ED) "THE
  WANDERER."* (T.P. DUNNING & A.J. BLISS,
  EDS)
  J. TORRINGA, 179(ES):FEB71-55
WANDOR, M., ED. THE BODY POLITIC.
  617(TLS):11MAY73-524
WANDRUSZKA, M., SPRACHEN - VERGLEICHBAR
  UND UNVERGLEICHLICH.
  H.H. CHRISTMANN, 343:BAND13HEFT2-212
  U.L. FIGGE, 490:JAN71-120
  J. JUHÁSZ, 657(WW):NOV/DEC70-421
  E. KÖNIG, 297(JL):OCT71-268
  H. RHEINFELDER, 430(NS):MAY70-250
WANG, H-H. HSIEN-T'UNG YUN-NAN HUI-MIN
  SHIH-PIEN (THE MOHAMMEDAN UPRISING IN
  YUNNAN 1856-1873).
  C-Y. CHEN, 293(JAST):NOV70-177
WANG, S-N. T'ANG-TAI FAN-CHEN YU CHUNG-
  YANG KUAN-HSI CHIH YEN-CHIU.
  R.J. KROMPART, 293(JAST):MAY71-659
WANG, W.S-Y. & A. LYOVIN. CLIBOC: CHI-
  NESE LINGUISTICS BIBLIOGRAPHY ON COM-
  PUTER.
  L. HAFT, 399(MLJ):MAY71-329
  205(FMLS):OCT71-414
WANGERMANN, E. THE AUSTRIAN ACHIEVEMENT
  1700-1800.
  617(TLS):14SEP73-1048
WANMALI, S. REGIONAL PLANNING FOR SOCIAL
  FACILITIES.
  J.E. BRUSH, 293(JAST):MAY71-703
WANTLING, W. SICK FLY.
  W.G. SHEPHERD, 493:SUMMER71-204
WARBURG, F. ALL AUTHORS ARE EQUAL.
  G. ANNAN, 362:22NOV73-715
  617(TLS):23NOV73-1449
WARD, A. OUR HUMAN CONSTITUTION. JEN-
  NY'S FIRST-CLASS JOURNEY.
  J. FREEMAN, 97(CQ):SPRING71-292
WARD, A.G., ED. THE QUEST FOR THESEUS.
  J. BOARDMAN, 90:OCT71-613
  J.M. COOK, 123:JUN72-288
  A.J. PODLECKI, 124:FEB72-206
WARD, B. & R. DUBOS. ONLY ONE EARTH.*
  617(TLS):30MAR73-359
WARD, C., ED. VANDALISM.
  617(TLS):26OCT73-1298
WARD, D. T.S. ELIOT BETWEEN TWO WORLDS.
  617(TLS):26OCT73-1308
WARD, D. JONATHAN SWIFT.
  617(TLS):23NOV73-1416
WARD, H.M. UNITE OR DIE.
  R.F. CAMPBELL, 432(NEQ):DEC71-683
WARD, J.A. THE SEARCH FOR FORM.*
  D. KRAMER, 573(SSF):SUMMER71-495
WARD, J.O. - SEE SCHOLES, P.A.
WARD, J.T. CHARTISM.
  617(TLS):28DEC73-1580
WARD, K. ETHICS AND CHRISTIANITY.
  A. MONTEFIORE, 479(PHQ):JAN71-90
WARD, M. ROBERT BROWNING AND HIS WORLD.*
  (VOL 1)
  M.B. CRAMER, 405(MP):FEB71-294

WARD, M. ROBERT BROWNING AND HIS WORLD.*
  (VOL 2)
  I. ARMSTRONG, 637(VS):DEC70-208
  M.B. CRAMER, 405(MP):FEB71-294
WARD, M. THE TRAGI-COMEDY OF PEN BROWN-
  ING (1849-1912).
  442(NY):13JAN73-92
  617(TLS):11MAY73-530
WARD, P. SPANISH LITERARY APPRECIATION.*
  205(FMLS):JAN71-100
WARD, R. - SEE LA MESLÉE, E.M.
WARD, W.R. - SEE BUNTING, J.
WARD, W.S., COMP. A BIBLIOGRAPHY OF
  LITERARY REVIEWS IN BRITISH PERIODI-
  CALS, 1798-1820.
  617(TLS):30MAR73-358
WARD, W.S., COMP. LITERARY REVIEWS IN
  BRITISH PERIODICALS 1798-1820.
  617(TLS):9FEB73-160
WARDEN, G.B. BOSTON, 1689-1776.*
  R.D. BROWN, 656(WMQ):APR71-334
WARDLE, R.M. HAZLITT.*
  J.H. ADAMSON, 651(WHR):AUTUMN72-384
  L. STEVENSON, 579(SAQ):SPRING72-268
  676(YR):SPRING72-VIII
WARDLE, R.M. - SEE GODWIN, W. & M. WOLL-
  STONECRAFT
WARDROPER, J. KINGS, LORDS AND WICKED
  LIBELLERS.
  617(TLS):19OCT73-1266
WARDROPPER, B.W., ED. TEATRO ESPAÑOL DEL
  SIGLO DE ORO.*
  A.L. MACKENZIE, 86(BHS):JAN72-73
WARE, C. THE INNOCENTS.
  B. CAPPS, 649(WAL):SUMMER70-161
WARES, A.C. A COMPARATIVE STUDY OF YUMAN
  CONSONANTISM.
  H.W. LAW, 353:NOV71-113
WARK, R.R. ISAAC CRUICKSHANK'S DRAWINGS
  FOR DROLLS.
  J. HAYES, 39:NOV71-421
WARK, R.R. EARLY BRITISH DRAWINGS IN THE
  HUNTINGTON COLLECTION, 1600-1750.*
  J. HAYES, 39:NOV71-421
  E. WATERHOUSE, 54:DEC71-538
WARMINGTON, B.H. NERO: REALITY AND
  LEGEND.*
  M. SWAN, 24:OCT72-626
WARNANT, L. DICTIONNAIRE DE LA PRONONCI-
  ATION FRANÇAISE.* (3RD ED) (J. DUCULOT,
  ED)
  A. BOILEAU, 556(RLV):1971/4-503
  L. BONDY, 209(FM):APR71-174
WARNER, F. LYING FIGURES. MAQUETTES.
  617(TLS):30MAR73-354
WARNER, M. THE DRAGON EMPRESS.
  617(TLS):5JAN73-16
WARNER, O. CHATTO AND WINDUS.
  617(TLS):5OCT73-1193
WARNER, P. BRITISH BATTLEFIELDS: THE
  MIDLANDS.
  617(TLS):23NOV73-1456
WARNER, P. THE MEDIEVAL CASTLE.*
  N. DOWNS, 589:OCT72-743
WARNICKE, R.M. WILLIAM LAMBARDE.
  617(TLS):23NOV73-1451
WARNKE, F.J. VERSIONS OF BAROQUE.
  R.L. COLIE, 676(YR):SUMMER72-591
WARNOCK, M. EXISTENTIALISM.
  F. ARMENGAUD, 53(AGP):BAND53HEFT3-321
  A. MANSER, 483:JUL71-270
  P.J.W. MILLER, 399(MLJ):OCT71-403
  F.A. OLAFSON, 479(PHQ):APR71-178
WARNOCK, R.G., ED. DIE PREDIGTEN JOHAN-
  NES PAULIS.*
  F.G. BANTA, 301(JEGP):APR72-297
  G.F. JONES, 406:SPRING72-83

WARR, B. ACKNOWLEDGMENT TO LIFE.* (L.
GASPARINI, ED)
F. COGSWELL, 529(QQ):SUMMER71-325
WARR, P. PSYCHOLOGY AND COLLECTIVE
BARGAINING.
617(TLS):2NOV73-1340
WARRACK, J. TCHAIKOVSKY.
617(TLS):30NOV73-1480
WARREN, A. CONNECTIONS.*
L. LEARY, 432(NEQ):MAR71-159
WARREN, J. & E. GERRY. A STUDY IN DIS-
SENT. (C.H. GARDINER, ED)
G.B. SKILLIN, 14:OCT70-413
WARREN, K. THE BRITISH IRON AND STEEL
SHEET INDUSTRY SINCE 1840.
A. BIRCH, 637(VS):JUN71-464
WARREN, K. MINERAL RESOURCES.
617(TLS):18MAY73-565
WARREN, R.P. MEET ME IN THE GREEN GLEN.*
M. COOKE, 676(YR):SUMMER72-599
42(AR):WINTER71/72-589
WARREN, R.P. JOHN GREENLEAF WHITTIER'S
POETRY.
S. FERGUSON, 569(SR):SUMMER72-493
L. LEARY, 579(SAQ):SPRING72-273
W. STAFFORD, 191(ELN):JUN72-312
WARREN, W.L. HENRY II.
617(TLS):21SEP73-1069
WARREN, W.P. - SEE SELLARS, R.W.
WARWICK, A.R. THE PHOENIX SUBURB.
617(TLS):9MAR73-277
WASHINGTON, B.T. THE BOOKER T. WASHING-
TON PAPERS. (L.R. HARLAN, ED)
J. ANDERSON, 453:9AUG73-34
J.H. BRACEY, JR., 441:4MAR73-34
E.K. WELSCH, 70(ANQ):FEB73-94
617(TLS):13APR73-414
WASILEWSKA, E. THE SILVER MADONNA.
J. WALKIN, 32:DEC72-902
WASIOLEK, E. - SEE DOSTOEVSKY, F.M.
WASKOW, A.I. THE BUSH IS BURNING.
S. KATZ, 390:DEC71-72
WASOWOSKI, S., ED. EAST-WEST TRADE AND
THE TECHNOLOGY GAP.
P.B. MAGGS, 550(RUSR):JAN71-89
WASSERMAN, E.R. SHELLEY.
K.N. CAMERON, 401(MLQ):DEC72-463
WASSERMAN, J.L., WITH J.M. LUKACH & A.
BEALE. DAUMIER SCULPTURE.
S.L. FAISON, JR., 54:JUN70-220
WASSING, R.S. AFRICAN ART.
F. WILLETT, 54:JUN71-277
WASSNER, S.O., ED & TRANS. TREASURY OF
RUSSIAN SHORT STORIES 1900-1966.
V.D. MIHAILOVICH, 573(SSF):FALL71-650
WASSON, R.G. SOMA.*
M. SULLIVAN, 318(JAOS):APR-JUN71-346
WÄSTBERG, P. THE AIR CAGE.*
V. CUNNINGHAM, 362:8FEB73-189
617(TLS):16FEB73-169
WATERBURY, J. NORTH FOR THE TRADE.
617(TLS):15JUN73-696
WATERER, J.W. LEATHER CRAFTSMANSHIP.*
E.T.J., 135:JUN70-133
WATERFIELD, G. PROFESSIONAL DIPLOMAT.
617(TLS):30NOV73-1472
WATERHOUSE, E. REYNOLDS.
617(TLS):14DEC73-1528
WATERMAN, J.T. A HISTORY OF THE GERMAN
LANGUAGE.*
W. BONDZIO, 682(ZPSK):BAND23HEFT2/3-
291
WATERMEIER, D.J. - SEE BOOTH, E. & W.
WINTER
WATERS, F. PIKE'S PEAK.
T.J. LYON, 649(WAL):SPRING71-62

WATERS, I. FOLKLORE AND DIALECT OF THE
LOWER WYE VALLEY.
617(TLS):31AUG73-1009
WATERS, M.L. & E.A. LITTLE, EDS. LA
PORTE OUVERTE.
D. NOAKES, 207(FR):DEC70-431
WATERS, T.A. THE LOST VICTIM.
N. CALLENDAR, 441:16DEC73-18
WATERS, W. BURNE-JONES.
617(TLS):31AUG73-1009
WATKIN, D. THOMAS HOPE, 1769-1831, AND
THE NEO-CLASSICAL IDEA.*
S. MILLIKIN, 576:MAY70-199
D. WIEBENSON, 56:SUMMER71-243
WATKIN, D.J., ED. SALE CATALOGUES OF
LIBRARIES OF EMINENT PERSONS. (VOL 4:
ARCHITECTS.)
617(TLS):19OCT73-1288
WATKINS, C. INDOGERMANISCHE GRAMMATIK.
(VOL 3, PT 1) (J. KURYŁOWICZ, ED)
F. BADER, 555:VOL45FASC2-304
J.W. POULTNEY, 24:APR72-343
W.F. WYATT, JR., 350:SEP72-687
WATKINS, F.C. THE FLESH AND THE WORD.
M.E. BRADFORD, 579(SAQ):SPRING72-277
S. DONALDSON, 27(AL):MAR72-171
H.F. GARLICK, 67:NOV72-233
WATKINS, J.W.N. HOBBES'S SYSTEM OF
IDEAS.
617(TLS):12OCT73-1250
WATKINS, L.W. MIDDLETON, MASSACHUSETTS.
W.M. WHITEHILL, 432(NEQ):SEP71-519
WATKINS, V. FIDELITIES.
F. LEFRANC, 189(EA):JUL-SEP70-349
WATKINSON, R. PRE-RAPHAELITE ART AND
DESIGN.
D.J. GORDON, 592:NOV70-218
R. LEBOWITZ, 58:NOV70-16
WATMOUGH, D. ASHES FOR EASTER AND OTHER
MONODRAMAS.
R.F. HASSAN, 296:FALL73-100
WATSON, A. JUAN DE LA CUEVA AND THE
PORTUGUESE SUCCESSION.
617(TLS):11MAY73-532
WATSON, A. THE LAW OF PROPERTY IN THE
LATER ROMAN REPUBLIC.*
H.D. EVJEN, 121(CJ):APR-MAY72-379
WATSON, A. THE LAW OF SUCCESSION IN THE
LATER ROMAN REPUBLIC.
F.C. BOURNE, 124:FEB72-206
S.I. OOST, 122:OCT72-296
WATSON, A.G. THE MANUSCRIPTS OF HENRY
SAVILE OF BANKE.*
P.D.A. HARVEY, 325:APR71-243
L. ROSTENBERG, 551(RENQ):AUTUMN71-394
WATSON, B. CHINESE LYRICISM.
639(VQR):AUTUMN71-CLXXIII
WATSON, C.P. & A.C. REYNELL - SEE OVID
WATSON, F.J.B. & C.C. DAUTERMAN. THE
WRIGHTSMAN COLLECTION. (VOLS 3&4)
G. DE BELLAIGUE, 39:DEC71-516
WATSON, G. THE ENGLISH IDEOLOGY.
J. VINCENT, 362:22MAR73-384
617(TLS):16MAR73-288
WATSON, G. THE ENGLISH PETRARCHANS.*
L. FORSTER, 179(ES):JUN71-265
F. MOURET, 549(RLC):JAN-MAR70-130
WATSON, G. GOODWIFE HOT AND OTHERS.
E.C. SMITH, 424:SEP71-214
WATSON, G., ED. LITERARY ENGLISH SINCE
SHAKESPEARE.
A. BRUTEN, 447(N&Q):AUG71-310
R.D. EAGLESON, 67:NOV72-276
R. FOWLER, 184(EIC):OCT71-398
566:AUTUMN71-28

WATSON, G., ED. THE NEW CAMBRIDGE BIBLI-
OGRAPHY OF ENGLISH LITERATURE. (VOL 2)
    J.M.P., 568(SCN):SPRING72-18
    D.T. TORCHIANA, 566:AUTUMN71-25
WATSON, G., ED. THE NEW CAMBRIDGE BIBLI-
OGRAPHY OF ENGLISH LITERATURE.* (VOL
3)
    D. CHAMBERS, 503:SUMMER70-95
    H.J. HEANEY, 445(NCF):DEC70-370
    W.G. LANE, 594:FALL70-380
WATSON, G. THE STUDY OF LITERATURE.*
    G. BOAS, 322(JHI):JAN-MAR70-148
    L.T. LEMON, 502(PRS):FALL70-263
    S.F. RENDALL, 131(CL):SUMMER72-260
WATSON, I. THE EMBEDDING.
    617(TLS):9NOV73-1378
WATSON, J.R. PICTURESQUE LANDSCAPE AND
ENGLISH ROMANTIC POETRY.
    J.D. JUMP, 148:SPRING71-87
    H. PESCHMANN, 175:SUMMER71-57
WATSON, L. SUPERNATURE.
    617(TLS):26OCT73-1318
WATSON, P. FASANELLA'S CITY.
    L. NOCHLIN, 441:2DEC73-44
WATSON, P., ED. PSYCHOLOGY AND RACE.
    617(TLS):6APR73-372
WATSON, R. CHRISTMAS IN LAS VEGAS.
    W.H. PRITCHARD, 249(HUDR):SPRING72-123
    F.D. REEVE, 491:MAR73-348
WATSON-WILLIAMS, H. ANDRÉ GIDE AND THE
GREEK MYTH.
    E.U. BERTALOT, 207(FR):OCT70-222
    D. MOUTOTE, 535(RHL):MAR-APR70-336
WATT, A. AUSTRALIAN DIPLOMAT.
    617(TLS):29JUN73-754
WATT, D.C., J. MAYALL & C. NAVARI, EDS.
DOCUMENTS ON INTERNATIONAL AFFAIRS,
1963.
    617(TLS):3AUG73-897
WATT, I., ED. CONRAD: "THE SECRET AGENT."
    617(TLS):15JUN73-664
WATT, I., ED. THE VICTORIAN NOVEL.
    K.T. VON ROSADOR, 72:BAND209HEFT4/6-
    413
WATT, J.A. THE CHURCH AND THE TWO
NATIONS IN MEDIEVAL IRELAND.
    F. BARLOW, 382(MAE):1972/2-176
WATTERS, P. DOWN TO NOW.*
    N. LEDERER, 584(SWR):SUMMER72-260
WATTERS, P. & S. GILLERS, EDS. INVESTI-
GATING THE FBI.
    M. ROGIN, 441:17JUN73-24
WATTERS, R.E., COMP. A CHECKLIST OF CAN-
ADIAN LITERATURE AND BACKGROUND MATERI-
ALS 1628-1960. (2ND ED)
    J.R. SORFLEET, 296:SPRING73-94
WATTS, A. IN MY OWN WAY.*
    617(TLS):8JUN73-630
WATTS, A.C. THE LYRE AND THE HARP.*
    F.M. COMBELLACK, 122:JAN72-69
    A. CRÉPIN, 189(EA):JUL-SEP70-274
    D.A.H. EVANS, 597(SN):VOL42#2-486
    H.L. ROGERS, 541(RES):NOV71-465
WATTS, A.J., ED. WARSHIPS AND NAVIES
1973.
    617(TLS):23FEB73-212
WATTS, A.J. - SEE RUGE, F.
WATTS, C.A.H. DEPRESSION.
    617(TLS):23NOV73-1456
WATTS, C.T. - SEE CONRAD, J.
WATTS, D.G. THE LEARNING OF HISTORY.
    617(TLS):20APR73-454
WATTS, E.R., ED. NEW HOPE FOR RURAL
AFRICA.
    W. ALLAN, 69:JAN71-78

WATTS, E.S. ERNEST HEMINGWAY AND THE
ARTS.
    J.E. CHAMBERLIN, 249(HUDR):WINTER
    72/73-698
    V.H. WINNER, 27(AL):MAY72-335
WATTS, M.T. THE COUNTRYSIDE AROUND YOU.
    617(TLS):20JUL73-842
WAUGH, A. BANGKOK.
    639(VQR):AUTUMN71-CLXXXVI
WAUGH, A. THE FATAL GIFT.
    S. HILL, 362:19JUL73-92
    M. LEVIN, 441:5AUG73-12
    E. WEEKS, 61:AUG73-102
WAUTHIER, C. THE LITERATURE AND THOUGHT
OF MODERN AFRICA.
    R.C. CLARK, 544:FALL71-246
LORD WAVELL. WAVELL: THE VICEROY'S
JOURNAL. (P. MOON, ED)
    R. CROSSMAN, 362:12JUL73-59
    617(TLS):13JUL73-795
WAYMAN, T. WAITING FOR WAYMAN.
    A.B. CAMERON, 99:AUG73-33
    J. SHERMAN, 198:FALL73-103
WAYNE, J. BROWN BREAD AND BUTTER IN THE
BASEMENT.
    617(TLS):10AUG73-920
WEAIT, C. BASSOON REED-MAKING.
    W. WATERHOUSE, 415:AUG72-776
WEALES, G. CLIFFORD ODETS, PLAYWRIGHT.
    T.F. MARSHALL, 27(AL):NOV72-514
    J.R. TAYLOR, 157:AUTUMN71-76
WEATHERBY, H.L. CARDINAL NEWMAN IN HIS
AGE.
    617(TLS):18MAY73-565
WEATHERHEAD, A.K. THE EDGE OF THE
IMAGE.*
    M.M., 502(PRS):FALL70-276
WEATHERS, W. THE LONESOME GAME.
    J.H. MATTHEWS, 219(GAR):WINTER71-519
WEAVER, H. & P. BERGERON - SEE POLK, J.K.
WEAVER, J.T., COMP. FORTY YEARS OF
SCREEN CREDITS.
    200:OCT70-500
WEAVER, K.D. LENIN'S GRANDCHILDREN.
    W.L. MATHES, 32:JUN72-449
    639(VQR):AUTUMN71-CLXXXVIII
WEAVER, M. WILLIAM CARLOS WILLIAMS.*
    K.L. GOODWIN, 67:NOV72-235
    P. MARIANI, 418(MR):AUTUMN72-672
    S. PAUL, 301(JEGP):OCT72-555
WEAVER, R., ED. CANADIAN SHORT STORIES.
    M. PAGE, 573(SSF):SPRING71-337
WEAVER, R. & W. TOYE, EDS. THE OXFORD
ANTHOLOGY OF CANADIAN LITERATURE.
    W.J. KEITH, 99:AUG73-31
WEBB, B. THE BRITISH INTERNAL-COMBUSTION
LOCOMOTIVE: 1894-1940.
    617(TLS):21DEC73-1574
WEBB, E. SAMUEL BECKETT.*
    D. HAYMAN, 454:WINTER72-183
WEBB, E. THE PLAYS OF SAMUEL BECKETT.
    617(TLS):12OCT73-1217
WEBB, P. THE SNOWBOYS.
    M. LEVIN, 441:4NOV73-81
WEBB, L. STRIBLING.
    M. LEVIN, 441:19AUG73-10
WEBB, P. SELECTED POEMS 1954-1965.*
    P. STEVENS, 102(CANL):SPRING72-82
WEBBER, J. THE ELOQUENT "I".*
    J.M. MUELLER, 405(MP):AUG70-109
WEBER, A. & J.M. BÄCHTOLD. ZÜRICHDEUT-
SCHES WÖRTERBUCH FÜR SCHULE UND HAUS.
(2ND ED)
    S. SONDEREGGER, 657(WW):SEP/OCT70-351
WEBER, D. DEUTSCHE LITERATUR SEIT 1945
IN EINZELDARSTELLUNGEN. (2ND ED)
    M.J. GONZÁLEZ, 202(FMOD):NOV71/FEB72-
    143
    C. SOMMER, 564:OCT70-238

WEBER, E. JOHN GOWER: DICHTER EINER
ETHISCH-POLITISCHEN REFORMATION.*
JOHN GOWER: ZUR LITERARISCHEN FORM
SEINER DICHTUNG.*
P.F. THEINER, 179(ES):JUN71-261
WEBER, E. A MODERN HISTORY OF EUROPE.
617(TLS):3AUG73-895
WEBER, G. & A. ROSENAUER, EDS. KUNST-
HISTORISCHE FORSCHUNGEN.
617(TLS):15JUN73-699
WEBER, H. DIE ZÜRCHERISCHEN LANDGEMEIN-
DEN IN DER HELVETIK 1798-1803.
R. HAUSWIRTH, 182:VOL24#19/20-761
WEBER, J-P. STENDHAL.
J. BOREL, 98:JUL70-604
K.A. READER, 402(MLR):JUL72-640
K. RINGGER, 224(GRM):BAND21HEFT3-361
F.W. SAUNDERS, 208(FS):APR72-210
WEBER, R. STEPHEN'S GREEN REVISITED.
H. SERGEANT, 175:SUMMER71-65
WEBER, R.W. DIE AUSSAGE DER FORM.*
H. HEUERMANN, 430(NS):NOV71-612
WEBER, S.A. THEOLOGY AND POETRY IN THE
MIDDLE ENGLISH LYRIC.*
R.T. DAVIES, 541(RES):AUG71-324
H. MUSURILLO, 613:SPRING70-129
R. WOOLF, 405(MP):MAY71-376
WEBSTER, H.C. AFTER THE TRAUMA.
J.O. BAILEY, 177(ELT):VOL13#4-305
WEBSTER, J. THE WHITE DEVIL. (J.R. MUL-
RYNE, ED)
F. LAGARDE, 189(EA):JUL-SEP71-325
"JOHN WEBSTER." (G.K. & S.K. HUNTER,
EDS)
L. DESVIGNES, 549(RLC):JAN-MAR71-108
A.L. FRENCH, 97(CQ):AUTUMN70-195
WEBSTER, M. FRANCIS WHEATLEY.
M.E., 135:OCT70-138
R. EDWARDS, 39:JAN71-69
W. PRESSLY, 54:SEP71-420
J. SUNDERLAND, 90:FEB71-102
WEBSTER, T.B.L. ATHENIAN CULTURE AND
SOCIETY.
617(TLS):22JUN73-710
WEBSTER, T.B.L. THE GREEK CHORUS.*
J. DIGGLE, 123:JUN72-230
WEBSTER, T.B.L. GREEK THEATRE PRODUCTION.
(2ND ED)
H. LLOYD-JONES, 123:JUN72-280
WEBSTER, T.B.L. AN INTRODUCTION TO
SOPHOCLES.* (2ND ED)
R. WEIL, 555:VOL45FASC2-335
WEBSTER, T.B.L. MONUMENTS ILLUSTRATING
OLD AND MIDDLE COMEDY. (2ND ED)
B.A. SPARKES, 303:VOL91-210
WEBSTER, T.B.L. POTTER AND PATRON IN
CLASSICAL ATHENS.
617(TLS):8JUN73-650
WEBSTER, T.B.L. - SEE SOPHOCLES
"WEBSTER'S DICTIONARY OF PROPER NAMES."
(G. PAYTON, COMP)
C.M. ROTHRAUFF, 424:SEP71-216
WECHSBERG, J. THE GLORY OF THE VIOLIN.
D. SCHOENBAUM, 441:28JAN73-22
WECHSBERG, J. THE OPERA.*
441:13MAY73-40
WECHSBERG, J. THE WALTZ EMPERORS.
442(NY):31DEC73-59
617(TLS):7DEC73-1517
WEDEKIND, F. SPRING AWAKENING.
G.P. BUTLER, 220(GL&L):OCT71-44
WEDGWOOD, C.V. OLIVER CROMWELL.
617(TLS):20JUL73-823
WEEKS, A.L. THE OTHER SIDE OF COEXIS-
TENCE.*
R.D. WARTH, 550(RUSR):JAN71-87
WEEKS, D. CORVO.*
P. JULLIAN, 441:28JAN73-32

WEES, W.C. VORTICISM AND THE ENGLISH
AVANT-GARDE.
G. WOODCOCK, 102(CANL):AUTUMN72-97
WEESNER, T. THE CAR THIEF.*
617(TLS):6APR73-369
"WEGE ZUM NEUEN VERSTÄNDNIS THEODOR
STORMS."
F.R. SAMMERN-FRANKENEGG, 597(SN):
VOL42#2-531
WEGNER, G. KIRCHENJAHR UND MESSFEIER IN
DER WÜRZBURGER DOMLITURGIE DES SPÄTEN
MITTELALTERS.
R. PFAFF, 589:JAN72-151
WEGNER, M. EXIL UND LITERATUR.
W. BERTHOLD, 433:APR70-205
WEGNER, M. MUSIK UND TANZ.*
P. CHANTRAINE, 555:VOL45FASC1-145
WEHLEN, W. GESCHICHTSSCHREIBUNG UND
STAATSAUFFASSUNG IM ZEITALTER LUDWIGS
DES FROMMEN.
R. FOLZ, 182:VOL24#13/14-570
WEHRLI, F. DIE SCHULE DES ARISTOTELES.
(2ND ED) (PT 5)
P. CHANTRAINE, 555:VOL45FASC1-155
WEHRLI, F. DIE SCHULE DES ARISTOTELES.
(2ND ED) (PT 7)
P. CHANTRAINE, 555:VOL45FASC1-155
G.B. KERFERD, 123:MAR72-104
WEHRLI, F. DIE SCHULE DES ARISTOTELES.*
(2ND ED) (PT 8)
P. CHANTRAINE, 555:VOL45FASC1-156
WEHRLI, F. DIE SCHULE DES ARISTOTELES.
(2ND ED) (PTS 9&10)
P. CHANTRAINE, 555:VOL45FASC1-156
G.B. KERFERD, 123:MAR72-104
WEHRLI, M. FORMEN MITTELALTERLICHER
ERZÄHLUNG.*
V. GÜNTHER, 182:VOL24#11/12-486
WEIDENFELD, W. DIE ENGLANDPOLITIK GUSTAV
STRESEMANNS.
617(TLS):29JUN73-739
WEIDHORN, M. RICHARD LOVELACE.*
H.M. RICHMOND, 551(RENQ):SUMMER71-285
WEIGAND, H.J. FÄHRTEN UND FUNDE.
W. SCHRÖDER, 680(ZDP):BAND90HEFT4-620
WEIGEL, H. KARL KRAUS.
E.F. TIMMS, 402(MLR):APR72-473
WEIGHTMAN, J. THE CONCEPT OF THE AVANT-
GARDE.
F. KERMODE, 362:7JUN73-766
617(TLS):25MAY73-573
WEIGLE, M. THE PENITENTES OF THE SOUTH-
WEST.
R. AHLBORN, 292(JAF):OCT-DEC71-463
WEIGUM, W. - SEE VEIRAS, H.F.
WEIL, A. THE NATURAL MIND.*
W.D.M. PATON, 362:9AUG73-190
WEIL, G.L. THE LONG SHOT.
M. JANEWAY, 61:OCT73-124
C. LYDON, 441:14OCT73-2
G. WILLS, 453:4OCT73-3
442(NY):29OCT73-182
WEIL, R. - SEE ARISTOTLE
WEIL, S. FIRST AND LAST NOTEBOOKS.* (R.
REES, ED & TRANS)
J.P. LITTLE, 208(FS):JUL72-357
L. REINHARDT, 483:JUL71-274
WEIL, S. OPPRESSION AND LIBERTY.
R. COLES, 31(ASCH):AUTUMN73-692
WEILER, G. MAUTHNER'S CRITIQUE OF LAN-
GUAGE.
R.D. EAGLESON, 67:NOV72-267
A.R.L., 319:JUL73-435
WEIMANN, R. SHAKESPEARE UND DIE TRADI-
TION DES VOLKSTHEATERS.*
G. AHRENDS, 224(GRM):MAY70-226
J.W. THOMAS, 599:SPRING70-189

WEIMAR, K. VERSUCH ÜBER DIE VORAUSSET-
ZUNG UND ENTSTEHUNG DER ROMANTIK.*
A. ANGER, 406:FALL72-303
W. EMMERICH, 221(GQ):JAN71-105
WEIMAR, K.S. & W. HOFFMEISTER. PRACTICE
AND PROGRESS. (2ND ED)
L.E. BRISTER, 221(GQ):MAR71-262
WEIN, H. KENTAURISCHE PHILOSOPHIE.
D. MISGELD, 154:DEC70-473
WEIN, H. PHILOSOPHIE ALS ERFAHRUNGSWIS-
SENSCHAFT.
G.K., 154:MAR71-210
H. SCHNELLE, 206:AUG70-427
WEIN, H. SPRACHPHILOSOPHIE DER GEGEN-
WART.
H. SCHNELLE, 206:AUG70-427
WEINBERG, B., ED. TRATTATI DI POETICA
E RETORICA DEL CINQUECENTO. (VOL 1)
A. BONGIORNO, 551(RENQ):SUMMER71-234
WEINBERG, H.A. THE NEW NOVEL IN AMERICA.*
M. BEEBE, 191(ELN):DEC71-161
B. GROSS, 405(MP):NOV71-186
M.G. PORTER, 594:FALL71-332
WEINBERG, H.G., COMP. THE COMPLETE
"GREED."*
442(NY):7APR73-152
WEINBERG, J.R. IDEAS AND CONCEPTS.
J.W. YOLTON, 154:JUN71-349
WEINBERG, W. DIE RESTE DES JÜDISCHDEUT-
SCHEN.*
M. CALIEBE, 657(WW):MAR/APR71-137
J. EICHHOFF, 406:SPRING72-58
J. WEISSBERG, 680(ZDP):BAND90HEFT1-
152
WEINBROT, H.D. THE FORMAL STRAIN.*
W. KINSLEY, 223:DEC71-348
R. LAWRENCE, 175:SPRING70-33
R. PARKIN, 173(ECS):SUMMER71-492
WEINER, J. MANTILLAS IN MUSCOVY.
A.V. KNOWLES, 86(BHS):APR72-189
A. ZVIGUILSKY, 549(RLC):OCT-DEC70-565
WEINER, J.B. THE MORNING AFTER.
C. LEHMANN-HAUPT, 441:18JAN73-43
R. YATES, 441:28JAN73-6
WEINFIELD, H. CARNIVAL CANTATA.
F.D. REEVE, 491:MAR73-348
WEINGART, R.E. THE LOGIC OF DIVINE LOVE.
J. LECLERCQ, 382(MAE):1972/1-59
WEINGARTEN, R. ALICE DANS LES JARDINS
DU LUXEMBOURG.
B. KAY, 207(FR):APR71-974
WEINGARTEN, R. L'ETÉ; AKARA; LES NOUR-
RICES.
M. SAKHAROFF, 207(FR):DEC70-426
WEINRICH, H. LINGUISTIK DER LÜGE.
R.F. BERG, 206:AUG70-433
WEINRICH, H. PHONOLOGISCHE STUDIEN ZUR
ROMANISCHEN SPRACHGESCHICHTE.
R. POSNER, 297(JL):OCT71-306
WEINSTEIN, A. PRELUDE TO POPULISM.
639(VQR):WINTER71-XXXIX
WEINSTEIN, D. SAVONAROLA AND FLORENCE.
G. BRUCKER, 589:JUL72-573
D. HAY, 402(MLR):OCT72-922
A. MOLHO, 551(RENQ):WINTER71-522
A. NOVOTNY, 182:VOL24#3-117
639(VQR):SUMMER71-CXVII
WEINSTEIN, F. & G.M. PLATT. THE WISH TO
BE FREE.
G.D. ROSS, 173(ECS):WINTER71/72-328
WEINSTEIN, M.A. WILLIAM EDMONDSTOUNE
AYTOUN AND THE SPASMODIC CONTROVERSY.*
K. ALLOTT, 447(N&Q):MAR71-117
E. FRYKMAN, 597(SN):VOL42#2-477
WEINSTEIN, M.E. JAPAN'S POSTWAR DEFENSE
POLICY, 1947-1968.
F.W. IKLÉ, 293(JAST):AUG71-899

WEINSTEIN, P.M. HENRY JAMES AND THE
REQUIREMENTS OF THE IMAGINATION.*
G. CORE, 385(MQR):WINTER73-82
W.T. STAFFORD, 27(AL):MAR72-160
WEINSTOCK, H. VINCENZO BELLINI.*
W. DEAN, 415:AUG72-772
L.G.O., 410(M&L):OCT72-454
WEINSTOCK, H. DIE FUNKTION ELISABETHAN-
ISCHER SPRACHWÖRTER UND PSEUDOSPRICH-
WÖRTER BEI SHAKESPEARE.
G.H.V. BUNT, 179(ES):OCT71-456
R. FRICKER, 570(SQ):SPRING70-178
WEINSTOCK, H. MITTELENGLISCHES ELEMEN-
TARBUCH.
G. BAUER, 72:BAND209HEFT1/3-142
WEINTRAUB, S. JOURNEY TO HEARTBREAK.
(BRITISH TITLE: BERNARD SHAW 1914-1918.)
F.P.W. MC DOWELL, 295:FEB73-120
M.J. MENDELSOHN, 572:SEP71-137
617(TLS):3AUG73-901
WEINTRAUB, S. - SEE SHAW, G.B.
WEINZWEIG, H. PASSING CEREMONY.
K. MULHALLEN, 99:NOV-DEC73-31
WEIR, M. A TOE ON THE LADDER.
617(TLS):2NOV73-1352
WEIS, E. & E. - SEE "THE NEW SCHÖFFLER-
WEIS COMPACT GERMAN AND ENGLISH DIC-
TIONARY"
WEISBEIN, W. & A. VERBA - SEE BOYER, P. &
N. SPERANSKI
WEISBERG, D.B. GUILD STRUCTURE AND POL-
ITICAL ALLEGIANCE IN EARLY ACHAEMENID
MESOPOTAMIA.
J. RENGER, 318(JAOS):OCT-DEC71-494
WEISBERGER, A.M. LE LETTERATURE DEL
BELGIO.
R.O.J. VAN NUFFEL, 549(RLC):JAN-MAR70-
125
WEISENBECK, J.D. ALFRED NORTH WHITEHEAD'S
PHILOSOPHY OF VALUES.
T.P.A., 543:SEP70-143
WEISER-AALL, L. SVANGERSKAP OG FØDSEL I
NYERE NORSK TRADISJON.
E. ETTLINGER, 203:WINTER71-339
WEISGERBER, J. FAULKNER ET DOSTOÏEVSKI.*
J. DE LABRIOLLE, 549(RLC):OCT-DEC70-
576
H-J. LOPE, 52:BAND6HEFT2-229
M. MOLINARI, 557(RSH):OCT-DEC70-653
WEISGERBER, J.L. DIE NAMEN DER UBIER.*
G. ALFÖLDY, 630(ZDP):BAND90HEFT1-130
K.H. SCHMIDT, 260(IF):BAND74-205
WEISGERBER, J.L. DIE SPRACHGEMEINSCHAFT
ALS GEGENSTAND SPRACHWISSENSCHAFTLICHER
FORSCHUNG.
U. EGLI, 343:BAND13HEFT2-179
WEISS, A. HÉROÏNES DU THÉÂTRE DE HENRY
DE MONTHERLANT.*
A. BLANC, 535(RHL):JAN-FEB71-141
WEISS, F.G. HEGEL'S CRITIQUE OF ARIS-
TOTLE'S PHILOSOPHY OF MIND.
H.S. HARRIS, 154:SEP70-251
WEISS, G. & C. ANDERSON. BEGEGNUNG MIT
DEUTSCHLAND.
H-C. KAYSER, 221(GQ):NOV71-619
L.J. RIPPLEY, 399(MLJ):OCT71-420
WEISS, P. PHILOSOPHY IN PROCESS.* (VOL
3)
R. NEVILLE, 543:DEC70-276
WEISS, P. PHILOSOPHY IN PROCESS. (VOL 4)
J. COLLINS, 613:AUTUMN70-461
R. NEVILLE, 543:DEC70-276
WEISS, P. SPORT.
J.S. ULLIAN, 311(JP):24MAY73-299
WEISS, R. THE RENAISSANCE DISCOVERY OF
CLASSICAL ANTIQUITY.*
M. GREENHALGH, 46:JUN70-454

WEISS, T. THE BREATH OF CLOWNS AND
KINGS.
    J-B. FORT, 189(EA):OCT-DEC71-522
    D. RIGGS, 651(WHR):WINTER72-85
WEISS, T. THE WORLD BEFORE US.*
    L. LIEBERMAN, 676(YR):AUTUMN71-82
    639(VQR):SUMMER71-CV
WEISSENBERGER, K. DIE ELEGIE BEI PAUL
CELAN.*
    G.T. GILLESPIE, 402(MLR):JUL72-712
WEISSENBERGER, K. FORMEN DER ELEGIE: VON
GOETHE BIS CELAN.*
    R. FURNESS, 220(GL&L):JUL72-400
    T. ZIOLKOWSKI, 222(GR):JAN71-77
WEISSKOPF, T. IMMANUEL KANT UND DIE
PÄDAGOGIK.
    T. BALLAUFF, 342:BAND62HEFT4-505
    W. RITZEL, 182:VOL24#9/10-393
WEISSTEIN, U. EINFÜHRUNG IN DIE VER-
GLEICHENDE LITERATURWISSENSCHAFT.
    G.R. KAISER, 224(GRM):BAND21HEFT4-467
    J. LINK, 490:JAN/APR70-315
WEISSTEIN, U. MAX FRISCH.
    H.F. GARTEN, 220(GL&L):OCT71-53
    H.D. OSTERLE, 221(GQ):NOV71-598
WEIT, E. EYEWITNESS.
    C. SERPELL, 362:22FEB73-248
    617(TLS):25MAY73-576
WEITZMAN, A.J. - SEE MARANA, G.P.
WEITZMANN, K., COMP. CATALOGUE OF THE
BYZANTINE AND EARLY MEDIEVAL ANTIQUI-
TIES IN THE DUMBARTON OAKS COLLECTION.
(VOL 3)
    617(TLS):12OCT73-1245
WEITZMANN, K. STUDIES IN CLASSICAL AND
BYZANTINE MANUSCRIPT ILLUMINATION.*
(H.L. KESSLER, ED)
    D.A. BULLOUGH, 182:VOL24#19/20-706
    S.G. DAITZ, 124:OCT71-61
WEKWERTH, M. SCHRIFTEN.
    617(TLS):28DEC73-1591
WELCH, D. MAIDEN VOYAGE. THE DENTON
WELCH JOURNALS. (J. BROOKE, ED)
    617(TLS):28SEP73-1131
WELCH, H. THE BUDDHIST REVIVAL IN CHINA.
    L.R. LANCASTER, 244(HJAS):VOL31-336
WELCH, J. RIDING THE EARTHBOY 40.
    F.D. REEVE, 491:MAR73-348
WELCH, R.E., JR. GEORGE FRISBIE HOAR AND
THE HALF-BREED REPUBLICANS.
    J.W. HESS, 432(NEQ):SEP71-503
WELCH, S.C. A KING'S BOOK OF KINGS.
    617(TLS):4MAY73-508
WELCH, W. AMERICAN IMAGES OF SOVIET
FOREIGN POLICY.*
    E.B. TOMPKINS, 550(RUSR):JUL71-300
WELCOME, J. THE CHELTENHAM GOLD CUP.
    617(TLS):23MAR73-333
WELDON, F. DOWN AMONG THE WOMEN.
    R.A. WEYR, 441:11FEB73-26
WELKE, K. UNTERSUCHUNGEN ZUM SYSTEM DER
MODALVERBEN IN DER DEUTSCHEN SPRACHE
DER GEGENWART.
    H. ZIMMERMANN, 657(WW):NOV/DEC70-423
WELKER, R.L. & H. GOWER, EDS. THE SENSE
OF FICTION.
    J.W. STEVENSON, 573(SSF):SUMMER71-475
WELLARD, J. THE SEARCH FOR THE ETRUS-
CANS.
    617(TLS):28DEC73-1584
WELLEK, A. WITZ, LYRIK, SPRACHE.*
    S. PRAWER, 220(GL&L):JAN72-192
WELLEK, R. DISCRIMINATIONS.*
    J-L. BACKÈS, 549(RLC):JUL-SEP71-400
    L. LERNER, 541(RES):AUG71-385
    E.N. TIGERSTEDT, 597(SN):VOL43#2-599
    J. VOISINE, 149:SEP72-331

WELLES, C.B. ALEXANDER AND THE HELLEN-
ISTIC WORLD.*
    E. BADIAN, 487:SUMMER71-176
    E.N. BORZA, 122:OCT72-308
WELLESZ, E. ARNOLD SCHOENBERG.* (NEW
ED)
    R.T. BECK, 447(N&Q):DEC71-480
    A. PAYNE, 415:MAY72-461
WELLFORD, H. SOWING THE WIND.
    S. LAZARUS & L. ROSS, 453:28JUN73-31
    R. SHERRILL, 441:4MAR73-3
WELLMAN, C. CHALLENGE AND RESPONSE.
    E. TELFER, 518:MAY72-31
    A.J. WATT, 63:DEC72-288
WELLS, D. JANE.
    E. FEINSTEIN, 362:25OCT73-572
    617(TLS):26OCT73-1324
WELLS, G.A. THE PLAYS OF GRILLPARZER.*
    I.V. MORRIS, 220(GL&L):JAN72-168
WELLS, H.G. THE WEALTH OF MR. WADDY.
(H. WILSON, ED)
    W.J. SCHEICK, 177(ELT):VOL13#1-86
WELLS, R.V. THREE CHRISTIAN TRANSCENDEN-
TALISTS.
    H.W. SCHNEIDER, 319:OCT73-561
WELLS, S. LITERATURE AND DRAMA.
    J.R. BROWN, 157:SPRING71-67
    E. QUINN, 551(RENQ):WINTER71-571
    N. RABKIN, 402(MLR):APR72-400
WELLS, S. SHAKESPEARE: A READING GUIDE.
    R.A. FOAKES, 175:AUTUMN70-98
WELMERS, B.F. & W.E. IGBO: A LEARNER'S
DICTIONARY.*
    M.M. GREEN, 69:APR71-180
WELSCH, R.L. SOD WALLS.
    R.V. FRANCAVIGLIA, 650(WF):JAN71-63
WELSH, A. THE CITY OF DICKENS.*
    M. PRICE, 676(YR):WINTER72-271
    M. SLATER, 445(NCF):MAR72-492
    G.J. WORTH, 301(JEGP):OCT72-551
WELTY, E. LOSING BATTLES.*
    C.Y. RICH, 577(SHR):WINTER71-85
    C. WEST, 219(GAR):FALL71-375
    42(AR):SPRING70-131
WELTY, E. THE OPTIMIST'S DAUGHTER.*
    S. HILL, 362:22MAR73-390
    P.M. SPACKS, 249(HUDR):AUTUMN72-508
    617(TLS):30MAR73-341
WELZIG, W. DER DEUTSCHE ROMAN IM 20.
JAHRHUNDERT. (2ND ED)
    M.J. GONZÁLEZ, 202(FMOD):NOV71/FEB72-
145
WELZIG, W., ED. ERASMUS-STUDIENAUSGABE.
(VOLS 1, 3, 4, 5, 6)
    E. GUTMANN, 657(WW):SEP/OCT70-351
WENCK VON HERRENBERG, J. DAS BÜCHLEIN
VON DER SEELE. (G. STEER, ED)
    N.T.J. VOORWINDEN, 433:JUL70-314
WENDLER, U. EICHENDORFF UND DAS MUSIKAL-
ISCHE THEATER.
    D.W. SCHUMANN, 221(GQ):NOV71-566
WENDT, H.F. SPRACHEN.
    G.F. MEIER, 682(ZPSK):BAND24HEFT1/2-
154
WENGER, K. GOTTFRIED KELLERS AUSEINANDER-
SETZUNG MIT DEM CHRISTENTUM.
    G. BENDA, 406:SUMMER72-184
WENKE, H. - SEE SPRANGER, E.
WENSINGER, A.S. & W.B. COLEY - SEE LICHT-
ENBERG, G.C.
WENTZEL, K. FORTOLKNING OG SKAEBNE.
    A. JØRGENSEN, 172(EDDA):1971/5-309
WENZEL, G. THOMAS MANNS BRIEFWERK.
    H. MATTER, 654(WB):10/1970-216
WERBA, H. EIN JAHR IN DEUTSCHLAND.
    A.W. BEERBAUM, 399(MLJ):MAR71-197
    W. HAAS, 221(GQ):MAY71-428

WERBIK, H. INFORMATIONSGEHALT UND EMO-
TIONALE WIRKUNG VON MUSIK.
  E. SAMS, 415:SEP72-871
VAN DER WERF, H. THE CHANSONS OF THE
TROUBADOURS AND TROUVÈRES.
  617(TLS):9FEB73-156
WERNER, A. CHAGALL, WATERCOLORS AND
GOUACHES.
  J. GUTMANN, 287:JUL/AUG71-27
  L. HAESSLE, 58:NOV70-18
WERNER, A. DEGAS PASTELS.
  P. POOL, 39:APR70-324
WERNER, H-G. GESCHICHTE DES POLITISCHEN
GEDICHTS IN DEUTSCHLAND VON 1815 BIS
1840.
  W. FEUDEL, 654(WB):4/1971-216
WERNER, O. EINFÜHRUNG IN DIE STRUKTUR-
ELLE BESCHREIBUNG DES DEUTSCHEN. (PT 1)
  D.A. BECKER, 406:SPRING72-60
WERNER, R. HETHITISCHE GERICHTSPROTO-
KOLLE.
  G. NEUMANN, 260(IF):BAND75-296
WERNSDÖRFER, T. DIE ENTFREMDETE WELT.
  G. PHILIPS, 182:VOL24#6-278
WESCHER, H. COLLAGE.
  R. LEBOWITZ, 58:DEC71/JAN72-24
WESLING, D. WORDSWORTH AND THE ADEQUACY
OF LANDSCAPE.
  J. COLMER, 402(MLR):JAN72-173
  H. PESCHMANN, 175:SUMMER71-57
  J.R. WATSON, 541(RES):AUG71-354
WESSEL, K. BYZANTINE ENAMELS FROM THE
5TH TO THE 13TH CENTURY.*
  J. BECKWITH, 39:JAN70-84
WESSÉN, E. DIE NORDISCHEN SPRACHEN.
  K. DÜWEL, 260(IF):BAND74-306
  P. HALLEUX, 556(RLV):1970/3-332
  G. KÖTZ, 343:BAND13HEFT2-220
WEST, A. - SEE BERKOVITS, I.
WEST, D. THE IMAGERY AND POETRY OF
LUCRETIUS.*
  E.M. MC LEOD, 487:AUTUMN71-292
WEST, D. READING HORACE.
  C.L. BABCOCK, 24:JUL72-501
WEST, G.A. TOBACCO, PIPES AND SMOKING
CUSTOMS OF THE AMERICAN INDIANS.
  E.P. HAMP, 269(IJAL):APR71-136
WEST, G.D. AN INDEX OF PROPER NAMES IN
FRENCH ARTHURIAN VERSE ROMANCES (1150-
1300).
  M.D. LEGGE, 382(MAE):1972/1-65
  E.C. SMITH, 424:DEC70-311
  H.F. WILLIAMS, 545(RPH):MAY72-475
WEST, J. CRIMSON RAMBLERS OF THE WORLD,
FAREWELL.
  L.T. LEMON, 502(PRS):WINTER71/72-367
WEST, J. EXCEPT FOR THEE AND ME.
  J.G., 502(PRS):SPRING70-86
WEST, J. HIDE AND SEEK.
  N. HALE, 441:13MAY73-10
WEST, J. RUSSIAN SYMBOLISM.*
  J-L. BACKÈS, 549(RLC):JUL-SEP71-433
  L.A. FOSTER, 399(MLJ):OCT71-406
  I. JONES, 619(TC):VOL179#1049-54
WEST, J.B., WITH M.L. KOTZ. UPSTAIRS AT
THE WHITE HOUSE.
  E. BOMBECK, 441:16DEC73-24
WEST, J.F. FAROE.
  617(TLS):21SEP73-1075
WEST, M. THE HERETIC.
  P. ROBERTS, 565:VOL12#2-72
WEST, M. THE SALAMANDER.
  R. BRYDEN, 362:2AUG73-155
  W. SCHOTT, 441:21OCT73-46
  442(NY):5NOV73-184
  617(TLS):3AUG73-911

WEST, M.L. EARLY GREEK PHILOSOPHY AND
THE ORIENT.
  F. LASSERRE, 182:VOL24#11/12-497
WEST, P. COLONEL MINT.*
  R. BRYDEN, 362:7JUN73-772
  P.M. SPACKS, 249(HUDR):AUTUMN72-502
  617(TLS):8JUN73-634
WEST, R. RIVER OF TEARS.*
  617(TLS):12JAN73-45
WEST, R.H. SHAKESPEARE AND THE OUTER
MYSTERY.*
  R.A. FOAKES, 175:SPRING70-22
  R. SOELLNER, 570(SQ):SPRING70-185
WESTBROOK, M. WALTER VAN TILBURG CLARK.
  L.L. LEE, 649(WAL):SUMMER70-153
WESTERINK, L.G. - SEE OLYMPIODORUS
WESTERMANN, D. & M.A. BRYAN. HANDBOOK OF
AFRICAN LANGUAGES. (PT 2) (NEW ED)
  H. JUNGRAITHMAYR, 315(JAL):VOL10PT2-
  62
WESTFAL, S. THE POLISH LANGUAGE.
  I. KUNERT, 343:BAND13HEFT1-89
WESTFALL, R.S. FORCE IN NEWTON'S PHYS-
ICS.
  617(TLS):1JUN73-615
WESTHEIMER, D. GOING PUBLIC.
  N. CALLENDAR, 441:14OCT73-47
WESTIN, A.F. & M.A. BAKER. DATABANKS IN
A FREE SOCIETY.
  H. SCHWARTZ, 441:8JUL73-19
WESTLAKE, D.E. COPS AND ROBBERS.*
  617(TLS):16MAR73-303
WESTLAKE, D.E. UNDER AN ENGLISH HEAVEN.*
  617(TLS):9MAR73-256
WESTLAKE, D.E. & B. GARFIELD. GANGWAY.
  N. CALLENDAR, 441:3JUN73-34
WESTLAKE, H.D. ESSAYS ON THE GREEK HIS-
TORIANS AND GREEK HISTORY.*
  V. EHRENBERG, 303:VOL91-196
  R. WEIL, 555:VOL45FASC2-339
WESTLAKE, H.D. INDIVIDUALS IN THUCY-
DIDES.*
  R. WEIL, 555:VOL45FASC2-337
WESTLAKE, N.M. - SEE SMITH, R.P.
WESTON, C. POOR, POOR, OPHELIA.*
  617(TLS):23FEB73-219
WESTON, P. CLARINET VIRTUOSI OF THE
PAST.
  N. O'LOUGHLIN, 415:APR72-366
WESTPHAL, F.A. THE ACTIVITY OF PHILOSO-
PHY.
  L.G., 543:JUN71-760
WESTPHALEN, T. BEOWULF 3150-3155.*
  F.C. ROBINSON, 38:BAND88HEFT3-363
WESTRICH, S.A. THE ORMÉE OF BORDEAUX.
  C. EYER, 568(SCN):FALL-WINTER72-70
  617(TLS):27APR73-468
WESTRUP, J. - SEE BLOM, E.
WESTWOOD, J.N. WITNESSES OF TSUSHIMA.*
  J.A. WHITE, 550(RUSR):APR71-194
  293(JAST):NOV70-245
WETHERILL, P.M. FLAUBERT ET LA CRITIQUE
LITTÉRAIRE.
  J. BRUNEAU, 535(RHL):JAN-FEB70-149
WETZEL, D. A BIRD IN THE HAND.
  C. LEHMANN-HAUPT, 441:18JAN73-43
  M. LEVIN, 441:28JAN73-34
  442(NY):27JAN73-93
WETZEL, H. KLANG UND BILD IN DEN DICH-
TUNGEN GEORG TRAKLS.*
  F. VAN INGEN, 433:JAN70-90
WEVILL, D. WHERE THE ARROW FALLS.
  A. MAC LEAN, 362:20DEC73-859
  617(TLS):1JUN73-610
WEYAND, N., ED. IMMORTAL DIAMOND.
  W.R. MUNDT, 598(SOR):AUTUMN73-1029
WEYDT, H. ABTÖNUNGSPARTIKEL.
  M.H. FOLSOM, 353:SEP70-112

WEYEMBERGH-BOUSSART, M. ALFRED DÖBLIN.
   K. MÜLLER-SALGET, 680(ZDP):BAND90
   HEFT2-301
WEYL, N. & W. MARINA. AMERICAN STATESMEN
   ON SLAVERY AND THE NEGRO.
   C. WILSON, 396(MODA):WINTER72-105
WEZLER, A. PARIBHĀṢĀ IV, V UND XV.
   R. ROCHER, 318(JAOS):APR-JUN71-314
WHALEN, P. ON BEAR'S HEAD.
   R.H. BAYES, 50(ARQ):WINTER70-377
WHALEN, P. SEVERANCE PAY.
   J.R. REED, 491:APR73-47
WHALEY, B. CODEWORD BARBAROSSA.
   A. BULLOCK, 453:28JUN73-30
   H.E. SALISBURY, 441:6MAY73-7
WHALLEY, J.I. ENGLISH HANDWRITING 1540-
   1853.
   N. BARKER, 78(BC):WINTER71-535
WHALLON, W. FORMULA, CHARACTER, AND
   CONTEXT.*
   K.R. BROOKS, 382(MAE):1972/1-50
   A. CRÉPIN, 189(EA):JUL-SEP70-274
   D.A.H. EVANS, 597(SN):VOL42#2-486
WHARTON, D.B. THE ALASKA GOLD RUSH.
   441:15APR73-32
WHATELY, R. ELEMENTS OF RHETORIC. (7TH
   ED)
   D. EHNINGER, 480(P&R):SPRING71-132
WHATMOUGH, J. THE DIALECTS OF ANCIENT
   GAUL.*
   R.J. CORMIER, 399(MLJ):MAY71-325
   D.E. EVANS, 123:JUN72-243
   E.P. HAMP, 215(GL):VOL11#1-56
   R.L. THOMSON, 447(N&Q):APR71-157
WHEAT, J.C. & C.F. BRUN. MAPS AND CHARTS
   PUBLISHED IN AMERICA BEFORE 1800.
   R.A. SKELTON, 354:SEP70-272
WHEATLEY, J. PROLEGOMENA TO PHILOSOPHY.
   R.F. LADENSON, 154:MAR71-170
WHEATLEY, J.H. PATTERNS IN THACKERAY'S
   FICTION.*
   J. ESPEY, 445(NCF):JUN70-123
   R. LAWRENCE, 175:SPRING70-33
WHEDON, J. GIRL OF THE GOLDEN WEST.
   C. LEHMANN-HAUPT, 441:28MAY73-13
WHEELER, C. HIGH RELIEF.
   M. EASTON, 39:JAN71-73
WHEELER, G. PIERPONT MORGAN AND FRIENDS.
   R.C. ALBERTS, 441:9DEC73-6
WHEELER, T. THE WRECK OF THE RAT TRAP.
   617(TLS):6JUL73-769
WHEELER-BENNETT, J., ED. ACTION THIS
   DAY.
   J.E. TALMADGE, 219(GAR):FALL71-385
WHEELOCK, C. THE MYTHMAKER.*
   R. CHRIST, 613:AUTUMN70-460
   Z. GERTEL, 238:MAR71-211
WHEELOCK, J.H. BY DAYLIGHT AND IN DREAM.*
   F.D. REEVE, 491:JAN73-234
   639(VQR):WINTER71-XVIII
WHEELWRIGHT, J. COLLECTED POEMS OF JOHN
   WHEELWRIGHT. (A.H. ROSENFELD, ED)
   J. ASHBERY, 453:22FEB73-3
   J.M. BRINNIN, 441:7JAN73-4
   R. HOWARD, 491:SEP73-351
WHEELWRIGHT, P. THE BURNING FOUNTAIN.
   METAPHOR AND REALITY.
   K.W. BRITTON, 447(N&Q):OCT71-388
WHIFFEN, M. AMERICAN ARCHITECTURE SINCE
   1780.
   J.M.D., 44:MAR70-59
   I. MC CALLUM, 46:OCT70-266
WHIGHAM, P. THE BLUE WINGED BEE.
   J. TIPTON, 661:SPRING71-64
WHINNEY, M. EARLY FLEMISH PAINTING.*
   R.A. KOCH, 54:JUN70-202
   G. MARTIN, 39:JAN70-88
   C. TALBOT, 56:WINTER71-485

WHINNEY, M. HOME HOUSE, NO. 20 PORTMAN
   SQUARE.*
   J. HARRIS, 46:SEP70-200
WHISTLER, L. PICTURES ON GLASS.
   617(TLS):31AUG73-998
WHITAKER, B., ED. THE FOURTH WORLD.
   617(TLS):26JAN73-82
WHITBOURN, C.J. THE "ARCIPRESTE DE TALA-
   VERA" AND THE LITERATURE OF LOVE.
   G.B. GYBBON-MONYPENNY, 402(MLR):APR72-
   439
   D.W. LOMAX, 86(BHS):APR72-177
   205(FMLS):JUL71-298
WHITBY, W.M. & R.R. ANDERSON - SEE LOPE
   DE VEGA
WHITCOMB, I. AFTER THE BALL.
   442(NY):2JUN73-124
WHITE, A.R. TRUTH.
   J.M. SHORTER, 518:JAN72-35
WHITE, C.C. & A.M. HOLLAND. NO QUITTIN'
   SENSE.
   G.F. ACKERMAN, 649(WAL):SPRING70-76
WHITE, D.H. POPE AND THE CONTEXT OF CON-
   TROVERSY.*
   M. KALLICH, 481(PQ):JUL71-470
   P.M. SPACKS, 173(ECS):FALL71-177
   H. TROWBRIDGE, 405(MP):NOV71-169
WHITE, D.M. & A.C. SEWTER. I DISEGNI DI
   G.B. PIAZZETTA NELLA BIBLIOTECA REALE
   DI TORINO.
   F.J.B. WATSON, 39:OCT70-318
WHITE, E. FORGETTING ELENA.
   A. FRIEDMAN, 441:25MAR73-2
WHITE, E.W. ANNE BRADSTREET.*
   R.B. DAVIS, 27(AL):MAR72-154
   J.A.L. LEMAY, 579(SAQ):SUMMER72-437
WHITE, E.W. BENJAMIN BRITTEN.*
   J.P., 376:APR71-124
WHITE, G. ENGLISH ILLUSTRATION: THE
   SIXTIES 1855-1870.
   R. GRAHAM, 503:SPRING71-46
WHITE, G.A. & C. NEWMAN, EDS. LITERATURE
   IN REVOLUTION.
   R.G. DAVIS, 441:14JAN73-21
WHITE, J. ART AND ARCHITECTURE IN ITALY,
   1250-1400.
   M. TRACHTENBERG, 576:OCT70-276
WHITE, J. DARK INFERNO.
   617(TLS):2FEB73-129
WHITE, J. NATIONAL GALLERY OF IRELAND.*
   D.T., 135:JUL70-213
WHITE, J. JOHN BUTLER YEATS AND THE
   IRISH RENAISSANCE.
   617(TLS):1JUN73-620
WHITE, J.J. MYTHOLOGY IN THE MODERN
   NOVEL.*
   J.B. VICKERY, 659:SUMMER73-392
WHITE, J.M. CORTÉS AND THE DOWNFALL OF
   THE AZTEC EMPIRE.
   639(VQR):SUMMER71-CXXVII
WHITE, J.M. THE GARDEN GAME.
   617(TLS):3AUG73-911
WHITE, J.W. THE SŌKAGAKKAI AND MASS
   SOCIETY.
   D.J. HESSELGRAVE, 293(JAST):AUG71-901
   M.B. YAMASHITA, 285(JAPQ):JUL-SEP71-
   344
WHITE, K.D. A BIBLIOGRAPHY OF ROMAN AGRI-
   CULTURE.
   J.A. RICHMOND, 123:DEC72-389
WHITE, K.D. ROMAN FARMING.
   F.C. BOURNE, 124:SEP71-27
   J.A. RICHMOND, 123:DEC72-389
WHITE, M., ED. DOCUMENTS IN THE HISTORY
   OF AMERICAN PHILOSOPHY.
   617(TLS):16NOV73-1396

WHITE, M. PRAGMATISM AND THE AMERICAN
MIND.
  617(TLS):16NOV73-1396
WHITE, M. SCIENCE AND SENTIMENT IN
AMERICA.*
  E.H. MADDEN, 319:APR73-277
  617(TLS):16NOV73-1396
WHITE, N. & E. WILLENSKY, EDS. AIA GUIDE
TO NEW YORK CITY.
  A. BURNHAM, 576:DEC70-356
WHITE, P. THE EYE OF THE STORM.
  T. O'KEEFFE, 362:27SEP73-427
  617(TLS):21SEP73-1072
WHITE, P. THE VIVISECTOR.*
  L. CANTRELL, 381:MAR71-125
WHITE, R.J. THE ANTI-PHILOSOPHERS.
  A. MONTEFIORE, 393(MIND):APR71-304
  N.T. PHILLIPSON, 483:APR71-172
WHITE, R.J. - SEE COLERIDGE, S.T.
WHITE, R.L., ED. THE ACHIEVEMENT OF
SHERWOOD ANDERSON.
  M. BRADBURY, 148:SUMMER71-185
WHITE, R.L., ED. TAR.
  D.B. KESTERSON, 573(SSF):SUMMER71-494
WHITE, R.L. - SEE ANDERSON, S.
WHITE, R.L. - SEE ANDERSON, S. & G.
STEIN
WHITE, T.D. THE DISTANCE AND THE DARK.
  S. HILL, 362:17MAY73-658
  T. LASK, 441:17FEB73-33
  M. LEVIN, 441:25FEB73-49
  617(TLS):25MAY73-575
WHITE, T.H. THE MAKING OF THE PRESIDENT
1972.
  T. BERGER, 441:5AUG73-1
  M. FRANKEL, 441:30JUL73-31
  M. JANEWAY, 61:OCT73-120
  G. WILLS, 453:4OCT73-3
  442(NY):8OCT73-171
WHITEHEAD, A.N. LA FONCTION DE LA RAISON
ET AUTRES ESSAIS.
  R. HÉBERT, 154:SEP70-291
WHITEHEAD, G.K. DEER OF THE WORLD.
  617(TLS):20APR73-453
WHITEHILL, W.M., ED. BOSTON PRINTS AND
PRINTMAKERS 1670-1775.
  617(TLS):12OCT73-1259
WHITEHOUSE, A. WINGS FOR THE CHARIOTS.
  M. LEVIN, 441:24JUN73-12
WHITEHOUSE, I. NEGOTIATIONS WITH THE
UNIVERSE.
  J. DITSKY, 628:SPRING72-108
WHITELEY, C.H. MIND IN ACTION.
  617(TLS):31AUG73-1004
WHITELEY, S., D. BRIGGS & M. TURNER.
DEALING WITH DEVIANTS.
  617(TLS):16FEB73-172
WHITELEY, W.H. SWAHILI.
  A.H.J. PRINS, 69:JUL70-281
WHITER, W. WALTER WHITER: A SPECIMEN OF
A COMMENTARY ON SHAKESPEARE. (A. OVER,
ED)
  M.A. SHAABER, 570(SQ):SPRING70-181
WHITEWAY, R.S. THE RISE OF THE PORTU-
GUESE POWER IN INDIA 1497-1550.
  R.A. CALLAHAN, 318(JAOS):JAN-MAR71-157
WHITFIELD, F.J. - SEE MIRSKY, D.S.
WHITFIELD, J.H. DISCOURSES ON MACHIA-
VELLI.
  T.K. RABB, 551(RENQ):SPRING71-65
  A. SCAGLIONE, 401(MLQ):JUN71-214
WHITFIELD, J.H. - SEE MACHIAVELLI, N.
WHITING, B.J., WITH H.W. WHITING, COMPS.
PROVERBS, SENTENCES, AND PROVERBIAL
PHRASES, FROM ENGLISH WRITINGS MAINLY
BEFORE 1500.*
  N. DAVIS, 382(MAE):1972/2-164
                            [CONTINUED]

[CONTINUING]
  H. GNEUSS, 38:BAND88HEFT4-529
  A.G. RIGG, 541(RES):AUG71-326
WHITING, C.G. - SEE VALÉRY, P.
WHITING, N. WHILE COURTING THE SERGEANT'S
DAUGHTER.
  W. CORBETT, 600:WINTER/SPRING70-233
WHITMAN, W. AN AMERICAN PRIMER.
  E. BUTSCHER, 646(WWR):DEC70-125
WHITMAN, W. THE CORRESPONDENCE OF WALT
WHITMAN.* (VOLS 4&5) (E.H. MILLER, ED)
  C.C. HOLLIS, 646(WWR):SEP70-93
WHITMAN, W. HOJAS DE HIERBA. (J.L.
BORGES, TRANS)
  E. BERNAL LABRADA, 263:JAN-MAR72-59
WHITMAN, W. THE TENDEREST LOVER.* (W.
LOWENFELS, ED)
  G.M. WHITE, 646(WWR):JUN71-67
WHITMAN, W. WALT WHITMAN'S LEAVES OF
GRASS. (C.M. BABCOCK, ED) MIRACLES.
LEAVES OF GRASS: A FACSIMILE OF THE
FIRST EDITION.
  W. WHITE, 646(WWR):MAR70-28
WHITNEY, J.B.R. CHINA.
  S-D. CHANG, 293(JAST):NOV70-169
  L. VEILLEUX, 302:JUL71-377
WHITNEY, J.D. TRACKS.*
  M. CZARNECKI, 648:JUN70-37
WHITNEY, M.S. - SEE DE MAGNY, O.
WHITROW, G.J., ED. EINSTEIN.
  J. ZINMAN, 441:23SEP73-44
WHITSON, W.W. & C-H. HUANG. THE CHINESE
HIGH COMMAND.
  617(TLS):17AUG73-948
WHITTAKER, C.R. - SEE HERODIAN
WHITTEMORE, L.H. THE SUPER COPS.
  M.P. NICHOLS, 441:27MAY73-3
WHITTEN, L.H. THE ALCHEMIST.
  M. LEVIN, 441:25NOV73-48
WHITTOCK, T. A READING OF THE "CANTER-
BURY TALES."*
  D. MEHL, 38:BAND89HEFT2-254
"WHO WROTE THE MOVIE...AND WHAT ELSE DID
HE WRITE?"
  C. NORTH, 200:AUG-SEP71-432
WHONE, H. THE SIMPLICITY OF PLAYING THE
VIOLIN.*
  J. MIDDLEMISS, 415:JUL72-672
"WHO'S WHO IN MUSIC." (6TH ED)
  A. JACOBS, 415:AUG72-774
WIATR, J.J. WSPÓŁCZESNY ANTYKOMUNIZM A
NAUKI SPOŁECZNE.
  Z.A. JORDAN, 32:JUN72-469
WIBBERLEY, L. THE TESTAMENT OF THEOPHIL-
US.
  C.E. SIMCOX, 441:7OCT73-34
WICHMANN, S. FRANZ VON LENBACH UND
SEINE ZEIT.
  617(TLS):7SEP73-1021
WICKBERG, E., COMP. HISTORICAL INTER-
ACTION OF CHINA AND VIETNAM.
  W. GUNGWU, 318(JAOS):OCT-DEC71-522
WICKER, T. FACING THE LIONS.
  P. ADAMS, 61:AUG73-103
  P. ANDERSON, 441:3JUN73-5
  C. LEHMANN-HAUPT, 441:13JUN73-55
  442(NY):2JUL73-76
  617(TLS):2NOV73-1334
WICKES, G. AMERICANS IN PARIS.*
  G.M. REEVES, 131(CL):SUMMER72-279
WICKHAM, G. EARLY ENGLISH STAGES, 1300
TO 1660.* (VOL 2, PT 2)
  R. STODDARD, 70(ANQ):SEP72-12
WICKHAM, G. SHAKESPEARE'S DRAMATIC HERI-
TAGE.*
  R.A. FOAKES, 175:SPRING70-22
  B. KURTH, 376:OCT71-131

WICKRAM, G. SÄMTLICHE WERKE. (VOL 11)
(H-G. ROLOFF, ED)
E. SOBEL, 301(JEGP):OCT72-573
WICKWIRE, F. & M. CORNWALLIS: THE AMERI-
CAN ADVENTURE.*
D.A. BAUGH, 656(WMQ):JAN71-133
WIDEMAN, J.E. THE LYNCHERS.
R.P. BRICKNER, 441:29APR73-25
A. BROYARD, 441:15MAY73-43
"WIDENER LIBRARY SHELFLIST 35-38: ENG-
LISH LITERATURE."
617(TLS):2MAR73-248
WIDJOJO NITISASTRO. POPULATION TRENDS IN
INDONESIA.
G.B. SIMMONS, 293(JAST):AUG71-916
WIDMER, K. THE WAYS OF NIHILISM.
R.H. FOGLE, 27(AL):NOV72-492
B.R. MC ELDERRY, JR., 573(SSF):SPRING
71-347
WIDSTRAND, C.G., ED. AFRICAN BOUNDARY
PROBLEMS.
A.H.M. KIRK-GREENE, 69:JUL71-260
WIEBE, R., ED. STORIES FROM WESTERN
CANADA.*
D. STEPHENS, 102(CANL):AUTUMN72-84
WIEBE, R. THE TEMPTATIONS OF BIG BEAR.
M.F. DIXON, 99:NOV-DEC73-30
A. DUECK, 296:FALL73-88
WIEBENSON, D. TONY GARNIER: THE CITÉ
INDUSTRIELLE.*
J.E. BURCHARD, 54:MAR71-133
H.H. WAECHTER, 44:SEP71-76
WIEBENSON, D. SOURCES OF GREEK REVIVAL
ARCHITECTURE.
J.M. COOK, 56:AUTUMN70-311
J. SUMMERSON, 54:DEC71-541
WIECKENBERG, E-P. ZUR GESCHICHTE DER
KAPITELÜBERSCHRIFT IM DEUTSCHEN ROMAN
VOM 15. JAHRHUNDERT BIS ZUM AUSGANG DES
BAROCK.
P. SKRINE, 402(MLR):OCT72-938
J.K. SOWDEN, 220(GL&L):JAN72-173
WIEDEMANN, C., ED. DER GALANTE STIL:
1680-1730.*
L.P. JOHNSON, 400(MLN):OCT71-721
R.M.G. NICKISCH, 224(GRM):AUG70-358
WIENER, J., ED. GREAT BRITAIN: FOREIGN
POLICY AND THE SPAN OF EMPIRE, 1689-
1971.*
R.W. NOBLE, 362:16AUG73-221
WIENOLD, G. GENUS UND SEMANTIK.
U. EGLI, 343:BAND13HEFT1-31
D. KASTOVSKY, 260(IF):BAND75-256
WIENOLD, G. - SEE BROCH, H.
WIENPAHL, P. ZEN DIARY.*
B. ZEUSCHNER, 485(PE&W):JUL71-344
WIERENGA, L. LA TROADE, DE ROBERT GAR-
NIER.
R. LEBÈGUE, 549(RLC):JUL-SEP71-417
WIERER, R. DER FÖDERALISMUS IM DONAUR-
AUM.
M. MOLNÁR, 98:JAN70-72
WIERLACHER, A. DAS BÜRGERLICHE DRAMA.*
K.L. BERGHAHN, 221(GQ):JAN71-109
WIERLACHER, A. - SEE VALDASTRI, I.
WIERSCHIN, M. MEISTER JOHANN LIECHTEN-
AUERS KUNST DES FECHTENS.
E. PLOSS, 680(ZDP):BAND89HEFT1-120
WIERZBICKA, A. O JĘZYKU DLA WSZYSTKICH.
I. BELLERT, 353:JAN70-111
VON WIESE, B., ED. DEUTSCHE DICHTER DER
MODERNE.* (2ND ED)
H. BOESCHENSTEIN, 182:VOL24#19/20-743
VON WIESE, B., ED. DEUTSCHE DICHTER DES
19. JAHRHUNDERTS.*
I.F., 191(ELN):SEP71(SUPP)-122
N.A. FURNESS, 220(GL&L):APR72-286
J. HERMAND, 680(ZDP):BAND89HEFT2-295

VON WIESE, B., ED. DEUTSCHE DRAMATURGIE
DES 19. JAHRHUNDERTS.*
E. MC INNES, 220(GL&L):JAN72-172
VON WIESE, B., ED. DEUTSCHE DRAMATURGIE
VOM NATURALISMUS BIS ZUR GEGENWART.
M.E. STEWART, 220(GL&L):JUL72-397
VON WIESE, B. KARL IMMERMANN.*
G.J. HOLST, 301(JEGP):OCT72-584
VON WIESE, B. & R. HENSS, EDS. NATIONAL-
ISMUS IN GERMANISTIK UND DICHTUNG.
L. HERMODSSON, 597(SN):VOL42#1-298
WEISE, C. SÄMTLICHE WERKE. (VOLS 1&3)
(J.D. LINDBERG, ED)
R.R. HEITNER, 301(JEGP):JUL72-418
WIESEL, E. A BEGGAR IN JERUSALEM.
L. ELKIN, 287:MAY70-34
WIESEL, E. LE MENDIANT DE JÉRUSALEM.
J. KOLBERT, 207(FR):OCT70-189
WIESEL, E. LA NUIT, L'AUBE, LE JOUR.
H.H. WEINBERG, 207(FR):APR71-975
WIESEL, E. THE OATH.
A. FRIEDMAN, 441:18NOV73-5
WIESEL, E. SOULS ON FIRE.*
617(TLS):29JUN73-755
WIESELGREN, T. LUNI SUL MIGNONE.* (VOL
2, FASC 1: THE IRON AGE SETTLEMENT ON
THE ACROPOLIS.)
A.R. NEUMANN, 182:VOL24#11/12-493
WIESMANN, L. GOTTFRIED KELLER.
W.E. YUILL, 205(FMLS):OCT70-413
WIESNER, J. FAHREN UND REITEN.*
P. CHANTRAINE, 555:VOL45FASC1-147
WIESSNER, E. DER WORTSCHATZ VON HEINRICH
WITTENWILERS "RING."* (B. BOESCH, ED)
J.S. GROSECLOSE, 406:WINTER72-399
G.F. JONES, 221(GQ):MAY71-405
WIGGINS, D. IDENTITY AND SPATIO-TEMPORAL
CONTINUITY.*
J. PERRY, 316:SEP70-447
WIGGINTON, E., ED. FOXFIRE 2.
442(NY):13AUG73-87
WIGHAM, E. THE POWER TO MANAGE.
617(TLS):27APR73-466
WIGHTMAN, E.M. ROMAN TRIER AND THE TRE-
VERI.
J.C. MANN, 313:VOL61-294
R. SCRANTON, 122:JUL72-219
S.E. SMETHURST, 529(QQ):AUTUMN71-481
WILBER, D.N. PERSEPOLIS.
T.C. YOUNG, JR., 487:SUMMER71-174
WILBERG VIGNAU-SCHUURMAN, T.A.G. DIE
EMBLEMATISCHEN ELEMENTE IM WERKE JORIS
HOEFNAGELS.*
H. MIELKE, 683:BAND34HEFT2-152
W. STECHOW, 54:SEP71-415
WILBERT, J. - SEE LOUKOTKA, Č.
WILBUR, R. WALKING TO SLEEP.*
P. CUMMINS, 134(CP):SPRING70-72
H. SERGEANT, 175:AUTUMN71-106
S. TOULSON, 493:SUMMER71-208
WILCKE, C. DAS LUGALBANDAEPOS.
J. KLEIN, 318(JAOS):APR-JUN71-295
WILCOCK, J. & J. TUCK. MEXICO ON $5 AND
$10 A DAY.
S.S. BENSON, 37:OCT71-42
WILCOX, C. HIDING PLACE.
N. CALLENDAR, 441:6MAY73-41
WILCZYŃSKI, J. THE ECONOMICS AND POLI-
TICS OF EAST-WEST TRADE.*
A. ZAUBERMAN, 497(POLR):SPRING71-118
WILCZYNSKI, J. THE ECONOMICS OF SOCIAL-
ISM.
J.S. PRYBYLA, 32:SEP72-691
WILCZYNSKI, J. PROFIT, RISK AND INCEN-
TIVES UNDER SOCIALIST ECONOMIC PLAN-
NING.
617(TLS):2FEB73-116

WILCZYNSKI, J. SOCIALIST ECONOMIC DEVEL-
OPMENT AND REFORMS.
  M. ELLMAN, 575(SEER):OCT72-629
  G. GROSSMAN, 32:SEP72-689
  617(TLS):2FEB73-116
WILD, G. BOGUMILEN UND KATHARER IN IHRER
SYMBOLIK. (PT 1)
  H-W. HAUSSIG, 182:VOL24#17/18-695
WILD, J. THE RADICAL EMPIRICISM OF WIL-
LIAM JAMES.*
  D.C. MATHUR, 484(PPR):DEC70-302
  J.K. ROTH, 319:APR73-280
WILD, P. TEXTILE MANUFACTURE IN THE
NORTHERN ROMAN PROVINCES.
  P. SALWAY, 123:JUN72-262
WILD, P. TERMS AND RENEWALS.
  J. GALASSI, 491:MAR73-344
WILDE, F-E. KIERKEGAARDS VERSTÄNDNIS DER
EXISTENZ.*
  G.J. STACK, 319:APR73-275
WILDE, O. THE ARTIST AS CRITIC.* (R.
ELLMANN, ED)
  E. ENGELBERG, 637(VS):DEC70-205
WILDENSTEIN, G. CHARDIN.*
  B. SCOTT, 39:JUN70-488
  D.T., 135:OCT70-139
WILDER, A. AMERICAN POPULAR SONG.*
(J.T. MAHER, ED)
  G. ISEMINGER, 109:SPRING/SUMMER73-165
WILDER, A.N. THE NEW VOICE.
  A.J. FRY, 433:APR71-221
WILDER, T. THEOPHILUS NORTH.
  A. BROYARD, 441:24OCT73-37
  G. HICKS, 441:21OCT73-1
  E. WEEKS, 61:NOV73-126
  442(NY):29OCT73-179
WILDING, M. ASPECTS OF THE DYING PROCESS.
  617(TLS):13JUL73-797
WILDING, M., ED. MARVELL.*
  P. LEGOUIS, 189(EA):JAN-MAR71-92
WILDING, M. MILTON'S "PARADISE LOST."*
  R.D. JORDAN, 568(SCN):FALL-WINTER72-
    66
  P. LEGOUIS, 189(EA):OCT-DEC71-532
WILDMAN, A.K. THE MAKING OF A WORKER'S
REVOLUTION.* (VOL 1)
  I. GETZLER, 575(SEER):JAN72-129
WILDMAN, E., ED. EXPERIMENTS IN PROSE.
  D.H. SULLIVAN, 648:OCT70-69
WILDMAN, E. NUCLEAR LOVE.
  A. OSTRIKER, 473(PR):SUMMER72-464
WILES, P.J.D., ED. PREDICTION OF COMMUN-
IST ECONOMIC PERFORMANCE.*
  G. GROSSMAN, 32:DEC72-905
  A. ZAUBERMAN, 575(SEER):JUL72-483
WILEY, P.E. NOVELIST OF THREE WORLDS.
  B. ROUSE, 599:SPRING71-193
WILH, R. - SEE "JAHRBUCH FÜR VOLKSLIED-
FORSCHUNG" (VOLS 13-16)
WILHELM, J.J., ED & TRANS. MEDIEVAL
SONG.*
  42(AR):WINTER71/72-601
WILHELM, J.J. SEVEN TROUBADOURS.
  F.R.P. AKEHURST, 207(FR):FEB71-626
  D. EVANS, 447(N&Q):JAN71-38
  J. VAN EERDE, 399(MLJ):FEB71-117
WILHELMSEN, F.D. THE PARADOXICAL STRUC-
TURE OF EXISTENCE.
  G.L. DONALDSON, 613:AUTUMN71-463
WILKEN, R.L. JUDAISM AND THE EARLY
CHRISTIAN MIND.
  M. SMITH, 328:SUMMER71-370
WILKES, J.J. DALMATIA.*
  J.P. WILD, 313:VOL61-294
WILKINS, E.H. & T.G. BERGIN, EDS. A CON-
CORDANCE TO THE "DIVINE COMEDY" OF
DANTE ALIGHIERI.
  G.C. LEPSCHY, 353:JUN70-112

WILKINS, N., ED. TWO MIRACLES: LA NONNE
QUI LAISSA SON ABBAIE; SAINT VALENTIN.
  617(TLS):18MAY73-564
WILKINS, N. - SEE DE MACHAUT, G.
WILKINSON, B., ED. THE CREATION OF
MEDIEVAL PARLIAMENTS.
  617(TLS):9MAR73-277
WILKINSON, D. MALRAUX.
  P-A. FORTIER, 188(ECR):WINTER70-346
WILKINSON, E. & L.A. WILLOUGHBY - SEE
SCHILLER, F.
WILKINSON, F. EDGED WEAPONS.
  J.F. HAYWARD, 90:JAN71-52
WILKINSON, L.P. THE "GEORGICS" OF VIR-
GIL.*
  W.S. ANDERSON, 121(CJ):OCT-NOV71-76
  R.B. LLOYD, 24:JUL72-491
  E. DE SAINT-DENIS, 555:VOL45FASC1-169
WILKINSON, R. THE BROKEN REBEL.
  617(TLS):11MAY73-524
WILKINSON, S. CALE.
  639(VQR):WINTER71-VIII
WILKS, J.H. TREES OF THE BRITISH ISLES
IN HISTORY AND LEGEND.
  617(TLS):2FEB73-133
WILKS, Y.A. GRAMMAR, MEANING, AND THE
MACHINE ANALYSIS OF LANGUAGE.*
  H.A. LEWIS, 518:OCT72-36
  J. LYONS, 402(MLR):OCT72-858
WILL, B. TRADING UNDER SAIL OFF JAPAN,
1860-99. (G.A. LENSEN, ED)
  B.B. SZCZESNIAK, 318(JAOS):JAN-MAR71-
    148
WILL, F. BRANDY IN THE SNOW.
  P.D. ZIVKOVIC, 109:SPRING/SUMMER73-144
WILLARD, N. TESTIMONY OF THE INVISIBLE
MAN.
  M. MARCUS, 502(PRS):SPRING71-88
WILLCOCK, M.M. A COMMENTARY ON HOMER'S
"ILIAD," BOOKS I-VI.
  F.M. COMBELLACK, 122:APR72-142
  J.B. HAINSWORTH, 123:JUN72-176
  J.W. SHUMAKER, 124:SEP71-24
WILLCOX, W.B. - SEE FRANKLIN, B.
WILLEFORD, W. THE FOOL AND HIS SCEPTER.*
  J.W. ASHTON, 292(JAF):JUL-SEP71-356
  R. LAWRENCE, 175:AUTUMN70-107
  G.A. TEST, 405(MP):MAY71-409
WILLET, J. EL ROMPECABEZAS EXPRESION-
ISTA.
  H. WALZ, 202(FMOD):JUN71-334
WILLETT, F. AFRICAN ART.
  D. DYCKES, 58:SUMMER71-10
  J. PICTON, 592:MAR71-132
WILLETT, F. IFE IN THE HISTORY OF WEST
AFRICAN SCULPTURE.
  E.L.R. MEYEROWITZ, 39:JUL70-81
  A. RUBIN, 54:SEP70-348
WILLETT, J. EXPRESSIONISM.
  W.M. JEWELL, 651(WHR):SPRING72-181
  F. WHITFORD, 402(MLR):JAN72-157
  F. WHITFORD, 592:JUL/AUG71-50
WILLETT, J. & R. MANHEIM - SEE BRECHT, B.
WILLETTS, P.J. THE HENRY LAWES MANU-
SCRIPT.
  F.W. STERNFELD, 354:SEP70-262
WILLIAM OF OCKHAM - SEE UNDER OCKHAM
WILLIAM OF SHERWOOD. WILLIAM OF SHER-
WOOD'S TREATISE ON SYNCATEGOREMATIC
WORDS.* (N. KRETZMANN, ED & TRANS)
  M. TWEEDALE, 316:SEP70-450
  E. WINANCE, 319:JUL73-403
WILLIAMS, A. THE BERIA PAPERS.
  N. CALLENDAR, 441:28OCT73-49
  C. LEHMANN-HAUPT, 441:19OCT73-47
  617(TLS):20APR73-437

WILLIAMS, A. & M.E. NOVAK. CONGREVE
CONSIDER'D.
566:SPRING72-89
WILLIAMS, A.W. A SOCIAL HISTORY OF THE
GREATER BOSTON CLUBS.
P.R. RITTER, 432(NEQ):MAR71-172
WILLIAMS, B. PROBLEMS OF THE SELF.
R. WOLLHEIM, 362:26JUL73-122
617(TLS):14DEC73-1536
WILLIAMS, B. & J.W. EHRLICH. A MATTER
OF CONFIDENCE.
N. CALLENDAR, 441:4MAR73-42
WILLIAMS, C. MAN ON A LEASH.
N. CALLENDAR, 441:30SEP73-18
WILLIAMS, C. WOMEN ON THE ROPE.
617(TLS):2NOV73-1352
WILLIAMS, C.B. STYLE AND VOCABULARY.
M.F. WAKELIN, 541(RES):MAY71-243
WILLIAMS, C.J. THEATRES AND AUDIENCES.
J.R. BROWN, 157:SPRING71-67
WILLIAMS, C.J. MADAME VESTRIS.
617(TLS):7SEP73-1020
WILLIAMS, C.K. I AM THE BITTER NAME.
J. KESSLER, 491:FEB73-292
WILLIAMS, C.K. - SEE HILL, B.H.
WILLIAMS, D. TOO QUICK DESPAIRER.
P.G. SCOTT, 637(VS):JUN71-465
WILLIAMS, D. TROUSERED APES.
A.E. DYSON, 148:SUMMER71-99
WILLIAMS, D.T. THE BATTLE OF BOSWORTH.
617(TLS):5OCT73-1195
WILLIAMS, E. EMLYN.
P. BLACK, 362:22NOV73-716
617(TLS):9NOV73-1367
WILLIAMS, E.B. THE BANTAM NEW COLLEGE
SPANISH AND ENGLISH DICTIONARY.
R.J. WIEZELL, 240(HR):JUL71-345
WILLIAMS, F., ED. LANGUAGE AND POVERTY.
J.L. DILLARD, 350:JUN72-479
WILLIAMS, F. NO FIXED ADDRESS.
617(TLS):16FEB73-173
WILLIAMS, G.C. ADAPTATION AND NATURAL
SELECTION.
W.C. WIMSATT, 486:DEC70-620
WILLIAMS, G.G. GUIDE TO LITERARY LONDON.
617(TLS):15JUN73-699
WILLIAMS, G.R. THE BLACK TREASURES OF
SCOTLAND YARD.
617(TLS):16NOV73-1409
WILLIAMS, G.W. - SEE CRASHAW, R.
WILLIAMS, G.W. - SEE "JACOB ECKHARD'S
CHOIRMASTER'S BOOK OF 1809".
WILLIAMS, H.F. LES LAIS DE MARIE DE
FRANCE.
B.J.M. ANGLES, 399(MLJ):FEB71-126
W.W. KIBLER, 207(FR):OCT70-161
WILLIAMS, I. EARLY ENGLISH WATERCOLOURS.
R. EDWARDS, 39:APR71-341
WILLIAMS, I. - SEE FIELDING, H.
WILLIAMS, I.M. THACKERAY.
P. ROBERTS, 541(RES):FEB71-107
WILLIAMS, J. AUGUSTUS.*
R. BLYTHE, 362:4OCT73-459
J. LEO, 441:8APR73-30
WILLIAMS, J. AN EAR IN BARTRAM'S TREE.
H. SERGEANT, 175:SUMMER71-65
WILLIAMS, J. STATE OF GRACE.
A. BROYARD, 441:7NOV73-39
G. GODWIN, 441:22APR73-2
WILLIAMS, J. STONER.
D. MAHON, 362:21JUN73-840
617(TLS):18MAY73-545
WILLIAMS, J. THE WINTERING.
P.M. SPACKS, 249(HUDR):SPRING72-166
639(VQR):SUMMER71-XCVI
WILLIAMS, J.A. FLASHBACKS.
P. COWAN, 441:6MAY73-34

WILLIAMS, J.A. THE MAN WHO CRIED I AM.
R.E. FLEMING, 659:SPRING73-186
WILLIAMS, J.A. THEMES OF ISLAMIC CIVILI-
ZATION.
R.E. ABU SHANAB, 319:JAN73-117
WILLIAMS, J.B. BRITISH COMMERCIAL POLICY
AND TRADE EXPANSION 1750-1850.
617(TLS):6APR73-399
WILLIAMS, J.C. & M., EDS. THE NEGRO
SPEAKS.
A.L. SMITH, 583:WINTER70-183
WILLIAMS, J.S. & M. STEPHENS, EDS. THE
LILTING HOUSE.
P.E. LEWIS, 565:VOL11#3-62
H. SERGEANT, 175:SPRING70-29
WILLIAMS, K. JONATHAN SWIFT AND THE AGE
OF COMPROMISE.
P. DANCHIN, 179(ES):APR71-178
WILLIAMS, K., ED. SWIFT: THE CRITICAL
HERITAGE.*
T. BROWN, 159(DM):WINTER70/71-123
WILLIAMS, M. THE ONLY WORLD THERE IS.*
639(VQR):SUMMER71-CIV
WILLIAMS, N. ALL THE QUEEN'S MEN.
617(TLS):19JAN73-62
WILLIAMS, P. BACH ORGAN MUSIC.*
W. EMERY, 415:AUG72-775
WILLIAMS, P. FIGURED BASS ACCOMPANI-
MENT.*
T. BORGIR, 317:FALL72-476
WILLIAMS, P. OUTLAW BLUES.
M. PETERSON, 470:JAN71-45
WILLIAMS, P.M. WARS, PLOTS AND SCANDALS
IN POST-WAR FRANCE.
N. HAMPSON, 208(FS):JUL72-369
H.G. THORBURN, 529(QQ):SUMMER71-332
WILLIAMS, P.M., WITH D. GOLDEY & M. HAR-
RISON. FRENCH POLITICIANS AND ELEC-
TIONS 1951-1969.
N. HAMPSON, 208(FS):JUL72-369
WILLIAMS, R. THE COUNTRY AND THE CITY.
M. BERMAN, 441:15JUL73-1
N. BLIVEN, 442(NY):13AUG73-83
P.N. FURBANK, 362:26APR73-548
617(TLS):7SEP73-1027
WILLIAMS, R. THE ENGLISH NOVEL FROM
DICKENS TO LAWRENCE.*
P. COLLINS, 155:JAN71-47
E. DELAVENAY, 189(EA):APR-JUN71-205
U.C. KNOEPFLMACHER, 637(VS):JUN71-455
W.D. SCHAEFER, 445(NCF):DEC70-377
WILLIAMS, R. GEORGE ORWELL.*
R. MC CORMACK, 606(TAMR):#58-77
WILLIAMS, R.J. HEBREW SYNTAX.
Y. HAYON, 215(GL):VOL10#3-199
WILLIAMS, R.L. THE FRENCH REVOLUTION OF
1870-1871.
F. BUSI, 207(FR):OCT70-197
WILLIAMS, R.R. FAITH AND THE FAITH.
617(TLS):23FEB73-221
WILLIAMS, R.T. THE SILVER COINAGE OF
THE PHOKIANS.
617(TLS):23MAR73-333
WILLIAMS, R.V. - SEE UNDER VAUGHAN WIL-
LIAMS, R.
WILLIAMS, S. CODICES PSEUDO-ISIDORIANI.
R.E. REYNOLDS, 589:OCT72-818
WILLIAMS, S. FREEDOM AND ORDER IN A
LIBERAL SOCIETY.
617(TLS):5OCT73-1196
WILLIAMS, T. MALLARMÉ AND THE LANGUAGE
OF MYSTICISM.
639(VQR):AUTUMN71-CLXIX
WILLIAMS, T.C. THE CONCEPT OF THE CATE-
GORICAL IMPERATIVE.*
A.R.C. DUNCAN, 154:DEC70-436
P. LASKA, 482(PHR):JAN71-126
G. NESSLER, 342:BAND62HEFT3-412

WILLIAMS, T.D., ED. SECRET SOCIETIES IN
IRELAND.
617(TLS):7SEP73-1029
WILLIAMS, W. MR. PENROSE.
P.G. ADAMS, 27(AL):NOV72-478
WILLIAMS, W.C. IMAGINATIONS. (W.
SCHOTT, ED)
G. BURNS, 584(SWR):SPRING72-162
J. DOLLAR, 590:SPRING72-12
S. FAUCHEREAU, 98:JUL71-626
639(VQR):WINTER71-XXVI
WILLIAMS, W.C. IN THE AMERICAN GRAIN.
S. FAUCHEREAU, 98:JUL71-626
WILLIAMS, W.E. ALLEN LANE.
C. DRIVER, 362:26APR73-551
617(TLS):20APR73-439
WILLIAMS-WOOD, C. STAFFORDSHIRE POT LIDS
AND THEIR POTTERS.
617(TLS):29JUN73-757
WILLIAMSEN, V.G. - SEE MIRA DE AMESCUA,
A.
WILLIAMSON, A. THOMAS PAINE.
617(TLS):7SEP73-1022
WILLIAMSON, G. A READER'S GUIDE TO THE
METAPHYSICAL POETS.
J-M. BENOIST, 98:AUG/SEP71-730
WILLIAMSON, G.A. - SEE CATULLUS
WILLIAMSON, H.N.H. FAREWELL TO THE DON.
(J. HARRIS, ED)
G.A. BRINKLEY, 32:JUN72-423
WILLIAMSON, H.R. CATHERINE DE' MEDICI.
W. BEAUCHAMP, 441:23DEC73-10
WILLIAMSON, J. CHARLES KEMBLE, MAN OF
THE THEATRE.*
S.C., 191(ELN):SEP71(SUPP)-17
J.C. TREWIN, 157:AUTUMN70-66
WILLIAMSON, J. H.G. WELLS.
T. STURGEON, 441:4NOV73-75
WILLIAMSON, J.G. KARL HELFFERICH.
617(TLS):19JAN73-61
WILLIAMSON, J.V. & V.M. BURKE, EDS. A
VARIOUS LANGUAGE.
R.E. COOLEY, 351(LL):DEC71-263
WILLIAMSON, K. THE ATLANTIC ISLANDS.
J. SIMPSON, 203:WINTER70-320
WILLIAMSON, M. ROBERT HARRIS 1849-1919.
R.L. BLOORE, 96:APR/MAY71-82
WILLIAMSON, S. THE MUNICH AIR DISASTER.
617(TLS):16MAR73-305
WILLIAMSON, S.R., JR. THE POLITICS OF
GRAND STRATEGY.*
R.A. COSGROVE, 50(ARQ):WINTER70-369
639(VQR):WINTER71-XXXVIII
VAN WILLIGEN, D.M. EXERCICES ORAUX.
M-L. MOREAU, 556(RLV):1971/2-237
WILLINGHAM, C. RAMBLING ROSE.*
617(TLS):6JUL73-783
WILLIS, A.J., COMP. CANTERBURY MARRIAGE
LICENCES 1781-1809.
E. WELCH, 325:APR71-245
WILLIS, A.J. GENEALOGY FOR BEGINNERS.
(2ND ED)
D. DAWE, 325:APR71-253
WILLIS, J.T., WITH H. RINGGREN - SEE
ENGNELL, I.
WILLIS, R.S. - SEE RUIZ, J.
WILLISON, I.R., ED. THE NEW CAMBRIDGE
BIBLIOGRAPHY OF ENGLISH LITERATURE.*
(VOL 4)
D. DONOGHUE, 453:19APR73-26
C. RICKS, 362:8FEB73-187
WILLS, G. JADE OF THE EAST.
617(TLS):6JUL73-766
WILLS, G. SILVER FOR PLEASURE AND IN-
VESTMENT.
C. OMAN, 39:MAY70-405
WILLS, P. FREE AS A BIRD.
617(TLS):29JUN73-756

WILLS, V., ED. REPORTS ON THE ANNEXED
ESTATES 1755-1769.
617(TLS):31AUG73-1001
WILLSMORE, A.W. MANAGING MODERN MAN.
617(TLS):21DEC73-1571
WILLSON, A.L., ED. A GÜNTER GRASS SYM-
POSIUM.
W.V. BLOMSTER, 406:WINTER72-385
WILMERDING, J., ED. THE GENIUS OF AMERI-
CAN PAINTING.
L. NOCHLIN, 441:2DEC73-4
WILMERDING, J. WINSLOW HOMER.*
E. WEEKS, 61:JAN73-99
WILMET, M. LE SYSTÈME DE L'INDICATIF EN
MOYEN FRANÇAIS.
M. LÉONARD, 320(CJL):FALL70-64
J. POHL, 209(FM):APR71-165
WILMOT, J. THE COMPLETE POEMS OF JOHN
WILMOT, EARL OF ROCHESTER.* (D.M.
VIETH, ED)
A. BARTON, 179(ES):DEC71-553
C.C. DOYLE, 173(ECS):FALL70-103
P. LEGOUIS, 189(EA):APR-JUN71-196
WILMOT, J. & OTHERS. THE GYLDENSTOLPE
MANUSCRIPT MISCELLANY OF POEMS BY JOHN
WILMOT, EARL OF ROCHESTER, AND OTHER
RESTORATION AUTHORS. (B. DANIELSSON &
D.M. VIETH, EDS)
A. BARTON, 179(ES):DEC71-553
WILSON, A. AS IF BY MAGIC.
P. ADAMS, 61:NOV73-128
D.A.N. JONES, 362:31MAY73-726
E. WHITE, 441:14OCT73-7
M. WOOD, 453:1NOV73-20
617(TLS):1JUN73-605
WILSON, A. THE CONCORDE FIASCO.
617(TLS):28DEC73-1595
WILSON, A. DEATH DANCE.
E. BALDESHWILER, 573(SSF):SUMMER71-
477
WILSON, A. THE WORLD OF CHARLES DICKENS.*
M. PRICE, 676(YR):WINTER72-271
S. WALL, 184(EIC):JUL71-261
WILSON, A. & P. JULLIAN. FOR WHOM THE
CLOCHE TOLLS.
G. DAVENPORT, 441:15APR73-5
WILSON, A.M. DIDEROT.*
J. STAROBINSKI, 453:22MAR73-18
617(TLS):19JAN73-59
WILSON, B.R. MAGIC AND THE MILLENNIUM.
617(TLS):16NOV73-1403
WILSON, B.R., ED. RATIONALITY.
W.V. DONIELA, 63:MAY72-97
A.C. MICHALOS, 154:DEC71-835
WILSON, C. QUEEN ELIZABETH AND THE
REVOLT OF THE NETHERLANDS.
639(VQR):SPRING71-LXXVI
WILSON, C. NEW PATHWAYS IN PSYCHOLOGY.
J.S. GORDON, 441:28JAN73-2
WILSON, C. SCOTTISH OPERA.
N. GOODWIN, 415:JUL72-671
WILSON, C. BERNARD SHAW.
S.P. ALBERT, 572:JAN70-38
WILSON, C. VOYAGE TO A BEGINNING.*
571:SUMMER70-114
WILSON, C.A. FOOD AND DRINK IN BRITAIN
FROM THE STONE AGE TO RECENT TIMES.
617(TLS):28DEC73-1583
WILSON, C.M. STARS IS GOD'S LANTERNS.
K.M. BRIGGS, 203:SPRING71-85
WILSON, D. THE FUTURE ROLE OF SINGAPORE.
617(TLS):6APR73-368
WILSON, D. MINORITY REPORT.
617(TLS):21DEC73-1563
WILSON, D.A. THE UNITED STATES AND THE
FUTURE OF THAILAND.
K.P. LANDON, 293(JAST):MAY71-729

WITTKOWER, R. & M. BORN UNDER SATURN.
  J.A. EMMENS, 54:SEP71-427
WITTKOWER, R. & M. THE DIVINE MICHELAN-
  GELO.
  O. BERENDSEN, 54:MAR70-102
WITTKOWSKI, W. DER JUNGE HEBBEL.
  L.W. KAHN, 222(GR):MAR71-141
WITTLIN, A.S. MUSEUMS.
  A.R. BLUMENTHAL, 127:FALL71-94
  P.J. KORSHIN, 481(PQ):JUL71-373
WITTLIN, C.J. - SEE LIVY
WITTLIN, T. COMMISSAR.
  617(TLS):12OCT73-1251
WITTRAM, R. RUSSIA AND EUROPE.
  617(TLS):27JUL73-865
WITTRAM, R. STUDIEN ZUM SELBSTVERSTÄND-
  NIS DES 1. UND 2. KABINETTS DER RUSSIS-
  CHEN PROVISORISCHEN REGIERUNG (MÄRZ
  BIS JULI 1917).
  W.E. MOSSE, 575(SEER):JUL72-474
WITTREICH, J.A., JR., ED. THE ROMANTICS
  ON MILTON.
  D.V.E., 191(ELN):SEP71(SUPP)-22
WITTROCK, W. DIE ÄLTESTEN MELODIETYPEN
  IM OSTDEUTSCHEN VOLKSGESANG.
  M. KOLINSKI, 187:SEP73-551
WLOSOK, A. ROME UND DIE CHRISTEN.*
  W.H.C. FREND, 123:JUN72-284
WODEHOUSE, P.G. BACHELORS ANONYMOUS.
  R. GARFITT, 362:18OCT73-528
  617(TLS):2NOV73-1338
WODEHOUSE, P.G. THE LITTLE NUGGET.
  PEARLS, GIRLS AND MONTY BODKIN.* SAM
  THE SUDDEN.
  617(TLS):26JAN73-84
WODEHOUSE, P.G. THE PLOT THAT THICKENED.
  M. LEVIN, 441:5AUG73-12
  M. WOOD, 453:1NOV73-20
  442(NY):13AUG73-86
WODEHOUSE, P.G. THE WORLD OF JEEVES.
  ALL ABOUT JEEVES.
  M. WOOD, 453:1NOV73-20
WODTKE, F.W. - SEE BENN, G.
WOEHRLIN, W.F. CHERNYSHEVSKII.*
  S. MONAS, 32:SEP72-667
  N.V. RIASANOVSKY, 319:JAN73-127
WOHLGEMUTH-BERGLUND, G. WORT FÜR WORT.
  H. BROCKHAUS, 406:SUMMER72-198
WOJTECKI, D. STUDIEN ZUR PERSONENGE-
  SCHICHTE DES DEUTSCHEN ORDENS IM 13.
  JAHRHUNDERT.
  R. FOLZ, 182:VOL24#3-120
WOLD, R. "EL DIARIO DE MÉXICO."*
  P.T. BRADLEY, 86(BHS):OCT72-415
WOLF, C. LESEN UND SCHREIBEN.
  617(TLS):6APR73-396
WOLF, C. THE QUEST FOR CHRISTA T.*
  E. GLOVER, 565:VOL12#4-53
WOLF, E. GENERALBASSÜBUNGEN.
  P. WILLIAMS, 415:FEB72-157
WOLF, E.R. PEASANT WARS OF THE TWENTIETH
  CENTURY.
  G. BENNETT, 293(JAST):NOV70-162
WOLF, F.O. DIE NEUE WISSENSCHAFT DES
  THOMAS HOBBES.
  G. GAWLICK, 53(AGP):BAND53HEFT3-310
WOLF, G.D. THE FAIR PLAY SETTLERS OF THE
  WEST BRANCH VALLEY, 1769-1784.
  R.S. KLEIN, 656(WMQ):JUL71-504
WOLF, H. - SEE ROTHE, J.
WOLF, J.B., ED. LOUIS XIV.
  617(TLS):2FEB73-133
WOLF, J.C. & G. FITZ GERALD, EDS. PAST,
  PRESENT AND FUTURE PERFECT.
  T. STURGEON, 441:4NOV73-75
WOLF, L. A DREAM OF DRACULA.
  P. ADAMS, 61:JAN73-100
  G. STADE, 441:14JAN73-2

WOLF, L. SPRACHGEOGRAPHISCHE UNTERSUCH-
  UNGEN ZU DEN BEZEICHNUNGEN FÜR HAUS-
  TIERE IM MASSIF CENTRAL.
  P. WUNDERLI, 260(IF):BAND74-291
WOLF, L., ED. TEXTE UND DOKUMENTE ZUR
  FRANZÖSISCHEN SPRACHGESCHICHTE: 16.
  JAHRHUNDERT.*
  M. SANDMANN, 545(RPH):AUG71-146
WOLF, P.M. EUGÈNE HÉNARD AND THE BEGIN-
  NING OF URBANISM IN PARIS 1900-1914.
  N. EVENSON, 576:MAY71-182
WOLF, R. MEIN FAMILI.
  617(TLS):12JAN73-36
WOLF-ROTTKAY, W-H. ALTNORDISCH-ISLÄNDIS-
  CHES LESEBUCH.
  G. KÖTZ, 343:BAND13HEFT2-203
WOLFE, B. MEMOIRS OF A NOT ALTOGETHER
  SHY PORNOGRAPHER.*
  C. QUIMBY, 109:SPRING/SUMMER73-171
WOLFE, D. THE IMAGE OF MAN IN AMERICA.
  L.B. CEBIK, 219(GAR):SPRING71-107
WOLFE, D.M. MILTON AND HIS ENGLAND.
  E. KEENELT, 568(SCN):SPRING72-7
WOLFE, G. THE FIFTH HEAD OF CERBERUS.
  617(TLS):18MAY73-562
WOLFE, M. THE FISCAL SYSTEM OF RENAIS-
  SANCE FRANCE.
  617(TLS):6JUL73-780
WOLFE, M. MAN ON A STRING.
  N. CALLENDAR, 441:23DEC73-16
WOLFE, M., ED. A SATURDAY NIGHT SCRAP-
  BOOK.
  C. BERGER, 99:NOV-DEC73-26
WOLFE, P. REBECCA WEST.
  617(TLS):21DEC73-1553
WOLFE, P.M. LINGUISTIC CHANGE AND THE
  GREAT VOWEL SHIFT IN ENGLISH.
  617(TLS):3AUG73-909
WOLFE, T. THE NOTEBOOKS OF THOMAS WOLFE.*
  (R.S. KENNEDY & P. REEVES, EDS)
  B.R. MC ELDERRY, JR., 219(GAR):FALL
    70-368
WOLFE, T. & E.W. JOHNSON, EDS. THE NEW
  JOURNALISM.
  C. LEHMANN-HAUPT, 441:27JUN73-63
  R. TODD, 61:JUL73-99
  M. WOOD, 441:22JUL73-20
WOLFE, T.W. SOVIET POWER AND EUROPE,
  1945-1970.*
  R.E. KANET, 550(RUSR):APR71-185
WÖLFEL, K., ED. LESSINGS LEBEN UND WERK
  IN DATEN UND BILDERN.
  S. SEIFERT, 654(WB):8/1971-181
WOLFENSBERGER, H. MUNDARTWANDEL IM 20.
  JAHRHUNDERT.*
  E. BAUER, 597(SN):VOL42#2-529
WOLFENSTEIN, E.V. THE REVOLUTIONARY
  PERSONALITY.
  R. COLES, 453:8MAR73-25
WOLFF, H.J. DAS JUSTIZWESEN DER PTOLE-
  MÄER. (2ND ED)
  A. POLAČEK, 182:VOL24#5-237
WOLFF, K. THE TEACHING OF ARTUR SCHNA-
  BEL.*
  H.F., 410(M&L):JUL72-326
WOLFF, L. KLEINERE SCHRIFTEN ZUR ALT-
  DEUTSCHEN PHILOLOGIE. (W. SCHRÖDER,
  ED)
  B. KRATZ, 133:1970/1-121
WOLFF, L. - SEE HARTMANN VON AUE
WOLFF, R.L. & H.W. HAZARD, EDS. A HIS-
  TORY OF THE CRUSADES. (VOL 2) (2ND ED)
  J.F. POWERS, 613:SPRING71-148
WOLFF, R.P. PHILOSOPHY.
  R.E. ABU SHANAB, 484(PPR):JUN72-585
WOLFF, R.P. THE POVERTY OF LIBERALISM.*
  R. PASOTTI, 321:SPRING71-136
WOLFF, T. - SEE PUSHKIN, A.S.

WOLFF-WINDEGG, P. SWIFT.*
    F. RAU, 224(GRM):JAN70-111
WOLFRAM, H. ROOT AND BRANCH.
    R.K. KAUL, 255(HAB):WINTER70-52
WOLFRAM VON ESCHENBACH, W. TITUREL.
  (W.J. SCHRÖDER & G. HOLLANDT, EDS)
    J. HEINZLE, 190:BAND65HEFT4-435
WOLFSON, A. SPINOZA.
    H.W. BRANN, 328:FALL70-492
WOLFSON, H.A. THE PHILOSOPHY OF THE
  CHURCH FATHERS. (VOL 1) (3RD ED)
    H. MUSURILLO, 613:AUTUMN71-457
    T.S.P., 543:MAR71-553
WOLFSON, L. LE SCHIZO ET LES LANGUES.
    A. REY, 98:AUG-SEP70-677
WOLFZETTEL, F. MICHEL BUTOR UND DER
  KOLLEKTIVROMAN.
    S.M. BELL, 208(FS):JUL72-362
WOLIN, S.S. HOBBES AND THE EPIC TRADI-
  TION OF POLITICAL THEORY.
    C. WALTON, 481(PQ):JUL71-441
WOLITZ, S.L. THE PROUSTIAN COMMUNITY.*
    617(TLS):13APR73-423
WOLKENFELD, J. JOYCE CARY.*
    B. HARDY, 447(N&Q):JUL71-279
WOLLHEIM, D.A. THE UNIVERSE MAKERS.*
    639(VQR):SUMMER71-CXI
WOLLHEIM, D.A., WITH A.W. SAHA, EDS. THE
  1973 ANNUAL WORLD'S BEST SF.
    617(TLS):9NOV73-1378
WOLLHEIM, R. ART AND ITS OBJECTS.*
    R. ARNHEIM, 54:DEC70-471
    D.T. WIECK, 290(JAAC):WINTER70-271
WOLLMAN, N. & G. BONEM. THE OUTLOOK FOR
  WATER.
    42(AR):SUMMER71-290
WOLOCH, I. JACOBIN LEGACY.
    E.L. EISENSTEIN, 207(FR):APR71-946
WOLOHOJIAN, A.M. - SEE PSEUDO-CALLISTHENES
WOLSKA-CONUS, W. - SEE COSMAS INDICOPLEUS-
  TÈS
WOLTERSTORFF, N. ON UNIVERSALS.
    D. HOLDCROFT, 518:MAY72-32
    R. MUEHLMANN, 154:SEP71-577
WOOD, A.K. TEXAS COASTAL BEND.
    W. GARD, 584(SWR):SPRING72-V
WOOD, A.W. KANT'S MORAL RELIGION.
    J.D.C., 543:JUN71-760
    D. WALSH, 479(PHQ):JAN71-75
    F.E. WILSON, 185:OCT70-79
WOOD, C. CHAUCER AND THE COUNTRY OF THE
  STARS.*
    N.C. CARPENTER, 219(GAR):WINTER70-511
    J.D. NORTH, 541(RES):NOV71-471
    J.M. STEADMAN, 301(JEGP):JAN72-113
    R.M. WILSON, 175:AUTUMN70-97
WOOD, C. H.
    A. RENDLE, 157:WINTER70-70
WOOD, G.B. THE NORTH COUNTRY.
    617(TLS):23FEB73-222
WOOD, J. NORTH BEAT.
    617(TLS):18MAY73-562
WOOD, J. THREE BLIND MICE.
    N. CALLENDAR, 441:9DEC73-50
WOOD, R.C. - SEE MILLER, H. & J.R. CHILDS
WOOD, R.E. MARTIN BUBER'S ONTOLOGY.
    S.J.B., 543:SEP70-143
WOOD, R.E., ED. THE FUTURE OF META-
  PHYSICS.
    M. LEBOWITZ, 598(SOR):SPRING73-452
WOOD, T. THE BRIGHTER SIDE OF BILLY
  WILDER, PRIMARILY.
    G. BARING, 200:MAY70-290
WOODBRIDGE, K. LANDSCAPE AND ANTIQUITY.
    J. LEES-MILNE, 39:MAY71-435
    A.J. SAMBROOK, 173(ECS):SPRING72-484

WOODBURY, C.J. TALKS WITH EMERSON. (H.L.
  FINCH, ED)
    D. ABEL, 432(NEQ):DEC71-679
WOODCOCK, G. THE CRYSTAL SPIRIT.
    R. MC CORMACK, 606(TAMR):#58-77
WOODCOCK, G., ED. WYNDHAM LEWIS IN
  CANADA.
    J. COLDWELL, 102(CANL):WINTER72-88
WOODCOCK, G., ED. MALCOLM LOWRY.*
    J. COLDWELL, 102(CANL):WINTER72-88
    A. ROBERTSON, 648:OCT71-53
WOODCOCK, G. HUGH MAC LENNAN.*
    B. NESBITT, 648:JAN71-68
WOODCOCK, G. THE REJECTION OF POLITICS.
    S. AJZENSTAT, 99:NOV-DEC73-45
WOODCOCK, G. - SEE DICKENS, C.
WOODESON, J. MARK GERTLER.
    617(TLS):26JAN73-96
WOODHEAD, A.G. THUCYDIDES ON THE NATURE
  OF POWER.*
    G.L. CAWKWELL, 123:JUN72-186
    M.F. MC GREGOR, 487:SPRING71-76
WOODHOUSE, A.S.P. THE HEAVENLY MUSE. (H.
  MAC CALLUM, ED)
    617(TLS):21SEP73-1090
WOODHOUSE, J.R. - SEE CALVINO, I.
WOODHOUSE, M. BLUE BONE.
    M. LEVIN, 441:22APR73-28
    617(TLS):17AUG73-959
WOODMAN, R.G. JAMES REANEY.*
    G. WARKENTIN, 296:WINTER73-88
WOODMAN, V. & A. KENT. GLOUCESTER AS
  IT WAS.
    617(TLS):21DEC73-1573
WOODRESS, J. WILLA CATHER.*
    S. ALLABACK, 401(MLQ):DEC71-445
    J.T. FLANAGAN, 301(JEGP):APR72-290
WOODRING, C. POLITICS IN ENGLISH ROMANTIC
  POETRY.*
    H. BLOOM, 639(VQR):SPRING71-314
    S.C., 191(ELN):SEP71(SUPP)-22
    C.J. MYERS, 150(DR):SUMMER71-274
    M.F. SCHULZ, 401(MLQ):MAR72-83
WOODRING, C. WORDSWORTH.*
    H. PESCHMANN, 175:AUTUMN70-104
WOODS, F. - SEE CHURCHILL, W.S.
WOODS, J. TURNING TO LOOK BACK.
    J.R. COOLEY, 398:AUTUMN73-221
    R. PINSKY, 491:JUN73-168
    V. YOUNG, 249(HUDR):WINTER72/73-669
WOODS, S. SERPENT'S TOOTH.
    N. CALLENDAR, 441:29JUL73-13
WOODS, S. YET SHE MUST DIE.
    617(TLS):16MAR73-303
WOODS, W.C. THE KILLING ZONE.
    42(AR):SUMMER70-262
WOODSIDE, A.B. VIETNAM AND THE CHINESE
  MODEL.*
    639(VQR):SUMMER71-CXXVII
WOODSTONE, A. NIXON'S HEAD.
    441:20MAY73-20
WOODSWORTH, J.S. MY NEIGHBOUR. STRANGERS
  WITH OUR GATES.
    G.W., 102(CANL):AUTUMN72-112
WOODWARD, C.A. THE GROWTH OF A PARTY
  SYSTEM IN CEYLON.
    G.J. LERSKI, 293(JAST):NOV70-222
WOODWARD, C.V. AMERICAN COUNTERPOINT.*
    676(YR):AUTUMN71-XXX
WOODWARD, G.S. POCAHONTAS.*
    B. TOELKEN, 650(WF):OCT70-268
WOODWARD, J.B. LEONID ANDREYEV.*
    P.A. FISCHER, 32:JUN72-512
    S. KARLINSKY, 550(RUSR):JAN71-76
    205(FMLS):OCT70-424
WOODY, R.J. "DANCE TO A LONELY TUNE."
    D. HERING, 151:OCT70-87
WOOF, R. - SEE THOMPSON, T.W.

WOOLDRIDGE, W.C. UNCLE SAM - THE MONO-
POLY MAN.
E. HOLLOWAY, 619(TC):VOL179#1049-51
WOOLF, J. & J. GANDON - SEE UNDER BADE-
SLADE, J. & J. ROCQUE
WOOLF, L. THE JOURNEY NOT THE ARRIVAL
MATTERS.
D. GERVAIS, 97(CQ):SPRING/SUMMER70-82
F.P.W. MC DOWELL, 177(ELT):VOL13#2-
174
H.H. SHAPLEY, 50(ARQ):AUTUMN70-272
T.F. STALEY, 295:NOV72-576
WOOLF, L. SOWING. GROWING. BEGINNING
AGAIN. DOWNHILL ALL THE WAY.
D. GERVAIS, 97(CQ):SPRING/SUMMER70-82
WOOLF, S.J., ED. THE REBIRTH OF ITALY
1943-50.
617(TLS):16FEB73-186
WOOLF, V. MRS. DALLOWAY'S PARTY. (S.
MC NICHOL, ED)
M. DRABBLE, 362:10MAY73-623
617(TLS):20JUL73-831
WOOLFORD, J., ED. SALE CATALOGUES OF
LIBRARIES OF EMINENT PERSONS. (VOL 6)
617(TLS):13JUL73-816
WOOLHOUSE, R.S. LOCKE'S PHILOSOPHY OF
SCIENCE AND KNOWLEDGE.
J.M. HUMBER, 484(PPR):JUN72-579
S.E. KINDRED, 311(JP):21JUN73-352
WOOLMAN, J. THE JOURNAL AND MAJOR ESSAYS
OF JOHN WOOLMAN. (P.P. MOULTON, ED)
D.B. SHEA, 165:FALL73-204
WORCESTRE, W. WILLIAM WORCESTRE "ITIN-
ERARIES."* (J.H. HARVEY, ED)
T. HASSALL, 382(MAE):1972/2-172
G.B. PARKS, 551(RENQ):SUMMER71-269
WORDSWORTH, J. THE LETTERS OF JOHN WORDS-
WORTH.* (C.H. KETCHAM, ED)
J.R. MAC GILLIVRAY, 627(UTQ):FALL70-73
C.L. MORRISON, 541(RES):MAY71-249
WORDSWORTH, W. & D. THE LETTERS OF WIL-
LIAM AND DOROTHY WORDSWORTH.* (VOL 1)
(2ND ED) (E. DE SELINCOURT, ED; REV BY
C.L. SHAVER)
J. WORDSWORTH, 38:BAND88HEFT3-401
WORDSWORTH, W. & D. THE LETTERS OF WIL-
LIAM AND DOROTHY WORDSWORTH.* (2ND ED)
(E. DE SELINCOURT, ED) (VOL 2 REV BY
M. MOORMAN; VOL 3 REV BY M. MOORMAN &
A.G. HILL)
C.L. MORRISON, 541(RES):NOV71-527
"WORK IN AMERICA."
M. KEMPTON, 453:8FEB73-11
R. SHERRILL, 441:8JUL73-2
"THE WORLD OF LEARNING 1972-73."
617(TLS):2FEB73-114
WORMALD, F. THE WINCHESTER PSALTER.
617(TLS):28SEP73-1140
WÖRNER, K.H. STOCKHAUSEN. (B. HOPKINS,
ED & TRANS)
617(TLS):2MAR73-239
WOROSZYLSKI, W. THE LIFE OF MAYAKOVSKY.*
E.J. BROWN, 550(RUSR):OCT71-398
WORSTHORNE, P. THE SOCIALIST MYTH.
L. CLARK, 619(TC):VOL179#1049-51
"WÖRTERBUCH DER DEUTSCHEN AUSSPRACHE."
(2ND ED)
K. KOHLER, 680(ZDP):BAND90HEFT1-147
WORTH, D.S. DICTIONARY OF WESTERN KAM-
CHADAL.
G.F. MEIER, 682(ZPSK):BAND23HEFT6-645
WORTH, D.S., A.S. KOZAK & D.B. JOHNSON.
RUSSIAN DERIVATIONAL DICTIONARY.*
T.J. BUTLER, 32:SEP72-738
H.H. KELLER, 350:MAR72-197
WORTH, K.J. REVOLUTIONS IN MODERN ENG-
LISH DRAMA.
617(TLS):6JUL73-775

WORTLEY, W.V. TALLEMANT DES RÉAUX.
G. BREMNER, 402(MLR):APR72-414
WOSIEN, M-G. THE RUSSIAN FOLK-TALE.*
E. STENBOCK-FERMOR, 550(RUSR):JAN71-84
WOTTON, H. THE ELEMENTS OF ARCHITECTURE.
(F. HARD, ED)
N. MILLER, 576:MAR70-64
WRANGLES, A., ED. THE COMPLETE GUIDE TO
SEA ANGLING. (REV)
617(TLS):16FEB73-189
WRAY, E., C. ROSENFIELD & D. BAILEY.
TEN LIVES OF THE BUDDHA.
617(TLS):17AUG73-944
WRIGGINS, W.H. THE RULER'S IMPERATIVE.
H. BIENEN, 293(JAST):FEB71-420
WRIGHT, A. FIRST PERSONS.
B. HAYES, 441:18NOV73-51
C. LEHMANN-HAUPT, 441:28NOV73-49
WRIGHT, C. ABSOLUTELY NOTHING TO GET
ALARMED ABOUT.
P. ADAMS, 61:APR73-128
A. BROYARD, 441:9APR73-41
D. FREEMAN, 441:11MAR73-34
442(NY):17MAR73-131
WRIGHT, C. THE LIBERAL CHRISTIANS.
L. BUELL, 432(NEQ):MAR71-163
WRIGHT, D., ED. BENJAMIN FRANKLIN.
M. HALL, 432(NEQ):JUN71-317
WRIGHT, D. - SEE DE QUINCEY, T.
WRIGHT, D.H. - SEE "THE VESPASIAN PSAL-
TER"
WRIGHT, D.M., ED. THE COUNTRYMAN GARDEN-
ING BOOK.
617(TLS):23NOV73-1456
WRIGHT, D.M. THE FLY-FISHER'S PLANTS.
617(TLS):10AUG73-937
WRIGHT, E.O. THE POLITICS OF PUNISHMENT.
D.J. ROTHMAN, 441:27MAY73-4
WRIGHT, F.L. AN ORGANIC ARCHITECTURE.
E.A. SÖVIK, 363:FEB71-53
VON WRIGHT, G.H. EXPLANATION AND UNDER-
STANDING.*
G.G. BRITTAN, JR., 311(JP):22NOV73-
759
R.G. SWINBURNE, 518:MAY72-34
VON WRIGHT, G.H. - SEE WITTGENSTEIN, L.
WRIGHT, H.B. & M.K. SPEARS - SEE PRIOR,
M.
WRIGHT, J. COLLECTED POEMS.*
R. OLIVER, 598(SOR):SPRING73-492
M.G. PERLOFF, 659:WINTER73-97
WRIGHT, J. SHALL WE GATHER AT THE RIVER.*
M. BROWN, 565:VOL11#2-57
WRIGHT, J. - SEE HESSE, H.
WRIGHT, J.W. SHELLEY'S MYTH OF METAPHOR.*
S-C., 191(ELN):SEP71(SUPP)-57
639(VQR):SPRING71-LXV
WRIGHT, K.A. GENTLE ARE ITS SONGS.
617(TLS):20JUL73-826
WRIGHT, L.B. GOLD, GLORY, AND THE GOS-
PEL.*
R. PIKE, 656(WMQ):JUL71-516
639(VQR):SPRING71-LXXIII
WRIGHT, M.C., ED. CHINA IN REVOLUTION:
THE FIRST PHASE, 1900-1913.*
I.C.Y. HSÜ, 318(JAOS):JAN-MAR71-149
WRIGHT, N. - SEE IRVING, W.
WRIGHT, P. KNIBB "THE NOTORIOUS."
617(TLS):4MAY73-493
WRIGHT, R.B. IN THE MIDDLE OF A LIFE.
R.P. BRICKNER, 441:23SEP73-7
B. DE MOTT, 61:DEC73-126
WRIGHT, R.B. THE WEEKEND MAN.*
M.J. EDWARDS, 102(CANL):WINTER72-91
L.T. LEMON, 502(PRS):FALL71-268
WRIGHT, R.C.M. A HANDBOOK OF PLANT
PROPAGATION.
617(TLS):19OCT73-1289

WRIGHT, W.A. - SEE ASCHAM, R.
WRIGHT, W.E. COLONEL EPHRAIM WILLIAMS.
R.D. BIRDSALL, 432(NEQ):SEP71-493
WRIGHT, W.F. THE SHAPING OF THE DYNASTS.*
J. DELBAERE-GARANT, 556(RLV):1970/1-
104
WRIGLEY, E.A., ED. IDENTIFYING PEOPLE IN
THE PAST.
617(TLS):12OCT73-1226
WROTH, L.C. THE VOYAGES OF GIOVANNIA DA
VERRAZANO, 1524-1528.
C. BRIDENBAUGH, 432(NEQ):MAR71-157
WU HSI-TSE. FEI CHENG-CH'ING LUN.
L.H.D. GORDON & S. CHANG, 293(JAST):
NOV70-137
WU, S.H.L. COMMUNICATION AND IMPERIAL
CONTROL IN CHINA.
A.Y-C. LUI, 302:JUL71-375
PEI HUANG, 244(HJAS):VOL31-323
WU, Y-L., ED. CHINA.
R. MURPHEY, 441:23SEP73-40
617(TLS):13JUL73-817
WU, Y-L. & R.B. SHEEKS. THE ORGANIZATION
AND SUPPORT OF SCIENTIFIC RESEARCH AND
DEVELOPMENT IN MAINLAND CHINA.
R.P. SUTTMEIER, 293(JAST):FEB71-448
WUL, S. THE TEMPLE OF THE PAST.
T. STURGEON, 441:23SEP73-39
WULBERN, J.H. BRECHT AND IONESCO.
J. FUEGI, 397(MD):FEB72-483
F. JONES, 401(MLQ):SEP72-346
V. WILLIAMS, 406:SUMMER72-166
WUNBERG, G. DER FRÜHE HOFMANNSTHAL.
R. MAJUT, 224(GRM):NOV70-474
WUNBERG, G. - SEE BAHR, H.
WUNDERLI, P. LA PLUS ANCIENNE TRADUCTION
PROVENÇALE (XIIE SIÈCLE) DES CHAPITRES
XIII À XVII DE L'ÉVANGILE DE SAINT
JEAN.
R. BAUM, 72:BAND209HEFT1/3-195
Å. GRAFSTRÖM, 597(SN):VOL43#1-278
WUNDERLICH, D., ED. PROBLEME UND FORT-
SCHRITTE DER TRANSFORMATIONSGRAMMATIK.
J. FELIXBERGER, 72:BAND209HEFT4/6-389
WURLITZER, R. FLATS.
639(VQR):WINTER71-IX
WURMAN, R., A. LEVY & J. KATZ. THE
NATURE OF RECREATION.
C. WISEMAN, 231:FEB73-105
WURMAN, R.S. MAKING THE CITY OBSERVABLE.
505:NOV71-138
WÜRZBACH, N., ED. THE NOVEL IN LETTERS.
R.A. DAY, 454:WINTER72-189
C.J. RAWSON, 447(N&Q):AUG71-314
G. ROHMANN, 430(NS):JUN70-311
"WÜRZBURGER PROSASTUDIEN I."*
P. OCHSENBEIN, 657(WW):JAN/FEB71-64
WÜST, J. DIE LEIS WILLELME.
W. ROTHWELL, 208(FS):APR72-185
WYATT, T. COLLECTED POEMS OF SIR THOMAS
WYATT.* (K. MUIR & P. THOMSON, EDS)
H.A. MASON, 97(CQ):SUMMER/AUTUMN71-
355
W. MAYNARD, 541(RES):MAY71-187
WYATT, W. TURN AGAIN, WESTMINSTER.
R. CROSSMAN, 362:22NOV73-713
617(TLS):30NOV73-1463
WYATT, W.F., JR. INDO-EUROPEAN /A/.*
N.E. COLLINGE, 320(CJL):FALL71-70
A. SIHLER, 215(GL):VOL11#3-155
O. SZEMERÉNYI, 350:MAR72-165
WYATT, W.F., JR. METRICAL LENGTHENING
IN HOMER.*
H.M. HOENIGSWALD, 350:DEC72-929
C.J. RUIJGH, 361:VOL27#2/3-263
M.M. WILLCOCK, 123:MAR72-68

WYCHERLEY, W. L'EPOUSE CAMPAGNARDE (THE
COUNTRY WIFE). (A. MAVROCORDATO, ED &
TRANS)
I. SIMON, 556(RLV):1971/2-230
WYCZYNSKI, P., J. MÉNARD & J. HARE, EDS.
RECHERCHE ET LITTÉRATURE CANADIENNE-
FRANCAISE.* [SHOWN IN PREV UNDER 1ST
ED ONLY]
R. MERCIER, 557(RSH):JUL-SEP70-499
B-Z. SHEK, 207(FR):DEC70-474
WYKA, K. MODERNIZM POLSKI.
J.T. BAER, 497(POLR):WINTER71-126
WYLDER, D.E. HEMINGWAY'S HEROES.
R.W. ETULAIN, 594:FALL70-382
WYLDER, E. THE LAST FACE.
G.W. ALLEN, 27(AL):MAY72-322
WYLER, S. DER BEGRIFF DER MACHT IN
CHRISTOPHER MARLOWES TAMBURLAINE I.
R. RIS, 343:BAND13HEFT2-205
WYLIE, L., A. BÉGUÉ & L. BÉGUÉ. LES
FRANÇAIS.*
W. WRAGE, 207(FR):OCT70-152
WYLIE, N.S. RUSSELL AND THE BED-BUGS.
617(TLS):30MAR73-361
WYLLER, E.A. DER SPÄTE PLATON.*
P.M. HUBY, 123:JUN72-198
WYND, O. THE FORTY DAYS.
M. LEVIN, 441:14JAN73-24
WYROZUMSKI, J. - SEE GRODECKI, R.
WYSLING, H. "MYTHOS UND PSYCHOLOGIE" BEI
THOMAS MANN.
I. FEUERLICHT, 221(GQ):NOV71-600
WYSS, H., ED. DAS LUZERNER OSTERSPIEL.*
H.R., 657(WW):MAR/APR70-138
H. STOPP, 680(ZDP):BAND90HEFT3-463
WYTRWAL, A. POLES IN AMERICAN HISTORY
AND TRADITION.
J. ZUBRZYCKI, 575(SEER):JAN72-145


XENOPHON. CYROPÉDIE. (VOL 1) (M. BIZOS,
ED & TRANS)
F.M. WASSERMANN, 124:NOV71-105
XENOPHON. MEMOIRS OF SOCRATES [AND] THE
SYMPOSIUM.* (H. TREDENNICK, TRANS)
D. SIDER, 399(MLJ):MAR71-188
XENOPHON. XÉNOPHON, "L'ART DE LA
CHASSE."* (É. DELEBECQUE, ED & TRANS)
P. LOUIS, 555:VOL45FASC2-343
J.A. RICHMOND, 123:JUN72-192
XHAUFFLAIRE, M. FEUERBACH ET LA THÉOLO-
GIE DE LA SÉCULARISATION.
L. BOUGIE, 154:JUN71-398


YAKIR, P. A CHILDHOOD IN PRISON.* (R.
CONQUEST, ED)
T. LASK, 441:3MAR73-35
YAMAGUCHI, M. THE INTUITION OF ZEN AND
BERGSON.
P.F. SCHMIDT, 485(PE&W):JAN71-92
P. WIENPAHL, 318(JAOS):OCT-DEC71-525
YÁÑEZ, A. THE LEAN LANDS.*
J.D. MC KEE, 649(WAL):SPRING70-65
YANG, M.M.C. SOCIOECONOMIC RESULTS OF
LAND REFORM IN TAIWAN.
S.P.S. HO, 293(JAST):FEB71-452
YANOVSKY, B. THE DARK FIELD OF VENUS.
P. ADAMS, 61:MAR73-107
W.H. AUDEN, 453:22FEB73-34
C. LEHMANN-HAUPT, 441:22JAN73-29
441:25FEB73-22
YANOVSKY, V.S. OF LIGHT AND SOUNDING
BRASS.*
442(NY):20JAN73-102

YAO HSIN-NUNG. THE MALICE OF EMPIRE.
  W.A. LYELL, 352(LE&W):VOL15#2-316
  A. RENDLE, 157:SUMMER70-75
  W. SCHULTZ, 50(ARQ):AUTUMN71-275
YARMOLINSKY, A. DOSTOEVSKY: WORKS AND
  DAYS.*
  V. TERRAS, 32:JUN72-507
YARMOLINSKY, A. THE MILITARY ESTABLISH-
  MENT.
  H.H. RANSOM, 639(VQR):SPRING71-278
YARMOLINSKY, A. - SEE CHEKHOV, A.
YARROW, P.J. A LITERARY HISTORY OF
  FRANCE. (VOL 2)
  R.E. TAYLOR, 551(RENQ):SPRING71-98
YARWOOD, D. ROBERT ADAM.
  J. LEES-MILNE, 39:JAN71-71
  S. SPECTOR, 58:SEP/OCT70-18
YAŚASVATSĀGARA, Ś. SYĀDVĀDAMUKTĀVALĪ OR
  JAINAVIŚEṢATARKA AND BHĀVASAPTATIKĀ BY
  ŚRĪ YAŚASVATSĀGARA. (S.A. UPADHYAYA,
  ED)
  L. ROCHER, 318(JAOS):JAN-MAR71-152
YASHPAL. SHORT STORIES OF YASHPAL,
  AUTHOR AND PATRIOT. (C. FRIEND, ED &
  TRANS)
  R.V. BAUMER, 352(LE&W):VOL15#2-329
  R.O. SWAN, 293(JAST):FEB71-514
YASUJI, T. - SEE UNDER TOITA YASUJI
YASUO, N. - SEE UNDER NAKAMURA YASUO
YATE, W. AN ACCOUNT OF NEW ZEALAND.
  F. SARGESON, 368:SEP71-299
YATES, F.A. THE ROSICRUCIAN ENLIGHTEN-
  MENT.
  C. HILL, 453:4OCT73-23
  H. TREVOR-ROPER, 362:18JAN73-87
  617(TLS):20APR73-445
YATES, F.A. THEATRE OF THE WORLD.*
  T. LAWRENSON, 402(MLR):JUL72-614
  S. ORGEL, 405(MP):NOV71-159
  502(PRS):FALL70-278
YATES, J.M. THE GREAT BEAR LAKE MEDITA-
  TIONS.*
  D. BARBOUR, 150(DR):SPRING71-133
  J. REID, 102(CANL):WINTER72-95
  R.S., 376:JAN71-131
YATES, J.M. PARALLAX.
  J. DITSKY, 628:SPRING72-108
YATES, J.V., ED. THE INTERNATIONAL YEAR
  BOOK AND STATESMEN'S WHO'S WHO 1973.
  617(TLS):21SEP73-1091
YATES, W.E. GRILLPARZER.*
  E. KRISPYN, 301(JEGP):OCT72-587
  A. OBERMAYER, 67:NOV72-251
YATES, W.E. - SEE GRILLPARZER, F.
YAVETZ, Z. PLEBS AND PRINCEPS.*
  J. HELLEGOUARC'H, 555:VOL45FASC1-182
YAZAKI, T. SOCIAL CHANGE AND THE CITY
  IN JAPAN.
  G. ROZMAN, 293(JAST):MAY71-681
YAZAKI, T. THE SOCIOECONOMIC STRUCTURE
  OF THE TOKYO METROPOLITAN COMPLEX.
  C.C. BRETT, 293(JAST):AUG71-902
"THE YEARBOOK OF ENGLISH STUDIES." (VOL
  1) (T.J.B. SPENCER & R.L. SMALLWOOD,
  EDS)
  C.J. HORNE, 67:MAY72-93
YEATS, W.B., ED. FAIRY AND FOLK TALES OF
  IRELAND.
  617(TLS):22JUN73-726
YEATS, W.B. MEMOIRS. (D. DONOGHUE, ED)
  P. ADAMS, 61:MAY73-122
  W. EMPSON, 453:13DEC73-43
  C. LEHMANN-HAUPT, 441:2APR73-33
  T. PARKINSON, 441:29APR73-2
  617(TLS):19JAN73-53

YEATS, W.B. JOHN SHERMAN & DHOYA.*
  (R.J. FINNERAN, ED)
  I. FLETCHER, 447(N&Q):JUL71-275
  N.H. MAC KENZIE, 529(QQ):AUTUMN71-462
  R.S., 376:APR71-129
  G.B. SAUL, 50(ARQ):SUMMER70-191
YEATS, W.B. A TOWER OF POLISHED BLACK
  STONES.* (D.R. CLARK & G. MAYHEW, EDS)
  R.J. FINNERAN, 295:FEB73-129
YEATS, W.B. UNCOLLECTED PROSE BY W.B.
  YEATS.* (VOL 1) (J.P. FRAYNE, ED)
  A.N. JEFFARES, 541(RES):AUG71-375
  N.H. MAC KENZIE, 529(QQ):AUTUMN71-462
  T. WEBB, 597(SN):VOL43#2-594
YEATS, W.B. & T. KINSELLA. DAVIS, MAN-
  GAN, FERGUSON?
  R.F., 189(EA):APR-JUN71-212
YEHOSHUA, A.B. THREE DAYS AND A CHILD.
  E.M. BRONER, 390:NOV70-78
  J. GREENFIELD, 287:DEC70-27
YÊKHAUN, M.L. - SEE UNDER MINN LATT YÊK-
  HAUN
YELLEN, S. THE CONVEX MIRROR.
  F.D. REEVE, 491:JAN73-234
YERUSHALMI, Y.H. FROM SPANISH COURT TO
  ITALIAN GHETTO.
  R.H. POPKIN, 319:JUL73-403
YETMAN, N.R., ED. LIFE UNDER THE "PECU-
  LIAR INSTITUTION."
  F.N. BONEY, 219(GAR):WINTER71-521
  C.W. JOYNER, 292(JAF):OCT-DEC71-453
YGLESIAS, H. HOW SHE DIED.*
  617(TLS):26JAN73-85
YIP, W-L. EZRA POUND'S "CATHAY."*
  D.B. GRAHAM, 352(LE&W):VOL15#1-157
  M. LOI, 549(RLC):JAN-MAR71-129
  H. SERGEANT, 175:SUMMER71-63
YOKOI, S. SAIGOTEKI NO NIHON NO HEITAI.
  R.L. BROWN, 270:VOL22#4-84
YOLTON, J.W. LOCKE AND THE COMPASS OF
  HUMAN UNDERSTANDING.*
  J. BENNETT, 479(PHQ):JUL71-265
  639(VQR):SUMMER71-CXXXVI
YOLTON, J.W., ED. JOHN LOCKE: PROBLEMS
  AND PERSPECTIVES.*
  P.J. WHITE, 154:DEC71-843
YOLTON, J.W. METAPHYSICAL ANALYSIS.*
  J.B.L., 543:SEP70-144
  F. WILSON, 486:SEP70-455
YOROI, K. GAṆEŚAGĪTĀ.
  H.V. GUENTHER, 318(JAOS):OCT-DEC71-554
YOSELOFF, M. REMEMBER ME TO MARCIE.
  M. LEVIN, 441:4FEB73-27
YOSHIDA, M. IN SEARCH OF PERSIAN POT-
  TERY.
  617(TLS):15JUN73-699
YOST, C. THE CONDUCT AND MISCONDUCT OF
  FOREIGN AFFAIRS.
  D.P. CALLEO, 441:25FEB73-44
  H. CLARK, 109:SPRING/SUMMER73-162
YOUNG, A.F., ED. DISSENT.
  K.J. HANSEN & J.A. NUECHTERLEIN,
    529(QQ):SPRING71-128
YOUNG, C.T. THE CAPTIVE.
  M. LEVIN, 441:23DEC73-16
YOUNG, D.C. THREE ODES OF PINDAR.
  W.J. SLATER, 487:SPRING71-70
YOUNG, D.P. SWEATING OUT THE WINTER.*
  L. HART, 661:SUMMER/FALL71-85
YOUNG, E. THE BOWES MUSEUM, BARNARD
  CASTLE CATALOGUE OF SPANISH AND ITALIAN
  PAINTINGS.
  T. CROMBIE, 39:FEB71-150
YOUNG, E. THE CORRESPONDENCE OF EDWARD
  YOUNG, 1683-1765.* (H. PETTIT, ED)
  J.A. HAY, 67:NOV72-225
  W.L. WALLACE, 651(WHR):AUTUMN72-375

YOUNG, E.R.  STORIES FROM INDIAN WIGWAMS
   AND NORTHERN CAMPFIRES.
      K. O'DONNELL, 296:SUMMER73-120
YOUNG, I.S.  UNCLE HERSCHEL, DR. PADIL-
   SKY, AND THE EVIL EYE.
      M. LEVIN, 441:25MAR73-48
YOUNG, J.  J.Y.: THE AUTOBIOGRAPHY OF
   JIMMY YOUNG.
      F. DILLON, 362:6DEC73-788
YOUNG, J.Z.  AN INTRODUCTION TO THE STUDY
   OF MAN.*
      C.P. HASKINS, 441:23DEC73-12
YOUNG, K.  CHAPEL.
      617(TLS):10AUG73-933
YOUNG, K. - SEE LOCKHART, R.B.
YOUNG, L.K.  BRITISH POLICY IN CHINA
   1895-1902.
      J.J. NOLDE, 293(JAST):FEB71-439
YOUNG, M. & P. WILLMOTT.  THE SYMMETRICAL
   FAMILY.
      W.G. RUNCIMAN, 362:25OCT73-570
      617(TLS):26OCT73-1307
YOUNG, P.  NAPOLEON'S MARSHALS.
      617(TLS):16NOV73-1390
YOUNG, P. - SEE HEMINGWAY, E.
YOUNG, P. & J.P. LAWFORD.  WELLINGTON'S
   MASTERPIECE.
      617(TLS):13JUL73-805
YOUNG, P.M.  THE BACHS, 1500-1850.*
      639(VQR):WINTER71-XXXVI
YOUNG, P.M.  HAYDN.
      M. PETERSON, 470:MAY71-35
YOUNG, P.M.  SIR ARTHUR SULLIVAN.*
      G.H., 410(M&L):APR72-213
      A. LAMB, 415:JAN72-44
YOUNG, R.E., A.L. BECKER & K.L. PIKE.
   RHETORIC.
      G. CANNON, 350:SEP72-751
YOUNG, R.M.  MIND, BRAIN AND ADAPTATION
   IN THE NINETEENTH CENTURY.
      B.J. LOEWENBERG, 637(VS):MAR71-343
YOUNG, S.Z.  TERMS OF ENTRY.
      617(TLS):23NOV73-1422
YOUNG, V.  ON FILM.
      D. BROMWICH, 441:20MAY73-5
YOUNG, W.  OBSESSIVE POISONER.
      617(TLS):2MAR73-249
YOUNGBLOOD, G.  EXPANDED CINEMA.
      P. GIDAL, 592:MAR71-136
YOUNGSON, A.J.  AFTER THE FORTY-FIVE.
      617(TLS):31AUG73-1001
YOUSKEVITCH, I. & OTHERS.  DANCE PERSPEC-
   TIVES 40.
      A. PAGE, 290(JAAC):SUMMER71-566
YOXALL, H.W.  THE ENJOYMENT OF WINE.
      R.A. SOKOLOV, 441:2DEC73-84
YU-SHEN, C. - SEE UNDER CHIEN YU-SHEN
YUAN, F.K.S. & MA CHING-HSIEN, COMPS.
   HUO-PI CHIN-YUNG LUN-WEN FEN-LEI SO-YIN.
      293(JAST):NOV70-245
YUAN, F.K.S. & MA CHING-HSIEN, COMPS.
   TSAI-CHENG LUN-WEN FEN-LEI SO-YIN.
   CHING-CHI LUN-WEN FEN-LEI SO-YIN.
      293(JAST):NOV70-244
YÜCEL, T.  L'IMAGINAIRE DE BERNANOS.
      E. BEAUMONT, 208(FS):APR72-223
      E.M. O'SHARKEY, 402(MLR):JUL72-657
YUILL, W.E. - SEE LENZ, J.M.R.
YUKICHI, F. - SEE UNDER FUKUZAWA YUKICHI
YURCHENKO, H.  A MIGHTY HARD ROAD.
      M. PETERSON, 470:JAN71-44
YURICK, S.  SOMEONE JUST LIKE YOU.*
      617(TLS):20JUL73-825
YURKIEVICH, S.  FUNDADORES DE LA NUEVA
   POESÍA LATINOAMERICANA.
      D.L. SHAW, 402(MLR):APR72-447

ZABEEH, F.  HUME.
      H.J. ALLEN, 321:WINTER70[VOL5#1]-75
ZABEEH, F. - SEE "AVICENNA'S TREATISE ON
   LOGIC"
ZABEL, M.D. - SEE ROBINSON, E.A.
ZAC, S.  SPINOZA ET L'INTERPRÉTATION DE
   L'ECRITURE.
      G. ISRAEL, 542:APR-JUN70-191
ZACEK, J.F.  PALACKÝ.
      F.L. CARSTEN, 575(SEER):JUL72-468
ZADDY, Z.P.  CHRÉTIEN STUDIES.
      617(TLS):13APR73-429
ZADKINE, O.  LE MAILLET ET LE CISEAU,
   SOUVENIRS DE MA VIE.
      H.R. HOPE, 54:MAR71-130
ZAGORIN, P.  THE COURT AND THE COUNTRY.
      M. CAMPBELL, 551(RENQ):WINTER71-553
      S.S. WEBB, 656(WMQ):JAN71-129
ZAHARIA, N., M. PETRESCU-DÎMBOVIŢA & E.
   ZAHARIA.  AŞEZĂRI DIN MOLDOVA.
      J. NANDRIŞ, 575(SEER):JUL72-486
      R. PITTIONI, 182:VOL24#13/14-560
ZAIMOV, I. & V. ZAIMOVA.  BITOLSKI NADPIS
   NA IVAN VLADISLAV SAMODŬRZHETS BŬLGAR-
   SKI.
      H.G. LUNT, 32:JUN72-499
ZAIONCHKOVSKY, P.A.  ROSSIISKOE SAMODER-
   ZHAVIE V KONTSE XIX STOLETIIA.
      V.D. MEDLIN, 32:MAR72-160
ZALL, P.M., ED.  A NEST OF NINNIES AND
   OTHER ENGLISH JESTBOOKS OF THE SEVEN-
   TEENTH CENTURY.
      173(ECS):SUMMER71-499
ZAMPETTI, P.  THE COMPLETE PAINTINGS OF
   GIORGIONE.
      G. ROBERTSON, 39:DEC71-524
ZAMPETTI, P. - SEE "LORENZO LOTTO"
ZAMYATIN, Y.  A SOVIET HERETIC.*  (M.
   GINSBURG, ED & TRANS)
      J. DELANEY, 550(RUSR):APR71-211
ZANER, R.M. - SEE SCHUTZ, A.
ZANKER, P.  FORUM AUGUSTUM.
      R. BRILLIANT, 54:MAR71-110
ZANZOTTO, A.  GLI SGUARDI I FATTI E SEN-
   HAL.
      J-M. GARDAIR, 98:JUL71-665
ZAOZERSKAIA, E.I.  U ISTOKOV KRUPNOGO
   PROIZVODSTVA V ROSSKOI PROMYSHLENNOSTI
   XVI-XVII VEKOV.
      J.T. FUHRMANN, 32:DEC72-884
ZAPF, H.  MANUALE TYPOGRAPHICUM.
      42(AR):SPRING71-138
ZARDOYA, C.  POESÍA ESPAÑOLA DEL 98 Y
   DEL 27.*
      H.T. YOUNG, 240(HR):JAN71-120
ZAREV, P.  PREOBRAZENA LITERATURA.
      270:VOL22#1-12
ZAREV, P., G. DIMOV & I. KONEV.  IZSLED-
   VANIIA V CHEST NA AKADEMIK MIKHAIL
   ARNAUDOV.
      P. SHASHKO, 32:MAR72-233
ZAREV, P., S. KAROLEV & G. TSANEV, EDS.
   ISTORIIA NA BŬLGARSKATA LITERATURA.
   (VOL 3)
      C-A. MOSER, 32:DEC72-932
ZARNECKI, G.  ROMANESQUE ART.
      R. LEBOWITZ, 58:MAR72-18
      617(TLS):2FEB73-128
ZASLOW, M.  THE OPENING OF THE CANADIAN
   NORTH, 1870-1914.*
      617(TLS):13JUL73-811
ZAUNERT, P.  WESTFÄLISCHE SAGEN.  (2ND
   ED)  RHEINLAND SAGEN.  (NEW ED)
      F. HARKORT, 196:BAND12HEFT2/3-284
ZAZOFF, P.  ETRUSKISCHE SKARABÄEN.*
      R. HIGGINS, 54:SEP71-396
ZEBEL, S.H.  BALFOUR.
      617(TLS):18MAY73-549

VAN DER ZEE, H. & B. WILLIAM AND MARY.
A. WHITMAN, 441:24JUL73-29
442(NY):9JUL73-71
617(TLS):19OCT73-1279
ZEHBE, J. - SEE KANT, I.
"ZEICHEN UND SYSTEM DER SPRACHE." (VOL
1)
U. EGLI, 343:BAND13HEFT2-180
ZEIGLER, J., COMP. WORLD WAR II.
D.F. HARRISON, 14:OCT71-388
ZELAZNY, R. JACK OF SHADOWS.
617(TLS):18MAY73-562
ZELDIN, T. FRANCE 1848-1945. (VOL 1)
D. CAUTE, 362:25OCT73-561
ZELINSKY, B. ROMAN UND ROMANCHRONIK.
T. EEKMAN, 32:JUN72-509
ZELLER, B. HERMANN HESSE.
617(TLS):31AUG73-989
ZELLER, B. PORTRAIT OF HESSE.
E. WEBB, 648:JAN72-75
ZELNIK, R.E. LABOR AND SOCIETY IN TSAR-
IST RUSSIA.*
W.L. BLACKWELL, 32:SEP72-665
ZEMAN, Z.A.B. THE BREAK-UP OF THE HABS-
BURG EMPIRE. ÖSTERREICH-UNGARN IN DER
WELTPOLITIK 1900 BIS 1918. DIE NATION-
ALE FRAGE IN DER ÖSTERREICH-UNGARISCHEN
MONARCHIE 1900-1918.
M. MOLNÁR, 98:JAN70-73
ZEMAN, Z.A.B. THE GENTLEMEN NEGOTIATORS.
S.D. SPECTOR, 32:DEC72-914
ZEMP, H. MUSIQUE DAN.
A.P. MERRIAM, 187:JAN73-139
ZEMSKY, R. MERCHANTS, FARMERS, AND RIVER
GODS.
M. FREIBERG, 432(NEQ):SEP71-500
ZENK, G. KONZENTRATIONSPOLITIK IN SCHWE-
DEN.
K. MELLEROWICZ, 182:VOL24#19/20-722
ZENKOVSKY, S.A. RUSSIA'S OLD BELIEVERS.*
(RUSSIAN TITLE: RUSSKOE STAROOBRIAD-
CHESTVO.)
G. IVASK, 550(RUSR):APR71-191
ZENKOVSKY, S.A. & D.L. ARMBRUSTER. A
GUIDE TO THE BIBLIOGRAPHIES OF RUSSIAN
LITERATURE.*
C.M. HOTIMSKY, 67:MAY72-116
J.S.G. SIMMONS, 402(MLR):APR72-478
ZENTNER, W. - SEE HEBEL, J.P.
ZÉPHIR, J.J. PSYCHOLOGIE DE SALAVIN DE
GEORGES DUHAMEL.
J. FOX, 208(FS):OCT72-478
S. RAPHAEL, 402(MLR):APR72-426
ZEPPI, S. PROTAGORA E LA FILOSOFIA DEL
SUO TEMPO.
L.M·P·, 543:MAR71-553
ZÉRAFFA, M. ROMAN ET SOCIÉTÉ.
P.P. CLARK, 454:SPRING72-257
ZERASCHI, H. DAS BUCH VON DER DREHORGEL.
P. WILLIAMS, 415:OCT72-980
ZERBE, J. HAPPY TIMES. (TEXT BY B. GILL)
S. SCHWARTZ, 441:2DEC73-95
ZERNER, H. THE SCHOOL OF FONTAINEBLEAU:
ETCHINGS AND ENGRAVINGS.*
G. MARTIN, 39:APR70-324
N. MILLER, 56:WINTER70-447
ZERNOV, N.M. & OTHERS. NA PERELOME.
I. KIRILLOVA, 575(SEER):JUL72-488
D. VON MOHRENSCHILDT, 550(RUSR):OCT
71-416
VON ZESEN, P. ASSENAT 1670. (V. MEID,
ED)
H. RÜDIGER, 52:BAND6HEFT1-77
ZETTERSTEN, A. THE ENGLISH OF TRISTAN DA
CUNHA.
R.B. LE PAGE, 361:VOL26#3-328
E. SIVERTSEN, 597(SN):VOL42#1-267

ZETZSCHE, R. DIE SÜDROUTE.
P. VOSSELER, 182:VOL24#3-125
ZEYDEL, E.H., ED & TRANS. VAGABOND VERSE.
L.J. FRIEDMAN, 545(RPH):AUG71-129
ZIEGENGEIST, G., ED. AKTUELLE PROBLEME
DER VERGLEICHENDEN LITERATURFORSCHUNG.
F. JOST, 149:SEP72-326
ZIEGLER, C. VON DEN MADRIGALEN.
M.K. SLOCUM, 406:SPRING72-82
ZIEGLER, J. ZUR RELIGÖSEN HALTUNG DER
GEGENKAISER IM 4. JH. N. CHR.
W.H.C. FREND, 123:JUN72-290
ZIEGLER, K. - SEE PLUTARCH
ZIEGLER, P. OMDURMAN.
617(TLS):26OCT73-1304
ZIERER, E. INTRODUCCIÓN A LA LENGUA
JAPONESA HABLADA.
G.F. MEIER, 682(ZPSK):BAND23HEFT4-428
ZIERER, E. LA LOGICA FORMAL EN LA LIN-
GÜISTICA.
J. CHAURAND, 209(FM):OCT70-460
ZIETARSKA, J. SZTUKA PRZEKŁADU W POGLĄ-
DACH LITERACKICH POLSKIEGO OŚWIECENIA.
H. JECHOVÁ, 549(RLC):JAN-MAR71-117
ZIFF, L. THE AMERICAN 1890'S.*
W.M. GIBSON, 405(MP):AUG70-119
H-J. LANG, 38:BAND88HEFT3-413
ZIFF, L. PURITANISM IN AMERICA.
Q. ANDERSON, 441:16DEC73-4
A. WHITMAN, 441:29DEC73-23
ZIFF, P. PHILOSOPHIC TURNINGS.*
B. CAMPBELL, 353:OCT71-85
ZILLMAN, L.J. - SEE SHELLEY, P.B.
ZIMMER, K.E. AFFIXAL NEGATION IN ENGLISH
AND OTHER LANGUAGES.
L.A. GYURKO, 545(RPH):NOV71-225
G. PRICE, 47(ARL):VOL17FASC1-38
ZIMMERMAN, D.R. RH: THE INTIMATE HISTORY
OF A DISEASE AND ITS CONQUEST.
H. SCHWARTZ, 441:18AUG73-19
ZIMMERMANN, G-D. SONGS OF IRISH REBEL-
LION.*
J.W. FOSTER, 650(WF):JUL70-210
ZIMMERMANN, R.C. DAS WELTBILD DES JUNGEN
GOETHE. (VOL 1)
H. FISCHER-LAMBERG, 190:BAND65HEFT2-
214
D. HARTH, 224(GRM):NOV70-472
H. REISS, 220(GL&L):JAN72-177
H. WALZ, 202(FMOD):JUN70-343
ZINBERG, N.E. & J.A. ROBERTSON. DRUGS
AND THE PUBLIC.*
P. STEINFELS & R.M. VEATCH, 441:
4FEB73-6
ZINGARELLI, N. VOCABOLARIO DELLA LINGUA
ITALIANA.
R-C. MELZI, 276:SUMMER71-262
ZINKIN, T. WEEDS GROW FAST.
P. BEER, 362:25JAN73-122
617(TLS):16MAR73-286
ZINSLI, P. WALSER VOLKSTUM IN DER
SCHWEIZ, IN VORARLBERG, LIECHTENSTEIN
UND PIEMONT.
R.M. KULLY, 657(WW):MAY/JUN70-211
ZIOLKOWSKI, T. DIMENSIONS OF THE MODERN
NOVEL.*
M. DURZAK, 680(ZDP):BAND89HEFT2-307
R.H. FARQUHARSON, 564:MAR71-73
H. STEINECKE, 405(MP):FEB71-315
B. VÖLKER-HEZEL, 556(RLV):1971/4-494
J.J. WHITE, 220(GL&L):JUL72-404
ZIOLKOWSKI, T. FICTIONAL TRANSFIGURA-
TIONS OF JESUS.
617(TLS):17AUG73-959
ZIOLKOWSKI, T. - SEE HESSE, H.
ZIPES, J.D. THE GREAT REFUSAL.
R.C. BALL, 131(CL):SPRING72-189
P. STENBERG, 564:OCT71-246

ZIRIN, R.A.  THE PHONOLOGICAL BASIS OF
  LATIN PROSODY.
    H.M. HOENIGSWALD, 124:NOV71-102
ZIRING, L.  THE AYUB KHAN ERA.
    H.K. SHERWANI, 273(IC):OCT71-296
ŽIRMUNSKIJ, V.  INTRODUCTION TO METRICS.
  (E. STANKIEWICZ & W.N. VICKERY, EDS)
    H. WODE, 353:JUN70-99
ŽIRMUNSKIJ, V. & N. SIGAL - SEE WALPOLE,
  H., J. CAZOTTE & W. BECKFORD
ZOBEL, F.  CUENCA.
    B. DYCKES, 58:APR71-18
ZOBEL, H.B.  THE BOSTON MASSACRE.*
    K. PREYER, 432(NEQ):JUN71-319
ZOBEL, K. & R. GRIFFEL.  KLEINE DEUTSCHE
  TYPOLOGIE.
    M.A.S. FIELDS, 399(MLJ):MAR71-192
ZODER, R.  FAMILIENNAMEN IN OSTFALEN.
    H. VON GADOW, 657(WW):NOV/DEC70-424
ZOHN, H.  DER FARBENVOLLE UNTERGANG.
    A.W. WONDERLEY, 399(MLJ):DEC71-529
ZOHN, H.  KARL KRAUS.
    E. HELLER, 453:3MAY73-21
ZOLA, E.  L'AFFAIRE DREYFUS, LA VÉRITÉ
  EN MARCHE.  (C. BECKER, ED)
    N. HAMPSON, 208(FS):JAN72-91
ZOLA, E.  L'ASSOMMOIR.  (J. DUBOIS, ED)
    T.G.S. COMBE, 208(FS):JUL72-349
ZOLA, E.  THÉRÈSE RAQUIN.  LA FORTUNE DES
  ROUGON.  LA CURÉE.  NANA.  POT-BOUILLE.
    F.W.J. HEMMINGS, 208(FS):OCT72-467
ZOLA, E.  ZOLA: MON SALON - MANET - ECRITS
  SUR L'ART.
    T. CLARK, 592:NOV71-212
ZOLDESTER, P.H.  ADALBERT STIFTERS WELT-
  ANSCHAUUNG.*
    J.M. MC GLATHERY, 221(GQ):NOV71-577
ZÖLLNER, E., ED.  GESCHICHTE DER FRANKEN
  BIS ZUR MITTE DES SECHSTEN JAHRHUN-
  DERTS.*
    W. GOFFART, 589:JUL72-578
ZOLTAI, D.  ETHOS UND AFFEKT.*
    J.S.W., 410(M&L):APR72-215
ZONG, I-S.  AN INTRODUCTION TO KOREAN
  LITERATURE.
    CHA CHU WHAN, 302:JUL71-380
ZORRILLA, F.D. - SEE UNDER DE ROJAS ZOR-
  RILLA, F.
ZOSIMUS.  ZOSIME: "HISTOIRE NOUVELLE."
  (VOL 1) (F. PASCHOUD, ED & TRANS)
    T.E. GREGORY, 124:MAR72-234
DE ZOUCHE HALL, R.  A BIBLIOGRAPHY ON
  VERNACULAR ARCHITECTURE.
    617(TLS):2FEB73-133
Z SCHOCKE, R.  DIE KULTURLANDSCHAFT DES
  HUNSRÜCKS UND SEINER RANDLANDSCHAFTEN
  IN DER GEGENWART UND IN IHRER HISTOR-
  ISCHEN ENTWICKLUNG.
    P. VOSSELER, 182:VOL24#7/8-381
ZSUPPÁN, M. - SEE ROBERTET, J.
ZUBERBÜHLER, R.  HÖLDERLINS ERNEUERUNG
  DER SPRACHE AUS IHREN ETYMOLOGISCHEN
  URSPRÜNGEN.*
    G.L. JONES, 220(GL&L):JAN72-198
    L. RYAN, 221(GQ):JAN71-100
ZUCCHELLI, B.  STUDI SULLE FORMAZIONI
  LATINE IN "-LO-" NON DIMINUTIVE E SUI
  LORO RAPPORTI CON I DIMINUTIVI.
    A.M. DAVIES, 123:DEC72-421
    J.W. POULTNEY, 350:MAR72-179
ZUCKERMAN, A.  TIGER KITTENS.
    N. CALLENDAR, 441:15APR73-35
ZUCKERMAN, G.  FAREWELL, FRANK MERRIWELL.
    M. LEVIN, 441:27MAY73-19
ZUCKERMAN, M.  PEACEABLE KINGDOMS.*
    J.J. WATERS, 432(NEQ):MAR71-153
ZUCKERMAN, S.  BEYOND THE IVORY TOWER.
    J. ROSENHEAD, 111:19FEB71-147

ZÜFLE, M.  PROSA DER WELT.*
    P. ROUBICZEK, 220(GL&L):OCT71-67
ZUK, G.  SELECTED VERSE.  (R. SKELTON,
  TRANS)
    E. FEINSOD, 114(CHIR):JAN-FEB71-156
    A. HUTCHINSON, 102(CANL):WINTER72-78
ZUK, W. & R.H. CLARK.  KINETIC ARCHITEC-
  TURE.
    R.P. BURNS, JR., 505:MAR71-135
ZUKOFSKY, C. & L. - SEE "CATULLUS"
DE ZULUETA, C.  NAVARRO LEDESMA, EL
  HOMBRE Y SU TIEMPO.
    R. PÉREZ DE LA DEHESA, 240(HR):OCT71-
    454
ZUMTHOR, P.  LE PUITS DE BABEL.
    M.G. ROSE, 207(FR):OCT70-190
"THE ZUÑIS: SELF PORTRAYALS." (A. QUAM,
  TRANS)
    R. COLES, 442(NY):10FEB73-109
ZUNTZ, G.  PERSEPHONE.*
    V. TEJERA, 319:OCT73-540
ZUTT, H. - SEE HARTMANN VON AUE
ZVIGUILSKY, A. - SEE BOTKINE, V.
ZWANENBURG, W.  RECHERCHES SUR LA PRO-
  SODIE DE LA PHRASE FRANÇAISE.*
    A. CLASSE, 47(ARL):VOL17FASC1-61
ZWEIG, P.  AGAINST EMPTINESS.*
    D. ROSOCHACKI, 600:FALL71-138
ZWEIG, P. - SEE GOLL, Y.
ZWEZ, R.E.  HACIA LA REVALORIZACIÓN DE LA
  SEGUNDA PARTE DEL LAZARILLO (1555).
  LAZARILLOS RAROS.
    R.O. JONES, 86(BHS):OCT72-403
ZWIERLEIN, O.  DER TERENZKOMMENTAR DES
  DONAT IM CODEX CHIGIANUS H VII 240.
    W.G. ARNOTT, 123:DEC72-347
ZWIRNER, E. & K. EZAWA, EDS.  PHONOMET-
  RIE.  (PT 2)
    G. HEIKE, 260(IF):BAND75-362
    A. WOLLMANN, 38:BAND89HEFT1-119
ZYCHLINSKA, R.  HERBSTIKE SKVERN.
    S. KREITER, 287:MAR70-27
ZYLA, W.T., ED.  JAMES JOYCE.
    E. KREUTZER, 52:BAND6HEFT1-115
ZYTARUK, G.J. - SEE LAWRENCE, D.H.

WITHDRAWAL